Responding to Literature

Responding
to
Literature

JUDITH A. STANFORD

Rivier College

Mayfield Publishing Company
Mountain View, California
London · Toronto

LIBRARY OF CONGRESS CATALOGING-IN-PUBLICATION DATA

Responding to literature / [edited by] Judith A. Stanford.
     p.   cm.
     Includes indexes.
     ISBN 1-55934-081-9 (pbk.)
     1. College readers. 2. English language — Rhetoric.
     3. Literature — Collections. I. Stanford, Judith A.
PE1417.R4745 1992
808 — dc20   91-40781
                                     CIP

Manufactured in the United States of America
10 9 8 7 6 5 4 3

Mayfield Publishing Company
1240 Villa Street
Mountain View, California 94041

Sponsoring editor, Janet Beatty; managing editor, Linda Toy; production editor, Carol Zafiropoulos; manuscript editor, Antonio Padial; text and cover design, David Bullen. This text was set in 10/12 Bembo by Thompson Type and printed by R. R. Donnelley & Sons Co. on 40# Restorecote Thin.

Cover: Pierre Bonnard, *The Window*. The Bridgeman Art Library/Copyright 1991 ARS, N.Y./ADAGP/SPADEM

Acknowledgments and copyrights continue at the back of the book on pages 1564–1568, which constitute an extension of the copyright page.

For Don, my best reader

PREFACE

Samuel Johnson's renowned biographer, James Boswell, reports a heated exchange of literary opinions that took place one late winter afternoon over cups of steaming, black coffee. Incensed by the proffered opinion that he "ought" to have read some particular work, Johnson replied, "A man ought to read just as inclination leads him; for what he reads as a task will do him little good." Most of us would agree with Johnson; what we read through our own motivation usually means more to us and stays with us longer than does something we are forced to read. Yet how do we discover what we want to read? Perhaps we walk into a bookstore and browse through the latest paperbacks, or we may listen to the recommendations of family members and friends. But these methods have their limits. At bookstores, for instance, many readers look only for writers with whom they are familiar or look only for the most recent arrivals in one particular section — perhaps mystery, science fiction, or romance.

Responding to Literature encourages readers to explore a richly diverse selection of literature, including the essay. Three introductory chapters use student papers to illustrate ways of responding to and writing about literature. Seven thematically arranged sections follow, each with five stories, ten or more poems, a play, and two essays. A final section offers 137 additional selections arranged by genre, chronologically. In all, the book provides 58 stories, 184 poems, 13 plays (4 of them short), and 26 essays.

Responding to Literature helps readers to develop a wide range of possibilities as they decide what they will read in the future. The text offers this encouragement to readers through these key features:

- *Emphasis on the reader's personal response.* The text stresses the importance of the readers' interaction with and response to what they read. Chapter 1 explores the difference between reading as a choice and reading as a requirement; this emphasis on the reader's engagement with the literary work is reflected throughout the text.
- *Examples of student writing.* The three introductory chapters provide many examples of students' notes, journal entries, sample drafts, and revised papers, including numerous examples of writers working collaboratively.
- *Informal introduction to literary terms.* Chapter 2 offers four works — a story, a poem, a brief play, and an essay — and student-written responses to them that incorporate key literary terms in a natural, informal way. The chapter stresses the similarities among literary genres, showing students, for example, that once they know how to talk about character in short stories, they also know how to discuss character in drama and persona in poetry.

The emphasis is always on how readers find meaning in a work—how they bring their own knowledge, experiences, and insights to bear on what they read.

• *Emphasis on the writing process.* Chapter 3 devotes special attention to the writing process, including strategies for discovering and exploring ideas, considering the audience, drafting, revising, and editing. This chapter provides five examples of students writing in different ways as they respond to Dylan Thomas's "Do not go gentle into that good night" and Joan Aleshire's "Slipping." The five papers—a personal response, a comparison, an explication, an evaluation, and a researched response—are accompanied by explanations of each student's process. Set off from the text throughout are summaries of many flexible, yet clear, guidelines of approaches to writing about literature. Chapter 3 also offers examples of students preparing for and participating in conferences with the instructor as well as with a writing center tutor.

• *Balance of new and classic selections.* The selections include an unusually strong representation of fresh voices, including women, minorities, and writers from other countries, as well as many familiar favorites.

• *Thought-provoking questions about the works.* The "Considerations" and "Connections" sections following the pieces in the thematic sections provide ways of thinking and writing about the selections that lead readers away from a single "correct" interpretation and instead suggest multiple possibilities—always, of course, to be supported by evidence in the work itself.

• *Full-color section inviting students to make connections between literature and art.* Eight poems are paired with works of art that inspired them (or vice versa); students are asked to reflect on their responses to both visual and verbal works.

To accompany the text, I've written a thorough and practical Instructor's Manual that provides suggestions for teaching the first class, working with small groups in class, and encouraging interaction in the classroom. Also included are suggested responses for each discussion or writing topic in the thematic anthology and a commentary and ideas for writing topics for each selection in the additional reading section.

ACKNOWLEDGMENTS

My own teaching and the inspiration for this text owe much to the writing of Louise Rosenblatt, Robert Scholes, Robert DiYanni, Nancie Atwell, and Mike Rose. My CCCC's roommates, Rebecca Burnett, Kathleen Shine Cain, and Bonnie Sunstein, who understand the value of long lunches and good conversations, have provided both intellectual and emotional support. Lynn Quitman Troyka deserves special thanks for encouraging me in many ways, especially in the world of textbook publishing. Writing and Learning Center faculty as well as many English Department faculty members at Rivier College have inspired me with lively literary discussions, a generous willingness to share ideas, and a keen understanding of the importance of positive reinforcement. I thank my husband, Don, and my sons, Aaron and David, for being people who like to read and who share with me their thoughts about what they read. My mother, Arline Dupras, earns praise for the endless support she gave researching and typing, but most especially for being the person who first taught me that reading was joyful.

The reviewers of this text offered helpful and wise suggestions which I greatly appreciate: Thomas Dukes, University of Akron; Cynthia A. Eby, James Madison University; Leonard Engel, Quinnipiac College; Jennifer W. Thompson, University of Kansas; James Wanless, Henry Ford Community College.

At Mayfield Publishing Company, Carol Zafiropoulos worked with amazing speed and grace during the production of the book, while Laurel Graziano and Pam Trainer attended to the difficult task of obtaining permissions. I would like to thank Tom Broadbent, Editorial Director, for his wise, sensible, and sensitive approach to publishing and for the ideas he shared over an unforgettable dinner in Boston. Finally, I thank Senior Editor Jan Beatty, whose vision, warmth, and wit have made this project possible. She is all that one could ask for in an editor — or a friend.

CONTENTS

ON BEING HUMAN: LITERARY THEMES

Innocence and Experience 109

Death *763*

CONNECTIONS: ART AND LITERATURE

Color Section (follows page 608)

ADDITIONAL READINGS

An Introduction to Short Fiction   892

An Anthology of Short Fiction

An Introduction to Poetry   *1090*

An Anthology of Poetry

An Introduction To Drama *1187*

An Anthology of Plays

An Introduction to Nonfiction *1489*

An Anthology of Nonfiction

ALTERNATE CONTENTS
BY GENRE

Poetry

Drama

Nonfiction

1

Why Read Literature?

At the first meeting of a course called "Literature and Writing," a professor asked students to respond to a question written on the forms she distributed to them. She explained that some students would receive Form A and some Form B. The question on each form was different, although the two questions differed by only one word.

Form A asked students, "Why do you read literature? (For the purposes of this response, please consider 'literature' to mean any and all fiction, poetry, drama, and essays.)"

Form B asked students, "Why do we read literature? (For the purposes of this response, please consider 'literature' to mean any and all fiction, poetry, drama, and essays.)"

Exercise

Before you read further, consider the two questions. Do you see any real difference between them? How would you respond to each question? Take a few minutes to jot down your thoughts. Then compare your responses with those that follow.

WHY DO YOU READ LITERATURE?

Students responded to this question in a wide variety of ways. The following comments are representative:

I read mostly fiction for pleasure. Poetry and drama I don't read much. When I read, I like to escape — to get away from all the pressures of everyday life. So, I don't want to read about a lot of the same troubles I have. And no unhappy endings. *Karin Estes*

I don't read what you call literature except that you said "any and all fiction, poetry, drama, or essays." So, if "any and all" can mean Stephen King (which a teacher I had said was not literature) then that's what I read. And the reason is his books always hold my interest because I get interested in the characters' lives. Then, when they get into totally weird situations, it's like I can really believe that. I don't know why I like to read stuff that scares me, but I do. I also like this kind of movie. *Jeff Pedino*

Literature to me has always meant a place to find someone else who goes through the same things I do. But seeing them and their problems or situations more in an objective way. When I was in middle school, I read a lot of Judy Blume's novels. I liked that she was honest and wrote about real feelings people have instead of what was some fantasy of how people should feel. She wasn't always teaching a lesson. Also, in high school I read *Tess of the D'Urbervilles* by Thomas Hardy. I thought Hardy was really honest, too, and Tess is not just the perfect little heroine. Then I read three more novels by Hardy because I liked how he wrote. I do that. Read a lot of one author when I find someone I like. *Kate Anstrom*

I read literature for two reasons: (1) it's assigned by a teacher, and (2) it's something that interests me. Most of the time these are not the same thing. Forget poetry, which is always a big puzzle to me. I don't want to have to figure out hidden meanings. I don't read drama because who buys drama in a book store? I like novels or short stories in some magazines. Adventures that move fast and have a good plot really keep my interest (mysteries are sometimes good, too, when you don't figure out on the second page who the killer was). *Dave Willette*

WHY DO WE READ LITERATURE?

The responses to this question were not so widely varied, but they were very different from the responses to the first question. Here are two samples; nearly all students gave a variation on one of these two themes:

We read literature to find the beauty of words of great writers. Literature teaches us the truth about our lives. We learn good values from literature like Shakespeare. *Elayne Mercier*

Literature is very important to read because those writers have lasted through a lot of years, and so what they say must be important. Otherwise they would have been forgotten. We read literature because it is an important part of our education. Like history is one part and math is one part and literature is one part. *Rick McDougal*

BRIDGING THE GAP

The differences students saw between personal reading (and the reasons for it) and "school reading" (and the reasons for it) show up clearly in these different responses. When answering the universally phrased question "Why do we read literature?" students dutifully answered with language that echoed pat textbook phrases, such as "beauty of words," "truth about our lives," and "lasted through . . . years." Few students mentioned whether they themselves found literature beautiful; few wondered why literature had "lasted through the years." Almost no one commented on any personal, individual reading choices. The only author consistently mentioned by name was Shakespeare.

By contrast, students' responses to the more individual question ("Why do I read literature?") varied widely and showed that literature was important to them for many different reasons. In addition, they noted some of the problems they encountered with traditionally defined "literature." For example, when Jeff Pedino comments that a teacher did not consider Stephen King's writing literature, he's beginning to search for a definition. In essence, Jeff is asking, "What makes a story, novel, poem, play, or essay 'literature'?"

Note, also, Dave Willette's comment that he doesn't enjoy poetry because he doesn't like reading that is a "puzzle." Dave cuts right to the heart of an issue that had always bothered him — the feeling that reading literature (and especially poetry) was basically a grueling search through a maze of difficult words to find a hidden meaning.

Some students made observations about their reading patterns. For instance, Kate Anstrom likes to read many novels by the same author (she mentions Judy Blume and Thomas Hardy). Kate's response is interesting because she bridges the gap between literature that is read in school and outside of school. She read *Tess of the D'Urbervilles* for a class and liked the novel because she thought Hardy was honest. He created a heroine who was far from perfect.

So, Kate makes a connection between her values (it's clear that truth, honesty, and realism are important to her) and the literature she reads. She looks at assigned books in a personal way and thus makes them part of her world. Of course, there's a reciprocal exchange involved, too. Hardy and his characters become part of Kate's world, but she also becomes part of theirs. When she reads Hardy's novels, she sees, senses, and experiences nineteenth-century England in a direct and detailed way. She doesn't read with detachment but instead becomes deeply involved with Hardy's creation.

This text invites you to make personal connections with various selections of literature that other readers have found important to their lives. A work of literature exists on the printed page, but it gains life and meaning only when individual readers bring their knowledge, beliefs, feelings, and values to the reading experience. You are not expected to like or to enjoy everything you read in this text (or everything that you read anywhere): no reader could honestly claim to do that. But you should be able to *respond* to every work that you read. Having a genuine response — and being willing to explore that response — is the key to opening new possibilities in whatever you read, in or out of class, both now and in the future.

RESPONDING TO WHAT YOU READ

The great thing about responding to literature is that there are no absolute answers. A response is a beginning point. You read a work through, keeping your mind and spirit open, and then jot down what you thought and felt as you read it. An initial response might include any of the following:

- A question (about the meaning of a word or sentence, the choice of a word, the reason why a particular character appears in the work; the reason the author chose to begin or end as he or she did)
- A comment on what you think the work is about and why you are interested or not interested in that idea
- An observation about a particular description, or line, or sentence to which you had a strong reaction (you liked it; you disliked it; it made you angry, happy, sad, puzzled, uncomfortable)
- A connection between this work and something else you have read, experienced, or observed in your own life

Remember that a response is a place to begin. Just as we often change our first impressions of a person or situation, readers often revise initial responses to a work of literature.

Exercise

Read the following poem by Robert Frost and then write down your responses. You don't have to interpret the poem (although interpretation can certainly be one part of response). Don't worry about what you are "supposed to get" from the reading. Just notice your reactions and then write them down. When you are finished, compare your responses to the students' comments that follow Frost's poem. If possible, compare your comments to those of students in your class.

ROBERT FROST (1874–1963)

The Road Not Taken

Two roads diverged in a yellow wood,
And sorry I could not travel both
And be one traveler, long I stood
And looked down one as far as I could
To where it bent in the undergrowth;   5

Then took the other, as just as fair,
And having perhaps the better claim,
Because it was grassy and wanted wear;
Though as for that the passing there
Had worn them really about the same,   10

And both that morning equally lay
In leaves no step had trodden black.
Oh, I kept the first for another day!
Yet knowing how way leads on to way,
I doubted if I should ever come back.   15

I shall be telling this with a sigh
Somewhere ages and ages hence:
Two roads diverged in a wood, and I —
I took the one less traveled by,
And that has made all the difference.   20

Sample Student Responses to "The Road Not Taken"

> This person is standing in the woods, and it's probably fall because the leaves are yellow. This is a nice time to take a walk, and it's a question which way he wants to go, because he would like to see all of the woods. He can go on only one path today. But I can't figure out why he says in lines 14 and 15 that he couldn't come back. Why does he doubt he'll come back if he wants to see what's on the other path? *Janice Angstrom, age 18*

> This is not a poem about Frost just taking some walk in the woods. It's about him making a choice to be a poet. Then in the last verse he is glad he made that choice, and he says it has made all the difference in his life. *Gilbert Brown, age 21*

> I see this as a poem about choices. The poet might be thinking about one choice, but I think it could mean many different possible decisions. I don't think the choice seems too big at first because I notice lines 9 and 10 say that the paths really had been traveled almost the same amount. To me, this is like a lot of life decisions. They may seem small

at the time, but as Frost says, one way leads on to another, and you can't go back and relive your life. *Anita Juarez, age 35*

In the poem, the poet is sorry he made a certain choice in his life. He calls the poem "The Road Not Taken," so he is looking at the choice he didn't make and thinking about it for some reason. Maybe wondering what life would be like if he took that other road. And that is why he sighs in the last stanza. He is regretting what he lost out on. I can understand this because I do this, too. I look back and see some choices I made — like dropping out of school and going into the army — and I can see what I missed. *David Furman, age 28*

Commentary

You may find one or more of these responses similar to yours, or they all may be very different. Some of the observations may have surprised you. And certainly you noticed that two of the student writers had reactions that were nearly opposite. Gilbert Brown thinks that the speaker in the poem is glad he made a certain choice, whereas David Furman thinks that the speaker regrets the choice.

Suppose those two students compared their responses to Frost's poem. Noticing the difference in their reactions, they might reread "The Road Not Taken." David Furman has already offered some evidence to back up what he says: he notes that the title focuses on the path that was not followed, and he reads the sigh as sad. But Gilbert Brown might well ask whether a sigh is always sad. A sigh might show pleasure, contentment, relief, or any number of other emotions. How can these two commentators resolve their differences?

The answer is that they don't have to find a single resolution. Both readings of this poem are possible. By listening to a number of responses and then rereading the work to see what evoked those responses, readers often discover multiple possibilities, new ways of looking at the work that they had not previously considered.

Of course, there is always the chance that returning to the work will cause a reader to rethink an initial reaction. For instance, how would Gilbert Brown support his idea that the poem is about Frost's decision to be a poet? Nothing in the poem directly backs up this reading; to the contrary, lines 9 and 10 suggest that the choice involves two rather similar alternatives. Nevertheless, nothing in the poem definitely rules out the possibility that the choice relates to careers. Gilbert Brown might decide, however, to broaden the scope of his initial reaction.

Notice that David Furman relates strongly to what he sees as the speaker's regret. David's response shows that he regrets several life choices he made, and so he believes that the speaker in the poem must be experiencing this emotion, too. Even if David Furman modifies his reading to include other possibilities (for example, that the speaker in the poem might be proud of or pleased with his choice), that revision does not lessen the importance of the personal connection David has made with the poem. His reading remains a possibility, but now he also sees a fuller context than he did at first.

And what about Janice Angstrom? She sees the poem as basically about taking a walk in the woods. Is she wrong or imperceptive? No. Her reading is a very useful first step. She sees clearly the picture the poet paints and, in addition, she sees that part of the picture is puzzling. In lines 14 and 15, Janice recognizes an element of contradiction. If the speaker in the poem were simply talking about a woodland walk, he would not be so concerned about being unable to backtrack and explore another path. Janice, then, uses her literal first response to raise questions that lead to a nonliteral reading of the poem. Janice shows that she is perceptive by recognizing those questions and by being willing to pursue them.

Anita Juarez makes an intriguing observation when she notes that lines 9 and 10 suggest that the choice was not between extreme opposites. The paths are almost equally worn, so the choice is probably not between, for instance, nonconformity and conformity. Because of her own experiences, Anita sees a valuable insight in Frost's poem: it's frequently the apparently minor decisions in life that end up making "all the difference." Because of her initial reaction to "The Road Not Taken," she decided to read the poem more closely and to use it for the following assignment:

> Choose a poem to which you have a strong personal response. Then reread the poem and come to class prepared with notes to help you explain your response. Be sure to refer to specific lines and stanzas in the poem as you explain your thoughts and feelings.

Exercise

After reading the example that follows, choose a poem from the anthology section of this text and take notes as though you were preparing for the assignment given to Anita.

CLOSE ACTIVE READING

Once you've read a work of literature — poem, story, novel, or play — and noted your initial response, you may decide (or be asked) to read more closely. As you read, you check on your first reactions, and you consider the reactions you've heard others express. Close active reading always means reading with a pen or pencil (rather than a highlighter) in your hand. You might use a highlighter during your first reading to mark passages that impress, puzzle, delight, or outrage you, but a close reading requires actually interacting with the work — writing down your questions and observations as you go.

Here is how Anita Juarez marked "The Road Not Taken":

The Road Not Taken

Why not "The Road Taken"?

Two roads diverged in a yellow wood,   *Why yellow? Could be fall or spring— New beginnings?*
And sorry I could not travel both
And be one traveler, long I stood
And looked down one as far as I could
To where it bent in the undergrowth;   *— maybe hard to get past.*   5

Then took the other, as just as fair,   *— are they the same?*
And having perhaps the better claim,
Because it was grassy and wanted wear;
Though as for that the passing there
Had worn them really about the same,   *Again— seems Similar*   10

And both that morning equally lay
In leaves no step had trodden black.
Oh, I kept the first for another day!
Yet knowing how way leads on to way,   *Like a lot of choices in life — lead you in many directions.*
I doubted if I should ever come back.   15

Happy or Sad About Choices?

I shall be telling this with a sigh
Somewhere ages and ages hence:
Two roads diverged in a wood, and I—
I took the one less traveled by,
And that has made all the difference.   20

Sample Oral Response to "The Road Not Taken"

Using these notes as a guide, Anita Juarez gave the following informal oral response in class:

> When I read this poem, I thought right away of the choice I made in high school not to study foreign languages. In the poem, the speaker makes his choice in either fall or spring—when the woods are yellow. I see both these seasons as times of new beginnings. In spring, everything new is growing. In fall (at least for students) it's the start of a new school year. I made my choice one fall when a guidance director told me I was not "college material" and recommended that I drop my French class. September should have been a beginning, but I saw it as an end to my dream for college. It's only now that I can begin to think it was—in a way—a beginning, too.
>
> Dropping French was desirable because I didn't do well in languages, but taking a language was also desirable because you had to

take a language to get into college. So, like the speaker in the poem, I made a choice between two possibilities — and just as the poem says, both these two choices had been made before by many people. As Frost says, "the passing there/Had worn them really about the same."

What really interested me about the poem is the way it says that "way leads on to way." Because I decided not to take a language, I knew I couldn't go to college — back then you had to have a language to get into college. So, after high school, I went to work at Sears, and at work I met my husband. So, working at Sears was what got me to meet that particular man. And then marrying him, I had children (that were of course different from those I might have had if I married somebody else). I could keep going on, but you get the idea about how "way led on to way" in my life.

In the poem the person doubts that he will "ever come back." Well, at first when I read this, I thought that in a way I have come back because now I am starting college, which I couldn't do out of high school. But I really know it's still not the same, because I am a different person than I was then. All those "ways that lead to other ways" have made me — or maybe helped me to become — somebody new. So, this is not about going back to an old fork in the road but being at a new one.

You can't really tell whether in the last stanza the speaker is entirely happy, entirely sad, or some mixture. But you can see he knows now how important life's choices can be. He knows he'll think back over one particular choice even when he is an old man ("somewhere ages and ages hence"). I feel the same way. Reading this poem has made me look at some of the choices I've made, and I know I'll still be looking at them years from now. And, whether for better or worse, those choices will have "made all the difference."

Commentary

Anita Juarez read "The Road Not Taken" carefully and related the speaker's experience to her own choices in life. Her observations show that she became genuinely interested in Frost's theme and was able to appreciate his poem more fully by bringing something of herself to her reading. You may think her commentary is very different from what you have previously thought of as "literary analysis." Certainly, her ideas are expressed informally and personally, yet she has indeed "analyzed" the poem (looked at how parts of it work to create the whole).

Chapter 2 introduces and explains terms that are useful when you talk or write about literature, and Chapter 3 demonstrates and explains five ways of writing about literature. As you read Chapters 2 and 3, remember that all real enjoyment and understanding of literature begins with your engagement as a reader and your willingness to discover and explore the kinds of responses introduced in this chapter.

Exercise

Using the notes you took for the exercise on page 7, plan an oral response similar to the one you just read. Remember to refer to specific parts of the poem to explain why you had the responses you describe.

KEEPING A READING JOURNAL

In addition to taking notes, keeping a reading journal is one of the best ways to explore your responses to literature as well as to discover ideas for papers you may write. The comments on pages 5 and 6 come from students' journals, as do the paragraphs that introduce each new section in Chapter 2 (see pages 25, 30, 39, 43, 49).

There are many different ways of keeping such a journal. If you write a journal for your class, the instructor may ask you to write a certain number of entries each week and may specify how long those entries should be. The instructor may also suggest topics or approaches to help you determine the focus of some or all of the entries.

For journal entries that you plan yourself, consider the following possibilities:

Guidelines: Keeping a Reading Journal

1. After you read a work, jot down several questions that come to mind. Then choose one question and explore it more fully.
2. List the emotions (anger, pity, envy, admiration, astonishment, and so on) the work evoked. Then explain the reasons you think you felt these emotions.
3. Copy one sentence, one line, or one phrase that struck you as especially beautiful, puzzling, enlightening, and so on. Then discuss how and why the sentence, line, or phrase evoked this response.
4. Write a letter to the author asking questions or making observations about the work.
5. Write a letter to one of the characters (or to the speaker in a poem) describing your response to a choice or decision he or she made.
6. Explain why you could—or couldn't—identify with a particular character or situation in the work.
7. Jot down your initial impression of a work. Then reread and write another entry describing new or changed impressions.
8. Make notes during class discussion of a particular work. Then respond to a comment made either by the instructor or by another student.

2

Joining the Conversation: Ways of Talking about Literature

People who start a new job or a new sport often find themselves surrounded by unfamiliar language. "Byte," "hard disk," and "system error" may not mean much to a newly hired office worker, but the new employee soon learns the terminology along with the practical steps required to use the office computer. Saying "monitor" instead of "the thing that looks like a TV" simplifies communication. The novice skier is in a similar situation. Someone who has never skied probably doesn't know or care about the difference between "new powder" and "packed, granular snow." As soon as a person rents skis and takes the first lesson, however, understanding the words that describe the condition of the ski slopes becomes important. It's much easier to warn a fellow skier of danger on the slopes by mentioning "moguls" than by describing "bumps and ridges with hard, icy coverings." In addition, learning new words to describe kinds of snow makes skiers more conscious of the natural world around them. They become aware of subtle distinctions they might not have noticed before.

Like computer users and skiers, many people who talk and write about literature use specialized terminology. Understanding the terms that describe various aspects of literature enriches the reader's experience. This vocabulary not only provides a shortcut for talking or writing about literature but also often suggests new ways of looking at poetry, fiction, drama, and nonfiction and at the connections between our lives and the literary works we read.

To begin learning about the language of literature, read the following selections. Each represents one genre of literature: fiction, poetry, drama, and nonfiction. As you read, make notes in the margins to keep track of your responses to each selection. (For note-taking suggestions, see Chapter 1, page 4). Following each selection are suggestions for writing to develop your responses further.

PATRICIA GRACE (1937–   )

Butterflies

The grandmother plaited her granddaughter's hair and then she said, "Get your lunch. Put it in your bag. Get your apple. You come straight back after school, straight home here. Listen to the teacher," she said. "Do what she say."

Her grandfather was out on the step. He walked down the path with her and out onto the footpath. He said to a neighbor, "Our granddaughter goes to school. She lives with us now."

"She's fine," the neighbor said. "She's terrific with her two plaits in her hair."

"And clever," the grandfather said. "Writes every day in her book."

"She's fine," the neighbor said.   5

The grandfather waited with his granddaughter by the crossing and then he said, "Go to school. Listen to the teacher. Do what she say."

When the granddaughter came home from school her grandfather was hoeing around the cabbages. Her grandmother was picking beans. They stopped their work.

"You bring your book home?" the grandmother asked.

"Yes."

"You write your story?"   10

"Yes."

"What's your story?"

"About the butterflies."

"Get your book then. Read your story."

The granddaughter took her book from her schoolbag and opened it.   15

"I killed all the butterflies," she read. "This is me and this is all the butterflies."

"And your teacher like your story, did she?"

"I don't know."

"What your teacher say?"

"She said butterflies are beautiful creatures. They hatch out and fly in   20
the sun. The butterflies visit all the pretty flowers, she said. They lay their
eggs and then they die. You don't kill butterflies, that's what she said."

The grandmother and the grandfather were quiet for a long time, and
their granddaughter, holding the book, stood quite still in the warm garden.

"Because you see," the grandfather said, "your teacher, she buy all her
cabbages from the supermarket and that's why."

Responding to "Butterflies"

1. Describe the relationship between the granddaughter and grandparents.
   Compare it to your own relationship to your grandparents or to other
   grandchild-grandparent relationships you know of.
2. What can you tell about the place where these people live? Can you make
   any guesses about the time period in which they live?
3. Even though the schoolteacher does not appear in the story, can you tell
   anything about her? What kind of a person do you think she is? How
   effective do you think she is as a teacher? Why?
4. What is your response to the advice the grandfather gives the granddaughter as she sets out for school? Do you think the grandfather might
   change his advice in response to his granddaughter's experience? Explain.
5. What was your response to the connection the grandfather makes between cabbages and butterflies? Explain.

LANGSTON HUGHES (1902–1967)

Theme for English B

The instructor said,

> Go home and write
> a page tonight.

> And let that page come out of you —
> Then, it will be true.   5

I wonder if it's that simple?

I am twenty-two, colored, born in Winston-Salem.
I went to school there, then Durham, then here
to this college on the hill above Harlem.
I am the only colored student in my class.   10
The steps from the hill lead down to Harlem,
through a park, then I cross St. Nicholas,

Eighth Avenue, Seventh, and I come to the Y,
the Harlem Branch Y, where I take the elevator
up to my room, sit down, and write this page: 15

It's not easy to know what is true for you or me
at twenty-two, my age. But I guess I'm what
I feel and see and hear. Harlem, I hear you:
hear you, hear me — we two — you, me talk on this page.
(I hear New York, too.) Me — who?   20

Well, I like to eat, sleep, drink, and be in love.
I like to work, read, learn, and understand life.
I like a pipe for a Christmas present,
or records — Bessie, bop, or Bach.

I guess being colored doesn't make me not like   25
the same things other folks like who are other races.
So will my page be colored that I write?
Being me, it will not be white.
But it will be
a part of you, instructor.   30
You are white —
yet a part of me, as I am a part of you.
That's American.
Sometimes perhaps you don't want to be a part of me.
Nor do I often want to be a part of you.   35
But we are, that's true!
As I learn from you,
I guess you learn from me —
although you're older — and white —
and somewhat more free.   40

This is my page for English B.

Responding to "Theme for English B"

1. Describe the thoughts and feelings that run through the speaker's mind as he considers the assignment for his English course. Does his process in any way remind you of the way you think about course assignments? Or do you work entirely differently? Explain.

2. What places seem significant to the speaker? How are they significant? For example, what differences does he suggest between the places he has lived (and the place he now lives) and the place he attends his classes? What comparisons can you make between places where you have lived and places where you have attended school?

3. What does the poem tell you about the speaker? Make two lists, one describing what might be called external facts (the speaker's age, for

example) and the other describing the inner speaker (his hopes, fears, motivations, personality traits, and so on).

4. What do you make of the question "So will my page be colored that I write?" (line 27)? What is the speaker's answer to his own question? What is your response to this answer?

5. If you were the instructor and received this poem in response to the assignment suggested in lines 2–5, how would you grade the paper? What comments would you write to explain your thoughts and feelings to the student?

WENDY WASSERSTEIN (1950–   )

The Man in a Case

Characters
BYELINKOV
VARINKA

Scene *A small garden in the village of Mironitski. 1898.*

(BYELINKOV *is pacing. Enter* VARINKA *out of breath.*)

BYELINKOV: You are ten minutes late.

VARINKA: The most amazing thing happened on my way over here. You know the woman who runs the grocery store down the road. She wears a black wig during the week, and a blond wig on Saturday nights. And she has the daughter who married an engineer in Moscow who is doing very well thank you and is living, God bless them, in a three-room apartment. But he really is the most boring man in the world. All he talks about is his future and his station in life. Well, she heard we were to be married and she gave me this basket of apricots to give to you.

BYELINKOV: That is a most amazing thing!

VARINKA: She said to me, "Varinka, you are marrying the most honorable man in the entire village. In this village he is the only man fit to speak with my son-in-law."

BYELINKOV: I don't care for apricots. They give me hives.

VARINKA: I can return them. I'm sure if I told her they give you hives she would give me a basket of raisins or a cake.

BYELINKOV: I don't know this woman or her pompous son-in-law. Why would she give me her cakes?

VARINKA: She adores you!

BYELINKOV: She is emotionally loose.

VARINKA: She adores you by reputation. Everyone adores you by reputation. I tell everyone I am to marry Byelinkov, the finest teacher in the county.

BYELINKOV: You tell them this?

VARINKA: If they don't tell me first.

BYELINKOV: Pride can be an imperfect value.

VARINKA: It isn't pride. It is the truth. You are a great man!

BYELINKOV: I am the master of Greek and Latin at a local school at the end of the village of Mironitski.

(VARINKA kisses him.)

VARINKA: And I am to be the master of Greek and Latin's wife!

BYELINKOV: Being married requires a great deal of responsibility. I hope I am able to provide you with all that a married man must properly provide a wife.

VARINKA: We will be very happy.

BYELINKOV: Happiness is for children. We are entering into a social contract, an amicable agreement to provide us with a secure and satisfying future.

VARINKA: You are so sweet! You are the sweetest man in the world!

BYELINKOV: I'm a man set in his ways who saw a chance to provide himself with a small challenge.

VARINKA: Look at you! Look at you! Your sweet round spectacles, your dear collar always starched, always raised, your perfectly pressed pants always creasing at right angles perpendicular to the floor, and my most favorite part, the sweet little galoshes, rain or shine, just in case. My Byelinkov, never taken by surprise. Except by me.

BYELINKOV: You speak about me as if I were your pet.

VARINKA: You are my pet! My little school mouse.

BYELINKOV: A mouse?

VARINKA: My sweetest dancing bear with galoshes, my little stale babka.

BYELINKOV: A stale babka?

VARINKA: I am not Pushkin.°

BYELINKOV *(Laughs)*: That depends what you think of Pushkin.

VARINKA: You're smiling. I knew I could make you smile today.

BYELINKOV: I am a responsible man. Every day I have for breakfast black bread, fruit, hot tea, and every day I smile three times. I am halfway into my translation of the *Aeneid*° from classical Greek hexameter° into Russian alexandrines.° In twenty years I have never been late to school. I am a responsible man, but no dancing bear.

VARINKA: Dance with me.

BYELINKOV: Now? It is nearly four weeks before the wedding!

Pushkin: A Russian poet and prose writer (1799–1837).   Aeneid: Epic poem written by Vergil (70–19 B.C.).   *hexameter:* A line of verse having six metric units.   *alexandrine:* A line of verse having six metric units.

VARINKA: It's a beautiful afternoon. We are in your garden. The roses are in full bloom.

BYELINKOV: The roses have beetles.

VARINKA: Dance with me!

BYELINKOV: You are a demanding woman.

VARINKA: You chose me. And right. And left. And turn. And right. And left.

BYELINKOV: And turn. Give me your hand. You dance like a school mouse. It's a beautiful afternoon! We are in my garden. The roses are in full bloom! And turn. And turn. (*Twirls* VARINKA *around*)

VARINKA: I am the luckiest woman!

(BYELINKOV *stops dancing.*)

Why are you stopping?

BYELINKOV: To place a lilac in your hair. Every year on this day I will place a lilac in your hair.

VARINKA: Will you remember?

BYELINKOV: I will write it down. (*Takes a notebook from his pocket*) Dear Byelinkov, don't forget the day a young lady, your bride, entered your garden, your peace, and danced on the roses. On that day every year you are to place a lilac in her hair.

VARINKA: I love you.

BYELINKOV: It is convenient we met.

VARINKA: I love you.

BYELINKOV: You are a girl.

VARINKA: I am thirty.

BYELINKOV: But you think like a girl. That is an attractive attribute.

VARINKA: Do you love me?

BYELINKOV: We've never spoken about housekeeping.

VARINKA: I am an excellent housekeeper. I kept house for my family on the farm in Gadyatchsky. I can make a beetroot soup with tomatoes and aubergines which is so nice. Awfully, awfully nice.

BYELINKOV: You are fond of expletives.

VARINKA: My beet soup, sir, is excellent!

BYELINKOV: Please don't be cross. I too am an excellent housekeeper. I have a place for everything in the house. A shelf for each pot, a cubby for every spoon, a folder for favorite recipes. I have cooked for myself for twenty years. Though my beet soup is not outstanding, it is sufficient.

VARINKA: I'm sure it's very good.

BYELINKOV: No. It is awfully, awfully not. What I am outstanding in, however, what gives me greatest pleasure, is preserving those things which are left over. I wrap each tomato slice I haven't used in a wet cloth and place it in the coolest corner of the house. I have had my shoes for seven years because I wrap them in the galoshes you are so fond of. And every night before I go to sleep I wrap my bed in quilts and curtains so I never catch a draft.

VARINKA: You sleep with curtains on your bed?

BYELINKOV: I like to keep warm.

VARINKA: I will make you a new quilt.

BYELINKOV: No. No new quilt. That would be hazardous.

VARINKA: It is hazardous to sleep under curtains.

BYELINKOV: Varinka, I don't like change very much. If one works out the arithmetic, the final fraction of improvement is at best less than an eighth of value over the total damage caused by disruption. I never thought of marrying till I saw your eyes dancing among the familiar faces at the headmaster's tea. I assumed I would grow old preserved like those which are left over, wrapped suitably in my case of curtains and quilts.

VARINKA: Byelinkov, I want us to have dinners with friends and summer country visits. I want people to say, "Have you spent time with Varinka and Byelinkov? He is so happy now that they are married. She is just what he needed."

BYELINKOV: You have already brought me some happiness. But I never was a sad man. Don't ever think I thought I was a sad man.

VARINKA: My sweetest darling, you can be whatever you want! If you are sad, they'll say she talks all the time, and he is soft-spoken and kind.

BYELINKOV: And if I am difficult?

VARINKA: Oh, they'll say he is difficult because he is highly intelligent. All great men are difficult. Look at Lermontov, Tchaikovsky, Peter the Great.

BYELINKOV: Ivan the Terrible.

VARINKA: Yes, him too.

BYELINKOV: Why are you marrying me? I am none of these things.

VARINKA: To me you are.

BYELINKOV: You have imagined this. You have constructed an elaborate romance for yourself. Perhaps you are the great one. You are the one with the great imagination.

VARINKA: Byelinkov, I am a pretty girl of thirty. You're right, I am not a woman. I have not made myself into a woman because I do not deserve that honor. Until I came to this town to visit my brother I lived on my family's farm. As the years passed I became younger and younger in fear that I would never marry. And it wasn't that I wasn't pretty enough or sweet enough, it was just that no man ever looked at me and saw a wife. I was not the woman who would be there when he came home. Until I met you I thought I would lie all my life and say I never married because I never met a man I loved. I will love you, Byelinkov. And I will help you to love me. We deserve the life everyone else has. We deserve not to be different.

BYELINKOV: Yes. We are the same as everyone else.

VARINKA: Tell me you love me.

BYELINKOV: I love you.

VARINKA *(Takes his hands)*: We will be very happy. I am very strong. *(Pauses)* It is time for tea.

BYELINKOV: It is too early for tea. Tea is at half past the hour.

VARINKA: Do you have heavy cream? It will be awfully nice with apricots.

BYELINKOV: Heavy cream is too rich for teatime.

VARINKA: But today is special. Today you placed a lilac in my hair. Write in your note pad. Every year we will celebrate with apricots and heavy cream. I will go to my brother's house and get some.

BYELINKOV: But your brother's house is a mile from here.

VARINKA: Today it is much shorter. Today my brother gave me his bicycle to ride. I will be back very soon.

BYELINKOV: You rode to my house by bicycle! Did anyone see you?

VARINKA: Of course. I had such fun. I told you I saw the grocery store lady with the son-in-law who is doing very well thank you in Moscow, and the headmaster's wife.

BYELINKOV: You saw the headmaster's wife!

VARINKA: She smiled at me.

BYELINKOV: Did she laugh or smile?

VARINKA: She laughed a little. She said, "My dear, you are very progressive to ride a bicycle." She said, "you and your fiancé Byelinkov must ride together sometime. I wonder if he'll take off his galoshes when he rides a bicycle."

BYELINKOV: She said that?

VARINKA: She adores you. We had a good giggle.

BYELINKOV: A woman can be arrested for riding a bicycle. That is not progressive, it is a premeditated revolutionary act. Your brother must be awfully, awfully careful on behalf of your behavior. He has been careless — oh so careless — in giving you the bicycle.

VARINKA: Dearest Byelinkov, you are wrapping yourself under curtains and quilts! I made friends on the bicycle.

BYELINKOV: You saw more than the headmaster's wife and the idiot grocery woman.

VARINKA: She is not an idiot.

BYELINKOV: She is a potato-vending, sausage-armed fool!

VARINKA: Shhhh! My school mouse. Shhh!

BYELINKOV: What other friends did you make on this bicycle?

VARINKA: I saw students from my brother's classes. They waved and shouted, "Anthropos in love! Anthropos in love!!"

BYELINKOV: Where is that bicycle?

VARINKA: I left it outside the gate. Where are you going?

BYELINKOV *(Muttering as he exits)*: Anthropos in love, anthropos in love.

VARINKA: They were cheering me on. Careful, you'll trample the roses.

BYELINKOV *(Returning with the bicycle)*: Anthropos is the Greek singular for man. Anthropos in love translates as the Greek and Latin master in love. Of course they cheered you. Their instructor, who teaches them the discipline and contained beauty of the classics, is in love with a sprite on a bicycle. It is a good giggle, isn't it? A very good giggle! I am returning this bicycle to your brother.

VARINKA: But it is teatime.

BYELINKOV: Today we will not have tea.

VARINKA: But you will have to walk back a mile.

BYELINKOV: I have my galoshes on. *(Gets on the bicycle)* Varinka, we deserve not to be different. *(Begins to pedal. The bicycle doesn't move.)*

VARINKA: Put the kickstand up.

BYELINKOV: I beg your pardon.

VARINKA *(Giggling)*: Byelinkov, to make the bicycle move, you must put the kickstand up.

(BYELINKOV *puts it up and awkwardly falls off the bicycle as it moves.)*

(Laughing) Ha ha ha. My little school mouse. You look so funny! You are the sweetest dearest man in the world. Ha ha ha!

(Pause)

BYELINKOV: Please help me up. I'm afraid my galosh is caught.

VARINKA *(Trying not to laugh)*: Your galosh is caught! *(Explodes in laughter again)* Oh, you are so funny! I do love you so. *(Helps* BYELINKOV *up)* You were right, my pet, as always. We don't need heavy cream for tea. The fraction of improvement isn't worth the damage caused by the disruption.

BYELINKOV: Varinka, it is still too early for tea. I must complete two stanzas of my translation before late afternoon. That is my regular schedule.

VARINKA: Then I will watch while you work.

BYELINKOV: No. You had a good giggle. That is enough.

VARINKA: Then while you work I will work too. I will make lists of guests for our wedding.

BYELINKOV: I can concentrate only when I am alone in my house. Please take your bicycle home to your brother.

VARINKA: But I don't want to leave you. You look so sad.

BYELINKOV: I never was a sad man. Don't ever think I was a sad man.

VARINKA: Byelinkov, it's a beautiful day, we are in your garden. The roses are in bloom.

BYELINKOV: Allow me to help you on to your bicycle. *(Takes* VARIN-KA's *hand as she gets on the bike)*

VARINKA: You are such a gentleman. We will be very happy.

BYELINKOV: You are very strong. Good day, Varinka.

> (VARINKA *pedals off.* BYELINKOV, *alone in the garden, takes out his pad and rips up the note about the lilac, strews it over the garden, then carefully picks up each piece of paper and places them all in a small envelope as lights fade to black.)*

Responding to *The Man in a Case*

1. Describe the relationship between the man and woman in the play. What seems important to each of them? Do any things seem important to them both? Explain. Does their relationship remind you of any relationships you know about? Describe the differences and similarities you see.
2. Did you find it important to know that this play takes place in 1898? Where do you think the village of Mironitski is located? Was knowing the location in any way connected to your response to the play?
3. Were you more sympathetic to one of the characters than to the other? Or did you find them both equally appealing (or lacking in appeal)? Explain.
4. What did you make of the bicycle episode? Why is Byelinkov so upset about Varinka's riding the bicycle? What is her response? How does this episode relate to other episodes in the play?
5. Write a short scene that takes place between Varinka and Byelinkov two weeks after the day of the play's action. What future do you predict for them? Why?

E. B. WHITE (1899–1985)

Education

I have an increasing admiration for the teacher in the country school where we have a third-grade scholar in attendance. She not only undertakes to instruct her charges in all the subjects of the first three grades, but she manages to function quietly and effectively as a guardian of their health, their clothes, their habits, their mothers, and their snowball engagements. She has been doing this sort of Augean° task for twenty years, and is both kind and wise. She cooks for the children on the stove that heats the room, and she can cool their passions or warm their soup with equal competence. She conceives their costumes, cleans up their messes, and shares their confi-

---

Augean task: A very difficult task. (King Augeas of Elis set the Greek hero Hercules to the task of cleaning the royal stables, which had been neglected for thirty years.)

dences. My boy already regards his teacher as his great friend, and I think tells her a great deal more than he tells us.

The shift from city school to country school was something we worried about quietly all last summer. I have always rather favored public school over private school, if only because in public school you meet a greater variety of children. This bias of mine, I suspect, is partly an attempt to justify my own past (I never knew anything but public schools) and partly an involuntary defense against getting kicked in the shins by a young ceramist on his way to the kiln. My wife was unacquainted with public schools, never having been exposed (in her early life) to anything more public than the washroom of Miss Winsor's. Regardless of our backgrounds, we both knew that the change in schools was something that concerned not us but the scholar himself. We hoped it would work out all right. In New York our son went to a medium-priced private institution with semi-progressive ideas of education, and modern plumbing. He learned fast, kept well, and we were satisfied. It was an electric, colorful, regimented existence with moments of pleasurable pause and giddy incident. The day the Christmas angel fainted and had to be carried out by one of the Wise Men was educational in the highest sense of the term. Our scholar gave imitations of it around the house for weeks afterward, and I doubt if it ever goes completely out of his mind.

His days were rich in formal experience. Wearing overalls and an old sweater (the accepted uniform of the private seminary), he sallied forth at morn accompanied by a nurse or a parent and walked (or was pulled) two blocks to a corner where the school bus made a flag stop. This flashy vehicle was as punctual as death: seeing us waiting at the cold curb, it would sweep to a halt, open its mouth, suck the boy in, and spring away with an angry growl. It was a good deal like a train picking up a bag of mail. At school the scholar was worked on for six or seven hours by a half a dozen teachers and a nurse, and was revived on orange juice in mid-morning. In a cinder court he played games supervised by an athletic instructor, and in a cafeteria he ate lunch worked out by a dietitian. He soon learned to read with gratifying facility and discernment and to make Indian weapons of a semi-deadly nature. Whenever one of his classmates fell low of a fever the news was put on the wires and there were breathless phone calls to physicians, discussing periods of incubation and allied magic.

In the country all one can say is that the situation is different, and somehow more casual. Dressed in corduroys, sweatshirt, and short rubber boots, and carrying a tin dinner-pail, our scholar departs at crack of dawn for the village school, two and a half miles down the road, next to the cemetery. When the road is open and the car will start, he makes the journey by motor, courtesy of his old man. When the snow is deep or the motor is dead or both, he makes it on the hoof. In the afternoons he walks or hitches all or part of the way home in fair weather, gets transported in foul. The schoolhouse is a two-room frame building, bungalow type, shingles stained a burnt brown with weather-resistant stain. It has a chemical toilet in the basement and two teachers above stairs. One takes the first three grades, the other the fourth, fifth, and sixth. They have little or no time for individual instruction, and no time at all for the esoteric. They teach what they know themselves, just as fast and as hard as they can manage. The pupils sit still at their desks in class, and do their milling around outdoors during recess.

There is no supervised play. They play cops and robbers (only they call it "Jail") and throw things at one another — snowballs in winter, rose hips in fall. It seems to satisfy them. They also construct darts, pinwheels, and "pick-up sticks" (jackstraws), and the school itself does a brisk trade in penny candy, which is for sale right in the classroom and which contains "surprises." The most highly prized surprise is a fake cigarette, made of cardboard, fiendishly lifelike.

The memory of how apprehensive we were at the beginning is still strong. The boy was nervous about the change too. The tension, on that first fair morning in September when we drove him to school, almost blew the windows out of the sedan. And when later we picked him up on the road, wandering along with his little blue lunch-pail, and got his laconic report "All right" in answer to our inquiry about how the day had gone, our relief was vast. Now, after almost a year of it, the only difference we can discover in the two school experiences is that in the country he sleeps better at night — and *that* probably is more the air than the education. When grilled on the subject of school-in-country *vs.* school-in-city, he replied that the chief difference is that the day seems to go so much quicker in the country. "Just like lightning," he reported.

Responding to "Education"

1. Make a list of the details the speaker provides to explain why he has "an increasing admiration for the teacher in the country school." Do you agree that these qualities are admirable? Explain.

2. How do the physical facilities of the city school compare with those of the country school? Which school would you prefer to attend (or to teach in)? Discuss your reasons.

3. Read paragraph 3 carefully and explain your response to the speaker's description of the school bus that takes his son to the city school.

4. In the final paragraph, the speaker says, "Now, after almost a year of it, the only difference we can discover in the two school experiences is that in the country he sleeps better at night — and *that* probably is more the air than the education." To what extent do the details in the rest of the essay suggest that the speaker does or does not favor one school over the other? Do you find evidence to suggest that the "third-grade scholar" prefers one school to the other?

5. The speaker says that he "always rather favored public school over private school." What is your response to this judgment? Have you attended

private schools? Public schools? Both? What differences do you believe exist between public and private schools?

___

THE VOCABULARY OF LITERATURE

As you look at your own responses to the four selections you've just read, you'll almost certainly find comments about actions and events, about people and places, about ideas and values. In addition, you'll probably note questions about the significance of particular objects, about the choice of certain words, or the use of references to people, places, and events outside the work itself.

Each of the following sections begins with observations, evaluations, or questions written by students — mostly freshmen and sophomores — who had just read the same selections you have. The commentary following their responses suggests how these students have provided insights both into the works themselves and into ways of reading, writing, thinking, and talking about literature.

ACTIONS AND EVENTS

In "Butterflies," the granddaughter is at a big point in her life — starting school. You can tell it's near the beginning because she writes a story in only two sentences. Also, you get the impression she has drawn a picture when she says, "This is me." Usually you only draw pictures like that very early in your school years. You can see she is not in agreement with her teacher because of the killing of the butterflies, which the teacher didn't understand. And I don't understand this, really. Why would the granddaughter want to kill butterflies? *Lisa Tisico*

I think the student in this poem ["Theme for English B"] is walking all the time that he is talking. In the lines where he talks about the steps that lead down the hill and "through a park" and then he even shows taking the elevator. Well, I guess once he's off the elevator and in his room, he's not walking then. But I liked the verse where he is walking because I could picture this. Probably because this is how I do a lot of my planning for classes and other things. I walk a lot and I am always putting my mind in gear and thinking while I do this. *Jim Belanger*

At first I thought that *The Man in a Case* was just all talking, but when I went back to read again, it was full of action. I love the way Varinka gets Byelinkov to dance. He is so stuffy and talks about how he is "a responsible man, but no dancing bear." Then two minutes later, he is dancing (and I could picture him like a dancing bear because Varinka counts off the steps like a bear trainer). This shows you that they really do seem to have fun together. But later the action with the bicycle makes everything fall apart. He is so jealous of her because she is free and not afraid to do things like riding a bicycle when she could be arrested or when other people might not approve. *Bonnie Dederian*

I can really understand the feelings of the third-grade kid that the father talks about. Changing schools is hard because you're the new kid and you have to get to know everything, like the teacher, the other kids, and how things are done, all over again. My father is in the military, so we moved all the time. The best part of the essay for me was when the father tells that the kid thinks his day goes by "Just like lightning." You can tell he must like that school because time usually goes by very slowly in school, and especially when you're young. *Ryan Berker*

When readers react to literature, among the first aspects they notice are actions and events. You can see how natural this response is when you think about talking to a friend who recommends a new film. You'd almost certainly ask some version of this question: "What's it about?" And your friend would almost certainly respond by giving you a brief summary of what happens in the film or perhaps (like Bonnie Dederian in her response to *The Man in a Case*) by singling out particular actions that seemed especially interesting, entertaining, moving, frightening, or significant in some way.

Plot

When you tell what happens in a film or in a work of literature, you are describing the **plot,** the sequence of events that take place. Most readers begin by describing *external* actions, those that, through the writer's description, we can see and hear. For instance, in her response to "Butterflies," Lisa Tisico begins by writing about the granddaughter's starting school and the drawing she includes in her story of killing butterflies. These are external plot actions. But Lisa also asks questions that indicate her interest in *internal* actions, those events that take place inside the mind and heart. For example, she sees that the granddaughter does not agree with the teacher; in addition, Lisa wonders why the child would want to kill butterflies. So, looking at the external actions carefully led Lisa to think about the internal changes that might be happening.

Structure

The sequence of external and internal actions and events in a literary work creates its **structure,** the pattern the plot follows. In most traditional plays and works of fiction, the plot structure is something like this:

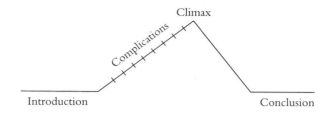

The work usually opens with an **introduction** that lets us know whom the action will concern and where the action will take place. Next, we are given a **complication** or a series of complications (small or large problems, sometimes comic, sometimes serious). For instance, in *The Man in a Case,* after Byelinkov and Varinka greet each other, they almost immediately have a series of small disagreements. He claims not to like the apricots she has received as a gift for him. She offers to return the apricots and try to exchange them for a different gift. He responds by attacking the character of the woman who gave Varinka the apricots.

It's easy to see that these two are not an entirely compatible couple, and most readers begin to wonder about the wisdom of their engagement. These early complications are revealed primarily through conversation, but, as Bonnie Dederian notes in her comment on this play, their incompatibility becomes even more obvious through two key actions in the play. The first action is the dance. Byelinkov protests that he is not a dancing bear, yet Varinka is able to lead him into a romantic, gently humorous noonday waltz in the garden. Now the two characters seem to come together, yet almost immediately they get into another squabble, this time over housekeeping styles. As Varinka talks about her fantasy of a marriage in which she and her husband will have "the life everyone has," Byelinkov appears to agree with her. So far in this play, the complications seem to follow a pattern of disagreement followed by reconciliation followed by new disagreement and further reconciliation.

The episode of the bicycle, however — which Bonnie Dederian sees as the action "that makes everything fall apart" — takes the play beyond complications and to the **climax** (the point of greatest tension or the turning point). Varinka has braved the law against women riding bicycles as well as the possible bad opinion of people who might see her. Byelinkov is shocked and particularly upset that some of his students have seen Varinka; he fears that they will laugh at him for being engaged to such a free-spirited woman. The turning point comes when Byelinkov tries to take charge by riding the bicycle back to the house of Varinka's brother. However, Byelinkov simply embarrasses himself by showing that he has no idea how to ride the bicycle. When Varinka first laughs and then rushes to help in response to his pleas, Byelinkov sends her away. Whether they will marry or not remains to be seen; however, the **conclusion,** the ending of the play, shows him ripping up and scattering the pieces of the note reminding him to put lilac in Varinka's hair. Byelinkov must wonder if he will ever again be able to feel totally in control of his life or whether he'll be able to rely so completely on his carefully kept lists and notes.

Conflict

As you read a literary work and think about the structure of the plot — and particularly as you focus on the complications and climax — keep in mind that nearly all fiction and drama, and many poems, focus on a **conflict,** a struggle between opposing forces. The conflict or conflicts in a literary work are usually reflected or accompanied by the external and internal action. For instance, in Langston Hughes's poem "Theme for English B," the speaker starts by introducing a complication: he has been assigned a topic for a theme. As Jim Belanger notes in his response to the poem, the first verse shows the speaker walking and thinking as he struggles to decide how to write this theme. The external actions (walking and taking the elevator) suggest the internal action (thoughts moving along and then suddenly upward with the idea of what to write in response to the assignment). The conflict here takes place *within the speaker's mind.* The speaker wonders what he can write that will fulfill the assignment, that his instructor will understand, and that will still remain true to himself.

In addition to conflicts inside the mind, literary works may also focus on conflicts *between individuals* (as with Varinka and Byelinkov), *between an individual and a social force* (a community, school, church, workplace), and *between an individual and a natural force* (disease, fire, flood, cold, famine). It's important to note that conflicts do not necessarily belong in just one category. For instance, in "Theme for English B," the speaker is definitely experiencing an internal conflict, yet he also demonstrates the conflicts he feels between himself and various social forces (for example, the discrepancy between his world and the world of his white instructor).

Sometimes you find conflict even in works of nonfiction, where you might not expect it. For example, Ryan Berker's comment on E. B. White's "Education" suggests some of the conflicts the third-grader might face as he changes schools. And, of course, the essay focuses on the conflict between the values and procedures of the public school and the values and procedures of the private school.

Whatever the nature of the conflict, it often forces characters to make a decision: to act or not to act, to behave according to a personal moral code or an external moral code, to compromise or to refuse to compromise, to grow and change or to remain more or less the same. The point at which characters make these choices is usually the climactic moment of the story, poem, or play. The effects or implications of this choice usually represent the conclusion of the literary work.

Irony of Situation

The actions and events in a work may generate a sense of irony. **Irony of situation** is a difference between what a character says and what a character does. For example, Bonnie Dederian notes that Byelinkov claims he is not a dancing bear yet a minute later is, in fact, performing just like the animal he claims to disdain. The discrepancy between what Byelinkov says and what he does is ironic. In this case, the irony is comic, but sometimes the ironic discrepancy can be sad or tragic. If a character claims to be brave, for instance, yet fails to act bravely in a crucial moment, that discrepancy is ironic. This irony, however, might well shock or sadden readers rather than amuse them.

Irony of situation also occurs when a character expects one thing to happen and instead something else happens. For instance, in "Butterflies," the granddaughter expected that her story of the butterflies would please her teacher. The teacher's reaction, however, was very different from the one the child expected. The grandfather's final comment, "Because, you see, your teacher, she buy all her cabbages from the supermarket and that's why," underlines the irony. To the child, the butterflies are pests whose eggs will hatch into worms that destroy the cabbage crop. When she kills butterflies in her grandfather's garden, she is acting practically and usefully. To the teacher, who does not have to grow her own food, the butterflies are simply beautiful creatures of nature.

Terms Related to Actions and Events

Plot: The sequence of events and actions in a literary work.

Structure: The pattern formed by the events and actions in a literary work. Traditional elements of structure are introduction, complications, climax, and conclusion.

Introduction: The beginning of a work, which usually suggests the setting (time and place) and shows one or more of the main characters.

Complications: Events or actions that establish the conflict in a literary work.

Climax: The turning point, often signified by a character's making a significant decision or taking action to resolve a conflict.

Conflict: A struggle between internal and external forces in a literary work.

Conclusion: The ending of a work, which often shows the effects of the climactic action or decision.

Irony of situation: A discrepancy between what is said and what is done or between what is expected and what actually happens.

Exercises: Actions and Events

1. Think about a television program or a film you have seen recently that shows a character facing a conflict. Describe the conflict, its resolution, and your response to that resolution. For instance, would you have made the same choice or choices as the character? Why? Do you find the character's reaction to the conflict realistic? Explain.

2. Think of an ironic situation you have observed or experienced. Briefly

describe the situation and then explain why you see it as ironic. Do you consider this ironic situation comic, sad, annoying, enlightening? Explain. Remember that irony always requires a discrepancy between two things (what is said and what is done, for instance).

3. Read any one of the following works from this book.

   "The Lady with the Pet Dog" page 910
   "The Revolt of 'Mother'" page 923
   "The Loudest Voice" page 677
   "Hills Like White Elephants" page 986
   "Ulysses" page 1121
   "Mending Wall" page 1142
   Trifles page 319

Then describe the complications that lead one character or speaker to the climactic action or decision. Explain your response to each complication. Do you see one particular complication as more important than any others? Why? Speculate on what might have happened if the character or speaker had responded differently than he or she did to any of the complications you identified.

PEOPLE

The grandfather and grandmother [in "Butterflies"] seem like very wise people to me even though they don't speak correct English. They try to give their granddaughter good advice, and I noticed that both of them tell her to do what the teacher says. What's really good and what makes me say they are wise is that when the granddaughter comes home they ask her about school and they really listen. They are quiet with her when they find out what the teacher said about the butterflies. I think this is because they know she must feel bad or at least confused. What's also good, and shows the grandfather to be wise, is that in the end he makes a comment about why the teacher said what she did. You get the feeling that maybe he will be thinking hard about his advice to "listen to the teacher." *Mark James*

You think about this poem ["Theme for English B"] and you don't right away think about a person or character because it's like the poet, Langston Hughes, is describing something that happened. But when you think about it, this could be something that happened to Hughes or not. Because a poem can be made up—and I think a lot of them are—just like the story we read about the butterflies, which didn't necessarily happen to the author. So when I stopped thinking about just the poet, I started to think about the person that was created in the poem. And you know a lot about him. He is black (but he says "colored," which isn't a word I'd expect him to use), he is 22 years old, and he is taking a class called "English B" that sounds to me like a freshman course from the assignment. So, he's a little old to be starting college, and he mentions his age again in line 16, so maybe he thinks about it a lot. He's on his own, too. Lives at the "Y"—not at home or in a dorm. Maybe being older and on your own would make you especially think about being free, which he talks about. But he doesn't feel completely free—you can see that in line 40 when he says his English instructor is "more free" than he is. *Carlene Indreasano*

At first I was totally sympathetic with Varinka [in the play *The Man in a Case*]. If I ask myself who I would rather spend the afternoon with, there's no contest. Varinka has a good sense of humor and a spirit of adventure (she's not afraid to ride the bicycle, even though it's illegal). Also, she seems to love life—she wants to enjoy apricots and dancing and flowers. Byelinkov, on the other hand, is just depressing. He is too concerned with what his students think—too uptight, not liking to have fun. But then I thought about some of the questions he asks Varinka about why she is marrying him. She sees him one way, and he sees himself another way. He may be boring, but he has a right to be himself, so by the end I have some sympathy for Byelinkov and I can see why he rips up the note—but I did wonder why he picked up the pieces again—maybe just he's so concerned with neatness? *Nathalie LaRochelle*

The father in "Education" has a good sense of humor, and you can see that he laughs at himself as well as at other people. He makes fun of the way parents in New York got on the telephone to each other and to the doctor whenever one of the children in the school got sick. But he also is sort of making fun of himself because he tells about things like picking his son up after his first day at the new school and being deeply relieved when he said his day had been "all right." Underneath almost every sentence, you can feel a father who cares a lot and thinks a lot about his son. *Dora DiFonzo*

Most of us are interested in other people. When we meet someone for the first time, we notice certain things: how the person looks, speaks, and acts, for example. We make judgments according to what we notice. Sometimes, as we get to know the person better, those evaluations are affirmed. Sometimes they are challenged. Interest in other people is more than just idle curiosity. We base our most important life decisions—whom we will work with, whom we will live with, whom we will love—on what we learn from observing, talking with, and interacting with other people.

It's not surprising, then, that when we watch television programs, see movies, or read literature, most of us pay close attention to the people—the **characters**—whose lives unfold before us. To stay interested in a film, a novel, a short story, or a play, we must find the characters interesting in some way. Some characters fascinate us by being very different—by living in a distant place or a time long past or by being wildly glamorous or consummately evil. Sometimes characters may capture our minds and hearts because they are people we can relate to. They may face circumstances similar to our own or may act in ways that make us feel as though we are looking in a mirror. Frequently a character intrigues us by displaying a special quality or style: a unique sense of humor, a gift for the absurd, or a profoundly wise way of looking at the world.

Characters: Listening and Observing

Just as we respond to the people in our lives according to what we notice when we look at them and when we listen to them, readers respond to the speech, actions, and appearance of literary characters.

LISTENING Sometimes characters speak with others **(dialogue).** For example, as Mark James observes, the grandparents in "Butterflies" speak kindly with their granddaughter. They show they want the best for her by encouraging her to do well in school. And they ask questions that indicate their concern when she returns from school. We learn a great deal about the grandparents from listening to what they say. It is also interesting to note Mark's comment that the grandparents "don't speak correct English." Debates about what is and is not "correct" English have been going on for centuries and will continue to go on, but, nonetheless, Mark has noticed something important. The grandparents speak a **dialect,** a language that is different from the form taught in school. Noticing the grandparents' speech patterns leads to seeing a gentle irony in their wisdom. They may not know how to speak the "proper" English of the schools, but unlike the schoolteacher, who buys "all her cabbages from the supermarket," they understand the point of their granddaughter's story. Further, they grasp the reason behind the teacher's different interpretation.

When characters speak to each other, they reveal certain qualities about themselves and about their relationships with the characters to whom they speak. The conversation between the grandparents and granddaughter provides one example; the dialogue between Varinka and Byelinkov provides another. He speaks primarily in an orderly, controlled manner, whereas she tends to be as extravagant in her language as she is in her behavior: to Varinka everything is "awfully, awfully nice" or "excellent" or "awfully not." We can learn a great deal about Varinka's and Byelinkov's personalities just by noticing how they speak to each other, and understanding their personalities leads to questions about their relationship, their conflicts, their hopes for the future.

In addition to speaking to others, characters sometimes talk to an absent or unspeaking listener **(monologue).** In a play, a character may address thoughts directly to the audience, or the character may speak thoughts aloud without any acknowledgment that an audience is there **(soliloquy)**. Such a strategy gives the audience a chance to hear the uncensored thoughts of the character, thoughts that have not been shaped by the interaction with another character in the play.

The character in "Theme for English B" reveals everything we know about him through a monologue: musings that he addresses to his instructor. The reader has a chance to "hear" the thoughts of this character (sometimes called the *persona* or *speaker*) and to learn certain things about him. Carlene Indreasano notices that the speaker mentions twice that he is twenty-two. Wondering why age might be important to him, she links his age with his concern for freedom. You may have noticed other details that the speaker reveals through his monologue, and you may have had a response quite different from Carlene's. For instance, many readers note the questions of race and of nationality that the speaker raises in lines 25–35. The point here is not that everyone should notice the same details — or that some details are necessarily more important than others — but rather that "listening" carefully to what the speaker says leads to learning more about him, to asking questions, and to speculating on the significance of the experience he describes.

OBSERVING Hearing what characters say leads to insights into who they are: what they believe, what they fear, what they hope for, and how they think about themselves and others. Observing characters provides further information. Just as you notice certain external characteristics about a person you meet, readers notice those qualities about a literary character. We know, for instance, that the granddaughter in "Butterflies" wears her hair in "two plaits" (braids) and that she carries a schoolbag, so we can create a picture of her in our minds. We know from Varinka's description that Byelinkov wears round spectacles, perfectly pressed pants, and galoshes (whether or not it's raining). These details allow us not only to visualize Byelinkov but also make some inferences about his personality.

If you've ever indulged in "people watching" (perhaps at an airport or in a supermarket), you are probably an expert at noticing characteristics (such as age, hair color, manner of dress) and at observing gestures, body movements, and other actions. Nathalie LaRochelle notes two significant actions in *The Man in a Case*. Varinka rides a bicycle (suggesting to Nathalie that Varinka has "a spirit of adventure"), and Byelinkov rips up the note he has written to remind himself to place lilacs in Varinka's hair. Byelinkov's action raises a question for Nathalie and leads her to think further about his **motivation** (the reason behind the action).

Seeing a play is like people watching. Your understanding of the characters is enriched by seeing their dress, gestures, and so on. When you read plays, it's important not to skip the **stage directions** (parenthetical notes by the playwright, at the beginning of the play or just before or just after a speech). These directions indicate what the characters are doing, describe their significant gestures and tone of voice, and often tell as much about the characters as do their words.

Although it may seem easier to notice gestures and movements of characters in plays or in works of fiction than in poetry, the speaker's words often indicate actions. In "Theme for English B," for example, the speaker's walk from the college "on the hill above Harlem" to his room at "the Harlem Branch Y" suggests the physical distance he must travel each day and also may hint at the distance he feels between himself and his white instructor.

By observing literary characters astutely and listening carefully to their words and thoughts, we bring them closer to our own lives. In much the same way, getting to know a person better may bring joy, pain, complication, challenge, frustration, and fulfillment.

Characters: Growing and Changing

In life, all of us grow and change every day. We often don't notice day-to-day changes because they are so small, but if we haven't seen someone for a while—for a year or two or even a few months—we usually notice differences, both in physical appearance and in the way the person thinks, speaks, and acts. To observe changes accurately, and to speculate on what brought about those changes, we have to know a person fairly well.

So it is with literary characters. Many times, a story, play, or poem shows a character who changes—a **dynamic character.** To be interested in the change, we need to know the character fairly well. He or she must come alive for us. To capture our interest, the author must create a **round** (well-developed) **character** rather than a **flat character** who shows only one or two characteristics. When Mark James talks about the grandparents in "Butterflies," he focuses on the qualities he observes: they try to give their granddaughter good advice; they listen to her; they show they are sensitive to her feelings by being quiet with her. Finally, Mark notes that the grandparents, particularly the grandfather, change at the end of the story. The grandfather sees that the teacher does not necessarily have all the right answers, or at least the only right answers. She does not know that butterflies can be harmful to cabbages, so she misunderstands the granddaughter's story. As Mark suggests, the grandfather's final comment strongly suggests that he will rethink his advice to "listen to the teacher."

Although "Butterflies" is a very short story, the grandfather comes alive as a round, dynamic character. The teacher, by contrast, is a flat character. She shows herself only in her single, rather rigid comment to the granddaughter. Flat characters are nearly always **static;** that is, they do not change. Round characters, however, may be either static or dynamic. And noting whether a round character changes or remains the same can lead you to ask significant questions about the work you are reading.

For example, consider Nathalie LaRochelle's observations about Byelinkov. She notices some negative qualities about Byelinkov, but she is also sympathetic to the questions he asks about Varinka's reasons for marrying him. She sees that Byelinkov is more than just a stereotypical fussy old schoolmaster; he shows more than one side to his character. When Nathalie comments on Byelinkov's action at the end of the play — ripping up the note and scattering the pieces — she wonders why he picks the pieces up again. She pushes the question further, speculating that the gathering up might reflect nothing more than Byelinkov's concern with neatness. According to this reading, Byelinkov has not been changed by the events of the afternoon. Now suppose the gathering up indicates that he wants to save the note, that he regrets his rejection both of Varinka and of the romantic gesture the note represents. If so, Byelinkov has grown and developed, and your response to him and to the play might be quite different from your response during the first reading.

Like our readings of the comments and actions of people we meet in everyday life, no single reading of literary characters' words or gestures is necessarily "correct." No one observation represents the "final answer." Instead, multiple possibilities exist. The important thing to remember is that all those possibilities must be suggested — and supported — by details in the text. Obviously we draw on our own life experiences and observations when we think about literary characters, but it's essential to keep in mind that the information that leads to our responses comes from what the work itself offers.

Characters: Point of View

Suppose you hear a friend talk angrily about an argument with a roommate and later hear the roommate describe the same disagreement. What are the chances that the two reports will be the same? Almost none. Accounts such as these are bound to be very different, primarily because they are being told from two distinct **points of view.** What information is offered? What is withheld? Which words are repeated? Which are suppressed? What significance is the incident given? The answers to all these questions depend on who is describing the argument. When you form your own opinion about the disagreement, you take into account who is recounting the incident. In much the same way, readers think carefully about point of view in literary works.

AUTHOR AND SPEAKER Distinguishing between author and speaker in a literary work is essential. Unlike roommates describing an argument, poets, playwrights, writers of fiction, and sometimes even writers of nonfiction are not necessarily telling personal stories. Although **authors** often do write about incidents or people from their own lives, they write through a created voice that is not necessarily identical to their own.

Carlene Indreasano points out this distinction between author and speaker. In her comment on "Theme for English B," she says that the events in the poem "could be something that happened to Hughes [the poet] or not." Carlene is absolutely right. In fact, Hughes did attend Columbia University (which does sit "on the hill above Harlem"), but it does not matter whether or not he received the assignment described and responded to it in the way described. What matters is that Hughes has created a **speaker (persona)** who describes receiving and responding to an assignment that asks students to "Go home and write / a page tonight. / And let that page come out of you— / Then, it will be true."

NARRATOR Just as the voice in a poem is called the speaker, the voice that tells a story (in a novel or short fiction) is called the **narrator.** (Sometimes a play has a narrator. For example, see the narrative sections in *The Glass Menagerie,* pages 173–223. Usually, however, a play unfolds directly from the character's dialogue, along with playwright's stage directions.)

In fiction, the narrator is sometimes **omniscient** (all-knowing), moving freely into the minds of all the characters. An omniscient narrator can report not only what characters look like, what they do, and what they say but also what they think. A variation is the **limited omniscient** narrator, who sees into the mind of only one character. Obviously, when the thoughts of only one character are reported, readers know more about that character than any other and see the events of the story — as well as the other characters — through that character's eyes.

Sometimes the narrator is also a character in the story. In this case, the narrator uses the **first person** ("I" or "we"). First-person narrators can, of course, report only what is in their own minds or what they see or hear. Omniscient, limited omniscient, and first-person narrators may also make evaluations — for example, they may state that a character is brave or silly or that an action was wise or foolhardy. As readers, we must consider the source of such judgments. Is the narrator **reliable** or **unreliable?** Is there reason to think that the narrator is suppressing information, is lying outright, or is simply incapable of seeing and understanding certain facts? Even if the narrator is reliable, keep in mind that the events are reported from that person's point of view — a different viewpoint might lead to a very different story. Consider, for example, how different the episode in "Butterflies" would be if it were told from the point of view of the teacher.

Sometimes the narrator is **objective,** like a sound camera that reports what it sees and hears. This point of view is used in the story "Butterflies." We are told what the characters do and say, but we are not taken inside their minds. Objective point of view leaves all evaluation and judgment to the reader. Even so, the narrator still has a great deal of power. This particular objective narrator, for example, shows us only the girl and her grandparents; we do not get to see the teacher and to observe for ourselves her response to the girl's story. It's always essential, then, to recognize that the speaker in a poem and the narrator (or characters) in a work of fiction or in drama show us only one way of looking at an experience, an object, a person, or an emotion. There are many other ways — left unexplored except in our own imaginations — of looking at that same experience, object, person, or emotion.

PEOPLE IN NONFICTION Nonfiction — essays, articles, letters, journals, documents — does not usually have fictional characters, yet in every work of nonfiction there is at least one very important point of view: the author's. Identifying and understanding the author's point of view help suggest the work's meaning. For instance, Dora DiFonzo notes that the father who talks about his son in "Education" uses humor. Yet behind the humor, Dora thinks, lie deep concern and — perhaps — a serious comment about the effect of school experiences not only on the child but also on the parents.

Terms Related to People

Characters: The fictional people who are part of the action of a literary work.

Dialogue: A conversation between two or more fictional characters.

Dialect: A variety of a language different from that generally taught in school; may include distinctive pronunciations of words, original vocabulary, or grammatical constructions that are not considered standard.

Monologue: A speech by one character addressed to a silent or absent listener.

Soliloquy: A speech by one character in a play, given while the character is alone on the stage or standing apart from other characters and intended to represent the inner thoughts of the character.

Motivation: The reason or reasons that cause a character to think, act, or speak in a certain way.

Stage directions: Comments by the playwright to provide actors (or readers) with information about actions and ways of speaking specific lines.

Dynamic character: A character who changes in some significant way during the course of the work.

Round character: A character who shows many different facets; often presented in depth and with great detail.

Flat character: A character who usually has only one outstanding trait or feature.

Static character: A character who does not change in any significant way during the course of the work.

Point of view: The position from which the details of the work are reported or described.

Author/speaker/persona/narrator: The *author* is the person who writes the literary work. Do not confuse the author with the *speaker* or *persona*, the voice that is heard in a poem, or the *narrator*, the voice that tells a work of fiction (or sometimes frames a play).

Omniscient narrator: A narrator who knows everything and can report both external actions and conversations as well as the internal thoughts of all characters and who often provides evaluations and judgments of characters and events.

Limited omniscient narrator: A narrator who can report external actions and conversations but who can describe the internal thoughts of only one character. A limited omniscient narrator may offer evaluations and judgments of characters and events.

First-person narrator: A narrator who is also a character in the work and who uses "I" or "we" to tell the story. First-person narrators can report their own thoughts but not the thoughts of others. They may offer evaluations and judgments of characters and events.

Reliable/unreliable narrators: A reliable narrator convinces readers that he or she is reporting events, actions, and conversations accurately and without prejudice. An unreliable narrator raises suspicions in the minds of readers that events, actions, and conversations may be reported inaccurately and that evaluations may reflect intentional or unintentional prejudice.

Objective narrator: A narrator who, like a camera, shows external events and conversations but cannot look inside the minds of characters or offer evaluations and judgments.

Exercises: People

1. Describe your first impressions of a person you now know well, noting what caused you to have these impressions. Then explain your current view of this person. Discuss what events, conversations, actions, or interactions either confirmed or changed your initial impression.

2. Think of a film you have seen or a book you have read in which the characters changed significantly. Explain what the characters were like both before and after the change. What motivated the change? What was your response to the change?

3. Read (or reread) any of the works listed in Exercise 3, page 29. Think about how the point of view of the speaker, narrator, or characters affects your response to that work. Try rewriting one section of the work from a different point of view. For example, if the poem or story uses the first-person point of view, try changing every instance of "I" to "he" or "she." Or, if the story or poem is told from an omniscient point of view, try retelling it through the eyes of one of the characters (consider minor characters as well as major characters). Explain how you think the work would change if it were told from this new point of view.

PLACES AND TIMES

This story ("Butterflies") makes me very confused. I can see the grandparents are farmers who probably grow their own food or maybe sell food, so it seems like they are in an isolated place. Also, I thought maybe this happened a long time ago because in some ways it sounds like a fairy tale or any story that might start like: "In a faraway place, long ago. . . ." But then they talk about the supermarket, so it's got to be modern and not too isolated. And I don't get the part about the teacher buying her cabbages in supermarkets. What does that have to do with the butterflies? *Lara Zoufally*

First I look at the introductory sentence under "Scene" [in *The Man in a Case*], and I see "1898" which, right away, makes me know I am not going to like this play because I like to read modern things. Then, I don't know where Mironitski is (but I figure that out from "Moscow" in the first speech of Varinka — Russia). So now I am totally turned off because it's also a country I don't know much about and am not really interested in. What is funny is that as I read even though there are things I don't know — like "little stale babka" — basically, Byelinkov and Varinka could be this couple I know! She is really crazy and does things that are wild and slightly illegal (driving too fast, etc.). He is — I know this is unbelievable — just like B. Even to the round glasses and the "being neat" stuff. But these people are still together, so maybe there's hope for V and B at the end. (He *could* learn to ride a bike!!!) So how much difference is there between love in Russia (1898) and love in the U.S. (1990)? *Tanya Elizah*

Places and Times in "Theme for English B": I would say the time is both past and present. You start in the present, jump to the past, then back to the present. Places? Well, the speaker is in one place — walking from his college to his room at the Harlem Branch Y — but, on the other hand, there is another place, too, which is inside his mind when he thinks back to the past. I looked up Winston-Salem and it's in the South, and there is also a Durham, N.C., so Durham could be (and probably is) south, too. I think this is important — the North and the South all together because the speaker seems to come to a point about being American and having all the parts (people and parts of the country, I think he means) connected. They have to interact whether they want to or not. *Paul Medino*

This essay ["Education"] must have been written quite a few years ago because I don't think that now even way out in the country they have schools where the teachers have to cook on a stove in the classroom (except for homemaking classes, I mean). And I think it would be a fire hazard to heat a school with a stove. But other than those things, both of the schools seemed like places that could exist today. I liked the way the author seemed to make the point that it didn't matter that the city school had all this fancy equipment. The country school was better because of the people. I think that's true now. There's too much push for more money to build schools and to make the *place* better, but what needs more attention is the people. *Ray Conover*

"Where do you come from?" You can expect new acquaintances to ask this question. Learning where others were born or grew up or discovering where they have lived or traveled helps us understand them better. In some cases, a new friend comes from a place where customs and values are different from ours. For instance, most people in the United States believe that not looking another person in the eye indicates shame or deceit. In some cultures, however, looking directly at another individual is a sign of boldness and lack of respect.

Time can be as important as place in determining the way a person thinks and acts. Consider the way people from different generations characteristically think about circumstances and ideas. For instance, many people who lived through the Great Depression of the 1930s attach more importance to saving money and achieving job security than people who have not experienced widespread poverty and unemployment. Although not all people who live in a particular time think exactly the same way, recognizing the influence of time helps us understand and appreciate the differences we observe in our daily lives.

In reading literature, it is just as important as it is in daily life to think about time and place, the **setting** of the work.

Place

Lara Zoufally raises important questions about the setting of "Butterflies." She notices that the grandparents seem to live in a somewhat isolated place where they farm and grow their own vegetables. But, Lara notes, they can't be too isolated because the grandfather talks about supermarkets. When Lara read this journal entry aloud in class, another student, Rolf Jensen, responded to her final question, "What does that have to do with the butterflies?" He explained that certain butterflies lay eggs on cabbages. The eggs hatch into caterpillars that eat the cabbages. For a farm family, killing the butterflies is a useful — even necessary — act. Like the teacher in the story, Lara (and many readers) may not immediately see the irony in the teacher's response to the granddaughter's story. Rolf, who grew up in a family that farmed, was able to provide the information, related to the setting, that made the story meaningful for Lara.

In addition to talking with others, readers can sometimes uncover information about setting by finding out something about the author's background. Reference books, such as *Contemporary Authors, Dictionary of Literary Biography,* and *American Authors, 1600–1900,* are useful resources. For instance, if you knew that Patricia Grace, the author of "Butterflies," was a Maori New Zealander, you could read about the Maori population. Although you can't assume that Grace is definitely writing about the Maori culture, you might find details that suggest a larger context for the grandparents' way of speaking, for their value of education, and for their relationship with their granddaughter.

So, as you read "Butterflies," it's helpful to think about the location — a somewhat isolated farm — and it's interesting to speculate that the farm may be part of a Maori village in New Zealand. Smaller details of setting are also important. For instance, in "Theme for English B," the speaker describes "the steps from the hill" that lead to the Harlem Y, where he takes the elevator (another detail of setting) and goes to his room (yet another setting). Paul Medino also notes an intriguing aspect of the setting in "Theme for English B." Much of the setting is inside the speaker's mind. The speaker recalls the Southern cities where he was born and went to school. Later, he talks directly to Harlem (lines 18 and 19) as though it were a person. The **exterior** (outside) **setting** in this poem in many ways reflects and enhances our understanding of the **interior setting:** the setting inside the speaker's mind and heart.

Sometimes place is the main focus of a work. For example, in E. B. White's "Education," the two schools, and their surroundings, are central. Details of setting fill the essay. The "cold curbs" and "cinder court" in the city contrast sharply with the country roads and unsupervised playground in the country. The settings imply the more important spiritual difference suggested by the author's final paragraph: his son now sleeps better, and his school day goes by "like lightning."

Time

Tanya Elizah was disappointed when she read the **stage directions** at the beginning of *The Man in a Case* and discovered that the play took place not only in a location she had never heard of but also during a time that she believed would not interest her. She discovered, however, that the conversations, conflicts, and actions of the characters transcended their own time. Varinka and Byelinkov reminded her of people she knew, leading her to ask how much difference there is between love in 1898 Russia and love in the present-day United States.

If Tanya had pursued this question, she might have noticed that, in spite of the many similarities, there are also real differences. In the United States today, a woman would hardly be regarded as revolutionary for riding a bicycle — and even if she were, there are few laws today that forbid to women actions allowed to men. Also, although there are certainly women today who are eager to marry, few of them would spend their 20s living on their parents' farm, apparently engaged in no occupation other than hoping that some man would finally look at them and "see a wife." Varinka's passive way of living seems to contradict her lively, unconventional spirit unless we remember that, in 1898, women of the upper and middle classes had very limited options. Most either married or were dependents of any male relative who would take them in.

The stage directions (essential to the understanding of a play) often provide details of setting; you can learn other details from the comments and observations the characters make. For example, Varinka and Byelinkov both talk about the lilacs and roses in bloom in the garden, so we can infer that the play takes place in the spring. How might this point be significant? Consider, for example, how the drama would change if it took place in a cavernous, dark, wood-paneled living room lit only by the flames in a large fireplace and if Byelinkov placed a sprig of holly instead of lilacs in Varinka's hair.

Writers understand the power of time and often use time in special ways. For instance, Paul Medino says that the time in "Theme for English B" is "both past and present," noting that the poem begins "in the present, jump(s) to the past, then back to the present." The events in the poem do not take place in chronological order, with the speaker telling us about his birth, his early education, then about his present education. Instead, the poem begins in the present, with the instructor's assignment; then there is a **flashback,** a description of events that occurred earlier. Whenever a writer chooses to change time sequence — to work with a structure other than chronological order — the reader should ask why. How is my response affected by the way time is used in this work? For instance, what if the instructor's words (and the question in line 6) were not given until after line 10?

Terms Related to Places and Times

Setting: The time and place of a literary work. Setting includes social, political, and economic background as well as geographic, physical locations.

Exterior setting: Aspects of setting that exist outside of the characters.

Interior setting: Aspects of setting that exist inside the minds and hearts of the characters.

Stage directions: Comments by the playwright to provide actors (or readers) with information about the times and places in which the play is set.

Flashback: An interruption in the chronological order of a work by description of earlier occurrences.

Exercises: Places and Times

1. Write a paragraph or two about an event that took place before you were born (for example, the passage of the 19th amendment, which gave women the right to vote; the Vietnam War; President Kennedy's assassination). Then interview someone who was alive then and remembers the event. After the interview, write another paragraph indicating anything new that you have learned, explaining which of your ideas and impressions were confirmed and which were changed.

2. Think about films and television programs you have seen recently. Then discuss one whose setting strikes you as especially important. First, explain the place and the time and then describe how the setting relates to the characters and their actions. What would happen if these characters and their story were transported to another time and/or place?

3. Read (or reread) any of the works listed in Exercise 3, page 29. Explain when and where the work takes place. How can you identify times and locations? Think about how the setting affects your response to that work. What aspects of the work would be greatly changed if the setting

were changed? Do any aspects seem "timeless" and "placeless" (aspects that would be meaningful and important in nearly any place or time)? Explain.

WORDS AND IMAGES, SOUNDS AND PATTERNS

You [the instructor] said "Theme for English B" is a poem, but it seems more like a speech or maybe a journal entry to me. The assignment from the speaker's teacher (lines 2–5) is like a poem with rhyme words at the end of lines. Also, I noticed a few other rhymes like "write"/"white" (lines 27–28), "true"/"you" (lines 36–37), and "me"/ "free"/"B" (line 38 and lines 40–41). But most of this "Theme," when you read it out loud and don't look at the way the lines are set up on the page, could be just a regular paragraph. So why is it a poem? Because it begins and ends with the rhyming lines? *Terence Sullivan*

The butterflies mean one thing to the grandparents and the grand-daughter and something else to the teacher. Now, I think I am supposed to sympathize with the granddaughter, and I do feel sorry for her that her teacher didn't like her story. But the teacher's view of butterflies is more like my own. I think they are beautiful, and I was really shocked to think about the granddaughter drawing a picture of killing them. When she said that, it really gave me a strange feeling because I thought it was very odd and not what I expected. So to the granddaughter the butterflies are one thing and to the teacher another (and I feel more or less like the teacher, but I see the granddaughter's reason). So who is right here about butterflies? This is something to think about. *Naomi Rousseau*

Just look at the way Byelinkov and Varinka talk and you know they are two opposite people. Varinka just goes on and on and uses lots of cute expressions like calling Byelinkov a "little school mouse" and talking about his "perfectly pressed pants" and his "sweet little galoshes." Byelinkov tells her, "You are fond of expletives" (which according to my dictionary means a word or phrase that is not needed for the sense of a sentence). Byelinkov likes to talk in short sentences and to give advice: "Pride can be an imperfect value" and "Being married requires a great deal of responsibility." Varinka likes to compare Byelinkov to things, like a mouse, a dancing bear, and a stale babka and to famous people in Russian history like Lermontov, Tchaikovsky, and Peter the Great. She sees that the roses are beautiful, but he sees beetles in the roses. To my mind, he talks about translating Greek and Latin poetry — which he probably thinks is beautiful — but Varinka sees things around her as beautiful and special and Byelinkov doesn't even really seem to look at those things. *Maureen Wimselski*

The absolute best thing in this essay is the school bus in the city. It's hilarious but it also shows a kind of terror. First White says the bus is "punctual as death." Then the school bus proceeds to "open its mouth" and apparently eat up the boy. Then it takes off like a vicious animal "with an angry growl." To me this says it all. Going to that school is like death — or like getting eaten up by a beast. You can just feel the dread of the kid (or maybe it's the father's dread, maybe he remembers his own school days). *Gerald Stryker*

One of the things that gives life to a fictional character is the way that character speaks. We come to identify certain words and expressions with that particular character.

Style

A character's style, then, is established by the way that person speaks and acts. Of course, authors choose the words and phrases that make up their characters' speech, describe their actions, and create the setting in which they speak and act. We need to keep this in mind when we consider exactly what it is that distinguishes the **style** of one writer from another. And, of course, it's essential to ask how a writer's style affects your response to that person's literary work. Why do you like one style better than another? Why does one style bore, puzzle, or annoy you whereas another delights, informs, and makes you want to read on? How does the author's style relate to the meaning or meanings you discover in the work or to the questions the work raises?

Tone

Tone, the attitude of the author to the characters and situations in the work, is closely related to style. For example, Gerald Stryker notes that, in "Education," E. B. White uses humorous images that are tinged with seriousness (even terror). The yellow city school bus that "swallows" the child in the story is funny, but White's words also suggest that a child can be overwhelmed by the trappings and demands of certain kinds of schooling. The tone here is complex, and it suggests the complexity the author sees in his subject.

Diction

Diction (choice of words) helps to establish a writer's style and tone. Some writers, for example, choose to use many descriptive words, whereas some use almost none. Consider the contrast between the speeches Wendy Wasserstein gives her characters in *The Man in a Case* and the language of the narrator and characters in Patricia Grace's "Butterflies." Wasserstein's play is filled with language that appeals to all the senses **(imagery);** we can easily conjure up the scent of the lilacs and roses; the anticipated delicious apricots and cream; the picture of Byelinkov wrapped in his "quilts and curtains" as he retires for the night. In contrast, Grace's story focuses on only one image: that of the butterflies. The description is spare and, as Lara Zoufally (page 37) notes, the story "sounds like a fairy tale or any story that might start like: 'In a faraway place, long ago. . . .'" Lara notices, then, that the language of "Butterflies" makes it sound like one of those childhood tales, perhaps a fable. The story's language raises questions about its meaning. Does it have a simple moral — or lesson — as a fable does? Or is Patricia Grace's story more complex than that?

Syntax

Syntax is the arrangement of words in phrases or sentences and the arrangement of phrases or sentences in paragraphs (fiction), speeches (plays), or lines and stanzas (poetry). Choices related to syntax are aspects of a writer's style. Terence Sullivan raises an important question when he notes that much of "Theme for English B" sounds like a paragraph of regular prose. Unless you look at the arrangement of the sentences and phrases into lines and stanzas, you might not be aware that you are reading a poem. Why does Langston Hughes choose this syntax to write about this experience? The speaker, after all, describes an assignment to which most students would respond by writing a carefully planned essay with an opening paragraph, thesis statement, body, and conclusion. Why, then, does he respond with a poem?

Rhythm and Rhyme

Closely connected to the syntax of a work — and also part of a writer's style — are **rhythm** (the pattern of sound) and **rhyme** (the matching of final sounds in two or more words). The rhythms of many parts of "Theme for English B," for example, are the rhythms of everyday prose speech. Yet, as Terence Sullivan notes, the instructor's assignment at the beginning sounds like a traditional poem. You can read these lines aloud in an exaggerated way to hear the regular beat:

> Gŏ hóme aňd wríte
> ă páge tŏníght.
> Aňd lét thăt páge cŏme oút ŏf yóu —
> Thén, ĭt wíll bĕ trúe.

It's intriguing that the instructor's words have such a regular pattern, seeming to lead logically to the speaker/student's otherwise unconventional essay poem. Perhaps this student sees and hears the world in terms of poetic sound and patterns?

Terence Sullivan also comments on rhyme; he wonders if a poem that doesn't rhyme in a regular pattern is really a poem, raising the question of how to distinguish between poetry and prose. Terence notes that the poem begins and ends with rhyming lines, creating, in a sense, bookends of strong end rhymes to frame the rest of the poem. In addition to using end rhymes, the poet also uses internal rhyme. Look at lines 16 and 17, for instance.

It's not easy to know what is **true** for **you** or me
at twenty-**two,** my age.

And the next three lines have six one-syllable words that rhyme with "you"; the repetition of these words and, of course, the fact that they rhyme contribute to a subtle, insistent poetic rhythm even while the speaker seems simply to be conversing in everyday speech.

Notice also, in line 24, the list of records the speaker likes: "Bessie, bop, or Bach." These choices represent a wide range of musical taste, and notice also that the words sound musical as you pronounce them. The identical initial sounds create **alliteration.**

Of course, alliteration is not a device used strictly by poets: the romantic Varinka, as Maureen Wimselski notes, describes Byelinkov's "perfectly pressed pants." The rhythmic sound of the initial "p's" underlines the extravagance of her speech and makes many readers smile in sympathy at Byelinkov's complaint that she is "fond of expletives."

Figurative Language

As they work, writers choose whether and when to use **figurative language:** words or expressions that carry more than their literal meaning. Wendy Wasserstein, for instance, fills Varinka's speeches with **metaphors** (comparisons of unlike objects). Varinka calls Byelinkov "my little school mouse," "my sweetest dancing bear," and "my little stale babka." Byelinkov also makes comparisons, but his are less direct; he uses **similes** (comparisons of unlike things using the words "like" or "as"), such as "You speak about me as if I were your pet" and "You dance like a school mouse."

Sometimes the writer's figurative language allows a reader to see an object in a new way. For example, in "Theme for English B," the speaker uses an **apostrophe** (he speaks directly to an inanimate object or place) when he says: "I feel and see and hear. Harlem, I hear you." The apostrophe seems to show that he feels connected to Harlem, perhaps as he would feel connected to a close friend or relative. During class discussion of this work, Terence Sullivan (whose response to the poem appears on page 42) wondered why, when the speaker says he also hears New York, he does not choose to speak directly to that city as he does to Harlem.

Personification means giving an inanimate object the characteristics of a person or animal. E. B. White's beastlike school bus is an excellent example of this kind of figurative language. We can see the bus bearing down on its innocent victim, and we certainly get the impression that city schooling, for White, has more to do with being a helpless captive than a willing participant.

A writer sometimes repeats a word or image so many times in a literary work that you begin to wonder why. Why, for instance, does Patricia Grace call her story "Butterflies" and use butterflies as the central image? Naomi Rousseau writes that the "butterflies mean one thing to the grandparents and the granddaughter and something else to the teacher." And, to the reader, the butterflies may come to have a different meaning from either of those two. The butterflies, then, become a **symbol,** standing for more than just winged creatures that lay eggs on cabbages. The butterflies may indicate the great diversity of ways to look at the world around us; they may suggest the need not to limit ourselves, but to stay open to many possibilities.

Verbal Irony

Just as there can be discrepancies between what a character says and what a character does or between what a character believes to be true and what the reader knows to be true (irony of situation, page 27), so, too, can there be discrepancies between what a character or author says and what he or she means **(verbal irony).** For example, when Varinka compares Byelinkov to Lermontov, Tchaikovsky, and Peter the Great (all respected Russian men), Byelinkov adds, "Ivan the Terrible." Of course, Byelinkov does not really mean he is like the merciless tyrant; he is being ironic. But Varinka either doesn't pick up on the irony or replies with an ironic statement of her own, "Yes, him too." Whether Varinka is intentionally ironic or not, the discrepancies underline the enormous differences between these two would-be lovers.

Allusions

To understand the irony just described, you have to know that Lermontov, Tchaikovsky, and Peter the Great are all admired figures from Russian history and that Ivan the Terrible (whose name should give him away) was a ruthless czar. When writers use **allusions** (references to events, people, and places outside the work itself), you can usually figure out what is going on from the context. However, if you are interested in adding an extra dimension to your reading, it's easy enough to find the references in a dictionary or encyclopedia. *Webster's New World Dictionary,* for instance, would let you know that Lermontov was a Russian poet and novelist, Tchaikovsky a composer, and Peter the Great a czar. Knowing these specific definitions underlines the extent of Varinka's exaggerations; she considers — or perhaps wishes — her fiancé to be the equal of the most outstanding writers, composers, and rulers of their country.

Terms Related to Words and Images, Sounds and Patterns

Style: The way an author chooses words; arranges them in lines, sentences, paragraphs, or stanzas; and conveys meaning through the use of imagery, rhythm, rhyme, figurative language, irony, and other devices.

Tone: The attitude of the author toward the subject of the work.

Diction: Choice of words.

Imagery: Words that appeal to the five senses: touch, taste, sight, hearing, and smell.

Syntax: The way words are arranged in phrases or sentences and the way phrases or sentences are arranged in paragraphs (fiction), speeches (plays), or lines and stanzas (poetry).

Rhythm: Pattern of sound.

Rhyme: The matching of final sounds in two or more words.

Alliteration: The repetition of identical initial sounds in neighboring words or syllables.

Figurative language: Words or expressions that carry more than their literal meaning.

Metaphor: Comparison of two unlike things.

Simile: Comparison of two unlike things, using the words "like" or "as."

Apostrophe: Addressing an inanimate object or place as if it were alive.

Personification: Giving an inanimate object the qualities of a person or animal.

Symbol: In a literary work, an object, action, person, or animal that stands for something more than its literal meaning.

Verbal irony: A discrepancy between what is said and what is meant or between what is said and what the reader knows to be true.

Allusion: A reference to a person, place, object, or event outside the work itself.

Exercises: Words and Images, Sounds and Patterns

1. Think of three friends or acquaintances who speak in a distinctive way. Imagine a conversation between these three people (even though they may not know each other). Write the conversation and then explain briefly what special qualities you notice in the way these three people speak. What would make you recognize these people if you could hear but not see them?

2. For one day, carry a small notebook with you and write down every example of figurative language you see or hear. Keep your mind open to all kinds of possibilities: explanations in textbooks, the language of sports reporters, the speeches of politicians, the exaggerations of advertising. And, of course, stay alert to overheard conversations as well as to your own speech. At the end of the day, write a brief comment describing your discoveries and your response to those discoveries.

3. Read, reread, or reconsider any of the works listed in Exercise 3, page 29. Try reading a section (a stanza, a paragraph or two) aloud and (if possible) have someone else read the same section aloud so that you can listen. What do you notice about sounds, images, words, patterns? Describe your response to the author's (or a character's) diction, to a particularly striking or strange image, to an intriguing use of figurative language, or to the rhythm (or rhyme) of a work.

IDEAS

The following excerpts from journal entries show the ideas students discovered as they read, discussed, and thought about "Butterflies," *The Man in a Case,* and "Theme for English B." The italicized sentences represent general statements that could apply beyond the work itself.

"Butterflies" shows how easy — and how dangerous — it is to look at the world around you in just one way. The teacher sees only the beauty in the butterfly and doesn't even consider any other possibility. Because she doesn't know about, or try to find out about, another possibility, her student goes home very puzzled and unhappy. *Lara Zoufally*

The butterflies symbolize destruction to the grandparents and beauty to the teacher. Who is right? Neither. *People see things according to their own perspective and sometimes this causes problems in communication.* Sure, maybe the teacher should have asked the granddaughter about her picture without making such a judgment. But, on the other hand, the grandparents maybe need to look more carefully and see that even though the butterflies cause problems, they are also beautiful. *Naomi Rousseau*

"Theme for English B" has ideas both of separation and of connection. The speaker is physically apart from his instructor. The instructor is at the college on the hill in NYC, and the speaker is back in his room in Harlem. But the speaker is writing an assignment for the instructor, so even though there's separation, there's connection. And I think this is very important and what is meant by "As I learn from you, / I guess you learn from me." The instructor learns from the student while the student learns from the teacher because both have different experiences and knowledge to give. *What is meant here is that everyone can gain from listening to someone else who is different from themselves. Paul Medino*

As the speaker walks and walks to his room in Harlem, it seems like his thoughts are walking, too. And you get the impression that those thoughts walk all over America. He's looking at what it means to be a black person in America, and he's arguing that white people have to see that black people are just as American as they are. Even for people who may not like it. As he says, the instructor is "a part of me, as I am a part of you." *Whites had better realize that blacks are part of America, too, and that there has to be some kind of connection between the two parts. Mark James*

Varinka makes fun of Byelinkov for being so stuffy and wearing galoshes all the time. True, he has a rather rigid way of looking at things, but Varinka is also rigid. For instance, she wants to get married to have "the life everyone else has" and to "not be different." And she wants Byelinkov to fit into one specific role — a hero, like Peter the Great. *To me, people have to let others be themselves. Love doesn't come from trying to change someone. You have to accept people as they are.* Nathalie LaRochelle

I kept thinking and thinking about the title: *The Man in a Case.* I saw the line where Byelinkov says that he thought he "would grow old preserved like those which are left over, wrapped suitably in my case of curtains and quilts." I realized that later Varinka tells him, "You are wrapping yourself under curtains and quilts." So, to me, some of the curtains and quilts were the real ones on his bed, but they were also a metaphor. Those curtains and quilts are like a cocoon, an outer case, that Byelinkov has to protect himself against experiences of the world. But you get the impression that Byelinkov will never "hatch" out into maturity. *Protection like that has a cost. Insulation against experiences of the world — even something simple like eating peaches and cream for lunch — means that a person may lose the chance of human connection (of love, in this case).* Maureen Wimselski

White may say that the only difference he sees in the two schools is that his son "sleeps better at night." It's clear to me, however, that he's really saying something quite different. *A simple and uncomplicated schooling is better in every way than a school that has too many trend-setting new programs.* In the city, his son gets "worked on," but in the country it seems to be the boy who does the work and the teacher is just there to help. She gives him food for his body and food for his mind. It's simple and direct — not planned by a dietician or other fancy experts. Marianne Bachmann

After reading a work carefully, with mind and spirit fully open to actions, events, people, places, times, sounds, images, words, and patterns, a reader may well feel overwhelmed. "What does it all mean?" "What's the point?" "What am I supposed to get from this?" "What's the lesson here?" "What's the author trying to say?" These questions — and others — often nag insistently at us, giving us the sense that even though the work evoked a definite response, something more has been left undiscovered.

These questions lead you to consider **theme,** the central idea you seek as you read a work and think about it. The theme of a work is a generalization: an idea that can be broadly applied both to the work itself and to real-life situations outside the work. For example, consider Maureen Wimselski's statement: *"Protection like that has a cost. Insulation against experiences of the world —* even something simple like eating peaches and cream for lunch — *means that a person may lose the chance of human connection (of love, in this* case)." The italicized words represent a general statement of theme that could apply to people and circumstances very different from those in Wasserstein's play. The details from the play are examples that demonstrate how Maureen arrived at her larger idea, her statement of theme.

It's important to understand that "meaning" is not fixed in literature. Two people reading the same work may see different themes. One person reading a work at age twenty and the same work at age thirty or forty-five may see different themes. Literary scholars reading the same work frequently see different themes. So, questions such as, "What am I supposed to get from this?" do not have a specific, easily defined answer. Although it's interesting — and often helpful — to know what others think about a work, their ideas should not define what any other reader is "supposed to get" from the work.

Some literary works, such as fables and biblical parables, do have a lesson or a moral that is directly stated by the writer. Most works, however, convey their meaning indirectly. Whether or not there is something to be learned — and what that something is — depends on what the reader discovers in the work and on how those discoveries interact with what the reader already knows, thinks, or feels about the subject of the work. Sometimes a work of literature causes us to think differently about something; sometimes it reinforces what we already believe, adding new details to support our current beliefs and emotions; sometimes we encounter a work whose main idea offends or angers us. A reader who is affronted by a work is likely to see a very different theme than the reader whose values are reaffirmed by the same work.

What a writer intended to say is not necessarily what the work "says" to various readers. So the question "What is the writer trying to say?" is not really very helpful. For example, a writer may convey one thing to an audience from her or his own time and something quite different to an audience reading the same work a century later. The reader — not the author — defines the theme, although, of course, the reader's ideas relate directly to what the author has written.

As you read the students' responses at the beginning of this section, you almost certainly noticed that those who commented on the same works had quite different views. For instance, Lara Zoufally focused on the teacher's narrow view in "Butterflies," whereas Naomi Rousseau thought that both the grandparents and the teacher lacked something in the way they looked at butterflies. As you read the story, you might have discovered still another theme. Notice that both Lara and Naomi use specific details and examples from the story to support their generalization (their statement of theme). Because they offer evidence from their reading, it's easy to see how they arrived at their ideas. Direct references to the work make these statements of theme convincing and thought-provoking.

As you think about a work and the main idea it conveys to you, remember to support your observations with specific references to the work.

Don't be intimidated by the thought that theme must be some hidden secret. Instead, look at what you know about the work, what you have felt, what you have observed as you read. Work from the strength of what you do know rather than assuming that you are faced with a mysterious puzzle.

Exercises: Theme

1. Choose a film that you have seen more than once and that you think is worth seeing again. Write a paragraph or two explaining why you feel so strongly about this film. As part of your explanation, include a brief discussion of the film's theme.
2. Write a response to one of the students' comments at the beginning of this section. Explain why you agree or disagree with the way that student sees the work in question.
3. Read, reread, or rethink any of the selections listed in Exercise 3, page 29. Write a response that includes your view of the work's theme. Be sure to make specific references to the work to explain what you say.

3

Writing about Literature

At first I hated that we have to keep journals for this class, but after a while what I noticed is that when I write about some poem or story that we've read, I find out ideas I didn't know I had. *Maurine Buckley*

For me reading has always been my best pleasure. Even when I was only five or six, people were always saying, "She's always got her nose in a book." Writing about what I read is not that hard for me. What I like best is starting a paper with what I think is a great idea and then finding out while I'm writing that a lot of other ideas are in my head, too. So it's a way to think about what I've read. *Nadine Nuñez*

No way will I ever "enjoy" writing a paper, but I do have to say that one thing that happens is this: When I start really thinking about an idea I have for a paper, and listening hard to class discussion, and pushing thoughts around in my brain and then trying out writing them, I sometimes find that I've changed my mind from my first reaction to the story, poem, or whatever. This is a big step because I don't usually change my mind. So for me, writing in this class has made me see that an idea might start out in one direction, but when you really think about it, it might take you some place entirely different. *Tim Janning*

Maurine, Nadine, and Tim, students in an introductory course called "Literature and Writing," reacted to writing about literature in different ways. Nadine found putting her ideas in writing rather easy. Maurine and Tim at first saw writing as an obstacle: a requirement to be dutifully carried out. As the semester progressed, however, they all discovered an important insight that Nadine suggests: Writing is a way of thinking. Maurine found that her journal entries helped her to discover ideas she didn't know she had; Tim saw that the mental energy required to really think through a topic for a paper often led him to modify his initial way of reading and responding to a work.

The value, then, of writing about literature is the same as the value of writing honestly and with emotional and intellectual vigor about any subject: the hard work brings new ways of understanding, of thinking and feeling. Both the process of writing and the final product provide the satisfaction of learning new ways to perceive, to speculate, to wonder, and to know.

This chapter explains strategies for and approaches to writing about literature by using samples of students' spoken and written responses to the following two poems. You'll find the samples of students' writing more meaningful if you take time now to read the poems and to respond to them through both discussion and writing.

DYLAN THOMAS (1914–1953)

Do Not Go Gentle into That Good Night

Do not go gentle into that good night,
Old age should burn and rave at close of day;
Rage, rage against the dying of the light.

Though wise men at their end know dark is right,
Because their words had forked no lightning they   5
Do not go gentle into that good night.

Good men, the last wave by, crying how bright
Their frail deeds might have danced in a green bay,
Rage, rage against the dying of the light.

Wild men who caught and sang the sun in flight,   10
And learn, too late, they grieved it on its way,
Do not go gentle into that good night.

Grave men, near death, who see with blinding sight
Blind eyes could blaze like meteors and be gay,
Rage, rage against the dying of the light.   15

And you, my father, there on the sad height,
Curse, bless, me now with your fierce tears, I pray,
Do not go gentle into that good night.
Rage, rage against the dying of the light.

Responding to "Do Not Go Gentle into That Good Night"

1. Given the details of the poem, how do you picture the speaker in the poem? How do you picture his father?
2. What advice does the speaker in this poem give to his father? What is your response to this advice?
3. Imagine that you are the father, hearing this advice. What might you say in a letter answering your son?
4. Read the poem aloud and, if possible, listen to the poem being read aloud. Try using a different tone of voice or emphasizing different phrases. Notice whether — and how — your response to the poem changes with these variations.

JOAN ALESHIRE (1947–   )

Slipping

Age comes to my father as a slow
slipping: the leg that weakens, will
barely support him, the curtain of mist
that falls over one eye. Years, like
pickpockets, lift his concentration,   5
memory, fine sense of direction. The car,
as he drives, drifts from lane to lane
like a raft on a river, speeds and slows
for no reason, keeps missing turns.

As my mother says, "He's never liked   10
to talk about feelings," but tonight
out walking, as I slow to match his pace —
his left leg trailing a little like
a child who keeps pulling on your hand — he says,
"I love you so much." Darkness, and the sense   15
we always have that each visit may be
the last, have pushed away years of restraint.

A photograph taken of him teaching—
white coat, stethoscope like a pet snake
around his neck, chair tipped back   20
against the lecture-room wall—shows
a man talking, love of his work lighting
his face—in a way we seldom saw at home.
I answer that I love him, too, but
hardly knowing him, what I love   25
is the way reserve has slipped from
his feeling, like a screen suddenly
falling, exposing someone dressing or
washing: how wrinkles ring a bent neck,
how soft and mutable is the usually hidden flesh.   30

Responding to "Slipping"

1. How did you respond to the description of the father in the first stanza? Was this response changed or reinforced after you finished reading the poem? Explain.
2. How do you imagine the relationships among the family members described in this poem? What facts about their lives do the details of the poem show? What can you infer from those details?
3. Explain your response to the speaker's attitude regarding the changes in her father.
4. Try writing this poem as though it were a prose paragraph. Copy the sentences and punctuation exactly as they appear, but arrange the sentences in a paragraph rather than in lines. Pay attention to the length of the sentences as you write them and to the way some of the sentences are punctuated with dashes. Does reading the new arrangement change your response to the poem? Explain.

THE PROCESS OF WRITING ABOUT LITERATURE

Understanding the Assignment

When you are writing about literature for a class, your writing assignments originate—at least to some extent—from your instructor. It's important to have a clear notion of what you are being asked to do. An assignment may be quite open ("Write an essay responding to any work we have read this semester"), or it may be structured in a number of ways. Read or listen to the assignment carefully before you begin planning how you will fulfill it.

Thinking about the Assignment

Keep in mind the following questions as you begin thinking about an assignment:

1. Does the assignment ask that your subject be a specific work or works?
2. Does the assignment ask that you focus on a specific genre (poetry, fiction, drama, essay)?
3. Does the assignment ask that you focus on a particular aspect of the literary work or works (for example, on the images of war or on the concept of honor)?
4. Does the assignment specify an audience, real (for instance, will you be reading part or all of the paper to the class?) or imagined (for example, will you be writing a fictional letter from one character to another?)?
5. Does the assignment ask for a particular approach or organization? For example, are you being asked to compare? To explicate? To evaluate? (These approaches and methods of organization are explained and demonstrated on pages 66–96.)
6. Does the assignment specify a length? (The focus of a two-page paper will be quite different from that of a ten-page paper.)
7. Does the assignment ask for (or allow) research?
8. Does the assignment ask that you discover a topic for yourself?

Keeping these questions in mind, read the following assignment. The instructor wants students to write a paper of two to four pages (typewritten, double-spaced). When they submit their papers, students are to give a brief talk (three to five minutes) explaining the most significant point of the paper.

Assignment Topics (Choose One)

1. Briefly summarize your response to one of these poems and then, using a personal narrative, explain that response, making references to the poem that show its connection to your narrative.
2. Explore the similarities and differences you see between these poems. Then write a paper explaining what you discovered and what significance you find in these similarities and differences.
3. What, exactly, does the speaker say in each poem? And how does he or she say it? Look carefully at the language in the poems. Then choose one poem and explain how the central idea of the poem unfolds as you read from one stanza to the next.
4. Consider the values and beliefs suggested by each of these poems. Choose one of the poems and explain those values and beliefs as well as your evaluation of them. Do you agree with them completely? Question them? Explain.
5. Discover a question related to Thomas's "Do Not Go Gentle" and do research to explore that question. In your paper, refer to at least three sources.

Writing to Respond

A response paper can take many different directions, but remember that part of the point of the paper is to help those who read it understand the connections you made. Why did this particular poem, short story, play, or essay evoke a sad memory or recall a triumph? What details affected you strongly? You need to show your audience exactly what you felt as you were reading the work. Avoid simply announcing that you liked or didn't like what you read. Showing means finding examples that will make sense to your readers. For this reason, you should reread the work carefully several times to find telling examples. To write a strong response paper, you need to make clear and frequent references to the work that evoked the thoughts and feelings you'll be discussing.

Topic 1

Briefly summarize your response to one of these poems and then, using a personal narrative, explain that response, making references to the poem that show its connection to your narrative.

This assignment asks for the reader's response, that is, for the personal and individual feelings and thoughts evoked by the experience of reading either Thomas's or Aleshire's poems. In this case, the topic asks for an example from the reader's experience that will support, develop, and explain that response.

DISCOVERING IDEAS: JOURNAL ENTRIES After reading the assignment sheet, Karen Angstrom decided that she would like to work with the first assignment. She read both poems twice and then wrote the following journal entry about her response to "Slipping." (For more information on journals, see page 10.)

> OK, first time through I kept thinking about this daughter who seems like she's glad her father is old and weak because now he tells her he loves her. I felt sympathy for the daughter. But the second time through, her response began to seem selfish to me. She seemed to me to be willing to have her father old and weak as long as he would say that he loved her. But what about how the father felt inside? Maybe he was acting the way he was because he was scared. The poem talks about the screen falling down, which seems to me like the person's protection against the world. That made me think about Mr. Gagnon and the way he was after his stroke—how he lost his protection. The poem looks from the daughter's point of view and she sees the change as positive. But from the point of view

of the person who is changing, losing part of what has been yourself has to be frightening. And I definitely see that as negative. So I see another side to this poem.

This journal entry shows Karen's changing response as she read "Slipping." In addition, she keeps the writing topic she has chosen in mind, remembering that she has to include a personal narrative to explain her response. As she thinks about her second reading, she focuses on one particular image (the screen suddenly falling) that triggered a strong memory for her and leads her to the observation that "losing part of what has been yourself has to be frightening."

CONSIDERING AUDIENCE After deciding to write about Aleshire's poem and to use the story of Mr. Gagnon to illustrate her response, Karen thought about the audience for her paper (and for the oral response that was part of the assignment). Her instructor would be reading the paper; both the instructor and her classmates would be listening to her report. Everyone in this audience would be familiar with "Slipping," so Karen knew she wouldn't have to give a detailed summary of the poem.

No one in her audience, however, knew Mr. Gagnon, a man who had lived in Karen's neighborhood for as long as she could remember. She knew she would have to give some background information to help her audience understand why the changes in Mr. Gagnon after his surgery were so important to her and how having known Mr. Gagnon affected her response to the poem.

Karen also thought about the different views various classmates held. She knew that some would not share her response to "Slipping." She realized she would need to choose her words and examples carefully to express herself honestly without alienating readers or listeners whose responses to the poem were different from her own. Her purpose in writing the paper was not to make her audience angry but rather to show clearly her own thoughts and feelings.

NARROWING THE TOPIC Having decided on a general topic — the way the change in Mr. Gagnon related to her response to "Slipping" — Karen realized that she needed to find a more specific focus before she began drafting her paper. To explore possibilities, she made the following lists:

"Slipping"
    father used to be full of energy
    "love of work lighting his face"
    now losing physical abilities
        can't drive
        can't walk easily
    used to be reserved about emotions
    now exposes emotions
    can't (or doesn't) control feelings

Mr. Gagnon
   always full of energy and life
   never praised or said thanks
   brain tumor
   surgery not successful
   changing — every day worse
   exposing emotions he never would have
   pain from exposing
   no control over feelings

As Karen looked at these lists, she paid special attention to the idea of exposing emotions and to the sense of losing control. She then made another list, this time with possible subjects for her response essay.

   emotions and old age
   old age: changing emotions
   emotions, control, and self

Karen decided that the third topic best fit her response both to the poem and to her former neighbor, Mr. Gagnon. She knew that she wanted to explore a view of the changes brought by old age and illness that differed from the view suggested by Aleshire.

DEVISING A PRELIMINARY THESIS STATEMENT Once Karen had a narrowed topic in mind, she thought about what she wanted to say about this subject. She came up with these possibilities. Remember that a **thesis statement** makes an assertion; it does not simply announce a subject but instead indicates what the writer plans to say about the subject. Remember also that a preliminary thesis statement is tentative. You may revise it or even change it completely during the drafting process. The benefit of having a preliminary thesis is that it provides the sense of a central idea as you begin writing.

When a person's "reserve has slipped from feeling," the main emotion revealed may be fear.
Losing control because of sickness or old age may make a person emotional because of fear.
Losing control over your life is frightening.

The first thesis seemed strongest to Karen because it focuses specifically on what she wanted to say about her response to the poem. The assertion in the second statement is not as clear or as straightforward as the first, and the third thesis is too broad and general. Also, the first thesis is strengthened by the specific reference to the poem, which supports the central idea she proposes.

PLANNING ORGANIZATION While evaluating possible thesis statements, Karen saw what direction she wanted to take. Also, she'd made a list of ideas to discuss in her response to the poem and in the narrative about Mr. Gagnon that would explain her response. She now thought about how to organize her material, how to present it most effectively to her audience. The opening paragraph, she decided, would briefly describe her response to Aleshire's poem. The story of Mr. Gagnon's relationship with her and her brother Cory would follow. It seemed logical to give the details in chronological order, beginning with Mr. Gagnon before he became sick and then explaining the changes after his surgery.

To help keep this organization clearly in mind, Karen wrote an informal outline.

1. Introduction (My response to "Slipping" — details on what the father has lost — driving, work, etc.)
2. Mr. Gagnon
   When I was young — always there, welcoming us, but also grouchy; never saying thanks
   Mr. G's illness and surgery
   Visiting Mr. G — his change
3. Conclusion???

DRAFTING After doing the preliminary reading, writing, and thinking described here, Karen realized that she knew how she wanted to start her paper and she had a plan for developing the narrative example. She did not, however, know how she was going to conclude.

At this point, writing a draft — putting her explorations together on paper — seemed the best strategy.

CHANGES
Karen Angstrom

The daughter in Joan Aleshire's poem "Slipping" is seeing her father become more open to expressing emotions as he becomes older. "Like a screen suddenly falling." The daughter sees this change as positive, and my first response was to agree with her view, then I thought about the changes the father has gone through. He can't do the things he loved anymore. Work as a teacher. Drive a car safely. Walk without limping. Everything that used to make up this man's self seems to be gone. Yes, he says words of love, but when a person's "reserve has slipped from feeling," because of old age or illness, the main emotion which is revealed may be fear.

There was a man in our neighborhood who reminds me of the father in "Slipping." He, too, loved to work. He sang at the top of his voice (usually off tune) whenever he worked outside and he was always demanding that we join in. Both in his songs and in his projects. "In the good old SUMMER-TI-IME," my brother Cory and I would bellow as we helped him rig up a pulley to lift stones over his garden fence. "Let me call you SWE-EE-THEART," we'd try to harmonize as we built a birdfeeder designed to completely baffle squirrels. Mr. G was always busy and was always trying to figure out some new way to do something.

When Cory and I worked with him, he didn't have too much patience. There might be a tool that we'd drop or we'd put something together wrong, he'd have some sharp comment for us. Sometimes he'd send us home. Or even tell us to "get lost." There were many years, however, when we were fascinated by his strange inventions, and we'd always go back when we got one of his semi-grouchy invitations to "stop staring at me and get over here to help." As we got older, we really were able to help, but Mr. Gagnon never said thank you. I guess he never thought about it. Because Cory and I were always there, willing to come.

One day, when I was twelve years old, I realized I hadn't seen Mr. G for two or three days. I was told by my mother that he'd been sick. A brain tumor was diagnosed by the doctors, they wanted to operate. I felt sick myself thinking about it. Mr. G didn't want the surgery because he was told all the things that could happen. His eyesight or his ability to walk could be lost. Not to mention his memory. Finally, however, he had the surgery.

When he came home, my mom, Cory, and I went to visit. It was horrible. Mr. G had been in the hospital for two weeks and he had lost lots of weight. Mrs. G said that he had bad dreams both when he was awake and when he was asleep. He just stared at us. He looked scared. Then he croaked in a little, tinny voice "Who's that? Who's that?" We said our names, and he called for me to come over. He grabbed at my hand and started to tell me how glad he was to see me; how much he liked Cory and me. He thanked us for coming to see him. And kept saying over and over to please come back.

Unlike the speaker in the poem, I didn't feel good about this change. There were times that I used to wish that Mr. G would at least acknowledge the good things Cory and I did. But, now as he talked, it just seemed that he didn't have any of himself left. I suppose, in a way, I was seeing behind a screen that suddenly fell away. I was seeing an intimate part of Mr. G, but I felt like he was forced into showing this part of himself. It wasn't like he just decided he wanted to express that he liked us. It seemed like he was forced into it by his sickness. It was the weakness and the fear of not being strong again. The fear that we wouldn't come to visit now that he was changed.

The speaker in "Slipping" says that what she loves about her aging father is "the way reserve has slipped from his feeling." But is emotion expressed under these circumstances really something to celebrate?

REVISING FOCUS: TITLES, OPENINGS, CONCLUSIONS After Karen had written her draft, she put it away for several days and then looked at it again with a fresh mind and "new eyes." As she read, Karen liked very much the way she had described Mr. Gagnon. For example, she saw that the specific details she had used — the songs he taught and the projects he worked on — showed the reader his life and energy.

But she was not happy with her title. She felt it was too general and did not really reflect what she hoped to say in the paper. Also, she thought the opening paragraph was somewhat confusing. She didn't explain the first quote she used; it just seemed to hang there without really making much sense. In addition, her tentative thesis needed added detail to make clear that the changing emotions she discussed resulted from the weakening that often accompanies aging and illness.

Karen also recognized that her conclusion was much too brief. Her question was a starting place, but she needed to develop her response more fully. Her list for revising looked like this:

1. Title — needs to be more specific
2. Opening paragraph
   Explain quote better
   Revise thesis
3. Conclusion — expand (maybe trying answering question?)

EDITING FOCUS: "TO BE," EXPLETIVES, PASSIVE VOICE As Karen reread her paper, she noticed that some of her sentences seemed awkward. They just didn't sound right as she read them aloud. With some help from a tutor at the writing center on her campus, she saw three problems she could correct:

1. Overuse of forms of the verb "to be." Karen replaced them with active verbs where possible.

   Mr. G. was always busy and was always trying to figure out some new way to do something.
   Edited: Mr. G. always kept busy trying to figure out some new way to do something.

2. Overuse of expletives such as "there is" and "there are."

   There was a man in our neighborhood who reminds me of the father in "Slipping."
   Edited: Mr. Gagnon, a man from our neighborhood, reminds me of the father in "Slipping."

3. Overuse of passive-voice constructions. (In passive-voice constructions, the subject of the sentence is acted upon; in active voice, the subject acts.)

A brain tumor was diagnosed by the doctors.
Edited: The doctors had diagnosed a brain tumor.

PROOFREADING FOCUS: FRAGMENTS AND COMMA
SPLICES The tutor at the writing center also told Karen that some of her
sentences were confusing because they were fragments or comma splices.

Fragment: Drive a car safely
Edited: He can't drive a car safely.

Comma splice: The daughter sees this change as positive, and my
first response was to agree with her view, then I thought about the
changes the father has gone through.
Edited: The daughter sees this change as positive, and my first response was to agree with her view. Then I thought about the
changes the father has gone through.

Exercise

Keeping in mind the revising, editing, and proofreading focuses just
discussed as well as your own evaluation of the draft, try rewriting Karen's
paper. Think carefully about the reasons for the changes you make. Then
compare your final version with the one that follows. Of course, each person's revision of this paper will be different. The point is not to duplicate
Karen's final paper but to think about the differences and similarities between the choices she made and the choices you made.

CHANGES: FOR BETTER OR WORSE?
Karen Angstrom

The daughter in Joan Aleshire's poem "Slipping" notices her father
becoming more open to expressing emotions as he becomes older. She
says his normal reserve is "like a screen suddenly falling." The daughter sees this change as positive, and my first response was to agree
with her view. Then I thought about the changes the father has gone
through. He can't do the things he loved anymore. He can't work as a
teacher or drive a car safely or walk without limping. Everything that
used to make up this man's self seems to be gone. Yes, he says words
of love, but when a person's "reserve has slipped from feeling," because of old age or illness, the main emotion revealed may be fear.

Mr. Gagnon, a man from our neighborhood, reminds me of the
father in "Slipping." Like the father, Mr. G, too, loved to work. He
sang at the top of his voice (usually off tune) whenever he worked
outside, and he frequently demanded that my brother Cory and I join
him, both in his songs and in his projects. "In the good old SUM-

MER-TI-IME," my brother and I would bellow as we helped Mr. G rig up a pulley to lift stones over his garden fence. "Let me call you SWE-EE-THEART," we'd try to harmonize as we built a birdfeeder designed to completely baffle squirrels. Mr. G always kept busy trying to figure out some new way to do something.

When Cory and I worked with him, he didn't have too much patience. If we dropped a tool or put something together wrong, he'd have some sharp comment for us. Sometimes he'd send us home or even tell us to "get lost." Nevertheless, for many years, we were fascinated by his strange inventions, and we'd always go back when we got one of his semi-grouchy invitations to "stop staring at me and get over here to help." As we got older, we really were able to help. We unloaded countless boxes of supplies from his old station wagon and picked up hundreds of scraps to store in what he called his "useful junk" pile. During all these years, Mr. Gagnon never said thank you or told us that we did a good job. He never told us he was glad to see us, either. I guess he never thought about it since Cory and I were always there, willing to come.

One day, when I was twelve years old, I realized I hadn't seen Mr. G for two or three days. My mother told me that he'd been sick. The doctors diagnosed a brain tumor, and they wanted to operate. I felt sick myself thinking about it. When he was told all the possible side-effects of the operation, Mr. G didn't want the surgery. He could have lost his eyesight or his ability to walk, not to mention his memory. Finally, however, he had the surgery.

When he came home, my mom, Cory, and I went to visit. It was horrible. Mr. G had been in the hospital for two weeks, and he had lost lots of weight. Mrs. G said that he had bad dreams both when he was awake and when he was asleep. He just stared at us, looking scared. Then he croaked in a little, tinny voice: "Who's that? Who's that?" We said our names, and he called for me to come over. He grabbed at my hand and started to tell me how glad he was to see me. He repeated several times how much he liked Cory and me. He thanked us for coming to see him and kept saying over and over to please come back.

Unlike the speaker in the poem, I didn't feel good about this change. Sometimes I used to wish that Mr. G would at least acknowledge the good things Cory and I did. But, now as he talked, it just seemed that he didn't have any of himself left. I suppose, in a way, like the daughter in "Slipping," I was seeing behind a screen that had suddenly fallen away. I was seeing an intimate part of Mr. G, but I felt like he was forced into showing this part of himself. He didn't have the chance to decide for himself that he wanted to express that he liked us. He seemed forced by his weakness, and the fear of not being strong again, to talk about his feelings. I believed he feared that we wouldn't come to visit now that he could no longer create intriguing projects or order us around.

The speaker in "Slipping" says that what she loves about her aging father is "the way reserve has slipped from his feeling." But is emotion expressed under these circumstances really something to celebrate? I don't think so. Yes, "years of restraint" may have been pushed away, yet the force that pushes them may be fear rather than love. The person who stands exposed like "someone dressing or washing" has lost all of his privacy and all of his personal power. That person has no more real self.

Exercise

Read a work from the anthology sections of this book and then, using the process demonstrated with Karen's paper, plan and write a response. Begin by briefly summarizing your response to the work and then use a personal narrative to explain that response. Make references to the story, poem, play, or essay that show its connection to your narrative.

As you write your response keep the following guidelines in mind:

Guidelines: Writing a Response

1. Read the work several times, making marginal notes and writing journal entries to explore your responses.
2. Focus on one response that seems particularly strong.
3. Explain that response, using examples from your own experience, but also make certain to refer to the work so that the connections between your experience and the work are clear.
4. Remember that a response asks for your own ideas and feelings, not simply a summary of the ideas and feelings in the work.

Writing to Compare

The second assignment topic asks the reader to make comparisons between "Slipping" and "Do Not Go Gentle."

Topic 2

Explore the similarities and differences you see between these poems. Then write a paper explaining what you discovered and what significance you find in these similarities and differences.

As Walter Johnson considered this topic, he thought that it was relatively simple to see several things that were the same about the two poems as well as several things that were different. But the topic also asked for an explanation of the significance of the similarities and differences. This step — making meaning from the comparisons and contrasts — seemed more difficult.

DISCOVERING IDEAS: DISCUSSION Walter read the poems several times and made these lists of similarities and differences to bring to a scheduled small-group discussion of paper topics.

	"Do Not Go Gentle"	"Slipping"
SUBJECT	old age of speaker's father	same
RHYME	regular rhyme pattern	no rhyme
IMAGES	mostly visual — (lots about light)	visual and physical — leg weakens, walking slowly; screen falling
SETTING	on a mountain? ("sad height"?)	in familiar places; walking near home; thinking of photograph (probably at home) — picture shows father at work
IDEA	changes in father seen as negative; he should fight old age (the "good night")	changes in father positive; becomes more loving, less reserved

Walter's instructor assigned him to a group of four students; all of them were working on the comparison topic. Several had brought lists of their own. Everyone agreed that finding the significance was the most difficult part of the assignment. The following edited excerpt from a taped transcript of their discussion illustrates the way talking about literature can lead to discovering possibilities for writing.

Walter: One poem — "Do Not Go Gentle" — says that the changes in old age are bad, but in "Slipping" the person seems to see those changes as good. So they're completely opposite.

Anna: Well, I don't see — I don't think that — in "Do Not Go" what you have to look at is that he says "*good* night." Why is old age — or, I think it's death — a "good night" if it's bad? But I agree he wants his father to fight it.

Tomás: Same thing to me about "Slipping." You can't — in my opinion, you can't just say that she — the person who's talking in the poem — is saying something like, "Old age is really great and it makes people change in a good way." I mean it's definitely under pretty awful circumstances. Like the guy — her father — is losing his memory and he can't even drive a car right. So I would say *some* changes in old age can be good.

Michelle: But what Anna was saying, I think "good night" could be just like saying "good-bye." So that it would be: "Don't go without a fight into that last 'good-bye.'" Don't just go through these changes without resisting what you lose.

Walter: Right. I can see what Anna says, but he says "rage, rage against the dying of the light" so many times. And like I wrote on the list here with the rhyme words — so many of them rhyme with "light" — it's like he really wants to emphasize that. To emphasize that the father should fight against the light going away — the light, I think, is like his life — his normal life. It's a metaphor or symbol — whatever — for life.

Anna: I can agree — but what I'm just saying — it's not the opposite of what you're saying — it's just that you can't totally ignore the "good" part.

Tomás: So does it matter whether this guy thinks that old age can be a little bit good or not? What I noticed was the way he was giving advice to his father. He's like really making a lot of decisions for his father, I think. Or trying to make them.

Walter: The person in "Slipping," she's not telling her father what to do — she's just glad he is changed.

Michelle: Right. The speaker in "Do Not Go Gentle" seems like he can't accept the changes in his father — or in anyone who gets old and is facing death. The daughter in "Slipping," you can see she's accepting the changes — and she even appreciates some of the changes.

CONSIDERING AUDIENCE, NARROWING THE TOPIC, AND DEVISING A PRELIMINARY THESIS After thinking about this discussion, Walter realized he needed to be careful not to make sweeping generalizations he couldn't support. For instance, he saw that Anna had a reasonable point about the ambiguity of the phrase "good night." To make what he said convincing to other students (and, of course, to the instructor) he could not simply say that one poem showed the changes of old age as bad and the other showed those changes as good.

The last part of the discussion printed here seemed particularly useful for discovering a specific topic and formulating a preliminary thesis. Walter thought about the speaker in "Do Not Go Gentle" giving advice to his father and compared that to the speaker in "Slipping" describing her thoughts. She seems to be much more accepting of the changes of old age than does the speaker in Thomas's poem.

This insight led to the following preliminary thesis:

> The speakers in Joan Aleshire's poem "Slipping" and Dylan Thomas's poem "Do Not Go Gentle into That Good Night" raise questions about the responses of those who must watch someone they love face the changes of old age.

PLANNING ORGANIZATION Walter now had a central idea to work with, and he had the list he'd made to bring to the group discussion. In addition, he had other notes written in the margins of the poem as well as notes taken in class and during and after the small-group discussion.

When he thought about organizing the information, he remembered from his composition course that there are two standard ways to write about comparisons and contrasts. He could talk about one poem first and then talk about the second, referring back to the first to note similarities and differences. Or he could talk about one point he wanted to make and discuss each poem in relationship to that point, then go on to a new point once again, discussing each poem in relationship to that point, and so on. Instead of deciding on one structure and then drafting, Walter decided to try writing two outlines to see which organization would work best with the ideas and information he had gathered.

RESPONSES
  I. Introduction — responses of person watching a parent face the changes of old age
 II. "Do Not Go Gentle"
     A. Speaker's tone — giving advice
     B. Rhyme and rhythm — emphasizes pattern; speaker wants order; wants listener to do what speaker wants
     C. Setting — general, symbolic, applies to many "old men" (people?) in various circumstances
     D. Images — mostly visual; focus on seeing, and on past actions
III. "Slipping"
     A. Speaker's tone — explaining, reassuring
     B. No rhyme — rhythm close to ordinary talking; not like planned speech
     C. Setting — real-life (a walk outside family house; a photo of the father in his classroom)
     D. Images — appeal to both sight and touch — more intimate
 IV. Conclusion: Speakers' responses different; themes of poems go in different directions. Contradictory? Agreeing in any way?

RESPONSES
  I. Introduction — responses of person watching a parent face the changes of old age
 II. Speaker's tone
     A. "Do Not Go Gentle" — giving advice, resisting
     B. "Slipping" — accepting
III. Rhyme and rhythm
     A. "Do Not Go Gentle" — emphasizes pattern; speaker wants order; wants listener to do what speaker wants
     B. "Slipping" — No rhyme — rhythm seems close to ordinary talking — not like planned speech
 IV. Setting
     A. "Do Not Go Gentle" — general, applies to many "old men" (people?) in various circumstances
     B. "Slipping" — specific: one father; individual experiences (teaching, going for walks)

V. Images
    A. "Do Not Go Gentle" — mostly visual; focuses on seeing, and on past actions
    B. "Slipping" — appeals to both sight and touch — more intimate
VI. Conclusion: Speakers' responses different; themes of poems go in different directions. Contradictory? Agreeing in any way?

DRAFTING After thinking about both possibilities for organizing, Walter decided to try the first arrangement. Like most successful writers, he revises throughout the process of working on the assignment. For instance, looking at the two outlines convinced him that his title needed to be more specific. He needed to connect his idea of responses to the theme he was working with, and so he came up with "Responses: Raging versus Slipping."

Note, too, that he doesn't expect to resolve every question about his topic completely before he starts drafting. For example, his outlines show that he still has questions about the paper's conclusion.

RESPONSES: RAGING VERSUS SLIPPING
Walter Johnson

The speakers in Joan Aleshire's poem "Slipping" and Dylan Thomas's poem "Do Not Go Gentle into That Good Night" describe their responses as their fathers face the changes of old age. The speakers in these two poems look at their aging parents in very different ways.

In "Do Not Go Gentle" the speaker is talking to his father and is telling him to fight against "the dying of the light." The speaker sounds like he is giving a speech that is meant to convey the conviction to his father, and a larger audience would be informed as well, that it's important to "rage, rage" against the changes of old age. This is advice given to all old men, not just to one old man. Then each of the stanzas that follows talks about one category of old men and showed that no matter what they may have done in life, in the end they all fight the changes that lead to death. They did not give in easily.

The regular rhythm and rhyme in the poem contributes to making it sound like an argument. This repetition emphasizes the speaker's plea. It sounds like a carefully planned speech that is designed to be very convincing to anyone who hears it, not just the father who is not spoken to directly until the last stanza.

It's hard to tell where this speaker is. He isn't clearly in a house or a work place or any building. In the middle four stanzas, the men described are related to parts of nature but these seemed to be general and not specific places. The father in the final stanza is on a "sad height," which doesn't seem like a real mountain. Instead, it may be a metaphor for the final place humans reach just before they die. All these setting elements emphasized that the speaker was arguing for an approach to old age that he thinks is best for many men. Of course, it was also best for his father as well.

Most of the images in the poem are visual. They are things you see or think about. Things you feel or experience are not pictured. For example, the speaker talks about words that "forked no lightning" and deeds that "might have danced in a green bay." The speaker talked about past deeds rather than about the present experience of aging and (possibly) illness that these old men, and the speaker's father, now face.

The speaker's tone in "Slipping" is explanatory and accepting. The speaker is describing the changes in her father with understanding. She sympathizes with her father and understands what he is facing, but she doesn't wish him back the way he was. She expresses, instead, her love for his new way of expressing his emotions.

In "Slipping" there are no rhymes, and the rhythm seems like an ordinary conversation and not like a planned speech that is making an argument. The speaker even uses direct quotations, giving the exact words of her mother and father.

In "Slipping" the settings are from real life. The father is shown driving a car, taking a walk with his daughter, and there is a picture of him teaching in his classroom.

The images in "Slipping" are personal and appeal to both sight and touch. The father's leg "trailing a little" and the "curtain of mist" that obscures his sight make the changes he faces specific. He is compared to "a child who keeps pulling on your hand," and his feelings are exposed like someone who was dressing behind a screen that suddenly falls down.

The speakers, who clearly love the aging fathers, have very different responses to the changes they see. The speaker in "Do Not Go Gentle" takes the responsibility for his father's life on his own shoulders. He tells his father how to approach old age. It seems like the speaker just thinks about death as the ultimate enemy which everyone should fight. On the other hand, the speaker in "Slipping" sees both the negative aspects of the changes and also the positive aspects. The speaker in "Do Not Go Gentle" rages against accepting his father's changes. On the other hand, the speaker in Aleshire's poem just slips into this new phase of life.

REVISING FOCUS: TRANSITIONS, DEVELOPMENT OF IDEAS When Walter read his paper to Anna, Tomás, and Michelle during an in-class workshop, he asked about the organization of his paper. As he reread his paper, the meaning didn't seem to flow smoothly from paragraph to paragraph. He wondered whether he should have used the organization shown in the second outline (page 69). Here's an excerpt from an edited transcript of the tape made during the discussion that followed:

Anna: I don't know — to me, the other organization — where you discuss each little bit separately — that could be just as jumpy.

Tomás: The main thing for me was that when you got to the part on "Slipping," it seemed really like a surprise. I didn't really see where you led in to it.

Michelle: We were talking the last time about similarities and differences — which is the subject or — well — the approach to the paper. But I don't see that.

Walter: Don't see what?

Michelle: Don't see that you are comparing. It's like two separate papers — except for the first paragraph and the conclusion.

After thinking about the comments of his writing group, Walter saw that he had not connected his thoughts clearly. He had not shown his readers how he got from one idea to the next. He knew that he needed to work on **transitions:** words, phrases, and sentences that provide a bridge from one paragraph to the next or from one section of the paper to the next. He had to show the relationship among his ideas and examples.

In addition, he noticed that some of his paragraphs seemed too short. As he read them, he saw that he needed to expand and explain his ideas more fully. He needed to be more specific: to give details, reasons, and examples that would convey his thoughts accurately to his audience.

EDITING FOCUS: NOMINALIZATIONS, PARALLEL STRUCTURE   The writing group also noticed several sentences that needed to be edited. Most of the sentences either used some form of the verb "to be" too much (see page 63) or relied too heavily on nouns that were formed from verbs (nominalizations). As an example, Tomás pointed out this sentence from the second paragraph:

> The speaker sounds like he is giving a speech that is meant to convey the conviction to his father, and a larger audience would be informed as well, that it's important to "rage, rage" against the changes of old age.

Notice that Walter uses some form of the verb "to be" three times. When a sentence sounds wordy and plodding, you can often improve it by getting rid of excess "to be" verbs. In addition, this sentence uses the nominalization "convey the conviction" instead of the simpler, more direct, active form of the verb "convince." Here's the sentence as Walter edited it.

> The speaker sounds like he is giving a speech meant to convince his father, and a larger audience would be informed as well, to "rage, rage" against the changes of old age.

Walter can improve the structure of this sentence further by using parallel phrases instead of the awkward "his father, and readers would be informed as well."

> The speaker sounds like he is giving a speech meant to convince not only his father but also a larger audience to "rage, rage" against the changes of old age.

Notice that the edited sentence is much leaner and sleeker than the original; the edited sentence uses thirty words, whereas the original uses forty.

PROOFREADING FOCUS: SUBJECT-VERB AGREEMENT, TENSE AGREEMENT As the writing group gave final consideration to Walter's paper, Michelle suggested that he proofread for two other problems:

1. Problem with subject-verb agreement.

   Plural subject   *Singular verb*
   The regular *rhythm and rhyme* in the poem *contributes* to making it sound like an argument.

   Edited: The regular *rhythm* and *rhyme* in the poem *contribute* to making it sound like an argument.

2. Problem with verb tense agreement. Verbs should all be in the same tense unless there is a reason to indicate a change to another time. Generally, papers about literature are written in present tense. In this sentence, "showed" marks an unneeded switch from present to past tense:

   Present
   Then each of the stanzas that follows *talks* about one category of

   Past   *Present perfect*
   old men and *showed* that no matter what they *may have done* in life,

   Present
   in the end they all *fight* the changes that lead to death.

   Edited: Then each of the stanzas that follows *talks* about one category of old man and *shows* that, no matter what they *may have done* in life, in the end they all *fight* the changes that lead to death.

Exercise

Keeping in mind the revising, editing, and proofreading focuses just discussed as well as your own evaluation of the draft, try rewriting Walter's paper. Think carefully about the reasons for the changes you make. Then compare your final version with the one that follows. Of course, each person's revision of this paper will be different. The point is not to duplicate Walter's final paper but to think about the differences and similarities between the choices he made and the choices you made.

RESPONSES: RAGING VERSUS SLIPPING
Walter Johnson

The speakers in Joan Aleshire's poem "Slipping" and Dylan Thomas's poem "Do Not Go Gentle into That Good Night" describe their responses as their fathers experience the changes of old age. Thomas's speaker sees his father as representative of all men facing old age and urges his father to fight old age. Aleshire's speaker, on the other hand, looks at her father's changes in a more personal way and sees some of the changes as being in some ways positive.

In "Do Not Go Gentle" the speaker talks to his father and tells him to struggle against "the dying of the light." The speaker sounds like he is giving a speech meant to convince not only his father but also a larger audience to "rage, rage" against death. For instance, he says in the first stanza, "Old age should burn and rave at close of day." Here the speaker advises all old men, not just one old man. Then each stanza that follows talks about one category of old man and shows that, no matter what they may have done in life, in the end they all fight death. They do not give in easily.

The regular rhythm and rhyme in the poem contribute to making it sound like an argument. Of the nineteen lines in the poem, thirteen either end with the word "light" or "night" or with a word that rhymes with "light" or "night." This repetition emphasizes the speaker's plea. It sounds like a carefully planned speech designed to convince not just the father, who is not directly addressed until the last stanza, but anyone who hears it.

The setting of the poem also indicates a larger audience than just the father. It's hard to tell where this speaker is. He isn't clearly in a building or in a specific outdoor location. In the middle four stanzas, the men described relate to parts of nature (lightning, a green bay, the sun, meteors) but these seem to be general and not specific places. The father in the final stanza stands on a "sad height," which doesn't seem like a real mountain but instead like a metaphor for the final place humans reach just before they die. All these setting elements emphasize that the speaker argues for an approach to old age that he considers best for many men as well as for his father.

The speaker's approach to old age seems to be highly idealistic and philosophical. Most of the images in the poem are visual. They show things you see or think about rather than things you feel or experience, for example, words that "forked no lightning" and deeds that "might have danced in a green bay." The speaker talks about past deeds rather than about the present experience of aging and (possibly) illness that these old men, and the speaker's father, now face.

In contrast to the formal, arguing tone of "Do Not Go Gentle," the speaker's tone in "Slipping" explains and accepts. The speaker describes the changes in her father with understanding. She sees that his legs can "barely support him" and that he is losing his memory. These details show that she sympathizes with her father and recognizes what he is facing, but she doesn't wish him back the way he was. She expresses, instead, her love for his new way of expressing his emotions. She describes this openness with a gentle image, noting "how soft and mutable is the usually hidden flesh."

The rhyme and rhythm also contrast sharply with those of "Do Not Go Gentle." In Thomas's poem, the rhythm and rhyme are regular and repetitive. In "Slipping," there are no rhymes, and the rhythm seems like everyday speech and not like a planned formal argument. The speaker even uses direct quotations, giving the exact words of her mother ("He's never liked to talk about feelings") and her father ("I love you"). This dialogue gives an intimate view of a specific family rather the formal picture conveyed by the language of "Do Not Go Gentle."

In "Do Not Go Gentle," there's no clear picture of the speaker's location, and his examples also have general, idealized settings. In "Slipping," however, the setting comes from real life. The father is shown driving a car, taking a walk with his daughter, and teaching in his classroom. Even the metaphor the daughter uses to describe his changes — the screen falling — gives a picture of a dressing room, like the ones in a doctor's office.

The images in "Slipping" also show the difference between this poem and "Do Not Go Gentle." While Thomas's images are visual and can be applied generally to large groups of men, the images in "Slipping" are personal and appeal to both sight and touch. The father's leg "trailing a little" and the "curtain of mist" that obscures his sight make the changes he faces specific. His trailing leg is compared to "a child who keeps pulling on your hand," and his feelings are exposed like someone who was dressing behind a screen that suddenly falls down. Both images give a physical sense of someone who has lost power.

The speakers, who clearly love their aging fathers, have very different responses to the changes they see. The speaker in "Do Not Go Gentle" takes the responsibility for his father's life on his own shoulders. He tells his father how to approach old age. It seems like the speaker just thinks about death as the ultimate enemy that everyone should fight. On the other hand, the speaker in "Slipping" sees both the negative and the positive aspects of the changes. The father no longer has the pleasure of his work, but he now has found a relationship with his family, which never seemed to be possible before. The speaker in "Do Not Go Gentle" rages against accepting his father's changes, whereas the speaker in Aleshire's poem seems, like her father, to slip gently into this new phase of life.

Exercise

Read several works from any one of the thematic anthology sections of this book. Then, using the process demonstrated with Walter's paper, choose two works and plan and write a comparison. Keep in mind the following guidelines:

Guidelines: Writing a Comparison

1. As you plan the paper by doing preliminary reading, writing, and thinking, remember that listing and outlining are useful strategies for planning a comparison paper.
2. Remember that a comparison should be made for a purpose. A comparison should not simply list the similarities and differences discovered during planning sessions.
3. Note which similarities or differences seem most significant and decide which you will emphasize.
4. Decide how you will organize your paper — for example, the "whole-subject" approach, the "point-by-point" approach, or a combination of these approaches.
5. Open with a paragraph that focuses on the purpose and point of the comparison. For example, do *not* say

    > In this paper "Slipping" will be compared to "Do Not Go Gentle into That Good Night."

    or

    > There are many similarities and differences between "Slipping" and "Do Not Go Gentle into That Good Night."

    Do say, for example

    > The speakers in Joan Aleshire's poem "Slipping" and Dylan Thomas's poem "Do Not Go Gentle into That Good Night" describe their responses as their fathers face the changes of old age.
6. Develop each subject (or each point) in a separate paragraph (or a series of carefully related and logically linked paragraphs).
7. Make certain that transitions between paragraphs and between sections of the paper show the connections — the comparisons and contrasts — you want to make.
8. Develop a conclusion that offers an analysis, evaluates the evidence the body of your paper provides, or in some other way shows the significance of the comparison you have made.

Writing to Analyze

When you analyze, you look at parts (or at a part) in relationship to the whole to which they belong. For example, a United States history exam might ask you to discuss and explain the significance of the economic causes of the American Revolution. Such a question requires that you look at part (the economic causes) of a whole (the American Revolution) and that you explain how knowing about that part contributes to understanding the whole. When you analyze a work of literature, you look carefully at its parts — or at one particular part — to see what they contribute to the meaning the whole work holds for you. For instance, you might look carefully at the language of a poem, a particular character in a short story, or a significant scene in a play.

Explication is one form of analysis. The word "explicate" comes from the Latin *explicare,* which means to unfold. When you write a paper that unfolds the meaning of a work, you are writing an explication. The third assignment topic asks for such an approach.

Topic 3

What, exactly, does the speaker say in "Do Not Go Gentle"? And how does he say it? How does the central idea of the poem unfold as you read from one stanza to the next?

Matt Cejak chose this topic. He noticed that the first part of the topic seemed relatively easy; he didn't think he'd have much trouble describing what the speaker says. He also felt confident that he could talk about the central idea of the poem (as required by the last part of the topic). Explaining both how the speaker conveys his meaning and how each stanza relates to the central idea of the poem seemed more difficult.

DISCOVERING IDEAS: PARAPHRASING To make certain he had a sense of what was going on in each stanza, Matt decided to write a **paraphrase.** That is, he decided to write a series of short paragraphs, putting each stanza into his own words.

Paraphrase of "Do Not Go Gentle" (by Dylan Thomas)
1. People who are old should not be resigned to dying. They should fight against it.
2. People who are wise may know that death is the right thing, but (????something about lightning???not sure) they still resist dying.
3. People who are good (seems to mean morally upright?) realize that their time on earth is nearly through, but they think about the things they have done and that makes them fight against death.
4. "Wild men" (outlaws? rebels? nonconformists? crazy people?) who did strange and brave things and acted like they didn't care if they were doing things that might kill them find out at the end of their lives that they regret having to give up life. They then fight against death.
5. Serious (sad?) men who are near death and nearly blind (with disease or old age?) realize (or think) they could still act in some special way (like meteors). These people fight death, too.
6. (Talks directly to his father) You are facing death. I want you to give me your blessing, even though you may curse me with your angry tears, so that you can fight against death.

As he read over the paraphrase, Matt saw that he had a place to begin. But he also saw that working on the explication was going to be harder than he had thought. The paraphrase of "Do Not Go Gentle" seemed matter-of-fact and overly simple. It had none of the energy of the original poem. In addition, the paraphrase raised questions: some of the stanzas were hard to put into prose. They didn't easily yield one thought or idea.

Matt looked closely again at the poem and compared it to his paraphrase. He made this list of what the paraphrase lacked:

1. sound — rhyme, rhythm
2. pattern — repetition, arrangement and number of lines in stanzas
3. figurative language — metaphors, symbols
4. many possible meanings to phrases and sentences

Matt decided to use this list as a guide when he drafted his explication. As he discussed each stanza, he would consider how each of the elements helped to convey meaning.

CONSIDERING AUDIENCE, NARROWING THE TOPIC, AND DEVISING A PRELIMINARY THESIS At this point, Matt thought about focusing his topic more clearly and about finding a preliminary thesis. Everything he came up with seemed too obvious. For example, here are some possibilities he tried:

Dylan Thomas's poem "Do Not Go Gentle into That Good Night" describes the words of a son pleading with his father to fight death.

The speaker in Dylan Thomas's poem "Do Not Go Gentle into That Good Night" urges his father to fight against the ending of his life.

In the poem "Do Not Go Gentle into That Good Night" by Dylan Thomas the idea is given that death is a force to fight.

Matt liked the third possibility better than the other two because the idea seemed more widely applicable than the other two, but he was not really satisfied. Looking back at the topic he'd chosen for this paper, he realized that none of his possible theses really addressed the question of how the ideas and feelings in the poem were conveyed.

Thinking of his instructor as an important part of the audience for this paper, Matt realized that he needed to work on all parts of the topic. Although he was not happy with any of his possible theses, he decided to write a draft to see whether he could discover a clear focus during writing.

PLANNING ORGANIZATION Because Matt was still not sure where he was going, he had trouble planning the organization of the draft. He didn't have any idea how to write an opening paragraph because he still didn't have a clear preliminary thesis. He remembered, however, that an explication is an unfolding of the meaning of a work. So, he decided to start by discussing the first stanza and then move chronologically through the other five stanzas. He hoped this process would help him to discover how the poem "worked"; then he could return during the revision process to write an introduction.

DRAFTING Matt began work on the draft, keeping in mind the four elements he'd listed as crucial to the way the poem conveys meaning.

EXPLICATION: "DO NOT GO GENTLE"
Matthew Cejak

In the first stanza, three lines give the speaker's plea to old people not to die easily. They should fight and be angry at "close of day." The first and third lines of the stanza rhyme — "night" and "light." The word "rage" is repeated twice. "Night" is a metaphor for death, and "day" or "light" are metaphors for life.

In the second stanza, there are three lines again. They have the same rhyme pattern as the first stanza. In this stanza, the speaker talks about wise men who "know dark is right." When they spoke during their lifetime maybe they didn't really get their message across. They didn't speak like lightning. So they don't want to die, they want to continue to live. The last line repeats the first line of the first stanza.

REVISING FOCUS: SUMMARIZING VERSUS ANALYZING At this point, Matt stopped and reread what he had written. He was happy with some aspects and unhappy with others. He had gone beyond the paraphrase he had written earlier and was paying attention to the list he'd made of elements to consider, but the draft still didn't seem to address the "how" part of the assignment. At this point, Matt asked his instructor for a conference. To prepare for the office conference, Matt consulted the guidelines the instructor had distributed at the beginning of the term.

Guidelines: Preparing for a Writing Conference

1. Gather all preliminary work (notes, drafts, books with your annotations, etc.) to bring with you.
2. List the strong points of your paper.
3. List the weak points of your paper. Focus first on large issues — such as organization or use of examples — rather than finer points — such as word choice or punctuation.
4. List approaches you have considered to revise the weaknesses you see.
5. Make a list of questions about your writing project.
6. Make your questions precise.

   Not this: How can I get a better grade on this paper?
   But this: This statement, I know, is too general. How can I make my point more specific?

The following conversation is an edited transcript of Matt's conference with his instructor:

Matt: I can't get started — I know this is wrong.

Instructor: Well, actually, you have a good start here. You've got a lot on paper. Try reading what you've written in this draft out loud.

Matt: (After finishing reading) I know it's not — not enough — or, somehow, doesn't answer the "how" part. But —

Instructor: I think you're right — do you see why?

Matt: No! If I saw why — I would — If I saw why, I'd change it.

Instructor: (Laughs) Right — yes — I see your point. OK. This time, listen to me read what you've said. Tell me what you're learning — new insights into the poem — whatever. *(Reads the draft)*

Matt: What it sounds like to me is a summary of the notes — here — I did this paraphrase and then this list.

Instructor: Good stuff here, Matt. You've done a lot of work — but now you need to go further. You said the word yourself. You've got mostly summary — either summary of meaning or summary of various elements. Take this paragraph, for instance:

> In the first stanza, three lines give the speaker's plea to old people not to die easily. They should fight and be angry at "close of day." The first and third lines of the stanza rhyme "night" and "light." The word "rage" is repeated twice. "Night" is a metaphor for death, and "day" or "light" are metaphors for life.

What's the point here?

Matt: I guess — mmm — it's just to tell what the aspects of the poem are.

Instructor: Can you put any of these sentences together — work on them in a connected way? How do they relate?

Matt: Well, I talk about "night" and "day" or "light" being metaphors and then there's this part about "night" and "light" rhyming and this part where I quote "close of day" — so — maybe — something about how they go together? Why they go together?

Instructor: Sounds like a good plan — let me hear you talk a little more about your idea.

Matt: Well, how about that "night" and "day" are really important to the poem and that this repeating — and the metaphor — and the rhyme — I would say maybe that's how Thomas makes you really notice the importance.

Instructor: See — now you're really getting away from summary and into the analysis — the explication. Good. See — you say "that's *how* Thomas makes you notice. . . ."

After talking with his instructor, Matt knew what direction he wanted his paper to take. He had to make the hard decision to discard most of the first draft. Keeping in mind the idea of making connections and of analyzing rather than summarizing, Matt wrote this second draft. He still was not sure of his central idea, so he again followed his plan of explicating each stanza in chronological order, planning to go back and write an introductory paragraph later.

EXPLICATION: "DO NOT GO GENTLE"
Matthew Cejak

The first stanza begins with the speaker's plea, addressed to old people. They should fight against going "into that good night," a metaphor for death. The words in this stanza set a tone of heat and passion. Those who face death should "burn," "rave," and "rage." The repetition of the word "rage" emphasizes the importance the speaker places on this fight against death.

The second stanza gives the first of three examples demonstrating why the speaker believes old people should resist death. Wise men may know that "dark" — another metaphor for death — "is right." But when these wise men spoke during their lifetime maybe they didn't really get their message across. They didn't speak like lightning. So they don't want to die, they want to continue to live. "Lightning" relates to "light" in the first stanza; both indicate something powerful and good. The lightning may be powerful words, while the light represents life itself. In this stanza, the rhyme scheme of the poem begins to underline the speaker's insistence on life. Like in the first stanza, the first and third lines rhyme. And all four of these lines (1, 3, 4, and 6) rhyme, too. The rhyme emphasizes the relationship between "light" (life) and "night" (death) and the struggle between the two.

"Good men" serve as the example in stanza three. They don't want to die because they think back on the actions of their lives, and they realize that these actions may not have been fully appreciated. These actions are described as "frail deeds." The word "frail" suggests the weakness often associated with old age, and the "good men" think about how those actions "might have danced in a green bay." This phrase shows the men's actions as lively and sparkling, like light on the water in a bay. Once again, the idea of light is emphasized as good and the idea of dark (death) as bad. The deeds could have been "bright" and so these "good men" fight against letting their light go out. The importance of life is stressed by the rhyming of "bright" and "light" at the ends of the first and last lines in the stanza.

"Wild men" are shown in the fourth stanza as the example of old people who fight death. They seem to be people who grabbed on to parts of life, and yet also let those same parts of life go with no regrets. They "caught" the sun, which may be a metaphor for a very intense and beautiful part of life, but they sung "the sun in flight." This singing indicates that they were able to say good-bye to these intense, beautiful times with joy. But now they realize that they also feel sorrow. They feel the loss of these strong experiences. Once again, the image of light (the sun) is good. It represents power, energy, and life.

Like the "wise men" wishing their words had been like lightning, and like the "good men" imagining their deeds dancing "in a green bay," the "wild men" seem to have a strong connection with the physical part of nature (in this case the sun). The final line repeats the ending line of the second stanza and the first line of the first stanza: "Do not go gentle into that good night." The repetition ties this example in with the others and shows that yet one more category of old people fight the ending of life.

The final example of those who "rage, rage against the dying of the light" are grave men. It's interesting to note that "grave" means serious, yet "grave" here could also maybe suggest the nearness to burial — the grave of the dead. These grave men may be nearly blind, but the speaker says they see with "blinding sight." This means that even though they might not have all their senses working in the same way as a younger person, they can still *see* meaning in life. Here again the imagery relates to a beautiful, strong, and spectacular part of nature — meteors. The blind eyes of the grave men could still "blaze" with commitment to the power of life.

The poem concludes with a stanza that returns to the plea of the first stanza. In the middle four stanzas that give examples, the lines "Rage, rage against the dying of the light" and "Do not go gentle into that good night" have been used to complete sentences of description. For example, "Good men rage against the dying of the light" or "Wild men do not go gentle into that good night." Now these lines are addressed directly to the speaker's father, so they would read more like this, "Father, I am asking you not to 'go gentle into that good night,'" or "Father, I am pleading with you to 'rage, rage against the dying of the light.'" The opening request is backed up by a series of examples, leading to a stronger plea (the only four-line stanza in the poem). The speaker builds an argument that he hopes will encourage his father to stay strong and brave even in the face of death. The frequent rhymes emphasize the opposing forces of "light"/"bright" (life) and "night" (death) and the repetition of the speaker's pleas ("Do not go . . ." and "Rage, rage . . .") underline the urgency of his message to his father.

Matt was much happier with this draft. He read it through and decided that what he talked about most was the repetition and the emphasis that repetition gave to the poem. He revised his title and — after several tries — wrote this opening paragraph to make the focus of his paper clear:

THE POWER OF SOUND AND SIGHT IN "DO NOT GO GENTLE"
Matthew Cejak

Dylan Thomas's poem "Do Not Go Gentle into That Good Night" gives a man's plea to his father to fight death. Images of strength, power, and life fill the poem, showing nature's beauty and energy and giving reasons for the father to fight death. The poem's rhythm and sound seem to oppose death, too. The rhymes and repetition of lines build a lively pattern to the speaker's final argument.

EDITING FOCUS: CONCISENESS One of the earlier versions of Matt's opening paragraph looked like this:

> In Dylan Thomas's poem "Do Not Go Gentle into That Good Night," he writes about the plea a man is making to his father to mount a gallant battle against the trials and tribulations of the finality of death. The poem is filled with images of strength, power, and life. These images show to the reader the beauty and energy of nature and give reasons for the father to fight the grim reaper. As a matter of fact, the poem has a rhythm and sound that seem to oppose the ghastly specter of death, too. The rhymes and repetition of lines build a lively pattern to the speaker's final argument.

With his instructor's help, Matt identified the following problems. Matt edited to make certain that he conveyed his meaning as directly and clearly as possible.

1. Unneeded words and phrases.

   Wordy: As a matter of fact, the poem has a rhythm and sound that seem to oppose the ghastly specter of death, too.
   Edited: The poem's rhythm and sound seem to oppose death, too.

2. Unnecessary repetition. Matt combined sentences, trying to eliminate repetition.

   Wordy: The poem is filled with images of strength, power, and life. These images show to the reader the beauty and energy of nature and give reasons for the father to fight the grim reaper.
   Edited: Images of strength, power, and life fill the poem, showing nature's beauty and energy and giving reasons for the father to fight death.

3. Clichés and overused phrases.

   Wordy: fight the grim reaper
   Edited: fight death

4. Redundancy.

   Wordy: the finality of death.
   Edited: death. (Death is obviously final, so "finality of death" is ineffectively repetitious.)

Exercise

Compare the two versions of Matt's paragraph on pages 82–83. Then, editing for conciseness, revise the following early version of another paragraph from Matt's paper. When you have completed the revision, compare your editing decisions with the editing decisions demonstrated by the second paragraph of Matt's paper, page 81.

The second stanza gives the first of three examples the speaker gives for the purpose of demonstrating why he believes old people should resist death. Wise men may know that "dark is right." Like "night" in the first stanza, "dark" is a metaphor for death. But these wise men, when they spoke during their lifetime maybe they didn't really get their message across. They didn't speak like lightning. So they don't want to die. Instead, continuing in life is their heart's desire. "Lightning" relates to "light" in the first stanza. Good is implied by these words, and they also suggest strong power. The lightning may be powerful words. Light, on the other hand, represents the liveliness of life itself. In this stanza, the type of rhyme scheme of the poem begins to underline the insistence of the speaker on life. As in the first stanza, the first and third lines rhyme. And all four of these lines (1, 3, 4, and 6) rhyme, too. The rhyme emphasizes the relationship between "light" (life) and "night" (death) and the struggle that is continually going on between these two archenemies.

PROOFREADING FOCUS: APOSTROPHES, QUOTATION MARKS TO INDICATE WORDS USED IN A SPECIAL WAY As he completed his draft, Matt noticed that he had questions about the use of apostrophes. In addition, when he discussed a word from the poem, he was not certain whether to underline it, put it in quotation marks, or use no punctuation.

A quick check with a grammar handbook told him that apostrophes are required in the following situations:

- To form possessive nouns:

  Singular: One author's opinion.
  Plural: Two authors' opinion.

  Note: Do not use apostrophes with possessive pronouns such as "his," "hers," "theirs," and "ours."

  Note: When a word does not form the plural by adding "s" or "es," form the possessive simply by adding apostrophe "s."
  No: The childrens' story.
  Yes: The children's story.

- To form contractions:

were not becomes weren't

Note: "It's" is the contraction for "it is"; "its" is a possessive pronoun. (The bird left its nest.)

Note: Do not use apostrophes with verbs that are not part of contractions.
  No: He read's well.
  Yes: He reads well.

The handbook gave the following rule for punctuating words used in special situations:

- Words being referred to as words can be either underlined or enclosed in quotation marks.

"Light" is used as a metaphor for life.

or

Light is used as a metaphor for life.

Be consistent throughout the paper; use either quotation marks or underlining, not a combination.

Exercises:

1. Applying these rules, proofread and correct the following earlier versions of sentences from Matt's paper. Add apostrophes where needed; delete incorrectly used apostrophes. Add either quotation marks or underlining to words used as words (be consistent; use either quotation marks or underlining, not both).

   The first stanza begins with the speakers plea, addressed to old people.
   The repetition of the word rage emphasizes the importance the speaker places on this fight against death.
   They didnt speak like lightning.
   This phrase shows the mens' actions as lively and sparkling, like light on the water in a bay.
   It represent's power, energy, and life.
   Its interesting to note that grave means serious, yet "grave" here could also maybe suggest the nearness to burial.
   Now these lines are addressed directly to the speakers' father.

2. Keeping in mind the revising, editing, and proofreading strategies described in this chapter (as well as other strategies you know), combine Matt's first paragraph (pages 82–83) with his draft (pages 81–82) to make a strong, unified essay. Be prepared to explain the choices you make as you revise, edit, and proofread.

3. Read several poems from the poetry anthology section and then, using the process demonstrated with Matt's paper, plan and write an explication. Keep in mind the following guidelines:

Guidelines: Writing an Explication

1. An analysis, or explication, "unfolds" the poem (or section of a short story, novel, play, or essay). That is, it explains in detail how the work communicates to the reader.
2. An explication considers significant details and suggestions in the poem, including — but not limited to — these elements:

   sound (rhyme and rhythm)
   structure (patterns of lines and stanzas)
   figurative language (metaphors, similes, symbols)
   irony
   definitions of words

3. An explication shows how each part contributes to the whole meaning of the work; each part of the discussion, therefore, must relate to a clear central idea.
4. An explication is not a paraphrase (a restatement of the ideas of the work in your own words); instead, it is an explanation of the way a work communicates.
5. An explication is easy to organize; working chronologically from first to last stanza of a poem (or from beginning to end of a section from a short story, novel, essay, or play) makes the most sense.
6. An explication begins with an introduction indicating the main idea of the work and suggesting the direction of the explication.
7. An explication concludes with a paragraph that sums up the meaning that has been unfolded for the reader.

Writing to Evaluate

A literary work can be judged in many ways. For instance, a reader may evaluate a work by asking questions such as these: "Is this poem beautiful?" "Are the motives of the characters in this short story convincing?" "Are the ideas in this play worthy of close, careful attention?" "What are the values supported by this work? And do I subscribe to those values?"

You are probably prompted to ask a question of your own: "According to what standards?" Any evaluation — whether of a literary work, a scientific theory, or a historical event — must be based on criteria. The next question, of course, is "Who sets these criteria?" The answers to these questions are not simple. Each reader must develop his or her own standards for evaluation, but where do these criteria come from? They come from what we have learned, what we have experienced, what we have observed or heard — not only in school but also at home, in our communities, in our religious institutions, at work.

A topic such as number 4 requires an evaluation of the values and beliefs expressed by the work, and — more importantly — asks for the reader to examine his or her own values and beliefs as a means of judging the work.

Topic 4

Consider the values and beliefs suggested by each of these poems. Choose one of the poems and explain those values and beliefs as well as your evaluation of them. Do you agree with them completely? Question them? Explain.

DISCOVERING IDEAS: INTERVIEWING After reading both poems, Josh Epstein wrote this journal entry:

> I read "Do Not Go Gentle" first and I thought how much this son loved his father, that he didn't want him to just die with no fight. I was thinking right away that I would write the paper on the values in this poem which I can relate to — not so much my father, but my grandfather — I really want him to keep going even though he does have emphysema. I hate to see him slow down. Then I read "Slipping." This was a hard poem for me to read because you can see she loves her father, but she in some ways really likes seeing him slow down. Now, this to me is almost the exact opposite of the idea in Thomas's poem. It's saying, "Don't fight the changes of old age, just accept them and look for the good." I didn't agree with this because I think you should always fight for every bit of life. But the more I thought about it, the more I wondered which way I would want my relatives to think or act if I was the person who was getting old.

After writing this journal entry and thinking about the topic for a while, Josh still wasn't sure what his own criteria were for judging the values suggested by the two poems. He decided to work on "Slipping" because he saw that the poem supported the ideas of love and commitment (which he also believed in). But the means of showing love — accepting and even welcoming debilitating changes — was something he found difficult to understand.

To think further about the issues raised by the poem, Josh decided to interview Norma Heath, a nurse who worked with elderly patients and their families at the hospital where Josh held a part-time job. He chose Norma because in the past they'd had conversations about some patients in the hospital. Josh knew Norma believed that families often distressed hospitalized relatives by pushing for more treatment rather than accepting the changes brought on by illness. To prepare Norma for the interview, Josh asked her to read the poem. He also wrote a list of questions he wanted to ask. After asking permission, Josh taped the interview so that he could review it at home and make certain he was accurate if he decided to quote Norma. The following is a transcript of part of that tape:

Josh: So, what did you think of the poem?

Norma: I'm not a great one for poetry — but this one I liked — I kept reading it — especially the last lines.

Josh: Why the last lines?

Norma: I think — I guess — well, for me the screen seems like the ones we have in some of the exam rooms. And it falls, and you really see the whole truth about this man — who, I think, was a doctor in his professional life. So he was used to examining people and seeing — maybe "the truth" about them. But nobody saw him in that way.

Josh: I see what you mean. But I still think it's weird that his daughter is, like, loving this change. Because, to me, what it shows is that her father is really not her father — I mean the way she always knew him. He's like weaker, but she likes that just because now he says he loves her.

Norma: To me it makes total sense — and I'm not sure what you mean by weaker. You mean the father is physically weak or emotionally weak because he says he loves her?

Josh: No, I — of course I don't mean to say "I love you" is emotionally weak, but it's because he's physically weak that he says it. I mean, would he say that if he still was totally well? I think the physical weakness has, sort of, broken him down.

Norma: I'm not sure I agree. Yes, his body is weak. But sometimes the inner change is not like breaking down. More like letting something go. Letting something go that has been preventing strength — hmm — preventing strong feelings. Like the poem says here "reserve has slipped" away from him. Now his loving of his daughter can be seen. And he is lucky she can accept that. And she's not just totally cynical about it.

Josh: What do you mean by totally cynical?

Norma: Well, some families, they just ignore changes like that because it's like they feel it's just another symptom of the person getting old. Or else they get angry with the person and it's like, "Well, it's too late!" I see a lot of bitterness.

Josh: But this daughter seems happy — she's not angry or bitter.

Norma: That's what I get — and I tell you, I wish we had more daughters like her who could say, "what I love" is this or that about some change they see in their parent — mother or father.

After the interview — and after spending more time rereading and rethinking the poem — Josh thought more about the speaker in the poem and about the implications of her responses to her father's changes. Norma's comment about the change showing strength rather than weakness really intrigued him.

CONSIDERING AUDIENCE, NARROWING THE TOPIC, AND DEVISING A PRELIMINARY THESIS Josh decided to focus on emotional strength as a central concept for evaluating the poem. He came up with this list of questions:

What does the poem say about emotional strength?
Who shows emotional strength?
Why is this person (or persons) showing emotional strength?
What is the definition of emotional strength in this poem?
What is my definition of emotional strength?
What does the poem say about the relationship between emotional strength and love?
What do I think about the relationship between emotional strength and love?

Josh knew that several people in the class had a strongly negative response to the values expressed in the poem. Just as he at first had questioned the daughter's motives for admiring the changes in her father, many students had seen her reaction as selfish. Josh realized that he was going to propose an alternative reading. He knew that he would have to work hard to find evidence that was convincing. He also knew he had to express his ideas so that people who did not share his views would not feel personally attacked.

Josh had no trouble coming up with a preliminary thesis. He knew he wanted to focus on the concept of emotional strength.

Both the speaker and the father in Joan Aleshire's poem "Slipping" show emotional strength and love as they face the changes brought by his aging.

PLANNING ORGANIZATION When he was ready to draft, Josh thought about how he wanted to start his essay and where he would go with it. He decided to focus on the questions he had listed and to use images and ideas from the poem to explore those questions. He rewrote the questions as statements and reordered the questions like this:

Introduction: focus on relationship of emotional strength and love.
1. Both father and daughter show emotional strength.
2. They show emotional strength in different ways and for a different reason.
   A. Father: physical changes cause him to drop his guard; wants to tell what has always been there.
   B. Daughter: accepts changes; does not act angry or judgmental.
3. Emotional strength means being able to change and to accept change.
4. Having the ability to change and accept change is a necessary part of loving and being loved.

DRAFTING Using the notes he had taken during the interview, notes he had made on a copy of the poem, journal entries, and the outline, Josh wrote several drafts. Here is his final copy:

LOVE AND STRENGTH
Josh Epstein

In Joan Aleshire's poem "Slipping," a daughter describes the changes old age has brought to her father. The father gradually loses his physical abilities and, in addition, becomes less reserved. The daughter accepts the physical changes and welcomes her father's loss of restraint. Although both the speaker and the father are weak in some ways, they also show emotional strength and love as they face the changes brought by his aging.

Many images in the first two stanzas suggest the father's physical weakness: "the leg that weakens . . . the curtain of mist that falls over one eye"; the lost concentration and "fine sense of direction." In addition, he has become dependent on other family members. When he takes a walk with his daughter, she has to slow down "to match his pace." She describes him as being similar to "a child who keeps pulling on your hand."

Another change that might be seen as weakening is the way he no longer keeps his feelings inside himself. For much of his life, this man has saved his emotional energy for his work. His daughter explains that a familiar photograph of him, teaching with his

> chair tipped back
> against the lecture-room wall — shows
> a man talking, love of his work lighting
> his face — in a way we seldom saw at home.

Now instead of putting his emotions into his work, he freely tells his daughter, "I love you so much." So his ability to keep up his reserve with his family is no longer there. True, in a way he has weakened, but also he now shows real feelings for his daughter, which is a kind of emotional strength. It's as if the weakening of the body has allowed his strong feelings to come out. They were simply trapped inside.

The daughter, too, shows her emotional strength. Recalling her mother's observation that "[your father] never liked / to talk about feelings," the speaker honestly describes the father she knew when she was growing up as someone who didn't show too much affection at home. However, she doesn't seem bitter and angry, which would show weakness. Instead, she loves her father the way he is now. She doesn't berate him for what happened in the past. Also, even though it seems like her father didn't spend too much time with the family in the past, she is still willing to take walks with him and to talk to him. She doesn't hold a grudge or retaliate by rejecting him.

The father has grown stronger in family relationships even though his body has grown weaker. The daughter shows that she is strong because she accepts the love her father has begun to express. Both the father and the daughter use the emotional strength brought about by his aging to express the connection they feel to each other. Both say, "I love you," which are words they may not have spoken out loud before.

REVISING FOCUS: LOGIC While he was drafting, Josh saw that he needed to work on presenting his ideas logically. He isolated these particular problems in earlier drafts of the final copy you just read.

1. Making **absolute statements** that could not be supported. For instance, he used words such as "all," "every," or "none" when he should have acknowledged exceptions.

   Illogical: All the images in the first two stanzas suggest the father's physical weakness. (Not every image in these stanzas suggests physical weakness; for example, the image of the darkness pushing "away years of restraint" suggests an emotional, not a physical change.)
   Revised: Many of the images in the first two stanzas suggest the father's physical weakness.

2. Using a **question-begging** approach, that is, stating that something "is obvious" or that "everyone knows" something rather than providing evidence to support the point.

   Illogical: It's obvious that the daughter, too, shows emotional strength. She really understands her father and herself. (It's not obvious to the reader of the paper; evidence is needed to demonstrate the daughter's emotional strength and to demonstrate — rather than simply announce — her understanding of her father and herself.)
   Revised: The daughter, too, shows her emotional strength. She honestly describes the father she knew when she was growing up as someone who didn't show too much affection at home. However, she doesn't seem bitter and angry, which would show weakness. Instead, she loves her father the way he is now. She doesn't berate him for what happened in the past. Also, even though it seems like her father didn't spend too much time with the family in the past, she is still willing to take walks with him and to talk to him. She doesn't hold a grudge or retaliate by rejecting him. (Here details and examples provide evidence to show the reader the validity of the draft paragraph's initial sentence and to replace the broad generalization of the second sentence in the draft version.)

3. Using a **non sequitur.** This Latin term means "it does not follow" and describes conclusions drawn from evidence that cannot logically support them—for example, saying that a certain point in a work of literature is true because the speaker states that it is so. (Because some speakers are unreliable, their statements cannot be taken as truth.)

Illogical: She honestly describes the father she knew when she was growing up as someone who didn't show too much affection at home. Of course, because he is her father, she knows that he really did love her and she is not bitter or angry. (It is not necessarily true that "because he is her father" she would know that he loved her. The mere fact of parenthood does not ensure love.)

Revised: She honestly describes the father she knew when she was growing up as someone who didn't show too much affection at home. However, she doesn't seem bitter and angry, which would show weakness. Instead, she loves her father the way he is now. (Here the transitional sentence beginning with "however" shows the logical relationship between the ideas expressed in the sentences that precede and follow it.)

The three fallacies in the preceding list are examples of problems with logic that can make a paper unclear or undermine an essential point. Consult an English handbook to review other possible problems with logic as well as strategies for revision.

EDITING FOCUS: INTEGRATING AND PUNCTUATING QUOTATIONS As Josh read through an early draft of his paper, he realized that he had problems with the quotations he had used. He edited his paper to conform to the following rules:

1. Make clear whose ideas you are quoting and whom you are talking about:

   Unclear: The poem talks about slowing down "to match his pace" and being similar to "a child who keeps pulling on your hand."
   Edited: When the father takes a walk with his daughter, she has to slow down "to match his pace." She describes his leg as dragging like "a child who keeps pulling on your hand."

2. Use quotation marks around short quotations (four lines or fewer) that are combined with your own sentences.

   When he takes a walk with his daughter, she has to slow down "to match his pace."

3. When you cite fewer than three lines of poetry, run the words or phrases into your own sentences. Indicate line breaks with a slash (/).

Recalling her mother's observation that "[your father] never liked/
to talk about feelings," the speaker honestly describes the father she
knew when she was growing up as someone who didn't show too
much affection at home.

4. Set off long quotations (more than four lines) in a separate block
    (called an extract) indented several spaces. Do not use quotation
    marks around the extract.

    His daughter explains that a familiar photograph of him teaching
    with his

    > chair tipped back
    > against the lecture-room wall — shows
    > a man talking, love of his work lighting
    > his face — in a way we seldom saw at home.

5. Integrate quotations into your own sentences to show the relation-
    ship of the quotation to the point you are making.

    Unclear: Now, he puts his emotions into his family instead of his
    work. "I love you so much."
    Edited: Now instead of putting his emotions into his work, he freely
    tells his daughter, "I love you so much."

    Unclear: Another change relates to his work.

    > A photograph taken of him teaching —
    > white coat, stethoscope like a pet snake
    > around his neck, chair tipped back
    > against the lecture-room wall — shows
    > a man talking, love of his work lighting
    > his face — in a way we seldom saw at home.

    Edited: Another change that might be seen as weakening is the way
    he no longer keeps his feelings inside himself. For much of his life,
    this man has saved his emotional energy for his work. His daughter
    explains that a familiar photograph of him, teaching with his

    > chair tipped back
    > against the lecture-room wall — shows
    > a man talking, love of his work lighting
    > his face — in a way we seldom saw at home.

6. Use the ellipsis (three spaced periods) to show that words are
    omitted.

    Many images in the first two stanzas suggest the father's physical
    weakness: "the leg that weakens . . . the curtain of mist that falls
    over one eye."

7. Use brackets to indicate a minor change that makes a quotation
    grammatically compatible with the rest of your sentence.

Original: As the daughter watches her father's changes, it's clear that "what I love is the way reserve has slipped from / feeling."

Edited: As the daughter watches her father's changes, it's clear that "what [she loves] is the way reserve has slipped from / [his] feeling."

8. Check carefully to make certain that quotations are accurate.
9. To make your quotations effective, use them sparingly. Overly long quotations often obscure the meaning they are intended to convey.

PROOFREADING FOCUS: PRONOUN REFERENCE, PRONOUN AGREEMENT, TREATMENT OF TITLES While proofreading, Josh realized he needed to work on revising pronoun references. For example, here's a sentence from an earlier draft of paragraph 4.

Her mother says that her father "never liked / to talk about feelings." She honestly describes him as someone who didn't show too much affection at home.

To whom does "her" in the phrase "her father" refer? To the mother or to the daughter? Almost certainly it refers to the daughter, but the reference needs to be made clear.

Edited: Recalling her mother's observation that "[your father] never liked / to talk about feelings," the speaker honestly describes the father she knew when she was growing up as someone who didn't show too much affection at home.

Of course, this sentence has also been revised in other ways — but the proofreading issue here is that a pronoun cannot convey its meaning accurately if the reader cannot tell who or what that pronoun represents.

Another problem with pronouns in the paper was their agreement with the nouns to which they referred.

It's as if the weakening of the body has allowed his strong feelings to come out. It was simply trapped inside. ("It" is singular, and the word referred to, "feelings," is plural. Pronouns must agree in number with the words to which they refer.)

Edited: It's as if the weakening of the body has allowed his strong feelings to come out. They were simply trapped inside.

As Josh proofread, he realized he wasn't sure how to treat titles, so he checked an English handbook and found these rules:

Treatment of Titles

1. When citing a poem, short story, or essay, put the title in quotation marks.

In Joan Aleshire's poem "Slipping," a daughter describes the changes old age has brought to her father.

2. When citing a novel or a play, underline the title (or use italics).

   Dickens's novel <u>A Tale of Two Cities</u> is often required reading for high school sophomores.

   or

   Dickens's novel *A Tale of Two Cities* is often required reading for high school sophomores.

3. When writing the title of your own paper, do not underline it or put it in quotation marks.

   Love and Strength

4. Always capitalize the first word in a title as well as all other important words. (Do not capitalize small, unimportant words such as "and," "the," "an," "a," "of," "to," "in," etc.)

   Dylan Thomas published "Do Not Go Gentle into That Good Night" in 1952.

Exercise

Read several works from the anthology section and then, using the process demonstrated with Josh's paper, plan and write an evaluation of the beliefs and values expressed in one of the poems. Keep the following guidelines in mind:

Guidelines: Writing an Evaluation of Beliefs and Values

1. Identify the beliefs and values expressed in the work, making note of specific details that demonstrate these beliefs and values.
2. Think about the criteria you will use to evaluate those beliefs and values.
3. Consider what questions might be raised concerning those beliefs and values. (If you share those values, imagine the response of someone who does not.)
4. To expand your thinking, consider interviewing others who might be particularly interested in the values and beliefs expressed in the work.
5. Decide whether your evaluation will support or question (perhaps even refute) the values and beliefs expressed in the work.
6. List your reasons for supporting, questioning, or refuting these values and beliefs.
7. Remember to reread the work frequently to make certain you are responding to values and beliefs actually expressed there.
8. Make certain the opening section of the paper makes clear both the values and beliefs expressed in the poem and the approach you are taking toward those values and beliefs.

9. Make certain the conclusion sums up the evaluation — the reasons you support and subscribe to (or do not support and subscribe to) the beliefs and values expressed in the work.

Writing a Research Paper

The fifth assignment topic calls for research. Here it is:

Topic 5

Discover a question related to Thomas's "Do Not Go Gentle" and do research to explore that question. In your paper, refer to at least three sources.

A paper that requires research can lead in many directions. In some courses, particularly the physical or social sciences, research may include experiments or observations you design and carry out yourself. Another research strategy is the interview: talking to experts who know about the subject you are considering. For this assignment, library resources — books, journals, newspapers — are most useful.

As Toni Jackmon considered writing about "Do Not Go Gentle," she became curious about many things. She wondered if the final stanza really did address Thomas's father. She wondered what relationship he had had with his father. In addition, she was confused about the different kinds of men who "do not go gentle" into death. What did wise men, good men, wild men, or grave men have to do with the father in the poem?

Toni saw that she did not yet have one question to explore, as the assignment asked. She decided to do some reading, hoping that her research would help her to focus on one particular consideration.

DISCOVERING IDEAS: RESEARCHING Toni went to the library and made an appointment to talk to a reference librarian. During her appointment with the librarian, David Bauer, she discovered many possibilities. The resources David suggested fell primarily into four categories:

1. **Special encyclopedias, reference works, handbooks, and general histories.** For Toni's project, David suggested the following:

   Annual Bibliography of English Language and Literature
   Dictionary of Literary Biography
   Dictionary of National Biography [British]

2. **Periodicals** (journals and magazines; in this case, journals and magazines relating to the field of English literature). David suggested that, to find articles relating to Dylan Thomas, Toni should use **periodical indexes** (guides compiled by organizations that research the most important journals and magazines in any field of

study and then publish indexes listing articles alphabetically according to their subject matter). For information on literary topics, David suggested these indexes:

Humanities Index
MLA International Bibliography

3. **Newspapers.** With David's help, Toni learned how to use the *New York Times Index* and also the microfilm reader/copier, because copies of the *Times* are stored on microfilm.
4. **Books.** Toni was already familiar with this source and knew how to use the library's card catalogue to find books relating to Thomas's work. David provided her with more options, however, by explaining the process of **interlibrary loan** so that Toni could have access to books not held by her library.

Toni decided to begin by reading some background information on Thomas. She used the *Dictionary of Literary Biography* and (at David's suggestion) she also checked the *New York Times Index* for 1953 (the year of Thomas's death), looking under the topic "Deaths" to find his obituary.

She discovered that Thomas apparently had a happy childhood growing up in Wales. Although he experienced the usual conflicts with his parents, the family remained close. "Do Not Go Gentle," she learned, was written during the months of Thomas's father's final illness, but what interested her more were the details of Thomas's own battle with alcoholism and his subsequent early death at the age of 39. She also found that he had published a volume of poetry called *Death and Entrances,* which suggested to her that death was a frequent theme in Thomas's work.

Toni then decided to look for information specifically related to "Do Not Go Gentle." She found a book, William York Tindall's *A Reader's Guide to Dylan Thomas,* that gave a reading of the poem. She was surprised to see that Tindall thought the "grave men" were poets and decided to look further to find out how other scholars might have interpreted the kinds of men Thomas said did not "go gentle" to their deaths.

Toni could not find any further references to this theme in the books she read. She turned next to the *Humanities Index* and discovered the titles of several articles that looked promising. After reading the articles, she decided that the most relevant was "Thomas' 'Do Not Go Gentle into That Good Night'" by Michael W. Murphy.

THOMAS' DO NOT GO GENTLE INTO THAT GOOD NIGHT
Michael W. Murphy, University of Wisconsin, Green Bay

Although there is widespread agreement about the theme of Dylan Thomas' "Do Not Go Gentle into That Good Night" (the need to affirm life emotionally at the hour of death, even when one rationally recognizes that death is both natural and inevitable), the references in the poem to "wise men," "good men," "wild men," and "grave men" have caused considerable difficulty. The only two critics who have ventured to explicate the references (most commentators simply ignore them) differ essentially in their interpretations: Clark Emery identifies the wise men as "philosophers who had thundered but lit no fires"; the good men as "saints, who at last see abstinence as *contra naturam*"; the wild men as "poets, whose best intentions were reversed"; and the grave men as "sober-sides, who realize they have lived half-lives" (*The World of Dylan Thomas*, p. 54). William York Tindall, on the other hand, agrees that the wise men are some kind of philosophers but interprets the good men as "moralists, Puritans perhaps, who, having avoided dancing waters in life's 'green bay,' cannot accept death after such a life," and considers the grave men, not the wild men, to be the poets; the wild men are "men of action and lovers of living" (*A Reader's Guide to Dylan Thomas*, p. 205). Both Emery's and Tindall's interpretations are not only unjustifiably narrow but, more importantly, fail to take account of the careful play of opposites — "my dialectical method," Thomas called it — which characterizes this poem, as it does so many of his others.

The contrast between the wise men of the second tercet and the good men of the third is specifically indicated by the placement of "words" and "deeds" in parallel positions in these stanzas as well as by the explicit contrast of "dark" and "bright" and the implicit contrast of the sky (where the lightning would appear) and the water ("green bay"). The wise men who have spent their lives preaching wisdom are contrasted with the good men who have spent their lives practicing it. Both rage against death because their work has not accomplished anything. The words of the wise have gone unheeded; they have not sparked or generated any change in the actions of men or brought any light into the world. The deeds of the good men have been similarly ignored, engulfed by the waves of the rough sea of life. Had that sea been more serene — "a green bay" — the frail deeds would have remained afloat, serving as a visible example for others to follow (like the "woodtongued virtue" of Ann Jones that Thomas called upon to "Babble like a bellbuoy" in "After the Funeral").

The fourth and fifth tercets present another pair of contrasting types, and again an active way of life is opposed to a more passive way, with neither proving satisfactory. Again, too, the contrast is expressed in terms of light and dark — or day and night — imagery, the wild men being associated with the light (the sun) and the grave men with the dark (blindness and meteors, which are only visible at night). The wild men are those who have taken a hedonistic, *carpe diem* (cf. "caught . . . the sun") approach to life, only to discover that it is time which has caught them, rather than *vice-versa* — a theme which occurs frequently in Thomas' poetry, most memorably at the end of "Fern Hill": "Time held me green and dying / Though I sang in my chains like the sea." Thus the songs the wild men sang extolling the sun appear now, in retrospect, to have been elegies lamenting its passing. In contrast to the Dionysian wild men, the grave men are the sober-minded Apollonians who have taken such an ascetic approach to life that all the joys of life have passed them by. Now, nearing death (the pun on "grave" is typical of Thomas), they are suddenly struck — like Saul on the road to Damascus — with a blinding revelation: though they are afflicted with all the infirmities of old age, not even blindness could keep them from enjoying life fully (and thus dying with meteor-like splendor) if they could only live a little longer.

Taken all together, the references to the wise, good, wild, and grave men suggest that life is always too brief and incomplete for everyone, regardless of how he has lived. Thus no one should "go gentle into that good night," especially someone like Thomas' father, who presumably represents a combination of all the types described in the poem.

Toni was particularly pleased to note that Murphy mentioned the reading by Tindall. She was a little surprised that another scholar Murphy mentioned, Clark Emery, thought that the "wild men" were poets. Here's the journal entry she wrote:

> When I read Tindall, and he said the grave men were poets, I was surprised because I didn't think of any of these people as having specific roles in life. They seemed like personality types. Then, in the article that I found, Michael W. Murphy quotes Clark Emery as saying that the wild men were "poets, whose best intentions were reversed." I know in class we keep talking about different readings, but it still threw me off guard to see this difference. Then Murphy has a whole other idea. I'm going to reread the poem (for the fifth time!!) to see if I see any poets there!

This journal entry shows how Toni used the research process to refine her questions about "Do Not Go Gentle" and about Thomas himself. She realized that she wanted to focus on the interpretation of the wise, good, wild, and grave men.

CONSIDERING AUDIENCE, NARROWING THE TOPIC, AND DEVISING A PRELIMINARY THESIS Toni realized that her instructor would probably be familiar with the background material and the literary criticism she had discovered, but most of the other students in the class would not. She knew that she would have to explain the views she was discussing, yet she also wanted to avoid simply summarizing the critical views she had read. She knew that the focus of the paper should be to pursue her own examination of this question she formulated: Do the wise, good, wild, and grave men, and their actions, relate in some way to poets and poetry?

Several rereadings of the poem, plus consideration of Michael Murphy's article and the ideas of several other scholars, led Toni to decide that there could very well be a poet—or rather several poets—in the poem. She was especially struck by Murphy's contention that the interpretation of any one of the groups of men as "poet" was too narrow, and she was also intrigued by his final statement that Thomas's father "presumably represents a combination of all the types described in the poem."

Here are several note cards she made as she worked toward developing a preliminary thesis statement. Note that Toni carefully put all the publishing information at the top of the first note card from a source. On subsequent note cards she simply used the author's last name. She used quotation marks to make clear which words were directly taken from the source. She also noted the page from which she took direct quotes. Toni needed all of this information to document her research properly.

Michael W. Murphy
"Thomas's 'Do Not Go Gentle
into That Good Night'"
Explication, 28, Feb. 1970, 55.

Claims interpretations seeing one
group of men as poets "unjustifiably
narrow."

Murphy, 55

(p.55) "Thus no one should 'go gentle into
That good night,' especially someone
like Thomas's father, who presumably
represents a combination of all the
types described in the poem."

Why "presumably"? Why do these types
relate mainly to Thomas's father?
Maybe instead to poet → Then to all
of us?

> *Horace Gregory, " The Black-Stock-*
> *inged Bait and Dylan Thomas " in*
> *Critical Essays on Dylan Thomas*
> *ed. Georg Gaston, G.K. Hall,*
> *Boston, 1989, 118-129*
>
> (p. 120)   *"denial of Spiritual death "*
> *" In one sense, the poem stands*
> *as Thomas's own epitaph."*

After thinking about the research she had gathered, Toni developed this preliminary thesis statement:

> Dylan Thomas's men are described as wise, good, wild, and grave. They could share qualities with poets. On the other hand, their lives and their views of life also represent us all.

PLANNING ORGANIZATION Toni decided to begin her paper by discussing some of the proposed interpretations of Thomas's wise, good, wild, and grave men. Then, after stating her own view in her thesis, she planned to move through the poem stanza by stanza, showing why she thought each type of man could represent both a poet and also a broad range of humans.

Toni did not have a conclusion firmly in mind, but she thought she might use, in some context, the phrase from Horace Gregory's article suggesting that the poem could stand "as Thomas's own epitaph."

DRAFTING Toni began her paper by considering the proposed interpretations, discovered through her research, of wise, good, wild, and grave men.

> William York Tindall describes the grave men in "Do Not Go Gentle" as poets. On the other hand, it may be that the wild men are the poets, but "Although there is widespread agreement about the theme of Dylan Thomas' "Do Not Go Gentle into That Good Night" (the need to affirm life emotionally at the hour of death, even when one rationally recognizes that death is both natural and inevitable), the references in the poem to "wise men," "good men," and "wild men" and "grave men" have caused considerable difficulty." "Taken all together, the references to the wise, good, wild, and grave men suggest that life is always too brief and incomplete for everyone, regardless of how he has lived. Thus no one should

"go gentle into that good night," especially someone like Thomas' father who presumably represents a combination of all the types described in the poem" (55). These interpretations all seem too narrow. Dylan Thomas's men are described as wise, good, wild, and grave. They could share qualities with poets. On the other hand, their lives and their views of life also represent us all.

REVISING FOCUS: USING QUOTATIONS EFFECTIVELY As she read over the paragraph, Toni found it confusing. It was hard to tell where the quotations started and ended. In fact, the paragraph seemed to be mostly quotations. Also, she saw that it wasn't clear whether William York Tindall was responsible for all the quotes and ideas or whether they came from other writers.

The following rules helped Toni with the revision process:

1. When quoted words appear within short quotations, enclose the quoted words in single quotation marks.

   Michael Murphy believes the poem argues that "no one should 'go gentle into that good night,' especially someone like Thomas' father" (55).

2. Document all direct quotations and paraphrases (someone else's ideas put in your own words). That is, give credit by indicating the source either in an introduction to the quotation or paraphrase or in parentheses following the quotation or paraphrase. Give the page number of the source in parentheses following the quotation or paraphrase.

   Clark Emery identifies the wild men as "poets, whose best intentions were reversed" (54).

   or

   On the other hand, the wild men may be identified as "poets, whose best intentions were reversed" (Emery, 54).

3. List your references according to an established format. For papers in the humanities (for example, English, music, art, foreign languages), document your sources according to the Modern Languages Association (MLA) format. See Appendix A, page 1550, for explanations and examples.

In addition to these points, Toni recognized another essential principle relating to quotations: *Do not overquote.* She saw that she needed to rely more on her own words and ideas, using the possibilities she had discovered in her research as ways to discover and explore — rather than replace — her own thoughts.

Keeping in mind the new approach she wanted to take — using primarily her own ideas and using quotations and paraphrases sparingly — Toni wrote this revision.

WE ARE ALL POETS
Toni Jackmon

In *A Reader's Guide to Dylan Thomas,* William York Tindall describes the grave men in "Do Not Go Gentle" as poets (205). Clark Emery beleives that the wild men are the poets (Murphy 55). Michael Murphy, on the other hand, does not identify any of the men as poets. He sees all of the men mentioned in stanzas 2–4 as having a broader interpretation, suggesting "that life is always too brief and incomplete for everyone, regardless of how he has lived" (55). Even Murphy's interpretation, however, seems too narrow. Dylan Thomas's men are described as wise, good, wild, and grave. They could share qualities with poets. On the other hand, there lives and there views of life also represent us all.

The wise men may be like poets. These would be poets who have not been heard. Their "words had forked no lightning." Of course they would not want to die in that situation. They would hope for a chance to have their words make a difference. The wise men do not need to just stand for poets, however. They could stand for any person who felt that he or she had not really had a chance to do anything in life that might make an inpact on others. People who felt they had not yet done something significant or useful might feel this way. They certainly would fight death.

The good men, too, could be poets. The "frail deeds" might refer to writing poems. Line 8 says that those deeds "might have danced in a green bay." This could mean that the poems had the possibility to cause a beautiful responce. They could have been bright, and they could have danced. For some reason they didn't. Many people besides poets also feel this way. They see their work and their actions as not having caused the reaction they would have hoped for.

The wild men might be poets who spent most of their time "singing" (writing) about the sun. The sun represents beautiful things in life. Maybe they didn't really take the time to appreciate those beautiful things. They didn't stop to think that nothing can last forever. Beauty started to go. Then they greived. These poets are certainly like many people. These are people who don't take the time to appreciate what they have. Then at the end of their lives they want want to fight death. They want to live longer to have a chance to appreciate "the sun in flight." Now they understand what they loose when that sun (beauty) has gone from them.

Thomas describes the grave men as seeing "with blinding sight." We often think of poets as being able to see things that others cannot see. The grave men, too, could be poets. These poets might be near death. They still, however, have the ability to see special things. They want to live so they can continue to enlighten others. This enlightenment of others is what could be meant by "blind eyes could blaze like meteors." Their knowledge could shine out still. So it's easy to see how the images in this stanza could apply specificaly to poets. It's also easy to see how they could apply to most people. Most of us beleive that we are special individuals. As special, unique beings we have special ways of seeing. Each of us sees the world in a slightly different way. In old age, near death, our phsyical sight might be failing. We would probably still, however, beleive that we had a special way to "see" (understand) the world around us. This beleif in being unique is one of the things that would keep a person fightting against dying.

It makes sence that Dylan Thomas, a poet, might have chosen examples of men who could be seen as poets. Horace Gregory suggests this possibility when he says that "Do Not Go Gentle" could be read "as Thomas's own epitaph" (129). On the other hand, a poet does not have to be somebody who stands entirely apart from the rest of human-ity. The examples also suggest that those who fight against death could be any of us who look back and see our actions as incomplete or as unappreciated. Those who fight could be any of us who failed to stop to fully acknowledge the beauty in our lives or any or us who consider our view of the world to be unique and special. Perhaps, in a way, we are all poets. Thomas may be speaking to us all when he says, "Do not go gentle into that good night."

Works Cited

Gregory, Horace. "The Black-Stockinged Bait and Dylan Thomas." *Critical Essays on Dylan Thomas.* Ed. Georg Gaston. Boston: G. K. Hall, 1989, 125–132.

Murphy, Michael. "Thomas' 'Do Not Go Gentle into That Good Night.'" *Explicator* 28 (1970): 55.

Tindall, William York. *A Reader's Guide to Dylan Thomas.* New York: Macmillan, 1962.

EDITING FOCUS: COMBINING SENTENCES Reading her re-vised draft, Toni was happy with the way she had used quotations, but felt that many of her sentences did not seem to flow together smoothly. Working with her instructor, she revised again according to the following rules for combining sentences:

1. Reduce information in one sentence to a group of words you can include in another sentence.

   Dylan Thomas was born and grew up in Wales. He was a poet.
   Edited: The poet Dylan Thomas was born and grew up in Wales.

2. Make one sentence into a clause; join the remaining sentence and the clause to show the relationship between the two.

   Dylan Thomas was married to a woman named Caitlin. She wrote a book about their life together.

Edited: Dylan Thomas was married to a woman named Caitlin, who wrote a book about their life together.

3. Join two short sentences with a word that shows the relationship between the two.

Dylan Thomas traveled widely to give poetry readings. His heart remained in Wales, however.
Edited: Dylan Thomas traveled widely to give poetry readings, but his heart remained in Wales.

Keeping these rules in mind, Toni edited her second paragraph this way:

The wise men may be like poets who have not been heard. Because their "words had forked no lightning," they do not want to die, but hope for a chance to have their words make a difference. The wise men do not need to stand just for poets, however. They could stand for any person who felt that he or she had not really had a chance to do anything in life that might make an inpact on others — people who felt they had not yet done something significant or useful might fight death.

Exercise

Edit the rest of Toni's paper, using the preceding sentence-combining strategies.

PROOFREADING FOCUS: SPELLING After working on her sentence structure, Toni ran a spelling checker program that was part of her word processing software. Although she found several spelling mistakes, she knew that she couldn't rely on it to find every mistake. She kept in mind the following points for using a spelling checker effectively:

1. Remember that a spelling checker cannot tell the difference between words that sound alike but are spelled differently (for instance, "their," "there," and "they're").
2. Remember that a spelling checker cannot read in context. For instance, it won't mark "run" as an error in "the run [sun] rose early."
3. Keep a notebook beside your computer. When your spelling checker discovers an error, write the correct version of the word in your notebook. Every time the spelling checker finds that same word incorrectly spelled, put a checkmark next to it in your notebook. If you accumulate five checkmarks, practice writing the word until you learn how to spell it.
4. Use your list of misspelled words to evaluate patterns of errors. For example, you may frequently misspell words with "ie" or "ei" in

them. Or you may have problems knowing whether to double a letter when adding an ending to a word. If you notice patterns like these, check an English handbook and learn the rules that will help to avoid such errors.

Exercises

1. Proofread Toni's paper for spelling errors. First, read the paper backward, beginning with the last sentence. Reading this way helps you to focus on spelling rather than on the meaning of the sentences. Then read the paper from beginning to end to pick up errors that depend on context. List the corrected versions of words that are misspelled, noting any patterns of errors that you discover.

2. Choose a poem, short story, or play from the anthology section. Then, using the process demonstrated with Toni's paper (as well as any other strategies explained in this chapter) plan and write a paper that integrates your ideas with the ideas of others (discovered through library research). Keep in mind the following guidelines:

Guidelines: Writing a Research Paper

1. Begin by reading the work carefully and by thinking of questions that outside reading might help you answer.

2. Become familiar with library resources.

> Books (and the cataloguing system used by your library)
> Specialized dictionaries and encyclopedias
> Periodical indexes
> > *The Humanities Index*
> > *The MLA International Bibliography*
> Newspaper indexes: *The New York Times Index*

3. Skim the sources you discover to find which might help to answer or focus your questions.

4. Decide on a preliminary thesis.

5. Take notes from sources that will help you to explore this thesis. (Make certain to note carefully bibliographic information, including author, title, date and place of publication, publisher, and page numbers, from each source.)

6. Organize your information and begin to draft.

7. Remember to use quotations and paraphrases sparingly. Your ideas, not those of your sources, should dominate the paper.

8. Lead in to quotations and paraphrases smoothly, so that the reader knows why they are important.

9. Provide accurate documentation for quoted and paraphrased material. (See Appendix A.)
10. Provide an accurate list of works cited. (See Appendix A.)

SUMMARY

Strategies for Discovering and Exploring Ideas

1. Write journal entries about the work (pages 58, 59, and 87).
2. Discuss the work with others (page 67).
3. Make lists of questions or observations about the work (pages 67, 78, and 89).
4. Write a paraphrase of a poem or of a complex section of a story, play, or essay (page 77).
5. Interview someone who has special interest or expertise in the theme or subject of the work (page 87).
6. Research the ideas of others on the work (page 96).

Strategies for Evaluating Your Audience

1. Consider the readers' interests (page 68).
2. Consider the readers' knowledge (pages 78, 99).
3. Consider the readers' opinions (page 89).
4. Consider the readers' values (page 89).

Strategies for Revising

1. Give the paper an accurate, inviting title (page 63).
2. Open with a paragraph that indicates the paper's purpose and intrigues the reader (page 63).
3. Conclude with a paragraph that follows logically from the rest of the paper and that does more than summarize (page 63).
4. Use clear transitions to show the relationship between sections of the paper, between paragraphs, and between sentences (page 71).
5. Use evidence — details, reasons, and examples — from the work to support your ideas (pages 72 and 91).
6. Keep summaries of works very short (no more than a few sentences at most). Know the difference between summarizing and discussing your own ideas (page 79).
7. Make sure your ideas are logically presented (page 91).
8. Make sure the organization of your paper is clear (pages 61, 68, 89, and 101).
9. Use quotations and paraphrases effectively. Lead in to quotations and paraphrases smoothly (pages 92 and 102).

10. Use quotations and paraphrases sparingly to support your points. Your own ideas should form the core of the paper (page 102).

Strategies for Editing

1. Avoid overuse of the verb "to be," expletives, passive voice, and nominalizations (pages 63, 64, and 72).
2. Use parallel structure effectively (page 72).
3. Be concise (page 83).
4. Integrate quotations well and punctuate them accurately (page 92).
5. Combine sentences to eliminate wordiness, repetition, and choppy structure (page 104).

Strategies for Proofreading

1. Rewrite fragments and comma splices as complete sentences (page 64).
2. Make subjects and verbs agree (page 73).
3. Make verb tenses agree (page 73).
4. Make sure that pronoun references are clear (page 94).
5. Make pronouns agree with the nouns to which they refer (page 94).
6. Punctuate lines of poetry correctly (page 92).
7. Use apostrophes correctly (page 84).
8. Use quotation marks correctly (page 84).
9. Format titles correctly (page 94).
10. Check for spelling or typographical errors (page 105).

Innocence and Experience

JAMES JOYCE (1882–1941)

Araby

North Richmond Street, being blind, was a quiet street except at the hour when the Christian Brothers' School set the boys free. An uninhabited house of two stories stood at the blind end, detached from its neighbors in a square ground. The other houses of the street, conscious of decent lives within them, gazed at one another with brown imperturbable faces.

The former tenant of our house, a priest, had died in the back drawing-room. Air, musty from having been long enclosed, hung in all the rooms, and the waste room behind the kitchen was littered with old useless papers. Among these I found a few paper-covered books, the pages of which were curled and damp: *The Abbot,* by Walter Scott, *The Devout Communicant* and *The Memoirs of Vidoca.* I liked the last best because its leaves were yellow. The wild garden behind the house contained a central apple-tree and a few straggling bushes under one of which I found the late tenant's rusty bicycle-pump. He had been a very charitable priest: in his will he had left all his money to institutions and the furniture of his house to his sister.

When the short days of winter came dusk fell before we had well eaten our dinners. When we met in the street the houses had grown somber. The space of sky above us was the color of ever-changing violet and towards it the lamps of the street lifted their feeble lanterns. The cold air stung us and we played till our bodies glowed. Our shouts echoed in the silent street. The career of our play brought us through the dark muddy lanes behind the houses where we ran the gantlet of the rough tribes from the cottages, to the back doors of the dark dripping gardens where odors arose from the ashpits, to the dark odorous stables where a coachman smoothed and combed the horse or shook music from the buckled harness. When we returned to the street light from the kitchen windows had filled the areas. If my uncle was seen turning the corner we hid in the shadow until we had seen him safely housed. Or if Mangan's sister came out on the doorstep to call her brother in to his tea we watched her from our shadow peer up and down the street. We waited to see whether she would remain or go in and, if she remained, we left our shadow and walked up to Mangan's steps resignedly. She was waiting for us, her figure defined by the light from the half-opened door. Her brother always teased her before he obeyed and I stood by the railings looking at her. Her dress swung as she moved her body and the soft rope of her hair tossed from side to side.

Every morning I lay on the floor in the front parlor watching her door. The blind was pulled down to within an inch of the sash so that I could not be seen. When she came out on the doorstep my heart leaped. I ran to the hall, seized my books and followed her. I kept her brown figure always in my eye and, when we came near the point at which our ways diverged, I quickened my pace and passed her. This happened morning after morning. I had never spoken to her, except for a few casual words, and yet her name was like a summons to all my foolish blood.

Her image accompanied me even in places the most hostile to romance. On Saturday evenings when my aunt went marketing I had to go to carry some of the parcels. We walked through the flaring streets, jostled by drunken men and bargaining women, amid the curses of laborers, the shrill litanies of shop-boys who stood on guard by the barrels of pigs' cheeks, the nasal chanting of street-singers, who sang a *come-all-you* about O'Donovan Rossa, or a ballad about the troubles in our native land. These noises converged in a single sensation of life for me: I imagined that I bore my chalice safely through a throng of foes. Her name sprang to my lips at moments in strange prayers and praises which I myself did not understand. My eyes were often full of tears (I could not tell why) and at times a flood from my heart seemed to pour itself out into my bosom. I thought little of the future. I did not know whether I would ever speak to her or not or, if I spoke to her, how I could tell her of my confused adoration. But my body was like a harp and her words and gestures were like fingers running upon the wires.

One evening I went into the back drawing-room in which the priest had died. It was a dark rainy evening and there was no sound in the house. Through one of the broken panes I heard the rain impinge upon the earth, the fine incessant needles of water playing in the sodden beds. Some distant lamp or lighted window gleamed below me. I was thankful that I could see so little. All my senses seemed to desire to veil themselves and, feeling that I was about to slip from them, I pressed the palms of my hands together until they trembled, murmering: *O love! O love!* many times.

At last she spoke to me. When she addressed the first words to me I was so confused that I did not know what to answer. She asked me was I going to *Araby.* I forget whether I answered yes or no. It would be a splendid bazaar, she said; she would love to go.

—And why can't you? I asked.

While she spoke she turned a silver bracelet round and round her wrist. She could not go, she said, because there would be a retreat that week in her convent. Her brother and two other boys were fighting for their caps and I was alone at the railings. She held one of the spikes, bowing her head towards me. The light from the lamp opposite our door caught the white curve of a neck, lit up her hair that rested there and, falling, lit up the hand upon the railing. It fell over one side of her dress and caught the white border of a petticoat, just visible as she stood at ease.

—It's well for you, she said.

—If I go, I said, I will bring you something.

What innumerable follies laid waste my waking and sleeping thoughts after that evening! I wished to annihilate the tedious intervening days. I chafed against the work of school. At night in my bedroom and by day in the classroom her image came between me and the page I strove to read. The syllables of the word *Araby* were called to me through the silence in which my soul luxuriated and cast an Eastern enchantment over me. I asked for leave to go to the bazaar on Saturday night. My aunt was surprised and hoped it was not some Freemason affair. I answered few questions in class, I watched my master's face pass from amiability to sternness; he hoped I was not beginning to idle. I could not call my wandering thoughts together. I had hardly any patience with the serious work of life which, now that it stood between me and my desire, seemed to me child's play, ugly monotonous child's play.

On Saturday morning I reminded my uncle that I wished to go to the bazaar in the evening. He was fussing at the hall-stand, looking for the hat-brush, and answered me curtly:

— Yes, boy, I know.

As he was in the hall I could not go into the front parlor and lie at the window. I left the house in bad humor and walked slowly towards the school. The air was pitilessly raw and already my heart misgave me.

When I came home to dinner my uncle had not yet been home. Still it was early. I sat staring at the clock for some time and, when its ticking began to irritate me, I left the room. I mounted the staircase and gained the upper part of the house. The high cold empty gloomy rooms liberated me and I went from room to room singing. From the front window I saw my companions playing below in the street. Their cries reached me weakened and indistinct and, leaning my forehead against the cool glass, I looked over at the dark house where she lived. I may have stood there for an hour, seeing nothing but the brown-clad figure cast by my imagination, touched discreetly by the lamplight at the curved neck, at the hand upon the railings and at the border below the dress.

When I came downstairs again I found Mrs. Mercer sitting at the fire. She was an old garrulous woman, a pawnbroker's widow, who collected used stamps for some pious purpose. I had to endure the gossip of the tea-table. The meal was prolonged beyond an hour and still my uncle did not come. Mrs. Mercer stood up to go: she was sorry she couldn't wait any longer, but it was after eight o'clock and she did not like to be out late, as the night air was bad for her. When she had gone I began to walk up and down the room, clenching my fists. My aunt said:

— I'm afraid you may put off your bazaar for this night of Our Lord.

At nine o'clock I heard my uncle's latchkey in the halldoor. I heard him talking to himself and heard the hall-stand rocking when it had received the weight of his overcoat. I could interpret these signs. When he was midway through his dinner I asked him to give me the money to go to the bazaar. He had forgotten.

— The people are in bed and after their first sleep now, he said.

I did not smile. My aunt said to him energetically:

—Can't you give him the money and let him go? You've kept him late enough as it is.

My uncle said he was very sorry he had forgotten. He said he believed in the old saying: *All work and no play makes Jack a dull boy.* He asked me where I was going and, when I had told him a second time he asked me did I know *The Arab's Farewell to His Steed.* When I left the kitchen he was about to recite the opening lines of the piece to my aunt.

I held a florin tightly in my hand as I strode down Buckingham Street towards the station. The sight of the streets thronged with buyers and glaring with gas recalled to me the purpose of my journey. I took my seat in a third-class carriage of a deserted train. After an intolerable delay the train moved out of the station slowly. It crept onward among ruinous houses and over the twinkling river. At Westland Row Station a crowd of people pressed to the carriage doors; but the porters moved them back, saying that it was a special train for the bazaar. I remained alone in the bare carriage. In a few minutes the train drew up beside an improvised wooden platform. I passed out on to the road and saw by the lighted dial of a clock that it was ten minutes to ten. In front of me was a large building which displayed a magical name.

I could not find any sixpenny entrance and, fearing that the bazaar 25 would be closed, I passed in quickly through a turnstile, handing a shilling to a weary-looking man. I found myself in a big hall girdled at half its height by a gallery. Nearly all the stalls were closed and the greater part of the hall was in darkness. I recognized a silence like that which pervades a church after a service. I walked into the center of the bazaar timidly. A few people were gathered about the stalls which were still open. Before a curtain, over which the words *Café Chantant* were written in colored lamps, two men were counting money on a salver. I listened to the fall of the coins.

Remembering with difficulty why I had come I went over to one of the stalls and examined porcelain vases and flowered tea-sets. At the door of the stall a young lady was talking and laughing with two young gentlemen. I remarked their English accents and listened vaguely to their conversation.

—O, I never said such a thing!

—O, but you did!

—O, but I didn't!

—Didn't she say that? 30

—Yes. I heard her.

—O, there's a . . . fib!

Observing me the young lady came over and asked me did I wish to buy anything. The tone of her voice was not encouraging; she seemed to have spoken to me out of a sense of duty. I looked humbly at the great jars that stood like eastern guards at either side of the dark entrance to the stall and murmured:

—No, thank you.

The young lady changed the position of one of the vases and went 35
back to the two young men. They began to talk of the same subject. Once
or twice the young lady glanced at me over her shoulder.

I lingered before her stall, though I knew my stay was useless, to make
my interest in her wares seem the more real. Then I turned away slowly and
walked down the middle of the bazaar. I allowed the two pennies to fall
against the sixpence in my pocket. I heard a voice call from one end of the
gallery that the light was out. The upper part of the hall was now completely
dark.

Gazing up into the darkness I saw myself as a creature driven and
derided by vanity; and my eyes burned with anguish and anger.

Considerations

1. Compare the adult narrator who tells the story with the younger self he
   describes. What differences do you see in the two? Similarities?
2. List several details relating to the story's setting and consider how those
   details relate to the changes the narrator experiences.
3. What does the narrator expect to find at Araby? What drives him so
   intensely to the bazaar? Why is he so intensely disappointed?
4. What is your response to the final passage describing the narrator's experience when he finally arrives at Araby?
5. Describe an experience you anticipated with pleasure but found the actual
   event disappointing. Provide specific details that show what you hoped
   for and why those hopes were not realized. In addition, show the difference between the way you looked at this experience as a child and the
   way you look at it now.

JEAN STAFFORD (1915–1979)

Bad Characters

Up until I learned my lesson in a very bitter way, I never had more than one friend at a time, and my friendships, though ardent, were short. When they ended and I was sent packing in unforgetting indignation, it was always my fault; I would swear vilely in front of a girl I knew to be pious and prim (by the time I was eight, the most grandiloquent gangster could have added nothing to my vocabulary — I had an awful tongue), or I would call a Tenderfoot Scout a sissy or make fun of athletics to the daughter of the high-school coach. These outbursts came without plan; I would simply one day, in the middle of a game of Russian bank or a hike or a conversation, be possessed with a passion to be by myself, and my lips instantly and without warning would accommodate me. My friend was never more surprised than I was when this irrevocable slander, this terrible, talented invective, came boiling out of my mouth.

Afterward, when I had got the solitude I had wanted, I was dismayed, for I did not like it. Then I would sadly finish the game of cards as if someone were still across the table from me; I would sit down on the mesa and through a glaze of tears would watch my friend departing with outraged strides; mournfully, I would talk to myself. Because I had already alienated everyone I knew, I then had nowhere to turn, so a famine set in and I would have no companion but Muff, the cat, who loathed all human beings except, significantly, me — truly. She bit and scratched the hands that fed her, she arched her back like a Halloween cat if someone kindly tried to pet her, she hissed, laid her ears flat to her skull, growled, fluffed up her tail into a great bush and flailed it like a bullwhack. But she purred for me, she patted me with her paws, keeping her claws in their velvet scabbards. She was not only an ill-natured cat, she was also badly dressed. She was a calico, and the distribution of her colors was a mess; she looked as if she had been left out in the rain and her paint had run. She had a Roman nose as the result of some early injury, her tail was skinny, she had a perfectly venomous look in her eye. My family said — my family discriminated against me — that I was much closer kin to Muff than I was to any of them. To tease me into a tantrum, my brother Jack and my sister Stella often called me Kitty instead of Emily. Little Tess did not dare, because she knew I'd chloroform her if she did. Jack, the meanest boy I have ever known in my life, called me Polecat and talked about my mania for fish, which, it so happened, I despised. The name would have been far more appropriate for *him,* since he trapped skunks up in the foothills — we lived in Adams, Colorado — and quite often, because he was careless and foolhardy, his clothes had to be buried, and even when that was done, he sometimes was sent home from school on the complaint of girls sitting next to him.

Along about Christmastime when I was eleven, I was making a snow-man with Virgil Meade in his backyard, and all of a sudden, just as we had got around to the right arm, I had to be alone. So I called him a son of a sea cook, said it was common knowledge that his mother had bedbugs and that his father, a dentist and the deputy marshal, was a bootlegger on the side. For a moment, Virgil was too aghast to speak — a little earlier we had agreed to marry someday and become millionaires — and then, with a bellow of fury, he knocked me down and washed my face in snow. I saw stars, and black balls bounced before my eyes. When finally he let me up, we were both crying, and he hollered that if I didn't get off his property that instant, his father would arrest me and send me to Canon City. I trudged slowly home, half frozen, critically sick at heart. So it was old Muff again for me for quite some time. Old Muff, that is, until I met Lottie Jump, although "met" is a euphemism for the way I first encountered her.

I saw Lottie for the first time one afternoon in our own kitchen, stealing a chocolate cake. Stella and Jack had not come home from school yet — not having my difficult disposition, they were popular, and they were at their friends' houses, pulling taffy, I suppose, making popcorn balls, playing casino, having fun — and my mother had taken Tess with her to visit a friend in one of the T.B. sanitariums. I was alone in the house, and making a funny-looking Christmas card, although I had no one to send it to. When I heard someone in the kitchen, I thought it was Mother home early, and I went out to ask her why the green pine tree I had pasted on a square of red paper looked as if it were falling down. And there, instead of Mother and my baby sister, was this pale, conspicuous child in the act of lifting the glass cover from the devil's-food my mother had taken out of the oven an hour before and set on the plant shelf by the window. The child had her back to me, and when she heard my footfall, she wheeled with an amazing look of fear and hatred on her pinched and pasty face. Simultaneously, she put the cover over the cake again, and then she stood motionless as if she were under a spell.

I was scared, for I was not sure what was happening, and anyhow it   5
gives you a turn to find a stranger in the kitchen in the middle of the afternoon, even if the stranger is only a skinny child in a moldy coat and sopping-wet basketball shoes. Between us there was a lengthy silence, but there was a great deal of noise in the room: the alarm clock ticked smugly; the teakettle simmered patiently on the back of the stove; Muff, cross at having been waked up, thumped her tail against the side of the terrarium in the window where she had been sleeping — contrary to orders — among the geraniums. This went on, it seemed to me, for hours and hours while that tall, sickly girl and I confronted each other. When, after a long time, she did open her mouth, it was to tell a prodigious lie. "I came to see if you'd like to play with me," she said. I think she sighed and stole a sidelong and regretful glance at the cake.

Beggars cannot be choosers, and I had been missing Virgil so sorely, as well as all those other dear friends forever lost to me, that in spite of her flagrance (she had never clapped eyes on me before, she had had no way of knowing there was a creature of my age in the house — she had come in like a hobo to steal my mother's cake), I was flattered and consoled. I asked her name and, learning it, believed my ears no better than my eyes: Lottie Jump. What on earth! What on earth — you surely will agree with me — and yet when I told her mine, Emily Vanderpool, she laughed until she coughed and gasped. "Beg pardon," she said. "Names like them always hit my funny bone. There was this towhead boy in school named Delbert Saxonfield." I saw no connection and I was insulted (what's so funny about Vanderpool, I'd like to know), but Lottie Jump was, technically, my guest and I *was* lonesome, so I asked her, since she had spoken of playing with me, if she knew how to play Andy-I-Over. She said "Naw." It turned out that she did not know how to play any games at all; she couldn't do anything and didn't want to do anything; her only recreation and her only gift was, and always had been, stealing. But this I did not know at the time.

As it happened, it was too cold and snowy to play outdoors that day anyhow, and after I had run through my list of indoor games and Lottie had shaken her head at all of them (when I spoke of Parcheesi, she went "Ugh!" and pretended to be sick), she suggested that we look through my mother's bureau drawers. This did not strike me as strange at all, for it was one of my favorite things to do, and I led the way to Mother's bedroom without a moment's hesitation. I loved the smell of the lavender she kept in gauze bags among her chamois gloves and linen handkerchiefs and filmy scarves; there was a pink fascinator knitted of something as fine as spider's thread, and it made me go quite soft — I wasn't soft as a rule, I was as hard as nails and I gave my mother a rough time — to think of her wearing it around her head as she waltzed on the ice in the bygone days. We examined stockings, nightgowns, camisoles, strings of beads, and mosaic pins, keepsake buttons from dresses worn on memorial occasions, tortoiseshell combs, and a transformation made from Aunt Joey's hair when she had racily had it bobbed. Lottie admired particularly a blue cloisonné perfume flask with ferns and peacocks on it. "Hey," she said, "this sure is cute. I like thing-daddies like this here." But very abruptly she got bored and said, "Let's talk instead. In the front room." I agreed, a little perplexed this time, because I had been about to show her a remarkable powder box that played *The Blue Danube*. We went into the parlor, where Lottie looked at her image in the pier glass for quite a while and with great absorption, as if she had never seen herself before. Then she moved over to the window seat and knelt on it, looking out at the front walk. She kept her hands in the pockets of her thin dark-red coat; once she took out one of her dirty paws to rub her nose for a minute and I saw a bulge in that pocket, like a bunch of jackstones. I know now that it wasn't jackstones, it was my mother's perfume flask; I thought at the time her hands were cold and that that was why she kept them put away, for I had noticed that she had no mittens.

Lottie did most of the talking, and while she talked, she never once looked at me but kept her eyes fixed on the approach to our house. She told me that her family had come to Adams a month before from Muskogee, Oklahoma, where her father, before he got tuberculosis, had been a brakeman on the Frisco. Now they lived down by Arapahoe Creek, on the west side of town, in one of the cottages of a wretched settlement made up of people so poor and so sick — for in nearly every ramshackle house someone was coughing himself to death — that each time I went past I blushed with guilt because my shoes were sound and my coat was warm and I was well. I wished that Lottie had not told me where she lived, but she was not aware of any pathos in her family's situation, and, indeed, it was with a certain boastfulness that she told me her mother was the short-order cook at the Comanche Café (she pronounced this word in one syllable), which I knew was the dirtiest, darkest, smelliest place in town, patronized by coal miners who never washed their faces and sometimes had such dangerous fights after drinking dago red that the sheriff had to come. Laughing, Lottie told me that her mother was half Indian, and, laughing even harder, she said that her brother didn't have any brains and had never been to school. She herself was eleven years old, but she was only in the third grade, because teachers had always had it in for her — making her go to the blackboard and all like that when she was tired. She hated school — she went to Ashton, on North Hill, and that was why I had never seen her, for I went to Carlyle Hill — and she especially hated the teacher, Miss Cudahy, who had a head shaped like a pine cone and who had killed several people with her ruler. Lottie loved the movies ("Not them Western ones or the ones with apes in," she said. "Ones about hugging and kissing. I love it when they die in that big old soft bed with the curtains up top, and he comes in and says 'Don't leave me, Marguerite de la Mar'"), and she loved to ride in cars. She loved Mr. Goodbars, and if there was one thing she despised worse than another it was tapioca. ("Pa calls it fish eyes. He calls floating island horse spit. He's a big piece of cheese. I hate him.") She did not like cats (Muff was now sitting on the mantelpiece, glaring like an owl); she kind of liked snakes — except cottonmouths and rattlers — because she found them kind of funny; she had once seen a goat eat a tin can. She said that one of these days she would take me downtown — it was a slowpoke town, she said, a one-horse burg (I had never heard such gaudy, cynical talk and was trying to memorize it all) — if I would get some money for the trolley fare: she hated to walk, and I ought to be proud that she had walked all the way from Arapahoe Creek today for the sole solitary purpose of seeing me.

Seeing our freshly baked dessert in the window was a more likely story, but I did not care, for I was deeply impressed by this bold, sassy girl from Oklahoma and greatly admired the poise with which she aired her prejudices. Lottie Jump was certainly nothing to look at. She was tall and made of skin and bones; she was evilly ugly, and her clothes were a disgrace, not just ill-fitting and old and ragged but dirty, unmentionably so; clearly she did not wash much or brush her teeth, which were notched like a saw, and small and brown (it crossed my mind that perhaps she chewed tobacco); her long, lank hair looked as if it might have nits. But she had personality. She made me think of one of those self-contained dogs whose home is where his handout is and who travels alone but, if it suits him to, will become the leader of a pack. She was aloof, never looking at me, but amiable in the way she kept calling me "kid." I liked her enormously, and presently I told her so.

At this, she turned around and smiled at me. Her smile was the smile   10
of a jack-o'-lantern — high, wide, and handsome. When it was over, no trace of it remained. "Well, that's keen, kid, and I like you, too," she said in her downright Muskogee accent. She gave me a long, appraising look. Her eyes were the color of mud. "Listen, kid, how much do you like me?"

"I like you loads, Lottie," I said. "Better than anybody else, and I'm not kidding."

"You want to be pals?"

"Do I!" I cried. So *there,* Virgil Meade, you big fat hootenanny, I thought.

"All right, kid, we'll be pals." And she held out her hand for me to shake. I had to go and get it, for she did not alter her position on the window seat. It was a dry, cold hand, and the grip was severe, with more a feeling of bones in it than friendliness.

Lottie turned and scanned our path and scanned the sidewalk beyond,   15
and then she said, in a lower voice, "Do you know how to lift?"

"Lift?" I wondered if she meant to lift *her.* I was sure I could do it, since she was so skinny, but I couldn't imagine why she would want me to.

"Shoplift, I mean. Like in the five-and-dime."

I did not know the term, and Lottie scowled at my stupidity.

"Steal, for crying in the beer!" she said impatiently. This she said so loudly that Muff jumped down from the mantel and left the room in contempt.

I was thrilled to death and shocked to pieces. "Stealing is a sin," I said.   20
"You get put in jail for it."

"Ish ka bibble! I should worry if it's a sin or not," said Lottie, with a shrug. "And they'll never put a smart old whatsis like *me* in jail. It's fun, stealing is — it's a picnic. I'll teach you if you want to learn, kid." Shamelessly she winked at me and grinned again. (That grin! She could have taken it off her face and put it on the table.) And she added, "If you don't, we can't be pals, because lifting is the only kind of playing I like. I hate those dumb games like Statues. Kick-the-Can — phooey!"

I was torn between agitation (I went to Sunday school and knew already about morality; Judge Bay, a crabby old man who loved to punish sinners, was a friend of my father's and once had given Jack a lecture on the criminal mind when he came to call and found Jack looking up an answer in his arithmetic book) and excitement over the daring invitation to misconduct myself in so perilous a way. My life, on reflection, looked deadly prim; all I'd ever done to vary the monotony of it was to swear. I knew that Lottie Jump meant what she said—that I could have her friendship only on her terms (plainly, she had gone it alone for a long time and could go it alone for the rest of her life)—and although I trembled like an aspen and my heart went pitapat, I said, "I want to be pals with you, Lottie."

"All right, Vanderpool," said Lottie, and got off the window seat. "I wouldn't go braggin' about it if I was you. I wouldn't go telling my ma and pa and the next-door neighbor that you and Lottie Jump are going down to the five-and-dime next Saturday aft and lift us some nice rings and garters and things like that. I mean it, kid." And she drew the back of her forefinger across her throat and made a dire face.

"I won't. I promise I won't. My *gosh,* why would I?"

"That's the ticket," said Lottie, with a grin. "I'll meet you at the trolley   25
shelter at two o'clock. You have the money. For both down and up. I ain't going to climb up that ornery hill after I've had my fun."

"Yes, Lottie," I said. Where was I going to get twenty cents? I was going to have to start stealing before she even taught me how. Lottie was facing the center of the room, but she had eyes in the back of her head, and she whirled around back to the window; my mother and Tess were turning in our front path.

"Back way," I whispered, and in a moment Lottie was gone; the swinging door that usually squeaked did not make a sound as she vanished through it. I listened and I never heard the back door open and close. Nor did I hear her, in a split second, lift the glass cover and remove that cake designed to feed six people.

I was restless and snappish between Wednesday afternoon and Saturday. When Mother found the cake was gone, she scolded me for not keeping my ears cocked. She assumed, naturally, that a tramp had taken it, for she knew I hadn't eaten it; I never ate anything if I could help it (except for raw potatoes, which I loved) and had been known as a problem feeder from the beginning of my life. At first it occurred to me to have a tantrum and bring her around to my point of view: my tantrums scared the living daylights out of her because my veins stood out and I turned blue and couldn't get my breath. But I rejected this for a more sensible plan. I said, "It just so happens I didn't hear anything. But if I had, I suppose you wish I had gone out in the kitchen and let the robber cut me up into a million little tiny pieces with his sword. You wouldn't even bury me. You'd just put me on the dump. *I* know who's wanted in this family and who isn't." Tears of sorrow, not of anger, came in powerful tides and I groped blindly to the bedroom I shared with Stella, where I lay on my bed and shook with big, silent *weltschmerzlich°* sobs. Mother followed me immediately, and so did Tess, and both of them comforted me and told me how much they loved me. I said they didn't; they said they did. Presently, I got a headache, as I always did when I cried, so I got to have an aspirin and a cold cloth on my head, and when Jack and Stella came home, they had to be quiet. I heard Jack say, "Emily Vanderpool is the biggest polecat in the U.S.A. Whyn't she go in the kitchen and say, 'Hands up'? He would lit out." And Mother said, "Sh-h-h! You don't want your sister to be sick, do you?" Muff, not realizing that Lottie had replaced her, came in and curled up at my thigh, purring lustily; I found myself glad that she had left the room before Lottie Jump made her proposition to me, and in gratitude I stroked her unattractive head.

Other things happened. Mother discovered the loss of her perfume flask and talked about nothing else at meals for two whole days. Luckily, it did not occur to her that it had been stolen—she simply thought she had mislaid it—but her monomania got on my father's nerves and he lashed out at her and at the rest of us. And because I was the cause of it all and my conscience was after me with red-hot pokers, I finally *had* to have a tantrum. I slammed my fork down in the middle of supper on the second day and yelled, "If you don't stop fighting, I'm going to kill myself. Yammer, yammer, nag, nag!" And I put my fingers in my ears and squeezed my eyes tight shut and screamed so the whole county could hear, "Shut *up!*" And then I lost my breath and began to turn blue. Daddy hastily apologized to everyone, and Mother said she was sorry for carrying on so about a trinket that had nothing but sentimental value—she was just vexed with herself for being careless, that was all, and she wasn't going to say another word about it.

I never heard so many references to stealing and cake, and even to Oklahoma (ordinarily no one mentioned Oklahoma once in a month of Sundays) and the ten-cent store as I did throughout those next days. I myself once made a ghastly slip and said something to Stella about "the five-and-dime." "The five-and-*dime!*" she exclaimed. "Where'd you get *that* kind of talk? Do you by any chance have reference to the *ten-cent store?*"

The worst of all was Friday night—the very night before I was to meet Lottie Jump—when Judge Bay came to play two-handed pinochle with Daddy. The Judge, a giant in intimidating haberdashery—for some reason, the white piping on his vest bespoke, for me, handcuffs and prison bars— and with an aura of disapproval for almost everything on earth except what pertained directly to himself, was telling Daddy, before they began their game, about the infamous vandalism that had been going on among the college students. "I have reason to believe that there are girls in this gang as well as boys," he said. "They ransack vacant houses and take everything. In one house on Pleasant Street, up there by the Catholic Church, there wasn't anything to take, so they took the kitchen sink. Wasn't a question of taking everything *but*—they took the kitchen sink."

weltschmerzlich: Reflecting the sorrow of the world.

"What ever would they want with a kitchen sink?" asked my mother.

"Mischief," replied the Judge. "If we ever catch them and if they come within my jurisdiction, I can tell you I will give them no quarter. A thief, in my opinion, is the lowest of the low."

Mother told about the chocolate cake. By now, the fiction was so factual in my mind that each time I thought of it I saw a funny-paper bum in baggy pants held up by rope, a hat with holes through which tufts of hair stuck up, shoes from which his toes protruded, a disreputable stubble on his face; he came up beneath the open window where the devil's food was cooling and he stole it and hotfooted it for the woods, where his companion was frying a small fish in a beat-up skillet. It never crossed my mind any longer that Lottie Jump had hooked that delicious cake.

Judge Bay was properly impressed. "If you will steal a chocolate cake,   35
if you will steal a kitchen sink, you will steal diamonds and money. The small child who pilfers a penny from his mother's pocketbook has started down a path that may lead him to holding up a bank."

It was a good thing I had no homework that night, for I could not possibly have concentrated. We were all sent to our rooms, because the pinochle players had to have absolute quiet. I spent the evening doing cross-stitch. I was making a bureau runner for a Christmas present; as in the case of the Christmas card, I had no one to give it to, but now I decided to give it to Lottie Jump's mother. Stella was reading *Black Beauty,* crying. It was an interminable evening. Stella went to bed first; I saw to that, because I didn't want her lying there awake listening to me talking in my sleep. Besides, I didn't want her to see me tearing open the cardboard box — the one in the shape of a church, which held my Christmas Sunday-school offering. Over the door of the church was this shaming legend: "My mite for the poor widow." When Stella had begun to grind her teeth in her first deep sleep, I took twenty cents away from the poor widow, whoever she was (the owner of the kitchen sink, no doubt), for the trolley fare, and secreted it and the remaining three pennies in the pocket of my middy. I wrapped the money well in a handkerchief and buttoned the pocket and hung my skirt over the middy. And then I tore the paper church into bits — the heavens opened and Judge Bay came toward me with a double-barreled shotgun — and hid the bits under a pile of pajamas. I did not sleep one wink. Except that I must have, because of the stupendous nightmares that kept wrenching the flesh off my skeleton and caused me to come close to perishing of thirst; once I fell out of bed and hit my head on Stella's ice skates. I would have waked her up and given her a piece of my mind for leaving them in such a lousy place, but then I remembered: I wanted *no* commotion of any kind.

I couldn't eat breakfast and I couldn't eat lunch. Old Johnny-on-the-spot Jack kept saying, *"Poor* Polecat. Polecat wants her fish for dinner." Mother made an abortive attempt to take my temperature. And when all that hullabaloo subsided, I was nearly in the soup because Mother asked me to mind Tess while she went to the sanitarium to see Mrs. Rogers, who, all of a sudden, was too sick to have anyone but grownups near her. Stella couldn't stay with the baby, because she had to go to ballet, and Jack couldn't, because he had to go up to the mesa and empty his traps. ("No, they *can't* wait. You want my skins to rot in this hot-one-day-cold-the-next weather?") I was arguing and whining when the telephone rang. Mother went to answer it and came back with a look of great sadness; Mrs. Rogers, she had learned, had had another hemorrhage. So Mother would not be going to the sanitarium after all and I needn't stay with Tess.

By the time I left the house, I was as cross as a bear. I felt awful about the widow's mite and I felt awful for being mean about staying with Tess, for Mrs. Rogers was a kind old lady, in a cozy blue hug-me-tight and an old-fangled boudoir cap, dying here all alone; she was a friend of Grandma's and had lived just down the street from her in Missouri, and all in the world Mrs. Rogers wanted to do was go back home and lie down in her own big bedroom in her own big, high-ceilinged house and have Grandma and other members of the Eastern Star come in from time to time to say hello. But they wouldn't let her go home; they were going to kill or cure her. I could not help feeling that my hardness of heart and evil intention had had a good deal to do with her new crisis; right at the very same minute I had been saying "Does that old Mrs. Methuselah *always* have to spoil my fun?" the poor wasted thing was probably coughing up her blood and saying to the nurse, "Tell Emily Vanderpool not to mind me, she can run and play."

I had a bad character, I know that, but my badness never gave me half the enjoyment Jack and Stella thought it did. A good deal of the time I wanted to eat lye. I was certainly having no fun now, thinking of Mrs. Rogers and of depriving that poor widow of bread and milk; what if this penniless woman without a husband had a dog to feed, too? Or a baby? And besides, I didn't want to go downtown to steal anything from the ten-cent store; I didn't want to see Lottie Jump again—not really, for I knew in my bones that that girl was trouble with a capital "T." And still, in our short meeting she had mesmerized me; I would think about her style of talking and the expert way she had made off with the perfume flask and the cake (how had she carried the cake through the streets without being noticed?) and be bowled over, for the part of me that did not love God was a black-hearted villain. And apart from these considerations, I had some sort of idea that if I did not keep my appointment with Lottie Jump, she would somehow get revenge; she had seemed a girl of purpose. So, revolted and fascinated, brave and lily-livered, I plodded along through the snow in my flopping galoshes up toward the Chautauqua, where the trolley stop was. On my way, I passed Virgil Meade's house; there was not just a snowman, there was a whole snow family in the back yard, and Virgil himself was throwing a stick for his dog. I was delighted to see that he was alone.

Lottie, who was sitting on a bench in the shelter eating a Mr. Goodbar, looked the same as she had the other time except that she was wearing an   40 amazing hat. I think I had expected her to have a black handkerchief over the lower part of her face or to be wearing a Jesse James waistcoat. But I had never thought of a hat. It was felt; it was the color of cooked meat; it had some flowers appliquéd on the front of it; it had no brim, but rose straight up to a very considerable height, like a monument. It sat so low on her forehead and it was so tight that it looked, in a way, like part of her.

"How's every little thing, bub?" she said, licking her candy wrapper.

"Fine, Lottie," I said, freshly awed.

A silence fell. I drank some water from the drinking fountain, sat down, fastened my galoshes, and unfastened them again.

"My mother's teeth grow wrong way to," said Lottie, and showed me what she meant: the lower teeth were in front of the upper ones. "That so-called trolley car takes its own sweet time. This town is blah."

To save the honor of my home town, the trolley came scraping and groaning up the hill just then, its bell clanging with an idiotic frenzy, and ground to a stop. Its broad, proud cowcatcher was filled with dirty snow, in the middle of which rested a tomato can, put there, probably, by somebody who was bored to death and couldn't think of anything else to do — I did a lot of pointless things like that on lonesome Saturday afternoons. It was the custom of this trolley car, a rather mysterious one, to pause at the shelter for five minutes while the conductor, who was either Mr. Jansen or Mr. Peck, depending on whether it was the A.M. run or the P.M., got out and stretched and smoked and spit. Sometimes the passengers got out, too, acting like sightseers whose destination was this sturdy stucco gazebo instead of, as it really was, the Piggly Wiggly or the Nelson Dry. You expected them to take snapshots of the drinking fountain or of the Chautauqua meeting house up on the hill. And when they all got back in the car, you expected them to exchange intelligent observations on the aborigines and the ruins they had seen.

Today there were no passengers, and as soon as Mr. Peck got out and began staring at the mountains as if he had never seen them before while he made himself a cigarette, Lottie, in her tall hat (was it something like the Inspector's hat in the Katzenjammer Kids?), got into the car, motioning me to follow. I put our nickels in the empty box and joined her on the very last double seat. It was only then that she mapped out the plan for the afternoon, in a low but still insouciant voice. The hat — she did not apologize for it, she simply referred to it as "my hat" — was to be the repository of whatever we stole. In the future, it would be advisable for me to have one like it. (How? Surely it was unique. The flowers, I saw on closer examination, were tulips, but they were blue, and a very unsettling shade of blue.) I was to engage a clerk on one side of the counter, asking her the price of, let's say, a tube of Daggett & Ramsdell vanishing cream, while Lottie would lift a round comb or a barrette or a hair net or whatever on the other side. Then, at a signal, I would decide against the vanishing cream and would move on to the next counter that she indicated. The signal was interesting; it was to be the raising

45

of her hat from the rear — "like I've got the itch and gotta scratch," she said. I was relieved that I was to have no part in the actual stealing, and I was touched that Lottie, who was going to do all the work, said we would "go halvers" on the take. She asked me if there was anything in particular I wanted — she herself had nothing special in mind and was going to shop around first — and I said I would like some rubber gloves. This request was entirely spontaneous; I had never before in my life thought of rubber gloves in one way or another, but a psychologist — or Judge Bay — might have said that this was most significant and that I was planning at that moment to go on from petty larceny to bigger game, armed with a weapon on which I wished to leave no fingerprints.

On the way downtown, quite a few people got on the trolley, and they all gave us such peculiar looks that I was chickenhearted until I realized it must be Lottie's hat they were looking at. No wonder. I kept looking at it myself out of the corner of my eye; it was like a watermelon standing on end. No, it was like a tremendous test tube. On this trip — a slow one, for the trolley pottered through that part of town in a desultory, neighborly way, even going into areas where no one lived — Lottie told me some of the things she had stolen in Muskogee and here in Adams. They included a white satin prayer book (think of it!), Mr. Goodbars by the thousands (she had probably never paid for a Mr. Goodbar in her life), a dinner ring valued at two dollars, a strawberry emery, several cans of corn, some shoelaces, a set of poker chips, countless pencils, four spark plugs ("Pa had this old car, see, and it was broke, so we took 'er to get fixed; I'll build me a radio with 'em sometime — you know? Listen in on them ear muffs to Tulsa?"), a Boy Scout knife, and a Girl Scout folding cup. She made a regular practice of going through the pockets of the coats in the cloakroom every day at recess, but she had never found anything there worth a red cent and was about to give that up. Once, she had taken a gold pencil from a teacher's desk and had got caught — she was sure that this was one of the reasons she was only in the third grade. Of this unjust experience, she said, "The old hoot owl! If I was drivin' in a car on a lonesome stretch and she was settin' beside me, I'd wait till we got to a pile of gravel and then I'd stop and say, 'Git out, Miss Priss.' She'd git out, all right."

Since Lottie was so frank, I was emboldened at last to ask her what she had done with the cake. She faced me with her grin; this grin, in combination with the hat, gave me a surprise from which I have never recovered. "I ate it up," she said. "I went in your garage and sat on your daddy's old tires and ate it. It was pretty good."

There were two ten-cent stores side by side in our town, Kresge's and Woolworth's, and as we walked down the main street toward them, Lottie played with a Yo-Yo. Since the street was thronged with Christmas shoppers and farmers in for Saturday, this was no ordinary accomplishment; all in all, Lottie Jump was someone to be reckoned with. I cannot say that I was proud to be seen with her; the fact is that I hoped I would not meet anyone I knew, and I thanked my lucky stars that Jack was up in the hills with his dead skunks because if he had seen her with that lid and that Yo-Yo, I would never have heard the last of it. But in another way I *was* proud to be with her; in a smaller hemisphere, in one that included only her and me, I was swaggering—I felt like Somebody, marching along beside this lofty Somebody from Oklahoma who was going to hold up the dime store.

There is nothing like Woolworth's at Christmastime. It smells of pea-   50
nut brittle and terrible chocolate candy, Djer-Kiss talcum powder and Ben Hur Perfume—smells sourly of tinsel and waxily of artificial poinsettias. The crowds are made up largely of children and women, with here and there a deliberative old man; the women are buying ribbons and wrappings and Christmas cards, and the children are buying asbestos pot holders for their mothers and, for their fathers, suède bookmarks with a burnt-in design that says "A good book is a good friend" or "Souvenir from the Garden of the Gods." It is very noisy. The salesgirls are forever ringing their bells and asking the floorwalker to bring them change for a five; babies in go-carts are screaming as parcels fall on their heads; the women, waving rolls of red tissue paper, try to attract the attention of the harried girl behind the counter. ("Miss! All I want is this one batch of the red. Can't I just give you the dime?" And the girl, beside herself, mottled with vexation, cries back, "Has to be rung up, Moddom, that's the rule.") There is pandemonium at the toy counter, where things are being tested by the customers—wound up, set off, tooted, pounded, made to say "Maaaah-Maaaah!" There is very little gaiety in the scene and, in fact, those baffled old men look as if they were walking over their own dead bodies, but there is an atmosphere of carnival, nevertheless, and as soon as Lottie and I entered the doors of Woolworth's golden-and-vermilion bedlam, I grew giddy and hot—not pleasantly so. The feeling, indeed, was distinctly disagreeable, like the beginning of a stomach upset.

Lottie gave me a nudge and said softly, "Go look at the envelopes. I want some rubber bands."

This counter was relatively uncrowded (the seasonal stationery supplies—the Christmas cards and wrapping paper and stickers—were at a separate counter), and I went around to examine some very beautiful letter paper; it was pale pink and it had a border of roses all around it. The clerk here was a cheerful middle-aged woman wearing an apron, and she was giving all her attention to a seedy old man who could not make up his mind between mucilage and paste. "Take your time, Dad," she said. "Compared to the rest of the girls, I'm on my vacation." The old man, holding a tube in one hand and a bottle in the other, looked at her vaguely and said, "I want it for stamps. Sometimes I write a letter and stamp it and then don't mail it and steam the stamp off. Must have ninety cents' worth of stamps like that." The woman laughed. "I know what you mean," she said. "I get mad and write a letter and then I tear it up." The old man gave her a condescending look and said, "That so? But I don't suppose yours are of a political nature." He bent his gaze again to the choice of adhesives.

This first undertaking was duck soup for Lottie. I did not even have to exchange a word with the woman; I saw Miss Fagin lift up *that hat* and give me the high sign, and we moved away, she down one aisle and I down the other, now and again catching a glimpse of each other through the throngs. We met at the foot of the second counter, where notions were sold.

"Fun, huh?" said Lottie, and I nodded, although I felt wholly dreary. "I want some crochet hooks," she said. "Price the rickrack."

This time the clerk was adding up her receipts and did not even look   55 at me or at a woman who was angrily and in vain trying to buy a paper of pins. Out went Lottie's scrawny hand, up went her domed chimney. In this way for some time she bagged sitting birds: a tea strainer (there was no one at all at that counter), a box of Mrs. Carpenter's All Purpose Nails, the rubber gloves I had said I wanted, and four packages of mixed seeds. Now you have some idea of the size of Lottie Jump's hat.

I was nervous, not from being her accomplice but from being in this crowd on an empty stomach, and I was getting tired — we had been in the store for at least an hour — and the whole enterprise seemed pointless. There wasn't a thing in her hat I wanted — not even the rubber gloves. But in exact proportion as my spirits descended, Lottie's rose; clearly she had only been target-practicing and now she was moving in for the kill.

We met beside the books of paper dolls, for reconnaissance. "I'm gonna get me a pair of pearl beads," said Lottie. "You go fuss with the hairpins, hear?"

Luck, combined with her skill, would have stayed with Lottie, and her hat would have been a cornucopia by the end of the afternoon if, at the very moment her hand went out for the string of beads, that idiosyncrasy of mine had not struck me full force. I had never known it to come with so few preliminaries; probably this was so because I was oppressed by all the masses of bodies poking and pushing me, and all the open mouths breathing in my face. Anyhow, right then, at the crucial time, I *had to be alone.*

I stood staring down at the bone hairpins for a moment, and when the girl behind the counter said, "What kind does Mother want, hon? What color is Mother's hair?" I looked past her and across at Lottie and I said, "Your brother isn't the only one in your family that doesn't have any brains." The clerk, astonished, turned to look where I was looking and caught Lottie in the act of lifting up her hat to put the pearls inside. She had unwisely chosen a long strand and was having a little trouble; I had the nasty thought that it looked as if her brains were leaking out.

The clerk, not able to deal with this emergency herself, frantically   60 punched her bell and cried, "Floorwalker! Mr. Bellamy! I've caught a thief!"

Momentarily there was a violent hush — then such a clamor as you have never heard. Bells rang, babies howled, crockery crashed to the floor as people stumbled in their rush to the arena.

Mr. Bellamy, nineteen years old but broad of shoulder and jaw, was instantly standing beside Lottie, holding her arm with one hand while with the other he removed her hat to reveal to the overjoyed audience that incredible array of merchandise. Her hair all wild, her face a mask of innocent bewilderment, Lottie Jump, the scurvy thing, pretended to be deaf and dumb. She pointed at the rubber gloves and then she pointed at me, and Mr. Bellamy, able at last to prove his mettle, said "Aha!" and, still holding Lottie, moved around the counter to me and grabbed *my* arm. He gave the hat to the clerk and asked her kindly to accompany him and his redhanded catch to the manager's office.

I don't know where Lottie is now — whether she is on the stage or in jail. If her performance after our arrest meant anything, the first is quite as likely as the second. (I never saw her again, and for all I know she lit out of town that night on a freight train. Or perhaps her whole family decamped as suddenly as they had arrived; ours was a most transient population. You can be sure I made no attempt to find her again, and for months I avoided going anywhere near Arapahoe Creek or North Hill.) She never said a word but kept making signs with her fingers, adlibbing the whole thing. They tested her hearing by shooting off a popgun right in her ear and she never batted an eyelid.

They called up my father, and he came over from the Safeway on the double. I heard very little of what he said because I was crying so hard, but one thing I did hear him say was "Well young lady, I guess you've seen to it that I'll have to part company with my good friend Judge Bay." I tried to defend myself, but it was useless. The manager, Mr. Bellamy, the clerk, and my father patted Lottie on the shoulder, and the clerk said, "Poor, afflicted child." For being a poor, afflicted child, they gave her a bag of hard candy, and she gave them the most fraudulent smile of gratitude, and slobbered a little, and shuffled out, holding her empty hat in front of her like a beggarman. I hate Lottie Jump to this day, but I have to hand it to her — she was a genius.

The floorwalker would have liked to see me sentenced to the reform   65
school for life, I am sure, but the manager said that considering this was my first offense, he would let my father attend to my punishment. The old-maid clerk, who looked precisely like Emmy Schmalz, clucked her tongue and shook her head at me. My father hustled me out of the office and out of the store and into the car and home, muttering the entire time; now and again I'd hear the words "morals" and "nowadays."

What's the use of telling the rest? You know what happened. Daddy on second thoughts decided not to hang his head in front of Judge Bay but to make use of his friendship in this time of need, and he took me to see the scary old curmudgeon at his house. All I remember of that long declamation, during which the Judge sat behind his desk never taking his eyes off me, was the warning "I want you to give this a great deal of thought, Miss. I want you to search and seek in the innermost corners of your conscience and root out every bit of badness." Oh, *him!* Why, listen, if I'd rooted out all the badness in me, there wouldn't have been anything left of me. My mother cried for days because she had nurtured an outlaw and was ashamed to show her face at the neighborhood store; my father was silent, and he often looked at me. Stella, who was a prig, said, "And to think you did it at *Christmas* time!" As for Jack — well, Jack a couple of times did not know how close he came to seeing glory when I had a butcher knife in my hand. It was Polecat this and Polecat that until I nearly went off my rocker. Tess, of course, didn't know what was going on, and asked so many questions that finally I told her to go to Helen Hunt Jackson in a savage tone of voice.

Good old Muff.

It is not true that you don't learn by experience. At any rate, I did that time. I began immediately to have two or three friends at a time — to be sure, because of the stigma on me, they were by no means the elite of Carlyle Hill Grade — and never again when that terrible need to be alone arose did I let fly. I would say, instead, "I've got a headache. I'll have to go home and take an aspirin," or "Gosh all hemlocks, I forgot — I've got to go to the dentist."

After the scandal died down, I got into the Campfire Girls. It was through pull, of course, since Stella had been a respected member for two years and my mother was a friend of the leader. But it turned out all right. Even Muff did not miss our periods of companionship, because about that time she grew up and started having literally millions of kittens.

Considerations

1. The story begins and ends with Emily discussing her sudden attacks of "needing to be alone." In addition, one of these "attacks" occurs at a crucial point in the story: while Lottie and Emily are in the midst of their shoplifting expedition. Speculate on the reasons for and the significance of these "attacks," keeping in mind Emily's interactions with other characters in the story.
2. Read the description of Muff (second paragraph). In what ways can Muff be compared to Emily? To Lottie Jump? What significance might be attached to Muff's changes as described in the final sentence of the story?
3. What values does Emily's family hold (what seems to be important to them)? What values does Lottie Jump hold? Do Lottie's and Emily's families hold any values in common? Imagine a conversation between a member of Emily's family and Lottie Jump after the shoplifting episode. How might this person accuse Lottie, and how might she respond?
4. Does Emily gain anything from knowing Lottie Jump? Does she lose anything? Explain.
5. To what extent does Emily's family control her and to what extent does she control them? Do you see the balance of power as changing in any significant way during the course of the story? Explain.

ALICE ADAMS (1926–   )

By the Sea

Because she looked older than she was, eighteen, and was very pretty, her two slightly crooked front teeth more than offset by wheat-blond hair and green eyes, Dylan Ballentyne was allowed to be a waitress at the Cypress Lodge without having been a bus girl first. She hated the work — loathed, despised it — but it was literally the only job in town, town being a cluster of houses and a couple of stores on the northern California coast. Dylan also hated the town and the wild, dramatically desolate landscape of the area, to which she and her mother had moved at the beginning of the summer, coming down from San Francisco, where Dylan had been happy in the sunny Mission District, out of sight of the sea.

Now she moved drearily through days of trays and dishes, spilled coffee and gelatinous ash-strewn food, fat cross guests or hyper-friendly ones. She was sustained by her small paycheck and somewhat more generous tips, and by her own large fantasies of ultimate rescue, or escape.

The Lodge, an ornately Victorian structure with pinnacles and turrets, was on a high bluff two miles south of town, surrounded by sharply sloping meadows which were edged with dark-green cypresses and pines, overlooking the turbulent, shark-infested, almost inaccessible sea. (One more disappointment: talking up the move, Dylan's mother, self-named Flower, had invented long beach days and picnics; they would both learn to surf, she had said.)

Breakfast was served at the Lodge from eight till ten-thirty, lunch from eleven-thirty until two, in a long glassed-in porch, the dining room. Supposedly between those two meals the help got a break, half an hour for a sandwich or a cigarette, but more often than not it was about five minutes, what with lingering breakfasters and early, eager lunchers. Dinner was at six, set up at five-thirty, and thus there really was a free hour or sometimes two, in the mid to late afternoon. Dylan usually spent this time in the "library" of the Lodge, a dim, musty room, paneled in fake mahogany. Too tired for books, although her reading habits had delighted English teachers in high school, she leafed through old *House Beautifuls, Gourmets* or *Vogues,* avidly drinking in all those ads for the accoutrements of rich and leisurely exotic lives.

Curiously, what she saw and read made her almost happy, for that limited time, like a drug. She could nearly believe that she saw herself in *Vogue,* in a Rolls-Royce ad: a tall thin blond woman (she was thin, if not very tall) in silk and careless fur, one jeweled hand on the fender of a silver car, and in the background a handsome man, dark, wearing a tuxedo.

Then there was dinner. Drinks. Wines. Specifics as to the doneness of steaks or roasts. Complaints. I ordered *medium* rare. Is this crab really *fresh?* And heavy trays. The woman who managed the restaurant saw to it that

5

waitresses and bus girls "shared" that labor, possibly out of some vaguely egalitarian sense that the trays were too heavy for any single group. By eight-thirty or so, Dylan and all the girls would be slow-witted with exhaustion, smiles stiffening on their very young faces, perspiration drying under their arms and down their backs. Then there would come the stentorian voice of the manageress: "*Dylan,* are you awake? You look a thousand miles away."

Actually, in her dreams, Dylan was less than two hundred miles away, in San Francisco.

One fantasy of rescue which Dylan recognized as childish, and unlikely, probably, was that a nice older couple (in their fifties, anyway; Flower was only thirty-eight) would adopt her. At the end of their stay at the Lodge, after several weeks, they would say, "Well, Dylan, we just don't see how we're going to get along without you. Do you think you could possibly . . . ?" There had in fact been several couples who could have filled that bill — older people from San Francisco, or even L.A., San Diego, Scottsdale — who stayed for a few weeks at the Lodge, who liked Dylan and tipped her generously. But so far none of them had been unable to leave without her; they didn't even send her postcards.

Another fantasy, a little more plausible, more grown up, involved a man who would come to the Lodge alone and would fall in love with Dylan and take her away. The man was as indistinct as the one in the Rolls-Royce ads, as vaguely handsome, dark and rich.

In the meantime, the local boys who came around to see the other   10
waitresses tried to talk to Dylan; their hair was too long and their faces splotchily sunburned from cycling and surfing, which were the only two things they did, besides drinking beer. Dylan ignored them, and went on dreaming.

The usual group of guests at the Lodge didn't offer much material for fantasy: youngish, well-off couples who arrived in big new station wagons with several children, new summer clothes and new sports equipment. Apart from these stylish parents, there were always two or three very young couples, perhaps just married or perhaps not, all with the look of not quite being able to afford where they were.

And always some very old people.

There was, actually, one unmarried man (almost divorced) among the guests, and although he was very nice, intelligent, about twenty-eight, he did not look rich, or, for that matter, handsome and dark. Whitney Iverson was a stocky red-blond man with a strawberry birthmark on one side of his neck. Deep-set blue eyes were his best feature. Probably he was not the one to fall in love and rescue Dylan, although he seemed to like her very much. Mr. Iverson, too, spent his late afternoons in the Lodge's library.

Exactly what Mr. Iverson did for a living was not clear; he mentioned the Peace Corps and VISTA, and then he said that he was writing; not novels—articles. His wife was divorcing him and she was making a lot of trouble about money, he said: a blow, he hadn't thought she was like that. (But how could he have enough money for anyone to make trouble about, Dylan wondered.) He had brought down a carload of books. When he wasn't reading in his room, or working on whatever he was writing, he took long, long walks, every day, miles over the meadows, back and forth to what there was of a town. Glimpsing him through a window as she set up tables, Dylan noted his stride, his strong shoulders. Sometimes he climbed down the steep perilous banks to the edge of the sea, to the narrow strip of coarse gray sand that passed for a beach. Perfectly safe, he said, if you checked the tides. Unlike Dylan, he was crazy about this landscape; he found the sea and the stretching hills of grass and rock, the acres of sky, all marvelous; even the billowing fog that threatened all summer he saw as lovely, something amazing.

Sometimes Dylan tried to see the local scenery with Whitney Iverson's eyes, and sometimes, remarkably, this worked. She was able to imagine herself a sojourner in this area, as he was, and then she could succumb to the sharp blue beauty of that wild Pacific, the dark-green, wind-bent feathery cypresses, and the sheer cliffs going down to the water, with their crevices of moss and tiny brilliant wild flowers.

But usually she just looked around in a dull, hating way. Usually she was miserably bored and hopelessly despondent.

They had moved down here to the seaside, to this tiny nothing town, Dylan and Flower, so that Flower could concentrate on making jewelry, which was her profession. Actually, the move was the idea of Zachery, Flower's boyfriend. Flower would make the jewelry and Zach would take it up to San Francisco to sell; someday he might even try L.A. And Zach would bring back new materials for Flower to use—gold and silver and pearls. Flower, who was several months behind in her rent, had agreed to this plan. Also, as Dylan saw it, Flower was totally dominated by Zach, who was big and dark and roughly handsome, and sometimes mean. Dylan further suspected that Zach wanted them out of town, wanted to see less of Flower, and the summer had borne out her theory: instead of his living with them and making occasional forays to the city, as Flower had imagined, it was just the other way around. Zach made occasional visits to them, and the rest of the time, when she wasn't working or trying to work on some earrings or a necklace, Flower sat sipping the harsh, local red wine and reading the used paperbacks that Zach brought down in big cartons along with the jewelry materials — "to keep you out of mischief," he had said.

Flower wore her graying blond hair long, in the non-style of her whole adult life, and she was putting on weight. When she wanted to work she took an upper, another commodity supplied by Zach, but this didn't do much to keep her weight down, just kept her "wired," as she sometimes said. Dylan alternated between impatience and the most tender sympathy for her mother, who was in some ways more like a friend; it was often clear to Dylan that actually she had to be the stronger person, the one in charge. But Flower was so nice, really, a wonderful cook and generous to her friends, and she could be funny. Some of the jewelry she made was beautiful — recently, a necklace of silver and stones that Zach said were real opals. Flower had talent, originality. If she could just dump Zach for good, Dylan thought, and then not replace him with someone worse, as she usually did. Always some mean jerk. If she could just not drink, not take speed.

From the start Flower had been genuinely sympathetic about Dylan's awful job. "Honey, I can hardly stand to think about it," she would say, and her eyes would fill. She had been a waitress several times herself. "You and those heavy trays, and the mess. Look, why don't you just quit? Honestly, we'll get by like we always have. I'll just tell Zach he's got to bring more stuff down, and sell more, too. And you can help me."

This seemed a dangerous plan to Dylan, possibly because it relied on   20 Zach, who Dylan was sure would end up in jail, or worse. She stubbornly stuck with her job, and on her two days off (Mondays and Tuesdays, of all useless days) she stayed in bed a lot, and read, and allowed her mother to "spoil" her, with breakfast trays ("Well, after all, who deserves her own tray more than you do, baby?") and her favorite salads for lunch, with every available fresh vegetable and sometimes shrimp.

When she wasn't talking to her mother or helping out with household chores, Dylan was reading a book that Mr. Iverson had lent her — *The Eustace Diamonds,* by Trollope.° This had come about because one afternoon, meeting him in the library, Dylan had explained the old *Vogues,* the *House Beautifuls* scattered near her lap, saying that she was too tired just then to read, and that she missed television. The winter before, she had loved *The Pallisers,* she said, and, before that, *Upstairs, Downstairs.* Mr. Iverson had recommended *The Eustace Diamonds.* "It's really my favorite of the Palliser novels,"° he said, and he went to get it for her — running all the way up to his room and back, apparently; he was out of breath as he handed her the book.

But why was he so eager to please her? She knew that she was pretty, but she wasn't all that pretty, in her own estimation; she was highly conscious of the two crooked front teeth, although she had perfected a radiant, slightly false smile that almost hid them.

"I wonder if he could be one of *the* Iversons," Flower mused, informed by Dylan one Monday of the source of her book.

Anthony Trollope: (1812–1882) British novelist whose novels satirically depict the lives of ordinary upper- or middle-class people. *Palliser novels:* A series of six novels by Trollope, concerned with politics and urban society.

"The Iversons?" In Flower's voice it had sounded like the Pallisers.

"One of the really terrific, old San Francisco families. You know, 25 Huntingtons, Floods, Crockers, Iversons. What does he look like, your Mr. Iverson?"

Dylan found this hard to answer, although usually with Flower she spoke very easily, they were so used to each other. "Well." She hesitated. "He's sort of blond, with nice blue eyes and a small nose. He has this birthmark on his neck, but it's not really noticeable."

Flower laughed. "In that case, he's not a real Iverson. They've all got dark hair and the most aristocratic beaky noses. And none of them could possibly have a birthmark — they'd drown it at birth."

Dylan laughed, too, although she felt an obscure disloyalty to Mr. Iverson.

And, looking at Flower, Dylan thought, as she had before, that Flower *could* change her life, take charge of herself. She was basically strong. But in the next moment Dylan decided, as she also had before, more frequently, that probably Flower wouldn't change; in her brief experience people didn't, or not much. Zach would go to jail and Flower would find somebody worse, and get grayer and fatter. And she, Dylan, had better forget about anything as childish as being adopted by rich old people; she must concentrate on marrying someone who really had *money*. Resolution made her feel suddenly adult.

"Honey," asked Flower, "are you sure you won't have a glass of wine?" 30

"My mother wonders if you're a real Iverson." Dylan had not quite meant to say this; the sentence spoke itself, leaving her slightly embarrassed, as she sat with Whitney Iverson on a small sofa in the library. It was her afternoon break; she was tired, and she told herself that she didn't know what she was saying.

Mr. Iverson, whose intense blue eyes had been staring into hers, now turned away, so that Dylan was more aware of the mark on his neck than she had been before. Or could it have deepened to a darker mulberry stain?

He said, "Well, I am and I'm not, actually. I think of them as my parents and I grew up with them, in the Atherton house, but actually I'm adopted."

"Really?" Two girls Dylan knew at Mission High had got pregnant and had given up their babies to be adopted. His real mother, then, could have been an ordinary highschool girl? The idea made her uncomfortable, as though he had suddenly moved closer to her.

"I believe they were very aware of it, my not being really theirs," 35 Whitney Iverson said, again looking away from her. "Especially when I messed up in some way, like choosing Reed, instead of Stanford. Then graduate school . . ."

As he talked on, seeming to search for new words for the feelings engendered in him by his adoptive parents, Dylan felt herself involuntarily retreat. No one had ever talked to her in quite that way, and she was uneasy. She looked through the long leaded windows to the wavering sunlight beyond; she stared at the dust-moted shafts of light in the dingy room where they were.

In fact, for Dylan, Whitney's very niceness was somehow against him; his kindness, his willingness to talk, ran against the rather austere grain of her fantasies.

Apparently sensing what she felt, or some of it, Whitney stopped short, and he laughed in a self-conscious way. "Well, there you have the poor-adopted-kid self-'pity trip of the month," he said. "'Poor,' Christ, they've drowned me in money."

Feeling that this last was not really addressed to her (and thinking of Flower's phrase about the birthmark, "drowned at birth"), Dylan said nothing. She stared at his hands, which were strong and brown, long-fingered, and she suddenly, sharply, wished that he would touch her. Touch, instead of all this awkward talk.

Later, considering that conversation, Dylan found herself moved, in spite of herself. How terrible to feel not only that you did not really belong with your parents but that they were disappointed in you. Whitney Iverson hadn't said anything about it, of course, but they must have minded about the birthmark, along with college and graduate school. 40

She and Flower were so clearly mother and daughter — obviously, ir-revocably so; her green eyes were Flower's, even her crooked front teeth. Also, Flower had always thought she was wonderful. "My daughter Dylan," she would say, in her strongest, proudest voice.

But what had he possibly meant about "drowned in money"? Was he really rich, or had that been a joke? His car was an old VW convertible, and his button-down shirts were frayed, his baggy jackets shabby. Would a rich person drive a car like that, or wear those clothes? Probably not, thought Dylan; on the other hand, he did not seem a man to say that he was rich if he was not.

In any case, Dylan decided that she was giving him too much thought, since she had no real reason to think that he cared about her. Maybe he was an Iverson, and a snob, and did not want anything to do with a waitress. If he had wanted to see her, he could have suggested dinner, a movie or driving down to Santa Cruz on one of her days off. Probably she would have said yes, and on the way home, maybe on a bluff overlooking the sea, he could have parked the car, have turned to her.

So far, Dylan had had little experience of ambiguity; its emerging presence made her both impatient and confused. She did not know what to do or how to think about the contradictions in Whitney Iverson.

Although over the summer Dylan and Whitney had met almost every day in the library, this was never a stated arrangement, and if either of them 45 missed a day, as they each sometimes did, nothing was said. This calculated diffidence seemed to suit them; they were like children who could not quite admit to seeking each other out.

One day, when Dylan had already decided that he would not come, and not caring really — she was too tired to care, what with extra guests and heavier trays — after she had been in the library for almost half an hour, she heard running steps, his, and then Whitney Iverson burst in, quite out of breath. "Oh . . . I'm glad you're still here," he got out, and he sat down heavily beside her. "I had some terrific news." But then on the verge of telling her, he stopped, and laughed, and said, "But I'm afraid it won't sound all that terrific to you."

Unhelpfully she looked at him.

"The *Yale Review,*" he said. "They've taken an article I sent them. I'm really pleased."

He had been right, in that the *Yale Review* was meaningless to Dylan, but his sense of triumph was real and visible to her. She *felt* his success, and she thought just then that he looked wonderful.

September, once Labor Day was past, was much clearer and warmer,   50
the sea a more brilliant blue, than during the summer. Under a light, fleece-clouded sky the water shimmered, all diamonds and gold, and the rocky cliffs in full sunlight were as pale as ivory. Even Dylan admitted to herself that it was beautiful; sometimes she felt herself penetrated by that scenery, her consciousness filled with it.

Whitney Iverson was leaving on the fifteenth; he had told Dylan so, naming the day as they sat together in the library. And then he said, "Would it be okay if I called you at home, sometime?"

The truth was, they didn't have a phone. Flower had been in so much trouble with the phone company that she didn't want to get into all that again. And so now Dylan blushed, and lied. "Well, maybe not. My mother's really strict."

He blushed, too, the birthmark darkening. "Well, I'll have to come back to see you," he said. "But will you still be here?"

How could she know, especially since he didn't even name a time when he would come? With a careless lack of tact she answered, "I hope not," and then she laughed.

Very seriously he asked, "Well, could we at least go for a walk or   55
something before I go? I could show you the beach." He gave a small laugh, indicating that the beach was really nothing much to see, and then he said, "Dylan, I've wanted so much to see you, I *care* so much for you — but here, there would have been . . . implications . . . you know . . ."

She didn't know; she refused to understand what he meant, unless he was confirming her old suspicion of snobbery; his not wanting to be seen with a waitress. She frowned slightly, and said, "Of course," and thought that she would not, after all, see him again. So much for Whitney Iverson.

But the next afternoon, during her break, in the brilliant September weather the library looked to her unbearably dingy, and all those magazines were so old. She stepped outside through the door at the end of the porch, and there was Mr. Iverson, just coming out through another door.

He smiled widely, said, "Perfect! We can just make it before the tide."

Wanting to say that she hadn't meant to go for a walk with him — she was just getting some air, and her shoes were wrong, canvas sandals — Dylan said neither of those things, but followed along, across the yellowing grass, toward the bluff.

He led her to a place that she hadn't known was there, a dip in the headland, from which the beach was only a few yards down, by a not steep, narrow path. Whitney went ahead, first turning back to reach for her hand, which she gave him. Making her way just behind, Dylan was more aware of his touch, of their firmly joined warm hands, than of anything else in the day: the sunlight, the sea, her poorly shod feet.

But as they reached the narrow strip of land, instead of turning to embrace her, although he still held her hand, Whitney cried out, "See? Isn't it fantastic?"

A small wave hit Dylan's left foot, soaking the fabric of her sandal. Unkissed, she stared at the back of his shirt collar, which was more frayed even than his usual shirts, below his slightly too long red-blond hair.

Then he turned to her; he picked up her other hand from her side, gazing intently down into her face. But it was somehow too late. Something within her had turned against him, whether from her wet foot or his worn-out collar, or sheer faulty timing, so that when he said, "You're so lovely, you make me shy," instead of being moved, as she might have been, Dylan thought he sounded silly (a grown man, shy?) and she stepped back a little, away from him.

He could still have kissed her, easily (she later thought), but he did not. Instead, he reached into one of the pockets of his jeans, fishing about, as he said, " . . . for something I wanted you to have."

Had he brought her a present, some small valuable keepsake? Prepared to relent, Dylan then saw that he had not; what he was handing her was a cardboard square, a card, on which were printed his name and telephone number. He said, "I just got these. My mother sent them. She's big on engraving." He grimaced as Dylan thought, Oh, your mother really is an Iverson. "The number's my new bachelor pad," he told her. "It's unlisted. Look, I really wish you'd call me. Any time. Collect. I'll be there." He looked away from her, for a moment out to sea, then down to the sand, where for the first time he seemed to notice her wet foot. "Oh Lord!" he exclaimed. "Will you have to change? I could run you home. . . ."

Not liking the fuss, and not at all liking the attention paid to those particular shoes (cheap, flimsy), somewhat coldly Dylan said no; the guests had thinned out and she was going home anyway as soon as the tables had been set up.

"Then I won't see you?"

She gave him her widest, most falsely shining smile, and turned and started up the path ahead of him. At the top she smiled again, and was about to turn away when Whitney grasped her wrist and said, with a startling, unfamiliar scowl, "*Call* me, you hear? I don't want to lose you."

What Dylan had said about being able to leave after setting up the tables was true; she had been told that she could then go home, which she did. The only problem, of course, was that she would earn less money; it could be a very lean, cold winter. Thinking about money, and, less clearly about Whitney Iverson, Dylan was not quite ready for the wild-eyed Flower, who greeted her at the door: "We're celebrating. Congratulate me! I've dumped Zach."

But Dylan had heard this before, and she knew the shape of the evening 70 that her mother's announcement presaged: strong triumphant statements along with a festive dinner, more and more wine, then tears. Sinkingly she listened as her mother described that afternoon's visit from Zach, how terrible he was and how firm she, Flower, had been, how final. "And we're celebrating with a really great fish soup," finished Flower, leading Dylan into the kitchen.

The evening did go more or less as Dylan had feared and imagined that it would. Ladling out the rich fish soup, Flower told Dylan how just plain fed up she was with men, and she repeated a line that she had recently heard and liked: "A woman without a man is like a mushroom without a bicycle."

Dylan did not find this as terrifically funny as Flower did, but she dutifully laughed.

A little later, sopping French bread into the liquid, Flower said, "But maybe it's just the guys I pick? I really seem to have some kind of instinct."

Flower had said that before, and Dylan always, if silently, agreed with her: it was too obvious to repeat. And then, maybe there really weren't any nice men around anymore, at her mother's age? Maybe they all got mean and terrible, the way a lot of women got fat? Dylan thought then of Whitney Iverson, who was only about ten years younger than Flower was; would he, too, eventually become impossible, cruel and unfaithful?

In a way that would have seemed alarmingly telepathic if Dylan had 75 not been used to having her thoughts read by her mother, Flower asked, "What ever happened to your new friend, Mr. Iverson? Was he really one of *them?*"

"I don't know. I guess so," Dylan muttered, wishing that she had never mentioned Whitney to her mother.

Over salad, Flower announced that she was going on a diet. "Tomorrow. First thing. Don't worry, I'll still have the stuff you like around for you, but from now on no more carbohydrates for me."

At least, this time, she didn't cry.

At some hour in the middle of the night, or early morning, Dylan woke up—a thing she rarely did. Her ears and her mind were full of the distant sound of the sea, and she could see it as it had been in the afternoon, vastly glittering, when she had been preoccupied with her wet shoe, with Whitney's not kissing her. And she felt a sudden closeness to him; suddenly she understood what he had not quite said. By "implications" he had meant that the time and place were wrong for them. He was shy and just then not especially happy, what with his divorce and all, but he truly cared about her. If he had felt less he probably would have kissed her, in the careless, meaningless way of a man on vacation kissing a pretty waitress and then going back to his own real life. Whitney was that rarity her mother despaired of finding: a truly nice man. On her way back to sleep Dylan imagined calling him. She could go up to see him on the bus, or he could come down, and they could go out together, nothing to do with the Lodge. Could talk, be alone.

However, Dylan woke up the next morning in quite another mood.   80 She felt wonderful, her own person, needing no one, certainly not a man who had not bothered, really, to claim her. Looking in the mirror, she saw herself as more than pretty, as almost beautiful; it was one of her very good days.

Flower, too, at breakfast seemed cheerful, not hung over. Maybe there was something in the air? Passing buttered English muffins to Dylan, Flower took none, although she loved them. "Tomato juice and eggs and black coffee, from here on in," she said. She did not take any pills.

Later, walking toward the Lodge, Dylan felt lighthearted, energetic. And how beautiful everything was! (Whitney Iverson had been right.) The sloping meadows, the pale clear sky, the chalky cliffs, the diamond-shining sea were all marvelous. She had a strong presentiment of luck; some good fortune would come to her at last.

At the sound of a car behind her she moved out of the way, turning then to look. She had had for a moment the crazy thought that it could be Whitney coming back for her, but of course it was not. It was a new gray Porsche, going slowly, looking for something. Walking a little faster, Dylan began to adjust her smile.

Considerations

1. As Dylan worked at her waitressing job, she dreamed of "rescue" or "escape." What do you see as the difference between the two words? How does this difference relate to the actions, reactions, and interactions of the main characters?

2. Imagine how Whitney would describe one episode in the story. Discuss and evaluate the differences you see between his point of view and Dylan's.

3. What irony do you find in the hopes and dreams of the three main characters as compared to the realities of their lives and the opportunities available to them?

4. Describe the work each of the three main characters does. Evaluate the significance of each character's attitude toward his or her work.

5. How are Dylan and Flower alike? How are they different? What do you find significant about their similarities and differences? Consider particularly the ending of the story: What is Flower looking for in life? What is Dylan seeking?

W. D. WETHERELL (1948–   )

The Bass, the River, and Sheila Mant

There was a summer in my life when the only creature that seemed lovelier to me than a largemouth bass was Sheila Mant. I was fourteen. The Mants had rented the cottage next to ours on the river; with their parties, their frantic games of softball, their constant comings and goings, they appeared to me denizens of a brilliant existence. "Too noisy by half," my mother quickly decided, but I would have given anything to be invited to one of their parties, and when my parents went to bed I would sneak through the woods to their hedge and stare enchanted at the candlelit swirl of white dresses and bright, paisley skirts.

Sheila was the middle daughter—at seventeen, all but out of reach. She would spend her days sunbathing on a float my Uncle Sierbert had moored in their cove, and before July was over I had learned all her moods. If she lay flat on the diving board with her hand trailing idly in the water, she was pensive, not to be disturbed. On her side, her head propped up by her arm, she was observant, considering those around her with a look that seemed queenly and severe. Sitting up, arms tucked around her long, sun-tanned legs, she was approachable, but barely, and it was only in those glorious moments when she stretched herself prior to entering the water that her various suitors found the courage to come near.

These were many. The Dartmouth heavyweight crew would scull by her house on their way upriver, and I think all eight of them must have been in love with her at various times during the summer; the coxswain would curse them through his megaphone, but without effect—there was always a pause in their pace when they passed Sheila's float. I suppose to these jaded twenty-year-olds she seemed the incarnation of innocence and youth, while to me she appeared unutterably suave, the epitome of sophistication. I was on the swim team at school, and to win her attention would do endless laps between my house and the Vermont shore, hoping she would notice the beauty of my flutter kick, the power of my crawl. Finishing, I would boost myself up onto our dock and glance casually over toward her, but she was never watching, and the miraculous day she was, I immediately climbed the diving board and did my best tuck and a half for her, and continued diving until she had left and the sun went down and my longing was like a madness and I couldn't stop.

It was late August by the time I got up the nerve to ask her out. The tortured will-I's, won't-I's, the agonized indecision over what to say, the false starts toward her house and embarrassed retreats—the details of these have been seared from my memory, and the only part I remember clearly is emerging from the woods toward dusk while they were playing softball on their lawn, as bashful and frightened as a unicorn.

Sheila was stationed halfway between first and second, well outside the   5
infield. She didn't seem surprised to see me — as a matter of fact, she didn't
seem to see me at all.

"If you're playing second base, you should move closer," I said.

She turned — I took the full brunt of her long red hair and well-spaced
freckles.

"I'm playing outfield," she said, "I don't like the responsibility of
having a base."

"Yeah, I can understand that," I said, though I couldn't. "There's a
band in Dixford tomorrow night at nine. Want to go?"

One of her brothers sent the ball sailing over the leftfielder's head; she   10
stood and watched it disappear toward the river.

"You have a car?" she asked, without looking up.

I played my master stroke. "We'll go by canoe."

I spent all of the following day polishing it. I turned it upside down on
our lawn and rubbed every inch with Brillo, hosing off the dirt, wiping it
with chamois until it gleamed as bright as aluminum ever gleamed. About
five, I slid it into the water, arranging cushions near the bow so Sheila could
lean on them if she was in one of her pensive moods, propping up my
father's transistor radio by the middle thwart so we could have music when
we came back. Automatically, without thinking about it, I mounted my
Mitchell reel on my Pfleuger spinning rod and stuck it in the stern.

I say automatically, because I never went anywhere that summer without a fishing rod. When I wasn't swimming laps to impress Sheila, I was
back in our driveway practicing casts, and when I wasn't practicing casts, I
was tying the line to Tosca, our springer spaniel, to test the reel's drag, and
when I wasn't doing any of those things, I was fishing the river for bass.

Too nervous to sit at home, I got in the canoe early and started pad-   15
dling in a huge circle that would get me to Sheila's dock around eight. As
automatically as I brought along my rod, I tied on a big Rapala plug, let it
down into the water, let out some line and immediately forgot all about it.

It was already dark by the time I glided up to the Mants' dock. Even
by day the river was quiet, most of the summer people preferring Sunapee
or one of the other nearby lakes, and at night it was a solitude difficult to
believe, a corridor of hidden life that ran between banks like a tunnel. Even
the stars were part of it. They weren't as sharp anywhere else; they seemed
to have chosen the river as a guide on their slow wheel toward morning,
and in the course of the summer's fishing, I had learned all their names.

I was there ten minutes before Sheila appeared. I heard the slam of
their screen door first, then saw her in the spotlight as she came slowly
down the path. As beautiful as she was on the float, she was even lovelier
now — her white dress went perfectly with her hair, and complimented her
figure even more than her swimsuit.

It was her face that bothered me. It had on its delightful fullness a very
dubious expression.

"Look," she said. "I can get Dad's car."

"It's faster this way," I lied. "Parking's tense up there. Hey, it's safe. I   20
won't tip it or anything."

She let herself down reluctantly into the bow. I was glad she wasn't
facing me. When her eyes were on me, I felt like diving in the river again
from agony and joy.

I pried the canoe away from the dock and started paddling upstream.
There was an extra paddle in the bow, but Sheila made no move to pick it
up. She took her shoes off, and dangled her feet over the side.

Ten minutes went by.

"What kind of band?" she said.

"It's sort of like folk music. You'll like it."   25

"Eric Caswell's going to be there. He strokes number four."

"No kidding?" I said. I had no idea who she meant.

"What's that sound?" she said, pointing toward the shore.

"Bass. That splashing sound?"

"Over there."   30

"Yeah, bass. They come into the shallows at night to chase frogs and
moths and things. Big largemouths. *Micropetrus salmonides,*" I added, showing off.

"I think fishing's dumb," she said, making a face. "I mean, it's boring
and all. Definitely dumb."

Now I have spent a great deal of time in the years since wondering
why Sheila Mant should come down so hard on fishing. Was her father a
fisherman? Her antipathy toward fishing nothing more than normal filial
rebellion? Had she tried it once? A messy encounter with worms? It doesn't
matter. What does, is that at that fragile moment in time I would have given
anything not to appear dumb in Sheila's severe and unforgiving eyes.

She hadn't seen my equipment yet. What I *should* have done, of course,
was push the canoe in closer to shore and carefully slide the rod into some
branches where I could pick it up again in the morning. Failing that, I could
have surreptitiously dumped the whole outfit overboard, written off the
forty or so dollars as love's tribute. What I actually *did* do was gently lean
forward, and slowly, ever so slowly, push the rod back through my legs
toward the stern where it would be less conspicuous.

It must have been just exactly what the bass was waiting for. Fish will   35
trail a lure sometimes, trying to make up their mind whether or not to
attack, and the slight pause in the plug's speed caused by my adjustment was
tantalizing enough to overcome the bass's inhibitions. My rod, safely out of
sight at last, bent double. The line, tightly coiled, peeled off the spool with
the shrill, tearing zip of a high-speed drill.

Four things occurred to me at once. One, that it was a bass. Two, that
it was a big bass. Three, that it was the biggest bass I had ever hooked.
Four, that Sheila Mant must not know.

"What was that?" she said, turning half around.

"Uh, what was what?"

"That buzzing noise."

"Bats."

She shuddered, quickly drew her feet back into the canoe. Every instinct I had told me to pick up the rod and strike back at the bass, but there was no need to—it was already solidly hooked. Downstream, an awesome distance downstream, it jumped clear of the water, landing with a concussion heavy enough to ripple the entire river. For a moment, I thought it was gone, but then the rod was bending again, the tip dancing into the water. Slowly, not making any motion that might alert Sheila, I reached down to tighten the drag.

While all this was going on, Sheila had begun talking and it was a few minutes before I was able to catch up with her train of thought.

"I went to a party there. These fraternity men. Katherine says I could get in there if I wanted. I'm thinking more of UVM or Bennington. Somewhere I can ski."

The bass was slanting toward the rocks on the New Hampshire side by the ruins of Donaldson's boathouse. It had to be an old bass—a young one probably wouldn't have known the rocks were there. I brought the canoe back into the middle of the river, hoping to head it off.

"That's neat," I mumbled. "Skiing. Yeah, I can see that."

"Eric said I have the figure to model, but I thought I should get an education first. I mean, it might be a while before I get started and all. I was thinking of getting my hair styled, more swept back? I mean, Ann-Margret? Like hers, only shorter?"

She hesitated. "Are we going backward?"

We were. I had managed to keep the bass in the middle of the river away from the rocks, but it had plenty of room there, and for the first time a chance to exert its full strength. I quickly computed the weight necessary to draw a fully loaded canoe backwards—the thought of it made me feel faint.

"It's just the current," I said hoarsely. "No sweat or anything."

I dug in deeper with my paddle. Reassured, Sheila began talking about something else, but all my attention was taken up now with the fish. I could feel its desperation as the water grew shallower. I could sense the extra strain on the line, the frantic way it cut back and forth in the water. I could visualize what it looked like—the gape of its mouth, the flared gills and thick, vertical tail. The bass couldn't have encountered many forces in its long life that it wasn't capable of handling, and the unrelenting tug at its mouth must have been a source of great puzzlement and mounting panic.

Me, I had problems of my own. To get to Dixford, I had to paddle up a sluggish stream that came into the river beneath a covered bridge. There was a shallow sandbar at the mouth of this stream—weeds on one side, rocks on the other. Without doubt, this is where I would lose the fish.

"I have to be careful with my complexion. I tan, but in segments. I can't figure out if it's even worth it. I shouldn't even do it probably. I saw Jackie Kennedy in Boston and she wasn't tan at all."

Taking a deep breath, I paddled as hard as I could for the middle, deepest part of the bar. I could have threaded the eye of a needle with the canoe, but the pull on the stern threw me off and I overcompensated — the canoe veered left and scraped bottom. I pushed the paddle down and shoved. A moment of hesitation . . . a moment more. . . . The canoe shot clear into the deeper water of the stream. I immediately looked down at the rod. It was bent in the same, tight arc — miraculously, the bass was still on.

The moon was out now. It was low and full enough that its beam shone directly on Sheila there ahead of me in the canoe, washing her in a creamy, luminous glow. I could see the lithe, easy shape of her figure. I could see the way her hair curled down off her shoulders, the proud, alert tilt of her head, and all these things were as a tug on my heart. Not just Sheila, but the aura she carried about her of parties and casual touchings and grace. Behind me, I could feel the strain of the bass, steadier now, growing weaker, and this was another tug on my heart, not just the bass but the beat of the river and the slant of the stars and the smell of the night, until finally it seemed I would be torn apart between longings, split in half. Twenty yards ahead of us was the road, and once I pulled the canoe up on shore, the bass would be gone, irretrievably gone. If instead I stood up, grabbed the rod and started pumping, I would have it — as tired as the bass was, there was no chance it could get away. I reached down for the rod, hesitated, looked up to where Sheila was stretching herself lazily toward the sky, her small breasts rising beneath the soft fabric of her dress, and the tug was too much for me, and quicker than it takes to write down, I pulled a penknife from my pocket and cut the line in half.

With a sick, nauseous feeling in my stomach, I saw the rod unbend.   55

"My legs are sore," Sheila whined. "Are we there yet?"

Through a superhuman effort of self-control, I was able to beach the canoe and help Sheila off. The rest of the night is much foggier. We walked to the fair — there was the smell of popcorn, the sound of guitars. I may have danced once or twice with her, but all I really remember is her coming over to me once the music was done to explain that she would be going home in Eric Caswell's Corvette.

"Okay," I mumbled.

For the first time that night she looked at me, really looked at me.

"You're a funny kid, you know that?"   60

Funny. Different. Dreamy. Odd. How many times was I to hear that in the years to come, all spoken with the same quizzical, half-accusatory tone Sheila used then. Poor Sheila! Before the month was over, the spell she cast over me was gone, but the memory of that lost bass haunted me all summer and haunts me still. There would be other Sheila Mants in my life, other fish, and though I came close once or twice, it was these secret, hidden tuggings in the night that claimed me, and I never made the same mistake again.

Considerations

1. Describe the differences between Sheila Mant's world and the world of the narrator. Consider their families, their actions, and their conversations. Compare what each character considers important and evaluate the significance of this comparison.
2. What are the relationships between the bass, the river, and Sheila Mant? What role does each play in the narrator's fourteenth summer?
3. Make a list of decisions or choices the narrator makes. Evaluate some or all of those decisions or choices. Speculate on why the narrator responds as he does and on the long- and short-term significance of his responses.
4. Reread the following passage carefully. Then, using the narrator's words as a model, write a paragraph using specific details to describe a place that was important to you during your early teenage years.

> It was already dark by the time I glided up to the Mants' dock. Even by day the river was quiet, most of the summer people preferring Sunapee or one of the other nearby lakes, and at night it was a solitude difficult to believe, a corridor of hidden life that ran between banks like a tunnel. Even the stars were part of it. They weren't as sharp anywhere else; they seemed to have chosen the river as a guide on their slow wheel toward morning, and in the course of the summer's fishing, I had learned all their names.

5. Evaluate the narrator's final comment: "I never made the same mistake again." What mistake does he believe he made? Explain and discuss the implications of that mistake.

JAMAICA KINCAID (1950–   )

The Circling Hand

During my holidays from school, I was allowed to stay in bed until long after my father had gone to work. He left our house every weekday at the stroke of seven by the Anglican church bell. I would lie in bed awake, and I could hear all the sounds my parents made as they prepared for the day ahead. As my mother made my father his breakfast, my father would shave, using his shaving brush that had an ivory handle and a razor that matched; then he would step outside to the little shed he had built for us as a bathroom, to quickly bathe in water that he had instructed my mother to leave outside overnight in the dew. That way, the water would be very cold, and he believed that cold water strengthened his back. If I had been a boy, I would have gotten the same treatment, but since I was a girl, and on top of that went to school only with other girls, my mother would always add some hot water to my bathwater to take off the chill. On Sunday afternoons, while I was in Sunday school, my father took a hot bath; the tub was half filled with plain water, and then my mother would add a large caldronful of water in which she had just boiled some bark and leaves from a bay-leaf tree. The bark and leaves were there for no reason other than that he liked the smell. He would then spend hours lying in this bath, studying his pool coupons or drawing examples of pieces of furniture he planned to make. When I came home from Sunday school, we would sit down to our Sunday dinner.

My mother and I often took a bath together. Sometimes it was just a plain bath, which didn't take very long. Other times, it was a special bath in which the barks and flowers of many different trees, together with all sorts of oils were boiled in the same large caldron. We would then sit in this bath in a darkened room with a strange-smelling candle burning away. As we sat in this bath, my mother would bathe different parts of my body; then she would do the same to herself. We took these baths after my mother had consulted with her obeah woman, and with her mother and a trusted friend, and all three of them had confirmed that from the look of things around our house — the way a small scratch on my instep had turned into a small sore, then a large sore, and how long it had taken to heal; the way a dog she knew, and a friendly dog at that, suddenly turned and bit her; how a porcelain bowl she had carried from one eternity and hoped to carry into the next suddenly slipped out of her capable hands and broke into pieces the size of grains of sand; how words she spoke in jest to a friend had been completely misunderstood — one of the many women my father had loved, had never married, but with whom he had had children was trying to harm my mother and me by setting bad spirits on us.

When I got up, I placed my bedclothes and my nightie in the sun to air out, brushed my teeth, and washed and dressed myself. My mother would then give me my breakfast, but since, during my holidays, I was not going to school, I wasn't forced to eat an enormous breakfast of porridge, eggs, an orange or half a grapefruit, bread and butter, and cheese. I could get away with just some bread and butter and cheese and porridge and cocoa. I spent the day following my mother around and observing the way she did everything. When we went to the grocer's, she would point out to me the reason she bought each thing. I was shown a loaf of bread or a pound of butter from at least ten different angles. When we went to market, if that day she wanted to buy some crabs she would inquire from the person selling them if they came from near Parham, and if the person said yes my mother did not buy the crabs. In Parham was the leper colony, and my mother was convinced that the crabs ate nothing but the food from the lepers' own plates. If we were then to eat the crabs, it wouldn't be long before we were lepers ourselves and living unhappily in the leper colony.

How important I felt to be with my mother. For many people, their wares and provisions laid out in front of them, would brighten up when they saw her coming and would try hard to get her attention. They would dive underneath their stalls and bring out goods even better than what they had on display. They were disappointed when she held something up in the air, looked at it, turning it this way and that, and then, screwing up her face, said, "I don't think so," and turned and walked away — off to another stall to see if someone who only last week had sold her some delicious christophine had something that was just as good. They would call out after her turned back that next week they expected to have eddoes or dasheen or whatever, and my mother would say, "We'll see," in a very disbelieving tone of voice. If then we went to Mr. Kenneth, it would be only for a few minutes, for he knew exactly what my mother wanted and always had it ready for her. Mr. Kenneth had known me since I was a small child, and he would always remind me of little things I had done then as he fed me a piece of raw liver he had set aside for me. It was one of the few things I liked to eat, and, to boot, it pleased my mother to see me eat something that was so good for me, and she would tell me in great detail the effect the raw liver would have on my red blood corpuscles.

We walked home in the hot midmorning sun mostly without event. 5 When I was much smaller, quite a few times while I was walking with my mother she would suddenly grab me and wrap me up in her skirt and drag me along with her as if in a great hurry. I would hear an angry voice saying angry things, and then, after we had passed the angry voice, my mother would release me. Neither my mother nor my father ever came straight out and told me anything, but I had put two and two together and I knew that it was one of the women that my father had loved and with whom he had had a child or children, and who never forgave him for marrying my mother and having me. It was one of those women who were always trying to harm my mother and me, and they must have loved my father very much, for not once did any of them ever try to hurt him, and whenever he passed them on the street it was as if he and these women had never met.

When we got home, my mother started to prepare our lunch (pumpkin soup with droppers, banana fritters with salt fish stewed in antroba and tomatoes, fungie with salt fish stewed in antroba and tomatoes, or pepper pot, all depending on what my mother had found at market that day). As my mother went about from pot to pot, stirring one, adding something to the other, I was ever in her wake. As she dipped into a pot of boiling something or other to taste for correct seasoning, she would give me a taste of it also, asking me what I thought. Not that she really wanted to know what I thought, for she had told me many times that my taste buds were not quite developed yet, but it was just to include me in everything. While she made our lunch, she would also keep an eye on her washing. If it was a Tuesday and the colored clothes had been starched, as she placed them on the line I would follow, carrying a basket of clothespins for her. While the starched colored clothes were being dried on the line, the white clothes were being whitened on the stone heap. It was a beautiful stone heap that my father had made for her; an enormous circle of stone, about six inches high, in the middle of our yard. On it the soapy white clothes were spread out; as the sun dried them, bleaching out all stains, they had to be made wet again by dousing them with buckets of water. On my holidays, I did this for my mother. As I watered the clothes, she would come up behind me, instructing me to get the clothes thoroughly wet, showing me a shirt that I should turn over so that the sleeves were exposed.

Over our lunch, my mother and father talked to each other about the houses my father had to build; how disgusted he had become with one of his apprentices, or with Mr. Oatie; what they thought of my schooling so far; what they thought of the noises Mr. Jarvis and his friends made for so many days when they locked themselves up inside Mr. Jarvis's house and drank rum and ate fish they had caught themselves and danced to the music of an accordion that they took turns playing. On and on they talked. As they talked, my head would move from side to side, looking at them. When my eyes rested on my father, I didn't think very much of the way he looked. But when my eyes rested on my mother, I found her beautiful. Her head looked as if it should be on a sixpence. What a beautiful long neck, and long plaited hair, which she pinned up around the crown of her head because when her hair hung down it made her too hot. Her nose was the shape of a flower on the brink of opening. Her mouth, moving up and down as she ate and talked at the same time, was such a beautiful mouth I could have looked at it forever if I had to and not mind. Her lips were wide and almost thin, and when she said certain words I could see small parts of big white teeth — so big, and pearly, like some nice buttons on one of my dresses. I didn't much care about what she said when she was in this mood with my father. She made him laugh so. She could hardly say a word before he would burst out laughing. We ate our food, I cleared the table, we said goodbye to my father as he went back to work, I helped my mother with the dishes, and then we settled into the afternoon.

When my mother, at sixteen, after quarreling with her father, left his house on Dominica and came to Antigua, she packed all her things in an enormous wooden trunk that she had bought in Roseau for almost six shillings. She painted the trunk yellow and green outside, and she lined the inside with wallpaper that had a cream background with pink roses printed all over it. Two days after she left her father's house, she boarded a boat and sailed for Antigua. It was a small boat, and the trip would have taken a day and a half ordinarily, but a hurricane blew up and the boat was lost at sea for almost five days. By the time it got to Antigua, the boat was practically in splinters, and though two or three of the passengers were lost overboard, along with some of the cargo, my mother and her trunk were safe. Now, twenty-four years later, this trunk was kept under my bed, and in it were things that had belonged to me, starting from just before I was born. There was the chemise, made of white cotton, with scallop edging around the sleeves, neck, and hem, and white flowers embroidered on the front — the first garment I wore after being born. My mother had made that herself, and once, when we were passing by, I was even shown the tree under which she sat as she made this garment. There were some of my diapers, with their handkerchief hemstitch that she had also done herself; there was a pair of white wool booties with matching jacket and hat; there was a blanket in white wool and a blanket in white flannel cotton; there was a plain white linen hat with lace trimming; there was my christening outfit; there were two of my baby bottles: one in the shape of a normal baby bottle, and the other shaped like a boat, with a nipple on either end; there was a thermos in which my mother had kept a tea that was supposed to have a soothing effect on me; there was the dress I wore on my first birthday: a yellow cotton with green smocking on the front; there was the dress I wore on my second birthday: pink cotton with green smocking on the front; there was also a photograph of me on my second birthday wearing my pink dress and my first pair of earrings, a chain around my neck, and a pair of bracelets, all specially made of gold from British Guiana; there was the first pair of shoes I grew out of after I knew how to walk; there was the dress I wore when I first went to school, and the first notebook in which I wrote; there were the sheets for my crib and the sheets for my first bed; there was my first straw hat, my first straw basket — decorated with flowers — my grandmother had sent me from Dominica; there were my report cards, my certificates of merit from school, and my certificates of merit from Sunday school.

From time to time, my mother would fix on a certain place in our house and give it a good cleaning. If I was at home when she happened to do this, I was at her side, as usual. When she did this with the trunk, it was a tremendous pleasure, for after she had removed all the things from the trunk, and aired them out, and changed the camphor balls, and then refolded the things and put them back in their places in the trunk, as she held each thing in her hand she would tell me a story about myself. Sometimes I knew the story first hand, for I could remember the incident quite well; sometimes what she told me had happened when I was too young to know anything; and sometimes it happened before I was even born. Whichever way, I knew exactly what she would say, for I had heard it so many times before, but I never got tired of it. For instance, the flowers on the chemise, the first garment I wore after being born, were not put on correctly, and that is because when my mother was embroidering them I kicked so much that her hand was unsteady. My mother said that usually when I kicked around in her stomach and she told me to stop I would, but on that day I paid no attention at all. When she told me this story, she would smile at me and say, "You see, even then you were hard to manage." It pleased me to think that, before she could see my face, my mother spoke to me in the same way she did now. On and on my mother would go. No small part of my life was so unimportant that she hadn't made a note of it, and now she would tell it to me over and over again. I would sit next to her and she would show me the very dress I wore on the day I bit another child my age with whom I was playing. "Your biting phase," she called it. Or the day she warned me not to play around the coal pot, because I liked to sing to myself and dance around the fire. Two seconds later, I fell into the hot coals, burning my elbows. My mother cried when she saw that it wasn't serious, and now, as she told me about it, she would kiss the little black patches of scars on my elbows.

As she told me the stories, I sometimes sat at her side, leaning against her, or I would crouch on my knees behind her back and lean over her shoulder. As I did this, I would occasionally sniff at her neck, or behind her ears, or at her hair. She smelled sometimes of lemons, sometimes of sage, sometimes of roses, sometimes of bay leaf. At times I would no longer hear what it was she was saying; I just liked to look at her mouth as it opened and closed over words, or as she laughed. How terrible it must be for all the people who had no one to love them so and no one whom they loved so, I thought. My father, for instance. When he was a little boy, his parents, after kissing him goodbye and leaving him with his grandmother, boarded a boat and sailed to South America. He never saw them again, though they wrote to him and sent him presents — packages of clothes on his birthday and at Christmas. He then grew to love his grandmother, and she loved him, for she took care of him and worked hard at keeping him well fed and clothed. From the beginning, they slept in the same bed, and as he became a young man they continued to do so. When he was no longer in school and had started working, every night, after he and his grandmother had eaten their dinner, my father would go off to visit his friends. He would then return home at around midnight and fall asleep next to his grandmother. In the morning, his grandmother would awake at half past five or so, a half hour before my father, and prepare his bath and breakfast and make everything proper and ready for him, so that at seven o'clock sharp he stepped out the door off to work. One morning, though, he overslept, because his grandmother didn't wake him up. When he awoke, she was still lying next to him. When he tried to wake her, he couldn't. She had died lying next to him sometime during the night. Even though he was overcome with grief, he built her coffin and made sure she had a nice funeral. He never slept in that bed again, and shortly afterward he moved out of that house. He was eighteen years old then.

When my father first told me this story, I threw myself at him at the end of it, and we both started to cry—he just a little, I quite a lot. It was a Sunday afternoon; he and my mother and I had gone for a walk in the botanical gardens. My mother had wandered off to look at some strange kind of thistle, and we could see her as she bent over the bushes to get a closer look and reach out to touch the leaves of the plant. When she returned to us and saw that we had both been crying, she started to get quite worked up, but my father quickly told her what had happened and she laughed at us and called us her little fools. But then she took me in her arms and kissed me, and she said that I needn't worry about such a thing as her sailing off or dying and leaving me all alone in the world. But if ever after that I saw my father sitting alone with a faraway look on his face, I was filled with pity for him. He had been alone in the world all that time, what with his mother sailing off on a boat with his father and his never seeing her again, and then his grandmother dying while lying next to him in the middle of the night. It was more than anyone should have to bear. I loved him so and wished that I had a mother to give him, for, no matter how much my own mother loved him, it could never be the same.

When my mother got through with the trunk, and I had heard again and again just what I had been like and who had said what to me at what point in my life, I was given my tea—a cup of cocoa and a buttered bun. My father by then would return home from work, and he was given his tea. As my mother went around preparing our supper, picking up clothes from the stone heap, or taking clothes off the clothesline, I would sit in a corner of our yard and watch her. She never stood still. Her powerful legs carried her from one part of the yard to the other, and in and out of the house. Sometimes she might call out to me to go and get some thyme or basil or some other herb for her, for she grew all her herbs in little pots that she kept in a corner of our little garden. Sometimes when I gave her the herbs, she might stoop down and kiss me on my lips and then on my neck. It was in such a paradise that I lived.

The summer of the year I turned twelve, I could see that I had grown taller; most of my clothes no longer fit. When I could get a dress over my head, the waist then came up to just below my chest. My legs had become more spindlelike, the hair on my head even more unruly than usual, small tufts of hair had appeared under my arms, and when I perspired the smell was strange, as if I had turned into a strange animal. I didn't say anything about it, and my mother and father didn't seem to notice, for they didn't say anything, either. Up to then, my mother and I had many dresses made out of the same cloth, though hers had a different, more grownup style, a boat neck or a sweetheart neckline, and a pleated or gored skirt, while my dresses had high necks with collars, a deep hemline, and, of course, a sash that tied in the back. One day, my mother and I had gone to get some material for new dresses to celebrate her birthday (the usual gift from my father), when I came upon a piece of cloth—a yellow background, with figures of men, dressed in a long-ago fashion, seated at pianos that they were playing, and all around them musical notes flying off into the air. I immediately said how much I loved this piece of cloth and how nice I thought it would look on us both, but my mother replied, "Oh, no. You are getting too old for that. It's time you had your own clothes. You just cannot go around the rest of your life looking like a little me." To say that I felt the earth swept away from under me would not be going too far. It wasn't just what she said, it was the way she said it. No accompanying little laugh. No bending over and kissing my little wet forehead (for suddenly I turned hot, then cold, and all my pores must have opened up, for fluids just flowed out of me). In the end, I got my dress with the men playing their pianos, and my mother got a dress with red and yellow overgrown hibiscus, but I was never able to wear my own dress or see my mother in hers without feeling bitterness and hatred, directed not so much toward my mother as toward, I suppose, life in general.

As if that were not enough, my mother informed me that I was on the verge of becoming a young lady, so there were quite a few things I would have to do differently. She didn't say exactly just what it was that made me on the verge of becoming a young lady, and I was so glad of that, because I didn't want to know. Behind a closed door, I stood naked in front of a mirror and looked at myself from head to toe. I was so long and bony that I more than filled up the mirror, and my small ribs pressed out against my skin. I tried to push my unruly hair down against my head so that it would lie flat, but as soon as I let it go it bounced up again. I could see the small tufts of hair under my arms. And then I got a good look at my nose. It had suddenly spread across my face, almost blotting out my cheeks, taking up my whole face, so that if I didn't know I was me standing there I would have wondered about that strange girl—and to think that only so recently my nose had been a small thing, the size of a rosebud. But what could I do? I thought of begging my mother to ask my father if he could build for me a set of clamps into which I could screw myself at night before I went to sleep and which would surely cut back on my growing. I was about to ask her this when I remembered that a few days earlier I had asked in my most pleasing, winning way for a look through the trunk. A person I did not recognize answered in a voice I did not recognize, "Absolutely not! You and I don't have time for that anymore." Again, did the ground wash out from under me? Again, the answer would have to be yes, and I wouldn't be going too far.

Because of this young-lady business, instead of days spent in perfect harmony with my mother, I trailing in her footsteps, she showering down on me her kisses and affection and attention, I was now sent off to learn one thing and another. I was sent to someone who knew all about manners and how to meet and greet important people in the world. This woman soon asked me not to come again, since I could not resist making farting-like noises each time I had to practice a curtsy, it made the other girls laugh so. I was sent for piano lessons. The piano teacher, a shriveled-up old spinster from Lancashire, England, soon asked me not to come back, since I seemed unable to resist eating from the bowl of plums she had placed on the piano purely for decoration. In the first case, I told my mother a lie — I told her that the manners teacher had found that my manners needed no improvement, so I needn't come anymore. This made her very pleased. In the second case, there was no getting around it — she had to find out. When the piano teacher told her of my misdeed, she turned and walked away from me, and I wasn't sure that if she had been asked who I was she wouldn't have said, "I don't know," right then and there. What a new thing this was for me: my mother's back turned on me in disgust. It was true that I didn't spend all my days at my mother's side before this, that I spent most of my days at school, but before this young-lady business I could sit and think of my mother, see her doing one thing or another, and always her face bore a smile for me. Now I often saw her with the corners of her mouth turned down in disapproval of me. And why was my mother carrying my new state so far? She took to pointing out that one day I would have my own house and I might want it to be a different house from the one she kept. Once, when showing me a way to store linen, she patted the folded sheets in place and said, "Of course, in your own house you might choose another way." That the day might actually come when we would live apart I had never believed. My throat hurt from the tears I held bottled up tight inside. Sometimes we would both forget the new order of things and would slip into our old ways. But that didn't last very long.

In the middle of all these new things, I had forgotten that I was to enter a new school that September. I had then a set of things to do, preparing for school. I had to go to the seamstress to be measured for new uniforms, since my body now made a mockery of the old measurements. I had to get shoes, a new school hat, and lots of new books. In my new school, I needed a different exercise book for each subject, and in addition to the usual — English, arithmetic, and so on — I now had to take Latin and French, and attend classes in a brand-new science building. I began to look forward to my new school. I hoped that everyone there would be new, that there would be no one I had ever met before. That way, I could put on a new set of airs; I could say I was something that I was not, and no one would ever know the difference.

On the Sunday before the Monday I started at my new school, my mother became cross over the way I had made my bed. In the center of my bedspread, my mother had embroidered a bowl overflowing with flowers and two lovebirds on either side of the bowl. I had placed the bedspread on my bed in a lopsided way so that the embroidery was not in the center of my bed, the way it should have been. My mother made a fuss about it, and I could see that she was right and I regretted very much not doing that one little thing that would have pleased her. I had lately become careless, she said, and I could only silently agree with her.

I came home from church, and my mother still seemed to hold the bedspread against me, so I kept out of her way. At half past two in the afternoon, I went off to Sunday school. At Sunday school, I was given a certificate for best student in my study-of-the-Bible group. It was a surprise that I would receive the certificate on that day, though we had known about the results of the test weeks before. I rushed home with my certificate in hand, feeling that with this prize I would reconquer my mother—a chance for her to smile on me again.

When I got to our house, I rushed into the yard and called out to her, but no answer came. I then walked into the house. At first, I didn't hear anything. Then I heard sounds coming from the direction of my parents' room. My mother must be in there, I thought. When I got to the door, I could see that my mother and father were lying in their bed. It didn't interest me what they were doing—only that my mother's hand was on the small of my father's back and that it was making a circular motion. But her hand! It was white and bony, as if it had long been dead and had been left out in the elements. It seemed not to be her hand, and yet it could only be her hand, so well did I know it. It went around and around in the same circular motion, and I looked at it as if I would never see anything else in my life again. If I were to forget everything else in the world, I could not forget her hand as it looked then. I could also make out that the sounds I had heard were her kissing my father's ears and his mouth and his face. I looked at them for I don't know how long.

When I next saw my mother, I was standing at the dinner table that I had just set, having made a tremendous commotion with knives and forks as I got them out of their drawer, letting my parents know that I was home. I had set the table and was now half standing near my chair, half draped over the table, staring at nothing in particular and trying to ignore my mother's presence. Though I couldn't remember our eyes having met, I was quite sure that she had seen me in the bedroom, and I didn't know what I would say if she mentioned it. Instead, she said in a voice that was sort of cross and sort of something else, "Are you going to just stand there doing nothing all day?" The something else was new; I had never heard it in her voice before.

20

I couldn't say exactly what it was, but I know that it caused me to reply, "And what if I do?" and at the same time to stare at her directly in the eyes. It must have been a shock to her, the way I spoke. I had never talked back to her before. She looked at me, and then, instead of saying some squelching thing that would put me back in my place, she dropped her eyes and walked away. From the back, she looked small and funny. She carried her hands limp at her sides. I was sure I could never let those hands touch me again; I was sure I could never let her kiss me again. All that was finished.

I was amazed that I could eat my food, for all of it reminded me of things that had taken place between my mother and me. A long time ago, when I wouldn't eat my beef, complaining that it involved too much chewing, my mother would first chew up pieces of meat in her own mouth and then feed it to me. When I had hated carrots so much that even the sight of them would send me into a fit of tears, my mother would try to find all sorts of ways to make them palatable for me. All that was finished now. I didn't think that I would ever think of any of it again with fondness. I looked at my parents. My father was just the same, eating his food in the same old way, his two rows of false teeth clop-clopping like a horse being driven off to market. He was regaling us with another one of his stories about when he was a young man and played cricket on one island or the other. What he said now must have been funny, for my mother couldn't stop laughing. He didn't seem to notice that I was not entertained.

My father and I then went for our customary Sunday-afternoon walk. My mother did not come with us. I don't know what she stayed home to do. On our walk, my father tried to hold my hand, but I pulled myself away from him, doing it in such a way that he would think I felt too big for that now.

That Monday, I went to my new school. I was placed in a class with girls I had never seen before. Some of them had heard about me, though, for I was the youngest among them and was said to be very bright. I liked a girl named Albertine, and I liked a girl named Gweneth. At the end of the day, Gwen and I were in love, and so we walked home arm in arm together.

When I got home, my mother greeted me with the customary kiss and inquiries. I told her about my day, going out of my way to provide pleasing details, leaving out, of course, any mention at all of Gwen and my overpowering feelings for her.

Considerations

1. Describe several of the items the speaker's mother stores in her trunk. What do these items represent to the speaker? To her mother?
2. How does the speaker's relationship with her mother change? List specific events that demonstrate the change and explain their significance.

3. What role does the speaker's father play in her life? At the end of the story, why does she pull away from her father as they walk together?
4. Choose any incident in the story and retell it from the mother's point of view. As you do this, explicate the mother's reasons for changing so greatly in the way she treats her daughter.
5. Suppose someone gave you a memory trunk and asked you to store in it five items emblematic of significant events, people, or places in your life. What items would you select? Describe the items and explain their significance both at the time you acquired them and to your life today.

A. E. HOUSMAN (1859–1936)

When I was one-and-twenty

When I was one-and-twenty
   I heard a wise man say,
'Give crowns and pounds and guineas
   But not your heart away;
Give pearls away and rubies   5
   But keep your fancy free.'
But I was one-and-twenty,
   No use to talk to me.

When I was one-and-twenty
   I heard him say again,   10
'The heart out of the bosom
   Was never given in vain;
'Tis paid with sighs a plenty
   And sold for endless rue.'
And I am two-and-twenty,   15
   And oh, 'tis true, 'tis true.

Considerations

1. Compare the advice given by the wise man in stanza 1 to the advice he gives in stanza 2. Is he saying the same thing both times? Or do you see the meaning as different? What might he mean, for instance, by "keep your fancy free"?
2. How does the attitude of the speaker change from stanza 1 to stanza 2? Pay particular attention to the last two lines in each stanza. What are the implications of the change?

3. Imagine the speaker at thirty-two (or at forty or at sixty-five). To what extent and in what ways do you think this early lesson might affect his later life? Create several possible scenarios.

COUNTEE CULLEN (1903–1946)

Incident

Once riding in old Baltimore,
    Heart-filled, head-filled with glee,
I saw a Baltimorean
    Keep looking straight at me.

Now I was eight and very small,   5
    And he was no whit bigger,
And so I smiled, but he poked out
    His tongue and called me, "Nigger."

I saw the whole of Baltimore
    From May until December: 10
Of all the things that happened there
    That's all that I remember.

Considerations

1. Read this poem aloud. How do the rhythm and rhyme in the poem relate to the picture given of the speaker and of his experience?
2. What is the significance of the final stanza? Why is this the only event that the speaker remembers about his eight-month stay in Baltimore?
3. Describe an incident from your past that you remember as vividly as the speaker remembers this one. Focus on one particular moment lasting no more than five or ten minutes. Explain both what happened and why it was so significant that you can still recall it in detail.

ELIZABETH BISHOP (1911–1979)

First Death in Nova Scotia

In the cold, cold parlor,
my mother laid out Arthur
beneath the chromographs:

Edward, Prince of Wales,
with Princess Alexandra,   5
and King George with Queen Mary.
Below them on the table
stood a stuffed loon
shot and stuffed by Uncle
Arthur, Arthur's father.   10

Since Uncle Arthur fired
a bullet into him,
he hadn't said a word.
He kept his own counsel
on his white, frozen lake,   15
the marble-topped table.
His breast was deep and white,
cold and caressable;
his eyes were red glass,
much to be desired.   20

"Come," said my mother,
"Come and say good-bye
to your little cousin Arthur."
I was lifted up and given
one lily of the valley   25
to put in Arthur's hand.
Arthur's coffin was
a little frosted cake,
and the red-eyed loon eyed it
from his white, frozen lake.   30

Arthur was very small.
He was all white, like a doll
that hadn't been painted yet.
Jack Frost had started to paint him
the way he always painted   35
the Maple Leaf (Forever).
He had just begun on his hair,
a few red strokes, and then
Jack Frost had dropped the brush
and left him white, forever.   40

The gracious royal couples
were warm in red and ermine;
their feet were well wrapped up
in the ladies' ermine trains.

They invited Arthur to be   45
the smallest page at court.
But how could Arthur go,
clutching his tiny lily,
with his eyes shut up so tight
and the roads deep in snow?   50

Considerations

1. List the images in the poem that impress you most. Then sort them into
   groups of sight, sound, and touch images. What do these images suggest
   about the speaker's childhood view of death?
2. What is the relationship between the stuffed loon and the dead child?
3. Consider the final lines in the poem. What does this question suggest to
   you? What do you think might have been going on in the mind of the
   child/speaker as she asks this question?

BETTIE SELLERS (1926–   )

In the Counselor's Waiting Room

The terra cotta girl
with the big flat farm feet
traces furrows in the rug
with her toes,
reads an existentialist paperback   5
from psychology class,
finds no ease there
from the guilt of loving
the quiet girl down the hall.
Their home soil has seen to this visit,   10
their Baptist mothers,
who weep for the waste of sturdy hips
ripe for grandchildren.

Considerations

1. What conflict (or conflicts) do you see in the poem? Why are the Baptist
   mothers so upset with their daughters? What values clash?
2. Consider the implications of the two settings — the college that the "terra
   cotta girl" and "the quiet girl down the hall" attend and the "home soil"
   of the Baptist mothers.

3. Why are these people sitting in a counselor's waiting room? What might motivate the girl (or girls) to be there? Their mothers?

———————

MAY SWENSON (1919–1989)

The Centaur°

The summer that I was ten —
Can it be there was only one
summer that I was ten? It must

have been a long one then —
each day I'd go out to choose   5
a fresh horse from my stable

which was a willow grove
down by the old canal.
I'd go on my two bare feet.

But when, with my brother's jack-knife,   10
I had cut me a long limber horse
with a good thick knob for a head,

and peeled him slick and clean
except a few leaves for the tail,
and cinched my brother's belt   15

around his head for a rein,
I'd straddle and canter him fast
up the grass bank to the path,

trot along in the lovely dust
that talcumed over his hoofs,   20
hiding my toes, and turning

his feet to swift half-moons.
The willow knob with the strap
jouncing between my thighs

———————

Centaur: A creature, half man, half horse, in Greek mythology; most followed Dionysus, the god of wine and celebration, but some were teachers of humans.

was the pommel and yet the poll   25
of my nickering pony's head.
My head and my neck were mine,

yet they were shaped like a horse.
My hair flopped to the side
like the mane of a horse in the wind.   30

My forelock swung in my eyes,
my neck arched and I snorted.
I shied and skittered and reared,
stopped and raised my knees,
pawed at the ground and quivered.   35
My teeth bared as we wheeled

and swished through the dust again.
I was the horse and the rider,
and the leather I slapped to his rump

spanked my own behind.   40
Doubled, my two hoofs beat
a gallop along the bank,

the wind twanged in my mane,
my mouth squared to the bit.
And yet I sat on my steed   45

quiet, negligent riding,
my toes standing the stirrups,
my thighs hugging his ribs.

At a walk we drew up to the porch.
I tethered him to a paling.   50
Dismounting, I smoothed my skirt

and entered the dusky hall.
My feet on the clean linoleum
left ghostly toes in the hall.

Where have you been? said my mother.   55
Been riding, I said from the sink,
and filled me a glass of water.

What's that in your pocket? she said.
Just my knife. It weighted my pocket
and stretched my dress awry.   60

Go tie back your hair, said my mother,
and *Why is your mouth all green?*
Rob Roy, he pulled some clover
as we crossed the field, I told her.

Considerations

1. Why does the speaker's tenth summer seem so long to her? Suggest as many possibilities as you can; provide details from the poem to support your ideas.
2. What is the significance of the conversation between mother and daughter in the final lines of the poem? Consider carefully the imagery the speaker uses to describe herself as you respond and, in addition, consider the meaning of the title.
3. Imagine that you are the speaker's mother. Then write a journal entry describing your daughter during her tenth summer. Use details and images from the poem to support your projection of the mother's thoughts and feelings.

ANNE SEXTON (1928–1975)

Snow White and the Seven Dwarfs

No matter what life you lead
the virgin is a lovely number:
cheeks as fragile as cigarette paper,
arms and legs made of Limoges,
lips like Vin Du Rhône,   5
rolling her china-blue doll eyes
open and shut.
Open to say,
Good Day Mama,
and shut for the thrust   10
of the unicorn.
She is unsoiled.
She is as white as a bonefish.

Once there was a lovely virgin
called Snow White.   15
Say she was thirteen.
Her stepmother,
a beauty in her own right,
though eaten, of course, by age,

would hear of no beauty surpassing her own.   20
Beauty is a simple passion,
but, oh my friends, in the end
you will dance the fire dance in iron shoes.
The stepmother had a mirror to which she referred —
something like the weather forecast —   25
a mirror that proclaimed
the one beauty of the land.
She would ask,
Looking glass upon the wall,
who is fairest of us all?   30
And the mirror would reply,
You are fairest of us all.
Pride pumped in her like poison.

Suddenly one day the mirror replied,
Queen, you are full fair, 'tis true,   35
but Snow White is fairer than you.
Until that moment Snow White
had been no more important
than a dust mouse under the bed.
But now the queen saw brown spots on her hand   40
and four whiskers over her lip
so she condemned Snow White
to be hacked to death.
Bring me her heart, she said to the hunter,
and I will salt it and eat it.   45
The hunter, however, let his prisoner go
and brought a boar's heart back to the castle.
The queen chewed it up like a cube steak.
Now I am fairest, she said,
lapping her slim white fingers.   50

Snow White walked in the wildwood
for weeks and weeks.
At each turn there were twenty doorways
and at each stood a hungry wolf,
his tongue lolling out like a worm.   55
The birds called out lewdly,
talking like pink parrots,
and the snakes hung down in loops,
each a noose for her sweet white neck.
On the seventh week   60
she came to the seventh mountain

and there she found the dwarf house.
It was as droll as a honeymoon cottage
and completely equipped with
seven beds, seven chairs, seven forks   65
and seven chamber pots.
Snow White ate seven chicken livers
and lay down, at last, to sleep.

The dwarfs, those little hot dogs,
walked three times around Snow White,   70
the sleeping virgin. They were wise
and wattled like small czars.
Yes. It's a good omen,
they said, and will bring us luck.
They stood on tiptoes to watch   75
Snow White wake up. She told them
about the mirror and the killer-queen
and they asked her to stay and keep house.
Beware of your stepmother,
they said.   80
Soon she will know you are here.
While we are away in the mines
during the day, you must not
open the door.

Looking glass upon the wall . . .   85
The mirror told
and so the queen dressed herself in rags
and went out like a peddler to trap Snow White.
She went across seven mountains.
She came to the dwarf house   90
and Snow White opened the door
and bought a bit of lacing.
The queen fastened it tightly
around her bodice,
as tight as an Ace bandage,   95
so tight that Snow White swooned.
She lay on the floor, a plucked daisy.
When the dwarfs came home they undid the lace
and she revived miraculously.
She was as full of life as soda pop.   100
Beware of your stepmother,
they said.
She will try once more.

Looking glass upon the wall . . .
Once more the mirror told   105
and once more the queen dressed in rags
and once more Snow White opened the door.
This time she bought a poison comb,
a curved eight-inch scorpion,
and put it in her hair and swooned again.   110
The dwarfs returned and took out the comb
and she revived miraculously.
She opened her eyes as wide as Orphan Annie.
Beware, beware, they said,
but the mirror told,   115
the queen came,
Snow White, the dumb bunny,
opened the door
and she bit into a poison apple
and fell down for the final time.   120
When the dwarfs returned
they undid her bodice,
they looked for a comb,
but it did no good.
Though they washed her with wine   125
and rubbed her with butter
it was to no avail.
She lay as still as a gold piece.

The seven dwarfs could not bring themselves
to bury her in the black ground   130
so they made a glass coffin
and set it upon the seventh mountain
so that all who passed by
could peek in upon her beauty.
A prince came one June day   135
and would not budge.
He stayed so long his hair turned green
and still he would not leave.
The dwarfs took pity upon him
and gave him the glass Snow White —   140
its doll's eyes shut forever —
to keep in his far-off castle.
As the prince's men carried the coffin
they stumbled and dropped it
and the chunk of apple flew out   145
of her throat and she woke up miraculously.

And thus Snow White became the prince's bride.
The wicked queen was invited to the wedding feast
and when she arrived there were
red-hot iron shoes,   150
in the manner of red-hot roller skates,
clamped upon her feet.
First your toes will smoke
and then your heels will turn black
and you will fry upward like a frog,   155
she was told.
And so she danced until she was dead,
a subterranean figure,
her tongue flicking in and out
like a gas jet.   160
Meanwhile Snow White held court,
rolling her china-blue doll eyes open and shut
and sometimes referring to her mirror
as women do.

WILLIAM BLAKE (1757–1827)

London

I wander thro' each charter'd street,
Near where the charter'd Thames does flow,
And mark in every face I meet
Marks of weakness, marks of woe.

In every cry of every man,   5
In every Infant's cry of fear,
In every voice, in every ban,
The mind-forg'd manacles I hear.

How the Chimney-sweeper's cry
Every blackning Church appalls;   10
And the hapless Soldier's sigh
Runs in blood down Palace walls.

But most thro' midnight streets I hear
How the youthful Harlot's curse
Blasts the new-born Infant's tear,   15
And blights with plagues the Marriage hearse.

GERARD MANLEY HOPKINS (1844–1889)

Spring and Fall
To a Young Child

Márgarét, are you gríeving
Over Goldengrove unleaving?
Leáves, líke the things of man, you
With your fresh thoughts care for, can you?
Ah! ás the heart grows older   5
It will come to such sights colder
By and by, nor spare a sigh
Though worlds of wanwood leafmeal lie;
And yet you wíll weep and know why.
Now no matter, child, the name: 10
Sórrow's spríngs áre the same.
Nor mouth had, no nor mind, expressed
What heart heard of, ghost guessed:
It ís the blight man was born for,
It is Margaret you mourn for.   15

ROBERT FROST (1874–1963)

Birches

When I see birches bend to left and right
Across the lines of straighter darker trees,
I like to think some boy's been swinging them.
But swinging doesn't bend them down to stay
As ice-storms do. Often you must have seen them   5
Loaded with ice a sunny winter morning
After a rain. They click upon themselves
As the breeze rises, and turn many-colored
As the stir cracks and crazes their enamel.
Soon the sun's warmth makes them shed crystal shells   10
Shattering and avalanching on the snow-crust —
Such heaps of broken glass to sweep away
You'd think the inner dome of heaven had fallen.
They are dragged to the withered bracken by the load,
And they seem not to break; though once they are bowed   15
So low for long, they never right themselves:

You may see their trunks arching in the woods
Years afterwards, trailing their leaves on the ground
Like girls on hands and knees that throw their hair
Before them over their heads to dry in the sun.   20
But I was going to say when Truth broke in
With all her matter-of-fact about the ice-storm,
I should prefer to have some boy bend them
As he went out and in to fetch the cows —
Some boy too far from town to learn baseball,   25
Whose only play was what he found himself,
Summer or winter, and could play alone.
One by one he subdued his father's trees
By riding them down over and over again
Until he took the stiffness out of them,   30
And not one but hung limp, not one was left
For him to conquer. He learned all there was
To learn about not launching out too soon
And so not carrying the tree away
Clear to the ground. He always kept his poise   35
To the top branches, climbing carefully
With the same pains you use to fill a cup
Up to the brim, and even above the brim.
Then he flung outward, feet first, with a swish,
Kicking his way down through the air to the ground.   40
So was I once myself a swinger of birches.
And so I dream of going back to be.
It's when I'm weary of considerations,
And life is too much like a pathless wood
Where your face burns and tickles with the cobwebs   45
Broken across it, and one eye is weeping
From a twig's having lashed across it open.
I'd like to get away from earth awhile
And then come back to it and begin over.
May no fate willfully misunderstand me   50
And half grant what I wish and snatch me away
Not to return. Earth's the right place for love:
I don't know where it's likely to go better.
I'd like to go by climbing a birch tree,
And climb black branches up a snow-white trunk   55
Toward heaven, till the tree could bear no more,
But dipped its top and set me down again.
That would be good both going and coming back.
One could do worse than be a swinger of birches.

JOHN CROWE RANSOM (1888–1974)

Blue Girls

Twirling your blue skirts, travelling the sward
Under the towers of your seminary,
Go listen to your teachers old and contrary
Without believing a word.

Tie the white fillets then about your hair   5
And think no more of what will come to pass
Than bluebirds that go walking on the grass
And chattering on the air.

Practise your beauty, blue girls, before it fail;
And I will cry with my loud lips and publish   10
Beauty which all our power shall never establish,
It is so frail.

For I could tell you a story which is true;
I know a woman with a terrible tongue,
Blear eyes fallen from blue,   15
All her perfections tarnished — yet it is not long
Since she was lovelier than any of you.

GWENDOLYN BROOKS (1917–   )

We Real Cool

The Pool Players.
Seven at the Golden Shovel.

We real cool. We
Left school. We

Lurk late. We
Strike straight. We

Sing sin. We   5
Thin gin. We

Jazz June. We
Die soon.

WILLIAM STAFFORD (1914–   )

Fifteen

South of the Bridge on Seventeenth
I found back of the willows one summer
day a motorcycle with engine running
as it lay on its side, ticking over
slowly in the high grass. I was fifteen.   5

I admired all that pulsing gleam, the
shiny flanks, the demure headlights
fringed where it lay; I led it gently
to the road and stood with that
companion, ready and friendly. I was fifteen.   10

We could find the end of a road, meet
the sky on out Seventeenth. I thought about
hills, and patting the handle got back a
confident opinion. On the bridge we indulged
a forward feeling, a tremble. I was fifteen.   15

Thinking, back farther in the grass I found
the owner, just coming to, where he had flipped
over the rail. He had blood on his hand, was pale —
I helped him walk to his machine. He ran his hand
over it, called me good man, roared away.   20

I stood there, fifteen.

MURIEL STUART (1889–   )

In the Orchard

'I thought you loved me.' 'No, it was only fun.'
'When we stood there, closer than all?' 'Well, the harvest moon
Was shining and queer in your hair, and it turned my head.'
'That made you?' 'Yes.' 'Just the moon and the light it made
Under the tree?' 'Well, your mouth, too.' 'Yes, my mouth?'   5
'And the quiet there that sang like the drum in the booth.
You shouldn't have danced like that.' 'Like what?' 'So close,
With your head turned up, and the flower in your hair, a rose
That smelt all warm.' 'I loved you. I thought you knew

I wouldn't have danced like that with any but you.'   10
'I didn't know. I thought you knew it was fun.'
'I thought it was love you meant.' 'Well, it's done.' 'Yes, it's done.
I've seen boys stone a blackbird, and watched them drown
A kitten . . . it clawed at the reeds, and they pushed it down
Into the pool while it screamed. Is that fun, too?'   15
'Well, boys are like that . . . Your brothers . . .' 'Yes, I know.
But you, so lovely and strong! Not you! Not you!'
'They don't understand it's cruel. It's only a game.'
'And are girls fun, too?' 'No, still in a way it's the same.
It's queer and lovely to have a girl . . .' 'Go on.'   20
'It makes you mad for a bit to feel she's your own,
And you laugh and kiss her, and maybe you give her a ring,
But it's only in fun.' 'But I gave you everything.'
'Well, you shouldn't have done it. You know what a fellow thinks
When a girl does that.' 'Yes, he talks of her over his drinks   25
And calls her a —' 'Stop that now. I thought you knew.'
'But it wasn't with anyone else. It was only you.'
'How did I know? I thought you wanted it too.
I thought you were like the rest. Well, what's to be done?'
'To be done?' 'Is it all right?' 'Yes.' 'Sure?' 'Yes, but why?'   30
'I don't know. I thought you were going to cry.
You said you had something to tell me.' 'Yes, I know.
It wasn't anything really . . . I think I'll go.'
'Yes, it's late. There's thunder about, a drop of rain
Fell on my hand in the dark. I'll see you again   35
At the dance next week. You're sure that everything's right?'
'Yes,' 'Well, I'll be going.' 'Kiss me . . . ' 'Good night.'. . . 'Good night.'

TENNESSEE WILLIAMS (1911–1983)

The Glass Menagerie

Characters

AMANDA WINGFIELD, *the mother. A little woman of great but confused vitality clinging frantically to another time and place. Her characterization must be carefully created, not copied from type. She is not paranoiac, but her life is paranoia. There is much to admire in* AMANDA, *and as much to love and pity as there is to laugh at. Certainly she has endurance and a kind of heroism, and though her foolishness makes her unwittingly cruel at times, there is tenderness in her slight person.*

LAURA WINGFIELD, *her daughter.* AMANDA, *having failed to establish contact with reality, continues to live vitally in her illusions, but* LAURA's *situation is even greater. A childhood illness has left her crippled, one leg slightly shorter than the other, and held in a brace. This defect need not be more than suggested on the stage. Stemming from this,* LAURA's *separation increases till she is like a piece of her own glass collection, too exquisitely fragile to move from the shelf.*

TOM WINGFIELD, *her son. And the narrator of the play. A poet with a job in a warehouse. His nature is not remorseless, but to escape from a trap he has to act without pity.*

JIM O'CONNOR, *the gentleman caller. A nice, ordinary, young man.*

Scene *An alley in St. Louis.*
Part I *Preparation for a Gentleman Caller.*
Part II *The Gentleman Calls.*
Time *Now and the Past.*

Scene I

The Wingfield apartment is in the rear of the building, one of those vast hive-like conglomerations of cellular living-units that flower as warty growths in overcrowded urban centers of lower middle-class population and are symptomatic of the impulse of this largest and fundamentally enslaved section of American society to avoid fluidity and differentiation and to exist and function as one interfused mass of automatism.

The apartment faces an alley and is entered by a fire-escape, a structure whose name is a touch of accidental poetic truth, for all of these huge buildings are always burning with the slow and implacable fires of human desperation. The fire-escape is included in the set — that is, the landing of it and steps descending from it.

The scene is memory and is therefore nonrealistic. Memory takes a lot of poetic license. It omits some details; others are exaggerated, according to the emotional value of the articles it touches, for memory is seated predominantly in the heart. The interior is therefore rather dim and poetic.

At the rise of the curtain, the audience is faced with the dark, grim rear wall of the Wingfield tenement. This building, which runs parallel to the footlights, is flanked on both sides by dark, narrow alleys which run into murky canyons of tangled clotheslines, garbage cans and the sinister latticework of neighboring fire-escapes. It is up and down these side alleys that exterior entrances and exits are made, during the play. At the end of TOM's *opening commentary, the dark tenement wall slowly reveals (by means of a transparency) the interior of the ground floor Wingfield apartment.*

Downstage is the living room, which also serves as a sleeping room for LAURA, *the sofa unfolding to make her bed. Upstage, center, and divided by a wide arch or second proscenium with transparent faded portieres (or second curtain), is the dining room. In an old-fashioned what-not in the living room are seen scores of transparent glass animals. A blown-up photograph of the father hangs on the wall of the living room, facing the audience, to the left of the archway. It is the face of a very handsome young man in a doughboy's° First World War cap. He is gallantly smiling, ineluctably smiling, as if to say, "I will be smiling forever."*

The audience hears and sees the opening scene in the dining room through both the transparent fourth wall of the building and the transparent gauze portieres of the dining-room arch. It is during this revealing scene that the fourth wall slowly ascends, out of sight. This transparent exterior wall is not brought down again until the very end of the play, during TOM's *final speech.*

The narrator is an undisguised convention of the play. He takes whatever license with dramatic convention as is convenient to his purposes.

TOM *enters dressed as a merchant sailor from the alley, stage left, and strolls across the front of the stage to the fire-escape. There he stops and lights a cigarette. He addresses the audience.*

TOM: Yes, I have tricks in my pocket, I have things up my sleeve. But I am the opposite of a stage magician. He gives you illusion that has the appearance of truth. I give you truth in the pleasant disguise of illusion. To begin with, I turn back time. I reverse it to that quaint period, the thirties, when the huge middle class of America was matriculating in a school for the blind. Their eyes had failed them, or they had failed their eyes, and so they were having their fingers pressed forcibly down on the fiery Braille alphabet of a dissolving economy. In Spain there was revolution. Here there was only shouting and confusion. In Spain there was Guernica.° Here there were disturbances of labor, sometimes pretty violent, in otherwise peaceful cities such as Chicago, Cleveland, Saint Louis. . . . This is the social background of the play.

(Music.)

The play is memory. Being a memory play, it is dimly lighted, it is sentimental, it is not realistic. In memory everything seems to happen

---

SCENE I. *doughboy:* soldier in World War I, usually indicating an infantryman. *Guernica:* Spanish town destroyed in 1937 by German bombers aiding Spanish dictator Franco during the Spanish Civil War.

to music. That explains the fiddle in the wings. I am the narrator of the play, and also a character in it. The other characters are my mother, Amanda, my sister, Laura, and a gentleman caller who appears in the final scenes. He is the most realistic character in the play, being an emissary from a world of reality that we were somehow set apart from. But since I have a poet's weakness for symbols, I am using this character also as a symbol; he is the long delayed but always expected something that we live for. There is a fifth character in the play who doesn't appear except in this larger-than-life photograph over the mantel. This is our father who left us a long time ago. He was a telephone man who fell in love with long distances; he gave up his job with the telephone company and skipped the light fantastic out of town . . . The last we heard of him was a picture post-card from Mazatlan, on the Pacific coast of Mexico, containing a message of two words — "Hello — Good-bye!" and an address. I think the rest of the play will explain itself. . . .

AMANDA*'s voice becomes audible through the portieres.*

(Legend on Screen: "Où Sont les Neiges.")°

He divides the portieres and enters the upstage area.

   AMANDA *and* LAURA *are seated at a drop-leaf table. Eating is indicated by gestures without food or utensils.* AMANDA *faces the audience.* TOM *and* LAURA *are seated in profile.*

   The interior has lit up softly and through the scrim we see AMANDA *and* LAURA *seated at the table in the upstage area.*

AMANDA *(calling)*: Tom?

TOM: Yes, Mother.

AMANDA: We can't say grace until you come to the table!

TOM: Coming, Mother. *(He bows slightly and withdraws, reappearing a few moments later in his place at the table.)*

AMANDA *(to her son)*: Honey, don't *push* with your *fingers*. If you have to push with something, the thing to push with is a crust of bread. And chew — chew! Animals have sections in their stomachs which enable them to digest food without mastication, but human beings are supposed to chew their food before they swallow it down. Eat food leisurely, son, and really enjoy it. A well-cooked meal has lots of delicate flavors that have to be held in the mouth for appreciation. So chew your food and give your salivary glands a chance to function!

TOM *deliberately lays his imaginary fork down and pushes his chair back from the table.*

Où Sont les Neiges [d'antan]: "Where are the snows of yesteryear?" Williams intended this quotation from the French poet François Villon to be projected on a screen at the back of the stage. The line focuses attention on aspects of life that have been lost in the past.

TOM: I haven't enjoyed one bite of this dinner because of your constant directions on how to eat it. It's you that makes me rush through meals with your hawk-like attention to every bite I take. Sickening — spoils my appetite — all this discussion of animals' secretion — salivary glands — mastication!

AMANDA *(lightly)*: Temperament like a Metropolitan star! *(He rises and crosses downstage.)* You're not excused from the table.

TOM: I am getting a cigarette.

AMANDA: You smoke too much.

> LAURA *rises.*

LAURA: I'll bring in the blanc mange.

> *He remains standing with his cigarette by the portieres during the following.*

AMANDA *(rising)*: No, sister, no, sister — you be the lady this time and I'll be the darky.

LAURA: I'm already up.

AMANDA: Resume your seat, little sister — I want you to stay fresh and pretty — for gentlemen callers!

LAURA: I'm not expecting any gentlemen callers.

AMANDA *(Crossing out to kitchenette. Airily.)*: Sometimes they come when they are least expected! Why, I remember one Sunday afternoon in Blue Mountain — *(Enters kitchenette.)*

TOM: I know what's coming!

LAURA: Yes. But let her tell it.

TOM: Again?

LAURA: She loves to tell it.

> AMANDA *returns with bowl of dessert.*

AMANDA: One Sunday afternoon in Blue Mountain — your mother received — *seventeen* — gentlemen callers! Why, sometimes there weren't chairs enough to accommodate them all. We had to send the nigger over to bring in folding chairs from the parish house.

TOM *(remaining at portieres)*: How did you entertain those gentlemen callers?

AMANDA: I understood the art of conversation!

TOM: I bet you could talk.

AMANDA: Girls in those days *knew* how to talk, I can tell you.

TOM: Yes?

(Image: Amanda as a Girl on a Porch Greeting Callers.)

AMANDA: They knew how to entertain their gentlemen callers. It wasn't enough for a girl to be possessed of a pretty face and a graceful figure — although I wasn't slighted in either respect. She also needed to have a nimble wit and a tongue to meet all occasions.

TOM: What did you talk about?

AMANDA: Things of importance going on in the world! Never anything coarse or common or vulgar. *(She addresses Tom as though he were seated in the vacant chair at the table though he remains by portieres. He plays this scene as though he held the book.)* My callers were gentlemen—all! Among my callers were some of the most prominent young planters of the Mississippi Delta—planters and sons of planters!

TOM *motions for music and a spot of light on* AMANDA. *Her eyes lift, her face glows, her voice becomes rich and elegiac.*

(Screen Legend: "Où Sont les Neiges.")

There was a young Champ Laughlin who later became vice-president of the Delta Planters Bank. Hadley Stevenson who was drowned in Moon Lake and left his widow one hundred and fifty thousand in Government Bonds. There were the Cutrere brothers, Wesley and Bates. Bates was one of my bright particular beaux! He got in a quarrel with that wild Wainright boy. They shot it out on the floor of Moon Lake Casino. Bates was shot through the stomach. Died in the ambulance on his way to Memphis. His widow was also well-provided for, came into eight or ten thousand acres, that's all. She married him on the rebound—never loved her—carried my picture on him the night he died! And there was that boy that every girl in the Delta had set her cap for! That beautiful, brilliant young Fitzhugh boy from Green County!

TOM: What did he leave his widow?

AMANDA: He never married! Gracious, you talk as though all of my old admirers had turned up their toes to the daisies!

TOM: Isn't this the first you mentioned that still survives?

AMANDA: That Fitzhugh boy went North and made a fortune—came to be known as the Wolf of Wall Street! He had the Midas touch, whatever he touched turned to gold! And I could have been Mrs. Duncan J. Fitzhugh, mind you! But—I picked your *father!*

LAURA *(rising)*: Mother, let me clear the table.

AMANDA: No dear, you go in front and study your typewriter chart. Or practice your shorthand a little. Stay fresh and pretty—It's almost time for our gentlemen callers to start arriving. *(She flounces girlishly toward the kitchenette.)* How many do you suppose we're going to entertain this afternoon?

TOM *throws down the paper and jumps up with a groan.*

LAURA *(alone in the dining room)*: I don't believe we're going to receive any, Mother.

AMANDA *(reappearing, airily)*: What? No one—not one? You must be joking! *(*LAURA *nervously echoes her laugh. She slips in a fugitive manner through the half-open portieres and draws them gently behind her. A shaft of very clear light is thrown on her face against the faded tapestry of the curtains.)*

(Music: "The Glass Menagerie" under Faintly.) (Lightly.) Not one gentleman caller? It can't be true! There must be a flood, there must have been a tornado!

LAURA: It isn't a flood, it's not a tornado, Mother. I'm just not popular like you were in Blue Mountain. . . . *(*TOM *utters another groan.* LAURA *glances at him with a faint, apologetic smile. Her voice catching a little.)* Mother's afraid I'm going to be an old maid.

(The Scene Dims Out with "Glass Menagerie" Music.)

Scene II

"Laura, Haven't You Ever Liked Some Boy?"

On the dark stage the screen is lighted with the image of blue roses.
Gradually LAURA*'s figure becomes apparent and the screen goes out.*
The music subsides.
LAURA is seated in the delicate ivory chair at the small clawfoot table.
She wears a dress of soft violet material for a kimono — her hair tied back from her forehead with a ribbon.
She is washing and polishing her collection of glass.
AMANDA appears on the fire-escape steps. At the sound of her ascent, LAURA *catches her breath, thrusts the bowl of ornaments away and seats herself stiffly before the diagram of the typewriter keyboard as though it held her spellbound. Something has happened to* AMANDA. *It is written in her face as she climbs to the landing: a look that is grim and hopeless and a little absurd.*
She has on one of those cheap or imitation velvety-looking cloth coats with imitation fur collar. Her hat is five or six years old, one of those dreadful cloche hats that were worn in the late twenties, and she is clasping an enormous black patent-leather pocketbook with nickel clasp and initials. This is her fulldress outfit, the one she usually wears to the D.A.R.
Before entering she looks through the door.
She purses her lips, opens her eyes wide, rolls them upward and shakes her head.
Then she slowly lets herself in the door. Seeing her mother's expression LAURA *touches her lips with a nervous gesture.*

LAURA: Hello, Mother, I was — *(She makes a nervous gesture toward the chart on the wall.* AMANDA *leans against the shut door and stares at* LAURA *with a martyred look.)*

AMANDA: Deception? Deception? *(She slowly removes her hat and gloves, continuing the swift suffering stare. She lets the hat and gloves fall on the floor — a bit of acting.)*

LAURA *(shakily)*: How was the D.A.R. meeting? *(*AMANDA *slowly opens her purse and removes a dainty white handkerchief which she shakes out delicately and delicately touches to her lips and nostrils.)* Didn't you go to the D.A.R. meeting, Mother?

AMANDA *(faintly, almost inaudibly)*: —No.—No. *(then more forcibly)* I did not have the strength—to go the D.A.R. In fact, I did not have the courage! I wanted to find a hole in the ground and hide myself in it forever! *(She crosses slowly to the wall and removes the diagram of the typewriter keyboard. She holds it in front of her for a second, staring at it sweetly and sorrowfully—then bites her lips and tears it in two pieces.)*

LAURA *(faintly)*: Why did you do that, Mother? *(AMANDA repeats the same procedure with the chart of the Gregg Alphabet.)* Why are you—

AMANDA: Why? Why? How old are you, Laura?

LAURA: Mother, you know my age.

AMANDA: I thought that you were an adult; it seems that I was mistaken. *(She crosses slowly to the sofa and sinks down and stares at LAURA.)*

LAURA: Please don't stare at me, Mother.

AMANDA *closes her eyes and lowers her head. Count ten.*

AMANDA: What are we going to do, what is going to become of us, what is the future?

Count ten.

LAURA: Has something happened, Mother? *(AMANDA draws a long breath and takes out the handkerchief again. Dabbing process.)* Mother, has—something happened?

AMANDA: I'll be all right in a minute. I'm just bewildered—*(count five)*—by life. . . .

LAURA: Mother, I wish that you would tell me what's happened.

AMANDA: As you know, I was supposed to be inducted into my office at the D.A.R. this afternoon. **(Image: A Swarm of Typewriters.)** But I stopped off at Rubicam's Business College to speak to your teachers about your having a cold and ask them what progress they thought you were making down there.

LAURA: Oh. . . .

AMANDA: I went to the typing instructor and introduced myself as your mother. She didn't know who you were. Wingfield, she said. We don't have any such student enrolled at the school! I assured her she did, that you had been going to classes since early in January. "I wonder," she said, "if you could be talking about that terribly shy little girl who dropped out of school after only a few days' attendance?" "No," I said, "Laura, my daughter, has been going to school every day for the past six weeks." "Excuse me," she said. She took the attendance book out and there was your name, unmistakably printed, and all the dates you were absent until they decided that you had dropped out of school. I still said, "No, there must have been some mistake! There must have been some mix-up in the records." And she said, "No—I remember her perfectly now. Her hand shook so that she couldn't hit the right keys! The first time we gave a speed-test, she broke down completely — was sick at the stomach and almost had to be carried into the wash-room! After that morning she never showed up any more. We phoned the house but never got any answer" — while I was working at Famous and Barr, I suppose, demonstrating those — Oh! I felt so weak I could barely keep on my feet. I had to sit down while they got me a glass of water! Fifty dollars' tuition, all of our plans — my hopes and ambitions for you — just gone up the spout, just gone up the spout like that. (LAURA *draws a long breath and gets awkwardly to her feet. She crosses to the victrola and winds it up.*) What are you doing?

LAURA: Oh! (*She releases the handle and returns to her seat.*)

AMANDA: Laura, where have you been going when you've gone out pretending that you were going to business college?

LAURA: I've just been going out walking.

AMANDA: That's not true.

LAURA: It is. I just went walking.

AMANDA: Walking? Walking? In winter? Deliberately courting pneumonia in that light coat? Where did you walk to, Laura?

LAURA: It was the lesser of two evils, Mother. **(Image: Winter Scene in Park.)** I couldn't go back up. I — threw up — on the floor!

AMANDA: From half past seven till after five every day you mean to tell me you walked around in the park, because you wanted to make me think that you were still going to Rubicam's Business College?

LAURA: It wasn't as bad as it sounds. I went inside places to get warmed up.

AMANDA: Inside where?

LAURA: I went in the art museum and the bird-houses at the Zoo. I visited the penguins every day! Sometimes I did without lunch and went to the movies. Lately I've been spending most of my afternoons in the Jewel-box, that big glass house where they raise the tropical flowers.

AMANDA: You did all this to deceive me, just for the deception? (LAURA *looks down.*) Why?

LAURA: Mother, when you're disappointed, you get that awful suffering look on your face, like the picture of Jesus' mother in the museum!

AMANDA: Hush!

LAURA: I couldn't face it.

Pause. A whisper of strings.

(Legend: "The Crust of Humility.")

AMANDA (*hopelessly fingering the huge pocketbook*): So what are we going to do the rest of our lives? Stay home and watch the parades go by? Amuse ourselves with the glass menagerie, darling? Eternally play those worn-out phonograph records your father left as a painful reminder of him? We won't have a business career — we've given that up because it gave us nervous indigestion! (*Laughs wearily.*) What is there left but dependency all our lives? I know so well what becomes of unmarried women who aren't prepared to occupy a position. I've seen such pitiful cases in the South — barely tolerated spinsters living upon the grudging patronage of sister's husband or brother's wife — stuck away in some little mouse-trap of a room — encouraged by one in-law to visit another — little birdlike women without any nest — eating the crust of humility all their life! Is that the future that we've mapped out for ourselves? I swear it's the only alternative I can think of! It isn't a very pleasant alternative, is it? Of course — some girls *do marry.* *(LAURA twists her hands nervously.)* Haven't you ever liked some boy?

LAURA: Yes I liked one once. *(rises)* I came across his picture a while ago.

AMANDA *(with some interest)*: He gave you his picture?

LAURA: No, it's in the year-book.

AMANDA *(disappointed)*: Oh — a high-school boy.

(Screen Image: Jim as a High-School Hero Bearing a Silver Cup.)

LAURA: Yes. His name was Jim. *(LAURA lifts the heavy annual from the clawfoot table.)* Here he is in *The Pirates of Penzance.*

AMANDA *(absently)*: The what?

LAURA: The operetta the senior class put on. He had a wonderful voice and we sat across the aisle from each other Mondays, Wednesdays and Fridays in the Aud. Here he is with the silver cup for debating! See his grin?

AMANDA *(absently)*: He must have had a jolly disposition.

LAURA: He used to call me — Blue Roses.

(Image: Blue Roses.)

AMANDA: Why did he call you such a name as that?

LAURA: When I had that attack of pleurosis — he asked me what was the matter when I came back. I said pleurosis — he thought that I said Blue Roses! So that's what he always called me after that. Whenever he saw me, he'd holler, "Hello, Blue Roses!" I didn't care for the girl that he went out with. Emily Meisenbach. Emily was the best-dressed girl at Soldan. She never struck me, though, as being sincere . . . It says in the Personal Section — they're engaged. That's — six years ago! They must be married by now.

AMANDA: Girls that aren't cut out for business careers usually wind up married to some nice man. *(Gets up with a spark of revival.)* Sister, that's what you'll do!

LAURA *utters a startled, doubtful laugh. She reaches quickly for a piece of glass.*

LAURA: But, Mother —

AMANDA: Yes? *(crossing to photograph)*

LAURA *(in a tone of frightened apology)*: I'm — crippled!

(Image: Screen.)

AMANDA: Nonsense! Laura, I've told you never, never to use that word. Why, you're not crippled, you just have a little defect — hardly noticeable, even! When people have some slight disadvantage like that, they cultivate other things to make up for it — develop charm — and vivacity — and — *charm!* That's all you have to do! *(She turns again to the photograph.)* One thing your father had *plenty of* — was *charm!*

TOM *motions to the fiddle in the wings.*

(The Scene Fades out with Music.)

Scene III

(Legend on the Screen: "After the Fiasco — ")

TOM *speaks from the fire-escape landing.*

TOM: After the fiasco at Rubicam's Business College, the idea of getting a gentleman caller for Laura began to play a more important part in Mother's calculations. It became an obsession. Like some archetype of the universal unconscious, the image of the gentleman caller haunted our small apartment. . . . **(Image: Young Man at Door with Flowers.)** An evening at home rarely passed without some allusion to this image, this spectre, this hope. . . . Even when he wasn't mentioned, his presence hung in Mother's preoccupied look and in my sister's frightened, apologetic manner — hung like a sentence passed upon the Wingfields! Mother was a woman of action as well as words. She began to take logical steps in the planned direction. Late that winter and in the early spring — realizing that extra money would be needed to properly feather the nest and plume the bird — she conducted a vigorous campaign on the telephone, roping in subscribers to one of those magazines for matrons called *The Home-maker's Companion,* the type of journal that features the serialized sublimations of ladies of letters who think in terms of delicate cup-like breasts, slim, tapering waists, rich, creamy thighs, eyes like wood-smoke in autumn, fingers that soothe and caress like strains of music, bodies as powerful as Etruscan sculpture.

(Screen Image: Glamour Magazine Cover.)

AMANDA *enters with phone on long extension cord. She is spotted in the dim stage.*

AMANDA: Ida Scott? This is Amanda Wingfield! We *missed* you at the D.A.R. last Monday! I said to myself: She's probably suffering with that sinus condition! How is that sinus condition? Horrors! Heaven have mercy! — You're a Christian martyr, yes, that's what you are, a Christian martyr! Well, I just now happened to notice that your subscription to the *Companion*'s about to expire! Yes, it expires with the next issue, honey!—just when that wonderful new serial by Bessie Mae Hopper is getting off to such an exciting start. Oh, honey, it's something that you can't miss! You remember how *Gone With the Wind* took everybody by storm? You simply couldn't go out if you hadn't read it. All everybody *talked* was Scarlett O'Hara. Well, this is a book that critics already compare to *Gone With the Wind*. It's the *Gone With the Wind* of the post-World War generation!—What?—Burning?—Oh, honey, don't let them burn, go take a look in the oven and I'll hold the wire! Heavens—I think she's hung up!

(Dim Out)

(Legend on Screen: "You Think I'm in Love with Continental Shoemakers?")

Before the stage is lighted, the violent voices of TOM *and* AMANDA *are heard. They are quarreling behind the portieres. In front of them stands* LAURA *with clenched hands and panicky expression.*
A clear pool of light on her figure throughout this scene.

TOM: What in Christ's name am I—

AMANDA *(shrilly)*: Don't you use that—

TOM: Supposed to do!

AMANDA: Expression! Not in my—

TOM: Ohhh!

AMANDA: Presence! Have you gone out of your senses?

TOM: I have, that's true, *driven* out!

AMANDA: What is the matter with you, you—big—big—IDIOT!

TOM: Look—I've got *no thing*, no single thing—

AMANDA: Lower your voice!

TOM: In my life here that I can call my OWN! Everything is—

AMANDA: Stop that shouting!

TOM: Yesterday you confiscated my books! You had the nerve to—

AMANDA: I took that horrible novel back to the libarary—yes! That hideous book by that insane Mr. Lawrence. *(*TOM *laughs wildly.)* I cannot control the output of diseased minds or people who cater to them— *(*TOM *laughs still more wildly.)* BUT I WON'T ALLOW SUCH FILTH BROUGHT INTO MY HOUSE! No, no, no, no, no!

TOM: House, house! Who pays rent on it, who makes a slave of himself to—

AMANDA *(fairly screeching)*: Don't you DARE to—

TOM: No, No, I musn't say things! *I've* got to just—

AMANDA: Let me tell you—

TOM: I don't want to hear any more! *(He tears the portieres open. The upstage area is lit with a turgid smoky red glow.)*

AMANDA*'s hair is in metal curlers and she wears a very old bathrobe, much too large for her slight figure, a relic of the faithless Mr. Wingfield.*

An upright typewriter and a wild disarray of manuscripts are on the drop-leaf table. The quarrel was probably precipitated by AMANDA*'s interruption of his creative labor. A chair is lying overthrown on the floor. Their gesticulating shadows are cast on the ceiling by the fiery glow.*

AMANDA: You *will* hear more, you—

TOM: No, I won't hear more, I'm going out!

AMANDA: You come right back in—

TOM: Out, out out! Because I'm—

AMANDA: Come back here, Tom Wingfield! I'm not through talking to you!

TOM: Oh, go—

LAURA *(desperately)*: Tom!

AMANDA: You're going to listen, and no more insolence from you! I'm at the end of my patience! *(He comes back toward her.)*

TOM: What do you think I'm at? Aren't I supposed to have any patience to reach the end of, Mother? I know, I know. It seems unimportant to you, what I'm *doing*—what I *want* to do—having a little *difference* between them! You don't think that—

AMANDA: I think you've been doing things that you're ashamed of. That's why you act like this. I don't believe you go every night to the movies. Nobody goes to the movies night after night. Nobody in their right minds goes to the movies as often as you pretend to. People don't go to the movies at nearly midnight, and movies don't let out at two A.M. Come in stumbling. Muttering to yourself like a maniac! You get three hours sleep and then go to work. Oh, I can picture the way you're doing down there. Moping, doping, because you're in no condition.

TOM *(wildly)*: No, I'm in no condition!

AMANDA: What right have you got to jeopardize your job? Jeopardize the security of us all? How do you think we'd manage if you were—

TOM: Listen! You think I'm crazy *about* the *warehouse*? *(He bends fiercely toward her slight figure.)* You think I'm in love with the Continental Shoemakers? You think I want to spend fifty-five *years* down there in that—*celotex interior!* with—*fluorescent—tubes!* Look! I'd rather somebody picked up a crowbar and battered out my brains—than go back mornings! I *go!* Every time you come in yelling that God damn *"Rise and Shine!" "Rise and Shine!"* I say to myself, "How *lucky dead* people are!" But I get up. I *go!* For sixty-five dollars a month I give up all that I dream of doing and being *ever!* And you say self—*self's* all I ever think of. Why, listen, if self is what I thought of, Mother, I'd be where he is— GONE! *(pointing to father's picture)* As far as the system of transportation reaches! *(He starts past her. She grabs his arm.)* Don't grab at me, Mother!

AMANDA: Where are you going?

TOM: I'm going to the *movies!*

AMANDA: I don't believe that lie!

TOM (*Crouching toward her, overtowering her tiny figure. She backs away, gasping*): I'm going to opium dens! Yes, opium dens, dens of vice and criminals' hang-outs, Mother. I've joined the Hogan gang, I'm a hired assassin, I carry a tommy-gun in a violin case! I run a string of cat-houses in the Valley! They call me Killer, Killer Wingfield, I'm leading a double-life, a simple, honest warehouse worker by day, by night a dynamic *czar* of the *underworld, Mother.* I go to gambling casinos, I spin away fortunes on the roulette table! I wear a patch over one eye and a false mustache, sometimes I put on green whiskers. On those occasions they call me—*El Diablo!* Oh, I could tell you things to make you sleepless! My enemies plan to dynamite this place. They're going to blow us all sky-high some night! I'll be glad, very happy, and so will you! You'll go, up on a broomstick, over Blue Mountain with seventeen gentlemen callers! You ugly—babbling old—*witch.* . . . (*He goes through a series of violent, clumsy movements, seizing his overcoat, lunging to the door, pulling it fiercely open. The women watch him, aghast. His arm catches in the sleeve of the coat as he struggles to pull it on. For a moment he is pinioned by the bulky garment. With an outraged groan he tears the coat off again, splitting the shoulders of it, and hurls it across the room. It strikes against the shelf of Laura's glass collection, there is a tinkle of shattering glass. Laura cries out as if wounded.*)

(Music Legend: "The Glass Menagerie.")

LAURA (*shrilly*): *My glass!*—menagerie. . . . (*She covers her face and turns away.*)

But AMANDA *is still stunned and stupefied by the "ugly witch" so that she barely notices this occurrence. Now she recovers her speech.*

AMANDA (*in an awful voice*): I won't speak to you—until you apologize! (*She crosses through portieres and draws them together behind her.* TOM *is left with* LAURA. LAURA *clings weakly to the mantel with her face averted.* TOM *stares at her stupidly for a moment. Then he crosses to shelf. Drops awkwardly to his knees to collect the fallen glass, glancing at* LAURA *as if he would speak but couldn't.*)

"The Glass Menagerie" steals in as

(The Scene Dims Out.)

Scene IV

The interior is dark. Faint in the alley.

A deep-voiced bell in a church is tolling the hour of five as the scene commences.

TOM *appears at the top of the alley. After each solemn boom of the bell in the tower, he shakes a little noise-maker or rattle as if to express the tiny spasm of man in contrast to the sustained power and dignity of the Almighty. This and the unsteadiness of his advance make it evident that he has been drinking.*

As he climbs the few steps to the fire-escape landing light steals up inside. LAURA *appears in night-dress, observing* TOM's *empty bed in the front room.*

TOM fishes in his pockets for the door-key, removing a motley assortment of articles in the search, including a perfect shower of movie-ticket stubs and an empty bottle. At last he finds the key, but just as he is about to insert it, it slips from his fingers. He strikes a match and crouches below the door.

TOM *(bitterly)*: One crack — and it falls through!

>   LAURA *opens the door.*

LAURA: Tom! Tom, what are you doing?

TOM: Looking for a door-key.

LAURA: Where have you been all this time?

TOM: I have been to the movies.

LAURA: All this time at the movies?

TOM: There was a very long program. There was a Garbo picture and a Mickey Mouse and a travelogue and a newsreel and a preview of coming attractions. And there was an organ solo and a collection for the milk-fund — simultaneously — which ended up in a terrible fight between a fat lady and an usher!

LAURA *(innocently)*: Did you have to stay through everything?

TOM: Of course! And, oh, I forgot! There was a big stage show! The headliner on this stage show was Malvolio the Magician. He performed wonderful tricks, many of them, such as pouring water back and forth between pitchers. First it turned to wine and then it turned to beer and then it turned to whiskey. I know it was whiskey it finally turned into because he needed somebody to come up out of the audience to help him, and I came up — both shows! It was Kentucky Straight Bourbon. A very generous fellow, he gave souvenirs. *(He pulls from his back pocket a shimmering rainbow-colored scarf.)* He gave me this. This is his magic scarf. You can have it, Laura. You wave it over a canary cage and you get a bowl of gold-fish. You wave it over the gold-fish bowl and they fly away canaries. . . . But the wonderfullest trick of all was the coffin trick. We nailed him into a coffin and he got out of the coffin without removing one nail. *(He has come inside.)* There is a trick that would come in handy for me — get me out of this 2 by 4 situation! *(flops onto bed and starts removing shoes)*

LAURA: Tom — Shhh!

TOM: What you shushing me for?

LAURA: You'll wake up Mother.

TOM: Goody, goody! Pay 'er back for all those "Rise an' Shines." *(lies down, groaning)* You know it don't take much intelligence to get yourself into a nailed-up coffin, Laura. But who in hell ever got himself out of one without removing one nail?

As if in answer, the father's grinning photograph lights up.

(Scene Dims Out.)

Immediately following: The church bell is heard striking six. At the sixth stroke the alarm clock goes off in AMANDA'*s room, and after a few moments we hear her calling: "Rise and Shine! Rise and Shine! Laura, go tell your brother to rise and shine!"*

TOM *(sitting up slowly)*: I'll rise — but I won't shine.

The light increases.

AMANDA: Laura, tell your brother his coffee is ready.

LAURA *slips into front room.*

LAURA: Tom! it's nearly seven. Don't make Mother nervous. *(He stares at her stupidly. Beseechingly.)* Tom, speak to Mother this morning. Make up with her, apologize, speak to her!

TOM: She won't to me. It's her that started not speaking.

LAURA: If you just say you're sorry she'll start speaking.

TOM: Her not speaking — is that such a tragedy?

LAURA: Please — please!

AMANDA *(calling from kitchenette)*: Laura, are you going to do what I asked you to do, or do I have to get dressed and go out myself?

LAURA: Going, going — soon as I get on my coat! *(She pulls on a shapeless felt hat with nervous, jerky movement, pleadingly glancing at* TOM. *Rushes awkwardly for coat. The coat is one of* AMANDA'*s inaccurately made-over, the sleeves too short for* LAURA.) Butter and what else?

AMANDA *(entering upstage)*: Just butter. Tell them to charge it.

LAURA: Mother, they make such faces when I do that.

AMANDA: Sticks and stones may break my bones, but the expression on Mr. Garfinkel's face won't harm us! Tell your brother his coffee is getting cold.

LAURA *(at door)*: Do what I asked you, will you, will you, Tom?

He looks sullenly away.

AMANDA: Laura, go now or just don't go at all!

LAURA *(rushing out)*: Going — going! *(A second later she cries out.* TOM *springs up and crosses to the door.* AMANDA *rushes anxiously in.* TOM *opens the door.)*

TOM: Laura?

LAURA: I'm all right. I slipped, but I'm all right.

AMANDA *(peering anxiously after her)*: If anyone breaks a leg on those fire-escape steps, the landlord ought to be sued for every cent he possesses! *(She shuts door. Remembers she isn't speaking and returns to other room.)*

As TOM *enters listlessly for his coffee, she turns her back to him and stands rigidly facing the window on the gloomy gray vault of the areaway. Its light on her face with its aged but childish features is cruelly sharp, satirical as a Daumier° print.*

(Music under: "Ave Maria.")

TOM *glances sheepishly but sullenly at her averted figure and slumps at the table. The coffee is scalding hot; he sips it and gasps and spits it back in the cup. At his gasp,* AMANDA *catches her breath and half turns. Then catches herself and turns back to window.*

   TOM *blows on his coffee, glancing sidewise at his mother. She clears her throat.* TOM *clears his. He starts to rise. Sinks back down again, scratches his head, clears his throat again.* AMANDA *coughs.* TOM *raises his cup in both hands to blow on it, his eyes staring over the rim of it at his mother for several moments. Then he slowly sets the cup down and awkwardly and hesitantly rises from the chair.*

TOM (*hoarsely*): Mother. I—I apologize. Mother. (AMANDA *draws a quick, shuddering breath. Her face works grotesquely. She breaks into childlike tears.*) I'm sorry for what I said, for everything that I said, I didn't mean it.

AMANDA (*sobbingly*): My devotion has made me a witch and so I make myself hateful to my children!

TOM: No, you *don't.*

AMANDA: I worry so much, don't sleep, it makes me nervous!

TOM (*gently*): I understand that.

AMANDA: I've had to put up a solitary battle all these years. But you're my right-hand bower! Don't fall down, don't fail!

TOM (*gently*): I try, Mother.

AMANDA (*with great enthusiasm*): Try and you will SUCCEED! (*The notion makes her breathless.*) Why, you—you're just *full* of natural endowments! Both of my children—they're *unusual* children! Don't you think I know it? I'm so—*proud!* Happy and—feel I've—so much to be thankful for but—Promise me one thing, son!

TOM: What, Mother?

AMANDA: Promise, son, you'll—never be a drunkard!

TOM (*turns to her grinning*): I will never be a drunkard, Mother.

AMANDA: That's what frightened me so, that you'd be drinking! Eat a bowl of Purina!

TOM: Just coffee, Mother.

AMANDA: Shredded wheat biscuit?

TOM: No. No, Mother, just coffee.

AMANDA: You can't put in a day's work on an empty stomach. You've got ten minutes—don't gulp! Drinking too-hot liquids makes cancer of the stomach. . . . Put cream in.

SCENE IV. *Daumier*: (1808–1879) French caricaturist, painter, and sculptor. He was known for his merciless irony in the realistic lithographs he created to ridicule bourgeois society.

TOM: No, thank you.

AMANDA: To cool it.

TOM: No! No, thank you, I want it black.

AMANDA: I know, but it's not good for you. We have to do all that we can to build ourselves up. In these trying times we live in, all that we have to cling to is — each other. . . . That's why it's so important to — Tom, I — I sent out your sister so I could discuss something with you. If you hadn't spoken I would have spoken to you. *(Sits down.)*

TOM *(gently)*: What is it, Mother, that you want to discuss?

AMANDA: Laura!

TOM *puts his cup down slowly.*

(Legend on Screen: "Laura.")

(Music: "The Glass Menagerie.")

TOM: — Oh. — Laura . . .

AMANDA *(touching his sleeve)*: You know how Laura is. So quiet but — still water runs deep! She notices things and I think she — broods about them. *(TOM looks up.)* A few days ago I came in and she was crying.

TOM: What about?

AMANDA: You.

TOM: Me?

AMANDA: She has an idea that you're not happy here.

TOM: What gave her that idea?

AMANDA: What gives her any idea? However, you do act strangely. I — I'm not criticizing, understand *that!* I know your ambitions do not lie in the warehouse, that like everybody in the whole wide world — you've had to — make sacrifices, but — Tom — Tom — life's not easy, it calls for — Spartan endurance! There's so many things in my heart that I cannot describe to you! I've never told you but I — *loved* your father. . . .

TOM *(gently)*: I know that, Mother.

AMANDA: And you — when I see you taking after his ways! Staying out late — and — well, you *had* been drinking the night you were in that — terrifying condition! Laura says that you hate the apartment and that you go out nights to get away from it! Is that true, Tom?

TOM: No. You say there's so much in your heart that you can't describe to me. That's true of me, too. There's so much in my heart that I can't describe to *you!* So let's respect each other's —

AMANDA: But, why — *why,* Tom — are you always so *restless?* Where do you go to, nights?

TOM: I — go to the movies.

AMANDA: Why do you go to the movies so much, Tom?

TOM: I go to the movies because — I like adventure. Adventure is something I don't have much of at work, so I go to the movies.

AMANDA: But, Tom, you go to the movies *entirely* too *much!*

TOM: I like a lot of adventure.

> AMANDA *looks baffled, then hurt. As the familiar inquisition resumes he becomes hard and impatient again.* AMANDA *slips back into her querulous attitude toward him.*

(Image on Screen: Sailing Vessel with Jolly Roger.)

AMANDA: Most young men find adventure in their careers.

TOM: Then most young men are not employed in a warehouse.

AMANDA: The world is full of young men employed in warehouses and offices and factories.

TOM: Do all of them find adventure in their careers?

AMANDA: They do or they do without it! Not everybody has a craze for adventure.

TOM: Man is by instinct a lover, a hunter, a fighter, and none of those instincts are given much play at the warehouse!

AMANDA: Man is by instinct! Don't quote instinct to me! Instinct is something that people have got away from! It belongs to animals! Christian adults don't want it!

TOM: What do Christian adults want, then, Mother?

AMANDA: Superior things! Things of the mind and the spirit! Only animals have to satisfy instincts! Surely your aims are somewhat higher than theirs! Than monkeys — pigs —

TOM: I reckon they're not.

AMANDA: You're joking. However, that isn't what I wanted to discuss.

TOM *(rising)*: I haven't much time.

AMANDA *(pushing his shoulders)*: Sit down.

TOM: You want me to punch in red at the warehouse, Mother?

AMANDA: You have five minutes. I want to talk about Laura.

(Legend: "Plans and Provisions.")

TOM: All right! What about Laura?

AMANDA: We have to be making plans and provisions for her. She's older than you, two years, and nothing has happened. She just drifts along doing nothing. It frightens me terribly how she just drifts along.

TOM: I guess she's the type that people call home girls.

AMANDA: There's no such type, and if there is, it's a pity! That is unless the home is hers, with a husband!

TOM: What?

AMANDA: Oh, I can see the handwriting on the wall as plain as I see the nose in front of my face! It's terrifying! More and more you remind me of your father! He was out all hours without explanation — Then *left! Goodbye!* And me with the bag to hold. I saw that letter you got from the Merchant Marine. I know what you're dreaming of. I'm not standing here blindfolded. Very well, then. Then *do* it! But not till there's somebody to take your place.

TOM: What do you mean?

AMANDA: I mean that as soon as Laura has got somebody to take care of her, married, a home of her own, independent — why, then you'll be free to go wherever you please, on land, on sea, whichever way the wind blows! But until that time you've got to look out for your sister. I don't say me because I'm old and don't matter! I say for your sister because she's young and dependent. I put her in business college — a dismal failure! Frightened her so it made her sick to her stomach. I took her over to the Young People's League at the church. Another fiasco. She spoke to nobody, nobody spoke to her. Now all she does is fool with those pieces of glass and play those worn-out records. What kind of a life is that for a girl to lead!

TOM: What can I do about it?

AMANDA: Overcome selfishness! Self, self, self is all that you ever think of! *(TOM springs up and crosses to get his coat. It is ugly and bulky. He pulls on a cap with earmuffs.)* Where is your muffler? Put your wool muffler on! *(He snatches it angrily from the closet and tosses it around his neck and pulls both ends tight.)* Tom! I haven't said what I had in mind to ask you.

TOM: I'm too late to —

AMANDA *(Catching his arms — very importunately. Then shyly)*: Down at the warehouse, aren't there some — nice young men?

TOM: No!

AMANDA: There *must* be — *some* . . .

TOM: Mother —

Gesture.

AMANDA: Find out one that's clean-living — doesn't drink and — ask him out for sister!

TOM: What?

AMANDA: For *sister!* To *meet!* Get *acquainted!*

TOM *(stamping to door)*: Oh, my go-osh!

AMANDA: Will you? *(He opens door. Imploringly.)* Will you? *(He starts down.)* Will you? *Will* you, dear?

TOM *(calling back)*: YES!

AMANDA *closes the door hesitantly and with a troubled but faintly hopeful expression.*

(Screen Image: Glamour Magazine Cover.)

Spot AMANDA *at phone.*

AMANDA: Ella Cartwright? This is Amanda Wingfield! How are you, honey? How is that kidney condition? *(count five)* Horrors! *(count five)* You're a Christian martyr, yes, honey, that's what you are, a Christian martyr! Well, I just happened to notice in my little red book that your subscription to the *Companion* has just run out! I knew that you wouldn't want to miss out on the wonderful serial starting in this new issue. It's by Bessie Mae Hopper, the first thing she's written since *Honeymoon for Three*. Wasn't that a strange and interesting story? Well, this one is even lovelier, I believe. It has a sophisticated society background. It's all about the horsey set on Long Island!

(Fade Out.)

Scene V

(Legend on Screen: "Annunciation.") *Fade with music.*

It is early dusk of a spring evening. Supper has just been finished in the Wingfield apartment. AMANDA *and* LAURA *in light colored dresses are removing dishes from the table, in the upstage area, which is shadowy, their movements formalized almost as a dance or ritual, their moving forms as pale and silent as moths.*

*   * TOM, *in white shirt and trousers, rises from the table and crosses toward the fire-escape.*

AMANDA *(as he passes her)*: Son, will you do me a favor?

TOM: What?

AMANDA: Comb your hair! You look so pretty when your hair is combed! *(*TOM *slouches on sofa with evening paper. Enormous caption "Franco Triumphs.")* There is only one respect in which I would like you to emulate your father.

TOM: What respect is that?

AMANDA: The care he always took of his appearance. He never allowed himself to look untidy. *(He throws down the paper and crosses to fire-escape.)* Where are you going?

TOM: I'm going out to smoke.

AMANDA: You smoke too much. A pack a day at fifteen cents a pack. How much would that amount to in a month? Thirty times fifteen is how much, Tom? Figure it out and you will be astounded at what you could save. Enough to give you a night-school course in accounting at Washington U! Just think what a wonderful thing that would be for you, son!

*   * TOM *is unmoved by the thought.*

TOM: I'd rather smoke. *(He steps out on landing, letting the screen door slam.)*

AMANDA *(sharply)*: I know! That's the tragedy of it. . . . *(Alone, she turns to look at her husband's picture.)*

(Dance Music: "All the World Is Waiting for the Sunrise.")

TOM *(to the audience)*: Across the alley from us was the Paradise Dance Hall. On evenings in spring the windows and doors were open and the music came outdoors. Sometimes the lights were turned out except for a large glass sphere that hung from the ceiling. It would turn slowly about and filter the dusk with delicate rainbow colors. Then the orchestra played a waltz or a tango, something that had a slow and sensuous rhythm. Couples would come outside, to the relative privacy of the alley. You could see them kissing behind ash-pits and telephone poles. This was the compensation for lives that passed like mine, without any change or adventure. Adventure and change were imminent in this year. They were waiting around the corner for all these kids. Suspended in the mist over Berchtesgaden,° caught in the folds of Chamberlain's° umbrella — In Spain there was Guernica! But here there was only hot swing music and liquor, dance halls, bars, and movies, and sex that hung in the gloom like a chandelier and flooded the world with brief, deceptive rainbows. . . . All the world was waiting for bombardments!

AMANDA *turns from the picture and comes outside.*

AMANDA *(sighing):* A fire-escape landing's a poor excuse for a porch. *(She spreads a newspaper on a step and sits down, gracefully and demurely as if she were settling into a swing on a Mississippi veranda.)* What are you looking at?

TOM: The moon.

AMANDA: Is there a moon this evening?

TOM: It's rising over Garfinkel's Delicatessen.

AMANDA: So it is! A little silver slipper of a moon. Have you made a wish on it yet?

TOM: Um-hum.

AMANDA: What did you wish for?

TOM: That's a secret.

AMANDA: A secret, huh? Well, I won't tell mine either. I will be just as mysterious as you.

TOM: I bet I can guess what yours is.

AMANDA: Is my head so transparent?

TOM: You're not a sphinx.

AMANDA: No, I don't have secrets. I'll tell you what I wished for on the moon. Success and happiness for my precious children! I wish for that whenever there's a moon, and when there isn't a moon, I wish for it, too.

TOM: I thought perhaps you wished for a gentleman caller.

AMANDA: Why do you say that?

TOM: Don't you remember asking me to fetch one?

AMANDA: I remember suggesting that it would be nice for your sister if you brought home some nice young man from the warehouse. I think I've made that suggestion more than once.

SCENE V. *Berchtesgaden:* A resort town in Bavaria, Germany, where Hitler built a fortress-like encampment. The leaders of the Third Reich met there with Hitler to plan sessions. *Chamberlain:* (1869–1940) British prime minister who believed that Hitler could be dealt with rationally and so followed a policy of appeasement. Many believed that this policy led to the outbreak of World War II.

TOM: Yes, you have made it repeatedly.

AMANDA: Well?

TOM: We are going to have one.

AMANDA: What?

TOM: A gentleman caller!

(The Annunciation Is Celebrated with Music.)

AMANDA *rises.*

(Image on Screen: Caller with Bouquet.)

AMANDA: You mean you have asked some nice young man to come over?

TOM: Yep. I've asked him to dinner.

AMANDA: You really did?

TOM: I did!

AMANDA: You did, and did he—*accept?*

TOM: He did!

AMANDA: Well, well—well, well! That's—lovely!

TOM: I thought that you would be pleased.

AMANDA: It's definite, then?

TOM: Very definite.

AMANDA: Soon?

TOM: Very soon.

AMANDA: For heaven's sake, stop putting on and tell me some things, will you?

TOM: What things do you want me to tell you?

AMANDA: Naturally I would like to know when he's *coming!*

TOM: He's coming tomorrow.

AMANDA: *Tomorrow?*

TOM: Yep. Tomorrow.

AMANDA: But, Tom!

TOM: Yes, Mother?

AMANDA: Tomorrow gives me no time!

TOM: Time for what?

AMANDA: Preparations! Why didn't you phone me at once, as soon as you asked him, the minute that he accepted? Then, don't you see, I could have been getting ready!

TOM: You don't have to make any fuss.

AMANDA: Oh, Tom, Tom, Tom, of course I have to make a fuss! I want things nice, not sloppy! Not thrown together. I'll certainly have to do some fast thinking, won't I?

TOM: I don't see why you have to think at all.

AMANDA: You just don't know. We can't have a gentleman caller in a pig-sty! All my wedding silver has to be polished, the monogrammed table linen ought to be laundered! The windows have to be washed and fresh curtains put up. And how about clothes? We have to *wear* something, don't we?

TOM: Mother, this boy is no one to make a fuss over!

AMANDA: Do you realize he's the first young man we've introduced to your sister? It's terrible, dreadful, disgraceful that poor little sister has never received a single gentleman caller! Tom, come inside! *(She opens the screen door.)*

TOM: What for?

AMANDA: I want to ask you some things.

TOM: If you're going to make such a fuss, I'll call it off, I'll tell him not to come.

AMANDA: You certainly won't do anything of the kind. Nothing offends people worse than broken engagements. It simply means I'll have to work like a Turk! We won't be brilliant, but we'll pass inspection. Come on inside. *(TOM follows, groaning.)* Sit down.

TOM: Any particular place you would like me to sit?

AMANDA: Thank heavens I've got that new sofa! I'm also making payments on a floor lamp I'll have sent out! And put the chintz covers on, they'll brighten things up! Of course I'd hoped to have these walls repapered. . . . What is the young man's name?

TOM: His name is O'Connor.

AMANDA: That, of course, means fish — tomorrow is Friday! I'll have that salmon loaf — with Durkee's dressing! What does he do? He works at the warehouse?

TOM: Of course! How else would I —

AMANDA: Tom, he — doesn't drink?

TOM: Why do you ask me that?

AMANDA: Your father *did!*

TOM: Don't get started on that!

AMANDA: He *does* drink, then?

TOM: Not that I know of!

AMANDA: Make sure, be certain! The last thing I want for my daughter's a boy who drinks!

TOM: Aren't you being a little premature? Mr. O'Connor has not yet appeared on the scene!

AMANDA: But will tomorrow. To meet your sister, and what do I know about his character? Nothing! Old maids are better off than wives of drunkards!

TOM: Oh, my God!

AMANDA: Be still!

TOM *(leaning forward to whisper)*: Lots of fellows meet girls whom they don't marry!

AMANDA: Oh, talk sensibly, Tom — and don't be sarcastic! *(She has gotten a hairbrush.)*

TOM: What are you doing?

AMANDA: I'm brushing that cow-lick down! What is this young man's position at the warehouse?

TOM (*submitting grimly to the brush and the interrogation*): This young man's position is that of a shipping clerk, Mother.

AMANDA: Sounds to me like a fairly responsible job, the sort of a job *you* would be in if you just had more *get-up*. What is his salary? Have you got any idea?

TOM: I would judge it to be approximately eighty-five dollars a month.

AMANDA: Well—not princely, but—

TOM: Twenty more than I make.

AMANDA: Yes, how well I know! But for a family man, eighty-five dollars a month is not much more than you can just get by on. . . .

TOM: Yes, but Mr. O'Connor is not a family man.

AMANDA: He might be, mightn't he? Some time in the future?

TOM: I see. Plans and provisions.

AMANDA: You are the only young man that I know of who ignores the fact that the future becomes the present, the present the past, and the past turns into everlasting regret if you don't plan for it!

TOM: I will think that over and see what I can make of it.

AMANDA: Don't be supercilious with your mother! Tell me some more about this—what do you call him?

TOM: James D. O'Connor. The D. is for Delaney.

AMANDA: Irish on *both* sides! *Gracious!* And doesn't drink?

TOM: Shall I call him up and ask him right this minute?

AMANDA: The only way to find out about those things is to make discreet inquiries at the proper moment. When I was a girl in Blue Mountain and it was suspected that a young man drank, the girl whose attentions he had been receiving, if any girl *was,* would sometimes speak to the minister of his church, or rather her father would if her father was living, and sort of feel him out on the young man's character. That is the way such things are discreetly handled to keep a young woman from making a tragic mistake!

TOM: Then how did you happen to make a tragic mistake?

AMANDA: That innocent look of your father's had everyone fooled! He *smiled*—the world was *enchanted!* No girl can do worse than put herself at the mercy of a handsome appearance! I hope that Mr. O'Connor is not too good-looking.

TOM: No, he's not too good-looking. He's covered with freckles and hasn't too much of a nose.

AMANDA: He's not right-down homely, though?

TOM: Not right-down homely. Just medium homely, I'd say.

AMANDA: Character's what to look for in a man.

TOM: That's what I've always said, Mother.

AMANDA: You've never said anything of the kind and I suspect you would never give it a thought.

TOM: Don't be suspicious of me.

AMANDA: At least I hope he's the type that's up and coming.

TOM: I think he really goes in for self-improvement.

AMANDA: What reason have you to think so?

TOM: He goes to night school.

AMANDA (*beaming*): Splendid! What does he do, I mean study?

TOM: Radio engineering and public speaking!

AMANDA: Then he has visions of being advanced in the world! Any young man who studies public speaking is aiming to have an executive job some day! And radio engineering? A thing for the future! Both of these facts are very illuminating. Those are the sort of things that a mother should know concerning any young man who comes to call on her daughter. Seriously or — not.

TOM: One little warning. He doesn't know about Laura. I didn't let on that we had dark ulterior motives. I just said, why don't you come have dinner with us? He said okay and that was the whole conversation.

AMANDA: I bet it was! You're eloquent as an oyster. However, he'll know about Laura when he gets here. When he sees how lovely and sweet and pretty she is, he'll thank his lucky stars he was asked to dinner.

TOM: Mother, you mustn't expect too much of Laura.

AMANDA: What do you mean?

TOM: Laura seems all those things to you and me because she's ours and we love her. We don't even notice she's crippled any more.

AMANDA: Don't say crippled! You know that I never allow that word to be used!

TOM: But face facts, Mother. She is and — that's not all —

AMANDA: What do you mean "not all"?

TOM: Laura is very different from other girls.

AMANDA: I think the difference is all to her advantage.

TOM: Not quite all — in the eyes of others — strangers — she's terribly shy and lives in a world of her own and those things make her seem a little peculiar to people outside the house.

AMANDA: Don't say peculiar.

TOM: Face the facts. She is.

(The Dance-hall Music Changes to a Tango That Has a Minor and Somewhat Ominous Tone.)

AMANDA: In what way is she peculiar — may I ask?

TOM (*gently*): She lives in a world of her own — a world of — little glass ornaments, Mother. . . . (*Gets up.* AMANDA *remains holding brush, looking at him, troubled.*) She plays old phonograph records and — that's about all — (*He glances at himself in the mirror and crosses to door.*)

AMANDA (*sharply*): Where are you going?

TOM: I'm going to the movies. (*out screen door*)

AMANDA: Not to the movies, every night to the movies! *(follows quickly to screen door)* I don't believe you always go to the movies! *(He is gone. AMANDA looks worriedly after him for a moment. Then vitality and optimism return and she turns from the door. Crossing to portieres.)* Laura! Laura! *(LAURA answers from kitchenette.)*

LAURA: Yes, Mother.

AMANDA: Let those dishes go and come in front! *(LAURA appears with dish towel. Gaily.)* Laura, come here and make a wish on the moon!

LAURA *(entering)*: Moon — moon?

AMANDA: A little silver slipper of a moon. Look over your left shoulder, Laura, and make a wish! *(LAURA looks faintly puzzled as if called out of sleep. AMANDA seizes her shoulders and turns her at an angle by the door.)* Now! Now, darling, *wish!*

LAURA: What shall I wish for, Mother?

AMANDA *(her voice trembling and her eyes suddenly filling with tears)*: Happiness! Good Fortune!

The violin rises and the stage dims out.

Scene VI

(Image: High-School Hero.)

TOM: And so the following evening I brought Jim home to dinner. I had known Jim slightly in high school. In high school Jim was a hero. He had tremendous Irish good nature and vitality with the scrubbed and polished look of white chinaware. He seemed to move in a continual spotlight. He was a star in basketball, captain of the debating club, president of the senior class and the glee club and he sang the male lead in the annual light operas. He was always running or bounding, never just walking. He seemed always at the point of defeating the law of gravity. He was shooting with such velocity through his adolescence that you would logically expect him to arrive at nothing short of the White House by the time he was thirty. But Jim apparently ran into more interference after his graduation from Soldan. His speed had definitely slowed. Six years after he left high school he was holding a job that wasn't much better than mine.

(Image: Clerk.)

He was the only one at the warehouse with whom I was on friendly terms. I was valuable to him as someone who could remember his former glory, who had seen him win basketball games and the silver cup in debating. He knew of my secret practice of retiring to a cabinet of the washroom to work on poems when business was slack in the warehouse. He called me Shakespeare. And while the other boys in the warehouse regarded me with suspicious hostility, Jim took a humorous attitude toward me. Gradually his attitude affected the others, their hostility wore off and they also began to smile at me as people smile at an oddly fashioned dog who trots across their path at some distance.

I knew that Jim and Laura had known each other at Soldan, and I had heard Laura speak admiringly of his voice. I didn't know if Jim remembered her or not. In high school Laura had been as unobtrusive as Jim had been astonishing. If he did remember Laura, it was not as my sister, for when I asked him to dinner, he grinned and said, "You know, Shakespeare, I never thought of you as having folks!"

He was about to discover that I did. . . .

(Light Up Stage.)

(Legend on Screen: "The Accent of a Coming Foot.")

Friday evening. It is about five o'clock of a late spring evening which comes "scattering poems in the sky."

A delicate lemony light is in the Wingfield apartment.

AMANDA *has worked like a Turk in preparation for the gentleman caller. The results are astonishing. The new floor lamp with its rose-silk shade is in place, a colored paper lantern conceals the broken light fixture in the ceiling, new billowing white curtains are at the windows, chintz covers are on chairs and sofa, a pair of new sofa pillows make their initial appearance.*

Open boxes and tissue paper are scattered on the floor.

LAURA *stands in the middle with lifted arms while* AMANDA *crouches before her, adjusting the hem of the new dress, devout and ritualistic. The dress is colored and designed by memory. The arrangement of Laura's hair is changed; it is softer and more becoming. A fragile, unearthly prettiness has come out in* LAURA: *she is like a piece of translucent glass touched by light, given a momentary radiance, not actual, not lasting.*

AMANDA *(impatiently)*: Why are you trembling?

LAURA: Mother, you've made me so nervous!

AMANDA: How have I made you nervous?

LAURA: By all this fuss! You make it seem so important!

AMANDA: I don't understand you, Laura. You couldn't be satisfied with just sitting home, and yet whenever I try to arrange something for you, you seem to resist it. *(She gets up.)* Now take a look at yourself. No, wait! Wait just a moment — I have an idea!

LAURA: What is it now?

AMANDA *produces two powder puffs which she wraps in handkerchiefs and stuffs in* LAURA's *bosom.*

LAURA: Mother, what are you doing?

AMANDA: They call them "Gay Deceivers"!

LAURA: I won't wear them!

AMANDA: You will!

LAURA: Why should I?

AMANDA: Because, to be painfully honest, your chest is flat.

LAURA: You make is seem like we were setting a trap.

AMANDA: All pretty girls are a trap, a pretty trap, and men expect them to be. *(Legend: "A Pretty Trap.")* Now look at yourself, young lady. This is the prettiest you will ever be! I've got to fix myself now! You're going to be surprised by your mother's appearance! *(She crosses through portieres, humming gaily.)*

LAURA *moves slowly to the long mirror and stares solemnly at herself.*
 A wind blows the white curtains inward in a slow, graceful motion and with a faint, sorrowful sighing.

AMANDA *(offstage)*: It isn't dark enough yet. *(She turns slowly before the mirror with a troubled look.)*

**(Legend on Screen: "This Is My Sister: Celebrate Her with Strings!"
Music.)**

AMANDA *(laughing off)*: I'm going to show you something. I'm going to make a spectacular appearance!

LAURA: What is it, Mother?

AMANDA: Possess your soul in patience — you will see! Something I've resurrected from that old trunk! Styles haven't changed so terribly much after all. . . . *(She parts the portieres.)* Now just look at your mother! *(She wears a girlish frock of yellowed voile with a blue silk sash. She carries a bunch of jonquils — the legend of her youth is nearly revived. Feverishly.)* This is the dress in which I led the cotillion. Won the cakewalk twice at Sunset Hill, wore one spring to the Governor's ball in Jackson! See how I sashayed around the ballroom, Laura? *(She raises her skirt and does a mincing step around the room.)* I wore it on Sundays for my gentlemen callers! I had it on the day I met your father — I had malaria fever all that spring. The change of climate from East Tennessee to the Delta — weakened resistance — I had a little temperature all the time — not enough to be serious — just enough to make me restless and giddy! Invitations poured in — parties all over the Delta! — "Stay in bed," said Mother, "you have fever!" — but I just wouldn't. — I took quinine but kept on going, going! — Evenings, dances! — Afternoons, long, long rides! Picnics — lovely! — So lovely, that country in May. — All lacy with dogwood, literally flooded with jonquils! — That was the spring I had the craze for jonquils. Jonquils became an absolute obsession. Mother said, "Honey, there's no more room for jonquils." And still I kept bringing in more jonquils. Whenever, wherever I saw them, I'd say, "Stop! Stop! I see jonquils." I made the young men help me gather the jonquils! It was a joke, Amanda and her jonquils! Finally there were no more vases to hold them, every available space was filled with jonquils. No vases to hold them? All right, I'll hold them myself! And then I — *(She stops in front of the picture.)* **(Music)** met your father! Malaria fever and jonquils and then — this — boy. . . . *(She switches on the rose-colored lamp.)* I hope they get here before it starts to rain. *(She crosses upstage and places the jonquils in bowl on table.)* I gave your brother a little extra change so he and Mr. O'Connor could take the service car home.

LAURA *(with altered look)*: What did you say his name was?

AMANDA: O'Connor.

LAURA: What is his first name?

AMANDA: I don't remember. Oh, yes, I do. It was — Jim!

Laura sways slightly and catches hold of a chair.

(Legend on Screen: "Not Jim!")

LAURA *(faintly)*: Not — Jim!

AMANDA: Yes, that was it, it was Jim! I've never known a Jim that wasn't nice!

(Music: Ominous.)

LAURA: Are you sure his name is Jim O'Connor?

AMANDA: Yes. Why?

LAURA: Is he the one that Tom used to know in high school?

AMANDA: He didn't say so. I think he just got to know him at the warehouse.

LAURA: There was a Jim O'Connor we both knew in high school — *(Then, with effort.)* If that is the one that Tom is bringing to dinner — you'll have to excuse me, I won't come to the table.

AMANDA: What sort of nonsense is this?

LAURA: You asked me once if I'd ever liked a boy. Don't you remember I showed you this boy's picture?

AMANDA: You mean the boy you showed me in the year book?

LAURA: Yes, that boy.

AMANDA: Laura, Laura, were you in love with that boy?

LAURA: I don't know, Mother. All I know is I couldn't sit at the table if it was him!

AMANDA: It won't be him. It isn't the least bit likely. But whether it is or not, you will come to the table. You will not be excused.

LAURA: I'll have to be, Mother.

AMANDA: I don't intend to humor your silliness, Laura. I've had too much from you and your brother, both! So just sit down and compose yourself till they come. Tom has forgotten his key so you'll have to let them in, when they arrive.

LAURA *(panicky)*: Oh, Mother — *you* answer the door!

AMANDA *(lightly)*: I'll be in the kitchen — busy!

LAURA: Oh, Mother, please answer the door, don't make me do it!

AMANDA *(crossing into kitchenette)*: I've got to fix the dressing for the salmon. Fuss, fuss — silliness! — over a gentleman caller!

Door swings, shut. LAURA *is left alone.*

(Legend: "Terror!")

She utters a low moan and turns off the lamp — sits stiffly on the edge of the sofa, knotting her fingers together.

(Legend on Screen: "The Opening of a Door!")

TOM *and* JIM *appear on the fire-escape steps and climb to landing. Hearing their approach,* LAURA *rises with a panicky gesture. She retreats to the portieres.*

The doorbell. Laura catches her breath and touches her throat. Low drums.

AMANDA *(calling)*: Laura, sweetheart! The door!

LAURA *stares at it without moving.*

JIM: I think we just beat the rain.

TOM: Uh-huh. *(He rings again, nervously.* JIM *whistles and fishes for a cigarette.)*

AMANDA *(very, very gaily)*: Laura, that is your brother and Mr. O'Connor! Will you let them in, darling?

LAURA *crosses toward kitchenette door.*

LAURA *(breathlessly)*: Mother — you go to the door!

AMANDA *steps out of kitchenette and stares furiously at Laura. She points imperiously at the door.*

LAURA: Please, please!

AMANDA *(in a fierce whisper)*: What is the matter with you, you silly thing?

LAURA *(desperately)*: Please, you answer it, *please!*

AMANDA: I told you I wasn't going to humor you, Laura. Why have you chosen this moment to lose your mind?

LAURA: Please, please, please, you go!

AMANDA: You'll have to go to the door because I can't!

LAURA *(despairingly)*: I can't either!

AMANDA: Why?

LAURA: I'm *sick!*

AMANDA: I'm sick too — of your nonsense! Why can't you and your brother be normal people? Fantastic whims and behavior! *(*TOM *gives a long ring.)* Preposterous goings on! Can you give me one reason — *(calls out lyrically)* COMING! JUST ONE SECOND! — why should you be afraid to open a door? Now you answer it, Laura!

LAURA: Oh, oh, oh . . . *(She returns through the portieres. Darts to the victrola and winds it frantically and turns it on.)*

AMANDA: Laura Wingfield, you march right to that door!

LAURA: Yes — yes, Mother!

A faraway, scratchy rendition of "Dardanella" softens the air and gives her strength to move through it. She slips to the door and draws it cautiously open. TOM *enters with the caller,* JIM O'CONNOR.

TOM: Laura, this is Jim. Jim, this is my sister, Laura.

JIM *(stepping inside)*: I didn't know that Shakespeare had a sister!

LAURA *(retreating stiff and trembling from the door)*: How — how do you do?

JIM *(heartily extending his hand)*: Okay!

LAURA *touches it hesitantly with hers.*

JIM: Your hand's *cold,* Laura!

LAURA: Yes, well — I've been playing the victrola. . . .

JIM: Must have been playing classical music on it! You ought to play a little hot swing music to warm you up!

LAURA: Excuse me — I haven't finished playing the victrola. . . .

She turns awkwardly and hurries into the front room. She pauses a second by the victrola. Then catches her breath and darts through the portieres like a frightened deer.

JIM *(grinning)*: What was the matter?

TOM: Oh — with Laura? Laura is — terribly shy.

JIM: Shy, huh? It's unusual to meet a shy girl nowadays. I don't believe you ever mentioned you had a sister.

TOM: Well, now you know. I have one. Here is the *Post Dispatch.* You want a piece of it?

JIM: Uh-huh.

TOM: What piece? The comics?

JIM: Sports! *(glances at it)* Ole Dizzy Dean is on his bad behavior.

TOM *(disinterest)*: Yeah? *(lights cigarette and crosses back to fire-escape door)*

JIM: Where are *you* going?

TOM: I'm going out on the terrace.

JIM *(goes after him)*: You know, Shakespeare — I'm going to sell you a bill of goods!

TOM: What goods?

JIM: A course I'm taking.

TOM: Huh?

JIM: In public speaking! You and me, we're not the warehouse type.

TOM: Thanks — that's good news. But what has public speaking got to do with it?

JIM: It fits you for — executive positions!

TOM: Awww.

JIM: I tell you it's done a helluva lot for me.

(Image: Executive at Desk.)

TOM: In what respect?

JIM: In every! Ask yourself what is the difference between you an' me and men in the office down front? Brains? — No! — Ability? — No! Then what? Just one little thing —

TOM: What is that one little thing?

JIM: Primarily it amounts to — social poise! Being able to square up to people and hold your own on any social level!

AMANDA *(offstage)*: Tom?

TOM: Yes, Mother?

AMANDA: Is that you and Mr. O'Connor?

TOM: Yes, Mother.

AMANDA: Well, you just make yourselves comfortable in there.

TOM: Yes, Mother.

AMANDA: Ask Mr. O'Connor if he would like to wash his hands.

JIM: Aw — no — thank you — I took care of that at the warehouse. Tom —

TOM: Yes?

JIM: Mr. Mendoza was speaking to me about you.

TOM: Favorably?

JIM: What do you think?

TOM: Well —

JIM: You're going to be out of a job if you don't wake up.

TOM: I am waking up —

JIM: You show no signs.

TOM: The signs are interior.

(Image on Screen: The Sailing Vessel with Jolly Roger Again.)

TOM: I'm planning to change. *(He leans over the rail speaking with quiet exhilaration. The incandescent marquees and signs of the first-run movie houses light his face from across the alley. He looks like a voyager.)* I'm right at the point of committing myself to a future that doesn't include the warehouse and Mr. Mendoza or even a night-school course in public speaking.

JIM: What are you gassing about?

TOM: I'm tired of the movies.

JIM: Movies!

TOM: Yes, movies! Look at them — *(a wave toward the marvels of Grand Avenue)* All of those glamorous people — having adventures — hogging it all, gobbling the whole thing up! You know what happens? People go to the *movies* instead of *moving!* Hollywood characters are supposed to have all the adventures for everybody in America, while everybody in America sits in a dark room and watches them have them! Yes, until there's a war. That's when adventure becomes available to the masses! *Everyone's* dish, not only Gable's! Then the people in the dark room come out of the dark room to have some adventures themselves — Goody, goody — It's our turn now, to go to the South Sea Island — to make a safari — to be exotic, far-off — But I'm not patient. I don't want to wait till then. I'm tired of the *movies* and I am *about to move!*

JIM *(incredulously)*: Move?

TOM: Yes.

JIM: When?

TOM: Soon!

JIM: Where? Where?

Theme three music seems to answer the question, while TOM *thinks it over. He searches among his pockets.*

TOM: I'm starting to boil inside. I know I seem dreamy, but inside — well, I'm boiling! Whenever I pick up a shoe, I shudder a little thinking how short life is and what I am doing! — Whatever that means. I know it doesn't mean shoes — except as something to wear on a traveler's feet! *(finds paper)* Look —

JIM: What?

TOM: I'm a member.

JIM *(reading)*: The Union of Merchant Seamen.

TOM: I paid my dues this month, instead of the light bill.

JIM: You will regret it when they turn the lights off.

TOM: I won't be here.

JIM: How about your mother?

TOM: I'm like my father. The bastard son of a bastard! See how he grins? And he's been absent going on sixteen years!

JIM: You're just talking, you drip. How does your mother feel about it?

TOM: Shhh — Here comes Mother! Mother is not acquainted with my plans!

AMANDA *(enters portieres)*: Where are you all?

TOM: On the terrace, Mother.

They start inside. She advances to them. TOM *is distinctly shocked at her appearance. Even* JIM *blinks a little. He is making his first contact with girlish Southern vivacity and in spite of the night-school course in public speaking is somewhat thrown off the beam by the unexpected outlay of social charm.*

Certain responses are attempted by JIM *but are swept aside by* AMANDA*'s gay laughter and chatter.* TOM *is embarrassed but after the first shock* JIM *reacts very warmly. Grins and chuckles, is altogether won over.*

(Image: Amanda as a Girl.)

AMANDA *(coyly smiling, shaking her girlish ringlets)*: Well, well, well, so this is Mr. O'Connor. Introductions entirely unnecessary. I've heard so much about you from my boy. I finally said to him, Tom — good gracious! — why don't you bring this paragon to supper? I'd like to meet this nice young man at the warehouse! — Instead of just hearing him sing your praises so much! I don't know why my son is so stand-offish — that's not Southern behavior! Let's sit down and — I think we could stand a little more air in here! Tom, leave the door open. I felt a nice fresh breeze a moment ago. Where has it gone? Mmm, so warm already! And not quite summer, even. We're going to burn up when summer really gets started. However, we're having — we're having a very light supper. I think light things are better fo' this time of year. The same as light clothes are. Light clothes an' light food are what warm weather calls fo'. You know our blood gets so thick during th' winter — it takes a while fo' us to *adjust* ou'selves! — when the season changes . . . It's come so quick this year. I wasn't prepared. All of a sudden — heavens! Already summer! — I ran to the trunk an' pulled out this light dress — Terribly old! Historical almost! But feels so good — so good an' co-ol, y'know. . . .

TOM: Mother —

AMANDA: Yes, honey?

TOM: How about — supper?

AMANDA: Honey, you go ask Sister if supper is ready! You know that Sister is in full charge of supper! Tell her you hungry boys are waiting for it. *(To* JIM.*)* Have you met Laura?

JIM: She —

AMANDA: Let you in? Oh, good, you've met already! It's rare for a girl as sweet an' pretty as Laura to be domestic! But Laura is, thank heavens, not only pretty but also very domestic. I'm not at all. I never was a bit. I never could make a thing but angel-food cake. Well, in the South we had so many servants. Gone, gone, gone. All vestiges of gracious living! Gone completely! I wasn't prepared for what the future brought me. All of my gentlemen callers were sons of planters and so of course I assumed that I would be married to one and raise my family on a large piece of land with plenty of servants. But man proposes — and woman accepts the proposal! — To vary that old, old saying a little bit — I married no planter! I married a man who worked for the telephone company! — that gallantly smiling gentleman over there! *(points to the picture)* A telephone man who — fell in love with long-distance! — Now he travels and I don't even know where! — But what am I going on for about my — tribulations? Tell me yours — I hope you don't have any! Tom?

TOM *(returning)*: Yes, Mother?

AMANDA: Is supper nearly ready?

TOM: It looks to me like supper is on the table.

AMANDA: Let me look — *(She rises prettily and looks through portieres.)* Oh, lovely — But where is Sister?

TOM: Laura is not feeling well and she says that she thinks she'd better not come to the table.

AMANDA: What?—Nonsense!—Laura? Oh, Laura!

LAURA (*offstage, faintly*): Yes, Mother.

AMANDA: You really must come to the table. We won't be seated until you come to the table! Come in, Mr. O'Connor. You sit over there and I'll—Laura? Laura Wingfield! You're keeping us waiting, honey! We can't say grace until you come to the table!

The back door is pushed weakly open and LAURA *comes in. She is obviously quite faint, her lips trembling, her eyes wide and staring. She moves unsteadily toward the table.*

(Legend: "Terror!")

Outside a summer storm is coming abruptly. The white curtains billow inward at the windows and there is a sorrowful murmer and deep blue dusk.
    LAURA *suddenly stumbles—She catches at a chair with a faint moan.*

TOM: Laura!

AMANDA: Laura! (*There is a clap of thunder.*) **(Legend: "Ah!")** (*despairingly*) Why, Laura, you *are* sick, darling! Tom, help your sister into the living room, dear! Sit in the living room, Laura—rest on the sofa. Well! (*to the gentleman caller*) Standing over the hot stove made her ill!—I told her that it was just too warm this evening, but—(TOM *comes back in.* LAURA *is on the sofa.*) Is Laura all right now?

TOM: Yes.

AMANDA: What *is* that? Rain? A nice cool rain has come up! (*She gives the gentleman caller a frightened look.*) I think we may—have grace—now . . . (TOM *looks at her stupidly.*) Tom, honey—you say grace!

TOM: Oh . . . "For these and all thy mercies—" (*They bow their heads,* AMANDA *stealing a nervous glance at Jim. In the living room* LAURA, *stretched on the sofa, clenches her hand to her lips, to hold back a shuddering sob.*) God's Holy Name be praised—

(The Scene Dims Out.)

Scene VII

A Souvenir.

Half an hour later. Dinner is just being finished in the upstage area which is concealed by the drawn portieres.

    As the curtain rises LAURA *is still huddled upon the sofa, her feet drawn under her, her head resting on a pale blue pillow, her eyes wide and mysteriously watchful. The new floor lamp with its shade of rose-colored silk gives a soft, becoming light to her face, bringing out the fragile, unearthly prettiness which usually escapes attention. There is a steady murmur of rain, but it is slackening and stops soon after the scene begins; the air outside becomes pale and luminous as the moon breaks out.*

    A moment after the curtain rises, the lights in both rooms flicker and go out.

JIM: Hey, there, Mr. Light Bulb!

AMANDA *laughs nervously.*

(Legend: "Suspension of a Public Service.")

AMANDA: Where was Moses when the lights went out? Ha-ha. Do you know the answer to that one, Mr. O'Connor?

JIM: No, Ma'am, what's the answer?

AMANDA: In the dark! (JIM *laughs appreciatively.*) Everybody sit still. I'll light the candles. Isn't it lucky we have them on the table? Where's a match? Which of you gentlemen can provide a match?

JIM: Here.

AMANDA: Thank you, sir.

JIM: Not at all, Ma'am!

AMANDA: I guess the fuse has burnt out. Mr. O'Connor, can you tell a burnt-out fuse? I know I can't and Tom is a total loss when it comes to mechanics. **(Sound: Getting Up: Voices Recede a Little to Kitchenette.)** Oh, be careful you don't bump into something. We don't want our gentleman caller to break his neck. Now wouldn't that be a fine howdy-do?

JIM: Ha-ha! Where is the fuse-box?

AMANDA: Right here next to the stove. Can you see anything?

JIM: Just a minute.

AMANDA: Isn't electricity a mysterious thing? Wasn't it Benjamin Franklin who tied a key to a kite? We live in such a mysterious universe, don't we? Some people say that science clears up all the mysteries for us. In my opinion it only creates more! Have you found it yet?

JIM: No, Ma'am. All these fuses look okay to me.

AMANDA: Tom!

TOM: Yes, Mother?

AMANDA: That light bill I gave you several days ago. The one I told you we got the notices about?

TOM: Oh. — Yeah.

(Legend: "Ha!")

AMANDA: You didn't neglect to pay it by any chance?

TOM: Why, I —

AMANDA: Didn't! I might have known it!

JIM: Shakespeare probably wrote a poem on that light bill, Mrs. Wingfield.

AMANDA: I might have known better than to trust him with it! There's such a high price for negligence in this world!

JIM: Maybe the poem will win a ten-dollar prize.

AMANDA: We'll just have to spend the remainder of the evening in the nineteenth century, before Mr. Edison made the Mazda° lamp!

SCENE VII. *Mazda lamp:* Electric lamp that replaced kerosene lamps or candles.

JIM: Candlelight is my favorite kind of light.

AMANDA: That shows you're romantic! But that's no excuse for Tom. Well, we got through dinner. Very considerate of them to let us get through dinner before they plunged us into everlasting darkness, wasn't it, Mr. O'Connor?

JIM: Ha-ha!

AMANDA: Tom, as a penalty for your carelessness you can help me with the dishes.

JIM: Let me give you a hand.

AMANDA: Indeed you will not!

JIM: I ought to be good for something.

AMANDA: Good for something? *(Her tone is rhapsodic.)* You? Why, Mr. O'Connor, nobody, *nobody's* given me this much entertainment in years — as you have!

JIM: Aw, now, Mrs. Wingfield!

AMANDA: I'm not exaggerating, not one bit! But Sister is all by her lonesome. You go keep her company in the parlor! I'll give you this lovely old candelabrum that used to be on the altar at the church of the Heavenly Rest. It was melted a little out of shape when the church burnt down. Lightning struck it one spring. Gypsy Jones was holding a revival at the time and he intimated that the church was destroyed because the Episcopalians gave card parties.

JIM: Ha-ha.

AMANDA: And how about coaxing Sister to drink a little wine? I think it would be good for her! Can you carry both at once?

JIM: Sure. I'm Superman!

AMANDA: Now, Thomas, get into this apron!

The door of kitchenette swings closed on AMANDA's *gay laughter; the flickering light approaches the portieres.*

LAURA sits up nervously as he enters. Her speech at first is low and breathless from the almost intolerable strain of being alone with a stranger.

(The Legend: "I Don't Suppose You Remember Me at All!")

In her first speeches in this scene, before JIM's *warmth overcomes her paralyzing shyness,* LAURA's *voice is thin and breathless as though she has run up a steep flight of stairs.*

JIM's attitude is gently humorous. In playing this scene it should be stressed that while the incident is apparently unimportant, it is to LAURA *the climax of her secret life.*

JIM: Hello, there, Laura.

LAURA *(faintly)*: Hello. *(She clears her throat.)*

JIM: How are you feeling now? Better?

LAURA: Yes. Yes, thank you.

JIM: This is for you. A little dandelion wine. *(He extends it toward her with extravagant gallantry.)*

LAURA: Thank you.

JIM: Drink it—but don't get drunk! *(He laughs heartily.* LAURA *takes the glass uncertainly; laughs shyly.)* Where shall I set the candles?

LAURA: Oh—oh, anywhere . . .

JIM: How about here on the floor? Any objections?

LAURA: No.

JIM: I'll spread a newspaper under to catch the drippings. I like to sit on the floor. Mind if I do?

LAURA: Oh, no.

JIM: Give me a pillow?

LAURA: What?

JIM: A pillow!

LAURA: Oh . . . *(hands him one quickly)*

JIM: How about you? Don't you like to sit on the floor?

LAURA: Oh—yes.

JIM: Why don't you, then?

LAURA: I—will.

JIM: Take a pillow! *(LAURA does. Sits on the other side of the candelabrum.* JIM *crosses his legs and smiles engagingly at her.)* I can't hardly see you sitting way over there.

LAURA: I can—see you.

JIM: I know, but that's not fair, I'm in the limelight. *(LAURA moves her pillow closer.)* Good! Now I can see you! Comfortable?

LAURA: Yes.

JIM: So am I. Comfortable as a cow. Will you have some gum?

LAURA: No, thank you.

JIM: I think that I will indulge, with your permission. *(Musingly unwraps it and holds it up.)* Think of the fortune made by the guy that invented the first piece of chewing gum. Amazing, huh? The Wrigley Building is one of the sights of Chicago.—I saw it summer before last when I went up to the Century of Progress. Did you take in the Century of Progress?

LAURA: No, I didn't.

JIM: Well, it was quite a wonderful exposition. What impressed me most was the Hall of Science. Gives you an idea of what the future will be in America, even more wonderful than the present time is! *(Pause. Smiling at her.)* Your brother tells me you're shy. Is that right, Laura?

LAURA: I—don't know.

JIM: I judge you to be an old-fashioned type of girl. Well, I think that's a pretty good type to be. Hope you don't think I'm being too personal—do you?

LAURA *(hastily, out of embarrassment)*: I believe I *will* take a piece of gum, if you—don't mind. *(Clearing her throat.)* Mr. O'Connor, have you—kept up with your singing?

JIM: Singing? Me?

LAURA: Yes. I remember what a beautiful voice you had.

JIM: When did you hear me sing?

(Voice Offstage in the Pause.)

VOICE *(offstage)*: O blow, ye winds, heigh-ho
A-roving I will go!
I'm off to my love
With a boxing glove —
Ten thousand miles away!

JIM: You say you've heard me sing?

LAURA: Oh, yes! Yes, very often . . . I — don't suppose you remember me — at all?

JIM *(smiling doubtfully)*: You know I have an idea I've seen you before. I had that idea soon as you opened the door. It seemed almost like I was about to remember your name. But the name that I started to call you — wasn't a name! And so I stopped myself before I said it.

LAURA: Wasn't it — Blue Roses?

JIM *(springs up, grinning)*: Blue Roses! My gosh, yes — Blue Roses! That's what I had on my tongue when you opened the door! Isn't it funny what tricks your memory plays? I didn't connect you with the high school somehow or other. But that's where it was; it was high school. I didn't even know you were Shakespeare's sister! Gosh, I'm sorry.

LAURA: I didn't expect you to. You — barely knew me!

JIM: But we did have a speaking acquaintance, huh?

LAURA: Yes, we — spoke to each other.

JIM: When did you recognize me?

LAURA: Oh, right away!

JIM: Soon as I came in the door?

LAURA: When I heard your name I thought it was probably you. I knew that Tom used to know you a little in high school. So when you came in the door — Well, then I was — sure.

JIM: Why didn't you *say* something, then?

LAURA *(breathlessly)*: I didn't know what to say, I was — too surprised!

JIM: For goodness' sakes! You know, this sure is funny!

LAURA: Yes! Yes, isn't it, though . . .

JIM: Didn't we have a class in something together?

LAURA: Yes, we did.

JIM: What class was that?

LAURA: It was — singing — Chorus!

JIM: Aw!

LAURA: I sat across the aisle from you in the Aud.

JIM: Aw.

LAURA: Mondays, Wednesdays and Fridays.

JIM: Now I remember — you always came in late.

LAURA: Yes, it was so hard for me, getting upstairs. I had that brace on my leg — it clumped so loud!

JIM: I never heard any clumping.

LAURA (*wincing at the recollection*): To me it sounded like — thunder!

JIM: Well, well, well. I never even noticed.

LAURA: And everybody was seated before I came in. I had to walk in front of all those people. My seat was in the back row. I had to go clumping all the way up the aisle with everyone watching!

JIM: You shouldn't have been self-conscious.

LAURA: I know, but I was. It was always such a relief when the singing started.

JIM: Aw, yes, I've placed you now! I used to call you Blue Roses. How was it that I got started calling you that?

LAURA: I was out of school a little while with pleurosis. When I came back you asked me what was the matter. I said I had pleurosis — you thought I said Blue Roses. That's what you always called me after that!

JIM: I hope you didn't mind.

LAURA: Oh, no — I liked it. You see, I wasn't acquainted with many — people. . . .

JIM: As I remember you sort of stuck by yourself.

LAURA: I — I — never had much luck at — making friends.

JIM: I don't see why you wouldn't.

LAURA: Well, I — started out badly.

JIM: You mean being —

LAURA: Yes, it sort of — stood between me —

JIM: You shouldn't have let it!

LAURA: I know, but it did, and —

JIM: You were shy with people!

LAURA: I tried not to be but never could —

JIM: Overcome it?

LAURA: No, I — I never could!

JIM: I guess being shy is something you have to work out of kind of gradually.

LAURA (*sorrowfully*): Yes — I guess it —

JIM: Takes time!

LAURA: Yes —

JIM: People are not so dreadful when you know them. That's what you have to remember! And everybody has problems, not just you, but practically everybody has got some problems. You think of yourself as having the only problems, as being the only one who is disappointed. But just look around you and you will see lots of people as disappointed as you are. For instance, I hoped when I was going to high school that I would be further along at this time, six years later, than I am now — You remember that wonderful write-up I had in *The Torch?*

LAURA: Yes! *(She rises and crosses to table.)*

JIM: It said I was bound to succeed in anything I went into! *(LAURA returns with the annual.)* Holy Jeez! *The Torch!* *(He accepts it reverently. They smile across it with mutual wonder.* LAURA *crouches beside him and they begin to turn though it.* LAURA*'s shyness is dissolving in his warmth.)*

LAURA: Here you are in *Pirates of Penzance!*

JIM *(wistfully)*: I sang the baritone lead in that operetta.

LAURA *(rapidly)*: So — *beautifully!*

JIM *(protesting)*: Aw —

LAURA: Yes, yes — beautifully — beautifully!

JIM: You heard me?

LAURA: All three times!

JIM: No!

LAURA: Yes!

JIM: All three performances?

LAURA *(looking down)*: Yes.

JIM: Why?

LAURA: I — wanted to ask you to — autograph my program.

JIM: Why didn't you ask me to?

LAURA: You were always surrounded by your own friends so much that I never had a chance to.

JIM: You should have just —

LAURA: Well, I — thought you might think I was —

JIM: Thought I might think you was — what?

LAURA: Oh —

JIM *(with reflective relish)*: I was beleaguered by females in those days.

LAURA: You were terribly popular!

JIM: Yeah —

LAURA: You had such a — friendly way —

JIM: I was spoiled in high school.

LAURA: Everybody — liked you!

JIM: Including you?

LAURA: I — yes, I — I did, too — *(She gently closes the book in her lap.)*

JIM: Well, well, well! — Give me that program, Laura. *(She hands it to him. He signs it with a flourish.)* There are you — better late than never!

LAURA: Oh, I — what a — surprise!

JIM: My signature isn't worth very much right now. But some day — maybe — it will increase in value! Being disappointed is one thing and being discouraged is something else. I am disappointed but I'm not discouraged. I'm twenty-three years old. How old are you?

LAURA: I'll be twenty-four in June.

JIM: That's not old age!

LAURA: No, but —

JIM: You finished high school?

LAURA *(with difficulty)*: I didn't go back.

JIM: You mean you dropped out?

LAURA: I made bad grades in my final examinations. *(She rises and replaces the book and the program. Her voice strained.)* How is — Emily Meisenbach getting along?

JIM: Oh, that kraut-head!

LAURA: Why do you call her that?

JIM: That's what she was.

LAURA: You're not still — going with her?

JIM: I never see her.

LAURA: It said in the Personal Section that you were — engaged!

JIM: I know, but I wasn't impressed by that — propaganda!

LAURA: It wasn't — the truth?

JIM: Only in Emily's optimistic opinion!

LAURA: Oh —

(Legend: "What Have You Done since High School?")

JIM *lights a cigarette and leans indolently back on his elbows smiling at* LAURA *with a warmth and charm which light her inwardly with altar candles. She remains by the table and turns in her hands a piece of glass to cover her tumult.*

JIM *(after several reflective puffs on a cigarette)*: What have you done since high school? *(She seems not to hear him.)* Huh? *(*LAURA *looks up.)* I said what have you done since high school, Laura?

LAURA: Nothing much.

JIM: You must have been doing something these six long years.

LAURA: Yes.

JIM: Well, then, such as what?

LAURA: I took a business course at business college —

JIM: How did that work out?

LAURA: Well, not very — well — I had to drop out, it gave me — indigestion —

JIM *laughs gently.*

JIM: What are you doing now?

LAURA: I don't do anything — much. Oh, please don't think I sit around doing nothing! My glass collection takes up a good deal of my time. Glass is something you have to take good care of.

JIM: What did you say — about glass?

LAURA: Collection I said — I have one — *(She clears her throat and turns away again, acutely shy).*

JIM *(abruptly)*: You know what I judge to be the trouble with you? Inferiority complex! Know what that is? That's what they call it when someone low-rates himself! I understand it because I had it, too. Although my case was not so aggravated as yours seems to be. I had it until I took up public speaking, developed my voice, and learned that I had an aptitude for science. Before that time I never thought of myself as being outstanding in any way whatsoever! Now I've never made a regular study of it, but I have a friend who says I can analyze people better than doctors that make a profession of it. I don't claim that to be necessarily true, but I can sure guess a person's psychology, Laura! *(takes out his gum)* Excuse me, Laura. I always take it out when the flavor is gone. I'll use this scrap of paper to wrap it in. I know how it is to get it stuck on a shoe. Yep—that's what I judge to be your principal trouble. A lack of confidence in yourself as a person. You don't have the proper amount of faith in yourself. I'm basing that fact on a number of your remarks and also on certain observations I've made. For instance that clumping you thought was so awful in high school. You say that you even dreaded to walk into class. You see what you did? You dropped out of school, you gave up an education because of a clump, which as far as I know was practically non-existent! A little physical defect is what you have. Hardly noticeable even! Magnified thousands of times by imagination! You know what my strong advice to you is? Think of yourself as *superior* in some way!

LAURA: In what way would I think?

JIM: Why, man alive, Laura! Just look about you a little. What do you see? A world full of common people. All of 'em born and all of 'em going to die! Which of them has one-tenth of your good points! Or mine! Or anyone else's, as far as that goes—Gosh! Everybody excels in some one thing. Some in many! *(unconsciously glances at himself in the mirror)* All you've got to do is discover in *what!* Take me, for instance. *(He adjusts his tie at the mirror.)* My interest happens to lie in electro-dynamics. I'm taking a course in radio engineering at night school, Laura, on top of a fairly responsible job at the warehouse. I'm taking that course and studying public speaking.

LAURA: Ohhhh.

JIM: Because I believe in the future of television! *(turning back to her)* I wish to be ready to go up right along with it. Therefore I'm planning to get in on the ground floor. In fact, I've already made the right connections and all that remains is for the industry itself to get under way! Full steam—*(His eyes are starry.)* Knowledge—Zzzzzp! Money—Zzzzzzp!—Power! That's the cycle democracy is built on! *(His attitude is convincingly dynamic.* LAURA *stares at him, even her shyness eclipsed in her absolute wonder. He suddenly grins.)* I guess you think I think a lot of myself!

LAURA: No—o-o-o, I—

JIM: Now how about you? Isn't there something you take more interest in than anything else?

LAURA: Well, I do—as I said—have my—glass collection—

A peal of girlish laughter from the kitchen.

JIM: I'm not right sure I know what you're talking about. What kind of glass is it?

LAURA: Little articles of it, they're ornaments mostly! Most of them are little animals made out of glass, the tiniest little animals in the world. Mother calls them a glass menagerie! Here's an example of one, if you'd like to see it! This one is one of the oldest. It's nearly thirteen. *(He stretches out his hand.)* **(Music: "The Glass Menagerie.")** Oh, be careful—if you breathe, it breaks!

JIM: I'd better not take it. I'm pretty clumsy with things.

LAURA: Go on, I trust you with him! *(places it in his palm)* There now— you're holding him gently! Hold him over the light, he loves the light! You see how the light shines through him?

JIM: It sure does shine!

LAURA: I shouldn't be partial, but he is my favorite one.

JIM: What kind of a thing is this one supposed to be?

LAURA: Haven't you noticed the single horn on his forehead?

JIM: A unicorn, huh?

LAURA: Mmm-hmmm!

JIM: Unicorns, aren't they extinct in the modern world?

LAURA: I know!

JIM: Poor little fellow, he must feel sort of lonesome.

LAURA *(smiling)*: Well, if he does he doesn't complain about it. He stays on a shelf with some horses that don't have horns and all of them seem to get along nicely together.

JIM: How do you know?

LAURA *(lightly)*: I haven't heard any arguments among them!

JIM *(grinning)*: No arguments, huh? Well, that's a pretty good sign! Where shall I set him?

LAURA: Put him on the table. They all like a change of scenery once in a while!

JIM *(stretching)*: Well, well, well, well—Look how big my shadow is when I stretch!

LAURA: Oh, oh, yes—it stretches across the ceiling!

JIM *(crossing to door)*: I think it's stopped raining. *(opens fire-escape door)* Where does the music come from?

LAURA: From the Paradise Dance Hall across the alley.

JIM: How about cutting the rug a little, Miss Wingfield?

LAURA: Oh, I—

JIM: Or is your program filled up? Let me have a look at it. *(grasps imaginary card)* Why, every dance is taken! I'll just have to scratch some out.

(Waltz Music: "La Golondrina.") Ahhh, a waltz! *(He executes some sweeping turns by himself, then holds his arms toward* LAURA.*)*

LAURA *(breathlessly)*: I—can't dance!

JIM: There you go, that inferiority stuff!

LAURA: I've never danced in my life!

JIM: Come on, try!

LAURA: Oh, but I'd step on you!

JIM: I'm not made out of glass.

LAURA: How—how—how do we start?

JIM: Just leave it to me. You hold your arms out a little.

LAURA: Like this?

JIM: A little bit higher. Right. Now don't tighten up, that's the main thing about it—relax.

LAURA *(laughing breathlessly)*: It's hard not to.

JIM: Okay.

LAURA: I'm afraid you can't budge me.

JIM: What do you bet I can't? *(He swings her into motion.)*

LAURA: Goodness, yes, you can!

JIM: Let yourself go, now, Laura, just let yourself go.

LAURA: I'm—

JIM: Come on!

LAURA: Trying?

JIM: Not so stiff—Easy does it!

LAURA: I know but I'm—

JIM: Loosen th' backbone! There now, that's a lot better.

LAURA: Am I?

JIM: Lots, lots better! *(He moves her about the room in a clumsy waltz.)*

LAURA: Oh, my!

JIM: Ha-ha!

LAURA: Goodness, yes you can!

JIM: Ha-ha-ha! *(They suddenly bump into the table. Jim stops.)* What did we hit on?

LAURA: Table.

JIM: Did something fall off it? I think—

LAURA: Yes.

JIM: I hope that it wasn't the little glass horse with the horn!

LAURA: Yes.

JIM: Aw, aw, aw. Is it broken?

LAURA: Now it is just like all the other horses.

JIM: It's lost its—

LAURA: Horn! It doesn't matter. Maybe it's a blessing in disguise.

JIM: You'll never forgive me. I bet that that was your favorite piece of glass.

LAURA: I don't have favorites much. It's no tragedy, Freckles. Glass breaks so easily. No matter how careful you are. The traffic jars the shelves and things fall off them.

JIM: Still I'm awfully sorry that I was the cause.

LAURA *(smiling)*: I'll just imagine he had an operation. The horn was removed to make him feel less — freakish! *(They both laugh.)* Now he
will feel more at home with the other horses, the ones that don't have
horns . . .

JIM: Ha-ha, that's very funny! *(suddenly serious)* I'm glad to see that you
have a sense of humor. You know — you're — well — very different!
Surprisingly different from anyone else I know! *(His voice becomes soft
and hesitant with a genuine feeling.)* Do you mind me telling you that?
(LAURA is abashed beyond speech.) You make me feel sort of — I don't
know how to put it! I'm usually pretty good at expressing things,
but — This is something that I don't know how to say! *(LAURA touches
her throat and clears it — turns the broken unicorn in her hands.)* *(even softer)*
Has anyone ever told you that you were pretty? **(Pause: Music.)**
(LAURA looks up slowly, with wonder, and shakes her head.) Well, you
are! In a very different way from anyone else. And all the nicer because
of the difference, too. *(His voice becomes low and husky. LAURA turns
away, nearly faint with the novelty of her emotions.)* I wish you were my
sister. I'd teach you to have some confidence in yourself. The different
people are not like other people, but being different is nothing to be
ashamed of. Because other people are not such wonderful people.
They're one hundred times one thousand. You're one times one! They
walk all over the earth. You just stay here. They're common as —
weeds, but — you — well, you're — *Blue Roses!*

(Image on Screen: Blue Roses.)

(Music Changes.)

LAURA: But blue is wrong for — roses . . .

JIM: It's right for you — You're — pretty!

LAURA: In what respect am I pretty?

JIM: In all respects — believe me! Your eyes — your hair — are pretty! Your
hands are pretty! *(He catches hold of her hand.)* You think I'm making
this up because I'm invited to dinner and have to be nice. Oh, I could
do that! I could put on an act for you, Laura, and say lots of things
without being very sincere. But this time I am. I'm talking to you
sincerely. I happened to notice you had this inferiority complex that
keeps you from feeling comfortable with people. Somebody needs to
build your confidence up and make you proud instead of shy and
turning away and — blushing — Somebody ought to — ought to — *kiss*
you, Laura! *(His hand slips slowly up her arm to her shoulder.)* **(Music
Swells Tumultuously.)** *(He suddenly turns her about and kisses her on the
lips. When he releases her LAURA sinks on the sofa with a bright, dazed
look. JIM backs away and fishes in his pocket for a cigarette.)* **(Legend on
Screen: "Souvenir.")** Stumble-john! *(He lights the cigarette, avoiding her
look. There is a peal of girlish laughter from AMANDA in the kitchen.*

LAURA *slowly raises and opens her hand. It still contains the little broken glass animal. She looks at it with a tender, bewildered expression.)* Stumble-john! I shouldn't have done that—That was way off the beam. You don't smoke, do you? *(She looks up, smiling, not hearing the question. He sits beside her a little gingerly. She looks at him speechlessly—waiting. He coughs decorously and moves a little farther aside as he considers the situation and senses her feelings, dimly, with perturbation. Gently.)* Would you—care for a—mint? *(She doesn't seem to hear him but her look grows brighter even.)* Peppermint—Life Saver? My pocket's a regular drug store—wherever I go . . . *(He pops a mint in his mouth. Then gulps and decides to make a clean breast of it. He speaks slowly and gingerly.)* Laura, you know, if I had a sister like you, I'd do the same thing as Tom, I'd bring out fellows—introduce her to them. The right type of boys of a type to—appreciate her. Only—well—he made a mistake about me. Maybe I've got no call to be saying this. That may not have been the idea in having me over. But what if it was? There's nothing wrong about that. The only trouble is that in my case—I'm not in a situation to—do the right thing. I can't take down your number and say I'll phone. I can't call up next week and—ask for a date. I thought I had better explain the situation in case you misunderstood it and—hurt your feelings. . . . *(Pause. Slowly, very slowly,* LAURA's *look changes, her eyes returning slowly from his to the ornament in her palm.)*

AMANDA *utters another gay laugh in the kitchen.*

LAURA *(faintly)*: You—won't—call again?

JIM: No, Laura, I can't. *(He rises from the sofa.)* As I was just explaining, I've—got strings on me, Laura, I've—been going steady! I go out all the time with a girl named Betty. She's a home-girl like you, and Catholic, and Irish, and in a great many ways we—get along fine. I met her last summer on a moonlight boat trip up the river to Alton, on the *Majestic.* Well—right away from the start it was—love! **(Legend: Love!)** *(*LAURA *sways slightly forward and grips the arm of the sofa. He fails to notice, now enrapt in his own comfortable being.)* Being in love has made a new man of me! *(Leaning stiffly forward, clutching the arm of the sofa,* LAURA *struggles visibly with her storm. But* JIM *is oblivious, she is a long way off.)* The power of love is really pretty tremendous! Love is something that—changes the whole world, Laura! *(The storm abates a little and* LAURA *leans back. He notices her again.)* It happened that Betty's aunt took sick, she got a wire and had to go to Centralia. So Tom—when he asked me to dinner—I naturally just accepted the invitation, not knowing that you—that he—that I—(He stops awkwardly.)* Huh—I'm a stumble-john! *(He flops back on the sofa. The holy candles in the altar of* LAURA's *face have been snuffed out! There is a look of almost infinite desolation. Jim glances at her uneasily.)* I wish that you would—say something. *(She bites her lip which was trembling and then bravely smiles. She opens her hand again on the broken glass ornament. Then* *she gently takes his hand and raises it level with her own. She carefully places the unicorn in the palm of his hand, then pushes his fingers closed upon it.)* What are you—doing that for? You want me to have him?—Laura? *(She nods.)* What for?

LAURA: A—souvenir . . .

She rises unsteadily and crouches beside the victrola to wind it up.

(Legend on Screen: "Things Have a Way of Turning Out So Badly.")

(Or Image: "Gentleman Caller Waving Good-bye!—Gaily.")

At this moment AMANDA *rushes brightly back in the front room. She bears a pitcher of fruit punch in an old-fashioned cut-glass pitcher and a plate of macaroons. The plate has a gold border and poppies painted on it.*

AMANDA: Well, well, well! Isn't the air delightful after the shower? I've made you children a little liquid refreshment. *(turns gaily to the gentleman caller)* Jim, do you know that song about lemonade?

"Lemonade, lemonade
Made in the shade and stirred with a spade—
Good enough for any old maid!"

JIM *(uneasily)*: Ha-ha! No—I never heard it.
AMANDA: Why, Laura! You look so serious!
JIM: We were having a serious conversation.
AMANDA: Good! Now you're better acquainted!
JIM *(uncertainly)*: Ha-ha! Yes.
AMANDA: You modern young people are much more serious-minded than my generation. I was so gay as a girl!
JIM: You haven't changed, Mrs. Wingfield.
AMANDA: Tonight I'm rejuvenated! The gaiety of the occasion, Mr. O'Connor! *(She tosses her head with a peal of laughter. Spills lemonade.)* Oooo! I'm baptizing myself!
JIM: Here—let me—.
AMANDA *(setting the pitcher down)*: There now. I discovered we had some maraschino cherries. I dumped them in, juice and all!
JIM: You shouldn't have gone to that trouble, Mrs. Wingfield.
AMANDA: Trouble, trouble? Why it was loads of fun! Didn't you hear me cutting up in the kitchen? I bet your ears were burning! I told Tom how outdone with him I was for keeping you to himself so long a time! He should have brought you over much, much sooner! Well, now that you've found your way, I want you to be a very frequent caller! Not just occasional but all the time. Oh, we're going to have a lot of gay times together! I see them coming! Mmm, just breathe that air! So fresh, and the moon's so pretty! I'll skip back out—I know where my place is when young folks are having a—serious conversation!

JIM: Oh, don't go out, Mrs. Wingfield. The fact of the matter is I've got to be going.

AMANDA: Going now? You're joking! Why, it's only the shank of the evening, Mr. O'Connor!

JIM: Well, you know how it is.

AMANDA: You mean you're a young workingman and have to keep working-men's hours. We'll let you off early tonight. But only on the condition that next time you stay later. What's the best night for you? Isn't Saturday the best night for you workingmen?

JIM: I have a couple of time-clocks to punch, Mrs. Wingfield. One at morning, another at night!

AMANDA: My, but you *are* ambitious! You work at night, too?

JIM: No, Ma'am, not work but — Betty! *(He crosses deliberately to pick up his hat. The band at the Paradise Dance Hall goes into a tender waltz.)*

AMANDA: Betty? Betty? Who's — Betty! *(There is an ominous cracking sound in the sky.)*

JIM: Oh, just a girl. The girl I go steady with! *(He smiles charmingly. The sky falls.)*

(Legend: "The Sky Falls.")

AMANDA *(a long-drawn exhalation)*: Ohhhh . . . Is it a serious romance, Mr. O'Connor?

JIM: We're going to be married the second Sunday in June.

AMANDA: Ohhhh — how nice! Tom didn't mention that you were engaged to be married.

JIM: The cat's not out of the bag at the warehouse yet. You know how they are. They call you Romeo and stuff like that. *(He stops at the oval mirror to put on his hat. He carefully shapes the brim and the crown to give a discreetly dashing effect.)* It's been a wonderful evening, Mrs. Wingfield. I guess this is what they mean by Southern hospitality.

AMANDA: It really wasn't anything at all.

JIM: I hope it don't seem like I'm rushing off. But I promised Betty I'd pick her up at the Wabash depot, an' by the time I get my jalopy down there her train'll be in. Some women are pretty upset if you keep 'em waiting.

AMANDA: Yes, I know — The tyranny of women! *(extends her hand)* Good-bye, Mr. O'Connor. I wish you luck — and happiness — and success! All three of them, and so does Laura! — Don't you, Laura?

LAURA: Yes!

JIM *(taking her hand)*: Goodbye, Laura. I'm certainly going to treasure that souvenir. And don't you forget the good advice I gave you. *(raises his voice to a cheery shout)* So long, Shakespeare! Thanks again, ladies — Good night!

He grins and ducks jauntily out.

Still bravely grimacing, AMANDA *closes the door on the gentleman caller. Then she turns back to the room with a puzzled expression. She and* LAURA *don't dare to face each other.* LAURA *crouches beside the victrola to wind it.*

AMANDA *(faintly)*: Things have a way of turning out so badly. I don't believe that I would play the victrola. Well, well—well—Our gentleman caller was engaged to be married! Tom!

TOM *(from back)*: Yes, Mother?

AMANDA: Come in here a minute. I want to tell you something awfully funny.

TOM *(enters with macaroon and a glass of lemonade)*: Has the gentleman caller gotten away already?

AMANDA: The gentleman caller has made an early departure. What a wonderful joke you played on us!

TOM: How do you mean?

AMANDA: You didn't mention that he was engaged to be married.

TOM: Jim? Engaged?

AMANDA: That's what he just informed us.

TOM: I'll be jiggered! I didn't know about that.

AMANDA: That seems very peculiar.

TOM: What's peculiar about it?

AMANDA: Didn't you call him your best friend down at the warehouse?

TOM: He is, but how did I know?

AMANDA: It seems extremely peculiar that you wouldn't know your best friend was going to be married!

TOM: The warehouse is where I work, not where I know things about people!

AMANDA: You don't know things anywhere! You live in a dream; you manufacture illusions! *(He crosses to door.)* Where are you going?

TOM: I'm going to the movies.

AMANDA: That's right, now that you've had us make such fools of ourselves. The effort, the preparations, all the expense! The new floor lamp, the rug, the clothes for Laura! All for what? To entertain some other girl's fiancé! Go to the movies, go! Don't think about us, a mother deserted, an unmarried sister who's crippled and has no job! Don't let anything interfere with your selfish pleasure! Just go, go, go—to the movies!

TOM: All right, I will! The more you shout about my selfishness to me the quicker I'll go, and I won't go to the movies!

AMANDA: Go, then! Then go to the moon—you selfish dreamer!

TOM *smashes his glass on the floor. He plunges out on the fire-escape, slamming the door.* LAURA *screams—cut by door.*

Dance-hall music up. TOM *goes to the rail and grips it desperately, lifting his face in the chill white moonlight penetrating the narrow abyss of the alley.*

(Legend on Screen: "And So Good-bye . . .")

T O M*'s closing speech is timed with the interior pantomime. The interior scene is played as though viewed through sound-proof glass.* A M A N D A *appears to be making a comforting speech to* L A U R A *who is huddled upon the sofa. Now that we cannot hear the mother's speech, her silliness is gone and she has dignity and tragic beauty.* L A U R A*'s dark hair hides her face until at the end of the speech she lifts it to smile at her mother.* A M A N D A*'s gestures are slow and graceful, almost dancelike, as she comforts the daughter. At the end of her speech she glances a moment at the father's picture — then withdraws through the portieres. At close of* T O M*'s speech,* L A U R A *blows out the candles, ending the play.*

T O M: I didn't go to the moon, I went much further — for time is the longest distance between two places — Not long after that I was fired for writing a poem on the lid of a shoe-box. I left Saint Louis. I descended the steps of this fire-escape for a last time and followed, from then on, in my father's footsteps, attempting to find in motion what was lost in space — I traveled around a great deal. The cities swept about me like dead leaves, leaves that were brightly colored but torn away from the branches. I would have stopped, but was pursued by something. It always came upon me unawares, taking me altogether by surprise. Perhaps is was a familiar bit of music. Perhaps it was only a piece of transparent glass. Perhaps I am walking along a street at night, in some strange city, before I have found companions. I pass the lighted window of a shop where perfume is sold. The window is filled with pieces of colored glass, tiny transparent bottles in delicate colors, like bits of a shattered rainbow. Then all at once my sister touches my shoulder. I turn around and look into her eyes . . . Oh, Laura, Laura, I tried to leave you behind me, but I am more faithful than I intended to be! I reach for a cigarette, I cross the street, I run into the movies or a bar, I buy a drink, I speak to the nearest stranger — anything that can blow your candles out! *(*L A U R A *bends over the candles.)* — for nowadays the world is lit by lightning! Blow out your candles, Laura — and so goodbye . . .

She blows the candles out.

(The Scene Dissolves.)

Considerations

1. Write a brief summary (no more than one paragraph) of the action in each of the play's seven scenes. Then explain what significant conflicts you see as being introduced, developed, or resolved in each of these scenes.

2. Tom, one of the play's main characters, also serves as the narrator. How would the play be changed if there were no narrator — or if one of the other characters served as narrator?

3. In what ways are dreams and fantasies important to Jim, to Amanda, and to Laura?

4. Evaluate the relationship between Jim and Amanda and between Laura and Amanda. What are the significant differences and similarities in these relationships?

5. Although Mr. Wingfield never appears on stage, his portrait dominates the action in several scenes. What do we know about Mr. Wingfield? How do we learn these things? Evaluate the effect Mr. Wingfield's absence has apparently had on his wife, son, and daughter.

LANGSTON HUGHES (1902–1967)

Salvation

I was saved from sin when I was going on thirteen. But not really saved. It happened like this. There was a big revival at my Auntie Reed's church. Every night for weeks there had been much preaching, singing, praying, and shouting, and some very hardened sinners had been brought to Christ, and the membership of the church had grown by leaps and bounds. Then just before the revival ended, they held a special meeting for children, "to bring the young lambs to the fold." My aunt spoke of it for days ahead. That night I was escorted to the front row and placed on the mourners' bench with all the other young sinners, who had not yet been brought to Jesus.

My aunt told me that when you were saved you saw a light, and something happened to you inside! And Jesus came into your life! And God was with you from then on! She said you could see and hear and feel Jesus in your soul. I believed her. I had heard a great many old people say the same thing and it seemed to me they ought to know. So I sat there calmly in the hot, crowded church, waiting for Jesus to come to me.

The preacher preached a wonderful rhythmical sermon, all moans and shouts and lonely cries and dire pictures of hell, and then he sang a song about the ninety and nine safe in the fold, but one little lamb was left out in the cold. Then he said: "Won't you come? Won't you come to Jesus? Young lambs, won't you come?" And he held out his arms to all us young sinners there on the mourners' bench. And the little girls cried. And some of them jumped up and went to Jesus right away. But most of us just sat there.

A great many old people came and knelt around us and prayed, old women with jet-black faces and braided hair, old men with work-gnarled hands. And the church sang a song about the lower lights are burning, some poor sinners to be saved. And the whole building rocked with prayer and song.

Still I kept waiting to *see* Jesus.

Finally all the young people had gone to the altar and were saved, but one boy and me. He was a rounder's son named Westley. Westley and I were surrounded by sisters and deacons praying. It was very hot in the church, and getting late now. Finally Westley said to me in a whisper: "God damn! I'm tired o' sitting here. Let's get up and be saved." So he got up and was saved.

Then I was left all alone on the mourners' bench. My aunt came and knelt at my knees and cried, while prayers and song swirled all around me in the little church. The whole congregation prayed for me alone, in a mighty wail of moans and voices. And I kept waiting serenely for Jesus, waiting, waiting — but he didn't come. I wanted to see him, but nothing

5

happened to me. Nothing! I wanted something to happen to me, but nothing happened.

I heard the songs and the minister saying: "Why don't you come? My dear child, why don't you come to Jesus? Jesus is waiting for you. He wants you. Why don't you come? Sister Reed, what is this child's name?"

"Langston," my aunt sobbed.

"Langston, why don't you come? Why don't you come and be saved? 10 Oh, Lamb of God! Why don't you come?"

Now it was really getting late. I began to be ashamed of myself, holding everything up so long. I began to wonder what God thought about Westley, who certainly hadn't seen Jesus either, but who was now sitting proudly on the platform, swinging his knickerbockered legs and grinning down at me, surrounded by deacons and old women on their knees praying. God had not struck Westley dead for taking his name in vain or for lying in the temple. So I decided that maybe to save further trouble, I'd better lie, too, and say that Jesus had come, and get up and be saved.

So I got up.

Suddenly the whole room broke into a sea of shouting, as they saw me rise. Waves of rejoicing swept the place. Women leaped in the air. My aunt threw her arms around me. The minister took me by the hand and led me to the platform.

When things quieted down, in a hushed silence, punctuated by a few ecstatic "Amens," all the new young lambs were blessed in the name of God. Then joyous singing filled the room.

That night, for the last time in my life but one — for I was a big boy 15 twelve years old — I cried. I cried, in bed alone, and couldn't stop. I buried my head under the quilts, but my aunt heard me. She woke up and told my uncle I was crying because the Holy Ghost had come into my life, and because I had seen Jesus. But I was really crying because I couldn't bear to tell her that I had lied, that I had deceived everybody in the church, that I hadn't seen Jesus, and that now I didn't believe there was a Jesus any more, since he didn't come to help me.

Considerations

1. Compare the narrator to Westley. Keep in mind the narrator's hopes, fears, and expectations and, using evidence provided by the words and actions of the two boys, speculate on how they might contrast with Westley's.
2. What is your definition of "salvation"? How many possible meanings of "salvation" are stated or implied in Hughes's memoir?
3. Evaluate Auntie Reed's motives and expectations. What does she want for the narrator? What does she want for herself?
4. Why does the narrator cry? Consider the reasons he states and speculate on other reasons (and on the implications of those reasons).

5. This essay describes a moment when a young man comes to doubt a strongly held belief. Notice that he recalls in detail the sights, sounds, and feelings of that moment. Think about a strongly held belief that you have come to question and describe an incident that led you to doubt that belief. Use Hughes's essay as an example; recreate for your readers the sights, sounds, and feelings of the moment you describe.

MAYA ANGELOU (1928–   )

Graduation in Stamps

The children in Stamps trembled visibly with anticipation. Some adults were excited too, but to be certain the whole young population had come down with graduation epidemic. Large classes were graduating from both the grammar school and the high school. Even those who were years removed from their own day of glorious release were anxious to help with preparations as a kind of dry run. The junior students who were moving into the vacating classes' chairs were tradition-bound to show their talents for leadership and management. They strutted through the school and around the campus exerting pressure on the lower grades. Their authority was so new that occasionally if they pressed a little too hard it had to be overlooked. After all, next term was coming, and it never hurt a sixth grader to have a play sister in the eighth grade, or a tenth-year student to be able to call a twelfth grader Bubba. So all was endured in a spirit of shared understanding. But the graduating classes themselves were the nobility. Like travelers with exotic destinations on their minds, the graduates were remarkably forgetful. They came to school without their books, or tablets or even pencils. Volunteers fell over themselves to secure replacements for the missing equipment. When accepted, the willing workers might or might not be thanked, and it was of no importance to the pre-graduation rites. Even teachers were respectful of the now quiet and aging seniors, and tended to speak to them, if not as equals, as beings only slightly lower than themselves. After tests were returned and grades given, the student body, which acted like an extended family, knew who did well, who excelled, and what piteous ones had failed.

Unlike the white high school, Lafayette County Training School distinguished itself by having neither lawn, nor hedges, nor tennis court, nor climbing ivy. Its two buildings (main classrooms, the grade school and home economics) were set on a dirt hill with no fence to limit either its boundaries or those of bordering farms. There was a large expanse to the left of the school which was used alternately as a baseball diamond or a basketball court. Rusty hoops on the swaying poles represented the permanent recreational equipment, although bats and balls could be borrowed from the P.E. teacher if the borrower was qualified and if the diamond wasn't occupied.

Over this rocky area relieved by a few shady tall persimmon trees the graduating class walked. The girls often held hands and no longer bothered to speak to the lower students. There was a sadness about them, as if this old world was not their home and they were bound for higher ground. The boys, on the other hand, had become more friendly, more outgoing. A decided change from the closed attitude they projected while studying for finals. Now they seemed not ready to give up the old school, the familiar paths and classrooms. Only a small percentage would be continuing on to college — one of the South's A & M (agricultural and mechanical) schools, which trained Negro youths to be carpenters, farmers, handymen, masons, maids, cooks and baby nurses. Their future rode heavily on their shoulders, and blinded them to the collective joy that had pervaded the lives of the boys and girls in the grammar school graduating class.

Parents who could afford it had ordered new shoes and ready-made clothes for themselves from Sears and Roebuck or Montgomery Ward. They also engaged the best seamstresses to make the floating graduating dresses and to cut down secondhand pants which would be pressed to a military slickness for the important event.

Oh, it was important, all right. Whitefolks would attend the cere-   5
mony, and two or three would speak of God and home, and the Southern way of life, and Mrs. Parsons, the principal's wife, would play the graduation march while the lower-grade graduates paraded down the aisles and took their seats below the platform. The high school seniors would wait in empty classrooms to make their dramatic entrance.

In the Store I was the person of the moment. The birthday girl. The center. Bailey had graduated the year before, although to do so he had had to forfeit all pleasures to make up for his time lost in Baton Rouge.

My class was wearing butter-yellow piqué dresses, and Momma launched out on mine. She smocked the yoke into tiny crisscrossing puckers, then shirred the rest of the bodice. Her dark fingers ducked in and out of the lemony cloth as she embroidered raised daisies around the hem. Before she considered herself finished she had added a crocheted cuff on the puff sleeves, and a pointy crocheted collar.

I was going to be lovely. A walking model of all the various styles of fine hand sewing and it didn't worry me that I was only twelve years old and merely graduating from the eighth grade. Besides, many teachers in Arkansas Negro schools had only that diploma and were licensed to impart wisdom.

The days had become longer and more noticeable. The faded beige of former times had been replaced with strong and sure colors. I began to see my classmates' clothes, their skin tones, and the dust that waved off pussy willows. Clouds that lazed across the sky were objects of great concern to me. Their shiftier shapes might have held a message that in my new happiness and with a little bit of time I'd soon decipher. During that period I looked at the arch of heaven so religiously my neck kept a steady ache. I had taken to smiling more often, and my jaws hurt from the unaccustomed activity. Between the two physical sore spots, I suppose I could have been uncomfortable, but that was not the case. As a member of the winning team (the graduating class of 1940) I had outdistanced unpleasant sensations by miles. I was headed for the freedom of open fields.

Youth and social approval allied themselves with me and we tram-   10
meled memories of slights and insults. The wind of our swift passage re-

modeled my features. Lost tears were pounded to mud and then to dust. Years of withdrawal were brushed aside and left behind, as hanging ropes of parasitic moss.

My work alone had awarded me a top place and I was going to be one of the first called in the graduating ceremonies. On the classroom blackboard, as well as on the bulletin board in the auditorium, there were blue stars and white stars and red stars. No absences, no tardinesses, and my academic work was among the best of the year. I could say the pre-amble to the Constitution even faster than Bailey. We timed ourselves often: "WethepeopleoftheUnitedStatesinordertoformamoreperfectunion . . ." I had memorized the Presidents of the United States from Washington to Roosevelt in chronological as well as alphabetical order.

My hair pleased me too. Gradually the black mass had lengthened and thickened, so that it kept at last to its braided pattern, and I didn't have to yank my scalp off when I tried to comb it.

Louise and I had rehearsed the exercises until we tired out ourselves. Henry Reed was class valedictorian. He was a small, very black boy with hooded eyes, a long, broad nose and an oddly shaped head. I had admired him for years because each term he and I vied for the best grades in our class. Most often he bested me, but instead of being disappointed, I was pleased that we shared top places between us. Like many Southern black children, he lived with his grandmother, who was as strict as Momma and as kind as she knew how to be. He was courteous, respectful and soft-spoken to elders, but on the playground he chose to play the roughest games. I admired him. Anyone, I reckoned, sufficiently afraid or sufficiently dull could be polite. But to be able to operate at a top level with both adults and children was admirable.

His valedictory speech was entitled "To Be or Not to Be." The rigid tenth-grade teacher had helped him write it. He'd been working on the dramatic stresses for months.

The weeks until graduation were filled with heady activities. A group of small children were to be presented in a play about buttercups and daisies and bunny rabbits. They could be heard throughout the building practicing their hops and their little songs that sounded like silver bells. The older girls (non-graduates, of course) were assigned the task of making refreshments for the night's festivities. A tangy scent of ginger, cinnamon, nutmeg and chocolate wafted around the home economics building as the budding cooks made samples for themselves and their teachers.

In every corner of the workshop, axes and saws split fresh timber as the woodshop boys made sets and stage scenery. Only the graduates were left out of the general bustle. We were free to sit in the library at the back of the building or look in quite detachedly, naturally, on the measures being taken for our event.

Even the minister preached on graduation the Sunday before. His sub-ject was, "Let your light so shine that men will see your good works and praise your Father, Who is in Heaven." Although the sermon was purported to be addressed to us, he used the occasion to speak to backsliders, gamblers and general ne'er-do-wells. But since he had called our names at the beginning of the service we were mollified.

Among Negros the tradition was to give presents to children going only from one grade to another. How much more important this was when the person was graduating at the top of the class. Uncle Willie and Momma had sent away for a Mickey Mouse watch like Bailey's. Louise gave me four embroidered handkerchiefs. (I gave her three crocheted doilies.) Mrs. Sneed, the minister's wife, made me an underskirt to wear for graduation, and nearly every customer gave me a nickel or maybe even a dime with the instruction "Keep on moving to higher ground," or some such encouragement.

Amazingly the great day finally dawned and I was out of bed before I knew it. I threw open the back door to see it more clearly, but Momma said, "Sister, come away from that door and put your robe on."

I hoped the memory of that morning would never leave me. Sunlight was itself still young, and the day had none of the insistence maturity would bring it in a few hours. In my robe and barefoot in the backyard, under cover of going to see about my new beans, I gave myself up to the gentle warmth and thanked God that no matter what evil I had done in my life He had allowed me to live to see this day. Somewhere in my fatalism I had expected to die, accidentally, and never have the chance to walk up the stairs in the auditorium and gracefully receive my hard-earned diploma. Out of God's merciful bosom I had won reprieve. 20

Bailey came out in his robe and gave me a box wrapped in Christmas paper. He said he had saved his money for months to pay for it. It felt like a box of chocolates, but I knew Bailey wouldn't save money to buy candy when we had all we could want under our noses.

He was as proud of the gifts as I. It was a soft-leather-bound copy of a collection of poems by Edgar Allan Poe,° or, as Bailey and I called him, "Eap." I turned to "Annabel Lee" and we walked up and down the garden rows, the cool dirt between our toes, reciting the beautifully sad lines.

Momma made a Sunday breakfast although it was only Friday. After we finished the blessing, I opened my eyes to find the watch on my plate. It was a dream of a day. Everything went smoothly and to my credit. I didn't have to be reminded or scolded for anything. Near evening I was too jittery to attend to chores, so Bailey volunteered to do all before his bath.

Days before, we had made a sign for the Store, and as we turned out the lights Momma hung the cardboard over the doorknob. It read clearly: CLOSED: GRADUATION.

Edgar Allan Poe: (1809–1849) American editor, critic, poet and short-story writer. A brilliant, haunted man, Poe created poems and stories that combined the beautiful with the grotesque, the real with the fantastic.

My dress fitted perfectly and everyone said that I looked like a sun- 25
beam in it. On the hill, going toward the school, Bailey walked behind with
Uncle Willie, who muttered, "Go on, Ju." He wanted him to walk ahead
with us because it embarrassed him to have to walk so slowly. Bailey said
he'd let the ladies walk together, and the men would bring up the rear. We
all laughed, nicely.

Little children dashed by out of the dark like fireflies. Their crepe paper
dresses and butterfly wings were not made for running and we heard more
than one rip, dryly, and the regretful "uh uh" that followed.

The school blazed without gaiety. The windows seemed cold and unfriendly from the lower hill. A sense of ill-fated timing crept over me, and
if Momma hadn't reached for my hand I would have drifted back to Bailey
and Uncle Willie, and possibly beyond. She made a few slow jokes about
my feet getting cold, and tugged me along to the now-strange building.

Around the front steps, assurance came back. There were my fellow
"greats," the graduating class. Hair brushed back, legs oiled, new dresses
and pressed pleats, fresh pocket handkerchiefs and little handbags, all home-
sewn. Oh, we were up to snuff, all right. I joined my comrades and didn't
even see my family go in to find seats in the crowded auditorium.

The school band struck up a march and all classes filed in as had been
rehearsed. We stood in front of our seats, as assigned, and on a signal from
the choir director, we sat. No sooner had this been accomplished than the
band started to play the national anthem. We rose again and sang the song,
after which we recited the pledge of allegiance. We remained standing for a
brief minute before the choir director and the principal signaled to us, rather
desperately I thought, to take our seats. The command was so unusual that
our carefully rehearsed and smooth-running machine was thrown off. For a
full minute we fumbled for our chairs and bumped into each other awkwardly. Habits change or solidify under pressure, so in our state of nervous
tension we had been ready to follow our usual assembly pattern: the American national anthem, then the pledge of allegiance, then the song every
Black person I knew called the Negro National Anthem. All done in the
same key, with the same passion and most often standing on the same foot.

Finding my seat at last, I was overcome with a presentiment of worse 30
things to come. Something unrehearsed, unplanned, was going to happen,
and we were going to be made to look bad. I distinctly remember being
explicit in the choice of pronoun. It was "we," the graduating class, the unit,
that concerned me then.

The principal welcomed "parents and friends" and asked the Baptist
minister to lead us in prayer. His invocation was brief and punchy, and for a
second I thought we were getting back on the high road to right action.
When the principal came back to the dais, however, his voice had changed.
Sounds always affected me profoundly and the principal's voice was one of
my favorites. During assembly it melted and lowed weakly into the audi-

ence. It had not been in my plan to listen to him, but my curiosity was piqued and I straightened up to give him my attention.

He was talking about Booker T. Washington,° our "late great leader," who said we can be as close as the fingers on the hand, etc. . . . Then he said a few vague things about friendship and the friendship of kindly people to those less fortunate than themselves. With that his voice nearly faded, thin, away. Like a river diminishing to a stream and then to a trickle. But he cleared his throat and said, "Our speaker tonight, who is also our friend, came from Texarkana to deliver the commencement address, but due to the irregularity of the train schedule, he's going to, as they say, 'speak and run.'" He said that we understood and wanted the man to know that we were most grateful for the time he was able to give us and then something about how we were willing always to adjust to another's program; and without more ado — "I give you Mr. Edward Donleavy."

Not one but two white men came through the door offstage. The shorter one walked to the speaker's platform, and the tall one moved over to the center seat and sat down. But that was our principal's seat, and already occupied. The dislodged gentleman bounced around for a long breath or two before the Baptist minister gave him his chair, then with more dignity than the situation deserved, the minister walked off the stage.

Donleavy looked at the audience once (on reflection, I'm sure that he wanted only to reassure himself that we were really there), adjusted his glasses and began to read from a sheaf of papers.

He was glad "to be here and to see the work going on just as it was in the other schools." 35

At the first "Amen" from the audience I willed the offender to immediate death by choking on the word. But Amens and Yes, sir's began to fall around the room like rain through a ragged umbrella.

He told us of the wonderful changes we children in Stamps had in store. The Central School (naturally, the white school was Central) had already been granted improvements that would be in use in the fall. A well-known artist was coming from Little Rock to teach art to them. They were going to have the newest microscopes and chemistry equipment for their laboratory. Mr. Donleavy didn't leave us long in the dark over who made these improvements available to Central High. Nor were we to be ignored in the general betterment scheme he had in mind.

He said that he had pointed out to people at a very high level that one of the first-line football tacklers at Arkansas Agricultural and Mechanical College had graduated from good old Lafayette County Training School.

Booker T. Washington: (1856–1915) Black American educator who founded Tuskegee Institute, a post-high school institution of learning for black students who were not, at that time, admitted to most colleges and universities. He was criticized by many black leaders because he argued that social equality could not be attained — and should not be a goal for black people — until they had, on their own, attained economic independence.

Here fewer Amen's were heard. Those few that did break through lay dully in the air with the heaviness of habit.

He went on to praise us. He went on to say how he had bragged that "one of the best basketball players at Fisk sank his first ball right here at Lafayette County Training School."

The white kids were going to have a chance to become Galileos° and Madame Curies° and Edisons° and Gauguins,° and our boys (the girls weren't even in on it) would try to be Jesse Owenses° and Joe Louises.° 4(

Owens and the Brown Bomber were great heroes in our world, but what school official in the white-goddom of Little Rock had the right to decide that those two men must be our only heroes? Who decided that for Henry Reed to become a scientist he had to work like George Washington Carver,° as a bootblack, to buy a lousy microscope? Bailey was obviously always going to be too small to be an athlete, so which concrete angel glued to what county seat had decided that if my brother wanted to become a lawyer he had to first pay penance for his skin by picking cotton and hoeing corn and studying correspondence books at night for twenty years?

The man's dead words fell like bricks around the auditorium and too many settled in my belly. Constrained by hard-learned manners I couldn't look behind me, but to my left and right the proud graduating class of 1940 had dropped their heads. Every girl in my row had found something new to do with her handkerchief. Some folded the tiny squares into love knots, some into triangles, but most were wadding them, then pressing them flat on their yellow laps.

On the dais, the ancient tragedy was being replayed. Professor Parsons sat, a sculptor's reject, rigid. His large, heavy body seemed devoid of will or willingness, and his eyes said he was no longer with us. The other teachers examined the flag (which was draped stage right) or their notes, or the windows which opened on our now-famous playing diamond.

Galileo: (1564–1642) Italian astronomer and physicist. He discovered many physical laws, constructed the first telescope, and confirmed the theory that the earth moves around the sun. *Madame Curie:* (1867–1934) Polish-born French physicist. She won the Nobel Prize in 1911 for the discovery of metallic radium. *Thomas Alva Edison:* (1847–1931) One of the most productive American inventors. Among his significant inventions were the record player, the motion picture, the incandescent lamp, and a system for the distribution of electricity. *Paul Gauguin:* (1848–1903) French painter, associated with the impressionists, noted especially for rejecting traditional naturalism and, instead, using nature as an inspiration for abstract symbols and figures. *Jesse Owens:* (1913–1981) Black American track star who won four gold medals at the 1936 Olympics, which were held in Berlin. Owens made a mockery of Hitler's contention that "Aryan" athletes were superior to all others. *Joe Lewis:* (b. 1914) Black American boxer. Holder of the heavyweight title, Lewis was known as the Brown Bomber. *George Washington Carver:* (1864–1943) Black American agricultural chemist. Born a slave, he later taught at Tuskegee Institute, where he carried out research that led to crop diversification in the South. He is particularly credited with discovering new uses for crops such as peanuts and soybeans.

Graduation, the hush-hush magic time of frills and gifts and congratulations and diplomas, was finished for me before my name was called. The accomplishment was nothing. The meticulous maps, drawn in three colors of ink, learning and spelling decasyllabic words, memorizing the whole of *The Rape of Lucrece*° — it was for nothing. Donleavy had exposed us.

We were maids and farmers, handymen and washerwomen, and anything higher that we aspired to was farcical and presumptuous.   45

Then I wished that Gabriel Prosser° and Nat Turner° had killed all whitefolks in their beds and that Abraham Lincoln had been assassinated before the signing of the Emancipation Proclamation, and that Harriet Tubman° had been killed by that blow on her head and Christopher Columbus had drowned in the *Santa Maria*.

It was awful to be Negro and have no control over my life. It was brutal to be young and already trained to sit quietly and listen to charges brought against my color with no chance of defense. We should all be dead. I thought I should like to see us all dead, one on top of the other. A pyramid of flesh with the whitefolks on the bottom, as the broad base, then the Indians with their silly tomahawks and tepees and wigwams and treaties, the Negroes with their mops and recipes and cotton sacks and spirituals sticking out of their mouths. The Dutch children should all stumble in their wooden shoes and break their necks. The French should choke to death on the Louisiana Purchase (1803) while silkworms ate all the Chinese with their stupid pigtails. As a species, we were an abomination. All of us.

Donleavy was running for election, and assured our parents that if he won we could count on having the only colored paved playing field in that part of Arkansas. Also — he never looked up to acknowledge the grunts of acceptance — also, we were bound to get some new equipment for the home economics building and the workshop.

He finished, and since there was no need to give any more than the most perfunctory thank-you's, he nodded to the men on the stage, and the tall white man who was never introduced joined him at the door. They left with the attitude that now they were off to something really important. (The graduation ceremonies at Lafayette County Training School had been a mere preliminary.)

The ugliness they left was palpable. An uninvited guest who wouldn't   50
leave. The choir was summoned and sang a modern arrangement of "On-

---

The Rape of Lucrece: A narrative poem, 1855 lines long, written by William Shakespeare. *Gabriel Prosser, Nat Turner:* Leaders of slave rebellions. In 1800, Prosser recruited several hundred slaves to attack Richmond. Before they could attack, they were betrayed, and the leaders of the rebellion were captured and executed. In 1831, Turner led a group of slaves who eventually killed 57 white men, women, and children as a protest against slavery. *Harriet Tubman* (1820–1913): A black American abolitionist who escaped from slavery in 1849 and worked with the underground railroad, leading more than 300 slaves north to freedom.

ward, Christian Soldiers," with new words pertaining to graduates seeking their place in the world. But it didn't work. Elouise, the daughter of the Baptist minister, recited "Invictus," and I could have cried at the impertinence of "I am the master of my fate, I am the captain of my soul."

My name had lost its ring of familiarity and I had to be nudged to go and receive my diploma. All my preparations had fled. I neither marched up to the stage like a conquering Amazon, nor did I look in the audience for Bailey's nod of approval. Marguerite Johnson, I heard the name again, my honors were read, there were noises in the audience of appreciation, and I took my place on the stage as rehearsed.

I thought about colors I hated: ecru, puce, lavender, beige and black.

There was shuffling and rustling around me, then Henry Reed was giving his valedictory address, "To Be or Not to Be." Hadn't he heard the whitefolks? We couldn't *be,* so the question was a waste of time. Henry's voice came clear and strong. I feared to look at him. Hadn't he got the message? There was no "nobler in the mind" for Negroes because the world didn't think we had minds, and they let us know it. "Outrageous fortune"? Now, that was a joke. When the ceremony was over I had to tell Henry Reed some things. That is, if I still cared. Not "rub," Henry, "erase." "Ah, there's the erase." Us.

Henry had been a good student in elocution. His voice rose on tides of promise and fell on waves of warnings. The English teacher had helped him to create a sermon winging through Hamlet's soliloquy. To be a man, a doer, a builder, a leader, or to be a tool, an unfunny joke, a crusher of funky toadstools. I marveled that Henry could go through the speech as if we had a choice.

I had been listening and silently rebutting each sentence with my eyes 55 closed; then there was a hush, which in an audience warns that something unplanned is happening. I looked up and saw Henry Reed, the conservative, the proper, the A student, turn his back to the audience and turn to us (the proud graduating class of 1940) and sing, nearly speaking,

> Lift ev'ry voice and sing
> Till earth and heaven ring
> Ring with the harmonies of Liberty . . .*

It was the poem written by James Weldon Johnson. It was the music composed by J. Rosamond Johnson. It was the Negro national anthem. Out of habit we were singing it.

Our mothers and fathers stood in the dark hall and joined the hymn of encouragement. A kindergarten teacher led the small children onto the stage

---

*"Lift Ev'ry Voice and Sing"—words by James Weldon Johnson and music by J. Rosamond Johnson. Copyright by Edward B. Marks Music Corporation. Used by permission.

and the buttercups and daisies and bunny rabbits marked time and tried to follow:

> Stony the road we trod
> Bitter the chastening rod
> Felt in the days when hope, unborn, had died.
> Yet with a steady beat
> Have not our weary feet
> Come to the place for which our fathers sighed?

Every child I knew had learned that song with his ABC's and along with "Jesus Loves Me This I Know." But I personally had never heard it before. Never heard the words, despite the thousands of times I had sung them. Never thought they had anything to do with me.

On the other hand, the words of Patrick Henry° had made such an impression on me that I had been able to stretch myself tall and trembling and say, "I know not what course others may take, but as for me, give me liberty or give me death."

And now I heard, really for the first time:

> We have come over a way that with tears has been watered,
> We have come, treading our path through the blood of the slaugh-
> tered.

While echoes of the song shivered in the air, Henry Reed bowed his   60
head, said "Thank you," and returned to his place in the line. The tears that slipped down many faces were not wiped away in shame.

We were on top again. As always, again. We survived. The depths had been icy and dark, but now a bright sun spoke to our souls. I was no longer simply a member of the proud graduating class of 1940; I was a proud member of the wonderful beautiful Negro race.

Considerations

1. Although the word "graduation" appears in the title, the first half of the work focuses on preparation for the event. What effect does Maya Angelou (pen name of Marguerite Johnson) create by describing in such detail the community's involvement in and anticipation of the ceremony? What—if anything—would be lost if the first half of the essay were abbreviated or omitted?

2. Describe the attitude of the white officials who attend the graduation. Provide details from the essay to explain your analysis of their actions, words, and responses.

Patrick Henry: (1726–1799) A leader of the American Revolution who was admired for his skills as a public speaker. The rallying cry, "Give me liberty or give me death," is attributed to him.

3. Henry Reed's speech is titled, "To Be or Not To Be." Using a dictionary of quotations, identify the allusion made by the title as well as by Angelou's comments on the title. Speculate on the irony suggested by the title and by Reed's speech as contrasted to Mr. Donleavy's speech.

4. Describe Marguerite Johnson's response when she is called to receive her diploma. How does the reality compare with the way she had imagined the moment? How can you explain this change and its implications?

5. Maya Angelou describes an incident related to her formal education that taught her lessons different from those she learned from books. Think of your own school experiences and describe an incident — apart from regular subject-matter study — that taught you something you consider valuable. As you write your essay, consider the strategies Angelou uses. For instance, notice her description of setting, her arrangement of events in chronological order, and her direct quotation of conversations and speeches.

CONNECTIONS: INNOCENCE AND EXPERIENCE

1. "The Circling Hand" and "Salvation" show children or young adults who become disillusioned through the words and actions of adults they have loved and trusted. Compare and comment on the experiences depicted in these works.

2. "Araby," "By the Sea," "The Bass, the River, and Sheila Mant," and "When I was one-and-twenty," relate to early experiences with romantic love. Comment on the changes experienced by the main characters in the short stories and the speaker in the poem.

3. Discuss the role of conflicts between parents and children as part of the passage from innocence to experience. Consider at least three of these works: "Bad Characters," "The Circling Hand," *The Glass Menagerie,* "In the Counselor's Waiting Room," "The Centaur."

4. What are the differences — if any — in the ways males and females move from innocence to experience? Consider any of the following works as you think about this question.

Works Relating to Males	Works Relating to Females
"Araby"	"Bad Characters"
"The Bass, the River, and Sheila Mant"	"By the Sea"
The Glass Menagerie	"The Circling Hand"
"Salvation"	"In the Counselor's Waiting Room"
	"The Centaur"

5. Consider the effect of prejudice experienced by young people as they grow and mature. Include both "Incident" and "Graduation" as part of your consideration. Although both works focus on the prejudice of whites against blacks, you may include other forms of prejudice in your discussion.

Work

WILLIAM CARLOS WILLIAMS (1883–1963)

The Use of Force

They were new patients to me, all I had was the name, Olson. Please come down as soon as you can, my daughter is very sick.

When I arrived I was met by the mother, a big startled looking woman, very clean and apologetic who merely said, Is this the doctor? and let me in. In the back, she added. You must excuse us, doctor, we have her in the kitchen where it is warm. It is very damp here sometimes.

The child was fully dressed and sitting on her father's lap near the kitchen table. He tried to get up, but I motioned for him not to bother, took off my overcoat and started to look things over. I could see that they were all very nervous, eyeing me up and down distrustfully. As often, in such cases, they weren't telling me more than they had to, it was up to me to tell them; that's why they were spending three dollars on me.

The child was fairly eating me up with her cold, steady eyes, and no expression to her face whatever. She did not move and seemed, inwardly, quiet; an unusually attractive little thing, and as strong as a heifer in appearance. But her face was flushed, she was breathing rapidly, and I realized that she had a high fever. She had magnificent blonde hair, in profusion. One of those picture children often reproduced in advertising leaflets and the photogravure sections of the Sunday papers.

She's had a fever for three days, began the father, and we don't know what it comes from. My wife has given her things, you know, like people do, but it don't do no good. And there's been a lot of sickness around. So we tho't you'd better look her over and tell us what is the matter.

As doctors often do I took a trial shot at it as a point of departure. Has she had a sore throat?

Both parents answered me together, No . . . No, she says her throat don't hurt her.

Does your throat hurt you? added the mother to the child. But the little girl's expression didn't change, nor did she move her eyes from my face.

Have you looked?

I tried to, said the mother, but I couldn't see.

As it happens, we had been having a number of cases of diphtheria in the school to which this child went during that month and we were all, quite apparently, thinking of that, though no one had as yet spoken of the thing.

Well, I said, suppose we take a look at the throat first. I smiled in my best professional manner and asking for the child's first name I said, come on, Mathilda, open your mouth and let's take a look at your throat.

Nothing doing.

Aw, come on, I coaxed, just open your mouth wide and let me take a look. Look, I said opening both hands wide, I haven't anything in my hands. Just open up and let me see.

Such a nice man, put in the mother. Look how kind he is to you. Come on, do what he tells you to. He won't hurt you.   15

At that I ground my teeth in disgust. If only they wouldn't use the word "hurt" I might be able to get somewhere. But I did not allow myself to be hurried or disturbed, but speaking quietly and slowly I approached the child again.

As I moved my chair a little nearer, suddenly with one catlike movement both her hands clawed instinctively for my eyes and she almost reached them too. In fact she knocked my glasses flying and they fell, though unbroken, several feet away from me on the kitchen floor.

Both the mother and father almost turned themselves inside out in embarrassment and apology. You bad girl, said the mother, taking her and shaking her by one arm. Look what you've done. The nice man. . . .

For heaven's sake, I broke in. Don't call me a nice man to her. I'm here to look at her throat on the chance that she might have diphtheria and possibly die of it. But that's nothing to her. Look here, I said to the child, we're going to look at your throat. You're old enough to understand what I'm saying. Will you open it now by yourself or shall we have to open it for you?

Not a move. Even her expression hadn't changed. Her breaths however   20
were coming faster and faster. Then the battle began. I had to do it. I had to have a throat culture for her own protection. But first I told the parents that it was entirely up to them. I explained the danger but said that I would not insist on a throat examination so long as they would take the responsibility.

If you don't do what the doctor says you'll have to go to the hospital, the mother admonished her severely.

Oh yeah? I had to smile to myself. After all, I had already fallen in love with the savage brat, the parents were contemptible to me. In the ensuing struggle they grew more and more abject, crushed, exhausted while she surely rose to magnificent heights of insane fury of effort bred of her terror of me.

The father tried his best, and he was a big man but the fact that she was his daughter, his shame at her behavior and his dread of hurting her made him release her just at the critical moment several times when I had almost achieved success, till I wanted to kill him. But his dread also that she might have diphtheria made him tell me to go on, go on though he himself was almost fainting, while the mother moved back and forth behind us raising and lowering her hands in an agony of apprehension.

Put her in front of you on your lap, I ordered, and hold both her wrists.

But as soon as he did the child let out a scream. Don't, you're hurting   25
me. Let go of my hands. Let them go I tell you. Then she shrieked terrifyingly, hysterically. Stop it! Stop it! You're killing me!

Do you think she can stand it, doctor! said the mother.

You get out, said the husband to his wife. Do you want her to die of diphtheria?

Come on now, hold her, I said.

Then I grasped the child's head with my left hand and tried to get the wooden tongue depressor between her teeth. She fought, with clenched teeth, desperately! But now I also had grown furious—at a child. I tried to hold myself down but I couldn't. I know how to expose a throat for inspection. And I did my best. When finally I got the wooden spatula behind the last teeth and just the point of it into the mouth cavity, she opened up for an instant but before I could see anything she came down again and gripping the wooden blade between her molars she reduced it to splinters before I could get it out again.

Aren't you ashamed, the mother yelled at her. Aren't you ashamed to   30
act like that in front of the doctor?

Get me a smooth-handled spoon of some sort, I told the mother. We're going through with this. The child's mouth was already bleeding. Her tongue was cut and she was screaming in wild hysterical shrieks. Perhaps I should have desisted and come back in an hour or more. No doubt it would have been better. But I have seen at least two children lying dead in bed of neglect in such cases, and feeling that I must get a diagnosis now or never I went at it again. But the worst of it was that I too had got beyond reason. I could have torn the child apart in my own fury and enjoyed it. It was a pleasure to attack her. My face was burning with it.

The damned little brat must be protected against her own idiocy, one says to one's self at such times. Others must be protected against her. It is social necessity. And all these things are true. But a blind fury, a feeling of adult shame, bred of a longing for muscular release are the operatives. One goes on to the end.

In a final unreasoning assault I overpowered the child's neck and jaws. I forced the heavy silver spoon back of her teeth and down her throat till she gagged. And there it was—both tonsils covered with membrane. She had fought valiantly to keep me from knowing her secret. She had been hiding that sore throat for three days at least and lying to her parents in order to escape just such an outcome as this.

Now truly she was furious. She had been on the defensive before but now she attacked. Tried to get off her father's lap and fly at me while tears of defeat blinded her eyes.

Considerations

1. What is your initial response to the characters in this story? Do you sympathize primarily with the doctor? With Mathilda? With the parents? Do your sympathies change throughout the story? Explain.
2. What is the doctor's attitude toward his work? What is his attitude toward

his patient? Look closely at the words he uses to describe her. How does the tone of those words change as the story progresses?

3. List as many conflicts as you can find in "The Use of Force." Explain how these conflicts relate to each other and how they are resolved (or why they are left unresolved).

4. Argue for or against the following proposition: The doctor's use of force was necessary and justified.

5. Think about a conflict you have encountered at work. Using both dialogue and descriptive details, explain the situation and discuss your response to it.

JAMES THURBER (1894–1961)

The Catbird Seat

Mr. Martin bought the pack of Camels on Monday night in the most crowded cigar store on Broadway. It was theater time and seven or eight men were buying cigarettes. The clerk didn't even glance at Mr. Martin, who put the pack in his overcoat pocket and went out. If any of the staff at F & S had seen him buy the cigarettes, they would have been astonished, for it was generally known that Mr. Martin did not smoke, and never had. No one saw him.

It was just a week to the day since Mr. Martin had decided to rub out Mrs. Ulgine Barrows. The term "rub out" pleased him because it suggested nothing more than the correction of an error — in this case an error of Mr. Fitweiler. Mr. Martin had spent each night of the past week working out his plan and examining it. As he walked home now he went over it again. For the hundredth time he resented the element of imprecision, the margin of guesswork that entered into the business. The project as he had worked it out was casual and bold, the risks were considerable. Something might go wrong anywhere along the line. And therein lay the cunning of his scheme. No one would ever see in it the cautious, painstaking hand of Erwin Martin, head of the filing department at F & S, of whom Mr. Fitweiler had once said, "Man is fallible but Martin isn't." No one would see his hand, that is, unless it were caught in the act.

Sitting in his apartment, drinking a glass of milk, Mr. Martin reviewed his case against Mrs. Ulgine Barrows, as he had every night for seven nights. He began at the beginning. Her quacking voice and braying laugh had first profaned the halls of F & S on March 7, 1941 (Mr. Martin had a head for dates). Old Roberts, the personnel chief, had introduced her as the newly appointed special adviser to the president of the firm, Mr. Fitweiler. The woman had appalled Mr. Martin instantly, but he hadn't shown it. He had given her his dry hand, a look of studious concentration, and a faint smile. "Well," she had said, looking at the papers on his desk, "are you lifting the oxcart out of the ditch?" As Mr. Martin recalled that moment, over his milk, he squirmed slightly. He must keep his mind on her crimes as a special adviser, not on her peccadillos as a personality. This he found difficult to do, in spite of entering an objection and sustaining it. The faults of the woman as a woman kept chattering on in his mind like an unruly witness. She had, for almost two years now, baited him. In the halls, in the elevator, even in his own office, into which she romped now and then like a circus horse, she was constantly shouting out these silly questions at him. "Are you lifting the oxcart out of the ditch? Are you tearing up the pea patch? Are you hollering down the rain barrel? Are you scraping around the bottom of the pickle barrel? Are you sitting in the catbird seat?"

It was Joey Hart, one of Mr. Martin's two assistants, who had explained what the gibberish meant. "She must be a Dodger fan," he had said. "Red Barber announces the Dodger games over the radio and he uses those expressions — picked 'em up down South." Joey had gone on to explain one or two. "Tearing up the pea patch" meant going on a rampage; "sitting in the catbird seat" meant sitting pretty, like a batter with three balls and no strikes on him. Mr. Martin dismissed all this with an effort. It had been annoying, it had driven him near to distraction, but he was too solid a man to be moved to murder by anything so childish. It was fortunate, he reflected as he passed on to the important charges against Mrs. Barrows, that he had stood up under it so well. He had maintained always an outward appearance of polite tolerance. "Why, I even believe you like the woman," Miss Paird, his other assistant, had once said to him. He had simply smiled.

A gavel rapped in Mr. Martin's mind and the case proper was resumed. Mrs. Ulgine Barrows stood charged with willful, blatant, and persistent attempts to destroy the efficiency and system of F & S. It was competent, material, and relevant to review her advent and rise to power. Mr. Martin had got the story from Miss Paird, who seemed always able to find things out. According to her, Mrs. Barrows had met Mr. Fitweiler at a party, where she had rescued him from the embraces of a powerfully built drunken man who had mistaken the president of F & S for a famous retired Middle Western football coach. She had led him to a sofa and somehow worked upon him a monstrous magic. The aging gentleman had jumped to the conclusion there and then that this was a woman of singular attainments, equipped to bring out the best in him and in the firm. A week later he had introduced her into F & S as his special adviser. On that day confusion got its foot in the door. After Miss Tyson, Mr. Brundage, and Mr. Bartlett had been fired and Mr. Munson had taken his hat and stalked out, mailing in his resignation later, old Roberts had been emboldened to speak to Mr. Fitweiler. He mentioned that Mr. Munson's department had been "a little disrupted" and hadn't they perhaps better resume the old system there? Mr. Fitweiler had said certainly not. He had the greatest faith in Mrs. Barrows' ideas. "They require a little seasoning, a little seasoning, is all," he had added. Mr. Roberts had given it up. Mr. Martin reviewed in detail all the changes wrought by Mrs. Barrows. She had begun chipping at the cornices of the firm's edifice and now she was swinging at the foundation stones with a pickaxe.

Mr. Martin came now, in his summing up, to the afternoon of Monday, November 2, 1942 — just one week ago. On that day, at 3 P.M., Mrs. Barrows had bounced into his office. "Boo!" she had yelled. "Are you scraping around the bottom of the pickle barrel?" Mr. Martin had looked at her from under his green eyeshade, saying nothing. She had begun to wander about the office, taking it in with her great, popping eyes. "Do you really need *all* these filing cabinets?" she had demanded suddenly. Mr. Martin's heart had jumped. "Each of these files," he had said, keeping his voice even, "plays an indispensable part in the system of F & S." She had brayed at him, "Well, don't tear up the pea patch!" and gone to the door. From there she had bawled, "But you sure have got a lot of fine scrap in here!" Mr. Martin could no longer doubt that the finger was on his beloved department. Her pickaxe was on the upswing, poised for the first blow. It had not come yet; he had received no blue memo from the enchanted Mr. Fitweiler bearing nonsensical instructions deriving from the obscene woman. But there was no doubt in Mr. Martin's mind that one would be forthcoming. He must act quickly. Already a precious week had gone by. Mr. Martin stood up in his living room, still holding his milk glass. "Gentlemen of the jury," he said to himself, "I demand the death penalty for this horrible person."

The next day Mr. Martin followed his routine, as usual. He polished his glasses more often and once sharpened an already sharp pencil but not even Miss Paird noticed. Only once did he catch sight of his victim; she swept past him in the hall with a patronizing "Hi!" At five-thirty he walked home, as usual, and had a glass of milk, as usual. He had never drunk anything stronger in his life — unless you could count ginger ale. The late Sam Schlosser, the S of F & S, had praised Mr. Martin at a staff meeting several years before for his temperate habits. "Our most efficient worker neither drinks nor smokes," he had said. "The results speak for themselves." Mr. Fitweiler had sat by, nodding approval.

Mr. Martin was still thinking about that red-letter day as he walked over to the Schrafft's on Fifth Avenue near Forty-sixth Street. He got there, as he always did, at eight o'clock. He finished his dinner and the financial page of the *Sun* at a quarter to nine, as he always did. It was his custom after dinner to take a walk. This time he walked down Fifth Avenue at a casual pace. His gloved hands felt moist and warm, his forehead cold. He transferred the Camels from his overcoat to a jacket pocket. He wondered, as he did so, if they did not represent an unnecessary note of strain. Mrs. Barrows smoked only Luckies. It was his idea to puff a few puffs on a Camel (after the rubbing-out), stub it out in the ashtray holding her lipstick-stained Luckies, and thus drag a small red herring across the trail. Perhaps it was not a good idea. It would take time. He might even choke, too loudly.

Mr. Martin had never seen the house on West Twelfth Street where Mrs. Barrows lived, but he had a clear enough picture of it. Fortunately, she had bragged to everybody about her ducky first-floor apartment in the perfectly darling three-story redbrick. There would be no doorman or other attendants; just the tenants of the second and third floors. As he walked along, Mr. Martin realized that he would get there before nine-thirty. He had considered walking north on Fifth Avenue from Schrafft's to a point from which it would take him until ten o'clock to reach the house. At that hour people were less likely to be coming in or going out. But the procedure would have made an awkward loop in the straight thread of his casualness, and he had abandoned it. It was impossible to figure when people would be entering or leaving the house, anyway. There was a great risk at any hour. If he ran into anybody, he would simply have to place the rubbing-out of Ulgine Barrows in the inactive file forever. The same thing would hold true if there were someone in her apartment. In that case he would just say that he had been passing by, recognized her charming house and thought to drop in.

It was eighteen minutes after nine when Mr. Martin turned into Twelfth Street. A man passed him, and a man and a woman talking. There was no one within fifty paces when he came to the house, halfway down the block. He was up the steps and in the small vestibule in no time, pressing the bell under the card that said "Mrs. Ulgine Barrows." When the clicking in the lock started, he jumped forward against the door. He got inside fast, closing the door behind him. A bulb in a lantern hung from the hall ceiling on a chain seemed to give a monstrously bright light. There was nobody on the stair, which went up ahead of him along the left wall. A door opened down the hall in the wall on the right. He went toward it swiftly, on tiptoe.

"Well, for God's sake, look who's here!" bawled Mrs. Barrows, and her braying laugh rang out like the report of a shotgun. He rushed past her like a football tackle, bumping her. "Hey, quit shoving!" she said, closing the door behind them. They were in her living room, which seemed to Mr. Martin to be lighted by a hundred lamps. "What's after you?" she said. "You're as jumpy as a goat." He found he was unable to speak. His heart was wheezing in his throat. "I — yes," he finally brought out. She was jabbering and laughing as she started to help him off with his coat. "No, no," he said. "I'll put it there." He took it off and put it on a chair near the door. "Your hat and gloves, too," she said. "You're in a lady's house." He put his hat on top of the coat. Mrs. Barrows seemed larger than he had thought. He kept his gloves on. "I was passing by," he said. "I recognized — is there anyone here?" She laughed louder than ever. "No," she said, "we're all alone. You're as white as a sheet, you funny man. Whatever *has* come over you? I'll mix you a toddy." She started toward a door across the room. "Scotch-and-soda be all right? But say, you don't drink, do you?" She turned and gave him her amused look. Mr. Martin pulled himself together. "Scotch-and-soda will be all right," he heard himself say. He could hear her laughing in the kitchen.

Mr. Martin looked quickly around the living room for the weapon. He had counted on finding one there. There were andirons and a poker and something in a corner that looked like an Indian club. None of them would do. It couldn't be that way. He began to pace around. He came to a desk. On it lay a metal paper knife with an ornate handle. Would it be sharp enough? He reached for it and knocked over a small brass jar. Stamps spilled out of it and it fell to the floor with a clatter. "Hey," Mrs. Barrows yelled from the kitchen, "are you tearing up the pea patch?" Mr. Martin gave a strange laugh. Picking up the knife, he tried its point against his left wrist. It was blunt. It wouldn't do.

When Mrs. Barrows reappeared, carrying two highballs, Mr. Martin, standing there with his gloves on, became acutely conscious of the fantasy he had wrought. Cigarettes in his pocket, a drink prepared for him — it was all too grossly improbable. It was more than that; it was impossible. Somewhere in the back of his mind a vague idea stirred, sprouted. "For heaven's sake; take off those gloves," said Mrs. Barrows. "I always wear them in the house," said Mr. Martin. The idea began to bloom, strange and wonderful. She put the glasses on a coffee table in front of a sofa and sat on the sofa. "Come over here, you odd little man," she said. Mr. Martin went over and sat beside her. It was difficult getting a cigarette out of the pack of Camels, but he managed it. She held a match for him, laughing. "Well," she said, handing him his drink, "this is perfectly marvelous. You with a drink and a cigarette."

Mr. Martin puffed, not too awkwardly, and took a gulp of the highball. "I drink and smoke all the time," he said. He clinked his glass against hers. "Here's nuts to that old windbag, Fitweiler," he said, and gulped again. The stuff tasted awful, but he made no grimace. "Really, Mr. Martin," she said, her voice and posture changing, "you are insulting our employer." Mrs. Barrows was now all special adviser to the president. "I am preparing a bomb," said Mr. Martin, "which will blow the old goat higher than hell." He had only had a little of the drink, which was not strong. It couldn't be that. "Do you take dope or something?" Mrs. Barrows asked coldly. "Heroin," said Mr. Martin. "I'll be coked to the gills when I bump that old buzzard off." "Mr. Martin!" she shouted, getting to her feet. "That will be all of that. You must go at once." Mr. Martin took another swallow of his drink. He tapped his cigarette out in the ashtray and put the pack of Camels on the coffee table. Then he got up. She stood glaring at him. He walked over and put on his hat and coat. "Not a word about this," he said, and laid an index finger against his lips. All Mrs. Barrows could bring out was "Really!" Mr. Martin put his hand on the doorknob. "I'm sitting in the catbird seat," he said. He stuck his tongue out at her and left. Nobody saw him go.

Mr. Martin got to his apartment, walking, well before eleven. No one saw him go in. He had two glasses of milk after brushing his teeth, and he felt elated. It wasn't tipsiness, because he hadn't been tipsy. Anyway, the walk had worn off all effects of the whisky. He got in bed and read a magazine for a while. He was asleep before midnight.

Mr. Martin got to the office at eight-thirty the next morning, as usual. At a quarter to nine, Ulgine Barrows, who had never before arrived at work before ten, swept into his office. "I'm reporting to Mr. Fitweiler now!" she shouted. "If he turns you over to the police, it's no more than you deserve!" Mr. Martin gave her a look of shocked surprise. "I beg your pardon?" he said. Mrs. Barrows snorted and bounced out of the room, leaving Miss Paird and Joey Hart staring after her. "What's the matter with that old devil now?" asked Miss Paird. "I have no idea," said Mr. Martin, resuming his work. The other two looked at him and then at each other. Miss Paird got up and went out. She walked slowly past the closed door of Mr. Fitweiler's office. Mrs. Barrows was yelling inside, but she was not braying. Miss Paird could not hear what the woman was saying. She went back to her desk.

Forty-five minutes later, Mrs. Barrows left the president's office and went into her own, shutting the door. It wasn't until half an hour later that Mr. Fitweiler sent for Mr. Martin. The head of the filing department, neat, quiet, attentive, stood in front of the old man's desk. Mr. Fitweiler was pale and nervous. He took his glasses off and twiddled them. He made a small, bruffing sound in his throat. "Martin," he said, "you have been with us more than twenty years." "Twenty-two, sir," said Mr. Martin. "In that time," pursued the president, "your work and your—uh—manner have been exemplary." "I trust so, sir," said Mr. Martin. "I have understood, Martin," said Mr. Fitweiler, "that you have never taken a drink or smoked." "That is correct, sir," said Mr. Martin. "Ah, yes." Mr. Fitweiler polished his glasses. "You may describe what you did after leaving the office yesterday, Martin," he said. Mr. Martin allowed less than a second for his bewildered pause. "Certainly, sir," he said. "I walked home. Then I went to Schrafft's for dinner. Afterward I walked home again. I went to bed early, sir, and read a magazine for a while. I was asleep before eleven." "Ah, yes," said Mr. Fitweiler again. He was silent for a moment, searching for the proper words to say to the head of the filing department. "Mrs. Barrows," he said finally, "Mrs. Barrows has worked hard, Martin, very hard. It grieves me to report that she has suffered a severe breakdown. It has taken the form of a persecution complex accompanied by distressing hallucinations." "I am very sorry, sir," said Mr. Martin. "Mrs. Barrows is under the delusion," continued Mr. Fitweiler, "that you visited her last evening and behaved yourself in an—uh—unseemly manner." He raised his hand to silence Mr. Martin's little pained outcry. "It is the nature of these psychological diseases," Mr. Fitweiler said, "to fix upon the least likely and most innocent party as the—uh—source of persecution. These matters are not for the lay mind to grasp, Martin. I've just had my psychiatrist, Doctor Fitch, on the phone. He would not, of course, commit himself, but he made enough generalizations to substantiate my suspicions. I suggested to Mrs. Barrows when she had completed her—uh—story to me this morning, that she visit Doctor Fitch, for I suspected a condition at once. She flew, I regret to say, into a rage, and demanded—uh—requested that I call you on the carpet. You may not know, Martin, but Mrs. Barrows had planned a reorganization of your department—subject to my approval, of course, subject to my approval. This brought you, rather than anyone else, to her mind—but again that is a phenomenon for Doctor Fitch and not for us. So, Martin, I am afraid Mrs. Barrows' usefulness here is at an end." "I am dreadfully sorry, sir," said Mr. Martin.

It was at this point that the door to the office blew open with the suddenness of a gas-main explosion and Mrs. Barrows catapulted through it. "Is the little rat denying it?" she screamed. "He can't get away with that!" Mr. Martin got up and moved discreetly to a point beside Mr. Fitweiler's chair. "You drank and smoked at my apartment," she bawled at Mr. Martin, "and you know it! You called Mr. Fitweiler an old windbag and said you were going to blow him up when you got coked to the gills on your heroin!" She stopped yelling to catch her breath and a new glint came into her popping eyes. "If you weren't such a drab, ordinary little man," she said. "I'd think you'd planned it all. Sticking your tongue out, saying you were sitting in the catbird seat, because you thought no one would believe me when I told it! My God, it's really too perfect!" She brayed loudly and hysterically, and the fury was on her again. She glared at Mr. Fitweiler. "Can't you see how he has tricked us, you old fool? Can't you see his little game?" But Mr. Fitweiler had been surreptitiously pressing all the buttons under the top of his desk and employees of F & S began pouring into the room. "Stockton," said Mr. Fitweiler, "you and Fishbein will take Mrs. Barrows to her home. Mrs. Powell, you will go with them." Stockton, who had played a little football in high school, blocked Mrs. Barrows as she made for Mr. Martin. It took him and Fishbein together to force her out of the door into the hall, crowded with stenographers and office boys. She was still screaming imprecations at Mr. Martin, tangled and contradictory imprecations. The hubbub finally died out down the corridor.

"I regret that this has happened," said Mr. Fitweiler. "I shall ask you to dismiss it from your mind, Martin." "Yes, sir," said Mr. Martin, anticipating his chief's "That will be all" by moving to the door. "I will dismiss it." He went out and shut the door, and his step was light and quick in the hall. When he entered his department he had slowed down to his customary gait, and he walked quietly across the room to the W20 file, wearing a look of studious concentration.

Considerations

1. Make a list of Mrs. Barrows's personal characteristics — how she looks, talks, acts, and thinks. Consider how other people in the office respond to these characteristics and comment on the significance of their responses.
2. Make a list of Mr. Martin's personal characteristics — how he looks, talks, acts, and thinks. Compare this list with the list you made describing Mrs. Barrows. Are Mr. Martin and Mrs. Barrows completely opposite? Do they share any similarities?
3. What is the effect of Thurber's decision to start the story right in the midst of things — with Mr. Martin planning to "rub out" Mrs. Barrows — rather than first explaining the events that led up to this situation?

How would the story be changed if the action took place in straight chronological order?

4. Do you think Mr. Martin goes to Mrs. Barrows's apartment with a serious intent to commit murder? What evidence might be offered to support the case that he does? That he does not?

5. In what ways is this story ironic? Consider how these ironies might suggest the story's theme (or themes).

SARAH ORNE JEWETT (1849–1909)

Tom's Husband

I shall not dwell long upon the circumstances that led to the marriage of my hero and heroine; though their courtship was to them, the only one that has ever noticeably approached the ideal, it had many aspects in which it was entirely commonplace in other people's eyes. While the world in general smiles at lovers with kindly approval and sympathy, it refuses to be aware of the unprecedented delight which is amazing to the lovers themselves.

But, as has been true in many other cases, when they were at last married, the most ideal of situations was found to have been changed to the most practical. Instead of having shared their original duties, and, as school-boys would say, going halves, they discovered that the cares of life had been doubled. This led to some distressing moments for both our friends; they understood suddenly that instead of dwelling in heaven they were still upon earth, and had made themselves slaves to new laws and limitations. Instead of being freer and happier than ever before, they had assumed new responsibilities; they had established a new household, and must fulfill in some way or another the obligations of it. They looked back with affection to their engagement; they had been longing to have each other to themselves, apart from the world, but it seemed that they never felt so keenly that they were still units in modern society. Since Adam and Eve were in Paradise, before the devil joined them, nobody has had a chance to imitate that unlucky couple. In some respects they told the truth when, twenty times a day, they said that life had never been so pleasant before; but there were mental reservations on either side which might have subjected them to the accusation of lying. Somehow, there was a little feeling of disappointment, and they caught themselves wondering — though they would have died sooner than confess it — whether they were quite so happy as they had expected. The truth was, they were much happier than people usually are, for they had an uncommon capacity for enjoyment. For a little while they were like a sailboat that is beating and has to drift a few minutes before it can catch the wind and start off on the other tack. And they had the same feeling, too, that any one is likely to have who has been long pursuing some object of his ambition or desire. Whether it is a coin, or a picture, or a stray volume of some old edition of Shakespeare, or whether it is an office under government or a lover, when fairly in one's grasp there is a loss of the eagerness that was felt in pursuit. Satisfaction, even after one has dined well, is not so interesting and eager a feeling as hunger.

My hero and heroine were reasonably well established to begin with: they each had some money, though Mr. Wilson had most. His father had at one time been a rich man, but with the decline, a few years before, of manufacturing interests, he had become, mostly through the fault of others, somewhat involved; and at the time of his death his affairs were in such a condition that it was still a question whether a very large sum or a moderately large one would represent his estate. Mrs. Wilson, Tom's step-mother, was somewhat of an invalid; she suffered severely at times with asthma, but she was almost entirely relieved by living in another part of the country. While her husband lived, she had accepted her illness as inevitable, and rarely left home; but during the last few years she had lived in Philadelphia with her own people, making short and wheezing visits only from time to time, and had not undergone a voluntary period of suffering since the occasion of Tom's marriage, which she had entirely approved. She had a sufficient property of her own, and she and Tom were independent of each other in that way. Her only other step-child was a daughter, who had married a navy officer, and had at this time gone out to spend three years (or less) with her husband, who had been ordered to Japan.

It is not unfrequently noticed that in many marriages one of the persons who choose each other as partners for life is said to have thrown himself or herself away, and the relatives and friends look on with dismal forebodings and ill-concealed submission. In this case it was the wife who might have done so much better, according to public opinion. She did not think so herself, luckily, either before marriage or afterward, and I do not think it occurred to her to picture to herself the sort of career which would have been her alternative. She had been an only child, and had usually taken her own way. Some one once said that it was a great pity that she had not been obliged to work for her living, for she had inherited a most uncommon business talent, and, without being disreputably keen at a bargain, her insight into the practical working of affairs was very clear and far-reaching. Her father, who had also been a manufacturer, like Tom's, had often said it had been a mistake that she was a girl instead of a boy. Such executive ability as hers is often wasted in the more contracted sphere of women, and is apt to be more a disadvantage than a help. She was too independent and self-reliant for a wife; it would seem at first thought that she needed a wife herself more than she did a husband. Most men like best the women whose natures cling and appeal to theirs for protection. But Tom Wilson, while he did not wish to be protected himself, liked these very qualities in his wife which would have displeased some other men; to tell the truth, he was very much in love with his wife just as she was. He was a successful collector of almost everything but money, and during a great part of his life he had been an invalid, and he had grown, as he laughingly confessed, very old-womanish. He had been badly lamed, when a boy, by being caught in some machinery in his father's mill, near which he was idling one afternoon, and though he had almost entirely outgrown the effect of his injury, it had not been until after many years. He had been in college, but his eyes had given out there, and he had been obliged to leave in the middle of his junior year, though he had kept up a pleasant intercourse with the members of his class, with whom he had been a great favorite. He was a good deal of an idler in the world. I do not think his ambition, except in the case of securing Mary Dunn for his wife, had ever been distinct; he seemed to make the most he could of each day as it came, without making all his days' works tend toward some grand result, and go toward the upbuilding of some grand plan and purpose. He consequently gave no promise of being either distinguished or great. When his eyes would allow, he was an indefatigable reader; and although he would have said that he read only for amusement, yet he amused himself with books that were well worth the time he spent over them.

The house where he lived nominally belonged to his step-mother, but she had taken for granted that Tom would bring his wife home to it, and assured him that it should be to all intents and purposes his. Tom was deeply attached to the old place, which was altogether the pleasantest in town. He had kept bachelor's hall there most of the time since his father's death, and he had taken great pleasure, before his marriage, in refitting it to some extent, though it was already comfortable and furnished in remarkably good taste. People said of him that if it had not been for his illnesses, and if he had been a poor boy, he probably would have made something of himself. As it was, he was not very well known by the townspeople, being somewhat reserved, and not taking much interest in their every-day subjects of conversation. Nobody liked him so well as they liked his wife, yet there was no reason why he should be disliked enough to have much said about him.

After our friends had been married for some time, and had outlived the first strangeness of the new order of things, and had done their duty to their neighbors with so much apparent willingness and generosity that even Tom himself was liked a great deal better than he ever had been before, they were sitting together one stormy evening in the library, before the fire. Mrs. Wilson had been reading Tom the letters which had come to him by the night's mail. There was a long one from his sister in Nagasaki, which had been written with a good deal of ill-disguised reproach. She complained of the smallness of the income of her share in her father's estate, and said that she had been assured by American friends that the smaller mills were starting up everywhere, and beginning to do well again. Since so much of their money was invested in the factory, she had been surprised and sorry to find by Tom's last letters that he had seemed to have no idea of putting in a proper person as superintendent, and going to work again. Four per cent on her other property, which she had been told she must soon expect instead of eight, would make a great difference to her. A navy captain in a foreign port was obliged to entertain a great deal, and Tom must know that it cost them much more to live than it did him, and ought to think of their interests. She hoped he would talk over what was best to be done with their mother (who had been made executor, with Tom, of his father's will).

Tom laughed a little, but looked disturbed. His wife had said something to the same effect, and his mother had spoken once or twice in her letters of the prospect of starting the mill again. He was not a bit of a business man, and he did not feel certain, with the theories which he had arrived at of the state of the country, that it was safe yet to spend the money which would have to be spent in putting the mill in order. "They think that the minute it is going again we shall be making money hand over hand, just as father did when we were children," he said. "It is going to cost us no end of money before we can make anything. Before father died he meant to put in a good deal of new machinery, I remember. I don't know anything about the business myself, and I would have sold out long ago if I had had an offer that came anywhere near the value. The larger mills are the only ones that are good for anything now, and we should have to bring a crowd of French Canadians here; the day is past for the people who live in this part of the country to go into the factory again. Even the Irish all go West when they come into the country, and don't come to places like this any more."

"But there are a good many of the old work-people down in the village," said Mrs. Wilson. "Jack Towne asked me the other day if you weren't going to start up in the spring."

Tom moved uneasily in his chair, "I'll put you in for superintendent, if you like," he said, half angrily, whereupon Mary threw the newspaper at him; but by the time he had thrown it back he was in good humor again.

"Do you know, Tom," she said, with amazing seriousness, "that I believe I should like nothing in the world so much as to be the head of a large business? I hate keeping house, — I always did; and I never did so much of it in all my life put together as I have since I have been married. I suppose it isn't womanly to say so, but if I could escape from the whole thing I believe I should be perfectly happy. If you get rich when the mill is going again, I shall beg for a housekeeper, and shirk everything. I give you fair warning. I don't believe I keep this house half so well as you did before I came here." 10

Tom's eyes twinkled. "I am going to have that glory, — I don't think you do, Polly; but you can't say that I have not been forbearing. I certainly have not told you more than twice how we used to have things cooked. I'm not going to be your kitchen-colonel."

"Of course it seemed the proper thing to do," said his wife, meditatively; "but I think we should have been even happier than we have if I had been spared it. I have had some days of wretchedness that I shudder to think of. I never know what to have for breakfast; and I ought not to say it, but I don't mind the sight of dust. I look upon housekeeping as my life's great discipline"; and at this pathetic confession they both laughed heartily.

"I've a great mind to take it off your hands," said Tom. "I always rather liked it, to tell the truth, and I ought to be a better housekeeper, — I have been at it for five years; though housekeeping for one is different from what it is for two, and one of them a woman. You see you have brought a different element into my family. Luckily, the servants are pretty well drilled. I do think you upset them a good deal at first!"

Mary Wilson smiled as if she only half heard what he was saying. She drummed with her foot on the floor and looked intently at the fire, and presently gave it a vigorous poking. "Well?" said Tom, after he had waited patiently as long as he could.

"Tom! I'm going to propose something to you. I wish you would really do as you said, and take all the home affairs under your care, and let me start the mill. I am certain I could manage it. Of course I should get people who understood the thing to teach me. I believe I was made for it; I should like it above all things. And this is what I will do: I will bear the cost of starting it, myself, — I think I have money enough, or can get it; and if I have not put affairs in the right trim at the end of a year I will stop, and you may make some other arrangement. If I have, you and your mother and sister can pay me back." 15

"So I am going to be the wife, and you the husband," said Tom, a little indignantly; "at least, that is what people will say. It's a regular Darby and Joan affair, and you think you can do more work in a day than I can do in three. Do you know that you must go to town to buy cotton? And do you know there are a thousand things about it that you don't know?"

"And never will?" said Mary, with perfect good humor. "Why, Tom, I can learn as well as you, and a good deal better, for I like business, and you don't. You forget that I was always father's right-hand man after I was a dozen years old, and that you have let me invest my money and some of your own, and I haven't made a blunder yet."

Tom thought that his wife had never looked so handsome or so happy. "I don't care. I should rather like the fun of knowing what people will say. It is a new departure, at any rate. Women think they can do everything better than men in these days, but I'm the first man, apparently, who has wished he were a woman."

"Of course people will laugh," said Mary, "but they will say that it's just like me, and think I am fortunate to have married a man who will let me do as I choose. I don't see why it isn't sensible: you will be living exactly as you were before you married, as to home affairs; and since it was a good thing for you to know something about housekeeping then, I can't imagine why you shouldn't go on with it now, since it makes me miserable, and I am wasting a fine business talent while I do it. What do we care for people's talking about it?"

"It seems to me that it is something like women's smoking: it isn't wicked, but it isn't the custom of the country. And I don't like the idea of your going among business men. Of course I should be above going with you, and having people think I must be an idiot; they would say that you married a manufacturing interest, and I was thrown in. I can foresee that my pride is going to be humbled to the dust in every way," Tom declared in mournful tones, and began to shake with laughter. "It is one of your lovely castles in the air, dear Polly, but an old brick mill needs a better foundation than the clouds. No, I'll look around, and get an honest, experienced man for agent. I suppose it's the best thing we can do, for the machinery ought not to lie still any longer; but I mean to sell the factory as soon as 20

I can. I devoutly wish it would take fire, for the insurance would be the best price we are likely to get. That is a famous letter from Alice! I am afraid the captain has been growling over his pay, or they have been giving too many little dinners on board ship. If we were rid of the mill, you and I might go out there this winter. It would be capital fun."

Mary smiled again in an absent-minded way. Tom had an uneasy feeling that he had not heard the end of it yet, but nothing more was said for a day or two. When Mrs. Tom Wilson announced, with no apparent thought of being contradicted, that she had entirely made up her mind, and she meant to see those men who had been overseers of the different departments, who still lived in the village, and have the mill put in order at once, Tom looked disturbed, but made no opposition; and soon after breakfast his wife formally presented him with a handful of keys, and told him there was some lamb in the house for dinner; and presently he heard the wheels of her little phaeton rattling off down the road. I should be untruthful if I tried to persuade any one that he was not provoked; he thought she would at least have waited for his formal permission, and at first he meant to take another horse, and chase her, and bring her back in disgrace, and put a stop to the whole thing. But something assured him that she knew what she was about, and he determined to let her have her own way. If she failed, it might do no harm, and this was the only ungallant thought he gave her. He was sure that she would do nothing unladylike, or be unmindful of his dignity; and he believed it would be looked upon as one of her odd, independent freaks, which always had won respect in the end, however much they had been laughed at in the beginning. "Susan," said he, as that estimable person went by the door with the dust-pan, "you may tell Catherine to come to me for orders about the house, and you may do so yourself. I am going to take charge again, as I did before I was married. It is no trouble to me, and Mrs. Wilson dislikes it. Besides, she is going into business, and will have a great deal else to think of."

"Yes, sir; very well, sir," said Susan, who was suddenly moved to ask so many questions that she was utterly silent. But her master looked very happy; there was evidently no disapproval of his wife; and she went on up the stairs, and began to sweep them down, knocking the dust-brush about excitedly, as if she were trying to kill a descending colony of insects.

Tom went out to the stable and mounted his horse, which had been waiting for him to take his customary after-breakfast ride to the post-office, and he galloped down the road in quest of the phaeton. He saw Mary talking with Jack Towne, who had been an overseer and a valued workman of his father's. He was looking much surprised and pleased.

"I wasn't caring so much about getting work, myself," he explained; "I've got what will carry me and my wife through; but it'll be better for the young folks about here to work near home. My nephews are wanting something to do; they were going to Lynn next week. I don't say but I should like to be to work in the old place again. I've sort of missed it, since we shut down."

"I'm sorry I was so long in overtaking you," said Tom, politely, to his   25
wife. "Well, Jack, did Mrs. Wilson tell you she's going to start the mill? You must give her all the help you can."

"'Deed I will," said Mr. Towne, gallantly, without a bit of astonishment.

"I don't know much about the business yet," said Mrs. Wilson, who had been a little overcome at Jack Towne's lingo of the different rooms and machinery, and who felt an overpowering sense of having a great deal before her in the next few weeks. "By the time the mill is ready, I will be ready, too," she said, taking heart a little; and Tom, who was quick to understand her moods, could not help laughing, as he rode alongside. "We want a new barrel of flour, Tom, dear," she said, by way of punishment for his untimely mirth.

If she lost courage in the long delay, or was disheartened at the steady call for funds, she made no sign; and after a while the mill started up, and her cares were lightened, so that she told Tom that before next pay day she would like to go to Boston for a few days, and go to the theatre, and have a frolic and a rest. She really looked pale and thin, and she said she never worked so hard in all her life; but nobody knew how happy she was, and she was so glad she had married Tom, for some men would have laughed at it.

"I laughed at it," said Tom, meekly. "All is, if I don't cry by and by, because I am a beggar, I shall be lucky." But Mary looked fearlessly serene, and said that there was no danger at present.

It would have been ridiculous to expect a dividend the first year,   30
though the Nagasaki people were pacified with difficulty. All the business letters came to Tom's address, and everybody who was not directly concerned thought that he was the motive power of the reawakened enterprise. Sometimes business people came to the mill, and were amazed at having to confer with Mrs. Wilson, but they soon had to respect her talents and her success. She was helped by the old clerk, who had been promptly recalled and reinstated, and she certainly did capitally well. She was laughed at, as she had expected to be, and people said they should think Tom would be ashamed of himself; but it soon appeared that he was not to blame, and what reproach was offered was on the score of his wife's oddity. There was nothing about the mill that she did not understand before very long, and at the end of the second year she declared a small dividend with great pride and triumph. And she was congratulated on her success, and every one thought of her project in a different way from the way they had thought of it in the beginning. She had singularly good fortune: at the end of the third year she was making money for herself and her friends faster than most people were, and approving letters began to come from Nagasaki. The Ashtons had been

ordered to stay in that region, and it was evident that they were continually being obliged to entertain more instead of less. Their children were growing fast, too, and constantly becoming more expensive. The captain and his wife had already begun to congratulate themselves secretly that their two sons would in all probability come into possession, one day, of their uncle Tom's handsome property.

For a good while Tom enjoyed life, and went on his quiet way serenely. He was anxious at first, for he thought that Mary was going to make ducks and drakes of his money and her own. And then he did not exactly like the looks of the thing, either; he feared that his wife was growing successful as a business person at the risk of losing her womanliness. But as time went on, and he found there was no fear of that, he accepted the situation philosophically. He gave up his collection of engravings, having become more interested in one of coins and medals, which took up most of his leisure time. He often went to the city in pursuit of such treasures, and gained much renown in certain quarters as a numismatologist of great skill and experience. But at last his house (which had almost kept itself, and had given him little to do beside ordering the dinners, while faithful old Catherine and her niece Susan were his aids) suddenly became a great care to him. Catherine, who had been the main-stay of the family for many years, died after a short illness, and Susan must needs choose that time, of all others, for being married to one of the second hands in the mill. There followed a long and dismal season of experimenting, and for a time there was a procession of incapable creatures going in at one kitchen door and out of the other. His wife would not have liked to say so, but it seemed to her that Tom was growing fussy about the house affairs, and took more notice of those minor details than he used. She wished more than once, when she was tired, that he would not talk so much about the housekeeping; he seemed sometimes to have no other thought.

In the early days of Mrs. Wilson's business life, she had made it a rule to consult her husband on every subject of importance; but it had speedily proved to be a formality. Tom tried manfully to show a deep interest which he did not feel, and his wife gave up, little by little, telling him much about her affairs. She said that she liked to drop business when she came home in the evening; and at last she fell into the habit of taking a nap on the library sofa, while Tom, who could not use his eyes much by lamp-light, sat smoking or in utter idleness before the fire. When they were first married his wife had made it a rule that she should always read him the evening papers, and afterward they had always gone on with some book of history or philosophy, in which they were both interested. These evenings of their early married life had been charming to both of them, and from time to time one would say to the other that they ought to take up again the habit of reading together. Mary was so unaffectedly tired in the evening that Tom never liked to propose a walk; for, though he was not a man of peculiarly social nature, he had always been accustomed to pay an occasional evening visit to his neighbors in the village. And though he had little interest in the business world, and still less knowledge of it, after a while he wished that his wife would have more to say about what she was planning and doing, or how things were getting on. He thought that her chief aid, old Mr. Jackson, was far more in her thoughts than he. She was forever quoting Jackson's opinions. He did not like to find that she took it for granted that he was not interested in the welfare of his own property; it made him feel like a sort of pensioner and dependent, though, when they had guests at the house, which was by no means seldom, there was nothing in her manner that would imply that she thought herself in any way the head of the family. It was hard work to find fault with his wife in any way, though, to give him his due, he rarely tried.

But, this being a wholly unnatural state of things, the reader must expect to hear of its change at last, and the first blow from the enemy was dealt by an old woman, who lived nearby, and who called to Tom one morning, as he was driving down to the village in a great hurry (to post a letter, which ordered his agent to secure a long-wished-for ancient copper coin, at any price), to ask him if they had made yeast that week, and if she could borrow a cupful, as her own had met with some misfortune. Tom was instantly in a rage, and he mentally condemned her to some undeserved fate, but told her aloud to go and see the cook. This slight delay, besides being killing to his dignity, caused him to lose the mail, and in the end his much-desired copper coin. It was a hard day for him, altogether; it was Wednesday, and the first days of the week having been stormy the washing was very late. And Mary came home to dinner provokingly good-natured. She had met an old schoolmate and her husband driving home from the mountains, and had first taken them over her factory, to their great amusement and delight, and then had brought them home to dinner. Tom greeted them cordially, and manifested his usual graceful hospitality; but the minute he saw his wife alone he said in a plaintive tone of rebuke, "I should think you might have remembered that the servants are unusually busy to-day. I do wish you would take a little interest in things at home. The women have been washing, and I'm sure I don't know what sort of a dinner we can give your friends. I wish you had thought to bring home some steak. I have been busy myself, and couldn't go down to the village. I thought we would only have a lunch."

Mary was hungry, but she said nothing, except that it would be all right, — she didn't mind; and perhaps they could have some canned soup.

She often went to town to buy or look at cotton, or to see some improvement in machinery, and she brought home beautiful bits of furniture and new pictures for the house, and showed a touching thoughtfulness in remembering Tom's fancies; but somehow he had an uneasy suspicion that she could get along pretty well without him when it came to the deeper wishes and hopes of her life, and that her most important concerns were all matters in which he had no share. He seemed to himself to have merged his life in his wife's; he lost his interest in things outside the house and grounds; he felt himself fast growing rusty and behind the times, and to have somehow missed a good deal in life; he had a suspicion that he was a failure. One day the thought rushed over him that his had been almost exactly the experience of most women, and he wondered if it really was any more disappointing and ignominious to him than it was to women themselves. "Some of them may be contented with it," he said to himself, soberly. "People think women are designed for such careers by nature, but I don't know why I ever made such a fool of myself."

Having once seen his situation in life from such a standpoint, he felt it day by day to be more degrading, and he wondered what he should do about it; and once, drawn by a new, strange sympathy, he went to the little family burying-ground. It was one of the mild, dim days that come sometimes in early November, when the pale sunlight is like the pathetic smile of a sad face, and he sat for a long time on the limp, frost-bitten grass beside his mother's grave.

But when he went home in the twilight his step-mother, who just then was making them a little visit, mentioned that she had been looking through some boxes of hers that had been packed long before and stowed away in the garret. "Everything looks very nice up there," she said, in her wheezing voice (which, worse than usual that day, always made him nervous), and added, without any intentional slight to his feelings. "I do think you have always been a most excellent housekeeper."

"I'm tired of such nonsense!" he exclaimed, with surprising indignation. "Mary, I wish you to arrange your affairs so that you can leave them for six months at least. I am going to spend this winter in Europe."

"Why, Tom, dear!" said his wife, appealingly. "I couldn't leave my business any way in the" —

But she caught sight of a look on his usually placid countenance that was something more than decision, and refrained from saying anything more. 40

And three weeks from that day they sailed.

Considerations

1. What are the qualities that led people to say of Mary "that it was a great pity that she had not been obliged to work for her living" and her father to observe that "it had been a mistake that she was a girl instead of a boy"? Do these comments reflect attitudes that have now been abandoned (the story was written in 1884), or are comments like these still made today? Give examples to support your response.

2. What conflicts arise in the Wilsons' marriage? How are those conflicts related to the work each wants to do? To what extent are the conflicts related to community opinion?

3. Comment on the way each of the Wilsons views the importance of holding power within the marriage.
4. What critique of traditional "women's work" is implied by Tom's growing dissatisfaction? What is your response to this critique?
5. Discuss your response to a situation in which you decided (or were required) to act in a role that has not been traditionally defined as "appropriate" for your sex.

RICHARD WRIGHT (1908–1960)

The Man Who Was Almost a Man

Dave struck out across the fields, looking homeward through paling light. Whut's the use talkin wid em niggers in the field? Anyhow, his mother was putting supper on the table. Them niggers can't understan nothing. One of these days he was going to get a gun and practice shooting, then they couldn't talk to him as though he were a little boy. He slowed, looking at the ground. Shucks, Ah ain scareda them even ef they are biggern me! Aw, Ah know whut Ahma do. Ahm going by ol Joe's sto n git that Sears Roebuck catlog n look at them guns. Mebbe Ma will lemme buy one when she gits mah pay from ol man Hawkins. Ahma beg her t gimme some money. Ahm ol ernough to hava gun. Ahm seventeen. Almost a man. He strode, feeling his long loose-jointed limbs. Shucks, a man oughta hava little gun aftah he done worked hard all day.

He came in sight of Joe's store. A yellow lantern glowed on the front porch. He mounted steps and went through the screen door, hearing it bang behind him. There was a strong smell of coal oil and mackerel fish. He felt very confident until he saw fat Joe walk in through the rear door, then his courage began to ooze.

"Howdy, Dave! Whutcha want?"

"How yuh, Mistah Joe? Aw, Ah don wanna buy nothing. Ah jus wanted t see ef yuhd lemme look at tha catlog erwhile."

"Sure! You wanna see it here?"   5

"Nawsuh. Ah wants t take it home wid me. Ah'll bring it back ter-morrow when Ah come in from the fiels."

"You plannin on buying something?"

"Yessuh."

"Your ma lettin you have your own money now?"

"Shucks. Mistah Joe, Ahm gittin t be a man like anybody else!"   10

Joe laughed and wiped his greasy white face with a red bandanna. "What you plannin on buyin?"

Dave looked at the floor, scratched his head, scratched his thigh, and smiled. Then he looked up shyly.

"Ah'll tell yuh, Mistah Joe, ef yuh promise yuh won't tell."

"I promise."   15

"Waal, Ahma buy a gun."

"A gun? What you want with a gun?"

"Ah wanna keep it."

"You ain't nothing but a boy. You don't need a gun."

"Aw, lemme have the catlog, Mistah Joe. Ah'll bring it back."   20

Joe walked through the rear door. Dave was elated. He looked around at barrels of sugar and flour. He heard Joe coming back. He craned his neck to see if he were bringing the book. Yeah, he's got it. Gawddog, he's got it!

"Here, but be sure you bring it back. It's the only one I got."

"Sho, Mistah Joe."

"Say, if you wanna buy a gun, why don't you buy one from me? I gotta gun to sell."

"Will it shoot?"

"Sure it'll shoot."

"Whut kind is it?"

"Oh, it's kinda old . . . a left-hand Wheeler. A pistol. A big one."

"Is it got bullets in it?"

"It's loaded."

"Kin Ah see it?"

"Where's your money?"

"What yuh wan fer it?"

"I'll let you have it for two dollars."

"Just two dollahs? Shucks. Ah could buy tha when Ah git mah pay."

"I'll have it here when you want it."

"Awright, suh. Ah be in fer it."

He went through the door, hearing it slam again behind him. Ahma git some money from Ma n buy me a gun! Only two dollahs! He tucked the thick catalogue under his arm and hurried.

"Where yuh been, boy?" His mother held a steaming dish of blackeyed peas.

"Aw, Ma, Ah just stopped down the road t talk wid the boys."

"Yuh know bettah t keep suppah waiting."

He sat down, resting the catalogue on the edge of the table.

"Yuh git up from there and git to the well n wash yosef! Ah ain feedin no hogs in mah house!"

She grabbed his shoulder and pushed him. He stumbled out of the room, then came back to get the catalogue.

"Whut this?"

"Aw, Ma, it's jusa catlog."

"Who yuh git it from?"

"From Joe, down at the sto."

"Waal, thas good. We kin use it in the outhouse."

"Naw, Ma." He grabbed for it. "Gimme ma catlog, Ma."

She held onto it and glared at him.

"Quit hollerin at me! Whut's wrong wid yuh? Yuh crazy?"

"But Ma, please. It ain mine! It's Joe's! He tol me t bring it back t im termorrow."

She gave up the book. He stumbled down the back steps, hugging the thick book under his arm. When he had splashed water on his face and hands, he groped back to the kitchen and fumbled in a corner for the towel. He bumped into a chair; it clattered to the floor. The catalogue sprawled at his feet. When he had dried his eyes he snatched up the book and held it again under his arms. His mother stood watching him.

25

30

35

40

45

50

"Now, ef yuh gonna act a fool over that ol book, Ah'll take it n burn   55
it up."

"Naw, Ma, please."

"Waal, set down n be still!"

He sat down and drew the oil lamp close. He thumbed page after
page, unaware of the food his mother set on the table. His father came in.
Then his small brother.

"Whutcha got there, Dave?" his father asked.

"Jusa catlog," he answered, not looking up.   60

"Yeah, here they is!" His eyes glowed at blue-and-black revolvers. He
glanced up, feeling sudden guilt. His father was watching him. He eased the
book under the table and rested it on his knees. After the blessing was asked,
he ate. He scooped up peas and swallowed fat meat without chewing. But-
termilk helped to wash it down. He did not want to mention money before
his father. He would do much better by cornering his mother when she was
alone. He looked at his father uneasily out of the edge of his eye.

"Boy, how come yuh don quit foolin wid tha book n eat yo suppah?"

"Yessuh."

"How you n ol man Hawkins gitten erlong?"

"Suh?"   65

"Can't yuh hear? Why don yuh listen? Ah ast yu how wuz yuh n ol
man Hawkins gittin erlong?"

"Oh, swell, Pa. Ah plows mo lan than anybody over there."

"Waal, yuh oughta keep you mind on whut yuh doin."

"Yessuh."

He poured his plate full of molasses and sopped it up slowly with a   70
chunk of cornbread. When his father and brother had left the kitchen, he
still sat and looked again at the guns in the catalogue, longing to muster
courage enough to present his case to his mother. Lawd, ef Ah only had tha
pretty one! He could almost feel the slickness of the weapon with his fingers.
If he had a gun like that he would polish it and keep it shining so it would
never rust. N Ah'd keep it loaded, by Gawd!

"Ma?" His voice was hesitant.

"Hunh?"

"Ol man Hawkins give yuh mah money yit?"

"Yeah, but ain no usa yuh thinking about throwin nona it erway. Ahm
keepin tha money sos yuh kin have cloes t go to school this winter."

He rose and went to her side with the open catalogue in his palms. She   75
was washing dishes, her head bent low over a pan. Shyly he raised the book.
When he spoke, his voice was husky, faint.

"Ma, Gawd knows Ah wans one of these."

"One of whut?" she asked, not raising her eyes.

"One of these," he said again, not daring even to point. She glanced
up at the page, then at him with wide eyes.

"Nigger, is yuh gone plumb crazy?"

"Aw, Ma —"   80

"Git outta here! Don yuh talk t me bout no gun! Yuh a fool!"

"Ma, Ah kin buy one fer two dollahs."

"Not ef Ah knows it, yuh ain!"

"But yuh promised me one—"

"Ah don care what Ah promised! Yuh ain nothing but a boy yit!"   85

"Ma ef yuh lemme buy one Ah'll *never* ast yuh fer nothing no mo."

"Ah tol yuh t git outta here! Yuh ain gonna toucha penny of tha money fer no gun! Thas how come Ah has Mistah Hawkins t pay yu wages t me, cause Ah knows yuh ain got no sense."

"But, Ma, we needa gun. Pa ain got no gun. We needa gun in the house. Yuh kin never tell whut might happen."

"Now don yuh try to maka fool outta me, boy! Ef we did hava gun, yuh wouldn't have it!"

He laid the catalogue down and slipped his arm around her waist.   90

"Aw, Ma, Ah done worked hard alla summer n ain ast yuh fer nothing, is Ah, now?"

"Thas whut yuh spose t do!"

"But Ma, Ah wans a gun. Yuh kin lemme have two dollahs outta mah money. Please, Ma. I kin give it to Pa . . . Please, Ma! Ah loves yuh, Ma."

When she spoke her voice came soft and low.

"What yu wan wida gun, Dave? Yuh don need no gun. Yuh'll git in   95
trouble. N ef yo pa jus thought Ah let yuh have money t buy a gun he'd hava fit."

"Ah'll hide it, Ma. It ain but two dollahs."

"Lawd, chil, whut's wrong wid yuh?"

"Ain nothin wrong, Ma. Ahm almos a man now. Ah wans a gun."

"Who gonna sell yuh a gun?"

"Ol Joe at the sto."   100

"N it don cos but two dollahs?"

"Thas all, Ma. Jus two dollahs. Please, Ma."

She was stacking the plates away; her hands moved slowly, reflectively. Dave kept an anxious silence. Finally, she turned to him.

"Ah'll let yuh git tha gun ef yuh promise me one thing."

"Whut's tha, Ma?"   105

"Yuh bring it straight back t me, yuh hear? It be fer Pa."

"Yessum! Lemme go now, Ma."

She stooped, turned slightly to one side, raised the hem of her dress, rolled down the top of her stocking, and came up with a slender wad of bills.

"Here," she said. "Lawd knows yuh don need no gun. But yer pa does. Yuh bring it right back t me, yuh hear? Ahma put it up. Now ef yuh don, Ahma have yuh pa lick yuh so hard yuh won fergit it."

"Yessum."   110

He took the money, ran down the steps, and across the yard.

"Dave! Yuuuuu Daaaaave!"

He heard, but he was not going to stop now. "Naw, Lawd!"

The first movement he made the following morning was to reach under his pillow for the gun. In the gray light of dawn he held it loosely, feeling a sense of power. Could kill a man with a gun like this. Kill anybody, black or white. And if he were holding his gun in his hand, nobody could run over him; they would have to respect him. It was a big gun, with a long barrel and a heavy handle. He raised and lowered it in his hand, marveling at its weight.

He had not come straight home with it as his mother had asked; in- 115 stead he had stayed out in the fields, holding the weapon in his hand, aiming it now and then at some imaginary foe. But he had not fired it; he had been afraid that his father might hear. Also he was not sure he knew how to fire it.

To avoid surrendering the pistol he had not come into the house until he knew that they were all asleep. When his mother had tiptoed to his bedside late that night and demanded the gun, he had first played possum; then he had told her that the gun was hidden outdoors, that he would bring it to her in the morning. Now he lay turning it slowly in his hands. He broke it, took out the cartridges, felt them, and then put them back.

He slid out of bed, got a long strip of old flannel from a trunk, wrapped the gun in it, and tied it to his naked thigh while it was still loaded. He did not go in to breakfast. Even though it was not yet daylight, he started for Jim Hawkins' plantation. Just as the sun was rising he reached the barns where the mules and plows were kept.

"Hey! That you, Dave?"

He turned. Jim Hawkins stood eying him suspiciously.

"What're yuh doing here so early?" 120

"Ah didn't know Ah wuz gittin up so early, Mistah Hawkins. Ah was fixin t hitch up ol Jenny n take her t the fiels."

"Good. Since you're so early, how about plowing that stretch down by the woods?"

"Suits me, Mistah Hawkins."

"O.K. Go to it!"

He hitched Jenny to a plow and started across the fields. Hot dog! This 125 was just what he wanted. If he could get down by the woods, he could shoot his gun and nobody would hear. He walked behind the plow, hearing the traces creaking, feeling the gun tied tight to his thigh.

When he reached the woods, he plowed two whole rows before he decided to take out the gun. Finally, he stopped, looked in all directions, then untied the gun and held it in his hand. He turned to the mule and smiled.

"Know whut this is, Jenny? Naw, yuh wouldn know! Yuhs jusa ol mule! Anyhow, this is a gun, n it kin shoot, by Gawd!"

He held the gun at arm's length. Whut t hell, Ahma shoot this thing! He looked at Jenny again.

"Lissen here, Jenny! When Ah pull this ol trigger, Ah don wan yuh to run n acka fool now?"

Jenny stood with head down, her short ears pricked straight. Dave   130
walked off about twenty feet, held the gun far out from him at arm's length,
and turned his head. Hell, he told himself, Ah ain afraid. The gun felt loose
in his fingers; he waved it wildly for a moment. Then he shut his eyes and
tightened his forefinger. Bloom! A report half deafened him and he thought
his right hand was torn from his arm. He heard Jenny whinnying and
galloping over the field, and he found himself on his knees, squeezing his
fingers hard between his legs. His hand was numb; he jammed it into his
mouth, trying to warm it, trying to stop the pain. The gun lay at his feet.
He did not quite know what had happened. He stood up and stared at the
gun as though it were a living thing. He gritted his teeth and kicked the
gun. Yuh almos broke mah arm! He turned to look for Jenny; she was far
over the fields, tossing her head and kicking wildly.

"Hol on there, ol mule!"

When he caught up with her she stood trembling, walling her big
white eyes at him. The plow was far away; the traces had broken. Then
Dave stopped short, looking, not believing. Jenny was bleeding. Her left
side was red and wet with blood. He went closer. Lawd, have mercy! Won-
dah did Ah shoot this mule? He grabbed for Jenny's mane. She flinched,
snorted, whirled, tossing her head.

"Hol on now! Hol on."

Then he saw the hole in Jenny's side, right between the ribs. It was
round, wet, red. A crimson stream streaked down the front leg, flowing
fast. Good Gawd! Ah wuzn't shootin at tha mule. He felt panic. He knew
he had to stop that blood, or Jenny would bleed to death. He had never seen
so much blood in all his life. He chased the mule for half a mile, trying to
catch her. Finally she stopped, breathing hard, stumpy tail half arched. He
caught her mane and led her back to where the plow and gun lay. Then he
stooped and grabbed handfuls of damp black earth and tried to plug the
bullet hole. Jenny shuddered, whinnied, and broke from him.

"Hol on! Hol on now!"   135

He tried to plug it again, but blood came anyhow. His fingers were
hot and sticky. He rubbed dirt into his palms, trying to dry them. Then
again he attempted to plug the bullet hole, but Jenny shied away, kicking
her heels high. He stood helpless. He had to do something. He ran at Jenny;
she dodged him. He watched a red stream of blood flow down Jenny's leg
and form a bright pool at her feet.

"Jenny . . . Jenny," he called weakly.

His lips trembled. She's bleeding t death! He looked in the direction of
home, wanting to go back, wanting to get help. But he saw the pistol lying
in the damp black clay. He had a queer feeling that if he only did something,
this would not be; Jenny would not be there bleeding to death.

When he went to her this time, she did not move. She stood with
sleepy, dreamy eyes; and when he touched her she gave a low-pitched
whinny and knelt to the ground, her front knees slopping in blood.

"Jenny . . . Jenny . . . " he whispered.   140

For a long time she held her neck erect; then her head sank, slowly. Her ribs swelled with a mighty heave and she went over.

Dave's stomach felt empty, very empty. He picked up the gun and held it gingerly between his thumb and forefinger. He buried it at the foot of a tree. He took a stick and tried to cover the pool of blood with dirt — but what was the use? There was Jenny lying with her mouth open and her eyes walled and glassy. He could not tell Jim Hawkins he had shot his mule. But he had to tell something. Yeah, Ah'll tell em Jenny started gittin ill n fell on the joint of the plow. . . . But that would hardly happen to a mule. He walked across the field slowly, head down.

It was sunset. Two of Jim Hawkins' men were over near the edge of the woods digging a hole in which to bury Jenny. Dave was surrounded by a knot of people, all of whom were looking down at the dead mule.

"I don't see how in the world it happened," said Jim Hawkins for the tenth time.

The crowd parted and Dave's mother, father, and small brother pushed   145
into the center.

"Where Dave?" his mother called.

"There he is," said Jim Hawkins.

His mother grabbed him.

"Whut happened, Dave? Whut yuh done?"

"Nothin."   150

"C'mon, boy, talk," his father said.

Dave took a deep breath and told the story he knew nobody believed.

"Waal," he drawled. "Ah brung ol Jenny down here sos Ah could do mah plowin. Ah plowed bout two rows, just like yuh see." He stopped and pointed at the long rows of upturned earth. "Then somethin musta been wrong wid ol Jenny. She wouldn ack right a-tall. She started snortin n kickin her heels. Ah tried t hol her, but she pulled erway, rearin n goin in. Then when the point of the plow was stickin up in the air, she swung erroun n twisted herself back on it . . . She stuck herself n started t bleed. N fo Ah could do anything, she wuz dead."

"Did you ever hear of anything like that in all your life?" asked Jim Hawkins.

There were white and black standing in the crowd. They murmured.   155
Dave's mother came close to him and looked hard into his face. "Tell the truth, Dave," she said.

"Looks like a bullet hole to me," said one man.

"Dave, whut yuh do wid tha gun?" his mother asked.

The crowd surged in, looking at him. He jammed his hands into his pockets, shook his head slowly from left to right, and backed away. His eyes were wide and painful.

"Did he hava gun?" asked Jim Hawkins.

"By Gawd, Ah tol yuh tha wuz a gun wound," said a man, slapping   160
his thigh.

His father caught his shoulders and shook him till his teeth rattled.

"Tell whut happened, yuh rascal! Tell whut . . . "

Dave looked at Jenny's stiff legs and began to cry.

"What yuh do wid tha gun?" his mother asked.

"Whut wuz he doin wida gun?" his father asked.   165

"Come on and tell the truth," said Hawkins. "Ain't nobody going to hurt you . . . "

His mother crowded close to him.

"Did yuh shoot tha mule, Dave?"

Dave cried, seeing blurred white and black faces.

"Ahh ddinn gggo tt sshooot hher . . . Ah sswear tt Gawd Ahh   170
ddin. . . . Ah wuz a-tryin t sssee ef the gggun would sshoot — "

"Where yuh git the gun from?" his father asked.

"Ah got it from Joe, at the sto."

"Where yuh git the money?"

"Ma give it t me."

"He kept worryin me, Bob. Ah had t. Ah tol im t bring the gun right   175
back t me . . . It was fer yuh, the gun."

"But how yuh happen to shoot that mule?" asked Jim Hawkins.

"Ah wuzn shootin at the mule, Mistah Hawkins! The gun jumped when Ah pulled the trigger . . . N fo Ah knowed anythin Jenny was there a-bleedin."

Somebody in the crowd laughed. Jim Hawkins walked close to Dave and looked into his face.

"Well, looks like you have bought you a mule, Dave."

"Ah swear to Gawd. Ah didn go t kill the mule, Mistah Hawkins!"   180

"But you killed her!"

All the crowd was laughing now. They stood on tiptoe and poked heads over one another's shoulders.

"Well, boy, looks like yuh done bought a dead mule! Hahaha!"

"Ain tha ershame."

"Hohohohoho."   185

Dave stood, head down, twisting his feet in the dirt.

"Well, you needn't worry about it, Bob," said Jim Hawkins to Dave's father. "Just let the boy keep on working and pay me two dollars a month."

"Whut yuh wan fer yo mule, Mistah Hawkins?"

Jim Hawkins screwed up his eyes.

"Fifty dollars."   190

"Whut yuh do wid tha gun?" Dave's father demanded.

Dave said nothing.

"Yuh wan me t take a tree n beat yuh till yuh talk!"

"Nawsuh!"

"Whut yuh do wid it?"   195

"Ah throwed it erway."

"Where?"

"Ah . . . Ah throwed it in the creek."

"Waal, c mon home. N firs thing in the mawnin git to tha creek n fin
tha gun."

"Yessuh."

"Whut yuh pay fer it?"

"Two dollahs."

"Take tha gun n git yo money back n carry it t Mistah Hawkins, yuh
hear? N don fergit Ahma lam you black bottom good fer this! Now march
yoself on home, suh!"

Dave turned and walked slowly. He heard people laughing. Dave
glared, his eyes welling with tears. Hot anger bubbled in him. Then he
swallowed and stumbled on.

That night Dave did not sleep. He was glad that he had gotten out of
killing the mule so easily, but he was hurt. Something hot seemed to turn
over inside him each time he remembered how they had laughed. He tossed
on his bed, feeling his hard pillow. *N Pa says he's gonna beat me . . .* He
remembered other beatings, and his back quivered. *Naw, naw, Ah sho don
wan im t beat me tha way no mo. Dam em all!* Nobody ever gave him
anything. All he did was work. *They treat me like a mule, n then they beat
me.* He gritted his teeth. *N Ma had t tell on me.*

Well, if he had to, he would take old man Hawkins that two dollars.
But that meant selling the gun. And he wanted to keep that gun. Fifty
dollars for a dead mule.

He turned over, thinking how he had fired the gun. He had an itch to
fire it again. *Ef other men kin shoota gun, by Gawd, Ah kin!* He was still,
listening. *Mebbe they all sleepin now.* The house was still. He heard the soft
breathing of his brother. *Yes, now!* He would go down and get that gun and
see if he could fire it! He eased out of bed and slipped into overalls.

The moon was bright. He ran almost all the way to the edge of the
woods. He stumbled over the ground, looking for the spot where he had
buried the gun. *Yeah, here it is.* Like a hungry dog scratching for a bone, he
pawed it up. He puffed his black cheeks and blew dirt from the trigger and
barrel. He broke it and found four cartridges unshot. He looked around; the
fields were filled with silence and moonlight. He clutched the gun stiff and
hard in his fingers. But, as soon as he wanted to pull the trigger, he shut his
eyes and turned his head. *Naw, Ah can't shoot wid mah eyes closed n mah
head turned.* With effort he held his eyes open; then he squeezed. *Blooooom!*
He was stiff, not breathing. The gun was still in his hands. *Dammit, he'd
done it!* He fired again. *Blooooom!* He smiled. *Blooooom! Blooooom! Click,
click.* There! It was empty. If anybody could shoot a gun, he could. He put
the gun into his hip pocket and started across the fields.

When he reached the top of a ridge he stood straight and proud in the
moonlight, looking at Jim Hawkins' big white house, feeling the gun sagging in his pocket. *Lawd, ef Ah had just one mo bullet Ah'd taka shot at tha
house. Ah'd like t scare ol man Hawkins jusa little . . . Jusa enough t let im
know Dave Saunders is a man.*

To his left the road curved, running to the tracks of the Illinois Central. 210 He jerked his head, listening. From far off came a faint *hoooof-hoooof; hoooof-hoooof*. . . He stood rigid. Two dollahs a mont. Les see now . . . Tha means it'll take bout two years. Shucks! Ah'll be dam!

He started down the road, toward the tracks. Yeah, here she comes. He stood beside the track and held himself stiffly. Here she comes erroun the ben . . . C mon, yuh slow poke! C mon! He had his hand on his gun; something quivered in his stomach. Then the train thundered past, the gray and brown box cars rumbling and clinking. He gripped the gun tightly; then he jerked his hand out of his pocket. Ah betcha Bill wouldn't do it! Ah betcha . . . The cars slid past, steel grinding upon steel. Ahm ridin yuh ternight, so hep me Gawd! He was hot all over. He hesitated just a moment; then he grabbed, pulled atop of a car, and lay flat. He felt his pocket; the gun was still there. Ahead the long rails were glinting in the moonlight, stretching away, away to somewhere, somewhere where he could be a man . . .

Considerations

1. Describe Dave's attitude toward his work, his employer, and the people with whom he works. To what extent do you think his complaints are justified?
2. Why does Dave's mother oppose his having a gun? Why does she ultimately give in? What is your response to his argument that he ought to have a gun because he's seventeen and "almost a man."
3. What values do Dave's parents hold? How are his values different from theirs? Speculate on the reasons for the differences between their values.
4. Analyze the episode where Dave shoots Jenny. Notice his language, his thoughts, and his actions. What significance do you see in this episode?
5. Some critics have argued that at the end of the story Dave has become a man. Do you agree? Explain.

HERMAN MELVILLE (1819–1891)

Bartleby, the Scrivener

A Story of Wall Street

I am a rather elderly man. The nature of my avocations, for the last thirty years, has brought me into more than ordinary contact with what would seem an interesting and somewhat singular set of men, of whom, as yet, nothing, that I know of, has ever been written—I mean, the law-copyists, or scriveners. I have known very many of them, professionally and privately, and, if I pleased, could relate divers histories, at which good-natured gentlemen might smile, and sentimental souls might weep. But I waive the biographies of all other scriveners, for a few passages in the life of Bartleby, who was a scrivener, the strangest I ever saw, or heard of. While, of other law-copyists, I might write the complete life, of Bartleby nothing of that sort can be done. I believe that no materials exist, for a full and satisfactory biography of this man. It is an irreparable loss to literature. Bartleby was one of those beings of whom nothing is ascertainable, except from the original sources, and, in his case, those are very small. What my own astonished eyes saw of Bartleby, *that* is all I know of him, except, indeed, one vague report, which will appear in the sequel.

Ere introducing the scrivener, as he first appeared to me, it is fit I make some mention of myself, my *employés,* my business, my chambers, and general surroundings, because some such description is indispensable to an adequate understanding of the chief character about to be presented. Im-primis:° I am a man who, from his youth upwards, has been filled with a profound conviction that the easiest way of life is the best. Hence, though I belong to a profession proverbially energetic and nervous, even to turbu-lence, at times, yet nothing of that sort have I ever suffered to invade my peace. I am one of those unambitious lawyers who never address a jury, or in any way draw down public applause; but, in the cool tranquility of a snug retreat, do a snug business among rich men's bonds, and mortgages, and title-deeds. All who know me, consider me an eminently *safe* man. The late John Jacob Astor, a personage little given to poetic enthusiasm, had no hesitation in pronouncing my first grand point to be prudence; my next, method. I do not speak it in vanity, but simply record the fact, that I was not unemployed in my profession by the late John Jacob Astor; a name which, I admit, I love to repeat; for it hath a rounded and orbicular sound to it, and rings like unto bullion. I will freely add, that I was not insensible to the late John Jacob Astor's good opinion.

Some time prior to the period at which this little history begins, my avocations had been largely increased. The good old office, now extinct in the State of New York, of a Master in Chancery, had been conferred upon

---

Imprimis: (Latin) In the first place.

me. It was not a very arduous office, but very pleasantly remunerative. I seldom lose my temper; much more seldom indulge in dangerous indignation at wrongs and outrages; but I must be permitted to be rash here and declare, that I consider the sudden and violent abrogation of the office of Master in Chancery, by the new Constitution, as a — premature act; inasmuch as I had counted upon a life-lease of the profits, whereas I only received those of a few short years. But this is by the way.

My chambers were up stairs, at No. — Wall Street. At one end, they looked upon the white wall of the interior of a spacious skylight shaft, penetrating the building from top to bottom.

This view might have been considered rather tame than otherwise, deficient in what landscape painters call "life." But, if so, the view from the other end of my chambers offered, at least, a contrast, if nothing more. In that direction, my windows commanded an unobstructed view of a lofty brick wall, black by age and everlasting shade; which wall required no spy-glass to bring out its lurking beauties, but, for the benefit of all near-sighted spectators, was pushed up to within ten feet of my window-panes. Owing to the great height of the surrounding buildings, and my chambers being on the second floor, the interval between this wall and mine not a little resembled a huge square cistern.

At the period just preceding the advent of Bartleby, I had two persons as copyists in my employment, and a promising lad as an office-boy. First, Turkey; second, Nippers; third, Ginger Nut. These may seem names, the like of which are not usually found in the Directory. In truth, they were nicknames, mutually conferred upon each other by my three clerks, and were deemed expressive of their respective persons or characters. Turkey was a short, pursy Englishman, of about my own age — that is, somewhere not far from sixty. In the morning, one might say, his face was of a fine florid hue, but after twelve o'clock, meridian — his dinner hour — it blazed like a grate full of Christmas coals; and continued blazing — but, as it were, with a gradual wane — till six o'clock, P.M., or thereabouts; after which, I saw no more of the proprietor of the face, which, gaining its meridian with the sun, seemed to set with it, to rise, culminate, and decline the following day, with the like regularity and undiminished glory. There are many singular coincidences I have known in the course of my life, not the least among which was the fact, that, exactly when Turkey displayed his fullest beams from his red and radiant countenance, just then, too, at that critical moment, began the daily period when I considered his business capacities as seriously disturbed for the remainder of the twenty-four hours. Not that he was absolutely idle, or averse to business then; far from it. The difficulty was, he was apt to be altogether too energetic. There was a strange, inflamed, flurried, flighty recklessness of activity about him. He would be incautious in dipping his pen into his inkstand. All his blots upon my documents were dropped there after twelve o'clock, meridian. Indeed, not only would he be reckless, and sadly given to making blots in the afternoon, but, some days, he went further, and was rather noisy. At such times, too, his face flamed with augmented blazonry, as if cannel coal had been heaped on anthracite. He made an unpleasant racket with his chair; spilled his sand-box; in mending his pens, impatiently split them all to pieces, and threw them on the floor in a sudden passion; stood up, and leaned over his table, boxing his papers about in a most indecorous manner, very sad to behold in an elderly man like him. Nevertheless, as he was in many ways a most valuable person to me, and all the time before twelve o'clock, meridian, was the quickest, steadiest creature, too, accomplishing a great deal of work in a style not easily to be matched—for these reasons, I was willing to overlook his eccentricities, though, indeed, occasionally, I remonstrated with him. I did this very gently, however, because, though the civilest, nay, the blandest and most reverential of men in the morning, yet, in the afternoon, he was disposed, upon provocation, to be slightly rash with his tongue—in fact, insolent. Now, valuing his morning services as I did, and resolved not to lose them—yet, at the same time, made uncomfortable by his inflamed ways after twelve o'clock—and being a man of peace, unwilling by my admonitions to call forth unseemly retorts from him, I took upon me, one Saturday noon (he was always worse on Saturdays) to hint to him, very kindly, that, perhaps, now that he was growing old, it might be well to abridge his labors; in short, he need not come to my chambers after twelve o'clock, but, dinner over, had best go home to his lodgings, and rest himself till tea-time. But no; he insisted upon his afternoon devotions. His countenance became intolerably fervid, as he oratorically assured me—gesticulating with a long ruler at the other end of the room—that if his services in the morning were useful, how indispensable, then, in the afternoon?

"With submission, sir," said Turkey, on this occasion, "I consider myself your right-hand man. In the morning I but marshal and deploy my columns; but in the afternoon I put myself at their head, and gallantly charge the foe, thus"—and he made a violent thrust with the ruler.

"But the blots, Turkey," intimated I.

"True; but, with submission sir, behold these hairs! I am getting old. Surely, sir, a blot or two of a warm afternoon is not to be severely urged against gray hairs. Old age—even if it blot the page—is honorable. With submission, sir, we *both* are getting old."

This appeal to my fellow-feeling was hardly to be resisted. At all   10
events, I saw that go he would not. So, I made up my mind to let him stay, resolving, nevertheless, to see to it that, during the afternoon, he had to do with my less important papers.

Nippers, the second on my list, was a whiskered, sallow, and, upon the whole, rather piratical-looking young man, of about five-and-twenty. I always deemed him the victim of two evil powers—ambition and indigestion. The ambition was evinced by a certain impatience of the duties of a mere copyist, an unwarrantable usurpation of strictly professional affairs such as the original drawing up of legal documents. The indigestion seemed

betokened in an occasional nervous testiness and grinning irritability, causing the teeth to audibly grind together over mistakes committed in copying;
unnecessary maledictions, hissed, rather than spoken, in the heat of business;
and especially by a continual discontent with the height of the table where
he worked. Though of a very ingenious mechanical turn, Nippers could
never get this table to suit him. He put chips under it, blocks of various
sorts, bits of pasteboard, and at last went so far as to attempt an exquisite
adjustment, by final pieces of folded blotting-paper. But no invention would
answer. If, for the sake of easing his back, he brought the table-lid at a sharp
angle well up towards his chin, and wrote there like a man using the steep
roof of a Dutch house for his desk, then he declared that it stopped the
circulation in his arms. If now he lowered the table to his waistbands, and
stooped over it in writing, then there was a sore aching in his back. In short,
the truth of the matter was, Nippers knew not what he wanted. Or, if he
wanted anything, it was to be rid of a scrivener's table altogether. Among
the manifestations of his diseased ambition was a fondness he had for receiving visits from certain ambiguous-looking fellows in seedy coats, whom he
called his clients. Indeed, I was aware that not only was he, at times, considerable of a ward-politician, but he occasionally did a little business at the
justices' courts, and was not unknown on the steps of the Tombs.° I have
good reason to believe, however, that one individual who called upon him
at my chambers, and who, with a grand air, he insisted was his client, was
no other than a dun, and the alleged title-deed, a bill. But, with all his
failings, and the annoyances he caused me, Nippers, like his compatriot
Turkey, was a very useful man to me; wrote a neat, swift hand; and, when
he chose, was not deficient in a gentlemanly sort of deportment. Added to
this, he always dressed in a gentlemanly sort of way; and so, incidentally,
reflected credit upon my chambers. Whereas, with respect to Turkey, I had
much ado to keep him from being a reproach to me. His clothes were apt to
look oily, and smell of eating-houses. He wore his pantaloons very loose
and baggy in summer. His coats were execrable, his hat not to be handled.
But while the hat was a thing of indifference to me, inasmuch as his natural
civility and deference, as a dependent Englishman, always led him to doff it
the moment he entered the room, yet his coat was another matter. Concerning his coats, I reasoned with him; but with no effect. The truth was, I
suppose, that a man with so small an income could not afford to sport such
a lustrous face and a lustrous coat at one and the same time. As Nippers
once observed, Turkey's money went chiefly for red ink. One winter day, I
presented Turkey with a highly respectable-looking coat of my own—a
padded gray coat, of a most comfortable warmth, and which buttoned
straight up from the knee to the neck. I thought Turkey would appreciate
the favor, and abate his rashness and obstreperousness of afternoons. But no;
I verily believe that buttoning himself up in so downy and blanket-like a

Tombs: A notoriously dark and heavily guarded prison in New York City.

coat had a pernicious effect upon him — upon the same principle that too much oats are bad for horses. In fact, precisely as a rash, restive horse is said to feel his oats, so Turkey felt his coat. It made him insolent. He was a man whom prosperity harmed.

Though, concerning the self-indulgent habits of Turkey, I had my own private surmises, yet, touching Nippers, I was well persuaded that, whatever might be his faults in other respects, he was, at least, a temperate young man. But, indeed, nature herself seemed to have been his vintner, and, at his birth, charged him so thoroughly with an irritable, brandy-like disposition, that all subsequent potations were needless. When I consider how, amid the stillness of my chambers, Nippers would sometimes impatiently rise from his seat, and stooping over his table, spread his arms wide apart, seize the whole desk, and move it, and jerk it, with a grim, grinding motion on the floor, as if the table were a perverse voluntary agent, intent on thwarting and vexing him, I plainly perceive that, for Nippers, brandy-and-water were altogether superfluous.

It was fortunate for me that, owing to its peculiar cause — indigestion — the irritability and consequent nervousness of Nippers were mainly observable in the morning, while in the afternoon he was comparatively mild. So that, Turkey's paroxysms only coming on about twelve o'clock, I never had to do with their eccentricities at one time. Their fits relieved each other, like guards. When Nippers' was on, Turkey's was off; and *vice versa*. This was a good natural arrangement, under the circumstances.

Ginger Nut, the third on my list, was a lad, some twelve years old. His father was a carman, ambitious of seeing his son on the bench instead of a cart, before he died. So he sent him to my office, as student at law, errand-boy, cleaner, and sweeper, at the rate of one dollar a week. He had a little desk to himself, but he did not use it much. Upon inspection, the drawer exhibited a great array of the shells of various sorts of nuts. Indeed, to this quick-witted youth, the whole noble science of the law was contained in a nutshell. Not the least among the employments of Ginger Nut, as well as one which he discharged with the most alacrity, was his duty as cake and apple purveyor for Turkey and Nippers. Copying lawpapers being proverbially a dry, husky sort of business, my two scriveners were fain to moisten their mouths very often with Spitzenbergs, to be had at the numerous stalls nigh the Custom House and Post Office. Also, they sent Ginger Nut very frequently for that peculiar cake — small, flat, round, and very spicy — after which he had been named by them. Of a cold morning, when business was but dull, Turkey would gobble up scores of these cakes, as if they were mere wafers — indeed, they sell them at the rate of six or eight for a penny — the scrape of his pen blending with the crunching of the crisp particles in his mouth. Of all the fiery afternoon blunders and flurried rashness of Turkey, was his once moistening a ginger-cake between his lips, and clapping it on to a mortgage, for a seal. I came within an ace of dismissing him then. But he mollified me by making an oriental bow, and saying —

"With submission, sir, it was generous of me to find you in stationery   15
on my own account."

Now my original business—that of a conveyancer and title hunter, and
drawer-up of recondite documents of all sorts—was considerably increased
by receiving the Master's office. There was now great work for scriveners.
Not only must I push the clerks already with me, but I must have additional
help.

In answer to my advertisement, a motionless young man one morning
stood upon my office threshold, the door being open, for it was summer. I
can see that figure now—pallidly neat, pitiably respectable, incurably forlorn! It was Bartleby.

After a few words touching his qualifications, I engaged him, glad to
have among my corps of copyists a man of so singularly sedate an aspect,
which I thought might operate beneficially upon the flighty temper of Turkey, and the fiery one of Nippers.

I should have stated before that ground-glass folding-doors divided
my premises into two parts, one of which was occupied by my scriveners,
the other by myself. According to my humor, I threw open these doors, or
closed them. I resolved to assign Bartleby a corner by the folding-doors,
but on my side of them, so as to have this quiet man within easy call, in
case any trifling thing was to be done. I placed his desk close up to a small
side-window in that part of the room, a window which originally had
afforded a lateral view of certain grimy brickyards and bricks, but which,
owing to subsequent erections, commanded at present no view at all, though
it gave some light. Within three feet of the panes was a wall, and the light
came down from far above, between two lofty buildings, as from a very
small opening in a dome. Still further to a satisfactory arrangement, I procured a high green folding screen, which might entirely isolate Bartleby
from my sight, though not remove him from my voice. And thus, in a
manner, privacy and society were conjoined.

At first, Bartleby did an extraordinary quantity of writing. As if long   20
famishing for something to copy, he seemed to gorge himself on my documents. There was no pause for digestion. He ran a day and night line,
copying by sunlight and by candle-light. I should have been quite delighted
with his application, had he been cheerfully industrious. But he wrote on
silently, palely, mechanically.

It is, of course, an indispensable part of a scrivener's business to verify
the accuracy of his copy, word by word. Where there are two or more
scriveners in an office, they assist each other in this examination, one reading
from the copy, the other holding the original. It is a very dull, wearisome,
and lethargic affair. I can readily imagine that, to some sanguine tempera-
ments, it would be altogether intolerable. For example, I cannot credit that
the mettlesome poet, Byron, would have contentedly sat down with Bartleby to examine a law document of, say five hundred pages, closely written
in a crimpy hand.

Now and then, in the haste of business, it had been my habit to assist in comparing some brief document myself, calling Turkey or Nippers for this purpose. One object I had, in placing Bartleby so handy to me behind the screen, was, to avail myself of his services on such trivial occasions. It was on the third day, I think, of his being with me, and before any necessity had arisen for having his own writing examined, that, being much hurried to complete a small affair I had in hand, I abruptly called to Bartleby. In my haste and natural expectancy of instant compliance, I sat with my head bent over the original on my desk, and my right hand sideways, and somewhat nervously extended with the copy, so that, immediately upon emerging from his retreat, Bartleby might snatch it and proceed to business without the least delay.

In this very attitude did I sit when I called to him, rapidly stating what it was I wanted him to do—namely, to examine a small paper with me. Imagine my surprise, nay, my consternation, when, without moving from his privacy, Bartleby, in a singularly mild, firm voice, replied, "I would prefer not to."

I sat awhile in perfect silence, rallying my stunned faculties. Immediately it occurred to me that my ears had deceived me, or Bartleby had entirely misunderstood my meaning. I repeated my request in the clearest tone I could assume; but in quite as clear a one came the previous reply, "I would prefer not to."

"Prefer not to," echoed I, rising in high excitement, and crossing the   25
room with a stride. "What do you mean? Are you moonstruck? I want you to help me compare this sheet here—take it," and I thrust it towards him.

"I would prefer not to," said he.

I looked at him steadfastly. His face was leanly composed; his gray eyes dimly calm. Not a wrinkle of agitation rippled him. Had there been the least uneasiness, anger, impatience, or impertinence in his manner; in other words, had there been anything ordinarily human about him, doubtless I should have violently dismissed him from the premises. But as it was, I should have as soon thought of turning my pale plaster-of-paris bust of Cicero° out of doors. I stood gazing at him awhile, as he went on with his own writing, and then reseated myself at my desk. This is very strange, thought I. What had one best do? But my business hurried me. I concluded to forget the matter for the present, reserving it for my future leisure. So, calling Nippers from the other room, the paper was speedily examined.

A few days after this, Bartleby concluded four lengthy documents, being quadruplicates of a week's testimony taken before me in my High Court of Chancery. It became necessary to examine them. It was an important suit, and great accuracy was imperative. Having all things arranged, I

Cicero: (106–43 B.C.) A Roman philosopher, orator, and senator; his philosophical writings are generally stoical (a school of thought that believed humans should set aside their own emotions, passions, and prejudices to perform their higher duty as reflected by the laws of nature).

called Turkey, Nippers, and Ginger Nut, from the next room, meaning to place the four copies in the hands of my four clerks, while I should read from the original. Accordingly, Turkey, Nippers, and Ginger Nut had taken their seats in a row, each with his document in his hand, when I called to Bartleby to join this interesting group.

"Bartleby! quick, I am waiting."

I heard a slow scrape of his chair legs on the uncarpeted floor, and soon   30
he appeared standing at the entrance of his hermitage.

"What is wanted?" said he, mildly.

"The copies, the copies," said I, hurriedly. "We are going to examine them. There" — and I held towards him the fourth quadruplicate.

"I would prefer not to," he said, and gently disappeared behind the screen.

For a few moments I was turned into a pillar of salt, standing at the head of my seated column of clerks. Recovering myself, I advanced towards the screen, and demanded the reason for such extraordinary conduct.

"*Why* do you refuse?"   35

"I would prefer not to."

With any other man I should have flown outright into a dreadful passion, scorned all further words, and thrust him ignominiously from my presence. But there was something about Bartleby that not only strangely disarmed me, but, in a wonderful manner, touched and disconcerted me. I began to reason with him.

"These are your own copies we are about to examine. It is labor saving to you, because one examination will answer for your four papers. It is common usage. Every copyist is bound to help examine his copy. Is it not so? Will you not speak? Answer!"

"I prefer not to," he replied in a flute-like tone. It seemed to me that, while I had been addressing him, he carefully revolved every statement that I made; fully comprehended the meaning; could not gainsay the irresistible conclusion; but, at the same time, some paramount consideration prevailed with him to reply as he did.

"You are decided, then, not to comply with my request — a request   40
made according to common usage and common sense?"

He briefly gave me to understand, that on that point my judgment was sound. Yes: his decision was irreversible.

It is not seldom the case that, when a man is browbeaten in some unprecedented and violently unreasonable way, he begins to stagger in his own plainest faith. He begins, as it were, vaguely to surmise that, wonderful as it may be, all the justice and all the reason is on the other side. Accordingly, if any disinterested persons are present, he turns to them for some reinforcement for his own faltering mind.

"Turkey," said I, "what do you think of this? Am I not right?"

"With submission, sir," said Turkey, in his blandest tone, "I think that you are."

"Nippers," said I, "what do *you* think of it?"   45

"I think I should kick him out of the office."

(The reader of nice perceptions will have perceived that, it being morning, Turkey's answer is couched in polite and tranquil terms, but Nippers replies in ill-tempered ones. Or, to repeat a previous sentence, Nippers' ugly mood was on duty, and Turkey's off.)

"Ginger Nut," said I, willing to enlist the smallest suffrage in my behalf, "what do *you* think of it?"

"I think, sir, he's a little *luny,*" replied Ginger Nut, with a grin.

"You hear what they say," said I, turning towards the screen, "come   50 forth and do your duty."

But he vouchsafed no reply. I pondered a moment in sore perplexity. But once more business hurried me. I determined again to postpone the consideration of this dilemma to my future leisure. With a little trouble we made out to examine the papers without Bartleby, though at every page or two Turkey deferentially dropped his opinion, that this proceeding was quite out of the common; while Nippers, twitching in his chair with a dyspeptic nervousness, ground out, between his set teeth, occasional hissing maledictions against the stubborn oaf behind the screen. And for his (Nippers') part, this was the first and the last time he would do another man's business without pay.

Meanwhile Bartleby sat in his hermitage, oblivious to everything but his own peculiar business there.

Some days passed, the scrivener being employed upon another lengthy work. His late remarkable conduct led me to regard his ways narrowly. I observed that he never went to dinner; indeed, that he never went anywhere. As yet I had never, of my personal knowledge, known him to be outside of my office. He was a perpetual sentry in the corner. At about eleven o'clock though, in the morning, I noticed that Ginger Nut would advance towards the opening in Bartleby's screen, as if silently beckoned thither by a gesture invisible to me where I sat. The boy would then leave the office, jingling a few pence, and reappear with a handful of ginger-nuts, which he delivered in the hermitage, receiving two of the cakes for his trouble.

He lives, then, on ginger-nuts, thought I; never eats a dinner, properly speaking; he must be a vegetarian, then, but no; he never eats even vegetables, he eats nothing but ginger-nuts. My mind then ran on in reveries concerning the probable effects upon the human constitution of living entirely on ginger-nuts. Ginger-nuts are so called, because they contain ginger as one of their peculiar constituents, and the final flavoring one. Now, what was ginger? A hot, spicy thing. Was Bartleby hot and spicy? Not at all. Ginger, then, had no effect upon Bartleby. Probably he preferred it should have none.

Nothing so aggravates an earnest person as a passive resistance. If the   55 individual so resisted be of a not inhumane temper, and the resisting one perfectly harmless in his passivity, then, in the better moods of the former, he will endeavor charitably to construe to his imagination what proves impossible to be solved by his judgment. Even so, for the most part, I regarded Bartleby and his ways. Poor fellow! thought I, he means no mischief; it is plain he intends no insolence; his aspect sufficiently evinces that his eccentricities are involuntary. He is useful to me. I can get along with him. If I turn him away, the chances are he will fall in with some less indulgent employer, and then he will be rudely treated, and perhaps driven forth miserably to starve. Yes. Here I can cheaply purchase a delicious self-approval. To befriend Bartleby; to humor him in his strange wilfulness, will cost me little or nothing, while I lay up in my soul what will eventually prove a sweet morsel for my conscience. But this mood was not invariable with me. The passiveness of Bartleby sometimes irritated me. I felt strangely goaded on to encounter him in new opposition—to elicit some angry spark from him answerable to my own. But, indeed, I might as well have essayed to strike fire with my knuckles against a bit of Windsor soap. But one afternoon the evil impulse in me mastered me, and the following little scene ensued:

"Bartleby," said I, "when those papers are all copied, I will compare them with you."

"I would prefer not to."

"How? Surely you do not mean to persist in that mulish vagary?"

No answer.

I threw open the folding-doors nearby, and turning upon Turkey and Nippers, exclaimed: 60

"Bartleby a second time says, he won't examine his papers. What do you think of it, Turkey?"

It was afternoon, be it remembered. Turkey sat glowing like a brass boiler; his bald head steaming; his hands reeling among his blotted papers.

"Think of it?" roared Turkey. "I think I'll just step behind his screen, and black his eyes for him!"

So saying, Turkey rose to his feet and threw his arms into a pugilistic position. He was hurrying away to make good his promise, when I detained him, alarmed at the effect of incautiously rousing Turkey's combativeness after dinner.

"Sit down, Turkey," said I, "and hear what Nippers has to say. What 65 do you think of it, Nippers? Would I not be justified in immediately dismissing Bartleby?"

"Excuse me, that is for you to decide, sir. I think his conduct quite unusual, and, indeed, unjust, as regards Turkey and myself. But it may only be a passing whim."

"Ah," exclaimed I, "you have strangely changed your mind, then—you speak very gently of him now."

"All beer," cried Turkey; "gentleness is effects of beer—Nippers and I dined together to-day. You see how gentle *I* am, sir. Shall I go and black his eyes?"

"You refer to Bartleby, I suppose. No, not to-day, Turkey," I replied; "pray, put up your fists."

I closed the doors, and again advanced towards Bartleby. I felt addi-   70
tional incentives tempting me to my fate. I burned to be rebelled against again. I remembered that Bartleby never left the office.

"Bartleby," said I, Ginger Nut is away; just step around to the Post Office, won't you?" (it was but a three minutes' walk) "and see if there is anything for me."

"I would prefer not to."

"You *will* not?"

"I *prefer* not."

I staggered to my desk, and sat there in a deep study. My blind invet-   75
eracy returned. Was there any other thing in which I could procure myself to be ignominiously repulsed by this lean, penniless wight? — my hired clerk? What added thing is there, perfectly reasonable, that he will be sure to refuse to do?

"Bartleby!"

No answer.

"Bartleby," in a louder tone.

No answer.

"Bartleby," I roared.   80

Like a very ghost, agreeably to the laws of magical invocation, at the third summons, he appeared at the entrance of his hermitage.

"Go to the next room, and tell Nippers to come to me."

"I prefer not to," he respectfully and slowly said, and mildly disappeared.

"Very good, Bartleby," said I, in a quiet sort of serenely-severe self-possessed tone, intimating the unalterable purpose of some terrible retribution very close at hand. At the moment I half intended something of the kind. But upon the whole, as it was drawing towards my dinner-hour, I thought it best to put on my hat and walk home for the day, suffering much from perplexity and distress of mind.

Shall I acknowledge it? The conclusion of this whole business was, that   85
it soon became a fixed fact of my chambers, that a pale young scrivener, by the name of Bartleby, had a desk there; that he copied for me at the usual rate of four cents a folio (one hundred words); but he was permanently exempt from examining the work done by him, that duty being transferred to Turkey and Nippers, out of compliment, doubtless, to their superior acuteness; moreover, said Bartleby was never, on any account, to be dispatched on the most trivial errand of any sort; and that even if entreated to take upon him such a matter, it was generally understood that he would "prefer not to" — in other words, that he would refuse point-blank.

As days passed on, I became considerably reconciled to Bartleby. His steadiness, his freedom from all dissipation, his incessant industry (except when he chose to throw himself into a standing revery behind his screen), his great stillness, his unalterableness of demeanor under all circumstances, made him a valuable acquisition. One prime thing was this — *he was always there* — first in the morning, continually through the day, and the last at night. I had a singular confidence in his honesty. I felt my most precious papers perfectly safe in his hands. Sometimes, to be sure, I could not, for the very soul of me, avoid falling into sudden spasmodic passions with him. For it was exceeding difficult to bear in mind all the time those strange peculiarities, privileges, and unheard-of exemptions, forming the tacit stipulations on Bartleby's part under which he remained in my office. Now and then, in the eagerness of dispatching pressing business, I would inadvertently summon Bartleby, in a short, rapid tone, to put his finger, say, on the incipient tie of a bit of red tape with which I was about compressing some papers. Of course, from behind the screen the usual answer, "I prefer not to," was sure to come; and then, how could a human creature, with the common infirmities of our nature, refrain from bitterly exclaiming upon such perverseness — such unreasonableness? However, every added repulse of this sort which I received only tended to lessen the probability of my repeating the inadvertence.

Here it must be said, that, according to the custom of most legal gentlemen occupying chambers in densely populated law buildings, there were several keys to my door. One was kept by a woman residing in the attic, which person weekly scrubbed and daily swept and dusted my apartments. Another was kept by Turkey for convenience sake. The third I sometimes carried in my own pocket. The fourth I knew not who had.

Now, one Sunday morning I happened to go to Trinity Church, to hear a celebrated preacher, and finding myself rather early on the ground I thought I would walk round to my chambers for a while. Luckily I had my key with me; but upon applying it to the lock, I found it resisted by something inserted from the inside. Quite surprised, I called out; when to my consternation a key was turned from within; and thrusting his lean visage at me, and holding the door ajar, the apparition of Bartleby appeared, in his shirt-sleeves, and otherwise in a strangely tattered *deshabille*,° saying quietly that he was sorry, but he was deeply engaged just then, and — preferred not admitting me at present. In a brief word or two, he moreover added, that perhaps I had better walk round the block two or three times, and by that time he would probably have concluded his affairs.

Now, the utterly unsurmised appearance of Bartleby, tenanting my law-chambers of a Sunday morning, with his cadaverously gentlemanly *nonchalance,* yet withal firm and self-possessed, had such a strange effect upon me, that incontinently I slunk away from my own door, and did as desired. But not without sundry twinges of impotent rebellion against the mild effrontery of this unaccountable scrivener. Indeed, it was his wonderful mildness chiefly, which not only disarmed me, but unmanned me, as it were.

---

deshabille: Partial dress or night clothes.

For I consider that one, for the time, is a sort of unmanned when he tranquilly permits his hired clerk to dictate to him, and order him away from his own premises. Furthermore, I was full of uneasiness as to what Bartleby could possibly be doing in my office in his shirt-sleeves, and in an otherwise dismantled condition of a Sunday morning. Was anything amiss going on? Nay, that was out of the question. It was not to be thought of for a moment that Bartleby was an immoral person. But what could he be doing there? — copying? Nay again, whatever might be his eccentricities, Bartleby was an eminently decorous person. He would be the last man to sit down to his desk in any state approaching to nudity. Besides, it was Sunday; and there was something about Bartleby that forbade the supposition that he would by any secular occupation violate the proprieties of the day.

Nevertheless, my mind was not pacified; and full of a restless curiosity, at last I returned to the door. Without hindrance I inserted my key, opened it, and entered. Bartleby was not to be seen. I looked round anxiously, peeped behind his screen; but it was very plain that he was gone. Upon more closely examining the place, I surmised that for an indefinite period Bartleby must have ate, dressed, and slept in my office, and that too without plate, mirror, or bed. The cushioned seat of a rickety old sofa in one corner bore the faint impress of a lean, reclining form. Rolled away under his desk, I found a blanket; under the empty grate, a blacking box and brush; on a chair, a tin basin, with soap and a ragged towel; in a newspaper a few crumbs of ginger-nuts and a morsel of cheese. Yes, thought I, it is evident enough that Bartleby has been making his home here, keeping bachelor's hall all by himself. Immediately then the thought came sweeping across me, what miserable friendlessness and loneliness are here revealed! His poverty is great; but his solitude, how horrible! Think of it. Of a Sunday, Wall Street is deserted as Petra;° and every night of every day it is an emptiness. This building, too, which of week-days hums with industry and life, at nightfall echoes with sheer vacancy, and all through Sunday is forlorn. And here Bartleby makes his home; sole spectator of a solitude which he has seen all populous — a sort of innocent and transformed Marius° brooding among the ruins of Carthage!

For the first time in my life a feeling of overpowering stinging melancholy seized me. Before, I had never experienced aught but a not unpleasing sadness. The bond of a common humanity now drew me irresistibly to gloom. A fraternal melancholy! For both I and Bartleby were sons of Adam. I remembered the bright silks and sparkling faces I had seen that day, in gala trim, swan-like sailing down the Mississippi of Broadway; and I contrasted them with the pallid copyist, and thought to myself, Ah, happiness courts the light, so we deem the world is gay; but misery hides aloof, so we deem

90

Petra: Ancient city in present-day Jordan; rediscovered in 1812 after being deserted for more than 1000 years.   *Gaius Marius:* (157?–186 B.C.) A Roman military leader who was elected consul but was later banished by his enemies, who forced him to flee to Carthage, a city in North Africa.

that misery there is none. These sad fancyings — chimeras, doubtless, of a sick and silly brain — led on to other and more special thoughts, concerning the eccentricities of Bartleby. Presentiments of strange discoveries hovered round me. The scrivener's pale form appeared to me laid out, among uncaring strangers, in its shivering winding-sheet.

Suddenly I was attracted by Bartleby's closed desk, the key in open sight left in the lock.

I mean no mischief, seek the gratification of no heartless curiosity, thought I; besides, the desk is mine, and its contents, too, so I will make bold to look within. Everything was methodically arranged, the papers smoothly placed. The pigeon-holes were deep, and removing the files of documents, I groped into their recesses. Presently I felt something there, and dragged it out. It was an old bandanna handkerchief, heavy and knotted. I opened it, and saw it was a saving's bank.

I now recalled all the quiet mysteries which I had noted in the man. I remembered that he never spoke but to answer; that, though at intervals he had considerable time to himself, yet I had never seen him reading — no, not even a newspaper; that for long periods he would stand looking out, at his pale window behind the screen, upon the dead brick wall; I was quite sure he never visited any refectory or eating-house; while his pale face clearly indicated that he never drank beer like Turkey; or tea and coffee even, like other men; that he never went anywhere in particular that I could learn; never went out for a walk, unless, indeed, that was the case at present; that he had declined telling who he was, or whence he came, or whether he had any relatives in the world; that though so thin and pale, he never complained of ill-health. And more than all, I remembered a certain unconscious air of pallid — how shall I call it? — of pallid haughtiness, say, or rather an austere reserve about him, which has positively awed me into my tame compliance with his eccentricities, when I had feared to ask him to do the slightest incidental thing for me, even though I might know, from his long-continued motionlessness, that behind his screen he must be standing in one of those dead-wall reveries of his.

Revolving all these things, and coupling them with the recently dis-   95
covered fact, that he made my office his constant abiding place and home, and not forgetful of his morbid moodiness; revolving all these things, a prudential feeling began to steal over me. My first emotions had been those of pure melancholy and sincerest pity; but just in proportion as the forlornness of Bartleby grew and grew to my imagination, did that same melancholy merge into fear, that pity into repulsion. So true it is, and so terrible, too, that up to a certain point the thought or sight of misery enlists our best affections; but, in certain special cases, beyond that point it does not. They err who would assert that invariably this is owing to the inherent selfishness of the human heart. It rather proceeds from a certain hopelessness of remedying excessive and organic ill. To a sensitive being, pity is not seldom pain. And when at last it is perceived that such pity cannot lead to effectual succor,

common sense bids the soul be rid of it. What I saw that morning persuaded me that the scrivener was the victim of innate and incurable disorder. I might give alms to his body; but his body did not pain him; it was his soul that suffered, and his soul I could not reach.

I did not accomplish the purpose of going to Trinity Church that morning. Somehow, the things I had seen disqualified me for the time from church-going. I walked homeward, thinking what I would do with Bartleby. Finally, I resolved upon this—I would put certain calm questions to him the next morning, touching his history, etc., and if he declined to answer them openly and unreservedly (and I supposed he would prefer not), then to give him a twenty dollar bill over and above whatever I might owe him, and tell him his services were no longer required; but that if in any other way I could assist him, I would be happy to do so, especially if he desired to return to his native place, wherever that might be, I would willingly help to defray the expenses. Moreover, if, after reaching home, he found himself at any time in want of aid, a letter from him would be sure of a reply.

The next morning came.

"Bartleby," said I, gently calling to him behind his screen.

No reply.

"Bartleby," said I, in a still gentler tone, "come here; I am not going to ask you to do anything you would prefer not to do—I simply wish to speak to you."

Upon this he noiselessly slid into view.

"Will you tell me, Bartleby, where you were born?"

"I would prefer not to."

"Will you tell me *anything* about yourself?"

"I would prefer not to."

"But what reasonable objection can you have to speak to me? I feel friendly towards you."

He did not look at me while I spoke, but kept his glance fixed upon my bust of Cicero, which, as I then sat, was directly behind me, some six inches above my head.

"What is your answer, Bartleby?" said I, after waiting a considerable time for a reply, during which his countenance remained immovable, only there was the faintest conceivable tremor of the white attenuated mouth.

"At present I prefer to give no answer," he said, and retired into his hermitage.

It was rather weak in me I confess, but his manner, on this occasion, nettled me. Not only did there seem to lurk in it a certain calm disdain, but his perverseness seemed ungrateful, considering the undeniable good usage and indulgence he had received from me.

Again I sat ruminating what I should do. Mortified as I was at his behavior, and resolved as I had been to dismiss him when I entered my office, nevertheless I strangely felt something superstitious knocking at my heart, and forbidding me to carry out my purpose, and denouncing me for a villain if I dared to breathe one bitter word against this forlornest of mankind. At last, familiarly drawing my chair behind his screen, I sat down and said: "Bartleby, never mind, then, about revealing your history; but let me entreat you, as a friend, to comply as far as may be with the usages of this office. Say now, you will help to examine papers tomorrow or next day: in short, say now, that in a day or two you will begin to be a little reasonable: — say so, Bartleby."

"At present I would prefer not to be a little reasonable," was his mildly cadaverous reply.

Just then the folding-doors opened, and Nippers approached. He seemed suffering from an unusually bad night's rest, induced by severer indigestion than common. He overheard those final words of Bartleby.

"*Prefer not,* eh?" gritted Nippers — "I'd *prefer* him, if I were you, sir," addressing me — "I'd *prefer* him; I'd give him preferences, the stubborn mule! What is it, sir, pray, that he *prefers* not to do now?"

Bartleby moved not a limb.   115

"Mr. Nippers," said I, "I'd prefer that you would withdraw for the present."

Somehow, of late, I had got into the way of involuntarily using this word "prefer" upon all sorts of not exactly suitable occasions. And I trembled to think that my contact with the scrivener had already and seriously affected me in a mental way. And what further and deeper aberration might it not yet produce? This apprehension had not been without efficacy in determining me to summary measures.

As Nippers, looking very sour and sulky, was departing, Turkey blandly and deferentially approached.

"With submission, sir," said he, "yesterday I was thinking about Bartleby here, and I think that if he would but prefer to take a quart of good ale every day, it would do much towards mending him, and enabling him to assist in examining his papers."

"So you have got the word, too," said I, slightly excited.   120

"With submission, what word, sir?" asked Turkey, respectfully crowding himself into the contracted space behind the screen, and by so doing, making me jostle the scrivener. "What word, sir?"

"I would prefer to be left alone here," said Bartleby, as if offended at being mobbed in his privacy.

"*That's* the word, Turkey," said I — "*that's* it."

"Oh, *prefer?* oh yes — queer word. I never use it myself. But, sir, as I was saying, if he would but prefer — "

"Turkey," interrupted I, "you will please withdraw."   125

"Oh certainly, sir, if you prefer that I should."

As he opened the folding-door to retire, Nippers at his desk caught a glimpse of me, and asked whether I would prefer to have a certain paper copied on blue paper or white. He did not in the least roguishly accent the word "prefer." It was plain that it involuntarily rolled from his tongue. I thought to myself, surely I must get rid of a demented man, who already has in some degree turned the tongues, if not the heads of myself and clerks. But I thought it prudent not to break the dismission at once.

The next day I noticed that Bartleby did nothing but stand at his window in his dead-wall revery. Upon asking him why he did not write, he said that he had decided upon doing no more writing.

"Why, how now? what next?" exclaimed I, "do no more writing?"

"No more."   130

"And what is the reason?"

"Do you not see the reason for yourself?" he indifferently replied.

I looked steadfastly at him, and perceived that his eyes looked dull and glazed. Instantly it occurred to me, that his unexampled diligence in copying by his dim window for the first few weeks of his stay with me might have temporarily impaired his vision.

I was touched. I said something in condolence with him. I hinted that of course he did wisely in abstaining from writing for a while; and urged him to embrace that opportunity of taking wholesome exercise in the open air. This, however, he did not do. A few days after this, my other clerks being absent, and being in a great hurry to dispatch certain letters by the mail, I thought that, having nothing else earthly to do, Bartleby would surely be less inflexible than usual, and carry these letters to the Post Office. But he blankly declined. So, much to my inconvenience, I went myself.

Still added days went by. Whether Bartleby's eyes improved or not, I   135
could not say. To all appearance, I thought they did. But when I asked him if they did, he vouchsafed no answer. At all events, he would do no copying. At last, in replying to my urgings, he informed me that he had permanently given up copying.

"What!" exclaimed I; "suppose your eyes should get entirely well— better than ever before—would you not copy then?"

"I have given up copying," he answered, and slid aside.

He remained as ever, a fixture in my chamber. Nay—if that were possible—he became still more of a fixture than before. What was to be done? He would do nothing in the office; why should he stay there? In plain fact, he had now become a millstone to me, not only useless as a necklace, but afflictive to bear. Yet I was sorry for him. I speak less than truth when I say that, on his own account, he occasioned me uneasiness. If he would but have named a single relative or friend, I would instantly have written, and urged their taking the poor fellow away to some convenient retreat. But he seemed alone, absolutely alone in the universe. A bit of wreck in the mid-Atlantic. At length, necessities connected with my business tyrannized over all other considerations. Decently as I could, I told Bartleby that in six days' time he must unconditionally leave the office. I warned him to take measures, in the interval, for procuring some other abode. I offered to assist him in this endeavor, if he himself would but take the first step towards a removal. "And when you finally quit me, Bartleby," added I, "I shall see that you go not away entirely unprovided. Six days from this hour, remember."

At the expiration of that period, I peeped behind the screen, and lo! Bartleby was there.

I buttoned up my coat, balanced myself; advanced slowly towards 140 him, touched his shoulder, and said, "The time has come; you must quit this place; I am sorry for you; here is money; but you must go."

"I would prefer not," he replied, with his back still towards me.

"You *must*."

He remained silent.

Now I had an unbounded confidence in this man's common honesty. He had frequently restored to me sixpences and shillings carelessly dropped upon the floor, for I am apt to be very reckless in such shirt-button affairs. The proceeding, then, which followed will not be deemed extraordinary.

"Bartleby," said I, "I owe you twelve dollars on account; here are 145 thirty-two; the odd twenty are yours — Will you take it?" and I handed the bills towards him.

But he made no motion.

"I will leave them here, then," putting them under a weight on the table. Then taking my hat and cane and going to the door, I tranquilly turned and added — "After you have removed your things from these offices, Bartleby, you will of course lock the door — since every one is now gone for the day but you — and if you please, slip your key underneath the mat, so that I may have it in the morning. I shall not see you again; so good-bye to you. If, hereafter, in your new place of abode, I can be of any service to you, do not fail to advise me by letter. Good-bye, Bartleby, and fare you well."

But he answered not a word; like the last column of some ruined temple, he remained standing mute and solitary in the middle of the otherwise deserted room.

As I walked home in a pensive mood, my vanity got the better of my pity. I could not but highly plume myself on my masterly management in getting rid of Bartleby. Masterly I call it, and such it must appear to any dispassionate thinker. The beauty of my procedure seemed to consist in its perfect quietness. There was no vulgar bullying, no bravado of any sort, no choleric hectoring, and striding to and fro across the apartment, jerking out vehement commands for Bartleby to bundle himself off with his beggarly traps. Nothing of the kind. Without loudly bidding Bartleby depart — as an inferior genius might have done — I *assumed* the ground that depart he must; and upon that assumption built all I had to say. The more I thought over my procedure, the more I was charmed with it. Nevertheless, next morning, upon awakening, I had my doubts — I had somehow slept off the fumes of vanity. One of the coolest and wisest hours a man has, is just after he awakes in the morning. My procedure seemed as sagacious as ever — but only in theory. How it would prove in practice — there was the rub. It was truly a beautiful thought to have assumed Bartleby's departure; but, after all, that assumption was simply my own, and none of Bartleby's. The great point was, not whether I had assumed that he would quit me, but whether he would prefer to do so. He was more a man of preferences than assumptions.

After breakfast, I walked down town, arguing the probabilities *pro* and   150
con. One moment I thought it would prove a miserable failure, and Bartleby would be found all alive at my office as usual; the next moment it seemed certain that I should find his chair empty. And so I kept veering about. At the corner of Broadway and Canal Street, I saw quite an excited group of people standing in earnest conversation.

"I'll take odds he doesn't," said a voice as I passed.

"Doesn't go? — done!" said I, "put up your money."

I was instinctively putting my hand in my pocket to produce my own, when I remembered that this was an election day. The words I had overheard bore no reference to Bartleby, but to the success or non-success of some candidate for the mayoralty. In my intent frame of mind, I had, as it were, imagined that all Broadway shared in my excitement, and were debating the same question with me. I passed on, very thankful that the uproar of the street screened my momentary absent-mindedness.

As I had intended, I was earlier than usual at my office door. I stood listening for a moment. All was still. He must be gone. I tried the knob. The door was locked. Yes, my procedure had worked to a charm; he indeed must be vanished. Yet a certain melancholy mixed with this: I was almost sorry for my brilliant success. I was fumbling under the door mat for the key, which Bartleby was to have left there for me, when accidentally my knee knocked against a panel, producing a summoning sound, and in response a voice came to me from within — "Not yet; I am occupied."

It was Bartleby.   155

I was thunderstruck. For an instant I stood like the man who, pipe in mouth, was killed one cloudless afternoon long ago in Virginia, by summer lightning; at his own warm open window he was killed, and remained leaning out there upon the dreamy afternoon, till some one touched him, when he fell.

"Not gone!" I murmured at last. But again obeying that wondrous ascendancy which the inscrutable scrivener had over me, and from which ascendancy, for all my chafing, I could not completely escape, I slowly went down stairs and out into the street, and while walking round the block, considered what I should next do in this unheard-of perplexity. Turn the man out by an actual thrusting I could not; to drive him away by calling him hard names would not do; calling in the police was an unpleasant idea; and yet, permit him to enjoy his cadaverous triumph over me — this, too, I could not think of. What was to be done? or, if nothing could be done, was there anything further that I could *assume* in the matter? Yes, as before I had prospectively assumed that Bartleby would depart, so now I might retrospectively assume that departed he was. In the legitimate carrying out of this assumption, I might enter my office in a great hurry, and pretending not to see Bartleby at all, walk straight against him as if he were air. Such a proceeding would in a singular degree have the appearance of a home-thrust. It was hardly possible that Bartleby could withstand such an application of the doctrine of assumption. But upon second thoughts the success of the plan seemed rather dubious. I resolved to argue the matter over with him again.

"Bartleby," said I, entering the office, with a quietly severe expression, "I am seriously displeased. I am pained, Bartleby. I had thought better of you. I had imagined you of such a gentlemanly organization, that in any delicate dilemma a slight hint would suffice — in short, an assumption. But it appears I am deceived. Why," I added, unaffectedly starting, "you have not even touched that money yet," pointing to it, just where I had left it the evening previous.

He answered nothing.

"Will you, or will you not, quit me?" I now demanded in a sudden passion, advancing close to him.   160

"I would prefer *not* to quit you," he replied, gently emphasizing the *not*.

"What earthly right have you to stay here? Do you pay any rent? Do you pay my taxes? Or is this property yours?"

He answered nothing.

"Are you ready to go on and write now? Are your eyes recovered? Could you copy a small paper for me this morning? or help examine a few lines? or step round to the Post Office? In a word, will you do anything at all, to give a coloring to your refusal to depart the premises?"

He silently retired into his hermitage.   165

I was now in such a state of nervous resentment that I thought it but prudent to check myself at present from further demonstrations. Bartleby and I were alone. I remembered the tragedy of the unfortunate Adams° and the still more unfortunate Colt° in the solitary office of the latter; and how poor Colt, being dreadfully incensed by Adams, and imprudently permitting himself to get wildly excited, was at unawares hurried into his fatal act — an act which certainly no man could possibly deplore more than the actor himself. Often it had occurred to me in my ponderings upon the subject that had that altercation taken place in the public street, or at a private residence, it would not have terminated as it did. It was the circumstance of being alone in a solitary office, up stairs, of a building entirely unhallowed by humanizing domestic associations — an uncarpeted office, doubtless, of a dusty, haggard sort of appearance — this it must have been, which greatly helped to enhance the irritable desperation of the hapless Colt.

But when this old Adam of resentment rose in me and tempted me concerning Bartleby, I grappled him and threw him. How? Why, simply by recalling the divine injunction: "A new commandment give I unto you, that

---

Adams, Colt: Samuel Adams was murdered by John C. Colt in 1842. After being convicted, Colt committed suicide shortly before his scheduled execution.

ye love one another." Yes, this it was that saved me. Aside from higher considerations, charity often operates as a vastly wise and prudent principle — a great safeguard to its possessor. Men have committed murder for jealousy's sake, and anger's sake, and hatred's sake, and selfishness' sake, and spiritual pride's sake; but no man, that ever I heard of, ever committed a diabolical murder for sweet charity's sake. Mere self-interest, then, if no better motive can be enlisted, should, especially with high-tempered men, prompt all beings to charity and philanthropy. At any rate, upon the occasion in question, I strove to drown my exasperated feelings towards the scrivener by benevolently construing his conduct. Poor fellow, poor fellow! thought I, he don't mean anything; and besides, he has seen hard times, and ought to be indulged.

I endeavored, also, immediately to occupy myself, and at the same time to comfort my despondency. I tried to fancy, that in the course of the morning, at such time as might prove agreeable to him, Bartleby, of his own free accord, would emerge from his hermitage and take up some decided line of march in the direction of the door. But no. Half-past twelve o'clock came; Turkey began to glow in the face, overturn his inkstand, and become generally obstreperous; Nippers abated down into quietude and courtesy; Ginger Nut munched his noon apple; and Bartleby remained standing at his window in one of his profoundest dead-wall reveries. Will it be credited? Ought I to acknowledge it? That afternoon I left the office without saying one further word to him.

Some days now passed, during which, at leisure intervals I looked a little into "Edwards° on the Will," and "Priestley° on Necessity." Under the circumstances, those books induced a salutary feeling. Gradually I slid into the persuasion that these troubles of mine, touching the scrivener, had been all predestined from eternity, and Bartleby was billeted upon me for some mysterious purpose of an all-wise Providence, which it was not for a mere mortal like me to fathom. Yes, Bartleby, stay there behind your screen, thought I; I shall persecute you no more; you are harmless and noiseless as any of these old chairs; in short, I never feel so private as when I know you are here. At last I see it, I feel it; I penetrate to the predestined purpose of my life. I am content. Others may have loftier parts to enact; but my mission in this world, Bartleby, is to furnish you with office-room for such period as you may see fit to remain.

I believe that this wise and blessed frame of mind would have contin- 170 ued with me, had it not been for the unsolicited and uncharitable remarks obtruded upon me by my professional friends who visited the rooms. But thus it often is, that the constant friction of illiberal minds wears out at last

Jonathan Edwards: (1703–1758) An American theologian whose *Freedom of the Will* (1754) supports the philosophy of predestination, a doctrine that claims human lives are pre-ordained and that humans do not have free will but act according to the plan set out by their creator. *Joseph Priestly:* (1733–1804) An English scientist and theologian who trained for the Presbyterian ministry but later adopted Unitarian views. Although his philosophy differed from that of Edwards, both believed that human nature was predetermined.

the best resolves of the more generous. Though to be sure, when I reflected upon it, it was not strange that people entering my office should be struck by the peculiar aspect of the unaccountable Bartleby, and so be tempted to throw out some sinister observations concerning him. Sometimes an attorney, having business with me, and calling at my office, and finding no one but the scrivener there, would undertake to obtain some sort of precise information from him touching my whereabouts; but without heeding his idle talk, Bartleby would remain standing immovable in the middle of the room. So after contemplating him in that position for a time, the attorney would depart, no wiser than he came.

Also, when a reference was going on, and the room full of lawyers and witnesses, and business driving fast, some deeply-occupied legal gentleman present, seeing Bartleby wholly unemployed, would request him to run round to his (the legal gentleman's) office and fetch some papers for him. Thereupon, Bartleby would tranquilly decline, and yet remain idle as before. Then the lawyer would give a great stare, and turn to me. And what could I say? At last I was made aware that all through the circle of my professional acquaintance, a whisper of wonder was running round, having reference to the strange creature I kept at my office. This worried me very much. And as the idea came upon me of his possibly turning out a long-lived man, and keeping occupying my chambers, and denying my authority; and perplexing my visitors; and scandalizing my professional reputation; and casting a general gloom over the premises; keeping soul and body together to the last upon his savings (for doubtless he spent but half a dime a day), and in the end perhaps outlive me, and claim possession of my office by right of his perpetual occupancy: as all these dark anticipations crowded upon me more and more, and my friends continually intruded their relentless remarks upon the apparition in my room; a great change was wrought in me. I resolved to gather all my faculties together, and forever rid me of this intolerable incubus.

Ere revolving any complicated project, however, adapted to this end, I first simply suggested to Bartleby the propriety of his permanent departure. In a calm and serious tone, I commended the idea to his careful and mature consideration. But, having taken three days to meditate upon it, he apprised me, that his original determination remained the same; in short, that he still preferred to abide with me.

What shall I do? I now said to myself, buttoning up my coat to the last button. What shall I do? what ought I to do? what does conscience say I *should* do with this man, or, rather, ghost. Rid myself of him, I must; go, he shall. But how? You will not thrust him, the poor, pale, passive mortal — you will not thrust such a helpless creature out of your door? you will not dishonor yourself by such cruelty? No, I will not, I cannot do that. Rather would I let him live and die here, and then mason up his remains in the wall. What, then, will you do? For all your coaxing, he will not budge. Bribes he leaves under your own paper-weight on your table; in short, it is quite plain that he prefers to cling to you.

Then something severe, something unusual must be done. What! surely you will not have him collared by a constable, and commit his innocent pallor to the common jail? And upon what ground could you procure such a thing to be done? — a vagrant, is he? What! he a vagrant, a wanderer, who refuses to budge? It is because he will *not* be a vagrant, then, that you seek to count him *as* a vagrant. That is too absurd. No visible means of support: there I have him. Wrong again: for indubitably he *does* support himself, and that is the only unanswerable proof that any man can show of his possessing the means so to do. No more, then. Since he will not quit me, I must quit him. I will change my offices; I will move elsewhere, and give him fair notice, that if I find him on my new premises I will then proceed against him as a common trespasser.

Acting accordingly, next day I thus addressed him: "I find these chambers too far from the City Hall; the air is unwholesome. In a word, I propose to remove my offices next week, and shall no longer require your services. I tell you this now, in order that you may seek another place." 175

He made no reply, and nothing more was said.

On the appointed day I engaged carts and men, proceeded to my chambers, and, having but little furniture, everything was removed in a few hours. Throughout, the scrivener remained standing behind the screen, which I directed to be removed the last thing. It was withdrawn; and, being folded up like a huge folio, left him the motionless occupant of a naked room. I stood in the entry watching him a moment, while something from within me upbraided me.

I re-entered, with my hand in my pocket — and — and my heart in my mouth.

"Good-bye, Bartleby; I am going — good-bye, and God some way bless you; and take that," slipping something in his hand. But it dropped upon the floor, and then — strange to say — I tore myself from him whom I had so longed to be rid of.

Established in my new quarters, for a day or two I kept the door locked, and started at every footfall in the passages. When I returned to my rooms, after any little absence, I would pause at the threshold for an instant, and attentively listen, ere applying my key. But these fears were needless. Bartleby never came nigh me. 180

I thought all was going well, when a perturbed-looking stranger visited me, inquiring whether I was the person who had recently occupied rooms at No. — Wall Street.

Full of forebodings, I replied that I was.

"Then, sir," said the stranger, who proved a lawyer, "you are responsible for the man you left there. He refuses to do any copying; he refuses to do anything; he says he prefers not to; and he refuses to quit the premises."

"I am very sorry, sir," said I, with assumed tranquillity, but an inward tremor, "but, really, the man you allude to is nothing to me — he is no relation or apprentice of mine, that you should hold me responsible for him."

"In mercy's name, who is he?" 185

"I certainly cannot inform you. I know nothing about him. Formerly I employed him as a copyist; but he has done nothing for me now for some time past."

"I shall settle him, then—good morning, sir."

Several days passed, and I heard nothing more; and, though I often felt a charitable prompting to call at the place and see poor Bartleby, yet a certain squeamishness, of I know not what, withheld me.

All is over with him, by this time, thought I, at last, when, through another week, no further intelligence reached me. But, coming to my room the day after, I found several persons waiting at my door in a high state of nervous excitement.

"That's the man—here he comes," cried the foremost one, whom I 190 recognized as the lawyer who had previously called upon me alone.

"You must take him away, sir, at once," cried a portly person among them, advancing upon me, and whom I knew to be the landlord of No. — Wall Street. "These gentlemen, my tenants, cannot stand it any longer; Mr. B——," pointing to the lawyer, "has turned him out of his room, and he now persists in haunting the building generally, sitting upon the banisters of the stairs by day, and sleeping in the entry by night. Everybody is concerned; clients are leaving the offices; some fears are entertained of a mob; something you must do, and that without delay."

Aghast at this torrent, I fell back before it, and would fain have locked myself in my new quarters. In vain I persisted that Bartleby was nothing to me—no more than to any one else. In vain—I was the last person known to have anything to do with him, and they held me to the terrible account. Fearful, then, of being exposed in the papers (as one person present obscurely threatened), I considered the matter, and, at length, said, that if the lawyer would give me a confidential interview with the scrivener, in his (the lawyer's) own room, I would, that afternoon, strive my best to rid them of the nuisance they complained of.

Going up stairs to my old haunt, there was Bartleby silently sitting upon the banister at the landing.

"What are you doing here, Bartleby?" said I.

"Sitting upon the banister," he mildly replied. 195

I motioned him into the lawyer's room, who then left us.

"Bartleby," said I, "are you aware that you are the cause of great tribulation to me, by persisting in occupying the entry after being dismissed from the office?"

No answer.

"Now one of two things must take place. Either you must do something, or something must be done to you. Now what sort of business would you like to engage in? Would you like to re-engage in copying for some one?"

"No, I would prefer not to make any change." 200

"Would you like a clerkship in a dry-goods store?"

"There is too much confinement about that. No, I would not like a clerkship; but I am not particular."

"Too much confinement," I cried, "why, you keep yourself confined all the time!"

"I would prefer not to take a clerkship," he rejoined, as if to settle that little item at once.

"How would a bar-tender's business suit you? There is no trying of the eye-sight in that." 205

"I would not like it at all; though, as I said before, I am not particular."

His unwonted wordiness inspirited me. I returned to the charge.

"Well, then, would you like to travel through the country collecting bills for the merchants? That would improve your health."

"No, I would prefer to be doing something else."

"How, then, would going as a companion to Europe, to entertain some 210 young gentleman with your conversation — how would that suit you?"

"Not at all. It does not strike me that there is anything definite about that. I like to be stationary. But I am not particular."

"Stationary you shall be, then," I cried, now losing all patience, and, for the first time in all my exasperating connection with him, fairly flying into a passion. "If you do not go away from these premises before night, I shall feel bound — indeed, I *am* bound — to — to — to quit the premises myself!" I rather absurdly concluded, knowing not with what possible threat to try to frighten his immobility into compliance. Despairing of all further efforts, I was precipitately leaving him, when a final thought occurred to me — one which had not been wholly unindulged before.

"Bartleby," said I, in the kindest tone I could assume under such exciting circumstances, "will you go home with me now — not to my office, but my dwelling — and remain there till we can conclude upon some convenient arrangement for you at our leisure? Come, let us start now, right away."

"No: at present I would prefer not to make any change at all."

I answered nothing; but, effectually dodging every one by the sudden- 215 ness and rapidity of my flight, rushed from the building, ran up Wall Street towards Broadway, and, jumping into the first omnibus, was soon removed from pursuit. As soon as tranquillity returned, I distinctly perceived that I had now done all that I possibly could, both in respect to the demands of the landlord and his tenants, and with regard to my own desire and sense of duty, to benefit Bartleby, and shield him from rude persecution. I now strove to be entirely care-free and quiescent; and my conscience justified me in the attempt; though, indeed, it was not so successful as I could have wished. So fearful was I of being again hunted out by the incensed landlord and his exasperated tenants, that, surrendering my business to Nippers, for a few days, I drove about the upper part of the town and through the suburbs, in my rockaway; crossed over to Jersey City and Hoboken, and paid fugitive visits to Manhattanville and Astoria. In fact, I almost lived in my rockaway for the time.

When again I entered my office, lo, a note from the landlord lay upon the desk. I opened it with trembling hands. It informed me that the writer had sent to the police, and had Bartleby removed to the Tombs as a vagrant. Moreover, since I knew more about him than any one else, he wished me to appear at that place, and make a suitable statement of the facts. These tidings had a conflicting effect upon me. At first I was indignant; but, at last, almost approved. The landlord's energetic, summary disposition, had led him to adopt a procedure which I do not think I would have decided upon myself; and yet, as a last resort, under such peculiar circumstances, it seemed the only plan.

As I afterwards learned, the poor scrivener, when told that he must be conducted to the Tombs, offered not the slightest obstacle, but, in his pale, unmoving way, silently acquiesced.

Some of the compassionate and curious by-standers joined the party; and headed by one of the constables arm-in-arm with Bartleby, the silent procession filed its way through all the noise, and heat, and joy of the roaring thoroughfares at noon.

The same day I received the note, I went to the Tombs, or, to speak more properly, the Halls of Justice. Seeking the right officer, I stated the purpose of my call, and was informed that the individual I described was, indeed, within. I then assured the functionary that Bartleby was a perfectly honest man, and greatly to be compassionated, however unaccountably eccentric. I narrated all I knew, and closed by suggesting the idea of letting him remain in as indulgent confinement as possible, till something less harsh might be done—though, indeed, I hardly knew what. At all events, if nothing else could be decided upon, the alms-house must receive him. I then begged to have an interview.

Being under no disgraceful charge, and quite serene and harmless in all his ways, they had permitted him freely to wander about the prison, and, especially, in the inclosed grass-platted yards thereof. And so I found him there, standing all alone in the quietest of the yards, his face towards a high wall, while all around, from the narrow slits of the jail windows, I thought I saw peering out upon him the eyes of murderers and thieves.

"Bartleby!"

"I know you," he said, without looking round—"and I want nothing to say to you."

"It was not I that brought you here, Bartleby," said I, keenly pained at his implied suspicion. "And to you, this should not be so vile a place. Nothing reproachful attaches to you by being here. And see, it is not so sad a place as one might think. Look, there is the sky, and here is the grass."

"I know where I am," he replied, but would say nothing more, and so I left him.

As I entered the corridor again, a broad meat-like man, in an apron, 225
accosted me, and, jerking his thumb over his shoulder, said—"Is that your
friend?"

"Yes."

"Does he want to starve? If he does, let him live on the prison fare,
that's all."

"Who are you?" asked I, not knowing what to make of such an unof-
ficially speaking person in such a place.

"I am the grub-man. Such gentlemen as have friends here, hire me to
provide them with something good to eat."

"Is this so?" said I, turning to the turnkey. 230

He said it was.

"Well, then," said I, slipping some silver into the grub-man's hands
(for so they called him), "I want you to give particular attention to my
friend there; let him have the best dinner you can get. And you must be as
polite to him as possible."

"Introduce me, will you?" said the grub-man, looking at me with an
expression which seemed to say he was all impatience for an opportunity to
give a specimen of his breeding.

Thinking it would prove of benefit to the scrivener, I acquiesced; and,
asking the grub-man his name, went up with him to Bartleby.

"Bartleby, this is a friend; you will find him very useful to you." 235

"Your sarvant, sir, your sarvant," said the grub-man, making a low
salutation behind his apron. "Hope you find it pleasant here, sir; nice
grounds—cool apartments—hope you'll stay with us some time—try to
make it agreeable. What will you have for dinner to-day?"

"I prefer not to dine to-day," said Bartleby, turning away. "It would
disagree with me; I am unused to dinners." So saying, he slowly moved
to the other side of the inclosure, and took up a position fronting the
dead-wall.

"How's this?" said the grub-man, addressing me with a stare of astonishment. "He's odd, ain't he?"

"I think he is a little deranged," said I, sadly.

"Deranged? deranged is it? Well, now, upon my word, I thought that 240
friend of yourn was a gentleman forger; they are always pale and genteel-
like, them forgers. I can't help pity 'em—can't help it, sir. Did you know
Monroe Edwards?" he added, touchingly, and paused. Then, laying his hand
piteously on my shoulder, sighed, "he died of consumption at Sing-Sing.
So you weren't acquainted with Monroe?"

"No, I was never socially acquainted with any forgers. But I cannot
stop longer. Look to my friend yonder. You will not lose by it. I will see
you again."

Some few days after this, I again obtained admission to the Tombs,
and went through the corridors in quest of Bartleby; but without finding
him.

"I saw him coming from his cell not long ago," said a turnkey, "may be he's gone to loiter in the yards."

So I went in that direction.

"Are you looking for the silent man?" said another turnkey, passing me. "Yonder he lies—sleeping in the yard there. 'Tis not twenty minutes since I saw him lie down." 245

The yard was entirely quiet. It was not accessible to the common prisoners. The surrounding walls, of amazing thickness, kept off all sounds behind them. The Egyptian character of the masonry weighed upon me with its gloom. But a soft imprisoned turf grew under foot. The heart of the eternal pyramids, it seemed, wherein, by some strange magic, through the clefts, grass-seed, dropped by birds, had sprung.

Strangely huddled at the base of the wall, his knees drawn up, and lying on his side, his head touching the cold stones, I saw the wasted Bartleby. But nothing stirred. I paused; then went close up to him; stooped over, and saw that his dim eyes were open; otherwise he seemed profoundly sleeping. Something prompted me to touch him. I felt his hand, when a tingling shiver ran up my arm and down my spine to my feet.

The round face of the grub-man peered upon me now. "His dinner is ready. Won't he dine to-day, either? Or does he live without dining?"

"Lives without dining," said I, and closed the eyes.

"Eh!—He's asleep, ain't he?" 250

"With kings and counselors,"° murmured I.

There would seem little need for proceeding further in this history. Imagination will readily supply the meagre recital of poor Bartleby's interment. But, ere parting with the reader, let me say, that if this little narrative has sufficiently interested him, to awaken curiosity as to who Bartleby was, and what manner of life he led prior to the present narrator's making his acquaintance, I can only reply, that in such curiosity I fully share, but am wholly unable to gratify it. Yet here I hardly know whether I should divulge one little item of rumor, which came to my ear a few months after the scrivener's decease. Upon what basis it rested, I could never ascertain; and hence, how true it is I cannot now tell. But, inasmuch as this vague report has not been without a certain suggestive interest to me, however sad, it may prove the same with some others; and so I will briefly mention it. The report was this: that Bartleby had been a subordinate clerk in the Dead Letter Office at Washington, from which he had been suddenly removed by a change in the administration. When I think over this rumor, hardly can I express the emotions which seize me. Dead letters! does it not sound like dead men? Conceive a man by nature and misfortune prone to a pallid hopelessness, can any business seem more fitted to heighten it than that of continually handling these dead letters, and assorting them for the flames?

kings and counselors: See Job 3:14. Crying out against a series of tragedies and misfortunes, Job wishes he had never been born so that he might have "been at rest with kings and counselors of the earth, which built desolate places for themselves."

For by the cart-load they are annually burned. Sometimes from out the folded paper the pale clerk takes a ring — the finger it was meant for, perhaps, moulders in the grave; a bank-note sent in swiftest charity — he whom it would relieve, nor eats nor hungers any more; pardon for those who died despairing; hope for those who died unhoping; good tidings for those who died stifled by unrelieved calamities. On errands of life, these letters speed to death.

Ah, Bartleby! Ah, humanity!

Considerations

1. Discuss the attitude of the narrator toward his profession. What details led you to your evaluation?
2. Consider the significance of the subtitle. Does this story seem to be an indictment of the American business world? Explain.
3. Make a list of facts that you know about Bartleby — his past life, his appearance, his actions, his words — then speculate on his increasingly resistant attitude toward his work. What do you think motivates him?
4. A scrivener never creates original material but only copies the words of others. How might this work affect those who do it? What jobs in our society share this quality with the now-obsolete job of scrivener?
5. Imagine yourself as an employer facing an employee like Bartleby. Create the dialogue that might take place after he or she has told you, "I prefer not to."

MARGE PIERCY (1936–   )

To Be of Use

The people I love the best
jump into work head first
without dallying in the shallows
and swim off with sure strokes almost out of sight.
They seem to become natives of that element,   5
the black sleek heads of seals
bouncing like half-submerged balls.

I love people who harness themselves, an ox to a heavy cart,
who pull like water buffalo, with massive patience,
who strain in the mud and the muck to move things forward,   10
who do what has to be done, again and again.

I want to be with people who submerge
in the task, who go into the fields to harvest

and work in a row and pass the bags along,
who stand in the line and haul in their places,   15
who are not parlor generals and field deserters
but move in a common rhythm
when the food must come in or the fire be put out.

The work of the world is common as mud.
Botched, it smears the hands, crumbles to dust.   20
But the thing worth doing well done
has a shape that satisfies, clean and evident.
Greek amphoras for wine or oil,
Hopi vases that held corn, are put in museums
but you know they were made to be used.   25
The pitcher cries for water to carry
and a person for work that is real.

Considerations

1. What kind of work and workers does the speaker say she admires? Consider the extended metaphor in the first stanza as you respond.
2. How does the speaker relate her views on art to her views on work? Can creating art be viewed as work — even if the object has no practical use or application? Explain.
3. Does the definition of admired workers apply only to physical laborers? In what way might it apply to those who work with their minds rather than their hands?

P. K. PAGE (1916–   )

Typists

They without message, having read
the running words on their machines,
know every letter as a stamp
cutting the stencils of their ears.
Deep in their hands, like pianists,   5
all longing gropes and moves, is trapped
behind the tensile gloves of skin.

Or blind, sit with their faces locked
away from work. Their varied eyes
are stiff as everlasting flowers.   10
While fingers on a different plane

perform the automatic act
as questions grope along the dark
and twisting corridors of brain.

Crowded together typists touch   15
softly as ducks and seem to sense
each others' anguish with the swift
sympathy of the deaf and dumb.

Considerations

1. Speculate on why the speaker describes the typists as being "without message." What are the implications of this phrase?
2. Explicate the image in the final stanza. Does the speaker seem sympathetic toward or critical of typists? Explain.
3. Imagine yourself as someone who has worked as a typist for many years. Write a letter to the poet, P. K. Page, explaining your response to the poem.

RICHARD WILBUR (1921–   )

The Writer

In her room at the prow of the house
Where light breaks, and the windows are tossed with linden,
My daughter is writing a story.

I pause in the stairwell, hearing
From her shut door a commotion of typewriter-keys   5
Like a chain hauled over a gunwale.

Young as she is, the stuff
Of her life is a great cargo, and some of it heavy:
I wish her a lucky passage.

But now it is she who pauses,   10
As if to reject my thought and its easy figure.
A stillness greatens, in which

The whole house seems to be thinking,
And then she is at it again with a bunched clamor
Of strokes, and again is silent.   15

I remember the dazed starling
Which was trapped in that very room, two years ago;
How we stole in, lifted a sash

And retreated, not to affright it;
And how for a helpless hour, through the crack of the door,   20
We watched the sleek, wild, dark

And iridescent creature
Batter against the brilliance, drop like a glove
To the hard floor, or the desk-top,

And wait then, humped and bloody,   25
For the wits to try it again; and how our spirits
Rose when, suddenly sure,

It lifted off from a chair-back,
Beating a smooth course for the right window
And clearing the sill of the world.   30

It is always a matter, my darling,
Of life or death, as I had forgotten. I wish
What I wished you before, but harder.

Considerations

1. The subject of the poem is a young girl — probably a child. Do you consider a child engaged in writing to be "working"? Explain.
2. Comment on the relationship of the "dazed starling" (described in lines 16–30) to the speaker's daughter.
3. Speculate on the significance of the final stanza. What is it that is "always a matter . . ./Of life or death"? And what is it that the speaker wished for his daughter (and now wishes even "harder")?

JUDY GRAHN (1940–   )

Ella, in a square apron, along Highway 80

She's a copperheaded waitress,
tired and sharp-worded, she hides
her bad brown tooth behind a wicked

smile, and flicks her ass
out of habit, to fend off the pass   5
that passes for affection.
She keeps her mind the way men
keep a knife — keen to strip the game
down to her size. She has a thin spine,
swallows her eggs cold, and tells lies.   10
She slaps a wet rag at the truck drivers
if they should complain. She understands
the necessity for pain, turns away
the smaller tips, out of pride, and
keeps a flask under the counter. Once,   15
she shot a lover who misused her child.
Before she got out of jail, the courts had pounced
and given the child away. Like some isolated lake,
her flat blue eyes take care of their own stark
bottoms. Her hands are nervous, curled, ready   20
to scrape.
The common woman is as common
as a rattlesnake.

Considerations

1. Cite specific images in the poem that relate to the simile in the final two
   lines. What is your response to this comparison? Do you see Ella as
   admirable? Frightening? Comic? Dangerous? Explain.
2. Look for word play in the poem. What words have more than one meaning? How does the word play relate to the central comparison of the
   poem?
3. Describe one scene or incident suggested by the poem as Ella might have
   written about it in her journal.

KRAFT ROMPF (1948–   )

Waiting Table

To serve, I wait and pluck
the rose, brush crumbs, carry

madly trays of oysters and
Bloody Marys. Swinging through

doors, I hear them: mouths   5
open, eyes bugging, choking;

they beat a white clothed
table for caffeine piping

hot and sweet, sweet sugar.
Oh, ' should pour it in   10

their eyes! And set their
tongues afire. How the chef

understands when I order
tartare and shout, "Let them

eat it raw!" Oh I would stuff   15
their noses with garlic

and the house pianist
could play the Hammer March

on their toes. But for a
tip — for a tip, for a tip —   20

I would work so very, very
hard, and so gladly let

them shine into my soul,
and bow to them and laugh

with them and sing. I would   25
gladly give them everything.

Considerations

1. Make a list of as many examples of repetition as you can find in the poem. How does the repetition relate to the tone the speaker uses to describe his work?
2. What images does the speaker use to describe the restaurant's customers? What do these images suggest about the way he sees himself and his work?
3. What is the speaker's primary motive for working? Explain your response to the values suggested by this motive.

ANNE BRADSTREET (1612?–1672)

A Letter to Her Husband, Absent upon Public Employment

My head, my heart, mine eyes, my life, nay, more,
My joy, my magazine of earthly store,
If two be one, as surely thou and I,
How stayest thou there, whilst I at Ipswich lie?
So many steps, head from the heart to sever,   5
If but a neck, soon should we be together.
I, like the Earth this season, mourn in black,
My Sun is gone so far in's zodiac,
Whom whilst I 'joyed, nor storms, nor frost I felt,
His warmth such frigid colds did cause to melt,   10
My chilled limbs now numbed lie forlorn;
Return, return, sweet Sol,° from Capricorn;°
In this dead time, alas, what can I more
Than view those fruits which through thy heat I bore?
Which sweet contentment yield me for a space,   15
True living pictures of their father's face.
O strange effect! now thou art southward gone,
I weary grow the tedious day so long;
But when thou northward to me shalt return,
I wish my Sun may never set, but burn   20
Within the Cancer° of my glowing breast,
The welcome house of him my dearest guest.
Where ever, ever stay, and go not thence,
Till nature's sad decree shall call thee hence;
Flesh of thy flesh, bone of thy bone,   25
I here, thou there, yet both but one.

12 *Sol:* Sun; *Capricorn:* Zodiac sign indicating winter.   21 *Cancer:* Zodiac sign indicating summer.

ROBERT FROST (1874–1963)

The Death of the Hired Man

Mary sat musing on the lamp-flame at the table
Waiting for Warren. When she heard his step,
She ran on tiptoe down the darkened passage
To meet him in the doorway with the news
And put him on his guard. "Silas is back."   5
She pushed him outward with her through the door
And shut it after her. "Be kind," she said.

She took the market things from Warren's arms
And set them on the porch, then drew him down
To sit beside her on the wooden steps.   10

"When was I ever anything but kind to him?
But I'll not have the fellow back," he said.
"I told him so last haying, didn't I?
If he left then, I said, that ended it.
What good is he? Who else will harbor him   15
At his age for the little he can do?
What help he is there's no depending on.
Off he goes always when I need him most.
He thinks he ought to earn a little pay,
Enough at least to buy tobacco with,   20
So he won't have to beg and be beholden.
'All right,' I say, 'I can't afford to pay
Any fixed wages, though I wish I could.'
'Someone else can.' 'Then someone else will have to.'
I shouldn't mind his bettering himself   25
If that was what it was. You can be certain,
When he begins like that, there's someone at him
Trying to coax him off with pocket money, —
In haying time, when any help is scarce.
In winter he comes back to us. I'm done."   30

"Sh! not so loud: he'll hear you," Mary said.

"I want him to: he'll have to soon or late."

"He's worn out. He's asleep beside the stove.
When I came up from Rowe's I found him here,
Huddled against the barn door fast asleep,   35
A miserable sight, and frightening, too —
You needn't smile — I didn't recognize him —
I wasn't looking for him — and he's changed.
Wait till you see."

          "Where did you say he'd been?"

"He didn't say. I dragged him to the house,   40
And gave him tea and tried to make him smoke.
I tried to make him talk about his travels.
Nothing would do: he just kept nodding off."

"What did he say? Did he say anything?"

"But little."   45

        "Anything? Mary, confess
He said he'd come to ditch the meadow for me."

"Warren!"

        "But did he? I just want to know."

"Of course he did. What would you have him say?
Surely you wouldn't grudge the poor old man
Some humble way to save his self-respect.   50
He added, if you really care to know,
He meant to clear the upper pasture, too.
That sounds like something you have heard before?
Warren, I wish you could have heard the way
He jumbled everything. I stopped to look   55
Two or three times — he made me feel so queer —
To see if he was talking in his sleep.
He ran on Harold Wilson — you remember —
The boy you had in haying four years since.
He's finished school, and teaching in his college.   60
Silas declares you'll have to get him back.
He says they two will make a team for work:
Between them they will lay this farm as smooth!
The way he mixed that in with other things.
He thinks young Wilson a likely lad, though daft   65
On education — you know how they fought
All through July under the blazing sun,
Silas up on the cart to build the load
Harold along beside to pitch it on."

"Yes, I took care to keep well out of earshot."   70

"Well, those days trouble Silas like a dream.
You wouldn't think they would. How some things linger!
Harold's young college boy's assurance piqued him.
After so many years he still keeps finding
Good arguments he sees he might have used.   75
I sympathize. I know just how it feels
To think of the right thing to say too late.
Harold's associated in his mind with Latin.
He asked me what I thought of Harold's saying
He studied Latin, like the violin,   80
Because he liked it — that an argument!

He said he couldn't make the boy believe
He could find water with a hazel prong —
Which showed how much good school had ever done him.
He wanted to go over that. But most of all   85
He thinks if he could have another chance
To teach him how to build a load of hay — "

"I know that's Silas' one accomplishment.
He bundles every forkful in its place,
And tags and numbers it for future reference,   90
So he can find and easily dislodge it
In the unloading. Silas does that well.
He takes it out in bunches like big birds' nests.
You never see him standing on the hay
He's trying to lift, straining to lift himself."   95

"He thinks if he could teach him that, he'd be
Some good perhaps to someone in the world.
He hates to see a boy the fool of books.
Poor Silas, so concerned for other folk,
And nothing to look backward to with pride,   100
And nothing to look forward to with hope,
So now and never any different."

Part of a moon was falling down the west,
Dragging the whole sky with it to the hills.
Its light poured softly in her lap. She saw it   105
And spread her apron to it. She put out her hand
Among the harp-like morning-glory strings,
Taut with the dew from garden bed to eaves,
As if she played unheard some tenderness
That wrought on him beside her in the night.   110
"Warren," she said, "he has come home to die:
You needn't be afraid he'll leave you this time."

"Home," he mocked gently.

                    "Yes, what else but home?
It all depends on what you mean by home.
Of course he's nothing to us, any more   115
Than was the hound that came a stranger to us
Out of the woods, worn out upon the trail."

"Home is the place where, when you have to go there,
They have to take you in."

"I should have called it
Something you somehow haven't to deserve." 120

Warren leaned out and took a step or two,
Picked up a little stick, and brought it back
And broke it in his hand and tossed it by.
"Silas has better claim on us you think
Than on his brother? Thirteen little miles 125
As the road winds would bring him to his door.
Silas has walked that far no doubt to-day.
Why doesn't he go there? His brother's rich,
A somebody — director in the bank."

"He never told us that." 130

"We know it though."

"I think his brother ought to help, of course.
I'll see to that if there is need. He ought of right
To take him in, and might be willing to —
He may be better than appearances.
But have some pity on Silas. Do you think 135
If he had any pride in claiming kin
Or anything he looked for from his brother,
He'd keep so still about him all this time?"

"I wonder what's between them."

"I can tell you.
Silas is what he is — we wouldn't mind him — 140
But just the kind that kinsfolk can't abide.
He never did a thing so very bad.
He don't know why he isn't quite as good
As anybody. Worthless though he is,
He won't be made ashamed to please his brother." 145

"*I* can't think Si ever hurt anyone."

"No, but he hurt my heart the way he lay
And rolled his old head on that sharp-edged chair-back.
He wouldn't let me put him on the lounge.
You must go in and see what you can do. 150
I made the bed up for him there tonight.
You'll be surprised at him — how much he's broken.
His working days are done; I'm sure of it."

"I'd not be in a hurry to say that."

"I haven't been. Go, look, see for yourself.   155
But, Warren, please remember how it is:
He's come to help you ditch the meadow.
He has a plan. You mustn't laugh at him.
He may not speak of it, and then he may.
I'll sit and see if that small sailing cloud   160
Will hit or miss the moon."

          It hit the moon.
Then there were three there, making a dim row,
The moon, the little silver cloud, and she.

Warren returned — too soon, it seemed to her,
Slipped to her side, caught up her hand and waited.   165
"Warren?" she questioned.

          "Dead," was all he answered.

EZRA POUND (1885–1972)

The River-Merchant's Wife: a Letter

While my hair was still cut straight across my forehead
I played about the front gate, pulling flowers.
You came by on bamboo stilts, playing horse,
You walked about my seat, playing with blue plums.
And we went on living in the village of Chōkan: 5
Two small people, without dislike or suspicion.

At fourteen I married My Lord you.
I never laughed, being bashful.
Lowering my head, I looked at the wall.
Called to, a thousand times, I never looked back.   10

At fifteen I stopped scowling,
I desired my dust to be mingled with yours
Forever and forever and forever.
Why should I climb the look out?

At sixteen you departed,   15
You went into far Ku-tō-yen, by the river of swirling eddies,
And you have been gone five months.
The monkeys make sorrowful noise overhead.

You dragged your feet when you went out.
By the gate now, the moss is grown, the different mosses,   20
Too deep to clear them away!

The leaves fall early this autumn, in wind.
The paired butterflies are already yellow with August
Over the grass in the West garden;
They hurt me. I grow older.   25

If you are coming down through the narrows of the river Kiang,
Please let me know before hand,
And I will come out to meet you
        As far as Chō-fū-Sa.   30

BY RIHAKU° (LI T' AI PO)

Rihaku: The Chinese poet translated by Pound.

W. H. AUDEN (1907–1973)

The Unknown Citizen
(To JS/07/M/378
This Marble Monument Is Erected by the State)

He was found by the Bureau of Statistics to be
One against whom there was no official complaint,
And all the reports on his conduct agree
That, in the modern sense of an old-fashioned word, he was a saint,
For in everything he did he served the Greater Community.   5
Except for the War till the day he retired
He worked in a factory and never got fired
But satisfied his employers, Fudge Motors Inc.
Yet he wasn't a scab or odd in his views,
For his Union reports that he paid his dues,   10
(Our report on his Union shows it was sound)
And our Social Psychology workers found
That he was popular with his mates and liked a drink.
The Press are convinced that he bought a paper every day
And that his reactions to advertisements were normal in every way.   15
Policies taken out in his name prove that he was fully insured,
And his Health-card shows he was once in hospital but left it cured.
Both Producers Research and High-Grade Living declare
He was fully sensible to the advantages of the Installment Plan
And had everything necessary to the Modern Man,   20

A phonograph, a radio, a car and a frigidaire.
Our researchers into Public Opinion are content
That he held the proper opinions for the time of year;
When there was peace, he was for peace; when there was war, he went.
He was married and added five children to the population,   25
Which our Eugenist° says was the right number for a parent of his gen-
    eration.
And our teachers report that he never interfered with their education.
Was he free? Was he happy? The question is absurd:
Had anything been wrong, we should certainly have heard.

26 *Eugenist:* A person who studies the improvement of a species through the control of hereditary factors.

ELIZABETH BISHOP (1911–1978)

Filling Station

Oh, but it is dirty!
—this little filling station,
oil-soaked, oil-permeated
to a disturbing, over-all
black translucency.   5
Be careful with that match!

Father wears a dirty,
oil-soaked monkey suit
that cuts him under the arms,
and several quick and saucy   10
and greasy sons assist him
(it's a family filling station),
all quite thoroughly dirty.

Do they live in the station?
It has a cement porch   15
behind the pumps, and on it
a set of crushed and grease-
impregnated wickerwork;
on the wicker sofa
a dirty dog, quite comfy.   20

Some comic books provide
the only note of color—
of certain color. They lie
upon a big dim doily

draping a taboret°   *a small stool* 25
(part of the set), beside
a big hirsute begonia.

Why the extraneous plant?
Why the taboret?
Why, oh why, the doily?   30
(Embroidered in daisy stitch
with marguerites, I think,
and heavy with gray crochet.)

Somebody embroidered the doily.
Somebody waters the plant,   35
or oils it, maybe. Somebody
arranges the rows of cans
so that they softly say:
ESSO — SO — SO — SO
to high-strung automobiles.   40
Somebody loves us all.

JOHN ASHBERY (1927–   )

The Instruction Manual

As I sit looking out of a window of the building
I wish I did not have to write the instruction manual on the uses of a new
    metal.
I look down into the street and see people, each walking with an inner
    peace,
And envy them — they are so far away from me!
Not one of them has to worry about getting out this manual on schedule.   5
And, as my way is, I begin to dream, resting my elbows on the desk and
    leaning out of the window a little,
Of dim Guadalajara!° City of rose-colored flowers!
City I wanted most to see, and most did not see, in Mexico!
But I fancy I see, under the press of having to write the instruction manual,
Your public square, city, with its elaborate little bandstand!   10
The band is playing *Scheherazade* by Rimsky-Korsakov.°
Around stand the flower girls, handing out rose- and lemon-colored flowers,

7 *Guadalajara:* Located 275 miles west-northwest of Mexico City, Guadalajara is the second-largest city in Mexico and the place where mariachi bands originated. 11 *Rimsky-Korsakov:* (1844–1908) A Russian composer, Rimsky-Korsakov wrote *Scheherazade* in 1888 for the Russian Ballet. The ballet tells the story of the title character, who, to keep her husband from killing her, entertained him with a tale a night for 1001 nights.

Each attractive in her rose-and-blue striped dress (Oh! such shades of rose and blue),

And nearby is the little white booth where women in green serve you green and yellow fruit.

The couples are parading; everyone is in a holiday mood.   15

First, leading the parade, is a dapper fellow

Clothed in deep blue. On his head sits a white hat

And he wears a mustache, which has been trimmed for the occasion.

His dear one, his wife, is young and pretty; her shawl is rose, pink, and white.

Her slippers are patent leather, in the American fashion,   20

And she carries a fan, for she is modest, and does not want the crowd to see her face too often.

But everybody is so busy with his wife or loved one

I doubt they would notice the mustachioed man's wife.

Here come the boys! They are skipping and throwing little things on the sidewalk

Which is made of gray tile. One of them, a little older, has a toothpick in   25
his teeth.

He is silenter than the rest, and affects not to notice the pretty young girls in white.

But his friends notice them, and shout their jeers at the laughing girls.

Yet soon all this will cease, with the deepening of their years,

And love bring each to the parade grounds for another reason.

But I have lost sight of the young fellow with the toothpick.   30

Wait — there he is — on the other side of the bandstand,

Secluded from his friends, in earnest talk with a young girl

Of fourteen or fifteen. I try to hear what they are saying

But it seems they are just mumbling something — shy words of love, probably.

She is slightly taller than he, and looks quietly down into his sincere eyes.   35

She is wearing white. The breeze ruffles her long fine black hair against her olive cheek.

Obviously she is in love. The boy, the young boy with the toothpick, he is in love too;

His eyes show it. Turning from this couple,

I see there is an intermission in the concert.

The paraders are resting and sipping drinks through straws   40

(The drinks are dispensed from a large glass crock by a lady in dark blue),

And the musicians mingle among them, in their creamy white uniforms, and talk

About the weather, perhaps, or how their kids are doing at school.

Let us take this opportunity to tiptoe into one of the side streets.

Here you may see one of those white houses with green trim   45

That are so popular here. Look — I told you!

It is cool and dim inside, but the patio is sunny.
An old woman in gray sits there, fanning herself with a palm leaf fan.
She welcomes us to her patio, and offers us a cooling drink.
"My son is in Mexico City," she says. "He would welcome you too   50
If he were here. But his job is with a bank there.
Look, here is a photograph of him."
And a dark-skinned lad with pearly teeth grins out at us from the worn
    leather frame.
We thank her for her hospitality, for it is getting late
And we must catch a view of the city, before we leave, from a good high   55
    place.
That church tower will do—the faded pink one, there against the fierce blue
    of the sky. Slowly we enter.
The caretaker, an old man dressed in brown and gray, asks us how long we
    have been in the city, and how we like it here.
His daughter is scrubbing the steps—she nods to us as we pass into the
    tower.
Soon we have reached the top, and the whole network of the city extends
    before us.
There is the rich quarter, with its houses of pink and white, and its   60
    crumbling, leafy terraces;
There is the poorer quarter, its homes a deep blue.
There is the market, where men are selling hats and swatting flies
And there is the public library, painted several shades of pale green and
    beige.
Look! There is the square we just came from, with the promenaders.
There are fewer of them, now that the heat of the day has increased,   65
But the young boy and girl still lurk in the shadows of the bandstand.
And there is the home of the little old lady—
She is still sitting in the patio, fanning herself.
How limited, but how complete withal, has been our experience of
    Guadalajara!
We have seen young love, married love, and the love of an aged mother for   70
    her son.
We have heard the music, tasted the drinks, and looked at colored houses.
What more is there to do, except stay? And that we cannot do.
And as a last breeze freshens the top of the weathered old tower, I turn my
    gaze
Back to the instruction manual which has made me dream of Guadalajara.

SUSAN GLASPELL (1852–1930)

Trifles

Characters

GEORGE HENDERSON, *county attorney*
HENRY PETERS, *sheriff*
LEWIS HALE, *a neighboring farmer*
MRS. PETERS
MRS. HALE

Scene *The kitchen in the now abandoned farmhouse of John Wright, a gloomy kitchen, and left without having been put in order—unwashed pans under the sink, a loaf of bread outside the breadbox, a dish towel on the table—other signs of incompleted work. At the rear the outer door opens and the* SHERIFF *comes in followed by the* COUNTY ATTORNEY *and* HALE. *The* SHERIFF *and* HALE *are men in middle life, the* COUNTY ATTORNEY *is a young man; all are much bundled up and go at once to the stove. They are followed by two women—the Sheriff's wife first; she is a slight wiry woman, a thin nervous face.* MRS. HALE *is larger and would ordinarily be called more comfortable looking, but she is disturbed now and looks fearfully about as she enters. The women have come in slowly, and stand close together near the door.*

COUNTY ATTORNEY *(rubbing his hands)*: This feels good. Come up to the fire, ladies.

MRS. PETERS *(after taking a step forward)*: I'm not—cold.

SHERIFF *(unbuttoning his overcoat and stepping away from the stove as if to mark the beginning of official business)*: Now, Mr. Hale, before we move things about, you explain to Mr. Henderson just what you saw when you came here yesterday morning.

COUNTY ATTORNEY: By the way, has anything been moved? Are things just as you left them yesterday?

SHERIFF *(looking about)*: It's just the same. When it dropped below zero last night I thought I'd better send Frank out this morning to make a fire for us—no use getting pneumonia with a big case on, but I told him not to touch anything except the stove—and you know Frank.

COUNTY ATTORNEY: Somebody should have been left here yesterday.

SHERIFF: Oh—yesterday. When I had to send Frank to Morris Center for that man who went crazy—I want you to know I had my hands full yesterday, I knew you could get back from Omaha by today and as long as I went over everything here myself—

COUNTY ATTORNEY: Well, Mr. Hale, tell just what happened when you came here yesterday morning.

HALE: Harry and I had started to town with a load of potatoes. We came along the road from my place and as I got here I said, "I'm going to

see if I can't get John Wright to go in with me on a party telephone."
I spoke to Wright about it once before and he put me off, saying folks
talked too much anyway, and all he asked was peace and quiet — I guess
you know about how much he talked himself; but I thought maybe if
I went to the house and talked about it before his wife, though I said
to Harry that I didn't know as what his wife wanted made such difference to John —

COUNTY ATTORNEY: Let's talk about that later, Mr. Hale. I do want to
talk about that, but tell now just what happened when you got to the
house.

HALE: I didn't hear or see anything; I knocked at the door, and still it was
all quiet inside. I knew they must be up, it was past eight o'clock. So
I knocked again, and I thought I heard somebody say, "Come in." I
wasn't sure, I'm not sure yet, but I opened the door — this door *(indicating the door by which the two women are still standing)* and there in that
rocker — *(pointing to it)* sat Mrs. Wright.

They all look at the rocker.

COUNTY ATTORNEY: What — was she doing?

HALE: She was rockin' back and forth. She had her apron in her hand and
was kind of — pleating it.

COUNTY ATTORNEY: And how did she — look?

HALE: Well, she looked queer.

COUNTY ATTORNEY: How do you mean — queer?

HALE: Well, as if she didn't know what she was going to do next. And
kind of done up.

COUNTY ATTORNEY: How did she seem to feel about your coming?

HALE: Why, I don't think she minded — one way or other. She didn't pay
much attention. I said, "How do, Mrs. Wright, it's cold, ain't it?" And
she said, "Is it?" — and went on kind of pleating at her apron. Well, I
was surprised; she didn't ask me to come up to the stove, or to set
down, but just sat there, not even looking at me, so I said, "I want to
see John." And then she — laughed. I guess you would call it a laugh. I
thought of Harry and the team outside, so I said a little sharp: "Can't
I see John?" "No," she says, kind o' dull like. "Ain't he home?" says I.
"Yes," says she, "he's home." "Then why can't I see him?" I asked her,
out of patience. "'Cause he's dead," says she. "*Dead?*" says I. She just
nodded her head, not getting a bit excited, but rockin' back and forth.
"Why — where is he?" says I, not knowing what to say. She just
pointed upstairs — like that *(himself pointing to the room above)*. I got up,
with the idea of going up there. I walked from there to here — then I
says, "Why, what did he die of?" "He died of a rope around his neck,"
says she, and just went on pleatin' at her apron. Well, I went out and
called Harry. I thought I might — need help. We went upstairs and there
he was lyin' —

COUNTY ATTORNEY: I think I'd rather have you go into that upstairs, where you can point it all out. Just go on now with the rest of the story.

HALE: Well, my first thought was to get that rope off. It looked . . . *(stops, his face twitches)* . . . but Harry, he went up to him, and he said, "No, he's dead all right, and we'd better not touch anything." So we went back down stairs. She was still sitting that same way. "Has anybody been notified?" I asked. "No," says she, unconcerned. "Who did this, Mrs. Wright?" said Harry. He said it businesslike — and she stopped pleatin' of her apron. "I don't know," she says. "You don't *know?*" says Harry. "No," says she. "Weren't you sleepin' in the bed with him?" says Harry. "Yes," says she, "but I was on the inside." "Somebody slipped a rope around his neck and strangled him and you didn't wake up?" says Harry. "I didn't wake up," she said after him. We must 'a looked as if we didn't see how that could be, for after a minute she said, "I sleep sound." Harry was going to ask her more questions but I said maybe we ought to let her tell her story first to the coroner, or the sheriff, so Harry went fast as he could to Rivers' place, where there's a telephone.

COUNTY ATTORNEY: And what did Mrs. Wright do when she knew that you had gone for the coroner?

HALE: She moved from that chair to this one over here *(pointing to a small chair in the corner)* and just sat there with her hands held together and looking down. I got a feeling that I ought to make some conversation, so I said I had come in to see if John wanted to put in a telephone, and at that she started to laugh, and then she stopped and looked at me — scared. *(The* COUNTY ATTORNEY, *who has had his notebook out, makes a note.)* I dunno, maybe it wasn't scared. I wouldn't like to say it was. Soon Harry got back, and then Dr. Lloyd came, and you, Mr. Peters, and so I guess that's all I know that you don't.

COUNTY ATTORNEY *(looking around)*: I guess we'll go upstairs first — and then out to the barn and around there. *(to the* SHERIFF) You're convinced that there was nothing important here — nothing that would point to any motive.

SHERIFF: Nothing here but kitchen things.

The COUNTY ATTORNEY, *after again looking around the kitchen, opens the door of a cupboard closet. He gets up on a chair and looks on a shelf. Pulls his hand away, sticky.*

COUNTY ATTORNEY: Here's a nice mess.

The women draw nearer.

MRS. PETERS *(to the other woman)*: Oh, her fruit; it did freeze. *(to the* COUNTY ATTORNEY) She worried about that when it turned so cold. She said the fire'd go out and her jars would break.

SHERIFF: Well, can you beat the women! Held for murder and worryin' about her preserves.

COUNTY ATTORNEY: I guess before we're through she may have something more serious than preserves to worry about.

HALE: Well, women are used to worrying over trifles.

The two women move a little closer together.

COUNTY ATTORNEY *(with the gallantry of a young politician)*: And yet, for all their worries, what would we do without the ladies? *(The women do not unbend. He goes to the sink, takes a dipperful of water from the pail and pouring it into a basin, washes his hands. Starts to wipe them on the roller towel, turns it for a cleaner place.)* Dirty towels! *(kicks his foot against the pans under the sink)* Not much of a housekeeper, would you say ladies?

MRS. HALE *(stiffly)*: There's a great deal of work to be done on a farm.

COUNTY ATTORNEY: To be sure. And yet *(with a little bow to her)* I know there are some Dickson county farmhouses which do not have such roller towels.

He gives it a pull to expose its full length again.

MRS. HALE: Those towels get dirty awful quick. Men's hands aren't always as clean as they might be.

COUNTY ATTORNEY: Ah, loyal to your sex, I see. But you and Mrs. Wright were neighbors. I suppose you were friends, too.

MRS. HALE *(shaking her head)*: I've not seen much of her of late years. I've not been in this house — it's more than a year.

COUNTY ATTORNEY: And why was that? You didn't like her?

MRS. HALE: I liked her all well enough. Farmers' wives have their hands full, Mr. Henderson. And then —

COUNTY ATTORNEY: Yes — ?

MRS. HALE *(looking about)*: It never seemed a very cheerful place.

COUNTY ATTORNEY: No — it's not cheerful. I shouldn't say she had the homemaking instinct.

MRS. HALE: Well, I don't know as Wright had, either.

COUNTY ATTORNEY: You mean that they didn't get on very well?

MRS. HALE: No, I don't mean anything. But I don't think a place'd be any cheerfuller for John Wright's being in it.

COUNTY ATTORNEY: I'd like to talk more of that a little later. I want to get the lay of things upstairs now.

He goes to the left, where three steps lead to a stair door.

SHERIFF: I suppose anything Mrs. Peters does'll be all right. She was to take in some clothes for her, you know, and a few little things. We left in such a hurry yesterday.

COUNTY ATTORNEY: Yes, but I would like to see what you take, Mrs. Peters, and keep an eye out for anything that might be of use to us.

MRS. PETERS: Yes, Mr. Henderson.

The women listen to the men's steps on the stairs, then look about the kitchen.

MRS. HALE: I'd hate to have men coming into my kitchen, snooping around and criticising.

She arranges the pans under sink which the COUNTY ATTORNEY *had shoved out of place.*

MRS. PETERS: Of course it's no more than their duty.

MRS. HALE: Duty's all right, but I guess that deputy sheriff that came out to make the fire might have got a little of this on. *(gives the roller towel a pull)* Wish I'd thought of that sooner. Seems mean to talk about her for not having things slicked up when she had to come away in such a hurry.

MRS. PETERS *(who has gone to a small table in the left rear corner of the room, and lifted one end of a towel that covers a pan)*: She had bread set.

Stands still.

MRS. HALE *(eyes fixed on a loaf of bread beside the breadbox, which is on a low shelf at the other side of the room. Moves slowly toward it.)*: She was going to put this in there. *(Picks up loaf, then abruptly drops it. In a manner of returning to familiar things.)* It's a shame about her fruit. I wonder if it's all gone. *(Gets up on the chair and looks.)* I think there's some here that's all right, Mrs. Peters. Yes — here; *(holding it toward the window)* this is cherries, too. *(looking again)* I declare I believe that's the only one. *(Gets down, bottle in her hand. Goes to the sink and wipes it off on the outside.)* She'll feel awful bad after all her hard work in the hot weather. I remember the afternoon I put up my cherries last summer.

She puts the bottle on the big kitchen table, center of the room. With a sigh, is about to sit down in the rocking-chair. Before she is seated realizes what chair it is; with a slow look at it, steps back. The chair which she has touched rocks back and forth.

MRS. PETERS: Well, I must get those things from the front room closet. *(She goes to the door at the right, but after looking into the other room, steps back.)* You coming with me, Mrs. Hale? You could help me carry them.

They go in the other room; reappear, MRS. PETERS *carrying a dress and skirt,* MRS. HALE *following with a pair of shoes.*

MRS. PETERS: My, it's cold in there.

She puts the clothes on the big table, and hurries to the stove.

MRS. HALE *(examining her skirt)*: Wright was close. I think maybe that's why she kept so much to herself. She didn't even belong to the Ladies

Aid. I suppose she felt she couldn't do her part, and then you don't enjoy things when you feel shabby. She used to wear pretty clothes and be lively, when she was Minnie Foster, one of the town girls singing in the choir. But that — oh, that was thirty years ago. This all you was to take in?

MRS. PETERS: She said she wanted an apron. Funny thing to want, for there isn't much to get you dirty in jail, goodness knows. But I suppose just to make her feel more natural. She said they was in the top drawer in this cupboard. Yes, here. And then her little shawl that always hung behind the door. *(opens stair door and looks)* Yes, here it is.

Quickly shuts door leading upstairs.

MRS. HALE *(abruptly moving toward her)*: Mrs. Peters?
MRS. PETERS: Yes, Mrs. Hale?
MRS. HALE: Do you think she did it?
MRS. PETERS *(in a frightened voice)*: Oh, I don't know.
MRS. HALE: Well, I don't think she did. Asking for an apron and her little shawl. Worrying about her fruit.
MRS. PETERS *(Starts to speak, glances up, where footsteps are heard in the room above. In a low voice.)*: Mr. Peters says it looks bad for her. Mr. Henderson is awful sarcastic in a speech and he'll make fun of her sayin' she didn't wake up.
MRS. HALE: Well, I guess John Wright didn't wake when they was slipping that rope under his neck.
MRS. PETERS: No, it's strange. It must have been done awful crafty and still. They say it was such a — funny way to kill a man, rigging it all up like that.
MRS. HALE: That's just what Mr. Hale said. There was a gun in the house. He says that's what he can't understand.
MRS. PETERS: Mr. Henderson said coming out that what was needed for the case was a motive; something to show anger, or — sudden feeling.
MRS. HALE *(who is standing by the table)*: Well, I don't see any signs of anger around here. *(She puts her hand on the dish towel which lies on the table, stands looking down at table, one half of which is clean, the other half messy.)* It's wiped to here. *(Makes a move as if to finish work, then turns and looks at loaf of bread outside the breadbox. Drops towel. In that voice of coming back to familiar things.)* Wonder how they are finding things upstairs. I hope she had it a little more red-up up there. You know, it seems kind of *sneaking.* Locking her up in town and then coming out here and trying to get her own house to turn against her!
MRS. PETERS: But Mrs. Hale, the law is the law.
MRS. HALE: I s'pose 'tis. *(unbuttoning her coat)* Better loosen up your things, Mrs. Peters. You won't feel them when you go out.

Mrs. Peters takes off her fur tippet, goes to hang it on hook at back of room, stands looking at the under part of the small corner table.

MRS. PETERS: She was piecing a quilt.

She brings the large sewing basket and they look at the bright pieces.

MRS. HALE: It's log cabin pattern. Pretty, isn't it? I wonder if she was goin' to quilt it or just knot it?

Footsteps have been heard coming down the stairs. The SHERIFF *enters followed by* HALE *and the* COUNTY ATTORNEY.

SHERIFF: They wonder if she was going to quilt it or just knot it!

The men laugh; the women look abashed.

COUNTY ATTORNEY (*rubbing his hands over the stove*): Frank's fire didn't do much up there, did it? Well, let's go out to the barn and get that cleared up.

The men go outside.

MRS. HALE (*resentfully*): I don't know as there's anything so strange, our takin' up our time with little things while we're waiting for them to get the evidence. (*She sits down at the big table smoothing out a block with decision.*) I don't see as it's anything to laugh about.

MRS. PETERS (*apologetically*): Of course they've got awful important things on their minds.

Pulls up a chair and joins Mrs. Hale at the table.

MRS. HALE (*examining another block*): Mrs. Peters, look at this one. Here, this is the one she was working on, and look at the sewing! All the rest of it has been so nice and even. And look at this! It's all over the place! Why, it looks as if she didn't know what she was about!

After she has said this they look at each other, then start to glance back at the door. After an instant MRS. HALE *has pulled at a knot and ripped the sewing.*

MRS. PETERS: Oh, what are you doing, Mrs. Hale?

MRS. HALE (*mildly*): Just pulling out a stitch or two that's not sewed very good. (*threading a needle*) Bad sewing always made me fidgety.

MRS. PETERS (*nervously*): I don't think we ought to touch things.

MRS. HALE: I'll just finish up this end. (*suddenly stopping and leaning forward*) Mrs. Peters?

MRS. PETERS: Yes, Mrs. Hale?

MRS. HALE: What do you suppose she was so nervous about?

MRS. PETERS: Oh—I don't know. I don't know as she was nervous. I sometimes sew awful queer when I'm just tired. (MRS. HALE *starts to say something, looks at* MRS. PETERS, *then goes on sewing.*) Well, I must get these things wrapped up. They may be through sooner than we think. (*putting apron and other things together*) I wonder where I can find a piece of paper, and string.

MRS. HALE: In that cupboard, maybe.

MRS. PETERS *(looking in cupboard)*: Why, here's a birdcage. *(holds it up)* Did she have a bird, Mrs. Hale?

MRS. HALE: Why, I don't know whether she did or not—I've not been here for so long. There was a man around last year selling canaries cheap, but I don't know as she took one; maybe she did. She used to sing real pretty herself.

MRS. PETERS *(glancing around)*: Seems funny to think of a bird here. But she must have had one, or why would she have a cage? I wonder what happened to it.

MRS. HALE: I s'pose maybe the cat got it.

MRS. PETERS: No, she didn't have a cat. She's got that feeling some people have about cats—being afraid of them. My cat got in her room and she was real upset and asked me to take it out.

MRS. HALE: My sister Bessie was like that. Queer, ain't it?

MRS. PETERS *(examining the cage)*: Why, look at this door. It's broke. One hinge is pulled apart.

MRS. HALE *(looking too)*: Looks as if someone must have been rough with it.

MRS. PETERS: Why, yes.

She brings the cage forward and puts it on the table.

MRS. HALE: I wish if they're going to find any evidence they'd be about it. I don't like this place.

MRS. PETERS: But I'm awful glad you came with me, Mrs. Hale. It would be lonesome for me sitting here alone.

MRS. HALE: It would, wouldn't it? *(dropping her sewing)* But I tell you what I do wish, Mrs. Peters. I wish I had come over sometimes when *she* was here. I—*(looking around the room)*—wish I had.

MRS. PETERS: But of course you were awful busy, Mrs. Hale—your house and your children.

MRS. HALE: I could've come. I stayed away because it weren't cheerful—and that's why I ought to have come. I—I've never liked this place. Maybe because it's down in a hollow and you don't see the road. I dunno what it is but it's a lonesome place and always was. I wish I had come over to see Minnie Foster sometimes. I can see now—

Shakes her head.

MRS. PETERS: Well, you mustn't reproach yourself, Mrs. Hale. Somehow we just don't see how it is with other folks until—something comes up.

MRS. HALE: Not having children makes less work—but it makes a quiet house, and Wright out to work all day, and no company when he did come in. Did you know John Wright, Mrs. Peters?

MRS. PETERS: Not to know him; I've seen him in town. They say he was a good man.

MRS. HALE: Yes — good; he didn't drink, and kept his word as well as most, I guess, and paid his debts. But he was a hard man, Mrs. Peters. Just to pass the time of day with him — *(shivers)* Like a raw wind that gets to the bone. *(pauses, her eye falling on the cage)* I should think she would 'a wanted a bird. But what do you suppose went with it?

MRS. PETERS: I don't know, unless it got sick and died.

She reaches over and swings the broken door, swings it again. Both women watch it.

MRS. HALE: You weren't raised round here, were you? *(Mrs. Peters shakes her head.)* You didn't know — her?

MRS. PETERS: Not till they brought her yesterday.

MRS. HALE: She — come to think of it, she was kind of like a bird herself — real sweet and pretty, but kind of timid and — fluttery. How — she — did — change. *(silence; then as if struck by a happy thought and relieved to get back to everyday things)* Tell you what, Mrs. Peters, why don't you take the quilt in with you? It might take up her mind.

MRS. PETERS: Why, I think that's a real nice idea, Mrs. Hale. There couldn't possibly be any objection to it, could there? Now, just what would I take? I wonder if her patches are in here — and her things.

They look in the sewing basket.

MRS. HALE: Here's some red. I expect this has got sewing things in it. *(brings out a fancy box.)* What a pretty box. Looks like something somebody would give you. Maybe her scissors are in here. *(Opens box. Suddenly puts her hand to her nose.)* Why — *(MRS. PETERS bends nearer, then turns her face away.)* There's something wrapped up in this piece of silk.

MRS. PETERS: Why, this isn't her scissors.

MRS. HALE *(lifting the silk)*: Oh, Mrs. Peters — it's —

MRS. PETERS *bends closer.*

MRS. PETERS: It's the bird.

MRS. HALE *(jumping up)*: But, Mrs. Peters — look at it! Its neck! Look at its neck! It's all — other side *to.*

MRS. PETERS: Somebody — wrung — its — neck.

Their eyes meet. A look of growing comprehension, of horror. Steps are heard outside. MRS. HALE *slips box under quilt pieces, and sinks into her chair. Enter* SHERIFF *and* COUNTY ATTORNEY. MRS. PETERS *rises.*

COUNTY ATTORNEY *(as one turning from serious things to little pleasantries)*: Well, ladies, have you decided whether she was going to quilt it or knot it?

MRS. PETERS: We think she was going to — knot it.

COUNTY ATTORNEY: Well, that's interesting, I'm sure. *(seeing the birdcage)* Has the bird flown?

MRS. HALE *(putting more quilt pieces over the box)*: We think the — cat got it.

COUNTY ATTORNEY *(preoccupied)*: Is there a cat?

MRS. HALE *glances in a quick covert way at* MRS. PETERS.

MRS. PETERS: Well, not *now*. They're superstitious, you know. They leave.

COUNTY ATTORNEY *(to* SHERIFF PETERS, *continuing an interrupted conversation)*: No sign at all of anyone having come from the outside. Their own rope. Now let's go up again and go over it piece by piece. *(They start upstairs.)* It would have to have been someone who knew just the —

MRS. PETERS sits down. The two women sit there not looking at one another, but as if peering into something and at the same time holding back. When they talk now it is in the manner of feeling their way over strange ground, as if afraid of what they are saying, but as if they can not help saying it.

MRS. HALE: She liked the bird. She was going to bury it in that pretty box.

MRS. PETERS *(in a whisper)*: When I was a girl — my kitten — there was a boy took a hatchet, and before my eyes — and before I could get there — *(covers her face an instant)* If they hadn't held me back I would have — *(catches herself, looks upstairs where steps are heard, falters weakly)* — hurt him.

MRS. HALE *(with a slow look around her)*: I wonder how it would seem never to have had any children around. *(pause)* No, Wright wouldn't like the bird — a thing that sang. She used to sing. He killed that, too.

MRS. PETERS *(moving uneasily)*: We don't know who killed the bird.

MRS. HALE: I knew John Wright.

MRS. PETERS: It was an awful thing was done in this house that night, Mrs. Hale. Killing a man while he slept, slipping a rope around his neck that choked the life out of him.

MRS. HALE: His neck. Choked the life out of him.

Her hand goes out and rests on the birdcage.

MRS. PETERS *(with rising voice)*: We don't know who killed him. We don't know.

MRS. HALE *(her own feeling not interrupted)*: If there'd been years and years of nothing, then a bird to sing to you, it would be awful — still, after the bird was still.

MRS. PETERS *(something within her speaking)*: I know what stillness is. When we homesteaded in Dakota, and my first baby died — after he was two years old, and me with no other then —

MRS. HALE *(moving)*: How soon do you suppose they'll be through, looking for the evidence?

MRS. PETERS: I know what stillness is. *(pulling herself back)* The law has got to punish crime, Mrs. Hale.

MRS. HALE *(not as if answering that)*: I wish you'd seen Minnie Foster when she wore a white dress with blue ribbons and stood up there in the choir and sang. *(a look around the room)* Oh, I *wish* I'd come over here once in a while! That was a crime! That was a crime! Who's going to punish that?

MRS. PETERS *(looking upstairs)*: We mustn't — take on.

MRS. HALE: I might have known she needed help! I know how things can be — for women. I tell you, it's queer, Mrs. Peters. We live close to-gether and we live far apart. We all go through the same things — it's all just a different kind of the same thing. *(brushes her eyes; noticing the bottle of fruit, reaches out for it)* If I was you I wouldn't tell her her fruit was gone. Tell her it *ain't*. Tell her it's all right. Take this in to prove it to her. She — she may never know whether it was broke or not.

MRS. PETERS *(Takes the bottle, looks about for something to wrap it in; takes petticoat from the clothes brought from the other room, very nervously begins winding this around the bottle. In a false voice)*: My, it's a good thing the men couldn't hear us. Wouldn't they just laugh! Getting all stirred up over a little thing like a — dead canary. As if that could have anything to do with — with — wouldn't they *laugh!*

The men are heard coming down stairs.

MRS. HALE *(under her breath)*: Maybe they would — maybe they wouldn't.

COUNTY ATTORNEY: No, Peters, it's all perfectly clear except a reason for doing it. But you know juries when it comes to women. If there was some definite thing. Something to show — something to make a story about — a thing that would connect up with this strange way of doing it —

The women's eyes meet for an instant. Enter HALE *from outer door.*

HALE: Well, I've got the team around. Pretty cold out there.

COUNTY ATTORNEY: I'm going to stay here a while by myself. *(to the* SHERIFF*)* You can send Frank out for me, can't you? I want to go over everything. I'm not satisfied that we can't do better.

SHERIFF: Do you want to see what Mrs. Peters is going to take in?

The COUNTY ATTORNEY *goes to the table, picks up the apron, laughs.*

COUNTY ATTORNEY: Oh, I guess they're not very dangerous things the ladies have picked out. *(Moves a few things about, disturbing the quilt pieces which cover the box. Steps back.)* No, Mrs. Peters doesn't need supervising. For that matter, a sheriff's wife is married to the law. Ever think of it that way, Mrs. Peters?

MRS. PETERS: Not — just that way.

SHERIFF *(chuckling)*: Married to the law. *(moves toward the other room)* I just want you to come in here a minute, George. We ought to take a look at these windows.

COUNTY ATTORNEY *(scoffingly)*: Oh, windows!

SHERIFF: We'll be right out, Mr. Hale.

> HALE *goes outside. The* SHERIFF *follows the* COUNTY ATTORNEY *into the other room. Then* MRS. HALE *rises, hands tight together, looking intensely at* MRS. PETERS, *whose eyes make a slow turn, finally meeting* MRS. HALE's. *A moment* MRS. HALE *holds her, then her own eyes point the way to where the box is concealed. Suddenly* MRS. PETERS *throws back quilt pieces and tries to put the box in the bag she is wearing. It is too big. She opens box, starts to take bird out, cannot touch it, goes to pieces, stands there helpless. Sound of a knob turning in the other room.* MRS. HALE *snatches the box and puts it in the pocket of her big coat. Enter* COUNTY ATTORNEY *and* SHERIFF.

COUNTY ATTORNEY *(facetiously)*: Well, Henry, at least we found out that she was not going to quilt it. She was going to—what is it you call it, ladies?

MRS. HALE *(her hand against her pocket)*: We call it—knot it, Mr. Henderson.

Considerations

1. Make a chronological list of the events that happened (or that you speculate might have happened) both before and during the action of the play. Begin with Mr. and Mrs. Wright sitting in their living room. How would the play be changed if Glaspell had chosen to show us the action that takes place before the investigation on which the drama focuses?
2. What work do the men in the play do? What work do the women do? Explain how the men and women view and value their own work and how they view and value the work of the opposite sex.
3. Susan Glaspell wrote a short story describing the same events and characters depicted in *Trifles*. The story is titled "A Jury of Her Peers." Discuss the significance of each title and explain which you prefer.
4. What is your response to the decision made by Mrs. Peters and Mrs. Hale to hide the dead bird from the men? What are their motives? What values do their actions imply?
5. Comment on the final line of the play. Suggest several possible meanings for Mrs. Hale's response to the County Attorney's question.

VIRGINIA WOOLF (1882–1941)

Professions for Women

When your secretary invited me to come here, she told me that your Society is concerned with the employment of women and she suggested that I might tell you something about my own professional experiences. It is true I am a woman; it is true I am employed, but what professional experiences have I had? It is difficult to say. My profession is literature; and in that profession there are fewer experiences for women than in any other, with the exception of the stage — fewer, I mean, that are peculiar to women. For the road was cut many years ago — by Fanny Burney, by Aphra Behn, by Harriet Martineau, by Jane Austen, by George Eliot° — many famous women, and many more unknown and forgotten, have been before me, making the path smooth, and regulating my steps. Thus, when I came to write, there were very few material obstacles in my way. Writing was a reputable and harmless occupation. The family peace was not broken by the scratching of a pen. No demand was made upon the family purse. For ten and sixpence one can buy paper enough to write all the plays of Shakespeare — if one has a mind that way. Pianos and models, Paris, Vienna and Berlin, masters and mistresses, are not needed by a writer. The cheapness of writing paper is, of course, the reason why women have succeeded as writers before they have succeeded in the other professions.

But to tell you my story — it is a simple one. You have only got to figure to yourselves a girl in a bedroom with a pen in her hand. She had only to move that pen from left to right — from ten o'clock to one. Then it occurred to her to do what is simple and cheap enough after all — to slip a few of those pages into an envelope, fix a penny stamp in the corner, and drop the envelope in the red box at the corner. It was thus that I became a journalist; and my effort was rewarded on the first day of the following month — a very glorious day it was for me — by a letter from an editor containing a check for one pound ten shillings and sixpence. But to show you how little I deserve to be called a professional woman, how little I know of the struggles and difficulties of such lives, I have to admit that instead of spending that sum upon bread and butter, rent, shoes and stockings, or butcher's bills, I went out and bought a cat — a beautiful cat, a Persian cat, which very soon involved me in bitter disputes with my neighbors.

What could be easier than to write articles and to buy Persian cats with the profits? But wait a moment. Articles have to be about something. Mine, I seem to remember, was about a novel by a famous man. And while I was writing this review, I discovered that if I were going to review books I should need to do battle with a certain phantom. And the phantom was a

---

Fanny Burney, Aphra Behn, Harriet Martineau, Jane Austen, and George Eliot (the pen name of Mary Ann Evans): All eighteenth- or nineteenth-century authors. These women often faced disapproval, ridicule, and lack of acceptance because they chose to write for publication.

woman, and when I came to know her better I called her after the heroine of a famous poem, The Angel in the House. It was she who used to come between me and my paper when I was writing reviews. It was she who bothered me and wasted my time and so tormented me that at last I killed her. You who come of a younger and happier generation may not have heard of her — you may not know what I mean by the Angel in the House. I will describe her as shortly as I can. She was intensely sympathetic. She was immensely charming. She was utterly unselfish. She excelled in the difficult arts of family life. She sacrificed herself daily. If there was chicken, she took the leg; if there was a draught she sat in it — in short she was so constituted that she never had a mind or a wish of her own, but preferred to sympathize always with the minds and wishes of others. Above all — I need not say it — she was pure. Her purity was supposed to be her chief beauty — her blushes, her great grace. In those days — the last of Queen Victoria — every house had its Angel. And when I came to write I encountered her with the very first words. The shadow of her wings fell on my page; I heard the rustling of her skirts in the room. Directly, that is to say, I took my pen in hand to review that novel by a famous man, she slipped behind me and whispered: "My dear, you are a young woman. You are writing about a book that has been written by a man. Be sympathetic; be tender; flatter; deceive; use all the arts and wiles of our sex. Never let anybody guess that you have a mind of your own. Above all, be pure." And she made as if to guide my pen. I now record the one act for which I take some credit to myself, though the credit rightly belongs to some excellent ancestors of mine who left me a certain sum of money — shall we say five hundred pounds a year? — so that it was not necessary for me to depend solely on charm for my living. I turned upon her and caught her by the throat. I did my best to kill her. My excuse, if I were to be had up in a court of law, would be that I acted in self-defense. Had I not killed her she would have killed me. She would have plucked the heart out of my writing. For, as I found, directly I put pen to paper, you cannot review even a novel without having a mind of your own, without expressing what you think to be the truth about human relations, morality, sex. And all these questions, according to the Angel in the House, cannot be dealt with freely and openly by women; they must charm, they must conciliate, they must — to put it bluntly — tell lies if they are to succeed. Thus, whenever I felt the shadow of her wing or the radiance of her halo upon my page, I took up the inkpot and flung it at her. She died hard. Her fictitious nature was of great assistance to her. It is far harder to kill a phantom than a reality. She was always creeping back when I thought I had despatched her. Though I flatter myself that I killed her in the end, the struggle was severe; it took much time that I had better have spent upon learning Greek grammar, or in roaming the world in search of adventures. But it was a real experience; it was an experience that was bound to befall all women writers at that time: Killing the Angel in the House was part of the occupation of a woman writer.

But to continue my story. The Angel was dead; what then remained? You may say that what remained was a simple and common object — a young woman in a bedroom with an inkpot. In other words, now that she had rid herself of falsehood, that young woman had only to be herself. Ah, but what is "herself"? I mean, what is a woman? I assure you, I do not know. I do not believe that you know. I do not believe that anybody can know until she has expressed herself in all the arts and professions open to human skill. That indeed is one of the reasons why I have come here — out of respect for you, who are in process of showing us by your experiments what a woman is, who are in process of providing us, by your failures and successes, with that extremely important piece of information.

But to continue the story of my professional experiences. I made one   5
pound ten and six by my first review; and I bought a Persian cat with the proceeds. Then I grew ambitious. A Persian cat is all very well, I said; but a Persian cat is not enough. I must have a motor car. And it was thus that I became a novelist — for it is a very strange thing that people will give you a motor car if you will tell them a story. It is a still stranger thing that there is nothing so delightful in the world as telling stories. It is far pleasanter than writing reviews of famous novels. And yet, if I am to obey your secretary and tell you my professional experiences as a novelist, I must tell you about a very strange experience that befell me as a novelist. And to understand it you must try first to imagine a novelist's state of mind. I hope I am not giving away professional secrets if I say that a novelist's chief desire is to be as unconscious as possible. He has to induce in himself a state of perpetual lethargy. He wants life to proceed with the utmost quiet and regularity. He wants to see the same faces, to read the same books, to do the same things day after day, month after month, while he is writing, so that nothing may break the illusion in which he is living — so that nothing may disturb or disquiet the mysterious nosings about, feelings round, darts, dashes and sudden discoveries of that very shy and illusive spirit, the imagination. I suspect that this state is the same both for men and women. Be that as it may, I want you to imagine me writing a novel in a state of trance. I want you to figure to yourselves a girl sitting with a pen in her hand, which for minutes, and indeed for hours, she never dips into the inkpot. The image that comes to my mind when I think of this girl is the image of a fisherman lying sunk in dreams on the verge of a deep lake with a rod held out over the water. She was letting her imagination sweep unchecked round every rock and cranny of the world that lies submerged in the depths of our unconscious being. Now came the experience, the experience that I believe to be far commoner with women writers than with men. The line raced through the girl's fingers. Her imagination had rushed away. It had sought the pools, the depths, the dark places where the largest fish slumber. And then there was a smash. There was an explosion. There was foam and confusion. The imagination had dashed itself against something hard. The girl was roused from her dream. She was indeed in a state of the most acute

and difficult distress. To speak without figure she had thought of something, something about the body, about the passions which it was unfitting for her as a woman to say. Men, her reason told her, would be shocked. The consciousness of what men will say of a woman who speaks the truth about her passions had roused her from her artist's state of unconsciousness. She could write no more. The trance was over. Her imagination could work no longer. This I believe to be a very common experience with women writers — they are impeded by the extreme conventionality of the other sex. For though men sensibly allow themselves great freedom in these respects, I doubt that they realize or can control the extreme severity with which they condemn such freedom in women.

These then were two very genuine experiences of my own. These were two of the adventures of my professional life. The first — killing the Angel in the House — I think I solved. She died. But the second, telling the truth about my own experiences as a body, I do not think I solved. I doubt that any woman has solved it yet. The obstacles against her are still immensely powerful — and yet they are very difficult to define. Outwardly, what is simpler than to write books? Outwardly, what obstacles are there for a woman rather than for a man? Inwardly, I think, the case is very different; she has still many ghosts to fight, many prejudices to overcome. Indeed it will be a long time still, I think, before a women can sit down to write a book without finding a phantom to be slain, a rock to be dashed against. And if this is so in literature, the freest of all professions for women, how is it in the new professions which you are now for the first time entering?

Those are the questions that I should like, had I time, to ask you. And indeed, if I have laid stress upon these professional experiences of mine, it is because I believe that they are, though in different forms, yours also. Even when the path is nominally open — when there is nothing to prevent a woman from being a doctor, a lawyer, a civil servant — there are many phantoms and obstacles, as I believe, looming in her way. To discuss and define them is I think of great value and importance; for thus only can the labor be shared, the difficulties be solved. But besides this, it is necessary also to discuss the ends and the aims for which we are fighting, for which we are doing battle with these formidable obstacles. Those aims cannot be taken for granted; they must be perpetually questioned and examined. The whole position, as I see it — here in this hall surrounded by women practicing for the first time in history I know not how many different professions — is one of extraordinary interest and importance. You have won rooms of your own in the house hitherto exclusively owned by men. You are able, though not without great labor and effort, to pay the rent. You are earning your five hundred pounds a year. But this freedom is only a beginning; the room is your own, but it is still bare. It has to be furnished; it has to be decorated; it has to be shared. How are you going to furnish it, how are you going to decorate it? With whom are you going to share it, and upon what terms? These, I think, are questions of the utmost importance and interest. For the first time in history you are able to ask them; for the first time you are able to decide for yourselves what the answers should be. Willingly would I stay and discuss those questions and answers — but not tonight. My time is up; and I must cease.

Considerations

1. What reasons does Woolf give for finding writing a comfortable profession for a woman to pursue? What do these reasons suggest about the relationship between women, their families, and the world of work?

2. What does Woolf mean when she says that she was hindered in writing reviews of men's writing by "The Angel in the House"? Who or what does the Angel represent?

   Make a list of the Angel's qualities and consider why Woolf believes those qualities to be dangerous to a writer.

   What does Woolf mean when she says she killed the Angel?

3. In paragraph 4, Woolf asks, "What is a woman?" Explain her response to this question and then work on your own definition.

   Try also to answer the question, "What is a man?" How is your definition different from your definition of a woman? How do you explain the discrepancies?

4. What problems did Woolf encounter when she moved from writing reviews to writing novels? Explain the metaphor she uses in paragraph 5 to describe this problem.

5. Woolf ends her essay with a series of questions about the rooms women occupy (or will occupy) "in the house hitherto exclusively owned by men." She wrote "Professions for Women" in 1931; how would you answer her questions today, from the perspective of the 1990s?

JOSEPH EPSTEIN (1937–   )

The Virtues of Ambition

Ambition is one of those Rorschach words: define it and you instantly reveal a great deal about yourself. Even that most neutral of works, *Webster's,* in its Seventh New Collegiate Edition, gives itself away, defining ambition first and foremost as "an ardent desire for rank, fame, or power." Ardent immediately assumes a heat incommensurate with good sense and stability, and rank, fame, and power have come under fairly heavy attack for at least a century. One can, after all, be ambitious for the public good, for the alleviation of suffering, for the enlightenment of mankind, though there are some who say that these are precisely the ambitious people most to be distrusted.

Surely ambition is behind dreams of glory, of wealth, of love, of distinction, of accomplishment, of pleasure, of goodness. What life does with our dreams and expectations cannot, of course, be predicted. Some dreams, begun in selflessness, end in rancor; other dreams, begun in selfishness, end in large-heartedness. The unpredictability of the outcome of dreams is no reason to cease dreaming.

To be sure, ambition, the sheer thing unalloyed by some larger purpose than merely clambering up, is never a pretty prospect to ponder. As drunks have done to alcohol, the single-minded have done to ambition — given it a bad name. Like a taste for alcohol, too, ambition does not always allow for easy satiation. Some people cannot handle it; it has brought grief to others, and not merely the ambitious alone. Still, none of this seems sufficient cause for driving ambition under the counter.

What is the worst that can be said — that has been said — about ambition? Here is a (surely) partial list:

To begin with, it, ambition, is often antisocial, and indeed is now outmoded, belonging to an age when individualism was more valued and useful than it is today. The person strongly imbued with ambition ignores the collectivity; socially detached, he is on his own and out for his own. Individuality and ambition are firmly linked. The ambitious individual, far from identifying himself and his fortunes with the group, wishes to rise above it. The ambitious man or woman sees the world as a battle; rivalrousness is his or her principal emotion: the world has limited prizes to offer, and he or she is determined to get his or hers. Ambition is, moreover, jesuitical; it can argue those possessed by it into believing that what they want for themselves is good for everyone — that the satisfaction of their own desires is best for the commonweal. The truly ambitious believe that it is a dog-eat-dog world, and they are distinguished by wanting to be the dogs that do the eating.

From here it is but a short hop to believe that those who have achieved the common goals of ambition — money, fame, power — have achieved them through corruption of a greater or lesser degree, mostly a greater. Thus all politicians in high places, thought to be ambitious, are understood to be, ipso facto, without moral scruples. How could they have such scruples — a weighty burden in a high climb — and still have risen as they have?

If ambition is to be well regarded, the rewards of ambition — wealth, distinction, control over one's destiny — must be deemed worthy of the sacrifices made on ambition's behalf. If the tradition of ambition is to have vitality, it must be widely shared; and it especially must be esteemed by people who are themselves admired, the educated not least among them. The educated not least because, nowadays more than ever before, it is they who have usurped the platforms of public discussion and wield the power of the spoken and written word in newspapers, in magazines, on television. In an odd way, it is the educated who have claimed to have given up on ambition as an ideal. What is odd is that they have perhaps most benefited from ambition — if not always their own then that of their parents and grandparents. There is a heavy note of hypocrisy in this; a case of closing the barn door after the horses have escaped — with the educated themselves astride them.

Certainly people do not seem less interested in success and its accoutrements now than formerly. Summer homes, European travel, BMWs — the locations, place names, and name brands may change, but such items do not seem less in demand today than a decade or two years ago. What has happened is that people cannot own up to their dreams, as easily and openly as once they could, lest they be thought pushing, acquisitive, vulgar. Instead we are treated to fine pharisaical spectacles, which now more than ever seem in ample supply: the revolutionary lawyer quartered in the $250,000 Manhattan condominium; the critic of American materialism with a Southampton summer home; the publisher of radical books who takes his meals in three-star restaurants; the journalist advocating participatory democracy in all phases of life, whose own children are enrolled in private schools. For such people and many more perhaps not so egregious, the proper formulation is, "Succeed at all costs but refrain from *appearing* ambitious."

The attacks on ambition are many and come from various angles; its public defenders are few and unimpressive, where they are not extremely unattractive. As a result, the support for ambition as a healthy impulse, a quality to be admired and inculcated in the young, is probably lower than it has ever been in the United States. This does not mean that ambition is at an end, that people no longer feel its stirrings and promptings, but only that, no longer openly honored, it is less often openly professed. Consequences follow from this, of course, some of which are that ambition is driven underground, or made sly, or perverse. It can also be forced into vulgarity, as witness the blatant pratings of its contemporary promoters. Such, then, is the way things stand: on the left angry critics, on the right obtuse supporters, and in the middle, as usual, the majority of earnest people trying to get on in life.

Many people are naturally distrustful of ambition, feeling that it represents something intractable in human nature. Thus John Dean entitled his book about his involvement in the Watergate affair during the Nixon administration *Blind Ambition,* as if ambition were to blame for his ignoble actions, and not the constellation of qualities that make up his rather shabby character. Ambition, it must once again be underscored, is morally a two-sided street. Place next to John Dean Andrew Carnegie, who, among other philanthropic acts, bought the library of Lord Acton, at a time when Acton was in financial distress, and assigned its custodianship to Acton, who never was told who his benefactor was. Need much more be said on the subject than that, important though ambition is, there are some things that one must not sacrifice to it?

But going at things the other way, sacrificing ambition so as to guard against its potential excesses, is to go at things wrongly. To discourage ambition is to discourage dreams of grandeur and greatness. All men and women are born, live, suffer, and die; what distinguishes us one from another is our dreams, whether they be dreams about wordly or unworldly things, and what we do to make them come about.

It may seem an exaggeration to say that ambition is the linchpin of society, holding many of its disparate elements together, but it is not an exaggeration by much. Remove ambition and the essential elements of society seem to fly apart. Ambition, as opposed to mere fantasizing about desires, implies work and discipline to achieve goals, personal and social, of a kind society cannot survive without. Ambition is intimately connected with family, for men and women not only work partly for their families; husbands and wives are often ambitious for each other, but harbor some of their most ardent ambitions for their children. Yet to have a family nowadays — with birth control readily available, and inflation a good economic argument against having children — is nearly an expression of ambition in itself. Finally, though ambition was once the domain chiefly of monarchs and aristocrats, it has, in more recent times, increasingly become the domain of the middle class. Ambition and futurity — and a sense of building for tomorrow — are inextricable. Working, saving, planning — these, the daily aspects of ambition — have always been the distinguishing marks of a rising middle class. The attack against ambition is not incidentally an attack on the middle class and what it stands for. Like it or not, the middle class has done much of society's work in America; and it, the middle class, has from the beginning run on ambition.

It is not difficult to imagine a world shorn of ambition. It would probably be a kinder world: without demands, without abrasions, without disappointments. People would have time for reflection. Such work as they did would not be for themselves but for the collectivity. Competition would never enter in. Conflict would be eliminated, tension become a thing of the past. The stress of creation would be at an end. Art would no longer be

10

troubling, but purely celebratory in its functions. The family would become superfluous as a social unit, with all its former power for bringing about neurosis drained away. Longevity would be increased, for fewer people would die of heart attack or stroke caused by tumultuous endeavor. Anxiety would be extinct. Time would stretch on and on, with ambition long departed from the human heart.

Ah, how unrelievedly boring life would be!

There is a strong view that holds that success is a myth, and ambition therefore a sham. Does this mean that success does not really exist? That achievement is at bottom empty? That the efforts of men and women are of no significance alongside the force of movements and events? Now not all success, obviously, is worth esteeming, nor all ambition worth cultivating. Which are and which are not is something one soon enough learns on one's own. But even the most cynical secretly admit that success exists; that achievement counts for a great deal; and that the true myth is that the actions of men and women are useless. To believe otherwise is to take on a point of view that is likely to be deranging. It is, in its implications, to remove all motive for competence, interest in attainment, and regard for posterity.

We do not choose to be born. We do not choose our parents. We do not choose our historical epoch, the country of our birth, or the immediate circumstances of our upbringing. We do not, most of us, choose to die; nor do we choose the time or conditions of our death. But within all this realm of choicelessness, we do choose how we shall live: courageously or in cowardice, honorably or dishonorably, with purpose or in drift. We decide what is important and what is trivial in life. We decide that what makes us significant is either what we do or what we refuse to do. But no matter how indifferent the universe may be to our choices and decisions, these choices and decisions are ours to make. We decide. We choose. And as we decide and choose, so are our lives formed. In the end, forming our own destiny is what ambition is about.

Considerations

1. How and why does Epstein challenge the dictionary definition of "ambition"?
2. Reread the first six paragraphs carefully and explain the assumptions about ambition that Epstein explains. How does he use these assumptions to develop his essay?
3. Epstein claims that ambition is essential to hold society together. Do you agree with him? Identify specific points in his argument that you might challenge.
4. In paragraph 13, Epstein describes a society without ambition, concluding with the observation: "Ah, how unrelievedly boring life would be!" Do you agree? Explain.

5. What is your own definition of "ambition"? How does your definition relate to the work — paid or unpaid — that you currently do or plan to do?

CONNECTIONS: WORK

1. Read Joseph Epstein's "The Virtues of Ambition." Then explain whether you see the concept of ambition, as Epstein defines it, as important in any of the following works:
   "The Use of Force"
   "Bartleby, the Scrivener"
   "The Catbird Seat"
   "Tom's Husband"
   Which characters in these works seem ambitious? Which seem to lack ambition? Explain.

2. Discuss issues related to women and work as suggested by "Tom's Husband," *Trifles,* and "Professions for Women."

3. Consider conflicts between workers and employers as suggested by "Bartleby, the Scrivener," "The Catbird Seat," and "The Man Who Was Almost a Man."

4. Compare Marge Piercy's view of workers she admires ("To Be of Use") with the views expressed by Joseph Epstein in "The Virtues of Ambition." Would Piercy and Epstein admire the same workers?

5. Compare the waiter in Kraft Rompf's "Waiting Table" to the waitress in Judy Grahn's "Ella in a square apron along Highway 80."

Men and Women

KATE CHOPIN (1851–1904)

The Storm

1

The leaves were so still that even Bibi thought it was going to rain. Bobinôt, who was accustomed to converse on terms of perfect equality with his little son, called the child's attention to certain sombre clouds that were rolling with sinister intention from the west, accompanied by a sullen, threatening roar. They were at Friedheimer's store and decided to remain there till the storm had passed. They sat within the door on two empty kegs. Bibi was four years old and looked very wise.

"Mama'll be 'fraid, yes," he suggested with blinking eyes.

"She'll shut the house. Maybe she got Sylvie helpin' her this evenin'," Bobinôt responded reassuringly.

"No; she ent got Sylvie. Sylvie was helpin' her yistiday," piped Bibi.

Bobinôt arose and going across to the counter purchased a can of   5
shrimps, of which Calixta was very fond. Then he returned to his perch on the keg and sat stolidly holding the can of shrimps while the storm burst. It shook the wooden store and seemed to be ripping great furrows in the distant field. Bibi laid his little hand on his father's knee and was not afraid.

2

Calixta, at home, felt no uneasiness for their safety. She sat at a side window sewing furiously on a sewing machine. She was greatly occupied and did not notice the approaching storm. But she felt very warm and often stopped to mop her face on which the perspiration gathered in beads. She unfastened her white sacque at the throat. It began to grow dark, and suddenly realizing the situation she got up hurriedly and went about closing windows and doors.

Out on the small front gallery she had hung Bobinôt's Sunday clothes to air and she hastened out to gather them before the rain fell. As she stepped outside, Alcée Laballière rode in at the gate. She had not seen him very often since her marriage, and never alone. She stood there with Bobinôt's coat in her hands, and the big rain drops began to fall. Alcée rode his horse under the shelter of a side projection where the chickens had huddled and there were plows and a harrow piled up in the corner.

"May I come and wait on your gallery till the storm is over, Calixta?" he asked.

"Come 'long in, M'sieur Alcée."

His voice and her own startled her as if from a trance, and she seized   10
Bobinôt's vest. Alcée, mounting to the porch, grabbed the trousers and snatched Bibi's braided jacket that was about to be carried away by a sudden gust of wind. He expressed an intention to remain outside, but it was soon apparent that he might as well have been out in the open: the water beat in

upon the boards in driving sheets, and he went inside, closing the door after him. It was even necessary to put something beneath the door to keep the water out.

"My! what a rain! It's good two years sence it rain' like that," exclaimed Calixta as she rolled up a piece of bagging and Alcée helped her to thrust it beneath the crack.

She was a little fuller of figure than five years before when she married; but she had lost nothing of her vivacity. Her blue eyes still retained their melting quality; and her yellow hair, dishevelled by the wind and rain, kinked more stubbornly than ever about her ears and temples.

The rain beat upon the low, shingled roof with a force and clatter that threatened to break an entrance and deluge them there. They were in the dining room — the sitting room — the general utility room. Adjoining was her bed room, with Bibi's couch along side her own. The door stood open, and the room with its white, monumental bed, its closed shutters, looked dim and mysterious.

Alcée flung himself into a rocker and Calixta nervously began to gather up from the floor the lengths of a cotton sheet which she had been sewing.

"If this keeps up, *Dieu sait*° if the levees goin' to stan' it!" she exclaimed.   15

"What have you got to do with the levees?"

"I got enough to do! An' there's Bobinôt with Bibi out in that storm — if he only didn' left Friedheimer's!"

"Let us hope, Calixta, that Bobinôt's got sense enough to come in out of a cyclone."

She went and stood at the window with a greatly disturbed look on her face. She wiped the frame that was clouded with moisture. It was stiflingly hot. Alcée got up and joined her at the window, looking over her shoulder. The rain was coming down in sheets obscuring the view of far-off cabins and enveloping the distant wood in a gray mist. The playing of the lightning was incessant. A bolt struck a tall chinaberry tree at the edge of the field. It filled all visible space with a blinding glare and the crash seemed to invade the very boards they stood upon.

Calixta put her hands to her eyes, and with a cry, staggered backward.   20 Alcée's arm encircled her, and for an instant he drew her close and spasmodically to him.

"*Bonté!*"° she cried, releasing herself from his encircling arm and retreating from the window, "the house'll go next! If I only knew w'ere Bibi was!" She would not compose herself; she would not be seated. Alcée clasped her shoulders and looked into her face. The contact of her warm, palpitating body when he had unthinkingly drawn her into his arms, had aroused all the old-time infatuation and desire for her flesh.

Dieu sait: God knows.   Bonté!: My goodness!

"Calixta," he said, "don't be frightened. Nothing can happen. The house is too low to be struck, with so many tall trees standing about. There! aren't you going to be quiet? say, aren't you?" He pushed her hair back from her face that was warm and steaming. Her lips were as red and moist as pomegranate seed. Her white neck and a glimpse of her full, firm bosom disturbed him powerfully. As she glanced up at him the fear in her liquid blue eyes had given place to a drowsy gleam that unconsciously betrayed a sensuous desire. He looked down into her eyes and there was nothing for him to do but to gather her lips in a kiss. It reminded him of Assumption.

"Do you remember—in Assumption. Calixta?" he asked in a low voice broken by passion. Oh! she remembered; for in Assumption he had kissed her and kissed and kissed her; until his senses would well nigh fail, and to save her he would resort to a desperate flight. If she was not an immaculate dove in those days, she was still inviolate; a passionate creature whose very defenselessness had made her defense, against which his honor forbade him to prevail. Now—well, now—her lips seemed in a manner free to be tasted, as well as her round, white throat and her whiter breasts.

They did not heed the crashing torrents, and the roar of the elements made her laugh as she lay in his arms. She was a revelation in that dim, mysterious chamber; as white as the couch she lay upon. Her firm, elastic flesh that was knowing for the first time its birthright, was like a creamy lily that the sun invites to contribute its breath and perfume to the undying life of the world.

The generous abundance of her passion, without guile or trickery, was like a white flame which penetrated and found response in depths of his own sensuous nature that had never yet been reached. 25

When he touched her breasts they gave themselves up in quivering ecstasy, inviting his lips. Her mouth was a fountain of delight. And when he possessed her, they seemed to swoon together at the very borderland of life's mystery.

He stayed cushioned upon her, breathless, dazed, enervated, with his heart beating like a hammer upon her. With one hand she clasped his head, her lips lightly touching his forehead. The other hand stroked with a soothing rhythm his muscular shoulders.

The growl of the thunder was distant and passing away. The rain beat softly upon the shingles, inviting them to drowsiness and sleep. But they dared not yield.

The rain was over; and the sun was turning the glistening green world into a palace of gems. Calixta, on the gallery, watched Alcée ride away. He turned and smiled at her with a beaming face; and she lifted her pretty chin in the air and laughed aloud.

3

Bobinôt and Bibi, trudging home, stopped without at the cistern to 30 make themselves presentable.

"My! Bibi, w'at will yo' mama say! You ought to be ashame'. You oughtn' put on those good pants. Look at 'em! An' that mud on yo' collar! How you got that mud on yo' collar, Bibi? I never saw such a boy!" Bibi was the picture of pathetic resignation. Bobinôt was the embodiment of serious solicitude as he strove to remove from his own person and his son's the signs of their tramp over heavy roads and through wet fields. He scraped the mud off Bibi's bare legs and feet with a stick and carefully removed all traces from his heavy brogans. Then, prepared for the worst — the meeting with an over-scrupulous housewife, they entered cautiously at the back door.

Calixta was preparing supper. She had set the table and was dripping coffee at the hearth. She sprang up as they came in.

"Oh, Bobinôt! You back! My! but I was uneasy. W'ere you been during the rain? An' Bibi? he ain't wet? he ain't hurt?" She had clasped Bibi and was kissing him effusively. Bobinôt's explanations and apologies which he had been composing all along the way, died on his lips as Calixta felt him to see if he were dry, and seemed to express nothing but satisfaction at their safe return.

"I brought you some shrimps, Calixta," offered Bobinôt, hauling the can from his ample side pocket and laying it on the table.

"Shrimps! Oh, Bobinôt! you too good fo' anything!" and she gave him a smacking kiss on the cheek that resounded. "*J'vous reponds,*° we'll have a feas' to-night! umph-umph!" 35

Bobinôt and Bibi began to relax and enjoy themselves, and when the three seated themselves at table they laughed much and so loud that anyone might have heard them as far away as Laballière's.

4

Alcée Laballière wrote to his wife, Clarisse, that night. It was a loving letter, full of tender solitude. He told her not to hurry back, but if she and the babies liked it at Biloxi, to stay a month longer. He was getting on nicely; and though he missed them, he was willing to bear the separation a while longer — realizing that their health and pleasure were the first things to be considered.

5

As for Clarisse, she was charmed upon receiving her husband's letter. She and the babies were doing well. The society was agreeable; many of her old friends and acquaintances were at the bay. And the first free breath since her marriage seemed to restore the pleasant liberty of her maiden days. Devoted as she was to her husband, their intimate conjugal life was something which she was more than willing to forego for a while.

So the storm passed and everyone was happy.

J'vous reponds: I assure you.

Considerations

1. Analyze Calixta and Bobinôt's marriage, using details from the story to back up your analysis. Would you describe the marriage as "good" or "bad" — or would you use a different word? What are the positive elements of the marriage? Does anything seem to be missing?

2. Look carefully at the words Chopin chooses to describe the scenes between Calixta and Alcée. What do the words and images suggest about the author's attitude toward her characters? Does she sympathize? Is she judging them? Explain.

3. What differences do you notice between Calixta's and Alcée's speech patterns? What might these differences suggest about their social, economic, and educational background? Given this analysis, write a narrative describing their last evening together in Assumption. Why might they have decided to part rather than to marry?

4. What purpose is served by the opening and ending sections of the story? How would the story be changed (and how would your response change) if they were omitted and the second section stood as the whole story? Consider how your evaluation of characters, actions, and choices might be affected.

5. Write an argument defending or criticizing Calixta's and Alcée's actions. As you plan your argument, consider the final line of the story, "So the storm passed and everyone was happy." Do you agree?

D. H. LAWRENCE (1885–1930)

The Horse Dealer's Daughter

"Well, Mabel, and what are you going to do with yourself?" asked Joe, with foolish flippancy. He felt quite safe himself. Without listening for an answer, he turned aside, worked a grain of tobacco to the tip of his tongue, and spat it out. He did not care about anything, since he felt safe himself.

The three brothers and the sister sat round the desolate breakfast table, attempting some sort of desultory consultation. The morning's post had given the final tap to the family fortune, and all was over. The dreary dining-room itself, with its heavy mahogany furniture, looked as if it were waiting to be done away with.

But the consultation amounted to nothing. There was a strange air of ineffectuality about the three men, as they sprawled at table, smoking and reflecting vaguely on their own condition. The girl was alone, a rather short, sullen-looking young woman of twenty-seven. She did not share the same life as her brothers. She would have been good-looking, save for the impassive fixity of her face, "bull-dog," as her brothers called it.

There was a confused tramping of horses' feet outside. The three men all sprawled round in their chairs to watch. Beyond the dark hollybushes that separated the strip of lawn from the high-road, they could see a cavalcade of shire horses swinging out of their own yard, being taken for exercise. This was the last time. These were the last horses that would go through their hands. The young men watched with critical, callous looks. They were all frightened at the collapse of their lives, and the sense of disaster in which they were involved left them no inner freedom.

Yet they were three fine, well-set fellows enough. Joe, the eldest, was   5
a man of thirty-three, broad and handsome in a hot, flushed way. His face was red, he twisted his black moustache over a thick finger, his eyes were shallow and restless. He had a sensual way of uncovering his teeth when he laughed, and his bearing was stupid. Now he watched the horses with a glazed look of helplessness in his eyes, a certain stupor of downfall.

The great draught-horses swung past. They were tied head to tail, four of them, and they heaved along to where a lane branched off from the highroad, planting their great hoofs floutingly in the fine black mud, swinging their great rounded haunches sumptuously, and trotting a few sudden steps as they were led into the lane, round the corner. Every movement showed a massive, slumbrous strength, and a stupidity which held them in subjection. The groom at the head looked back, jerking the leading rope. And the cavalcade moved out of sight up the lane, the tail of the last horse bobbed up tight and stiff, held out taut from the swinging great haunches as they rocked behind the hedges in a motion like sleep.

Joe watched with glazed hopeless eyes. The horses were almost like his own body to him. He felt he was done for now. Luckily he was engaged to a woman as old as himself, and therefore her father, who was steward of a neighbouring estate, would provide him with a job. He would marry and go into harness. His life was over, he would be a subject animal now.

He turned uneasily aside, the retreating steps of the horses echoing in his ears. Then, with foolish restlessness, he reached for the scraps of bacon-rind from the plates, and making a faint whistling sound, flung them to the terrier that lay against the fender. He watched the dog swallow them, and waited till the creature looked into his eyes. Then a faint grin came on his face, and in a high, foolish voice he said:

"You won't get much more bacon, shall you, you little bitch?"

The dog faintly and dismally wagged its tail, then lowered its   10 haunches, circled round, and lay down again.

There was another helpless silence at the table. Joe sprawled uneasily in his seat, not willing to go till the family conclave was dissolved. Fred Henry, the second brother, was erect, clean-limbed, alert. He had watched the passing of the horses with more sangfroid. If he was an animal, like Joe, he was an animal which controls, not one which is controlled. He was master of any horse, and he carried himself with a well-tempered air of mastery. But he was not master of the situations of life. He pushed his coarse brown moustache upwards, off his lip, and glanced irritably at his sister, who sat impassive and inscrutable.

"You'll go and stop with Lucy for a bit, shan't you?" he asked. The girl did not answer.

"I don't see what else you can do," persisted Fred Henry.

"Go as a skivvy," Joe interpolated laconically.

The girl did not move a muscle.   15

"If I was her, I should go in for training for a nurse," said Malcolm, the youngest of them all. He was the baby of the family, a young man of twenty-two, with a fresh, jaunty *museau*.°

But Mabel did not take any notice of him. They had talked at her and round her for so many years, that she hardly heard them at all.

The marble clock on the mantelpiece softly chimed the half-hour, the dog rose uneasily from the hearthrug and looked at the party at the breakfast table. But still they sat on in ineffectual conclave.

"Oh, all right," said Joe suddenly, apropos of nothing. "I'll get a move on."

He pushed back his chair, straddled his knees with a downward jerk,   20 to get them free, in horsey fashion, and went to the fire. Still he did not go out of the room; he was curious to know what the others would do or say.

---

museau: muzzle or snout; slang for "face."

He began to charge his pipe, looking down at the dog and saying, in a high, affected voice:

"Going wi' me? Going wi' me are ter? Tha'rt goin' further than tha counts on just now, dost hear?"

The dog faintly wagged its tail, the man stuck out his jaw and covered his pipe with his hands, and puffed intently, losing himself in the tobacco, looking down all the while at the dog with an absent brown eye. The dog looked up at him in mournful distrust. Joe stood with his knees stuck out, in real horsey fashion.

"Have you had a letter from Lucy?" Fred Henry asked of his sister.

"Last week," came the neutral reply.

"And what does she say?"   25

There was no answer.

"Does she *ask* you to go and stop there?" persisted Fred Henry.

"She says I can if I like."

"Well, then, you'd better. Tell her you'll come on Monday."

This was received in silence.   30

"That's what you'll do then, is it?" said Fred Henry, in some exasperation.

But she made no answer. There was a silence of futility and irritation in the room. Malcolm grinned fatuously.

"You'll have to make up your mind between now and next Wednesday," said Joe loudly, "or else find yourself lodgings on the kerbstone."

The face of the young woman darkened, but she sat on immutable.

"Here's Jack Fergusson!" exclaimed Malcolm, who was looking aim-   35
lessly out of the window.

"Where?" exclaimed Joe, loudly.

"Just gone past."

"Coming in?"

Malcolm craned his neck to see the gate.

"Yes," he said.   40

There was a silence. Mabel sat on like one condemned, at the head of the table. Then a whistle was heard from the kitchen. The dog got up and barked sharply. Joe opened the door and shouted:

"Come on."

After a moment a young man entered. He was muffled up in overcoat and a purple woollen scarf, and his tweed cap, which he did not remove, was pulled down on his head. He was of medium height, his face was rather long and pale, his eyes looked tired.

"Hello, Jack! Well, Jack!" exclaimed Malcolm and Joe. Fred Henry merely said, "Jack."

"What's doing?" asked the newcomer, evidently addressing Fred   45
Henry.

"Same. We've got to be out by Wednesday. Got a cold?"

"I have — got it bad, too."

"Why don't you stop in?"

"*Me* stop in? When I can't stand on my legs, perhaps I shall have a chance." The young man spoke huskily. He had a slight Scotch accent.

"It's a knock-out, isn't it?" said Joe, boisterously, "if a doctor goes round croaking with a cold. Looks bad for the patients, doesn't it?"

The young doctor looked at him slowly.

"Anything the matter with *you*, then?" he asked sarcastically.

"Not as I know of. Damn your eyes, I hope not. Why?"

"I thought you were very concerned about the patients, wondered if you might be one yourself."

"Damn it, no, I've never been patient to no flaming doctor, and hope I never shall be," returned Joe.

At this point Mabel rose from the table, and they all seemed to become aware of her existence. She began putting the dishes together. The young doctor looked at her, but did not address her. He had not greeted her. She went out of the room with the tray, her face impassive and unchanged.

"When are you off then, all of you?" asked the doctor.

"I'm catching the eleven-forty," replied Malcolm. "Are you goin' down wi' th' trap, Joe?"

"Yes, I've told you I am going down wi' th' trap, haven't I?"

"We'd better be getting her in then. So long, Jack, if I don't see you before I go," said Malcolm, shaking hands.

He went out, followed by Joe, who seemed to have his tail between his legs.

"Well, this is the devil's own," exclaimed the doctor, when he was left alone with Fred Henry. "Going before Wednesday, are you."

"That's the orders," replied the other.

"Where, to Northampton?"

"That's it."

"The devil!" exclaimed Fergusson, with quiet chagrin.

And there was silence between the two.

"All settled up, are you?" asked Fergusson.

"About."

There was another pause.

"Well, I shall miss yer, Freddy, boy," said the young doctor.

"And I shall miss thee, Jack," returned the other.

"Miss you like hell," mused the doctor.

Fred Henry turned aside. There was nothing to say. Mabel came in again, to finish clearing the table.

"What are *you* going to do, then, Miss Pervin?" asked Fergusson. "Going to your sister's, are you?"

Mabel looked at him with her steady, dangerous eyes, that always made him uncomfortable, unsettling his superficial ease.

"No," she said.

"Well, what in the name of fortune are *you* going to do? Say what you mean to do," cried Fred Henry, with futile intensity.

But she only averted her head, and continued her work. She folded the white table-cloth, and put on the chenile cloth.

"The sulkiest bitch that ever trod!" muttered her brother.   80

But she finished her task with perfectly impassive face, the young doctor watching her interestedly all the while. Then she went out.

Fred Henry stared after her, clenching his lips, his blue eyes fixing in sharp antagonism, as he made a grimace of sour exasperation.

"You could bray her into bits, and that's all you'd get out of her," he said in a small, narrowed tone.

The doctor smiled faintly.

"What's she *going* to do, then?" he asked.   85

"Strike me if I know!" returned the other.

There was a pause. Then the doctor stirred.

"I'll be seeing you to-night, shall I?" he said to his friend.

"Ay — where's it to be? Are we going over to Jessdale?"

"I don't know. I've got such a cold on me. I'll come round to the Moon   90
and Stars, anyway."

"Let Lizzie and May miss their night for once, eh?"

"That's it — if I feel as I do now."

"All's one — "

The two young men went through the passage and down to the back door together. The house was large, but it was servantless now, and desolate. At the back was a small bricked house-yard, and beyond that a big square, gravelled fine and red, and having stables on two sides. Sloping, dank, winter-dark fields stretched away on the open sides.

But the stables were empty. Joseph Pervin, the father of the family,   95
had been a man of no education, who had become a fairly large horse dealer. The stables had been full of horses, there was a great turmoil and come-and-go of horses and of dealers and grooms. Then the kitchen was full of servants. But of late things had declined. The old man had married a second time, to retrieve his fortunes. Now he was dead and everything was gone to the dogs, there was nothing but debt and threatening.

For months, Mabel had been servantless in the big house, keeping the home together in penury for her ineffectual brothers. She had kept house for ten years. But previously it was with unstinted means. Then, however brutal and coarse everything was, the sense of money had kept her proud, confident. The men might be foul-mouthed, the women in the kitchen might have bad reputations, her brothers might have illegitimate children. But so long as there was money, the girl felt herself established and brutally proud, reserved.

No company came to the house, save dealers and coarse men. Mabel had no associates of her own sex, after her sister went away. But she did not mind. She went regularly to church, she attended to her father. And she lived in the memory of her mother, who had died when she was fourteen, and whom she had loved. She had loved her father, too, in a different way, depending upon him, and feeling secure in him, until at the age of fifty-four he married again. And then she had set hard against him. Now he had died and left them all hopelessly in debt.

She had suffered badly during the period of poverty. Nothing, however, could shake the curious sullen, animal pride that dominated each member of the family. Now, for Mabel, the end had come. Still she would not cast about her. She would follow her own way just the same. She would always hold the keys of her own situation. Mindless and persistent, she endured from day to day. What should she think? Why should she answer anybody? It was enough that this was the end and there was no way out. She need not pass any more darkly along the main street of the small town, avoiding every eye. She need not demean herself any more, going into the shops and buying the cheapest food. This was at an end. She thought of nobody, not even of herself. Mindless and persistent, she seemed in a sort of ecstasy to be coming nearer to her fulfillment, her own glorification, approaching her dead mother, who was glorified.

In the afternoon she took a little bag, with shears and sponge and a small scrubbing brush, and went out. It was a grey, wintry day, with saddened, dark green fields and an atmosphere blackened by the smoke of foundries not far off. She went quickly, darkly along the causeway, heeding nobody, through the town to the churchyard.

There she always felt secure, as if no one could see her, although as a matter of fact she was exposed to the stare of every one who passed along under the churchyard wall. Nevertheless, once under the shadow of the great looming church, among the graves, she felt immune from the world, reserved within the thick churchyard wall as in another country. 100

Carefully she clipped the grass from the grave, and arranged the pinky white, small chrysanthemums in the tin cross. When this was done, she took an empty jar from a neighbouring grave, brought water, and carefully, most scrupulously sponged the marble head-stone and the coping-stone.

It gave her sincere satisfaction to do this. She felt in immediate contact with the world of her mother. She took minute pains, went through the park in a state bordering on pure happiness, as if in performing this task she came into a subtle, intimate connection with her mother. For the life she followed here in the world was far less real than the world of death she inherited from her mother.

The doctor's house was just by the church. Fergusson, being a mere hired assistant, was slave to the country-side. As he hurried now to attend to the out-patients in the surgery, glancing across the graveyard with his quick eye, he saw the girl at her task at the grave. She seemed so intent and remote, it was like looking into another world. Some mystical element was touched in him. He slowed down as he walked, watching her as if spellbound.

She lifted her eyes, feeling him looking. Their eyes met. And each looked away again at once, each feeling, in some way, found out by the other. He lifted his cap and passed on down the road. There remained distinct in his consciousness, like a vision, the memory of her face, lifted from the tombstone in the churchyard, and looking at him with slow, large, portentous eyes. It *was* portentous, her face. It seemed to mesmerize him. There was a heavy power in her eyes which laid hold of his whole being, as if he had drunk some powerful drug. He had been feeling weak and done before. Now the life came back into him, he felt delivered from his own fretted, daily self.

He finished his duties at the surgery as quickly as might be, hastily filling up the bottle of the waiting people with cheap drugs. Then, in perpetual haste, he set off again to visit several cases in another part of his round, before tea-time. At all times he preferred to walk if he could, but particularly when he was not well. He fancied the motion restored him.

The afternoon was falling. It was grey, deadened, and wintry, with a slow, moist, heavy coldness sinking in and deadening all the faculties. But why should he think or notice? He hastily climbed the hill and turned across the dark green fields, following the black cindertrack. In the distance, across a shallow dip in the country, the small town was clustered like smouldering ash, a tower, a spire, a heap of low, raw, extinct houses. And on the nearest fringe of the town, sloping into the dip, was Oldmeadow, the Pervins' house. He could see the stables and the outbuildings distinctly, as they lay towards him on the slope. Well, he would not go there many more times! Another resource would be lost to him, another place gone: the only company he cared for in the alien, ugly little town he was losing. Nothing but work, drudgery, constant hastening from dwelling to dwelling among the colliers and the ironworkers. It wore him out, but at the same time he had a craving for it. It was a stimulant to him to be in the homes of the working people, moving as it were through the innermost body of their life. His nerves were excited and gratified. He could come so near, into the very lives of the rough, inarticulate, powerfully emotional men and women. He grumbled, he said he hated the hellish hole. But as a matter of fact it excited him, the contact with the rough, strongly-feeling people was a stimulant applied direct to his nerves.

Below Oldmeadow, in the green, shallow, soddened hollow of fields lay a square, deep pond. Roving across the landscape, the doctor's quick eye detected a figure in black passing through the gate of the field, down towards the pond. He looked again. It would be Mabel Pervin. His mind suddenly became alive and attentive.

Why was she going down there? He pulled up on the path on the slope above, and stood staring. He could just make sure of the small black figure moving in the hollow of the failing day. He seemed to see her in the midst of such obscurity, that he was like a clairvoyant, seeing rather with the mind's eye than with ordinary sight. Yet he could see her positively enough, whilst he kept his eye attentive. He felt, if he looked away from her, in the thick, ugly falling dusk, he would lose her altogether.

He followed her minutely as she moved, direct and intent, like something transmitted rather than stirring in voluntary activity, straight down the field towards the pond. There she stood on the bank for a moment. She never raised her head. Then she waded slowly into the water.

He stood motionless as the small black figure walked slowly and delib- 110 erately towards the centre of the pond, very slowly, gradually moving deeper into the motionless water, and still moving forward as the water got up to her breast. Then he could see her no more in the dusk of the dead afternoon.

"There!" he exclaimed. "Would you believe it?"

And he hastened straight down, running over the wet, soddened fields, pushing through the hedges, down into the depression of callous wintry obscurity. It took him several minutes to come to the pond. He stood on the bank, breathing heavily. He could see nothing. His eyes seemed to penetrate the dead water. Yes, perhaps that was the dark shadow of her black clothing beneath the surface of the water.

He slowly ventured into the pond. The bottom was deep, soft clay, he sank in, and the water clasped dead cold round his legs. As he stirred he could smell the cold, rotten clay that fouled up into the water. It was objectionable in his lungs. Still, repelled and yet not heeding, he moved deeper into the pond. The cold water rose over his thighs, over his loins, upon his abdomen. The lower part of his body was all sunk in the hideous cold element. And the bottom was so deeply soft and uncertain, he was afraid of pitching with his mouth underneath. He could not swim, and was afraid.

He crouched a little, spreading his hands under the water and moving them round, trying to feel for her. The dead cold pond swayed upon his chest. He moved again, a little deeper, and again, with his hands underneath, he felt all around the water. And he touched her clothing. But it evaded his fingers. He made a desperate effort to grasp it.

And so doing he lost his balance and went under, horribly, suffocating 115 in the foul earthy water, struggling madly for a few moments. At last, after what seemed an eternity, he got his footing, rose again into the air and looked around. He gasped, and knew he was in the world. Then he looked at the water. She had risen near him. He grasped her clothing, and drawing her nearer, turned to take his way to land again.

He went very slowly, carefully, absorbed in the slow progress. He rose higher, climbing out of the pond. The water was now only about his legs; he was thankful, full of relief to be out of the clutches of the pond. He lifted her and staggered on to the bank, out of the horror of wet, grey clay.

He laid her down on the bank. She was quite unconscious and running with water. He made the water come from her mouth, he worked to restore her. He did not have to work very long before he could feel the breathing begin again in her; she was breathing naturally. He worked a little longer.

He could feel her live beneath his hands; she was coming back. He wiped her face, wrapped her in his overcoat, looked round into the dim, dark grey world, then lifted her and staggered down the bank and across the fields.

It seemed an unthinkably long way, and his burden so heavy he felt he would never get to the house. But at last he was in the stable-yard, and then in the house-yard. He opened the door and went into the house. In the kitchen he laid her down on the hearth-rug, and called. The house was empty. But the fire was burning in the grate.

Then again he kneeled to attend to her. She was breathing regularly, her eyes were wide open and as if conscious, but there seemed something missing in her look. She was conscious in herself, but unconscious of her surroundings.

He ran upstairs, took blankets from a bed, and put them before the fire to warm. Then he removed her saturated, earthy-smelling clothing, rubbed her dry with a towel, and wrapped her naked in the blankets. Then he went into the dining room, to look for spirits. There was a little whisky. He drank a gulp himself, and put some into her mouth.

The effect was instantaneous. She looked full into his face, as if she had been seeing him for some time, and yet had only just become conscious of him.

"Dr. Fergusson?" she said.

"What?" he answered.

He was divesting himself of his coat, intending to find some dry clothing upstairs. He could not bear the smell of the dead, clayey water, and he was mortally afraid for his own health.

"What did I do?" she asked.

"Walked into the pond," he replied. He had begun to shudder like one sick, and could hardly attend to her. Her eyes remained full on him, he seemed to be going dark in his mind, looking back at her helplessly. The shuddering became quieter in him, his life came back in him, dark and unknowing, but strong again.

"Was I out of my mind?" she asked, while her eyes were fixed on him all the time.

"Maybe, for the moment," he replied. He felt quiet, because his strength had come back. The strange fretful strain had left him.

"Am I out of my mind now?" she asked.

"Are you?" he reflected a moment. "No," he answered truthfully. "I don't see that you are." He turned his face aside. He was afraid now, because he felt dazed, and felt dimly that her power was stronger than his, in this issue. And she continued to look at him fixedly all the time. "Can you tell me where I shall find some dry things to put on?" he asked.

"Did you dive into the pond for me?" she asked.

"No," he answered. "I walked in. But I went in overhead as well."

There was silence for a moment. He hesitated. He very much wanted to go upstairs to get into dry clothing. But there was another desire in him.

And she seemed to hold him. His will seemed to have gone to sleep, and left him, standing there slack before her. But he felt warm inside himself. He did not shudder at all, though his clothes were sodden on him.

"Why did you?" she asked.

"Because I didn't want you to do such a foolish thing," he said. 135

"It wasn't foolish," she said, still gazing at him as she lay on the floor, with a sofa cushion under her head. "It was the right thing to do. *I* knew best, then."

"I'll go and shift these wet things," he said. But still he had not the power to move out of her presence, until she sent him. It was as if she had the life of his body in her hands, and he could not extricate himself. Or perhaps he did not want to.

Suddenly she sat up. Then she became aware of her own immediate condition. She felt the blankets about her, she knew her own limbs.

For a moment it seemed as if her reason were going. She looked round, with wild eye, as if seeking something. He stood still with fear. She saw her clothing lying scattered.

"Who undressed me?" she asked, her eyes resting full and inevitable on his face.

"I did," he replied, "to bring you round." 140

For some moments she sat and gazed at him awfully, her lips parted.

"Do you love me, then?" she asked.

He only stood and stared at her, fascinated. His soul seemed to melt.

She shuffled forward on her knees, and put her arms around him, round his legs, as he stood there, pressing her breasts against his knees and thighs, clutching him with strange, convulsive certainty, pressing his thighs against her, drawing him to her face, her throat, as she looked up at him with flaring, humble eyes of transfiguration, triumphant in first possession.

"You love me," she murmured, in strange transport, yearning and 145
triumphant and confident. "You love me. I know you love me, I know."

And she was passionately kissing his knees, through the wet clothing, passionately and indiscriminately kissing his knees, his legs, as if unaware of everything.

He looked down at the tangled wet hair, the wild, bare, animal shoulders. He was amazed, bewildered, and afraid. He had never thought of loving her. He had never wanted to love her. When he rescued her and restored her, he was a doctor, and she was a patient. He had had no single personal thought of her. Nay, this introduction of the personal element was very distasteful to him, a violation of his professional honour. It was horrible to have her there embracing his knees. It was horrible. He revolted from it, violently. And yet—and yet—he had not the power to break away.

She looked at him again, with the same supplication of powerful love, and that same transcendent, frightening light of triumph. In view of the delicate flame which seemed to come from her face like a light, he was powerless. And yet he had never intended to love her. He had never intended. And something stubborn in him could not give way.

"You love me," she repeated, in a murmur of deep rhapsodic assurance. "You love me."

Her hands were drawing him, drawing him down to her. He was afraid, even a little horrified. For he had, really, no intention of loving her. Yet her hands were drawing him towards her. He put out his hand quickly to steady himself, and grasped her bare shoulder. A flame seemed to burn the hand that grasped her soft shoulder. He had no intention of loving her: his whole will was against his yielding. It was horrible. And yet wonderful was the touch of her shoulders, beautiful the shining of her face. Was she perhaps mad? He had a horror of yielding to her. Yet something in him ached also.

He had been staring away at the door, away from her. But his hand remained on her shoulder. She had gone suddenly very still. He looked down at her. Her eyes were now wide with fear, with doubt, the light was dying from her face, a shadow of terrible greyness was returning. He could not bear the touch of her eyes' question upon him, and the look of death behind the question.

With an inward groan he gave way, and let his heart yield towards her. A sudden gentle smile came on his face. And her eyes, which never left his face, slowly, slowly filled with tears. He watched the strange water rise in her eyes, like some slow fountain coming up. And his heart seemed to burn and melt away in his breast.

He could not bear to look at her any more. He dropped on his knees and caught her head with his arms and pressed her face against his throat. She was very still. His heart, which seemed to have broken, was burning with a kind of agony in his breast. And he felt her slow, hot tears wetting his throat. But he could not move.

He felt the hot tears wet his neck and the hollows of his neck, and he remained motionless, suspended through one of man's eternities. Only now it had become indispensable to him to have her face pressed close to him; he could never let her go again. He could never let her head go away from the close clutch of his arm. He wanted to remain like that for ever, with his heart hurting him in a pain that was also life to him. Without knowing, he was looking down on her damp, soft brown hair.

Then, as it were suddenly, he smelt the horrid stagnant smell of that water. And at the same moment she drew away from him and looked at him. Her eyes were wistful and unfathomable. He was afraid of them, and he fell to kissing her, not knowing what he was doing. He wanted her eyes not to have that terrible, wistful, unfathomable look.

When she turned her face to him again, a faint delicate flush was glowing, and there was again dawning that terrible shining of joy in her eyes, which really terrified him, and yet which he now wanted to see, because he feared the look of doubt still more.

"You love me?" she said, rather faltering.

"Yes." The word cost him a painful effort. Not because it wasn't true. But because it was too newly true, the *saying* seemed to tear open again his newly torn heart. And he hardly wanted it to be true, even now.

She lifted her face to him, and he bent forward and kissed her on the mouth, gently, with the one kiss that is an eternal pledge. And as he kissed her his heart strained again in his breast. He never intended to love her. But now it was over. He had crossed over the gulf to her, and all that he had left behind had shrivelled and become void.

After the kiss, her eyes again slowly filled with tears. She sat still,   160 away from him, with her face drooped aside, and her hands folded in her lap. The tears fell very slowly. There was complete silence. He too sat there motionless and silent on the hearthrug. The strange pain of his heart that was broken seemed to consume him. That he should love her? That this was love! That he should be ripped open in this way! Him, a doctor! How they would all jeer if they knew! It was agony to him to think they might know.

In the curious naked pain of the thought he looked again to her. She was sitting there drooped into a muse. He saw a tear fall, and his heart flared hot. He saw for the first time that one of her shoulders was quite uncovered, one arm bare, he could see one of her small breasts; dimly, because it had become almost dark in the room.

"Why are you crying?" he asked, in an altered voice.

She looked up at him, and behind her tears the consciousness of her situation for the first time brought a dark look of shame to her eyes.

"I'm not crying, really," she said, watching him half frightened.

He reached his hand, and softly closed it on her bare arm.   165

"I love you! I love you!" he said in a soft, low vibrating voice, unlike himself.

She shrank, and dropped her head. The soft, penetrating grip of his hand on her arm distressed her. She looked up at him.

"I want to go," she said. "I want to go and get you some dry things."

"Why?" he said. "I'm all right."

"But I want to go," she said. "And I want you to change your things."   170

He released her arm, and she wrapped herself in the blanket, looking at him rather frightened. And still she did not rise.

"Kiss me," she said wistfully.

He kissed her, but briefly, half in anger.

Then, after a second, she rose nervously, all mixed up in the blanket. He watched her in confusion, as she tried to extricate herself and wrap herself up so that she could walk. He watched her relentlessly, as she knew. And as she went, the blanket trailing, and as he saw a glimpse of her feet and her white leg, he tried to remember her as she was when he had wrapped her in the blanket. But then he didn't want to remember, because she had been nothing to him then, and his nature revolted from remembering her as she was when she was nothing to him.

A tumbling, muffled noise from within the dark house startled him.   175 Then he heard her voice: — "There are clothes." He rose and went to the foot of the stairs, and gathered up the garments she had thrown down. Then he came back to the fire, to rub himself down and dress. He grinned at his own appearance when he had finished.

The fire was sinking, so he put on coal. The house was now quite dark, save for the light of a street-lamp that shone in faintly from beyond the holly trees. He lit the gas with matches he found on the mantlepiece. Then he emptied the pockets of his own clothes, and threw all his wet things in a heap into the scullery. After which he gathered up her sodden clothes, gently, and put them in a separate heap on the copper-top in the scullery.

It was six o'clock on the clock. His own watch had stopped. He ought to go back to the surgery. He waited, and still she did not come down. So he went to the foot of the stairs and called:

"I shall have to go."

Almost immediately he heard her coming down. She had on her best dress of black voile, and her hair was tidy, but still damp. She looked at him — and in spite of herself, smiled.

"I don't like you in those clothes," she said. 180

"Do I look a sight?" he answered.

They were shy of one another.

"I'll make you some tea," she said.

"No, I must go."

"Must you?" And she looked at him again with the wide, strained, 185 doubtful eyes. And again, from the pain of his breast, he knew how he loved her. He went and bent to kiss her, gently, passionately, with his heart's painful kiss.

"And my hair smells so horrible," she murmured in distraction. "And I'm so awful, I'm so awful! Oh, no, I'm too awful." And she broke into bitter, heartbroken sobbing. "You can't want to love me, I'm horrible."

"Don't be silly, don't be silly," he said, trying to comfort her, kissing her, holding her in his arms. "I want you, I want to marry you, we're going to be married, quickly, quickly — tomorrow if I can."

But she only sobbed terribly, and cried:

"I feel awful. I feel awful. I feel I'm horrible to you."

"No, I want you, I want you," was all he answered, blindly, with that 190 terrible intonation which frightened her almost more than her horror lest he should *not* want her.

Considerations

1. Read the first five paragraphs of the story carefully and list descriptive words and phrases from these paragraphs. What do these words and phrases suggest about the relationship between Mabel and her brothers?

2. What is your response to the climactic moment — and the subsequent resolution — of the story. Are you able to believe that Jack Fergusson could recognize his love for Mabel so swiftly and so completely? Cite evidence from the story to support your view.

3. The point of view changes as the story progresses. At first, the scenes in the house are described quite objectively, yet later both Mabel's and Jack's thoughts and emotions are revealed. What is the effect of this change in

point of view? Why not, for instance, let the reader see into Mabel's mind from the beginning?

4. This story was originally titled "The Miracle." Do you think Lawrence made a wise choice in changing it to "The Horse Dealer's Daughter"? As you respond to this question, consider whether or not you see any part of the action as a miracle.

5. To what extent does this story belong to Jack Fergusson as well as to Mabel? What conflicts does he face? How does he resolve them?

BOBBIE ANN MASON (1940–   )

Shiloh

Leroy Moffitt's wife, Norma Jean, is working on her pectorals. She lifts three-pound dumbbells to warm up, then progresses to a twenty-pound barbell. Standing with her legs apart, she reminds Leroy of Wonder Woman.

"I'd give anything if I could just get these muscles to where they're real hard," says Norma Jean. "Feel this arm. It's not as hard as the other one."

"That's 'cause you're right-handed," says Leroy, dodging as she swings the barbell in an arc.

"Do you think so?"

"Sure."

Leroy is a truckdriver. He injured his leg in a highway accident four months ago, and his physical therapy, which involves weights and a pulley, prompted Norma Jean to try building herself up. Now she is attending a body-building class. Leroy has been collecting temporary disability since his tractor-trailer jackknifed in Missouri, badly twisting his left leg in its socket. He has a steel pin in his hip. He will probably not be able to drive his rig again. It sits in the backyard, like a gigantic bird that has flown home to roost. Leroy has been home in Kentucky for three months, and his leg is almost healed, but the accident frightened him and he does not want to drive any more long hauls. He is not sure what to do next. In the meantime, he makes things from craft kits. He started by building a miniature log cabin from notched Popsicle sticks. He varnished it and placed it on the TV set, where it remains. It reminds him of a rustic Nativity scene. Then he tried string art (sailing ships on black velvet), a macramé owl kit, a snap-together B-17 Flying Fortress, and a lamp made out of a model truck, with a light fixture screwed in the top of the cab. At first the kits were diversions, something to kill time, but now he is thinking about building a full-scale log house from a kit. It would be considerably cheaper than building a regular house, and besides, Leroy has grown to appreciate how things are put together. He has begun to realize that in all the years he was on the road he never took time to examine anything. He was always flying past scenery.

"They won't let you build a log cabin in any of the new subdivisions," Norma Jean tells him.

"They will if I tell them it's for you," he says, teasing her. Ever since they were married, he has promised Norma Jean he would build her a new home one day. They have always rented, and the house they live in is small and nondescript. It does not even feel like a home, Leroy realizes now.

Norma Jean works at the Rexall drugstore, and she has acquired an amazing amount of information about cosmetics. When she explains to Leroy the three stages of complexion care, involving creams, toners, and moisturizers, he thinks happily of other petroleum products—axle grease, diesel fuel. This is a connection between him and Norma Jean. Since he has been home, he has felt unusually tender about his wife and guilty over his long absences. But he can't tell what she feels about him. Norma Jean has never complained about his traveling; she has never made hurt remarks, like calling his truck a "widow-maker." He is reasonably certain she has been faithful to him, but he wishes she would celebrate his permanent homecoming more happily. Norma Jean is often startled to find Leroy at home, and he thinks she seems a little disappointed about it. Perhaps he reminds her too much of the early days of their marriage, before he went on the road. They had a child who died as an infant, years ago. They never speak about their memories of Randy, which have almost faded, but now that Leroy is home all the time, they sometimes feel awkward around each other, and Leroy wonders if one of them should mention the child. He has the feeling that they are waking up out of a dream together — that they must create a new marriage, start afresh. They are lucky they are still married. Leroy has read that for most people losing a child destroys the marriage — or else he heard this on *Donahue*. He can't always remember where he learns things anymore.

At Christmas, Leroy bought an electric organ for Norma Jean. She   10
used to play the piano when she was in high school. "It don't leave you," she told him once. "It's like riding a bicycle."

The new instrument had so many keys and buttons that she was bewildered by it at first. She touched the keys tentatively, pushed some buttons, then pecked out "Chopsticks." It came out in an amplified fox-trot rhythm, with marimba sounds.

"It's an orchestra!" she cried.

The organ had a pecan-look finish and eighteen preset chords, with optional flute, violin, trumpet, clarinet, and banjo accompaniments. Norma Jean mastered the organ almost immediately. At first she played Christmas songs. Then she bought *The Sixties Songbook* and learned every tune in it, adding variations to each with the rows of brightly colored buttons.

"I didn't like these old songs back then," she said. "But I have this crazy feeling I missed something."

"You didn't miss a thing," said Leroy.   15

Leroy likes to lie on the couch and smoke a joint and listen to Norma Jean play "Can't Take My Eyes Off You" and "I'll Be Back." He is back again. After fifteen years on the road, he is finally settling down with the woman he loves. She is still pretty. Her skin is flawless. Her frosted curls resemble pencil trimmings.

Now that Leroy has come home to stay, he notices how much the town has changed. Subdivisions are spreading across western Kentucky like an oil slick. The sign at the edge of town says "Pop: 11,500" — only seven hundred more than it said twenty years before. Leroy can't figure out who is living in all the new houses. The farmers who used to gather around the court-house square on Saturday afternoons to play checkers and spit tobacco juice have gone. It has been years since Leroy has thought about the farmers, and they have disappeared without his noticing.

Leroy meets a kid named Stevie Hamilton in the parking lot at the new shopping center. While they pretend to be strangers meeting over a stalled car, Stevie tosses an ounce of marijuana under the front seat of Leroy's car. Stevie is wearing orange jogging shoes and a T-shirt that says CHATTAHOO-CHEE SUPER-RAT. His father is a prominent doctor who lives in one of the expensive subdivisions in a new white-columned brick house that looks like a funeral parlor. In the phone book under his name there is a separate number, with the listing "Teenagers."

"Where do you get this stuff?" asks Leroy. "From your pappy?"

"That's for me to know and you to find out," Stevie says. He is slit-   20
eyed and skinny.

"What else you got?"

"What you interested in?"

"Nothing special. Just wondered."

Leroy used to take speed on the road. Now he has to go slowly. He needs to be mellow. He leans back against the car and says, "I'm aiming to build me a log house, soon as I get time. My wife, though, I don't think she likes the idea."

"Well, let me know when you want me again," Stevie says. He has a   25
cigarette in his cupped palm, as though sheltering it from the wind. He takes a long drag, then stomps it on the asphalt and slouches away.

Stevie's father was two years ahead of Leroy in high school. Leroy is thirty-four. He married Norma Jean when they were both eighteen, and their child Randy was born a few months later, but he died at the age of four months and three days. He would be about Stevie's age now. Norma Jean and Leroy were at the drive-in, watching a double feature (*Dr. Strangelove* and *Lover Come Back*), and the baby was sleeping in the back seat. When the first movie ended, the baby was dead. It was the sudden infant death syndrome. Leroy remembers handing Randy to a nurse at the emergency room, as though he were offering her a large doll as a present. A dead baby feels like a sack of flour. "It just happens sometimes," said the doctor, in what Leroy always recalls as a nonchalant tone. Leroy can hardly remember the child anymore, but he still sees vividly a scene from *Dr. Strangelove* in which the President of the United States was talking in a folksy voice on the hot line to the Soviet premier about the bomber accidentally headed toward Russia. He was in the War Room, and the world map was lit up. Leroy remembers Norma Jean standing catatonically beside him in the hospital and himself thinking: Who is this strange girl? He had forgotten who she was. Now scientists are saying that crib death is caused by a virus. Nobody knows anything, Leroy thinks. The answers are always changing.

When Leroy gets home from the shopping center, Norma Jean's mother, Mabel Beasley, is there. Until this year, Leroy has not realized how much time she spends with Norma Jean. When she visits, she inspects the closets and then the plants, informing Norma Jean when a plant is droopy or yellow. Mabel calls the plants "flowers," although there are never any blooms. She always notices if Norma Jean's laundry is piling up. Mabel is a short, overweight woman whose tight, brown-dyed curls look more like a wig than the actual wig she sometimes wears. Today she has brought Norma Jean an off-white dust ruffle she made for the bed; Mabel works in a custom-upholstery shop.

"This is the tenth one I made this year," Mabel says. "I got started and couldn't stop."

"It's real pretty," says Norma Jean.

"Now we can hide things under the bed," says Leroy, who gets along   30
with his mother-in-law primarily by joking with her. Mabel has never really forgiven him for disgracing her by getting Norma Jean pregnant. When the baby died, she said that fate was mocking her.

"What's that thing?" Mabel says to Leroy in a loud voice, pointing to a tangle of yarn on a piece of canvas.

Leroy holds it up for Mabel to see. "It's my needlepoint," he explains. "This is a *Star Trek* pillow cover."

"That's what a woman would do," says Mabel. "Great day in the morning!"

"All the big football players on TV do it," he says.

"Why, Leroy, you're always trying to fool me. I don't believe you for   35
one minute. You don't know what to do with yourself—that's the whole trouble. Sewing!"

"I'm aiming to build us a log house," says Leroy. "Soon as my plans come."

"Like *heck* you are," says Norma Jean. She takes Leroy's needlepoint and shoves it into a drawer. "You have to find a job first. Nobody can afford to build now anyway."

Mabel straightens her girdle and says, "I still think before you get tied down y'all ought to take a little run to Shiloh."

"One of these days, Mama," Norma Jean says impatiently.

Mabel is talking about Shiloh, Tennessee. For the past few years, she   40
has been urging Leroy and Norma Jean to visit the Civil War battleground there. Mabel went there on her honeymoon—the only real trip she ever took. Her husband died of a perforated ulcer when Norma Jean was ten, but Mabel, who was accepted into the United Daughters of the Confederacy in 1975, is still preoccupied with going back to Shiloh.

"I've been to kingdom come and back in that truck out yonder," Leroy says to Mabel, "but we never yet set foot in that battleground. Ain't that something? How did I miss it?"

"It's not even that far," Mabel says.

After Mabel leaves, Norma Jean reads to Leroy from a list she has made. "Things you could do," she announces. "You could get a job as a guard at Union Carbide, where they'd let you set on a stool. You could get on at the lumberyard. You could do a little carpenter work, if you want to build so bad. You could — "

"I can't do something where I'd have to stand up all day."

"You ought to try standing up all day behind a cosmetics counter. It's   45 amazing that I have strong feet, coming from two parents that never had strong feet at all." At the moment Norma Jean is holding on to the kitchen counter, raising her knees one at a time as she talks. She is wearing two-pound ankle weights.

"Don't worry," says Leroy. "I'll do something."

"You could truck calves to slaughter for somebody. You wouldn't have to drive any big old truck for that."

"I'm going to build you this house," says Leroy. "I want to make you a real home."

"I don't want to live in any log cabin."

"It's not a cabin. It's a house."   50

"I don't care. It looks like a cabin."

"You and me together could lift those logs. It's just like lifting weights."

Norma Jean doesn't answer. Under her breath, she is counting. Now she is marching through the kitchen. She is doing goose steps.

Before his accident, when Leroy came home he used to stay in the house with Norma Jean, watching TV in bed and playing cards. She would cook fried chicken, picnic ham, chocolate pie — all his favorites. Now he is home alone much of the time. In the mornings, Norma Jean disappears, leaving a cooling place in the bed. She eats a cereal called Body Buddies, and she leaves the bowl on the table, with the soggy tan balls floating in a milk puddle. He sees things about Norma Jean that he never realized before. When she chops onions, she stares off into a corner, as if she can't bear to look. She puts on her house slippers almost precisely at nine o'clock every evening and nudges her jogging shoes under the couch. She saves bread heels for the birds. Leroy watches the birds at the feeder. He notices the peculiar way goldfinches fly past the window. They close their wings, then fall, then spread their wings to catch and lift themselves. He wonders if they close their eyes when they fall. Norma Jean closes her eyes when they are in bed. She wants the lights turned out. Even then, he is sure she closes her eyes.

He goes for long drives around town. He tends to drive a car rather   55 carelessly. Power steering and an automatic shift make a car feel so small and inconsequential that his body is hardly involved in the driving process. His injured leg stretches out comfortably. Once or twice he has almost hit something, but even the prospect of an accident seems minor in a car. He cruises the new subdivisions, feeling like a criminal rehearsing for a robbery. Norma Jean is probably right about a log house being inappropriate here in the new subdivisions. All the houses look grand and complicated. They depress him.

One day when Leroy comes home from a drive he finds Norma Jean in tears. She is in the kitchen making a potato and mushroom–soup casserole, with grated-cheese topping. She is crying because her mother caught her smoking.

"I didn't hear her coming. I was standing here puffing away pretty as you please," Norma Jean says, wiping her eyes.

"I knew it would happen sooner or later," says Leroy, putting his arm around her.

"She don't know the meaning of the word 'knock,'" says Norma Jean. "It's a wonder she hadn't caught me years ago."

"Think of it this way," Leroy says. "What if she caught me with a   60 joint?"

"You better not let her!" Norma Jean shrieks. "I'm warning you, Leroy Moffitt!"

"I'm just kidding. Here, play me a tune. That'll help you relax."

Norma Jean puts the casserole in the oven and sets the timer. Then she plays a ragtime tune, with horns and banjo, as Leroy lights up a joint and lies on the couch, laughing to himself about Mabel's catching him at it. He thinks of Stevie Hamilton—a doctor's son pushing grass. Everything is funny. The whole town seems crazy and small. He is reminded of Virgil Mathis, a boastful policeman Leroy used to shoot pool with. Virgil recently led a drug bust in a back room at a bowling alley, where he seized ten thousand dollars' worth of marijuana. The newspaper had a picture of him holding up the bags of grass and grinning widely. Right now, Leroy can imagine Virgil breaking down the door and arresting him with a lungful of smoke. Virgil would probably have been alerted to the scene because of all the racket Norma Jean is making. Now she sounds like a hard-rock band. Norma Jean is terrific. When she switches to a Latin-rhythm version of "Sunshine Superman," Leroy hums along. Norma Jean's foot goes up and down, up and down.

"Well, what do you think?" Leroy says, when Norma Jean pauses to search through her music.

"What do I think about what?"   65

His mind has gone blank. Then he says, "I'll sell my rig and build us a house." That wasn't what he wanted to say. He wanted to know what she thought — what she *really* thought — about them.

"Don't start in on that again," says Norma Jean. She begins playing "Who'll Be the Next in Line?"

Leroy used to tell hitchhikers his whole life story — about his travels, his hometown, the baby. He would end with a question: "Well, what do you think?" It was just a rhetorical question. In time, he had the feeling that he'd been telling the same story over and over to the same hitchhikers. He quit talking to hitchhikers when he realized how his voice sounded — whining and self-pitying, like some teenage-tragedy song. Now Leroy has the sudden impulse to tell Norma Jean about himself, as if he had just met her. They have known each other so long they have forgotten a lot about each other. They could become reacquainted. But when the oven timer goes off and she runs to the kitchen, he forgets why he wants to do this.

The next day, Mabel drops by. It is Saturday and Norma Jean is cleaning. Leroy is studying the plans of his log house, which have finally come in the mail. He has them spread out on the table — big sheets of stiff blue paper, with diagrams and numbers printed in white. While Norma Jean runs the vacuum, Mabel drinks coffee. She sets her coffee cup on a blueprint.

"I'm just waiting for time to pass," she says to Leroy, drumming her   70
fingers on the table.

As soon as Norma Jean switches off the vacuum, Mabel says in a loud voice, "Did you hear about the datsun dog that killed the baby?"

Norma Jean says, "The word is 'dachshund.'"

"They put the dog on trial. It chewed the baby's legs off. The mother was in the next room all the time." She raises her voice. "They thought it was neglect."

Norma Jean is holding her ears. Leroy manages to open the refrigerator and get some Diet Pepsi to offer Mabel. Mabel still has some coffee and she waves away the Pepsi.

"Datsuns are like that," Mabel says. "They're jealous dogs. They'll   75
tear a place to pieces if you don't keep an eye on them."

"You better watch out what you're saying, Mabel," says Leroy.

"Well, facts is facts."

Leroy looks out the window at his rig. It is like a huge piece of furniture gathering dust in the backyard. Pretty soon it will be an antique. He hears the vacuum cleaner. Norma Jean seems to be cleaning the living room rug again.

Later, she says to Leroy, "She just said that about the baby because she caught me smoking. She's trying to pay me back."

"What are you talking about?" Leroy says, nervously shuffling   80
blueprints.

"You know good and well," Norma Jean says. She is sitting in a kitchen chair with her feet up and her arms wrapped around her knees. She looks small and helpless. She says, "The very idea, her bringing up a subject like that! Saying it was neglect."

"She didn't mean that," Leroy says.

"She might not have *thought* she meant it. She always says things like that. You don't know how she goes on."

"But she didn't really mean it. She was just talking."

Leroy opens a king-sized bottle of beer and pours it into two glasses,   85
dividing it carefully. He hands a glass to Norma Jean and she takes it from

him mechanically. For a long time, they sit by the kitchen window watching the birds at the feeder.

Something is happening. Norma Jean is going to night school. She has graduated from her six-week body-building course and now she is taking an adult-education course in composition at Paducah Community College. She spends her evenings outlining paragraphs.

"First you have a topic sentence," she explains to Leroy. "Then you divide it up. Your secondary topic has to be connected to your primary topic."

To Leroy, this sounds intimidating. "I never was any good in English," he says.

"It makes a lot of sense."

"What are you doing this for, anyhow?"   90

She shrugs. "It's something to do." She stands up and lifts her dumb-bells a few times.

"Driving a rig, nobody cared about my English."

"I'm not criticizing your English."

Norma Jean used to say, "If I lose ten minutes' sleep, I just drag all day." Now she stays up late, writing compositions. She got a B on her first paper—a how-to theme on soup-based casseroles. Recently Norma Jean has been cooking unusual foods—tacos, lasagna, Bombay chicken. She doesn't play the organ anymore, though her second paper was called "Why Music Is Important to Me." She sits at the kitchen table, concentrating on her outlines, while Leroy plays with his log house plans, practicing with a set of Lincoln Logs. The thought of getting a truckload of notched, numbered logs scares him, and he wants to be prepared. As he and Norma Jean work together at the kitchen table, Leroy has the hopeful thought that they are sharing something, but he knows he is a fool to think this. Norma Jean is miles away. He knows he is going to lose her. Like Mabel, he is just waiting for time to pass.

One day, Mabel is there before Norma Jean gets home from work, and   95
Leroy finds himself confiding in her. Mabel, he realizes, must know Norma Jean better than he does.

"I don't know what's got into that girl," Mabel says. "She used to go to bed with the chickens. Now you say she's up all hours. Plus her a-smoking. I like to died."

"I want to make her this beautiful home," Leroy says, indicating the Lincoln Logs. "I don't think she even wants it. Maybe she was happier with me gone."

"She don't know what to make of you, coming home like this."

"Is that it?"

Mabel takes the roof off his Lincoln Log cabin. "You couldn't get *me*   100
in a log cabin," she says. "I was raised in one. It's no picnic, let me tell you."

"They're different now," says Leroy.

"I tell you what," Mabel says, smiling oddly at Leroy.

"What?"

"Take her on down to Shiloh. Y'all need to get out together, stir a little. Her brain's all balled up over them books."

Leroy can see traces of Norma Jean's features in her mother's face. 105 Mabel's worn face has the texture of crinkled cotton, but suddenly she looks pretty. It occurs to Leroy that Mabel has been hinting all along that she wants them to take her with them to Shiloh.

"Let's all go to Shiloh," he says. "You and me and her. Come Sunday."

Mabel throws up her hands in protest. "Oh, no, not me. Young folks want to be by theirselves."

When Norma Jean comes in with groceries, Leroy says excitedly, "Your mama here's been dying to go to Shiloh for thirty-five years. It's about time we went, don't you think?"

"I'm not going to butt in on anybody's second honeymoon," Mabel says.

"Who's going on a honeymoon, for Christ's sake?" Norma Jean says 110 loudly.

"I never raised no daughter of mine to talk that-a-way," Mabel says.

"You ain't seen nothing yet," says Norma Jean. She starts putting away boxes and cans, slamming cabinet doors.

"There's a log cabin at Shiloh," Mabel says. "It was there during the battle. There's bullet holes in it."

"When are you going to *shut up* about Shiloh, Mama?" asks Norma Jean.

"I always thought Shiloh was the prettiest place, so full of history," 115 Mabel goes on. "I just hoped y'all could see it once before I die, so you could tell me about it." Later, she whispers to Leroy, "You do what I said. A little change is what she needs."

"Your name means 'the king,'" Norma Jean says to Leroy that evening. He is trying to get her to go to Shiloh, and she is reading a book about another century.

"Well, I reckon I ought to be right proud."

"I guess so."

"Am I still king around here?"

Norma Jean flexes her biceps and feels them for hardness. "I'm not 120 fooling around with anybody, if that's what you mean," she says.

"Would you tell me if you were?"

"I don't know."

"What does *your* name mean?"

"It was Marilyn Monroe's real name."

"No kidding!" 125

"Norma comes from the Normans. They were invaders," she says. She closes her book and looks hard at Leroy. "I'll go to Shiloh with you if you'll stop staring at me."

On Sunday, Norma Jean packs a picnic and they go to Shiloh. To Leroy's relief, Mabel says she does not want to come with them. Norma Jean drives, and Leroy, sitting beside her, feels like some boring hitchhiker she has picked up. He tries some conversation, but she answers him in monosyllables. At Shiloh, she drives aimlessly through the park, past bluffs and trails and steep ravines. Shiloh is an immense place, and Leroy cannot see it as a battleground. It is not what he expected. He thought it would look like a golf course. Monuments are everywhere, showing through the thick clusters of trees. Norma Jean passes the log cabin Mabel mentioned. It is surrounded by tourists looking for bullet holes.

"That's not the kind of log house I've got in mind," says Leroy apologetically.

"I know *that*."

"This is a pretty place. Your mama was right."   130

"It's O.K.," says Norma Jean. "Well, we've seen it. I hope she's satisfied."

They burst out laughing together.

At the park museum, a movie on Shiloh is shown every half hour, but they decide that they don't want to see it. They buy a souvenir Confederate flag for Mabel, and then they find a picnic spot near the cemetery. Norma Jean has brought a picnic cooler, with pimiento sandwiches, soft drinks, and Yodels. Leroy eats a sandwich and then smokes a joint, hiding it behind the picnic cooler. Norma Jean has quit smoking altogether. She is picking cake crumbs from the cellophane wrapper, like a fussy bird.

Leroy says, "So the boys in gray ended up in Corinth. The Union soldiers zapped 'em finally. April 7, 1862."

They both know that he doesn't know any history. He is just talking   135
about some of the historical plaques they have read. He feels awkward, like a boy on a date with an older girl. They are still just making conversation.

"Corinth is where Mama eloped to," says Norma Jean.

They sit in silence and stare at the cemetery for the Union dead and, beyond, at a tall cluster of trees. Campers are parked nearby, bumper to bumper, and small children in bright clothing are cavorting and squealing. Norma Jean wads up the cake wrapper and squeezes it tightly in her hand. Without looking at Leroy, she says, "I want to leave you."

Leroy takes a bottle of Coke out of the cooler and flips off the cap. He holds the bottle poised near his mouth but cannot remember to take a drink. Finally he says, "No, you don't."

"Yes, I do."

"I won't let you."   140

"You can't stop me."

"Don't do me that way."

Leroy knows Norma Jean will have her own way. "Didn't I promise to be home from now on?" he says.

"In some ways, a woman prefers a man who wanders," says Norma Jean. "That sounds crazy, I know."

"You're not crazy."   145

Leroy remembers to drink from his Coke. Then he says, "Yes, you *are* crazy. You and me could start all over again. Right back at the beginning."

"We *have* started all over again," says Norma Jean. "And this is how it turned out."

"What did I do wrong?"

"Nothing."

"Is this one of those women's lib things?" Leroy asks.   150

"Don't be funny."

The cemetery, a green slope dotted with white markers, looks like a subdivision site. Leroy is trying to comprehend that his marriage is breaking up, but for some reason he is wondering about white slabs in a graveyard.

"Everything was fine till Mama caught me smoking," says Norma Jean, standing up. "That set something off."

"What are you talking about?"

"She won't leave me alone — *you* won't leave me alone." Norma Jean   155
seems to be crying, but she is looking away from him. "I feel eighteen again. I can't face that all over again." She starts walking away. "No, it *wasn't* fine. I don't know what I'm saying. Forget it."

Leroy takes a lungful of smoke and closes his eyes as Norma Jean's words sink in. He tries to focus on the fact that thirty-five hundred soldiers died on the grounds around him. He can only think of that war as a board game with plastic soldiers. Leroy almost smiles, as he compares the Confederates' daring attack on the Union camps and Virgil Mathis's raid on the bowling alley. General Grant, drunk and furious, shoved the Southerners back to Corinth, where Mabel and Jet Beasley were married years later, when Mabel was still thin and good-looking. The next day, Mabel and Jet visited the battleground, and then Norma Jean was born, and then she married Leroy and they had a baby, which they lost, and now Leroy and Norma Jean are here at the same battleground. Leroy knows he is leaving out a lot. He is leaving out the insides of history. History was always just names and dates to him. It occurs to him that building a house out of logs is similarly empty — too simple. And the real inner workings of a marriage, like most of history, have escaped him. Now he sees that building a log house is the dumbest idea he could have had. It was clumsy of him to think Norma Jean would want a log house. It was a crazy idea. He'll have to think of something else, quickly. He will wad the blueprints into tight balls and fling them into the lake. Then he'll get moving again. He opens his eyes. Norma Jean has moved away and is walking through the cemetery, following a serpentine brick path.

Leroy gets up to follow his wife, but his good leg is asleep and his bad leg still hurts him. Norma Jean is far away, walking rapidly toward the bluff by the river, and he tries to hobble toward her. Some children run past him, screaming noisily. Norma Jean has reached the bluff, and she is looking out over the Tennessee River. Now she turns toward Leroy and waves her arms. Is she beckoning to him? She seems to be doing an exercise for her chest muscles. The sky is unusually pale — the color of the dust ruffle Mabel made for their bed.

Considerations

1. The story's title, the site of a famous Civil War battle, raises expectations of conflict. List the various "battles" you see taking place, both between characters and within characters. What connections might there be between these battles?

2. History — particularly the history of the South — is extremely important to the characters in "Shiloh." Notice that Leroy develops his own definition of history — both public and private. Do you agree with his view? Explain.

3. Both Leroy and Norma Jean refuse to talk about the death of their infant son. In what way might Randy's death contribute to the conflicts you see in the story? To what extent do you think Leroy and Norma Jean have dealt successfully with this loss?

4. Leroy and Norma Jean pursue very different activities. How do these activities help to define the fears and hopes of each character?

5. Read the final paragraph of the story. Do you see it as hopeful? Ominous? Ambiguous? Or something else? What do you see as the future possibilities for Leroy and Norma Jean? Explain.

ALBERTO MORAVIA (1907–1990)

The Chase

I have never been a sportsman — or, rather, I have been a sportsman only once, and that was the first and last time. I was a child, and one day, for some reason or other, I found myself together with my father, who was holding a gun in his hand, behind a bush, watching a bird that had perched on a branch not very far away. It was a large, gray bird — or perhaps it was brown — with a long — or perhaps a short — beak; I don't remember. I only remember what I felt at that moment as I looked at it. It was like watching an animal whose vitality was rendered more intense by the very fact of my watching it and of the animal's not knowing that I was watching it.

At that moment, I say, the notion of wildness entered my mind, never again to leave it: everything is wild which is autonomous and unpredictable and does not depend upon us. Then all of a sudden there was an explosion; I could no longer see the bird and I thought it had flown away. But my father was leading the way, walking in front of me through the under-growth. Finally he stooped down, picked up something, and put it in my hand. I was aware of something warm and soft and I lowered my eyes: there was the bird in the palm of my hand, its dangling, shattered head crowned with a plume of already-thickening blood. I burst into tears and dropped the corpse on the ground, and that was the end of my shooting experience.

I thought again of this remote episode in my life this very day after watching my wife, for the first and also the last time, as she was walking through the streets of the city. But let us take things in order.

What had my wife been like; what was she like now? She once had been, to put it briefly, "wild" — that is, entirely autonomous and unpredict-able; latterly she had become "tame" — that is, predictable and dependent. For a long time she had been like the bird that, on that far-off morning in my childhood, I had seen perching on the bough; latterly, I am sorry to say, she had become like a hen about which one knows everything in advance — how it moves, how it eats, how it lays eggs, how it sleeps, and so on.

Nevertheless I would not wish anyone to think that my wife's wildness consisted of an uncouth, rough, rebellious character. Apart from being ex-tremely beautiful, she is the gentlest, politest, most discreet person in the world. Rather her wildness consisted of the air of charming unpredictability, of independence in her way of living, with which during the first years of our marriage she acted in my presence, both at home and abroad. Wildness signified intimacy, privacy, secrecy. Yes, my wife as she sat in front of her dressing table, her eyes fixed on the looking glass, passing the hairbrush with a repeated motion over her long, loose hair, was just as wild as the solitary quail hopping forward along a sun-filled furrow or the furtive fox coming out into a clearing and stopping to look around before running on.

5

She was wild because I, as I looked at her, could never manage to foresee when she would give a last stroke with the hairbrush and rise and come toward me; wild to such a degree that sometimes when I went into our bedroom the smell of her, floating in the air, would have something of the acrid quality of a wild beast's lair.

Gradually she became less wild, tamer. I had had a fox, a quail, in the house, as I have said; then one day I realized that I had a hen. What effect does a hen have on someone who watches it? It has the effect of being, so to speak, an automaton in the form of a bird; automatic are the brief, rapid steps with which it moves about; automatic its hard, terse pecking; automatic the glance of the round eyes in its head that nods and turns; automatic its ready crouching down under the cock; automatic the dropping of the egg wherever it may be and the cry with which it announces that the egg has been laid. Good-by to the fox; good-by to the quail. And her smell — this no longer brought to my mind, in any way, the innocent odor of a wild animal; rather I detected in it the chemical suavity of some ordinary French perfume.

Our flat is on the first floor of a big building in a modern quarter of town; our windows look out on a square in which there is a small public garden, the haunt of nurses and children and dogs. One day I was standing at the window, looking in a melancholy way at the garden. My wife, shortly before, had dressed to go out; and once again, watching her, I had noticed the irrevocable and, so to speak, invisible character of her gestures and personality: something which gave one the feeling of a thing already seen and already done and which therefore evaded even the most determined observation. And now, as I stood looking at the garden and at the same time wondering why the adorable wildness of former times had so completely disappeared, suddenly my wife came into my range of vision as she walked quickly across the garden in the direction of the bus stop. I watched her and then I almost jumped for joy; in a movement she was making to pull down a fold of her narrow skirt and smooth it over her thigh with the tips of her long, sharp nails, in this movement I recognized the wildness that in the past had made me love her. It was only an instant, but in that instant I said to myself: She's become wild again because she's convinced that I am not there and am not watching her. Then I left the window and rushed out.

But I did not join her at the bus stop; I felt that I must not allow myself to be seen. Instead I hurried to my car, which was standing nearby, got in, and waited. A bus came and she got in together with some other people; the bus started off again and I began following it. Then there came back to me the memory of that one shooting expedition in which I had taken part as a child, and I saw that the bus was the undergrowth with its bushes and trees, my wife the bird perching on the bough while I, unseen, watched it living before my eyes. And the whole town, during this pursuit, became, as though by magic, a fact of nature like the countryside: the houses were hills, the streets valleys, the vehicles hedges and woods, and even the passersby on the pavements had something unpredictable and autonomous — that is, wild — about them. And in my mouth, behind my clenched teeth, there was the acrid, metallic taste of gunfire; and my eyes, usually listless and wandering, had become sharp, watchful, attentive.

These eyes were fixed intently upon the exit door when the bus came to the end of its run. A number of people got out, and then I saw my wife getting out. Once again I recognized, in the manner in which she broke free of the crowd and started off toward a neighboring street, the wildness that pleased me so much. I jumped out of the car and started following her.

She was walking in front of me, ignorant of my presence, a tall woman   10 with an elegant figure, long-legged, narrow-hipped, broad-backed, her brown hair falling on her shoulders.

Men turned around as she went past; perhaps they were aware of what I myself was now sensing with an intensity that quickened the beating of my heart and took my breath away: the unrestricted, steadily increasing, irresistible character of her mysterious wildness.

She walked hurriedly, having evidently some purpose in view, and even the fact that she had a purpose of which I was ignorant added to her wildness; I did not know where she was going, just as on that far-off morning I had not known what the bird perching on the bough was about to do. Moreover I thought the gradual, steady increase in this quality of wildness came partly from the fact that as she drew nearer to the object of this mysterious walk there was an increase in her — how shall I express it? — of biological tension, of existential excitement, of vital effervescence. Then, unexpectedly, with the suddenness of a film, her purpose was revealed.

A fair-haired young man in a leather jacket and a pair of corduroy trousers was leaning against the wall of a house in that ancient, narrow street. He was idly smoking as he looked in front of him. But as my wife passed close to him, he threw away his cigarette with a decisive gesture, took a step forward, and seized her arm. I was expecting her to rebuff him, to move away from him, but nothing happened: evidently obeying the rules of some kind of erotic ritual, she went on walking beside the young man. Then after a few steps, with a movement that confirmed her own complicity, she put her arm around her companion's waist and he put his around her.

I understood then that this unknown man who took such liberties with my wife was also attracted by wildness. And so, instead of making a conventional appointment with her, instead of meeting in a café with a handshake, a falsely friendly and respectful welcome, he had preferred, by agreement with her, to take her by surprise — or, rather, to pretend to do so — while she was apparently taking a walk on her own account. All this I perceived by intuition, noticing that at the very moment when he stepped forward and took her arm her wildness had, so to speak, given an upward bound. It was years since I had seen my wife so alive, but alas, the source of this life could not be traced to me.

They walked on thus entwined and then, without any preliminaries,   15
just like two wild animals, they did an unexpected thing: they went into one
of the dark doorways in order to kiss. I stopped and watched them from a
distance, peering into the darkness of the entrance. My wife was turned
away from me and was bending back with the pressure of his body, her hair
hanging free. I looked at that long, thick mane of brown hair, which as she
leaned back fell free of her shoulders, and I felt at that moment her vitality
reached its diapason, just as happens with wild animals when they couple
and their customary wildness is redoubled by the violence of love. I watched
for a long time and then, since the kiss went on and on and in fact seemed
to be prolonged beyond the limits of my power of endurance, I saw that I
would have to intervene.

I would have to go forward, seize my wife by the arm — or actually by
that hair, which hung down and conveyed so well the feeling of feminine
passivity — then hurl myself with clenched fists upon the blond young man.
After this encounter I would carry off my wife, weeping, mortified,
ashamed, while I was raging and brokenhearted, upbraiding her and pouring
scorn upon her.

But what else would this intervention amount to but the shot my
father fired at that free, unknowing bird as it perched on the bough? The
disorder and confusion, the mortification, the shame, that would follow
would irreparably destroy the rare and precious moment of wildness that I
was witnessing inside the dark doorway. It was true that this wildness was
directed against me; but I had to remember that wildness, always and everywhere, is directed against everything and everybody. After the scene of my
intervention it might be possible for me to regain control of my wife, but I
should find her shattered and lifeless in my arms like the bird that my father
placed in my hand so that I might throw it into the shooting bag.

The kiss went on and on: well, it was a kiss of passion — that could not
be denied. I waited until they finished, until they came out of the doorway,
until they walked on again still linked together. Then I turned back.

Considerations

1. Read the opening section carefully. How does this section suggest the
   way the narrator sees himself in relation to others? What role does he play
   in his world?
2. How well does the narrator think he knows his wife? How well does he
   actually know her? What do the discrepancies between these two views
   suggest about their relationship?
3. How does the narrator's wife apparently feel about the narrator's responses to her and about his actions? What effects does he seem to expect
   his actions to have on the marriage? What effects do you think his actions
   will have?

4. Describe the final incident—the meeting with the "fair-haired young man"—from the wife's point of view. Explain her feelings and motivations as she walks toward, meets, and embraces her lover.
5. What is the significance of the title? How does the image of the hunt—and the narrator's memories of his childhood hunting incident—suggest possible themes?

YASHAR KEMAL (1922–   )

A Dirty Story

The three of them were sitting on the damp earth, their backs against the dung-daubed brush wall and their knees drawn up to their chests, when another man walked up and crouched beside them.

"Have you heard?" said one of them excitedly. "Broken-Nose Jabbar's done it again! You know Jabbar, the fellow who brings all those women from the mountain villages and sells them in the plain? Well, this time he's come down with a couple of real beauties. The lads of Misdik have got together and bought one of them on the spot, and now they're having fun and making her dance and all that . . . It's unbelievable! Where does the fellow find so many women? How does he get them to come with him? He's the devil's own son, he is . . ."

"Well, that's how he makes a living," commented one of the men. "Ever since I can remember, this Jabbar's been peddling women for the villagers of the Chukurova plain. Allah provides for all and sundry . . ."

"He's still got the other one," said the newcomer, "and he's ready to give her away for a hundred liras."

"He'll find a customer soon enough," put in another man whose head   5
was hunched between his shoulders. "A good woman's worth more than a team of oxen, at least, in the Chukurova plain she is. You can always put her to the plow and, come summer, she'll bind and carry the sheaves, hoe, do anything. What's a hundred liras? Why, a woman brings in that much in one single summer. In the fields, at home, in bed. There's nothing like a woman. What's a hundred liras?"

Just then, Hollow Osman came up mumbling to himself and flopped down beside them without a word of greeting. He was a tall, broad-shouldered man with a rather shapeless potbellied body. His lips drooped foolishly and his eyes had an odd squintlike gaze.

"Hey, Osman," the man who had been talking addressed him. "Broken-Nose Jabbar's got a woman for sale again. Only a hundred liras. Tell Mistress Huru to buy her for you and have done with living alone and sleeping in barns like a dog."

Osman shrugged his shoulders doubtfully.

"Look here, man," pursued the other, "this is a chance in a million. What's a hundred liras? You've been slaving for that Huru since you dropped out of your mother's womb and she's never paid you a lira. She owes you this. And anyway she'll get back her money's worth in just one summer. A woman's good for everything, in the house, in the fields, in bed . . ."

Osman rose abruptly.   10

"I'll ask the Mistress," he said. "How should I know? . . ."

A couple of days later, a short, broad-hipped girl with blue beads strung into her plaited hair was seen at the door of Huru's barn in which

Hollow Osman always slept. She was staring out with huge wondering eyes.

A month passed. Two months . . . And passersby grew familiar with the sight of the strange wide-eyed girl at the barn door.

One day, a small dark boy with a face the size of a hand was seen pelting through the village. He rushed up to his mother where she sat on the threshold of her hut gossiping with Seedy Doneh.

"Mother," he screeched, "I've seen them! It's the truth, I swear it is. Uncle Osman's wife with . . . May my eyes drop out right here if I'm telling a lie."

Seedy Doneh turned to him sharply.

"What?" she cried. "Say it again. What's that about Fadik?"

"She was with the Agha's son. I saw them with my own eyes. He went into the barn with her. They couldn't see me where I was hiding. Then he took off his boots, you know the shiny yellow boots he wears . . . And then they lay down and . . . Let my two eyes drop out if . . ."

"I knew it!" crowed Seedy Doneh. "I knew it would turn out this way."

"Hollow Osman never had any manhood in him anyway," said the child's mother. "Always under that viper-tongued Huru's petticoats . . ."

"Didn't I tell you, Ansha, the very first day she came here that this would happen?" said Doneh. "I said this girl's ready to play around. Pretending she was too bashful to speak to anyone. Ah, still waters run deep . . ."

She rose quickly and hurried off to spread the news.

"Have you heard? Just as I foretold . . . Still waters . . . The Agha's son . . . Fadik . . ."

In a trice all the neighboring women had crowded at Ansha's door, trying to squeeze the last drop of information out of the child.

"Come on, tell us," urged one of the women for perhaps the hundredth time; "How did you see them?"

"Let my two eyes drop out right here if I'm lying," the child repeated again and again with unabated excitement. "The Agha's son came in, and then they lay down, both of them, and did things . . . I was watching through a chink in the wall. Uncle Osman's wife, you know, was crying. I can't do it, she was saying, and she was sobbing away all the time. Then the Agha's son pulled off those shiny yellow boots of his . . . Then I ran right here to tell Mother."

The news spread through the village like wildfire. People could talk about nothing else. Seedy Doneh, for one, seemed to have made it her job to leave no man or woman uninformed. As she scoured the village for new listeners, she chanced upon Osman himself.

"Haven't you heard what's come upon you?" she said, drawing him aside behind the wall of a hut. "You're disgraced, you jackass. The Agha's son has got his fingers up your wife's skirt. Try and clear your good name now if you can!"

Osman did not seem to understand.

"I don't know . . ." he murmured, shrugging his shoulders. "I'll have   30
to ask the Mistress. What would the Agha's son want with my wife?"

Doneh was incensed.

"What would he want with her, blockhead?" she screamed. "Damn
you, your wife's become a whore, that's what! She's turned your home into
a brothel. Anyone can come in and have her." She flounced off still screaming. "I spit on you! I spit on your manhood . . ."

Osman was upset.

"What are you shouting for, woman?" he called after her. "People will
think something's wrong. I have to ask the Mistress. She knows everything.
How should I know?"

He started walking home, his long arms dangling at his sides as though   35
they had been hitched to his shoulders as an afterthought, his fingers sticking out wide apart as was his habit. This time he was waylaid by their next-
door neighbor, Zeynep, who planted herself before him and tackled him at
the top of her voice.

"Ah Osman! You'd be better off dead! Why don't you go and bury
yourself? The whole village knows about it. Your wife . . .The Agha's son
. . . Ah Osman, how could you have brought such a woman into your
home? Where's your honor now? Disgraced . . . Ah Osman!"

He stared at her in bewilderment.

"How should I know?" he stammered, his huge hands opening out
like pitchforks. "The Mistress knows all about such things. I'll go and
ask her."

Zeynep turned her back on him in exasperation, her large skirt bal-
looning about her legs.

"Go bury yourself, Osman! I hope I see you dead after this."   40

A group of children were playing tipcat nearby. Suddenly one of them
broke into a chant.

"Go bury yourself, Osman . . . See you dead, Osman . . ."

The other children joined in mechanically without interrupting their
game.

Osman stared at them and turned away.

"How should I know?" he muttered. "I must go to the Mistress."   45

He found Huru sitting at her spinning wheel. Fadik was there too,
squatting near the hearth and listlessly chewing mastic gum.

"Mistress," said Osman, "have you heard what Seedy Doneh's saying?
She's saying I'm disgraced . . ."

Huru stepped on the pedal forcefully and brought the wheel to a stop.

"What's that?" she said. "What about Seedy Doneh?"

"I don't know . . . She said Fadik . . ."   50

"Look here," said Huru, "you mustn't believe those lying bitches.
You've got a good wife. Where would you find such a woman?"

"I don't know. Go bury yourself, they said. The children too . . ."

"Shut up," cried Huru, annoyed. "People always gossip about a beautiful woman. They go looking for the mote in their neighbor's eye without seeing the beam in their own. They'd better hold their peace because I've got a tongue in my head too . . ."

Osman smiled with relief.

"How could I know?" he said.   55

Down in the villages of the Chukurova plain, a sure sign of oncoming spring is when the women are seen with their heads on one another's lap, picking the lice out of one another's hair. So it was, on one of the first warm days of the year. A balmy sun shone caressingly down on the fields and village, and not a leaf stirred. A group of women were sitting before their huts on the dusty ground, busy with the lice and wagging their tongues for all they were worth. An acrid odor of sweat hung about the group. Seedy Doneh was rummaging in the hair of a large woman who was stretched full length on the ground. She decided that she had been silent long enough.

"No," she declared suddenly, "it's not as you say, sister! He didn't force her or any such thing. She simply fell for him the minute she saw those shiny yellow boots. If you're going to believe Huru! . . . She's got to deny it, of course."

"That Huru was born with a silver spoon in her mouth," said white-haired, toothless old Zala, wiping her bloodstained fingers on her ragged skirt. "Hollow Osman's been slaving for her like twenty men ever since she took him in, a kid the size of your hand! And all for a mere pittance of food. And now there's the woman too. Tell me, what's there left for Huru to do?"

"Ah," sighed another woman, "fortune has smiled on Huru, she has indeed! She's got two people serving her now."

"And both for nothing," old Zala reminded her.   60

"What it amounts to," said Seedy Doneh spitefully, "is that Huru used to have one wife and now she's got two. Osman was always a woman, and as for Fadik she's a real woman. He-he!"

"That she is, a real woman!" the others agreed.

"Huru says the Agha's son took her by force," pursued Doneh. "All right, but what about the others? What about those lining up at her door all through the night, eh? She never says no to any one of them, does she? She takes in everyone, young and old."

"The Lady Bountiful, that's what she is," said Elif. "And do you know something? Now that Fadik's here, the young men are leaving Omarja's yellow bitch in peace . . ."

"They've got somewhere better to go!" cackled the others.   65

Omarja's dumpy wife jumped up from where she was sitting on the edge of the group.

"Now look here, Elif!" she cried. "What's all this about our yellow dog? Stop blackening people's characters, will you?"

"Well, it's no lie, is it?" Doneh challenged her. "When was that bitch ever at your door where she should be all night? No, instead, there she came trotting up a-mornings with a rope dangling from her neck!"

"Don't go slandering our dog," protested Omarja's wife. "Why, if Omarja hears this, he'll kill the poor creature. Upon my word he will!"

"Go on!" said Doneh derisively. "Don't you come telling me that Omarja doesn't know his yellow bitch is the paramour of all the village youths! What about that time when Stumpy Veli caught some of them down by the river, all taking it in turns over her? Is there anyone in this village who didn't hear of that? It's no use trying to whitewash your bitch to us!"

Omarja's wife was alarmed.

"Don't, sister," she pleaded. "Omarja'll shoot the dog, that's sure . . ."

"Well, I'm not to blame for that, sister," retorted Doneh tartly. "Anyway, the bitch'll be all right now that Fadik's around. And so will Kurdish Velo's donkey . . ."

Kurdish Velo's wife began to fidget nervously.

"Not our fault," she blurted out in her broken Turkish. "We lock our donkey in, but they come and break the door! Velo furious. Velo say people round here savage. He say, with an animal deadly sin! He say he kill someone. Then he complain to the Headman. Velo going sell this donkey."

"You know what I think?" interposed Seedy Doneh. "They're going to make it hot for her in this village. Yes, they'll do what they did to Esheh."

"Poor Esheh," sighed old Zala. "What a woman she was before her man got thrown into prison! She would never have come to that, but she had no one to protect her. May they rot in hell, those that forced her into it! But she is dead and gone, poor thing."

"Eh!" said Doneh. "How could she be otherwise after the youths of five villages had done with her?" She straightened up. "Look here, sister," she said to the woman whose head was on her lap, "I couldn't get through your lice in days! They say the Government's invented some medicine for lice which they call Dee-Dee. Ah, if only we had a spoonful of that . . . Do you know, women, that Huru keeps watch over Fadik at night? She tells the youths when to come in and then drives them out with a stick. Ha-ha, and she wants us to believe in Fadik's virtue . . ."

"That's because it suits her. Where will she find people who'll work for nothing like those two?"

"Well, the lads are well provided for this year," snickered Doneh. "Who knows but that Huru may hop in and help Fadik out!"

Just then, Huru loomed up from behind a hut. She was a large woman with a sharp chin and a wrinkled face. Her graying hair was always carefully dyed with henna.

"Whores!" she shouted at the top of her voice, as she bore down upon them with arms akimbo. "City trollops! You get hold of a poor fellow's wife and let your tongues go wagging away. Tell me, are you any better than she? What do you want of this harmless mountain girl?" She pounced on Doneh who cringed back. "As for you, you filthy shitty-assed bitch, you'll shut your mouth or I'll start telling the truth about you and that husband of yours who pretends he's a man. You know me, don't you?"

Doneh blenched.

"Me, sister?" she stammered. "Me? I never . . . Other people's good name . . ."

The women were dispersing hastily. Only Kurdish Velo's wife, un- 85
aware of what was going on, continued picking lice out of her companion's hair.

"Velo says in our country women like this burnt alive. He says there no virtue in this Chukurova. No honor . . ."

The eastern sky had only just begun to pale as, with a great hullabaloo and calls and cries, the women and children drove the cattle out to pasture. Before their houses, red-aproned matrons were busy at the churns beating yogurt. The damp air smelled of spring.

Osman had long ago yoked the oxen and was waiting at Huru's door. She appeared in the doorway.

"Osman, my lion," she said, "you're not to come back until you've 90
plowed through the whole field. The girl Aysheh will look after your food and get you some bedding. Mind you do the sowing properly, my child. Husneh's hard pressed this year. And there's your wife to feed too now . . ."

Husneh was Huru's only child, whom in a moment of aberration she had given in marriage to Ali Efendi, a low-salaried tax collector. All the product of her land, everything Huru had, was for this daughter.

Osman did not move or say a word. He stood there in the half-light, a large black shadow near the yoked oxen whose tails were flapping their legs in slow rhythm.

Huru stepped up to him.

"What's the matter with you, Osman, my child," she said anxiously. "Is anything wrong?"

"Mistress," whispered Osman, "It's what Seedy Doneh's saying. And 95
Zeynep too . . . That my house . . . I don't know . . ."

Huru flared up.

"Shut up, you spineless dolt," she cried. "Don't you come babbling to me about the filthy inventions of those city trollops. I paid that broken-nosed thief a hundred good bank notes for the girl, didn't I? Did I ask you for as much as a lira? You listen to me. You can find fault with pure gold, but not with Fadik. Don't let me hear such nonsense from you again!"

Osman hesitated.

"I don't know . . ." he murmured, as he turned at last and drove the oxen off before him.

It was midmorning. A bright sun glowed over the sparkling fields. 100

Osman was struggling with the lean, emaciated oxen, which after plowing through only one acre had stretched themselves on the ground and simply refused to budge. Flushed and breathless, he let himself drop onto a mound and took his head in his hands. After a while, he rose and tried pulling the animals up by the tail.

"Accursed beasts," he muttered. "The Mistress says Husneh's in need this year. Get up this minute, accursed beasts!"

He pushed and heaved, but to no avail. Suddenly in a burst of fury, he flung himself on the black ox, dug his teeth into its nose, and shook it with all his might. Then he straightened up and looked about him sheepishly.

"If anyone saw me . . ." He swore as he spat out blood. "What can I do? Husneh's in need and there's Fadik to feed too. And now these heathen beasts . . . I don't know."

It was in this state of perplexity that Stumpy Veli found him when he strolled over from a neighboring field. 105

"So the team's collapsed, eh?" he commented. "Well, it was to be expected. Look at how their ribs are sticking out. You won't be able to get anything out of them."

"I don't know," muttered Osman faintly. "Husneh's in a bad way and I got married . . ."

"And a fine mess that's landed you in," burst out Veli angrily. "You'd have been better off dead!"

"I don't know," said Osman. "The Mistress paid a hundred liras for her . . ."

Stumpy Veli took hold of his arm and made him sit down. 110

"Look, Osman," he said, "the villagers told me to talk to you. They say you're giving the village a bad name. Ever since the Agha's son took up with your wife, all the other youths have followed suit and your house is just like a brothel now. The villagers say you've got to repudiate her. If you don't, they'll drive you both out. The honor of the whole village is at stake, and you know honor doesn't grow on trees . . ."

Osman, his head hanging down, was as still as a statue. A stray ant had caught his eye.

What's this ant doing around here at this time of day, he wondered to himself. Where can its nest be?

Veli nudged him sharply.

"Damn you, man!" he cried. "Think what'll happen if the police get 115 wind of this. She hasn't got any papers. Why, if the gendarmes once lay their hands on her, you know how it'll be. They'll play around with her for months, poor creature."

Osman started as though an electric current had been sent through his large frame.

"I haven't got any papers either," he whispered.

Veli drew nearer. Their shoulders touched. Osman's were trembling fitfully.

"Papers are the business of the Government," Veli said. "You and me, we can't understand such things. If we did, then what would we need a Government for? Now, listen to me. If the gendarmes get hold of her, we'll be the laughingstock of villages for miles around. We'll never be able to hold up our heads again in the Chukurova. You mustn't trifle with the honor of the whole village. Get rid of her before she drags you into more trouble."

"But where will I be without her?" protested Osman. "I'll die, that's all. Who'll do my washing? Who'll cook bulgur pilaf for me? I'll starve to death if I have to eat gruel again every day. I just can't do without her."

"The villagers will buy you another woman," said Veli. "We'll collect the money among us. A better woman, an honorable one, and beautiful too . . . I'll go up into the mountain villages and pick one for you myself. Just you pack this one off quickly . . ."

"I don't know," said Osman. "It's the Mistress knows about these things."

Veli was exasperated.

"Damn the Mistress!" he shouted. "It's up to you, you idiot!"

Then he softened. He tried persuasion again. He talked and talked. He talked himself hoarse, but Osman sat there immovable as a rock, his mouth clamped tight. Finally Veli spat in his face and stalked off.

It was well on in the afternoon when it occurred to Osman to unyoke the team. He had not stirred since Veli's departure. As for the oxen, they had just lain there placidly chewing the cud. He managed to get them to their feet and let them wander about the field, while he walked back to the village. He made straight for the Agha's house and waited in the yard, not speaking to anyone, until he saw the Agha's son riding in, the bridle of his horse lathered with sweat.

The Agha's son was taken aback. He dismounted quickly, but Osman waylaid him.

"Listen," he pleaded, "you're the son of our all-powerful Agha. What do you want with my wife?"

The Agha's son became the color of his famous boots. He hastily pulled a five-lira note out of his pocket and thrust it into Osman's hand.

"Take this," he mumbled and hurried away.

"But you're a great big Agha's son!" cried Osman after him. "Why do you want to drive her away? What harm has she done you? You're a great big . . ."

He was crushed. He stumbled away towards Huru's house, the five-lira note still in his hand.

At the sight of Osman, Huru blew her top.

"What are you doing here, you feebleminded ass?" she shouted. "Didn't I tell you not to come back until you'd finished all the plowing? Do you want to ruin me, you idiot?"

"Wait, Mistress," stammered Osman. "Listen . . ."

"Listen, he says! Damn the fool!"

"Mistress," he pleaded, "let me explain . . ."

Huru glared at him.

"Mistress, you haven't heard. You don't know what the villagers are going to do to me. They're going to throw me out of this village. Stumpy Veli said so. He said the police . . . He said papers . . . We haven't got any papers. Fadik hasn't and I haven't either. He said the gendarmes would carry Fadik away and do things to her. He said I must repudiate her because my house is a brothel. That's what he said. I said the Mistress knows these things . . . She paid the hundred liras . . ."

Huru was dancing with fury. She rushed out into the village square   140
and began howling at the top of her voice.

"Bastards! So she's a thorn in your flesh, this poor fellow's wife! If you want to drive whores out of this village why don't you start with your own wives and daughters? You'd better look for whores in your own homes, pimps that you are, all of you! And tell your sons to leave poor folks' women alone . . ."

Then she turned to Osman and gave him a push.

"Off you go! To the fields! No one's going to do anything to your wife. Not while I'm alive."

The villagers had gathered in the square and had heard Huru out in profound silence. As soon as she was gone, though, they started muttering among themselves.

"Who does that bitch think she is, abusing the whole village like that?   145
. . ."

The Agha, Wolf Mahmut, had heard her too.

"You just wait, Huru," he said grinding his teeth. "If you think you're going to get away with this . . ."

The night was dark, a thick damp darkness that seemed to cling to the face and hands. Huru had been waiting for some time now, concealed in the blackest shadow of the barn, when suddenly she perceived a stirring in the darkness, and a voice was calling softly at the door.

"Fadik! Open up, girl. It's me . . ."

The door creaked open and a shadow glided in. An uncontrollable   150
trembling seized Huru. She gripped her stick and flung herself on the door. It was unbolted and went crashing back against the wall. As she stood there trying to pierce the darkness, a few vague figures hustled by and made their escape. Taken by surprise, she hurled out a vitriolic oath and started groping about until she discovered Fadik crouching in à corner. She seized her by the hair and began to beat her with the stick.

"Bitch!" she hissed. "To think I was standing up for you . . ."

Fadik did not utter a sound as the blows rained down on her. At last Huru, exhausted, let go of her.

"Get up," she ordered, "and light some kindling."

Fadik raked out the dying embers and with much puffing and blowing managed to light a stick of torchwood. A pale honeyed light fell dimly over the stacked hay. There was an old pallet in one corner and a few kitchen utensils, but nothing else to show that the place was lived in.

Huru took Fadik's hand and looked at her sternly.   155

"Didn't you promise me, girl, that you'd never do it again?"

Fadik's head hung low.

"Do you know, you bitch," continued Huru, "what the villagers are going to do? They're going to kick you out of the village. Do you hear me?"

Fadik stirred a little. "Mistress, I swear I didn't go after them! They just came in spite of everything."

"Listen to me, girl," said Huru. "Do you know what happened to Esheh? That's what you'll come to if you're not careful. They're like ravening wolves, these men. If you fall into their clutches, they'll tear you to shreds. To shreds, I tell you!"

"But Mistress, I swear I never did anything to — "

"You must bolt your door because they'll be after you whether you do anything or not, and their pimps of fathers will put the blame on me. It's my hundred liras they can't swallow. They're dying to see it go to pot . . . Just like Esheh you'll be. They had no one in the world, she and her man, and when Ali was thrown into jail she was left all alone. He'd lifted a sheep from the Agha's flock and bought clothes and shoes for their son. A lovely child he was, three years old . . . Ali doted on him. But there he was in jail, and that yellow-booted good-for-nothing was soon after Esheh like the plague. She kept him at arm's length for as long as she could, poor Esheh, but he got what he wanted in the end. Then he turned her over to those ravening wolves . . . They dragged her about from village to village, from mountain to mountain. Twenty, thirty good-for-nothings . . . Her child was left among strangers, the little boy she had loved so. He died . . . Those who saw her said she was like a consumptive, thin and gray, but still they wouldn't let her go, those scoundrels. Then one day the village dogs came in all smeared with blood, and an eagle was circling over the plain. So the men went to look, and they found Esheh, her body half devoured by the dogs . . . They'd made her dance naked for them . . . They'd done all sorts of things to her. Yes, they as good as killed her. That's what the police said when they came up from the town. And when Ali heard of it, he died of grief in jail. Yes, my girl, you've got Esheh's fate before you. It isn't my hundred liras that I care for, it's you. As for Osman, I can always find another woman for him. Now I've warned you. Just call me if they come again. Esheh was all alone in the world. You've got me, at least. Do you swear to do as I'm telling you?"

"I swear it, Mistress," said Fadik.

Huru was suddenly very tired.

"Well, I'm going. You'll call me, won't you?"

As soon as she was gone, the youths crept out of the darkness and sneaked into the barn again.

"Hey, Fadik," they whispered. "Huru was lying to you, girl. Esheh just killed herself . . ."

There was a stretch of grass in front of the Agha's house, and on one side of it dung had been heaped to the size of a small hillock. The dung steamed in the early morning sun and not a breath stirred the warm air. A cock climbed to the top of the heap. It scraped the dung, stretched its neck, and crowed triumphantly, flapping its wings.

The group of villagers squatting about on the grass silently eyed the angry Agha. Wolf Mahmut was a huge man whose shadow when he was sitting was as large as that of an average man standing up. He was never seen without a frayed, checked overcoat, the only one in the village, that he had been wearing for years now.

He was toying irritably with his metal-framed glasses when Stumpy   170
Veli, who had been sent for a while ago, made his appearance. The Agha glared at him.

"Is this the way you get things done, you fraud?" he expostulated. "So you'd have Hollow Osman eating out of your hand in no time, eh?"

Stumpy Veli seemed to shrink to half his size.

"Agha," he said, "I tried everything. I talked and talked. I told him the villagers would drive them both out. I warned him of the gendarmes. All right, he said, I'll send her away. And then he didn't . . . If you ask me, Huru's at the bottom of it all."

The others stirred. "That she is!" they agreed.

Mahmut Agha jumped up. "I'll get even with her," he growled.   175

"That, you will, Agha," they assented. "But . . ."

"We've put up with that old whore long enough," continued the Agha, sitting down again.

"Yes, Agha," said Stumpy Veli, "but, you see, she relies on her son-in-law Ali, the tax collector. They'd better stop treading on my toes, she said, or I'll have Ali strip this village bare . . ."

"He can't do anything," said the Agha. "I don't owe the Government a bean."

"But we do, Agha," interposed one of the men. "He can come here   180
and take away our blankets and rugs, whatever we have . . ."

"It's because of Huru that he hasn't fleeced this village up to now," said another. "We owe a lot of money, Agha."

"Well, what are we to do then?" cried Mahmut Agha angrily. "All our youths have left the plow and the fields and are after the woman night and day like rutting bulls. At this rate, the whole village'll starve this year."

An old man spoke up in a tremulous voice. "I'm dead, for one," he wailed. "That woman's ruined my hearth. High morning it is already. Go to the plow, my son, I beg the boy. We'll starve if you don't plow. But he won't listen. He's always after that woman. I've lost my son because of that whore. I'm too old to plow any more. I'll starve this year. I'll go and throw myself at Huru's feet. There's nothing else to do . . ."

The Agha rose abruptly. "That Huru!" He gritted his teeth. "I'll settle her account."

He strode away.   185

The villagers looked up hopefully. "Mahmut Agha'll settle her account," they muttered. "He'll find a way . . ."

The Agha heard them and swelled with pride. "Yes, Mahmut Agha'll settle her account," he repeated grimly to himself.

He stopped before a hut and called out.
"Hatije Woman! Hatije!"
A middle-aged woman rushed out wiping her hands on her apron.   190
"Mahmut Agha!" she cried. "Welcome to our home. You never visit us these days." Then she whirled back. "Get up, you damned lazybones," she shouted angrily. "It's high morning, and look who's here."
Mahmut Agha followed her inside.
"Look, Agha," she complained, pointing to her son, "it's high morning and Halil still abed!"
Startled at the sight of the Agha, Halil sprang up and drew on his black *shalvar* trousers shamefacedly, while his mother continued with her lamentations.
"Ah, Mahmut Agha, you don't know what's befallen us! You don't   195 know, may I kiss your feet, my Agha, or you wouldn't have us on your land any longer . . . Ah, Mahmut Agha! This accursed son of mine . . . I would have seen him dead and buried, yes, buried in this black earth before . . ."
"What are you cursing the lad for?" Mahmut Agha interrupted her. "Wait, just tell me first."
"Ah, Agha, if you knew! It was full day when he came home this night. And it's the same every night, the same ever since Hollow Osman's woman came to the village. He lies abed all through the livelong day. Who'll do the plowing, I ask you? We'll starve this year. Ah, Mahmut Agha, do something! Please do something . . ."
"You go outside a little, will you, Hatije," said the Agha. Then he turned to Halil, stretching out his long, wrinkled neck which had become as red as a turkey's. "Listen to me, my boy, this has got to end. You must get this whore out of our village and give her to the youths of another village, any village. She's got to go and you'll do it. It's an order. Do you hear me?"
"Why, Agha!" Halil said ingratiatingly. "Is that what's worrying you? I'll get hold of her this very night and turn her over to Jelil from Ortakli village. You can count on me."
The Agha's spirits rose.   200
"Hatije," he called out, "come in here. See how I'm getting you out of this mess? And all the village too . . . Let that Huru know who she's dealing with in the future. They call me Wolf Mahmut and I know how to put her nose out of joint."

Long before dawn, piercing shrieks startled the echoes in the village.
"Bastards! Pimps!" Huru was howling. "You won't get away with this, not on your life you won't. My hundred liras were too much for you to swallow, eh, you fiends? You were jealous of this poor fellow's wife, eh?

But you just wait and see, Wolf Mahmut! I'll set the tax collector after you all in no time. I'll get even with you if I have to spend my last penny! I'll bribe the Mudir, the Kaymakam, all the officials. I'll send telegrams to Ankara, to Ismet Pasha, to the head of the Democrats. I'll have you all dragged into court, rotting away in police stations. I'll get my own back on you for Fadik's sake."

She paused to get her breath and was off again even louder than before.

Fadik had disappeared, that was the long and the short of it. Huru   205
soon found out that someone else was missing too. Huseyin's half-witted son, The Tick.

"Impossible," she said. "The Tick ravishing women? Not to save his life, he couldn't! This is just another trick of those good-for-nothings . . ."

"But really, Huru," the villagers tried to persuade her, "he was after her all the time. Don't you know he gathered white snails in the hills, threaded them into a necklace, and offered it to Fadik, and she hung it up on her wall as a keepsake? That's the plain truth, Huru."

"I don't believe it," Huru said stubbornly. "I wouldn't even if I saw them together with my own eyes . . ."

The next day it started raining, that sheer, plumb-line torrent which sets in over the Chukurova for days. The minute the bad news had reached him, Osman had abandoned his plow and had rushed back to the village. He was standing now motionless at Huru's door, the peak of his cap drooping over his eyes. His wet clothes clung to his flesh, glistening darkly, and his rawhide boots were clogged with mud.

"Come in out of the rain, Osman, do!" Huru kept urging him.   210

"I can't. I don't know . . ." was all he could say.

"Now, look here, Osman," said Huru. "She's gone, so what? Let them have that bitch. I'll find you a good woman, my Osman. Never mind the money. I'll spend twice as much on a new wife for you. Just you come in out of the rain."

Osman never moved.

"Listen, Osman. I've sent word to Ali. Come and levy the taxes at once, I said. Have no mercy on these ungrateful wretches. If you don't fleece them to their last rag, I said, you needn't count on me as a mother again. You'll see what I'm going to do to them, my Osman. You just come inside . . ."

The rain poured down straight and thick as the warp in a loom, and   215
Osman still stood there, his chin resting on his staff, like a thick tree whose branches have been lopped off.

Huru appealed to the neighbors. Two men came and pulled and pushed, but he seemed nailed to the ground. It was well in the afternoon when he stirred and began to pace the village from one end to the other, his head sunk between his shoulders and the rain streaming down his body.

"Poor fellow, he's gone mad," opined the villagers.

A few strong men finally carried him home. They undressed him and put him to bed.

Huru sat down beside him. "Look, Osman, I'll get you a new woman even if it costs me a thousand liras. You mustn't distress yourself so. Just for a woman . . ."

The next morning he was more his normal self, but no amount of reasoning or pleading from Huru could induce him to go back to the field. He left the house and resumed his pacing up and down.

The villagers had really begun to feel sorry for him now.

"Alas, poor Osman!" they murmured as he passed between the huts.

Osman heard them and heaved deep, heartrending sighs. And still he roamed aimlessly round and round.

Wolf Mahmut should have known better. Why, the whole village saw with half an eye what a rascal Halil was! How could he be trusted to give up a woman once he had got her into his hands? He had indeed got Fadik out of the way, but what he had done was to shut her up in one of the empty sheep pens in the hills beyond the village, and there he had posted The Tick to guard her.

"Play around with her if you like," he had told him contemptuously. "But if you let her give you the slip — " and he had seized The Tick's wrist and squeezed it until it hurt — "you're as good as dead."

Though twenty years old, The Tick was so scraggy and undersized that at first glance people would take him to be only ten. His arms and legs were as thin as matchsticks and he walked sideways like a crab. He had always had a way of clinging tenaciously to people or objects he took a fancy to, which even as a child had earned him his nickname. No one had ever called him by his real name and it looked as though his own mother had forgotten it too . . .

Halil would come every evening bringing food for Fadik and The Tick, and he would leave again just before dawn. But it was not three days before the village youths found out what was going on. After that there was a long queue every night outside the sheep pen. They would take it in turns, heedless of Fadik's tears and howls, and at daybreak, singing and firing their guns as though in a wedding procession, they would make their way back to the village.

Night was falling and Fadik began to tremble like a leaf. They would not be long now. They would come again and torture her. She was weak with fear and exhaustion. For the past two days, her gorge had risen at the very sight of food, and she lay there on the dirt floor, hardly able to move, her whole body covered with bruises and wounds.

The Tick was dozing away near the door of the pen.

Fadik tried to plead with him. "Let me go, brother," she begged. "I'll die if I have to bear another night of this."

The Tick half-opened his eyes. "I can't," he replied.

"But if I die, it'll be your fault. Before God it will . . . Please let me go."

"Why should it be my fault?" said The Tick. "I didn't bring you here, did I?"

"They'll never know. You'll say you fell asleep. I'll go off and hide somewhere. I'll go back to my mother . . ."

"I can't," said The Tick. "Halil would kill me if I let you go."   235

"But I want to go to my mother," she cried desperately. "You must let me go. Please let me go . . ."

It was dark now and the sound of singing drifted up from the village.

Fadik was seized with a violent fit of trembling. "They're coming," she said. "Let me get away now, brother. Save me! If you save me, I'll be your woman. I'll do anything . . ."

But The Tick had not been nicknamed for nothing.

"They'd kill me," he said. "Why should I die because of you? And   240 Halil's promised to buy me a pair of shoes, too. I'm not going to go without shoes because of you."

Fadik broke into wild sobbing. There was no hope now.

"Oh, God," she wept, "what shall I do now? Oh, Mother, why was I ever born?"

They lined up as usual at the entrance to the pen. The first one went in and a nerve-racking scream rose from Fadik, a scream that would have moved the most hardened of hearts. But the youths were deaf to everything. In they went, one after the other, and soon Fadik's screams died down. Not even a moan came out of her.

There were traces of blood on the ground at the back of the sheep pen. Halil and the Agha's son had had a fight the night before and the Agha's son had split open Halil's head.

"The woman's mine," Halil had insisted. "I've a right to go in first."   245

"No, you haven't," the Agha's son had contended. "I'm going to be the first."

The other youths had taken sides and joined the fray which had lasted most of the night, and it was a bedraggled band that wended back to the village that night.

Bowed down with grief, Hatije Woman came weeping to the Muhtar.

"My son is dying," she cried. "He's at his last gasp, my poor Halil, and it's the Agha's son who did it, all because of that whore of Huru's. Ah, Muhtar, if my son dies what's to become of me? There he lies struggling for life, the only hope of my hearth. But I won't let the Agha get away with this. I'll go to the Government. An old woman's only prop, I'll say . . ."

The Muhtar had great difficulty in talking Hatije out of her purpose.   250

"You go back home, Hatije Woman," he said when she had calmed down a little, "and don't worry. I'll deal with this business."

He summoned the Agha and the elders, and a long discussion ensued. It would not do to hand over the woman to the police station. These rapacious gendarmes! . . . The honor of the whole village was at stake. And if they passed her on to the youths of another village, Huru was sure to find out and bring her back. She would not rest until she did.

After long deliberation, they came to a decision at last. The woman would be returned to Osman, but on one condition. He would take himself off with her to some distant place and never appear in the village again. They had no doubt that Osman, grateful to have Fadik back to himself, would accept. And that would cook Huru's goose too. She would lose both the woman and Osman. It would teach her to insult a whole village!

A couple of men went to find Osman and brought him back with them to the Muhtar's house.

"Sit down," they urged him, but he just stood there grasping his staff, 255 staring about him with bloodshot eyes. His clothes hung down torn and crumpled and stained yellow from his lying all wet on the hay. His hair was a tangled, clotted mass and bits of straw clung to the stubble on his chin.

Wolf Mahmut took off his glasses and fidgeted with them.

"Osman, my lad," he remonstrated, "what's this state you're in? And all for a woman! Does a man let himself break down like this just for a woman? You'll die if you go on like this . . ."

"I don't know," said Osman. "I'll die . . ."

"See here, Osman," said the Agha. "We're here to help you. We'll get your woman back for you from out of those rascals' hands. Then you'll take her and go. You'll both get away from here, as far as possible. But you're not to tell Huru. She mustn't know where you are."

"You see, Osman," said Stumpy Veli, "how good the Agha's being 260 to you. Your own father wouldn't have done more."

"But you're not to tell Huru," the Agha insisted. "If you do, she'll never let you go away. And then the youths will come and take your woman away from you again. And how will you ever get yourself another woman?"

"And who'll wash your clothes then?" added Stumpy Veli. "Who'll cook your bulgur pilaf for you? You mustn't breathe a word to Huru. Just take Fadik and go off to the villages around Antep. Once there, you'll be sure to get a job on a farm. You'll be much better off than you ever were with Huru, and you'll have your woman with you too . . ."

"But how can I do that?" protested Osman. "The Mistress paid a hundred liras for Fadik."

"We'll collect that much among us," the Agha assured him. "Don't you worry about that. We'll see that Huru gets her money back. You just take the woman and go."

"I don't know," said Osman. His eyes filled with tears and he swal- 265 lowed. "The Mistress has always been so good to me . . . How can I . . . Just for a woman . . ."

"If you tell Huru, you're lost," said the Agha. "Is Huru the only mistress in the world? Aren't there other villages in this country? Take the woman and go. You'll never find another woman like Fadik. Listen, Veli'll tell you where she is and tomorrow you'll take her and go."

Osman bowed his head. He thought for a long time. Then he looked up at them.

"I won't tell her," he said at last. "Why should I want to stay here? There are other villages . . ."

Before dawn the next day, he set out for the sheep pen which Stumpy Veli had indicated.

"I don't know . . ." he hesitated at the door. "I don't know . . ." Then 270 he called out softly, "Fadik? Fadik, girl . . ."

There was no answer. Trembling with hope and fear, he stepped in, then stopped aghast. Fadik was lying there on the dirt floor with only a few tatters left to cover her naked body. Her huge eyes were fixed vacantly on the branches that roofed the pen.

He stood frozen, his eyes filling with tears. Then he bent his large body over her.

"Fadik," he whispered, "are you all right?"

Her answering moan shook him to the core. He slipped off his shirt and helped her into it. Then he noticed The Tick who had shrunk back into a corner, trying to make himself invisible. Osman moved on him threateningly.

"Uncle Osman," cried The Tick shaking with fear, "I didn't do it. It 275 was Halil. He said he'd buy me a pair of shoes . . . And Fadik would have died if I hadn't been here . . ."

Osman turned away, heaved Fadik onto his back swiftly, and threw himself out of the pen.

The mountain peaks were pale and the sun was about to rise. A few white clouds floated in the sky and a cool breeze caressed his face. The earth was wet with dew.

The Tick was scurrying off towards the village.

"Brother," Osman called after him, "go to the Mistress and tell her I thank her for all she's done for me, but I have to go. Tell her to forgive me . . ."

He set out in the opposite direction with Fadik on his back. He walked 280 without a break until the sun was up the height of two minarets. Then he lowered Fadik to the ground and sat down opposite her. They looked at each other for a long while without speaking.

"Tell me," said Osman. "Where shall we go now? I don't know . . ."

Fadik moaned.

The air smelled of spring and the earth steamed under the sun.

Considerations

1. Do you consider the title appropriate? In what ways can this be considered a "dirty story"? Explore as many possibilities as possible.
2. In paragraphs 1–11, a group of men express their views about women.

Who are these men? Do the actions and events of the rest of the story suggest that others in their society share this view? Explain.

3. Speculate on reasons why women would participate in and even encourage the degradation and exploitation of other women. Use examples from the story as well as examples from your own experience.

4. "A Dirty Story" takes places in a poor, rural Eastern culture. What are the qualities by which males are judged to be "real men" — both by themselves and by others — in this culture? How are females judged to be "real women"? How does this view compare with the standards used to judge "real men" or "real women" in our culture? Are the two cultures entirely different? Or do you see some similarities?

5. What motivates Osman to make the decision to rescue Fadik? What future do you predict for the two of them?

ANDREW MARVELL (1621–1678)

To His Coy Mistress

Had we but world enough, and time,
This coyness, lady, were no crime.
We would sit down, and think which way
To walk, and pass our long love's day.
Thou by the Indian Ganges'° side   5
Shoudst rubies find; I by the tide
Of Humber° would complain. I would
Love you ten years before the flood,
And you should, if you please, refuse
Till the conversion of the Jews.   10
My vegetable love should grow
Vaster than empires and more slow;
An hundred years should go to praise
Thine eyes, and on thy forehead gaze;
Two hundred to adore each breast,   15
But thirty thousand to the rest;
An age at least to every part,
And the last age should show your heart.
For, lady, you deserve this state,
Nor would I love at lower rate.   20
   But at my back I always hear
Time's wingéd chariot hurrying near;
And yonder all before us lie

5 *Ganges:* River in northern India.   7 *Humber:* Estuary in northern England formed by the Ouse and Trent rivers.

Deserts of vast eternity.
Thy beauty shall no more be found;   25
Nor, in thy marble vault, shall sound
My echoing song; then worms shall try
That long-preserved virginity,
And your quaint honor turn to dust,
And into ashes all my lust: 30
The grave's a fine and private place,
But none, I think, do there embrace.
   Now therefore, while the youthful hue
Sits on thy skin like morning dew
And while thy willing soul transpires   35
At every pore with instant fires,
Now let us sport us while we may,
And now, like amorous birds of prey,
Rather at once our time devour
Than languish in his slow-chapped power.   40
Let us roll all our strength and all
Our sweetness up into one ball,
And tear our pleasures with rough strife
Thorough the iron gates of life:
Thus, though we cannot make our sun   45
Stand still, yet we will make him run.

Considerations

1. What subject—love or time—is the main theme of this poem? How do the images of the poem connect and relate the two?
2. Write a prose version of this argument, listing each new point separately. How convincing do you find the argument? Explain your reasons.
3. Imagine that you are the woman to whom this poem is addressed. Write a letter giving the speaker your answer. Consider each point of his argument in your response.

APHRA BEHN (1640–1689)

The Willing Mistress

Amyntas led me to a grove,
   Where all the trees did shade us;
The sun itself, though it had strove,
   It could not have betrayed us.
The place secured from human eyes   5
   No other fear allows

But when the winds that gently rise
　　Do kiss the yielding boughs.

Down there we sat upon the moss,
　　And did begin to play   10
A thousand amorous tricks, to pass
　　The heat of all the day.
A many kisses did he give
　　And I returned the same,
Which made me willing to receive   15
　　That which I dare not name.

His charming eyes no aid required
　　To tell their softening tale;
On her that was already fired
　　'Twas easy to prevail.   20
He did but kiss and clasp me round,
　　Whilst those his thoughts expressed:
And laid me gently on the ground;
　　Ah who can guess the rest?

Considerations

1. What does the language of the poem suggest about the speaker's attitude toward sexual love? Cite specific images to support your view.
2. Compare the view of women suggested by this poem to the view of women suggested by "To His Coy Mistress."
3. This poem is part of a play, where it is sung by a maidservant to her mistress. Create the scene that leads up to the maid's decision to reveal this love affair to the woman who employs her.

ALAN DUGAN (1923–   )

Love Song: I and Thou

Nothing is plumb, level or square:
　　the studs are bowed, the joists
are shaky by nature, no piece fits
　　any other piece without a gap
or pinch, and bent nails   5
　　dance all over the surfacing
like maggots. By Christ
　　I am no carpenter, I built
the roof for myself, the walls

for myself, the floors   10
for myself, and got
    hung up in it myself. I
danced with a purple thumb
    at this house-warming, drunk
with my prime whiskey: rage.   15
    Oh I spat rage's nails
into the frame-up of my work:
    it held. It settled plumb,
level, solid, square and true
    for that great moment. Then   20
it screamed and went on through,
    skewing as wrong the other way.
God damned it. This is hell,
    but I planned it, I sawed it,
I nailed it, and I   25
    will live in it until it kills me.
I can nail my left palm
    to the left-hand cross-piece but
I can't do everything myself.
    I need a hand to nail the right,   30
a help, a love, a you, a wife.

Considerations

1. Describe the house suggested by the central image of the poem. What
   might the house represent? What meanings are suggested by the details
   relating to building the house?
2. Is the title ironic? In what way can this poem be considered a love song?
3. What role does the speaker suggest for the woman to whom this poem
   is addressed? How do you evaluate the implications of that role?

ANNE SEXTON (1928–1974)

For My Lover, Returning to His Wife

She is all there.
She was melted carefully down for you
and cast up from your childhood,
cast up from your one hundred favorite aggies.

She has always been there, my darling.   5
She is, in fact, exquisite.
Fireworks in the dull middle of February
and as real as a cast-iron pot.

Let's face it, I have been momentary.
A luxury. A bright red sloop in the harbor.   10
My hair rising like smoke from the car window.
Littleneck clams out of season.

She is more than that. She is your have to have,
has grown you your practical your tropical growth.
This is not an experiment. She is all harmony.   15
She sees to oars and oarlocks for the dinghy,

has placed wild flowers at the window at breakfast,
sat by the potter's wheel at midday,
set forth three children under the moon,
three cherubs drawn by Michelangelo,   20

done this with her legs spread out
in the terrible months in the chapel.
If you glance up, the children are there
like delicate balloons resting on the ceiling.

She has also carried each one down the hall   25
after supper, their heads privately bent,
two legs protesting, person to person,
her face flushed with a song and their little sleep.

I give you back your heart.
I give you permission —   30

for the fuse inside her, throbbing
angrily in the dirt, for the bitch in her
and the burying of her wound —
for the burying of her small red wound alive —

for the pale flickering flare under her ribs,   35
for the drunken sailor who waits in her left pulse,
for the mother's knee, for the stockings,
for the garter belt, for the call —

the curious call
when you will burrow in arms and breasts   40
and tug at the orange ribbon in her hair
and answer the call, the curious call.

She is so naked and singular.
She is the sum of yourself and your dream.
Climb her like a monument, step after step.   45
She is solid.

As for me, I am a watercolor.
I wash off.

Considerations

1. List the images that the speaker uses in the first 30 lines to describe the wife as well as the images she uses to describe herself. What do these images suggest about the role she sees the wife and herself playing in her lover's life?
2. Discuss the reference in lines 19–24 to Michelangelo. How is the wife like this artist?
3. How do the images of the wife in lines 31–46 contrast with the images in earlier lines? Why might the speaker use both the earlier and later images in describing the wife to her lover?

ELIZABETH LIBBEY (1947–   )

The Gesture

*In every parting there comes a moment when
    the beloved is already no longer with us.*
        Flaubert, *Sentimental Education*

He leans forward in his chair.
She gazes
over the rim of her wine glass, at the candle
unlit between them.
From the formal red earth of the tablecloth,   5
a continent begins to spread itself:
the arrivals and departures
in separate airports, the sumptuous bars
they will visit, each
without the other. That darkness which   10
fills the room one shares
with a stranger, darkness more inclusive
than sleep.

It has been a long trip
into and out of that closeness   15
which softens the set of face, softens
even that withdrawal of hands
into themselves. There is

nothing to say. And yet, as the waiter
refolds his towel   20
deftly over his arm as a sign to begin,
those delicious possibilities
sweeten each small
gesture of goodbye. Each anonymous, misplaced smile.

For him   25
she will leave her spectacles folded
in her lap, she will smooth
her speckled hair, and drink
whatever he chooses.
For her   30
he will look upon that face as if
it were not growing indistinct. He will order
for them both, with usual aplomb,
the specialty of the house.
He will request   35
that the candle be lit.

Considerations

1. How does the opening quotation relate to the ideas and images of the
    poem?
2. What is the relationship between these two people? What role has each
    played and does each play?
3. What future can you predict for these people? Will they be together in a
    year? In ten years? What leads you to your speculation?

ADRIENNE RICH (1929–   )

Aunt Jennifer's Tigers

Aunt Jennifer's tigers prance across a screen,
Bright topaz denizens of a world of green.
They do not fear the men beneath the tree;
They pace in sleek chivalric certainty.

Aunt Jennifer's fingers fluttering through her wool   5
Find even the ivory needle hard to pull.
The massive weight of Uncle's wedding band
Sits heavily upon Aunt Jennifer's hand.

When Aunt is dead, her terrified hands will lie
Still ringed with ordeals she was mastered by.   10
The tigers in the panel that she made
Will go on prancing, proud and unafraid.

Considerations

1. Make two lists, one of the images describing Aunt Jennifer and another of the images describing her tigers. In what ways is Aunt Jennifer like her tigers? In what ways is she different? What significance do you see in these similarities and differences?
2. What dreams might Aunt Jennifer's creations suggest? What world does she envision for her tigers?
3. What do the details of the poem suggest about Uncle? What are the possible roles he might play in Aunt Jennifer's life — and in her dreams?

SAPPHO (fl. ca. 610–ca. 580 B.C.)

To me he seems like a god

To me he seems like a god
as he sits facing you and
hears you near as you speak
softly and laugh
in a sweet echo that jolts   5
the heart in my ribs. For now
as I look at you my voice
is empty and

can say nothing as my tongue
cracks and slender fire is quick   10
under my skin. My eyes are dead
to light, my ears

pound, and sweat pours over me.
I convulse, paler than grass,
and feel my mind slip as I   15
go close to death

[but must suffer all, being poor.]

TRANSLATED BY WILLIS BARNSTONE

CHRISTOPHER MARLOWE (1564–1593)

The Passionate Shepherd to His Love

Come live with me and be my love,
And we will all the pleasures prove
That valleys, groves, hills, and fields,
Woods, or steepy mountain yields.

And we will sit upon the rocks,   5
Seeing the shepherds feed their flocks,
By shallow rivers to whose falls
Melodious birds sing madrigals.

And I will make thee beds of roses
And a thousand fragrant posies,   10
A cap of flowers, and a kirtle
Embroidered all with leaves of myrtle;

A gown made of the finest wool
Which from our pretty lambs we pull;
Fair lined slippers for the cold,   15
With buckles of the purest gold;

A belt of straw and ivy buds,
With coral clasps and amber studs:
And if these pleasures may thee move
Come live with me, and be my love.   20

The shepherds' swains shall dance and sing
For thy delight each May morning:
If these delights thy mind may move,
Then live with me and be my love.

SIR WALTER RALEIGH (1552?–1618)

The Nymph's Reply to the Shepherd

If all the world and love were young,
And truth in every shepherd's tongue,
These pretty pleasures might me move
To live with thee and be thy love.

Time drives the flocks from field to fold 5
When rivers rage and rocks grow cold,
And Philomel becometh dumb;
The rest complains of cares to come.

The flowers do fade, and wanton fields
To wayward winter reckoning yields; 10
A honey tongue, a heart of gall,
Is fancy's spring, but sorrow's fall.

Thy gowns, thy shoes, thy beds of roses,
Thy cap, thy kirtle, and thy posies
Soon break, soon wither, soon forgotten — 15
In folly ripe, in reason rotten.

Thy belt of straw and ivy buds,
Thy coral clasps and amber studs,
All these in me no means can move
To come to thee and be thy love. 20

But could youth last and love still breed,
Had joys no date nor age no need,
Then these delights my mind might move
To live with thee and be thy love.

JOHN DONNE (1572?–1631)

A Valediction: Forbidding Mourning

As virtuous men pass mildly away,
    And whisper to their souls to go,
Whilst some of their sad friends do say,
    "The breath goes now," and some say, "No,"

So let us melt, and make no noise, 5
    No tear-floods, nor sigh-tempests move;
'Twere profanation of our joys
    To tell the laity our love.

Moving of the earth brings harms and fears,
    Men reckon what it did and meant; 10
But trepidation of the spheres,
    Though greater far, is innocent.

Dull sublunary lovers' love
  (Whose soul is sense) cannot admit
Absence, because it doth remove   15
  Those things which elemented it.

But we, by a love so much refined
  That our selves know not what it is;
Inter-assured of the mind,
  Care less, eyes, lips, and hands to miss.   20

Our two souls therefore, which are one,
  Though I must go, endure not yet
A breach, but an expansion,
  Like gold to airy thinness beat.

If they be two, they are two so   25
  As stiff twin compasses are two:
Thy soul, the fixed foot, makes no show
  To move, but doth, if the other do;

And though it in the center sit,
  Yet when the other far doth roam,   30
It leans, and hearkens after it,
  And grows erect, as that comes home.

Such wilt thou be to me, who must,
  Like the other foot, obliquely run;
Thy firmness makes my circle just,   35
  And makes me end where I begun.

ROBERT HERRICK (1591–1674)

To the Virgins, to Make Much of Time

Gather ye rosebuds while ye may:
  Old Time is still a-flying;
And this same flower that smiles today,
  Tomorrow will be dying.

The glorious lamp of heaven, the sun,   5
  The higher he's a-getting,
The sooner will his race be run,
  And nearer he's to setting.

That age is best which is the first,
When youth and blood are warmer;   10
But being spent, the worse, and worst
    Times, still succeed the former.

Then be not coy, but use your time;
    And while ye may, go marry:
For, having lost but once your prime,   15
    You may for ever tarry.

ELIZABETH BARRETT BROWNING (1806–1861)

How do I love thee? (Sonnet 43)

How do I love thee? Let me count the ways.
I love thee to the depth and breadth and height
My soul can reach, when feeling out of sight
For the ends of Being and ideal Grace.
I love thee to the level of everyday's   5
Most quiet need, by sun and candle-light.
I love thee freely, as men strive for Right;
I love thee purely, as they turn from Praise.
I love thee with the passion put to use
In my old griefs, and with my childhood's faith.   10
I love thee with a love I seemed to lose
With my lost saints — I love thee with the breath,
Smiles, tears, of all my life! — and, if God choose,
I shall but love thee better after death.

ROBERT BROWNING (1812–1889)

My Last Duchess

Ferrara

That's my last duchess painted on the wall,
Looking as if she were alive. I call
That piece a wonder, now: Frà Pandolf's hands
Worked busily a day, and there she stands.
Will't please you sit and look at her? I said   5
"Frà Pandolf" by design, for never read

Strangers like you that pictured countenance,
The depth and passion of its earnest glance,
But to myself they turned (since none puts by
The curtain I have drawn for you, but I)   10
And seemed as they would ask me, if they durst,
How such a glance came there; so, not the first
Are you to turn and ask thus. Sir, 'twas not
Her husband's presence only, called that spot
Of joy into the Duchess' cheek: perhaps   15
Frà Pandolf chanced to say "Her mantle laps
Over my lady's wrist too much," or "Paint
Must never hope to reproduce the faint
Half-flush that dies along her throat": such stuff
Was courtesy, she thought, and cause enough   20
For calling up that spot of joy. She had
A heart — how shall I say? — too soon made glad,
Too easily impressed; she liked whate'er
She looked on, and her looks went everywhere.
Sir, 'twas all one! My favor at her breast,   25
The dropping of the daylight in the West,
The bough of cherries some officious fool
Broke in the orchard for her, the white mule
She rode with round the terrace — all and each
Would draw from her alike the approving speech,   30
Or blush, at least. She thanked men — good! but thanked
Somehow — I know not how — as if she ranked
My gift of a nine-hundred-years-old name
With anybody's gift. Who'd stoop to blame
This sort of trifling? Even had you skill   35
In speech — which I have not — to make your will
Quite clear to such an one, and say, "Just this
Or that in you disgusts me; here you miss,
Or there exceed the mark" — and if she let
Herself be lessoned so, nor plainly set   40
Her wits to yours, forsooth, and made excuse,
— E'en then would be some stooping; and I choose
Never to stoop. Oh sir, she smiled, no doubt,
Whene'er I passed her; but who passed without
Much the same smile? This grew; I gave commands;   45
Then all smiles stopped together. There she stands
As if alive. Will 't please you rise? We'll meet
The company below, then. I repeat,
The Count your master's known munificence
Is ample warrant that no just pretense   50

Of mine for dowry will be disallowed;
Though his fair daughter's self, as I avowed
At starting, is my object. Nay, we'll go
Together down, sir. Notice Neptune, though,
Taming a sea-horse, thought a rarity,   55
Which Claus of Innsbruck cast in bronze for me!

MAY SWENSON (1919–   )

Women

Women	Or they
should be	should be
pedestals	little horses
moving	those wooden
pedestals	sweet

Women   Or they
  should be   should be
    pedestals   little horses
     moving   those wooden
      pedestals   sweet   5
     moving   oldfashioned
    to the   painted
     motions   rocking
    of men   horses

      the gladdest things in the toyroom.   10

    The   feelingly
   pegs   and then
  of their   unfeelingly
  ears   To be
  so familiar   joyfully   15
and dear   ridden
to the trusting   rockingly
fists   ridden until
To be chafed   the restored

egos dismount and the legs stride away   20

Immobile   willing
  sweetlipped   to be set
  sturdy   into motion
  and smiling   Women
   women   should be   25
    should always   pedestals
    be waiting   to men

KRISTINE BATEY (1951–   )

Lot's Wife

While Lot, the conscience of a nation,
struggles with the Lord,
she struggles with the housework.
The City of Sin is where
she raises the children.   5
Ba'al° or Adonai°—
Whoever is God—
the bread must still be made
and the doorsill swept.
The Lord may kill the children tomorrow,   10
but today they must be bathed and fed.
Well and good to condemn your neighbors' religion;
but weren't they there
when the baby was born,
and when the well collapsed?   15
While her husband communes with God
she tucks the children into bed.
In the morning, when he tells her of the judgment,
she puts down the lamp she is cleaning
and calmly begins to pack.   20
In between bundling up the children
and deciding what will go,
she runs for a moment
to say goodbye to the herd,
gently patting each soft head   25
with tears in her eyes for the animals that will not understand.
She smiles blindly to the woman
who held her hand at childbed.
It is easy for eyes that have always turned to heaven
not to look back;   30
those that have been—by necessity—drawn to earth
cannot forget that life is lived from day to day.
Good, to a God, and good in human terms
are two different things.
On the breast of the hill, she chooses to be human,   35
and turns, in farewell—
and never regrets
the sacrifice.

6 *Ba'al:* Old Testament name for the chief god of the Canaanites whose cult practiced prostitution and child sacrifice. This cult was denounced by Jewish prophets; *Adonai:* Hebrew term for God.

AUGUST STRINDBERG (1849–1912)

The Stronger

Characters

MRS. X., *an actress, married*
MISS Y., *an actress, unmarried*
A WAITRESS

Scene

The corner of a ladies' café. Two little iron tables, a red velvet sofa, several chairs.
Enter MRS. X., *dressed in winter clothes, carrying a Japanese basket on her arm.*

MISS Y.: *sits with a half-empty beer bottle before her, reading an illustrated paper,*
which she changes later for another.

MRS. X.: Good afternoon, Amelia. You're sitting here alone on Christmas
eve like a poor bachelor!

MISS Y.: *(Looks up, nods, and resumes her reading.)*

MRS. X.: Do you know it really hurts me to see you like this, alone, in a
café, and on Christmas eve, too. It makes me feel as I did one time
when I saw a bridal party in a Paris restaurant, and the bride sat reading
a comic paper, while the groom played billiards with the witnesses.
Huh, thought I, with such a beginning, what will follow, and what
will be the end? He played billiards on his wedding eve! *(MISS Y. starts*
to speak) And she read a comic paper, you mean? Well, they are not
altogether the same thing.

(A WAITRESS enters, places a cup of chocolate before MRS. X. and
goes out.)

MRS. X.: You know what, Amelia! I believe you would have done better
to have kept him! Do you remember, I was the first to say "Forgive
him?" Do you remember that? You would be married now and have a
home. Remember that Christmas when you went out to visit your
fiancé's parents in the country? How you gloried in the happiness of
home life and really longed to quit the theater forever? Yes, Amelia
dear, home is the best of all — next to the theater — and as for children —
well, you don't understand that.

MISS Y.: *(Looks up scornfully.)*

(MRS. X. sips a few spoonfuls out of the cup, then opens her basket and
shows Christmas presents.)

MRS. X.: Now you shall see what I bought for my piggywigs. *(Takes up a*
doll.) Look at this! This is for Lisa, ha! Do you see how she can roll
her eyes and turn her head, eh? And here is Maja's popgun.

(Loads it and shoots at MISS Y.)

MISS Y.: *(Makes a startled gesture.)*

MRS. X.: Did I frighten you? Do you think I would like to shoot you, eh? On my soul, if I don't think you did! If you wanted to shoot *me* it wouldn't be so surprising, because I stood in your way — and I know you can never forget that — although I was absolutely innocent. You still believe I intrigued and got you out of the Stora theater, but I didn't. I didn't do that, although you think so. Well, it doesn't make any difference what I say to you. You still believe I did it. *(Takes up a pair of embroidered slippers.)* And these are for my better half. I embroidered them myself—I can't bear tulips, but he wants tulips on everything.

MISS Y.: *(Looks up ironically and curiously.)*

MRS. X.: *(putting a hand in each slipper.)* See what little feet Bob has! What? And you should see what a splendid stride he has! You've never seen him in slippers! *(*MISS Y. *laughs aloud.)* Look! *(She makes the slippers walk on the table.* MISS Y. *laughs loudly.)* And when he is grumpy he stamps like this with his foot. "What! damn those servants who can never learn to make coffee. Oh, now those creatures haven't trimmed the lamp wick properly!" And then there are drafts on the floor and his feet are cold. "Ugh, how cold it is; the stupid idiots can never keep the fire going." *(She rubs the slippers together, one sole over the other.)*

MISS Y.: *(Shrieks with laughter.)*

MRS. X.: And then he comes home and has to hunt for his slippers which Marie has stuck under the chiffonier — oh, but it's sinful to sit here and make fun of one's husband this way when he is kind and a good little man. You ought to have had such a husband, Amelia. What are you laughing at? What? What? And you see he's true to me. Yes, I'm sure of that, because he told me himself — what are you laughing at? — that when I was touring in Norway that brazen Frederika came and wanted to seduce him! Can you fancy anything so infamous? *(pause)* I'd have torn her eyes out if she had come to see him when I was at home. *(pause)* It was lucky that Bob told me about it himself and that it didn't reach me through gossip. *(pause)* But would you believe it, Frederika wasn't the only one! I don't know why, but the women are crazy about my husband. They must think he has influence about getting them theatrical engagements, because he is connected with the government. Perhaps you were after him yourself. I didn't use to trust you any too much. But now I know he never bothered his head about you, and you always seemed to have a grudge against him someway.

(Pause. They look at each other in a puzzled way.)

MRS. X.: Come and see us this evening, Amelia, and show us that you're not put out with us — not put out with me at any rate. I don't know, but I think it would be uncomfortable to have you for an enemy. Perhaps it's because I stood in your way *(more slowly)* or — I really — don't know why — in particular.

(Pause. MISS Y. *stares at* MRS. X. *curiously.)*

MRS. X.: *(thoughtfully).* Our acquaintance has been so queer. When I saw you for the first time I was afraid of you, so afraid that I didn't dare let you out of my sight; no matter when or where, I always found myself near you — I didn't dare have you for an enemy, so I became your friend. But there was always discord when you came to our house, because I saw that my husband couldn't endure you, and the whole thing seemed as awry to me as an ill-fitting gown — and I did all I could to make him friendly toward you, but with no success until you became engaged. Then came a violent friendship between you, so that it looked all at once as though you both dared show your real feelings only when you were secure — and then — how was it later? I didn't get jealous — strange to say! And I remember at the christening, when you acted as godmother, I made him kiss you — he did so, and you became so confused — as it were; I didn't notice it then — didn't think about it later, either — have never thought about it until — now! *(Rises suddenly.)* Why are you silent? You haven't said a word this whole time, but you have let me go on talking! You have sat there, and your eyes have reeled out of me all these thoughts which lay like raw silk in its cocoon — thoughts — suspicious thoughts, perhaps. Let me see — why did you break your engagement? Why do you never come to our house any more? Why won't you come to see us tonight?

*(*MISS Y.*appears as if about to speak.)*

MRS. X.: Hush, you needn't speak — I understand it all! It was because — and because — and because! Yes, yes! Now all the accounts balance. That's it. Fie, I won't sit at the same table with you. *(Moves her things to another table.)* That's the reason I had to embroider tulips — which I hate — on his slippers, because you are fond of tulips; that's why *(throws slippers on the floor)* we go to Lake Mälarn in the summer, because you don't like salt water; that's why my boy is named Eskil — because it's your father's name; that's why I wear your colors, read your authors, eat your favorite dishes, drink your drinks — chocolate, for instance; that's why — oh — my God — it's terrible, when I think about it; it's terrible. Everything, everything came from you to me, even your passions. Your soul crept into mine, like a worm into an apple, ate and ate, bored and bored, until nothing was left but the rind and a little black dust within. I wanted to get away from you, but I couldn't; you lay like a snake and charmed me with your black eyes; I felt that when I lifted my wings they only dragged me down; I lay in the water with bound feet, and the stronger I strove to keep up the deeper I worked myself down, down, until I sank to the bottom, where you lay like a giant crab to clutch me in your claws — and there I am lying now.

    I hate you, hate you, hate you! And you only sit there silent — silent and indifferent; indifferent whether it's new moon or waning moon, Christmas or New Year's, whether others are happy or unhappy; without power to hate or to love; as quiet as a stork by a rat hole—you couldn't scent your prey and capture it, but you could lie in wait for it! You sit here in your corner of the café—did you know it's called "The Rat Trap" for you?—and read the papers to see if misfortune hasn't befallen someone, to see if someone hasn't been given notice at the theater, perhaps; you sit here and calculate about your next victim and reckon on your chances of recompense like a pilot in a shipwreck. Poor Amelia, I pity you, nevertheless, because I know you are unhappy, unhappy like one who has been wounded, and angry because you are wounded. I can't be angry with you, no matter how much I want to be—because you come out the weaker one. Yes, all that with Bob doesn't trouble me. What is that to me, after all? And what difference does it make whether I learned to drink chocolate from you or some one else. *(Sips a spoonful from her cup)* Besides, chocolate is very healthful. And if you taught me how to dress—*tant mieux!*°—that has only made me more attractive to my husband; so you lost and I won there. Well, judging by certain signs, I believe you have already lost him; and you certainly intended that I should leave him—do as you did with your fiancé and regret as you now regret; but, you see, I don't do that—we mustn't be too exacting. And why should I take only what no one else wants?

Perhaps, take it all in all, I am at this moment the stronger one. You received nothing from me, but you gave me much. And now I seem like a thief since you have awakened and find I possess what is your loss. How could it be otherwise when everything is worthless and sterile in your hands? You can never keep a man's love with your tulips and your passions—but I can keep it. You can't learn how to live from your authors, as I have learned. You have no little Eskil to cherish, even if your father's name was Eskil. And why are you always silent, silent, silent? I thought that was strength, but perhaps it is because you have nothing to say! Because you never think about anything! *(Rises and picks up slippers.)* Now I'm going home—and take the tulips with me—*your* tulips! You are unable to learn from another; you can't bend—therefore, you broke like a dry stalk. But I won't break! Thank you, Amelia, for all your good lessons. Thanks for teaching my husband how to love. Now I'm going home to love him. *(Goes.)*

Considerations

1. No man appears in this play, yet Mr. X (Bob) plays a significant role. What kind of person do you think he is? Speculate on his feelings toward each of the women.

tant mieux! So much the better!

---

women at Feast Day, at Grab Days,° the women in the kitchen of my Cubero home, the women I grew up with; none of them appeared weak or helpless, none of them presented herself tentatively. I remember a certain reserve on those lovely brown faces; I remember the direct gaze of eyes framed by bright-colored shawls draped over their heads and cascading down their backs. I remember the clean cotton dresses and carefully pressed handembroidered aprons they always wore; I remember laughter and good food, especially the sweet bread and the oven bread they gave us. Nowhere in my mind is there a foolish woman, a dumb woman, a vain woman, or a plastic woman, though the Indian women I have known have shown a wide range of personal style and demeanor.

My memory includes the Navajo woman who was badly beaten by her Sioux husband; but I also remember that my grandmother abandoned her Sioux husband long ago. I recall the stories about the Laguna woman beaten regularly by her husband in the presence of her children so that the children would not believe in the strength and power of femininity. And I remember the women who drank, who got into fights with other women and with the men, and who often won those battles. I have memories of tired women, partying women, stubborn women, sullen women, amicable women, selfish women, shy women, and aggressive women. Most of all I

2. As Mrs. X. tells the story of her relationship with Bob, do you find what she says believable? Does she rationalize Bob's actions or does she seem to acknowledge the truth? Explain.

3. Strindberg calls this play *The Stronger*. Why? Do you see one character as stronger than the other? Do you see either of them as more deserving of admiration or of sympathy than the other? Explain.

4. Imagine the play in another setting — at another time of year, for example, or at a crowded party. How would these changes affect the play's action and themes?

5. Imagine the time immediately following Mrs. X.'s final speech. Assume that she does not leave, but instead acquiesces to Miss Y.'s (Amelie's) request that she sit down and listen to the other side of the story. Write Miss Y.'s dialogue as well as stage directions to indicate Mrs. X.'s silent responses.

PAULA GUNN ALLEN (1939–)

Where I Come from Is Like This

I

Modern American Indian women, like their non-Indian sisters, are deeply engaged in the struggle to redefine themselves. In their struggle they must reconcile traditional tribal definitions of women with industrial and postindustrial non-Indian definitions. Yet while these definitions seem to be more or less mutually exclusive, Indian women must somehow harmonize and integrate both in their own lives.

An American Indian woman is primarily defined by her tribal identity. In her eyes, her destiny is necessarily that of her people, and her sense of herself as a woman is first and foremost prescribed by her tribe. The definitions of woman's roles are as diverse as tribal cultures in the Americas. In some she is devalued, in others she wields considerable power. In some she is a familial/clan adjunct, in some she is as close to autonomous as her economic circumstances and psychological traits permit. But in no tribal definitions is she perceived in the same way as are women in western industrial and postindustrial cultures.

In the west, few images of women form part of the cultural mythos, and these are largely sexually charged. Among Christians, the madonna is the female prototype, and she is portrayed as essentially passive: her contribution is simply that of birthing. Little else is attributed to her and she certainly possesses few of the characteristics that are attributed to mythic figures among Indian tribes. This image is countered (rather than balanced) by the witch-goddess/whore characteristics designed to reinforce cultural beliefs about women, as well as western adversarial and dualistic perceptions of reality.

The tribes see women variously, but they do not question the power of femininity. Sometimes they see women as fearful, sometimes peaceful, sometimes omniscient and omnipotent, but they never portray women as mindless, helpless, simple, or oppressed. And while the women in a given tribe, clan, or band may be all these things, the individual woman is provided with a variety of im...s of women from the interconnected superna-...de she lives in

gradually been weakened and torn. But the oral tradition has prevented the complete destruction of the web, the ultimate disruption of tribal ways. The oral tradition is vital; it heals itself and the tribal web by adapting to the flow of the present while never relinquishing its connection to the past. Its adaptability has always been required, as many generations have experienced. Certainly the modern American Indian woman bears slight resemblance to her forebears — at least on superficial examination — but she is still a tribal woman in her deepest being. Her tribal sense of relationship to all that is continues to flourish. And though she is at times beset by her knowledge of the enormous gap between the life she lives and the life she was raised to live, and while she adapts her mind and being to the circumstances of her present life, she does so in tribal ways, mending the tears in the web of being from which she takes her existence as she goes.

My mother told me stories all the time, though I often did not recognize them as that. My mother told me stories about cooking and childbearing; she told me stories about menstruation and pregnancy; she told me stories about gods and heroes, about fairies and elves, about goddesses and spirits; she told me stories about the land and the sky, about cats and dogs, about snakes and spiders; she told me stories about climbing trees and exploring the mesas; she told me stories about going to dances and getting married; she told me stories about dressing and undressing, about sleeping and waking; she told me stories about herself, about her mother, about her grandmother. She told me stories about grieving and laughing, about thinking and doing; she told me stories about school and about people; about darning and mending; she told me stories about turquoise and about gold; she told me European stories and Laguna stories; she told me Catholic stories and Presbyterian stories; she told me city stories and country stories; she told me political stories and religious stories. She told me stories about living and stories about dying. And in all of those stories she told me who I was, who I was supposed to be, whom I came from, and who would follow me. In this way she taught me the meaning of the words she said, that all life is a circle and everything has a place within it. That's what she said and what she showed me in the things she did and the way she lives.

Of course, through my formal, white, Christian education, I discovered that other people had stories of their own — about women, about Indians, about fact, about reality — and I was amazed by a number of startling suppositions that others made about tribal customs and beliefs. According to the un-Indian, non-Indian view, for instance, Indians barred menstruating women from ceremonies and indeed segregated them from the rest of the people, consigning them to some space specially designed for them. This showed that Indians considered menstruating women unclean and not fit to enjoy the company of decent (nonmenstruating) people, that is, men. I was surprised and confused to hear this because my mother had taught me that white people had strange attitudes toward menstruation: they thought something was bad about it, that it meant you were sick, cursed, sinful, and weak

10

and that you had to be very careful during that time. She taught me that menstruation was a normal occurrence, that I could go swimming or hiking or whatever else I wanted to do during my period. She actively scorned women who took to their beds, who were incapacitated by cramps, who "got the blues."

As I struggled to reconcile these very contradictory interpretations of American Indians' traditional beliefs concerning menstruation, I realized that the menstrual taboos were about power, not about sin or filth. My conclusion was later borne out by some tribes' own explanations, which, as you may well imagine, came as quite a relief to me.

The truth of the matter as many Indians see it is that women who are at the peak of their fecundity are believed to possess power that throws male power totally out of kilter. They emit such force that, in their presence, any male-owned or -dominated ritual or sacred object cannot do its usual task. For instance, the Lakota say that a menstruating woman anywhere near a yuwipi man, who is a special sort of psychic, spirit-empowered healer, for a day or so before he is to do his ceremony will effectively disempower him. Conversely, among many if not most tribes, important ceremonies cannot be held without the presence of women. Sometimes the ritual woman who empowers the ceremony must be unmarried and virginal so that the power she channels is unalloyed, unweakened by sexual arousal and penetration by a male. Other ceremonies require tumescent women, others the presence of mature women who have borne children, and still others depend for empowerment on post-menopausal women. Women may be segregated from the company of the whole band or village on certain occasions, but on certain occasions men are also segregated. In short, each ritual depends on a certain balance of power, and the positions of women within the phases of womanhood are used by tribal people to empower certain rites. This does not derive from a male-dominant view; it is not a ritual observance imposed on women by men. It derives from a tribal view of reality that distinguishes tribal people from feudal and industrial people.

Among the tribes, the occult power of women, inextricably bound to our hormonal life, is thought to be very great; many hold that we possess innately the blood-given power to kill — with a glance, with a step, or with a judicious mixing of menstrual blood into somebody's soup. Medicine women among the Pomo of California cannot practice until they are sufficiently mature; when they are immature, their power is diffuse and is likely to interfere with their practice until time and experience have it under control. So women of the tribes are not especially inclined to see themselves as poor helpless victims of male domination. Even in those tribes where something akin to male domination was present, women are perceived as powerful, socially, physically, and metaphysically. In times past, as in times present, women carried enormous burdens with aplomb. We were far indeed from the "weaker sex," the designation that white aristocratic sisters unhappily earned for us all.

I remember my mother moving furniture all over the house when she wanted it changed. She didn't wait for my father to come home and help — she just went ahead and moved the piano, a huge upright from the old days, the couch, the refrigerator. Nobody had told her she was too weak to do such things. In imitation of her, I would delight in loading trucks at my father's store with cases of pop or fifty-pound sacks of flour. Even when I was quite small I could do it, and it gave me a belief in my own physical strength that advancing middle age can't quite erase. My mother used to tell me about the Acoma Pueblo women she had seen as a child carrying huge ollas (water pots) on their heads as they wound their way up the tortuous stairwell carved into the face of the "Sky City" mesa, a feat I tried to imitate with books and tin buckets. ("Sky City" is the term used by the Chamber of Commerce for the mother village of Acoma, which is situated atop a high sandstone table mountain.) I was never very successful, but even the attempt reminded me that I was supposed to be strong and balanced to be a proper girl.

Of course, my mother's Laguna people are Keres Indian, reputed to be   15
the last extreme mother-right people on earth. So it is no wonder that I got notably nonwhite notions about the natural strength and prowess of women. Indeed, it is only when I am trying to get non-Indian approval, recognition, or acknowledgment that my "weak sister" emotional and intellectual ploys get the better of my tribal woman's good sense. At such times I forget that I just moved the piano or just wrote a competent paper or just completed a financial transaction satisfactorily or have supported myself and my children for most of my adult life.

Nor is my contradictory behavior atypical. Most Indian women I know are in the same bicultural bind: we vacillate between being dependent and strong, self-reliant and powerless, strongly motivated and hopelessly insecure. We resolve the dilemma in various ways: some of us party all the time; some of us drink to excess; some of us travel and move around a lot; some of us land good jobs and then quit them; some of us engage in violent exchanges; some of us blow our brains out. We act in these destructive ways because we suffer from the societal conflicts caused by having to identify with two hopelessly opposed cultural definitions of women. Through this destructive dissonance we are unhappy prey to the self-disparagement common to, indeed demanded of, Indians living in the United States today. Our situation is caused by the exigencies of a history of invasion, conquest, and colonization whose searing marks are probably ineradicable. A popular bumper sticker on many Indian cars proclaims: "If You're Indian You're In," to which I always find myself adding under my breath, "Trouble."

III

No Indian can grow to any age without being informed that her people were "savages" who interfered with the march of progress pursued by respectable, loving, civilized white people. We are the villains of the scenario wher- we are mentioned at all. We are absent from much of white history except when we are calmly, rationally, succinctly, and systematically dehumanized. On the few occasions we are noticed in any way other than as howling, bloodthirsty beings, we are acclaimed for our noble quaintness. In this definition, we are exotic curios. Our ancient arts and customs are used to d-aw tourist money to state coffers, into the pocketbooks and bank accounts of scholars, and into support of the American-in-Disneyland promoters' dream.

As a Roman Catholic child I was treated to bloody tales of how the savage Indians martyred the hapless priests and missionaries who went among them in an attempt to lead them to the one true path. By the time I was through high school I had the idea that Indians were people who had benefited mightily from the advanced knowledge and superior morality of the Anglo-Europeans. At least I had, perforce, that idea to lay beside the other one that derived from my daily experience of Indian life, an idea less dehumanizing and more accurate because it came from my mother and the other Indian people who raised me. That idea was that Indians are a people who don't tell lies, who care for their children and their old people. You never see an Indian orphan, they said. You always know when you're old that someone will take care of you — one of your children will. Then they'd list the old folks who were being taken care of by this child or that. No child is ever considered illegitimate among the Indians, they said. If a girl gets pregnant, the baby is still part of the family, and the mother is too. That's what they said, and they showed me real people who lived according to those principles.

Of course the ravages of colonization have taken their toll; there are orphans in Indian country now, and abandoned, brutalized old folks; there are even illegitimate children, though the very concept still strikes me as absurd. There are battered children and neglected children, and there are battered wives and women who have been raped by Indian men. Proximity to the "civilizing" effects of white Christians has not improved the moral quality of life in Indian country, though each group, Indian and white, explains the situation differently. Nor is there much yet in the oral tradition that can enable us to adapt to these inhuman changes. But a force is growing in that direction, and it is helping Indian women reclaim their lives. Their power, their sense of direction and of self will soon be visible. It is the force of the women who speak and work and write, and it is formidable.

Through all the centuries of war and death and cultural and psychic 20 destruction have endured the women who raise the children and tend the fires, who pass along the tales and the traditions, who weep and bury the dead, who are the dead, and who never forget. There are always the women, who make pots and weave baskets, who fashion clothes and cheer their children on at powwow, who make fry bread and piki bread, and corn soup and chili stew, who dance and sing and remember and hold within their hearts the dream of their ancient peoples — that one day the woman who thinks will speak to us again, and everywhere there will be peace. Meanwhile we tell the stories and write the books and trade tales of anger and woe and stories of fun and scandal and laugh over all manner of things that happen every day. We watch and we wait.

My great-grandmother told my mother: Never forget you are Indian. And my mother told me the same thing. This, then, is how I have gone about remembering, so that my children will remember too.

Considerations

1. How does the view of women suggested by this essay compare with the view of women held in your community?
2. What does Allen mean when she speaks of the "bicultural bind" faced by Native American women? How does this relate to the struggle of Native American women "to redefine themselves"?
3. How are Native American men portrayed in this essay? What roles do they play in the lives of the women described? What is the men's relationship to the current struggle of the women for new identity?
4. In what ways are stories significant to the author? How does she see stories and story-telling as particularly important in the lives of Native American women?
5. How does Allen's essay address and challenge the stereotypes of Native Americans? Cite examples and explanations she uses to refute specific negative images.

PAUL THEROUX (1941–   )

Being a Man

There is a pathetic sentence in the chapter "Fetishism" in Dr. Norman Cameron's book *Personality Development and Psychopathology.* It goes, "Fetishists are nearly always men; and their commonest fetish is a woman's shoe." I cannot read that sentence without thinking that it is just one more awful thing about being a man—and perhaps it is an important thing to know about us.

I have always disliked being a man. The whole idea of manhood in America is pitiful, in my opinion. This version of masculinity is a little like having to wear an ill-fitting coat for one's entire life (by contrast, I imagine femininity to be an oppressive sense of nakedness). Even the expression "Be a man!" strikes me as insulting and abusive. It means: Be stupid, be unfeeling, obedient, soldierly and stop thinking. Man means "manly"—how can one think about men without considering the terrible ambition of manliness? And yet it is part of every man's life. It is a hideous and crippling lie; it not only insists on difference and connives at superiority, it is also by its very nature destructive—emotionally damaging and socially harmful.

The youth who is subverted, as most are, into believing in the masculine idea is effectively separated from women and he spends the rest of his life finding women a riddle and a nuisance. Of course, there is a female version of this male affliction. It begins with mothers encouraging little girls to say (to other adults) "Do you like my new dress?" In a sense, little girls are traditionally urged to please adults with a kind of coquettishness, while boys are enjoined to behave like monkeys toward each other. The nine-year-old coquette proceeds to become womanish in a subtle power game in which she learns to be sexually indispensable, socially decorative and always alert to a man's sense of inadequacy.

Femininity—being lady-like—implies needing a man as witness and seducer; but masculinity celebrates the exclusive company of men. That is why it is so grotesque; and that is also why there is no manliness without inadequacy—because it denies men the natural friendship of women.

It is very hard to imagine any concept of manliness that does not   5
belittle women, and it begins very early. At an age when I wanted to meet girls—let's say the treacherous years of thirteen to sixteen—I was told to take up a sport, get more fresh air, join the Boy Scouts, and I was urged not to read so much. It was the 1950s and if you asked too many questions about sex you were sent to camp—boy's camp, of course: the nightmare. Nothing is more unnatural or prison-like than a boy's camp, but if it were not for them we would have no Elks' Lodges, no pool rooms, no boxing matches, no Marines.

And perhaps no sports as we know them. Everyone is aware of how few in number are the athletes who behave like gentlemen. Just as high school basketball teaches you how to be a poor loser, the manly attitude towards sports seems to be little more than a recipe for creating bad marriages, social misfits, moral degenerates, sadists, latent rapists and just plain louts. I regard high school sports as a drug far worse than marijuana, and it is the reason that the average tennis champion, say, is a pathetic oaf.

Any objective study would find the quest for manliness essentially right-wing, puritanical, cowardly, neurotic and fueled largely by a fear of women. It is also certainly philistine. There is no book-hater like a Little League coach. But indeed all the creative arts are obnoxious to the manly ideal, because at their best the arts are pursued by uncompetitive and essentially solitary people. It makes it very hard for a creative youngster, for any boy who expresses the desire to be alone seems to be saying that there is something wrong with him.

It ought to be clear by now that I have something of an objection to the way we turn boys into men. It does not surprise me that when the President of the United States has his customary weekend off he dresses like a cowboy—it is both a measure of his insecurity and his willingness to please. In many ways, American culture does little more for a man than prepare him for modeling clothes in the L. L. Bean catalogue. I take this as a personal insult because for many years I found it impossible to admit to myself that I wanted to be a writer. It was my guilty secret, because being a writer was incompatible with being a man.

There are people who might deny this, but that is because the American writer, typically, has been so at pains to prove his manliness that we have come to see literariness and manliness as mingled qualities. But first there was a fear that writing was not a manly profession—indeed, not a profession at all. (The paradox in American letters is that it has always been easier for a woman to write and for a man to be published.) Growing up, I had thought of sports as wasteful and humiliating, and the idea of manliness was a bore. My wanting to become a writer was not a flight from that oppressive role-playing, but I quickly saw that it was at odds with it. Everything in stereotyped manliness goes against the life of the mind. The Hemingway personality is too tedious to go into here, and in any case his exertions are well-known, but certainly it was not until this aberrant behavior was examined by feminists in the 1960s that any male writer dared question the pugnacity in Hemingway's fiction. All the bullfighting and arm wrestling and elephant shooting diminished Hemingway as a writer, but it is consistent with a prevailing attitude in American writing: one cannot be a male writer without first proving that one is a man.

It is normal in America for a man to be dismissive or even somewhat apologetic about being a writer. Various factors make it easier. There is a heartiness about journalism that makes it acceptable—journalism is the manliest form of American writing and, therefore, the profession the most independent-minded women seek (yes, it is an illusion, but that is my point). Fiction-writing is equated with a kind of dispirited failure and is only manly

10

when it produces wealth—money is masculinity. So is drinking. Being a drunkard is another assertion, if misplaced, of manliness. The American male writer is traditionally proud of his heavy drinking. But we are also a very literal-minded people. A man proves his manhood in America in old-fashioned ways. He kills lions, like Hemingway; or he hunts ducks, like Nathanael West; or he makes pronouncements like, "A man should carry enough knife to defend himself with," as James Jones once said to a *Life* interviewer. Or he says he can drink you under the table. But even tiny drunken William Faulkner loved to mount a horse and go fox hunting, and Jack Kerouac roistered up and down Manhattan in a lumberjack shirt (and spent every night of *The Subterraneans* with his mother in Queens). And we are familiar with the lengths to which Norman Mailer is prepared, in his endearing way, to prove that he is just as much a monster as the next man.

When the novelist John Irving was revealed as a wrestler, people took him to be a very serious writer; and even a bubble reputation like Eric *(Love Story)* Segal's was enhanced by the news that he ran the marathon in a respectable time. How surprised we would be if Joyce Carol Oates were revealed as a sumo wrestler or Joan Didion active in pumping iron. "Lives in New York City with her three children" is the typical woman writer's biographical note, for just as the male writer must prove he has achieved a sort of muscular manhood, the woman writer—or rather her publicists—must prove her motherhood.

There would be no point in saying any of this if it were not generally accepted that to be a man is somehow—even now in feminist-influenced America—a privilege. It is on the contrary an unmerciful and punishing burden. Being a man is bad enough; being manly is appalling (in this sense, women's lib has done much more for men than for women). It is the sinister silliness of men's fashions, and a clubby attitude in the arts. It is the subversion of good students. It is the so-called "Dress Code" of the Ritz-Carlton Hotel in Boston, and it is the institutionalized cheating in college sports. It is the most primitive insecurity.

And this is also why men often object to feminism but are afraid to explain why: of course women have a justified grievance, but most men believe—and with reason—that their lives are just as bad.

Considerations

1. What is your response to the example in the opening paragraph? Speculate on the reasons why Theroux chose to begin with this example rather than with the second paragraph, where he explains the central idea of the essay.
2. In paragraph 3, Theroux suggests that the current American view of "manliness" encourages boys to feel distinctly apart from women and, therefore, "separated from women" for "the rest of . . . life." Such a man

finds "women a riddle and nuisance." Do you agree with this observation? Support your view with specific examples from your observations, experiences, or reading.

3. Summarize Theroux's view of high school sports. Respond to his view, using specific examples that support or challenge his points.

4. Much of Theroux's essay discusses the attitude he believes Americans hold toward men who choose to be writers. What is your attitude toward writing as a profession for men? What have you observed the attitudes of others to be?

5. Compare Theroux's discussion of writing as a profession for men with Virginia Woolf's discussion of writing as a profession for women ("Professions for Women," page 331).

CONNECTIONS: MEN AND WOMEN

1. Compare the views of male and female sexuality as suggested by these works: "The Storm," "A Dirty Story," "To His Coy Mistress," and "The Willing Mistress."

2. Compare the way roles of men and women are defined by the cultures represented in "The Chase," "A Dirty Story," "Where I Come from Is Like This," and "Being a Man."

3. Consider how economic issues affect relationships between men and women in "The Horse Dealer's Daughter" and "A Dirty Story."

4. Consider the theme of fidelity (and infidelity) in marriage in "The Storm," "The Chase," "For My Lover, Returning to His Wife," and *The Stronger.*

5. "Shiloh," "The Gesture," and "For My Lover, Returning to His Wife," all depict relationships that are failing for one reason or another. Compare the roles played by the men and women and the way those roles relate to the failure of the relationships.

Parents and Children

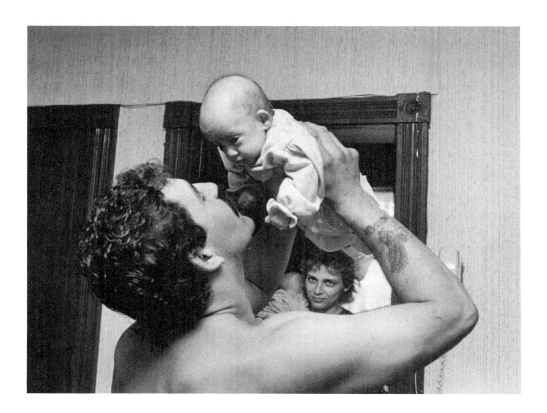

BERNARD MALAMUD (1914–1986)

Idiots First

The thick ticking of the tin clock stopped. Mendel, dozing in the dark, awoke in fright. The pain returned as he listened. He drew on his cold embittered clothing, and wasted minutes sitting at the edge of the bed.

"Isaac," he ultimately sighed.

In the kitchen, Isaac, his astonished mouth open, held six peanuts in his palm. He placed each on the table. "One . . . two . . . nine."

He gathered each peanut and appeared in the doorway. Mendel, in loose hat and long overcoat, still sat on the bed. Isaac watched with small eyes and ears, thick hair graying the sides of his head.

"Schlaf," he nasally said.   5

"No," muttered Mendel. As if stifling he rose. "Come, Isaac."

He wound his old watch though the sight of the stopped clock nauseated him.

Isaac wanted to hold it to his ear.

"No, it's late." Mendel put the watch carefully away. In the drawer he found the little paper bag of crumpled ones and fives and slipped it into his overcoat pocket. He helped Isaac on with his coat.

Isaac looked at one dark window, then at the other. Mendel stared at   10
both blank windows.

They went slowly down the darkly lit stairs, Mendel first, Isaac watching the moving shadows on the wall. To one long shadow he offered a peanut.

"Hungrig."

In the vestibule the old man gazed through the thin glass. The November night was cold and bleak. Opening the door he cautiously thrust his head out. Though he saw nothing he quickly shut the door.

"Ginzburg, that he came to see me yesterday," he whispered in Isaac's ear.

Isaac sucked air.   15

"You know who I mean?"

Isaac combed his chin with his fingers.

"That's the one, with the black whiskers. Don't talk to him or go with him if he asks you."

Isaac moaned.

"Young people he don't bother so much," Mendel said in afterthought.   20

It was suppertime and the street was empty but the store windows dimly lit their way to the corner. They crossed the deserted street and went on. Isaac, with a happy cry, pointed to the three golden balls. Mendel smiled but was exhausted when they got to the pawnshop.

The pawnbroker, a red-bearded man with black horn-rimmed glasses, was eating a whitefish at the rear of the store. He craned his head, saw them, and settled back to sip his tea.

In five minutes he came forward, patting his shapeless lips with a large white handkerchief.

Mendel, breathing heavily, handed him the worn gold watch. The pawnbroker, raising his glasses, screwed in his eyepiece. He turned the watch over once. "Eight dollars."

The dying man wet his cracked lips. "I must have thirty-five."   25

"So go to Rothschild."

"Cost me myself sixty."

"In 1905." The pawnbroker handed back the watch. It had stopped ticking. Mendel wound it slowly. It ticked hollowly.

"Isaac must go to my uncle that he lives in California."

"It's a free country," said the pawnbroker.   30

Isaac, watching a banjo, snickered.

"What's the matter with him?" the pawnbroker asked.

"So let be eight dollars," muttered Mendel, "but where will I get the rest till tonight?"

"How much for my hat and coat?" he asked.

"No sale." The pawnbroker went behind the cage and wrote out a   35
ticket. He locked the watch in a small drawer but Mendel still heard it ticking.

In the street he slipped the eight dollars into the paper bag, then searched in his pockets for a scrap of writing. Finding it, he strained to read the address by the light of the street lamp.

As they trudged to the subway, Mendel pointed to the sprinkled sky.

"Isaac, look how many stars are tonight."

"Eggs," said Isaac.

"First we will go to Mr. Fishbein, after we will eat."   40

They got off the train in upper Manhattan and had to walk several blocks before they located Fishbein's house.

"A regular palace," Mendel murmured, looking forward to a moment's warmth.

Isaac stared uneasily at the heavy door of the house.

Mendel rang. The servant, a man with long sideburns, came to the door and said Mr. and Mrs. Fishbein were dining and could see no one.

"He should eat in peace but we will wait till he finishes."   45

"Come back tomorrow morning. Tomorrow morning Mr. Fishbein will talk to you. He don't do business or charity at this time of the night."

"Charity I am not interested — "

"Come back tomorrow."

"Tell him it's life or death — "

"Whose life or death?"   50

"So if not his, then mine."

"Don't be such a big smart aleck."

"Look me in my face," said Mendel, "and tell me if I got time till tomorrow morning?"

The servant stared at him, then at Isaac, and reluctantly let them in.

The foyer was a vast high-ceilinged room with many oil paintings on the walls, voluminous silken draperies, a thick flowered rug at foot, and a marble staircase.

Mr. Fishbein, a paunchy bald-headed man with hairy nostrils and small patent leather feet, ran lightly down the stairs, a large napkin tucked under a tuxedo coat button. He stopped on the fifth step from the bottom and examined his visitors.

"Who comes on Friday night to a man that he has guests, to spoil him his supper?"

"Excuse me that I bother you, Mr. Fishbein," Mendel said. "If I didn't come now I couldn't come tomorrow."

"Without more preliminaries, please state your business. I'm a hungry man."

"Hungrig," wailed Isaac.

Fishbein adjusted his pince-nez. "What's the matter with him?"

"This is my son Isaac. He is like this all his life."

Isaac mewled.

"I am sending him to California."

"Mr. Fishbein don't contribute to personal pleasure trips."

"I am a sick man and he must go tonight on the train to my Uncle Leo."

"I never give to unorganized charity," Fishbein said, "but if you are hungry I will invite you downstairs in my kitchen. We are having tonight chicken with stuffed derma."

"All I ask is thirty-five dollars for the train ticket to my uncle in California. I have already the rest."

"Who is your uncle? How old a man?"

"Eighty-one years, a long life to him."

Fishbein burst into laughter. "Eighty-one years and you are sending him this half-wit."

Mendel, flailing both arms, cried, "Please, without names."

Fishbein politely conceded.

"Where is open the door there we go in the house," the sick man said. "If you will kindly give me thirty-five dollars, God will bless you. What is thirty-five dollars to Mr. Fishbein? Nothing. To me, for my boy, is everything."

Fishbein drew himself up to his tallest height.

"Private contributions I don't make — only to institutions. This is my fixed policy."

Mendel sank to his creaking knees on the rug.

"Please, Mr. Fishbein, if not thirty-five, give maybe twenty."

"Levinson!" Fishbein angrily called.

The servant with the long sideburns appeared at the top of the stairs.

"Show this party where is the door — unless he wishes to partake food before leaving the premises."

"For what I got chicken won't cure it," Mendel said.

"This way if you please," said Levinson, descending.

Isaac assisted his father up.

"Take him to an institution," Fishbein advised over the marble balus- 85
trade. He ran quickly up the stairs and they were at once outside, buffeted
by winds.

The walk to the subway was tedious. The wind blew mournfully.
Mendel, breathless, glanced furtively at shadows. Isaac, clutching his peanuts in his frozen fist, clung to his father's side. They entered a small park
to rest for a minute on a stone bench under a leafless two-branched tree. The
thick right branch was raised, the thin left one hung down. A very pale
moon rose slowly. So did a stranger as they approached the bench.

"Gut yuntif," he said hoarsely.

Mendel, drained of blood, waved his wasted arms. Isaac yowled sickly.
Then a bell chimed and it was only ten. Mendel let out a piercing anguished
cry as the bearded stranger disappeared into the bushes. A policeman came
running, and though he beat the bushes with his nightstick, could turn up
nothing. Mendel and Isaac hurried out of the little park. When Mendel
glanced back the dead tree had its thin arm raised, the thick one down. He
moaned.

They boarded a trolley, stopping at the home of a former friend, but
he had died years ago. On the same block they went into a cafeteria and
ordered two fried eggs for Isaac. The tables were crowded except where a
heavy-set man sat eating soup with kasha. After one look at him they left in
haste, although Isaac wept.

Mendel had another address on a slip of paper but the house was too 90
far away, in Queens, so they stood in a doorway shivering.

What can I do, he frantically thought, in one short hour?

He remembered the furniture in the house. It was junk but might
bring a few dollars. "Come, Isaac." They went once more to the pawnbroker's to talk to him, but the shop was dark and an iron gate — rings and gold
watches glinting through it — was drawn tight across his place of business.

They huddled behind a telephone pole, both freezing. Isaac whimpered.

"See the big moon, Isaac. The whole sky is white."

He pointed but Isaac wouldn't look. 95

Mendel dreamed for a minute of the sky lit up, long sheets of light in
all directions. Under the sky, in California, sat Uncle Leo drinking tea with
lemon. Mendel felt warm but woke up cold.

Across the street stood an ancient brick synagogue.

He pounded on the huge door but no one appeared. He waited till he
had breath and desperately knocked again. At last there were footsteps
within, and the synagogue door creaked open on its massive brass hinges.

A darkly dressed sexton, holding a dripping candle, glared at them.

"Who knocks this time of night with so much noise on the synagogue 100
door?"

Mendel told the sexton his troubles. "Please, I would like to speak to the rabbi."

"The rabbi is an old man. He sleeps now. His wife won't let you see him. Go home and come back tomorrow."

"To tomorrow I said goodbye already. I am a dying man."

Though the sexton seemed doubtful he pointed to an old wooden house next door. "In there he lives." He disappeared into the synagogue with his lit candle casting shadows around him.

Mendel, with Isaac clutching his sleeve, went up the wooden steps and   105
rang the bell. After five minutes a big-faced, gray-haired bulky woman came out on the porch with a torn robe thrown over her nightdress. She emphatically said the rabbi was sleeping and could not be waked.

But as she was insisting, the rabbi himself tottered to the door. He listened a minute and said, "Who wants to see me let them come in."

They entered a cluttered room. The rabbi was an old skinny man with bent shoulders and a wisp of white beard. He wore a flannel nightgown and black skullcap; his feet were bare.

"Vey is mir," his wife muttered. "Put on shoes or tomorrow comes sure pneumonia." She was a woman with a big belly, years younger than her husband. Staring at Isaac, she turned away.

Mendel apologetically related his errand. "All I need more is thirty-five dollars."

"Thirty-five?" said the rabbi's wife. "Why not thirty-five thousand?   110
Who has so much money? My husband is a poor rabbi. The doctors take away every penny."

"Dear friend," said the rabbi, "if I had I would give you."

"I got already seventy," Mendel said, heavy-hearted. "All I need more is thirty-five."

"God will give you," said the rabbi.

"In the grave," said Mendel. "I need tonight. Come, Isaac."

"Wait," called the rabbi.   115

He hurried inside, came out with a fur-lined caftan, and handed it to Mendel.

"Yascha," shrieked his wife, "not your new coat!"

"I got my old one. Who needs two coats for one body?"

"Yascha, I am screaming—"

"Who can go among poor people, tell me, in a new coat?"   120

"Yascha," she cried, "what can this man do with your coat? He needs tonight the money. The pawnbrokers are asleep."

"So let him wake them up."

"No." She grabbed the coat from Mendel.

He held on to a sleeve, wrestling her for the coat. Her I know, Mendel thought. "Shylock," he muttered. Her eyes glittered.

The rabbi groaned and tottered dizzily. His wife cried out as Mendel   125
yanked the coat from her hands.

"Run," cried the rabbi.

"Run, Isaac."

They ran out of the house and down the steps.

"Stop, you thief," called the rabbi's wife. The rabbi pressed both hands to his temples and fell to the floor.

"Help!" his wife wept. "Heart attack! Help!"   130

But Mendel and Isaac ran through the streets with the rabbi's new fur-lined caftan. After them noiselessly ran Ginzburg.

It was very late when Mendel bought the train ticket in the only booth open.

There was no time to stop for a sandwich so Isaac ate his peanuts and they hurried to the train in the vast deserted station.

"So in the morning," Mendel gasped as they ran, "there comes a man that he sells sandwiches and coffee. Eat but get change. When reaches California the train, will be waiting for you on the station Uncle Leo. If you don't recognize him he will recognize you. Tell him I send best regards."

But when they arrived at the gate to the platform it was shut, the   135
light out.

Mendel, groaning, beat on the gate with his fists.

"Too late," said the uniformed ticket collector, a bulky, bearded man with hairy nostrils and a fishy smell.

He pointed to the station clock. "Already past twelve."

"But I see standing there still the train," Mendel said, hopping in his grief.

"It just left—in one more minute."   140

"A minute is enough. Just open the gate."

"Too late I told you."

Mendel socked his bony chest with both hands. "With my whole heart I beg you this little favor."

"Favors you had enough already. For you the train is gone. You shoulda been dead already at midnight. I told you that yesterday. This is the best I can do."

"Ginzburg!" Mendel shrank from him.   145

"Who else?" The voice was metallic, eyes glittered, the expression amused.

"For myself," the old man begged, "I don't ask a thing. But what will happen to my boy?"

Ginzburg shrugged slightly. "What will happen happens. This isn't my responsibility. I got enough to think about without worrying about somebody on one cylinder."

"What then is your responsibility?"

"To create conditions. To make happen what happens. I ain't in the   150
anthropomorphic business."

"Whatever business you in, where is your pity?"

"This ain't my commodity. The law is the law."

"Which law is this?"

"The cosmic universal law, goddamit, the one I got to follow myself."

"What kind of a law is it?" cried Mendel. "For God's sake, don't you understand what I went through in my life with this poor boy? Look at him. For thirty-nine years, since the day he was born, I wait for him to grow up, but he don't. Do you understand what this means in a father's heart? Why don't you let him go to his uncle?" His voice had risen and he was shouting.

Isaac mewled loudly.

"Better calm down or you'll hurt somebody's feelings," Ginzburg said with a wink toward Isaac.

"All my life," Mendel cried, his body trembling, "what did I have? I was poor. I suffered from my health. When I worked I worked too hard. When I didn't work was worse. My wife died a young woman. But I didn't ask from anybody nothing. Now I ask a small favor. Be so kind, Mr. Ginzburg."

The ticket collector was picking his teeth with a match stick.

"You ain't the only one, my friend, some got it worse than you. That's how it goes in this country."

"You dog you." Mendel lunged at Ginzburg's throat and began to choke. "You bastard, don't you understand what it means human?"

They struggled nose to nose. Ginzburg, though his astonished eyes bulged, began to laugh. "You pipsqueak nothing. I'll freeze you to pieces."

His eyes lit in rage and Mendel felt an unbearable cold like an icy dagger invading his body, all of his parts shriveling.

Now I die without helping Isaac.

A crowd gathered. Isaac yelped in fright.

Clinging to Ginzburg in his last agony, Mendel saw reflected in the ticket collector's eyes the depth of his terror. But he saw that Ginzburg, staring at himself in Mendel's eyes, saw mirrored in them the extent of his own awful wrath. He beheld a shimmering, starry, blinding light that produced darkness.

Ginzburg looked astounded. "Who me?"

His grip on the squirming old man slowly loosened, and Mendel, his heart barely beating, slumped to the ground.

"Go," Ginzburg muttered, "take him to the train."

"Let pass," he commanded a guard.

The crowd parted. Isaac helped his father up and they tottered down the steps to the platform where the train waited, lit and ready to go.

Mendel found Isaac a coach seat and hastily embraced him. "Help Uncle Leo, Isaac. Also remember your father and mother."

"Be nice to him," he said to the conductor. "Show him where everything is."

He waited on the platform until the train began slowly to move. Isaac sat at the edge of his seat, his face strained in the direction of his journey.

When the train was gone, Mendel ascended the stairs to see what had become of Ginzburg.

Considerations

1. Ginzburg claims that Mendel is a "pipsqueak." What does he mean by this term? Given the evidence in the story, do you agree with Ginzburg's accusation? Explain.
2. Read the scene with Fishbein carefully. How does Fishbein regard Isaac? How does this view conflict with Mendel's view of his son? What does this scene suggest about each man's values?
3. What role does the Rabbi play in the story? How is he similar to or different from Fishbein? Do these similarities and differences suggest a significant theme?
4. What is Mendel's response to meeting Ginzburg at the train station? How does his response relate to his relationship with Isaac?
5. Make a list of all the references to time that you find in this story. Pay particular attention to the opening and closing paragraphs. What theme might these references to time suggest?

FRANK O'CONNOR (1903–1966)

My Oedipus Complex

Father was in the army all through the war—the first war, I mean—so, up to the age of five, I never saw much of him, and what I saw did not worry me. Sometimes I woke and there was a big figure in khaki peering down at me in the candlelight. Sometimes in the early morning I heard the slamming of the front door and the clatter of nailed boots down the cobbles of the lane. These were Father's entrances and exits. Like Santa Claus he came and went mysteriously.

In fact, I rather liked his visits, though it was an uncomfortable squeeze between Mother and him when I got into the big bed in the early morning. He smoked, which gave him a pleasant musty smell, and shaved, an operation of astounding interest. Each time he left a trail of souvenirs—model tanks and Gurkha knives with handles made of bullet cases, and German helmets and cap badges and buttonsticks, and all sorts of military equipment—carefully stowed away in a long box on top of the wardrobe, in case they ever came in handy. There was a bit of the magpie about Father; he expected everything to come in handy. When his back was turned, Mother let me get a chair and rummage through his treasures. She didn't seem to think so highly of them as he did.

The war was the most peaceful period of my life. The window of my attic faced southeast. My mother had curtained it, but that had small effect. I always woke with the first light and, with all the responsibilities of the previous day melted, feeling myself rather like the sun, ready to illumine and rejoice. Life never seemed so simple and clear and full of possibilities as then. I put my feet out from under the clothes—I called them Mrs. Left and Mrs. Right—and invented dramatic situations for them in which they discussed the problems of the day. At least Mrs. Right did; she was very demonstrative, but I hadn't the same control of Mrs. Left, so she mostly contented herself with nodding agreement.

They discussed what Mother and I should do during the day, what Santa Claus should give a fellow for Christmas, and what steps should be taken to brighten the home. There was that little matter of the baby, for instance. Mother and I could never agree about that. Ours was the only house in the terrace without a new baby, and Mother said we couldn't afford one till Father came back from the war because they cost seventeen and six. That showed how simple she was. The Geneys up the road had a baby, and everyone knew they couldn't afford seventeen and six. It was probably a cheap baby, and Mother wanted something really good, but I felt she was too exclusive. The Geneys' baby would have done us fine.

Having settled my plans for the day, I got up, put a chair under the attic window, and lifted the frame high enough to stick out my head. The window overlooked the front gardens of the terrace behind ours, and beyond these it looked over a deep valley to the tall, red-brick houses terraced up

5

the opposite hillside, which were all still in shadow, while those at our side of the valley were all lit up, though with long strange shadows that made them seem unfamiliar; rigid and painted.

After that I went into Mother's room and climbed into the big bed. She woke and I began to tell her of my schemes. By this time, though I never seem to have noticed it, I was petrified in my nightshirt, and I thawed as I talked until, the last frost melted. I fell asleep beside her and woke again only when I heard her below in the kitchen, making the breakfast.

After breakfast we went into town; heard Mass at St. Augustine's and said a prayer for Father, and did the shopping. If the afternoon was fine we either went for a walk in the country or a visit to Mother's great friend in the convent, Mother St. Dominic. Mother had them all praying for Father, and every night, going to bed, I asked God to send him back safe from the war to us. Little, indeed, did I know what I was praying for!

One morning, I got into the big bed, and there, sure enough, was Father in his usual Santa Claus manner, but later, instead of uniform, he put on his best blue suit, and Mother was as pleased as anything. I saw nothing to be pleased about, because, out of uniform, Father was altogether less interesting, but she only beamed, and explained that our prayers had been answered, and off we went to Mass to thank God for having brought Father safely home.

The irony of it! That very day when he came in to dinner he took off his boots and put on his slippers, donned the dirty old cap he wore about the house to save him from colds, crossed his legs, and began to talk gravely to Mother, who looked anxious. Naturally, I disliked her looking anxious, because it destroyed her good looks, so I interrupted him.

"Just a moment, Larry!" she said gently.   10

This was only what she said when we had boring visitors, so I attached no importance to it and went on talking.

"Do be quiet, Larry!" she said impatiently. "Don't you hear me talking to Daddy?"

This was the first time I had heard those ominous words, "talking to Daddy," and I couldn't help feeling that if this was how God answered prayers, he couldn't listen to them very attentively.

"Why are you talking to Daddy?" I asked with as great a show of indifference as I could muster.

"Because Daddy and I have business to discuss. Now, don't interrupt   15 again!"

In the afternoon, at Mother's request, Father took me for a walk. This time we went into town instead of out in the country, and I thought at first, in my usual optimistic way, that it might be an improvement. It was nothing of the sort. Father and I had quite different notions of a walk in town. He had no proper interest in trams, ships, and horses, and the only thing that seemed to divert him was talking to fellows as old as himself. When I wanted to stop he simply went on, dragging me behind him by the hand;

when he wanted to stop I had no alternative but to do the same. I noticed that it seemed to be a sign that he wanted to stop for a long time whenever he leaned against a wall. The second time I saw him do it I got wild. He seemed to be settling himself forever. I pulled him by the coat and trousers, but, unlike Mother who, if you were too persistent, got into a wax and said: "Larry, if you don't behave yourself, I'll give you a good slap," Father had an extraordinary capacity for amiable inattention. I sized him up and wondered would I cry, but he seemed to be too remote to be annoyed even by that. Really, it was like going for a walk with a mountain! He either ignored the wrenching and pummeling entirely, or else glanced down with a grin of amusement from his peak. I had never met anyone so absorbed in himself as he seemed.

At teatime, "talking to Daddy" began again, complicated this time by the fact that he had an evening paper, and every few minutes he put it down and told Mother something new out of it. I felt this was foul play. Man for man. I was prepared to compete with him any time for Mother's attention, but when he had it all made up for him by other people it left me no chance. Several times I tried to change the subject without success.

"You must be quiet while Daddy is reading, Larry," Mother said impatiently.

It was clear that she either genuinely liked talking to Father better than talking to me, or else that he had some terrible hold on her which made her afraid to admit the truth.

"Mummy," I said that night when she was tucking me up, "do you think if I prayed hard God would send Daddy back to the war?"

She seemed to think about that for a moment.

"No, dear," she said with a smile. "I don't think he would."

"Why wouldn't he, Mummy?"

"Because there isn't a war any longer, dear."

"But, Mummy, couldn't God make another war, if He liked?"

"He wouldn't like to, dear. It's not God who makes wars, but bad people."

"Oh!" I said.

I was disappointed about that. I began to think that God wasn't quite what he was cracked up to be.

Next morning I woke at my usual hour, feeling like a bottle of champagne. I put out my feet and invented a long conversation in which Mrs. Right talked of the trouble she had with her own father till she put him in the Home. I didn't quite know what the Home was but it sounded the right place for Father. Then I got my chair and stuck my head out of the attic window. Dawn was just breaking, with a guilty air that made me feel I had caught it in the act. My head bursting with stories and schemes, I stumbled in next door, and in the half-darkness scrambled into the big bed. There was no room at Mother's side so I had to get between her and Father. For the time being I had forgotten about him, and for several minutes I sat bolt

upright, racking my brains to know what I could do with him. He was
taking up more than his fair share of the bed, and I couldn't get comfortable,
so I gave him several kicks that made him grunt and stretch. He made room
all right, though. Mother waked and felt for me. I settled back comfortably
in the warmth of the bed with my thumb in my mouth.

"Mummy!" I hummed, loudly and contentedly.   30

"Sssh! dear," she whispered. "Don't wake Daddy!"

This was a new development, which threatened to be even more serious than "talking to Daddy." Life without my early-morning conferences
was unthinkable.

"Why?" I asked severely.

"Because poor Daddy is tired."

This seemed to me a quite inadequate reason, and I was sickened by   35
the sentimentality of her "poor Daddy." I never liked that sort of gush, it
always struck me as insincere.

"Oh!" I said lightly. Then in my most winning tone: "Do you know
where I want to go with you today, Mummy?"

"No, dear," she sighed.

"I want to go down the Glen and fish for thornybacks with my new
net, and then I want to go out to the Fox and Hounds, and — "

"Don't-wake-Daddy!" she hissed angrily, clapping her hand across my
mouth.

But it was too late. He was awake, or nearly so. He grunted and   40
reached for the matches. Then he stared incredulously at his watch.

"Like a cup of tea, dear?" asked Mother in a meek, hushed voice I had
never heard her use before. It sounded almost as though she were afraid.

"Tea?" he exclaimed indignantly. "Do you know what the time is?"

"And after that I want to go up the Rathcooney Road," I said loudly,
afraid I'd forget something in all those interruptions.

"Go to sleep at once, Larry!" she said sharply.

I began to snivel. I couldn't concentrate, the way that pair went on,   45
and smothering my early-morning schemes was like burying a family from
the cradle.

Father said nothing, but lit his pipe and sucked it, looking out into the
shadows without minding Mother or me. I knew he was mad. Every time I
made a remark Mother hushed me irritably. I was mortified. I felt it wasn't
fair; there was even something sinister in it. Every time I had pointed out to
her the waste of making two beds when we could both sleep in one, she had
told me it was healthier like that, and now here was this man, this stranger,
sleeping with her without the least regard for her health!

He got up early and made tea, but though he brought Mother a cup
he brought none for me.

"Mummy," I shouted. "I want a cup of tea, too."

"Yes, dear," she said patiently. "You can drink from Mummy's
saucer."

That settled it. Either Father or I would have to leave the house. I 50
didn't want to drink from Mother's saucer; I wanted to be treated as an equal
in my own home, so, just to spite her, I drank it all and left none for her.
She took that quietly, too.

But that night when she was putting me to bed she said gently:

"Larry, I want you to promise me something."

"What is it?" I asked.

"Not to come in and disturb poor Daddy in the morning. Promise?"

"Poor Daddy" again! I was becoming suspicious of everything involv- 55
ing that quite impossible man.

"Why?" I asked.

"Because poor Daddy is worried and tired and he doesn't sleep well."

"Why doesn't he, Mummy?"

"Well, you know, don't you, that while he was at the war Mummy
got the pennies from the Post Office?"

"From Miss MacCarthy?" 60

"That's right. But now, you see, Miss MacCarthy hasn't any more
pennies, so Daddy must go out and find us some. You know what would
happen if he couldn't?"

"No," I said, "tell us."

"Well, I think we might have to go out and beg for them like the poor
old woman on Fridays. We wouldn't like that, would we?"

"No," I agreed. "We wouldn't."

"So you'll promise not to come in and wake him?" 65

"Promise."

Mind you, I meant that. I knew pennies were a serious matter, and I
was all against having to go out and beg like the old woman on Fridays.
Mother laid out all my toys in a complete ring round the bed so that,
whatever way I got out, I was bound to fall over one of them.

When I woke I remembered my promise all right. I got up and sat on
the floor and played — for hours, it seemed to me. Then I got my chair and
looked out the attic window for more hours. I wished it was time for Father
to wake; I wished someone would make me a cup of tea. I didn't feel in the
least like the sun; instead, I was bored and so very, very cold! I simply
longed for the warmth and depth of the big featherbed.

At last I could stand it no longer. I went into the next room. As there
was still no room at Mother's side I climbed over her and she woke with a
start.

"Larry," she whispered, gripping my arm very tightly, "what did you 70
promise?"

"But I did, Mummy," I wailed, caught in the very act. "I was quiet
for ever so long."

"Oh, dear, and you're perished!" she said sadly, feeling me all over.
"Now, if I let you stay will you promise not to talk?"

"But I want to talk, Mummy," I wailed.

"That has nothing to do with it," she said with a firmness that was new to me. "Daddy wants to sleep. Now, do you understand that?"

I understood it only too well. I wanted to talk, he wanted to sleep — whose house was it, anyway? 75

"Mummy," I said with equal firmness. "I think it would be healthier for Daddy to sleep in his own bed."

That seemed to stagger her, because she said nothing for a while.

"Now, once for all," she went on, "you're to be perfectly quiet or go back to your own bed. Which is it to be?"

The injustice of it got me down. I had convicted her out of her own mouth of inconsistency and unreasonableness, and she hadn't even attempted to reply. Full of spite, I gave Father a kick, which she didn't notice but which made him grunt and open his eyes in alarm.

"What time is it?" he asked in a panic-stricken voice, not looking at 80 Mother but at the door, as if he saw someone there.

"It's early yet," she replied soothingly. "It's only the child. Go to sleep again. . . . Now, Larry," she added, getting out of bed, "you've wakened Daddy and you must go back."

This time, for all her quiet air, I knew she meant it, and knew that my principal rights and privileges were as good as lost unless I asserted them at once. As she lifted me, I gave a screech, enough to wake the dead, not to mind Father. He groaned.

"That damn child! Doesn't he ever sleep?"

"It's only a habit, dear," she said quietly, though I could see she was vexed.

"Well, it's time he got out of it," shouted Father, beginning to heave in 85 the bed. He suddenly gathered all the bedclothes about him, turned to the wall, and then looked back over his shoulder with nothing showing only two small, spiteful, dark eyes. The man looked very wicked.

To open the bedroom door, Mother had to let me down, and I broke free and dashed for the farthest corner, screeching. Father sat bolt upright in bed.

"Shut up, you little puppy!" he said in a choking voice.

I was so astonished that I stopped screeching. Never, never had anyone spoken to me in that tone before. I looked at him incredulously and saw his face convulsed with rage. It was only then that I fully realized how God had codded me, listening to my prayers for the safe return of this monster.

"Shut up, you!" I bawled, beside myself.

"What's that you said?" shouted Father, making a wild leap out of 90 the bed.

"Mick, Mick!" cried Mother. "Don't you see the child isn't used to you?"

"I see he's better fed than taught," snarled Father, waving his arms wildly. "He wants his bottom smacked."

All his previous shouting was as nothing to these obscene words referring to my person. They really made my blood boil.

"Smack your own!" I screamed hysterically. "Smack your own! Shut up! Shut up!"

At this he lost his patience and let fly at me. He did it with the lack of conviction you'd expect of a man under Mother's horrified eyes, and it ended up as a mere tap, but the sheer indignity of being struck at all by a stranger, a total stranger who had cajoled his way back from the war into our big bed as a result of my innocent intercession, made me completely dotty. I shrieked and shrieked, and danced in my bare feet, and Father, looking awkward and hairy in nothing but a short grey army shirt, glared down at me like a mountain out for murder. I think it must have been then that I realized he was jealous too. And there stood Mother in her nightdress, looking as if her heart was broken between us. I hoped she felt as she looked. It seemed to me that she deserved it all. 95

From that morning out my life was a hell. Father and I were enemies, open and avowed. We conducted a series of skirmishes against one another, he trying to steal my time with Mother and I his. When she was sitting on my bed, telling me a story, he took to looking for some pair of old boots which he alleged he had left behind him at the beginning of the war. While he talked to Mother I played loudly with my toys to show my total lack of concern. He created a terrible scene one evening when he came in from work and found me at his box, playing with his regimental badges, Gurkha knives and button-sticks. Mother got up and took the box from me.

"You mustn't play with Daddy's toys unless he lets you, Larry," she said severely. "Daddy doesn't play with yours."

For some reason Father looked at her as if she had struck him and then turned away with a scowl.

"Those are not toys," he growled, taking down the box again to see had I lifted anything. "Some of those curios are very rare and valuable."

But as time went on I saw more and more how he managed to alienate Mother and me. What made it worse was that I couldn't grasp his method or see what attraction he had for Mother. In every possible way he was less winning than I. He had a common accent and made noises at his tea. I thought for a while that it might be the newspapers she was interested in, so I made up bits of news of my own to read to her. Then I thought it might be the smoking, which I personally thought attractive, and took his pipes and went round the house dribbling into them till he caught me. I even made noises at my tea, but Mother only told me I was disgusting. It all seemed to hinge round that unhealthy habit of sleeping together, so I made a point of dropping into their bedroom and nosing around, talking to myself, so that they wouldn't know I was watching them, but they were never up to anything that I could see. In the end it beat me. It seemed to depend on being grown-up and giving people rings, and I realized I'd have to wait. 100

But at the same time I wanted him to see that I was only waiting, not giving up the fight. One evening when he was being particularly obnoxious, chattering away well above my head, I let him have it.

"Mummy," I said, "do you know what I'm going to do when I grow up?"

"No, dear," she replied. "What?"

"I'm going to marry you," I said quietly.

Father gave a great guffaw out of him, but he didn't take me in. I knew   105
it must only be pretence. And Mother, in spite of everything, was pleased. I felt she was probably relieved to know that one day Father's hold on her would be broken.

"Won't that be nice?" she said with a smile.

"It'll be very nice," I said confidently. "Because we're going to have lots and lots of babies."

"That's right, dear," she said placidly. "I think we'll have one soon, and then you'll have plenty of company."

I was no end pleased about that because it showed that in spite of the way she gave in to Father she still considered my wishes. Besides, it would put the Geneys in their place.

It didn't turn out like that, though. To begin with, she was very   110
preoccupied—I supposed about where she would get the seventeen and six—and though Father took to staying out late in the evenings it did me no particular good. She stopped taking me for walks, became as touchy as blazes, and smacked me for nothing at all. Sometimes I wished I'd never mentioned the confounded baby—I seemed to have a genius for bringing calamity on myself.

And calamity it was! Sonny arrived in the most appalling hullabaloo—even that much he couldn't do without a fuss—and from the first moment I disliked him. He was a difficult child—so far as I was concerned he was always difficult—and demanded far too much attention. Mother was simply silly about him, and couldn't see when he was only showing off. As company he was worse than useless. He slept all day, and I had to go round the house on tiptoe to avoid waking him. It wasn't any longer a question of not waking Father. The slogan now was "Don't-wake-Sonny!" I couldn't understand why the child wouldn't sleep at the proper time, so whenever Mother's back was turned I woke him. Sometimes to keep him awake I pinched him as well. Mother caught me at it one day and gave me a most unmerciful flaking.

One evening, when Father was coming in from work, I was playing trains in the front garden. I let on not to notice him; instead, I pretended to be talking to myself, and said in a loud voice: "If another bloody baby comes into this house, I'm going out."

Father stopped dead and looked at me over his shoulder.

"What's that you said?" he asked sternly.

"I was only talking to myself," I replied, trying to conceal my panic. 115
"It's private."

He turned and went in without a word. Mind you, I intended it as a
solemn warning, but its effect was quite different. Father started being quite
nice to me. I could understand that, of course. Mother was quite sickening
about Sonny. Even at mealtimes she'd get up and gawk at him in the cradle
with an idiotic smile, and tell Father to do the same. He was always polite
about it, but he looked so puzzled you could see he didn't know what she
was talking about. He complained of the way Sonny cried at night, but she
only got cross and said that Sonny never cried except when there was something up with him — which was a flaming lie, because Sonny never had
anything up with him, and only cried for attention. It was really painful to
see how simple-minded she was. Father wasn't attractive, but he had a fine
intelligence. He saw through Sonny, and now he knew that I saw through
him as well.

One night I woke with a start. There was someone beside me in the
bed. For one wild moment I felt sure it must be Mother, having come to her
senses and left Father for good, but then I heard Sonny in convulsions in the
next room, and Mother saying: "There! There! There!" and I knew it wasn't
she. It was Father. He was lying beside me, wide awake, breathing hard and
apparently as mad as hell.

After a while it came to me what he was mad about. It was his turn
now. After turning me out of the big bed, he had been turned out himself.
Mother had no consideration now for anyone but that poisonous pup, Sonny.
I couldn't help feeling sorry for Father. I had been through it all myself, and
even at that age I was magnanimous. I began to stroke him down and say:
"There! There!" He wasn't exactly responsive.

"Aren't you asleep either?" he snarled.

"Ah, come on and put your arm around us, can't you?" I said, and he 120
did, in a sort of way. Gingerly, I suppose, is how you'd describe it. He was
very bony but better than nothing.

At Christmas he went out of his way to buy me a really nice model
railway.

Considerations

1. This story falls into three sections: father's absence; father's return; Sonny's arrival. Consider the relationships among these three sections by
   evaluating the conflicts that are introduced and resolved (or left unresolved) in each.
2. Consider carefully the language of the narrator. What phrases seem like
   those of a five-year-old? What phrases are clearly those of an older person? What do you make of this combination? What effect does this

changing language have on the evaluation of the narrator's relationship with his parents?

3. Trace the changing relationship between Larry and his mother. Discuss and explain your responses to this change.

4. Trace the changing relationship between Larry and his father. Discuss and explain your responses to this change.

5. Write a dialogue that takes place at a holiday dinner, twenty years from the time of the story. Imagine the conversation between Larry, Sonny, the father, and the mother as Larry reminisces about this incident.

DORIS LESSING (1919–   )

Through the Tunnel

Going to the shore on the first morning of the holiday, the young English boy stopped at a turning of the path and looked down at a wild and rocky bay, and then over to the crowded beach he knew so well from other years. His mother walked on in front of him, carrying a bright-striped bag in one hand. Her other arm, swinging loose, was very white in the sun. The boy watched that white, naked arm, and turned his eyes, which had a frown behind them, toward the bay and back again to his mother. When she felt he was not with her, she swung around. "Oh, there you are, Jerry!" she said. She looked impatient, then smiled. "Why, darling, would you rather not come with me? Would you rather — " She frowned, conscientiously worrying over what amusements he might secretly be longing for which she had been too busy or too careless to imagine. He was very familiar with that anxious, apologetic smile. Contrition sent him running after her. And yet, as he ran, he looked back over his shoulder at the wild bay; and all morning, as he played on the safe beach, he was thinking of it.

Next morning, when it was time for the routine of swimming and sunbathing, his mother said, "Are you tired of the usual beach, Jerry? Would you like to go somewhere else?"

"Oh, no!" he said quickly, smiling at her out of that unfailing impulse of contrition — a sort of chivalry. Yet, walking down the path with her, he blurted out, "I'd like to go and have a look at those rocks down there."

She gave the idea her attention. It was a wild-looking place, and there was no one there, but she said, "Of course, Jerry. When you've had enough, come to the big beach. Or just go straight back to the villa, if you like." She walked away, that bare arm, now slightly reddened from yesterday's sun, swinging. And he almost ran after her again, feeling it unbearable that she should go by herself, but he did not.

She was thinking, Of course he's old enough to be safe without me. 5 Have I been keeping him too close? He mustn't feel he ought to be with me. I must be careful.

He was an only child, eleven years old. She was a widow. She was determined to be neither possessive nor lacking in devotion. She went worrying off to her beach.

As for Jerry, once he saw that his mother had gained her beach, he began the steep descent to the bay. From where he was, high up among red-brown rocks, it was a scoop of moving bluish green fringed with white. As he went lower, he saw that it spread among small promontories and inlets of rough, sharp rock, and the crisping, lapping surface showed stains of purple and darker blue. Finally, as he ran sliding and scraping down the last few yards, he saw an edge of white surf, and the shallow, luminous movement of water over white sand, and, beyond that, a solid, heavy blue.

He ran straight into the water and began swimming. He was a good swimmer. He went out fast over the gleaming sand, over a middle region where rocks lay like discoloured monsters under the surface, and then he was in the real sea — a warm sea where irregular cold currents from the deep water shocked his limbs.

When he was so far out that he could look back not only on the little bay but past the promontory that was between it and the big beach, he floated on the buoyant surface and looked for his mother. There she was, a speck of yellow under an umbrella that looked like a slice of orange peel. He swam back to shore, relieved at being sure she was there, but all at once very lonely.

On the edge of a small cape that marked the side of the bay away from the promontory was a loose scatter of rocks. Above them, some boys were stripping off their clothes. They came running, naked, down to the rocks. The English boy swam towards them, and kept his distance at a stone's throw. They were of that coast, all of them burned smooth dark brown, and speaking a language he did not understand. To be with them, of them, was a craving that filled his whole body. He swam a little closer; they turned and watched him with narrowed, alert dark eyes. Then one smiled and waved. It was enough. In a minute, he had swum in and was on the rocks beside them, smiling with a desperate, nervous supplication. They shouted cheerful greetings at him, and then, as he preserved his nervous, uncomprehending smile, they understood that he was a foreigner strayed from his own beach, and they proceeded to forget him. But he was happy. He was with them.

They began diving again and again from a high point into a well of blue sea between rough, pointed rocks. After they had dived and come up, they swam around, hauled themselves up, and waited their turn to dive again. They were big boys — men to Jerry. He dived, and they watched him, and when he swam around to take his place, they made way for him. He felt he was accepted, and he dived again, carefully, proud of himself.

Soon the biggest of the boys poised himself, shot down into the water, and did not come up. The others stood about, watching. Jerry, after waiting for the sleek brown head to appear, let out a yell of warning; they looked at him idly and turned their eyes back towards the water. After a long time, the boy came up on the other side of a big dark rock, letting the air out of his lungs in a sputtering gasp and a shout of triumph. Immediately, the rest of them dived in. One moment, the morning seemed full of chattering boys; the next, the air and the surface of the water were empty. But through the heavy blue, dark shapes could be seen moving and groping.

Jerry dived, shot past the school of underwater swimmers, saw a black wall of rock looming at him, touched it, and bobbed up at once to the surface, where the wall was a low barrier he could see across. There was no one visible; under him, in the water, the dim shapes of the swimmers had disappeared. Then one, and then another of the boys came up on the far side of the barrier of rock, and he understood that they had swum through some

10

gap or hole in it. He plunged down again. He could see nothing through the stinging salt water but the blank rock. When he came up, the boys were all on the diving rock, preparing to attempt the feat again. And now, in a panic of failure, he yelled up, in English, "Look at me! Look!" and he began splashing and kicking in the water like a foolish dog.

They looked down gravely, frowning. He knew the frown. At moments of failure, when he clowned to claim his mother's attention, it was with just this grave, embarrassed inspection that she rewarded him. Through his hot shame, feeling the pleading grin on his face like a scar that he could never remove, he looked up at the group of big brown boys on the rock and shouted, *"Bonjour! Merci! Au revoir! Monsieur, monsieur!"* while he hooked his fingers round his ears and waggled them.

Water surged into his mouth; he choked, sank, came up. The rock, lately weighted with boys, seemed to rear up out of the water as their weight was removed. They were flying down past him, now, into the water; the air was full of falling bodies. Then the rock was empty in the hot sunlight. He counted one, two, three. . . .   15

At fifty, he was terrified. They must all be drowning beneath him, in the watery caves of the rock! At a hundred, he stared around him at the empty hillside, wondering if he should yell for help. He counted faster, faster, to hurry them up, to bring them to the surface quickly, to drown them quickly—anything rather than the terror of counting on and on into the blue emptiness of the morning. And then, at a hundred and sixty, the water beyond the rock was full of boys blowing like brown whales. They swam back to the shore without a look at him.

He climbed back to the diving rock and sat down, feeling the hot roughness of it under his thighs. The boys were gathering up their bits of clothing and running off along the shore to another promontory. They were leaving to get away from him. He cried openly, fists in his eyes. There was no one to see him, and he cried himself out.

It seemed to him that a long time had passed, and he swam out to where he could see his mother. Yes, she was still there, a yellow spot under an orange umbrella. He swam back to the big rock, climbed up, and dived into the blue pool among the fanged and angry boulders. Down he went, until he touched the wall of rock again. But the salt was so painful in his eyes that he could not see.

He came to the surface, swam to shore and went back to the villa to wait for his mother. Soon she walked slowly up the path, swinging her striped bag, the flushed, naked arm dangling beside her. "I want some swimming goggles," he panted, defiant and beseeching.

She gave him a patient, inquisitive look as she said casually, "Well, of   20 course, darling."

But now, now, now! He must have them this minute, and no other time. He nagged and pestered until she went with him to a shop. As soon as she had bought the goggles, he grabbed them from her hand as if she were going to claim them for herself, and was off, running down the steep path to the bay.

Jerry swam out to the big barrier rock, adjusted the goggles, and dived. The impact of the water broke the rubber-enclosed vacuum, and the goggles came loose. He understood that he must swim down to the base of the rock from the surface of the water. He fixed the goggles tight and firm, filled his lungs, and floated, face down, on the water. Now he could see. It was as if he had eyes of a different kind—fish-eyes that showed everything clear and delicate and wavering in the bright water.

Under him, six or seven feet down, was a floor of perfectly clean, shining white sand, rippled firm and hard by the tides. Two greyish shapes steered there, like long, rounded pieces of wood or slate. They were fish. He saw them nose towards each other, poise motionless, make a dart forward, swerve off, and come around again. It was like a water dance. A few inches above them, the water sparkled as if sequins were dropping through it. Fish again—myriads of minute fish, the length of his fingernail, were drifting through the water, and in a moment he could feel the innumerable tiny touches of them against his limbs. It was like swimming in flaked silver. The great rock the big boys had swum through rose sheer out of the white sand, black, tufted lightly with greenish weed. He could see no gap in it. He swam down to its base.

Again and again he rose, took a big chestful of air, and went down. Again and again he groped over the surface of the rock, feeling it, almost hugging it in the desperate need to find the entrance. And then, once, while he was clinging to the black wall, his knees came up and he shot his feet out forward and they met no obstacle. He had found the hole.

He gained the surface, clambered about the stones that littered the   25
barrier rock until he found a big one, and, with this in his arms, let himself down over the side of the rock. He dropped, with the weight, straight to the sandy floor. Clinging tight to the anchor of stone, he lay on his side and looked in under the dark shelf at the place where his feet had gone. He could see the hole. It was an irregular, dark gap, but he could not see deep into it. He let go of his anchor, clung with his hands to the edges of the hole, and tried to push himself in.

He got his head in, found his shoulders jammed, moved them in sidewise, and was inside as far as his waist. He could see nothing ahead. Something soft and clammy touched his mouth, he saw a dark frond moving against the greyish rock, and panic filled him. He thought of octopuses, of clinging weed. He pushed himself out backward and caught a glimpse, as he retreated, of a harmless tentacle of seaweed drifting in the mouth of the tunnel. But it was enough. He reached the sunlight, swam to shore, and lay on the diving rock. He looked down into the blue well of water. He knew he must find his way through that cave, or hole, or tunnel, and out the other side.

First, he thought, he must learn to control his breathing. He let himself down into the water with another big stone in his arms, so that he could lie effortlessly on the bottom of the sea. He counted. One, two, three. He counted steadily. He could hear the movement of blood in his chest. Fifty-one, fifty-two. . . . His chest was hurting. He let go of the rock and went up into the air. He saw that the sun was low. He rushed to the villa and found his mother at her supper. She said only "Did you enjoy yourself?" and he said "Yes."

All night, the boy dreamed of the water-filled cave in the rock, and as soon as breakfast was over he went to the bay.

That night, his nose bled badly. For hours he had been underwater, learning to hold his breath, and now he felt weak and dizzy. His mother said, "I shouldn't overdo things, darling, if I were you."

That day and the next, Jerry exercised his lungs as if everything, the whole of his life, all that he would become, depended upon it. And again his nose bled at night, and his mother insisted on his coming with her the next day. It was a torment to him to waste a day of his careful self-training, but he stayed with her on that other beach, which now seemed a place for small children, a place where his mother might lie safe in the sun. It was not his beach.

He did not ask for permission, on the following day, to go to his beach. He went, before his mother could consider the complicated rights and wrongs of the matter. A day's rest, he discovered, had improved his count by ten. The big boys had made the passage while he counted a hundred and sixty. He had been counting fast, in his fright. Probably now, if he tried, he could get through that long tunnel, but he was not going to try yet. A curious, most unchildlike persistence, a controlled impatience, made him wait. In the meantime, he lay underwater on the white sand, littered now by stones he had brought down from the upper air, and studied the entrance to the tunnel. He knew every jut and corner of it, as far as it was possible to see. It was as if he already felt its sharpness about his shoulders.

He sat by the clock in the villa, when his mother was not near, and checked his time. He was incredulous and then proud to find he could hold his breath without strain for two minutes. The words "two minutes," authorized by the clock, brought the adventure that was so necessary to him close.

In another four days, his mother said, casually one morning, they must go home. On the day before they left, he would do it. He would do it if it killed him, he said defiantly to himself. But two days before they were to leave—a day of triumph when he increased his count by fifteen—his nose bled so badly that he turned dizzy and had to lie limply over the big rock like a bit of seaweed, watching the thick red blood flow on to the rock and trickle slowly down to the sea. He was frightened. Supposing he turned dizzy in the tunnel? Supposing he died there, trapped? Supposing—his head went around, in the hot sun, and he almost gave up. He thought he would return to the house and lie down, and next summer, perhaps, when he had another year's growth in him — *then* he would go through the hole.

But even after he had made the decision, or thought he had, he found himself sitting up on the rock and looking down into the water, and he knew that now, this moment, when his nose had only just stopped bleeding, when his head was still sore and throbbing — this was the moment when he would try. If he did not do it now, he never would. He was trembling with fear that he would not go, and he was trembling with horror at that long, long tunnel under the rock, under the sea. Even in the open sunlight, the barrier rock seemed very wide and very heavy; tons of rock pressed down on where he would go. If he died there, he would lie until one day — perhaps not before next year — those big boys would swim into it and find it blocked.

He put on his goggles, fitted them tight, tested the vacuum. His hands   35
were shaking. Then he chose the biggest stone he could carry and slipped over the edge of the rock until half of him was in the cool, enclosing water and half in the hot sun. He looked up once at the empty sky, filled his lungs once, twice, and then sank fast to the bottom with the stone. He let it go and began to count. He took the edges of the hole in his hands and drew himself into it, wriggling his shoulders in sidewise as he remembered he must, kicking himself along with his feet.

Soon he was clear inside. He was in a small rock-bound hole filled with yellowish-grey water. The water was pushing him up against the roof. The roof was sharp and pained his back. He pulled himself along with his hands — fast, fast — and used his legs as levers. His head knocked against something; a sharp pain dizzied him. Fifty, fifty-one, fifty-two. . . . He was without light, and the water seemed to press upon him with the weight of rock. Seventy-one, seventy-two. . . . There was no strain on his lungs. He felt like an inflated balloon, his lungs were so light and easy, but his head was pulsing.

He was being continually pressed against the sharp roof, which felt slimy as well as sharp. Again he thought of octopuses, and wondered if the tunnel might be filled with weed that could tangle him. He gave himself a panicky, convulsive kick forward, ducked his head, and swam. His feet and hands moved freely, as if in open water. The hole must have widened out. He thought he must be swimming fast, and he was frightened of banging his head if the tunnel narrowed.

A hundred, a hundred and one. . . . The water paled. Victory filled him. His lungs were beginning to hurt. A few more strokes and he would be out. He was counting wildly; he said a hundred and fifteen, and then, a long time later, a hundred and fifteen again. The water was a clear jewel-green all around him. Then he saw, above his head, a crack running up through the rock. Sunlight was falling through it, showing the clean dark rock of the tunnel, a single mussel shell, and darkness ahead.

He was at the end of what he could do. He looked up at the crack as if it were filled with air and not water, as if he could put his mouth to it to draw in air. A hundred and fifteen, he heard himself say inside his head — but he had said that long ago. He must go on into the blackness ahead, or he would drown. His head was swelling, his lungs cracking. A hundred and fifteen, a hundred and fifteen pounded through his head, and he feebly clutched at rocks in the dark, pulling himself forward, leaving the brief space of sunlit water behind. He felt he was dying. He was no longer quite conscious. He struggled on in the darkness between lapses into unconsciousness. An immense, swelling pain filled his head, and then the darkness cracked with an explosion of green light. His hands, groping forward, met nothing, and his feet, kicking back, propelled him out into the open sea.

He drifted to the surface, his face turned up to the air. He was gasping   40
like a fish. He felt he would sink now and drown; he could not swim the few feet back to the rock. Then he was clutching it and pulling himself up on to it. He lay face down, gasping. He could see nothing but a red-veined, clotted dark. His eyes must have burst, he thought; they were full of blood. He tore off his goggles and a gout of blood went into the sea. His nose was bleeding, and the blood had filled the goggles.

He scooped up handfuls of water from the cool, salty sea, to splash on his face, and did not know whether it was blood or salt water he tasted. After a time, his heart quieted, his eyes cleared, and he sat up. He could see the local boys diving and playing half a mile away. He did not want them. He wanted nothing but to get back home and lie down.

In a short while, Jerry swam to shore and climbed slowly up the path to the villa. He flung himself on his bed and slept, waking at the sound of feet on the path outside. His mother was coming back. He rushed to the bathroom, thinking she must not see his face with bloodstains, or tearstains, on it. He came out of the bathroom and met her as she walked into the villa, smiling, her eyes lighting up.

"Have a nice morning?" she asked, laying her hand on his warm brown shoulder a moment.

"Oh, yes, thank you," he said.

"You look a bit pale." And then, sharp and anxious, "How did you   45
bang your head?"

"Oh, just banged it," he told her.

She looked at him closely. He was strained. His eyes were glazed-looking. She was worried. And then she said to herself, "Oh, don't fuss! Nothing can happen. He can swim like a fish."

They sat down to lunch together.

"Mummy," he said. "I can stay under water for two minutes — three minutes, at least." It came bursting out of him.

"Can you, darling?" she said. "Well, I shouldn't overdo it. I don't   50
think you ought to swim any more today."

She was ready for a battle of wills, but he gave in at once. It was no longer of the least importance to go to the bay.

Considerations

1. List several details from the opening section of the story that indicate the relationship between Jerry and his mother. Then, using these details as evidence, evaluate the relationship.
2. What comparison does Jerry make between his relationship with his mother and his relationship to the boys who dive from the rocks? Speculate on the ways this comparison might contribute to his decision to find and swim through the tunnel.
3. Trace the changes in Jerry's attitude toward his mother — and in her attitude toward him — throughout the story. Consider not only words and thoughts but also gestures and other actions.
4. What motivates Jerry's swim through the tunnel? When you were reading about the swim, did you think he might drown, or were you quite certain he would live? What details in the story led you to either prediction?
5. Describe a risk (physical, emotional, or intellectual) that you have taken. Explain your motives as well as the results of the risk-taking.

TILLIE OLSEN (1913–   )

I Stand Here Ironing

I stand here ironing, and what you asked me moves tormented back and forth with the iron.

"I wish you would manage the time to come in and talk with me about your daughter. I'm sure you can help me understand her. She's a youngster who needs help and whom I'm deeply interested in helping."

"Who needs help." . . . Even if I came, what good would it do? You think because I am her mother I have a key, or that in some way you could use me as a key? She has lived for nineteen years. There is all that life that has happened outside of me, beyond me.

And when is there time to remember, to sift, to weigh, to estimate, to total? I will start and there will be an interruption and I will have to gather it all together again. Or I will become engulfed with all I did or did not do, with what should have been and what cannot be helped.

She was a beautiful baby. The first and only one of our five that was beautiful at birth. You do not guess how new and uneasy her tenancy in her now-loveliness. You did not know her all those years she was thought homely, or see her poring over her baby pictures, making me tell her over and over how beautiful she had been — and would be, I would tell her — and was now, to the seeing eye. But the seeing eyes were few or nonexistent. Including mine.

I nursed her. They feel that's important nowadays. I nursed all the children, but with her, with all the fierce rigidity of first motherhood, I did like the books then said. Though her cries battered me to trembling and my breasts ached with swollenness, I waited till the clock decreed.

Why do I put that first? I do not even know if it matters, or if it explains anything.

She was a beautiful baby. She blew shining bubbles of sound. She loved motion, loved light, loved color and music and textures. She would lie on the floor in her blue overalls patting the surface so hard in ecstasy her hands and feet would blur. She was a miracle to me, but when she was eight months old I had to leave her daytimes with the woman downstairs to whom she was no miracle at all, for I worked or looked for work and for Emily's father, who "could no longer endure" (he wrote in his good-bye note) "sharing want with us."

I was nineteen. It was the pre-relief, pre-WPA world of the depression. I would start running as soon as I got off the streetcar, running up the stairs, the place smelling sour, and awake or asleep to startle awake, when she saw me she would break into a clogged weeping that could not be comforted, a weeping I can hear yet.

After a while I found a job hashing at night so I could be with her days, and it was better. But it came to where I had to bring her to his family and leave her.

It took a long time to raise the money for her fare back. Then she got chicken pox and I had to wait longer. When she finally came, I hardly knew her, walking quick and nervous like her father, looking like her father, thin, and dressed in a shoddy red that yellowed her skin and glared at the pockmarks. All the baby loveliness gone.

She was two. Old enough for nursery school they said, and I did not know then what I know now — the fatigue of the long day, and the lacerations of group life in the kinds of nurseries that are only parking places for children.

Except that it would have made no difference if I had known. It was the only place there was. It was the only way we could be together, the only way I could hold a job.

And even without knowing, I knew. I knew the teacher that was evil because all these years it has curdled into my memory, the little boy hunched in the corner, her rasp, "why aren't you outside, because Alvin hits you? that's no reason, go out, scaredy." I knew Emily hated it even if she did not clutch and implore "don't go Mommy" like the other children, mornings.

She always had a reason why we should stay home. Momma, you look sick. Momma, I feel sick. Momma, the teachers aren't there today, they're sick. Momma, we can't go, there was a fire there last night. Momma, it's a holiday today, no school, they told me.

But never a direct protest, never rebellion. I think of our others in their three-, four-year-oldness — the explosions, the tempers, the denunciations, the demands — and I feel suddenly ill. I put the iron down. What in me demanded that goodness in her? And what was the cost, the cost to her of such goodness?

The old man living in the back once said in his gentle way: "You should smile at Emily more when you look at her." What *was* in my face when I looked at her? I loved her. There were all the acts of love.

It was only with the others I remembered what he said, and it was the face of joy, and not of care or tightness or worry I turned to them — too late for Emily. She does not smile easily, let alone almost always as her brothers and sisters do. Her face is closed and sombre, but when she wants, how fluid. You must have seen it in her pantomimes, you spoke of her rare gift for comedy on the stage that rouses a laughter out of the audience so dear they applaud and applaud and do not want to let her go.

Where does it come from, that comedy? There was none of it in her when she came back to me that second time, after I had had to send her away again. She had a new daddy now to learn to love, and I think perhaps it was a better time.

Except when we left her alone nights, telling ourselves she was old enough.

"Can't you go some other time, Mommy, like tomorrow?" she would ask. "Will it be just a little while you'll be gone? Do you promise?"

The time we came back, the front door open, the clock on the floor in the hall. She rigid awake. "It wasn't just a little while. I didn't cry. Three times I called you, just three times, and then I ran downstairs to open the door so you could come faster. The clock talked loud. I threw it away, it scared me what it talked."

She said the clock talked loud again that night I went to the hospital to have Susan. She was delirious with the fever that comes before red measles, but she was fully conscious all the week I was gone and the week after we were home when she could not come near the new baby or me.

She did not get well. She stayed skeleton thin, not wanting to eat, and night after night she had nightmares. She would call for me, and I would rouse from exhaustion to sleepily call back: "You're all right, darling, go to sleep, it's just a dream," and if she still called, in a sterner voice, "now go to sleep, Emily, there's nothing to hurt you." Twice, only twice, when I had to get up for Susan anyhow, I went in to sit with her.

Now when it is too late (as if she would let me hold and comfort her   25 like I do the others) I get up and go to her at once at her moan or restless stirring. "Are you awake, Emily? Can I get you something?" And the answer is always the same: "No, I'm all right, go back to sleep, Mother."

They persuaded me at the clinic to send her away to a convalescent home in the country where "she can have the kind of food and care you can't manage for her, and you'll be free to concentrate on the new baby." They still send children to that place. I see pictures on the society page of sleek young women planning affairs to raise money for it, or dancing at the affairs, or decorating Easter eggs or filling Christmas stockings for the children.

They never have a picture of the children so I do not know if the girls still wear those gigantic red bows and the ravaged looks on the every other Sunday when the parents can come to visit "unless otherwise notified" — as we were notified the first six weeks.

Oh it is a handsome place, green lawns and tall trees and fluted flower beds. High up on the balconies of each cottage the children stand, the girls in their red bows and white dresses, the boys in white suits and giant red ties. The parents stand below shrieking up to be heard and the children shriek down to be heard, and between them the invisible wall "Not To Be Contaminated by Parental Germs or Physical Affection."

There was a tiny girl who always stood hand in hand with Emily. Her parents never came. One visit she was gone. "They moved her to Rose Cottage" Emily shouted in explanation. "They don't like you to love anybody here."

She wrote once a week, the labored writing of a seven-year-old. "I am   30 fine. How is the baby. If I write my leter nicely I will have a star. Love." There never was a star. We wrote every other day, letters she could never hold or keep but only hear read — once. "We simply do not have room for children to keep any personal possessions," they patiently explained when we pieced one Sunday's shrieking together to plead how much it would mean to Emily, who loved so to keep things, to be allowed to keep her letters and cards.

Each visit she looked frailer. "She isn't eating," they told us.

(They had runny eggs for breakfast or mush with lumps, Emily said later, I'd hold it in my mouth and not swallow. Nothing ever tasted good, just when they had chicken.)

It took us eight months to get her released home, and only the fact that she gained back so little of her seven lost pounds convinced the social worker.

I used to try to hold and love her after she came back, but her body would stay stiff, and after a while she'd push away. She ate little. Food sickened her, and I think much of life too. Oh she had physical lightness and brightness, twinkling by on skates, bouncing like a ball up and down up and down over the jump rope, skimming over the hill; but these were momentary.

She fretted about her appearance, thin and dark and foreign-looking at a time when every little girl was supposed to look or thought she should look a chubby blonde replica of Shirley Temple. The doorbell sometimes rang for her, but no one seemed to come and play in the house or be a best friend. Maybe because we moved so much.   35

There was a boy she loved painfully through two school semesters. Months later she told me how she had taken pennies from my purse to buy him candy. "Licorice was his favorite and I brought him some every day, but he still liked Jennifer better'n me. Why, Mommy?" The kind of question for which there is no answer.

School was a worry to her. She was not glib or quick in a world where glibness and quickness were easily confused with ability to learn. To her overworked and exasperated teachers she was an overconscientious "slow learner" who kept trying to catch up and was absent entirely too often.

I let her be absent, though sometimes the illness was imaginary. How different from my now-strictness about attendance with the others. I wasn't working. We had a new baby, I was home anyhow. Sometimes, after Susan grew old enough, I would keep her home from school, too, to have them all together.

Mostly Emily had asthma, and her breathing, harsh and labored, would fill the house with a curiously tranquil sound. I would bring the two old dresser mirrors and her boxes of collections to her bed. She would select beads and single earrings, bottle tops and shells, dried flowers and pebbles, old postcards and scraps, all sorts of oddments; then she and Susan would play Kingdom, setting up landscapes and furniture, peopling them with action.

Those were the only times of peaceful companionship between her and   40
Susan. I have edged away from it, that poisonous feeling between them, that

terrible balancing of hurts and needs I had to do between the two, and did so badly, those earlier years.

Oh there are conflicts between the others too, each one human, needing, demanding, hurting, taking — but only between Emily and Susan, no, Emily toward Susan that corroding resentment. It seems so obvious on the surface, yet it is not obvious. Susan, the second child, Susan, golden- and curly-haired and chubby, quick and articulate and assured, everything in appearance and manner Emily was not; Susan, not able to resist Emily's precious things, losing or sometimes clumsily breaking them; Susan telling jokes and riddles to company for applause while Emily sat silent (to say to me later; that was *my* riddle, Mother, I told it to Susan); Susan, who for all the five years' difference in age was just a year behind Emily in developing physically.

I am glad for that slow physical development that widened the difference between her and her contemporaries, though she suffered over it. She was too vulnerable for that terrible world of youthful competition, of preening and parading, of constant measuring of yourself against every other, of envy, "If I had that copper hair," "If I had that skin. . . ." She tormented herself enough about not looking like the others, there was enough of the unsureness, the having to be conscious of words before you speak, the constant caring — what are they thinking of me? without having it all magnified by the merciless physical drives.

Ronnie is calling. He is wet and I change him. It is rare there is such a cry now. That time of motherhood is almost behind me when the ear is not one's own but must always be racked and listening for the child cry, the child call. We sit for a while and I hold him, looking out over the city spread in charcoal with its soft aisles of light. *"Shoogily,"* he breathes and curls closer. I carry him back to bed, asleep. *Shoogily.* A funny word, a family word, inherited from Emily, invented by her to say: *comfort.*

In this and other ways she leaves her seal, I say aloud. And startle at my saying it. What do I mean? What did I start to gather together, to try and make coherent? I was at the terrible, growing years. War years. I do not remember them well. I was working, there were four smaller ones now, there was not time for her. She had to help be a mother, and housekeeper, and shopper. She had to set her seal. Mornings of crisis and near hysteria trying to get lunches packed, hair combed, coats and shoes found, everyone to school or Child Care on time, the baby ready for transportation. And always the paper scribbled on by a smaller one, the book looked at by Susan then mislaid, the homework not done. Running out to that huge school where she was one, she was lost, she was a drop; suffering over the unpreparedness, stammering and unsure in her classes.

There was so little time left at night after the kids were bedded down. She would struggle over books, always eating (it was in those years she developed her enormous appetite that is legendary in our family) and I would be ironing, or preparing food for the next day, or writing V-mail to

Bill, or tending the baby. Sometimes, to make me laugh, or out of her despair, she would imitate happenings or types at school.

I think I said once: "Why don't you do something like this in the school amateur show?" One morning she phoned me at work, hardly understandable through the weeping: "Mother, I did it. I won, I won; they gave me first prize; they clapped and clapped and wouldn't let me go."

Now suddenly she was Somebody, and as imprisoned in her difference as she had been in anonymity.

She began to be asked to perform at other high schools, even in colleges, then at city and statewide affairs. The first one we went to, I only recognized her that first moment when thin, shy, she almost drowned herself into the curtains. Then: Was this Emily? The control, the command, the convulsing and deadly clowning, the spell, then the roaring, stamping audience, unwilling to let this rare and precious laughter out of their lives.

Afterwards: You ought to do something about her with a gift like that — but without money or knowing how, what does one do? We have left it all to her, and the gift has as often eddied inside, clogged and clotted, as been used and growing.

She is coming. She runs up the stairs two at a time with her light graceful step, and I know she is happy tonight. Whatever it was that occasioned your call did not happen today. 50

"Aren't you ever going to finish the ironing, Mother? Whistler painted his mother in a rocker. I'd have to paint mine standing over an ironing board." This is one of her communicative nights and she tells me everything and nothing as she fixes herself a plate of food out of the icebox.

She is so lovely. Why did you want me to come in at all? Why were you concerned? She will find her way.

She starts up the stairs to bed. "Don't get me up with the rest in the morning." "But I thought you were having midterms." "Oh, those," she comes back in, kisses me, and says quite lightly, "in a couple of years when we'll all be atom-dead they won't matter a bit."

She has said it before. She *believes* it. But because I have been dredging the past, and all that compounds a human being is so heavy and meaningful in me, I cannot endure it tonight.

I will never total it all. I will never come in to say: She was a child 55 seldom smiled at. Her father left me before she was a year old. I had to work her first six years when there was work, or I sent her home and to his relatives. There were years she had care she hated. She was dark and thin and foreign-looking in a world where the prestige went to blondeness and curly hair and dimples, she was slow where glibness was prized. She was a child of anxious, not proud, love. We were poor and could not afford for her the soil of easy growth. I was a young mother, I was a distracted mother. There were the other children pushing up, demanding. Her younger sister seemed all that she was not. There were years she did not want me to touch her. She kept too much in herself, her life was such she had to keep too much in herself. My wisdom came too late. She has much to her and prob-ably little will come of it. She is a child of her age, of depression, of war, of fear.

Let her be. So all that is in her will not bloom — but in how many does it? There is still enough left to live by. Only help her to know — help make it so there is cause for her to know — that she is more than this dress on the ironing board, helpless before the iron.

Considerations

1. What incident prompts the mother's long meditation as she stands at the ironing board? How does this incident suggest the relationship between the mother, her daughter, and the authority figures who have, to one degree or another, controlled the lives of both mother and daughter?
2. Make a list of the circumstances the mother sees as having prevented her from taking care of her children as she would have liked. To what extent do you find her explanations valid? To what extent do you find her explanations to be rationalizations?
3. The act of ironing is mentioned in the title, in the opening section, and in the conclusion. How does ironing serve as a metaphor for the mother's life? How does the mother use ironing as a metaphor to suggest the hopes she holds for her daughter's life?
4. How has Emily been affected by the circumstances of her life? Have the effects of these circumstances been entirely negative? Entirely positive?
5. Imagine that you are Emily and you have come across "I Stand Here Ironing" written as a meditation in the diary your mother has left open on the dining room table. Write a response to the feelings and ideas she has expressed.

LESLIE MARMON SILKO (1948–   )

Lullaby

The sun had gone down but the snow in the wind gave off its own light. It came in thick tufts like new wool — washed before the weaver spins it. Ayah reached out for it like her own babies had, and she smiled when she remembered how she had laughed at them. She was an old woman now, and her life had become memories. She sat down with her back against the wide cottonwood tree, feeling the rough bark on her back bones; she faced east and listened to the wind and snow sing a high-pitched Yeibechei° song. Out of the wind she felt warmer, and she could watch the wide fluffy snow fill in her tracks, steadily, until the direction she had come from was gone. By the light of the snow she could see the dark outline of the big arroyo a few feet away. She was sitting on the edge of Cebolleta Creek, where in the springtime the thin cows would graze on grass already chewed flat to the ground. In the wide deep creek bed where only a trickle of water flowed in the summer, the skinny cows would wander, looking for new grass along winding paths splashed with manure.

Ayah pulled the old Army blanket over her head like a shawl. Jimmie's blanket — the one he had sent to her. That was a long time ago and the green wool was faded, and it was unraveling on the edges. She did not want to think about Jimmie. So she thought about the weaving and the way her mother had done it. On the tall wooden loom set into the sand under a tamarack tree for shade. She could see it clearly. She had been only a little girl when her grandma gave her the wooden combs to pull the twigs and burrs from the raw, freshly washed wool. And while she combed the wool, her grandma sat beside her, spinning a silvery strand of yarn around the smooth cedar spindle. Her mother worked at the loom with yarns dyed bright yellow and red and gold. She watched them dye the yarn in boiling black pots full of beeweed petals, juniper berries, and sage. The blankets her mother made were soft and woven so tight that rain rolled off them like birds' feathers. Ayah remembered sleeping warm on cold windy nights, wrapped in her mother's blankets on the hogan's sandy floor.

The snow drifted now, with the northwest wind hurling it in gusts. It drifted up around her black overshoes — old ones with little metal buckles. She smiled at the snow which was trying to cover her little by little. She could remember when they had no black rubber overshoes; only the high buckskin leggings that they wrapped over their elkhide moccasins. If the snow was dry or frozen, a person could walk all day and not get wet; and in the evenings the beams of the ceiling would hang with lengths of pale buckskin leggings, drying out slowly.

Yeibechei: A night chant sung for healing.

She felt peaceful remembering. She didn't feel cold any more. Jimmie's blanket seemed warmer than it had ever been. And she could remember the morning he was born. She could remember whispering to her mother, who was sleeping on the other side of the hogan°, to tell her it was time now. She did not want to wake the others. The second time she called to her, her mother stood up and pulled on her shoes; she knew. They walked to the old stone hogan together, Ayah walking a step behind her mother. She waited alone, learning the rhythms of the pains while her mother went to call the old woman to help them. The morning was already warm even before dawn and Ayah smelled the bee flowers blooming and the young willow growing at the springs. She could remember that so clearly, but his birth merged into the births of the other children and to her it became all the same birth. They named him for the summer morning and in English they called him Jimmie.

It wasn't like Jimmie died. He just never came back, and one day a   5 dark blue sedan with white writing on its doors pulled up in front of the boxcar shack where the rancher let the Indians live. A man in a khaki uniform trimmed in gold gave them a yellow piece of paper and told them that Jimmie was dead. He said the Army would try to get the body back and then it would be shipped to them; but it wasn't likely because the helicopter had burned after it crashed. All of this was told to Chato because he could understand English. She stood inside the doorway holding the baby while Chato listened. Chato spoke English like a white man and he spoke Spanish too. He was taller than the white man and he stood straighter too. Chato didn't explain why; he just told the military man they could keep the body if they found it. The white man looked bewildered; he nodded his head and he left. Then Chato looked at her and shook his head, and then he told her, "Jimmie isn't coming home anymore," and when he spoke, he used the words to speak of the dead. She didn't cry then, but she hurt inside with anger. And she mourned him as the years passed, when a horse fell with Chato and broke his leg, and the white rancher told them he wouldn't pay Chato until he could work again. She mourned Jimmie because he would have worked for his father then; he would have saddled the big bay horse and ridden the fence lines each day, with wire cutters and heavy gloves, fixing the breaks in the barbed wire and putting the stray cattle back inside again.

She mourned him after the white doctors came to take Danny and Ella away. She was at the shack alone that day they came. It was back in the days before they hired Navajo women to go with them as interpreters. She recognized one of the doctors. She had seen him at the children's clinic at Cañoncito about a month ago. They were wearing khaki uniforms and they waved papers at her and a black ball-point pen, trying to make her understand their English words. She was frightened by the way they looked at the

---

hogan: Traditional Navajo dwelling.

children, like the lizard watches the fly. Danny was swinging on the tire swing on the elm tree behind the rancher's house, and Ella was toddling around the front door, dragging the broomstick horse Chato made for her. Ayah could see they wanted her to sign the papers, and Chato had taught her to sign her name. It was something she was proud of. She only wanted them to go, and to take their eyes away from her children.

She took the pen from the man without looking at his face and she signed the papers in three different places he pointed to. She stared at the ground by their feet and waited for them to leave. But they stood there and began to point and gesture at the children. Danny stopped swinging. Ayah could see his fear. She moved suddenly and grabbed Ella into her arms; the child squirmed, trying to get back to her toys. Ayah ran with the baby toward Danny; she screamed for him to run and then she grabbed him around his chest and carried him too. She ran south into the foothills of juniper trees and black lava rock. Behind her she heard the doctors running, but they had been taken by surprise, and as the hills became steeper and the cholla cactus were thicker, they stopped. When she reached the top of the hill, she stopped to listen in case they were circling around her. But in a few minutes she heard a car engine start and they drove away. The children had been too surprised to cry while she ran with them. Danny was shaking and Ella's little fingers were gripping Ayah's blouse.

She stayed up in the hills for the rest of the day, sitting on a black lava boulder in the sunshine where she could see for miles all around her. The sky was light blue and cloudless, and it was warm for late April. The sun warmth relaxed her and took the fear and anger away. She lay back on the rock and watched the sky. It seemed to her that she could walk into the sky, stepping through clouds endlessly. Danny played with little pebbles and stones, pretending they were birds eggs and then little rabbits. Ella sat at her feet and dropped fistfuls of dirt into the breeze, watching the dust and particles of sand intently. Ayah watched a hawk soar high above them, dark wings gliding; hunting or only watching, she did not know. The hawk was patient and he circled all afternoon before he disappeared around the high volcanic peak the Mexicans called Guadalupe.

Late in the afternoon, Ayah looked down at the gray boxcar shack with the paint all peeled from the wood; the stove pipe on the roof was rusted and crooked. The fire she had built that morning in the oil drum stove had burned out. Ella was asleep in her lap now and Danny sat close to her, complaining that he was hungry; he asked when they would go to the house. "We will stay up here until your father comes," she told him, "because those white men were chasing us." The boy remembered then and he nodded at her silently.

If Jimmie had been there he could have read those papers and explained to her what they said. Ayah would have known then, never to sign them. The doctors came back the next day and they brought a BIA° policeman   10

BIA: Bureau of Indian Affairs.

with them. They told Chato they had her signature and that was all they needed. Except for the kids. She listened to Chato sullenly; she hated him when he told her it was the old woman who died in the winter, spitting blood; it was her old grandma who had given the children this disease. "They don't spit blood," she said coldly. "The whites lie." She held Ella and Danny close to her, ready to run to the hills again. "I want a medicine man first," she said to Chato, not looking at him. He shook his head. "It's too late now. The policeman is with them. You signed the paper." His voice was gentle.

It was worse than if they had died: to lose the children and to know that somewhere, in a place called Colorado, in a place full of sick and dying strangers, her children were without her. There had been babies that died soon after they were born, and one that died before he could walk. She had carried them herself, up to the boulders and great pieces of the cliff that long ago crashed down from Long Mesa; she laid them in the crevices of sandstone and buried them in fine brown sand with round quartz pebbles that washed down the hills in the rain. She had endured it because they had been with her. But she could not bear this pain. She did not sleep for a long time after they took her children. She stayed on the hill where they had fled the first time, and she slept rolled up in the blanket Jimmie had sent her. She carried the pain in her belly and it was fed by everything she saw: the blue sky of their last day together and the dust and pebbles they played with; the swing in the elm tree and broomstick horse choked life from her. The pain filled her stomach and there was no room for food or for her lungs to fill with air. The air and the food would have been theirs.

She hated Chato, not because he let the policeman and doctors put the screaming children in the government car, but because he had taught her to sign her name. Because it was like the old ones always told her about learning their language or any of their ways: it endangered you. She slept alone on the hill until the middle of November when the first snows came. Then she made a bed for herself where the children had slept. She did not lie down beside Chato again until many years later, when he was sick and shivering and only her body could keep him warm. The illness came after the white rancher told Chato he was too old to work for him anymore, and Chato and his old woman should be out of the shack by the next afternoon because the rancher had hired new people to work there. That had satisfied her. To see how the white man repaid Chato's years of loyalty and work. All of Chato's fine-sounding English talk didn't change things.

It snowed steadily and the luminous light from the snow gradually diminished into the darkness. Somewhere in Cebolleta a dog barked and other village dogs joined with it. Ayah looked in the direction she had come, from the bar where Chato was buying the wine. Sometimes he told her to go on ahead and wait; and then he never came. And when she finally went back looking for him, she would find him passed out at the bottom of the wooden steps to Azzie's Bar. All the wine would be gone and most of the money too, from the pale blue check that came to them once a month in a government envelope. It was then that she would look at his face and his hands, scarred by ropes and the barbed wire of all those years, and she would think, this man is a stranger; for forty years she had smiled at him and cooked his food, but he remained a stranger. She stood up again, with the snow almost to her knees, and she walked back to find Chato.

It was hard to walk in the deep snow and she felt the air burn in her lungs. She stopped a short distance from the bar to rest and readjust the blanket. But this time he wasn't waiting for her on the bottom step with his old Stetson hat pulled down and his shoulders hunched up in his long wool overcoat.

She was careful not to slip on the wooden steps. When she pushed the door open, warm air and cigarette smoke hit her face. She looked around slowly and deliberately, in every corner, in every dark place that the old man might find to sleep. The bar owner didn't like Indians in there, especially Navajos, but he let Chato come in because he could talk Spanish like he was one of them. The men at the bar stared at her, and the bartender saw that she left the door open wide. Snowflakes were flying inside like moths and melting into a puddle on the oiled wood floor. He motioned to her to close the door, but she did not see him. She held herself straight and walked across the room slowly, searching the room with every step. The snow in her hair melted and she could feel it on her forehead. At the far corner of the room, she saw red flames at the mica window of the old stove door; she looked behind the stove just to make sure. The bar got quiet except for the Spanish polka music playing on the jukebox. She stood by the stove and shook the snow from her blanket and held it near the stove to dry. The wet wool smell reminded her of new-born goats in early March, brought inside to warm near the fire. She felt calm.

In past years they would have told her to get out. But her hair was white now and her face was wrinkled. They looked at her like she was a spider crawling slowly across the room. They were afraid; she could feel the fear. She looked at their faces steadily. They reminded her of the first time the white people brought her children back to her that winter. Danny had been shy and hid behind the thin white woman who brought them. And the baby had not known her until Ayah took her into her arms, and then Ella had nuzzled close to her as she had when she was nursing. The blonde woman was nervous and kept looking at a dainty gold watch on her wrist. She sat on the bench near the small window and watched the dark snow clouds gather around the mountains; she was worrying about the unpaved road. She was frightened by what she saw inside too: the strips of venison drying on a rope across the ceiling and the children jabbering excitedly in a language she did not know. So they stayed for only a few hours. Ayah watched the government car disappear down the road and she knew they

15

were already being weaned from these lava hills and from this sky. The last time they came was in early June, and Ella stared at her the way the men in the bar were now staring. Ayah did not try to pick her up; she smiled at her instead and spoke cheerfully to Danny. When he tried to answer her, he could not seem to remember and he spoke English words with the Navajo. But he gave her a scrap of paper that he had found somewhere and carried in his pocket; it was folded in half, and he shyly looked up at her and said it was a bird. She asked Chato if they were home for good this time. He spoke to the white woman and she shook her head. "How much longer?" he asked, and she said she didn't know; but Chato saw how she stared at the boxcar shack. Ayah turned away then. She did not say good-bye.

She felt satisfied that the men in the bar feared her. Maybe it was her face and the way she held her mouth with teeth clenched tight, like there was nothing anyone could do to her now. She walked north down the road, searching for the old man. She did this because she had the blanket, and there would be no place for him except with her and the blanket in the old adobe barn near the arroyo. They always slept there when they came to Cebolleta. If the money and the wine were gone, she would be relieved because then they could go home again; back to the old hogan with a dirt roof and rock walls where she herself had been born. And the next day the old man could go back to the few sheep they still had, to follow along behind them, guiding them, into dry sandy arroyos where sparse grass grew. She knew he did not like walking behind old ewes when for so many years he rode big quarter horses and worked with cattle. But she wasn't sorry for him; he should have known all along what would happen.

There had not been enough rain for their garden in five years; and that was when Chato finally hitched a ride into the town and brought back brown boxes of rice and sugar and big tin cans of welfare peaches. After that, at the first of the month they went to Cebolleta to ask the postmaster for the check; and then Chato would go to the bar and cash it. They did this as they planted the garden every May, not because anything would survive the summer dust, but because it was time to do this. The journey passed the days that smelled silent and dry like the caves above the canyon with yellow painted buffaloes on their walls.

He was walking along the pavement when she found him. He did not stop or turn around when he heard her behind him. She walked beside him and she noticed how slowly he moved now. He smelled strong of wood-smoke and urine. Lately he had been forgetting. Sometimes he called her by his sister's name and she had been gone for a long time. Once she had found him wandering on the road to the white man's ranch, and she asked him why he was going that way; he laughed at her and said, "You know they can't run that ranch without me," and he walked on determined, limping on the leg that had been crushed many years before. Now he looked at her curiously, as if for the first time, but he kept shuffling along, moving slowly along the side of the highway. His gray hair had grown long and spread out on the shoulders of the long overcoat. He wore the old felt hat pulled down over his ears. His boots were worn out at the toes and he had stuffed pieces of an old red shirt in the holes. The rags made his feet look like little animals up to their ears in snow. She laughed at his feet; the snow muffled the sound of her laugh. He stopped and looked at her again. The wind had quit blowing and the snow was falling straight down; the southeast sky was beginning to clear and Ayah could see a star.

"Let's rest awhile," she said to him. They walked away from the road and up the slope to the giant boulders that had tumbled down from the red sandrock mesa throughout the centuries of rainstorms and earth tremors. In a place where the boulders shut out the wind, they sat down with their backs against the rock. She offered half of the blanket to him and they sat wrapped together.

The storm passed swiftly. The clouds moved east. They were massive and full, crowding together across the sky. She watched them with the feeling of horses — steely blue-gray horses startled across the sky. The powerful haunches pushed into the distances and the tail hairs streamed white mist behind them. The sky cleared. Ayah saw that there was nothing between her and the stars. The light was crystalline. There was no shimmer, no distortion through earth haze. She breathed the clarity of the night sky; she smelled the purity of the half moon and the stars. He was lying on his side with his knees pulled up near his belly for warmth. His eyes were closed now, and in the light from the stars and the moon, he looked young again.

She could see it descend out of the night sky: an icy stillness from the edge of the thin moon. She recognized the freezing. It came gradually, sinking snowflake by snowflake until the crust was heavy and deep. It had the strength of the stars in Orion, and its journey was endless. Ayah knew that with the wine he would sleep. He would not feel it. She tucked the blanket around him, remembering how it was when Ella had been with her; and she felt the rush so big inside her heart for the babies. And she sang the only song she knew to sing for babies. She could not remember if she had ever sung it to her children, but she knew that her grandmother had sung it and her mother had sung it:

> *The earth is your mother,*
>   *she holds you.*
> *The sky is your father,*
>   *he protects you.*
> *Sleep,*
> *sleep.*
> *Rainbow is your sister,*
>   *she loves you.*

The winds are your brothers,
   they sing to you.
Sleep,
sleep.
We are together always
We are together always
There never was a time
when this
was not so.

Considerations

1. Read the opening paragraphs closely. Evaluate Ayah's memories, and speculate on what these memories tell about her and why they are so important to her.
2. Where and when does this story take place? What details indicate this setting? How important is the setting to the conflicts, actions, and character development of the story?
3. Why does Ayah hate Chato "because he had taught her to sign her name"? What does she mean by this? How does her response relate to her feelings about her husband and about her children?
4. How do the children change while they are away at the tuberculosis hospital? How does Ayah change? How do her memories of these changes relate to her going into the bar to bring Chato home and to her satisfaction that those inside the bar fear her?
5. What significance do you see in the lullaby Ayah sings at the end of the story?

THEODORE ROETHKE (1908–1963)

My Papa's Waltz

The whiskey on your breath
Could make a small boy dizzy;
But I hung on like death
Such waltzing was not easy.

We romped until the pans
Slid from the kitchen shelf;
My mother's countenance
Could not unfrown itself.

5

The hand that held my wrist
Was battered on one knuckle;
At every step you missed
My right ear scraped a buckle.

You beat time on my head
With a palm caked hard by dirt,
Then waltzed me off to bed
Still clinging to your shirt.

Considerations

1. List the images describing the father and his bedtime dance with his son. Do these words suggest the experience was positive? Negative? A mix? Explain.
2. Why is the mother frowning? Speculate on her reasons for refusing to join in the kitchen romp.
3. Rewrite this poem as a prose description of the same scene. Evaluate the changes that you make and comment on the way these changes alter the view of the experience described in the poem.

MAXINE W. KUMIN (1925–   )

Making the Jam without You

for Judy

Old daughter, small traveler
asleep in a German featherbed
under the eaves in a postcard town
of turrets and towers,
I am putting a dream in your head.

Listen! Here it is afternoon.
The rain comes down like bullets.
I stand in the kitchen,
that harem of good smells
where we have bumped hips and
cracked the cupboards with our talk
while the stove top danced with pots
and it was not clear who did
the mothering. Now I am

5

10

crushing blackberries   15
to make the annual jam
in a white cocoon of steam.

Take it, my sleeper. Redo it
in any of your three
languages and nineteen years.   20
Change the geography.
Let there be a mountain,
the fat cows on it belled
like a cathedral. Let
there be someone beside you   25
as you come upon the ruins
of a schloss°, all overgrown   *castle*
with a glorious thicket,
its brambles soft as wool.
Let him bring the buckets   30
crooked on his angel arms
and may the berries, vaster
than any forage in
the mild hills of New Hampshire,
drop in your pail, plum size,   35
heavy as the eyes
of an honest dog
and may you bear them
home together to a square
white unreconstructed kitchen   40
not unlike this one.

Now may your two heads
touch over the kettle,
over the blood of the berries
that drink up sugar and sun,   45
over that tar-thick boil
love cannot stir down.
More plainly than
the bric-a-brac of shelves
filling with jelly glasses,   50
more surely than
the light driving through them
trite as rubies, I see him
as pale as paraffin beside you.
I see you cutting   55
fresh baked bread to spread it
with the bright royal fur.

At this time
I lift the flap of your dream
and slip out thinner than a sliver   60
as your two mouths open
for the sweet stain of purple.

Considerations

1. What do the details of this poem tell you about the mother? About the
   daughter? How old would you guess each of these women is?
2. Write a brief summary of the dream the mother builds for her daughter.
   Why does she choose to leave that dream?
3. How might making jam serve as a metaphor for the relationship between
   this mother and her daughter?

JUDITH ORTIZ COFER (1952–   )

My Father in the Navy: A Childhood Memory

Stiff and immaculate
in the white cloth of his uniform
and a round cap on his head like a halo,
he was an apparition on leave from a shadow-world
and only flesh and blood when he rose from below   5
the waterline where he kept watch over the engines
and dials making sure the ship parted the waters
on a straight course.
Mother, brother and I kept vigil
on the nights and dawns of his arrivals,   10
watching the corner beyond the neon sign of a quasar
for the flash of white our father like an angel
heralding a new day.
His homecomings were the verses
we composed over the years making up   15
the siren's song that kept him coming back
from the bellies of iron whales
and into our nights
like the evening prayer.

Considerations

1. Make a list of the images describing the father. Then make a list of the
   images describing the way the speaker, her mother, and brother waited

for the father's return. Evaluate the speaker's view of her father and her view of the relationship between him and the rest of the family.

2. Imagine that you are the mother in the poem. Write a journal entry describing the emotions you experience and the thoughts you have as you wait for your husband's return from sea duty.

3. Both Frank O'Connor's "My Oedipus Complex" and Judith Ortiz Cofer's "My Father in the Navy" describe the experience of absent fathers and of their homecomings. What similarities and differences do you see between the two works?

ROBERT MEZEY (1935–   )

My Mother

My mother writes from Trenton,
a comedian to the bone
but underneath, serious
and all heart. "Honey," she says,
"be a mensch and Mary too,   5
it's no good to worry, you
are doing the best you can
your Dad and everyone
thinks you turned out very well
as long as you pay your bills   10
nobody can say a word
you can tell them to drop dead
so save a dollar it can't
hurt—remember Frank you went
to highschool with? he still lives   15
with his wife's mother, his wife
works while he writes his books and
did he ever sell a one
the four kids run around naked
36 and he's never had,   20
you'll forgive my expression
even a pot to piss in
or a window to throw it,
such a smart boy he couldn't
read the footprints on the wall   25
honey you think you know all
the answers you don't, please try
to put some money away
believe me it wouldn't hurt

artist shmartist life's too short   30
for that kind of, forgive me,
horseshit, I know what you want
better than you, all that counts
is to make a good living
and the best of everything,   35
as Sholem Aleichem said
he was a great writer did
you ever read his books dear,
you should make what he makes a year
anyway he says some place   40
Poverty is no disgrace
but it's no honor either
that's what I say,
love,
Mother"   45

Considerations

1. How do you respond to the mother in the poem? How does your response compare with her son's response (as suggested by his description of her)?
2. List several phrases from the poem that describe the mother. Then write a paragraph explaining what you can infer from those details.
3. What is the mother in this poem trying to convince her son to do? What strategies does she use to persuade her son to accept her point of view? How convincing do you find her argument?

ELLEN WOLFE (1948–   )

Amniocentesis°
for Yona

Lie up under the umbrella of my ribs
my new island
Sleep while the thin throat
samples your lake
First planting in my old body   5
they worry about you

Amniocentesis: Surgical procedure performed on a pregnant woman to determine the presence of disease or genetic defects in the fetus.

These people who fear monsters
will be looking for monsters
They will be looking for the skewed pattern
the aberrant piece   10
of your chromosome puzzle
Love
they will be listening
Sing for them
your perfect song   15

Considerations

1. Whom is the speaker addressing? What is her message?
2. Who are the "people who fear monsters"? What is the attitude of the speaker toward these people? What is your response toward this attitude?
3. Discuss the hopes and fears implied by the images and theme of this poem.

SEAMUS HEANEY (1939–   )

Digging

Between my finger and my thumb
The squat pen rests; snug as a gun.

Under my window, a clean rasping sound
When the spade sinks into gravelly ground:
My father, digging. I look down   5

Till his straining rump among the flowerbeds
Bends low, comes up twenty years away
Stooping in rhythm through potato drills
Where he was digging.

The coarse boot nestled on the lug, the shaft   10
Against the inside knee was levered firmly.
He rooted out tall tops, buried the bright edge deep
To scatter new potatoes that we picked
Loving their cool hardness in our hands.

By God, the old man could handle a spade.   15
Just like his old man.

My grandfather cut more turf in a day
Than any other man on Toner's bog.
Once I carried him milk in a bottle
Corked sloppily with paper. He straightened up   20
To drink it, then fell to right away

Nicking and slicing neatly, heaving sods
Over his shoulder, going down and down
For the good turf. Digging.

The cold smell of potato mould, the squelch and slap   25
Of soggy peat, the curt cuts of an edge
Through living roots awaken in my head.
But I've no spade to follow men like them.

Between my finger and my thumb
The squat pen rests.   30
I'll dig with it.

Considerations

1. What do the speaker, his father, and his grandfather have in common?
2. Can digging peat (fuel to be burned) or potatoes be considered a creative activity? Do you see manual labor as an art? A skill? A combination? Something else? Explain.
3. What is the tone of the poem? Does the speaker seem to regret that he cannot (or will not) follow the paths of his father and grandfather? Does he respect them? Pity them? Envy them? Explain.

ANONYMOUS

Lord Randal

"O where ha' you been, Lord Randal, my son?
And where ha' you been, my handsome young man?"
"I ha' been at the greenwood; mother, mak my bed soon,
For I'm wearied wi' hunting, and fain wad° lie down."   *would*

"An wha' met ye there, Lord Randal, my son?   5
An wha' met you there, my handsome young man?"
"O I met wi' my true-love; mother, mak my bed soon,
For I'm wearied wi' huntin', and fain wad lie down."

"And what did she give you, Lord Randal, my son?
And what did she give you, my handsome young man?"   10
"Eels fried in a pan; mother, mak my bed soon,
For I'm wearied wi' huntin', and fain wad lie down."

"And wha' gat your leavins, Lord Randal, my son?
And wha' gat your leavins, my handsome young man?"
"My hawks and my hounds; mother, mak my bed soon,   15
For I'm wearied wi' hunting, and fain wad lie down."

"And what becam of them, Lord Randal, my son?
And what becam of them, my handsome young man?"
"They stretched their legs out and died; mother, mak my bed soon,
For I'm wearied wi' huntin', and fain wad lie down."   20

"O I fear you are poisoned, Lord Randal, my son!
I fear you are poisoned, my handsome young man!"
"O yes, I am poisoned: mother, mak my bed soon,
For I'm sick at the heart, and I fain wad lie down."

"What d'ye leave to your mother, Lord Randal, my son?   25
What d'ye leave to your mother, my handsome young man?"
"Four and twenty milk kye°; mother, mak my bed soon,   *cows*
For I'm sick at the heart, and I fain wad lie down."

"What d'ye leave to your sister, Lord Randal, my son?
What d'ye leave to your sister, my handsome young man?"   30
"My gold and my silver; mother, mak my bed soon,
For I'm sick at the heart, and I fain wad lie down."

"What d'ye leave to your brother, Lord Randal, my son?
What d'ye leave to your brother, my handsome young man?"
"My houses and my lands; mother, mak my bed soon,   35
For I'm sick at the heart, and I fain wad lie down."

"What d'ye leave to your true-love, Lord Randal, my son?
What d'ye leave to your true-love, my handsome young man?"
"I leave her hell and fire; mother, make my bed soon,
For I'm sick at the heart, and I fain wad lie down."   40

GWENDOLYN BROOKS (1917–   )

The Mother

Abortions will not let you forget.
You remember the children you got that you did not get,
The damp small pulps with a little or with no hair,

The singers and workers that never handled the air.
You will never neglect or beat   5
Them, or silence or buy with a sweet.
You will never wind up the sucking-thumb
Or scuttle off ghosts that come.
You will never leave them, controlling your luscious sigh,
Return for a snack of them, with gobbling mother-eye.   10

I have heard in the voices of the wind the voices of my dim killed children.
I have contracted. I have eased
My dim dears at the breasts they could never suck.
I have said, Sweets, if I sinned, if I seized
Your luck   15
And your lives from your unfinished reach,
If I stole your births and your names,
Your straight baby tears and your games,
Your stilted or lovely loves, your tumults, your marriages, aches, and your
    deaths,
If I poisoned the beginnings of your breaths,   20
Believe that even in my deliberateness I was not deliberate.
Though why should I whine,
Whine that the crime was other than mine? —
Since anyhow you are dead.
Or rather, or instead,   25
You were never made.
But that too, I am afraid,
Is faulty: oh, what shall I say, how is the truth to be said?
You were born, you had body, you died.
It is just that you never giggled or planned or cried.   30

Believe me, I loved you all.
Believe me, I knew you, though faintly, and I loved,
    I loved you all.

SYLVIA PLATH (1932–1963)

Metaphors

I'm a riddle in nine syllables,
An elephant, a ponderous house,
A melon strolling on two tendrils.
O red fruit, ivory, fine timbers!
This loaf's big with its yeasty rising.   5
Money's new-minted in this fat purse.

I'm a means, a stage, a cow in calf.
I've eaten a bag of green apples,
Boarded the train there's no getting off.

MARGARET ATWOOD (1939–   )

Today

Today the lawn holds
my daughter like a hostage
where she walks, not as high
as the wrecked picnic table,
through the scant grass, burdock leaves   5
made ragged by the mower,
tripping, stopping
to pick up and put down.

(Watch the slope, hard clay with bladed
stones, posing   10
innocuous as daisies:
it leads down to the pond,
where the ducks beckon, eleven
of them, they are saying:
     feathers.   feathers.)   15

The lure of eleven birds
on water, the glitter
and true shine, how can I tell her
that white, that bluegreen gold
is treachery?   20

Each of these rescues
costs me something,
a loss, a dulling
of this bluegold eye.

Later she will learn   25
about edges. Or better, find
by luck or a longer journey
the shadow of that liquid
gold place, which can be
so single and clear for her   30
only now, when it means danger
only to me.

ARTHUR MILLER (1915–   )

All My Sons

Characters

FRANK LUBEY, *the Kellers' next-door neighbor*
JOE KELLER, *a factory owner*
DR. JIM BAYLISS, *friend of the Kellers*
SUE BAYLISS, *his wife*
LYDIA LUBEY, *Frank's wife*
CHRIS KELLER, *Joe's son*
BERT, *a little boy*
KATE KELLER (MOTHER), *Joe's wife*
ANN DEEVER, *their house guest*
GEORGE DEEVER, *her brother*

ACT I

Scene *The back yard of the Keller home in the outskirts of an American town. August of our era.*

The stage is hedged on right and left by tall, closely planted poplars which lend the yard a secluded atmosphere. Upstage is filled with the back of the house and its open porch, which extends into the yard some six feet. The house is two stories high and has seven rooms. It would have cost perhaps fifteen thousand in the early twenties when it was built. Now it is nicely painted, looks tight and comfortable, and the yard is green with sod, here and there plants whose season is gone.

At the right, beside the house, the entrance of the driveway can be seen, but the poplars cut off view of its continuation downstage. In the right corner, downstage, stands the four-foot-high stump of a slender apple tree whose upper trunk and branches lie toppled beside it, fruit still clinging to its branches.

Downstage left is a small, trellised arbor, shaped like a sea shell, with a decorative bulb hanging from its forward-curving roof. Garden chairs and a table are scattered about. A garbage pail is on the ground next to the porch steps, a wire leaf-burner near it.

As the curtain rises, it is early Sunday morning. JOE KELLER *is sitting in the sun reading the want ads of the Sunday paper, the other sections of which lie neatly on the ground beside him. Behind his back, inside the arbor,* DOCTOR JIM BAYLISS *is reading part of the paper at the table.*

KELLER *is nearing sixty. A heavy man of stolid mind and build, a business-man these many years, but with the imprint of the machine-shop worker and boss still upon him. When he reads, when he speaks, when he listens, it is with the terrible concentration of the uneducated man for whom there is still wonder in many commonly known things, a man whose judgments must be dredged out of experience and a peasantlike common sense. A man among men.*

DOCTOR BAYLISS *is nearing forty. A wry self-controlled man, an easy talker, but with a wisp of sadness that clings even to his self-effacing humor.*

They sit reading in peace. In a moment FRANK LUBEY *enters, from the right, through a small space between the poplars.* FRANK *is thirty-two but balding. A pleasant, opinionated man, uncertain of himself, with a tendency toward peevishness when crossed, but always wanting it pleasant and neighborly. He rather saunters in, leisurely, nothing to do. He does not notice* JIM *in the arbor. On his greeting,* JIM *does not bother to look up.*

FRANK: Hya.

KELLER: Hello, Frank. What's doin'?

FRANK: Nothin'. Walking off my breakfast. *(Looks up at the sky.)* That beautiful? Not a cloud.

KELLER *(looks up)*: Yeah, nice.

FRANK: Every Sunday ought to be like this.

KELLER *(indicating the sections beside him)*: Want the paper?

FRANK: What's the difference, it's all bad news. What's today's calamity?

KELLER: I don't know, I don't read the news part any more. It's more interesting in the want ads.

FRANK: Why, you trying to buy something?

KELLER: No, I'm just interested. To see what people want, y'know? For instance, here's a guy is lookin' for two Newfoundland dogs. Now what's he want with two Newfoundland dogs?

FRANK: That is funny.

KELLER: Here's another one. Wanted—old dictionaries. High prices paid. Now what's a man going to do with an old dictionary?

FRANK: Why not? Probably a book collector.

KELLER: You mean he'll make a living out of that?

FRANK: Sure, there's a lot of them.

KELLER *(shakes his head)*: All the kinds of business goin' on. In my day, either you were a lawyer, or a doctor, or you worked in a shop. Now . . .

FRANK: Well, I was going to be a forester once.

KELLER: Well, that shows you; in my day, there was no such thing. *(Scanning the page, sweeping it with his hand.)* You look at a page like this you realize how ignorant you are. *(Softly, with wonder.)* Psss!

FRANK: Hey, what happened to your tree?

KELLER: Ain't that awful? The wind must've got it last night. You heard the wind, didn't you?

FRANK: Oh yes, I got a mess in my yard too. *(Goes to the tree.)* Ts, what a pity. What'd Kate say?

KELLER: They're all asleep yet. I'm just waiting for her to see it.

FRANK: You know—it's funny.

KELLER: What?

FRANK: Larry was born in November. He'd been twenty-seven this fall. And his tree blows down.

KELLER *(touched)*: I'm surprised you remember his birthday, Frank. That's nice.

FRANK: Well, I'm working on his horoscope.

KELLER: How can you make him a horoscope? That's for the future, ain't it?

FRANK: Well, what I'm doing is this, see. Larry was reported missing on February ninth, right?

KELLER: Yeah?

FRANK: Well, then, we assume that if he was killed it was on February ninth. Now, what Kate wants . . .

KELLER: Oh, Kate asked you to make a horoscope?

FRANK: Yeah, what she wants to find out is whether February ninth was a favorable day for Larry.

KELLER: What is that, favorable day?

FRANK: Well, a favorable day for a person is a fortunate day, according to his stars. In other words it would be practically impossible for him to have died on his favorable day.

KELLER: Well, was that his favorable day? — February ninth?

FRANK: That's what I'm working on to find out. It takes time! *(With inner excitement, he moves downstage.)* See, the point is, if February ninth was his favorable day, then it's completely possible he's alive somewhere, because . . .

(He notices JIM *now.* JIM *is looking at him as though at an idiot. To* JIM — *with an uncertain laugh:)*

FRANK: I mean it's possible! I didn't even see you.

KELLER *(to* JIM*)*: Is he talkin' sense?

JIM: Him? He's all right. He's just completely out of his mind, that's all.

FRANK: The trouble with you is, you don't believe in anything.

JIM: And your trouble is that you believe in *anything.* You didn't see my kid this morning, did you?

FRANK: No.

KELLER: Imagine? He walked off with his thermometer. Right out of his bag.

JIM *(gets up)*: What a problem. He can't look at a girl without taking her temperature. *(Goes to the driveway, looks upstage toward the street.)*

FRANK: That boy's going to be a doctor; he's smart.

JIM: Over my dead body he'll be a doctor. A good beginning, too.

FRANK: Why? It's an honorable profession.

JIM *(looks at him tiredly)*: Frank, will you stop talking like a civics book?

(KELLER laughs.)

FRANK: Why, I saw a movie a couple of weeks ago, reminded me of you. There was a doctor in that picture . . .

KELLER: Don Ameche!

FRANK: I think it was, yeah. And he worked in his basement discovering things. That's what you ought to do; you could help humanity, instead of . . .

JIM: I would love to help humanity on a Warner Brothers salary.

KELLER *(points at him, laughing)*: That's very good, Jim.

JIM *(looks toward the house)*: Well, where's the beautiful girl was supposed to be here?

FRANK *(excited)*: Annie came?

KELLER: Sure, sleepin' upstairs. We picked her up on the one o'clock train last night. *(To JIM.)* Wonderful thing. Girl leaves here a scrawny kid. Couple of years go by, she's a regular woman. Hardly recognized her, and she was running in and out of this yard all her life. That was a very happy family used to live in your house, Jim.

JIM: Like to meet her. The block can use a pretty girl. In the whole neighborhood there's not a damned thing to look at. *(Enter SUE, JIM'S wife, from left. She is rounding forty, an overweight woman who fears it. On seeing her, JIM wryly adds:)* Except my wife, of course.

SUE *(in the same spirit)*: Mrs. Adams is on the phone, you dog.

JIM *(to KELLER, going to embrace his wife)*: Such is the condition which prevails.

SUE *(brushing him off, laughing, but meaning it)*: Don't sniff around me.

JIM: My love, my light . . .

SUE: Go to hell. *(Points to their house, left.)* And give her a nasty answer. I can smell her perfume over the phone.

JIM: What's the matter with her now?

SUE: I don't know, dear. She sounds like she's in terrible pain — unless her mouth is full of candy.

JIM: Why don't you just tell her to lay down?

SUE: She enjoys it more when you tell her to lay down. And when are you going to see Mr. Hubbard?

JIM: My dear, Mr. Hubbard is not sick, and I have better things to do than to sit there and hold his hand.

SUE: It seems to me that for ten dollars you could hold his hand.

JIM *(to KELLER)*: If your son wants to play golf tell him I'm ready. *(Going to the left.)* Or if he'd like to take a trip around the world for about thirty years. *(He exits by the left.)*

KELLER: Why do you needle him? He's a doctor, women are supposed to call him up.

SUE: All I said was Mrs. Adams is on the phone.

KELLER: You were a nurse too long, Susie. You're too . . . too . . . realistic.

SUE *(laughing, points at him)*: Now you said it!

(Enter LYDIA LUBEY from the right. She is a robust, laughing girl of twenty-seven.)

LYDIA: Frank, the toaster . . . *(Sees the others.)* Hya. *(To* FRANK.*)* The toaster is off again.

FRANK: Well, plug it in, I just fixed it.

LYDIA *(kindly, but insistently)*: Please, dear, fix it back like it was before.

FRANK *(peeved, going off by the right)*: I don't know why you can't learn to turn on a simple thing like a toaster! *(*FRANK *exits right.)*

SUE *(laughs)*: Thomas Edison.

LYDIA *(apologetically)*: He's really very handy.

KELLER: Left-handy.

LYDIA: Oh, the wind get your tree?

KELLER: Yeah, last night.

LYDIA: What a pity. Annie get in?

KELLER: She'll be down soon. Wait'll you meet her, Sue, she's a knockout.

SUE: I should've been a man. People are always introducing me to beautiful women. *(To* JOE.*)* Tell her to come over later; I imagine she'd like to see what we did with her house.

KELLER: Sad. Last night when she got out of the car she looked at your house and . . . she looked sad, y'know?

SUE: Well . . . everything is sad, Joe. See you later. *(*SUE *exits by the left.)*

LYDIA: Is she still unhappy, Joe?

KELLER: Annie? I don't suppose she goes around dancing on her toes, but she seems to be over it.

LYDIA: She going to get married? Is there anybody? . . .

KELLER: I suppose . . . say, it's a couple years already. She can't mourn a boy forever.

LYDIA: It's so strange . . . Annie's here and not even married. And I've got three babies. I always thought it'd be the other way round.

KELLER: Well, that's what a war does. I had two sons, now I got one. It changed all the tallies. In my day when you had sons it was an honor. Today a doctor could make a million dollars if he could figure out a way to bring a boy into the world without a trigger finger.

(Enter CHRIS KELLER *from the house.)*

LYDIA: Hya, Chris . . .

*(*FRANK *shouts from off right.)*

FRANK: Lydia, come in here! If you want the toaster to work don't plug in the malted mixer.

LYDIA *(embarrassed, laughs)*: Did I? . . .

FRANK: The next time I fix something don't tell me I'm crazy! Come in here!

LYDIA *(going to the right)*: I'll never hear the end of this one.

KELLER *(calling to* FRANK*)*: So what's the difference? Instead of toast have a malted!

(LYDIA exits laughing. CHRIS descends smiling from the porch. He is thirty-two, like his father solidly built, a listener, a man capable of immense affection and loyalty.)

KELLER: You want the paper? *(Offers the whole paper.)*

CHRIS *(coming down to him)*: That's all right, just the book section.

KELLER *(giving him the paper)*: You're always reading the book section and you never buy a book.

CHRIS *(sitting, opening the section)*: I like to keep abreast of my ignorance.

KELLER: What is that, every week a new book comes out?

CHRIS: Lot of new books.

KELLER: All different.

CHRIS: All different.

KELLER *(shakes his head)*: Psss! Annie up yet?

CHRIS: Mother's giving her breakfast in the dining room.

KELLER: See what happened to the tree?

CHRIS *(without looking up)*: Yeah.

KELLER: What's Mother going to say?

(Enter BERT from the driveway. He is about six.)

BERT: You're finally up.

KELLER: Ha! Bert's here! Where's Tommy? He's got his father's thermometer again.

BERT: He's taking a reading . . . but it's only oral.

KELLER: Oh, well, there's no harm in oral. So what's new this morning, Bert?

BERT: Nothin'.

KELLER: Then you couldn't've made a complete inspection of the block. In the beginning, when I first made you a policeman, you used to come in every morning with something new. Now, nothin's ever new.

BERT: Except some kids from Thirtieth Street. They started kicking a can down the block, and I made them go away because you were sleeping.

KELLER: Now you're talkin', Bert. Now you're on the ball. First thing you know I'm liable to make you a detective.

BERT: Can I see the jail now?

KELLER: Seein' the jail ain't allowed, Bert. You know that.

BERT: I betcha there isn't even a jail. I don't see any bars on the cellar windows.

KELLER: Bert, on my word of honor, there's a jail in the basement. I showed you my gun, didn't I?

BERT: But that's a hunting gun.

KELLER: That's an arresting gun!

BERT: Then why don't you ever arrest anybody? Tommy said another dirty word to Doris yesterday, and you didn't even demote him.

KELLER: Yeah, that's a dangerous character, that Tommy. *(Beckons him closer.)* What word does he say?

BERT *(blushing)*: Oh, I can't say that.

KELLER: Well, gimme an idea.

BERT: I can't. It's not a nice word.

KELLER: Just whisper it in my ear. I'll close my eyes. Maybe I won't even hear it.

BERT *(on tiptoe, puts his lips to* KELLER'S *ear, then in unbearable embarrassment steps away)*: I can't, Mr. Keller.

CHRIS *(looks up)*: Don't make him do that.

KELLER: Okay, Bert. I take your word. Now go out, and keep both eyes peeled.

BERT *(interested)*: For what?

KELLER: For what! Bert, the whole neighborhood is depending on you. A policeman don't ask questions. Now peel them eyes!

BERT *(mystified, but willing)*: Okay.

KELLER: And mum's the word, Bert.

BERT: About what?

KELLER: Just in general. Be v-e-r-y careful.

BERT *(nods in bewilderment)*: Okay. *(*BERT *exits up the driveway.)*

KELLER *(laughs)*: I got all the kids crazy!

CHRIS *(smiles, looks up toward the tree)*: One of these days, they'll all come in here and beat your brains out. *(He gets up, goes leisurely to the tree, touches the break in the stump.)*

KELLER: What's she going to say? Maybe we ought to tell her before she sees it.

CHRIS: She saw it.

KELLER: How could she see it? I was the first one up. She was still in bed.

CHRIS: She was out here when it broke.

KELLER: When?

CHRIS: About four this morning. *(Indicating the window above them.)* I heard it cracking and I woke up and looked out. She was standing right here when it cracked.

KELLER: What was she doing out here four in the morning?

CHRIS: I don't know. When it cracked she ran back into the house and cried in the kitchen.

KELLER: Did you talk to her?

CHRIS: No, I . . . I figured the best thing was to leave her alone. *(Pause.)*

KELLER *(deeply touched)*: She cried hard?

CHRIS: I could hear her right through the floor of my room. *(Slight pause.)*

KELLER: What was she doing out here at that hour? *(An undertone of anger showing.)* She's dreaming about him again. She's walking around at night.

CHRIS: I guess she is.

KELLER: She's getting just like after he died. *(Slight pause.)* What's the meaning of that?

CHRIS: I don't know the meaning of it. *(Slight pause.)* But I know one thing, Dad. We've made a terrible mistake with Mother.

KELLER: What?

CHRIS: Being dishonest with her. That kind of thing always pays off, and now it's paying off.

KELLER: What do you mean, dishonest?

CHRIS: You know Larry's not coming back and I know it. Why do we allow her to go on thinking that we believe with her?

KELLER: What do you want to do, argue with her?

CHRIS: I don't want to argue with her, but it's time she realized that nobody believes Larry is alive any more.

(KELLER simply moves away, thinking, looking at the ground.)

CHRIS: Why shouldn't she dream of him, walk the nights waiting for him? Do we contradict her? Do we say straight out that we have no hope any more? That we haven't had any hope for years now?

KELLER *(frightened at the thought)*: You can't say that to her.

CHRIS: We've got to say it to her.

KELLER: How're you going to prove it? Can you prove it?

CHRIS: For God's sake, three years! Nobody comes back after three years. It's insane.

KELLER: To you it is, and to me. But not to her. You can talk yourself blue in the face, but there's no body and there's no grave, so where are you?

CHRIS: Sit down, Dad. I want to talk to you.

KELLER *(looks at him searchingly a moment, and sitting . . .)*: The trouble is the goddam newspapers. Every month some boy turns up from nowhere, so the next one is going to be Larry, so . . .

CHRIS: All right, listen to me. *(Slight pause.)* You know why I asked Annie here, don't you?

KELLER *(he knows, but)*: . . . Why?

CHRIS: You know.

KELLER: Well, I got an idea, but . . . What's the story?

CHRIS: I'm going to ask her to marry me. *(Slight pause.)*

KELLER *(nods)*: Well, that's only your business, Chris.

CHRIS: You know it's not only my business.

KELLER: What do you want me to do? You're old enough to know your own mind.

CHRIS *(asking, annoyed)*: Then it's all right, I'll go ahead with it.

KELLER: Well, you want to be sure Mother isn't going to . . .

CHRIS: Then it isn't just my business.

KELLER: I'm just sayin' . . .

CHRIS: Sometimes you infuriate me, you know that? Isn't it your business, too, if I tell this to Mother and she throws a fit about it? You have such a talent for ignoring things.

KELLER: I ignore what I gotta ignore. The girl is Larry's girl . . .

CHRIS: She's not Larry's girl.

KELLER: From Mother's point of view he is not dead and you have no right to take his girl. *(Slight pause.)* Now you can go on from there if you know where to go, but I'm tellin' you I don't know where to go. See? I don't know. Now what can I do for you?

CHRIS *(gets up)*: I don't know why it is, but every time I reach out for something I want, I have to pull back because other people will suffer. My whole bloody life, time after time after time.

KELLER: You're a considerate fella, there's nothing wrong in that.

CHRIS: To hell with that.

KELLER: Did you ask Annie yet?

CHRIS: I wanted to get this settled first.

KELLER: How do you know she'll marry you? Maybe she feels the same way Mother does.

CHRIS: Well if she does then that's the end of it. From her letters I think she's forgotten him. I'll find out. And then we'll thrash it out with Mother. Right? Dad, don't avoid me.

KELLER: The trouble is you don't see enough women. You never did.

CHRIS: So what? I'm not fast with women.

KELLER: I don't see why it has to be Annie. . . .

CHRIS: Because it is.

KELLER: That's a good answer, but it don't answer anything. You haven't seen her since you went to war. It's five years.

CHRIS: I can't help it. I know her best. I was brought up next door to her. These years when I think of someone for my wife, I think of Annie. What do you want, a diagram?

KELLER: I don't want a diagram . . . I . . . I'm . . . She thinks he's coming back, Chris. You marry that girl and you're pronouncing him dead. Now what's going to happen to Mother? Do you know? I don't! *(Pause.)*

CHRIS: All right then, Dad.

KELLER *(thinking* CHRIS *has retreated)*: Give it some more thought.

CHRIS: I've given it three years of thought. I'd hoped that if I waited, Mother would forget Larry and then we'd have a regular wedding and everything happy. But if that can't happen here, then I'll have to get out.

KELLER: What the hell is *this?*

CHRIS: I'll get out. I'll get married and live some place else. Maybe in New York.

KELLER: Are you crazy?

CHRIS: I've been a good son too long, a good sucker. I'm through with it.

KELLER: You've got a business here, what the hell is . . .

CHRIS: The business doesn't inspire me.

KELLER: Must you be inspired?

CHRIS: I like it an hour a day. If I have to grub for money all day long, at least at evening I want it beautiful. I want a family, I want some kids, I want to build something I can give myself to. Annie is in the middle of that. Now . . . where do I find it?

KELLER: You mean . . . *(Goes to him.)* Tell me something, you mean you'd leave the business?

CHRIS: Yes. On this I would. *(Pause.)*

KELLER: Well . . . you don't want to think like that.

CHRIS: Then help me stay here.

KELLER: All right, but . . . but don't think like that. Because what the hell did I work for? That's only for you, Chris, the whole shootin' match is for you!

CHRIS: I know that, Dad. Just help me stay here.

KELLER *(puts a fist up to* CHRIS's *jaw)*: But don't think that way, you hear me?

CHRIS: I'm thinking that way.

KELLER *(lowering his hand)*: I don't understand you, do I?

CHRIS: No, you don't. I'm a pretty tough guy.

KELLER: Yeah. I can see that.

(MOTHER appears on the porch. She is in her early fifties, a woman of uncontrolled inspirations, and an overwhelming capacity for love.)

MOTHER: Joe?

CHRIS *(going toward the porch)*: Hello, Mom.

MOTHER *(indicating the house behind her; to* KELLER*)*: Did you take a bag from under the sink?

KELLER: Yeah, I put it in the pail.

MOTHER: Well, get it out of the pail. That's my potatoes.

(CHRIS bursts out laughing.)

KELLER *(laughing)*: I thought it was garbage. *(KELLER retrieves the bag wryly.)*

MOTHER: Will you do me a favor, Joe? Don't be helpful.

KELLER *(with distaste, lifting out the bag)*: I can afford another bag of potatoes.

MOTHER: Minnie scoured that pail in boiling water last night. It's cleaner than your teeth. Give me the bag.

KELLER *(as he gives her the bag)*: And I don't understand why, after I worked forty years and I got a maid, why I have to take out the garbage.

MOTHER: If you would make up your mind that every bag in the kitchen isn't full of garbage you wouldn't be throwing out my vegetables. Last time it was the onions.

KELLER: I don't like garbage in the house.

MOTHER: Then don't eat. *(She goes into the kitchen with the bag.)*

CHRIS: That settles you for today.

KELLER: Yeah, I'm in last place again. I don't know, once upon a time I used to think that when I got money again I would have a maid and my wife would take it easy. Now I got money, and I got a maid, and my wife is workin' for the maid. *(He sits in one of the chairs.)*

(MOTHER comes out on the last line.)

MOTHER: It's her day off, what are you crabbing about?

CHRIS *(to MOTHER)*: Isn't Annie finished eating?

MOTHER *(looking around preoccupiedly at the yard)*: She'll be right out. *(Moves.)* That wind did some job on this place. *(Of the tree.)* So much for that, thank God.

KELLER *(indicating the chair beside him)*: Sit down, take it easy.

MOTHER *(moving toward the border of plants, downstage, left; she presses her hand to the top of her head)*: I've got such a funny pain on the top of my head.

CHRIS: Can I get you an aspirin?

MOTHER *(picks a few petals off the ground, stands there smelling them in her hand, then sprinkles them over the plants)*: No more roses. It's so funny . . . *(She sits, then continues.)* . . . everything decides to happen at the same time. It'll be his birthday soon; his tree blows down, Annie comes. Everything that happened seems to be coming back. I was just down the cellar and what do I stumble over? His baseball glove. I haven't seen that baseball glove in a century.

CHRIS: Don't you think Annie looks well?

MOTHER: Fine. There's no question about it. She's a beauty . . . I still don't know what brought her here. Not that I'm not glad to see her, but . . .

CHRIS: I just thought we'd all like to see each other again.

(MOTHER just looks at him, nodding ever so slightly.)

CHRIS *(almost as though admitting something)*: And I wanted to see her myself.

MOTHER *(her nods halt; to KELLER)*: The only thing is I think her nose got longer. But I'll always love that girl. She's one that didn't jump into bed with somebody else as soon as it happened with her fella.

KELLER *(as though that were impossible for ANNIE)*: Oh, what're you . . .

MOTHER: Never mind. Most of them didn't wait till the telegrams were opened. I'm just glad she came so you can see I'm not *completely* out of my mind.

CHRIS: Just because she isn't married doesn't mean she's been mourning him.

MOTHER *(with an undercurrent of observation)*: Why then isn't she?

CHRIS *(a little flustered)*: Well . . . it could've been any number of things.

MOTHER *(directly at him)*: Like what, for instance?

CHRIS *(embarrassed, but standing his ground)*: I don't know. Whatever it is.

*(*MOTHER *gets up, pressing her palm to the top of her head.)*

CHRIS: Can I get you an aspirin?

MOTHER *(she goes aimlessly toward the tree)*: It's not like a headache.

KELLER: You don't sleep, that's why. You're wearing out more bedroom slippers than shoes.

MOTHER: I had a terrible night. *(She stops moving.)* I never had a night like that.

CHRIS *(goes to her)*: What was it, Mom? Did you dream?

MOTHER: More, more than a dream.

CHRIS *(hesitantly)*: About Larry?

MOTHER: I was fast asleep, and . . . *(Raising her arm over the audience.)* Remember the way he used to fly low past the house when he was in training? When we used to see his face in the cockpit going by? That's the way I saw him. Only high up. Way, way up, where the clouds are. He was so real I could reach out and touch him. And suddenly he started to fall. And crying, crying to me . . . Mom, Mom! I could hear him like he was in the room. Mom!—it was his voice! If I could touch him I knew I could stop him, if I could only . . . *(Breaks off, allowing her outstretched hand to fall.)* I woke up and it was so funny. . . . The wind . . . it was like the roaring of his engine. I came out here . . . I must've still been half asleep. I could hear that roaring like he was going by. The tree snapped right in front of me . . . and I like . . . came awake. *(She is looking at the tree. She suddenly realizes something, turns with a reprimanding finger shaking slightly at* KELLER.*)* See? We should never have planted that tree. I said so in the first place; it was too soon to plant a tree for him.

CHRIS *(alarmed)*: Too soon!

MOTHER *(angering)*: We rushed into it. Everybody was in such a hurry to bury him. I *said* not to plant it yet. *(To* KELLER.*)* I *told* you to! . . .

CHRIS *(grasping her by the arm)*: Mother, Mother! *(She looks into his face.)* The wind blew it down. What significance has that got? What are you talking about? *(He releases her. Unconvinced, she moves from him, and stands stroking her own cheek.* CHRIS *goes to her)*. Mother, please . . . Don't go through it all again, will you? It's no good, it doesn't accomplish anything. I've been thinking, y'know—maybe we ought to put our minds to forgetting him.

MOTHER: That's the third time you've said that this week.

CHRIS: Because it's not right; we never took up our lives again. We're like at a railroad station waiting for a train that never comes in.

MOTHER *(presses the top of her head)*: Get me an aspirin, heh?

CHRIS *(goes to her, smooths her cheek)*: And let's break out of this, heh, Mom? I thought the four of us might go out to dinner a couple of nights, maybe go dancing out at the shore.

MOTHER: Fine. *(To* KELLER.*)* We can do it tonight.

KELLER: Swell with me!

CHRIS: Sure, let's have some fun. *(To* MOTHER.*)* You'll start with this aspirin. *(He goes up and into the house with new spirit.)*

(Her smile vanishes.)

MOTHER *(with an accusing undertone)*: Why did he invite her here?

KELLER: Why does that bother you?

MOTHER: She's been in New York three and a half years, why all of a sudden? . . .

KELLER: Well, maybe . . . maybe he just wanted to see her . . .

MOTHER: Nobody comes seven hundred miles "just to see."

KELLER: What do you mean? He lived next door to the girl all his life, why shouldn't he want to see her again? *(*MOTHER *looks at him critically.)* Don't look at me like that, he didn't tell me any more than he told you.

MOTHER *(a warning and a question)*: He's not going to marry her.

KELLER: How do you know he's even thinking of it?

MOTHER: It's got that about it.

KELLER *(sharply watching her reaction)*: Well? So what?

MOTHER: What do you mean, so what? *(Alarmed, she glances toward the house.)* What's going on here, Joe?

KELLER: Now listen, kid . . .

MOTHER *(avoiding contact with him)*: She's not his girl, Joe; she knows she's not.

KELLER: You can't read her mind.

MOTHER: Then why is she still single? New York is full of men, why isn't she married? *(Pause.)* Probably a hundred people told her she's foolish, but she's waited.

KELLER: How do you know why she waited?

MOTHER: She knows what I know, that's why. She's faithful as a rock. In my worst moments, I think of her waiting, and I know again that I'm right.

KELLER: Look, it's a nice day. What are you arguing for?

MOTHER: I don't like the way Chris is behaving to her, and you too!

KELLER: I haven't said ten words to her.

MOTHER *(warningly)*: Nobody in this house dast take her faith away, Joe. Strangers might. But not his father, not his brother.

KELLER *(exasperated)*: What do you want me to do? What do you want?

MOTHER: I want you to act like he's coming back. Both of you. *(She moves about.)* Don't think I haven't noticed you since Chris invited her. I won't stand for any nonsense.

KELLER: But Kate . . .

MOTHER: Because if he's not coming back, then I'll kill myself! *(She sobs.)* Laugh. Laugh at me. *(She points to the tree.)* But why did that happen the very night she came back? Laugh, but there are meanings in such things. She goes to sleep in his room and his memorial breaks in pieces. Look at it, look. *(She goes to him.)* Joe . . .

KELLER: Calm yourself.

MOTHER: Believe with me, Joe. I can't stand all alone.

KELLER *(stroking her hand helplessly)*: Calm yourself.

MOTHER: Only last week a man turned up in Detroit, missing longer than Larry. You read it yourself.

KELLER *(noncommittally)*: All right, all right, calm yourself.

MOTHER: You above all have got to believe, you . . .

KELLER *(suddenly stops stroking her hand)*: Why me above all?

MOTHER *(to cover herself she touches his hair)*: Just don't stop believing . . .

KELLER *(brushing her hand away, but gently)*: What does that mean, me above all?

(Little BERT comes rushing down the driveway, at the right.)

BERT: Mr. Keller! Say, Mr. Keller . . . *(Pointing up the driveway.)* . . . Tommy just said it again!

KELLER *(not remembering any of it)*: Said what? . . . Who? . . .

BERT: The dirty word.

KELLER: Oh. Well . . . *(He preoccupiedly flicks his hand to dismiss BERT.)*

BERT: Gee, aren't you going to arrest him? I warned him.

MOTHER *(with suddenness)*: Stop that, Bert. Go home.

(BERT backs up as she advances.)

MOTHER: There's no jail here.

KELLER *(as thugh to say, Oh-what-the-hell-let-him-believe-there-is)*: Kate . . .

MOTHER *(turning on KELLER furiously)*: There's no jail here! I want you to stop that jail business!

KELLER *(as though to say, Oh-what-the-hell-let-him-believe-there-is)*: Kate . . .

MOTHER: Go home, Bert!

(BERT looks at her in astonishment, and at KELLER, turns around, and goes up the driveway.)

MOTHER *(she is shaken; her speech is bitten off, extremely urgent)*: I want you to stop that, Joe. That whole jail business!

KELLER *(alarmed, therefore angered)*: Look at you. Look at you shaking.

MOTHER *(trying to control herself, moving about, clasping her hands)*: I can't help it.

KELLER: What have I got to hide? What the hell is the matter with you, Kate?

MOTHER: I didn't say you had anything to hide, I'm just telling you to stop it! Now stop it!

(ANN and CHRIS appear on the porch. ANN is twenty-six, gentle, but despite herself capable of holding fast to what she knows.)

ANN: Ain't love grand!

(She leads off a general laugh that is not self-conscious because they know one another too well.)

CHRIS *(bringing* ANN *down, with an outstretched, chivalric arm)*: How about this kid?

MOTHER *(genuinely overcome with it)*: Annie, where did you get that dress!

ANN: I couldn't resist. I'm taking it right off before I ruin it. *(Swings around.)* How's that for three weeks' salary?

MOTHER *(to* KELLER*)*: Isn't she the most . . . *(To* ANN.*)* It's gorgeous, simply gor . . .

CHRIS *(to* MOTHER*)*: No kidding now, isn't she the prettiest gal you ever saw?

MOTHER *(caught short by his obvious admiration, she finds herself reaching out for a glass of water and aspirin in his hand, and . . .)*: I'm just afraid you gained a little weight, didn't you, darling? *(She gulps the pill and drinks.)*

ANN *(disappointed)*: It comes and goes. *(She walks left, toward the poplars.)*

KELLER: Look how nice her legs turned out!

ANN: Boy, the poplars got thick, didn't they?

KELLER: Well, it's three years, Annie. We're gettin old, kid.

(She parts branches, looks toward JIM's *yard.)*

MOTHER: How does Mom like New York?

ANN: Why'd they take our hammock away?

KELLER: Oh no, it broke. Couple of years ago.

MOTHER *(with gay, loving sarcasm, at* KELLER*)*: What broke? He had one of his light lunches and flopped into it.

ANN *(she laughs and turns back toward* JIM's *yard)*: Oh, excuse me!

*(*JIM *enters from in front of her.)*

JIM: How do you do. *(To* KELLER.*)* I found my thermometer . . . don't ask me where. *(To* CHRIS.*)* She looks very intelligent.

CHRIS: Ann, this is Jim . . . Doctor Bayliss.

ANN *(shaking* JIM's *hand)*: Oh sure, he writes a lot about you.

JIM: Don't believe it. He likes everybody. In Luxembourg he was known as Mother McKeller.

ANN: I can believe it. . . . You know? *(To the others.)* It's so strange seeing him come out of that yard. *(To* CHRIS.*)* I guess I never grew up. It almost seems that Mom and Pop are in there now. And you and my brother doing algebra, and Larry trying to copy my homework. Gosh, those dear dead days beyond recall.

JIM: Well, I hope that doesn't mean you want me to move out.

SUE *(calling from the left)*: Jim, come here! Mr. Hubbard is on the phone!

JIM: I told you I don't want . . .

SUE *(commandingly sweet)*: Please, dear!

JIM *(resigned)*: All right, Susie, *(Trailing off)* all right, all right . . . *(He takes* ANN's *hand.)* I've only met you, Ann, but if I may offer you a piece of advice — when you marry, never — even in your mind — never count your husband's money.

SUE *(from off)*: Jim?

JIM: At once! *(Turns and goes to the left.)* At once. *(He exits by the left.)*

MOTHER: I told her to take up the guitar. It'd be a common interest for them. *(They laugh.)* He loves the guitar.

ANN *(she becomes suddenly lively, grasps* MOTHER'S *hands)*: Let's eat at the shore tonight! Raise some hell around here, like we used to before Larry went!

MOTHER *(emotionally)*: You think of him! *(Hugs* ANN'S *head.)* You see? *(Triumphantly.)* She thinks of him!

ANN *(with an uncomprehending smile)*: What do you mean, Kate?

MOTHER: Nothing. Just that you . . . remember him, he's in your thoughts.

ANN: That's a funny thing to say; how could I help remembering him?

MOTHER *(it is drawing to a head the wrong way for her; she starts anew; she circles* ANN's *waist, and walks her to a chair, fixing the girl's hair)*: Sit down, dear.

*(*ANN *sits, watching her.)*

MOTHER: Did you hang up your things?

ANN: Yeah . . . *(To* CHRIS.*)* Say, you've sure gone in for clothes. I could hardly find room in the closet.

MOTHER: No. *(Sits.)* Don't you remember? That's Larry's room.

ANN: You mean . . . they're Larry's?

MOTHER: Didn't you recognize them?

ANN *(a little embarrassed)*: Well, it never occurred to me that you'd . . . I mean the shoes are all shined.

MOTHER: Yes, dear.

(Slight pause. ANN *can't stop staring at her.* MOTHER *breaks it by clasping her hands comfortably in her lap, and speaking with the relish of gossip.)*

MOTHER: For so long I've been aching for a nice conversation with you, Annie. Tell me something.

ANN: What?

MOTHER: I don't know. Something nice.

CHRIS *(wryly)*: She means do you go out much.

MOTHER: Oh, shut up.

KELLER: And are any of them serious?

MOTHER *(laughing)*: Why don't you both choke?

KELLER: Annie, you can't go into a restaurant with that woman any more. In five minutes thirty-nine strange people are sitting at the table telling her their life story.

MOTHER: If I can't ask Annie a personal question . . .

KELLER: Askin' is all right, but don't beat her over the head. You're beatin' her, you're beatin' her.

(They are laughing.)

ANN *(to* MOTHER*)*: Don't let them bulldoze you. Ask me anything you like. What do you want to know, Kate? Come on, let's gossip.

MOTHER *(to* CHRIS *and* KELLER*)*: She's the only one's got any sense. *(To* ANN.*)* Your mother . . . she's not getting a divorce, heh?

ANN: No, she's calmed down about it now. I think when he gets out they'll probably live together. In New York, of course.

MOTHER: That's fine. Because your father is still . . . I mean he's a decent man after all is said and done.

ANN: I don't care. She can take him back if she likes.

MOTHER: And you? You . . . *(Shakes her head negatively.)* . . . go out much? *(Slight pause.)*

ANN *(delicately)*: You mean am I waiting for him?

MOTHER: Well, no, I don't expect you to wait for him but . . .

ANN *(kindly)*: But that's what you mean, isn't it?

MOTHER: . . . Well . . . yes.

ANN: Well, I'm not, Kate.

MOTHER *(faintly)*: You're not.

ANN: Isn't it ridiculous? You don't really imagine he's . . .

MOTHER: I know, dear, but don't say it's ridiculous, because the papers were full of it. I don't know about New York but there was half a page about a man in Detroit missing longer than Larry and he turned up from Burma.

CHRIS: He couldn't have wanted to come home very badly, Mom.

MOTHER: Don't be so smart. Why couldn't he of lost his memory? Or . . . or . . . it could've been a million things. What is impossible that hasn't already happened in this world? Who is smart enough to say what can happen?

CHRIS *(going to her with a condescending laugh)*: Mother, you're absolutely . . .

MOTHER *(waving him off)*: Don't be so damned smart! Now stop it! *(Slight pause.)* There are just a few things you *don't* know. All of you. And I'll tell you one of them, Annie. Deep, deep in your heart you've always been waiting for him.

ANN *(resolutely)*: No, Kate.

MOTHER *(with increasing demand)*: But deep in your heart, Annie!

CHRIS: She ought to know, shouldn't she?

MOTHER *(looking at* ANN, *pointing at her)*: Don't let them tell you what to think. Listen to your heart. Only your heart.

ANN *(gets up, goes to her)*: Why does your heart tell you he's alive?

MOTHER: Because he has to be.

ANN: But why, Kate?

MOTHER: Because certain things have to be, and certain things can never be. Like the sun has to rise, it has to be. That's why there's God. Otherwise anything could happen. But there's God, so certain things can never happen. I would know, Annie — just like I knew the day he *(Indicates* CHRIS.*)* went into that terrible battle. Did he write me? Was it in the papers? No, but that morning I couldn't raise my head off the pillow. Ask Joe. Suddenly, I knew. I knew! And he was nearly killed that day. Annie, you know I'm right! *(Turns, trembling, going upstage.)*

ANN: No, Kate.

MOTHER *(stands there in silence)*: I have to have some tea.

*(*FRANK *appears from the right, carrying a ladder.)*

FRANK: Annie! *(Coming down.)* How are you, gee whiz.

ANN *(taking his hand)*: Why, Frank, you're losing your hair.

KELLER: He's got responsibility. Without Frank the stars wouldn't know when to come out.

FRANK *(laughs. To* ANN*)*: You look womanly. You've matured. You . . .

KELLER: Take it easy, Frank, you're a married man.

ANN *(as they laugh)*: You still haberdashering?

FRANK: Why not? Maybe I too can get to be president. How's your brother? Got his degree, I hear.

ANN: Oh, George has his own office now!

FRANK: Don't say. *(Funereally.)* And your dad? Is he? . . .

ANN *(abruptly)*: Fine. I'll be in to see Lydia.

FRANK *(sympathetically)*: How about it, does Dad expect a parole soon?

ANN *(with growing ill-ease)*: I really don't know, I . . .

FRANK *(stanchly defending her father for her sake)*: I mean because I feel, y'know, that if an intelligent man like your father is put in prison, there ought to be a law that says either you execute him, or let him go after a year. Because if you look at your statistics . . .

CHRIS: Want a hand with that ladder?

FRANK *(taking the cue)*: That's all right, I'll . . . *(Picks up the ladder.)* . . . I'll finish the horoscope tonight, Kate. *(Embarrassed.)* See you later, Ann, you look wonderful.

(She nods to him as he exits right. They look at ANN, *who has not moved.)*

CHRIS *(approaches her)*: Don't feel that way, he only asked about him.

ANN *(to all)*: Haven't they stopped talking about Dad?

CHRIS: Nobody talks about him any more.

KELLER: Gone and forgotten, kid. Here, sit down.

ANN *(as he seats her)*: Tell me. Because I don't want to meet anybody on the block if they're going to . . .

CHRIS: I don't want you to worry about it.

ANN *(to KELLER)*: Do they still remember the case? Do they talk about you?

KELLER: The only one still talks about it is my wife.

MOTHER: Because you keep playing policeman with the kids. All their parents hear out of you is jail, jail, jail. *(To ANN.)* I do everything I know to make people forget the damned thing and he . . .

KELLER: Actually what happened was that when I got home from the penitentiary the kids got very interested in me. You know kids. I was *(Laughs.)* like the expert on the jail situation. And as time passed they got it confused and . . . I ended up a detective. *(Laughs.)*

MOTHER: Except that *they* didn't get it confused. *(To ANN.)* He hands out police badges from the Post Toasties boxes.

(They laugh.)

ANN *(wondrously at them, happily)*: Gosh, it's wonderful to hear you laughing about it.

CHRIS: Why, what'd you expect?

ANN: The last thing I remember on this block was one word — "Murderers!" Remember that, Kate? . . . Mrs. Hammond standing in front of our house and yelling that word? . . . She's still around, I suppose.

MOTHER: They're all still around.

KELLER: Don't listen to her. Every Saturday night the whole gang is playin' poker in this yard. All the ones who yelled murder takin' my money now.

MOTHER: Don't, Joe, she's a sensitive girl, don't fool her. *(To ANN.)* They still remember about Dad. It's different with him — *(Indicates JOE.)* — he was exonerated, your father's still there. That's why I wasn't so enthusiastic about you coming. Honestly, I know how sensitive you are, and I told Chris, I said . . .

KELLER: Listen, you do like I did and you'll be all right. The day I come home, I got out of my car — but not in front of the house . . . on the corner. You should've been here, Annie, and you too, Chris; you'd 'a' seen something. Everybody knew I was getting out that day; the porches were loaded. Picture it now; none of them believed I was really innocent. The story was, I pulled a fast one getting myself exonerated. So I get out of my car, and I walk down the street. But very slow. And with a smile. The beast. I was the beast; the guy who sold cracked cylinder heads to the Army Air Force; the guy who made twenty-one P-40's crash in Australia. Kid, walkin' down the street that day I was guilty as hell. Except I wasn't, and there was a court paper in my pocket to prove I wasn't . . . and I walked . . . past . . . the porches.

Result? Fourteen months later I had one of the best shops in the state again, a respected man again, bigger than ever.

CHRIS *(with admiration)*: Joe McGuts.

KELLER *(now with great force)*: That's the only way you lick 'em, is guts! *(To* ANN.*)* The worst thing you did was to move away from here. You made it tough for your father when he gets out, and you made it tough for me. Sure, they play poker, but behind their eyes is that dirty thought — Keller, you were very intimate with a murderer. That's why I tell you, I like to see him move back right on this block.

MOTHER *(pained)*: How could they move back?

KELLER: It ain't gonna end *till* they move back! *(To* ANN.*)* Till people play cards with him again, and talk with him, and smile with him — you play cards with a man you know he can't be a murderer. And the next time you write him I like you to tell him just what I said.

*(*ANN *simply stares at him.)*

KELLER: You hear me?

ANN *(surprised)*: Don't you hold anything against him?

KELLER: Annie, I never believed in crucifying people.

ANN *(mystified)*: But he was your partner, he dragged you through the mud . . .

KELLER: Well, he ain't my sweetheart, but you gotta forgive, don't you?

ANN: You either, Kate? Don't you feel any . . . ? I mean I'm just curious.

KELLER: The next time you write Dad . . .

ANN: I don't write him.

KELLER *(struck)*: Well, every now and then you . . .

ANN *(a little ashamed, but determined)*: No, I've never written to him. Neither has my brother. *(To* CHRIS.*)* Say, do you feel this way too?

CHRIS: He murdered twenty-one pilots.

KELLER: What the hell kinda talk is that?

MOTHER: That's not a thing to say about a man.

ANN: What else can you say? When they took him away I followed him, went to him every visiting day. I was crying all the time. Until the news came about Larry. Then I realized. It's wrong to pity a man like that. Father or no father, there's only one way to look at him. He knowingly shipped out parts that would crash an airplane. And how do you know Larry wasn't one of them?

MOTHER: I was waiting for that. *(Going to her.)* As long as you're here, Annie, I want to ask you never to say that again.

ANN: I don't understand. I thought you'd be . . . at least mad at him.

MOTHER: What your father did had nothing to do with Larry. Nothing.

ANN: But we can't know that.

MOTHER *(striving for control)*: As long as you're here!

ANN *(perplexed)*: But Kate . . .

MOTHER: Put that out of your head!

KELLER: Because . . .

MOTHER *(quickly to* KELLER*)*: That's all, that's enough! *(Places her hand on her head.)* Come inside now, and have some tea with me. *(She turns and goes toward the house.)*

KELLER *(to* ANN*)*: The one thing you . . .

MOTHER *(sharply)*: He's not dead, so there's no argument! Now come!

KELLER *(angrily)*: In a minute!

*(*MOTHER *turns and goes into the house.)*

KELLER: Now look, Annie . . .

CHRIS: All right, Dad, forget it.

KELLER: No, she dasn't feel that way. Annie . . .

CHRIS: I'm sick of the whole subject, now cut it out.

KELLER: You want her to go on like this? *(To* ANN.*)* Now listen. Those cylinder heads went into P-40's only. What's the matter with you? You know Larry never flew a P-40.

CHRIS: So who flew those P-40's, pigs?

KELLER *(with great anxiety, a growing note of plea)*: The man was a fool, but don't make a murderer out of him. You got no sense? Look what it does to her! *(To* ANN.*)* You gotta appreciate what was doin' in that shop in the war. It was a madhouse. Every half hour the Major callin' for cylinder heads, they were whippin' us with the telephone. The trucks were hauling them away hot, damn near. I mean just try to see it human, see it human. All of a sudden a batch comes out with a crack. That happens, that's the business. A fine hairline crack. All right, so . . . so he's a little man, your father, always scared of loud voices. What'll the Major say?—Half a day's production shot. What'll I say? You know what I mean? Human. *(Slight pause.)* So he takes out his tools and he . . . covers over the cracks. All right . . . that's bad, it's wrong, but that's what a little man does. If I could've gone in that day I'd a told him—junk 'em, Herb, we can afford it. But alone he was afraid. But I know he meant no harm. He believed they'd hold up a hundred per cent. And a lot of them did. That's a mistake, but it ain't murder. You mustn't feel that way about him. You understand me? I don't like to see a girl eating out her heart.

ANN *(she regards him a moment)*: Joe, let's forget it.

KELLER: Annie, the day the news came about Larry he was in the next cell to mine . . . Dad. And he cried, Annie . . . he cried half the night.

ANN *(touched)*: He should have cried all night.

KELLER *(almost angered)*: Annie, I do not understand why you . . . !

CHRIS *(breaking in—with nervous urgency)*: Are you going to stop it?

ANN: Don't yell at him. He just wants everybody happy.

KELLER: That's my sentiments. I'll call Swanson's for a table. We'll have steaks.

CHRIS: And champagne.

KELLER: Now you're talkin'! Big time tonight, Annie!

ANN: Can't scare me.

KELLER *(to* CHRIS, *pointing at* ANNIE*)*: I like that girl. Wrap her up. *(They laugh. Goes up the porch.)* I want to see everybody drunk tonight. . . . You got nice legs, Annie. *(To* CHRIS.*)* Look at him, he's blushin'.

CHRIS: Drink your tea, Casanova.

*(*KELLER *laughs tauntingly, but warmly, pointing at* CHRIS, *and goes into the house.)*

CHRIS: Isn't he a great guy?

ANN: You're the only one I know who loves his parents!

CHRIS: I know. It went out of style, didn't it?

ANN *(with a sudden touch of sadness)*: It's all right. It's a good thing. *(She goes to a chair, looks about.)* You know? It's lovely here. The air is sweet.

CHRIS *(hopefully)*: You're not sorry you came?

ANN: Not sorry, no. But I'm . . . not going to stay . . .

CHRIS: Why?

ANN: In the first place, your mother as much as told me to go.

CHRIS: Well . . .

ANN: You saw that . . . and then you . . . you've been . . .

CHRIS: What?

ANN: Well . . . kind of embarrassed ever since I got here.

CHRIS: The trouble is I planned on sneaking up on you over a period of a week or so. But they take it for granted that we're all set.

ANN: I knew they would. Your mother anyway.

CHRIS: How did you know?

ANN: From her point of view, why else would I come?

CHRIS: Well . . . would you want to? *(*ANN *studies him.)* I guess you know this is why I asked you to come.

ANN: I guess this is why I came.

CHRIS: Ann, I love you. I love you a great deal. *(Finally.)* I love you. *(Pause. She waits.)* I have no imagination . . . that's all I know to tell you. I'm embarrassing you. I didn't want to tell it to you here. I wanted some place with trees around . . . some new place, we'd never been; a place where we'd be brand-new to each other. . . .

ANN *(she touches his arm)*: What's the matter?

CHRIS: You feel it's wrong here, don't you? This yard, this chair.

ANN: It's not wrong, Chris.

CHRIS: I don't want to win you away from anything. I want you to be ready for me.

ANN: Oh, Chris, I've been ready a long, long time.

CHRIS: Then he's gone forever. You're sure.

ANN: I almost got married two years ago.

CHRIS: . . . Why didn't you?

ANN: You started to write to me . . . *(Slight pause.)*

CHRIS: You felt something that far back?

ANN: M-hm.

CHRIS: Ann, why didn't you let me know?

ANN: I was waiting for you, Chris. Till then you never wrote. And when you did, what did you say? You sure can be ambiguous, you know.

CHRIS *(he looks toward the house, then at her, trembling)*: Give me a kiss, Ann. Give me a . . . *(They kiss.)* God, I kissed you, Annie, I kissed Annie. How long, how long I've been waiting to kiss you!!

ANN: I'll never forgive you. Why did you wait all these years? All I've done is sit and wonder if I was crazy for thinking of you.

CHRIS: Annie, we're going to live now! I'm going to make you so happy. *(He kisses her, but without their bodies touching.)*

ANN: Not like that you're not.

CHRIS *(laughs)*: Why? I kissed you . . .

ANN: Like Larry's brother. Do it like you, Chris.

(He moves from her.)

ANN: What is it?

CHRIS: Let's drive some place. . . . I want to be alone with you.

ANN: No . . . what is it, Chris, your mother?

CHRIS: No . . . nothing like that . . .

ANN: Then what's wrong? . . . You've got to tell me, mustn't you? It wouldn't work this way, would it . . . *(Slight pause.)* Even in your letters, there was something ashamed.

CHRIS: Yes. I suppose I've been ashamed. I . . . I don't know how to start to tell you. It's mixed up with so many other things, it goes so far back. You remember I was in command of a company.

ANN: Ya, sure.

CHRIS: Well, I lost them.

ANN: How many?

CHRIS: Just about all.

ANN: Oh gee.

CHRIS: It takes a little time to toss that off. Because they weren't just men. For instance, one time it'd been raining several days and this kid came to me and gave me his last pair of dry socks. Put them in my pocket. That's only a little thing . . . but . . . that's the kind of guys I had. They didn't die; they killed themselves for each other. I mean that exactly; a little more selfish and they'd've been here today. And I got an idea — watching them go down. Everything was being destroyed, see, but it seemed to me that one new thing was made. A kind of responsibility. Man for man. You understand me? — To show that, to bring that onto the earth again like some kind of a monument, and everyone would feel it standing there, behind him, and it would make a difference to him. *(Pause.)* And then I came home and it was incredible. I . . . there was no meaning in it here; the whole thing to them was a kind of a—bus accident. Like when I went to work with Dad, and that rat race again. I felt . . . ashamed somehow. Because nobody was changed at all. It seemed to make suckers out of a lot of guys. I felt wrong to be alive, to open the bankbook, to drive the new car, to see the new refrigerator. I mean you can take those things out of a war, but when you drive that car you've got to know that it came out of the love a man can have for a man, you've got to be a little better because of that. Otherwise what you have is really loot, and there's blood on it. I didn't want to take any of it. And I guess that included you.

ANN: And you still feel that way . . .

CHRIS: No . . .

ANN: Because you mustn't feel that way any more.

CHRIS: I want you now, Annie.

ANN: Because you have a right to whatever you have. Everything, Chris, understand that?

CHRIS: I'm glad you feel that way.

ANN: To me too. . . . And the money, there's nothing wrong in your money. Joe put hundreds of planes in the air, you should be proud. A man should be paid for that. . . .

CHRIS: Oh Annie, Annie. . . . I'm going to make a fortune for you!

ANN *(laughing softly)*: What'll I do with a fortune? . . .

(They kiss.)

CHRIS *(rocking with her)*: Believe me, Annie, we'll be fine, fine . . .

(KELLER enters from the house.)

KELLER *(thumbing toward the house)*: Hey, Ann, your brother . . . *(They step apart shyly. KELLER comes down, and wryly.)* What is this, Labor Day?

CHRIS *(waving him away, knowing the kidding will be endless)*: All right, all right . . .

ANN *(gaily)*: You shouldn't burst out like that.

KELLER: Well, nobody told me it was Labor Day. *(Looks around.)* Where's the hot dogs?

CHRIS *(loving it)*: All right. You said it once.

KELLER: Well, as long as I know it's Labor Day from now on, I'll wear a bell around my neck.

ANN *(affectionately)*: He's so subtle!

CHRIS: George Bernard Shaw as an elephant.

KELLER: George!—hey, that reminds me, your brother's on the phone.

ANN *(surprised)*: My brother?

KELLER: Yeah, George. Long-distance.

502 PARENTS AND CHILDREN

ANN (*she is strangely upset*): What's the matter, is anything wrong?

KELLER: I don't know, Kate's talking to him. Hurry up, she'll cost him five dollars.

ANN (*she takes a step upstage, then comes down toward* CHRIS): I wonder if we ought to tell your mother yet. She doesn't seem to . . . I mean I'd hate to argue with her.

CHRIS: We'll wait till tonight. After dinner. Now don't get tense, just leave it to me.

KELLER: What're you telling her?

CHRIS: Go ahead, Ann.

(*With misgivings,* ANN *goes up and into the house.*)

CHRIS: We're getting married, Dad.

(KELLER *nods indecisively.*)

CHRIS: Don't you say anything?

KELLER (*distracted*): I'm glad, Chris, I'm just . . . George is calling from Columbus.

CHRIS (*surprised*): Columbus!

KELLER: Did Annie tell you he was going to see his father today?

CHRIS: No, I don't think she knew anything about it.

KELLER (*asking uncomfortably*): Chris, you . . . you think you knew her pretty good?

CHRIS: What kind of a question . . . ?

KELLER: I'm just wondering. All these years George don't go to see his father. Suddenly he goes . . . and she comes here.

CHRIS (*a frown growing on his face*): Well, what about it?

KELLER: It's crazy, but it comes to my mind. She don't hold nothin' against me, does she?

CHRIS: I don't know what you're talking about.

KELLER: I'm just talkin'. To his last day in court the man blamed it all on me; and this is his daughter. I mean if she was sent here to find out something.

CHRIS (*angered*): Why? What is there to find out?

ANN (*on the phone, from within*): Why are you so excited, George? What happened there?

KELLER (*glancing at the house*): I mean if they want to open up the case again, for the nuisance value, to hurt us.

CHRIS: Dad . . . how could you think that of her?

ANN (*from within*): But what did he say to you?

KELLER: It couldn't be, heh. You know.

CHRIS: Dad, you amaze me . . .

KELLER (*breaking in*): All right, forget it, forget it. (*With great force, moving about.*) I want a clean start for you, Chris. I want a new sign over the plant — Christopher Keller, Incorporated.

CHRIS (*a little uneasily*): J. O. Keller is good enough.

KELLER: We'll talk about it. I'm going to build you a house, stone, with a driveway from the road. I want you to spread out, Chris, I want you to use what I made for you . . . (*He is close to him now.*) . . . I mean, with joy, Chris, without shame . . . with joy.

CHRIS (*touched*): I will, Dad.

KELLER (*with deep emotion*): . . . Say it to me.

CHRIS: . . . Why?

KELLER: Because sometimes I think you're . . . ashamed of the money.

CHRIS (*pained*): No, don't feel that.

KELLER: Because it's good money, there's nothing wrong with that money.

CHRIS (*a little frightened*): Dad, you don't have to tell me this.

KELLER (*with overriding affection and self-confidence now. He grips* CHRIS *by the back of the neck, and with laughter between his determined jaws*): Oh, you're going to have a life now, Chris! We'll get Mother so drunk tonight we'll all get married! (*Steps away, with a wide gesture of his arm.*) There's gonna be a wedding, kid, like there never was seen! Champagne, tuxedos . . . !

(*Breaks off as* MOTHER *comes out, listening to:*)

ANN (*from within*): Well, what did he tell you, for God's sake? All right, come then. Yes, they'll all be here, nobody's running away from you! And try to get hold of yourself, will you? All right, all right, good-by!

(*ANN comes out. She is somber with nervousness. Comes down, and manages an everyday smile as:*)

CHRIS: Something wrong?

ANN: He'll be in on the seven o'clock. He's in Columbus.

KELLER (*carefully*): What is it, your father took sick?

ANN (*mystified*): No, George didn't say he was sick. I . . . (*Shaking it off.*) . . . I don't know, I suppose it's something stupid, you know my brother. . . . (*She turns suddenly toward the house. Then comes to* CHRIS.) Let's go for a drive, or something.

CHRIS (*studies her for a troubled instant, then nods*): Sure — (*To his parents.*) Be back right away.

KELLER: Take your time.

(*A guitar begins to play off left, in* JIM'S *house as:*)

MOTHER (*to* ANN): You hear? Sue is playing the guitar. It keeps him in the house. They married too young.

(CHRIS, *sensing her nervousness, her appeal to him, kisses her and, with* ANN, *goes up the driveway and out.* MOTHER *comes down toward* KELLER, *her eyes fixed upon him.*)

KELLER (*with his heartbeat in it, softly*):   What happened? What does George want?

MOTHER: He's been in Columbus since this morning with Herb. He's gotta see Annie right away, he says.

KELLER: What for?

MOTHER: I don't know. (*She keeps watching him. He moves, looking at the ground, thinking. She speaks with warning.*) He's a lawyer now, Joe. George is a lawyer.

KELLER: So what?

MOTHER: All these years he wouldn't even send a post card to Herb. Since he got back from the war, not a postcard.

KELLER (*angering*): So what?

MOTHER (*her tension breaking out*): Suddenly he takes an airplane from New York to see him. An airplane!

KELLER: Well? So?

MOTHER (*trembling*): Why?

KELLER: I don't read minds. Do you?

MOTHER: Why, Joe? What has Herb suddenly got to tell him that he takes an airplane to see him?

KELLER: What do I care what Herb's got to tell him?

MOTHER: You're sure, Joe?

KELLER (*frightened, but angry*): Yes, I'm sure.

MOTHER (*she sits stiffly in a chair*): Be smart now, Joe. The boy is coming. Be smart.

KELLER (*leans over her — into her face; desperately*): Once and for all, did you hear what I said? I said I'm sure!

MOTHER (*she nods weakly*): All right, Joe. (*He straightens up.*) Just . . . be smart.

(KELLER, *in hopeless fury, looks at her, turns around, goes up to the porch and into the house, slamming the screen door violently behind him.* MOTHER *sits in the chair downstage, stiffly, staring, seeing.*)

ACT II

Scene *as before. The same evening, as twilight falls.*

As the curtain rises, CHRIS *is discovered at the right, pulling the broken-off tree up the alley, leaving the stump standing alone. He is dressed in good pants, white shoes, but without a shirt. He disappears with the tree up the alley when* MOTHER *appears on the porch. She comes down and stands at the mouth of the alley watching him. She has on a dressing gown, carries a tray of grape-juice drink in a pitcher, and glasses.*

MOTHER (*calling up to the alley*): Did you have to put on good pants to do that?

(*There is no answer, but the sound of the tree being dragged. She comes downstage and sets the tray on the table. Then looks around uneasily, then feels the pitcher for coolness, then picks up a scrap of paper and crumples it, and sits down. In a moment she gets up nervously with her hands clasped together, and moves about touching the chairs, a bush. . . .* CHRIS *enters from the alley, brushing off his hands.)*

MOTHER: You notice there's more light with that thing gone?

CHRIS: Why aren't you dressing?

MOTHER: It's suffocating upstairs. I made a grape drink for Georgie. He always liked grape.

CHRIS: Well, come on, get dressed. And what's Dad sleeping so much for?

MOTHER: He's worried. When he's worried he sleeps. *(She looks into his eyes.)* We're dumb, Chris. Dad and I are stupid people. We don't know anything. You've got to protect us.

CHRIS: You're silly; what's there to be afraid of?

MOTHER: To his last day in court Herb never gave up the idea that Dad made him do it. If he's coming to reopen the case I won't live through it. We can't go through that thing again.

CHRIS: George is just a damned fool, Mother, how can you take him so seriously?

MOTHER: That family hates us. Maybe even Annie . . .

CHRIS: Oh now, Mother . . .

MOTHER: You think just because you like everybody, they like you! You don't realize how people can hate. Chris, we've got a nice life here, everything was going so nice. Why do you bring them into it? We struggled all our lives for a little something, and now . . .

CHRIS: All right, stop working yourself up. Just leave everything to me.

MOTHER: When George goes home, tell her to go with him.

CHRIS *(noncommittally)*: Don't worry about Annie.

MOTHER: Herb is her father too.

CHRIS: Are you going to cut it out? Now come.

MOTHER *(going upstage with him)*: You don't realize how people can hate, Chris, they can hate so much they'll tear the world to pieces. . . .

(ANN, *dressed up, appears on the porch.)*

CHRIS: See? She's dressed already. *(As he and* MOTHER *mount the porch, to* ANN.*)* I've just got to put on a shirt.

ANN *(in a preoccupied way)*: Are you feeling well, Kate?

MOTHER *(laughs weakly)*: What's the difference, dear? There are certain people, y'know, the sicker they get the longer they live. *(She goes into the house.)*

CHRIS *(softly, touching her nose)*: You look nice.

ANN: We're going to tell her tonight.

CHRIS: Absolutely, don't worry about it.

ANN: I wish we could tell her now. I can't stand scheming. My stomach gets hard.

CHRIS: It's not scheming, we'll just get her in a better mood.

ANN: The only one who's relaxed is your father. *(Laughs.)* He's fast asleep.

CHRIS: I'm relaxed.

ANN: Are you?

CHRIS: Look. *(Holds out his hand and makes it shake violently. They laugh. He smacks her fanny.)* Let me know when George gets here.

(He goes into the house. ANN *comes down off the porch. She moves aimlessly, and then is drawn toward the tree stump. She goes to it, hesitantly touches the broken top in the hush of her thoughts. From the left,* SUE *enters and halts, seeing* ANN. ANN *is not aware of her.)*

SUE: Is my husband . . . ?

ANN *(turns, startled)*: Oh!

SUE *(comes toward her, concerned)*: I'm terribly sorry.

ANN *(laughs, embarrassed)*: It's all right, I . . . I'm a little silly about the dark.

SUE *(looks about)*: It is getting dark.

ANN: Are you looking for your husband?

SUE: As usual. *(Laughs tiredly.)* He spends so much time here they'll be charging him rent.

ANN: Nobody was dressed, so he drove over to the depot to pick up my brother.

SUE: Oh, your brother's in?

ANN: Ya, they ought to be here any minute now. Will you have a cold drink?

SUE: I will, thanks. *(*SUE *sits, strangely distressed, as* ANN *goes to the table, pours.)* My husband. Too hot to drive me to the beach. But for the Kellers?—Men are like little boys; for the neighbors they'll always cut the grass.

ANN: People like to do things for the Kellers. Been that way since I can remember.

SUE *(with an edge)*: It's amazing. I guess your brother's coming to give you away, heh?

ANN *(giving her the drink, burdened)*: I don't know. I suppose.

SUE: You must be all nerved up.

ANN: It's always a problem getting yourself married, isn't it? *(She sits.)*

SUE: That depends on your shape, of course. *(She laughs.)* I don't see why you should have had a problem.

ANN: Oh, I had chances.

SUE: I'll bet. It's romantic . . . it's very unusual to me, marrying the brother of your sweetheart.

ANN: I don't know. I think it's mostly that whenever I need somebody to tell me the truth I've always thought of Chris. When he tells you something you know it's so. He relaxes me.

SUE: And he's got money. That's important, you know.

ANN: It wouldn't matter to me.

SUE: You'd be surprised. It changes everything. I married an interne. On my salary. And that was bad, because as soon as a woman supports a man he owes her something. You can never owe somebody without resenting them.

(ANN *laughs.*)

SUE: That's true, you know.

ANN: Underneath, I think the doctor is very devoted.

SUE: Oh, certainly. But it's bad when a man always sees the bars in front of him. Jim thinks he's in jail all the time.

ANN *(deprecating)*: Oh . . .

SUE: That's why I've been intending to ask you a small favor, Ann. . . . It's something very important to me.

ANN: Certainly, if I can do it.

SUE: You can. When you take up housekeeping, try to find a place away from here.

ANN: Are you fooling?

SUE: I've very serious. My husband is unhappy with Chris around.

ANN *(amazed)*: How is that?

SUE: My husband is a successful doctor. But he's got an idea that he'd like to do medical research. Discover things. You see?

ANN: Well, isn't that good?

SUE: It's fine. For a small monk. Research pays twenty-five dollars a week minus laundering the hair shirt. You've got to give up your life to go into it.

ANN: How does Chris . . . ?

SUE *(gets up; with growing feeling)*: Now don't take it that way. I like Chris. If I didn't, I'd let him know. I don't butter people. But there's something about him that makes people want to be better than it's possible to be. He does that to people.

ANN: Why is that bad?

SUE: My husband has a family, dear. Every time he has a session with Chris he feels as though he's compromising himself by not giving up everything for research. As though Chris or anybody else isn't compromising. It happens with Jim every couple of years. He meets a man and makes a statue out of him.

ANN: Maybe he's right. I don't mean that Chris is a statue, but . . .

SUE: Now darling, you know he's not right.

ANN: I don't agree with you. Chris . . .

SUE: Let's face it, dear. The man is working with his father, isn't he? He's taking money out of that business every week in the year.

ANN: What of it?

SUE: *You* ask me what of it?

ANN: I certainly do ask you. (*Pause. She seems about to burst out.*) You oughtn't cast aspersions like that. I'm surprised at you.

SUE: You're surprised at *me*.

ANN: He'd never take five cents out of that plant if there was anything wrong in it.

SUE: You know that.

ANN: I know it. I resent everything you've said.

SUE *(moving toward her)*: You know what I resent, dear?

ANN *(troubled and afraid)*: Please, I don't want to argue.

SUE: I resent living next door to the Holy Family. It makes me look like a bum, you understand?

ANN: I can't do anything about that.

SUE: Who is he to ruin a man's life? Everybody knows Joe pulled a fast one to get out of jail.

ANN: That's not true!

SUE: Then why don't you go out and talk to people? Go on, talk to them. There's not a person on the block who doesn't know the truth.

ANN: That's a lie. They're on the best terms with the block. People come here all the time for cards and . . .

SUE: So what? They give him credit for being smart. I do too. I've got nothing against Joe. But if Chris wants people to put on the hair shirt, let him take off his broadcloth. He's driving my husband crazy with that phony idealism of his, and I'm at the end of my rope on it!

(CHRIS enters the porch, wearing shirt and tie now. She turns quickly, hearing:)

SUE *(with a smile)*: Hello, darling. How's Mother?

CHRIS: I thought George came.

SUE: No, it was just us.

CHRIS *(coming down to them)*: Susie, do me a favor, heh? Go up to Mother and see if you can calm her. She's all worked up.

SUE: She still doesn't know about you two?

CHRIS *(laughs a little)*: Well, she senses it, I guess. You know my mother.

SUE *(going up to the porch)*: Oh, yeah, she's psychic.

CHRIS: Maybe there's something in the medicine chest.

SUE: I'll give her one of everything. *(On the porch.)* Don't worry about Kate; couple of drinks, dance her around a little . . . she'll love Ann. *(To* ANN.*)* Because you're the female version of him. *(Indicates* CHRIS. CHRIS *laughs.)* Don't be alarmed, I said version. *(As they laugh* SUE *goes into house.)*

CHRIS: Interesting woman, isn't she?

ANN *(moving from him, uneasily)*: Ya, she's very interesting.

CHRIS: She's a great nurse, you know, she . . .

ANN *(in tension, but trying to control it)*: Are you still doing that?

CHRIS *(sensing something wrong, but still smiling)*: Doing what?

ANN: As soon as you get to know somebody you find a distinction for them. How do you know she's a great nurse?

CHRIS: What's the matter, Ann?

ANN: The woman hates you. She despises you!

CHRIS: Hey . . . what's hit you?

ANN *(weakly, sits)*: Gee, Chris.

CHRIS: What happened here?

ANN *(she looks at him mystified, alarmed)*: You never . . . Why didn't you tell me?

CHRIS: Tell you what?

ANN: She says they think Joe is guilty.

CHRIS *(looks away)*: Yes. Well . . . *(Looks at her.)* What of it?

ANN: Why did you say there was no feeling any more?

CHRIS: What difference does it make what they think?

ANN: I don't care what they think, I just don't understand why you took the trouble to deny it. You said it was all forgotten.

CHRIS: I didn't want you to feel there was anything wrong in you coming here, that's all. I know a lot of people think my father was guilty. I suppose I assumed there might be some question in your mind.

ANN: But I never once said I suspected him.

CHRIS: Nobody says it.

(Pause. Their eyes meet.)

CHRIS *(attempting a laugh)*: What's come over you? All of a sudden you . . .

ANN *(she goes up to him)*: I know how much you love him.

CHRIS: Do you think I could forgive him if he'd done that thing?

ANN: I'm not here out of a blue sky, Chris. I turned my back on my father; if there's anything wrong here now . . .

CHRIS: I know that, Ann.

ANN: George is coming from my father, and I don't think it's with a blessing.

CHRIS: You've got nothing to fear from George.

ANN: Tell me that. Just tell me that.

CHRIS *(takes her hands)*: The man is innocent, Ann. I know he seems afraid, but he was falsely accused once and it put him through hell. How would you behave if you were faced with the same thing again? Believe me, Ann, there's nothing wrong for you here! Believe me, kid!

ANN *(a hesitation, then she embraces him)*: All right.

(They kiss as KELLER appears quietly on the porch. He watches them.)

KELLER: What is this, still Labor Day?

(They break and laugh in embarrassment. KELLER comes down.)

KELLER: I got a regular Playland back here.

CHRIS: I thought you were going to shave.

KELLER *(sitting)*: In a minute. I woke up, I can't see nothin'.

ANN: You look shaved.

KELLER: Oh no. *(Massages his jaw.)* Gotta be extra special tonight. Big night, Annie. *(Crosses his legs.)* So how's it feel to be a married woman?

ANN *(laughs)*: I don't know yet.

KELLER *(to* CHRIS*)*: What's the matter, you slippin'?

CHRIS: The great roué!

KELLER: What is that roué?

CHRIS: It's French.

KELLER: Don't talk dirty.

(They laugh.)

CHRIS *(to* ANN*)*: You ever meet a bigger ignoramus?

KELLER: Well, *somebody's* got to make a living.

ANN *(as they laugh)*: That's telling him.

KELLER: I don't know, everybody's gettin' so goddam educated in this country there'll be nobody to take away the garbage.

(They laugh.)

KELLER: It's gettin' so the only dumb ones left are the bosses.

ANN: You're not so dumb, Joe.

KELLER: I know, but you go into our plant, for instance. I got so many lieutenants, majors, and colonels, when I want somebody to sweep the floor I gotta be careful, I'll insult somebody. No kiddin'. It's a tragedy; you stand on the street today and spit, you're gonna hit a college man.

CHRIS: Well, don't spit.

KELLER: I mean to say, it's comin' to a pass. *(He takes a breath.)* I been thinkin', Annie. *(They wait for him. He comforts himself, squints thoughtfully ahead.)* Your brother George. I been thinking about your brother George. When he comes I like you to brooch something to him.

CHRIS: Broach.

KELLER: What's the matter with brooch?

CHRIS *(smiling)*: It's not English.

KELLER: When I went to night school it was brooch.

ANN *(laughs)*: Well, in day school it's broach.

KELLER: Don't surround me, will you? Seriously, Ann . . . You say he's not well . . . George. I been thinkin', why should he knock himself out in New York with that cutthroat competition when I got so many friends here. I'm very friendly with some big lawyers in town. I could do something for George; I like to set him up here.

ANN: That's awfully nice of you, Joe.

KELLER: No, kid, it ain't nice of me. I want you to understand me. I'm thinking of Chris. *(Slight pause.)* See . . . this is what I mean. I ain't got the vocabulary, but this is the thought, see. You're young yet. You get older, you want to feel that you . . . accomplished something. In your life. My only accomplishment is my son. I ain't brainy. That's all I accomplished. What I want to know, Annie, is no matter what happens, my son is my son. That there's nothin' going to come between me and him. You follow me?

ANN: No. Why do you say that?

KELLER: Because . . . face the facts, facts is facts . . . your father hates me. I don't have to tell you to his last day in court he blamed the whole thing on me, that I put him there . . . and the rest of it. You know that.

ANN: Well, he'll say anything.

KELLER: Right. He'll say anything. But let's face it, a year, eighteen months, he'll be a free man. Who is he going to come to, Annie? His baby. You. He'll come old, mad, into your house.

ANN: That can't matter any more, Joe.

KELLER: *Now* you say that, but believe me, Annie, blood is blood. A man harps long enough in your ears and you're going to listen. And . . . my son is in your house and . . . What I'm drivin' at, I don't want that hate to come between us. *(Gestures between* CHRIS *and himself.)*

ANN: I can only tell you that that could never happen.

KELLER: You're in love now, Annie, but believe me, I'm older than you; a daughter is a daughter, and a father is a father. And it could happen. *(Slight pause.)* What I like to see you do is this. Your father wouldn't talk to me. But he'll talk to you and he'll talk to your brother. I like you both to go to him in prison and tell him . . . "Dad, Joe wants to bring you into the business when you get out."

ANN *(surprised, even shocked)*: You'd have him as a partner?

KELLER: No, no partner. A good job. *(Pause. He sees she is shocked, a little mystified. He gets up, speaks more nervously.)* I want him to know, Annie . . . while he's sitting there I want him to know that when he gets out he's got a place waitin' for him. It'll take his bitterness away. To know you got a place . . . it sweetens you.

ANN *(with an edge of fear, but the stress upon the reprimand)*: Joe, you owe him nothing.

KELLER: No, no . . . I owe him a good kick in the teeth, but . . .

CHRIS: Then kick him in the teeth. I don't want him in the plant, so that's that. And don't talk like that about him — people misunderstand you.

KELLER: And I don't understand why she has to crucify the man!

CHRIS: Well, it's her father, if she feels . . .

KELLER: No, no . . .

CHRIS *(almost angrily)*: What's it to you? Why? . . .

KELLER *(a commanding outburst in high nervousness)*: A father is a father! *(His hand goes to his cheek.)* I better . . . I better shave. *(He goes upstage a few yards, then turns, and a smile is on his face. Pointing at* ANN.*)* Didn't mean to yell at you, Annie.

ANN: Let's forget the whole thing, Joe.

KELLER: Right. *(To* CHRIS.*)* She's likable.

CHRIS: Shave, will you?

KELLER: Right again.

(As he turns to the porch, LYDIA *comes hurrying from her house, at the right.)*

LYDIA *(to* JOE*)*: I forgot all about it . . . *(Seeing* CHRIS *and* ANN.*)* Hya. *(To* JOE.*)* I promised to fix Kate's hair for tonight. Did she comb it yet?

KELLER: Always a smile, hey, Lydia?

LYDIA: Sure, why not?

KELLER *(going up the porch)*: Come on up and comb my Katie's hair.

*(*LYDIA *mounts the porch.)*

KELLER: She's got a big night, make her beautiful. *(At the door, turns to* CHRIS *and* ANN *below.)* Hey, that could be a song. *(Sings nicely, softly.)* "Come on up and comb my Katie's hair . . . " *(*LYDIA *goes into the house before him.)* "Oh, come on up 'cause she's my lady fair." *(To* ANN.*)* How's that for one year of night school? *(Sings, going in.)* "Oh come on up, come on up, and comb my lady's hair; oh . . . "

(He is half in the doorway when JIM *enters from the driveway.* KELLER *waits there.* JIM *has been walking fast, now comes to a halt, an air of excitement on him.)*

CHRIS *(after* JIM *has not ventured to speak, but only looked at them)*: What's the matter. Where is he?

JIM: Where are the folks?

CHRIS: Upstairs, dressing.

ANN: What happened to George?

JIM: I asked him to wait in the car. Listen to me now. *(Takes her hand, walks downstage with her, away from the house, speaks quietly, with running excitement.)* Can you take some advice?

*(*ANN *waits.)*

JIM: Don't bring him in here.

ANN: Why?

JIM: Kate is in bad shape, you can't explode this in front of her.

ANN: Explode what?

JIM: You know why he's here, don't try to kid it away. There's blood in his eye; drive him somewhere and talk to him alone.

CHRIS *(shaken, therefore angered)*: Don't be an old lady.

(He starts up toward the driveway. JIM *stops him.)*

JIM: He's come to take her home. *(His eyes meet* CHRIS'S.*)* What does that mean? *(Turns to* ANN.*)* You know what that means. Fight it out with him some place else.

ANN *(with difficulty, to* CHRIS*)*: I'll drive . . . him somewhere. *(She makes a move to go upstage.)*

CHRIS: No. *(She stops.)*

JIM: Will you stop being an idiot?

CHRIS *(indignantly)*: Cut that out! Nobody's afraid of him here.

> *(He goes to the driveway and is brought up short by* GEORGE, *who enters there.* GEORGE *is* CHRIS'S *age, but a paler man, now on the edge of his self-restraint. He speaks quietly, as though afraid to find himself screaming. An instant's hesitation and* CHRIS *steps up to him, hand extended, smiling. With an attempt at heartiness:)*

CHRIS: Helluva way to do. What're you sitting out there for?

GEORGE: Doctor said your mother isn't well, I . . .

CHRIS: So what? She'd want to see you, wouldn't she? *(Bringing him downstage.)* We've been waiting for you all afternoon.

ANN *(touching his collar)*: This is filthy, didn't you bring another shirt?

> *(*SUE *comes out of the house.)*

SUE: How about the beach, Jim?

JIM: Oh, it's too hot to drive.

SUE: How'd you get to the station—zeppelin?

CHRIS: This is Ann's brother, Sue. George—Mrs. Bayliss.

SUE *(takes his hand)*: How do you do.

GEORGE *(removes his hat)*: You're the people who bought our house, aren't you?

SUE: That's right. Come and see what we did with it before you leave.

GEORGE: I liked it the way it was.

SUE *(to* ANN*)*: He's frank, isn't he?

JIM: No, he's George. *(Takes her hand.)* See you later. *(To* GEORGE, *as he and* SUE *go left.)* Take it easy, fella.

CHRIS *(as* SUE *and* JIM *exit)*: Thanks for driving him! How about some grape juice? Mother made it especially for you.

GEORGE *(with forced appreciation)*: Good old Kate, remembered my grape juice.

> *(*ANN *goes to pour.)*

CHRIS: You drank enough of it in this house. How've you been, George?—Sit down.

GEORGE *(in a breathless way, he never stops moving)*: It takes me a minute. *(He looks around.)* It seems impossible.

CHRIS: What?

GEORGE: I'm back here.

CHRIS: Say, you've gotten nervous, haven't you?

GEORGE: Ya, toward the end of the day. What're you, big executive now?

CHRIS: Just kind of medium. How's the law?

GEORGE *(laughs in a strained way)*: I don't know. When I was studying in the hospital it seemed sensible, but outside there doesn't seem to be much of a law. The trees got thick, didn't they? *(Points to the stump.)* What's that?

CHRIS: Blew down last night. We had it there for Larry. You know.

GEORGE: Why — afraid you'll forget him?

CHRIS: What kind of remark is that?

ANN *(breaking in)*: When did you start wearing a hat? *(She goes to him with the glass.)*

GEORGE *(discovers the hat in his hand)*: Today. *(Directly at her, his fury almost bursting out.)* From now on I decided to look like a lawyer, anyway. *(Holds it up to her.)* Don't you recognize it?

ANN: Why? Where? . . .

GEORGE: Your father's. *(Tosses it into a chair.)* He asked me to wear it.

ANN *(out of duty, but fearfully)*: . . . How is he?

GEORGE: He got smaller. *(Laughs with his lips shut.)*

ANN: Smaller?

GEORGE: Yeah, little. *(Holds out his hand to measure.)* He's a little man. That's what happens to suckers, you know. It's good I went to him in time — another year there'd be nothing left but his smell.

CHRIS *(with an edge of combativeness)*: What's the matter, George, what's the trouble?

GEORGE *(puts down the glass; a smile comes onto his face, a sardonic grin)*: The trouble. The trouble is when you make suckers out of people once you shouldn't try to do it twice.

CHRIS: What does that mean?

GEORGE *(to ANN)*: You're not married yet, are you?

ANN *(frightened)*: George, will you sit down and stop being . . .

GEORGE: Are you married yet?

ANN: No, I'm not married yet.

GEORGE: You're not going to marry him.

ANN *(bridling)*: Why aren't I going to marry him?

GEORGE: Because his father destroyed your family.

(Pause. ANN does not move. CHRIS begins:)

CHRIS: Now look, George . . .

GEORGE: Cut it short, Chris. Tell her to come home with me. Let's not argue, you know what I've got to say.

CHRIS: George, you don't want to be the voice of God, do you?

GEORGE: I'm . . .

CHRIS: That's been your trouble all your life, George, you dive into things. What kind of a statement is that to make? You're a big boy now.

GEORGE *(as though "you're damned right")*: I'm a big boy now.

CHRIS: Don't come bulling in here. If you've got something to say, be civilized about it. You haven't even said hello to me.

GEORGE *(as though astonished)*: Don't civilize me!

CHRIS: Are you going to talk like a grown man or aren't you?

ANN *(quickly, to forestall an outburst from* GEORGE*)*: Sit down, dear. Don't be angry, what's the matter? *(He allows her to seat him, looking at her.)* Now what happened? You kissed me when I left, now you . . .

GEORGE *(breathlessly, to her alone)*: My life turned upside since then. I couldn't go back to work when you left. I wanted to go to Dad and tell him you were going to be married. It seemed impossible not to tell him. He loved you so much. *(Slight pause.)* Annie . . . we did a terrible thing. We can never be forgiven. Not even to send him a card at Christmas. I didn't see him once since I got home from the war! Annie, you don't know what was done to that man. You don't know what happened.

ANN *(afraid)*: Of course I know.

GEORGE: You can't know, you wouldn't be here. Dad came to work that day. The night foreman came to him and showed him the cylinder heads . . . they were coming out of the process with defects. There was something wrong with the process. So Dad went directly to the phone and called here and told Joe to come down right away. But the morning passed. No sign of Joe. So Dad called again. By this time he had over a hundred defectives. The Army was screaming for stuff and Dad didn't have anything to ship. So Joe told him . . . on the phone he told him to weld, cover up the crack in any way he could, and ship them out.

CHRIS: Are you through now?

GEORGE: I'm not through now! *(To* ANN.*)* Dad was afraid. He didn't know if they'd hold up in the air. Or maybe an Army inspector would catch him. But Joe told him they'd hold up, and swore to him . . . swore to him on the phone, Annie, that if anything happened he would take the whole responsibility. But Dad still wanted him there if he was going to do it. But he can't come down . . . he's sick. Sick! He suddenly gets the flu! Suddenly! But he promised to take responsibility. Do you understand what I'm saying? On the telephone you can't *have* responsibility! In a court you can always deny a phone call and that's exactly what he did. They knew he was a liar the first time, but in the appeal they believed that rotten lie and now Joe is a big shot and your father is the patsy. *(He gets up.)* Now what're you going to do? Answer me, what're you going to do — eat his food, sleep in his bed? You didn't even send your own father a card at Christmas, now what're you going to do?

CHRIS: What're *you* going to do, George?

GEORGE: He's too smart for me; I can't prove a phone call.

CHRIS *(gets up)*: Then how dare you come in here with that rot?

ANN: George, the court . . .

GEORGE: The court didn't know your father! But you know him. You know in your heart Joe did it.

CHRIS: Lower your voice or I'll throw you out of here!

ANN: George, I know everything you've said. Dad told that whole thing in court and they . . .

GEORGE *(almost weeping)*: The court did not know him, Annie! *(Now with deliberation he turns to* CHRIS.*)* I'll ask you something, and look me in the eye when you answer me.

CHRIS *(defiantly)*: I'll look you in the eye.

GEORGE: You know your father . . .

CHRIS *(with growing fear, and therefore anger)*: I know him well.

GEORGE: And he's the kind of boss to let a hundred and twenty-one cylinder heads be repaired and shipped out of his shop without even knowing about it?

CHRIS: He's that kind of boss.

GEORGE: And that's the same Joe Keller who never left his shop without first going around to see that all the lights were out.

CHRIS *(with growing fury)*: The same Joe Keller.

GEORGE: The same man who knows how many minutes a day his workers spend in the toilet.

CHRIS: The same man.

GEORGE: And my father, that frightened mouse who'd never buy a shirt without somebody along — that man would dare do such a thing on his own?

CHRIS: On his own. And because he's a frightened mouse this is another thing he'd do: throw the blame on somebody else because he's not man enough to take it himself. This is *exactly* what he'd do. He tried it in court but it didn't work, but with a fool like you it works!

GEORGE: Oh, Chris, you're a liar to yourself.

ANN *(deeply shaken)*: Don't talk like that!

CHRIS: Tell me, George. What happened? The court record was good enough for you all these years, why isn't it good now? Why did you believe it all these years? *(Slight pause.)*

GEORGE: I had no reason not to believe it. And besides — I thought you believed it. That meant something, too, you know. *(*CHRIS *stops moving.)* But today I heard it from his mouth. From his mouth it's altogether different than the record. Anyone who knows him, and knows your father, will believe it from his mouth. Your father tricked him. He took everything we have. I can't beat that. But this I can. She's one item he's not going to grab. *(Turns to* ANN.*)* Get your things. *(*ANN *stares at him.)* Everything they have is covered with blood. You're not the kind of girl who can live with that.

(ANN *turns her eyes on* CHRIS, *mystified and wondering.)*

CHRIS: Ann . . . you're not going to believe that, are you?

ANN *(she goes to him)*: You know it's not true, don't you?

GEORGE: How can he tell you? It's his father.

ANN (to GEORGE, *angrily*): Don't, please!

GEORGE: *He knows,* Annie . . .

CHRIS: The voice of God!

GEORGE: Then why isn't your name on the business? Explain that to her!

CHRIS: What the hell has that got to do with . . . ?

GEORGE: Annie, add it up. Why isn't his name on it?

CHRIS (*furiously*): Even when I don't own it?

GEORGE: Who're you kidding? Who gets it when he dies? (*To* ANN.) Open your eyes, you know the both of them, isn't that the first thing they'd do, the way they love each other? — J. O. Keller and Son?

(*Pause.* ANN *looks from him to* CHRIS. CHRIS *watches her face, waits.*)

GEORGE: None of these things ever even crossed your mind?

CHRIS: Yes, they crossed my mind. Anything can cross your mind!

GEORGE: I'll settle it. Do you want to settle it or are you afraid to?

CHRIS: . . . What . . . what do you mean?

GEORGE: Let me go up and talk to your father. In ten minutes you'll have the answer. Or are you afraid of the answer?

CHRIS: I'm not afraid of the answer. I know the answer. But my mother isn't well and I don't want a fight here now, and all you're going to do is fight with him.

GEORGE: Let me go to him.

CHRIS: You're not going to start a fight here now.

GEORGE (*to* ANN): What more do you want!

ANN (*turns her head suddenly toward the house. Apprehensively*): Someone's coming.

CHRIS (*glances toward the house; to* GEORGE, *quietly*): You won't say anything now.

ANN: Don't, George, not now. You'll go soon. I'll call a cab.

GEORGE: You're coming with me.

ANN: Please, leave it to me. And don't mention marriage, because we haven't told her yet. You understand? Don't . . . (*She sees a plan in his eyes. Alarmed,*) George, you're not going to start anything now!

(*Enter* MOTHER *on the porch. She is dressed almost formally, her hair is fixed. They are all turned toward her. On seeing* GEORGE *she raises both hands, comes down toward him, and in a voice meant to indicate her ill-health as well as her compassion for him:*)

MOTHER: Georgie, Georgie. (*She has paused in front of him.*)

GEORGE (*a little abashed — he always liked her*): Hello, Kate.

MOTHER (*she cups his face in her hands*): Georgie. They made an old man out of you. (*Touches his hair.*) Look, you're gray.

GEORGE (*her pity, open and unabashed, reaches into him, and he smiles sadly*): I know, I . . .

MOTHER *(shakes her finger at him)*: I told you when you went away, don't try for medals.

GEORGE *(he laughs, tiredly)*: I didn't try, Kate. They made it very easy for me.

MOTHER *(actually angry)*: Go on. *(Taking in* CHRIS.*)* You're all alike. *(To* ANN.*)* Look at him, why did you say he's fine? He looks like a ghost.

GEORGE *(relishing her solicitude)*: I feel all right.

MOTHER: I'm sick to look at you. What's the matter with your mother, why don't she feed you?

ANN: He just hasn't any appetite.

MOTHER: If he ate in my house he'd have an appetite. *(They laugh.)* I pity your husband! *(To* GEORGE.*)* Sit down, I'll make you a sandwich.

GEORGE *(taking her hand with an embarrassed laugh)*: I'm really not hungry.

MOTHER *(shaking her head)*: Honest to God, it breaks my heart to see what happened to all the children. How we worked and planned for you, and you end up no better than us.

GEORGE *(with deep feeling for her)*: You . . . you haven't changed, you know that, Kate?

MOTHER: None of us changed, Georgie. We all love you. Joe was just talking about the day you were born and the water got shut off. People were carrying basins from a block away — *(Laughs.)* — a stranger would think the whole neighborhood was on fire! *(They laugh. She sees the juice. To* ANN.*)* Why didn't you give him some juice!

ANN *(defensively)*: I offered it to him.

MOTHER *(scoffingly)*: You *offered* it. *(Thrusting the glass into* GEORGE'S *hand.)* Give it to him! *(To* GEORGE, *who is laughing.)* Sit down, and drink and . . . and *look* like something!

GEORGE *(sitting)*: Kate, I feel hungry already.

CHRIS *(proudly)*: She could turn Mahatma Gandhi into a heavyweight.

MOTHER *(to* CHRIS, *with great energy)*: Listen, to hell with the restaurant! I got a ham in the icebox, and frozen strawberries, and avocados and . . .

ANN: Swell, I'll help you!

GEORGE: The train leaves at eight-thirty, Ann.

MOTHER *(to* ANN*)*: You're leaving?

CHRIS: No, Mother, she's not . . .

ANN *(breaking through it, going to* GEORGE *quickly)*: You hardly got here; give yourself a chance to get acquainted again.

CHRIS: Sure, you don't even know us any more.

MOTHER: Well, Chris, if they can't stay, don't . . .

CHRIS: No, it's just a question of George, Mother, he planned on . . .

GOERGE *(he gets up — and politely, nicely, for* KATE'S *sake)*: Now wait a minute, Chris . . .

CHRIS *(smiling and full of command, cutting him off)*: If you want to go, I'll drive you to the station now, but if you're staying, no arguments while you're here.

MOTHER (*at last confessing the tension*): Why should he argue? (*She goes to him. With desperation and command and compassion, stroking his hair.*) Georgie and us have no argument. How could we have an argument, Georgie? We all got hit by the same lightning, how can you . . . ? Did you see what happened to Larry's tree, Georgie? (*She has taken his arm, and unwillingly he moves across stage toward it with her.*) Imagine? While I was dreaming of him in the middle of the night, the wind came along and . . .

(*Enter* LYDIA *onto the porch. As soon as she sees him:*)

LYDIA: Hey, Georgie! (*She comes down to him eagerly. She has a flowered hat in her hand.*)

GEORGE (*they shake hands warmly*): Hello, Laughy. What'd you do, grow?

LYDIA: I'm a big girl now.

MOTHER (*taking the hat from her*): Look what she can do to a hat!

ANN (*to* LYDIA, *admiring the hat*): Did you make that?

MOTHER: In ten minutes! (*She puts it on.*)

LYDIA (*fixing it on her head*): I only rearranged it.

GEORGE: You still make your own clothes?

CHRIS (*of* MOTHER): Ain't she classy? All she needs is a wolfhound dog.

LYDIA: You work in one of those big skyscrapers?

MOTHER (*moving her head right and left*): It feels like somebody is sitting on me.

ANN: It's beautiful, Kate.

MOTHER (*she kisses* LYDIA — *to* GEORGE): She's a genius! *You* should've married her. (*They laugh.*) *This* one can *feed* you!

LYDIA (*strangely embarrassed*): Oh, stop that, Kate.

GEORGE (*to* LYDIA): Didn't I hear you had a baby?

MOTHER: You don't hear so good. She's got three babies.

GEORGE (*a little hurt by it — to* LYDIA): No kidding, three?

LYDIA: Yeah, it was one-two-three. You've been away a long time, Georgie.

GEORGE: I'm beginning to realize.

MOTHER (*to* CHRIS *and* GEORGE): The trouble with you kids is you *think* too much.

(*They laugh.*)

LYDIA: Well, we think too.

MOTHER (*slaps* LYDIA'S *backside*): Yes, but not all the time.

GEORGE (*with almost obvious envy*): They never took Frank, heh?

LYDIA (*a little apologetically*): No, he was always one year ahead of the draft.

MOTHER: It's amazing. When they were calling boys twenty-seven Frank was just twenty-eight, when they made it twenty-eight he was just twenty-nine. That's why he took up astrology. It's all in when you were born, it just goes to show.

CHRIS: What does it go to show?

MOTHER *(to* CHRIS*)*: Don't be so intelligent. Some superstitions are very nice! *(To* LYDIA*.)* Did he finish Larry's horoscope?

LYDIA: I'll ask him now, I'm going in. *(To* GEORGE, *a little sadly, almost embarrassed.)* Would you like to see my babies? Come on.

GEORGE: I don't think so, Lydia. *(Slight pause.)*

LYDIA *(understanding)*: All right. Good luck to you, George.

GEORGE: Thanks. And to you . . . and Frank.

(She smiles at him, turns, and goes off right to her house. GEORGE *stands staring in that direction.)*

MOTHER *(reading his thoughts)*: She got pretty, heh?

GEORGE *(sadly)*: Very pretty.

MOTHER *(as a reprimand)*: She's beautiful, you damn fool.

GEORGE *(looks around longingly; and softly, with a catch in his throat)*: She makes it seem so nice around here. *(He walks slowly across the stage, looking at the ground as:)*

MOTHER *(shaking her finger, almost weeping)*: Look what happened to you because you wouldn't listen to me. I told you to marry that girl and stay out of that goddamned war!

GEORGE *(laughs at himself)*: She used to laugh too much.

MOTHER: And you didn't laugh enough. While you were getting mad about Fascism Frank was getting into her bed.

GEORGE *(with a bitter smile, to* CHRIS*)*: He won the war, Frank.

CHRIS: All the battles.

MOTHER *(in pursuit of this mood)*: The day they started the draft, Georgie, I told you you loved that girl.

CHRIS *(laughs)*: And truer love hath no man.

GEORGE *(laughs)*: She's wonderful!

MOTHER: I'm smarter than any of you, and now you're going to listen to me, George. You had big principles, Eagle Scouts the three of you; so now I got a tree, and this one *(Of* CHRIS.*)* when the weather gets bad he can't stand on his feet. *(Indicates* LYDIA'S *house.)* And that big dope next door who never reads anything but Andy Gump has three children and his house paid off. Stop being a philosopher. Look after *yourself.* Like Joe was just saying — you move back here, he'll help you get set, and I'll find you a girl and put a smile on your face.

GEORGE: Joe? Joe wants me here?

ANN *(eagerly)*: He asked me to tell you, and I think it's a good idea.

MOTHER: Certainly. Why must you make-believe you hate us? Is that another principle — that you have to hate us? You don't hate us, George, not in your heart. I know you, you can't fool me. I diapered you. *(Suddenly, to* ANN.*)* You remember Mr. Marcy's daughter?

ANN *(laughing)*: She's got you hooked already!

(And GEORGE *laughs, is excited.)*

MOTHER: You look her over, George; you'll see she's the most beautiful . . .

CHRIS: She's got warts, George.

MOTHER *(to* CHRIS*)*: She hasn't got warts! *(To* GEORGE.*)* So the girl has a little beauty mark on her chin . . .

CHRIS: And two on her nose.

MOTHER: Will you . . . ? *(As though this destroys the warts — to* GEORGE.*)* You remember. Her father's the retired police inspector.

CHRIS: Sergeant, George. He looks like a gorilla.

MOTHER: He's a very kind man! *(To* GEORGE.*)* He never shot anybody!

(They all burst out laughing as KELLER *enters onto the porch.)*

KELLER *(as he appears the laughter stops; coming down, with strained joviality)*: Well! Look who's here. *(Extending his hand.)* Georgie, good to see ya.

GEORGE *(shakes hands — somberly)*: How're you, Joe?

KELLER: So-so. Gettin' old. You comin' out to dinner with us?

GEORGE: No, got to be back in New York.

ANN: I'll call a cab for you. *(She goes up and into the house as:)*

KELLER: Too bad you can't stay, George. Sit down. *(To* KATE.*)* He looks fine.

MOTHER: He looks terrible.

KELLER: That's what I said, you look terrible, George. *(They laugh.)* I wear the pants and she beats me with the belt.

GEORGE: I saw your factory on the way from the station. It looks like General Motors.

KELLER: I wish it was General Motors, but it ain't, George. *(Crossing his legs easily.)* So you finally went to see your father, I hear.

GEORGE: Yes, this morning. What kind of stuff do you make now?

KELLER: Oh, little of everything. Pressure cookers, an assembly for washing machines. Got a nice, flexible plant now. So how'd you find Dad? Feel all right?

GEORGE *(searching* KELLER, *he speaks indecisively)*: No, he's not well, Joe.

KELLER: Not his heart again, is it?

GEORGE: It's everything, Joe. It's his soul.

CHRIS *(beginning to rise)*: How about seeing what they did with your house?

KELLER: Leave him be.

GEORGE: I'd like to talk to him.

KELLER: Sure, he just got here. That's the way they do, George. A little man makes a mistake and they hang him by the thumbs; the big ones become ambassadors. I wish you'd 'a' told me you were going to see Dad.

GEORGE *(studying him)*: I didn't know you were interested.

KELLER: In a way, I am. I would like him to know, George, that as far as I'm concerned, any time he wants he's got a place with me. I would like him to know that.

GEORGE *(he looks at* MOTHER*)*: He hates your guts, Joe. Don't you know that?

KELLER: I . . . imagined it. But that can change, too.

MOTHER: Herb was never like that.

GEORGE: He's like that now. He'd like to take every man who made money in the war and put him up against a wall.

KELLER: He'll need a lot of bullets.

GEORGE: And he'd better not get any.

KELLER: That's a sad thing to hear.

GEORGE *(now with his bitterness dominant)*: Why? What'd you expect him to think of you?

KELLER *(the force of his nature rising, but under control)*: A thing can be sad even if you expect it. I expected it because I know your father. And I'm sad to see he hasn't changed. *(He gets up.)* As long as I know him, twenty-five years, that part of him made me sad. The man never learned how to take the blame. You know that, George.

GEORGE *(he does)*: Well, I . . .

KELLER: But you do know it. Because the way you come in here you don't look like you remember it. I mean like in 1937 when we had the shop on Flood Street. And he damn near blew us all up with that heater he left burning for two days without water. He wouldn't admit that was his fault either. I had to fire a mechanic to save his face. You remember that.

GEORGE: Yes, but . . .

KELLER: I'm just mentioning it, George. Because this is just another one of a lot of things. Like when he gave Frank that money to invest in oil stock.

GEORGE *(distressed)*: I know that, I . . .

KELLER *(driving in, but restrained)*: But it's good to remember those things, kid. The way he cursed Frank because the stock went down. Was that Frank's fault? To listen to him Frank was a swindler. And all the man did was give him a bad tip.

GEORGE *(gets up, moves away)*: I know those things . . .

KELLER: Then remember them, remember them. *(ANN comes from the house, halts as KELLER continues.)* There are certain men in the world who rather see everybody hung before they'll take blame. You understand me, George?

(They stand facing each other, GEORGE *trying to judge him.)*

ANN *(coming downstage)*: The cab's on its way. Would you like to wash?

MOTHER *(with the thrust of hope)*: Why must he go? Make the midnight, George.

KELLER: Sure, you'll have dinner with us!

ANN: How about it? Why not? We're eating at the lake; we could have a swell time.

GEORGE (*looks at* KELLER, *then back to her*): All right. (*To* MOTHER.) Is Lydia . . . I mean Frank and Lydia coming?

MOTHER: I'll get you a date that'll make her look like a . . . ! (*She starts upstage.*)

GEORGE (*laughs*): No, I don't want a date.

CHRIS: I know somebody just for you! (*To* MOTHER.) Charlotte Tanner!

MOTHER: Sure, call her up!

(CHRIS *exits.*)

MOTHER (*to* GEORGE): Come upstairs and pick out a shirt and tie!

GEORGE (*they grow silent at his sudden emotion; he looks around at them and the place*): I never felt at home . . . anywhere but here. I feel so . . . (*He nearly laughs, and turns away from them.*) Kate, you look so young, you know? You didn't change at all. It . . . rings an old bell. (*Turns to* JOE.) You too, Joe, you're amazingly the same. The whole atmosphere is.

KELLER: Say, I ain't got time to get sick.

MOTHER: He hasn't been laid up in fifteen years . . .

KELLER (*quickly*): Except my flu during the war.

MOTHER: Heh?

KELLER: My flu, when I was sick during . . .

MOTHER (*quickly*): Well, sure . . . (*To* GEORGE.) . . . except for that flu, I mean. (*Pause.* GEORGE *stands perfectly still.* MOTHER, *a little desperately.*) I just forgot it, George. (GEORGE *doesn't move.*) I mean he's so rarely sick it slipped my mind. I thought he had pneumonia, he couldn't get off the bed.

GEORGE: Why did you say he's never . . . ?

KELLER: I know how you feel, kid, but I couldn't help it; I'll never forgive myself, because if I could've gone in that day I'd never allow Dad to touch those heads.

GEORGE: She said you'd never been sick.

MOTHER: I said he *was* sick!

GEORGE (*to* ANN): Didn't you hear her say . . . ?

MOTHER: Do you remember every time you were sick?

GEORGE: I'd remember pneumonia . . .

ANN: Now, George!

GEORGE: Especially if I got it the day my partner was going to patch up cylinder heads! What happened that day, Joe?

(MOTHER *sees* FRANK *coming into the yard holding a sheet of paper.*)

MOTHER: Frank! — did you see George?

FRANK (*extending his hand*): Lydia told me, I'm glad to . . . (*Breaks off in emotion.*) You'll have to pardon me. I've got something amazing for you, Kate, I finished Larry's horoscope.

MOTHER *(desperately)*: You'd be interested in this, George! *(Draws* GEORGE *over to* FRANK *while* GEORGE *stares at* KELLER*.)* It's wonderful the way he can understand the . . .

*(*CHRIS *enters from the house.)*

CHRIS: Charlotte's on the phone, George, go in and talk to her. *(He notices the sudden tension.)* What's . . . ?

MOTHER *(to* CHRIS*)*: He finished Larry's horoscope!

FRANK: Listen! It's amazing!

ANN *(to* CHRIS*)*: I don't think George wants to go.

GEORGE: You don't think *I* want to go!

ANN *(going to* CHRIS, *addressing* GEORGE*)*: Let me talk to him alone.

CHRIS: What happened now?

MOTHER: Nothing, nothing! *(Quickly, to* FRANK*.)* What did you find out?

FRANK: Larry is alive! Follow it now, you see the Milky Way? . . .

CHRIS: Will you stop filling her head with that junk?

FRANK: Is it junk to feel there's a greater power than ourselves?

MOTHER: Listen to him! Maybe you'll change your mind about things. *(To* ANN*.)* Both of you!

GEORGE *(to* ANN*)*: Can't you understand what she's telling you?

CHRIS: What is she telling her? *(To* MOTHER*.)* What did you say to her?

MOTHER *(of* FRANK, *avoiding his question)*: Chris—he could be right!

CHRIS: Frank, you're going to cut out this nonsense.

FRANK: I've studied the stars of his life, Chris, and I'm not going to argue with you. I'm telling you. He was reported missing on February ninth, but February ninth was his favorable day! You can laugh at a lot of it; I can understand you laughing. But the odds are a million to one that a man won't die on his favorable day. That's known, that's known, Chris! Somewhere in this world your brother is alive!

MOTHER: Why isn't it possible? Maybe you're doing a terrible thing with her! *(A car horn is heard from the street.)* Oh, that's their cab. Will you tell him to wait, Frank? And I want to talk about it with you later.

FRANK: Sure thing.

*(*FRANK *trots up the alley.* MOTHER *calls after him.)*

MOTHER: They'll be right out, driver!

CHRIS: She is not leaving, Mother.

GEORGE *(to* ANN*)*: She told you to go, get your things.

CHRIS: Nobody can tell her to go.

GEORGE: My darling sister, she told you to go! What are you waiting for now? He was never sick . . .

MOTHER: I didn't say that!

GEORGE: . . . He simply told your father to kill pilots and covered himself in bed!

CHRIS *(to* MOTHER*)*: What's this about?

MOTHER: It just happened to slip my mind that Dad . . .

ANN *(breaking in, to* GEORGE*)*: Go now, I want to see Chris alone.

GEORGE: But she told you to go!

ANN: I . . . I can't go.

GEORGE: But, Annie!

ANN: No . . . *(Of* CHRIS.*)* . . . he's the only one can tell me, George.

MOTHER: I packed your bag, darling . . .

CHRIS *(shocked)*: What?

MOTHER: I packed your bag, all you've got to do is close it.

ANN *(on the verge of weeping)*: I'm not closing anything. He asked me here and I'm staying till he tells me to go. Till he tells me!

MOTHER *(of* GEORGE*)*: But if that's how he feels . . .

CHRIS *(suddenly bursting out)*: That's all! Nothing more till Christ comes, about the case or Larry; not another word as long as I'm here!

*(*ANN *has been pressing* GEORGE *up toward the driveway.)*

GEORGE: Say no to them, Annie, somebody's got to say no to them. . . .

ANN *(pleading, yet forcing him, trying to comfort him)*: Please, dear, please . . . Don't, George, you mustn't cry, please. . . .

(They go up the driveway. CHRIS *turns to* MOTHER.*)*

CHRIS: What do you mean, you packed her bag? How dare you pack her bag?

MOTHER *(sobbing, she reaches out for him)*: Chris . . .

CHRIS *(refusing his mother's embrace)*: How dare you pack her bag?

MOTHER: She doesn't belong here.

CHRIS: Then I don't belong here.

MOTHER: She's Larry's girl, she's Larry's girl.

CHRIS: And I'm his brother and he's dead, and I'm marrying his girl.

MOTHER: Never, never in this world!

KELLER: You lost your mind?

MOTHER *(violently, pointing into* KELLER'S *face)*: You have nothing to say!

KELLER *(cruelly)*: I got plenty to say! Three and a half years you been talking like a maniac and I'm . . . !

MOTHER *(she smashes him across the face. Everything stops. Her hand remains suspended, trembling. She whispers)*: Nothing. You have nothing to say. Now I say. He's coming back. He's on his way. A boat is bringing him. Maybe a plane. He'll walk down the driveway. He'll come and say hello. And then we'll have a wedding, dear; he'll call her back and then she'll come. My boy is on his way, a long way home, and we . . . everybody has got to wait.

CHRIS *(about to weep)*: Mother dear, Mother . . .

MOTHER *(shaking her head, absolutely)*: Wait, wait . . .

CHRIS: How long? How long!

MOTHER *(rolling out of her)*: Till he comes; forever and ever till he comes; he's not dead, darling, till we're all in the ground, till all of us are gone.

CHRIS *(as an ultimatum)*: Mother, I'm going ahead with it.

MOTHER: Chris, I've never said no to you in my life, now I say no!

CHRIS: You'll never let him go till I do it.

MOTHER: I'll never let him go and you'll never let him go!

CHRIS: I've let him go a long . . .

MOTHER *(with no less force, but turning from him)*: Then let your father go.

(Pause. CHRIS *stands transfixed.)*

KELLER *(softly)*: She's out of her mind.

MOTHER: Altogether! *(To* CHRIS, *but not facing them.)* Let him go too. Is that possible? Then the boy is alive. God does not do such things; the boy is alive. *(She turns to* CHRIS.*)* You understand me now? As long as you live that boy is alive. *(She bursts into sobs.)* You understand me? *(Beyond control, she hurries up and into the house.)*

*(*CHRIS *has not moved.)*

KELLER *(he speaks insinuatingly, questioningly)*: She's out of her mind.

CHRIS *(a broken whisper)*: Then . . . you did it?

KELLER *(the beginning of a plea in his voice)*: He never flew a P-40.

CHRIS: But the others.

KELLER *(insistently)*: She's out of her mind. *(He takes a step toward* CHRIS, *pleadingly.)*

CHRIS *(unyielding)*: Dad . . . you did it?

KELLER: He never flew a P-40, what's the matter with you?

CHRIS *(still asking, and saying)*: Then you did it. To the others.

KELLER *(afraid of him, his deadly insistence)*: What's the matter with you? *(Comes nervously closer to him, and, seeing wildness in his eyes.)* What the hell is the matter with you?

CHRIS *(quietly, incredulously)*: How . . . how could you do that?

KELLER *(lost, he raises his fists)*: What's the matter with you?

CHRIS *(his passion beginning to flow)*: Dad . . . Dad, you killed twenty-one men.

KELLER: What, killed?

CHRIS: You killed them, you murdered them.

KELLER *(as though throwing his whole nature open before* CHRIS*)*: How could I kill anybody?

CHRIS: Dad! Dad!

KELLER *(trying to hush him)*: I didn't kill anybody!

CHRIS: Then explain it to me. What did you do? Explain it to me, or I'll tear you to pieces! What did you do, then? What did you do? Now tell me what you did. What did you do?

KELLER *(horrified at his overwhelming fury)*: Don't, Chris, don't . . .

CHRIS: I want to know what you did, now what did you do? You had a hundred and twenty-one cracked engine heads, now what did you do?

KELLER: If you're going to hang me, then I . . .

CHRIS: I'm listening, God almighty, I'm listening!

(Their movements now are those of subtle pursuit and escape. KELLER *keeps a step out of* CHRIS'S *range, as he talks.)*

KELLER: You're a boy—what could I do? I'm in business, a man is in business; a hundred and twenty-one cracked, you're out of business; you got a process, the process don't work you're out of business; you don't know how to operate, your stuff is no good; they close you up, they tear up your contracts, what the hell's it to them? You lay forty years into a business and they knock you out in five minutes—what could I do, let them take forty years, let them take my life away? *(His voice cracking.)* I never thought they'd install them. I swear to God. I thought they'd stop 'em before anybody took off.

CHRIS: Then why'd you ship them out?

KELLER: By the time they could spot them I thought I'd have the process going again, and I could show them they needed me and they'd let it go by. But weeks passed and I got no kickback, so I was going to tell them.

CHRIS: Then why didn't you tell them?

KELLER: It was too late. The paper, it was all over the front page, twenty-one went down, it was too late. They came with handcuffs into the shop, what could I do? *(Weeping, he approaches* CHRIS.*)* Chris . . . Chris, I did it for you, it was a chance and I took it for you. I'm sixty-one years old, when would I have another chance to make something for you? Sixty-one years old you don't get another chance, do ya?

CHRIS: You even knew they wouldn't hold up in the air.

KELLER: I didn't say that . . .

CHRIS: But you were going to warn them not to use them . . .

KELLER: But that don't mean . . .

CHRIS: It means you knew they'd crash.

KELLER: It don't mean that.

CHRIS: Then you *thought* they'd crash.

KELLER: I was afraid maybe . . .

CHRIS: You were afraid maybe! Almighty God in Heaven, what kind of man are you? Kids were hanging in the air by those heads. You knew that!

KELLER: For you, a business for you!

CHRIS *(with burning fury)*: For me! Where do you live, where have you come from? For me!—I was dying every day and you were killing my boys and you did it for me? I was so proud you were helping us win and you did it for me? What the hell do you think I was thinking of, the goddam business? Is that as far as your mind can see, the business?

What is that, the world—the business? What are you made of, dollar bills? What the hell do you mean, you did it for me? Don't you have a country? Don't you live in the world? What the hell are you? You're not even an animal, no animal kills his own, what are you? What must I do to you? I ought to tear the tongue out of your mouth, what must I do?

(He is weeping, and with his fist he begins to pound down upon his father's shoulder, and KELLER *stands there and weeps.)*

CHRIS *(with each blow)*: What? What! What! What! *(He stumbles away, covering his face as he weeps.)* What must I do, Jesus God, what must I do?

(He falls into a chair and cries. KELLER *raises a hand weakly, and comes toward him weeping, saying:)*

KELLER: Chris . . . My Chris . . .

ACT III

Scene *as before. Two o'clock the following morning.* MOTHER *is discovered as the curtain rises, rocking ceaselessly in a chair, staring at her thoughts. It is an intense, slight sort of rocking. A light shows from the upstairs bedroom, the lower-floor windows being dark. The moon is strong and casts its bluish light.* KELLER *stands inside the screen door staring at the right.*

Presently JIM, *dressed in jacket and hat, appears from the left, notices* KELLER, *goes up beside* MOTHER.

JIM: Any news?

MOTHER: No news.

JIM *(he takes another look at her and sits beside her and takes her hand)*: You can't sit up all night, dear, why don't you go to bed?

MOTHER: I'm waiting for Chris. *(Withdraws her hand.)* Don't worry about me, Jim, I'm perfectly all right.

JIM: But it's almost two o'clock.

MOTHER: Then it's two o'clock. I can't sleep. *(Slight pause.)* You had an emergency?

JIM *(tiredly)*: Somebody had a headache and thought he was dying. *(Slight pause.)* Half of my patients are quite mad. Nobody realizes how many people are walking around loose, and they're as cracked as coconuts. Money. Money-money-money-money. You say it long enough it doesn't mean anything. *(She smiles, makes a silent laugh.)* Oh, how I'd love to be around when that happens.

MOTHER *(shakes her head)*: Never. You're so childish, Jim! Sometimes you are.

*(*KELLER *disappears inside the house.)*

JIM *(looks at her a moment)*: Kate. *(Pause.)* What happened?

MOTHER: I told you. He had an argument with Joe. Then he got in the car and drove away.

JIM: What kind of argument?

MOTHER: An argument. Joe . . . he was crying like a child, before.

JIM: They argued about Ann?

MOTHER *(slight hesitation)*: No, not Ann. Imagine? *(Indicates the lighted window above.)* She hasn't come out of that room since he left. All night in that room.

JIM *(looks at the window, then at her)*. What'd Joe do, tell him?

MOTHER *(she stops rocking)*: Tell him what?

JIM: Don't be afraid, Kate. I know. I've always known.

MOTHER: How?

JIM: It occurred to me a long time ago. *(Pause.)*

MOTHER: I always had the feeling that in the back of his head, Chris . . . almost knew. I didn't think it would be such a shock.

JIM *(gets up)*: You don't know your own son. Chris would never know how to live with a thing like that. It takes a certain talent . . . for lying. You have it, and I do. But not him.

MOTHER: What do you mean — he's not coming back?

JIM: Oh, no, he'll come back. We all come back, Kate. These private little revolutions always die. The compromise is always made. In a peculiar way. Frank is right — every man does have a star. The star of one's honesty. And you spend your life groping for it, but once it's out it never lights again. I don't think he went very far. He probably just wanted to be alone to watch his star go out.

MOTHER: Just as long as he comes back.

JIM: I wish he wouldn't, Kate. One year I simply took off, went to New Orleans; for two months I lived on bananas and milk, and studied a certain disease. It was beautiful. And then she came, and she cried. And I went back home with her. And now I live in the usual darkness; I can't find myself; it's even hard sometimes to remember the kind of man I wanted to be. I'm a good husband, Chris is a good son — he'll come back.

(KELLER comes out on the porch.)

JIM *(going upstage — to MOTHER)*: I have a feeling he's in the park. I'll look around for him. Put her to bed, Joe; this is no good for what she's got. *(JIM exits up the driveway.)*

KELLER *(coming down)*: What does he want here?

MOTHER: His friend is not home.

KELLER *(his voice is husky; comes down to her)*: I don't like him mixing in so much.

MOTHER: It's too late, Joe. He knows.

KELLER *(apprehensively)*: How does he know?

MOTHER: He guessed a long time ago.

KELLER: I don't like that.

MOTHER *(laughs dangerously, quietly, into the line)*: What you don't like . . .

KELLER: Yes, what I don't like.

MOTHER: You can't bull yourself through this one, Joe, you better be smart now. This is not over yet.

KELLER *(indicating the lighted window above)*. And what is she doing up there? She don't come out of the room.

MOTHER: I don't know, what is she doing? Sit down, stop being mad. You want to live? You better figure out your life.

KELLER: She don't know, does she?

MOTHER: She saw Chris storming out of here. It's one and one, she knows how to add.

KELLER: Maybe I ought to talk to her.

MOTHER: Don't ask me, Joe.

KELLER *(almost an outburst)*: Then who do I ask! (MOTHER *remains silent.* KELLER, *asking for confirmation.)* But I don't think she'll do anything about it.

MOTHER: You're asking me again.

KELLER: I'm askin' you! Am I a stranger? *(Slight pause. He moves.)* I thought I had a family here. What the hell happened to my family?

MOTHER: You've got a family. I'm simply telling you that I have no strength to think any more.

KELLER: You have no strength. The minute there's trouble you have no strength!

MOTHER: Joe, you're doing the same thing again. All your life whenever there's trouble you yell at me and you think that settles it.

KELLER: Then what do I do? Tell me, talk to me, what do I do?

MOTHER: Joe . . . I've been thinking this way. If he comes back . . .

KELLER: He's comin' back, what do you mean "if"? . . . He's comin' back, what do I do?

MOTHER: I think if you sit him down and you . . . explain yourself. I mean you ought to make it clear to him that you *know* you did a terrible thing. *(Not looking into his eyes.)* I mean if he saw that you realize what you did. You see?

KELLER: What ice does that cut?

MOTHER *(a little fearfully)*: I mean if you told him that you want to pay for what you did.

KELLER *(sensing . . . quietly)*: How can I pay?

MOTHER *(she gets up, nervously)*: Tell him . . . you're willing to go to prison. *(Pause.)*

KELLER *(amazed, angering)*: I'm willing to . . . ?

MOTHER *(quickly)*: You wouldn't go, he wouldn't ask you to go. But if you told him you wanted to, if he could feel that you wanted to pay, maybe he would forgive you.

KELLER *(to her, as though she has spoken for herself too)*: He would forgive me! For what?

MOTHER *(moving away)*: Joe, you know what I mean.

KELLER: I don't know what you mean! You wanted money, so I made money. What must I be forgiven? You wanted money, didn't you?

MOTHER: I didn't want it that way.

KELLER: I didn't want it that way either! What difference is it what you want? I spoiled the both of you. I should've put him out when he was ten like I was put out, and made him earn his keep. Then he'd know how a buck is made in this world. Forgiven! I could live on a quarter a day myself, but I got a family so I . . .

MOTHER: Joe, Joe . . . it don't excuse it that you did it for the family.

KELLER: It's got to excuse it!

MOTHER: There's something bigger than the family to him.

KELLER: Nothin' is bigger!

MOTHER: There is to him.

KELLER: There's nothin' he could do that I wouldn't forgive. Because he's my son. Because I'm his father and he's my son.

MOTHER: Joe, I tell you . . .

KELLER: Nothin' is bigger than that. And you're going to tell him, you understand? I'm his father and he's my son, and if there's something bigger than that I'll put a bullet in my head!

MOTHER: You stop that!

KELLER: You heard me. Now you know what to tell him. *(Pause. He moves from her — halts.)* But he wouldn't put me away though. . . . He wouldn't do that. . . . Would he?

MOTHER: He loved you, Joe, you broke his heart.

KELLER: But to put me away . . .

MOTHER: I don't know. I'm beginning to think we don't really know him. They say in the war he was such a killer. Here he was always afraid of mice. I don't know him. I don't know what he'll do.

KELLER: Goddamn, if Larry was alive he wouldn't act like this. He understood the way the world is made. He listened to me. To him the world had a forty-foot front, it ended at the building line. This one, everything bothers him. You make a deal, overcharge two cents, and his hair falls out. He don't understand money. Too easy, it came too easy. Yes sir. Larry. That was a boy we lost. Larry. Larry. *(With an impatient cry.)* Where the hell is he?

MOTHER: Joe, Joe, please . . . you'll be all right, nothing is going to happen. . . .

KELLER *(desperately, lost)*: For you Kate, for both of you, that's all I ever lived for . . .

MOTHER: I know, darling, I know . . .

(ANN enters from the house. They say nothing, waiting for her to speak.)

ANN: Why do you stay up? I'll tell you when he comes.

KELLER *(apprehensively)*: You didn't eat supper, did you. *(To MOTHER.)* Why don't you make her something?

MOTHER: Sure, I'll . . .

ANN: Never mind, Kate, I'm all right. *(They're unable to speak to each other.)* I'll go upstairs. *(She starts, then halts.)* I'm not going to do anything about it . . .

MOTHER: Oh, she's a good girl! *(To KELLER.)* You see? She's a . . .

ANN: I'll do nothing about Joe, but you're going to do something for me. *(Directly to MOTHER.)* You made Chris feel guilty with me. Whether you wanted to or not, you've crippled him in front of me. I'd like you to tell him that Larry is dead and that you know it. You understand me? I'm not going out of here alone. There's no life for me that way. I want you to set him free. And then I promise you everything will end, and we'll go away, and that's all.

KELLER: You'll do that. You'll tell him.

ANN: I know what I'm asking, Kate. You had two sons. But you've only got one now.

KELLER: You'll tell him . . .

ANN: And you've got to say it to him so he knows you mean it.

MOTHER: My dear, if the boy was dead, it wouldn't depend on my words to make Chris know it. . . . The night he gets into your bed, his heart will dry up. Because he knows and you know. To his dying day he'll wait for his brother! No, my dear, no such thing. You're going in the morning, and you're going alone. That's your life, that's your lonely life. *(She starts for the house.)*

ANN: Larry is dead, Kate.

MOTHER: Don't speak to me.

ANN: He crashed off the coast of China, February ninth. His engine didn't fail him, but he died. I know.

(MOTHER stops moving.)

MOTHER: How . . . how did he die? . . .

(ANN is silent.)

MOTHER: How did he die? You're lying to me. If you know, how did he die?

ANN: I loved him. You know I loved him, don't you? Would I have looked at anyone else if I wasn't sure? That's enough for you.

MOTHER *(moving on her)*: What's enough for me? What're you talking about?

ANN: You're hurting my wrists.

MOTHER: What are you talking about?

(Pause. ANN looks at JOE.)

MOTHER: Joe, please go in the house . . .

KELLER: Why should I? . . .

MOTHER: Go, dear. *(She goes to him, caresses his cheek, and leads him upstage.)* Go.

KELLER *(glancing at* ANN*)*: I'll lay down. I'm tired. Lemme know when he comes. *(*KELLER *goes into the house.)*

ANN: Sit down . . . go on . . .

*(*MOTHER *sits slowly.)*

ANN: First you've got to understand. When I came, I didn't have any idea that Joe . . . I had nothing against him or you. I came to get married. I hoped . . . *(She brings out a letter from her pocket.)* So I didn't bring this to hurt you. I thought I'd show it to you only if there was no other way to settle Larry in your mind.

MOTHER: What is that?

ANN: He wrote me a letter just before he . . .

MOTHER: Larry?

ANN *(extending the letter)*: I'm not trying to hurt you, Kate. You're making me do this, now remember you're . . .

*(*MOTHER *takes the letter.)*

ANN: Remember.

*(*MOTHER *reads.)*

ANN: I've been so lonely, Kate . . . I can't leave here alone again.

(A long, low groan comes from MOTHER'S *throat as she reads.)*

ANN: You made me show it to you. You wouldn't believe me. I told you a hundred times — why didn't you believe me?

MOTHER: Oh, my God . . .

ANN *(with pity and fear)*: Kate, please, please . . .

MOTHER: Oh, my God, my God . . .

ANN: Oh, Kate dear, I'm so sorry . . .

*(*CHRIS *enters from the driveway. He seems exhausted.)*

CHRIS: What's the matter? . . .

ANN: Nothing, darling. Where were you? . . . You're all perspired . . .

*(*MOTHER *doesn't move.)*

ANN: Where were you?

CHRIS: Just drove around a little. I thought you'd be gone.

ANN: Where do I go? I have nowhere to go.

CHRIS *(to* MOTHER*)*: Where's Dad?

ANN: Inside lying down.

*(*MOTHER *has crumpled the letter in her hand.)*

CHRIS: Sit down, both of you. I'll say what there is to say.

MOTHER: I didn't hear the car . . .

CHRIS: I left it in the garage.

MOTHER: Chris, you look so . . . *(Takes his hand.)* You smashed your watch?

CHRIS: Against the steering wheel. I had a little accident. It's nothing, just a fender . . . I wasn't looking. Mother . . . I'm going away. For good. *(To* ANN *alone.)* I know what you're thinking, Annie. It's true. I'm yellow. I was made yellow here. In this house. Because I've suspected my father and I did nothing about it. If I knew the night I came home what I know now, he'd be in the district attorney's office by this time, and I'd have brought him there. Now if I look at him, all I'm able to do is cry.

MOTHER: What are you talking about? What else can you do?

CHRIS: I could jail him! I tell it to you with your teary eyes. I could jail him, if I were human any more. But I'm like everybody else now. I'm practical now. You made me practical.

MOTHER: But you have to be.

CHRIS: The cats in the alley are practical, the bums who ran away when we were fighting were practical. Only the dead weren't practical. But now I'm practical, and I spit on myself. I'm going away. I'm going now.

ANN: I'm coming with you . . .

CHRIS: No, Ann, I can't make that.

ANN: I don't ask you to do anything about Joe. I swear I never will!

CHRIS: Yes you do. In your heart you always will.

ANN: Take me with you. No one will understand why you're . . .

CHRIS: Maybe a few . . . in some hospital somewhere, there's a few will understand.

ANN: Then do what you have to do!

CHRIS: Do what? What is there to do? I've looked all night for a reason to make him suffer . . .

ANN: There is reason!

CHRIS: What? Do I raise the dead when I put him behind bars? Then what'll I do it for? We used to shoot a man who acted like a dog, but honor was real there, you were protecting something. But here? This is the land of the great *big* dogs, you don't love a man here, you eat him. *That's* the principle, the only one we really live by. — It just happened to kill a few people this time, that's all. The world's that way; how can I take it out on him? What sense does that make? This is a zoo, a zoo!

ANN *(to* MOTHER*)*: Why are you standing there? *You* know what he's got to do! — Tell him!

MOTHER *(clutching the letter tighter)*: Let him go.

ANN: I won't let him go, you'll tell him! . . .

MOTHER *(warning)*: Annie! . . .

ANN: Then I will!

(KELLER enters from the house. CHRIS sees him, goes up to the house, and starts past KELLER.)

KELLER *(worn, brokenhearted)*: What the hell is the matter with you? *(CHRIS halts and is silent.)* What's the matter with you? *(CHRIS remains silent.)* I want to talk to you.

CHRIS: I've got nothing to . . .

KELLER *(he pushes him toward the steps of the porch)*: I want to talk to you!

CHRIS: Don't do that, Dad. I'm going to hurt you if you do that.

KELLER *(quietly, with a break in his voice)*: Go down.

CHRIS *(after an instant)*: There's nothing to say, so say it quick.

(CHRIS comes down from the porch. KELLER then comes down, walks past him.)

KELLER: Exactly what's the matter? Without the philosophy involved. What's the matter? You got too much money? Is that what bothers you?

CHRIS *(with an edge of sarcasm)*: It bothers me.

KELLER: Then what's the difficulty? When something bothers you you either get used to it or you get rid of it. If you can't get used to it, then throw it away. You hear me? Take every cent and give it to charity, throw it in the sewer. Does that settle it? In the sewer, that's all. *(CHRIS is silent.)* What's the matter, you think I'm kidding? I'm tellin' you what to do; if it's dirty, then burn it. It's your money, that's not my money. I'm a dead man, I'm an old dead man, nothing's mine. Well, talk to me! — What do you want to do!

CHRIS *(trembling)*: It's not what I want to do. It's what you want to do.

KELLER: What should I want to do? *(CHRIS is silent.)* Jail? You want me to go to jail? *(CHRIS's eyes filling with tears, he remains silent. KELLER, himself near weeping.)* What're you crying for? If you want me to go say so, don't cry! Is that where I belong? — Then tell me so! *(Slight pause.)* What's the matter, why can't you tell me? *(Furiously.)* You say everything else to me, say that! *(Slight pause.)* I'll tell you why you can't say it. Because you know I don't belong there. Because you know! *(He is moving around CHRIS, jerkily, with growing emphasis and passion, and a persistent tone of desperation.)* If my money's dirty there ain't a clean nickel in the United States. Who worked for nothin' in that war? When they work for nothin', I'll work for nothin'. Did they ship a gun or a truck outa Detroit before they got their price? Is that clean? Nothin's clean. It's dollars and cents, nickels and dimes; war and peace, it's nickels and dimes, what's clean? The whole goddam country is gotta go if I go! That's why you can't tell me.

CHRIS: That's exactly why.

KELLER: Then . . . why am *I* bad?

CHRIS: I don't call you bad. *I* know you're no worse than most, but I thought you were better. I never saw you as a man. I saw you as my father. *(Almost breaking.)* I can't look at you this way, and I can't look at myself!

(He turns quickly and goes directly toward the porch. On this movement ANN *goes quickly to* MOTHER, *snatching the letter from her hand, and starts for* CHRIS. MOTHER *instantly rushes to intercept her.)*

MOTHER: Give me that!

ANN: He's going to read it! *(She gets away from* MOTHER *and thrusts the letter into* CHRIS'S *hand as:)*

MOTHER *(grasping for it in* CHRIS'S *hand)*: Give it to me, Chris, give that to me!

CHRIS *(looking from her to* ANN, *holding the letter clenched in his fist; looking from one to the other)*: What . . . ?

ANN: Larry. He wrote that to me the day he died . . .

KELLER: Larry?

MOTHER: Chris, it's not for you. Give it to me, please. . . . *(He unlocks her fingers from his wrist. In terror she backs from him as he starts to read.)* Joe . . . go away. . . .

KELLER *(mystified, frightened)*: Why'd she say, Larry, what . . . ?

MOTHER *(she desperately pushes him toward the alley, glancing at* CHRIS*)*: Go to the street! . . . *(He is resisting her, starting to speak; she leaves him and starts alone toward the driveway.)* Jim! Where's Jim . . . ! *(As she passes* CHRIS, *a little weeping laugh escapes him. She stops.)* Don't . . . *(Pleading from her whole soul.)* Don't tell him. . . .

CHRIS *(deadly quiet, through his teeth to his father)*: Three and one-half years . . . talking, talking. Now you tell me what you must do. . . . This is how he died, now tell me where you belong.

KELLER *(backing, now in deadly fear)*: Chris, a man can't be a Jesus in this world!

CHRIS: I know all about the world. I know the whole crap story. Now listen to this, and tell me what a man's got to be! *(Reads.)* "My dear Ann . . . " You listening? He wrote this the day he died. Listen, don't cry . . . listen! "My dear Ann: It is impossible to put down the things I feel. But I've got to tell you something. Yesterday they flew in a load of papers from the States and I read about Dad and your father being convicted. I can't express myself. I can't face the other men . . . I can't bear to live any more. Last night I circled the base for twenty minutes before I could bring myself in. How could he have done that? Every day three or four men never return and he sits back there 'doing business.' I can't face anybody . . . I don't know how to tell you what I feel. . . . I'm going out on a mission in a few minutes. They'll probably report me missing. If they do, I want you to know that you mustn't wait for me. I tell you, Ann, if I had him here now I could kill him."

(KELLER grabs letter from CHRIS and reads. Pause.)

CHRIS *(after a long pause)*: Now blame the world. Do you understand that letter?

KELLER *(almost inaudibly, staring)*: I think so. Get the car. I'll put on my jacket.

(He turns and seems about to fall. MOTHER reaches out quickly to support him.)

MOTHER *(with a pleading, lost cry)*: Joe . . .

KELLER *(with complete self-disgust)*: No, let me go; I want to go. . . . I'm sorry, Kate.

MOTHER: You're so foolish. Larry was your son too, wasn't he? You know he'd never tell you to do this!

KELLER *(indicating the letter)*: What is this if it isn't telling me? Sure, he was my son. But I think to him they were all my sons. And I guess they were, kid . . . I guess they were. *(Quietly, to CHRIS.)* I'll be down . . . in a minute. *(He turns and goes into the house.)*

MOTHER: He'll stay if you tell him to. Go to him!

CHRIS: Mother, he's got to go.

MOTHER: You both gone crazy? *(She presses CHRIS to go into the house.)* Tell him to sleep!

CHRIS: No, Mom.

MOTHER: God in Heaven, what is accomplished if he goes?

CHRIS: I thought you read that!

MOTHER: The war is over, didn't you hear? — It's over!

CHRIS: Then what was Larry to you, a stone that fell into the water? It's *not* enough to be sorry. Larry didn't kill himself so you and Dad would be "sorry"!

MOTHER: What more can we be?

CHRIS *(with all his power, beyond all restraint)*: You can be better! Once and for all you can know now that the whole earth comes in through those fences; there's a universe outside and you're responsible to it, and if you're not, you threw your son away, because that's why he died! He's got to go, and I'm . . .

(A shot is heard from the house. They leap in shock.)

CHRIS: Find Jim! *(He rushes into the house.)*

(ANN runs off, toward JIM'S house. MOTHER has not moved. Facing the house:)

MOTHER *(over and over)*: Joe . . . Joe . . . Joe.

(CHRIS comes out of the house.)

CHRIS *(apologetically)*: Mother . . .

MOTHER: Sssh.

(CHRIS comes to her, trying to speak. Weeping, she embraces him.)

CHRIS *(going to her arms)*: I didn't mean that he . . . *(CHRIS breaks into a sob.)*

MOTHER: Sssh. Sssh . . . Don't, don't, dear; you mustn't take it on yourself. Forget now. Live.

(She moves from him, and as she mounts the porch he hears the growing sound of her weeping. She goes inside. Alone, he comes erect, moves away from the sound, does not turn to it, as the curtain falls.)

CURTAIN

Considerations

1. Consider the incident between Bert and Joe Keller in Act I. Retell the incident from the point of view of six-year-old Bert. Then imagine Bert twenty or thirty years later, again telling of the incident as well as of Joe Keller's suicide the next day.
2. Joe Keller claims that he is not "brainy," and Kate tells Chris that both she and his father are "stupid." Do you agree with these characterizations? Are Joe and Kate unintelligent? As you answer, consider your definition of intelligence.
3. Compare Joe Keller's values with those of Chris. Explain your responses, positive and negative, to each character's values.
4. At one point in the play, Joe urges Ann Deever to forgive her father because "a father is a father." Do you agree with Joe? Should relatives forgive one another because of the strength of blood ties? Should family loyalties outweigh all others? Explain.
5. When *All My Sons* was first performed (a few years after the end of World War II), it was bitterly criticized by some as an unfair attack on the American business world. What is your response to this criticism? Do you think the play would have received similar criticism if (in an updated form) it had opened shortly after the close of the war with Iraq? Explain.

NANCY MAIRS (1943–   )

On Being Raised by a Daughter

Mothering. I didn't know how to do it. Does anyone? If there really were a maternal instinct, as a good many otherwise quite responsible human beings have claimed, then would we need men like Dr. Alan Guttmacher and Dr. Benjamin Spock to teach us how to mother, and would we be forever scrambling to keep up with the shifts in their child-bearing and child-rearing theories? Would we turn, shaken by our sense of our female incapacity, to the reassuring instructive voices of the fathers, who increasingly come in both sexes, murmuring how much weight to gain or lose, how long to offer the breast, how soon to toilet train, to send to school? Does the salmon ask for a map to the spawning ground? Does the bee send to the Department of Agriculture for a manual on honeymaking?

No, I came with no motherly chromosomes to pattern my gestures comfortably. Not only did I not know how to do it, I'm not even sure now that I wanted to do it. These days people choose whether or not to have children. I am not so very old — my forty-first birthday falls this month — yet I can say with the verity of a wrinkled granny that we did things differently in my day. I no more chose to have children than I had chosen to get married. I simply did what I had been raised to do. Right on schedule (or actually a little ahead of schedule, since I hadn't yet finished college) I wrapped myself in yards of white taffeta and put orange blossoms in my hair and marched myself, in front of the fond, approving gaze of a couple of hundred people, into the arms of a boy in a morning coat who was doing what he had been raised to do. After a year or so, the fond, approving gaze shifted to my belly, which I made swell to magnificent proportions before expelling an unpromising scrap of human flesh on whom the gaze could turn. This was Anne, created in a heedless gesture as close to instinctual as any I would ever perform: satisfaction of the social expectation that I, young, vigorous, equipped with functioning uterus and ovaries and breasts, would sanctify my union with George by bringing forth a son. (I missed, though I had better luck next time.)

The birth of Anne was dreadful, and at the beginning I hated her, briefly, more fiercely than I had ever hated anyone. My doctor, a small round elderly GP who delivered whatever babies came along in Bath, Maine, told me that my protracted pelvis might necessitate a Caesarian section, but he never instructed me what to do during this birth by whatever means. I guess I was supposed not to do but to endure. I remember, hours into a lengthy and complicated labor that ended in Dr. Fichtner's extracting Anne with forceps like a six-pound thirteen-ounce wisdom tooth, twisting my fingers through my hair, yanking, raking my face with my nails, shrieking at the nurse beside me, "Get this thing out of me! I hate it!" Until then I had rather liked Anne, as she humped up bigger and bigger each night under the bedsheet, her wriggles and thumps giving a constant undertone of companionship to my often solitary daily activities. But now I was sure she was killing me. The nurse loosened my fingers and soothed, "You'll feel differently in a little while."

She was right. In a rather long while I did feel differently. I was no longer in pain. But I didn't feel motherly. In fact, Anne on the outside wasn't half so companionable as Anne on the inside, and I think I felt a little lonely. And frightened. I hadn't the faintest idea what I was doing with this mite with the crossed blue eyes and the whoosh of hair sticking straight up. And now, more than eighteen years later, I still have the frequent sense that I don't know what I'm doing, complicated now, of course, by the guilt that I don't know what I've done and the terror that I don't know what I'm going to do. How, I wonder when a young woman comes into my room and speaks to me, her hair blown dry to casual elegance and her eyes uncrossed behind round brown frames, how did you get here? And where, when you turn and walk out of here, out of my house and out of the dailiness of my life, where will you go?

I have been mystified by motherhood largely because motherhood itself has been mystified. Perhaps before Freud I might have raised my children without knowing consciously my power to damage their spirits beyond human repair, but the signs have always been there: the Good Mother and the Terrible Mother; the dead saint and the wicked stepmother waiting to offer disguised poisons, shoes of hellfire. The one is as alien as the other. If you live in a culture where all children are raised by mothers, Nancy Chodorow points out in *The Reproduction of Mothering,* and if half those children are males who must separate with some violence from the mother in order to establish their different gender, and if the males have the power to determine, through the creation of symbolic systems like language and art, what culture itself is, then you will get a cultural view of mothers as others, on whom are projected traits that even they (who speak some form of the language, who look at the pictures even if they don't paint them) come to assume are their own. We live in a culture of object-mothers. The subject-mothers, culturally silenced for millennia, are only just beginning to speak.

The voices of authority tell me I may harm, even ruin my daughter (in large measure by spoiling her for the pleasurable uses of men). At first they issue from the eminences of science, in measured tones like those of Carl Jung: "Thus, if the child of an over-anxious mother regularly dreams that she is a terrifying animal or a witch, these experiences point to a split in the child's psyche that predisposes it to a neurosis." I am the stuff of my daughter's nightmares. Gradually the pronouncements trickle down into the market place and are reformulated for popular consumption by voices like Nancy Friday's in that long whine of sexual anxiety *My Mother/My Self,* which was on the bestseller list some years back: "When mother's silent and threatening disapproval adds dark colors to the girl's emergent sexuality, this fear be-

5

comes eroticized in such strange forms as masochism, love of the brute, rape fantasies—the thrill of whatever is most forbidden." I make of my daughter's life a waking nightmare as well. A book like *My Mother/My Self,* in dealing with our earliest relationship, out of which our ability to form all other relationships grows, taps a rich subterranean vein of desire and disappointment, but it does so only to portray daughter as victim.

The real danger these voices pose lies not so much in what they say as in what they leave out about motherhood, whether through ignorance or through incapacity. Jung was not a woman at all, at least socially speaking (archetypally, of course, he had an anima, which doesn't seem to have caused him much trouble). And Friday refused to have children on the grounds that if she chanced to have a daughter, she'd ruin her child just as her mother had ruined her (such an assumption suggests that her choice was a wise one). But neither these two nor the vast crowd of fellow motherhood-mystifiers between them take into adequate account the persistence of human development, which keeps the personality malleable indefinitely, if it is allowed to, or the implacable power of six pounds thirteen ounces of human flesh from the moment it draws a breath and wails its spirit out into the world.

Among all the uncertainties I have experienced about myself as a mother, of one point I feel sure: that I am not today the woman I would have been had Anne not been born one September evening almost nineteen years ago. I cannot prove this hypothesis, there being no control in this experiment, no twenty-two-year-old Nancy Mairs that night who had a son instead, whose baby died, who had had a miscarriage, who had not been able to get pregnant at all, who never married and lives now in a small, well-appointed apartment on the Marina in San Francisco, walking her Burmese cats on leashes in Golden Gate Park. There is only this Nancy Mairs who, for nearly half her life, has in raising been raised by a daughter.

Anne can't have found her job an easy one. Raising a mother is difficult enough under the best of circumstances. But when you get one who's both crippled and neurotic—who doesn't do her fair share of the housework, who lurches around the house and crashes to the floor in front of your friends, whose spirits flag and crumple unpredictably, who gets attacks of anxiety in the middle of stores and has to be cajoled into finishing simple errands—then you have your work cut out for you. Of all the things Anne has taught me, perhaps the most important is that one can live under difficult circumstances with a remarkable amount of equanimity and good humor. It's a lesson I need daily.

My education began, no doubt, from the moment of her birth. Perhaps even before. Perhaps from the moment I perceived her presence in the absence of my period, or from the instant (Christmas Eve, I'm convinced) of her conception, or even from the time I began to dream her. But then she was anonymous. As soon as she appeared, she took me firmly in diminutive hand and trained me much as I've come to see that my cats have trained me,

10

rewarding my good behavior (what difference a smile or a purr?) and punishing my bad (they've both tended to bite). But I don't think of my education as being under way till about nine months later when one day she heaved herself up in her car-bed, raised one arm in a stiff wave, and called, "Hi there!" A baby who could talk with me was beyond my ken. After all, I was raised before the days when dolls had electronic voice-boxes in their tummies and quavered "Hi there!" when you pulled the string. And anyway, Anne didn't have a string. *She* chose to speak to *me*.

I've never been the same.

Birth is, I think, an attenuated process, though we tend to use the word to describe only the physical separation of the baby from the mother. Fortunately, those first hours of birth were the worst, in terms of pain, or I don't think I'd have lasted. Each phase of the process involves separation, which may or may not be physical but always carries heavy psychic freight. For me, Anne's speech was a major step. It set her apart from me, over there, an entity with whom I could, literally, have a dialogue. It made her an other.

Feminist psychologists note that psychical birth, the process of differentiating self from other, is particularly problematic for female children. As Chodorow writes,

> Because they are the same gender as their daughters and have been girls, mothers of daughters tend not to experience these infant daughters as separate from them in the same way as do mothers of infant sons. . . . Primary identification and symbiosis with daughters tend to be stronger and cathexis of daughters is more likely to retain and emphasize narcissistic elements, that is, to be based on experiencing a daughter as an extension or double of a mother herself, with cathexis of the daughter as a sexual other usually remaining a weaker, less significant theme.

The consequence of this feeling of continuity between mother and daughter is that "separation and individuation remain particularly female developmental issues." But "problematic" doesn't mean "bad," a leap that Friday makes when she lifts "symbiosis" out of the psychoanalytic context in which Chodorow uses it and applies it to noninfantile relationships, giving it then not its full range of meaning but that portion of meaning which suits her program: symbiosis as a kind of perverse parasitism: a large but weak organism feeding on a smaller but strong host, which, as it grows, weakens until the two are evenly matched in size and incapacity. According to Friday, the mother limits her daughter's autonomy and independence, extinguishes her sexuality, terrifies her witless of men, then packages her in Saran Wrap to keep her fresh and hands her over to some man who, if she's not careful, will get on her a daughter on whom she will perform the same hideous rites.

I'm not saying that no mother does such things. Apparently Nancy Friday's mother did, and I recognize any number of my own experiences in hers. Nor am I saying that, through some virtue or miracle, I have avoided doing them to Anne. Of course I would want to think so; but God and Anne alone know what horrors I've perpetrated. All I can be sure of is that if Anne handed me a list of grievances, most of them would probably surprise me. If they didn't, I'd be a monster, not a mother.

What I am saying is that such things are not intrinsic to the mother-daughter relationship. As Chodorow notes in her study "Family Structure and Female Personality," women in societies as various as those in Atjeh, Java, and East London, where their "kin role, and in particular the mother role, is central and positively valued," have experiences and develop self-images very different from those of Western middle-class women:

> There is another important aspect of the situation in these societies. The continuing structural and practical importance of the mother-daughter tie not only ensures that a daughter develops a positive personal and role identification with her mother, but also requires that the close psychological tie between mother and daughter become firmly grounded in real role expectations. These provide a certain constraint and limitation upon the relationship, as well as an avenue for its expression through common spheres of interest based in the external social world.

Thus, although the problem of differentiation exists wherever mothers mother daughters, its implications vary from one social setting to another. If a woman like Friday's mother teaches her daughter that sex is risky at best and in general downright nasty, she does so not because she is a mother but because she is the product of a patriarchal order that demands that its women be chaste and compliant so that men may be sure of their paternity. In fact, such a concern is extrinsic to the mother-daughter relationship, which exists in essence outside the sphere of men. As soon as one can identify it for what it is, the concern of a particular group of human beings for maintaining a particular kind of power, one is free to choose whether or not to perpetuate it.

Thus, Friday's rationale for refusing to bear children, that she would inevitably visit upon her daughter the same evils her mother visited upon her, is off the mark, rooted in a sense of powerlessness in the face of the existing social order which seems to stem from belief in a biologically predetermined parasitism. Mothers, inexorably, must eat out the hearts of their daughters alive. Neither a mother nor a daughter has the power to avoid the dreadful outcome. They are only helpless women. But if we step outside socially imposed injunctions, then Friday is wrong, and daughters and their mothers wield powers for one another's help as well as harm. They may even make of one another revolutionaries.

Symbiosis is a spacious word. It may encompass parasitism and helotism (though the *Shorter Oxford Dictionary* disallows this meaning by requiring that the entities involved be mutually supportive). But it also — even chiefly — means commensalism, mutualism, "the intimate living together,"

15

says *Webster's Third,* "of two dissimilar organisms in any of various mutually beneficial relationships." The crux is the living-withness the word demands: We may live with one another well or badly. To live together reciprocally, each contributing to the other's support, in the figurative sense in which symbiosis represents human relationship, requires delicate balance, difficult to establish and to maintain. Both partners must give to it and take from it. Both must flourish under its influence, or it is no longer symbiotic. For these reasons, a symbiotic relationship between a mother and her growing daughter — or between any other two people, for that matter — may be rather rare. For these reasons, also, emotional symbiosis is not an ascribed characteristic of a relationship; rather, it is the outcome of the dynamics of some relationships between some people some of the time.

Symbiosis as I am now using the word — not like Chodorow to represent the phase of total infantile dependence or like Friday to suggest emotional vampirism but rather as a metaphor for the interdependence characteristic of living together well — does not result in identity. On the contrary, every definition I've found requires the difference of the entities involved. Thus, after the demands of infancy have been made and met, individuation is necessary if a true symbiotic system is to be maintained. Otherwise you get something else, some solid lump of psychic flesh whose name I do not know.

All the analyses I've read of mother-daughter relationships fail to account for my experience of Anne's power in our mutual life. The assumption seems to be that I'm the one in control, not just because I'm older than she is and, until recently, bigger and stronger, but because I have society's acknowledgment and support in the venture and she doesn't. I'm engaged in the honorable occupation of child-rearing, and if I can't figure the procedures out for myself, I can find shelves of manuals in any bookstore or library. No one even notices that Anne is engaged in mother-rearing, much less offers her any hot tips; indeed, books like *My Mother/My Self* only reinforce her powerlessness, making her out a victim of maternal solicitude and submerged rage, whose only recourse is more rage, rebellion, rejection: not an actor but a reactor. Such lopsided accounts arise, I suppose, from the premise — the consequence of a hierarchical view of human development — that adulthood signifies completion. But the fluidity, the pains and delights, the spurts of growth and sluggish spells of childhood never cease, though we may cease to acknowledge them in an effort to establish difference from, and hence authority over, our children. Out of the new arrivals in our lives — the odd word stumbled upon in a difficult text, the handsome black stranger who bursts in one night through the cat door, the telephone call out of a friend's silence of years, the sudden greeting from the girl-child — we constantly make of ourselves our selves.

When Anne waved and called out to me, she made an other not only   20
of herself but of me. Language is the ultimate alienator. When she spoke she created for herself a self so remote from me that it could communicate with

me only — imprecisely, imperfectly — through words. Shortly thereafter she named me, and went on naming me, into place, a slowish process. When she was not quite two, I left the world. I went into a state mental hospital and stayed there six months. During that time Anne lived with my mother, another Anne, and the two of them built a life around a space that they both expected me to come back to and fill. One afternoon, sitting in a basket in the checkout line at the IGA, Anne struck up a conversation with the man behind her who, gesturing toward Mother, said something about her mummy. "That's not my Mummy," Anne informed him, drawing herself high and fixing him with one crossed eye. "It's my Grandma. My Mummy is in the hospital." When Mother told me this story, I heard the message as I've heard it ever since: I'm the Mummy, the only Mummy (though I've grown up to be Mom, that hearty jokey apple-pie name, for reasons known only to my children), and that's who I've got to be.

As Mummy I have emphatically never been permitted to be Anne. Whatever fantasies I may have had, at some subliminal level, of my new daughter as a waxen dolly that I could pinch and pat into my likeness, Anne scotched them early, probably when she first spat puréed liver into my face (not to mention when she became the only one in the family who today eats liver in any form), certainly by the time she shouted out "Hi there!" (not "Mama" or "Dada," no private communiqué, but a greeting to all the world). Nor can I ever make her me. She wouldn't let me. Hence the possibility for our symbiosis, a state that demands two creatures for its establishment and maintenance. Anne has schooled me in the art of living well together by letting go.

Like any daughter's, hers hasn't been a simple task, but I don't think that the kind of gritty spirit it's called up in her will stand her in bad stead. She has been hampered by my own terror of separation, brought on perhaps by my early separation from my mother because of illness or my somewhat later permanent separation from my father through death. She has been helped, I think, by my curiosity to see what she would do next and by the fact that I've worked at jobs I enjoy since she was nine months old and that I've remained married, in considerable contentment, to her father, for as Chodorow points out, when "women do meaningful productive work, have ongoing adult companionship while they are parenting, and have satisfying emotional relationships with other adults, they are less likely to overinvest in children." And at least I've always *wanted* to let go. I just haven't always known how or when. Anne, through her peculiar quiet stubborn self-determination, has time after time peeled my white-knuckled fingers loose and shrugged away from my grasp.

Neither of us has had a whole lot of help from the world at large. We live in a society that still expects, even demands, that mothers control and manipulate their children's actions right into adulthood; that judges them according to the acceptability or unacceptability of their children's appearance and behavior; and that ensures their dependence on maternity for a sense, however diffuse, of self by giving them precious little else of interest to do. The mother who does let go, especially of a daughter, is still often considered irresponsible at best, unnatural at worst.

When Anne was sixteen, for instance, she decided to join a volunteer organization called Amigos de las Americas, training in Spanish and public health for several months and then going to Honduras to vaccinate pigs against hog cholera. United States policies in Central America hadn't yet created thoroughgoing chaos, and George and I thought this a wonderful way for her to begin inserting herself into the world. But George's parents, on a visit during her preparations, challenged me about Anne's plans. She ought not to be allowed to go, they said. It would be too much for her. The shock of entering a new culture would make her emotionally ill. "Ugh," Mum Mairs shuddered, "girls shouldn't have to dig latrines." (At that time, Anne hadn't yet received her assignment, but I presume that girls shouldn't have to slog around in pigshit either.) I was so startled by this attack, in terms I had not thought of before, that I doubt I said much to allay their fears, though I did ask Anne to tell them about her training in order to reassure them that she wasn't being thrust into the jungle naked and naive. Meanwhile, I thought about those terms, those feminine terms, forgotten at least momentarily by me, foreign as a source of motivation to Anne: nicety, physical and emotional frailty, passivity: all rolled into that statement that girls shouldn't have to dig latrines. (The logical extension of this attitude, I suppose, is that if a girl is all you've got, then you don't get a latrine. Ugh.)

Later, comparing notes with George, I learned that his parents had never mentioned the matter to him. I was at first hurt, angry, feeling picked on; later I came to understand that I was the natural target of their misgivings. George couldn't be counted on to know what girls should or shouldn't do, or to communicate his knowledge if he did. But I could. I was Anne's mother. And in letting her go to Latin America to live, if only briefly, in poverty, perhaps in squalor, and to perform manual labor, I was derelict in my duty.

Thus challenged, I had to rethink this duty. To Mum and Dad Mairs, obviously, it entailed the same protection I received growing up: keeping Anne safe and comfortable, even keeping her pure, at bottom probably protecting her maidenhead, though this mission is buried so deep in our cultural unconscious that I think they would be shocked at the mention of it. I recognized a different duty, a harsher one: to promote Anne's intellectual and spiritual growth even if it meant her leaving me. I didn't think that safety and comfort tended to lead to growth. As for protecting her maidenhead, I figured that was her responsibility, since she was the one who had it, or didn't have it, as the case might be. My duty, I saw, might in fact *be* dereliction, in the form of releasing her into the flood of choice and chance that would be her life. I thought she could swim. More important, she thought she could swim. Nonetheless, while she was gone I ran around

25

distracted and stricken with guilt, mumbling primitive prayers to Our Lady of Guadalupe to take up the watch I had left off. Then she came home, bearing rum and machetes wide-eyed right through customs, with a new taste for mangoes and a new delight in hot showers but without even the lice and dysentery and other gruesome manifestations of tropical fauna she had been promised.

She came back but never, of course, all the way back. Each departure contains an irrevocable element of private growth and self-sufficiency. For the most part I have thought her departures thrilling: the month she spent in New England with her grandparents when she was eight, flying back to Tucson alone; her first period; the first night she spent (quite chastely) with a boy, and later her first lover; her excellence at calculus; her choice to leave lover and family and lifelong friends to go to college on the other side of the country. As long as her new flights give her joy, I rejoice. Where I balk — and balk badly — is at those junctures where the growing hurts her.

One night a couple of winters ago, I woke from heavy early sleep to a young man standing in the dark by my bed: David, Anne's boyfriend. "Mrs. Mairs," he whispered, "I think you'd better come. Anne is drunk and she's really sick and I think you should take care of her." Clearly David wasn't drunk, hadn't been at the same party, he explained, but had met up with Anne afterward. He'd taken her to a friend's house, and though Chris wasn't at home, his mother had kindly taken them in, given them some tea, let Anne throw up in her toilet. But it was getting late, and David had a deadline. He had to bring Anne home, but he didn't dare leave her alone.

I hauled myself out of bed and padded to the other end of the cold house, where Anne was in her bathroom washing her face. When she heard my voice, she hissed, "David, I'll kill you," then came out and burst into tears. I sent David along as I held and rocked her, listening to her wretched tale. She certainly was drunk. The fumes rising from my sodden lap were enough to make me tiddly. Gradually I got her quieted and tucked into bed. The next day she felt suitably miserable. To this day she prefers milk to alcohol.

The children were surprised that I wasn't angry about this episode. In a way I was surprised myself. After all, I had forbidden Anne to drink alcohol outside our house, and she had disobeyed me. Wasn't anger the appropriate response to a disobedient child? But though I specialize in appropriate responses, I did not feel angry. Instead, I felt overwhelmingly sad. For days I was stabbed to the heart by the thought of Anne reeling and stumbling along a darkened street, her emotions black and muddled, abandoned by the group of nasty little boys who had given her beer and vodka and then gone off to have some other fun.

By that one act she stripped me of whatever vestiges of magical thinking I was clinging to about mothers and daughters. Until then, I think, I had still believed that through my wisdom and love I could protect her from the pains I had endured as a child. Suddenly my shield was in tatters. It was

30

a thing of gauze and tissue anyway. She has taught me the bitterest lesson in child-rearing I've yet had to learn: that she will have pain, must have it if she is to get to — and through — this place I am now and the places to which I have yet to go. For, as Juliet Mitchell writes, "pain and lack of satisfaction are the point, the triggers that evoke desire," that essential longing which marks our being in the world, both Anne's and mine, as human.

In teaching me to be her mother, Anne has, among all her other gifts, given me my own mother in ways that have often surprised me. For, as the French theorist Julia Kristeva writes in *Desire in Language,* "By giving birth, the woman enters into contact with her mother; she becomes, she is her own mother; they are the same continuity differentiating itself." Old rebellions have softened, old resentments cooled, now that I see my mother stereoscopically, the lense of motherhood superimposed on that of daughterhood. Every child, I'm sure, takes stern and secret vows along these lines: "When I grow up, I'm never going to make my child clean her room every Saturday, wear orange hair ribbons, babysit her sister, eat pea soup . . . "; and every mother must experience those moments of startlement and sometimes horror when she opens her mouth and hears issue forth not her own voice but the voice of her mother. Surprisingly often, I have found, my mother's voice speaks something that I, as a mother, want to say. I can remember that, when I had accepted a date with Fred — squat, chubby, a little loud, a French kisser, the bane of my high-school love life — and then got a better offer, Mother told me I had only two choices, to go with Fred or to stay home. I vowed then that I would never interfere with my child's social life. But I have had occasion to issue the same injunction, not because I can't tell where my mother ends and I begin, nor because I want Anne to suffer the same horrors I endured in the course of becoming a woman, but because I believe that the habit of courtesy toward one's fellow creatures is more durable than a fabulous night at the prom. Mother may have thought so too.

I gave Mother more trouble throughout my years at home than Anne has given me because, through some psychic and/or biochemical aberration, I was a depressive, though neither she nor I knew so at the time. I recognized that my behavior was erratic and that she got very angry with me for it. What I didn't see, and maybe she didn't either, was that behind her anger lay the anxiety and frustration caused by her helplessness to protect me from my pain. When, finally, I cracked up sufficiently to be sent to a mental hospital, I sensed that she was blaming herself for my troubledness (and no wonder in the disastrous wake of Freud), and I felt impatient with her for believing such silliness. But she was only exhibiting that reflexive maternal guilt which emerges at the infant's first wail: "I'm sorry. I'm sorry. I'm sorry I pushed you from this warm womb into the arms of strangers, me among them. I'm sorry I can't keep you perfectly full, perfectly dry, perfectly free from gas and fear, perfectly, perfectly happy." Any mother knows that if she could do these things, her infant would die more surely than if she covered its face with a rose-printed pillow. Still, part of her desire is to prevent the replication of desire.

Because I knew I had so often infuriated and wearied her, when I left for college I thought only of Mother's relief, never of the possibility that she might miss me. Why should she? The house was still crammed without me, my sister Sally still there, and my stepfather and the babies, and my grandmother too, not to mention an elderly Irish setter and a marmalade cat. As soon as I'd gone, Mother bought a dishwasher, and I figured that took care of any gap I'd left. Not until Anne began the process of selecting a college, finding a summer job in Wisconsin, packing away her mementoes, filling her suitcases did I think that Mother's first-born daughter (and not just a pair of hands in the dishpan) had once left her, and she must have grieved at the separation too. I love to visit her now because I know at last that she is delighted to have me there—not just glad of the company, but warmed and entertained by *me,* one of the daughters who raised her.

I am aware, too, that she once raised a mother, Granna, who lived   35
with us for many years. And Granna raised a mother, Grandma Virchow, with whom she and Mother lived for many years. And Grandma must have raised a mother as well, left behind in Germany in the 1890s, who must herself have raised a mother. "For we think back through our mothers if we are women," writes Virginia Woolf in *A Room of One's Own.* Anne has helped me in that backward dreaming. When she tells me that she doesn't plan to have children, I feel sad, but not because I won't have grandchildren. I mean, I'd welcome them, but I have quite enough characters populating my life to keep me entertained. Rather, I would like her to have this particular adventure, this becoming that a daughter forces.

Overall, I think Anne has done a pretty good job with me. Even without encouragement, in a society that doesn't consider her task authentic, she's done her share of leaning and hauling, shaping me to her needs, forcing me to learn and practice a role I have often found wearing and frightening. Maybe some women are mothers by nature, needing only an infant in their arms to bloom. I'm not. I've needed a lot of nurture. And still I hate it sometimes, especially when she makes me into an authoritarian ogre rumbling disapproval (just as I did to Mother, oh, how many times?). But she's firm and often fair. She doesn't coddle me. Years ago, before I got my brace, I used to have a lot of trouble putting on my left shoe and she would help me with it; the right shoe she'd hand me, saying, "You can do this one yourself." But on my birthday she bakes me lemon bread and, when I ask her what I smell, tells me she's washing dishes in lemon-scented detergent. I believe her and so am surprised by my birthday party. She is tolerant when I stamp my feet (figuratively speaking—if I really stamped my feet I'd fall in a heap and then we'd both get the giggles) and refuse to let her take my peach-colored gauze shirt to Honduras. But she is severe about suicide attempts. She has no use for my short stories, in which she says nothing ever happens, but she likes my essays, especially the ones she appears in, and sometimes my poems. She admires my clothing (especially my peach-colored gauze shirt), my hair, my cooking, but not my taste in music or in men. When my black cat, Bête Noire, the beast of my heart, was killed, she let me weep, hunched over, my tears splashing on the linoleum, and she never said, "Don't cry."

Before long Anne will have to consider the job done. A daughter can't spend a lifetime raising her mother any more than a mother can spend a lifetime raising her daughter; they both have other work to get on with. I can remember the liberating moment when I recognized that it was no longer my task to educate my mother in the ways of the real world; she'd just have to make the best of what she'd learned and muddle along on her own. Mother muddles well, I like to think because I gave her a good start. Anne deserves such a moment.

And I deserve her having it. It's what we've come this way for. Last summer, when George was visiting his parents, his mother sighed, "Life is never so good after the children have gone." George is her only child, and he's been gone for twenty-five years. I can't imagine sustaining a quarter of a century of anticlimax. Anne and I both confront transformation into women with wholly new sets of adventures as we learn to live well apart. I feel pretty well prepared now for muddling along on my own.

Considerations

1. After reading the whole essay, return to the parts where Mairs discusses the months just prior to and after Anne's birth. Make notes on her feelings and thoughts during this time. Compare Mairs's response to her daughter before birth, during birth, and in the first few months after birth. What is your reaction to her descriptions?

2. List several of the authorities on mothering and motherhood whom Mairs mentions, quotes, or paraphrases in this essay. How does she view these authorities? What impact have they (as a group) had on her own experiences, actions, and decisions as a mother?

3. Summarize Nancy Friday's view of the mother-daughter relationship as Mairs explains it. What is Mairs's response to this view? What is your response?

4. Mairs claims that Anne's job is more difficult because there are no books on "mother-rearing." Write a proposal for such a book, listing the chapters you would include and giving brief summaries of the contents of each chapter.

5. Summarize briefly the passage describing the opposition of Mum and Dad Mairs to Anne's proposed work in Honduras. Explain Mairs's response to their opposition; how does she evaluate the reasons behind what they say and the person to whom they choose to say it. Do you agree with her evaluation? Explain.

HARRY DOLAN (1927–   )

I Remember Papa

The other night after attending a gratifying function which had been initiated to help the black man, specifically to help build a nursery for children of working mothers, and after seeing and hearing white people make speeches professing their understanding and desire to go to any length to help, I found myself suddenly cornered and forced to defend the fabled laziness of the black man.

What was especially surprising was the fact that I assumed this white acquaintance—since he had paid thirty dollars to attend this dinner held for the purpose of helping the black man—did, at least in part, have some sympathy with what his, the white people, had tried to accomplish.

As I stood there watching his eyes I became suspect of my own sincerity, for I stood attentively nodding my head and smiling. I lit a cigarette, raised an eyebrow, performed all of the white man's laws of etiquette, and all the while I knew if it had been others of my black brothers, they would have cursed him for his smugness and invited him outside to test his theory of black man's courage and laziness. Of course I did none of these things. I grinned as he indicated in no uncertain terms that as soon as the black man got off his lazy butt and took advantage of all the blessings that had been offered him for the last two hundred years, then he, the white man, would indeed be willing to help.

I could have answered him—and was tempted to, for he was obviously sincere. Instead, I found an excuse to slip away and let a white man fight my battle, a friend, even a close friend. I went to a far corner and blindly played a game of pool by myself as the voices of this man and my friend dissected me. I stacked the pool balls, leaned over the table, and remembered a black man I had known.

It was said of him later in his life that he had let his family down. He'd been lazy, no-account, a troublemaker. Maybe so, maybe so, but I can't help remembering nights of his pacing the squeaking floor muttering to himself, coming back across the floor, sitting down, his legs trembling as he listened to the woman plead for him not to do anything bad.

"I'll go to hell first before I'll let you and the children starve." God, how many times had I heard him say that! How many other men standing bunched in helpless stagnation have I heard vow to take a gun and get some food for their children! Yes, they were planning to commit a crime; yes, they were potential criminals. Then. They are usually black too—another crime, it seems.

I remember that man, but more I remember his woman, my mother. Curiously though, I never remember her dancing, running, playing; always lying down, the smell of disinfectant strong, the deep continuous coughing, the brown paper bag filled with the toilet paper red with bubbly spit and blood, lying half concealed under the bed.

I never remember her eating food such as bread, meat, potatoes; only apples and only Delicious apples. In those days five cents apiece. She was a small woman, barely five foot.

"Junior," she would say softly. She never spoke above a whisper. "Go to the store and get me an apple." The thin trembling hand would reverse itself and slide up and under the covers and under the pillow and then return as though of its own volition, the weight almost too much, and as I'd start out the door, she would always smile and say, "Hurry, Junior."

I'd nod, and always, always there seemed to be a need to hurry. Those   10
trips were always made with a feeling of breathless fear. I didn't know why then, only that for some reason I must always come back as soon as possible.

I was returning with an especially large apple, walking along, tempted to bite just a tiny piece, when I turned the corner and saw the black police ambulance standing in front of my door. Suddenly I had to go to the bathroom so bad I couldn't move. I stood watching as two uniformed men came out with the stretcher, and then the sound of my mother's shrill voice hit me.

"Mama, Mama," she was screaming. I could see her twisting and swinging at the lady next door as she was held back. I stood there feeling the hot piss run down my trembling legs, feeling cold chills spatter through my body, causing frozen limbs to spasmodically begin to move. I forced myself toward the police wagon as the men opened the doors and slid the stretcher along the bare metal. I saw my mother's head bounce on the floor.

"Wait," I moaned, "don't hurt her." Then I was running, screaming, "Please don't hurt her."

I looked down at her pain-filled face, and she smiled, even then she smiled. I showed her the apple. The effort to nod seemed a terrible effort but she did, her eyes so very bright, so very shiny.

"You eat it, Junior, you and sis."   15

"What's wrong, Mama?" I asked softly. "You really, really sick now?" She nodded.

"Your father will be home soon. Tell him I'm at the General Hospital. Tell him to — to hurry."

"I'll tell him, Mama," I promised. "I'll tell him to hurry, Mama." She nodded sadly and puckered her lips as she always did since we weren't allowed to kiss her.

That was the last time I saw my mother except at the grave. My father   20
came to the funeral with two white men who stood on each side of him all the time. There were people crying all around us. My grandmother kept squeezing me and moaning. I saw my father try to cover his face but one of the men said something and he stood up stiffly after that. I didn't cry, because my mother seemed to look happier, more rested than I had ever seen her. For some reason, I was glad she was dead. I think maybe, except for us, she was too.

I was nine, my sister five. It was not until ten years later that I saw my father again.

We sat on opposite sides of a screen and talked into telephones. I had come there to tell him that in spite of my beginning, I had made it. I was nineteen, and a radioman in the U.S. Coast Guard, ready to fight and die for my country. There had been something mysterious about his smile.

"I'm proud of you, boy," he said. "You're a real man. You know I volunteered for the front lines too, but they turned me down."

We don't want you, I thought, we're not criminals, we're honest, strong. Then I looked again at this thief, this "Loaf-of-bread gunman" as the papers had tagged him. He had taken five loaves of bread, along with twelve dollars. Suddenly I could not stay there condemning this man, my father. It seemed such a waste, this magnificently strong man sitting there, his tremendous chest barely moving, hands resting quietly, talking to me, his whole being showering torrents of words about me.

"Be careful, boy, there are so many ways to fail, the pitfall sometimes   25
seems to be the easiest way out. Beware of my future, for you must continue, you must live. You must, for in you are all the dreams of my nights, all the ambitions of my days."

A bell rang and we stood up and a man pointed me toward a heavy door. I looked back, and saw him standing easy, hands at his side, so very calm, yet my mind filled to overflowing with the many things he had not said. It was to be ten years before he walked again as a free man, that is, as a physically free man.

I remember an earlier time, an earlier chapter of my growing up. I remember the first time my mother said we were taking lunch to my father's job. We had been down to the welfare line and I had stood with her, our feet burning against the hot pavement, and slowly moved forward in the sun. Years later I stood in chow lines over half of the world, but no desert, no burning deck was as hot as that day.

At last we reached the man sitting at the desk and my mother handed him the book of stamps. She smiled, a weak almost timid smile, as he checked her name and thumbed her to the food line.

As we headed home, my wagon was loaded with cans of corned beef, powdered milk, powdered eggs, and white margarine that she would later color yellow to look like butter.

At home we made sandwiches and off we went to my father's job, to   30
take him his lunch. I pulled my sister along in my wagon, a Red Flyer.

It was to be a picnic, a celebration really, my father's new job.

I remember the wagon did not have a tongue or handle but only a rope with which I pulled it wobbling along. We were excited, my sister and I, as we left our district of dirt streets and unpaved sidewalks and began to make our way along roads called boulevards and malls we had never had occasion to travel. The streets themselves were fascinating, so different. They were twice as wide, and there were exotic trees along the sidewalks and lo and behold trees down the center of the street as far as I could see and then we turned the corner and before us stretched an overwhelming sight. An overhead highway was being built. Columns rose to staggering heights, bull-dozers thrust what seemed to me mountains of dirt before them, and hundreds, no thousands of men seemed to be crawling like ants hurrying from one point to another. Cranes lifted nets of steel and laid them in rows on the crushed rock.

I stared in awe at important-looking white men in metal hats, carrying rolls of papers which they intermittently studied, then pointing into space at what to me seemed only emptiness.

And then I saw my father. He sat among fifty other black men, all surrounded by great boulders marked with red paint. They all held steel chisels with which they cut along the marked lines. They would strike a certain point and the boulder would split into smaller pieces and as we approached there was a silence around them except for the pinging of the hammer against the chisel. In all the noise it was a lonely sound, futile, lost, oppressive. My father seemed to be concentrating, his tremendous arm whipping the air. He was stripped to the waist, black muscles popping sweat, goggled eyes for the metal and stone only. We stood there, the three of us, my mother, my sister, and I, and watched my father work for us, and as he conquered the huge boulder my chest filled with pride. Each stroke shouted for all the world to hear: This is my family and I love them! No one can tell me this was the act of a lazy man.

Suddenly a white man walked up and blew a whistle and the black   35
men all looked up and stopped working. My father glanced over at me, grinned and winked. He was glistening with sweat, the smell strong and powerful. He dropped his big hand on my shoulder and guided me to a large boulder.

"Hey, boy, you see me beat that thing to bits? This one's next," he said, indicating the one that shaded us from the sun. "I'll pound it to gravel by nightfall." It was a challenge he expected, he welcomed. That was my lazy, shiftless father.

And then one day they brought him home, his thumb, index, and middle finger gone from his left hand. They sat him in the kitchen chair and mumbled something about carelessness. He sat there for two hours before he answered our pleadings.

"Chain broke, I—I was guiding boulder. I couldn't, I just couldn't get my hand out from under in time—I, goddam it, Jean, they took my fingers off. I layed right there, my hand under the rock, and they nipped them like butchering a hog. Look at my goddam hand."

My mother held him in her arms and talked to him. She spoke softly, so softly my sister and I, standing in the corner, couldn't hear the words, only the soothing softness of her voice.

"Joe, Joe, we can." And then he began to cry like—like I sometimes   40
did when I was hurt deep inside and couldn't do anything about it.

After that there was a change in him. My father had been a fighter. He had feared no man white or black. I remember the time we were sitting on a streetcar and a woman had forgotten her fare—or maybe she never had any in the first place. Anyway, the driver slammed the doors on her and held her squeezed between them.

My father jumped up, snatched the driver out of the seat, and let the woman out. He and the driver had words that led to battle and Pop knocked the driver down just as a patrolman arrived. The patrolman didn't listen to any of the people that tried to explain what had happened. He just began to swing his night stick at my father's head. It was a mistake. My father hit him once and even today I can see all the people laughing at the funny look on the policeman's face as he staggered back all the way across the street and up against a building, slowly sagging down.

The police wagon arrived with four other policemen and one told him they were going to beat his brains in when they got him down town.

My pop had laughed then and backed against the building.

"I guess ain't no sense me going peaceable then."   45

They knocked out all his upper front teeth that day, but as he said later, "Them four white boys will think of me every time they shave."

They finally overpowered him and dragged him, still struggling, to the wagon. One of them kept muttering, "He's one fighting son of a black bitch, he's a fighting son of a bitch."

All the time I hadn't said a word or cried or yelled as they stomped and kicked him. I had shut my eyes and held my lips tightly pressed together and I had done just as he'd always told me.

"You stay out of it, boy, stay real quiet, and when that wagon leaves, you run behind and keep it in sight. If they lose you, you ask someone where the closest police station is—that's where I'll be. You go home and tell your mother."

That's the way he had been before losing his left hand. Afterwards,   50 well, it took a lot from him. He told me one day, laughing and shaking the nub as he called it, "If I'd only had the thumb, just the lousy thumb, I'd have it made."

Gradually he lost the ability to see humor in the nub. I think the whole thing came to a head the night I killed the kitten.

We hadn't had meat or potatoes for over two weeks. Even the grease drippings were gone and my mother was too sick to raise her head from the pillow. So I had gotten the skillet and put it in the open grate. We had two cups of flour so I mixed water with it and poured it into the greasy skillet. I can still recall the coldness of the room on my back and the warmth from the grate on my face as my sister and I knelt and hungrily watched the flour brown.

You know, today my wife marvels at how, no matter what she puts before me, I eat with relish. My children say that I eat very fast. I pray to God they never have to experience the causes of my obsession. But back to the story—the flour finally hardened and I broke a piece for my sister and a piece for my mother and left mine in the skillet on the table.

I took my mother's piece over to the bed and put it in her hand. She didn't move so I raised her hand to her mouth and she began to suck on it. Then I heard my sister scream, "Topsy is eating your food, Junior, Topsy's eating your food!" I turned around to see the cat tearing at my tiny piece of hard dough. I went wild. I leaped across the room and grabbed the kitten by the tail and began slamming her against the wall.

"That's my food," I kept yelling, "my food!" At last I heard my sister screaming, "She's bleeding, you're killing Topsy. Here, here, eat my bread. Please don't kill her."   55

I stopped, horrified, staring at the limp nothing I now held. It was two weeks later that they got me to speak and that same night my father left the house for the last time. I don't say that what he did was right. No, it most assuredly was wrong. But what I do ask is, what else could he have done? I need an answer quickly now, today, right away, for I tell you this, my children will not starve, not here, not in this time of millions to foreign countries and fountains to throw tons of water upward to the sky, and nothing to the hungry, thirsty multitudes a stone's throw away.

Considerations

1. Consider carefully the advice Dolan's father gives him (paragraph 25). Comment on that advice by referring to your own observations and experiences.
2. Describe the father's attitude when he first begins the job splitting boulders. Why and how does that attitude change? Evaluate the effect this change has on Dolan.
3. Make a list of details Dolan uses to describe his mother. What can you infer about her and about Dolan's feelings for her?
4. What is Dolan's response when he first visits his father in prison? How does his view of his father change later in life? What significance can you see in these changes?
5. Dolan emphasizes poverty as a motivation for crime. To what extent does he use this evaluation to justify his father's choices and actions? Explain why (and to what extent) you agree or disagree with Dolan.

CONNECTIONS: PARENTS AND CHILDREN

1. In this section, all of the short stories, the play, several of the poems, and both the essays deal in some way with children who are separated from (or are becoming separate from) their parents. Consider issues relating to separation as part of the parent-child relationship. In what ways do you see separation as harmful? As necessary? Important for growth?

2. Consider the role played by outside authorities in the parent-child relationship. To what extent do you see outside help and intervention as helpful? To what extent as detrimental? Refer to your own experiences and observations as well as to any of these works: "I Stand Here Ironing," "Lullaby," "Amniocentesis," "On Being Raised by a Daughter," and "I Remember Papa."

3. The works in this section focus on many different relationships among parents and children. Consider, for example, the following classifications:

Mother–daughter relationships:	"I Stand Here Ironing" "Making the Jam without You" "On Being Raised by a Daughter"
Mother–son relationships:	"Through the Tunnel" "My Mother"
Father–daughter relationships:	"My Father in the Navy"
Father–son relationships:	"My Oedipus Complex" "Idiots First" "My Papa's Waltz" "I Remember Papa" *All My Sons*

Examining these relationships, can you see any significant similarities or differences within the groups? Among the groups? Explain.

4. Consider the impact of economic circumstances on the parent-child relationship as suggested by "I Stand Here Ironing," "Idiots First," *All My Sons*, and "I Remember Papa."

5. What is your concept of the ideal mother, father, son, or daughter? Use characters, incidents, conflicts, and decisions from any of the works (either as positive or negative examples) to develop your definition.

War

MARK TWAIN (1835–1910)

The War Prayer

It was a time of great and exalting excitement. The country was up in arms, the war was on, in every breast burned the holy fire of patriotism; the drums were beating, the bands playing, the toy pistols popping, the bunched firecrackers hissing and spluttering; on every hand and far down the receding and fading spread of roofs and balconies a fluttering wilderness of flags flashed in the sun; daily the young volunteers marched down the wide avenue gay and fine in their new uniforms, the proud fathers and mothers and sisters and sweethearts cheering them with voices choked with happy emotion as they swung by; nightly the packed mass meetings listened, panting, to patriot oratory which stirred the deepest deeps of their hearts and which they interrupted at briefest intervals with cyclones of applause, the tears running down their cheeks the while; in the churches the pastors preached devotion to flag and country and invoked the God of Battles, beseeching His aid in our good cause in outpouring of fervid eloquence which moved every listener. It was indeed a glad and gracious time, and the half-dozen rash spirits that ventured to disapprove of the war and cast a doubt upon its righteousness straightway got such a stern and angry warning that for their personal safety's sake they quickly shrank out of sight and offended no more in that way.

Sunday morning came — next day the battalions would leave for the front; the church was filled; the volunteers were there, their young faces alight with martial dreams — visions of the stern advance, the gathering momentum, the rushing charge, the flashing sabers, the flight of the foe, the tumult, the enveloping smoke, the fierce pursuit, the surrender! — then home from the war, bronzed heroes, welcomed, adored, submerged in golden seas of glory! With the volunteers sat their dear ones, proud, happy, and envied by the neighbors and friends who had no sons and brothers to send forth to the field of honor, there to win for the flag or, failing, die the noblest of noble deaths. The service proceeded; a war chapter from the Old Testament was read; the first prayer was said; it was followed by an organ burst that shook the building, and with one impulse the house rose, with glowing eyes and beating hearts, and poured out that tremendous invocation —

> God the all-terrible! Thou who ordainest,
> Thunder thy clarion and lightning thy sword!

Then came the "long" prayer. None could remember the like of it for passionate pleading and moving and beautiful language. The burden of its supplication was that an ever-merciful and benignant Father of us all would watch over our noble young soldiers and aid, comfort, and encourage them in their patriotic work; bless them, shield them in the day of battle and the hour of peril, bear them in His mighty hand, make them strong and confident, invincible in the bloody onset; help them to crush the foe, grant to them and to their flag and country imperishable honor and glory —

An aged stranger entered and moved with slow and noiseless step up the main aisle, his eyes fixed upon the minister, his long body clothed in a robe that reached to his feet, his head bare, his white hair descending in a frothy cataract to his shoulders, his seamy face unnaturally pale, pale even to ghastliness. With all eyes following him and wondering, he made his silent way; without pausing, he ascended to the preacher's side and stood there, waiting. With shut lids the preacher, unconscious of his presence, continued his moving prayer, and at last finished it with the words, uttered in fervent appeal, "Bless our arms, grant us the victory, O Lord our God, Father and Protector of our land and flag!"

The stranger touched his arm, motioned him to step aside — which the startled minister did — and took his place. During some moments he surveyed the spellbound audience with solemn eyes in which burned an uncanny light; then in a deep voice he said:

"I come from the Throne — bearing a message from Almighty God!" 5 The words smote the house with a shock; if the stranger perceived it he gave no attention. "He has heard the prayer of His servant your shepherd and will grant it if such shall be your desire after I, His messenger, shall have explained to you its import — that is to say, its full import. For it is like unto many of the prayers of men, in that it asks for more than he who utters it is aware of — except he pause and think.

"God's servant and yours has prayed his prayer. Has he paused and taken thought? Is it one prayer? No, it is two — one uttered, the other not. Both have reached the ear of Him Who heareth all supplications, the spoken and the unspoken. Ponder this — keep it in mind. If you would beseech a blessing upon yourself, beware! lest without intent you invoke a curse upon a neighbor at the same time. If you pray for the blessing of rain upon your crop which needs it, by that act you are possibly praying for a curse upon some neighbor's crop which may not need rain and can be injured by it.

"You have heard your servant's prayer — the uttered part of it. I am commissioned of God to put into words the other part of it — that part which the pastor, and also you in your hearts, fervently prayed silently. And ignorantly and unthinkingly? God grant that it was so! You heard these words: 'Grant us the victory, O Lord our God!' That is sufficient. The *whole* of the uttered prayer is compact into those pregnant words. Elaborations were not necessary. When you have prayed for victory you have prayed for many unmentioned results which follow victory — *must* follow it, cannot help but follow it. Upon the listening spirit of God the Father fell also the unspoken part of the prayer. He commandeth me to put it into words. Listen!

"O Lord our Father, our young patriots, idols of our hearts, go forth to battle — be Thou near them! With them, in spirit, we also go forth from the sweet peace of our beloved firesides to smite the foe. O Lord our God, help us to tear their soldiers to bloody shreds with our shells; help us to cover their smiling fields with the pale forms of their patriot dead; help us to drown the thunder of the guns with the shrieks of their wounded, writhing in pain; help us to lay waste their humble homes with a hurricane of fire; help us to wring the hearts of their unoffending widows with unavailing grief; help us to turn them out roofless with their little children to wander unfriended the wastes of their desolated land in rags and hunger and thirst, sports of the sun flames of summer and the icy winds of winter, broken in spirit, worn with travail, imploring Thee for the refuge of the grave and denied it — for our sakes who adore Thee, Lord, blast their hopes, blight their lives, protract their bitter pilgrimage, make heavy their steps, water their way with their tears, stain the white snow with the blood of their wounded feet! We ask it, in the spirit of love, of Him Who is the Source of Love, and Who is the ever-faithful refuge and friend of all that are sore beset and seek His aid with humble and contrite hearts. Amen.

(*After a pause*) "Ye have prayed it; if ye still desire it, speak! The messenger of the Most High waits."

It was believed afterward that the man was a lunatic, because there was   10
no sense in what he said.

Considerations

1. Read the first two paragraphs. List the phrases used to describe the time during which the story is set. Then list the phrases used to describe the people. What do these phrases suggest about the author's attitude toward his subject? Use specific examples to support your view.
2. What does the man who claims to be a messenger from God mean when he says that the minister's prayer is like many human prayers because it "asks for more than he who utters it is aware of — except he pause and think"? Can you think of other examples of prayers that might fit this description? Explain.
3. What might the messenger hope to accomplish by insisting that the congregation listen to his interpretation of the prayer? What do you think of the approach he takes to his audience? What chance does he have of convincing them to listen?
4. What conclusion do the members of the congregation reach? Do you agree with them? Explain why or why not.
5. To what extent do modern nations call on God in times of war? How might those nations respond to the messenger's interpretation of their prayers?

LUIGI PIRANDELLO (1867–1936)

War

The passengers who had left Rome by the night express had had to stop until dawn at the small station of Fabriano in order to continue their journey by the small old-fashioned local joining the main line with Sulmona.

At dawn, in a stuffy and smoky second-class carriage in which five people had already spent the night, a bulky woman in deep mourning was hoisted in — almost like a shapeless bundle. Behind her, puffing and moaning, followed her husband — a tiny man, thin and weakly, his face death-white, his eyes small and bright and looking shy and uneasy.

Having at last taken a seat he politely thanked the passengers who had helped his wife and who had made room for her; then he turned round to the woman trying to pull down the collar of her coat, and politely inquired:

"Are you all right, dear?"

The wife, instead of answering, pulled up her collar again to her eyes,   5
so as to hide her face.

"Nasty world," muttered the husband with a sad smile.

And he felt it his duty to explain to his traveling companions that the poor woman was to be pitied, for the war was taking away from her her only son, a boy of twenty to whom both had devoted their entire life, even breaking up their home at Sulmona to follow him to Rome, where he had to go as a student, then allowing him to volunteer for war with an assurance, however, that at least for six months he would not be sent to the front and now, all of a sudden, receiving a wire saying that he was due to leave in three days' time and asking them to go and see him off.

The woman under the big coat was twisting and wriggling, at times growling like a wild animal, feeling certain that all those explanations would not have aroused even a shadow of sympathy from those people who — most likely — were in the same plight as herself. One of them, who had been listening with particular attention, said:

"You should thank God that your son is only leaving now for the front. Mine has been sent there the first day of the war. He has already come back twice wounded and been sent back again to the front."

"What about me? I have two sons and three nephews at the front," said   10
another passenger.

"Maybe, but in our case it is our *only* son," ventured the husband.

"What difference can it make? You may spoil your only son with excessive attentions, but you cannot love him more than you would all your other children if you had any. Paternal love is not like bread that can be broken into pieces and split amongst the children in equal shares. A father gives *all* his love to each one of his children without discrimination, whether it be one or ten, and if I am suffering now for my two sons, I am not suffering half for each of them but double . . . "

"True . . . true . . . " sighed the embarrassed husband, "but suppose (of course we all hope it will never be your case) a father has two sons at the front and he loses one of them, there is still one left to console him . . . while . . . "

"Yes," answered the other, getting cross, "a son left to console him but also a son left for whom he must survive, while in the case of the father of an only son if the son dies the father can die too and put an end to his distress. Which of the two positions is the worse? Don't you see how my case would be worse than yours?"

"Nonsense," interrupted another traveler, a fat, red-faced man with   15 bloodshot eyes of the palest gray.

He was panting. From his bulging eyes seemed to spurt inner violence of an uncontrolled vitality which his weakened body could hardly contain.

"Nonsense," he repeated, trying to cover his mouth with his hand so as to hide the two missing front teeth. "Nonsense. Do we give life to our children for our own benefit?"

The other travelers stared at him in distress. The one who had had his son at the front since the first day of the war sighed: "You are right. Our children do not belong to us, they belong to the Country . . . "

"Bosh," retorted the fat traveler. "Do we think of the Country when we give life to our children? Our sons are born because . . . well, because they must be born and when they come to life they take our own life with them. This is the truth. We belong to them but they never belong to us. And when they reach twenty they are exactly what we were at their age. We too had a father and mother, but there were so many other things as well . . . girls, cigarettes, illusions, new ties . . . and the Country, of course, whose call we would have answered — when we were twenty — even if father and mother had said no. Now at our age, the love of our Country is still great, of course, but stronger than it is the love for our children. Is there any one of us here who wouldn't gladly take his son's place at the front if he could?"

There was a silence all round, everybody nodding as to approve.   20

"Why then," continued the fat man, "shouldn't we consider the feelings of our children when they are twenty? Isn't it natural that at their age they should consider the love for their Country (I am speaking of decent boys, of course) even greater than the love for us? Isn't it natural that it should be so, as after all they must look upon us as upon old boys who cannot move any more and must stay at home? If Country exists, if Country is a natural necessity, like bread, of which each of us must eat in order not to die of hunger, somebody must go to defend it. And our sons go, when they are twenty, and they don't want tears, because if they die, they die inflamed and happy (I am speaking, of course, of decent boys). Now, if one dies young and happy, without having the ugly sides of life, the boredom of it, the pettiness, the bitterness of disillusion . . . what more can we ask for him? Everyone should stop crying; everyone should laugh, as I do . . . or at least thank God — as I do — because my son, before dying, sent me a message saying that he was dying satisfied at having ended his life in the best way he could have wished. That is why, as you see, I do not even wear mourning . . . "

He shook his light fawn coat as to show it; his livid lip over his missing teeth was trembling, his eyes were watery and motionless, and soon after he ended with a shrill laugh which might well have been a sob.

"Quite so . . . quite so . . . " agreed the others.

The woman who, bundled in a corner under her coat, had been sitting and listening had — for the last three months — tried to find in the words of her husband and her friends something to console her in her deep sorrow, something that might show her how a mother should resign herself to send her son not even to death but to a probably dangerous life. Yet not a word had she found amongst the many which had been said . . . and her grief had been greater in seeing that nobody — as she thought — could share her feelings.

But now the words of the traveler amazed and almost stunned her. She suddenly realized that it wasn't the others who were wrong and could not understand her but herself who could not rise up to the same height of those fathers and mothers willing to resign themselves, without crying, not only to the departure of their sons but even to their death.   25

She lifted her head, she bent over from her corner trying to listen with great attention to the details which the fat man was giving to his companions about the way his son had fallen as a hero, for his King and his Country, happy and without regrets. It seemed to her that she had stumbled into a world she had never dreamt of, a world so far unknown to her and she was so pleased to hear everyone joining in congratulating that brave father who could so stoically speak of his child's death.

Then suddenly, just as if she had heard nothing of what had been said and almost as if waking up from a dream, she turned to the old man, asking him:

"Then . . . is your son really dead?"

Everybody stared at her. The old man, too, turned to look at her, fixing his great, bulging, horribly watery light gray eyes, deep in her face. For some little time he tried to answer, but words failed him. He looked and looked at her, almost as if only then — at that silly, incongruous question — he had suddenly realized at last that his son was really dead — gone for ever — for ever. His face contracted, became horribly distorted, then he snatched in haste a handkerchief from his pocket and, to the amazement of everyone, broke into harrowing, heart-rending, uncontrollable sobs.

Considerations

1. The story is titled "War," yet it focuses on a scene in a railroad car. To what extent does the story address the issues of war and battle? Consider, for example, what battles take place within the railroad car itself.

2. How is irony an integral part of the story? How does irony help to define characters as well as suggest theme?

3. What is the effect of changing points of view in this story? (At the beginning we know the thoughts of the woman, and at the end we see also into the mind and heart of the man whose son has been killed at the front.) How would the story be different if the reader knew this man's thoughts from the beginning?

4. The red-faced man believes that most young men feel more devoted to their country and to patriotic values than they do to their parents. What is your response to this observation? Do you consider this premise to be true today? How would young women fit into the picture? Would most of them value country over family? Or would something else entirely take precedence?

5. Throughout the story, nearly every character speaks of the necessity and nobility of parents letting their sons go off to fight for their country. How convincing do you find their arguments? How does the ending of the story relate to these earlier pronouncements?

FRANK O'CONNOR (1903–1966)

Guests of the Nation

I

At dusk the big Englishman, Belcher, would shift his long legs out of the ashes and say "Well, chums, what about it?" and Noble or me would say "All right, chum" (for we had picked up some of their curious expressions), and the little Englishman, Hawkins, would light the lamp and bring out the cards. Sometimes Jeremiah Donovan would come up and supervise the game and get excited over Hawkins's cards, which he always played badly, and shout at him as if he was one of our own "Ah, you divil, you, why didn't you play the tray?"

But ordinarily Jeremiah was a sober and contented poor devil like the big Englishman, Belcher, and was looked up to only because he was a fair hand at documents, though he was slow enough even with them. He wore a small cloth hat and big gaiters over his long pants, and you seldom saw him with his hands out of his pockets. He reddened when you talked to him, tilting from toe to heel and back, and looking down all the time at his big farmer's feet. Noble and me used to make fun of his broad accent, because we were from the town.

I couldn't at the time see the point of me and Noble guarding Belcher and Hawkins at all, for it was my belief that you could have planted that pair down anywhere from this to Claregalway and they'd have taken root there like a native weed. I never in my short experience seen two men to take to the country as they did.

They were handed on to us by the Second Battalion when the search for them became too hot, and Noble and myself, being young, took over with a natural feeling of responsibility, but Hawkins made us look like fools when he showed that he knew the country better than we did.

"You're the bloke they calls Bonaparte," he says to me. "Mary Brigid   5
O'Connell told me to ask you what you done with the pair of her brother's socks you borrowed."

For it seemed, as they explained it, that the Second used to have little evenings, and some of the girls of the neighbourhood turned in, and, seeing they were such decent chaps, our fellows couldn't leave the two Englishmen out of them. Hawkins learned to dance "The Walls of Limerick," "The Siege of Ennis," and "The Waves of Tory" as well as any of them, though, naturally, he couldn't return the compliment, because our lads at that time did not dance foreign dances on principle.

So whatever privileges Belcher and Hawkins had with the Second they just naturally took with us, and after the first day or two we gave up all pretence of keeping a close eye on them. Not that they could have got far, for they had accents you could cut with a knife and wore khaki tunics and overcoats with civilian pants and boots. But it's my belief that they never had any idea of escaping and were quite content to be where they were.

It was a treat to see how Belcher got off with the old woman of the house where we were staying. She was a great warrant to scold, and cranky even with us, but before ever she had a chance of giving our guests, as I may call them, a lick of her tongue, Belcher had made her his friend for life. She was breaking sticks, and Belcher, who hadn't been more than ten minutes in the house, jumped up from his seat and went over to her.

"Allow me, madam," he says, smiling his queer little smile, "please allow me"; and he takes the bloody hatchet. She was struck too paralytic to speak, and after that, Belcher would be at her heels, carrying a bucket, a basket, or a load of turf, as the case might be. As Noble said, he got into looking before she leapt, and hot water, or any little thing she wanted, Belcher would have it ready for her. For such a huge man (and though I am five foot ten myself I had to look up at him) he had an uncommon shortness — or should I say lack? — of speech. It took us some time to get used to him, walking in and out, like a ghost, without a word. Especially because Hawkins talked enough for a platoon, it was strange to hear big Belcher with his toes in the ashes come out with a solitary "Excuse me, chum," or "That's right, chum." His one and only passion was cards, and I will say for him that he was a good card-player. He could have fleeced myself and Noble, but whatever we lost to him Hawkins lost to us, and Hawkins played with the money Belcher gave him.

Hawkins lost to us because he had too much old gab, and we probably   10
lost to Belcher for the same reason. Hawkins and Noble would spit at one another about religion into the early hours of the morning, and Hawkins worried the soul out of Noble, whose brother was a priest, with a string of questions that would puzzle a cardinal. To make it worse even in treating of holy subjects, Hawkins had a deplorable tongue. I never in all my career met a man who could mix such a variety of cursing and bad language into an argument. He was a terrible man, and a fright to argue. He never did a stroke of work, and when he had no one else to talk to, he got stuck in the old woman.

He met his match in her, for one day when he tried to get her to complain profanely of the drought, she gave him a great come-down by blaming it entirely on Jupiter Pluvius (a deity neither Hawkins nor I had ever heard of, though Noble said that among the pagans it was believed that he had something to do with the rain). Another day he was swearing at the capitalists for starting the German war° when the old lady laid down her iron, puckered up her little crab's mouth, and said: "Mr. Hawkins, you can say what you like about the war, and think you'll deceive me because I'm only a simple poor countrywoman, but I know what started the war. It was the Italian Count that stole the heathen divinity out of the temple in Japan.

German war: World War I.

Believe me, Mr. Hawkins, nothing but sorrow and want can follow the people that disturb the hidden powers."

A queer old girl, all right.

II

We had our tea one evening, and Hawkins lit the lamp and we all sat into cards. Jeremiah Donovan came in too, and sat down and watched us for a while, and it suddenly struck me that he had no great love for the two Englishmen. It came as a great surprise to me, because I hadn't noticed anything about him before.

Late in the evening a really terrible argument blew up between Hawkins and Noble, about capitalists and priests and love of your country.

"The capitalists," says Hawkins with an angry gulp, "pays the priests   15 to tell you about the next world so as you won't notice what the bastards are up to in this."

"Nonsense, man!" says Noble, losing his temper. "Before ever a capitalist was thought of, people believed in the next world."

Hawkins stood up as though he was preaching a sermon.

"Oh, they did, did they?" he says with a sneer. "They believed all the things you believe, isn't that what you mean? And you believe that God created Adam, and Adam created Shem, and Shem created Jehoshophat. You believe all that silly old fairytale about Eve and Eden and the apple. Well, listen to me, chum. If you're entitled to hold a silly belief like that, I'm entitled to hold my silly belief—which is that the first thing your God created was a bleeding capitalist, with morality and Rolls-Royce complete. Am I right, chum?" he says to Belcher.

"You're right, chum," says Belcher with his amused smile, and got up from the table to stretch his long legs into the fire and stroke his moustache. So, seeing that Jeremiah Donovan was going, and that there was no knowing when the argument about religion would be over, I went out with him. We strolled down to the village together, and then he stopped and started blushing and mumbling and saying I ought to be behind, keeping guard on the prisoners. I didn't like the tone he took with me, and anyway I was bored with life in the cottage, so I replied by asking him what the hell we wanted guarding them at all for. I told him I'd talked it over with Noble, and that we'd both rather be out with a fighting column.

"What use are those fellows to us?" says I.   20

He looked at me in surprise and said: "I thought you knew we were keeping them as hostages."

"Hostages?" I said.

"The enemy have prisoners belonging to us," he says, "and now they're talking of shooting them. If they shoot our prisoners, we'll shoot theirs."

"Shoot them?" I said.

"What else did you think we were keeping them for?" he says.   25

"Wasn't it very unforeseen of you not to warn Noble and myself of that in the beginning?" I said.

"How was it?" says he. "You might have known it."

"We couldn't know it, Jeremiah Donovan," says I. "How could we when they were on our hands so long?"

"The enemy have our prisoners as long and longer," says he.

"That's not the same thing at all," says I.   30

"What difference is there?" says he.

I couldn't tell him, because I knew he wouldn't understand. If it was only an old dog that was going to the vet's, you'd try and not get too fond of him, but Jeremiah Donovan wasn't a man that would ever be in danger of that.

"And when is this thing going to be decided?" says I.

"We might hear tonight," he says. "Or tomorrow or the next day at latest. So if it's only hanging round here that's a trouble to you, you'll be free soon enough."

It wasn't the hanging round that was a trouble to me at all by this   35
time. I had worse things to worry about. When I got back to the cottage the argument was still on. Hawkins was holding forth in his best style, maintaining that there was no next world, and Noble was maintaining that there was; but I could see that Hawkins had had the best of it.

"Do you know what, chum?" he was saying with a saucy smile. "I think you're just as big a bleeding unbeliever as I am. You say you believe in the next world, and you know just as much about the next world as I do, which is sweet damn-all. What's heaven? You don't know. Where's heaven? You don't know. You know sweet damn-all! I ask you again, do they wear wings?"

"Very well, then," says Noble, "they do. Is that enough for you? They do wear wings."

"Where do they get them, then? Who makes them? Have they a factory for wings? Have they a sort of store where you hands in your chit and takes your bleeding wings?"

"You're an impossible man to argue with," says Noble. "Now, listen to me — " And they were off again.

It was long after midnight when we locked up and went to bed. As I   40
blew out the candle I told Noble what Jeremiah Donovan was after telling me. Noble took it very quietly. When we'd been in bed about an hour he asked me did I think we ought to tell the Englishmen. I didn't think we should, because it was more than likely that the English wouldn't shoot our men, and even if they did, the brigade officers, who were always up and down with the Second Battalion and knew the Englishmen well, wouldn't be likely to want them plugged. "I think so too," says Noble. "It would be great cruelty to put the wind up them now."

"It was very unforeseen of Jeremiah Donovan anyhow," says I.

It was next morning that we found it so hard to face Belcher and Hawkins. We went about the house all day scarcely saying a word. Belcher didn't seem to notice; he was stretched into the ashes as usual, with his usual look of waiting in quietness for something unforeseen to happen, but Hawkins noticed and put it down to Noble's being beaten in the argument of the night before.

"Why can't you take a discussion in the proper spirit?" he says severely. "You and your Adam and Eve! I'm a Communist, that's what I am. Communist or anarchist, it all comes to much the same thing." And for hours he went round the house, muttering when the fit took him. "Adam and Eve! Adam and Eve! Nothing better to do with their time than picking bleeding apples!"

III

I don't know how we got through that day, but I was very glad when it was over, the tea things were cleared away, and Belcher said in his peaceable way: "Well, chums, what about it?" We sat round the table and Hawkins took out the cards, and just then I heard Jeremiah Donovan's footstep on the path and a dark presentiment crossed my mind. I rose from the table and caught him before he reached the door.

"What do you want?" I asked.   45

"I want those two soldier friends of yours," he says, getting red.

"Is that the way, Jeremiah Donovan?" I asked.

"That's the way. There were four of our lads shot this morning, one of them a boy of sixteen."

"That's bad," I said.

At that moment Noble followed me out, and the three of us walked   50
down the path together, talking in whispers. Feeney, the local intelligence officer, was standing by the gate.

"What are you going to do about it?" I asked Jeremiah Donovan.

"I want you and Noble to get them out; tell them they're being shifted again; that'll be the quietest way."

"Leave me out of that," says Noble under his breath.

Jeremiah Donovan looks at him hard.

"All right," he says. "You and Feeney get a few tools from the shed   55
and dig a hole by the far end of the bog. Bonaparte and myself will be after you. Don't let anyone see you with the tools. I wouldn't like it to go beyond ourselves."

We saw Feeney and Noble go round to the shed and went in ourselves. I left Jeremiah Donovan to do the explanations. He told them that he had orders to send them back to the Second Battalion. Hawkins let out a mouthful of curses, and you could see that though Belcher didn't say anything, he was a bit upset too. The old woman was for having them stay in spite of us, and she didn't stop advising them until Jeremiah Donovan lost his temper and turned on her. He had a nasty temper, I noticed. It was pitch-dark in the cottage by this time, but no one thought of lighting the lamp, and in the darkness the two Englishmen fetched their topcoats and said good-bye to the old woman.

"Just as a man makes a home of a bleeding place, some bastard at headquarters thinks you're too cushy and shunts you off," says Hawkins, shaking her hand.

"A thousand thanks, madam," says Belcher. "A thousand thanks for everything" — as though he'd made it up.

We went round to the back of the house and down towards the bog. It was only then that Jeremiah Donovan told them. He was shaking with excitement.

"There were four of our fellows shot in Cork this morning and now   60 you're to be shot as a reprisal."

"What are you talking about?" snaps Hawkins. "It's bad enough being mucked about as we are without having to put up with your funny jokes."

"It isn't a joke," says Donovan. "I'm sorry, Hawkins, but it's true," and begins on the usual rigmarole about duty and how unpleasant it is.

I never noticed that people who talk a lot about duty find it much of a trouble to them.

"Oh, cut it out!" says Hawkins.

"Ask Bonaparte," says Donovan, seeing that Hawkins isn't taking him   65 seriously. "Isn't it true, Bonaparte?"

"It is," I say, and Hawkins stops.

"Ah, for Christ's sake, chum!"

"I mean it, chum," I say.

"You don't sound as if you meant it."

"If he doesn't mean it, I do," says Donovan, working himself up.   70

"What have you against me, Jeremiah Donovan?"

"I never said I had anything against you. But why did your people take out four of our prisoners and shoot them in cold blood?"

He took Hawkins by the arm and dragged him on, but it was impossible to make him understand that we were in earnest. I had the Smith and Wesson in my pocket and I kept fingering it and wondering what I'd do if they put up a fight for it or ran, and wishing to God they'd do one or the other. I knew if they did run for it, that I'd never fire on them. Hawkins wanted to know was Noble in it, and when we said yes, he asked us why Noble wanted to plug him. Why did any of us want to plug him? What had he done to us? Weren't we all chums? Didn't we understand him and didn't he understand us? Did we imagine for an instant that he'd shoot us for all the so-and-so officers in the so-and-so British Army?

By this time we'd reached the bog, and I was so sick I couldn't even answer him. We walked along the edge of it in the darkness, and every now and then Hawkins would call a halt and begin all over again, as if he was wound up, about our being chums, and I knew that nothing but the sight of the grave would convince him that we had to do it. And all the time I was hoping that something would happen; that they'd run for it or that Noble would take over the responsibility from me. I had the feeling that it was worse on Noble than on me.

IV

At last we saw the lantern in the distance and made towards it. Noble   75
was carrying it, and Feeney was standing somewhere in the darkness behind him, and the picture of them so still and silent in the bogland brought it home to me that we were in earnest, and banished the last bit of hope I had.

Belcher, on recognizing Noble, said: "Hallo, chum," in his quiet way, but Hawkins flew at him at once, and the argument began all over again, only this time Noble had nothing to say for himself and stood with his head down, holding the lantern between his legs.

It was Jeremiah Donovan who did the answering. For the twentieth time, as though it was haunting his mind, Hawkins asked if anybody thought he'd shoot Noble.

"Yes, you would," says Jeremiah Donovan.

"No, I wouldn't, damn you!"

"You would, because you'd know you'd be shot for not doing it."   80

"I wouldn't, not if I was to be shot twenty times over. I wouldn't shoot a pal. And Belcher wouldn't — isn't that right, Belcher?"

"That's right, chum," Belcher said, but more by way of answering the question than of joining in the argument. Belcher sounded as though whatever unforeseen thing he'd always been waiting for had come at last.

"Anyway, who says Noble would be shot if I wasn't? What do you think I'd do if I was in his place, out in the middle of a blasted bog?"

"What would you do?" asks Donovan.

"I'd go with him wherever he was going, of course. Share my last bob   85
with him and stick by him through thick and thin. No one can ever say of me that I let down a pal."

"We had enough of this," says Jeremiah Donovan, cocking his revolver. "Is there any message you want to send?"

"No, there isn't."

"Do you want to say your prayers?"

Hawkins came out with a cold-blooded remark that even shocked me and turned on Noble again.

"Listen to me, Noble," he says. "You and me are chums. You can't   90
come over to my side, so I'll come over to your side. That show you I mean what I say? Give me a rifle and I'll go along with you and the other lads."

Nobody answered him. We knew that was no way out.

"Hear what I'm saying?" he says. "I'm through with it. I'm a deserter or anything else you like. I don't believe in your stuff, but it's no worse than mine. That satisfy you?"

Noble raised his head, but Donovan began to speak and he lowered it again without replying.

"For the last time, have you any messages to send?" says Donovan in a cold, excited sort of voice.

"Shut up, Donovan! You don't understand me, but these lads do. 95 They're not the sort to make a pal and kill a pal. They're not the tools of any capitalist."

I alone of the crowd saw Donovan raise his Webley to the back of Hawkins's neck, and as he did so I shut my eyes and tried to pray. Hawkins had begun to say something else when Donovan fired, and as I opened my eyes at the bang, I saw Hawkins stagger at the knees and lie out flat at Noble's feet, slowly and as quiet as a kid falling asleep, with the lantern-light on his lean legs and bright farmer's boots. We all stood very still, watching him settle out in the last agony.

Then Belcher took out a handkerchief and began to tie it about his own eyes (in our excitement we'd forgotten to do the same for Hawkins), and, seeing it wasn't big enough, turned and asked for the loan of mine. I gave it to him and he knotted the two together and pointed with his foot at Hawkins.

"He's not quite dead," he says. "Better give him another."

Sure enough, Hawkins's left knee is beginning to rise. I bend down and put my gun to his head; then, recollecting myself, I get up again. Belcher understands what's in my mind.

"Give him his first," he says. "I don't mind. Poor bastard, we don't 100 know what's happening to him now."

I knelt and fired. By this time I didn't seem to know what I was doing. Belcher, who was fumbling a bit awkwardly with the handkerchiefs, came out with a laugh as he heard the shot. It was the first time I heard him laugh and it sent a shudder down my back; it sounded so unnatural.

"Poor bugger!" he said quietly. "And last night he was so curious about it all. It's very queer, chums, I always think. Now he knows as much about it as they'll ever let him know, and last night he was all in the dark."

Donovan helped him to tie the handkerchiefs about his eyes. "Thanks, chum," he said. Donovan asked if there were any messages he wanted sent.

"No, chum," he says. "Not for me. If any of you would like to write to Hawkins's mother, you'll find a letter from her in his pocket. He and his mother were great chums. But my missus left me eight years ago. Went away with another fellow and took the kid with her. I like the feeling of a home, as you may have noticed, but I couldn't start again after that."

It was an extraordinary thing, but in those few minutes Belcher said 105 more than in all the weeks before. It was just as if the sound of the shot had started a flood of talk in him and he could go on the whole night like that, quite happily, talking about himself. We stood round like fools now that he couldn't see us any longer. Donovan looked at Noble, and Noble shook his head. Then Donovan raised his Webley, and at that moment Belcher gives his queer laugh again. He may have thought we were talking about him, or perhaps he noticed the same thing I'd noticed and couldn't understand it.

"Excuse me, chums," he says. "I feel I'm talking the hell of a lot, and so silly, about my being so handy about a house and things like that. But this thing came on me suddenly. You'll forgive me, I'm sure."

"You don't want to say a prayer?" asks Donovan.

"No, chum," he says. "I don't think it would help. I'm ready, and you boys want to get it over."

"You understand that we're only doing our duty?" says Donovan.

Belcher's head was raised like a blind man's, so that you could only see   110 his chin and the tip of his nose in the lantern-light.

"I never could make out what duty was myself," he said. "I think you're all good lads, if that's what you mean. I'm not complaining."

Noble, just as if he couldn't bear any more of it, raised his fist at Donovan, and in a flash Donovan raised his gun and fired. The big man went over like a sack of meal, and this time there was no need of a second shot.

I don't remember much about the burying, but that it was worse than all the rest because we had to carry them to the grave. It was all mad lonely with nothing but a patch of lantern-light between ourselves and the dark, and birds hooting and screeching all round, disturbed by the guns. Noble went through Hawkins's belongings to find the letter from his mother, and then joined his hands together. He did the same with Belcher. Then, when we'd filled in the grave, we separated from Jeremiah Donovan and Feeney and took our tools back to the shed. All the way we didn't speak a word. The kitchen was dark and cold as we'd left it, and the old woman was sitting over the hearth, saying her beads. We walked past her into the room, and Noble struck a match to light the lamp. She rose quietly and came to the doorway with all her cantankerousness gone.

"What did ye do with them?" she asked in a whisper, and Noble started so that the match went out in his hand.

"What's that?" he asked without turning round.   115

"I heard ye," she said.

"What did you hear?" asked Noble.

"I heard ye. Do ye think I didn't hear ye, putting the spade back in the houseen?"

Noble struck another match and this time the lamp lit for him.

"Was that what ye did to them?" she asked.   120

Then, by God, in the very doorway, she fell on her knees and began praying, and after looking at her for a minute or two Noble did the same by the fireplace. I pushed my way out past her and left them at it. I stood at the door, watching the stars and listening to the shrieking of the birds dying out over the bogs. It is so strange what you feel at times like that you can't describe it. Noble says he saw everything ten times the size, as though there were nothing in the whole world but that little patch of bog with the two Englishmen stiffening into it, but with me it was as if the patch of bog where the Englishmen were was a million miles away, and even Noble and the old woman, mumbling behind me, and the birds and the bloody stars were all far away, and I was somehow very small and very lost and lonely like a child astray in the snow. And anything that happened to me afterwards, I never felt the same about again.

Considerations

1. List the details that suggest the setting (both time and place) of this story. How important is this specific setting to the story's action and theme? Might a story like this take place in a different time and location? Explain.
2. The four major characters demonstrate striking similarities and differences. How do these suggest the story's theme(s)?
3. What roles are played by the minor characters — the old woman and Donovan? How would the story be different if these characters were absent (or different)?
4. Throughout the story, several characters talk about "duty." What possible definitions of the word does the story suggest? How would you define the term? Consider, for example, different kinds of duty and evaluate whether one kind should take precedence over another.
5. Reread the details of the executions (Part IV). What effect does O'Connor achieve — and what questions does he raise — by including the gory description of the prisoners' agonizing deaths as well as Belcher's and Hawkins's responses to the executions?

KATHERINE MANSFIELD (1888–1923)

The Fly

"Y'are very snug in here," piped old Mr. Woodifield, and he peered out of the great, green leather armchair by his friend the boss's desk as a baby peers out of its pram. His talk was over; it was time for him to be off. But he did not want to go. Since he had retired, since his . . . stroke, the wife and the girls kept him boxed up in the house every day of the week except Tuesday. On Tuesday he was dressed up and brushed and allowed to cut back to the City for the day. Though what he did there the wife and girls couldn't imagine. Made a nuisance of himself to his friends, they supposed. . . . Well, perhaps so. All the same, we cling to our last pleasures as the tree clings to its last leaves. So there sat old Woodifield, smoking a cigar and staring almost greedily at the boss, who rolled in his office chair, stout, rosy, five years older than he, and still going strong, still at the helm. It did one good to see him.

Wistfully, admiringly, the old voice added, "It's snug in here, upon my word!"

"Yes, it's comfortable enough," agreed the boss, and he flipped the *Financial Times* with a paper-knife. As a matter of fact he was proud of his room; he liked to have it admired, especially by old Woodifield. It gave him a feeling of deep, solid satisfaction to be planted there in the midst of it in full view of that frail old figure in the muffler.

"I've had it done up lately," he explained, as he had explained for the past — how many? — weeks. "New carpet," and he pointed to the bright red carpet with a pattern of large white rings. "New furniture," and he nodded towards the massive bookcase and the table with legs like twisted treacle. "Electric heating!" He waved almost exultantly towards the five transparent, pearly sausages glowing so softly in the tilted copper pan.

But he did not draw old Woodifield's attention to the photograph over the table of a grave-looking boy in uniform standing in one of those spectral photographers' parks with photographers' storm-clouds behind him. It was not new. It had been there for over six years.

"There was something I wanted to tell you," said old Woodifield, and his eyes grew dim remembering. "Now what was it? I had it in my mind when I started out this morning." His hands began to tremble, and patches of red showed above his beard.

Poor old chap, he's on his last pins, thought the boss. And, feeling kindly, he winked at the old man, and said jokingly, "I tell you what. I've got a little drop of something here that'll do you good before you go out into the cold again. It's beautiful stuff. It wouldn't hurt a child." He took a key off his watch-chain, unlocked a cupboard below his desk, and drew forth a dark, squat bottle. "That's the medicine," said he. "And the man

5

from whom I got it told me on the strict Q. T.° it came from the cellars at Windsor Castle."

Old Woodifield's mouth fell open at the sight. He couldn't have looked more surprised if the boss had produced a rabbit.

"It's whisky, ain't it?" he piped, feebly.

The boss turned the bottle and lovingly showed him the label. Whisky   10
it was.

"D'you know," said he, peering up at the boss wonderingly, "they won't let me touch it at home." And he looked as though he was going to cry.

"Ah, that's where we know a bit more than the ladies," cried the boss, swooping across for two tumblers that stood on the table with the water-bottle, and pouring a generous finger into each. "Drink it down. It'll do you good. And don't put any water with it. It's sacrilege to tamper with stuff like this. Ah!" He tossed off his, pulled out his handkerchief, hastily wiped his moustaches, and cocked an eye at old Woodifield, who was rolling his in his chaps.

The old man swallowed, was silent a moment, and then said faintly, "It's nutty!"

But it warmed him; it crept into his chill old brain—he remembered.

"That was it," he said, heaving himself out of his chair. "I thought   15
you'd like to know. The girls were in Belgium last week having a look at poor Reggie's grave, and they happened to come across your boy's. They're quite near each other, it seems."

Old Woodifield paused, but the boss made no reply. Only a quiver in his eyelids showed that he heard.

"The girls were delighted with the way the place is kept," piped the old voice. "Beautifully looked after. Couldn't be better if they were at home. You've not been across, have yer?"

"No, no!" For various reasons the boss had not been across.

"There's miles of it," quavered old Woodifield, "and it's all as neat as a garden. Flowers growing on all the graves. Nice broad paths." It was plain from his voice how much he liked a nice broad path.

The pause came again. Then the old man brightened wonderfully.   20

"D'you know what the hotel made the girls pay for a pot of jam?" he piped. "Ten francs! Robbery, I call it. It was a little pot, so Gertrude says, no bigger than a half-crown. And she hadn't taken more than a spoonful when they charged her ten francs. Gertrude brought the pot away with her to teach 'em a lesson. Quite right, too; it's trading on our feelings. They think because we're over there having a look around we're ready to pay anything. That's what it is." And he turned towards the door.

Q. T.: Quiet, in secret (slang).

"Quite right, quite right!" cried the boss, though what was quite right he hadn't the least idea. He came round by his desk, followed the shuffling footsteps to the door, and saw the old fellow out. Woodifield was gone.

For a long moment the boss stayed, staring at nothing, while the grey-haired office messenger, watching him, dodged in and out of his cubby-hole like a dog that expects to be taken for a run. Then: "I'll see nobody for half an hour, Macey," said the boss. "Understand? Nobody at all."

"Very good, sir."

The door shut, the firm heavy steps recrossed the bright carpet, the fat body plumped down in the spring chair, and leaning forward, the boss covered his face with his hands. He wanted, he intended, he had arranged to weep. . . . 25

It had been a terrible shock to him when old Woodifield sprang that remark upon him about the boy's grave. It was exactly as though the earth had opened and he had seen the boy lying there with Woodifield's girls staring down at him. For it was strange. Although over six years had passed away, the boss never thought of the boy except as lying unchanged, unblemished in his uniform, asleep for ever. "My son!" groaned the boss. But no tears came yet. In the past, in the first months and even years after the boy's death, he had only to say those words to be overcome by such grief that nothing short of a violent fit of weeping could relieve him. Time, he had declared then, he had told everybody, could make no difference. Other men perhaps might recover, might live their loss down, but not he. How was it possible? His boy was an only son. Ever since his birth the boss had worked at building up this business for him; it had no other meaning if it was not for the boy. Life itself had come to have no other meaning. How on earth could he have slaved, denied himself, kept going all those years without the promise for ever before him of the boy's stepping into his shoes and carrying on where he left off?

And that promise had been so near being fulfilled. The boy had been in the office learning the ropes for a year before the war. Every morning they had started off together; they had come back by the same train. And what congratulations he had received as the boy's father! No wonder; he had taken to it marvellously. As to his popularity with the staff, every man jack of them down to old Macey couldn't make enough of the boy. And he wasn't in the least spoilt. No, he was just his bright, natural self, with the right word for everybody, with that boyish look and his habit of saying, "Simply splendid!"

But all that was over and done with as though it never had been. The day had come when Macey had handed him the telegram that brought the whole place crashing about his head. "Deeply regret to inform you . . . " And he had left the office a broken man, with his life in ruins.

Six years ago, six years . . . How quickly time passed! It might have happened yesterday. The boss took his hands from his face; he was puzzled. Something seemed to be wrong with him. He wasn't feeling as he wanted to feel. He decided to get up and have a look at the boy's photograph. But it wasn't a favorite photograph of his; the expression was unnatural. It was cold, even stern-looking. The boy had never looked like that.

At that moment the boss noticed that a fly had fallen into his broad 30 inkpot, and was trying feebly but desperately to clamber out again. Help! help! said those struggling legs. But the sides of the inkpot were wet and slippery; it fell back again and began to swim. The boss took up a pen, picked the fly out of the ink, and shook it on to a piece of blotting-paper. For a fraction of a second it lay still on the dark patch that oozed round it. Then the front legs waved, took hold, and, pulling its small sodden body up, it began the immense task of cleaning the ink from its wings. Over and under, over and under, went a leg along a wing, as the stone goes over and under the scythe. Then there was a pause, while the fly, seeming to stand on the tips of its toes, tried to expand first one wing and then the other. It succeeded at last, and, sitting down, it began, like a minute cat, to clean its face. Now one could imagine that the little front legs rubbed against each other lightly, joyfully. The horrible danger was over; it had escaped; it was ready for life again.

But just then the boss had an idea. He plunged his pen back into the ink, leaned his thick wrist on the blotting-paper, and as the fly tried its wings down came a great heavy blot. What would it make of that? What indeed! The little beggar seemed absolutely cowed, stunned, and afraid to move because of what would happen next. But then, as if painfully, it dragged itself forward. The front legs waved, caught hold, and, more slowly this time, the task began from the beginning.

He's a plucky little devil, thought the boss, and he felt a real admiration for the fly's courage. That was the way to tackle things; that was the right spirit. Never say die; it was only a question of . . . But the fly had again finished its laborious task, and the boss had just time to refill his pen, to shake fair and square on the new-cleaned body yet another dark drop. What about it this time? A painful moment of suspense followed. But behold, the front legs were again waving; the boss felt a rush of relief. He leaned over the fly and said to it tenderly, "You artful little b . . . " And he actually had the brilliant notion of breathing on it to help the drying process. All the same, there was something timid and weak about its efforts now, and the boss decided that this time should be the last, as he dipped the pen into the inkpot.

It was. The last blot on the soaked blotting-paper, and the draggled fly lay in it and did not stir. The back legs were stuck to the body; the front legs were not to be seen.

"Come on," said the boss. "Look sharp!" And he stirred it with his pen — in vain. Nothing happened or was likely to happen. The fly was dead.

The boss lifted the corpse on the end of the paper-knife and flung it 35 into the waste-paper basket. But such a grinding feeling of wretchedness seized him that he felt positively frightened. He started forward and pressed the bell for Macey.

"Bring me some fresh blotting-paper," he said, sternly, "and look sharp about it." And while the old dog padded away he fell to wondering what it was he had been thinking about before. What was it? It was . . . He took out his handkerchief and passed it inside his collar. For the life of him he could not remember.

Considerations

1. What are the three scenes into which this story is divided? What connections and relationships do you see among these scenes?
2. How are Old Woodifield and his boss similar? Different? What significance do you see in these similarities and differences?
3. Comment on the changes in the boss's feelings and responses to his loss since the son's death.
4. What is the significance of the boss's encounter with the fly? How does this encounter relate to the son's death?
5. Consider these lines from Shakespeare's *King Lear:*

   > As flies to wanton boys are we to the gods.
   > They kill us for their sport.

   How might these lines relate to the conflict and action in "The Fly"?

TIM O'BRIEN (1947–   )

The Things They Carried

First Lieutenant Jimmy Cross carried letters from a girl named Martha, a junior at Mount Sebastian College in New Jersey. They were not love letters, but Lieutenant Cross was hoping, so he kept them folded in plastic at the bottom of his rucksack. In the late afternoon, after a day's march, he would dig his foxhole, wash his hands under a canteen, unwrap the letters, hold them with the tips of his fingers, and spend the last hour of light pretending. He would imagine romantic camping trips into the White Mountains in New Hampshire. He would sometimes taste the envelope flaps, knowing her tongue had been there. More than anything, he wanted Martha to love him as he loved her, but the letters were mostly chatty, elusive on the matter of love. She was a virgin, he was almost sure. She was an English major at Mount Sebastian, and she wrote beautifully about her professors and roommates and midterm exams, about her respect for Chaucer and her great affection for Virginia Woolf. She often quoted lines of poetry; she never mentioned the war, except to say, Jimmy, take care of yourself. The letters weighed ten ounces. They were signed "Love, Martha," but Lieutenant Cross understood that "Love" was only a way of signing and did not mean what he sometimes pretended it meant. At dusk, he would carefully return the letters to his rucksack. Slowly, a bit distracted, he would get up and move among his men, checking the perimeter, then at full dark he would return to his hole and watch the night and wonder if Martha was a virgin.

The things they carried were largely determined by necessity. Among the necessities or near necessities were P-38 can openers, pocket knives, heat tabs, wrist watches, dog tags, mosquito repellent, chewing gum, candy, cigarettes, salt tablets, packets of Kool-Aid, lighters, matches, sewing kits, Military Payment Certificates, C rations, and two or three canteens of water. Together, these items weighed between fifteen and twenty pounds, depending upon a man's habits or rate of metabolism. Henry Dobbins, who was a big man, carried extra rations; he was especially fond of canned peaches in heavy syrup over pound cake. Dave Jensen, who practiced field hygiene, carried a toothbrush, dental floss, and several hotel-size bars of soap he'd stolen on R&R° in Sydney, Australia. Ted Lavender, who was scared, carried tranquilizers until he was shot in the head outside the village of Than Khe in mid-April. By necessity, and because it was SOP,° they all carried steel helmets that weighed five pounds including the liner and camouflage cover. They carried the standard fatigue jackets and trousers. Very few carried underwear. On their feet they carried jungle boots — 2.1 pounds — and Dave

---

R&R: Rest and recreation.   *SOP:* Standard operating procedure.

Jensen carried three pairs of socks and a can of Dr. Scholl's foot powder as a precaution against trench foot. Until he was shot, Ted Lavender carried six or seven ounces of premium dope, which for him was a necessity. Mitchell Sanders, the RTO, carried condoms. Norman Bowker carried a diary. Rat Kiley carried comic books. Kiowa, a devout Baptist, carried an illustrated New Testament that had been presented to him by his father, who taught Sunday school in Oklahoma City, Oklahoma. As a hedge against bad times, however, Kiowa also carried his grandmother's distrust of the white man, his grandfather's old hunting hatchet. Necessity dictated. Because the land was mined and booby-trapped, it was SOP for each man to carry a steel-centered, nylon-covered flak jacket, which weighed 6.7 pounds, but which on hot days seemed much heavier. Because you could die so quickly, each man carried at least one large compress bandage, usually in the helmet band for easy access. Because the nights were cold, and because the monsoons were wet, each carried a green plastic poncho that could be used as a raincoat or ground sheet or makeshift tent. With its quilted liner, the poncho weighed almost two pounds, but it was worth every ounce. In April, for instance, when Ted Lavender was shot, they used his poncho to wrap him up, then to carry him across the paddy, then to lift him into the chopper that took him away.

They were called legs or grunts.

To carry something was to "hump" it, as when Lieutenant Jimmy Cross humped his love for Martha up the hills and through the swamps. In its intransitive form, "to hump" meant "to walk," or "to march," but it implied burdens far beyond the intransitive.

Almost everyone humped photographs. In his wallet, Lieutenant Cross   5
carried two photographs of Martha. The first was a Kodachrome snapshot signed "Love," though he knew better. She stood against a brick wall. Her eyes were gray and neutral, her lips slightly open as she stared straight-on at the camera. At night, sometimes, Lieutenant Cross wondered who had taken the picture, because he knew she had boyfriends, because he loved her so much, and because he could see the shadow of the picture taker spreading out against the brick wall. The second photograph had been clipped from the 1968 Mount Sebastian yearbook. It was an action shot — women's volley-ball — and Martha was bent horizontal to the floor, reaching, the palms of her hands in sharp focus, the tongue taut, the expression frank and compet-itive. There was no visible sweat. She wore white gym shorts. Her legs, he thought, were almost certainly the legs of a virgin, dry and without hair, the left knee cocked and carrying her entire weight, which was just over one hundred pounds. Lieutenant Cross remembered touching that left knee. A dark theater, he remembered, and the movie was *Bonnie and Clyde,* and Martha wore a tweed skirt, and during the final scene, when he touched her knee, she turned and looked at him in a sad, sober way that made him pull his hand back, but he would always remember the feel of the tweed skirt

and the knee beneath it and the sound of the gunfire that killed Bonnie and Clyde, how embarrassing it was, how slow and oppressive. He remembered kissing her good night at the dorm door. Right then, he thought, he should've done something brave. He should've carried her up the stairs to her room and tied her to the bed and touched that left knee all night long. He should've risked it. Whenever he looked at the photographs, he thought of new things he should've done.

What they carried was partly a function of rank, partly of field specialty.

As a first lieutenant and platoon leader, Jimmy Cross carried a compass, maps, code books, binoculars, and a .45-caliber pistol that weighed 2.9 pounds fully loaded. He carried a strobe light and the responsibility for the lives of his men.

As an RTO, Mitchell Sanders carried the PRC-25 radio, a killer, twenty-six pounds with its battery.

As a medic, Rat Kiley carried a canvas satchel filled with morphine and plasma and malaria tablets and surgical tape and comic books and all the things a medic must carry, including M&M's for especially bad wounds, for a total weight of nearly twenty pounds.

As a big man, therefore a machine gunner, Henry Dobbins carried the   10
M-60, which weighed twenty-three pounds unloaded, but which was almost always loaded. In addition, Dobbins carried between ten and fifteen pounds of ammunition draped in belts across his chest and shoulders.

As PFCs or Spec 4s, most of them were common grunts and carried the standard M-16 gas-operated assault rifle. The weapon weighed 7.5 pounds unloaded, 8.2 pounds with its full twenty-round magazine. Depending on numerous factors, such as topography and psychology, the riflemen carried anywhere from twelve to twenty magazines, usually in cloth bandoliers, adding on another 8.4 pounds at minimum, fourteen pounds at maximum. When it was available, they also carried M-16 maintenance gear — rods and steel brushes and swabs and tubes of LSA oil — all of which weighed about a pound. Among the grunts, some carried the M-79 grenade launcher, 5.9 pounds unloaded, a reasonably light weapon except for the ammunition, which was heavy. A single round weighed ten ounces. The typical load was twenty-five rounds. But Ted Lavender, who was scared, carried thirty-four rounds when he was shot and killed outside Than Khe, and he went down under an exceptional burden, more than twenty pounds of ammunition, plus the flak jacket and helmet and rations and water and toilet paper and tranquilizers and all the rest, plus the unweighed fear. He was dead weight. There was no twitching or flopping. Kiowa, who saw it happen, said it was like watching a rock fall, or a big sandbag or something — just boom, then down — not like the movies where the dead guy rolls around and does fancy spins and goes ass over teakettle — not like that, Kiowa said, the poor bastard just flat-fuck fell. Boom. Down. Nothing else.

It was a bright morning in mid-April. Lieutenant Cross felt the pain. He blamed himself. They stripped off Lavender's canteens and ammo, all the heavy things, and Rat Kiley said the obvious, the guy's dead, and Mitchell Sanders used his radio to report one U.S. KIA and to request a chopper. Then they wrapped Lavender in his poncho. They carried him out to a dry paddy, established security, and sat smoking the dead man's dope until the chopper came. Lieutenant Cross kept to himself. He pictured Martha's smooth young face, thinking he loved her more than anything, more than his men, and now Ted Lavender was dead because he loved her so much and could not stop thinking about her. When the dust-off arrived, they carried Lavender aboard. Afterward they burned Than Khe. They marched until dusk, then dug their holes, and that night Kiowa kept explaining how you had to be there, how fast it was, how the poor guy just dropped like so much concrete. Boom-down, he said. Like cement.

In addition to the three standard weapons — the M-60, M-16, and M-79 — they carried whatever presented itself, or whatever seemed appropriate as a means of killing or staying alive. They carried catch-as-catch-can. At various times, in various situations, they carried M-14s and CAR-15s and Swedish Ks and grease guns and captured AK-47s and Chi-Coms and RPGs and Simonov carbines and black-market Uzis and .38-caliber Smith & Wesson handguns and 66 mm LAWs and shotguns and silencers and blackjacks and bayonets and C-4 plastic explosives. Lee Strunk carried a slingshot; a weapon of last resort, he called it. Mitchell Sanders carried brass knuckles. Kiowa carried his grandfather's feathered hatchet. Every third or fourth man carried a Claymore antipersonnel mine — 3.5 pounds with its firing device. They all carried fragmentation grenades — fourteen ounces each. They all carried at least one M-18 colored smoke grenade — twenty-four ounces. Some carried CS or tear gas grenades. Some carried white-phosphorus grenades. They carried all they could bear, and then some, including a silent awe for the terrible power of the things they carried.

In the first week of April, before Lavender died, Lieutenant Jimmy Cross received a good-luck charm from Martha. It was a simple pebble, an ounce at most. Smooth to the touch, it was a milky-white color with flecks of orange and violet, oval-shaped, like a miniature egg. In the accompanying letter, Martha wrote that she had found the pebble on the Jersey shoreline, precisely where the land touched water at high tide, where things came together but also separated. It was this separate-but-together quality, she wrote, that had inspired her to pick up the pebble and to carry it in her breast pocket for several days, where it seemed weightless, and then to send it through the mail, by air, as a token of her truest feelings for him. Lieutenant Cross found this romantic. But he wondered what her truest feelings were, exactly, and what she meant by separate-but-together. He wondered how the tides and waves had come into play on that afternoon along the Jersey shoreline when Martha saw the pebble and bent down to rescue it from geology. He imagined bare feet. Martha was a poet, with the poet's sensibilities, and her feet would be brown and bare, the toenails unpainted, the eyes chilly and somber like the ocean in March, and though it was painful, he wondered who had been with her that afternoon. He imagined a pair of shadows moving along the strip of sand where things came together but also separated. It was phantom jealousy, he knew, but he couldn't help himself. He loved her so much. On the march, through the hot days of early April, he carried the pebble in his mouth, turning it with his tongue, tasting sea salts and moisture. His mind wandered. He had difficulty keeping his attention on the war. On occasion he would yell at his men to spread out the column, to keep their eyes open, but then he would slip away into daydreams, just pretending, walking barefoot along the Jersey shore, with Martha, carrying nothing. He would feel himself rising. Sun and waves and gentle winds, all love and lightness.

What they carried varied by mission.

When a mission took them to the mountains, they carried mosquito   15 netting, machetes, canvas tarps, and extra bug juice.

If a mission seemed especially hazardous, or if it involved a place they knew to be bad, they carried everything they could. In certain heavily mined AOs, where the land was dense with Toe Poppers and Bouncing Betties, they took turns humping a twenty-eight-pound mine detector. With its headphones and big sensing plate, the equipment was a stress on the lower back and shoulders, awkward to handle, often useless because of the shrapnel in the earth, but they carried it anyway, partly for safety, partly for the illusion of safety.

On ambush, or other night missions, they carried peculiar little odds and ends. Kiowa always took along his New Testament and a pair of moccasins for silence. Dave Jensen carried night-sight vitamins high in carotin. Lee Strunk carried his slingshot; ammo, he claimed, would never be a problem. Rat Kiley carried brandy and M&M's. Until he was shot, Ted Lavender carried the starlight scope, which weighed 6.3 pounds with its aluminum carrying case. Henry Dobbins carried his girlfriend's pantyhose wrapped around his neck as a comforter. They all carried ghosts. When dark came, they would move out single file across the meadows and paddies to their ambush coordinates, where they would quietly set up the Claymores and lie down and spend the night waiting.

Other missions were more complicated and required special equipment. In mid-April, it was their mission to search out and destroy the elaborate tunnel complexes in the Than Khe area south of Chu Lai. To blow the tunnels, they carried one-pound blocks of pentrite high explosives, four blocks to a man, sixty-eight pounds in all. They carried wiring, detonators, and battery-powered clackers. Dave Jensen carried earplugs. Most often, before blowing the tunnels, they were ordered by higher command to search them, which was considered bad news, but by and large they just shrugged and carried out orders. Because he was a big man, Henry Dobbins was excused from tunnel duty. The others would draw numbers. Before Lavender died there were seventeen men in the platoon, and whoever drew the number seventeen would strip off his gear and crawl in head first with a flashlight and Lieutenant Cross's .45-caliber pistol. The rest of them would fan out as security. They would sit down or kneel, not facing the hole, listening to the ground beneath them, imagining cobwebs and ghosts, whatever was down there — the tunnel walls squeezing in — how the flashlight seemed impossibly heavy in the hand and how it was tunnel vision in the very strictest sense, compression in all ways, even time, and how you had to wiggle in — ass and elbows — a swallowed-up feeling — and how you found yourself worrying about odd things — will your flashlight go dead? Do rats carry rabies? If you screamed, how far would the sound carry? Would your buddies hear it? Would they have the courage to drag you out? In some respects, though not many, the waiting was worse than the tunnel itself. Imagination was a killer.

On April 16, when Lee Strunk drew the number seventeen, he laughed and muttered something and went down quickly. The morning was hot and very still. Not good, Kiowa said. He looked at the tunnel opening, then out across a dry paddy toward the village of Than Khe. Nothing moved. No clouds or birds or people. As they waited, the men smoked and drank Kool-Aid, not talking much, feeling sympathy for Lee Strunk but also feeling the luck of the draw. You win some, you lose some, said Mitchell Sanders, and sometimes you settle for a rain check. It was a tired line and no one laughed.

Henry Dobbins ate a tropical chocolate bar. Ted Lavender popped a 20 tranquilizer and went off to pee.

After five minutes, Lieutenant Jimmy Cross moved to the tunnel, leaned down, and examined the darkness. Trouble, he thought — a cave-in maybe. And then suddenly, without willing it, he was thinking about Martha. The stresses and fractures, the quick collapse, the two of them buried alive under all that weight. Dense, crushing love. Kneeling, watching the hole, he tried to concentrate on Lee Strunk and the war, all the dangers, but his love was too much for him, he felt paralyzed, he wanted to sleep inside her lungs and breathe her blood and be smothered. He wanted her to be a virgin and not a virgin, all at once. He wanted to know her. Intimate secrets — why poetry? Why so sad? Why that grayness in her eyes? Why so alone? Not lonely, just alone — riding her bike across campus or sitting off by herself in the cafeteria. Even dancing, she danced alone — and it was the aloneness that filled him with love. He remembered telling her that one evening. How she nodded and looked away. And how, later, when he kissed her, she received the kiss without returning it, her eyes wide open, not afraid, not a virgin's eyes, just flat and uninvolved.

Lieutenant Cross gazed at the tunnel. But he was not there. He was buried with Martha under the white sand at the Jersey shore. They were pressed together, and the pebble in his mouth was her tongue. He was smiling. Vaguely, he was aware of how quiet the day was, the sullen paddies, yet he could not bring himself to worry about matters of security. He was beyond that. He was just a kid at war, in love. He was twenty-two years old. He couldn't help it.

A few moments later Lee Strunk crawled out of the tunnel. He came up grinning, filthy but alive. Lieutenant Cross nodded and closed his eyes while the others clapped Strunk on the back and made jokes about rising from the dead.

Worms, Rat Kiley said. Right out of the grave. Fuckin' zombie.

The men laughed. They all felt great relief.   25

Spook City, said Mitchell Sanders.

Lee Strunk made a funny ghost sound, a kind of moaning, yet very happy, and right then, when Strunk made that high happy moaning sound, when he went *Ahhooooo,* right then Ted Lavender was shot in the head on his way back from peeing. He lay with his mouth open. The teeth were broken. There was a swollen black bruise under his left eye. The cheekbone was gone. Oh shit, Rat Kiley said, the guy's dead. The guy's dead, he kept saying, which seemed profound — the guy's dead. I mean really.

The things they carried were determined to some extent by superstition. Lieutenant Cross carried his good-luck pebble. Dave Jensen carried a rabbit's foot. Norman Bowker, otherwise a very gentle person, carried a thumb that had been presented to him as a gift by Mitchell Sanders. The thumb was dark brown, rubbery to the touch, and weighed four ounces at most. It had been cut from a VC corpse, a boy of fifteen or sixteen. They'd found him at the bottom of an irrigation ditch, badly burned, flies in his mouth and eyes. The boy wore black shorts and sandals. At the time of his death he had been carrying a pouch of rice, a rifle, and three magazines of ammunition.

You want my opinion, Mitchell Sanders said, there's a definite moral here.

He put his hand on the dead boy's wrist. He was quiet for a time, as if   30 counting a pulse, then he patted the stomach, almost affectionately, and used Kiowa's hunting hatchet to remove the thumb.

Henry Dobbins asked what the moral was.

Moral?

You know. *Moral.*

Sanders wrapped the thumb in toilet paper and handed it across to Norman Bowker. There was no blood. Smiling, he kicked the boy's head, watched the flies scatter, and said, It's like with that old TV show — Paladin. Have gun, will travel.

Henry Dobbins thought about it.   35

Yeah, well, he finally said. I don't see no moral.

There it *is,* man.

Fuck off.

They carried USO stationery and pencils and pens. They carried Sterno, safety pins, trip flares, signal flares, spools of wire, razor blades, chewing tobacco, liberated joss sticks and statuettes of the smiling Buddha, candles, grease pencils, *The Stars and Stripes,* fingernail clippers, Psy Ops leaflets, bush hats, bolos, and much more. Twice a week, when the resupply choppers came in, they carried hot chow in green Mermite cans and large canvas bags filled with iced beer and soda pop. They carried plastic water containers, each with a two-gallon capacity. Mitchell Sanders carried a set of starched tiger fatigues for special occasions. Henry Dobbins carried Black Flag insecticide. Dave Jensen carried empty sandbags that could be filled at night for added protection. Lee Strunk carried tanning lotion. Some things they carried in common. Taking turns, they carried the big PRC-77 scrambler radio, which weighed thirty pounds with its battery. They shared the weight of memory. They took up what others could no longer bear. Often, they carried each other, the wounded or weak. They carried infections. They carried chess sets, basketballs, Vietnamese-English dictionaries, insignia of rank, Bronze Stars and Purple Hearts, plastic cards imprinted with the Code of Conduct. They carried diseases, among them malaria and dysentery. They carried lice and ringworm and leeches and paddy algae and various rots and molds. They carried the land itself — Vietnam, the place, the soil — a powdery orange-red dust that covered their boots and fatigues and faces. They carried the sky. The whole atmosphere, they carried it, the humidity, the monsoons, the stink of fungus and decay, all of it, they carried gravity. They moved like mules. By daylight they took sniper fire, at night they were mortared, but it was not battle, it was just the endless march, village to village, without purpose, nothing won or lost. They marched for the sake of the march. They plodded along slowly, dumbly, leaning forward against the heat, unthinking, all blood and bone, simple grunts, soldiering with their legs, toiling up the hills and down into the paddies and across the rivers and up again and down, just humping, one step and then the next and then another, but no volition, no will, because it was automatic, it was anatomy, and the war was entirely a matter of posture and carriage, the hump was everything, a kind of inertia, a kind of emptiness, a dullness of desire and intellect and conscience and hope and human sensibility. Their principles were in their feet. Their calculations were biological. They had no sense of strategy or mission. They searched the villages without knowing what to look for, not caring, kicking over jars of rice, frisking children and old men, blowing tunnels, sometimes setting fires and sometimes not, then forming up and moving on to the next village, then other villages, where it would always be the same. They carried their own lives. The pressures were enormous. In the heat of early afternoon, they would remove their helmets and flak jackets, walking bare, which was dangerous but which helped ease the strain. They would often discard things along the route of march. Purely for comfort, they would throw away rations, blow their Claymores and grenades, no matter, because by nightfall the resupply choppers would arrive with more of the same, then a day or two later still more, fresh watermelons and crates of ammunition and sunglasses and woolen sweaters — the resources were stunning — sparklers for the Fourth of July, colored eggs for Easter. It was the great American war chest — the fruits of science, the smokestacks, the canneries, the arsenals at Hartford, the Minnesota forests, the machine shops, the vast fields of corn and wheat — they carried like freight trains; they carried it on their backs and shoulders — and for all the ambiguities of Vietnam, all the mysteries and unknowns, there was at least the single abiding certainty that they would never be at a loss for things to carry.

After the chopper took Lavender away, Lieutenant Jimmy Cross led   40
his men into the village of Than Khe. They burned everything. They shot chickens and dogs, they trashed the village well, they called in artillery and watched the wreckage, then they marched for several hours through the hot afternoon, and then at dusk, while Kiowa explained how Lavender died, Lieutenant Cross found himself trembling.

He tried not to cry. With his entrenching tool, which weighed five pounds, he began digging a hole in the earth.

He felt shame. He hated himself. He had loved Martha more than his men, and as a consequence Lavender was now dead, and this was something he would have to carry like a stone in his stomach for the rest of the war.

All he could do was dig. He used his entrenching tool like an ax, slashing, feeling both love and hate, and then later, when it was full dark, he sat at the bottom of his foxhole and wept. It went on for a long while. In part, he was grieving for Ted Lavender, but mostly it was for Martha, and for himself, because she belonged to another world, which was not quite real, and because she was a junior at Mount Sebastian College in New Jersey, a poet and a virgin and uninvolved, and because he realized she did not love him and never would.

Like cement, Kiowa whispered in the dark. I swear to God — boom-down. Not a word.

I've heard this, said Norman Bowker.   45

A pisser, you know? Still zipping himself up. Zapped while zipping.

All right, fine. That's enough.

Yeah, but you had to see it, the guy just —

I *heard,* man. Cement. So why not shut the fuck *up?*

Kiowa shook his head sadly and glanced over at the hole where Lieu-   50
tenant Jimmy Cross sat watching the night. The air was thick and wet. A warm, dense fog had settled over the paddies and there was the stillness that precedes rain.

After a time Kiowa sighed.

One thing for sure, he said. The Lieutenant's in some deep hurt. I mean that crying jag — the way he was carrying on — it wasn't fake or anything, it was real heavy-duty hurt. The man cares.

Sure, Norman Bowker said.

Say what you want, the man does care.

We all got problems.   55

Not Lavender.

No, I guess not, Bowker said. Do me a favor, though.

Shut up?

That's a smart Indian. Shut up.

Shrugging, Kiowa pulled off his boots. He wanted to say more, just   60
to lighten up his sleep, but instead he opened his New Testament and arranged it beneath his head as a pillow. The fog made things seem hollow and unattached. He tried not to think about Ted Lavender, but then he was thinking how fast it was, no drama, down and dead, and how it was hard to feel anything except surprise. It seemed un-Christian. He wished he could find some great sadness, or even anger, but the emotion wasn't there and he couldn't make it happen. Mostly he felt pleased to be alive. He liked the smell of the New Testament under his cheek, the leather and ink and paper and glue, whatever the chemicals were. He liked hearing the sounds of night. Even his fatigue, it felt fine, the stiff muscles and the prickly awareness of his own body, a floating feeling. He enjoyed not being dead. Lying there, Kiowa admired Lieutenant Jimmy Cross's capacity for grief. He wanted to share the man's pain, he wanted to care as Jimmy Cross cared. And yet when he closed his eyes, all he could think was Boom-down, and all he could feel was the pleasure of having his boots off and the fog curling in around him and the damp soil and the Bible smells and the plush comfort of night.

After a moment Norman Bowker sat up in the dark.

What the hell, he said. You want to talk, *talk*. Tell it to me.

Forget it.

No, man, go on. One thing I hate, it's a silent Indian.

For the most part they carried themselves with poise, a kind of dignity.   65
Now and then, however, there were times of panic, when they squealed or wanted to squeal but couldn't, when they twitched and made moaning sounds and covered their heads and said Dear Jesus and flopped around on the earth and fired their weapons blindly and cringed and sobbed and begged for the noise to stop and went wild and made stupid promises to themselves and to God and to their mothers and fathers, hoping not to die. In different ways, it happened to all of them. Afterward, when the firing ended, they would blink and peek up. They would touch their bodies, feeling shame, then quickly hiding it. They would force themselves to stand. As if in slow motion, frame by frame, the world would take on the old logic — absolute silence, then the wind, then sunlight, then voices. It was the burden of being

alive. Awkwardly, the men would reassemble themselves, first in private, then in groups, becoming soldiers again. They would repair the leaks in their eyes. They would check for casualties, call in dust-offs, light cigarettes, try to smile, clear their throats and spit and begin cleaning their weapons. After a time someone would shake his head and say, No lie, I almost shit my pants, and someone else would laugh, which meant it was bad, yes, but the guy had obviously not shit his pants, it wasn't that bad, and in any case nobody would ever do such a thing and then go ahead and talk about it. They would squint into the dense, oppressive sunlight. For a few moments, perhaps, they would fall silent, lighting a joint and tracking its passage from man to man, inhaling, holding in the humiliation. Scary stuff, one of them might say. But then someone else would grin or flick his eyebrows and say, Roger-dodger, almost cut me a new asshole, *almost*.

There were numerous such poses. Some carried themselves with a sort of wistful resignation, others with pride or stiff soldierly discipline or good humor or macho zeal. They were afraid of dying but they were even more afraid to show it.

They found jokes to tell.

They used a hard vocabulary to contain the terrible softness. *Greased*, they'd say. *Offed, lit up, zapped while zipping*. It wasn't cruelty, just stage presence. They were actors and the war came at them in 3-D. When someone died, it wasn't quite dying, because in a curious way it seemed scripted, and because they had their lines mostly memorized, irony mixed with tragedy, and because they called it by other names, as if to encyst and destroy the reality of death itself. They kicked corpses. They cut off thumbs. They talked grunt lingo. They told stories about Ted Lavender's supply of tranquilizers, how the poor guy didn't feel a thing, how incredibly tranquil he was.

There's a moral here, said Mitchell Sanders.

They were waiting for Lavender's chopper, smoking the dead man's dope. 70

The moral's pretty obvious, Sanders said, and winked. Stay away from drugs. No joke, they'll ruin your day every time.

Cute, said Henry Dobbins.

Mind-blower, get it? Talk about wiggy — nothing left, just blood and brains.

They made themselves laugh.

There it is, they'd say, over and over, as if the repetition itself were an 75 act of poise, a balance between crazy and almost crazy, knowing without going. There it is, which meant be cool, let it ride, because oh yeah, man, you can't change what can't be changed, there it is, there it absolutely and positively and fucking well *is*.

They were tough.

They carried all the emotional baggage of men who might die. Grief, terror, love, longing — these were intangibles, but the intangibles had their own mass and specific gravity, they had tangible weight. They carried shameful memories. They carried the common secret of cowardice barely restrained, the instinct to run or freeze or hide, and in many respects this was the heaviest burden of all, for it could never be put down, it required perfect balance and perfect posture. They carried their reputations. They carried the soldier's greatest fear, which was the fear of blushing. Men killed, and died, because they were embarrassed not to. It was what had brought them to the war in the first place, nothing positive, no dreams of glory or honor, just to avoid the blush of dishonor. They died so as not to die of embarrassment. They crawled into tunnels and walked point and advanced under fire. Each morning, despite the unknowns, they made their legs move. They endured. They kept humping. They did not submit to the obvious alternative, which was simply to close the eyes and fall. So easy, really. Go limp and tumble to the ground and let the muscles unwind and not speak and not budge until your buddies picked you up and lifted you into the chopper that would roar and dip its nose and carry you off to the world. A mere matter of falling, yet no one ever fell. It was not courage, exactly; the object was not valor. Rather, they were too frightened to be cowards.

By and large they carried these things inside, maintaining the masks of composure. They sneered at sick call. They spoke bitterly about guys who had found release by shooting off their own toes or fingers. Pussies, they'd say. Candyasses. It was fierce, mocking talk, with only a trace of envy or awe, but even so, the image played itself out behind their eyes.

They imagined the muzzle against flesh. They imagined the quick, sweet pain, then the evacuation to Japan, then a hospital with warm beds and cute geisha nurses.

They dreamed of freedom birds.

At night, on guard, staring into the dark, they were carried away by jumbo jets. They felt the rush of takeoff. *Gone!* they yelled. And then velocity, wings and engines, a smiling stewardess — but it was more than a plane, it was a real bird, a big sleek silver bird with feathers and talons and high screeching. They were flying. The weights fell off, there was nothing to bear. They laughed and held on tight, feeling the cold slap of wind and altitude, soaring, thinking *It's over, I'm gone!* — they were naked, they were light and free — it was all lightness, bright and fast and buoyant, light as light, a helium buzz in the brain, a giddy bubbling in the lungs as they were taken up over the clouds and the war, beyond duty, beyond gravity and mortification and global entanglements — *Sin loi!* they yelled, *I'm sorry, moth-erfuckers, but I'm out of it, I'm goofed, I'm on a space cruise, I'm gone!* — and it was a restful, disencumbered sensation, just riding the light waves, sailing that big silver freedom bird over the mountains and oceans, over America, over the farms and great sleeping cities and cemeteries and highways and the golden arches of McDonald's. It was flight, a kind of fleeing, a kind of falling, falling higher and higher, spinning off the edge of the earth and

80

beyond the sun and through the vast, silent vacuum where there were no burdens and where everything weighed exactly nothing. *Gone!* they screamed, *I'm sorry but I'm gone!* And so at night, not quite dreaming, they gave themselves over to lightness, they were carried, they were purely borne.

On the morning after Ted Lavender died, First Lieutenant Jimmy Cross crouched at the bottom of his foxhole and burned Martha's letters. Then he burned the two photographs. There was a steady rain falling, which made it difficult, but he used heat tabs and Sterno to build a small fire, screening it with his body, holding the photographs over the tight blue flame with the tips of his fingers.

He realized it was only a gesture. Stupid, he thought. Sentimental, too, but mostly just stupid.

Lavender was dead. You couldn't burn the blame.

Besides, the letters were in his head. And even now, without photo-   85
graphs, Lieutenant Cross could see Martha playing volleyball in her white gym shorts and yellow T-shirt. He could see her moving in the rain.

When the fire died out, Lieutenant Cross pulled his poncho over his shoulders and ate breakfast from a can.

There was no great mystery, he decided.

In those burned letters Martha had never mentioned the war, except to say, Jimmy, take care of yourself. She wasn't involved. She signed the letters "Love," but it wasn't love, and all the fine lines and technicalities did not matter.

The morning came up wet and blurry. Everything seemed part of everything else, the fog and Martha and the deepening rain.

It was a war, after all.   90

Half smiling, Lieutenant Jimmy Cross took out his maps. He shook his head hard, as if to clear it, then bent forward and began planning the day's march. In ten minutes, or maybe twenty, he would rouse the men and they would pack up and head west, where the maps showed the country to be green and inviting. They would do what they had always done. The rain might add some weight, but otherwise it would be one more day layered upon all the other days.

He was realistic about it. There was that new hardness in his stomach.

No more fantasies, he told himself.

Henceforth, when he thought about Martha, it would be only to think that she belonged elsewhere. He would shut down the daydreams. This was not Mount Sebastian, it was another world, where there were no pretty poems or midterm exams, a place where men died because of carelessness and gross stupidity. Kiowa was right. Boom down, and you were dead, never partly dead.

Briefly, in the rain, Lieutenant Cross saw Martha's gray eyes gazing   95
back at him.

He understood.

It was very sad, he thought. The things men carried inside. The things men did or felt they had to do.

He almost nodded at her, but didn't.

Instead he went back to his maps. He was now determined to perform his duties firmly and without negligence. It wouldn't help Lavender, he knew that, but from this point on he would comport himself as a soldier. He would dispose of his good-luck pebble. Swallow it, maybe, or use Lee Strunk's slingshot, or just drop it along the trail. On the march he would impose strict field discipline. He would be careful to send out flank security, to prevent straggling or bunching up, to keep his troops moving at the proper pace and at the proper interval. He would insist on clean weapons. He would confiscate the remainder of Lavender's dope. Later in the day, perhaps, he would call the men together and speak to them plainly. He would accept the blame for what had happened to Ted Lavender. He would be a man about it. He would look them in the eyes, keeping his chin level, and he would issue the new SOPs in a calm, impersonal tone of voice, an officer's voice, leaving no room for argument or discussion. Commencing immediately, he'd tell them, they would no longer abandon equipment along the route of march. They would police up their acts. They would get their shit together, and keep it together, and maintain it neatly and in good working order.

He would not tolerate laxity. He would show strength, distancing himself. 100

Among the men there would be grumbling, of course, and maybe worse, because their days would seem longer and their loads heavier, but Lieutenant Cross reminded himself that his obligation was not to be loved but to lead. He would dispense with love; it was not now a factor. And if anyone quarreled or complained, he would simply tighten his lips and arrange his shoulders in the correct command posture. He might give a curt little nod. Or he might not. He might just shrug and say Carry on, then they would saddle up and form into a column and move out toward the villages of Than Khe.

Considerations

1. List the "things" carried by the men as they move through the Vietnamese countryside. Write a brief response to several of these "things," discussing what the men's choices suggest about their hopes, their fears, and their values.
2. To what extent is Lieutenant Cross responsible for Ted Lavender's death? Why does he think he is responsible? How does his response to Lavender's death change his attitude toward his command?
3. Evaluate the responses of the men to Lavender's death.

4. Mitchell Sanders says, "There's a moral here." Do you see any moral to the story of Lavender's death? To the story of the others' responses to his death?
5. How do Lieutenant Cross's fantasies about Martha change throughout the story? What significance do you see in these changes? Do you see them as negative? Positive? Or something else?

THOMAS HARDY (1840–1928)

The Man He Killed

Had he and I but met
By some old ancient inn,
We should have sat us down to wet
Right many a nipperkin!

But ranged as infantry,   5
And staring face to face,
I shot at him as he at me,
And killed him in his place.

I shot him dead because—
Because he was my foe.   10
Just so: my foe of course he was;
That's clear enough; although

He thought he'd list, perhaps,
Off-hand like—just as I—
Was out of work—had sold his traps—   15
No other reason why.

Yes; quaint and curious war is!
You shoot a fellow down
You'd treat, if met where any bar is,
Or help to half-a-crown.   20

Considerations

1. Describe the speaker. What kind of man is he? What kind of work does he do? What does he enjoy in his free time? What are his values?
2. Reread lines 9 and 10. What is the effect of the repeated word "because"? How would the meaning change if one "because" were omitted?

3. What questions does the poem raise about war? Does it suggest any answers to those questions? Explain.

AMY LOWELL (1874–1925)

Patterns

I walk down the garden paths,
And all the daffodils
Are blowing, and the bright blue squills.
I walk down the patterned garden paths
In my stiff, brocaded gown. 5
With my powdered hair and jewelled fan,
I too am a rare
Pattern. As I wander down
The garden paths.

My dress is richly figured, 10
And the train
Makes a pink and silver stain
On the gravel, and the thrift
Of the borders.
Just a plate of current fashion, 15
Tripping by in high-heeled, ribboned shoes.
Not a softness anywhere about me,
Only whalebone and brocade.
And I sink on a seat in the shade
Of a lime tree. For my passion 20
Wars against the stiff brocade.
The daffodils and squills
Flutter in the breeze
As they please.
And I weep; 25
For the lime-tree is in blossom
And one small flower has dropped upon my bosom.

And the plashing of waterdrops
In the marble fountain
Comes down the garden paths. 30
The dripping never stops.
Underneath my stiffened gown

Is the softness of a woman bathing in a marble basin,
A basin in the midst of hedges grown
So thick, she cannot see her lover hiding,   35
But she guesses he is near,
And the sliding of the water
Seems the stroking of a dear
Hand upon her.
What is Summer in a fine brocaded gown!   40
I should like to see it lying in a heap upon the ground.
All the pink and silver crumpled up on the ground.

I would be the pink and silver as I ran along the paths,
And he would stumble after,
Bewildered by my laughter.   45
I should see the sun flashing from his sword-hilt and the buckles on his
    shoes.
I would choose
To lead him in a maze along the patterned paths,
A bright and laughing maze for my heavy-booted lover.
Till he caught me in the shade.   50
And the buttons of his waistcoat bruised my body as he clasped me,
Aching, melting, unafraid.
With the shadows of the leaves and the sundrops,
And the plopping of the waterdrops,
All about us in the open afternoon —   55
I am very like to swoon
With the weight of this brocade,
For the sun sifts through the shade.

Underneath the fallen blossom
In my bosom,   60
Is a letter I have hid.
It was brought to me this morning by a rider from the Duke.
'Madam, we regret to inform you that Lord Hartwell
Died in action Thursday se'nnight.'
As I read it in the white, morning sunlight,   65
The letters squirmed like snakes.
'Any answer, Madam,' said my footman.
'No,' I told him.
'See that the messenger takes some refreshment.
No, no answer.'   70
And I walked into the garden,
Up and down the patterned paths,

In my stiff, correct brocade.
The blue and yellow flowers stood up proudly in the sun,
Each one.   75
I stood upright too,
Held rigid to the pattern
By the stiffness of my gown.
Up and down I walked,
Up and down.   80

In a month he would have been my husband.
In a month, here, underneath this lime,
We would have broke the pattern;
He for me, and I for him,
He as Colonel, I as Lady,   85
On this shady seat.
He had a whim
That sunlight carried blessing.
And I answered, 'It shall be as you have said.'
Now he is dead.   90

In Summer and in Winter I shall walk
Up and down
The patterned garden paths
In my stiff, brocaded gown.
The squills and daffodils   95
Will give place to pillared roses, and to asters, and to snow.
I shall go
Up and down,
In my gown.
Gorgeously arrayed,   100
Boned and stayed.
And the softness of my body will be guarded from embrace
By each button, hook, and lace.
For the man who should loose me is dead,
Fighting with the Duke in Flanders,   105
In a pattern called a war.
Christ! What are patterns for?

Considerations

1. Consider the many ways the characters and actions in the poem suggest
   and relate to the title.
2. How does the speaker respond to the patterns in her life?

3. What patterns do you see in modern life? Are today's patterns as clearly defined as the patterns suggested by Lowell's poem? Do people today still feel limited and restricted by the patterns of their lives? Explain.

WILFRED OWEN (1893–1918)

Dulce et Decorum Est°

Bent double, like old beggars under sacks,
Knock-kneed, coughing like hags, we cursed through sludge,
Till on the haunting flares we turned our backs
And towards our distant rest began to trudge.
Men marched asleep. Many had lost their boots   5
But limped on, blood-shod. All went lame; all blind;
Drunk with fatigue; deaf even to the hoots
Of tired, outstripped Five-Nines° that dropped behind.

Gas! GAS! Quick, boys! — An ecstasy of fumbling,
Fitting the clumsy helmets just in time;   10
But someone still was yelling out and stumbling
And flound'ring like a man in fire or lime° . . .
Dim, through the misty panes and thick green light,
As under a green sea I saw him drowning.

In all my dreams, before my helpless sight,   15
He plunges at me, guttering, choking, drowning.

If in some smothering dreams you too could pace
Behind the wagon that we flung him in,
And watch the white eyes writhing in his face,
His hanging face, like a devil's sick of sin;   20
If you could hear, at every jolt, the blood
Come gargling from the froth-corrupted lungs,
Obscene as cancer, bitter as the cud

Dulce et Decorum Est: "It is sweet and fitting." The words come from Horace's *Odes*, II, ii, 13. The full quotation, given in the poem's final line, means, "It is sweet and fitting to die for one's country."   8 *Five-Nines:* Gas bombs used by Germans in World War I.   12 *Lime:* Quick-lime, a chemical that dissolves flesh and bones.

Of vile, incurable sores on innocent tongues, —
My friend, you would not tell with such high zest   25
To children ardent for some desperate glory,
The old Lie: *Dulce et decorum est*
Pro patria mori.

Considerations

1. Who are the people described in the opening stanza? What do the images Owen chooses suggest about their response to the circumstances they must face?
2. What purpose is served by the graphic details of the gas attack and, particularly, of the death of the soldier?
3. The Latin sentence, *Dulce et decorum est pro patria mori,* means "It is sweet and fitting to die for one's country." Owen, along with other British schoolchildren, would have learned this motto in his Latin classes. Do children today receive similar messages in school? Explain.

KARL SHAPIRO (1913–   )

The Conscientious Objector

The gates clanged and they walked you into jail
More tense than felons but relieved to find
The hostile world shut out, flags that dripped
From every mother's windowpane, obscene
The bloodlust sweating from the public heart,   5
The dog authority slavering at your throat.
A sense of quiet, of pulling down the blind
Possessed you. Punishment you felt was clean.

The decks, the catwalks, and the narrow light
Composed a ship. This was a mutinous crew   10
Troubling the captains for plain decencies,
A *Mayflower* brim with pilgrims headed out
To establish new theocracies to west,
A Noah's ark coasting the topmost seas
Ten miles above the sodomites and fish.   15
These inmates loved the only living doves.

Like all men hunted from the world you made
A good community, voyaging the storm
To no safe Plymouth or green Ararat;°

19 *Ararat:* The highest peak in Turkey, the landing place of Noah's ark.

Trouble or calm, the men with Bibles prayed,   20
The gaunt politicals construed our hate.
The opposite of all armies, you were best
Opposing uniformity and yourselves;
Prison and personality were your fate.

You suffered not so physically but knew   25
Maltreatment, hunger, ennui of the mind.
Well might the soldier kissing the hot beach
Erupting in his face damn all your kind.
Yet you who saved neither yourselves nor us
Are equally with those who shed the blood   30
The heroes of our cause. Your conscience is
What we come back to in the armistice.

Considerations

1. Why have the men in this poem been imprisoned? What are their different responses to that imprisonment?
2. Who is the speaker in the poem? What is his attitude toward the conscientious objector he describes?
3. What is your response to the comparisons of the prison, filled with conscientious objectors, to Noah's ark and to the *Mayflower?*

ELIZABETH BARRETT BROWNING (1806–1861)

Mother and Poet°
(Turin, After News from Gaeta, 1861)

1

DEAD! One of them shot by the sea in the east,
    And one of them shot in the west by the sea.
Dead! both my boys! When you sit at the feast
    And are wanting a great song for Italy free,
        Let none look at *me!*   5

2

Yet I was a poetess only last year,
    And good at my art, for a woman, men said;
But *this* woman, *this,* who is agonised here,
    —The east sea and west sea rhyme on in her head
        For ever instead.   10

Mother and Poet: The persona in this poem is Laura Savio, Italian poet and patriot. Her sons were both killed in the battle over the unification of Italy in 1861.

3

What art can a woman be good at? Oh, vain!
  What art *is* she good at, but hurting her breast
With the milk-teeth of babes, and a smile at the pain?
  Ah boys, how you hurt! you were strong as you pressed,
    And I proud, by that test.   15

4

What art's for a woman? To hold on her knees
  Both darlings! to feel all their arms round her throat,
Cling, strangle a little! to sew by degrees
  And 'broider the long-clothes and neat little coat;
    To dream and to doat.   20

5

To teach them . . . It stings there! *I* made them indeed
  Speak plain the word *country.* I taught them, no doubt,
That a country's a thing men should die for at need.
  I prated of liberty, rights, and about
    The tyrant cast out.   25

6

And when their eyes flashed . . . Oh my beautiful eyes! . . .
  I exulted; nay, let them go forth at the wheels
Of the guns, and denied not. But then the surprise
  When one sits quite alone! Then one weeps, then one kneels!
    God, how the house feels!   30

7

At first, happy news came, in gay letters moiled
  With my kisses, — of camp-life and glory, and how
They both loved me; and, soon coming home to be spoiled
  In return would fan off every fly from my brow
    With their green laurel-bough.   35

8

Then was triumph at Turin: "Ancona was free!"
  And some one came out of the cheers in the street,
With a face pale as stone, to say something to me.
  My Guido was dead! I fell down at his feet,
    While they cheered in the street.   40

9

I bore it; friends soothed me; my grief looked sublime
  As the ransom of Italy. One boy remained
To be leant on and walked with, recalling the time

When the first grew immortal, while both of us strained
  To the height he had gained.   45

10

And letters still came, shorter, sadder, more strong,
  Writ now but in one hand, "I was not to faint, —
One loved me for two — would be with me ere long:
  And *Viva l'Italia!*° — *he* died for, our saint,
    Who forbids our complaint."   50

11

My Nanni would add, "he was safe, and aware
  Of a presence that turned off the balls, — was imprest
It was Guido himself, who knew what I could bear,
  And how 'twas impossible, quite dispossessed
    To live on for the rest."   55

12

On which, without pause, up the telegraph line
  Swept smoothly the next news from Gaeta: — *Shot.*
Tell his mother. Ah, ah, "his," "their" mother, — not "mine,"
  No voice says "*My* mother" again to me. What!
    You think Guido forgot?   60

13

Are souls straight so happy that, dizzy with Heaven,
  They drop earth's affections, conceive not of woe?
I think not. Themselves were too lately forgiven
  Through THAT Love and Sorrow which reconciled so
    The Above and Below.   65

14

O Christ of the five wounds, who look'dst through the dark
  To the face of thy mother! consider, I pray,
How we common mothers stand desolate, mark,
  Whose sons, not being Christs, die with eyes turned away
    And no last word to say!   70

15

Both boys dead? but that's out of nature. We all
  Have been patriots, yet each house must always keep one.
'Twere imbecile, hewing out roads to a wall;
  And, when Italy's made, for what end is it done
    If we have not a son?   75

49 Viva L'Italia!: Long live (united) Italy!

16

Ah, ah, ah! when Gaeta's taken, what then?
    When the fair wicked queen° sits no more at her sport
Of the fire-balls of death crashing souls out of men?
    When the guns of Cavalli° with final retort
        Have cut the game short?   80

17

When Venice and Rome keep their new jubilee°
    When your flag takes all heaven for its white, green, and red,
When *you* have your country from mountain to sea,
    When King Victor has Italy's crown on his head,
        (And *I* have my Dead) —   85

18

What then? Do not mock me. Ah, ring your bells low,
    And burn your lights faintly! *My* country is *there,*
Above the star pricked by the last peak of snow:
    My Italy's THERE, with my brave civic Pair,
        To disfranchise despair!   90

19

Forgive me. Some women bear children in strength,
    And bite back the cry of their pain in self-scorn;
But the birth-pangs of nations will wring us at length
    Into wail such as this — and we sit on forlorn
        When the man-child is born.   95

20

Dead! One of them shot by the sea in the east,
    And one of them shot in the west by the sea.
Both! both my boys! If in keeping the feast
    You want a great song for your Italy free,
        Let none look at *me!*   100

Considerations

1. In this poem, the speaker is the Italian poet and patriot, Laura Savio.
   Both her sons died fighting in the war for the unification of Italy. One
   was killed in the attack on the fortress at Ancona and the other at the

---

77 *fair wicked queen:* Maria, wife of Frances II, the last king of the Neapolitan government, a
force that opposed unification.   79 *Cavalli:* General who commanded the siege of Gaeta, where
Nanni, Laura Savio's second son, was killed.   81 *new jubilee:* In 1861, when the poem was
written, Venice and Rome were still not part of united Italy.

siege of Gaeta. How does knowing this historical background affect your response to the poem? Or do you find your response unchanged? Explain.
2. What is the speaker's initial attitude toward the war? How and why does her attitude change?
3. What is your response toward the mother's changing position? Are you sympathetic? Critical? Something else? Explain.

RICHARD LOVELACE (1618–1658)

To Lucasta, Going to the Wars

Tell me not, sweet, I am unkind
That from the nunnery
Of thy chaste breast and quiet mind,
To war and arms I fly.

True, a new mistress now I chase,   5
The first foe in the field;
And with a stronger faith embrace
A sword, a horse, a shield.

Yet this inconstancy is such
As you too shall adore;   10
I could not love thee, dear, so much,
Loved I not honor more.

CAROLYN FORCHÉ (1950–   )

The Colonel

What you have heard is true. I was in his house. His wife carried a tray of coffee and sugar. His daughter filed her nails, his son went out for the night. There were daily papers, pet dogs, a pistol on the cushion beside him. The moon swung bare on its black cord over the house. On the television was a cop show. It was in English. Broken bottles were embedded in the walls around the house to scoop the kneecaps from a man's legs or cut his hands to lace. On the windows there were gratings like those in liquor stores. We had dinner, rack of lamb, good wine, a gold bell was on the table for calling the maid. The maid brought green mangoes, salt, a type of bread. I was asked how I enjoyed the country. There was a brief commercial in Spanish. His wife took everything away. There was some talk then of how difficult it had become to govern. The parrot said hello on the terrace. The colonel told it to shut up, and pushed himself from the table. My friend said to me with his eyes: say nothing. The colonel returned with a sack used to bring groceries home. He spilled many human ears on the table. They were like dried peach halves. There is no other way to say this. He took one of them in his hands, shook it in our faces, dropped it into a water glass. It came alive there. I am tired of fooling around he said. As for the rights of anyone, tell your people they can go fuck themselves. He swept the ears to the floor with his arm and held the last of his wine in the air. Something for your poetry, no? he said. Some of the ears on the floor caught this scrap of his voice. Some of the ears on the floor were pressed to the ground.

RANDALL JARRELL (1914–1965)

Gunner

Did they send me away from my cat and my wife
To a doctor who poked me and counted my teeth,
To a line on a plain, to a stove in a tent?
Did I nod in the flies of the schools?

And the fighters rolled into the tracer like rabbits,   5
The blood froze over my splints like a scab–
Did I snore, all still and grey in the turret,
Till the palms rose out of the sea with my death?

And the world ends here, in the sand of a grave,
All my wars over? . . . It was easy as that!   10
Has my wife a pension of so many mice?
Did the medals go home to my cat?

WALT WHITMAN (1819–1892)

Cavalry Crossing a Ford

A line in long array where they wind betwixt green islands,
They take a serpentine course, their arms flash in the sun — hark to the
    musical clank,
Behold the silvery river, in it the splashing horses loitering stop to drink,
Behold the brown-faced men, each group, each person a picture, the
    negligent rest on the saddles,
Some emerge on the opposite bank, others are just entering the ford — while,   5
Scarlet and blue and snowy white,
The guidon flags flutter gayly in the wind.

RICHARD EBERHART (1904–   )

The Fury of Aerial Bombardment

You would think the fury of aerial bombardment
Would rouse God to relent; the infinite spaces
Are still silent. He looks on shock-pried faces.
History, even, does not know what is meant.

You would feel that after so many centuries   5
God would give man to repent; yet he can kill
As Cain could, but with multitudinous will,
No farther advanced than in his ancient furies.

Was man made stupid to see his own stupidity?
Is God by definition indifferent, beyond us all?   10
Is the eternal truth man's fighting soul
Wherein the Beast ravens in its own avidity?

Of Van Wettering I speak, and Averill,
Names on a list, whose faces I do not recall
But they are gone to early death, who late in school   15
Distinguished the belt feed lever from the belt holding pawl.

DENISE LEVERTOV (1923–   )

What Were They Like?
(Questions and Answers)

1) Did the people of Viet Nam
   use lanterns of stone?

2) Did they hold ceremonies
   to reverence the opening of buds?
3) Were they inclined to rippling laughter?   5
4) Did they use bone and ivory,
   jade and silver, for ornament?
5) Had they an epic poem?
6) Did they distinguish between speech and singing?

1) Sir, their light hearts turned to stone.   10
   It is not remembered whether in gardens
   stone lanterns illumined pleasant ways.
2) Perhaps they gathered once to delight in blossom,
   but after the children were killed
   there were no more buds.   15
3) Sir, laughter is bitter to the burned mouth.
4) A dream ago, perhaps. Ornament is for joy.
   All the bones were charred.
5) It is not remembered. Remember,
   most were peasants; their life   20
   was in rice and bamboo.
   When peaceful clouds were reflected in the paddies
   and the water-buffalo stepped surely along terraces,
   maybe fathers told their sons old tales.
   When bombs smashed the mirrors   25
   there was time only to scream.
6) There is an echo yet, it is said,
   of their speech which was like a song.
   It is reported their singing resembled
   the flight of moths in moonlight.   30
   Who can say? It is silent now.

CONNECTIONS: ART AND LITERATURE

Poets create with words, while artists work with a variety of media including paint, ink, paper, canvas, clay, and metal. Yet both poets and artists offer us pictures reflecting their responses to images, experiences, people, places, emotions—observed, remembered, or imagined.

On the pages that follow, you will find poems paired with works of art. In two instances, the artist responds to the poem (Demuth's *I Saw the Figure 5 in Gold* and Williams' "The Great Figure"; Hunt's and Tennyson's *The Lady of Shallott*). In the other pairs, the poet writes in response to the artist's work.

As you read the poems and look at the art work, notice the connections you see. Begin by considering these questions:
- What is your initial response to each work considered separately?
- Does your response change when you consider the two works together?
- Can each work be appreciated on its own or is one entirely dependent on the other?
- How are the works of art similar to the poems?
- How are they different?
  - What details appear in the poem, but not in the art work?
  - What details appear in the art work, but not in the poem?
  - If the poem responds to a work of art, what has the poet chosen to add or alter?
  - If the painting responds to a poem, what has the artist chosen to add or alter?
  - What similarities and differences do you see in the artist's style and the poet's style?
  - What similarities and differences do you see in the way the artist and the poet have chosen to organize and present the details of the work?
- What significance do you see in the similarities and differences you have observed?
- How do the similarities and differences you have observed affect your response either to the poem or to the work of art?

Albrecht Dürer. *Knight, Death, and the Devil*. 1513. Engraving, 250 x 192 mm. Courtesy of The Fogg Art Museum, Harvard University, Cambridge, MA. Gift of William Gray from the Collection of Francis Calley Gray.

RANDALL JARRELL (1914–1965)

The Knight, Death, and the Devil

Cowhorn-crowned, shockheaded, cornshuck-bearded,
Death is a scarecrow—his death's-head a teetotum
That tilts up toward man confidentially
But trimmed with adders; ringlet-maned, rope-bridled,
The mare he rides crops herbs beside a skull.   5
He holds up, warning, the crossed cones of time:
Here, narrowing into now, the Past and Future
Are quicksand.
               A hoofed pikeman trots behind.
His pike's claw-hammer mocks—in duplicate, inverted—   10
The pocked, ribbed, soaring crescent of his horn.
A scapegoat aged into a steer; boar-snouted;
His great limp ears stuck sidelong out in air;
A dewlap bunched at his breast; a ram's-horn wound
Beneath each ear; a spur licked up and out   15
From the hide of his forehead; bat-winged, but in bone;
His eye a ring inside a ring inside a ring
That leers up, joyless, vile, in meek obscenity—
This is the devil. Flesh to flesh, he bleats
The herd back to the pit of being.   20

In fluted mail; upon his lance the bush
Of that old fox; a sheep-dog bounding at his stirrup,
In its eyes the cast of faithfulness (our help,
Our foolish help); his dun war-horse pacing
Beneath in strength, in ceremonious magnificence;   25
His castle—some man's castle—set on every crag:
So, companioned so, the knight moves through this world.
The fiend moos in amity, Death mouths, reminding:
He listens in assurance, has no glance
To spare for them, but looks past steadily   30
At—at—
            a man's look completes itself.

The death of his own flesh, set up outside him;
The flesh of his own soul, set up outside him—
Death and the devil, what are these to him?   35
His being accuses him—and yet his face is firm
In resolution, in absolute persistence;
The folds of smiling do for steadiness;
The face is its own fate—*a man does what he must*—
And the body underneath it says: *I am.*   40

Henri Matisse. *Two Girls, Red and Green Background*. 1947. Oil on canvas, 22 1/8 x 18 1/4 in. (56.2 x 46.4 cm.). The Baltimore Museum of Art: The Cone Collection, formed by Dr. Claribel Cone and Miss Etta Cone of Baltimore, MD. BMA 1950.264.

MOLLY PEACOCK (1947–   )

Matisse: Two Girls

I know who they are. That one's me,
the brunette on the right. The blond
in the yellow dress is you.

It's a picture without protection
like the snaps of us on our vacations   5
with the sun in our eyes. But here we are inside

a perfect summer house, like mine
when I was married and rich, with cool walls
and enormous windows flung open behind us

to the tops of old maples. They are not maples   10
in the *picture*—they are green clouds slashed
with brown stripes—but don't you like to look

at the places and faces in pictures to find out
where and which you are? I must be
the frightened one in blue, after my affair   15

with your husband. By the indictment of
your pointed nose, chin, elbows thrust
from that yellow dress, I know. Is yellow

the fiercer color? Or blue.
Well, the figure I chose as you—   20
her hair's too short, for one thing.

I thought it was you, since neither girl
will look at the other, but it is not us.
There is no wine, no cigarettes,

and the flowers on the table are too fresh.   25
I just cut them from my mother's garden,
having gotten up and dressed and almost

beaten my mother to the breakfast table.
But evidently she had eaten long before,
since there, in the picture,   30

the table's set only for one. The late one.
She has already watched the sunrise and has turned
away from the window to stare at the floor.

But her body sits toward me,
my arms stuck under my breasts, anticipating   35
the explosion—for having slept, for having cut...

for having what? A blue dress?
I wait for the hair to toss or
the figure to turn. It does not.

In fact, my mother turns to me quite often.   40
The blowsy head in the picture can't be her.
Look how young the girl in blue is,

how carefully she holds herself.
Her hair is parted so nicely,
as though she cared for it.   45

It is the color of the antlered branches
behind her, and her dress matches the sky.
What a burden she has to distinguish herself!

She must be a younger sister. Mine.
So the woman in yellow is me,   50
the pointed nose, the pointed chin,

the angularity in the summer room.
And my frightened younger sister,
newly married in this lovely summer house,

with such first luck at flowers   55
that she cannot be sure it is her talent,
has cut these roses to placate me,

because she cannot see my face
and watches only the points
seeming to pivot toward her.   60

But I am standing here,
and I do not mistake
where the rude lines originate.

Vincent van Gogh. *The Starry Night.* 1889. Oil on canvas, 29 x 36 1/4 in. Collection,
The Museum of Modern Art, New York. Acquired through the Lillie P. Bliss Bequest.

ANNE SEXTON (1928–1975)

The Starry Night

That does not keep me from having a terrible need of—shall I say the word—religion.
Then I go out at night to paint the stars.   Vincent van Gogh in a letter to his brother

The town does not exist
except where one black-haired tree slips
up like a drowned woman into the hot sky.
The town is silent.   The night boils with eleven stars
Oh starry starry night!   This is how   5
I want to die.

It moves.   They are all alive.
Even the moon bulges in its orange irons
to push children, like a god, from its eye.
The old unseen serpent swallows up the stars.   10
Oh starry starry night!   This is how
I want to die:

into that rushing beast of the night,
sucked up by that great dragon, to split
from my life with no flag,   15
no belly,
no cry.

Edwin Romanzo Elmer. *Mourning Picture*. 1890. Oil on canvas, 28 x 36 in. (71.1 x 91.5 cm.). Smith College Museum of Art, Northampton, Massachusetts. Purchased 1953.

ADRIENNE RICH (1929–   )

Mourning Picture

They have carried the mahogany chair and the cane rocker
out under the lilac bush,
and my father and my mother darkly sit there, in black clothes.
Our clapboard house stands fast on its hill,
my doll lies in her wicker pram   5
gazing at western Massachusetts.
This was our world.
I could remake each shaft of grass
feeling its rasp on my fingers,
draw out the map of every lilac leaf   10
of the net of veins on my father's
grief-tranced hand.

Out of my head, half-bursting,
still filling, the dream condenses—
shadows, crystals, ceilings, meadows, globes of dew.   15
Under the dull green of the lilacs, out in the light
carving each spoke of the pram the turned porch-pillars,
under high early-summer clouds,
I am Effie, visible and invisible,
remembering and remembered.   20

They will move from the house,
give the toys and pets away.
Mute and rigid with loss my mother
will ride the train to Baptist Corner,
the silk-spool will run bare.   25
I tell you, the thread that bound us lies
faint as a web in the dew.
Should I make you, world, again,
could I give back the leaf its skeleton, the air
its early-summer cloud, the house   30
its noonday presence, shadowless,
and leave *this* out? I am Effie, you were my dream.

William Holman Hunt. *The Lady of Shalott*. 1886–1905. Oil on canvas, 74 1/8 x 57 5/8 in.
Wadsworth Atheneum, Hartford, CT. The Ella Gallup Sumner and Mary Catlin Sumner Collection.

ALFRED, LORD TENNYSON (1809–1892)

The Lady of Shalott*

Part 2

There she weaves by night and day
A magic web with colors gay.
She has heard a whisper say,
A curse is on her if she stay
    To look down to Camelot.   5
She knows not what the curse may be,
And so she weaveth steadily,
And little other care hath she,
    The Lady of Shalott.

And moving through a mirror clear   10
That hangs before her all the year,
Shadows of the world appear.
There she sees the highway near
    Winding down to Camelot;
There the river eddy whirls,   15
And there the surly village churls,
And the red cloaks of market girls,
    Pass onward from Shalott.

Sometimes a troop of damsels glad,
An abbott on an ambling pad,   20
Sometimes a curly shepherd lad,
Or long-haired page in crimson clad,
    Goes by to towered Camelot;
And sometimes through the mirror blue
The knights come riding two and two: 25
She hath no loyal knight and true,
    The Lady of Shalott.

But in her web she still delights
To weave the mirror's magic sights,
For often through the silent nights   30
A funeral, with plumes and lights
    And music, went to Camelot;
Or when the moon was overhead,
Came two young lovers lately wed:
"I am half sick of shadows," said   35
    The Lady of Shalott.

*This poem may be found in its entirety in the poetry anthology section of this book.

Part 3

A bowshot from her bower eaves,
He rode between the barley sheaves,
The sun came dazzling through the leaves,
And flamed upon the brazen greaves
    Of bold Sir Lancelot.   40
A red-cross knight forever kneeled
To a lady in his shield,
That sparkled on the yellow field,
    Beside remote Shalott.   45

The gemmy bridle glittered free,
Like to some branch of stars we see
Hung in the golden Galaxy.
The bridle bells rang merrily
    As he rode down to Camelot;   50
And from his blazoned baldric slung
A mighty silver bugle hung,
And as he rode his armor rung,
    Beside remote Shalott.

All in the blue unclouded weather   55
Thick-jeweled shone the saddle leather,
The helmet and the helmet-feather
Burned like one burning flame together,
    As he rode down to Camelot;
As often through the purple night,   60
Below the starry clusters bright,
Some bearded meteor, trailing light,
    Moves over still Shalott.

His broad clear brow in sunlight glowed;
On burnished hooves his war horse trode;   65
From underneath his helmet flowed
His coal-black curls as on he rode,
    As he rode down to Camelot.
From the bank and from the river
He flashed into the crystal mirror,   70
"Tirra lirra," by the river
    Sang Sir Lancelot.

She left the web, she left the loom,
She made three paces through the room,
She saw the water lily bloom,   75

She saw the helmet and the plume,
      She looked down to Camelot.
Out flew the web and floated wide;
The mirror cracked from side to side;
"The curse is come upon me," cried   80
      The Lady of Shalott.

Pieter Breughel the Elder. *The Kermess*. c. 1567. Art Resource.

WILLIAM CARLOS WILLIAMS (1883–1963)

The Dance

In Breughel's great picture, The Kermess,
the dancers go round, they go round and
around, the squeal and the blare and the
tweedle of bagpipes, a bugle and fiddles
tipping their bellies (round as the thick-   5
sided glasses whose wash they impound)
their hips and their bellies off balance
to turn them. Kicking and rolling about
the Fair Grounds, swinging their butts, those
shanks must be sound to bear up under such   10
rollicking measures, prance as they dance
in Breughel's great picture, The Kermess.

RICHARD WILBUR (1921–   )

Giacometti

Rock insults us, hard and so boldly browed
Its scorn needs not to focus, and with fists
Which still unstirring strike:
Collected it resists
Until its buried glare begets a like   5
Anger in us, and finds our hardness. Proud,

Then, and armed, and with a patient rage
We carve cliff, shear stone to blocks,
And down to the image of man
Batter and shape the rock's   10
Fierce composure, closing its veins within
That outside man, itself its captive cage.

So we can baffle rock, and in our will
Can clothe and keep it. But if our will, though locked
In stone it clutches, change,   15
Then are we much worse mocked
Than cliffs can do: then we ourselves are strange
To what we were, which lowers on us still.

High in the air those habitants of stone
Look heavenward, lean to a thought, or stride   20
Toward some concluded war,
While we on every side,
Random as shells the sea drops down ashore,
Are walking, walking, many and alone.

What stony shape could hold us now, what hard   25
Bent can we bulk in air, where shall our feet
Come to a common stand?
Follow along this street
(Where rock recovers carven eye and hand),
Open the gate, and cross the narrow yard   30

And look where Giacometti in a room
Dim as a cave of the sea, has built the man
We are, and made him walk:
Towering like a thin
Coral, out of a reef of plaster chalk,   35
This is the single form we can assume.

We are this man unspeakably alone
Yet stripped of the singular utterly, shaved and scraped
Of all but being there,
Whose fullness is escaped   40
Like a burst balloon's: no nakedness so bare
As flesh gone in inquiring of the bone.

He is pruned of every gesture, saving only
The habit of coming and going. Every pace
Shuffles a million feet.   45
The faces in this face
Are all forgotten faces of the street
Gathered to one anonymous and lonely.

No prince and no Leviathan, he is made
Of infinite farewells. Oh never more   50
Diminished, nonetheless
Embodied here, we are
This starless walker, one who cannot guess
His will, his keel his nose's bony blade.

And volumes hover round like future shades   55
This least of man, in whom we join and take
A pilgrim's step behind,
And in whose guise we make
Our grim departures now, walking to find
What railleries of rock, what palisades?   60

Alberto Giacometti. *Walking Man II*. 1948. Bronze, 27
in. (69 cm) high. Hirshhorn Museum and Sculpture
Garden, Smithsonian Institution, Washington D.C.,
Gift of Joseph H. Hirshhorn, 1966. Photograph by
Lee Stalsworth.

Charles Demuth. *I Saw the Figure 5 in Gold.* 1928. Oil on composition board, 36 x 29 3/4". The Metropolitan Museum of Art, New York (The Alfred Stieglitz Collection, 1949).

WILLIAM CARLOS WILLIAMS (1883–1963)

The Great Figure

Among the rain
and lights
I saw the figure 5
in gold
on a red   5
fire truck
moving
tense
unheeded
to gong clangs   10
siren howls
and wheels rumbling
through the dark city

ARISTOPHANES (448?–380? B.C.)

Lysistrata

TRANSLATED BY WHITNEY OATES
AND CHARLES T. MURPHY

Characters

LYSISTRATA, *an Athenian woman*
CALONICE, *an Athenian woman*
MYRRHINE, *an Athenian woman*
LAMPITO, *a Spartan woman*
LEADER OF CHORUS OF OLD MEN
CHORUS OF OLD MEN
LEADER OF CHORUS OF OLD WOMEN
CHORUS OF OLD WOMEN
ATHENIAN MAGISTRATE
THREE ATHENIAN WOMEN
CINESIAS, *an Athenian, husband of Myrrhine*
SPARTAN HERALD
SPARTAN AMBASSADORS
ATHENIAN AMBASSADORS
TWO ATHENIAN CITIZENS
CHORUS OF ATHENIANS
CHORUS OF SPARTANS

Scene *In Athens, beneath the Acropolis. In the center of the stage is the propylaea, or gate-way to the Acropolis; to one side is a small grotto, sacred to Pan°. The orchestra represents a slope leading up to the gate-way. It is early in the morning.* LYSISTRATA *is pacing impatiently up and down.*

LYSISTRATA: If they'd been summoned to worship the God of Wine, or Pan, or to visit the Queen of Love, why, you couldn't have pushed your way through the streets for all the timbrels. But now there's not a single woman here — except my neighbour; here she comes.

(Enter CALONICE*)*

Good day to you, Calonice.

CALONICE: And to you, Lysistrata. *(Noticing* LYSISTRATA'S *impatient air.)* But what ails you? Don't scowl, my dear; it's not becoming to you to knit your brows like that.

LYSISTRATA *(sadly)*: Ah, Calonice, my heart aches; I'm so annoyed at us women. For among men we have a reputation for sly trickery —

CALONICE: And rightly too, on my word!

Pan: God of fields, forests, and wild animals.

LYSISTRATA: —but when they were told to meet here to consider a matter of no small importance, they lie abed and don't come.

CALONICE: Oh, they'll come all right, my dear. It's not easy for a woman to get out, you know. One is working on her husband, another is getting up the maid, another has to put the baby to bed, or wash and feed it.

LYSISTRATA: But after all, there are other matters more important than all that.

CALONICE: My dear Lysistrata, just what is this matter you've summoned us women to consider! What's up? Something big?

LYSISTRATA: Very big.

CALONICE (interested): Is it stout, too?

LYSISTRATA (smiling): Yes indeed—both big and stout.

CALONICE: What? And the women still haven't come?

LYSISTRATA: It's not what you suppose; they'd have come soon enough for *that.* But I've worked up something, and for many a sleepless night I've turned it this way and that.

CALONICE (in mock disapppointment): Oh, I guess it's pretty fine and slender, if you've turned it this way and that.

LYSISTRATA: So fine that the safety of the whole of Greece lies in us women.

CALONICE: In us women? It depends on a very slender reed then.

LYSISTRATA: Our country's fortunes are in our hands; and whether the Spartans shall perish—

CALONICE: Good! Let them perish, by all means.

LYSISTRATA: —and the Boeotians shall be completely annihilated.

CALONICE: Not completely! Please spare the eels.°

LYSISTRATA: As for Athens, I won't use any such unpleasant words. But you understand what I mean. But if the women will meet here—the Spartans, the Boeotians, and we Athenians—then all together we will save Greece.°

CALONICE: But what could women do that's clever or distinguished? We just sit around all dolled up in silk robes, looking pretty in our sheer gowns and evening slippers.

LYSISTRATA: These are just the things I hope will save us; these silk robes, perfumes, evening slippers, rouge, and our chiffon blouses.

CALONICE: How so?

LYSISTRATA: So never a man alive will lift a spear against the foe—

CALONICE: I'll get a silk gown at once.

LYSISTRATA: —or take up his shield—

CALONICE: I'll put on my sheerest gown!

LYSISTRATA: —or sword.

---

eels: Boeotian eels were a delicacy. . . . *save Greece:* At the time the play was written, Athens, Sparta, and several other Greek city-states had been at war for twenty years.

CALONICE: I'll buy a pair of evening slippers.

LYSISTRATA: Well then, shouldn't the women have come?

CALONICE: Come? Why, they should have *flown* here.

LYSISTRATA: Well, my dear, just watch: they'll act in true Athenian fashion—everything too late! And now there's not a woman here from the shore or from Salamis.

CALONICE: They're coming, I'm sure; at daybreak they were laying-to their oars to cross the straits.

LYSISTRATA: And those I expected would be the first to come—the women of Acharnae—they haven't arrived.

CALONICE: Yet the wife of Theagenes means to come; she consulted Hecate° about it. *(Seeing a group of women approaching.)* But look! Here come a few. And there are some more over here. Hurray! Where do they come from?

LYSISTRATA: From Anagyra.

CALONICE: Yes indeed! We've raised up quite a stink from Anagyra anyway.

(Enter MYRRHINE *in haste, followed by several other women.)*

MYRRHINE *(breathlessly)*: Have we come in time, Lysistrata? What do you say? Why so quiet?

LYSISTRATA: I can't say much for you, Myrrhine, coming at this hour on such important business.

MYRRHINE: Why, I had trouble finding my girdle in the dark. But if it's so important, we're here now; tell us.

LYSISTRATA: No. Let's wait a little for the women from Boeotia and the Peloponnesus.

MYRRHINE: That's a much better suggestion. Look! Here comes Lampito now.

(Enter LAMPITO *with two other women.)*

LYSISTRATA: Greetings, my dear Spartan friend. How pretty you look, my dear. What a smooth complexion and well-developed figure! You could throttle an ox.

LAMPITO: Faith, yes, I think I could. I take exercises and kick my heels against my bum. *(She demonstrates with a few steps of the Spartan "bottom-kicking" dance.)*

LYSISTRATA: And what splendid breasts you have.

LAMPITO: La! You handle me like a prize steer.

LYSISTRATA: And who is this young lady with you?

LAMPITO: Faith, she's an Ambassadress from Boeotia.

LYSISTRATA: Oh yes, a Boeotian, and blooming like a garden too.

CALONICE *(lifting up her skirt)*: My word! How neatly her garden's weeded!

Hecate: Goddess of witchcraft and sorcery.

LYSISTRATA: And who is the other girl?

LAMPITO: Oh, she's a Corinthian swell.

MYRRHINE *(after a rapid examination)*: Yes indeed. She swells very nicely *(pointing)* here and here.

LAMPITO: Who has gathered together this company of women?

LYSISTRATA: I have.

LAMPITO: Speak up, then. What do you want?

MYRRHINE: Yes, my dear, tell us what this important matter is.

LYSISTRATA: Very well, I'll tell you. But before I speak, let me ask you a little question.

MYRRHINE: Anything you like.

LYSISTRATA *(earnestly)*: Tell me: don't you yearn for the fathers of your children, who are away at the wars? I know you all have husbands abroad.

CALONICE: Why, yes; mercy me! my husband's been away for five months in Thrace keeping guard on — Eucrates.

MYRRHINE: And mine for seven whole months in Pylus.

LAMPITO: And mine, as soon as ever he returns from the fray, readjusts his shield and flies out of the house again.

LYSISTRATA: And as for lovers, there's not even a ghost of one left. Since the Milesians revolted from us, I've not even seen an eight-inch dingus to be a leather consolation for us widows. Are you willing, if I can find a way, to help me end the war?

MYRRHINE: Goodness, yes! I'd do it, even if I had to pawn my dress and — get drunk on the spot!

CALONICE: And I, even if I had to let myself be split in two like a flounder.

LAMPITO: I'd climb up Mt. Taygetus if I could catch a glimpse of peace.

LYSISTRATA: I'll tell you, then, in plain and simple words. My friends, if we are going to force our men to make peace, we must do without —

MYRRHINE: Without what? Tell us.

LYSISTRATA: Will you do it?

MYRRHINE: We'll do it, if it kills us.

LYSISTRATA: Well then, we must do without sex altogether. *(General consternation.)* Why do you turn away? Where go you? Why turn so pale? Why those tears? Will you do it or not? What means this hesitation?

MYRRHINE: I won't do it! Let the war go on.

CALONICE: Nor I! Let the war go on.

LYSISTRATA: So, my little flounder? Didn't you say just now you'd split yourself in half?

CALONICE: Anything else you like. I'm willing, even if I have to walk through fire. Anything rather than sex. There's nothing like it, my dear.

LYSISTRATA *(to MYRRHINE)*: What about you?

MYRRHINE *(sullenly)*: I'm willing to walk through fire, too.

LYSISTRATA: Oh vile and cursed breed! No wonder they make tragedies about us: we're naught but "love-affairs and bassinets." But you, my dear Spartan friend, if you alone are with me, our enterprise might yet succeed. Will you vote with me?

LAMPITO: 'Tis cruel hard, by my faith, for a woman to sleep alone without her nooky; but for all that, we certainly do need peace.

LYSISTRATA: Oh my dearest friend! You're the only real woman here.

CALONICE *(wavering)*: Well, if we do refrain from — *(shuddering)* what you say (God forbid!), would that bring peace?

LYSISTRATA: My goodness, yes! If we sit at home all rouged and powdered, dressed in our sheerest gowns, and neatly depilated, our men will get excited and want to take us; but if you don't come to them and keep away, they'll soon make a truce.

LAMPITO: Aye; Menelaus caught sight of Helen's° naked breast and dropped his sword, they say.

CALONICE: What if the men give us up?

LYSISTRATA: "Flay a skinned dog," as Pherecrates says.

CALONICE: Rubbish! These make-shifts are not good. But suppose they grab us and drag us into the bedroom?

LYSISTRATA: Hold on to the door.

CALONICE: And if they beat us?

LYSISTRATA: Give in with a bad grace. There's no pleasure in it for them when they have to use violence. And you must torment them in every possible way. They'll give up soon enough; a man gets no joy if he doesn't get along with his wife.

MYRRHINE: If this is your opinion, we agree.

LAMPITO: As for our men, we can persuade them to make a just and fair peace; but what about the Athenian rabble? Who will persuade them not to start any more monkey-shines?

LYSISTRATA: Don't worry. We guarantee to convince them.

LAMPITO: Not while their ships are rigged so well and they have that mighty treasure in the temple of Athene.°

LYSISTRATA: We've taken good care for that too; we shall seize the Acropolis today. The older women have orders to do this, and while we are making our arrangements, they are to pretend to make a sacrifice and occupy the Acropolis.°

LAMPITO: All will be well then. That's a very fine idea.

LYSISTRATA: Let's ratify this, Lampito, with the most solemn oath.

LAMPITO: Tell us what oath we shall swear.

Helen: The wife of Menelaus, King of Sparta. Helen's abduction by Paris precipitated the Trojan War. *Athene:* Pallas Athene is the goddess of wisdom. *Acropolis:* The fortified area of the city where the Parthenon (the temple of the gods) is located.

LYSISTRATA: Well said. Where's our Policewoman? *(to a Scythian slave)* What are you gaping at? Set a shield upside-down here in front of me, and give me the sacred meats.

CALONICE: Lysistrata, what sort of an oath are we to take?

LYSISTRATA: What oath? I'm going to slaughter a sheep over the shield, as they do in Aeschylus.

CALONICE: Don't, Lysistrata! No oaths about peace over a shield.

LYSISTRATA: What shall the oath be, then?

CALONICE: How about getting a white horse somewhere and cutting out its entrails for the sacrifice?

LYSISTRATA: White horse indeed!

CALONICE: Well then, how shall we swear?

MYRRHINE: I'll tell you: let's place a large black bowl upside-down and then slaughter — a flask of Thasian wine. And then let's swear — not to pour in a single drop of water.

LAMPITO: Lord! How I like that oath!

LYSISTRATA: Someone bring out a bowl and a flask.

(A slave brings the utensils for the sacrifice.)

CALONICE: Look, my friends! What a big jar! Here's a cup that 'twould give me joy to handle. *(She picks up the bowl.)*

LYSISTRATA: Set it down and put your hands on our victim. *(As CALONICE places her hands on the flask.)* Oh Lady of Persuasion and dear Loving Cup, graciously vouchsafe to receive this sacrifice from us women. *(She pours the wine into the bowl.)*

CALONICE: The blood has a good colour and spurts out nicely.

LAMPITO: Faith, it has a pleasant smell, too.

MYRRHINE: Oh, let me be the first to swear, ladies!

CALONICE: No, by our Lady! Not unless you're allotted the first turn.

LYSISTRATA: Place all your hands on the cup, and one of you repeat on behalf of all what I say. Then all will swear and ratify the oath. *I will suffer no man, be he husband or lover,*

CALONICE: *I will suffer no man, be he husband or lover,*

LYSISTRATA: *To approach me all hot and horny. (As* CALONICE *hesitates.)* Say it!

CALONICE *(slowly and painfully): To approach me all hot and horny.* O Lysistrata, I feel so weak in the knees!

LYSISTRATA: *I will remain at home unmated,*

CALONICE: *I will remain at home unmated,*

LYSISTRATA: *Wearing my sheerest gown and carefully adorned,*

CALONICE: *Wearing my sheerest gown and carefully adorned,*

LYSISTRATA: *That my husband may burn with desire for me,*

CALONICE: *That my husband may burn with desire for me,*

LYSISTRATA: *And if he takes me by force against my will,*

CALONICE: *And if he takes me by force against my will,*

LYSISTRATA: *I shall do it badly and keep from moving.*

CALONICE: *I shall do it badly and keep from moving.*

LYSISTRATA: *I will not stretch my slippers toward the ceiling,*

CALONICE: *I will not stretch my slippers toward the ceiling,*

LYSISTRATA: *Nor will I take the posture of the lioness on the knife-handle.*

CALONICE: *Nor will I take the posture of the lioness on the knife-handle.*

LYSISTRATA: *If I keep this oath, may I be permitted to drink from this cup,*

CALONICE: *If I keep this oath, may I be permitted to drink from this cup,*

LYSISTRATA: *But if I break it, may the cup be filled with water.*

CALONICE: *But if I break it, may the cup be filled with water.*

LYSISTRATA: Do you all swear to this?

ALL: I do, so help me!

LYSISTRATA: Come then, I'll just consummate this offering.

(She takes a long drink from the cup.)

CALONICE *(snatching the cup away)*: Shares, my dear! Let's drink to our continued friendship.

(A shout is heard from off-stage.)

LAMPITO: What's that shouting?

LYSISTRATA: That's what I was telling you: the women have just seized the Acropolis. Now, Lampito, go home and arrange matters in Sparta; and leave these two ladies here as hostages. We'll enter the Acropolis to join our friends and help them lock the gates.

CALONICE: Don't you suppose the men will come to attack us?

LYSISTRATA: Don't worry about them. Neither threats nor fire will suffice to open the gates, except on the terms we've stated.

CALONICE: I should say not! Else we'd belie our reputation as unmanageable pests.

(LAMPITO leaves the stage. The other women retire and enter the Acropolis through the Propylaea. Enter the CHORUS OF OLD MEN, carrying firepots and a load of heavy sticks.)

LEADER OF MEN: Onward, Draces, step by step, though your shoulder's aching.

Cursèd logs of olive-wood, what a load you're making!

FIRST SEMI-CHORUS OF OLD MEN *(singing)*:

Aye, many surprises await a man who lives to a ripe old age;

For who could suppose, Strymodorus my lad, that the women we've nourished (alas!),

Who sat at home to vex our days,

Would seize the holy image here,

And occupy this sacred shrine,

With bolts and bars, with fell design,

To lock the Propylaea?

LEADER OF MEN: Come with speed, Philourgus, come! to the temple
  hast'ning.
 There we'll heap these logs about in a circle round them,
 And whoever has conspired, raising this rebellion,
 Shall be roasted, scorched, and burnt, all without exception,
 Doomed by one unanimous vote—but first the wife of Lycon.
SECOND SEMI-CHORUS (singing):
 No, no! by Demeter,° while I'm alive, no woman shall mock at me.
 Not even the Spartan Cleomenes, our citadel first to seize,
  Got off unscathed; for all his pride
  And haughty Spartan arrogance;
  He left his arms and sneaked away,
  Stripped to his shirt, unkempt, unshav'd,
 With six years' filth still on him.
LEADER OF MEN: I besieged that hero bold, sleeping at my station,
 Marshalled at these holy gates sixteen deep against him.
 Shall I not these cursèd pests punish for their daring,
 Burning these Euripides-and-God-detested° women?
 Aye! or else may Marathon overturn my trophy.
FIRST SEMI-CHORUS (singing): There remains of my road
  Just this brow of the hill;
   There I speed on my way.
 Drag the logs up the hill, though we've got no ass to help.
 (God! my shoulder's bruised and sore!)
  Onward still must we go.
  Blow the fire! Don't let it go out
 Now we're near the end of our road.
ALL (blowing on the fire-pots): Whew! Whew! Drat the smoke!
SECOND SEMI-CHORUS (singing): Lord, what smoke rushing forth
  From the pot, like a dog
  Running mad, bites my eyes!
 This must be Lemnos-fire. What a sharp and stinging smoke!
  Rushing onward to the shrine
  Aid the gods. Once for all
  Show your mettle, Laches my boy!
  To the rescue hastening all!
ALL (blowing on the fire-pots): Whew! Whew! Drat the smoke!

 (The CHORUS has now reached the edge of the Orchestra nearest the stage,
 in front of the propylaea. They begin laying their logs and fire-pots on the
 ground.)

LEADER OF MEN: Thank heaven, this fire is still alive. Now let's first put
  down these logs here and place our torches in the pots to catch; then

---

Demeter: Goddess of agriculture and fertility.   Euripides: Among the greatest Greek writers of
tragedies.

let's make a rush for the gates with a battering-ram. If the women don't unbar the gate at our summons, we'll have to smoke them out.

Let me put down my load. Ouch! That hurts! *(to the audience)* Would any of the generals in Samos like to lend a hand with this log? *(Throwing down a log.)* Well, *that* won't break my back any more, at any rate. *(Turning to his fire-pot.)* Your job, my little pot, is to keep those coals alive and furnish me shortly with a red-hot torch.

O mistress Victory, be my ally and grant me to rout these audacious women in the Acropolis.

(While the MEN *are busy with their logs and fires, the* CHORUS OF OLD WOMEN *enters, carrying pitchers of water.)*

LEADER OF WOMEN: What's this I see? Smoke and flames? Is that a fire ablazing?

Let's rush upon them. Hurry up! They'll find us women ready.

FIRST SEMI-CHORUS OF OLD WOMEN *(singing)*:
> With wingèd foot onward I fly,
> Ere the flames consume Neodice;
> Lest Critylla be overwhelmed
By a lawless, accurst herd of old men.
I shudder with fear. Am I too late to aid them?
At break of the day filled we our jars with water
Fresh from the spring, pushing our way straight through the crowds.
> Oh, what a din!
> Mid crockery crashing, jostled by slave-girls,
> Sped we to save them, aiding our neighbours,
> Bearing this water to put out the flames.

SECOND SEMI-CHORUS OF OLD WOMEN *(singing)*:
> Such news I've heard; doddering fools
> Come with logs, like furnace-attendants,
> Loaded down with three hundred pounds,
> Breathing many a vain, blustering threat,
> That all these abhorred sluts will be burnt to charcoal.
> O goddess, I pray never may they be kindled;
Grant them to save Greece and our men, madness and war help them to end.
> With this as our purpose, golden-plumed Maiden,
> Guardian of Athens, seized we thy precinct.
> Be my ally, Warrior-maiden,
> 'Gainst these old men, bearing water with me.

(The WOMEN *have now reached their position in the Orchestra, and their* LEADER *advances toward the* LEADER OF THE MEN.)*

LEADER OF WOMEN: Hold on there! What's this, you utter scoundrels? No decent, God-fearing citizens would act like this.

LEADER OF MEN: Oho! Here's something unexpected: a swarm of women have come out to attack us.

LEADER OF WOMEN: What, do we frighten you? Surely you don't think we're too many for you. And yet there are ten thousand times more of us whom you haven't even seen.

LEADER OF MEN: What say, Phaedria? Shall we let these women wag their tongues? Shan't we take our sticks and break them over their backs?

LEADER OF WOMEN: Let's set our pitchers on the ground; then if anyone lays a hand on us, they won't get in our way.

LEADER OF MEN: By God! If someone gave them two or three smacks on the jaw, like Bupalus, they wouldn't talk so much!

LEADER OF WOMEN: Go on, hit me, somebody! Here's my jaw! But no other bitch will bite a piece out of you before me.

LEADER OF MEN: Silence! or I'll knock out your — senility!

LEADER OF WOMEN: Just lay one finger on Stratyllis, I dare you!

LEADER OF MEN: Suppose I dust you off with this fist? What will you do?

LEADER OF WOMEN: I'll tear the living guts out of you with my teeth.

LEADER OF MEN: No poet is more clever than Euripides: "There is no beast so shameless as a woman."

LEADER OF WOMEN: Let's pick up our jars of water, Rhodippe.

LEADER OF MEN: Why have you come here with water, you detestable slut?

LEADER OF WOMEN: And why have you come with fire, you funeral vault? To cremate yourself?

LEADER OF MEN: To light a fire and singe your friends.

LEADER OF WOMEN: And I've brought water to put out your fire.

LEADER OF MEN: What? You'll put out my fire?

LEADER OF WOMEN: Just try and see!

LEADER OF MEN: I wonder: shall I scorch you with this torch of mine?

LEADER OF WOMEN: If you've got any soap, I'll give you a bath.

LEADER OF MEN: Give *me* a bath, you stinking hag?

LEADER OF WOMEN: Yes — a bridal bath!

LEADER OF MEN: Just listen to her! What crust!

LEADER OF WOMEN: Well, I'm a free citizen.

LEADER OF MEN: I'll put an end to your brawling.

(The MEN *pick up their torches.)*

LEADER OF WOMEN: You'll never do jury-duty again.

(The WOMEN *pick up their pitchers.)*

LEADER OF MEN: Singe her hair for her!

LEADER OF WOMEN: Do your duty, water!

(The WOMEN *empty their pitchers on the* MEN.*)*

LEADER OF MEN: Ow! Ow! For heaven's sake!

LEADER OF WOMEN: Is it too hot?

LEADER OF MEN: What do you mean "hot"? Stop! What are you doing?

LEADER OF WOMEN: I'm watering you, so you'll be fresh and green.

LEADER OF MEN: But I'm all withered up with shaking.

LEADER OF WOMEN: Well, you've got a fire; why don't you dry yourself?

(Enter an ATHENIAN MAGISTRATE, *accompanied by* FOUR SCYTHIAN POLICEMEN.*)*

MAGISTRATE: Have these wanton women flared up again wtih their timbrels and their continual worship of Sabazius? Is this another Adonis-dirge upon the roof-tops — which we heard not long ago in the Assembly? That confounded Demostratus was urging us to sail to Sicily, and the whirling women shouted, "Woe for Adonis!"° And then Demostratus said we'd best enroll the infantry from Zacynthus, and a tipsy woman on the roof shrieked, "Beat your breasts for Adonis!" And that vile and filthy lunatic forced his measure through. Such license do our women take.

LEADER OF MEN: What if you heard of the insolence of these women here? Besides their other violent acts, they threw water all over us, and we have to shake out our clothes just as if we'd leaked in them.

MAGISTRATE: And rightly, too, by God! For we ourselves lead the women astray and teach them to play the wanton; from these roots such notions blossom forth. A man goes into the jeweler's shop and says, "About that necklace you made for my wife, goldsmith: last night, while she was dancing, the fastening-bolt slipped out of the hole. I have to sail over to Salamis today; if you're free, do come around tonight and fit a new bolt for her." Another goes to the shoe-maker, a strapping young fellow with manly parts, and says, "See here, cobbler, the sandalstrap chafes my wife's little — toe; it's so tender. Come around during the siesta and stretch it a little, so she'll be more comfortable." Now we see the results of such treatment: here I'm a special Councillor and need money to procure oars for the galleys; and I'm locked out of the Treasury by these women.

But this is no time to stand around. Bring up crow-bars there! I'll put an end to their insolence *(to one of the policemen)*. What are you gaping at, you wretch! What are you staring at? Got an eye out for a tavern, eh? Set your crow-bars here to the gates and force them open. *(Retiring to a safe distance)* I'll help from over here.

(The gates are thrown open and LYSISTRATA *comes out followed by several other* WOMEN.*)*

Adonis: A handsome young man loved by Aphrodite. The women mean that war is disastrous for young men.

LYSISTRATA: Don't force the gates; I'm coming out of my own accord. We don't need crow-bars here. What we need is good sound common-sense.

MAGISTRATE: Is that so, you strumpet? Where's my policeman? Officer, arrest her and tie her arms behind her back.

LYSISTRATA: By Artemis,° if he lays a finger on me, he'll pay for it, even if he is a public servant.

(The POLICEMAN *retires in terror.)*

MAGISTRATE: You there, are you afraid? Seize her round the waist — and you, too. Tie her up, both of you!

FIRST WOMAN *(as the* SECOND POLICEMAN *approaches* LYSISTRATA*)*: By Pandrosus, if you but touch her with your hand, I'll kick the stuffings out of you.

(The SECOND POLICEMAN *retires in terror.)*

MAGISTRATE: Just listen to that: "kick the stuffings out." Where's another policeman? Tie *her* up first, for her chatter.

SECOND WOMAN: By the Goddess of the Light, if you lay the tip of your finger on her, you'll soon need a doctor.

(The THIRD POLICEMAN *retires in terror.)*

MAGISTRATE: What's this? Where's my policemen? Seize *her* too. I'll soon stop your sallies.

THIRD WOMAN: By the Goddess of Tauros, if you go near her, I'll tear out your hair until it shrieks with pain.

(The FOURTH POLICEMAN *retires in terror.)*

MAGISTRATE: Oh, damn it all! I've run out of policemen. But women must never defeat us. Officers, let's charge them all together. Close up your ranks!

(The POLICEMEN *rally for a mass attack.)*

LYSISTRATA: By heaven, you'll soon find out that we have four companies of warrior-women, all fully equipped within!

MAGISTRATE *(advancing)*: Twist their arms off, men!

LYSISTRATA *(shouting)*: To the rescue, my valiant women!
    O sellers-of-barley-green-stuffs-and-eggs,
    O sellers-of-garlic, ye keepers-of-taverns, and vendors-of-bread,
      Grapple! Smite! Smash!
    Won't you heap filth on them? Give them a tongue-lashing!

(The WOMEN *beat off the* POLICEMEN*.)*

Artemis: Goddess of the moon, wild animals, and hunting.

Halt! Withdraw! No looting on the field.

MAGISTRATE: Damn it! My police-force has put up a very poor show.

LYSISTRATA: What did you expect? Did you think you were attacking slaves?

Didn't you know that women are filled with passion?

MAGISTRATE: Aye, passion enough — for a good strong drink!

LEADER OF MEN: O chief and leader of this land, why spend your words in vain?

Don't argue with these shameless beasts. You know not how we've fared:

A soapless bath they've given us; our clothes are soundly soaked.

LEADER OF WOMEN: Poor fool! You never should attack or strike a peaceful girl.

But if you do, your eyes must swell. For I am quite content

To sit unmoved, like modest maids, in peace and cause no pain;

But let a man stir up my hive, he'll find me like a wasp.

CHORUS OF MEN (*singing*):

Oh God, whatever shall we do with creatures like Womankind?

This can't be endured by any man alive. Question them!

Let us try to find out what this means.

To what end have they seized on this shrine,

This steep and rugged, high and holy, Undefiled Acropolis?

LEADER OF MEN: Come, put your questions; don't give in, and probe her every statement.

For base and shameful it would be to leave this plot untested.

MAGISTRATE: Well then, first of all I wish to ask her this: for what purpose have you barred us from the Acropolis?

LYSISTRATA: To keep the treasure safe, so you won't make war on account of it.

MAGISTRATE: What? Do we make war on account of the treasure?

LYSISTRATA: Yes, and you cause all our other troubles for it, too. Peisander and those greedy office-seekers keep things stirred up so they can find occasions to steal. Now let them do what they like: they'll never again make off with any of this money.

MAGISTRATE: What will you do?

LYSISTRATA: What a question! We'll administer it ourselves.

MAGISTRATE: *You* will administer the treasure?

LYSISTRATA: What's so strange in that? Don't we administer the household money for you?

MAGISTRATE: That's different.

LYSISTRATA: How is it different?

MAGISTRATE: We've got to make war with this money.

LYSISTRATA: But that's the very first thing: you mustn't make war.

MAGISTRATE: How else can we be saved?

LYSISTRATA: We'll save you.

MAGISTRATE: *You?*

LYSISTRATA: Yes, we!

MAGISTRATE: God forbid!

LYSISTRATA: We'll save you, whether you want it or not.

MAGISTRATE: Oh! This is terrible!

LYSISTRATA: You don't like it, but we're going to do it none the less.

MAGISTRATE: Good God! it's illegal!

LYSISTRATA: We *will* save you, my little man!

MAGISTRATE: Suppose I don't want you to?

LYSISTRATA: That's all the more reason.

MAGISTRATE: What business have you with war and peace?

LYSISTRATA: I'll explain.

MAGISTRATE *(shaking his fist)*: Speak up, or you'll smart for it.

LYSISTRATA: Just listen, and try to keep your hands still.

MAGISTRATE: I can't. I'm so mad I can't stop them.

FIRST WOMAN: Then you'll be the one to smart for it.

MAGISTRATE: Croak to yourself, old hag! *(to* LYSISTRATA*)* Now then, speak up.

LYSISTRATA: Very well. Formerly we endured the war for a good long time with our usual restraint, no matter what you men did. You wouldn't let us say "boo," although nothing you did suited us. But we watched you well, and though we stayed at home we'd often hear of some terribly stupid measure you'd proposed. Then, though grieving at heart, we'd smile sweetly and say, "What was passed in the Assembly today about writing on the treaty-stone?" "What's that to you?" my husband would say. "Hold your tongue!" and I held my tongue.

FIRST WOMAN: But I wouldn't have—not I!

MAGISTRATE: You'd have been soundly smacked, if you hadn't kept still.

LYSISTRATA: So I kept still at home. Then we'd hear of some plan still worse than the first; we'd say, "Husband, how could you pass such a stupid proposal!" He'd scowl at me and say, "If you don't mind your spinning, your head will be sore for weeks. *War shall be the concern of men.*"

MAGISTRATE: And he was right, upon my word!

LYSISTRATA: Why right, you confounded fool, when your proposals were so stupid and we weren't allowed to make any suggestions?

"There's not a *man* left in the country," says one. "No, not one," says another. Therefore all we women have decided in council to make a common effort to save Greece. How long should we have waited? Now, if you're willing to listen to our excellent proposals and keep silence for us in your turn, we still may save you.

MAGISTRATE: We men keep silence for you? That's terrible; I won't endure it!

LYSISTRATA: Silence!

MAGISTRATE: Silence for *you,* you wench, when you're wearing a snood? I'd rather die!

LYSISTRATA: Well, if that's all that bothers you—here! Take my snood and tie it round your head. *(During the following words the* WOMEN *dress up the* MAGISTRATE *in women's garments.)* And *now* keep quiet! Here, take this spinning-basket, too, and card your wool with robes tucked up, munching on beans. *War shall be the concern of Women!*

LEADER OF WOMEN: Arise and leave your pitchers, girls; no time is this to falter.

We too must aid our loyal friends; our turn has come for action.

CHORUS OF WOMEN *(singing)*:

I'll never tire of aiding them with song and dance; never may
Faintness keep my legs from moving to and fro endlessly.
　For I yearn to do all for my friends;
　　They have charm, they have wit, they have grace,
　　　With courage, brains, and best of virtues—Patriotic sapience.

LEADER OF WOMEN: Come, child of manliest ancient dames, offspring of stinging nettles,

Advance with rage unsoftened; for fair breezes speed you onward.

LYSISTRATA: If only sweet Eros° and the Cyprian Queen of Love shed charm over our breasts and limbs and inspire our men with amorous longing and priapic spasms, I think we may soon be called Peacemakers among the Greeks.

MAGISTRATE: What will you do?

LYSISTRATA: First of all, we'll stop those fellows who run madly about the Marketplace in arms.

FIRST WOMAN: Indeed we shall, by the Queen of Paphos.

LYSISTRATA: For now they roam about the market, amid the pots and greenstuffs, armed to the teeth like Corybantes.°

MAGISTRATE: That's what manly fellows ought to do!

LYSISTRATA: But it's so silly: a chap with a Gorgon-emblazoned shield buying pickled herring.

FIRST WOMAN: Why, just the other day I saw one of those long-haired dandies who command our cavalry ride up on horseback and pour into his bronze helmet the egg-broth he'd bought from an old dame. And there was a Thracian slinger too, shaking his lance like Tereus;° he'd scared the life out of the poor fig-peddler and was gulping down all her ripest fruit.

MAGISTRATE: How can you stop all the confusion in the various states and bring them together?

Eros: God of love.　*Corybantes:* Dancers who follow the goddess Cybale and engage in frenzied dancing and orgies.　*Tereus:* A king of Thrace.

LYSISTRATA: Very easily.

MAGISTRATE: Tell me how.

LYSISTRATA: Just like a ball of wool, when it's confused and snarled: we take it thus, and draw out a thread here and a thread there with our spindles; thus we'll unsnarl this war, if no one prevents us, and draw together the various states with embassies here and embassies there.

MAGISTRATE: Do you suppose you can stop this dreadful business with balls of wool and spindles, you nit-wits?

LYSISTRATA: Why, if *you* had any wits, you'd manage all affairs of state like our wool-working.

MAGISTRATE: How so?

LYSISTRATA: First you ought to treat the city as we do when we wash the dirt out of a fleece: stretch it out and pluck and thrash out of the city all those prickly scoundrels; aye, and card out those who conspire and stick together to gain office, pulling off their heads. Then card the wool, all of it, into one fair basket of goodwill, mingling in the aliens residing here, any loyal foreigners, and anyone who's in debt to the Treasury; and consider that all our colonies lie scattered round about like remnants; from all of these collect the wool and gather it together here, wind up a great ball, and then weave a good stout cloak for the democracy.

MAGISTRATE: Dreadful! Talking about thrashing and winding balls of wool, when you haven't the slightest share in the war!

LYSISTRATA: Why, you dirty scoundrel, we bear more than twice as much as you. First, we bear children and send off our sons as soldiers.

MAGISTRATE: Hush! Let bygones be bygones!

LYSISTRATA: Then, when we ought to be happy and enjoy our youth, we sleep alone because of your expeditions abroad. But never mind us married women: I grieve most for the maids who grow old at home unwed.

MAGISTRATE: Don't men grow old, too?

LYSISTRATA: For heaven's sake! That's not the same thing. When a man comes home, no matter how grey he is, he soon finds a girl to marry. But woman's bloom is short and fleeting; if she doesn't grasp her chance, no man is willing to marry her and she sits at home a prey to every fortune-teller.

MAGISTRATE *(coarsely)*: But if a man can still get it up —

LYSISTRATA: See here, you: what's the matter? Aren't you dead yet? There's plenty of room for you. Buy yourself a shroud and I'll bake you a honey-cake. *(Handing him a copper coin for his passage across the Styx.°)* Here's your fare! Now get yourself a wreath.

(During the following dialogue the WOMEN *dress up the* MAGISTRATE *as a corpse.)*

Styx: The river that encircles Hades, the world of the dead.

FIRST WOMAN: Here, take these fillets.

SECOND WOMAN: Here, take this wreath.

LYSISTRATA: What do you want? What's lacking? Get moving; off to the ferry! Charon° is calling you; don't keep him from sailing.

MAGISTRATE: Am I to endure these insults? By God! I'm going straight to the magistrates to show them how I've been treated.

LYSISTRATA: Are you grumbling that you haven't been properly laid out? Well, the day after tomorrow we'll send around all the usual offerings early in the morning.

(The MAGISTRATE *goes out still wearing his funeral decorations.* LYSISTRATA *and the* WOMEN *retire into the Acropolis.)*

LEADER OF MEN: Wake, ye sons of freedom, wake! 'Tis no time for sleeping. Up and at them, like a man! Let us strip for action.

(The CHORUS OF MEN *remove their outer cloaks.)*

CHORUS OF MEN *(singing)*:
Surely there is something here greater than meets the eye;
For without a doubt I smell Hippias' tyrany.
Dreadful fear assails me lest certain bands of Spartan men,
Meeting here with Cleisthenes, have inspired through treachery
All these god-detested women secretly to seize
Athens' treasure in the temple, and to stop that pay
        Whence I live at my ease.

LEADER OF MEN: Now isn't it terrible for them to advise the state and chatter about shields, being mere women?

And they think to reconcile us with the Spartans — men who hold nothing sacred any more than hungry wolves. Surely this is a web of deceit, my friends, to conceal an attempt at tyrany. But they'll never lord it over me; I'll be on my guard from now on,

"The blade I bear, A myrtle spray shall wear."

I'll occupy the market under arms and stand next to Aristogeiton.

Thus I'll stand beside him *(He strikes the pose of the famous statue of the tyrannicides, with one arm raised.)* And here's my chance to take this accurst old hag and — *(striking the* LEADER OF WOMEN*)* smack her on the jaw!

LEADER OF WOMEN: You'll go home in such a state your Ma won't recognize you!

Ladies all, upon the ground let us place these garments.

(The CHORUS OF WOMEN *remove their outer garments.)*

CHORUS OF WOMEN *(singing)*:
Citizens of Athens, hear useful words for the state.
Rightly; for it nurtured me in my youth royally.

Charon: Boatman who ferries souls of the dead across the river Styx.

As a child of seven years carried I the sacred box;
Then I was a Miller-maid, grinding at Athene's shrine;
Next I wore the saffron robe and played Brauronia's Bear;
And I walked as a Basket-bearer, wearing chains of figs,
      As a sweet maiden fair.

LEADER OF WOMEN: Therefore, am I not bound to give good advice to the city?

Don't take it ill that I was born a woman, if I contribute something better than our present troubles. I pay my share; for I contribute MEN. But you miserable old fools contribute nothing, and after squandering our ancestral treasure, the fruit of the Persian Wars, you make no contribution in return. And now, all on account of you, we're facing ruin.

What, muttering, are you? If you annoy me, I'll take this hard, rough slipper and — (*striking the* LEADER OF MEN) smack you on the jaw!

CHORUS OF MEN (*singing*):
This is outright insolence! Things go from bad to worse.
If you're men with any guts, prepare to meet the foe.
Let us strip our tunics off! We need the smell of male
Vigour. And we cannot fight all swaddled up in clothes.

(*They strip off their tunics.*)

Come then, my comrades, on to the battle, ye once to Leipsydrion came;
Then ye were MEN. Now call back your youthful vigour.
With light, wingèd footstep advance,
      Shaking old age from your frame.

LEADER OF MEN: If any of us give these wenches the slightest hold, they'll stop at nothing; such is their cunning.

They will even build ships and sail against us, like Artemisia. Or if they turn to mounting, I count our Knights as done for: a woman's such a tricky jockey when she gets astraddle, with a good firm seat for trotting. Just look at those Amazons° that Micon painted, fighting on horseback against men!

But we must throw them all in the pillory — (*seizing and choking the* LEADER OF WOMEN) grabbing hold of yonder neck!

CHORUS OF WOMEN (*singing*):
'Ware my anger! Like a boar 'twill rush upon you men.
Soon you'll bawl aloud for help, you'll be so soundly trimmed!
Come, my friends, let's strip with speed, and lay aside these robes;
Catch the scent of women's rage. Attack with tooth and nail!

(*They strip off their tunics.*)

Amazons: Race of female warriors.

Now then, come near me, you miserable man!
    You'll never eat garlic or black beans again.
And if you utter a single hard word, in rage I will "nurse" you as once
    The beetle requited her foe.

LEADER OF WOMEN: For you don't worry me; no, not so long as my
    Lampito lives and our Theban friend, the noble Ismenia.
      You can't do anything, not even if you pass a dozen — decrees!
    You miserable fool, all our neighbours hate you. Why, just the other
    day when I was holding a festival for Hecate, I invited as playmate
    from our neighbours the Boeotians a charming, wellbred Copiac —
    eel. But they refused to send me one on account of your decrees.
      And you'll never stop passing decrees until I grab your foot and —
    (tripping up the LEADER OF MEN) toss you down and break your
    neck!

(Here an interval of five days is supposed to elapse. LYSISTRATA *comes
out from the Acropolis.)*

LEADER OF WOMEN *(dramatically):*   Empress of this great emprise and
    undertaking,
    Why come you forth, I pray, with frowning brow?

LYSISTRATA: Ah, these cursèd women! Their deeds and female notions
    make me pace up and down in utter despair.

LEADER OF WOMEN: Ah, what sayest thou?

LYSISTRATA: The truth, alas! the truth.

LEADER OF WOMEN: What dreadful tale hast thou to tell thy friends?

LYSISTRATA: 'Tis shame to speak, and not to speak is hard.

LEADER OF WOMEN: Hide not from me whatever woes we suffer.

LYSISTRATA: Well then, to put it briefly, we want — laying!

LEADER OF WOMEN: O Zeus, Zeus!°

LYSISTRATA: Why call on Zeus? That's the way things are. I can no
    longer keep them away from the men, and they're all deserting. I
    caught one wriggling through a hole near the grotto of Pan, another
    sliding down a rope, another deserting her post; and yesterday I found
    one getting on a sparrow's back to fly off to Orsilochus, and had to
    pull her back by the hair. They're digging up all sorts of excuses to get
    home. Look, here comes one of them now.

(A WOMAN *comes hastily out of the Acropolis.)*

Here you! Where are you off to in such a hurry?

FIRST WOMAN: I want to go home. My very best wool is being devoured
    by moths.

LYSISTRATA: Moths? Nonsense! Go back inside.

FIRST WOMAN: I'll come back; I swear it. I just want to lay it out on the
    bed.

Zeus: King of Greek gods.

LYSISTRATA: Well, you won't lay it out, and you won't go home, either.

FIRST WOMAN: Shall I let my wool be ruined?

LYSISTRATA: If necessary, yes.

(ANOTHER WOMAN comes out.)

SECOND WOMAN: Oh, dear! Oh dear! My precious flax! I left it at home all unpeeled.

LYSISTRATA: Here's another one, going home for her "flax." Come back here!

SECOND WOMAN: But I just want to work it up a little and then I'll be right back.

LYSISTRATA: No indeed! If you start this, all other women will want to do the same.

(A THIRD WOMAN comes out.)

THIRD WOMAN: O Eilithyia, goddess of travail, stop my labour till I come to a lawful spot!

LYSISTRATA: What's this nonsense?

THIRD WOMAN: I'm going to have a baby — right now!

LYSISTRATA: But you weren't even pregnant yesterday.

THIRD WOMAN: Well, I am today. O Lysistrata, do send me home to see a midwife, right away.

LYSISTRATA: What are you talking about? *(Putting her hand on her stomach)* What's this hard lump here?

THIRD WOMAN: A little boy.

LYSISTRATA: My goodness, what have you got there? It seems hollow; I'll just find out. *(Pulling aside her robe)* Why, you silly goose, you've got Athene's sacred helmet there. And you said you were having a baby!

THIRD WOMAN: Well, I *am* having one, I swear!

LYSISTRATA: Then what's this helmet for?

THIRD WOMAN: If the baby starts coming while I'm still in the Acropolis, I'll creep into this like a pigeon and give birth to it there.

LYSISTRATA: Stuff and nonsense! It's plain enough what you're up to. You just wait here for the christening of this — helmet.

THIRD WOMAN: But I can't sleep in the Acropolis since I saw the sacred snake.

FIRST WOMAN: And I'm dying for lack of sleep: the hooting of owls keep me awake.

LYSISTRATA: Enough of these shams, you wretched creatures. You want your husbands, I suppose. Well, don't you think they want us? I'm sure they're spending miserable nights. Hold out, my friends, and endure for just a little while. There's an oracle that we shall conquer, if we don't split up. *(Producing a roll of paper.)* Here it is.

FIRST WOMAN: Tell us what it says.

LYSISTRATA: Listen.

"When in the length of time the Swallows shall gather together,
Fleeing the Hoopoe's amorous flight and the Cockatoo shunning,
Then shall your woes be ended and Zeus who thunders in heaven
Set what's below on top—"

FIRST WOMAN: What? Are we going to be on top?

LYSISTRATA: "But if the Swallows rebel and flutter away from the temple,
Never a bird in the world shall seem more wanton and worthless."

FIRST WOMAN: That's clear enough, upon my word!

LYSISTRATA: By all that's holy, let's not give up the struggle now. Let's go back inside. It would be a shame, my dear friends, to disobey the oracle.

(The WOMEN *all retire to the Acropolis again.)*

CHORUS OF MEN *(singing)*:
I have a tale to tell,
Which I know full well.
   It was told me
   In the nursery.

Once there was a likely lad,
   Melanion they name him;
The thought of marriage made him mad,
   For which I cannot blame him.

So off he went to mountains fair;
   (No women to upbraid him!)
A mighty hunter of the hare,
   He had a dog to aid him.

He never came back home to see
   Detested women's faces.
He showed a shrewd mentality.
   With him I'd fain change places!

ONE OF THE MEN *(to* ONE OF THE WOMEN*)*:   Come here, old dame;
   give me a kiss.

WOMAN: You'll ne'er eat garlic, if you dare!

MAN: I want to kick you—just like this!

WOMAN: Oh, there's a leg with bushy hair!

MAN: Myronides and Phormio
   Were hairy—and they thrashed the foe.

CHORUS OF WOMEN *(singing)*:
    I have another tale,
    With which to assail
        Your contention
        'Bout Melanion.

    Once upon a time a man
        Named Timon left our city,
    To live in some deserted land.
        (We thought him rather witty.)

    He dwelt alone amidst the thorn;
        In solitude he brooded.
    From some grim Fury he was born:
        Such hatred he exuded.

    He cursed you men, as scoundrels through
        And through, till life he ended.
    He couldn't stand the sight of you!
        But women he befriended.

WOMAN *(to* ONE OF THE MEN*)*: I'll smash your face in, if you like.
MAN: Oh no, please don't! You frighten me.
WOMAN: I'll lift my foot—and thus I'll strike.
MAN: Aha! Look there! What's that I see?
WOMAN: Whate'er you see, you cannot say
    That I'm not neatly trimmed today.

*(*LYSISTRATA *appears on the wall of the Acropolis.)*

LYSISTRATA: Hello! Hello! Girls, come here quick!

*(*SEVERAL WOMEN *appear beside her.)*

WOMAN: What is it? Why are you calling?
LYSISTRATA: I see a man coming: he's in a dreadful state. He's mad with passion. O Queen of Cyprus, Cythera, and Paphos, just keep on this way!
WOMAN: Where is the fellow?
LYSISTRATA: There beside the shrine of Demeter.
WOMAN: Oh yes, so he is. Who is he?
LYSISTRATA: Let's see. Do any of you know him?
MYRRHINE: Yes indeed. That's my husband, Cinesias.
LYSISTRATA: It's up to you, now: roast him, rack him, fool him, love him—and leave him! Do everything, except what our oath forbids.
MYRRHINE: Don't worry; I'll do it.
LYSISTRATA: I'll stay here to tease him and warm him up a bit. Off with you.

(The OTHER WOMEN *retire from the wall. Enter* CINESIAS *followed by* A SLAVE *carrying a baby.* CINESIAS *is obviously in great pain and distress.)*

CINESIAS *(groaning)*: Oh-h! Oh-h-h! This is killing me! Oh God, what tortures I'm suffering!

LYSISTRATA *(from the wall)*: Who's that within our lines?

CINESIAS: Me.

LYSISTRATA: A *man?*

CINESIAS *(pointing)*: A *man,* indeed!

LYSISTRATA: Well, go away!

CINESIAS: Who are you to send me away?

LYSISTRATA: The captain of the guard.

CINESIAS: Oh, for heaven's sake, call out Myrrhine for me.

LYSISTRATA: Call Myrrhine? Nonsense! Who are you?

CINESIAS: Her husband, Cinesias of Paionidai.

LYSISTRATA *(appearing much impressed)*: Oh, greetings, friend. Your name is not without honour here among us. Your wife is always talking about you, and whenever she takes an egg or an apple, she says, "Here's to my dear Cinesias!"

CINESIAS *(quivering with excitement)*: Oh, ye gods in heaven!

LYSISTRATA: Indeed she does! And whenever our conversations turn to men, your wife immediately says, "All others are mere rubbish compared with Cinesias."

CINESIAS *(groaning)*: Oh! Do call her for me.

LYSISTRATA: Why should I? What will you give me?

CINESIAS: Whatever you want. All I have is yours — and you see what I've got.

LYSISTRATA: Well then, I'll go down and call her. *(She descends.)*

CINESIAS: And hurry up! I've had no joy of life ever since she left home. When I go in the house, I feel awful: everything seems so empty and I can't enjoy my dinner. I'm in such a state all the time!

MYRRHINE *(from behind the wall)*: I *do* love him so. But he won't let me love him. No, no! Don't ask me to see him!

CINESIAS: O my darling, O Myrrhine honey, why do you do this to me?

*(*MYRRHINE *appears on the wall.)*

Come down here!

MYRRHINE: No, I won't come down.

CINESIAS: Won't you come, Myrrhine, when I call you?

MYRRHINE: No; you don't want me.

CINESIAS: *Don't want you?* I'm in agony!

MYRRHINE: I'm going now.

CINESIAS: Please don't. At least, listen to your baby. *(to the baby)* Here you, call your mamma! *(Pinching the baby.)*

BABY: Ma-ma! Ma-ma! Ma-ma!

CINESIAS *(to Myrrhine)*: What's the matter with you? Have you no pity for your child, who hasn't been washed or fed for five whole days?

MYRRHINE: Oh, poor child; your father pays no attention to you.

CINESIAS: Come down then, you heartless wretch, for the baby's sake.

MYRRHINE: Oh, what it is to be a mother! I've got to come down, I suppose.

(She leaves the wall and shortly reappears at the gate.)

CINESIAS *(to himself)*: She seems much younger, and she has such a sweet look about her. Oh, the way she teases me! And her pretty, provoking ways make me burn with longing.

MYRRHINE *(coming out of the gate and taking the baby)*: O my sweet little angel. Naughty papa! Here, let Mummy kiss you, Mamma's little sweetheart!

(She fondles the baby lovingly.)

CINESIAS *(in despair)*: You heartless creature, why do you do this? Why follow these other women and make both of us suffer so?

(He tries to embrace her.)

MYRRHINE: Don't touch me!

CINESIAS: You're letting all our things at home go to wrack and ruin.

MYRRHINE: I don't care.

CINESIAS: You don't care that your wool is being plucked to pieces by the chickens?

MYRRHINE: Not in the least.

CINESIAS: And you haven't celebrated the rites of Aphrodite for ever so long. Won't you come home?

MYRRHINE: Not on your life, unless you men make a truce and stop the war.

CINESIAS: Well, then, if that pleases you, we'll do it.

MYRRHINE: Well then, if that pleases *you*, I'll come home — afterwards! Right now I'm on oath not to.

CINESIAS: Then just lie down here with me for a moment.

MYRRHINE: No — *(in a teasing voice)* and yet I won't say I don't love you.

CINESIAS: You love me? Oh, do lie down here, Myrrhine dear!

MYRRHINE: What, you silly fool! in front of the baby?

CINESIAS *(hastily thrusting the baby at the slave)*: Of course not. Here — home! Take him, Manes! *(The SLAVE goes off with the baby.)* See, the baby's out of the way. Now won't you lie down?

MYRRHINE: But where, my dear?

CINESIAS: Where? The grotto of Pan's a lovely spot.

MYRRHINE: How could I purify myself before returning to the shrine?

CINESIAS: Easily: just wash here in the Clepsydra.

MYRRHINE: And then, shall I go back on my oath?

CINESIAS: On my head be it! Don't worry about the oath.

MYRRHINE: All right, then. Just let me bring out a bed.

CINESIAS: No, don't. The ground's all right.

MYRRHINE: Heavens, no! Bad as you are, I won't let you lie on the bare ground.

(She goes into the Acropolis.)

CINESIAS: Why, she really loves me; it's plain to see.

MYRRHINE *(returning with a bed)*: There! Now hurry up and lie down. I'll just slip off this dress. But—let's see: oh yes, I must fetch a mattress.

CINESIAS: Nonsense! No mattress for me.

MYRRHINE: Yes indeed! It's not nice on the bare springs.

CINESIAS: Give me a kiss.

MYRRHINE *(giving him a hasty kiss)*: There!

(She goes.)

CINESIAS *(in mingled distress and delight)*: Oh-h! Hurry back!

MYRRHINE *(returning with a mattress)*: Here's the mattress: lie down on it. I'm taking my things off now—but—let's see: you have no pillow.

CINESIAS: I don't *want* a pillow.

MYRRHINE: But I do.

(She goes.)

CINESIAS: Cheated again, just like Heracles and his dinner!

MYRRHINE *(returning with a pillow)*: Here, lift your head. *(to herself, wondering how else to tease him)* Is that all?

CINESIAS: Surely that's all! Do come here, precious!

MYRRHINE: I'm taking off my girdle. But remember: don't go back on your promise about the truce.

CINESIAS: I hope to die, if I do.

MYRRHINE: You don't have a blanket.

CINESIAS *(shouting in exasperation)*: *I don't want one!* I WANT TO—

MYRRHINE: Sh-h! There, there, I'll be back in a minute.

(She goes.)

CINESIAS: She'll be the death of me with these bedclothes.

MYRRHINE *(returning with a blanket)*: Here, get up.

CINESIAS: I've got *this* up!

MYRRHINE: Would you like some perfume?

CINESIAS: Good heavens, no! I won't have it!

MYRRHINE: Yes, you shall, whether you want it or not.

(She goes.)

CINESIAS: O lord! Confound all perfumes anyway!

MYRRHINE *(returning with a flask)*: Stretch out your hand and put some on.

CINESIAS *(suspiciously)*: By God, I don't much like this perfume. It smacks of shilly-shallying, and has no scent of the marriage-bed.

MYRRHINE: Oh dear! This is Rhodian perfume I've brought.

CINESIAS: It's quite all right, dear. Never mind.

MYRRHINE: Don't be silly!

(She goes out with the flask.)

CINESIAS: Damn the man who first concocted perfumes!

MYRRHINE *(returning with another flask)*: Here, try this flask.

CINESIAS: I've got another one all ready for you. Come, you wretch, lie down and stop bringing me things.

MYRRHINE: All right; I'm taking off my shoes. But, my dear, see that you vote for peace.

CINESIAS *(absently)*: I'll consider it.

(MYRRHINE runs away to the Acropolis.)

I'm ruined! The wench has skinned me and run away! *(chanting, in tragic style)* Alas! Alas! Deceived, deserted by this fairest of women, whom shall I—lay? Ah, my poor little child, how shall I nurture thee? Where's Cynalopex? I needs must hire a nurse!

LEADER OF MEN *(chanting)*: Ah, wretched man, in dreadful wise beguiled, bewrayed, thy soul is sore distressed. I pity thee, alas! What soul, what loins, what liver could stand this strain? How firm and unyielding he stands, with naught to aid him of a morning.

CINESIAS: O lord! O Zeus! What tortures I endure!

LEADER OF MEN: This is the way she's treated you, that vile and cursèd wanton.

LEADER OF WOMEN: Nay, not vile and cursèd, but sweet and dear.

LEADER OF MEN: Sweet, you say? Nay, hateful, hateful!

CINESIAS: Hateful indeed! O Zeus, Zeus!

Seize her and snatch her away,
Like a handful of dust, in a mighty,
Fiery tempest! Whirl her aloft, then let her drop
Down to the earth, with a crash, as she falls—
On the point of this waiting
Thingummybob!

(He goes out. Enter a SPARTAN HERALD in an obvious state of excitement, which he is doing his best to conceal.)

HERALD: Where can I find the Senate or the Prytanes? I've got an important message.

(The Athenian MAGISTRATE enters.)

MAGISTRATE: Say there, are you a man or Priapus?

HERALD *(in annoyance)*: I'm a herald, you lout! I've come from Sparta about the truce.

MAGISTRATE: Is that a spear you've got under your cloak?

HERALD: No, of course not!

MAGISTRATE: Why do you twist and turn so? Why hold your cloak in front of you? Did you rupture yourself on the trip?

HERALD: By gum, the fellow's an old fool.

MAGISTRATE *(pointing)*: Why, you dirty rascal, you're excited.

HERALD: Not at all. Stop this tom-foolery.

MAGISTRATE: Well, what's that I see?

HERALD: A Spartan message-staff.

MAGISTRATE: Oh, certainly! That's just the kind of message-staff I've got. But tell me the honest truth: how are things going in Sparta?

HERALD: All the land of Sparta is up in arms—and our allies are up, too. We need Pellene.

MAGISTRATE: What brought this trouble on you? A sudden Panic?

HERALD: No, Lampito started it and then all the other women in Sparta with one accord chased their husbands out of their beds.

MAGISTRATE: How do you feel?

HERALD: Terrible. We walk around the city bent over like men lighting matches in a wind. For our women won't let us touch them until we all agree and make peace throughout Greece.

MAGISTRATE: This is a general conspiracy of the women; I see it now. Well, hurry back and tell the Spartans to send ambassadors here with full powers to arrange a truce. And I'll go tell the Council to choose ambassadors from here; I've got something here that will soon persuade them!

HERALD: I'll fly there; for you've made an excellent suggestion.

(The HERALD *and the* MAGISTRATE *depart on opposite sides of the stage.)*

LEADER OF MEN: No beast or fire is harder than womankind to tame,
Nor is the spotted leopard so devoid of shame.

LEADER OF WOMEN: Knowing this, you dare provoke us to attack?
I'd be your steady friend, if you'd but take us back.

LEADER OF MEN: I'll never cease my hatred keen of womankind.

LEADER OF WOMEN: Just as you will. But now just let me help you find
That cloak you threw aside. You look so silly there
Without your clothes. Here, put it on and don't go bare.

LEADER OF MEN: That's very kind, and shows you're not entirely bad.
But I threw off my things when I was good and mad.

LEADER OF WOMEN: At last you seem a man, and won't be mocked, my lad.
If you'd been nice to me, I'd take this little gnat
That's in your eye and pluck it out for you, like that.

LEADER OF MEN: So that's what bothered me and bit my eye so long!
   Please dig it out for me. I own that I've been wrong.
LEADER OF WOMEN: I'll do so, though you've been a most ill-natured
      brat.
   Ye gods! See here! A huge and monstrous little gnat!
LEADER OF MEN: Oh, how that helps! For it was digging wells in me.
   And now it's out. My tears can roll down hard and free.
LEADER OF WOMEN: Here, let me wipe them off, although you're such
      a knave,
   And kiss me.
LEADER OF MEN: No!
LEADER OF WOMEN: Whate'er you say, a kiss I'll have.

   (She kisses him.)

LEADER OF MEN: Oh, confound these women! They've a coaxing way
      about them.
   He was wise and never spoke a truer word, who said,
   "We can't live with women, but we cannot live without them."
   Now I'll make a truce with you. We'll fight no more; instead,
      I will not injure you if you do me no wrong.
   And now let's join our ranks and then begin a song.
COMBINED CHORUS *(singing)*:
      Athenians, we're not prepared,
      To say a single ugly word
      About our fellow-citizens.
   Quite the contrary: we desire but to say and to do
   Naught but good. Quite enough are the ills now on hand.

      Men and women, be advised:
         If anyone requires
      Money — minae two or three —
         We've got what he desires.

      My purse is yours, on easy terms:
         When Peace shall reappear,
      Whate'er you've borrowed will be due.
         So speak up without fear.

      You needn't pay me back, you see,
      If you can get a cent from me!

      We're about to entertain
         Some foreign gentlemen;
      We've soup and tender, fresh-killed pork.
         Come round to dine at ten.

> Come early; wash, and dress with care,
>> And bring the children, too.
> Then step right in, no "by your leave."
>> We'll be expecting you.
>
> Walk in as if you owned the place.
> You'll find the door — shut in your face!

(Enter a group of SPARTAN AMBASSADORS; *they are in the same desperate condition as the* HERALD *in the previous scene.)*

LEADER OF CHORUS: Here come the envoys from Sparta, sprouting long beards and looking for the world as if they were carrying pig-pens in front of them.

> Greetings, gentlemen of Sparta. Tell me, in what state have you come?

SPARTAN: Why waste words? You can plainly see what state we've come in!

LEADER OF CHORUS: Wow! You're in a pretty high-strung condition, and it seems to be getting worse.

SPARTAN: It's indescribable. Won't someone please arrange a peace for us — in any way you like.

LEADER OF CHORUS: Here come our own, native ambassadors, crouching like wrestlers and holding their clothes in front of them; this seems an athletic kind of malady.

(Enter several ATHENIAN AMBASSADORS.*)*

ATHENIAN: Can anyone tell us where Lysistrata is? You see our condition.

LEADER OF CHORUS: Here's another case of the same complaint. Tell me, are the attacks worse in the morning?

ATHENIAN: No, we're always afflicted this way. If someone doesn't soon arrange this truce, you'd better not let me get my hands on — Cleisthenes!

LEADER OF CHORUS: If you're smart, you'll arrange your cloaks so none of these fellows who smashed the Hermae can see you.

ATHENIAN: Right you are; a very good suggestion.

SPARTAN: Aye, by all means. Here, let's hitch up our clothes.

ATHENIAN: Greetings, Spartan. We've suffered dreadful things.

SPARTAN: My dear fellow, we'd have suffered still worse if one of those fellows had seen us in this condition.

ATHENIAN: Well, gentlemen, we must get down to business. What's your errand here?

SPARTAN: We're ambassadors about peace.

ATHENIAN: Excellent; so are we. Only Lysistrata can arrange things for us; shall we summon her?

SPARTAN: Aye, and Lysistratus too, if you like.

LEADER OF CHORUS: No need to summon her, it seems. She's coming out of her own accord.

(Enter LYSISTRATA *accompanied by a statue of a nude female figure, which represents Reconciliation.)*

Hail, noblest of women; now must thou be
A judge shrewd and subtle, mild and severe,
Be sweet yet majestic; all manners employ.
The leaders of Hellas, caught by thy love-charms,
Have come to thy judgment, their charges submitting.

LYSISTRATA: This is no difficult task, if one catch them still in amorous passion, before they've resorted to each other. But I'll soon find out. Where's Reconciliation? Go, first bring the Spartans here, and don't seize them rudely and violently, as our tactless husbands used to do, but as befits a woman, like an old, familiar friend; if they won't give you their hands, take them however you can. Then go fetch these Athenians here, taking hold of whatever they offer you. Now then, men of Sparta, stand here beside me, and you Athenians on the other side, and listen to my words.

 I am a woman, it is true, but I have a mind; I'm not badly off in native wit, and by listening to my father and my elders, I've had a decent schooling.

 Now I intend to give you a scolding which you both deserve. With one common font you worship at the same altars, just like brothers, at Olympia, at Thermopylae, at Delphi — how many more might I name, if time permitted; — and the Barbarians stand by waiting with their armies; yet you are destroying the men and towns of Greece.

ATHENIAN: Oh, this tension is killing me!

LYSISTRATA: And now, men of Sparta, — to turn to you — don't you remember how the Spartan Pericleidas came here once as a suppliant, and sitting at our altar, all pale with fear in his crimson cloak, begged us for an army? For all Messene had attacked you and the god sent an earthquake too? Then Cimon went forth with four thousand hoplites and saved all Lacedaemon. Such was the aid you received from Athens, and now you lay waste the country which once treated you so well.

ATHENIAN *(hotly)*: They're in the wrong, Lysistrata, upon my word, they are!

SPARTAN *(absently, looking at the statue of Reconciliation)*: We're in the wrong. What hips! How lovely they are!

LYSISTRATA: Don't think I'm going to let you Athenians off. Don't you remember how the Spartans came in arms when you were wearing the rough, sheepskin cloak of slaves and slew the host of Thessalians, the comrades and allies of Hippias? Fighting with you on that day, alone of all the Greeks, they set you free and instead of a sheepskin gave your folk a handsome robe to wear.

SPARTAN *(looking at* LYSISTRATA*)*: I've never seen a more distinguished woman.

ATHENIAN *(looking at Reconciliation)*: I've never seen a more voluptuous body!

LYSISTRATA: Why then, with these many noble deeds to think of, do you fight each other? Why don't you stop this villainy? Why not make peace? Tell me, what prevents it?

SPARTAN *(waving vaguely at Reconciliation)*: We're willing, if you're willing to give up your position on yonder flank.

LYSISTRATA: What position, my good man?

SPARTAN: Pylus, I've been panting for it for ever so long.

ATHENIAN: No, by God! You shan't have it!

LYSISTRATA: Let them have it, my friend.

ATHENIAN: Then what shall we have to rouse things up?

LYSISTRATA: Ask for another place in exchange.

ATHENIAN: Well, let's see: first of all *(pointing to various parts of Reconciliation's anatomy)* give us Echinus here, this Maliac Inlet in back there, and these two Megarian legs.

SPARTAN: No, by heavens! You can't have *everything,* you crazy fool!

LYSISTRATA: Let it go. Don't fight over a pair of legs.

ATHENIAN *(taking off his cloak)*: I think I'll strip and do a little planting now.

SPARTAN *(following suit)*: And I'll just do a little fertilizing, by gosh!

LYSISTRATA: Wait until the truce is concluded. Now if you've decided on this course, hold a conference and discuss the matter with your allies.

ATHENIAN: Allies? Don't be ridiculous. They're in the same state we are. Won't our allies want the same thing we do — to jump in bed with their women?

SPARTAN: Ours will, I know.

ATHENIAN: Especially the Carystians, by God!

LYSISTRATA: Very well. Now purify yourselves, that your wives may feast and entertain you in the Acropolis; we've provisions by the basketfull. Exchange your oaths and pledges there, and then each of you may take his wife and go home.

ATHENIAN: Let's go at once.

SPARTAN: Come on, where you will.

ATHENIAN: For God's sake, let's hurry!

(They all go into the Acropolis.)

CHORUS *(singing)*:
    Whate'er I have of coverlets
        And robes of varied hue
    And golden trinkets — without stint
        I offer them to you.

Take what you will and bear it home,
  Your children to delight,
Or if your girl's a Basket-maid;
  Just choose whate'er's in sight.

There's naught within so well secured
  You cannot break the seal
And bear it off; just help yourselves;
  No hesitation feel.

But you'll see nothing, though you try,
Unless you've sharper eyes than I!

If anyone needs bread to feed
  A growing family,
I've lots of wheat and full-grown loaves;
  So just apply to me.

Let every poor man who desires
  Come round and bring a sack
To fetch the grain; my slave is there
  To load it on his back.

But don't come near my door, I say:
Beware the dog, and stay away!

(An ATHENIAN *enters carrying a torch; he knocks at the gate.)*

ATHENIAN: Open the door! *(to the* CHORUS, *which is clustered around the gate)* Make way, won't you! What are you hanging around for? Want me to singe you with this torch? *(to himself)* No; it's a stale trick, I won't do it! *(to the audience)* Still if I've got to do it to please *you*, I suppose I'll have to take the trouble.

(A SECOND ATHENIAN *comes out of the gate.)*

SECOND ATHENIAN: And I'll help you.

FIRST ATHENIAN *(waving his torch at the* CHORUS): Get out! Go bawl your heads off! Move on there, so the Spartans can leave in peace when the banquet's over.

(They brandish their torches until the CHORUS *leaves the Orchestra.)*

SECOND ATHENIAN: I've never seen such a pleasant banquet: the Spartans are charming fellows, indeed they are! And we Athenians are very witty in our cups.

FIRST ATHENIAN: Naturally: for when we're sober we're never at our best. If the Athenians would listen to me, we'd always get a little tipsy

on our embassies. As things are now, we go to Sparta when we're
sober and look around to stir up trouble. And then we don't hear what
they say—and as for what they *don't* say, we have all sorts of suspicions. And then we bring back varying reports about the mission. But
this time everything is pleasant; even if a man should sing the Telamon-
song when he ought to sing "Cleitagorus," we'd praise him and swear
it was excellent.

(The two CHORUSES *return, as a* CHORUS OF ATHENIANS *and a*
CHORUS OF SPARTANS.)

Here they come back again. Go to the devil, you scoundrels!

SECOND ATHENIAN: Get out, I say! They're coming out from the feast.

(Enter the SPARTAN *and* ATHENIAN ENVOYS, *followed by*
LYSISTRATA *and all the* WOMEN.)

SPARTAN *(to one of his fellow-envoys)*: My good fellow, take up your pipes;
I want to do a fancy two-step and sing a jolly song for the Athenians.

ATHENIAN: Yes, do take your pipes, by all means. I'd love to see you
dance.

SPARTAN *(singing and dancing with the* CHORUS OF SPARTANS):
These youths inspire
To song and dance, O Memory;
Stir up my Muse, to tell how we
And Athens' men, in our galleys clashing
At Artemisium, 'gainst foemen dashing in godlike ire,
Conquered the Persian and set Greece free.

Leonidas
Led on his valiant warriors
Whetting their teeth like angry boars.
Abundant foam on their lips was flow'ring,
A stream of sweat from their limbs was show'ring.
The Persian was
Numberless as the sand on the shores.

O Huntress who slayest the beasts in the glade,
O Virgin divine, hither come to our truce,
Unite us in bonds which all time will not loose.
Grant us to find in this treaty, we pray,
An unfailing source of true friendship today,
And all of our days, helping us to refrain
From weaseling tricks which bring war in their train.
Then hither, come hither! O huntress maid.

LYSISTRATA: Come then, since all is fairly done, men of Sparta, lead
away your wives, and you, Athenians, take yours. Let every man stand

beside his wife, and every wife beside her man, and then, to celebrate our fortune, let's dance. And in the future, let's take care to avoid these misunderstandings.

CHORUS OF ATHENIANS *(singing and dancing):*
Lead on the dances, your graces revealing.
Call Artemis hither, call Artemis' twin,
Leader of dances, Apollo the Healing,°
Kindly God—hither! Let's summon him in!
   Nysian Bacchus call,
Who with his Maenads, his eyes flashing fire,
   Dances, and last of all
Zeus of the thunderbolt flaming, the Sire,
   And Hera° in majesty,
   Queen of prosperity.
   Come, ye Powers who dwell above
   Unforgetting, our witnesses be
Of Peace with bonds of harmonious love—
The Peace which Cypris has wrought for me.
   Alleluia! Io Paean!
   Leap in joy—hurrah! hurrah!
   'Tis victory—hurrah! hurrah!
   Euoi! Euoi! Euai! Euai!

LYSISTRATA *(to the* SPARTANS*):*   Come now, sing a new song to cap ours.

CHORUS OF SPARTANS *(singing and dancing):*
Leaving Taygetus fair and renown'd
Muse of Laconia, hither come:
Amyclae's god in hymns resound.
Athene of the Brazen Home,
And Castor and Pollux, Tyndareus' sons,
Who sport where Eurotas murmuring runs.

   On with the dance! Heia! Ho!
     All leaping along,
   Mantles a-swinging as we go!
     Of Sparta our song.
There the holy chorus ever gladdens,
There the beat of stamping feet,
As our winsome fillies, lovely maidens,
Dance, beside Eurotas, banks a–skipping, —
Nimbly go to and fro
Hast'ning, leaping feet in measures tripping,

Apollo: The god of music, poetry, and prophecy; he exemplifies manly youth and beauty.
Hera: Queen of the gods; goddess of women and marriage.

Like the Bacchae's revels, hair a–streaming.
Leda's child, divine and mild,
Leads the holy dance, her fair face beaming.
    On with the dance! as your hand
      Presses the hair
    Streaming away unconfined.
      Leap in the air
    Light as the deer; footsteps resound
      Aiding our dance, beating the ground.
Praise Athene, Maid divine, unrivalled in her might,
Dweller in the Brazen Home, unconquered in the fight.

(All go out singing and dancing.)

Considerations

1. Identify and discuss the sources of humor in *Lysistrata*. Can any parts of the play be taken seriously? Explain.
2. Contrast the Chorus of Men with the Chorus of Women (include the Leader of Men and Leader of Women). What opposing attitudes and views do they suggest?
3. In what ways — and to what effect — does the play make fun of women as well as of men?
4. At the time that *Lysistrata* was written and performed (411 B.C.), Athenian audiences would have agreed that women should remain in the home, well away from the spheres of war or politics. Given those values, how can you account for the popularity of the play (which was presented many times — an unusual occurrence in ancient Greece)?
5. What comments does the play make on war? To what extent do you find those comments relevant today?

DONALD HALL (1928–   )

Purpose, Blame, and Fire
An eight-year-old's introduction to war horror

My father was too young for the Great War, not fifteen when it ended, and both of my grandfathers were too old. Their fathers fought in the Civil War — archaic blue figures, stiff-bearded in photographs — but in 1937, when I was eight, Gettysburg might have been Agincourt or Marathon. As a second world war came closer, I understood that my father felt guilty about missing the Great War; but I understood that he wanted to miss the new one as well.

Everyone was nervous, the Depression hanging on and war approaching. I was an only child, alert to my parents' anxiety. My mother was thin and attentive. She had come to Connecticut from a remote farm in New Hampshire, and as I grew up I became aware that she felt lonely in the suburbs; she paid more attention to her child, in her displacement, than she would have done if she had stayed up north with her sisters.

Sometimes she took me on excursions to New Haven — Saturdays during the school year, weekdays in summer. We walked up Ardmore Street to Whitney Avenue and waited for the bus that came every ten minutes to roll us four miles down Whitney and drop us at Church and Chapel outside Liggett's across from the New Haven Green. While I tagged along, she shopped at Shartenberg's and Malley's. When we had done shopping, we ate lunch at a place where I ordered franks and beans — two grilled hot dogs and a tiny crock of pea beans dark with molasses; dessert was Jell-O with real whipped cream or dry yellow cake with white frosting. Lunch cost thirty-nine cents.

Then we went to the movies. At the theater we would see a first-run film, a B-movie, one or two shorts, previews of coming attractions, and a newsreel. In the year 1937 I am almost sure that I watched Spencer Tracy in *Captains Courageous;* maybe Paul Muni in *The Life of Emile Zola,* probably *Lost Horizon* and *A Star Is Born.* But the only movie I remember seeing for certain, some fifty-four years later, is *The Last Train From Madrid.* After we took the bus home to Ardmore Street, I burned my collection of war cards and put away my toy soldiers forever.

In 1937 we boys wore long woolen stockings pulled up over the bottoms of corduroy knickers as we walked to Spring Glen Grammar School. There were no school buses. Children from my neighborhood took several different routes to school — for variety or to avoid a bully — but always passed the Glendower Drug Store, only two short blocks from the school.

If we had change in our pockets, we spent it there. For a nickel, we bought big candy bars or flat pieces of gum creased into five sticks and pink as a dog's tongue. With the gum came cards that illustrated our different

5

obsessions: Of course there were baseball cards, and I seem to recall cards for football as well; I remember G-man cards, each of which illustrated a triumph of law and order such as J. Edgar Hoover's agents flushing out Dillinger — shooting him in the lobby of a movie theater — or Pretty Boy Floyd. Although G-man cards were violent, they might have been the Society of Friends alongside another series that we bought and collected. We called them war cards, and they thrived in the bellicose air of 1937.

It was a time when the war in Spain shrieked from the front pages of newspapers, along with the Japanese invasion of China. In 1937 Stalin kept discovering to his astonishment that old colleagues had betrayed him; he shot seven of his best generals that year, doubtless a great advantage when Hitler invaded. In 1937 Trotsky found his way to Mexico, the UAW invented the sit-down strike, Neville Chamberlain asked Hitler for his cooperation in the interest of peace, the *Hindenburg* exploded and burned in New Jersey, and thousands of American progressives joined the Lincoln Brigade to fight fascism in Spain.

Even in the fourth grade we knew about Hitler, whose troops and planes fought alongside Franco against the Loyalists, who were aided by Stalin's troops and planes. Germany was again the enemy, less than twenty years after the Armistice of 1918. We were good, brave, loyal, outnumbered, and victorious against all odds; they were evil, cruel, cowardly, vicious, dumb, shrewd, and doomed. We knew who was right and who was wrong. (My father's mother's family had emigrated from Germany to New Haven in the 1880s, which was confusing.) In 1937 all of us — parents, teachers, children — understood that there would be another war and that America would join this war sooner than it had the Great War. Isolationists and pacifists campaigned against the war, but everyone knew that war was inevitable — whether it was or wasn't. A phenomenon like war cards makes it now seem as if we were being prepared, as if the adults were making sure that we grew up expecting to become soldiers, accepting the guns and the bombing and the death.

At least no one — so soon after the Great War — had the temerity to present war as a Cub Scout expedition. When we went to the movies, we saw a newsreel and sometimes even *The March of Time.* The late 1930s were endless parades in black and white, soldiers marching, weapons rolling past reviewing stands. I remember the bombing and strafing of refugees. I remember Hitler addressing rallies.

War cards used a lot of red ink. On the back of each card a short text [10] described a notorious incident, and on the front an artist illustrated what had happened. I remember one card that showed a Japanese bomb hitting a crowded Chinese bus, maybe in Shanghai: Bodies being torn apart hurtled through the air, intestines stretched and tangled, headless bodies littering the ground. I don't believe these cards were particularly ideological; as I recollect, the cards claimed to be educational, illustrating the Horrors of War. Blood was the whole matter.

We cherished our war cards, chewing gum as we walked home to add a new one to our collections: Blood of war was the food on which we nurtured our boyish death-love. If you got a duplicate you could swap, maybe the exploded bus for a card that showed the shelling of a boat. We collected war cards as we collected ourselves for war.

Surely, at eight, my imagination was filled by war. I loved airplanes and read pulp stories about dogfights over the trenches. I loved the pilot heroes of the era — Wiley Post, Amelia Earhart, later Wrong-Way Corrigan. When I imagined myself going to war it was to join the Lafayette Escadrille, fly Spads, and shoot down Fokker triplanes.

Then I saw *The Last Train From Madrid*. Did it really change my life? As I commit it to paper, the phrase sounds exaggerated, melodramatic. I never registered as a C.O.° (Nor did I serve in the military.) Although I worked in Ann Arbor with the movement against the Vietnam War, I was never a leader. Neither did I spell the country Amerika. It was war horror that filled my chest, not political commitment: A horror is not an idea, as a shudder is not a conviction. Certain horrors of war retain the power to burst me into tears, especially the random slaughter of civilians. And my first experience of such horrors, I now believe, must have occurred on the day in 1937 when I saw *The Last Train From Madrid*.

In September of 1990 — as another war approached — I saw *The Last Train From Madrid* again. Over the years I had thought of the film often and assumed that it was antifascist, popular front. It is no such thing; the film is astonishingly without political ideology. The plot is derivative, built of romantic clichés and stereotypes, and is impossible to take seriously: a *Grand Hotel* on wheels. The writing is ghastly, from clumsy exposition to flat dialogue. Its single import is the randomness of war horror.

The film opens with the hurtling image of a locomotive and train. A radio newscast tells us that tonight the last train will leave Madrid, after which — we understand — the city will be overrun by the nameless army that is besieging it. The army lacks not only name but idea, and its only purpose is death. As characters speak of the train's terminus in Valencia, Valencia becomes pure symbol: The destination is Arcadian peace in a countryside antithetical to the city's panic, chaos, and violent death. Naturally, everyone wants a seat on the train. The plot of the movie turns on separate and intermingled stories of people seeking passage on the train — their stratagems, their failures and successes. At the end of the movie the train steams out of Madrid carrying some of the people we've been introduced to and leaving others behind — not only behind but dead.

A noble young officer (noble because he is handsome and stands straight; noble because he is Anthony Quinn) listens at the film's beginning

15

C.O.: Conscientious objector, a person who refuses military service because of moral principles.

to impassioned pleas for passes, and in his dutiful nobility refuses them. We dwell on an old lady, well played, who begs for a pass and is refused. Most of our central figures are in couples, two by two like the ark's animals: the romantic interest, which I doubtless ignored in 1937 and found myself ignoring last fall. Love between two men (Anthony Quinn and Gilbert Roland) who swore blood brotherhood as soldiers in Africa years before is standard *Beau Geste* stuff, but it does provide the strongest human bond in the film—stronger for sure than the bonds each seeks to establish with Dorothy Lamour.

In one of the subplots a slaphappy American journalist (Lew Ayres) picks up a girl (Olympe Bradna) who wants to get to Madrid to see her father before the firing squad kills him. (Naturally, they fall in love; later, this pair makes it onto the Valencia-bound train.) She sees her father, he is shot—and we never receive an inkling, not a *notion,* of what he did or stood for that led to his cold-blooded execution. The killing feels wholly arbitrary: No motive is supplied or suggested. In this film's eerie political emptiness, execution by firing squad is not a political act (and thus in some way purposeful) but routine, everyday—like sunrise and sunset.

One soldier on the firing squad (Robert Cummings) is tender-hearted and will not fire his gun. For his sensitivity he will be sent to the front. He runs away—and runs into an unbelievable love. We see two people parting, a man and a woman whom we do not know. We understand that they have just made love, and that she is a prostitute. They seem fond of each other, happy, making plans for their next encounter. As the man walks into the street, we suddenly spy his shape down the sight of a rifle—a sniper's rifle. The sniper shoots him dead. Although we may assume that the sniper waited for this particular man, the film provides not one detail to support this assumption. We know nothing of this man or his killer or any motive; we know nothing about the shooting except the brute fact. Like the earlier execution by firing squad, this street killing—idyll destroyed by bullet—presents itself as wholly arbitrary.

It is this young prostitute (Helen Mack) with whom Cummings falls in love—and she with him—immediately. After Mack and Cummings drag her dead lover's body into her flat, they talk; Cummings wants the dead man's pass for the last train. Soon enough, they scheme a double escape. During their brief courtship, the couple construct of their lovers' talk the Arcadian Valencia to which the train will deliver them. Cummings eventually makes it to the train, but alone. Mack dies on the way—again arbitrarily.

By today's standards, of course, there are actually few deaths in *The Last Train From Madrid.* Channel-surfing the television—happening, say, upon a Chuck Norris movie—you will see more carnage before you can switch channels than you'll observe in eighty-five minutes of this old film. But the deaths I witnessed in 1937 stuck with me, as those I see in movies today for the most part do not. One in particular: Near the film's end, before the train leaves the station, guards move through the cars rechecking passes. As they demand papers from everyone, our anxiety mounts because they are approaching a vulnerable protagonist. Suddenly, looking at one man's pass — a stranger to us — the guards ask him to step outside. He looks nervous; he tries to run — and they shoot him down. They kill him *on purpose,* aiming their guns, yet they kill him *for no reason* that we will ever understand.

Murderous paradox drives the film: Malignity exists everywhere, yet most of the time it appears motiveless. To an eight-year-old in New Haven, the particular individuals shot and killed in the film suffered deaths as arbitrary as if they had been killed by bombs from the sky. An air raid takes place at the center of the film, a riot of civilian panic, people running and frightened. The sound track plays fear music, camera shots are jumpy and angular, and in one quick shot nervous pigeons scurry.

In Robert Frost's "Design" he writes about the malign coincidence of an invisible spider haply arranged to kill a fly; the poet asks what could have caused this coming-together except for "design of darkness to appall." Then he qualifies the question in a further line: "If design govern in a thing so small." In *The Last Train From Madrid* we are surrounded by fear of imminent death, but, horribly, we lack design. As humans, we wish or perhaps even need to understand the cause or to place blame — on an enemy, on politicians who betrayed us, on the cupidity or moral squalor of a person or a class of people — because blame implies purpose, and purpose, meaning. *The Last Train From Madrid* suggests that design may not govern in a thing so small as human life and death.

Printed words at the very start of the film scroll its neutrality: This movie will not uphold or defend either side of the war. When we read of battles in old histories we study the motives of each side, although the cause may mean little to us: We want to make sense. We may not keep with us the ideas behind a conflict — what we tend to remember are stories of heroism, cowardice, and suffering; "The river ran red with blood for seven days," we remember, not "Thus Centerville retained its access to the sea." Yet we make the effort to understand the history and politics, if only to satisfy ourselves that there appeared to be reasons for the blood: a design. By eschewing history and politics, *The Last Train From Madrid* leeches war of its particular temporal context, providing an eight-year-old with his first glimpse of war as eternal anonymous suffering. The film scrolls war's utter panic and sorrow. Oh, sorrow, sorrow, sorrow — the ripe life cut by hate without purpose, by anger lacking reason, by murder without blame.

How did my mother happen to take an eight-year-old to such a movie? Microfilm of the *New Haven Register* explains. The newspaper printed paragraphs of studio puffery that wholly misrepresented the film: "With but two pictures to her credit, both of which were outstanding successes, Dorothy

Lamour, the glamorous brunette, one of the season's most sensational 'finds,' moves into the ranks of the screen's charming leading ladies. The event takes place in 'The Last Train from Madrid,' the romance laid in war-torn Spain." I find it breathtaking to read this notice of the film that horrified me. "In this story Miss Lamour appears as a beautiful patrician girl, who is the beloved of a young lieutenant in the government forces and his best friend." When I read Frank S. Nugent's *New York Times* review (6/19/37), I am almost as astonished. He notes the lack of politics in this "glib little fiction," but for Nugent also there was no horror. "True, it treats of the Spanish revolution, but merely as Hollywood has, in the past, regarded the melo-dramatic turmoils of Ruritania and Zenda." He calls the film "a pre-tested melodrama which should suit the average palate," and in his conclusion makes a joke: "Its sympathies, neither Loyalist nor Rebel, are clearly on the side of the Ruritanians."

Frank S. Nugent was not eight years old. Was Nugent's cynicism more   25
appropriate than my horror? At eight, I ignored the silly romance at the film's center and registered only the panic of unmotivated murder. When I returned home after the Saturday matinee, I packed my lead toy soldiers with their flattish Great War helmets into a shoebox and tucked it deep in the long closet of my bedroom. I performed the ritual with so much sol-emnity that I might have played taps for background music. By this time I felt not panic but a sadness that would not relent, which may have derived from another melancholy that absorbed me that weekend. The film opened in New Haven on Saturday, July 10, 1937, while Amelia Earhart was missing over the Pacific. I remember playing outside the house, keeping the window open and a radio near the window; I remember a report that the Navy had spotted her plane on an atoll; I remember the correction of the report. In my mind's eye, Amelia Earhart circled continually, high in the air, the hum of the Lockheed's engine distant and plaintive, gas almost gone, the pilot in her leather helmet peering for land as she circled . . .

A day or two later, alone in the house, I carried my war cards down to the coal furnace in the cellar. I was not allowed to open the furnace door, but I opened it anyway and threw the cards onto the red coals. At first they smoldered and turned brown, and I feared that they would not burn — would give me away when my father came home and stoked the furnace. Then one card burst into bright yellow flame, then another, then all together flared briefly in the shadow-and-red hellfire of the furnace on Ardmore Street.

Considerations

1. Hall describes watching a movie that profoundly affected him. If you have had a similar experience, describe both the time and the place where you saw the movie. Then explain your response to the movie. How did it change the way you thought or acted?

2. Compare the responses (in schools, at home, on the playground) to World War II Hall describes to the responses you remember observing or experiencing during the 1991 war with Iraq. Do the differences or the similarities seem more striking? Explain.

3. Hall says, "A phenomenon like war cards makes it now seem as if we were being prepared, as if the adults were making sure that we grew up expecting to become soldiers, accepting the guns and the bombing and the death." What is your response to this statement? To what extent do you believe that the purpose (or effect) of war toys is to prepare the new generation to fight wars?

4. Read Hall's evaluation of *Last Train From Madrid*. Describe the roles played by male characters and the roles played by female characters. Which male characters seem admirable? Which female characters seem admirable? Explain your response. Would you expect similar roles to be played by men and women living under similar circumstances today? Explain.

5. Read Robert Frost's "Design" (page 1146). Then read Hall's reference to this poem (paragraph 22). Explain connections you see between Frost's poem and Hall's response to *Last Train From Madrid*.

ERNEST HEMINGWAY (1899–1961)

A New Kind of War

Madrid. — The window of the hotel is open and, as you lie in bed, you hear the firing in the front line seventeen blocks away. There is a rifle fire all night long. The rifles go tacrong, capong, craang, tacrong, and then a machine gun opens up. It has a bigger calibre and is much louder, rong, cararong, rong, rong. Then there is the incoming boom of a trench mortar shell and a burst of machine gun fire. You lie and listen to it and it is a great thing to be in bed with your feet stretched out gradually warming the cold foot of the bed and not out there in University City or Carabanchel. A man is singing hard-voiced in the street below and three drunks are arguing when you fall asleep.

In the morning, before your call comes from the desk, the roaring burst of a high explosive shell wakes you and you go to the window and look out to see a man, his head down, his coat collar up, sprinting desperately across the paved square. There is the acrid smell of high explosive you hoped you'd never smell again, and, in a bathrobe and bedroom slippers, you hurry down the marble stairs and almost into a middle-aged woman, wounded in the abdomen, who is being helped into the hotel entrance by two men in blue workmen's smocks. She has her two hands crossed below her big, old-style Spanish bosom and from between her fingers the blood is spurting in a thin stream. On the corner, twenty yards away, is a heap of rubble, smashed cement and thrown up dirt, a single dead man, his torn clothes dusty, and a great hole in the sidewalk from which the gas from a broken main is rising, looking like a heat mirage in the cold morning air.

"How many dead?" you ask a policeman.

"Only one," he says. "It went through the sidewalk and burst below. If it would have burst on the solid stone of the road there might have been fifty."

A policeman covers the top of the trunk, from which the head is   5
missing; they send for someone to repair the gas main and you go in to breakfast. A charwoman, her eyes red, is scrubbing the blood off the marble floor of the corridor. The dead man wasn't you nor anyone you know and everyone is very hungry in the morning after a cold night and a long day the day before up at the Guadalajara front.

"Did you see him?" asked someone else at breakfast.

"Sure," you say.

"That's where we pass a dozen times a day. Right on that corner." Someone makes a joke about missing teeth and someone else says not to make that joke. And everyone has the feeling that characterizes war. It wasn't me, see? It wasn't me.

The Italian dead up on the Guadalajara front weren't you, although Italian dead, because of where you had spent your boyhood, always seemed, still, like our dead. No. You went to the front early in the morning in a miserable little car with a more miserable little chauffeur who suffered visibly the closer he came to the fighting. But at night, sometimes late, without lights, with the big trucks roaring past, you came on back to sleep in a bed with sheets in a good hotel, paying a dollar a day for the best rooms on the front. The smaller rooms in the back, on the side away from the shelling, were considerably more expensive. After the shell that lit on the sidewalk in front of the hotel you got a beautiful double corner room on that side, twice the size of the one you had had, for less than a dollar. It wasn't me they killed. See? No. Not me. It wasn't me anymore.

Then, in a hospital given by the American Friends of Spanish Democracy, located out behind the Morata front along the road to Valencia, they said, "Raven wants to see you."   10

"Do I know him?"

"I don't think so," they said, "but he wants to see you."

"Where is he?"

"Upstairs."

In the room upstairs they are giving a blood transfusion to a man with   15
a very gray face who lay on a cot with his arm out, looking away from the gurgling bottle and moaning in a very impersonal way. He moaned mechanically and at regular intervals and it did not seem to be him that made the sound. His lips did not move.

"Where's Raven?" I asked.

"I'm here," said Raven.

The voice came from a high mound covered by a shoddy gray blanket. There were two arms crossed on the top of the mound and at one end there was something that had been a face, but now was a yellow scabby area with a wide bandage cross where the eyes had been.

"Who is it?" asked Raven. He didn't have lips, but he talked pretty well without them and with a pleasant voice.

"Hemingway," I said. "I came up to see how you were doing."   20

"My face was pretty bad," he said. "It got sort of burned from the grenade, but it's peeled a couple of times and it's doing better."

"It looks swell," I said. "It's doing fine."

I wasn't looking at it when I spoke.

"How are things in America?" he asked. "What do they think of us over there?"

"Sentiment's changed a lot," I said. "They're beginning to realize the   25
government is going to win this war."

"Do you think so?"

"Sure," I said.

"I'm awfully glad," he said. "You know, I wouldn't mind any of this if I could just watch what was going on. I don't mind the pain, you know. It never seemed important really. But I was always awfully interested in things and I really wouldn't mind the pain at all if I could just sort of follow things intelligently. I could even be some use. You know, I didn't mind the war at all. I did all right in the war. I got hit once before and I was back and rejoined the battalion in two weeks. I couldn't stand to be away. Then I got this."

He had put his hand in mine. It was not a worker's hand. There were no callouses and the nails on the long, spatulate fingers were smooth and rounded.

"How did you get it?" I asked.   30

"Well, there were some troops that were routed and we went over to sort of reform them and we did and then we had quite a fight with the fascists and we beat them. It was quite a bad fight, you know, but we beat them and then someone threw this grenade at me."

Holding his hand and hearing him tell it, I did not believe a word of it. What was left of him did not sound like the wreckage of a soldier somehow. I did not know how he had been wounded, but the story did not sound right. It was the sort of way everyone would like to have been wounded. But I wanted him to think I believed it.

"Where did you come from?" I asked.

"From Pittsburgh. I went to the University there."

"What did you do before you joined up here?"   35

"I was a social worker," he said. Then I knew it couldn't be true and I wondered how he had really been so frightfully wounded and I didn't care. In the war that I had known, men often lied about the manner of their wounding. Not at first; but later. I'd lied a little myself in my time. Especially late in the evening. But I was glad he thought I believed it, and we talked about books, he wanted to be a writer, and I told him about what happened north of Guadalajara and promised to bring some things from Madrid next time we got out that way. I hoped maybe I could get a radio.

"They tell me Dos Passos and Sinclair Lewis are coming over, too," he said.

"Yes," I said. "And when they come I'll bring them up to see you."

"Gee, that will be great," he said. "You don't know what that will mean to me."

"I'll bring them," I said.   40

"Will they be here pretty soon?"

"Just as soon as they come I'll bring them."

"Good boy, Ernest," he said. "You don't mind if I call you Ernest, do you?"

The voice came very clear and gentle from that face that looked like some hill that had been fought over in muddy weather and then baked in the sun.

"Hell, no," I said. "Please. Listen, old-timer, you're going to be fine.   45
You'll be a lot of good, you know. You can talk on the radio."

"Maybe," he said. "You'll be back?"

"Sure," I said. "Absolutely."

"Goodbye, Ernest," he said.

"Goodbye," I told him.

Downstairs they told me he'd lost both eyes as well as his face and was   50
also badly wounded all through the legs and in the feet.

"He's lost some toes, too," the doctor said, "but he doesn't know
that."

"I wonder if he'll ever know it."

"Oh, sure he will," the doctor said. "He's going to get well."

And it still isn't you that gets hit but it is your countryman now. Your
countryman from Pennsylvania, where once we fought at Gettysburg.

Then, walking along the road, with his left arm in an airplane splint,   55
walking with the gamecock walk of the professional British soldier that
neither ten years of militant party work nor the projecting metal wings of
the splint could destroy, I met Raven's commanding officer, Jock Cunningham, who had three fresh rifle wounds through his upper left arm (I
looked at them, one was septic) and another rifle bullet under his shoulder
blade that had entered his left chest, passed through, and lodged there. He
told me, in military terms, the history of the attempt to rally retiring troops
on his battalion's right flank, of his bombing raid down a trench which was
held at one end by the fascists and at the other end by the government
troops, of the taking of this trench and, with six men and a Lewis gun,
cutting off a group of some eighty fascists from their own lines, and of the
final desperate defense of their impossible position his six men put up until
the government troops came up and, attacking, straightened out the line
again. He told it clearly, completely convincingly, and with a strong Glas-
gow accent. He had deep, piercing eyes sheltered like an eagle's, and, hearing
him talk, you could tell the sort of soldier he was. For what he had done he
would have had a V.C. in the last war. In this war there are no decorations.
Wounds are the only decorations and they do not award wound stripes.

"Raven was in the same show," he said. "I didn't know he'd been hit.
Ay, he's a good mon. He got his after I got mine. The fascists we'd cut off
were very good troops. They never fired a useless shot when we were in
that bad spot. They waited in the dark there until they had us located and
then opened with volley fire. That's how I got four in the same place."

We talked for a while and he told me many things. They were all
important, but nothing was as important as what Jay Raven, the social
worker from Pittsburgh with no military training, had told me was true.
This is a strange new kind of war where you learn just as much as you are
able to believe.

Considerations

1. This essay, published in April 1937, describes Hemingway's work as a
   correspondent during the Spanish Civil War. From the details provided,
   what impressions do you get of this war? Why does Hemingway call it
   "a new kind of war"?

2. Hemingway writes the first part of the essay using second person ("you," as in "You lie and listen to it and it is a great thing to be in bed . . . "). Then he switches, mid-essay, to first person ("I" or "me," as in "It wasn't me they killed.") What is the effect of this switch? How would the essay be different if Hemingway had chosen to use either first or second person throughout?

3. The essay relies heavily on dialogue, especially in the hospital scenes with Jay Raven. What do you learn about Raven from the dialogue? About Hemingway?

4. Why do you think Hemingway was skeptical about Raven's story when he first heard it? How does Jock Cunningham's description of the same incident relate to Raven's explanation?

5. From reading this essay, what conjectures can you make about Hemingway's attitude toward this war? Cite specific details on which you base your evaluation.

CONNECTIONS: WAR

1. Considering any of the following works, discuss the implications of the way women's and men's roles in war have traditionally been defined: "The Things They Carried," *Lysistrata,* "The Man He Killed," "Patterns," "Mother and Poet," and "Purpose, Blame, and Fire."

2. "The War Prayer," "Guests of the Nation," and "The Man He Killed" suggest that defining the "enemy" isn't always easy. Discuss your response to the implications of these works.

3. Discuss the contrasting views of young and old, of those who go and those who wait, as suggested by "The Fly," "Dulce et Decorum Est," "Mother and Poet," "Purpose, Blame, and Fire," and "A New Kind of War."

4. Consider the concepts of loyalty and duty as suggested by "Guests of the Nation," "The Things They Carried," "The Conscientious Objector," and "Purpose, Blame, and Fire."

5. Choose any three works in this section and compare or contrast your responses to these works with your responses to any war (or armed conflict) you have lived through (either as a participant or as an observer at home).

Learning and Teaching

JAMES ALAN McPHERSON (1943–   )
Why I Like Country Music

No one will believe that I like country music. Even my wife scoffs when told such a possibility exists. "Go on!" Gloria tells me. "I can see blues, bebop, maybe even a little buckdancing. But not bluegrass." Gloria says, "Hillbilly stuff is not just music. It's like the New York Stock Exchange. The minute you see a sharp rise in it, you better watch out."

I tend to argue the point, but quietly, and mostly to myself. Gloria was born and raised in New York; she has come to believe in the stock exchange as the only index of economic health. My perceptions were shaped in South Carolina; and long ago I learned there, as a waiter in private clubs, to gauge economic flux by the tips people gave. We tend to disagree on other matters too, but the thing that gives me most frustration is trying to make her understand why I like country music. Perhaps it is because she hates the South and has capitulated emotionally to the horror stories told by refugees from down home. Perhaps it is because Gloria is third generation Northern-born. I do not know. What I do know is that, while the two of us are black, the distance between us is sometimes as great as that between Ibo and Yoruba.° And I do know that, despite her protestations, I like country music.

"You are crazy," Gloria tells me.

I tend to argue the point, but quietly, and mostly to myself.

Of course I do not like all country stuff; just pieces that make the right   5
connections. I like banjo because sometimes I hear ancestors in the strumming. I like the fiddlelike refrain in "Dixie" for the very same reason. But most of all I like square dancing—the interplay between fiddle and caller, the stomping, the swishing of dresses, the strutting, the proud turnings, the laughter. Most of all I like the laughter. In recent months I have wondered why I like this music and this dance. I have drawn no general conclusions, but from time to time I suspect it is because the square dance is the only dance form I ever mastered.

"I wouldn't say that in public," Gloria warns me.

I agree with her, but still affirm the truth of it, although quietly, and mostly to myself.

Dear Gloria: This is the truth of how it was:

In my youth in that distant country, while others learned to strut, I grew stiff as a winter cornstalk. When my playmates harmonized their rhythms, I stood on the sidelines in atonic detachment. While they shimmied, I merely jerked in lackluster imitation. I relate these facts here, not in remorse or self-castigation, but as a true confession of my circumstances. In those days, down in our small corner of South Carolina, proficiency in dance was a form of storytelling. A boy could say, "I traveled here and there,

---

Ibo and Yoruba: Two distinct African cultures.

saw this and fought that, conquered him and made love to her, lied to them, told a few others the truth, just so I could come back here and let you know what things out there are really like." He could communicate all this with smooth, graceful jiggles of his round bottom, synchronized with intricately coordinated sweeps of his arms and small, unexcited movements of his legs. Little girls could communicate much more.

But sadly, I could do none of it. Development of these skills depended   10
on the ministrations of family and neighbors. My family did not dance; our closest neighbor was a true-believing Seventh Day Adventist. Moreover, most new dances came from up North, brought to town usually by people returning to riff on the good life said to exist in those far Northern places. They prowled our dirt streets in rented Cadillacs; paraded our brick side-walks exhibiting styles abstracted from the fullness of life in Harlem, South Philadelphia, Roxbury, Baltimore and the South Side of Chicago. They confronted our provincial clothes merchants with the arrogant reminder, "But people ain't wearin' this in New Yo*kkk!*" Each of their movements, as well as their world-weary smoothness, told us locals meaningful tales of what was missing in our lives. Unfortunately, those of us under strict paren-tal supervision, or those of us without Northern connections, could only stand at a distance and worship these envoys of culture. We stood on the sidelines — styleless, gestureless, danceless, doing nothing more than an im-provised one-butt shuffle — hoping for one of them to touch our lives. It was my good fortune, during my tenth year on the sidelines, to have one of these Northerners introduce me to the square dance.

My dear, dear Gloria, her name was Gweneth Lawson:

She was a pretty, chocolate brown little girl with dark brown eyes and two long black braids. After all these years, the image of these two braids evokes in me all there is to remember about Gweneth Lawson. They were plaited across the top of her head and hung to a point just above the back of her Peter Pan collar. Sometimes she wore two bows, one red and one blue, and these tended to sway lazily near the place on her neck where the smooth brown of her skin and the white of her collar met the ink-bottle black of her hair. Even when I cannot remember her face, I remember the rainbow of deep, rich colors in which she lived. This is so because I watched them, every weekday, from my desk directly behind her in our fourth-grade class. And she wore the most magical perfume, or lotion, smelling just slightly of fresh-cut lemons, that wafted back to me whenever she made the slightest movement at her desk. Now I must tell you this much more, dear Gloria: whenever I smell fresh lemons, whether in the market or at home, I look around me — not for Gweneth Lawson, but for some quiet corner where I can revive in private certain memories of her. And in pursuing these mem-ories across such lemony bridges, I rediscover that I loved her.

Gweneth was from the South Carolina section of Brooklyn. Her par-ents had sent her south to live with her uncle, Mr. Richard Lawson, the brick mason, for an unspecified period of time. Just why they did this I do not know, unless it was their plan to have her absorb more of South Carolina folkways than conditions in Brooklyn would allow. She was a gentle, soft-spoken girl; I recall no condescension in her manner. This was all the more admirable because our unrestrained awe of a Northern-born black person usually induced in him some grand sense of his own importance. You must know that in those days older folks would point to someone and say, "He's from the North," and the statement would be sufficient in itself. Mothers made their children behave by advising that, if they led exemplary lives and attended church regularly, when they died they would go to New York. Only someone who understands what London meant to Dick Whittington,° or how California and the suburbs function in the national mind, could appreciate the mythical dimensions of this Northlore.

But Gweneth Lawson was above regional idealization. Though I might haved loved her partly because she was a Northerner, I loved her more because of the world of colors that seemed to be suspended about her head. I loved her glowing forehead and I loved her bright, dark brown eyes; I loved the black braids, the red and blue and sometimes yellow and pink ribbons; I loved the way the deep, rich brown of her neck melted into the pink or white cloth of her Peter Pan collar; I loved the lemony vapor on which she floated and from which, on occasion, she seemed to be inviting me to be buoyed up, up, up into her happy world; I loved the way she caused my heart to tumble whenever, during a restless moment, she seemed about to turn her head in my direction; I loved her more, though torturously, on the many occasions when she did not turn. Because I was a shy boy, I loved the way I could love her silently, at least six hours a day, without ever having to disclose my love.

My platonic state of mind might have stretched onward into a bliss- 15 ful infinity had not Mrs. Esther Clay Boswell, our teacher, made it her business to pry into the affair. Although she prided herself on being a strict disciplinarian, Mrs. Boswell was not without a sense of humor. A round, full-breasted woman in her early forties, she liked to amuse herself, and sometimes the class as well, by calling the attention of all eyes to whomever of us violated the structure she imposed on classroom activities. She was particularly hard on people like me who could not contain an impulse to daydream, or those who allowed their eyes to wander too far away from lessons printed on the blackboard. A black and white sign posted under the electric clock next to the door summed up her attitude toward this kind of truancy: NOTICE TO ALL CLOCKWATCHERS, it read, TIME PASSES. WILL YOU? Nor did she abide timidity in her students. Her voice booming, "Speak up, boy!" was more than enough to cause the more emotional among us, including me, to break into convenient flows of warm tears. But by

Dick Whittington: (1358?–1423) Born into poverty, Whittington became a wealthy merchant and later was three times elected to the office of Lord Mayor of London. A popular legend of the time claimed that, as a boy, Whittington had heard his future political success proclaimed in the ringing of church bells.

doing this we violated yet another rule, one on which depended our very survival in Mrs. Esther Clay Boswell's class. She would spell out this rule for us as she paced before her desk, slapping a thick, homemade ruler against the flat of her brown palm. "There ain't no *babies* in here," she would recite. *Thaap!* "Anybody thinks he's still a *baby* . . . " *Thaap!* ". . . should crawl back home to his mama's *titty.*" *Thaap!* "You little bunnies shed your *last water . . .* " *Thaap!* ". . . the minute you left home to come in here." *Thaap!* "From now on, you g'on do all your *cryin'* . . . " *Thaap!* ". . . in *church!*" *Thaap!* Whenever one of us compelled her to make this speech it would seem to me that her eyes paused overlong on my face. She would seem to be daring me, as if suspicious that, in addition to my secret passion for Gweneth Lawson, which she might excuse, I was also in the habit of throwing fits of temper.

She had read me right. I was the product of too much attention from my father. He favored me, paraded me around on his shoulder, inflated my ego constantly with what, among us at least, was a high compliment: "You my nigger if you don't get no bigger." This statement, along with my father's generous attentions, made me selfish and used to having my own way. I *expected* to have my own way in most things, and when I could not, I tended to throw tantrums calculated to break through any barrier raised against me.

Mrs. Boswell was also perceptive in assessing the extent of my infatuation with Gweneth Lawson. Despite my stealth in telegraphing emissions of affection into the back part of Gweneth's brain, I could not help but observe, occasionally, Mrs. Boswell's cool glance pausing on the two of us. But she never said a word. Instead, she would settle her eyes momentarily on Gweneth's face and then pass quickly to mine. But in that instant she seemed to be saying, "Don't look back now, girl, but I *know* that bald-headed boy behind you has you on his mind." She seemed to watch me daily, with a combination of amusement and absolute detachment in her brown eyes. And when she stared, it was not at me but at the normal focus of my attention: the end of Gweneth Lawson's black braids. Whenever I sensed Mrs. Boswell watching I would look away quickly, either down at my brown desk top or across the room to the blackboard. But her eyes could not be eluded this easily. Without looking at anyone in particular, she could make a specific point to one person in a manner so general that only long afterward did the real object of her attention realize it had been intended for him.

"Now you little brown bunnies," she might say, "and you black buck rabbits and you few cottontails mixed in, some of you starting to smell yourselves under the arms without knowing what it's all about." And here, it sometimes seemed to me, she allowed her eyes to pause casually on me before resuming their sweep of the entire room. "Now I know your mamas already made you think life is a bed of roses, but in *my* classroom you got to know the footpaths through the *sticky* parts of the rosebed." It was her custom during this ritual to prod and goad those of us who were developing reputations for meekness and indecision; yet her method was Socratic in that she compelled us, indirectly, to supply our own answers by exploiting one person as the walking symbol of the error she intended to correct. Clarence Buford, for example, an oversized but good-natured boy from a very poor family, served often as the helpmeet in this exercise.

"Buford," she might begin, slapping the ruler against her palm, "how does a tongue-tied country boy like you expect to get a wife?"

"I don't want no wife," Buford might grumble softly.   20

Of course the class would laugh.

"Oh yes you do," Mrs. Boswell would respond. "All you buck rabbits want wives." *Thaap!* "So how do you let a girl know you not just a bump on a log?"

"I know! I know!" a high voice might call from a seat across from mine. This, of course, would be Leon Pugh. A peanut-brown boy with curly hair, he seemed to know everything. Moreover, he seemed to take pride in being the only one who knew answers to life questions and would wave his arms excitedly whenever our attentions were focused on such matters. It seemed to me his voice would be extra loud and his arms waved more strenuously whenever he was certain that Gweneth Lawson, seated across from him, was interested in an answer to Mrs. Esther Clay Boswell's question. His eager arms, it seemed to me, would be reaching out to grasp Gweneth instead of the question asked.

"Buford, you twisted-tongue, bunion-toed country boy," Mrs. Boswell might say, ignoring Leon Pugh's hysterical arm-waving, "you gonna let a cottontail like Leon get a girlfriend before you?"

"I don't want no girlfriend," Clarence Buford would almost sob. "I   25
don't like no girls."

The class would laugh again while Leon Pugh manipulated his arms like a flight navigator under battle conditions. "I know! I know! I swear to *God* I know!"

When at last Mrs. Boswell would turn in his direction, I might sense that she was tempted momentarily to ask me for an answer. But as in most such exercises, it was the wordly-wise Leon Pugh who supplied this. "What do *you* think, Leon?" she would ask inevitably, but with a rather lifeless slap of the ruler against her palm.

"My daddy told me . . . " Leon would shout, turning slyly to beam at Gweneth, ". . . my daddy and my big brother from the Bronx New York told me that to git *anythin'* in this world you gotta learn how to blow your own horn."

"Why, Leon?" Mrs. Boswell might ask in a bored voice.

"Because," the little boy would recite, puffing out his chest, "because   30
if you don't blow your own horn ain't nobody else g'on blow it for you. That's what my daddy said."

"What do you think about that, Buford?" Mrs. Boswell would ask.

"I don't want no girlfriend anyhow," the puzzled Clarence Buford might say.

And then the cryptic lesson would suddenly be dropped.

This was Mrs. Esther Clay Boswell's method of teaching. More than anything written on the blackboard, her questions were calculated to make us turn around in our chairs and inquire in guarded whispers of each other, and especially of the wise and confident Leon Pugh, "What does she mean?" But none of us, besides Pugh, seemed able to comprehend what it was we ought to know but did not know. And Mrs. Boswell, plump brown fox that she was, never volunteered any more in the way of confirmation than was necessary to keep us interested. Instead, she paraded around us, methodically slapping that homemade ruler against her palm, suggesting by her silence more depth to her question, indeed, more implications in Leon's answer, than we were then able to perceive. And during such moments, whether inspired by selfishness or by the peculiar way Mrs. Boswell looked at me, I felt that finding answers to such questions was a task she had set for me, of all the members of the class.

Of course Leon Pugh, among other lesser lights, was my chief rival   35 for the affections of Gweneth Lawson. All during the school year, from September through the winter rains, he bested me in my attempts to look directly into her eyes and say a simple, heartfelt "hey." This was my ambition, but I never seemed able to get close enough to her attention. At Thanksgiving I helped draw a bounteous yellow cornucopia on the blackboard, with fruits and flowers matching the colors that floated around Gweneth's head; Leon Pugh made one by himself, a masterwork of silver paper and multicolored crepe, which he hung on the door. Its silver tail curled upward to a point just below the face of Mrs. Boswell's clock. At Christmas, when we drew names out of a hat for the exchange of gifts, I drew the name of Queen Rose Phipps, a fairly unattractive squash-yellow girl of absolutely no interest to me. Pugh, whether through collusion with the boy who handled the lottery or through pure luck, pulled forth from the hat the magic name of Gweneth Lawson. He gave her a set of deep purple bows for her braids and a basket of pecans from his father's tree. Uninterested now in the spirit of the occasion, I delivered to Queen Rose Phipps a pair of white socks. Each time Gweneth wore the purple bows she would glance over at Leon and smile. Each time Queen Rose wore my white socks I would turn away in embarrassment, lest I should see them pulling down into her shoes and exposing her skinny ankles.

After class, on wet winter days, I would trail along behind Gweneth to the bus stop, pause near the steps while she entered, and follow her down the aisle until she chose a seat. Usually, however, in clear violation of the code of conduct to which all gentlemen were expected to adhere, Leon Pugh would already be on the bus and shouting to passersby, "Move off! Get away! This here seat by me is reserved for the girl from Booklyn New York." Discouraged but not defeated, I would swing into the seat next nearest her and cast calf-eyed glances of wounded affection at the back of her head or at the brown, rainbow profile of her face. And at her stop, some eight or nine blocks from mine, I would disembark behind her along with a crowd of other love-struck boys. There would then follow a well-rehearsed scene in which all of us, save Leon Pugh, pretended to have gotten off the bus either too late or too soon to wend our proper paths homeward. And at slight cost to ourselves we enjoyed the advantage of being able to walk close by her as she glided toward her uncle's green-frame house. There, after pausing on the wooden steps and smiling radiantly around the crowd like a spring sun in that cold winter rain, she would sing, "Bye, y'all," and disappear into the structure with the mystery of a goddess. Afterward I would walk away, but slowly, much slower than the other boys, warmed by the music and light in her voice against the sharp, wet winds of the February afternoon.

I loved her, dear Gloria, and I danced with her and smelled the lemony youth of her and told her that I loved her, all this in a way you would never believe:

You would not know or remember, as I do, that in those days, in our area of the country, we enjoyed a pleasingly ironic mixture of Yankee and Confederate folkways. Our meals and manners, our speech, our attitudes toward certain ambiguous areas of history, even our acceptance of tragedy as the normal course of life — these things and more defined us as Southern. Yet the stern morality of our parents, their toughness and penny-pinching and attitudes toward work, their covert allegiance toward certain ideals, even the directions toward which they turned our faces, made us more Yankee than Cavalier. Moreover, some of our schools were named for Confederate men of distinction, but others were named for the stern-faced believers who had swept down from the North to save a people back, back long ago, in those long forgotten days of once upon a time. Still, our schoolbooks, our required classroom songs, our flags, our very relation to the statues and monuments in public parks, negated the story that these dreamers from the North had ever come. We sang the state song, memorized the verses of homegrown poets, honored in our books the names and dates of historical events both before and after that Historical Event which, in our region, supplanted even the division of the millennia introduced by the followers of Jesus Christ. Given the silent circumstances of our cultural environment, it was ironic, and perhaps just, that we maintained a synthesis of two traditions no longer supportive of each other. Thus it became traditional at our school to celebrate the arrival of spring on May first by both the ritual plaiting of the Maypole and square dancing.

On that day, as on a few others, the Superintendent of Schools and several officials were likely to visit our schoolyard and stand next to the rusty metal swings, watching the fourth, fifth, and sixth graders bob up and down and behind and before each other, around the gaily painted Maypoles. These happy children would pull and twist long runs of billowy crepe paper into wondrous, multicolored plaits. Afterward, on the edges of thunderous applause from teachers, parents and visiting dignitaries, a wave of elaborately costumed children would rush out onto the grounds in groups of eight and proceed with the square dance. "Dog*gone!*" the Superintendent of Schools was heard to exclaim on one occasion. "Y'all do it so good it just makes your *bones* set up and take notice."

Such was the schedule two weeks prior to May first, when Mrs. Bos-   40
well announced to our class that as fourth graders we were now eligible to participate in the festivities. The class was divided into two general sections of sixteen each, one group preparing to plait the pole and a second group, containing an equal number of boys and girls, practicing turns for our part in the square dance. I was chosen to square dance; so was Leon Pugh. Gweneth Lawson was placed with the pole plaiters. I was depressed until I remembered, happily, that I could not dance a lick. I reported this fact to Mrs. Boswell just after the drawing, during recess, saying that my lack of skill would only result in our class making a poor showing. I asked to be reassigned to the group of Maypole plaiters. Mrs. B. looked me over with considerable amusement tugging at the corners of her mouth. "Oh, you don't have to *dance* to do the square dance," she said. "That's a dance that was made up to mock folks that couldn't dance." She paused a second before adding thoughtfully: "The worse you are at dancing, the better you can square dance. It's just about the best dance in the world for a stiff little bunny like you."

"I want to plait the Maypole," I said.

"You'll square dance or I'll grease your little butt," Mrs. Esther Clay Boswell said.

"I ain't gonna do *nothin'!*" I muttered. But I said this quietly, and mostly to myself, while walking away from her desk. For the rest of the day she watched me closely, as if she knew what I was thinking.

The next morning I brought a note from my father. "Dear Mrs. Boswell:" I had watched him write earlier that morning, "My boy does not square dance. Please excuse him as I am afraid he will break down and cry and mess up the show. Yours truly . . . "

Mrs. Boswell said nothing after she had read the note. She merely   45
waved me to my seat. But in the early afternoon, when she read aloud the lists of those assigned to dancing and Maypole plaiting, she paused as my name rolled off her tongue. "You don't have to stay on the square dance team," she called to me. "You go on out in the yard with the Maypole team."

I was ecstatic. I hurried to my place in line some three warm bodies behind Gweneth Lawson. We prepared to march out.

"Wait a minute," Mrs. Boswell called. "Now it looks like we got seventeen bunnies on the Maypole team and fifteen on the square dance. We have to even things up." She made a thorough examination of both lists, scratching her head. Then she looked carefully up and down the line of stomping Maypoleites. "Miss Gweneth Lawson, you cute little cottontail you, it looks like you gonna have to go over to the square dance team. That'll give us eight sets of partners for the square dance . . . but now we have another problem." She made a great display of counting the members of the two squads of square dancers. "Now there's sixteen square dancers all right, but when we pair them off we got a problem of higher mathematics. With nine girls and only seven *boys,* looks like we gotta switch a girl from square dancing to Maypole and a boy from Maypole to square dancing."

I waited hopefully for Gweneth Lawson to volunteer. But just at that moment the clever Leon Pugh grabbed her hand and began jitterbugging as though he could hardly wait for the record player to be turned on and the dancing to begin.

"What a cute couple," Mrs. Boswell observed absently. "Now which one of you other girls wants to join up with the Maypole team?"

Following Pugh's example, the seven remaining boys grabbed the girls they wanted as partners. Only skinny Queen Rose Phipps and shy Beverly Hankins remained unclaimed. Queen Rose giggled nervously.

"Queen Rose," Mrs. B. called, "I know you don't mind plaiting the Maypole." She waved her ruler in a gesture of casual dismissal. Queen Rose raced across the room and squeezed into line.

"*Now,*" Mrs. Boswell said, "I need a boy to come across to the square dancers."

I was not unmindful of the free interchange of partners involved in square dancing, even though Leon Pugh had beat me in claiming the partner of my choice. All I really wanted was one moment swinging Gweneth Lawson in my arms. I raised my hand slowly.

"Oh, not *you,* little bunny," Mrs. Boswell said. "You and your daddy claim you don't like to square dance." She slapped her ruler against her palm. *Thaap! Thaap!* Then she said, "Clarence Buford, I *know* a big-footed country boy like you can square dance better than anybody. Come on over here and kiss cute little Miss Beverly Hankins."

"I don't like no girls *noway,*" Buford mumbled. But he went over and stood next to the giggling Beverly Hankins.

"Now!" said Mrs. B. "March on out in that yard and give that pole a good plaiting!"

We started to march out. Over my shoulder, as I reached the door, I glimpsed the overjoyed Leon Pugh whirling lightly on his toes. He sang in a confident tone:

> I saw the Lord give Moses a pocketful of roses.
> I skid Ezekiel's wheel on a ripe banana peel.
> I rowed the Nile, flew over a stile,
> Saw Jack Johnson pick his teeth
> With toenails from Jim Jeffries'° feets . . .

"Grab your partners!" Mrs. Esther Clay Boswell was saying as the oak door slammed behind us.

I had been undone. For almost two weeks I was obliged to stand on the sidelines and watch Leon Pugh allemande left and do-si-do my beloved

Jack Johnson/Jim Jeffries: Johnson, the first black world heavyweight champion, knocked out Jeffries, the former champion.

Gweneth. Worse, she seemed to be enjoying it. But I must give Leon proper credit: he was a dancing fool. In a matter of days he had mastered, and then improved on, the various turns and bows and gestures of the square dance. He leaped while the others plodded, whirled each girl through his arms with lightness and finesse, chattered playfully at the other boys when they tumbled over their own feet. Mrs. Boswell stood by the record player calling, "Put some *strut* in it, Buford, you big potato sack. Watch Leon and see how *he* does it." I leaned against the classroom wall and watched the dancers, my own group having already exhausted the limited variations possible in matters of Maypole plaiting.

At home each night I begged my father to send another note to Mrs.   60
Boswell, this time stating that I had no interest in the Maypole. But he resisted my entreaties and even threatened me with a whipping if I did not participate and make him proud of me. The real cause of his irritation was the considerable investment he had already made in purchasing an outfit for me. Mrs. Boswell had required all her students, square dancers and Maypole plaiters alike, to report on May first in outfits suitable for square dancing. My father had bought a new pair of dungarees, a blue shirt, a red and white polka-dot bandanna and a cowboy hat. He was in no mood to bend under the emotional weight of my new demands. As a matter of fact, early in the morning of May first he stood beside my bed with the bandanna in his left hand and his leather belt in his right hand, just in case I developed a sudden fever.

I dragged myself heavily through the warm, blue spring morning toward school, dressed like a carnival cowboy. When I entered the classroom I sulked against the wall, being content to watch the other children. And what happy buzzings and jumping and excitement they made as they compared costumes. Clarence Buford wore a Tom Mix hat° and a brown vest over a green shirt with red six-shooter patterns embossed on its collar. Another boy, Paul Carter, was dressed entirely in black, with a fluffly white handkerchief puffing from his neck. But Leon Pugh caught the attention of all our eyes. He wore a red and white checkered shirt, a loose green bandanna clasped at his throat by a shining silver buffalo head, brown chaps sewed onto his dungarees, and shiny brown cowboy boots with silver spurs that clanked each time he moved. In his hand he carried a carefully creased brown cowboy hat. He announced his fear that it would lose its shape and planned to put it on only when the dancing started. He would allow no one to touch it. Instead, he stood around clanking his feet and smoothing the crease in his fabulous hat and saying loudly, "My daddy says it pays to look good no matter what you put on."

The girls seemed prettier and much older than their ages. Even Queen Rose Phipps wore rouge on her cheeks that complemented her pale color.

Tom Mix hat: Like most early film, comic book, and television cowboy heroes, Tom Mix wore a white, broad-brimmed hat.

Shy Beverly Hankins had come dressed in a blue and white checkered bonnet and a crisp blue apron; she looked like a frontier mother. But Gweneth Lawson, my Gweneth Lawson, dominated the group of girls. She wore a long red dress with sheaves and sheaves of sparkling white crinoline belling it outward so it seemed she was floating. On her honey-brown wrists golden bracelets sparkled. A deep blue bandanna enclosed her head with the wonder of a summer sky. Black patent leather shoes glistened like half-hidden stars beneath the red and white of her hemline. She stood smiling before us and we marveled. At that moment I would have given the world to have been able to lead her about on my arm.

Mrs. Boswell watched us approvingly from behind her desk. Finally, at noon, she called, "Let's go on out!" Thirty-two living rainbows cascaded toward the door. Pole plaiters formed one line. Square dancers formed another. Mrs. Boswell strolled officiously past us in review. It seemed to me she almost paused while passing the spot where I stood on line. But she brushed past me, straightening an apron here, applying spittle and a rub to a rouged cheek there, waving a wary finger at an overanxious boy. Then she whacked her ruler against her palm and led us out into the yard. The fifth and sixth graders had already assembled. On one end of the playground were a dozen or so tall painted poles with long, thin wisps of green and blue and yellow and rustbrown crepe floating lazily on the sweet spring breezes.

"Maypole teams *up!*" called Mr. Henry Lucas, our principal, from his platform by the swings. Beside him stood the white Superintendent of Schools (who said later of the square dance, it was reported to all the classes, "Lord, y'all square dance so *good* it makes me plumb *ashamed* us white folks ain't takin' better care of our art stuff.") "Maypole teams up!" Mr. Henry Lucas shouted again. Some fifty of us, screaming shrilly, rushed to grasp our favorite color crepe. Then, to the music of "Sing Praise for All the Brightness and the Joy of Spring," we pulled and plaited in teams of six or seven until every pole was twisted as tight and as colorfully as the braids on Gweneth Lawson's head. Then, to the applause of proud teachers and parents and the whistles of the Superintendent of Schools, we scattered happily back under the wings of our respective teachers. I stood next to Mrs. Boswell, winded and trembling but confident I had done my best. She glanced down at me and said in a quiet voice, "I do believe you are learning the rhythm of the thing."

I did not respond.   65

"Let's *go!*" Leon Pugh shouted to the other kids, grabbing Gweneth Lawson's arm and taking a few clanking steps forward.

"Wait a minute, Leon," Mrs. Boswell hissed. "Mr. Lucas has to change the record."

Leon sighed. "But if we don't git out there first, all them other teams will take the best spots."

"Wait!" Mrs. Boswell ordered.

Leon sulked. He inched closer to Gweneth. I watched him swing her   70
hand impatiently. He stamped his feet and his silver spurs jangled.

Mrs. Boswell looked down at his feet. "Why, Leon," she said, "you can't go out there with razors on your shoes."

"These ain't razors," Leon muttered. "These here are spurs my brother in Bronx New York sent me just for this here dance."

"You have to take them off," Mrs. Boswell said.

Leon growled. But he reached down quickly and attempted to jerk the silver spurs from the heels of his boots. They did not come off. "No time!" he called, standing suddenly. "Mr. Lucas done put the record on."

"Leon, you might *cut* somebody with those things," Mrs. Boswell said. "Miss Gweneth Lawson's pretty red dress could get caught in those things and then she'll fall as surely as I'm standin' here."

"I'll just go out with my boots off," Leon replied.

But Mrs. Boswell shook her head firmly. "You just run on to the lunchroom and ask cook for some butter or mayo. That'll help 'em slip off." She paused, looking out over the black dirt playground. "And if you miss this first dance, why there'll be a second and maybe even a third. We'll get a Maypole plaiter to sub for you."

My heart leaped. Leon sensed it and stared at me. His hand tightened on Gweneth's as she stood radiant and smiling in the loving spring sunlight. Leon let her hand drop and bent quickly, pulling at the spurs with the fury of a Samson.

"Square dancers *up!*" Mr. Henry Lucas called.

"Sonofa*bitch!*" Leon grunted.

"Square dancers *up!*" called Mr. Lucas.

The fifth and sixth graders were screaming and rushing toward the center of the yard. Already the record was scratching out the high, slick voice of the caller. "*Sonofabitch!*" Leon moaned.

Mrs. Boswell looked directly at Gweneth, standing alone and abandoned next to Leon. "Miss Gweneth Lawson," Mrs. Boswell said in a cool voice, "it's a cryin' shame there ain't no prince to take you to that ball out there."

I do not remember moving, but I know I stood with Gweneth at the center of the yard. What I did there I do not know, but I remember watching the movements of others and doing what they did just after they had done it. Still, I cannot remember just when I looked into my partner's face or what I saw there. The scratchy voice of the caller bellowed directions and I obeyed:

Allemande left with your left hand
Right to your partner with a right and left grand . . .

Although I was told later that I made an allemande right instead of left, I have no memory of the mistake.

When you get to your partner pass her by
And pick up the next girl on the sly . . .

Nor can I remember picking up any other girl. I only remember that during many turns and do-si-dos I found myself looking into the warm brown eyes of Gweneth Lawson. I recall that she smiled at me. I recall that she laughed on another turn. I recall that I laughed with her an eternity later.

> . . . promenade that dear old thing
> Throw your head right back and sing *be*-cause, just *be*-cause . . .

I do remember quite well that during the final promenade before the record ended, Gweneth stood beside me and I said to her in a voice much louder than that of the caller, "When I get up to Brooklyn I hope I see you." But I do not remember what she said in response. I want to remember that she smiled.

I know I smiled, dear Gloria. I smiled with the lemonness of her and   85
the loving of her pressed deep into those saving places of my private self. It was my plan to savor these, and I did savor them. But when I reached New York, many years later, I did not think of Brooklyn. I followed the old, beaten, steady paths into uptown Manhattan. By then I had learned to dance to many other kinds of music. And I had forgotten the savory smell of lemon. But I think sometimes of Gweneth now when I hear country music. And although it is difficult to explain to you, I still maintain that I am no mere arithmetician in the art of the square dance. I am into the calculus of it.

"Go on!" you will tell me, backing into your Northern mythology. "I can see the hustle, the hump, maybe even the Ibo highlife. But no hillbilly."

These days I am firm about arguing the point, but, as always, quietly, and mostly to myself.

Considerations

1. Why does the narrator tell this story to Gloria? What do you imagine Gloria to be like? What might she learn from hearing this story? What might the narrator learn by telling it?
2. How does the narrator characterize himself in paragraphs 9 and 10? How does he characterize Gweneth Lawson (paragraphs 12–14)? How does his picture of her compare and contrast to his picture of himself?
3. Describe your response to Mrs. Esther Clay Boswell. Would you call her a good teacher? Would you like to be one of her students? Explain.
4. Explain the challenges and conflicts Leon Pugh brings into the narrator's life. What does he learn from facing these challenges and conflicts?
5. Comment on the story's final sentence. Why does the narrator continue to "argue the point," especially since he does so "quietly and mostly to [himself]"?

TONI CADE BAMBARA (1939–   )

The Lesson

Back in the days when everyone was old and stupid or young and foolish and me and Sugar were the only ones just right, this lady moved on our block with nappy hair and proper speech and no makeup. And quite naturally we laughed at her, laughed the way we did at the junk man who went about his business like he was some big-time president and his sorry-ass horse his secretary. And we kinda hated her too, hated the way we did the winos who cluttered up our parks and pissed on our handball walls and stank up our hallways and stairs so you couldn't halfway play hide-and-seek without a goddamn gas mask. Miss Moore was her name. The only woman on the block with no first name. And she was black as hell, cept for her feet, which were fish-white and spooky. And she was always planning these boring-ass things for us to do, us being my cousin, mostly, who lived on the block cause we all moved North the same time and to the same apartment then spread out gradual to breathe. And our parents would yank our heads into some kinda shape and crisp up our clothes so we'd be presentable for travel with Miss Moore, who always looked like she was going to church, though she never did. Which is just one of the things the grownups talked about when they talked behind her back like a dog. But when she came calling with some sachet she'd sewed up or some gingerbread she'd made or some book, why then they'd all be too embarrassed to turn her down and we'd get handed over all spruced up. She'd been to college and said it was only right that she should take responsibility for the young ones' education, and she not even related by marriage or blood. So they'd go for it. Specially Aunt Gretchen. She was the main gofer in the family. You got some ole dumb shit foolishness you want somebody to go for, you send for Aunt Gretchen. She been screwed into the go-along for so long, it's a blood-deep natural thing with her. Which is how she got saddled with me and Sugar and Junior in the first place while our mothers were in a la-de-da apartment up the block having a good ole time.

So this one day Miss Moore rounds us all up at the mailbox and it's puredee hot and she's knockin herself out about arithmetic. And school suppose to let up in summer I heard, but she don't never let up. And the starch in my pinafore scratching the shit outta me and I'm really hating this nappy-head bitch and her goddamn college degree. I'd much rather go to the pool or to the show where it's cool. So me and Sugar leaning on the mailbox being surly, which is a Miss Moore word. And Flyboy checking out what everybody brought for lunch. And Fat Butt already wasting his peanut-butter-and-jelly sandwich like the pig he is. And Junebug punchin on Q.T.'s arm for potato chips. And Rosie Giraffe shifting from one hip to the other waiting for somebody to step on her foot or ask her if she from

Georgia so she can kick ass, preferably Mercedes'. And Miss Moore asking us do we know what money is, like we a bunch of retards. I mean real money, she say, like it's only poker chips or monopoly papers we lay on the grocer. So right away I'm tired of this and say so. And would much rather snatch Sugar and go to the Sunset and terrorize the West Indian kids and take their hair ribbons and their money too. And Miss Moore files that remark away for next week's lesson on brotherhood, I can tell. And finally I say we oughta get to the subway cause it's cooler and besides we might meet some cute boys. Sugar done swiped her mama's lipstick, so we ready.

So we heading down the street and she's boring us silly about what things cost and what our parents make and how much goes for rent and how money ain't divided up right in this country. And then she gets to the part about we all poor and live in the slums, which I don't feature. And I'm ready to speak on that, but she steps out in the street and hails two cabs just like that. Then she hustles half the crew in with her and hands me a five-dollar bill and tells me to calculate 10 percent tip for the driver. And we're off. Me and Sugar and Junebug and Flyboy hangin out the window and hollering to everybody, putting lipstick on each other cause Flyboy a faggot anyway, and making farts with our sweaty armpits. But I'm mostly trying to figure how to spend this money. But they all fascinated with the meter ticking and Junebug starts laying bets as to how much it'll read when Flyboy can't hold his breath no more. Then Sugar lays bets as to how much it'll be when we get there. So I'm stuck. Don't nobody want to go for my plan, which is to jump out at the next light and run off to the first bar-b-que we can find. Then the driver tells us to get the hell out cause we there already. And the meter reads eighty-five cents. And I'm stalling to figure out the tip and Sugar say give him a dime. And I decide he don't need it bad as I do, so later for him. But then he tries to take off with Junebug foot still in the door so we talk about his mama something ferocious. Then we check out that we on Fifth Avenue and everybody dressed up in stockings. One lady in a fur coat, hot as it is. White folks crazy.

"This is the place," Miss Moore say, presenting it to us in the voice she uses at the museum. "Let's look in the windows before we go in."

"Can we steal?" Sugar asks very serious like she's getting the ground   5
rules squared away before she plays. "I beg your pardon," say Miss Moore, and we fall out. So she leads us around the windows of the toy store and me and Sugar screamin, "This is mine, that's mine, I gotta have that, that was made for me, I was born for that," till Big Butt drowns us out.

"Hey, I'm going to buy that there."

"That there? You don't even know what it is, stupid."

"I do so," he say punchin on Rosie Giraffe. "It's a microscope."

"Whatcha gonna do with a microscope, fool?"

"Look at things."   10

"Like what, Ronald?" ask Miss Moore. And Big Butt ain't got the first notion. So here go Miss Moore gabbing about the thousands of bacteria in a drop of water and the somethinorother in a speck of blood and the million and one living things in the air around us is invisible to the naked eye. And what she say that for? Junebug go to town on that "naked" and we rolling. Then Miss Moore ask what it cost. So we all jam into the window smudgin it up and the price tag say $300. So then she ask how long'd take for Big Butt and Junebug to save up their allowances. "Too long," I say. "Yeh," adds Sugar, "outgrown it by that time." And Miss Moore say no, you never outgrow learning instruments. "Why, even medical students and interns and," blah, blah, blah. And we ready to choke Big Butt for bringing it up in the first damn place.

"This here costs four hundred eighty dollars," say Rosie Giraffe. So we pile up all over her to see what she pointin out. My eyes tells me it's a chunk of glass cracked with something heavy, and different-color inks dripped into the splits, then the whole thing put into a oven or something. But for $480 it don't make sense.

"That's a paperweight made of semi-precious stones fused together under tremendous pressure," she explains slowly, with her hands doing the mining and all the factory work.

"So what's a paperweight?" asks Rosie Giraffe.

"To weigh paper with, dumbbell," say Flyboy, the wise man from   15
the East.

"Not exactly," say Miss Moore, which is what she say when you warm or way off too. "It's to weigh paper down so it won't scatter and make your desk untidy." So right away me and Sugar curtsy to each other and then to Mercedes who is more the tidy type.

"We don't keep paper on top of the desk in my class," say Junebug, figuring Miss Moore crazy or lyin one.

"At home, then," she say. "Don't you have a calendar and a pencil case and a blotter and a letter-opener on your desk at home where you do your homework?" And she know damn well what our homes look like cause she nosys around in them every chance she gets.

"I don't even have a desk," say Junebug. "Do we?"

"No. And I don't get no homework neither," says Big Butt.   20

"And I don't even have a home," say Flyboy like he do at school to keep the white folks off his back and sorry for him. Send this poor kid to camp posters, is his specialty.

"I do," says Mercedes. "I have a box of stationery on my desk and a picture of my cat. My godmother bought the stationery and the desk. There's a big rose on each sheet and the envelopes smell like roses."

"Who wants to know about your smelly-ass stationery," say Rosie Giraffe fore I can get my two cents in.

"It's important to have a work area all your own so that . . . "

"Will you look at this sailboat, please," say Flyboy, cuttin her off and   25 pointin to the thing like it was his. So once again we tumble all over each other to gaze at this magnificent thing in the toy store which is just big enough to maybe sail two kittens across the pond if you strap them to the posts tight. We all start reciting the price tag like we in assembly. "Hand-crafted sailboat of fiberglass at one thousand one hundred ninety-five dollars."

"Unbelievable," I hear myself say and am really stunned. I read it again for myself just in case the group recitation put me in a trance. Same thing. For some reason this pisses me off. We look at Miss Moore and she lookin at us, waiting for I dunno what.

"Who'd pay all that when you can buy a sailboat set for a quarter at Pop's, a tube of glue for a dime, and a ball of string for eight cents? It must have a motor and a whole lot else besides," I say. "My sailboat cost me about fifty cents."

"But will it take water?" say Mercedes with her smart ass.

"Took mine to Alley Pond Park once," say Flyboy. "String broke. Lost it. Pity."

"Sailed mine in Central Park and it keeled over and sank. Had to ask   30
my father for another dollar."

"And you got the strap," laugh Big Butt. "The jerk didn't even have a string on it. My old man wailed on his behind."

Little Q.T. was staring hard at the sailboat and you could see he wanted it bad. But he too little and somebody'd just take it from him. So what the hell. "This boat for kids, Miss Moore?"

"Parents silly to buy something like that just to get all broke up," say Rosie Giraffe.

"That much money it should last forever," I figure.

"My father'd buy it for me if I wanted it."   35

"Your father, my ass," say Rosie Giraffe getting a chance to finally push Mercedes.

"Must be rich people shop here," say Q.T.

"You are a very bright boy," say Flyboy. "What was your first clue?" And he rap him on the head with the back of his knuckles, since Q.T. the only one he could get away with. Though Q.T. liable to come up behind you years later and get his licks in when you half expect it.

"What I want to know is," I says to Miss Moore though I never talk to her, I wouldn't give the bitch that satisfaction, "is how much a real boat costs? I figure a thousand'd get you a yacht any day."

"Why don't you check that out," she says, "and report back to the   40
group?" Which really pains my ass. If you gonna mess up a perfectly good swim day least you could do is have some answers. "Let's go in," she say like she got something up her sleeve. Only she don't lead the way. So me and Sugar turn the corner to where the entrance is, but when we get there I kinda hang back. Not that I'm scared, what's there to be afraid of, just a toy

store. But I feel funny, shame. But what I got to be shamed about? Got as much right to go in as anybody. But somehow I can't seem to get hold of the door, so I step away from Sugar to lead. But she hangs back too. And I look at her and she looks at me and this is ridiculous. I mean, damn, I have never ever been shy about doing nothing or going nowhere. But then Mercedes steps up and then Rosie Giraffe and Big Butt crowd in behind and shove, and next thing we all stuffed into the doorway with only Mercedes squeezing past us, smoothing out her jumper and walking right down the aisle. Then the rest of us tumble in like a glued-together jigsaw done all wrong. And people lookin at us. And it's like the time me and Sugar crashed into the Catholic church on a dare. But once we got in there and everything so hushed and holy and the candles and the bowin and the handkerchiefs on all the drooping heads, I just couldn't go through with the plan. Which was for me to run up to the altar and do a tap dance while Sugar played the nose flute and messed around in the holy water. And Sugar kept givin me the elbow. Then later teased me so bad I tied her up in the shower and turned it on and locked her in. And she'd be there till this day if Aunt Gretchen hadn't finally figured I was lyin about the boarder takin a shower.

Same thing in the store. We all walkin on tiptoe and hardly touchin the games and puzzles and things. And I watched Miss Moore who is steady watchin us like she waitin for a sign. Like Mama Drewery watches the sky and sniffs the air and takes note of just how much slant is in the bird formation. Then me and Sugar bump smack into each other, so busy gazing at the toys, 'specially the sailboat. But we don't laugh and go into our fat-lady bump-stomach routine. We just stare at that price tag. Then Sugar run a finger over the whole boat. And I'm jealous and want to hit her. Maybe not her, but I sure want to punch somebody in the mouth.

"Watcha bring us here for, Miss Moore?"

"You sound angry, Sylvia. Are you mad about something?" Givin me one of them grins like she tellin a grown-up joke that never turns out to be funny. And she's lookin very closely at me like maybe she plannin to do my portrait from memory. I'm mad, but I won't give her that satisfaction. So I slouch around the store bein very bored and say, "Let's go."

Me and Sugar at the back of the train watchin the tracks whizzin by large then small then gettin gobbled up in the dark. I'm thinkin about this tricky toy I saw in the store. A clown that somersaults on a bar then does chin-ups just cause you yank lightly at his leg. Cost $35. I could see me askin my mother for a $35 birthday clown. "You wanna who that costs what?" she'd say, cocking her head to the side to get a better view of the hole in my head. Thirty-five dollars could buy new bunk beds for Junior and Gretchen's boy. Thirty-five dollars and the whole household could go visit Granddaddy Nelson in the country. Thirty-five dollars would pay for the rent and the piano bill too. Who are these people that spend that much for performing clowns and $1000 for toy sailboats? What kinda work they do and how they live and how come we ain't in on it? Where we are is who we are, Miss Moore always pointin out. But it don't necessarily have to be that way, she always adds then waits for somebody to say that poor people have to wake up and demand their share of the pie and don't none of us know what kind of pie she talking about in the first damn place. But she ain't so smart cause I still got her four dollars from the taxi and she sure ain't gettin it. Messin up my day with this shit. Sugar nudges me in my pocket and winks.

Miss Moore lines us up in front of the mailbox where we started from,   45 seem like years ago, and I got a headache for thinkin so hard. And we lean all over each other so we can hold up under the draggy-ass lecture she always finishes us off with at the end before we thank her for borin us to tears. But she just looks at us like she readin tea leaves. Finally she say, "Well, what did you think of F.A.O. Schwarz?"

Rosie Giraffe mumbles, "White folks crazy."

"I'd like to go there again when I get my birthday money," says Mercedes, and we shove her out the pack so she has to lean on the mailbox by herself.

"I'd like a shower. Tiring day," say Flyboy.

Then Sugar surprises me by sayin, "You know, Miss Moore, I don't think all of us here put together eat in a year what that sailboat costs." And Miss Moore lights up like somebody goosed her. "And?" she say, urging Sugar on. Only I'm standin on her foot so she don't continue.

"Imagine for a minute what kind of society it is in which some people   50 can spend on a toy what it would cost to feed a family of six or seven. What do you think?"

"I think," say Sugar pushing me off her feet like she never done before, cause I whip her ass in a minute, "that this is not much of a democracy if you ask me. Equal chance to pursue happiness means an equal crack at the dough, don't it?" Miss Moore is beside herself and I am disgusted with Sugar's treachery. So I stand on her foot one more time to see if she'll shove me. She shuts up, and Miss Moore looks at me, sorrowfully I'm thinkin. And somethin weird is goin on, I can feel it in my chest.

"Anybody else learn anything today?" lookin dead at me. I walk away and Sugar has to run to catch up and don't even seem to notice when I shrug her arm off my shoulder.

"Well, we got four dollars anyway," she says.

"Uh hunh."

"We could go to Hascombs and get half a chocolate layer and then go   55 to the Sunset and still have plenty money for potato chips and ice cream sodas."

"Uh hunh."

"Race you to Hascombs," she say.

We start down the block and she gets ahead which is O.K. by me cause

I'm going to the West End and then over to the Drive to think this day through. She can run if she want to and even run faster. But ain't nobody gonna beat me at nuthin.

Considerations

1. Although Miss Moore does not teach Sugar, Sylvia, and their friends in a traditional classroom, in what ways does she fit the stereotype of an elementary schoolteacher? In what ways does she challenge or escape the stereotype?
2. Explain Miss Moore's attitude toward the children she teaches and toward their parents. How is her attitude reflected by her teaching methods?
3. What do you see as Miss Moore's purpose for bringing Sugar, Sylvia, and their friends to F.A.O. Schwartz? What speculations do the children make about the trip and its purpose?
4. Identify and discuss some of the comic elements in the story. Do you find these elements distracting, or do they in some way contribute to the theme(s) you see?
5. Sugar and Sylvia react differently to the trip to F.A.O. Schwartz. What do you think each learns? Based on their different reactions to Miss Moore's lesson, what future can you predict for each girl?

GRACE PALEY (1922–   )

The Loudest Voice

There is a certain place where dumb-waiters boom, doors slam, dishes crash; every window is a mother's mouth bidding the street shut up, go skate somewhere else, come home. My voice is the loudest.

There, my own mother is still as full of breathing as me and the grocer stands up to speak to her. "Mrs. Abramowitz," he says, "people should not be afraid of their children."

"Ah, Mr. Bialik," my mother replies, "if you say to her or her father 'Ssh,' they say, 'In the grave it will be quiet.'"

"From Coney Island to the cemetery," says my papa. "It's the same subway; it's the same fare."

I am right next to the pickle barrel. My pinky is making tiny whirl-   5
pools in the brine. I stop a moment to announce: "Campbell's Tomato Soup. Campbell's Vegetable Beef Soup. Campbell's S-c-otch Broth . . ."

"Be quiet," the grocer says, "the labels are coming off."

"Please, Shirley, be a little quiet," my mother begs me.

In that place the whole street groans: Be quiet! Be quiet! but steals from the happy chorus of my inside self not a tittle or a jot.

There, too, but just around the corner, is a red brick building that has been old for many years. Every morning the children stand before it in double lines which must be straight. They are not insulted. They are waiting anyway.

I am usually among them. I am, in fact, the first, since I begin with   10
"A."

One cold morning the monitor tapped me on the shoulder. "Go to Room 409, Shirley Abramowitz," he said. I did as I was told. I went in a hurry up a down staircase to Room 409, which contained sixth-graders. I had to wait at the desk without wiggling until Mr. Hilton, their teacher, had time to speak.

After five minutes he said, "Shirley?"

"What?" I whispered.

He said, "My! My! Shirley Abramowitz! They told me you had a particularly loud, clear voice and read with lots of expression. Could that be true?"

"Oh yes," I whispered.   15

"In that case, don't be silly; I might very well be your teacher someday. Speak up, speak up."

"Yes," I shouted.

"More like it," he said. "Now, Shirley, can you put a ribbon in your hair or a bobby pin? It's too messy."

"Yes!" I bawled.

"Now, now, calm down." He turned to the class. "Children, not a 20
sound. Open at page 39. Read till 52. When you finish, start again." He
looked me over once more. "Now, Shirley, you know, I suppose, that Christmas is coming. We are preparing a beautiful play. Most of the parts have
been given out. But I still need a child with a strong voice, lots of stamina.
Do you know what stamina is? You do? Smart kid. You know, I heard you
read 'The Lord is my shepherd' in Assembly yesterday. I was very impressed. Wonderful delivery. Mrs. Jordan, your teacher, speaks highly of
you. Now listen to me, Shirley Abramowitz, if you want to take the part
and be in the play repeat after me, 'I swear to work harder than I ever did
before.'"

I looked to heaven and said at once, "Oh, I swear." I kissed my pinky
and looked at God.

"That is an actor's life, my dear," he explained. "Like a soldier's, never
tardy or disobedient to his general, the director. Everything," he said, "absolutely everything will depend on you."

That afternoon, all over the building, children scraped and scrubbed
the turkeys and the sheaves of corn off the schoolroom windows. Goodbye
Thanksgiving. The next morning a monitor brought red paper and green
paper from the office. We made new shapes and hung them on the walls and
glued them to the doors.

The teachers became happier and happier. Their heads were ringing
like the bells of childhood. My best friend Evie was prone to evil, but she
did not get a single demerit for whispering. We learned "Holy Night"
without an error. "How wonderful!" said Miss Glacé, the student teacher.
"To think that some of you don't even speak the language!" We learned
"Deck the Halls" and "Hark! The Herald Angels." . . . They weren't
ashamed and we weren't embarrassed.

Oh, but when my mother heard about it all, she said to my father: 25
"Misha, you don't know what's going on there. Cramer is the head of the
Tickets Committee."

"Who?" asked my father. "Cramer? Oh yes, an active woman."

"Active? Active has to have a reason. Listen," she said sadly, "I'm
surprised to see my neighbors making tra-la-la for Christmas."

My father couldn't think of what to say to that. Then he decided:
"You're in America! Clara, you wanted to come here. In Palestine the Arabs
would be eating you alive. Europe you had pogroms. Argentina is full of
Indians. Here you got Christmas. . . . Some joke, ha?"

"Very funny, Misha. What is becoming of you? If we came to a new
country a long time ago to run away from tyrants, and instead we fall into
a creeping pogrom, that our children learn a lot of lies, so what's the joke?
Ach, Misha, your idealism is going away."

"So is your sense of humor." 30

"That I never had, but idealism you had a lot of."

"I'm the same Misha Abramovitch, I didn't change an iota. Ask
anyone."

"Only ask me," says my mama, may she rest in peace. "I got the answer."

Meanwhile the neighbors had to think of what to say too.

Marty's father said: "You know, he has a very important part, my   35
boy."

"Mine also," said Mr. Sauerfeld.

"Not my boy!" said Mrs. Klieg. "I said to him no. The answer is no. When I say no! I mean no!"

The rabbi's wife said, "It's disgusting!" But no one listened to her. Under the narrow sky of God's great wisdom she wore a strawberry-blond wig.

Every day was noisy and full of experience. I was Right-hand Man. Mr. Hilton said: "How could I get along without you, Shirley?"

He said: "Your mother and father ought to get down on their knees   40
every night and thank God for giving them a child like you."

He also said: "You're absolutely a pleasure to work with, my dear, dear child."

Sometimes he said: "For God's sakes, what did I do with the script? Shirley! Shirley! Find it."

Then I answered quietly: "Here it is, Mr. Hilton."

Once in a while, when he was very tired, he would cry out: "Shirley, I'm just tired of screaming at those kids. Will you tell Ira Pushkov not to come in till Lester points to that star the second time?"

Then I roared: "Ira Pushkov, what's the matter with you? Dope! Mr.   45
Hilton told you five times already, don't come in till Lester points to that star the second time."

"Ach, Clara," my father asked, "what does she do there till six o'clock she can't even put the plates on the table?"

"Christmas," said my mother coldly.

"Ho! Ho!" my father said. "Christmas. What's the harm? After all, history teaches everyone. We learn from reading this is a holiday from pagan times also, candles, lights, even Chanukah. So we learn it's not altogether Christian. So if they think it's a private holiday, they're only ignorant, not patriotic. What belongs to history, belongs to all men. You want to go back to the Middle Ages? Is it better to shave your head with a secondhand razor? Does it hurt Shirley to learn to speak up? It does not. So maybe someday she won't live between the kitchen and the shop. She's not a fool."

I thank you, Papa, for your kindness. It is true about me to this day. I am foolish but I am not a fool.

That night my father kissed me and said with great interest in my   50
career, "Shirley, tomorrow's your big day. Congrats."

"Save it," my mother said. Then she shut all the windows in order to prevent tonsillitis.

In the morning it snowed. On the street corner a tree had been decorated for us by a kind city administration. In order to miss its chilly shadow our neighbors walked three blocks east to buy a loaf of bread. The butcher pulled down black window shades to keep the colored lights from shining on his chickens. Oh, not me. On the way to school, with both hands I tossed it a kiss of tolerance. Poor thing, it was a stranger in Egypt.

I walked straight into the auditorium past the staring children. "Go ahead, Shirley!" said the monitors. Four boys, big for their age, had already started work as propmen and stagehands.

Mr. Hilton was very nervous. He was not even happy. Whatever he started to say ended in a sideward look of sadness. He sat slumped in the middle of the first row and asked me to help Miss Glacé. I did this, although she thought my voice too resonant and said, "Showoff!"

Parents began to arrive long before we were ready. They wanted to   55
make a good impression. From among the yards of drapes I peeked out at the audience. I saw my embarrassed mother.

Ira, Lester, and Meyer were pasted to their beards by Miss Glacé. She almost forgot to thread the star on its wire, but I reminded her. I coughed a few times to clear my throat. Miss Glacé looked around and saw that everyone was in costume and on line waiting to play his part. She whispered, "All right . . ." Then:

Jackie Sauerfeld, the prettiest boy in first grade, parted the curtains with his skinny elbow and in a high voice sang out:

Parents dear
We are here
To make a Christmas play in time.
It we give
In narrative
And illustrate with pantomime.

He disappeared.

My voice burst immediately from the wings to the great shock of Ira, Lester, and Meyer, who were waiting for it but were surprised all the same.

"I remember, I remember, the house were I was born . . ."   60

Miss Glacé yanked the curtain open and there it was, the house—an old hayloft, where Celia Kornbluh lay in the straw with Cindy Lou, her favorite doll. Ira, Lester, and Meyer moved slowly from the wings toward her, sometimes pointing to a moving star and sometimes ahead to Cindy Lou.

It was a long story and it was a sad story. I carefully pronounced all the words about my lonesome childhood, while little Eddie Braunstein wandered upstage and down with his shepherd's stick, looking for sheep. I brought up lonesomeness again, and not being understood at all except by some women everybody hated. Eddie was too small for that and Marty Groff took his place, wearing his father's prayer shawl. I announced twelve friends, and half the boys in the fourth grade gathered round Marty, who stood on an orange crate while my voiced harangued. Sorrowful and loud, I declaimed about love and God and Man, but because of the terrible deceit

of Abie Stock we came suddenly to a famous moment. Marty, whose remembering tongue I was, waited at the foot of the cross. He stared desperately at the audience. I groaned, "My God, my God why hast thou forsaken
me?" The soldiers who were sheiks grabbed poor Marty to pin him up to
die, but he wrenched free, turned again to the audience, and spread his arms
aloft to show despair and the end. I murmured at the top of my voice, "The
rest is silence, but as everyone in this room, in this city—in this world—
now knows, I shall have life eternal."

That night Mrs. Kornbluh visited our kitchen for a glass of tea.

"How's the virgin?" asked my father with a look of concern.

"For a man with a daughter, you got a fresh mouth, Abramovitch."   65

"Here," said my father kindly, "have some lemon, it'll sweeten your
disposition."

They debated a little in Yiddish, then fell in a puddle of Russian and
Polish. What I understood next was my father, who said, "Still and all, it
was certainly a beautiful affair, you have to admit, introducing us to the
beliefs of a different culture."

"Well, yes," said Mrs. Kornbluh. "The only thing . . . you know
Charlie Turner—that cute boy in Celia's class—a couple others? They got
very small parts or no part at all. In very bad taste, it seemed to me. After
all, it's their religion."

"Ach," explained my mother, "what could Mr. Hilton do? They got
very small voices; after all, why should they holler? The English language
they know from the beginning by heart. They're blond like angels. You
think it's so important they should get in the play? Christmas . . . the whole
piece of goods . . . they own it."

I listened and listened until I couldn't listen any more. Too sleepy, I   70
climbed out of bed and kneeled. I made a little church of my hands and said,
"Hear, O Israel . . ." Then I called out in Yiddish, "Please, good night,
good night. Ssh." My father said, "Ssh yourself," and slammed the kitchen
door.

I was happy. I fell asleep at once. I had prayed for everybody: my
talking family, cousins far away, passersby, and all the lonesome Christians.
I expected to be heard. My voice was certainly the loudest.

Considerations

1. What differences do you see between the mother's and father's views on
   raising their daughter? What does each apparently want Shirley to learn?
2. What qualities does Mr. Hilton value in Shirley? What kind of advice
   does he give her? What do you think Shirley learns from her experiences
   with Mr. Hilton?
3. Consider the comments of Miss Glacé. What attitude does she have
   toward her students and their cultural background? To what extent do

you see the Miss Glacés of this world as positive educators? To what extent do you see them as negative?

4. Why do some people object to Shirley's loud voice? What does Shirley, herself, think about her loud voice? How does the concept of a "loud voice" serve as a metaphor for the relationships and circumstances Shirley may face in real life rather than on the stage?

5. What does Shirley mean when she says she is "foolish but not a fool"? Do you agree with her evaluation? Explain.

RALPH ELLISON (1914–   )

Battle Royal

It goes a long way back, some twenty years. All my life I had been looking for something, and everywhere I turned someone tried to tell me what it was. I accepted their answers too, though they were often in contradiction and even self-contradictory. I was naive. I was looking for myself and asking everyone except myself questions which I, and only I, could answer. It took me a long time and much painful boomeranging of my expectations to achieve a realization everyone else appears to have been born with: That I am nobody but myself. But first I had to discover that I am an invisible man!

And yet I am no freak of nature, nor of history. I was in the cards, other things having been equal (or unequal) eighty-five years ago. I am not ashamed of my grandparents for having been slaves. I am only ashamed of myself for having at one time been ashamed. About eighty-five years ago they were told that they were free, united with others of our country in everything pertaining to the common good, and, in everything social, separate like the fingers of the hand. And they believed it. They exulted in it. They stayed in their place, worked hard, and brought up my father to do the same. But my grandfather is the one. He was an odd old guy, my grandfather, and I am told I take after him. It was he who caused the trouble. On his deathbed he called my father to him and said, "Son, after I'm gone I want you to keep up the fight. I never told you, but our life is a war and I have been a traitor all my born days, a spy in the enemy's country ever since I give up my gun back in the Reconstruction. Live with your head in the lion's mouth. I want you to overcome 'em with yeses, undermine 'em with grins, agree 'em to death and destruction, let 'em swoller you till they vomit or bust wide open." They thought the old man had gone out of his mind. He had been the meekest of men. The younger children were rushed from the room, the shades drawn and the flame of the lamp turned so low that it sputtered on the wick like the old man's breathing. "Learn it to the young-uns," he whispered fiercely; then he died.

But my folks were more alarmed over his last words than over his dying. It was as though he had not died at all, his words caused so much anxiety. I was warned emphatically to forget what he had said and, indeed, this is the first time it has been mentioned outside the family circle. It had a tremendous effect upon me, however. I could never be sure of what he meant. Grandfather had been a quiet old man who never made any trouble, yet on his deathbed he had called himself a traitor and a spy, and he had spoken of his meekness as a dangerous activity. It became a constant puzzle which lay unanswered in the back of my mind. And whenever things went well for me I remembered my grandfather and felt guilty and uncomfortable. It was as though I was carrying out his advice in spite of myself. And to make it worse, everyone loved me for it. I was praised by the most lily-white men of the town. I was considered an example of desirable conduct — just as my grandfather had been. And what puzzled me was that the old man had defined it as *treachery*. When I was praised for my conduct I felt a guilt that in some way I was doing something that was really against the wishes of the white folks, that if they had understood they would have desired me to act just the opposite, that I should have been sulky and mean, and that that really would have been what they wanted, even though they were fooled and thought they wanted me to act as I did. It made me afraid that some day they would look upon me as a traitor and I would be lost. Still I was more afraid to act any other way because they didn't like that at all. The old man's words were like a curse. On my graduation day I delivered an oration in which I showed that humility was the secret, indeed, the very essence of progress. (Not that I believed this — how could I, remembering my grandfather? — I only believed that it worked.) It was a great success. Everyone praised me and I was invited to give the speech at a gathering of the town's leading white citizens. It was a triumph for our whole community.

It was in the main ballroom of the leading hotel. When I got there I discovered that it was on the occasion of a smoker, and I was told that since I was to be there anyway I might as well take part in the battle royal to be fought by some of my schoolmates as part of the entertainment. The battle royal came first.

All of the town's big shots were there in their tuxedos, wolfing down the buffet foods, drinking beer and whiskey and smoking black cigars. It was a large room with a high ceiling. Chairs were arranged in neat rows around three sides of a portable boxing ring. The fourth side was clear, revealing a gleaming space of polished floor. I had some misgivings over the battle royal, by the way. Not from a distaste for fighting, but because I didn't care too much for the other fellows who were to take part. They were tough guys who seemed to have no grandfather's curse worrying their minds. No one could mistake their toughness. And besides, I suspected that fighting a battle royal might detract from the dignity of my speech. In those pre-invisible days I visualized myself as a potential Booker T. Washington. But the other fellows didn't care too much for me either, and there were nine of them. I felt superior to them in my way, and I didn't like the manner in which we were all crowded together into the servants' elevator. Nor did they like my being there. In fact, as the warmly lighted floors flashed past the elevator we had words over the fact that I, by taking part in the fight, had knocked one of their friends out of a night's work.

We were led out of the elevator through a rococo hall into an anteroom and told to get into our fighting togs. Each of us was issued a pair of boxing gloves and ushered out into the big mirrored hall, which we entered looking cautiously about us and whispering, lest we might accidentally be heard above the noise of the room. It was foggy with cigar smoke. And already the whiskey was taking effect. I was shocked to see some of the most important men of the town quite tipsy. They were all there — bankers, lawyers, judges, doctors, fire chiefs, teachers, merchants. Even one of the more fashionable pastors. Something we could not see was going on up front. A clarinet was vibrating sensuously and the men were standing up and moving eagerly forward. We were a small tight group, clustered together, our bare upper bodies touching and shining with anticipatory sweat; while up front the big shots were becoming increasingly excited over something we still could not see. Suddenly I heard the school superintendent, who had told me to come, yell, "Bring up the shines, gentlemen! Bring up the little shines!"

We were rushed up to the front of the ballroom, where it smelled even more strongly of tobacco and whiskey. Then we were pushed into place. I almost wet my pants. A sea of faces, some hostile, some amused, ringed around us, and in the center, facing us, stood a magnificent blonde — stark naked. There was a dead silence. I felt a blast of cold air chill me. I tried to back away, but they were behind me and around me. Some of the boys stood with lowered heads, trembling. I felt a wave of irrational guilt and fear. My teeth chattered, my skin turned to goose flesh, my knees knocked. Yet I was strongly attracted and looked in spite of myself. Had the price of looking been blindness, I would have looked. The hair was yellow like that of a circus kewpie doll, the face heavily powdered and rouged, as though to form an abstract mask, the eyes hollow and smeared a cool blue, the color of a baboon's butt. I felt a desire to spit upon her as my eyes brushed slowly over her body. Her breasts were firm and round as the domes of East Indian temples, and I stood so close as to see the fine skin texture and beads of pearly perspiration glistening like dew around the pink and erected buds of her nipples. I wanted at one and the same time to run from the room, to sink through the floor, or go to her and cover her from my eyes and the eyes of the others with my body; to feel the soft thighs, to caress her and destroy her, to love her and murder her, to hide from her, and yet to stroke where below the small American flag tattooed upon her belly her thighs formed a capital V. I had a notion that of all in the room she saw only me with her impersonal eyes.

And then she began to dance, a slow sensuous movement; the smoke of a hundred cigars clinging to her like the thinnest of veils. She seemed like a fair bird-girl girdled in veils calling to me from the angry surface of some gray and threatening sea. I was transported. Then I became aware of the clarinet playing and the big shots yelling at us. Some threatened us if we looked and others if we did not. On my right I saw one boy faint. And now a man grabbed a silver pitcher from a table and stepped close as he dashed ice water upon him and stood him up and forced two of us to support him as his head hung and moans issued from his thick bluish lips. Another boy began to plead to go home. He was the largest of the group, wearing dark red fighting trunks much too small to conceal the erection which projected from him as though in answer to the insinuating low-registered moaning of the clarinet. He tried to hide himself with his boxing gloves.

And all the while the blonde continued dancing, smiling faintly at the big shots who watched her with fascination, and faintly smiling at our fear. I noticed a certain merchant who followed her hungrily, his lips loose and drooling. He was a large man who wore diamond studs in a shirtfront which swelled with the ample paunch underneath, and each time the blonde swayed her undulating hips he ran his hand through the thin hair of his bald head and, with his arms upheld, his posture clumsy like that of an intoxicated panda, wound his belly in a slow and obscene grind. This creature was completely hypnotized. The music had quickened. As the dancer flung herself about with a detached expression on her face, the men began reaching out to touch her. I could see their beefy fingers sink into the soft flesh. Some of the others tried to stop them and she began to move around the floor in graceful circles, as they gave chase, slipping and sliding over the polished floor. It was mad. Chairs went crashing, drinks were spilt, as they ran laughing and howling after her. They caught her just as she reached a door, raised her from the floor, and tossed her as college boys are tossed at a hazing, and above her red, fixed-smiling lips I saw the terror and disgust in her eyes, almost like my own terror and that which I saw in some of the other boys. As I watched, they tossed her twice and her soft breasts seemed to flatten against the air and her legs flung wildly as she spun. Some of the more sober ones helped her to escape. And I started off the floor, heading for the anteroom with the rest of the boys.

Some were still crying and in hysteria. But as we tried to leave we were stopped and ordered to get into the ring. There was nothing to do but what we were told. All ten of us climbed under the ropes and allowed ourselves to be blindfolded with broad bands of white cloth. One of the men seemed to feel a bit sympathetic and tried to cheer us up as we stood with our backs against the ropes. Some of us tried to grin. "See that boy over there?" one of the men said. "I want you to run across at the bell and give it to him right in the belly. If you don't get him, I'm going to get you. I don't like his looks." Each of us was told the same. The blindfolds were put on. Yet even then I had been going over my speech. In my mind each word was as bright as flame. I felt the cloth pressed into place, and frowned so that it would be loosened when I relaxed.

But now I felt a sudden fit of blind terror. I was unused to darkness. It was as though I had suddenly found myself in a dark room filled with poisonous cottonmouths. I could hear the bleary voices yelling insistently for the battle royal to begin.

"Get going in there!"

"Let me at the big nigger!"

I strained to pick up the school superintendent's voice, as though to squeeze some security out of that slightly more familiar sound.

"Let me at those black sonsabitches!" someone yelled.   15

"No, Jackson, no!" another voice yelled. "Here, somebody, help me hold Jack."

"I want to get at that ginger-colored nigger. Tear him limb from limb," the first voice yelled.

I stood against the ropes trembling. For in those days I was what they called ginger-colored, and he sounded as though he might crunch me between his teeth like a crisp ginger cookie.

Quite a struggle was going on. Chairs were being kicked about and I could hear voices grunting as with a terrific effort. I wanted to see, to see more desperately than ever before. But the blindfold was as tight as a thick skin-puckering scab and when I raised my gloved hands to push the layers of white aside a voice yelled, "Oh, no you don't, black bastard! Leave that alone!"

"Ring the bell before Jackson kills him a coon!" someone boomed in   20
the sudden silence. And I heard the bell clang and the sound of feet scuffling forward.

A glove smacked against my head. I pivoted, striking out stiffly as someone went past, and felt the jar ripple along the length of my arm to my shoulder. Then it seemed as though all nine of the boys had turned upon me at once. Blows pounded me from all sides while I struck out as best I could. So many blows landed upon me that I wondered if I were not the only blindfolded fighter in the ring, or if the man called Jackson hadn't succeeded in getting me after all.

Blindfolded, I could no longer control my motions. I had no dignity. I stumbled about like a baby or a drunken man. The smoke had become thicker and with each new blow it seemed to sear and further restrict my lungs. My saliva became like hot bitter glue. A glove connected with my head, filling my mouth with warm blood. It was everywhere. I could not tell if the moisture I felt upon my body was sweat or blood. A blow landed hard against the nape of my neck. I felt myself going over, my head hitting the floor. Streaks of blue light filled the black world behind the blindfold. I lay prone, pretending that I was knocked out, but felt myself seized by hands and yanked to my feet. "Get going, black boy! Mix it up!" My arms were like lead, my head smarting from blows. I managed to feel my way to the ropes and held on, trying to catch my breath. A glove landed in my midsection and I went over again, feeling as though the smoke had become a knife jabbed into my guts. Pushed this way and that by the legs milling around me, I finally pulled erect and discovered that I could see the black, sweat-washed forms weaving in the smoky-blue atmosphere like drunken dancers weaving to the rapid drumlike thuds of blows.

Everyone fought hysterically. It was complete anarchy. Everybody fought everybody else. No group fought together for long. Two, three, four, fought one, then turned to fight each other, were themselves attacked. Blows landed below the belt and in the kidney, with the gloves open as well as closed, and with my eye partly opened now there was not so much terror. I moved carefully, avoiding blows, although not too many to attract attention, fighting from group to group. The boys groped about like blind, cautious crabs crouching to protect their mid-sections, their heads pulled in short against their shoulders, their arms stretched nervously before them, with their fists testing the smoke-filled air like the knobbed feelers of hypersensitive snails. In the corner I glimpsed a boy violently punching the air and heard him scream in pain as he smashed his hand against a ring post. For a second I saw him bent over holding his hand, then going down as a blow caught his unprotected head. I played one group against the other, slipping in and throwing a punch then stepped out of range while pushing the others into the melee to take the blows blindly aimed at me. The smoke was agonizing and there were no rounds, no bells at three minute intervals to relieve our exhaustion. The room spun around me, a swirl of lights, smoke, sweating bodies surrounded by tense white faces. I bled from both nose and mouth, the blood spattering upon my chest.

The men kept yelling, "Slug him, black boy! Knock his guts out!"

"Uppercut him! Kill him! Kill that big boy!"   25

Taking a fake fall, I saw a boy going down heavily beside me as though we were felled by a single blow, saw a sneaker-clad foot shoot into his groin as the two who had knocked him down stumbled upon him. I rolled out of range, feeling a twinge of nausea.

The harder we fought the more threatening the men became. And yet, I had begun to worry about my speech again. How would it go? Would they recognize my ability? What would they give me?

I was fighting automatically when suddenly I noticed that one after another of the boys was leaving the ring. I was surprised, filled with panic, as though I had been left alone with an unknown danger. Then I understood. The boys had arranged it among themselves. It was custom for the two men left in the ring to slug it out for the winner's prize. I discovered this too late. When the bell sounded two men in tuxedos leaped into the ring and removed the blindfold. I found myself facing Tatlock, the biggest of the gang. I felt sick at my stomach. Hardly had the bell stopped ringing in my ears than it clanged again and I saw him moving swiftly toward me. Thinking of nothing else to do I hit him smash on the nose. He kept coming, bringing the rank sharp violence of stale sweat. His face was a black blank of a face, only his eyes alive — with hate of me and aglow with a feverish terror from what had happened to us all. I became anxious. I wanted to deliver my speech and he came at me as though he meant to beat it out of me. I smashed him again and again, taking his blows as they came. Then on a sudden impulse I struck him lightly and as we clinched, I whispered, "Fake like I knocked you out, you can have the prize."

"I'll break your behind," he whispered hoarsely.

"For *them?*"   30

"For *me,* sonofabitch."

They were yelling for us to break it up and Tatlock spun me half around with a blow, and as a joggled camera sweeps in a reeling scene, I saw the howling red faces crouching tense beneath the cloud of blue-gray smoke. For a moment the world wavered, unraveled, flowed, then my head cleared and Tatlock bounced before me. The fluttering shadow before my eyes was his jabbing left hand. Then falling forward, my head against his damp shoulder, I whispered.

"I'll make it five dollars more."

"Go to hell!"

But his muscles relaxed a trifle beneath my pressure and I breathed.   35 "Seven?"

"Give it to your ma," he said, ripping me beneath the heart.

And while I still held him I butted him and moved away. I felt myself bombarded with punches. I fought back with hopeless desperation. I wanted to deliver my speech more than anything else in the world, because I felt only these men could judge truly my ability, and now this stupid clown was ruining my chances. I began fighting carefully now, moving in to punch him and out again with my greater speed. A lucky blow to his chin and I had him going too — until I heard a loud voice yell, "I got my money on the big boy."

Hearing this, I almost dropped my guard. I was confused: Should I try to win against the voice out there? Would not this go against my speech, and was not this a moment for humility, for nonresistance? A blow to my head as I danced about sent my right eye popping like a jack-in-the-box and settled my dilemma. The room went red as I fell. It was a dream fall, my body languid and fastidious as to where to land, until the floor became impatient and smashed up to meet me. A moment later I came to. An hypnotic voice said FIVE emphatically. And I lay there, hazily watching a dark red spot of my own blood shaping itself into a butterfly, glistening and soaking into the soiled gray world of the canvas.

When the voice drawled TEN I was lifted up and dragged to a chair. I sat dazed. My eye pained and swelled with each throb of my pounding heart and I wondered if now I would be allowed to speak. I was wringing wet, my mouth still bleeding. We were grouped along the wall now. The other boys ignored me as they congratulated Tatlock and speculated as to how much they would be paid. One boy whimpered over his smashed hand. Looking up front, I saw attendants in white jackets rolling the portable ring away and placing a small square rug in the vacant space surrounded by chairs. Perhaps, I thought, I will stand on the rug to deliver my speech.

Then the M.C. called to us, "Come on up here boys and get your   40 money."

We ran forward to where the men laughed and talked in their chairs, waiting. Everyone seemed friendly now.

"There it is on the rug," the man said. I saw the rug covered with coins of all dimensions and a few crumpled bills. But what excited me, scattered here and there, were the gold pieces.

"Boys, it's all yours," the man said. "You get all you grab."

"That's right, Sambo," a blond man said, winking at me confidentially.

I trembled with excitement, forgetting my pain. I would get the gold   45 and the bills, I thought. I would use both hands. I would throw my body against the boys nearest to me block them from the gold.

"Get down around the rug now," the man commanded, "and don't anyone touch it until I give the signal."

"This ought to be good," I heard.

As told, we got around the square rug on our knees. Slowly the man raised his freckled hand as we followed it upward with our eyes.

I heard, "These niggers look like they're about to pray!"

Then, "Ready," the man said. "Go!"   50

I lunged for a yellow coin lying on the blue design on the carpet, touching it and sending a surprised shriek to join those rising around me. I tried frantically to remove my hand but could not let go. A hot, violent force tore through my body, shaking me like a wet rat. The rug was electrified. The hair bristled up on my head as I shook myself free. My muscles jumped, my nerves jangled, writhed. But I saw that this was not stopping the other boys. Laughing in fear and embarrassment, some were holding back and scooping up the coins knocked off by the painful contortions of the others. The men roared above us as we struggled.

"Pick it up, goddammit, pick it up!" someone called like a bass-voiced parrot. "Go on, get it!"

I crawled rapidly around the floor, picking up the coins, trying to avoid the coppers and to get greenbacks and the gold. Ignoring the shock by laughing, as I brushed the coins off quickly, I discovered that I could contain the electricity — a contradiction, but it works. Then the men began to push us onto the rug. Laughing embarrassedly, we struggled out of their hands and kept after the coins. We were all wet and slippery and hard to hold. Suddenly I saw a boy lifted into the air, glistening with sweat like a circus seal, and dropped, his wet back landing flush upon the charged rug, heard him yell and saw him literally dance upon his back, his elbows beating a frenzied tattoo upon the floor, his muscles twitching like the flesh of a horse stung by many flies. When he finally rolled off, his face was gray and no one stopped him when he ran from the floor amid booming laughter.

"Get the money," the M.C. called "That's good hard American cash!"

And we snatched and grabbed, snatched and grabbed. I was careful   55 not to come too close to the rug now, and when I felt the hot whiskey breath descend upon me like a cloud of foul air I reached out and grabbed the leg of a chair. It was occupied and I held on desperately.

"Leggo nigger! Leggo!"

The huge face wavered down to mine as he tried to push me free. But my body was slippery and he was too drunk. It was Mr. Colcord, who owned a chain of movie houses and "entertainment palaces." Each time he grabbed me I slipped out of his hands. It became a real struggle. I feared the rug more than I did the drunk, so I held on, surprising myself for a moment by trying to topple *him* upon the rug. It was such an enormous idea that I found myself actually carrying it out. I tried not to be obvious, yet when I grabbed his leg, trying to tumble him out of the chair, he raised up roaring with laughter, and, looking at me with soberness dead in the eye, kicked me viciously in the chest. The chair leg flew out of my hand and I felt myself going and rolled. It was as though I had rolled through a bed of hot coals. It seemed a whole century would pass before I would roll free, a century in which I was seared through the deepest levels of my body to the fearful breath within me and the breath seared and heated to the point of explosion. It'll all be over in a flash, I thought as I rolled clear. It'll all be over in a flash.

But not yet, the men on the other side were waiting, red faces swollen as though from apoplexy as they bent forward in their chairs. Seeing their fingers coming toward me I rolled away as a fumbled football rolls off the receiver's fingertips, back into the coals. That time I luckily sent the rug sliding out of place and heard the coins ringing against the floor and the boys scuffling to pick them up and the M.C. calling, "All right, boys, that's all. Go get dressed and get your money."

I was limp as a dish rag. My back felt as though it had been beaten with wires.

When we had dressed the M.C. came in and gave us each five dollars, 60 except Tatlock, who got ten for being last in the ring. Then he told us to leave. I was not to get a chance to deliver my speech, I thought. I was going out into the dim alley in despair when I was stopped and told to go back. I returned to the ballroom, where the men were pushing back their chairs and gathering in groups to talk.

The M.C. knocked on a table for quiet. "Gentlemen," he said, "we almost forgot an important part of the program. A most serious part, gentlemen. This boy was brought here to deliver a speech which he made at his graduation yesterday . . ."

"Bravo!"

"I'm told that he is the smartest boy we've got out there in Greenwood. I'm told that he knows more big words than a pocket-sized dictionary."

Much applause and laughter.

"So now, gentlemen, I want you to give him your attention." 65

There was still laughter as I faced them, my mouth dry, my eye throbbing. I began slowly, but evidently my throat was tense, because they began shouting, "Louder! Louder!"

"We of the younger generation extol the wisdom of that great leader and educator," I shouted, "who first spoke these flaming words of wisdom.

'A ship lost at sea for many days suddenly sighted a friendly vessel. From the mast of the unfortunate vessel was seen a signal: "Water, water; we die of thirst!" The answer from the friendly vessel came back: "Cast down your bucket where you are." The captain of the distressed vessel, at last heeding the injunction, cast down his bucket, and it came up full of fresh sparkling water from the mouth of the Amazon River.' And like him I say, and in his words, 'To those of my race who depend upon bettering their condition in a foreign land, or who underestimate the importance of cultivating friendly relations with the Southern white man, who is his next-door neighbor, I would say: "Cast down your bucket where you are" — cast it down in making friends in every manly way of the people of all races by whom we are surrounded. . . .'"

I spoke automatically and with such fervor that I did not realize that the men were still talking and laughing until my dry mouth, filling up with blood from the cut, almost strangled me. I coughed, wanting to stop and go to one of the tall brass, sand–filled spittoons to relieve myself, but a few of the men, especially the superintendent, were listening and I was afraid. So I gulped it down, blood, saliva, and all, and continued. (What powers of endurance I had during those days! What enthusiasm! What a belief in the rightness of things!) I spoke even louder in spite of the pain. But still they talked and still they laughed, as though deaf with cotton in dirty ears. So I spoke with greater emotional emphasis. I closed my ears and swallowed blood until I was nauseated. The speech seemed a hundred times as long as before, but I could not leave out a single word. All had to be said, each memorized nuance considered, rendered. Nor was that all. Whenever I uttered a word of three or more syllables a group of voices would yell for me to repeat it. I used the phrase "social responsibility" and they yelled:

"What's that word you say, boy?"

"Social responsibility," I said.   70

"What?"

"Social . . ."

"Louder."

". . . responsibility."

"More!"   75

"Respon — "

"Repeat!"

" — sibility."

The room filled with the uproar of laughter until, no doubt, distracted by having to gulp down my blood, I made a mistake and yelled a phrase I had often seen denounced with newspaper editorials, heard debated in private.

"Social . . ."   80

"What?" they yelled.

". . . equality — "

The laughter hung smokelike in the sudden stillness. I opened my eyes puzzled. Sounds of displeasure filled the room. The M.C. rushed forward. They shouted hostile phrases at me. But I did not understand.

A small dry mustached man in the front row blared out, "Say that slowly, son!"

"What sir?"

"What you just said!"

"Social responsibility, sir," I said.

"You weren't being smart, were you, boy?" he said, not unkindly.

"No, sir!"

"You sure that about 'equality' was a mistake?"

"Oh, yes, sir," I said. "I was swallowing blood."

"Well, you had better speak more slowly so we can understand. We mean to do right by you, but you've got to know your place at all times. All right, now, go on with your speech."

I was afraid. I wanted to leave but I wanted also to speak and I was afraid they'd snatch me down.

"Thank you, sir," I said, beginning where I had left off, and having them ignore me as before.

Yet when I finished there was a thunderous applause. I was surprised to see the superintendent come forth with a package wrapped in white tissue paper, and, gesturing for quiet, address the men.

"Gentlemen, you see that I did not overpraise this boy. He makes a good speech and some day he'll lead his people in the proper paths. And I don't have to tell you that that is important in these days and times. This is a good, smart boy, and so to encourage him in the right direction, in the name of the Board of Education I wish to present him a prize in the form of this . . ."

He paused, removing the tissue paper and revealing a gleaming calfskin briefcase.

". . . in the form of this first-class article from Shad Whitmore's shop."

"Boy," he said, addressing me, "take this prize and keep it well. Consider it a badge of office. Prize it. Keep developing as you are and some day it will be filled with important papers that will help shape the destiny of your people."

I was so moved that I could hardly express my thanks. A rope of bloody saliva forming a shape like an undiscovered continent drooled upon the leather and I wiped it quickly away. I felt an importance that I had never dreamed.

"Open it and see what's inside," I was told.

My fingers a-tremble, I complied, smelling the fresh leather and finding an official-looking document inside. It was a scholarship to the state college for Negroes. My eyes filled with tears and I ran awkwardly off the floor.

I was so overjoyed; I did not even mind when I discovered that the gold pieces I had scrambled for were brass pocket tokens advertising a certain make of automobile.

When I reached home everyone was excited. Next day the neighbors came to congratulate me. I even felt safe from grandfather, whose deathbed curse usually spoiled my triumphs. I stood beneath his photograph with my briefcase in hand and smiled triumphantly into his stolid black peasant's face. It was a face that fascinated me. The eyes seemed to follow everywhere I went.

That night I dreamed I was at a circus with him and that he refused to   105 laugh at the clowns no matter what they did. Then later he told me to open my briefcase and read what was inside and I did, finding an official envelope stamped with the state seal; and inside the envelope I found another and another, endlessly, and I thought I would fall of weariness. "Them's years," he said. "Now open that one." And I did and in it I found an engraved document containing a short message in letters of gold. "Read it," my grandfather said. "Out loud."

"To Whom It May Concern," I intoned. "Keep This Nigger-Boy Running."

I awoke with the old man's laughter ringing in my ears.

(It was a dream I was to remember and dream again for many years after. But at that time I had no insight into its meaning. First I had to attend college.)

Considerations

1. "Battle Royal" can be divided into six sections. Identify these sections and explain what the narrator learns in each section and how he changes in response to what he learns.
2. Consider the deathbed scene that opens the story. What lesson does the grandfather try to teach his grandchildren? What motivates him to change during the last moments of his life from "a quiet old man who never made any trouble" to an agitator whose words sound, in his family's ears, radical and alarming? Why is the family so disturbed by the final message? Why do they tell the children to forget what he said?
3. What achievement led to the narrator's invitation to speak before the town's white citizens? What are his expectations of the evening? What does he learn from the contrast between his expectations and the reality of the "battle royal"?
4. What lesson do the white men teach by their responses to the blond stripper?
5. Discuss the significance of the "slip" the narrator makes when he finally delivers his speech. Consider the relationship between the slip and the response of the audience. Pay particular attention to the white superintendent of schools and to the prize he awards the narrator.

EDNA O'BRIEN (1930–   )

Sister Imelda

Sister Imelda did not take classes on her first day back in the convent but we spotted her in the grounds after the evening Rosary. Excitement and curiosity impelled us to follow her and try to see what she looked like, but she thwarted us by walking with head bent and eyelids down. All we could be certain of was that she was tall and limber and that she prayed while she walked. No looking at nature for her, or no curiosity about seventy boarders in gaberdine coats and black shoes and stockings. We might just as well have been crows, so impervious was she to our stares and to abortive attempts at trying to say "Hello, Sister."

We had returned from our long summer holiday and we were all wretched. The convent, with its high stone wall and green iron gates enfolding us again, seemed more of a prison than ever — for after our spell in the outside world we all felt very much older and more sophisticated, and my friend Baba and I were dreaming of our final escape, which would be in a year. And so, on that damp autumn evening when I saw the chrysanthemums and saw the new nun intent on prayer I pitied her and thought how alone she must be, cut off from her friends and conversation, with only God as her intangible spouse.

The next day she came into our classroom to take geometry. Her pale, slightly long face I saw as formidable, but her eyes were different, being blue-black and full of verve. Her lips were very purple, as if she had put puce pencil on them. They were the lips of a woman who might sing in a cabaret, and unconsciously she had formed the habit of turning them inward, as if she, too, was aware of their provocativeness. She had spent the last four years — the same span that Baba and I had spent in the convent — at the university in Dublin, where she studied languages. We couldn't understand how she had resisted the temptations of the hectic world and willingly come back to this. Her spell in the outside world made her different from the other nuns; there was more bounce in her walk, more excitement in the way she tackled teaching, reminding us that it was the most important thing in the world as she uttered the phrase "Praise be the Incarnate World." She began each day's class by reading from Cardinal Newman,° who was a favorite of hers. She read how God dwelt in light unapproachable, and how with Him there was neither change nor shadow of alteration. It was amazing how her looks changed. Some days, when her eyes were flashing, she looked almost profane and made me wonder what events inside the precincts of the convent caused her to be suddenly so excited. She might have been a girl going to a dance, except for her habit.

Cardinal Newman: John Henry Newman (1801–1890), Roman Catholic theologian, cardinal, and author.

"Hasn't she wonderful eyes," I said to Baba. That particular day they were like blackberries, large and soft and shiny.

"Something wrong in her upstairs department," Baba said, and added   5
that with makeup Imelda would be a cinch.

"Still, she has a vocation!" I said, and even aired the idiotic view that I might have one. At certain moments it did seem enticing to become a nun, to lead a life unspotted by sin, never to have to have babies, and to wear a ring that singled one out as the Bride of Christ. But there was the other side to it, the silence, the gravity of it, having to get up two or three times a night to pray and, above all, never having the opportunity of leaving the confines of the place except for the funeral of one's parents. For us boarders it was torture, but for the nuns it was nothing short of doom. Also, we could complain to each other, and we did, food being the source of the greatest grumbles. Lunch was either bacon and cabbage or a peculiar stringy meat followed by tapioca pudding; tea consisted of bread dolloped with lard and occasionally, as a treat, fairly green rhubarb jam, which did not have enough sugar. Through the long curtainless windows we saw the conifer trees and a sky that was scarcely ever without the promise of rain or a downpour.

She was a right lunatic, then, Baba said, having gone to university for four years and willingly come back to incarceration, to poverty, chastity, and obedience. We concocted scenes of agony in some Dublin hostel, while a boy, or even a young man, stood beneath her bedroom window throwing up chunks of clay or whistles or a supplication. In our version of it he was slightly older than her, and possibly a medical student, since medical students had a knack with women, because of studying diagrams and skeletons. His advances, like those of a sudden storm, would intermittently rise and overwhelm her, and the memory of these sudden flaying advances of his would haunt her until she died, and if ever she contracted fever, these secrets would out. It was also rumored that she possessed a fierce temper and that, while a postulant,° she had hit a girl so badly with her leather strap that the girl had to be put to bed because of wounds. Yet another black mark against Sister Imelda was that her brother Ambrose had been sued by a nurse for breach of promise.°

That first morning when she came into our classroom and modestly introduced herself, I had no idea how terribly she would infiltrate my life, how in time she would be not just one of those teachers or nuns but rather a special one, almost like a ghost who passed the boundaries of common exchange and who crept inside one, devouring so much of one's thoughts, so much of one's passion, invading the place that was called one's heart. She talked in a low voice, as if she did not want her words to go beyond the

postulant: Candidate to become a member of a religious order for women.   *breach of promise:* At this time, some countries allowed women to sue men who had promised to marry them and then broken the engagement.

bounds of the wall, and constantly she stressed the value of work both to enlarge the mind and to discipline the thought. One of her eyelids was red and swollen, as if she was getting a sty. I reckoned that she overmortified° herself by not eating at all. I saw in her some terrible premonition of sacrifice which I would have to emulate. Then, in direct contrast, she absently held the stick of chalk between her first and second fingers, the very same as if it were a cigarette, and Baba whispered to me that she might have been a smoker when in Dublin. Sister Imelda looked down sharply at me and said what was the secret and would I like to share it, since it seemed so comical. I said, "Nothing, Sister, nothing," and her dark eyes exuded such vehemence that I prayed she would never have occasion to punish me.

November came and the tiled walls of the recreation hall oozed moisture and gloom. Most girls had sore throats and were told to suffer this inconvenience to mortify themselves in order to lend a glorious hand in that communion of spirit that linked the living with the dead. It was the month of the Suffering Souls in Purgatory, and as we heard of their twofold agony, the yearning for Christ and the ferocity of the leaping flames that burned and charred their poor limbs, we were asked to make acts of mortification. Some girls gave up jam or sweets and some gave up talking, and so in recreation time they were like dummies making signs with thumb and finger to merely say "How are you?" Baba said that saner people were locked in the lunatic asylum, which was only a mile away. We saw them in the grounds, pacing back and forth, with their mouths agape and dribble coming out of them, like melting icicles. Among our many fears was that one of those lunatics would break out and head straight for the convent and assault some of the girls.

Yet in the thick of all these dreads I found myself becoming dreadfully 10
happy. I had met Sister Imelda outside of class a few times and I felt that there was an attachment between us. Once it was in the grounds, when she did a reckless thing. She broke off a chrysanthemum and offered it to me to smell. It had no smell, or at least only something faint that suggested autumn, and feeling this to be the case herself, she said it was not a gardenia, was it? Another time we met in the chapel porch, and as she drew her shawl more tightly around her body, I felt how human she was, and prey to the cold.

In the classroom things were not so congenial between us. Geometry was my worst subject, indeed, a total mystery to me. She had not taught more than four classes when she realized this and threw a duster at me in a rage. A few girls gasped as she asked me to stand up and make a spectacle of myself. Her face had reddened, and presently she took out her handkerchief and patted the eye which was red and swollen. I not only felt a fool but felt in imminent danger of sneezing as I inhaled the smell of chalk that had fallen onto my gym frock. Suddenly she fled from the room, leaving us ten

---

overmortified: Mortification (physical punishment or deprivation) was practiced by some religious and laypeople as atonement for sins they believed they had committed.

minutes free until the next class. Some girls said it was a disgrace, said I should write home and say I had been assaulted. Others welcomed the few minutes in which to gabble. All I wanted was to run after her and say that I was sorry to have caused her such distemper, because I knew dimly that it was as much to do with liking as it was with dislike. In me then there came a sort of speechless tenderness for her, and I might have known that I was stirred.

"We could get her defrocked,"° Baba said, and elbowed me in God's name to sit down.

That evening at Benediction I had the most overwhelming surprise. It was a particularly happy evening, with the choir nuns in full soaring form and the rows of candles like so many little ladders to the golden chalice that glittered all the more because of the beams of fitful flame. I was full of tears when I discovered a new holy picture had been put in my prayer book, and before I dared look on the back to see who had given it to me, I felt and guessed that this was no ordinary picture from an ordinary girl friend, that this was a talisman and a peace offering from Sister Imelda. It was a pale-blue picture, so pale that it was almost gray, like the down of a pigeon, and it showed a mother looking down on the infant child. On the back, in her beautiful ornate handwriting, she had written a verse:

> Trust Him when dark doubts assail thee,
> Trust Him when thy faith is small,
> Trust Him when to simply trust Him
> Seems the hardest thing of all.

This was her atonement. To think that she had located the compartment in the chapel where I kept my prayer book and to think that she had been so naked as to write in it and give me a chance to boast about it and to show it to the other girls. When I thanked her next day, she bowed but did not speak. Mostly the nuns were on silence and only permitted to talk during class.

In no time I had received another present, a little miniature prayer book with a leather cover and gold edging. The prayers were in French and the lettering so minute it was as if a tiny insect had fashioned them. Soon I was publicly known as her pet. I opened the doors for her, raised the blackboard two pegs higher (she was taller than other nuns), and handed out the exercise books which she had corrected. Now in the margins of my geometry propositions I would find "Good" or "Excellent," when in the past she used to splash "Disgraceful." Baba said it was foul to be a nun's pet and that any girl who sucked up to a nun could not be trusted.

About a month later Sister Imelda asked me to carry her books up   15
four flights of stairs to the cookery kitchen. She taught cookery to a junior

---

defrocked: Literally, taken out of the religious garb; expelled from the religious community.

class. As she walked ahead of me, I thought how supple she was and how thoroughbred, and when she paused on the landing to look out through the long curtainless window, I too paused. Down below, two women in suede boots were chatting and smoking as they moved along the street with shopping baskets. Nearby a lay nun was on her knees scrubbing the granite steps, and the cold air was full of the raw smell of Jeyes Fluid. There was a potted plant on the landing, and Sister Imelda put her fingers in the earth and went "Tch tch tch," saying it needed water. I said I would water it later on. I was happy in my prison then, happy to be near her, happy to walk behind her as she twirled her beads and bowed to the servile nun. I no longer cried for my mother, no longer counted the days on a pocket calendar until the Christmas holidays.

"Come back at five," she said as she stood on the threshold of the cookery kitchen door. The girls, all in white overalls, were arranged around the long wooden table waiting for her. It was as if every girl was in love with her. Because, as she entered, their faces broke into smiles, and in different tones of audacity they said her name. She must have liked cookery class, because she beamed and called to someone, anyone, to get up a blazing fire. Then she went across to the cast-iron stove and spat on it to test its temperature. It was hot, because her spit rose up and sizzled.

When I got back later, she was sitting on the edge of the table swaying her legs. There was something reckless about her pose, something defiant. It seemed as if any minute she would take out a cigarette case, snap it open, and then archly offer me one. The wonderful smell of baking made me realize how hungry I was, but far more so, it brought back to me my own home, my mother testing orange cakes with a knitting needle and letting me lick the line of half-baked dough down the length of the needle. I wondered if she had supplanted my mother, and I hoped not, because I had aimed to outstep my original world and take my place in a new and hallowed one.

"I bet you have a sweet tooth," she said, and then she got up, crossed the kitchen, and from under a wonderful shining silver cloche she produced two jam tarts with a crisscross design on them where the pastry was latticed over the dark jam. They were still warm.

"What will I do with them?" I asked.

"Eat them, you goose," she said, and she watched me eat as if she herself derived some peculiar pleasure from it, whereas I was embarrassed about the pastry crumbling and the bits of blackberry jam staining my lips. She was amused. It was one of the most awkward yet thrilling moments I had lived, and inherent in the pleasure was the terrible sense of danger. Had we been caught, she, no doubt, would have had to make massive sacrifice. I looked at her and thought how peerless and how brave, and I wondered if she felt hungry. She had a white overall over her black habit and this made her warmer and freer, and caused me to think of the happiness that would be ours, the laissez-faire if we were away from the convent in an ordinary kitchen doing something easy and customary. But we weren't. It was clear to me then that my version of pleasure was inextricable from pain, that they existed side by side and were interdependent, like the two forces of an electric current.

"Had you a friend when you were in Dublin at university?" I asked daringly.

"I shared a desk with a sister from Howth and stayed in the same hostel," she said.

But what about boys? I thought, and what of your life now and do you long to go out into the world? But could not say it.

We knew something about the nuns' routine. It was rumored that they wore itchy wool underwear, ate dry bread for breakfast, rarely had meat, cakes, or dainties, kept certain hours of strict silence with each other, as well as constant vigil on their thoughts; so that if their minds wandered to the subject of food or pleasure, they would quickly revert to thoughts of God and their eternal souls. They slept on hard beds with no sheets and hairy blankets. At four o'clock in the morning while we slept, each nun got out of bed, in her habit — which was also her death habit — and chanting, they all flocked down the wooden stairs like ravens, to fling themselves on the tiled floor of the chapel. Each nun—even the Mother Superior — flung herself in total submission, saying prayers in Latin and offering up the moment to God. Then silently back to their cells for one more hour of rest. It was not difficult to imagine Sister Imelda face downward, arms outstretched, prostrate on the tiled floor. I often heard their chanting when I wakened suddenly from a nightmare, because, although we slept in a different building, both adjoined, and if one wakened one often heard that monotonous Latin chanting, long before the birds began, long before our own bell summoned us to rise at six.

"Do you eat nice food?" I asked.   25

"Of course," she said, and smiled. She sometimes broke into an eager smile, which she did much to conceal.

"Have you ever thought of what you will be?" she asked.

I shook my head. My design changed from day to day.

She looked at her man's silver pocket watch, closed the damper of the range, and prepared to leave. She checked that all the wall cupboards were locked by running her hand over them.

"Sister," I called, gathering enough courage at last — we must have   30 some secret, something to join us together — "what color hair have you?"

We never saw the nuns' hair, or their eyebrows, or ears, as all that part was covered by a stiff white wimple.

"You shouldn't ask such a thing," she said, getting pink in the face, and then she turned back and whispered, "I'll tell you on your last day here, provided your geometry has improved."

She had scarcely gone when Baba, who had been lurking behind some pillar, stuck her head in the door and said, "Christsake, save me a bit." She finished the second pastry, then went around looking in kitchen drawers. Because of everything being locked, she found only some castor sugar in a china shaker. She ate a little and threw the remainder into the dying fire, so that it flared up for a minute with a yellow spluttering flame. Baba showed her jealousy by putting it around the school that I was in the cookery kitchen every evening, gorging cakes with Sister Imelda and telling tales.

I did not speak to Sister Imelda again in private until the evening of our Christmas theatricals. She came to help us put on makeup and get into our stage clothes and fancy headgear. These clothes were kept in a trunk from one year to the next, and though sumptuous and strewn with braiding and gold, they smelled of camphor. Yet as we donned them we felt different, and as we sponged pancake makeup onto our faces, we became saucy and emphasized these new guises by adding dark pencil to the eyes and making the lips bright carmine. There was only one tube of lipstick and each girl clamored for it. The evening's entertainment was to comprise scenes from Shakespeare and laughing sketches. I had been chosen to recite Mark Antony's lament° over Caesar's body, and for this I was to wear a purple toga, white knee-length socks, and patent buckle shoes. The shoes were too big and I moved in them as if in clogs. She said to take them off, to go barefoot. I realized that I was getting nervous and that in an effort to memorize my speech, the words were getting all askew and flying about in my head, like the separate pieces of a jigsaw puzzle. She sensed my panic and very slowly put her hand on my face and enjoined me to look at her. I looked into her eyes, which seemed fathomless, and saw that she was willing me to be calm and obliging me to be master of my fears, and I little knew that one day she would have to do the same as regards the swoop of my feelings for her. As we continued to stare I felt myself becoming calm and the words were restored to me in their right and fluent order. The lights were being lowered out in the recreation hall, and we knew now that all the nuns had arrived, had settled themselves down, and were eagerly awaiting this annual hotchpotch of amateur entertainment. There was that fearsome hush as the hall went dark and the few spotlights were turned on. She kissed her crucifix and I realized that she was saying a prayer for me. Then she raised her arm as if depicting the stance of a Greek goddess, walking onto the stage, I was fired by her ardor.

Baba could say that I bawled like a bloody bull, but Sister Imelda, who   35 stood in the wings, said that temporarily she had felt the streets of Rome, had seen the corpse of Caesar, as I delivered those poignant, distempered lines. When I came off stage she put her arms around me and I was encased in a shower of silent kisses. After we had taken down the decorations and put the fancy clothes back in the trunk, I gave her two half-pound boxes of chocolates — bought for me illicitly by one of the day girls — and she gave me a casket made from the insides of match boxes and covered over with gilt paint and gold dust. It was like holding moths and finding their powder adhering to the fingers.

Mark Antony's lament: From Shakespeare's *Julius Caesar;* Act 3, scene 2, lines 73–107.

"What will you do on Christmas Day, Sister?" I said.

"I'll pray for you," she said.

It was useless to say, "Will you have turkey?" or "Will you have plum pudding?" or "Will you loll in bed?" because I believed that Christmas Day would be as bleak and deprived as any other day in her life. Yet she was radiant as if such austerity was joyful. Maybe she was basking in some secret realization involving her and me.

On the cold snowy afternoon three weeks later when we returned from our holidays, Sister Imelda came up to the dormitory to welcome me back. All the others girls had gone down to the recreation hall to do barn dances and I could hear someone banging on the piano. I did not want to go down and clump around with sixty other girls, having nothing to look forward to, only tea and the Rosary and early bed. The beds were damp after our stay at home, and when I put my hand between the sheets, it was like feeling dew but did not have the freshness of outdoors. What depressed me further was that I had seen a mouse in one of the cupboards, seen its tail curl with terror as it slipped away into a crevice. If there was one mouse, there were God knows how many, and the cakes we hid in secret would not be safe. I was still unpacking as she came down the narrow passage between the rows of iron beds and I saw in her walk such agitation.

"Tut, tut, tut, you've curled your hair," she said, offended. 40

Yes, the world outside was somehow declared in this perm, and for a second I remembered the scalding pains the trickles of ammonia dribbled down my forehead and then the joy as the hairdresser said that she would make me look like Movita, a Mexican star. Now suddenly that world and those aspirations seemed trite and I wanted to take a brush and straighten my hair and revert to the dark gawky somber girl that I had been. I offered her iced queen cakes that my mother had made, but she refused them and said she could only stay a second. She lent me a notebook of hers, which she had had as a pupil, and into which she had copied favorite quotations, some religious, some not. I read at random:

Twice or thrice had I loved thee,
Before I knew thy face or name.
So in a voice, so in a shapeless flame,
Angels affect us oft . . .

"Are you well?" I asked.

She looked pale. It may have been the day, which was wretched and gray with sleet, or it may have been the white bedspreads, but she appeared to be ailing.

"I missed you," she said.

"Me too," I said. 45

At home, gorging, eating trifle at all hours, even for breakfast, having little ratafias to dip in cups of tea, fitting on new shoes and silk stockings, I wished that she could be with us, enjoying the fire and the freedom.

"You know it is not proper for us to be so friendly."

"It's not wrong," I said.

I dreaded that she might decide to turn away from me, that she might stamp on our love and might suddenly draw a curtain over it, a black crepe curtain that would denote its death. I dreaded it and knew it was going to happen.

"We must not become attached," she said, and I could not say we   50 already were, no more than I could remind her of the day of the revels and the intimacy between us. Convents were dungeons and no doubt about it.

From then on she treated me as less of a favorite. She said my name sharply in class, and once she said if I must cough, could I wait until class had finished. Baba was delighted, as were the other girls, because they were glad to see me receding in her eyes. Yet I knew that the crispness was part of her love, because no matter how callously she looked at me, she would occasionally soften. Reading her notebook helped me, and I copied out her quotations into my own book, trying as accurately as possible to imitate her handwriting.

But some little time later when she came to supervise our study one evening, I got a smile from her as she sat on the rostrum looking down at us all. I continued to look up at her and by slight frowning indicated that I had a problem with my geometry. She beckoned to me lightly and I went up, bringing my copybook and the pen. Standing close to her, and also because her wimple was crooked, I saw one of her eyebrows for the first time. She saw that I noticed it and said did that satisfy my curiosity. I said not really. She said what else did I want to see, her swan's neck perhaps, and I went scarlet. I was amazed that she would say such a thing in the hearing of other girls, and then she said a worse thing, she said that G. K. Chesterton° was very forgetful and had once put on his trousers backward. She expected me to laugh. I was so close to her that a rumble in her stomach seemed to be taking place in my own, and about this she also laughed. It occurred to me for one terrible moment that maybe she had decided to leave the convent, to jump over the wall. Having done the theorem for me, she marked it "100 out of 100" and then asked if I had any other problems. My eyes filled with tears, I wanted her to realize that her recent coolness had wrought havoc with my nerves and my peace of mind.

"What is it?" she said.

I could cry, or I could tremble to try to convey the emotion, but I could not tell her. As if on cue, the Mother Superior came in and saw this glaring intimacy and frowned as she approached the rostrum.

"Would you please go back to your desk," she said, "and in future   55 kindly allow Sister Imelda to get on with her duties."

I tiptoed back and sat with head down, bursting with fear and shame. Then she looked at a tray on which the milk cups were laid, and finding one cup of milk untouched, she asked which girl had not drunk her milk.

G. K. Chesterton: (1874–1936) English essayist, novelist, and poet.

"Me, sister," I said, and I was called up to drink it and stand under the clock as a punishment. The milk was tepid and dusty, and I thought of cows on the fairs days at home and the farmers hitting them as they slid and slithered over the muddy streets.

For weeks I tried to see my nun in private; I even lurked outside doors where I knew she was due, only to be rebuffed again and again. I suspected the Mother Superior had warned her against making a favorite of me. But I still clung to a belief that a bond existed between us and that her coldness and even some glares which I had received were a charade, a mask. I would wonder how she felt alone in bed and what way she slept and if she thought of me, or refusing to think of me, if she dreamed of me as I did of her. She certainly got thinner, because her nun's silver ring slipped easily and sometimes unavoidably off her marriage finger. It occurred to me that she was having a nervous breakdown.

One day in March the sun came out, the radiators were turned off, and, though there was a lashing wind, we were told that officially spring had arrived and that we could play games. We all trooped up to the games field and, to our surprise, saw that Sister Imelda was officiating that day. The daffodils in the field tossed and turned; they were a very bright shocking yellow, but they were not as fetching as the little timid snowdrops that trembled in the wind. We played rounders,° and when my turn came to hit the ball with the long wooden pound, I crumbled and missed, fearing that the ball could hit me.

"Champ . . ." said Baba, jeering.

After three such failures Sister Imelda said that if I liked I could sit and watch, and when I was sitting in the greenhouse swallowing my shame, she came in and said that I must not give way to tears, because humiliation was the greatest test of Christ's love, or indeed *any* love.

"When you are a nun you will know that," she said, and instantly I made up my mind that I would be a nun and that though we might never be free to express our feelings, we would be under the same roof, in the same cloister, in mental and spiritual conjunction all our lives.

"Is it very hard at first?" I said.

"It's awful," she said, and she slipped a little medal into my gym-frock pocket. It was warm from being in her pocket, and as I held it, I knew that once again we were near and that in fact we had never severed. Walking down from the playing field to our Sunday lunch of mutton and cabbage, everyone chattered to Sister Imelda. The girls milled around her, linking her, trying to hold her hand, counting the various keys on her bunch of keys, and asking impudent questions.

"Sister, did you ever ride a motorbicycle?"

"Sister, did you ever wear seamless stockings?"

"Sister, who's your favorite film star — male?"

60

65

rounders: Sport similar to baseball; played mainly by girls.

"Sister, what's your favorite food?"

"Sister, if you had a wish, what would it be?"

"Sister, what do you do when you want to scratch your head?"   70

Yes, she had ridden a motorbicycle, and she had worn silk stockings, but they were seamed. She liked bananas best, and if she had a wish, it would be to go home for a few hours to see her parents and her brother.

That afternoon as we walked through the town, the sight of closed shops with porter barrels outside and mongrel dogs did not dispel my refound ecstasy. The medal was in my pocket, and every other second I would touch it for confirmation. Baba saw a Swiss roll in a confectioner's window laid on a doily and dusted with castor sugar, and it made her cry out with hunger and rail against being in a bloody reformatory, surrounded by drips and mopes. On impulse she took her nail file out of her pocket and dashed across to the window to see if she could cut the glass. The prefect rushed up from the back of the line and asked Baba if she wanted to be locked up.

"I am anyhow," Baba said, and sawed at one of her nails, to maintain her independence and vent her spleen. Baba was the only girl who could stand up to a prefect. When she felt like it, she dropped out of a walk, sat on a stone wall, and waited until we all came back. She said that if there was one thing more boring than studying it was walking. She used to roll down her stockings and examine her calves and say that she could see varicose veins coming from this bloody daily walk. Her legs, like all our legs, were black from the dye of the stockings; we were forbidden to bathe, because baths were immoral. We washed each night in an enamel basin beside our beds. When girls splashed cold water onto their chests, they let out cries, though this was forbidden.

After the walk we wrote home. We were allowed to write home once a week; our letters were always censored. I told my mother that I had made up my mind to be a nun, and asked if she could send me bananas when a batch arrived at our local grocery shop. That evening, perhaps as I wrote to my mother on the ruled white paper, a telegram arrived which said that Sister Imelda's brother had been killed in a van while on his way home from a hurling match. The Mother Superior announced it, and asked us to pray for his soul and write letters of sympathy to Sister Imelda's parents. We all wrote identical letters, because in our first year at school we had been given specimen letters for various occasions, and we all referred back to our specimen letter of sympathy.

Next day the town hire-car drove up to the convent, and Sister Imelda,   75 accompanied by another nun, went home for the funeral. She looked as white as a sheet, with eyes swollen, and she wore a heavy knitted shawl over her shoulders. Although she came back that night (I stayed awake to hear the car), we did not see her for a whole week, except to catch a glimpse of her back, in the chapel. When she resumed class, she was peaky and distant, making no reference at all to her recent tragedy.

The day the bananas came I waited outside the door and gave her a bunch wrapped in tissue paper. Some were still a little green, and she said that Mother Superior would put them in the glasshouse to ripen. I felt that Sister Imelda would never taste them; they would be kept for a visiting priest or bishop.

"Oh, Sister, I'm sorry about your brother," I said in a burst.

"It will come to us all, sooner or later," Sister Imelda said dolefully.

I dared to touch her wrist to communicate my sadness. She went quickly, probably for fear of breaking down. At times she grew irritable and had a boil on her cheek. She missed some classes and was replaced in the cookery kitchen by a younger nun. She asked me to pray for her brother's soul and to avoid seeing her alone. Each time as she came down a corridor toward me, I was obliged to turn the other way. Now Baba or some other girl moved the blackboard two pegs higher and spread her shawl, when wet, over the radiator to dry.

I got flu and was put to bed. Sickness took the same bleak course, a cup of hot senna delivered in person by the head nun, who stood there while I drank it, tea at lunchtime with thin slices of brown bread (because it was just after the war, food was still rationed, so the butter was mixed with lard and had white streaks running through it and a faintly rancid smell), hours of just lying there surveying the empty dormitory, the empty iron beds with white counterpanes on each one, and metal crucifixes laid on each white, frilled pillow slip. I knew that she would miss me and hoped that Baba would tell her where I was. I counted the number of tiles from the ceiling to the head of my bed, thought of my mother at home on the farm mixing hen food, thought of my father, losing his temper perhaps and stamping on the kitchen floor with nailed boots, and I recalled the money owing for my school fees and hoped that Sister Imelda would never get to hear of it. During the Christmas holiday I had seen a bill sent by the head nun to my father which said, "Please remit this week without fail." I hated being in bed causing extra trouble and therefore reminding the head nun of the unpaid liability. We had no clock in the dormitory, so there was no way of guessing the time, but the hours dragged.

Marigold, one of the maids, came to take off the counterpanes at five and brought with her two gifts from Sister Imelda—an orange and a pencil sharpener. I kept the orange peel in my hand, smelling it, and planning how I would thank her. Thinking of her I fell into a feverish sleep and was wakened when the girls came to bed at ten and switched on the various ceiling lights.

At Easter Sister Imelda warned me not to give her chocolates, so I got her a flashlamp instead and spare batteries. Pleased with such a useful gift (perhaps she read her letters in bed), she put her arms around me and allowed one cheek to adhere but not to make the sound of a kiss. It made up for the seven weeks of withdrawal, and as I drove down the convent drive with Baba, she waved to me, as she had promised, from the window of her cell.

In the last term at school, studying was intensive because of the examinations which loomed at the end of June. Like all the other nuns, Sister

Imelda thought only of these examinations. She crammed us with knowledge, lost her temper every other day, and gritted her teeth whenever the
blackboard was too greasy to take the imprint of the chalk. If ever I met her
in the corridor, she asked if I knew such and such a thing, and coming down
from Sunday games, she went over various questions with us. The fateful
examination day arrived and we sat at single desks supervised by some
strange woman from Dublin. Opening a locked trunk, she took out the
pink examination papers and distributed them around. Geometry was on
the fourth day. When we came out from it, Sister Imelda was in the hall
with all the answers, so that we could compare our answers with hers. Then
she called me aside and we went up toward the cookery kitchen and sat on
the stairs while she went over the paper with me, question for question. I
knew that I had three right and two wrong, but did not tell her so.

"It is black," she said then, rather suddenly. I thought she meant the
dark light where we were sitting.

"It's cool, though," I said.   85

Summer had come; our white skins baked under the heavy uniform,
and dark violet pansies bloomed in the convent grounds. She looked well
again, and her pale skin was once more unblemished.

"My hair," she whispered, "is black." And she told me how she had
spent her last night before entering the convent. She had gone cycling with
a boy and ridden for miles; and they'd lost their way up a mountain, and she
became afraid she would be so late home that she would sleep it out the next
morning. It was understood between us that I was going to enter the convent in September and that I could have a last fling, too.

Two days later we prepared to go home. There were farewells and
outlandish promises, and autograph books signed, and girls trudging up the
recreation hall, their cases bursting open with clothes and books. Baba
scattered biscuit crumbs in the dormitory for the mice and stuffed all her
prayer books under a mattress. Her father promised to collect us at four. I
had arranged with Sister Imelda secretly that I would meet her in one of the
summerhouses around the walks, where we would spend our last half hour
together. I expected that she would tell me something of what my life as a
postulant would be like. But Baba's father came an hour early. He had
something urgent to do later and came at three instead. All I could do was
ask Marigold to take a note to Sister Imelda.

Remembrance is all I ask,
But if remembrance should prove a task,
Forget me.

I hated Baba, hated her busy father, hated the thought of my mother
standing in the doorway in her good dress, welcoming me home at last. I
would have become a nun that minute if I could.

I wrote to my nun that night and again the next day and then every   90
week for a month. Her letters were censored, so I tried to convey my
feelings indirectly. In one of her letters to me (they were allowed one letter a
month) she said that she looked forward to seeing me in September. But by
September Baba and I had left for the university in Dublin. I stopped writing to Sister Imelda then, reluctant to tell her that I no longer wished to be
a nun.

In Dublin we enrolled at the college where she had surpassed herself. I
saw her maiden name on a list, for having graduated with special honors,
and for days was again sad and remorseful. I rushed out and bought batteries
for the flashlamp I'd given her, and posted them without any note enclosed.
No mention of my missing vocation, no mention of why I had stopped
writing.

One Sunday about two years later, Baba and I were going out to
Howth on a bus. Baba had met some businessmen who played golf there
and she had done a lot of scheming to get us invited out. The bus was
packed, mostly mothers with babies and children on their way to Dolly-
mount Strand. We drove along the coast road and saw the sea, bright green
and glinting in the sun, and because of the way the water was carved up into
millions of little wavelets, its surface seemed like an endless heap of dark-
green broken bottles. Near the shore the sand looked warm and was biscuit-
colored. We never swam or sunbathed, we never did anything that was good
for us. Life was geared to work and to meeting men, and yet one knew that
mating could only lead to one's being a mother and hawking obstreperous
children out to the seaside on Sunday. "They know not what they do" could
surely be said of us.

We were very made up; even the conductor seemed to disapprove and
snapped at having to give change of ten shillings. For no reason at all I
thought of our makeup rituals before the school play and how innocent it
was in comparison, because now our skins were smothered beneath layers
of it and we never took it off at night. Thinking of the convent, I suddenly
thought of Sister Imelda, and then, as if prey to a dream, I heard the rustle
of serge, smelled the Jeyes Fluid and the boiled cabbage, and saw her pale
shocked face in the months after her brother died. Then I looked around and
saw her in earnest, and at first thought I was imagining things. But no, she
had got on accompanied by another nun and they were settling themselves
in the back seat nearest the door. She looked older, but she had the same
aloof quality and the same eyes, and my heart began to race with a mixture
of excitement and dread. At first it raced with a prodigal strength, and then
it began to falter and I thought it was going to give out. My fear of her and
my love came back in one fell realization. I would have gone through the
window except that it was not wide enough. The thing was how to escape
her. Baba gurgled with delight, stood up, and in the most flagrant way
looked around to make sure that it was Imelda. She recognized the other
nun as one with the nickname of Johnny who taught piano lessons. Baba's

first thought was revenge, as she enumerated the punishments they had meted out to us and said how nice it would be to go back and shock them and say, "Mud in your eye, Sisters," or "Get lost," or something worse. Baba could not understand why I was quaking, no more than she could understand why I began to wipe off the lipstick. Above all, I knew that I could not confront them.

"You're going to have to," Baba said.

"I can't," I said.   95

It was not just my attire; it was the fact of my never having written and of my broken promise. Baba kept looking back and said they weren't saying a word and that children were gawking at them. It wasn't often that nuns traveled in buses, and we speculated as to where they might be going.

"They might be off to meet two fellows," Baba said, and visualized them in the golf club getting blotto and hoisting up their skirts. For me it was no laughing matter. She came up with a strategy: it was that as we approached our stop and the bus was still moving, I was to jump up and go down the aisle and pass them without even looking. She said most likely they would not notice us, as their eyes were lowered and they seemed to be praying.

"I can't run down the bus," I said. There was a matter of shaking limbs and already a terrible vertigo.

"You're going to," Baba said, and though insisting that I couldn't, I had already begun to rehearse an apology. While doing this, I kept blessing myself over and over again, and Baba kept reminding me that there was only one more stop before ours. When the dreadful moment came, I jumped up and put on my face what can only be called an apology of a smile. I followed Baba to the rear of the bus. But already they had gone. I saw the back of their two sable, identical figures with their veils being blown wildly about in the wind. They looked so cold and lost as they hurried along the pavement and I wanted to run after them. In some way I felt worse than if I had confronted them. I cannot be certain what I would have said. I knew that there is something sad and faintly distasteful about love's ending, particularly love that has never been fully realized. I might have hinted at that, but I doubt it. In our deepest moments we say the most inadequate things.

Considerations

1. Contrast the character of the narrator with the character of her friend Baba. What view does each take of the school? Of authority figures? Of Sister Imelda?

2. Describe Sister Imelda's classroom strategies. In addition to geometry or cookery, what values does she convey to her students?

3. Summarize the development of the relationship between Sister Imelda and the narrator. Focus particularly on the incident at the Christmas revels. What significance does the narrator see in this incident?

4. Imagine the conversations between Baba and the narrator as she tries to make up her mind whether to go back to the convent or to enroll at the university. Write a series of journal entries the narrator might have written at this time.

5. What do you think the narrator gained from knowing Sister Imelda? What did she lose?

HENRY REED (1914–1986)

Naming of Parts

Today we have naming of parts. Yesterday,
We had daily cleaning. And tomorrow morning,
We shall have what to do after firing. But today,
Today we have naming of parts. Japonica
Glistens like coral in all of the neighboring gardens,   5
    And today we have naming of parts.

This is the lower sling swivel. And this
Is the upper sling swivel, whose use you will see,
When you are given your slings. And this is the piling swivel,
Which in your case you have not got. The branches   10
Hold in the gardens their silent, eloquent gestures,
    Which in our case we have not got.

This is the safety-catch, which is always released
With an easy flick of the thumb. And please do not let me
See anyone using his finger. You can do it quite easy   15
If you have any strength in your thumb. The blossoms
Are fragile and motionless, never letting anyone see
    Any of them using their finger.

And this you can see is the bolt. The purpose of this
Is to open the breech, as you see. We can slide it   20
Rapidly backwards and forwards: we call this
Easing the spring. And rapidly backwards and forwards
The early bees are assaulting and fumbling the flowers:
    They call it easing the Spring.

They call it easing the Spring: it is perfectly easy   25
If you have any strength in your thumb: like the bolt,
And the breech, and the cocking-piece, and the point of balance,

Which in our case we have not got; and the almond-blossom
Silent in all of the gardens and the bees going backwards and forwards,
      For today we have naming of parts.   30

Considerations

1. Identify the two distinct voices in this poem. Which voice is trying to teach? What is he teaching?
2. What is the contrast between what the teacher says and what the learner hears and thinks? What significance do you see in this contrast?
3. Read the final stanza, in which the two voices mix. What is the effect of this merging?

WILLIAM BUTLER YEATS (1865–1939)

The Scholars

Bald heads forgetful of their sins,
Old, learned, respectable bald heads
Edit and annotate the lines
That young men, tossing on their beds,
Rhymed out in love's despair   5
To flatter beauty's ignorant ear.

All shuffle there; all cough in ink;
All wear the carpet with their shoes;
All think what other people think;
All know the man their neighbor knows.   10
Lord, what would they say
Did their Catullus walk that way?

Considerations

1. Who might the "bald heads" mentioned in the first line represent? How are they contrasted with the "young men"? What does the contrast suggest about teaching and learning?
2. Isolate an image you find particularly intriguing, puzzling, powerful— or in some other way interesting. Copy the image and explain your response to it. How does it work in connection with the rest of the poem?
3. Who was Catullus? What does the final question suggest about the speaker's attitude toward the scholars?

WALT WHITMAN (1819–1892)

There Was a Child Went Forth

There was a child went forth every day,
And the first object he looked upon, that object he became,
And that object became part of him for the day or a certain part of the day,
Or for many years or stretching cycles of years.

The early lilacs became part of this child, 5
And grass and white and red morning-glories, and white and red clover, and
    the song of the phoebe-bird,
And the Third-month lambs and the sow's pink-faint litter, and the mare's
    foal and the cow's calf,
And the noisy brood of the barnyard or by the mire of the pond-side,
And the fish suspending themselves so curiously below there, and the
    beautiful curious liquid,
And the water-plants with their graceful flat heads, all became part of him. 10

The field-sprouts of Fourth-month and Fifth-month became part of him,
Winter-grain sprouts and those of the light-yellow corn, and the esculent
    roots of the garden,
And the apple-trees covered with blossoms and the fruit afterward, and the
    wood-berries, and the commonest weeds by the road,
And the old drunkard staggering home from the outhouse of the tavern
    whence he had lately risen,
And the schoolmistress that passed on her way to the school, 15
And the friendly boys that passed, and the quarrelsome boys,
And the tidy and fresh-cheeked girls, and the barefoot negro boy and girl,
And all the changes of city and country wherever he went.

His own parents, he that had fathered him and she that had conceived him
    in her womb and birthed him,
They gave this child more of themselves than that, 20
They gave him afterward every day, they became part of him.

The mother at home quietly placing the dishes on the supper-table,
The mother with mild words, clean her cap and grown, a wholesome odor
    falling off her person and clothes as she walks by,
The father, strong, self-sufficient, manly, mean, angered, unjust, 25
The blow, the quick loud word, the tight bargain, the crafty lure,
The family usages, the language, the company, the furniture, the yearning
    and swelling heart,

Affection that will not be gainsayed, the sense of what is real, the thought if
    after all it should prove unreal,
The doubts of day-time and the doubts of night-time, the curious whether
    and how,
Whether that which appears so is so, or is it all flashes and specks?   30
Men and women crowding fast in the streets, if they are not flashes and
    specks, what are they?
The streets themselves and the façades of houses, and goods in the windows,
Vehicles, teams, the heavy-planked wharves, the huge crossing at the ferries,
The village on the highland seen from afar at sunset, the river between,
Shadows, aureola and mist, the light falling on roofs and gables of white or 35
    brown two miles off,
The schooner near by sleepily dropping down the tide, the little boat slack-
    towed astern,
The hurrying tumbling waves, quick-broken crests, slapping,
The strata of colored clouds, the long bar of maroon-tint away solitary by
    itself, the spread of purity it lies motionless in,
The horizon's edge, the flying sea-crow, the fragrance of salt marsh and 40
    shore mud,
These became part of that child who went forth every day, and who now
    goes, and will always go forth every day.

Considerations

1. Discuss the poem's first stanza. In what ways do children — or any of
   us — "become" the objects that we "look upon"? When, how, and why
   do those objects sometimes become part of us for days, weeks, or years?
   How does this stanza relate to the final line of the poem?
2. This child has learned lessons both from his mother and father. Contrast
   those lessons. Comment on the significance of this contrast.
3. Make a list of significant "objects" that you can remember seeing as you
   "went forth" during your own childhood. Write a response to one or
   more of those "objects" from your current, adult perspective.

MARIANNE MOORE (1887–1972)

The Student

"In America," began
the lecturer, "everyone must have a
degree. The French do not think that

all can have it, they don't say everyone
    must go to college." We   5
incline to feel, here,
    that although it may be unnecessary

to know fifteen languages,
one degree is not too much. With us, a
school — like the singing tree of which   10
the leaves were mouths that sang in concert —
    is both a tree of knowledge
and of liberty, —
    seen in the unanimity of college

mottoes, *lux et veritas*,°   15
Christo et ecclesiae,° *sapiet*
felici.° It may be that we
have not knowledge, just opinions, that we
    are undergraduates,
not students; we know   20
    we have been told with smiles, by expatriates

of whom we had asked "When will
your experiment be finished?" "Science
is never finished." Secluded
from domestic strife, Jack Bookworm led a   25
    college life, says Goldsmith;°
and here also as
    in France or Oxford, study is beset with

dangers — with bookworms, mildews,
and complaisancies. But someone in New   30
England has known enough to say
that the student is patience personified,
    a variety
of hero, "patient
    of neglect and of reproach," — who can "hold by   35

himself." You can't beat hens to
make them lay. Wolf's wool is the best of wool,
but it cannot be sheared, because

---

15 *lux et veritas:* Light and truth.   16 *Christo et ecclesiae:* Christ and the Church; *sapiet/felici:*
Knowledge makes one happy.   26 *Oliver Goldsmith:* (1730?–1774) Anglo-Irish poet, essayist,
and playwright.

the wolf will not comply. With knowledge as
    with wolves' surliness,   40
the student studies
    voluntarily, refusing to be less

than individual. He
    "gives his opinion and then rests upon it";
he renders service when there is   45
no reward, and is too reclusive for
    some things to seem to touch
him; not because he
    has no feeling but because he has so much.

Considerations

1. The lecturer contrasts America with other cultures, claiming that in America it is assumed that everyone should have a college degree. Do you agree with this observation? Should everyone be given the opportunity for higher education? Can everyone benefit from higher education? Defend your point of view with specific examples.
2. What is your response to the "someone in New/England" who says that "the student is patience personified,/a variety/of hero." Why must a student be patient? Does that make a student a "variety/of hero"? Explain. (Consider here your definition of "hero.")
3. Explain the paradox (apparent contradiction) implied by the final four lines of the poem.

LOUISE GLÜCK (1943–   )

The School Children

The children go forward with their little satchels.
And all morning the mothers have labored
to gather the late apples, red and gold,
like words of another language.

And on the other shore   5
are those who wait behind great desks
to receive these offerings.

How orderly they are — the nails
on which the children hang
their overcoats of blue or yellow wool.   10

And the teachers shall instruct them in silence
and the mothers shall scour the orchards for a way out,
drawing to themselves the gray limbs of the fruit trees
bearing so little ammunition.

Considerations

1. Look carefully at the language of the poem. What does it imply about the distance between the homes of these children and the schools the children attend? Speculate on how many kinds of "distance" might be implied.
2. What does the poem suggest the mothers are doing in the orchards? Suggest possible motives for their actions.
3. Does the poem give you a negative, positive, or neutral image of the school the children attend? Refer to specific images from the poem as you respond.

ANNA LEE WALTERS (1946–   )

A Teacher Taught Me

I

a teacher taught me
more than she knew
patting me on the head
putting words in my hand
— "pretty little *Indian* girl!"   5
saving them —
going to give them
back to her one day . . .
show them around too
cousins and friends   10
laugh and say — "aye"

II

binding by sincerity
hating that kindness
eight years' worth
third graders heard her   15
putting words in my hand
— "we should bow our heads
in shame for what we did
to the American Indian"
saving them —   20
going to give them

III

in jr. hi
a boy no color
transparent skin
except sprinkled freckles
followed me around   30
putting words in my hand
—"squaw, squaw, squaw"
(not that it mattered,
hell, man, I didn't know
what squaw meant . . .)   35
saving them —
going to give them
back to him one day . . .
show them around too
cousins and friends   40
laugh and say — "aye"

back to her one day . . .
show them around too
cousins and friends
laugh and say — "aye"   25

IV

slapping open handed
transparent boy
across freckled face
knocking glasses down   45
he finally sees
recollect a red
handprint over minutes
faded from others
he wears it still   50
putting words in my hand
—"sorry, so sorry"
saving them —
going to give them
back to him one day   55
show them around too
cousins and friends
laugh and say — "aye"

LINDA PASTAN (1932–   )

Ethics

In ethics class so many years ago
our teacher asked this question every fall:
if there were a fire in a museum
which would you save, a Rembrandt painting
or an old woman who hadn't many   5
years left anyhow? Restless on hard chairs
caring little for pictures or old age
we'd opt one year for life, the next for art
and always half-heartedly. Sometimes

the woman borrowed my grandmother's face 10
leaving her usual kitchen to wander
some drafty, half-imagined museum.
One year, feeling clever, I replied
why not let the woman decide herself?
Linda, the teacher would report, eschews 15
the burdens of responsibility.
This fall in a real museum I stand
before a real Rembrandt, old woman,
or nearly so, myself. The colors
within this frame are darker than autumn, 20
darker even than winter — the browns of earth,
though earth's most radiant elements burn
through the canvas. I know now that woman
and painting and season are almost one
and all beyond saving by children. 25

GARY GILDNER (1938–   )

First Practice

After the doctor checked to see
we weren't ruptured,
the man with the short cigar took us
under the grade school,
where we went in case of attack 5
or storm, and said
he was Clifford Hill, he was
a man who believed dogs
ate dogs, he had once killed
for his country, and if 10
there were any girls present
for them to leave now.
                        No one
left. OK, he said, he said I take
that to mean you are hungry
men who hate to lose as much 15
as I do. OK. Then
he made two lines of us
facing each other,
and across the way, he said,
is the man you hate most 20
in the world,
and if we are to win
that title I want to see how.

But I don't want to see
any marks when you're dressed,   25
he said. He said, *Now*.

e. e. cummings (1894–1962)

plato told

plato told

him:he couldn't
believe it(jesus

told him;he
wouldn't believe   5
it)lao

tsze
certainly told
him,and general
(yes   10

mam)
sherman;
and even
(believe it
or   15

not)you
told him:i told
him;we told him
(he didn't believe it,no

sir)it took   20
a nipponized bit° of
the old sixth

avenue
el;in the top of his head:to tell

him   25

---

21 *nipponized bit:* During World War II, some Japanese bullets were made from scrap metal sold
to Japan by the U.S.A. prior to the war.

FRANCES E. W. HARPER (1825–1911)

Learning to Read

Very soon the Yankee teachers
    Came down and set up school;
But, oh! how the Rebs did hate it, —
    It was agin' their rule.

Our masters always tried to hide   5
    Book learning from our eyes;
Knowledge didn't agree with slavery —
    'Twould make us all too wise.

But some of us would try to steal
    A little from the book,   10
And put the words together,
    And learn by hook or crook.

I remember Uncle Caldwell,
    Who took pot liquor fat
And greased the pages of his book,   15
    And hid it in his hat

And had his master ever seen
    The leaves upon his head,
He'd have thought them greasy papers,
    But nothing to be read.   20

And there was Mr. Turner's Ben,
    Who heard the children spell,
And picked the words right up by heart,
    And learned to read 'em well.

Well, the Northern folks kept sending   25
    The Yankee teachers down;
And they stood right up and helped us,
    Though Rebs did sneer and frown.

And, I longed to read my Bible,
    For precious words it said;   30
But when I begun to learn it,
    Folks just shook their heads,

And said there is no use trying,
   Oh! Chloe, you're too late;
But as I was rising sixty,   35
   I had no time to wait.

So I got a pair of glasses,
   And straight to work I went,
And never stopped till I could read
   The hymns and Testament.   40

Then I got a little cabin
   A place to call my own —
And I felt as independent
   As the queen upon her throne.

                                 1872

EUGÈNE IONESCO (1912–   )

The Lesson

TRANSLATED BY DONALD M. ALLEN

Characters
THE PROFESSOR, *aged 50 to 60*
THE YOUNG PUPIL, *aged 18*
THE MAID, *aged 45 to 50*

Scene *The office of the old professor, which also serves as a dining room. To the left, a door opens onto the apartment stairs; upstage, to the right, another door opens onto a corridor of the apartment. Upstage, a little left of center, a window, not very large, with plain curtains; on the outside sill of the window are ordinary potted plants. The low buildings with red roofs of a small town can be seen in the distance. The sky is grayish-blue. On the right stands a provincial buffet. The table doubles as a desk, it stands at stage center. There are three chairs around the table, and two more stand on each side of the window. Light-colored wallpaper, some shelves with books.*

(When the curtain rises the stage is empty, and it remains so for a few moments. Then we hear the doorbell ring.)

VOICE OF THE MAID *(from the corridor)*: Yes. I'm coming.

> *(The MAID comes in, after having run down the stairs. She is stout, aged 45 to 50, red-faced, and wears a peasant woman's cap. She rushes in, slamming the door to the right behind her, and dries her hands on her apron as she runs towards the door on the left. Meanwhile we hear the doorbell ring again.)*

MAID: Just a moment, I'm coming.

> *(She opens the door. A young PUPIL, aged 18, enters. She is wearing a gray student's smock, a small white collar, and carries a student's satchel under her arm.)*

MAID: Good morning, miss.
PUPIL: Good morning, madam. Is the Professor at home?
MAID: Have you come for the lesson?
PUPIL: Yes, I have.
MAID: He's expecting you. Sit down for a moment. I'll tell him you're here.
PUPIL: Thank you.

> *(She seats herself near the table, facing the audience; the hall door is to her left; her back is to the other door, through which the MAID hurriedly exits, calling:)*

MAID: Professor, come down please, your pupil is here.

VOICE OF THE PROFESSOR *(rather reedy)*: Thank you. I'm coming . . . in just a moment . . .

(The MAID *exits; the* PUPIL *draws in her legs, holds her satchel on her lap, and waits demurely. She casts a glance or two around the room, at the furniture, at the ceiling too. Then she takes a notebook out of her satchel, leafs through it, and stops to look at a page for a moment as though reviewing a lesson, as though taking a last look at her homework. She seems to be a well-brought-up girl, polite, but lively, gay, dynamic; a fresh smile is on her lips. During the course of the play she progressively loses the lively rhythm of her movement and her carriage, she becomes withdrawn. From gay and smiling she becomes progressively sad and morose; from very lively at the beginning, she becomes more and more fatigued and somnolent. Towards the end of the play her face must clearly express a nervous depression; her way of speaking shows the effects of this, her tongue becomes thick, words come to her memory with difficulty and emerge from her mouth with as much difficulty; she comes to have a manner vaguely paralyzed, the beginning of aphasia. Firm and determined at the beginning, so much so as to appear to be almost aggressive, she becomes more and more passive, until she is almost a mute and inert object, seemingly inanimate in the* PROFESSOR'S *hands, to such an extent that when he makes his final gesture, she no longer reacts. Insensible, her reflexes deadened, only her eyes in an expressionless face will show inexpressible astonishment and fear. The transition from one manner to the other must of course be made imperceptibly.*

The PROFESSOR *enters. He is a little old man with a little white beard. He wears pince-nez, a black skullcap, a long black schoolmaster's coat, trousers and shoes of black, detachable white collar, a black tie. Excessively polite, very timid, his voice deadened by his timidity, very proper, very much the teacher. He rubs his hands together constantly; occasionally a lewd gleam comes into his eyes and is quickly repressed.*

During the course of the play his timidity will disappear progressively, imperceptibly; and the lewd gleams in his eyes will become a steady devouring flame in the end. From a manner that is inoffensive at the start, the PROFESSOR *becomes more and more sure of himself, more and more nervous, aggressive, dominating, until he is able to do as he pleases with the* PUPIL, *who has become, in his hands, a pitiful creature. Of course, the voice of the* PROFESSOR *must change too, from thin and reedy, to stronger and stronger, until at the end it is extremely powerful, ringing, sonorous, while the* PUPIL'S *voice changes from the very clear and ringing tones that she has at the beginning of the play until it is almost inaudible. In these first scenes the* PROFESSOR *might stammer very slightly.)*

PROFESSOR: Good morning, young lady. You . . . I expect that you . . . that you are the new pupil?

PUPIL *(turns quickly with a lively and self-assured manner; she gets up, goes toward the* PROFESSOR, *and gives him her hand)*: Yes, Professor. Good morning, Professor. As you see, I'm on time. I didn't want to be late.

PROFESSOR: That's fine, miss. Thank you, you didn't really need to hurry. I am very sorry to have kept you waiting . . . I was just finishing up . . . well . . . I'm sorry . . . You will excuse me, won't you? . . .

PUPIL: Oh, certainly, Professor. It doesn't matter at all, Professor.

PROFESSOR: Please excuse me . . . Did you have any trouble finding the house?

PUPIL: No . . . Not at all. I just asked the way. Everybody knows you around here.

PROFESSOR: For thirty years I've lived in this town. You've not been here for long? How do you find it?

PUPIL: It's all right. The town is attractive and even agreeable, there's a nice park, a boarding school, a bishop, nice shops and streets . . .

PROFESSOR: That's very true, young lady. And yet, I'd just as soon live somewhere else. In Paris, or at least Bordeaux.

PUPIL: Do you like Bordeaux?

PROFESSOR: I don't know. I've never seen it.

PUPIL: But you know Paris?

PROFESSOR: No, I don't know it either, young lady, but if you'll permit me, can you tell me, Paris is the capital city of . . . miss?

PUPIL *(searching her memory for a moment, then, happily guessing)*: Paris is the capital city of . . . France?

PROFESSOR: Yes, young lady, bravo, that's very good, that's perfect. My congratulations. You have your French geography at your finger tips. You know your chief cities.

PUPIL: Oh! I don't know them all yet, Professor, it's not quite that easy, I have trouble learning them.

PROFESSOR: Oh! it will come . . . you mustn't give up . . . young lady . . . I beg your pardon . . . have patience . . . little by little . . . You will see, it will come in time . . . What a nice day it is today . . . or rather, not so nice . . . Oh! but then yes it is nice. In short, it's not too bad a day, that's the main thing . . . ahem . . . ahem . . . it's not raining and it's not snowing either.

PUPIL: That would be most unusual, for it's summer now.

PROFESSOR: Excuse me, miss, I was just going to say so . . . but as you will learn, one must be ready for anything.

PUPIL: I guess so, Professor.

PROFESSOR: We can't be sure of anything, young lady, in this world.

PUPIL: The snow falls in the winter. Winter is one of the four seasons. The other three are . . . uh . . . spr . . .

PROFESSOR: Yes?

PUPIL: . . . ing, and then summer . . . and . . . uh . . .

PROFESSOR: It begins like "automobile," miss.

PUPIL: Ah, yes, autumn . . .

PROFESSOR: That's right, miss. That's a good answer, that's perfect. I am convinced that you will be a good pupil. You will make real progress. You are intelligent, you seem to me to be well informed, and you've a good memory.

PUPIL: I know my seasons, don't I, Professor?

PROFESSOR: Yes, indeed, miss . . . or almost. But it will come in time. In any case, you're coming along. Soon you'll know all the seasons, even with your eyes closed. Just as I do.

PUPIL: It's hard.

PROFESSOR: Oh, no. All it takes is a little effort, a little good will, miss. You will see. It will come, you may be sure of that.

PUPIL: Oh, I do hope so, Professor. I have a great thirst for knowledge. My parents also want me to get an education. They want me to specialize. They consider a little general culture, even if it is solid, is no longer enough, in these times.

PROFESSOR: Your parents, miss, are perfectly right. You must go on with your studies. Forgive me for saying so, but it is very necessary. Our contemporary life has become most complex.

PUPIL: And so very complicated too . . . My parents are fairly rich, I'm lucky. They can help me in my work, help me in my very advanced studies.

PROFESSOR: And you wish to qualify for . . . ?

PUPIL: Just as soon as possible, for the first doctor's orals. They're in three weeks' time.

PROFESSOR: You already have your high school diploma, if you'll pardon the question?

PUPIL: Yes, Professor, I have my science diploma and my arts diploma, too.

PROFESSOR: Ah, you're very far advanced, even perhaps too advanced for your age. And which doctorate do you wish to qualify for? In the physical sciences or in moral philosophy?

PUPIL: My parents are very much hoping — if you think it will be possible in such a short time — they very much hope that I can qualify for the total doctorate.

PROFESSOR: The total doctorate? . . . You have great courage, young lady, I congratulate you sincerely. We will try, miss, to do our best. In any case, you already know quite a bit, and at so young an age too.

PUPIL: Oh, Professor.

PROFESSOR: Then, if you'll permit me, pardon me, please, I do think that we ought to get to work. We have scarcely any time to lose.

PUPIL: Oh, but certainly, Professor, I want to. I beg you to.

PROFESSOR: Then, may I ask you to sit down . . . there . . . Will you permit me, miss, that is if you have no objections, to sit down opposite you?

PUPIL: Oh, of course, Professor, please do.

PROFESSOR: Thank you very much, miss. *(They sit down facing each other at the table, their profiles to the audience.)* There we are. Now have you brought your books and notebooks?

PUPIL *(taking notebooks and books out of her satchel)*: Yes, Professor. Certainly, I have brought all that we'll need.

PROFESSOR: Perfect, miss. This is perfect. Now, if this doesn't bore you . . . shall we begin?

PUPIL: Yes, indeed, Professor, I am at your disposal.

PROFESSOR: At my disposal? *(A gleam comes into his eyes and is quickly extinguished; he begins to make a gesture that he suppresses at once.)* Oh, miss, it is I who am at *your* disposal. I am only your humble servant.

PUPIL: Oh, Professor . . .

PROFESSOR: If you will . . . now . . . we . . . we . . . I . . . I will begin by making a brief examination of your knowledge, past and present, so that we may chart our future course . . . Good. How is your perception of plurality?

PUPIL: It's rather vague . . . confused.

PROFESSOR: Good. We shall see.

> *(He rubs his hands together. The MAID enters, and this appears to irritate the PROFESSOR. She goes to the buffet and looks for something, lingering.)*

PROFESSOR: Now, miss, would you like to do a little arithmetic, that is if you want to . . .

PUPIL: Oh, yes, Professor. Certainly, I ask nothing better.

PROFESSOR: It is rather a new science, a modern science, properly speaking, it is more a method than a science . . . And it is also a therapy. *(To the MAID:)* Have you finished, Marie?

MAID: Yes, Professor, I've found the plate. I'm just going . . .

PROFESSOR: Hurry up then. Please go along to the kitchen, if you will.

MAID: Yes, Professor, I'm going. *(She starts to go out.)* Excuse me, Professor, but take care, I urge you to remain calm.

PROFESSOR: You're being ridiculous, Marie. Now, don't worry.

MAID: That's what you always say.

PROFESSOR: I will not stand for your insinuations. I know perfectly well how to comport myself. I am old enough for that.

MAID: Precisely, Professor. You will do better not to start the young lady on arithmetic. Arithmetic is tiring, exhausting.

PROFESSOR: Not at my age. And anyhow, what business is it of yours? This is my concern. And I know what I'm doing. This is not your department.

MAID: Very well, Professor. But you can't say that I didn't warn you.

PROFESSOR: Marie, I can get along without your advice.

MAID: As you wish, Professor. *(She exits.)*

PROFESSOR: Miss, I hope you'll pardon this absurd interruption . . . Excuse this woman . . . She is always afraid that I'll tire myself. She fusses over my health.

PUPIL: Oh, that's quite all right, Professor. It shows that she's very devoted. She loves you very much. Good servants are rare.

PROFESSOR: She exaggerates. Her fears are stupid. But let's return to our arithmetical knitting.

PUPIL: I'm following you, Professor.

PROFESSOR *(wittily)*: Without leaving your seat!

PUPIL *(appreciating his joke)*: Like you, Professor.

PROFESSOR: Good. Let us arithmetize a little now.

PUPIL: Yes, gladly, Professor.

PROFESSOR: It wouldn't be too tiresome for you to tell me . . .

PUPIL: Not at all, Professor, go on.

PROFESSOR: How much are one and one?

PUPIL: One and one make two.

PROFESSOR *(marveling at the* PUPIL'S *knowledge)*: Oh, but that's very good. You appear to me to be well along in your studies. You should easily achieve the total doctorate, miss.

PUPIL: I'm so glad. Especially to have someone like you tell me this.

PROFESSOR: Let's push on: how much are two and one?

PUPIL: Three.

PROFESSOR: Three and one?

PUPIL: Four.

PROFESSOR: Four and one?

PUPIL: Five.

PROFESSOR: Five and one?

PUPIL: Six.

PROFESSOR: Six and one?

PUPIL: Seven.

PROFESSOR: Seven and one?

PUPIL: Eight.

PROFESSOR: Seven and one?

PUPIL: Eight again.

PROFESSOR: Very well answered. Seven and one?

PUPIL: Eight once more.

PROFESSOR: Perfect. Excellent. Seven and one?

PUPIL: Eight again. And sometimes nine.

PROFESSOR: Magnificent. You are magnificent. You are exquisite. I congratulate you warmly, miss. There's scarcely any point in going on. At addition you are a past master. Now, let's look at subtraction. Tell me, if you are not exhausted, how many are four minus three?

PUPIL: Four minus three? . . . Four minus three?

PROFESSOR: Yes. I mean to say: subtract three from four.

PUPIL: That makes . . . seven?

PROFESSOR: I am sorry but I'm obliged to contradict you. Four minus three does not make seven. You are confused: four plus three makes seven, four minus three does not make seven . . . This is not addition anymore, we must subtract now.

PUPIL (*trying to understand*): Yes . . . yes . . .

PROFESSOR: Four minus three makes . . . How many? . . . How many?

PUPIL: Four?

PROFESSOR: No, miss, that's not it.

PUPIL: Three, then.

PROFESSOR: Not that either, miss . . . Pardon, I'm sorry . . . I ought to say, that's not it . . . excuse me.

PUPIL: Four minus three . . . Four minus three . . . Four minus three? . . . But now doesn't that make ten?

PROFESSOR: Oh, certainly not, miss. It's not a matter of guessing, you've got to think it out. Let's try to deduce it together. Would you like to count?

PUPIL: Yes, Professor. One . . . two . . . uh . . .

PROFESSOR: You know how to count? How far can you count up to?

PUPIL: I can count to . . . to infinity.

PROFESSOR: That's not possible, miss.

PUPIL: Well then, let's say to sixteen.

PROFESSOR: That is enough. One must know one's limits. Count then, if you will, please.

PUPIL: One . . . two . . . and after two, comes three . . . then four . . .

PROFESSOR: Stop there, miss. Which number is larger? Three or four?

PUPIL: Uh . . . three or four? Which is the larger? The larger of three or four? In what sense larger?

PROFESSOR: Some numbers are smaller and others are larger. In the larger numbers there are more units than in the small . . .

PUPIL: Than in the small numbers?

PROFESSOR: Unless the small ones have smaller units. If they are very small, then there might be more units in the small numbers than in the large . . . if it is a question of other units . . .

PUPIL: In that case, the small numbers can be larger than the large numbers?

PROFESSOR: Let's not go into that. That would take us much too far. You must realize simply that more than numbers are involved here . . . there are also magnitudes, totals, there are groups, there are heaps, heaps of such things as plums, trucks, geese, prune pits, etc. To facilitate our work, let's merely suppose that we have only equal numbers, then the bigger numbers will be those that have the most units.

PUPIL: The one that has the most is the biggest? Ah, I understand, Professor, you are identifying quality with quantity.

PROFESSOR: That is too theoretical, miss, too theoretical. You needn't concern yourself with that. Let us take an example and reason from a definite case. Let's leave the general conclusions for later. We have the number four and the number three, and each has always the same number of units. Which number will be larger, the smaller or the larger?

PUPIL: Excuse me, Professor . . . What do you mean by the larger number? Is it the one that is not so small as the other?

PROFESSOR: That's it, miss, perfect. You have understood me very well.

PUPIL: Then, it is four.

PROFESSOR: What is four—larger or smaller than three?

PUPIL: Smaller . . . no, larger.

PROFESSOR: Excellent answer. How many units are there between three and four? . . . Or between four and three, if you prefer?

PUPIL: There aren't any units, Professor, between three and four. Four comes immediately after three; there is nothing at all between three and four!

PROFESSOR: I haven't made myself very well understood. No doubt, it is my fault. I've not been sufficiently clear.

PUPIL: No, Professor, it's my fault.

PROFESSOR: Look here. Here are three matches. And here is another one, that makes four. Now watch carefully—we have four matches. I take one away, now how many are left?

(We don't see the matches, nor any of the objects that are mentioned. The PROFESSOR *gets up from the table, writes on the imaginary blackboard with an imaginary piece of chalk, etc.)*

PUPIL: Five. If three and one make four, four and one make five.

PROFESSOR: That's not it. That's not it at all. You always have a tendency to add. But one must be able to subtract too. It's not enough to integrate, you must also disintegrate. That's the way life is. That's philosophy. That's science. That's progress, civilization.

PUPIL: Yes, Professor.

PROFESSOR: Let's return to our matches. I have four of them. You see, there are really four. I take one away, and there remain only . . .

PUPIL: I don't know, Professor.

PROFESSOR: Come now, think. It's not easy, I admit. Nevertheless, you've had enough training to make the intellectual effort required to arrive at an understanding. So?

PUPIL: I can't get it, Professor. I don't know, Professor.

PROFESSOR: Let us take a simpler example. If you had two noses, and I pulled one of them off . . . how many would you have left?

PUPIL: None.

PROFESSOR: What do you mean, none?

PUPIL: Yes, it's because you haven't pulled off any, that's why I have one now. If you had pulled it off, I wouldn't have it anymore.

PROFESSOR: You've not understood my example. Suppose that you have only one ear.

PUPIL: Yes, and then?

PROFESSOR: If I gave you another one, how many would you have then?

PUPIL: Two.

PROFESSOR: Good. And if I gave you still another ear. How many would you have then?

PUPIL: Three ears.

PROFESSOR: Now, I take one away . . . and there remain . . . how many ears?

PUPIL: Two.

PROFESSOR: Good. I take away still another one, how many do you have left?

PUPIL: Two.

PROFESSOR: No. You have two, I take one away, I eat one up, then how many do you have left?

PUPIL: Two.

PROFESSOR: I eat one of them . . . one.

PUPIL: Two.

PROFESSOR: One.

PUPIL: Two.

PROFESSOR: One!

PUPIL: Two!

PROFESSOR: One!!!

PUPIL: Two!!!

PROFESSOR: One!!!

PUPIL: Two!!!

PROFESSOR: One!!!

PUPIL: Two!!!

PROFESSOR: No. No. That's not right. The example is not . . . it's not convincing. Listen to me.

PUPIL: Yes, Professor.

PROFESSOR: You've got . . . you've got . . . you've got . . .

PUPIL: Ten fingers!

PROFESSOR: If you wish. Perfect. Good. You have then ten fingers.

PUPIL: Yes, Professor.

PROFESSOR: How many would you have if you had only five of them?

PUPIL: Ten, Professor.

PROFESSOR: That's not right!

PUPIL: But it is, Professor.

PROFESSOR: I tell you it's not!

PUPIL: You just told me that I had ten . . .

PROFESSOR: I also said, immediately afterwards, that you had five!

PUPIL: I don't have five, I've got ten!

PROFESSOR: Let's try another approach . . . for purposes of subtraction let's limit ourselves to the numbers from one to five . . . Wait now, miss, you'll soon see. I'm going to make you understand.

(The PROFESSOR *begins to write on the imaginary blackboard. He moves it closer to the* PUPIL, *who turns around in order to see it.)*

PROFESSOR: Look here, miss . . . *(He pretends to draw a stick on the black-board and the number 1 below the stick; then two sticks and the number 2 below, then three sticks and the number 3 below, then four sticks with the number 4 below.)* You see . . .

PUPIL: Yes, Professor.

PROFESSOR: These are sticks, miss, sticks. This is one stick, these are two sticks, and three sticks, then four sticks, then five sticks. One stick, two sticks, three sticks, four and five sticks, these are numbers. When we count the sticks, each stick is a unit, miss . . . What have I just said?

PUPIL: "A unit, miss! What have I just said?"

PROFESSOR: Or a figure! Or a number! One, two, three, four, five, these are the elements of numeration, miss.

PUPIL *(hesitant)*: Yes, Professor. The elements, figures, which are sticks, units and numbers . . .

PROFESSOR: At the same time . . . that's to say, in short — the whole of arithmetic is there.

PUPIL: Yes, Professor. Good, Professor. Thanks, Professor.

PROFESSOR: Now, count, if you will please, using these elements . . . add and subtract . . .

PUPIL *(as though trying to impress them on her memory)*: Sticks are really figures and numbers are units?

PROFESSOR: Hmm . . . so to speak. And then?

PUPIL: One could subtract two units from three units, but can one subtract two twos from three threes? And two figures from four numbers? And three numbers from one unit?

PROFESSOR: No, miss.

PUPIL: Why, Professor?

PROFESSOR: Because, miss.

PUPIL: Because why, Professor? Since one is the same as the other?

PROFESSOR: That's the way it is, miss. It can't be explained. This is only comprehensible through internal mathematical reasoning. Either you have it or you don't.

PUPIL: So much the worse for me.

PROFESSOR: Listen to me, miss, if you don't achieve a profound under-standing of these principles, these arithmetical archetypes, you will never be able to perform correctly the functions of a polytechnician. Still less will you be able to teach a course in a polytechnical school . . . or the primary grades. I realize that this is not easy, it is very, very abstract . . . obviously . . . but unless you can comprehend the pri-mary elements, how do you expect to be able to calculate mentally — and this is the least of the things that even an ordinary engineer must be able to do—how much, for example, are three billion seven hundred fifty-five million nine hundred ninety-eight thousand two hundred fifty-one, multiplied by five billion one hundred sixty-two million three hundred and three thousand five hundred and eight?

PUPIL *(very quickly)*: That makes nineteen quintillion three hundred ninety quadrillion two trillion eight hundred forty-four billion two hundred nineteen million one hundred sixty-four thousand five hundred and eight . . .

PROFESSOR *(astonished)*: No. I don't think so. That must make nineteen quintillion three hundred ninety quadrillion two trillion eight hundred forty-four billion two hundred nineteen million one hundred sixty-four thousand five hundred and nine . . .

PUPIL: . . . No . . . five hundred and eight . . .

PROFESSOR *(more and more astonished, calculating mentally)*: Yes . . . you are right . . . the result is indeed . . . *(He mumbles unintelligibly:)* . . . quintillion, quadrillion, trillion, billion, million . . . *(Clearly:)* one hundred sixty-four thousand five hundred and eight . . . *(Stupefied:)* But how did you know that, if you don't know the principles of arithmetical reasoning?

PUPIL: It's easy. Not being able to rely on my reasoning, I've memorized all the products of all possible multiplications.

PROFESSOR: That's pretty good . . . However, permit me to confess to you that that doesn't satisfy me, miss, and I do not congratulate you: in mathematics and in arithmetic especially, the thing that counts—for in arithmetic it is always necessary to count—the thing that counts is, above all, understanding . . . It is by mathematical reasoning, simultaneously inductive and deductive, that you ought to arrive at this result—as well as at any other result. Mathematics is the sworn enemy of memory, which is excellent otherwise, but disastrous, arithmetically speaking! . . . That's why I'm not happy with this . . . this won't do, not at all . . .

PUPIL *(desolated)*: No, Professor.

PROFESSOR: Let's leave it for the moment. Let's go on to another exercise . . .

PUPIL: Yes, Professor.

MAID *(entering)*: Hmm, hmm, Professor . . .

PROFESSOR *(who doesn't hear her)*: It is unfortunate, miss, that you aren't further along in specialized mathematics . . .

MAID *(taking him by the sleeve)*: Professor! Professor!

PROFESSOR: I hear that you will not be able to qualify for the total doctor's orals . . .

PUPIL: Yes, Professor, it's too bad!

PROFESSOR: Unless you . . . *(To the* MAID:*)* Let me be, Marie . . . Look here, why are you bothering me? Go back to the kitchen! To your pots and pans! Go away! Go away! *(To the* PUPIL:*)* We will try to prepare you at least for the partial doctorate . . .

MAID: Professor! . . . Professor! . . . *(She pulls his sleeve.)*

PROFESSOR *(to the* MAID*)*: Now leave me alone! Let me be! What's the meaning of this? . . . *(To the* PUPIL:*)* I must therefore teach you, if you really do insist on attempting the partial doctorate . . .

PUPIL: Yes, Professor.

PROFESSOR: . . . The elements of linguistics and of comparative philology . . .

MAID: No, Professor, no! . . . You mustn't do that! . . .

PROFESSOR: Marie, you're going too far!

MAID: Professor, especially not philology, philology leads to calamity . . .

PUPIL *(astonished)*: To calamity? *(Smiling, a little stupidly:)* That's hard to believe.

PROFESSOR *(to the* MAID*)*: That's enough now! Get out of here!

MAID: All right, Professor, all right. But you can't say that I didn't warn you! Philology leads to calamity!

PROFESSOR: I'm an adult, Marie!

PUPIL: Yes, Professor.

MAID: As you wish.

(She exits.)

PROFESSOR: Let's continue, miss.

PUPIL: Yes, Professor.

PROFESSOR: I want you to listen now with the greatest possible attention to a lecture I have prepared . . .

PUPIL: Yes, Professor!

PROFESSOR: . . . Thanks to which, in fifteen minutes' time, you will be able to acquire the fundamental principles of the linguistic and comparative philology of the neo-Spanish languages.

PUPIL: Yes, Professor, oh good!

(She claps her hands.)

PROFESSOR *(with authority)*: Quiet! What do you mean by that?

PUPIL: I'm sorry, Professor.

(Slowly, she replaces her hands on the table.)

PROFESSOR: Quiet! *(He gets up, walks up and down the room, his hands behind his back; from time to time he stops at stage center or near the* PUPIL, *and underlines his words with a gesture of his hand; he orates, but without being too emotional. The* PUPIL *follows him with her eyes, occasionally with some difficulty, for she has to turn her head far around; once or twice, not more, she turns around completely.)* And now, miss, Spanish is truly the mother tongue which gave birth to all the neo-Spanish languages, of which Spanish, Latin, Italian, our own French, Portuguese, Romanian, Sardinian or Sardanapalian, Spanish and neo-Spanish — and also, in certain of its aspects, Turkish which is otherwise very close to Greek, which is only logical, since it is a fact that Turkey is a neighbor of Greece and Greece is even closer to Turkey than you are to me — this is only one more illustration of the very important linguistic law which states that geography and philology are twin sisters . . . You may take notes, miss.

PUPIL *(in a dull voice)*: Yes, Professor!

PROFESSOR: That which distinguishes the neo-Spanish languages from each other and their idioms from the other linguistic groups, such as the group of languages called Austrian and neo-Austrian or Hapsburgian, as well as the Esperanto, Helvetian, Monacan, Swiss, Andorran, Basque, and jai alai groups, and also the groups of diplomatic and technical languages — that which distinguishes them, I repeat, is their striking resemblance which makes it so hard to distinguish them from each other — I'm speaking of the neo-Spanish languages which one is able to distinguish from each other, however, only thanks to their distinctive characteristics, absolutely indisputable proofs of their extraordinary resemblance, which renders indisputable their common origin, and which, at the same time, differentiates them profoundly — through the continuation of the distinctive traits which I've just cited.

PUPIL: Oooh! Ye-e-e-s-s-s, Professor!

PROFESSOR: But let's not linger over generalities . . .

PUPIL *(regretfully, but won over)*: Oh, Professor . . .

PROFESSOR: This appears to interest you. All the better, all the better.

PUPIL: Oh, yes, Professor . . .

PROFESSOR: Don't worry, miss. We will come back to it later . . . That is if we come back to it at all. Who can say?

PUPIL *(enchanted in spite of everything)*: Oh, yes, Professor.

PROFESSOR: Every tongue — you must know this, miss, and remember it *until the hour of your death* . . .

PUPIL: Oh! yes, Professor, until the hour of my death . . . Yes, Professor . . .

PROFESSOR: . . . And this, too, is a fundamental principle, every tongue is at bottom nothing but language, which necessarily implies that it is composed of sounds, or . . .

PUPIL: Phonemes . . .

PROFESSOR: Just what I was going to say. Don't parade your knowledge. You'd do better to listen.

PUPIL: All right, Professor. Yes, Professor.

PROFESSOR: The sounds, miss, must be seized on the wing as they fly so that they'll not fall on deaf ears. As a result, when you set out to articulate, it is recommended, insofar as possible, that you lift up your neck and chin very high, and rise up on the tips of your toes, you see, this way . . .

PUPIL: Yes, Professor.

PROFESSOR: Keep quiet. Remain seated, don't interrupt me . . . And project the sounds very loudly with all the force of your lungs in conjunction with that of your vocal cords. Like this, look: "Butterfly," "Eureka," "Trafalgar," "Papaya." This way, the sounds become filled with a warm air that is lighter than the surrounding air so that they can fly without danger of falling on deaf ears, which are veritable voids, tombs of sonorities. If you utter several sounds at an accelerated speed, they will automatically cling to each other, constituting thus syllables, words, even sentences, that is to say groupings of various importance, purely irrational assemblages of sounds, denuded of all sense, but for that very reason the more capable of maintaining themselves without danger at a high altitude in the air. By themselves, words charged with significance will fall, weighted down by their meaning, and in the end they always collapse, fall . . .

PUPIL: . . . On deaf ears.

PROFESSOR: That's it, but don't interrupt . . . and into the worst confusion . . . Or else burst like balloons. Therefore, miss . . . *(The* PUPIL *suddenly appears to be unwell.)* What's the matter?

PUPIL: I've got a toothache, Professor.

PROFESSOR: That's not important. We're not going to stop for anything so trivial. Let us go on . . .

PUPIL *(appearing to be in more and more pain)*: Yes, Professor.

PROFESSOR: I draw your attention in passing to the consonants that change their nature in combinations. In this case *f* becomes *v, d* becomes *t, g* becomes *k,* and vice versa, as in these examples that I will cite for you: "That's all right," "hens and chickens," "Welsh rabbit," "lots of nothing," "not at all."

PUPIL: I've got a toothache.

PROFESSOR: Let's continue.

PUPIL: Yes.

PROFESSOR: To resume: it takes years and years to learn to pronounce. Thanks to science, we can achieve this in a few minutes. In order to project words, sounds and all the rest, you must realize that it is necessary to pitilessly expel air from the lungs, and make it pass delicately, caressingly, over the vocal cords, which, like harps or leaves in the wind, will suddenly shake, agitate, vibrate, vibrate, vibrate or uvulate, or fricate or jostle against each other, or sibilate, sibilate, placing everything in movement, the uvula, the tongue, the palate, the teeth . . .

PUPIL: I have a toothache.

PROFESSOR: . . . And the lips . . . Finally the words come out through the nose, the mouth, the ears, the pores, drawing along with them all the organs that we have named, torn up by the roots, in a powerful, majestic flight, which is none other than what is called, improperly, the voice, whether modulated in singing or transformed into a terrible symphonic storm with a whole procession . . . of garlands of all kinds of flowers, of sonorous artifices: labials, dentals, occlusives, palatals, and others, some caressing, some bitter or violent.

PUPIL: Yes, Professor, I've got a toothache.

PROFESSOR: Let's go on, go on. As for the neo-Spanish languages, they are closely related, so closely to each other, that they can be considered as true second cousins. Moreover, they have the same mother: Span-ishe, with a mute *e*. That is why it is so difficult to distinguish them from one another. That is why it is so useful to pronounce carefully, and to avoid errors in pronunciation. Pronunciation itself is worth a whole language. A bad pronunciation can get you into trouble. In this connection, permit me, parenthetically, to share a personal experience with you. *(Slight pause. The* PROFESSOR *goes over his memories for a moment; his features mellow, but he recovers at once.)* I was very young, little more than a child. It was during my military service. I had a friend in the regiment, a vicomte, who suffered from a rather serious defect in his pronunciation: he could not pronounce the letter *f*. Instead of *f,* he said *f*. Thus, instead of "Birds of a feather flock together," he said: "Birds of a feather flock together." He pronounced filly instead of filly, Firmin instead of Firmin, French bean instead of French bean, go frig yourself instead of go frig yourself, farrago instead of farrago, fee fi fo fum instead of fee fi fo fum, Philip instead of Philip, fictory instead of fictory, February instead of February, March-April instead of March-April, Gerard de Nerval and not as is correct — Gerard de Nerval, Mirabeau instead of Mirabeau, etc., instead of etc., and thus instead of etc., instead of etc., and thus and so forth. However, he managed to conceal his fault so effectively that, thanks to the hats he wore, no one ever noticed it.

PUPIL: Yes, I've got a toothache.

PROFESSOR *(abruptly changing his tone, his voice hardening)*: Let's go on. We'll first consider the points of similarity in order the better to appre-hend, later on, that which distinguishes all these languages from each other. The differences can scarcely be recognized by people who are not aware of them. Thus, all the words of all the languages . . .

PUPIL: Uh, yes? . . . I've got a toothache.

PROFESSOR: Let's continue . . . are always the same, just as all the suf-fixes, all the prefixes, all the terminations, all the roots . . .

PUPIL: Are the roots of words square?

PROFESSOR: Square or cube. That depends.

PUPIL: I've got a toothache.

PROFESSOR: Let's go on. Thus, to give you an example which is little more than an illustration, take the word "front" . . .

PUPIL: How do you want me to take it?

PROFESSOR: However you wish, so long as you take it, but above all do not interrupt.

PUPIL: I've got a toothache.

PROFESSOR: Let's continue . . . I said: Let's continue. Take now the word "front." Have you taken it?

PUPIL: Yes, yes, I've got it. My teeth, my teeth . . .

PROFESSOR: The word "front" is the root of "frontispiece." It is also to be found in "affronted." "Ispiece" is the suffix, and "af" the prefix. They are so called because they do not change. They don't want to.

PUPIL: I've got a toothache.

PROFESSOR: Let's go on. *(Rapidly:)* These prefixes are of Spanish origin. I hope you noticed that, did you?

PUPIL: Oh, how my tooth aches.

PROFESSOR: Let's continue. You've surely also noticed that they've not changed in French. And now, young lady, nothing has succeeded in changing them in Latin either, nor in Italian, nor in Portuguese, nor in Sardanapalian, nor in Sardanapali, nor in Romanian, nor in neo-Spanish, nor in Spanish, nor even in the Oriental: front, frontispiece, affronted, always the same word, invariably with the same root, the same suffix, the same prefix, in all the languages I have named. And it is always the same for all words.

PUPIL: In all languages, these words mean the same thing? I've got a toothache.

PROFESSOR: Absolutely. Moreover, it's more a notion than a word. In any case, you have always the same signification, the same composition, the same sound structure, not only for this word, but for all conceivable words, in all languages. For one single notion is expressed by one and the same word, and its synonyms, in all countries. Forget about your teeth.

PUPIL: I've got a toothache. Yes, yes, yes.

PROFESSOR: Good, let's go on. I tell you, let's go on . . . How would you say, for example, in French: the roses of my grandmother are as yellow as my grandfather who was Asiatic?

PUPIL: My teeth ache, ache, ache.

PROFESSOR: Let's go on, let's go on, go ahead and answer, anyway.

PUPIL: In French?

PROFESSOR: In French.

PUPIL: Uhh . . . I should say in French: the roses of my grandmother are . . . ?

PROFESSOR: As yellow as my grandfather who was Asiatic . . .

PUPIL: Oh well, one would say, in French, I believe, the roses . . . of my . . . how do you say "grandmother" in French?

PROFESSOR: In French? Grandmother.

PUPIL: The roses of my grandmother are as yellow—in French, is it "yellow"?

PROFESSOR: Yes, of course!

PUPIL: Are as yellow as my grandfather when he got angry.

PROFESSOR: No . . . who was A . . .

PUPIL: . . . siatic . . . I've got a toothache.

PROFESSOR: That's it.

PUPIL: I've got a tooth . . .

PROFESSOR: Ache . . . so what . . . let's continue! And now translate the same sentence into Spanish, then into neo-Spanish . . .

PUPIL: In Spanish . . . this would be: the roses of my grandmother are as yellow as my grandfather who was Asiatic.

PROFESSOR: No. That's wrong.

PUPIL: And in neo-Spanish: the roses of my grandmother are as yellow as my grandfather who was Asiatic.

PROFESSOR: That's wrong. That's wrong. That's wrong. You have inverted it, you've confused Spanish with neo-Spanish, and neo-Spanish with Spanish . . . Oh . . . no . . . it's the other way around . . .

PUPIL: I've got a toothache. You're getting mixed up.

PROFESSOR: You're the one who is mixing me up. Pay attention and take notes. I will say the sentence to you in Spanish, then in neo-Spanish, and finally, in Latin. You will repeat after me. Pay attention, for the resemblances are great. In fact, they are identical resemblances. Listen, follow carefully . . .

PUPIL: I've got a tooth . . .

PROFESSOR: . . . Ache.

PUPIL: Let us go on . . . Ah! . . .

PROFESSOR: . . . In Spanish: the roses of my grandmother are as yellow as my grandfather who was Asiatic; in Latin: the roses of my grandmother are as yellow as my grandfather who was Asiatic. Do you detect the differences? Translate this into . . . Romanian.

PUPIL: The . . . how do you say "roses" in Romanian?

PROFESSOR: But "roses," what else?

PUPIL: It's not "roses"? Oh, how my tooth aches!

PROFESSOR: Certainly not, certainly not, since "roses" is a translation in Oriental of the French word "roses," in Spanish "roses," do you get it? In Sardanapali, "roses" . . .

PUPIL: Excuse me, Professor, but . . . Oh, my toothache! . . . I don't get the difference.

PROFESSOR: But it's so simple! So simple! It's a matter of having a certain experience, a technical experience and practice in these diverse languages, which are so diverse in spite of the fact that they present wholly identical characteristics. I'm going to try to give you a key . . .

PUPIL: Toothache . . .

PROFESSOR: That which differentiates these languages, is neither the words, which are absolutely the same, nor the structure of the sentence which is everywhere the same, nor the intonation, which does not offer any differences, nor the rhythm of the language . . . that which differentiates them . . . are you listening?

PUPIL: I've got a toothache.

PROFESSOR: Are you listening to me, young lady? Aah! We're going to lose our temper.

PUPIL: You're bothering me, Professor. I've got a toothache.

PROFESSOR: Son of a cocker spaniel! Listen to me!

PUPIL: Oh well . . . yes . . . yes . . . go on . . .

PROFESSOR: That which distinguishes them from each other, on the one hand, and from their mother, Spanishe with its mute *e,* on the other hand . . . is . . .

PUPIL *(grimacing)*: Is what?

PROFESSOR: Is an intangible thing. Something intangible that one is able to perceive only after very long study, with a great deal of trouble and after the broadest experience . . .

PUPIL: Ah?

PROFESSOR: Yes, young lady. I cannot give you any rule. One must have a feeling for it, and well, that's it. But in order to have it, one must study, study, and then study some more.

PUPIL: Toothache.

PROFESSOR: All the same, there are some specific cases where words differ from one language to another . . . but we cannot base our knowledge on these cases, which are, so to speak, exceptional.

PUPIL: Oh, yes? . . . Oh, Professor, I've got a toothache.

PROFESSOR: Don't interrupt! Don't make me lose my temper! I can't answer for what I'll do. I was saying, then . . . Ah, yes, the exceptional cases, the so-called easily distinguished . . . or facilely distinguished . . . or conveniently . . . if you prefer . . . I repeat, if you prefer, for I see that you're not listening to me . . .

PUPIL: I've got a toothache.

PROFESSOR: I say then: in certain expressions in current usage, certain words differ totally from one language to another, so much so that the language employed is, in this case, considerably easier to identify. I'll give you an example: the neo-Spanish expression, famous in Madrid: "My country is the new Spain," becomes in Italian: "My country is . . .

PUPIL: The new Spain.

PROFESSOR: No! "My country is Italy." Tell me now, by simple deduction, how do you say "Italy" in French?

PUPIL: I've got a toothache.

PROFESSOR: But it's so easy: for the word "Italy," in French we have the word "France," which is an exact translation of it. My country is

France. And "France" in Oriental: "Orient!" My country is the Orient. And "Orient" in Portuguese: "Portugal!" The Oriental expression: My country is the Orient is translated then in the same fashion into Portuguese: My country is Portugal! And so on . . .

PUPIL: Oh, no more, no more. My teeth . . .

PROFESSOR: Ache! ache! ache! . . . I'm going to pull them out, I will! One more example. The word "capital"—it takes on, according to the language one speaks, a different meaning. That is to say that when a Spaniard says: "I reside in the capital," the word "capital" does not mean at all the same thing that a Portuguese means when he says: "I reside in the capital." All the more so in the case of a Frenchman, a neo-Spaniard, a Romanian, a Latin, a Sardanapali . . . Whenever you hear it, young lady—young lady, I'm saying this for you! Pooh! Whenever you hear the expression: "I reside in the capital," you will immediately and easily know whether this is Spanish or Spanish, neo-Spanish, French, Oriental, Romanian, or Latin, for it is enough to know which metropolis is referred to by the person who pronounces the sentence . . . at the very moment he pronounces it . . . But these are almost the only precise examples that I can give you . . .

PUPIL: Oh dear! My teeth . . .

PROFESSOR: Silence! Or I'll bash in your skull!

PUPIL: Just try to! Skulldugger!

(The PROFESSOR seizes her wrist and twists it.)

PUPIL: Oww!

PROFESSOR: Keep quiet now! Not a word!

PUPIL *(whimpering)*: Toothache . . .

PROFESSOR: One thing that is the most . . . how shall I say it? . . . the most paradoxical . . . yes . . . that's the word . . . the most paradoxical thing, is that a lot of people who are completely illiterate speak these different languages . . . do you understand? What did I just say?

PUPIL: . . . "Speak these different languages! What did I just say?"

PROFESSOR: You were lucky that time! . . . The common people speak a Spanish full of neo-Spanish words that they are entirely unaware of, all the while believing that they are speaking Latin . . . or they speak Latin, full of Oriental words, all the while believing that they're speaking Romanian . . . or Spanish, full of neo-Spanish, all the while believing that they're speaking Sardanapali, or Spanish . . . Do you understand?

PUPIL: Yes! yes! yes! yes! What more do you want? . . .

PROFESSOR: No insolence, my pet, or you'll be sorry . . . *(In a rage:)* But the worst of all, young lady, is that certain people, for example, in a Latin that they suppose is Spanish, say: "Both my kidneys are of the same kidney," in addressing themselves to a Frenchman who does not know a word of Spanish, but the latter understands it as if it were his own language. For that matter he thinks it is his own language. And the Frenchman will reply, in French: "Me too, sir, mine are too," and this will be perfectly comprehensible to a Spaniard, who will feel certain that the reply is in pure Spanish and that Spanish is being spoken . . . when, in reality, it was neither Spanish nor French, but Latin in the neo-Spanish dialect . . . Sit still, young lady, don't fidget, stop tapping your feet . . .

PUPIL: I've got a toothache.

PROFESSOR: How do you account for the fact that, in speaking without knowing which language they speak, or even while each of them believes that he is speaking another, the common people understand each other at all?

PUPIL: I wonder.

PROFESSOR: It is simply one of the inexplicable curiosities of the vulgar empiricism of the common people — not to be confused with experience! — a paradox, a non-sense, one of the aberrations of human nature, it is purely and simply instinct — to put it in a nutshell . . . That's what is involved here.

PUPIL: Hah! hah!

PROFESSOR: Instead of staring at the flies while I'm going to all this trouble . . . you would do much better to try to be more attentive . . . it is not I who is going to qualify for the partial doctor's orals . . . I passed mine a long time ago . . . and I've won my total doctorate, too . . . and my supertotal diploma . . . Don't you realize that what I'm saying is for your own good?

PUPIL: Toothache!

PROFESSOR: Ill-mannered . . . It can't go on like this, it won't do, it won't do, it won't do . . .

PUPIL: I'm . . . listening . . . to you . . .

PROFESSOR: Ahah! In order to learn to distinguish all the different languages, as I've told you, there is nothing better than practice . . . Let's take them up in order. I am going to try to teach you all the translations of the word "knife."

PUPIL: Well, all right . . . if you want . . .

PROFESSOR *(calling the* MAID*)*: Marie! Marie! She's not there . . . Marie! Marie! . . . Marie, where are you? *(He opens the door on the right.)* Marie! . . .

(He exits. The PUPIL *remains alone several minutes, staring into space, wearing a stupefied expression.)*

PROFESSOR *(offstage, in a shrill voice)*: Marie! What are you up to? Why don't you come! When I call you, you must come! *(He re-enters, followed by* MARIE.*)* It is I who gives the orders, do you hear? *(He points at the* PUPIL:*)* She doesn't understand anything, that girl. She doesn't understand!

MAID: Don't get into such a state, sir, you know where it'll end! You're going to go too far, you're going to go too far.

PROFESSOR: I'll be able to stop in time.

MAID: That's what you always say. I only wish I could see it.

PUPIL: I've got a toothache.

MAID: You see, it's starting, that's the symptom!

PROFESSOR: What symptom? Explain yourself? What do you mean?

PUPIL *(in a spiritless voice)*: Yes, what do you mean? I've got a toothache.

MAID: The final symptom! The chief symptom!

PROFESSOR: Stupid! stupid! stupid! *(The* MAID *starts to exit.)* Don't go away like that! I called you to help me find the Spanish, neo-Spanish, Portuguese, French, Oriental, Romanian, Sardanapali, Latin and Spanish knives.

MAID *(severely)*: Don't ask me. *(She exits.)*

PROFESSOR *(makes a gesture as though to protest, then refrains, a little helpless. Suddenly, he remembers)*: Ah! *(He goes quickly to the drawer where he finds a big knife, invisible or real according to the preference of the director. He seizes it and brandishes it happily.)* Here is one, young lady, here is a knife. It's too bad that we only have this one, but we're going to try to make it serve for all the languages, anyway! It will be enough if you will pronounce the word "knife" in all the languages, while looking at the object, very closely, fixedly, and imagining that it is in the language that you are speaking.

PUPIL: I've got a toothache.

PROFESSOR *(almost singing, chanting)*: Now, say "kni," like "kni," "fe," like "fe" . . . And look, look, look at it, watch it . . .

PUPIL: What is this one in? French, Italian or Spanish?

PROFESSOR: That doesn't matter now . . . That's not your concern. Say: "kni."

PUPIL: "Kni."

PROFESSOR: . . . "fe" . . . Look.

(He brandishes the knife under the PUPIL's *eyes.)*

PUPIL: "fe" . . .

PROFESSOR: Again . . . Look at it.

PUPIL: Oh, no! My God! I've had enough. And besides, I've got a toothache, my feet hurt me, I've got a headache.

PROFESSOR *(abruptly)*: Knife . . . look . . . knife . . . look . . . knife . . . look . . .

PUPIL: You're giving me an earache, too. Oh, your voice! It's so piercing!

PROFESSOR: Say: knife . . . kni . . . fe . . .

PUPIL: No! My ears hurt, I hurt all over . . .

PROFESSOR: I'm going to tear them off, your ears, that's what I'm going to do to you, and then they won't hurt you anymore, my pet.

PUPIL: Oh . . . you're hurting me, oh, you're hurting me . . .

PROFESSOR: Look, come on, quickly, repeat after me: "kni" . . .

PUPIL: Oh, since you insist . . . knife . . . knife . . . *(In a lucid moment, ironically:)* Is that neo-Spanish? . . .

PROFESSOR: If you like, yes, it's neo-Spanish, but hurry up . . . we haven't got time . . . And then, what do you mean by that insidious question? What are you up to?

PUPIL *(becoming more and more exhausted, weeping, desperate, at the same time both exasperated and in a trance)*: Ah!

PROFESSOR: Repeat, watch. *(He imitates a cuckoo:)* Knife, knife . . . knife, knife . . . knife, knife . . . knife, knife . . .

PUPIL: Oh, my head . . . aches . . . *(With her hand she caressingly touches the parts of her body as she names them:)* . . . My eyes . . .

PROFESSOR *(like a cuckoo)*: Knife, knife . . . knife, knife . . .

(They are both standing. The PROFESSOR *still brandishes his invisible knife, nearly beside himself, as he circles around her in a sort of scalp dance, but it is important that this not be exaggerated and that his dance steps be only suggested. The* PUPIL *stands facing the audience, then recoils in the direction of the window, sickly, languid, victimized.)*

PROFESSOR: Repeat, repeat: knife . . . knife . . . knife . . .

PUPIL: I've got a pain . . . my throat, neck . . . oh, my shoulders . . . my breast . . . knife . . .

PROFESSOR: Knife . . . knife . . . knife . . .

PUPIL: My hips . . . knife . . . my thighs . . . kni . . .

PROFESSOR: Pronounce it carefully . . . knife . . . knife . . .

PUPIL: Knife . . . my throat . . .

PROFESSOR: Knife . . . knife . . .

PUPIL: Knife . . . my shoulders . . . my arms, my breast, my hips . . . knife . . . knife . . .

PROFESSOR: That's right . . . Now, you're pronouncing it well . . .

PUPIL: Knife . . . my breast . . . my stomach . . .

PROFESSOR *(changing his voice)*: Pay attention . . . don't break my window . . . the knife kills . . .

PUPIL *(in a weak voice)*: Yes, yes . . . the knife kills?

PROFESSOR *(striking the* PUPIL *with a very spectacular blow of the knife)*: Aaah! That'll teach you!

*(*PUPIL *also cries "Aah!" then falls, flopping in an immodest position onto a chair which, as though by chance, is near the window. The murderer and his victim shout "Aaah!" at the same moment. After the first blow of the knife, the* PUPIL *flops onto the chair, her legs spread wide and hanging over both sides of the chair. The* PROFESSOR *remains standing in front of her, his back to the audience. After the first blow, he strikes her dead with a second slash of the knife, from bottom to top. After that blow a noticeable convulsion shakes his whole body.)*

PROFESSOR *(winded, mumbling)*: Bitch . . . Oh, that's good, that does me good . . . Ah! Ah! I'm exhausted . . . I can scarcely breathe . . . Aah! *(He breathes with difficulty; he falls — fortunately a chair is there; he mops his brow, mumbles some incomprehensible words; his breathing becomes normal. He gets up, looks at the knife in his hand, looks at the young girl, then as though he were waking up, in a panic:)* What have I done! What's going to happen to me now! What's going to happen! Oh! dear! Oh dear, I'm in trouble! Young lady, young lady, get up! *(He is agitated, still holding onto the invisible knife, which he doesn't know what to do with.)* Come now, young lady, the lesson is over . . . you may go . . . you can pay another time . . . Oh! she is dead . . . dea-ead . . . And by my knife . . . She is dea-ead . . . It's terrible. *(He calls the* MAID*:)* Marie! Marie! My good Marie, come here! Ah! ah! *(The door on the right opens a little and* MARIE *appears.)* No . . . don't come in . . . I made a mistake . . . I don't need you, Marie . . . I don't need you anymore . . . do you understand? . . .

*(*MAID *enters wearing a stern expression, without saying a word. She sees the corpse.)*

PROFESSOR *(in a voice less and less assured)*: I don't need you, Marie . . .

MAID *(sarcastic)*: Then, you're satisfied with your pupil, she's profited by your lesson?

PROFESSOR *(holding the knife behind his back)*: Yes, the lesson is finished . . . but . . . she . . . she's still there . . . she doesn't want to leave . . .

MAID *(very harshly)*: Is that a fact? . . .

PROFESSOR *(trembling)*: It wasn't I . . . it wasn't I . . . Marie . . . No . . . I assure you . . . it wasn't I, my little Marie . . .

MAID: And who was it? Who was it then? Me?

PROFESSOR: I don't know . . . maybe . . .

MAID: Or the cat?

PROFESSOR: That's possible . . . I don't know . . .

MAID: And today makes it the fortieth time! . . . And every day it's the same thing! Every day! You should be ashamed, at your age . . . and you're going to make yourself sick! You won't have any pupils left. That will serve you right.

PROFESSOR *(irritated)*: It wasn't my fault! She didn't want to learn! She was disobedient! She was a bad pupil! She didn't want to learn!

MAID: Liar! . . .

PROFESSOR *(craftily approaching the* MAID, *holding the knife behind his back)*: It's none of your business! *(He tries to strike her with a great blow of the knife; the* MAID *seizes his wrist in mid-gesture and twists it; the* PROFESSOR *lets the knife fall to the floor)*: . . . I'm sorry!

MAID *(gives him two loud, strong slaps; the* PROFESSOR *falls onto the floor, on his prat; he sobs)*: Little murderer! bastard! You're disgusting! You wanted to do that to me? I'm not one of your pupils, not me! *(She pulls him up by the collar, picks up his skullcap and puts it on his head; he's afraid she'll slap him again and holds his arm up to protect his face, like a child.)* Put the knife back where it belongs, go on! *(The* PROFESSOR *goes and puts it back in the drawer of the buffet, then comes back to her.)* Now didn't I warn you, just a little while ago: arithmetic leads to philology, and philology leads to crime . . .

PROFESSOR: You said "to calamity"!

MAID: It's the same thing.

PROFESSOR: I didn't understand you. I thought that "calamity" was a city and that you meant that philology leads to the city of Calamity . . .

MAID: Liar! Old fox! An intellectual like you is not going to make a mistake in the meanings of words. Don't try to pull the wool over my eyes.

PROFESSOR *(sobbing)*: I didn't kill her on purpose!

MAID: Are you sorry at least?

PROFESSOR: Oh, yes, Marie, I swear it to you!

MAID: I can't help feeling sorry for you! Ah! you're a good boy in spite of everything! I'll try to fix this. But don't start it again . . . It could give you a heart attack . . .

PROFESSOR: Yes, Marie! What are we going to do, now?

MAID: We're going to bury her . . . along with the thirty-nine others . . . that will make forty coffins . . . I'll call the undertakers and my lover, Father Auguste . . . I'll order the wreaths . . .

PROFESSOR: Yes, Marie, thank you very much.

MAID: Well, that's that. And perhaps it won't be necessary to call Auguste, since you yourself are something of a priest at times, if one can believe the gossip.

PROFESSOR: In any case, don't spend too much on the wreaths. She didn't pay for her lesson.

MAID: Don't worry . . . The least you can do is cover her up with her smock, she's not decent that way. And then we'll carry her out . . .

PROFESSOR: Yes, Marie, yes. *(He covers up the body.)* There's a chance that we'll get pinched . . . with forty coffins . . . Don't you think . . . people will be surprised . . . Suppose they ask us what's inside them?

MAID: Don't worry so much. We'll say that they're empty. And besides, people won't ask questions, they're used to it.

PROFESSOR: Even so . . .

MAID *(she takes out an armband with an insignia, perhaps the Nazi swastika)*: Wait, if you're afraid, wear this, then you won't have anything more to be afraid of. *(She puts the armband around his arm.)* . . . That's good politics.

PROFESSOR: Thanks, my little Marie. With this, I won't need to worry . . . You're a good girl, Marie . . . very loyal . . .

MAID: That's enough. Come on, sir. Are you all right?

PROFESSOR: Yes, my little Marie. *(The MAID and the PROFESSOR take the body of the young girl, one by the shoulders, the other by the legs, and move towards the door on the right.)* Be careful. We don't want to hurt her.

(They exit. The stage remains empty for several moments. We hear the doorbell ring at the left.)

VOICE OF THE MAID: Just a moment, I'm coming!

(She appears as she was at the beginning of the play, and goes towards the door. The doorbell rings again.)

MAID *(aside)*: She's certainly in a hurry, this one! *(Aloud:)* Just a moment! *(She goes to the door on the left, and opens it.)* Good morning, miss! You are the new pupil? You have come for the lesson? The Professor is expecting you. I'll go tell him that you've come. He'll be right down. Come in, miss, come in!

Considerations

1. Describe your initial responses to the Professor and explain how and why those responses change as you read the play.
2. *The Lesson* makes fun of certain types of teaching and learning. Identify three absurd or comic episodes and explain what aspects of teaching and learning they satirize.
3. What role does the Maid play? How would the drama change if the Professor and the young Pupil were the only characters?
4. What changes do you see in the young Pupil? What is the Professor trying to teach her? What does she learn?
5. Consider the significance of the title. For example, what lesson (or lessons) does Ionesco teach his audience?

LOREN EISELEY (1913–   )

The Hidden Teacher

*Sometimes the best teacher teaches only once to a single child or to
a grownup past hope.*
— Anonymous

I

The putting of formidable riddles did not arise with today's philosophers. In fact, there is a sense in which the experimental method of science
might be said merely to have widened the area of man's homelessness. Over
two thousand years ago, a man named Job, crouching in the Judean desert,
was moved to challenge what he felt to be the injustice of his God. The
voice in the whirlwind, in turn, volleyed pitiless questions upon the suppli-
cant — questions that have, in truth, precisely the ring of modern science.
For the Lord asked of Job by whose wisdom the hawk soars, and who had
fathered the rain, or entered the storehouses of the snow.

A youth standing by, one Elihu, also played a role in this drama, for
he ventured diffidently to his protesting elder that it was not true that God
failed to manifest Himself. He may speak in one way or another, though
men do not perceive it. In consequence of this remark perhaps it would be
well, whatever our individual beliefs, to consider what may be called the
hidden teacher, lest we become too much concerned with the formalities of
only one aspect of the education by which we learn.

We think we learn from teachers, and we sometimes do. But the teachers are not always to be found in school or in great laboratories. Sometimes
what we learn depends upon our own powers of insight. Moreover, our
teachers may be hidden, even the greatest teacher. And it was the young
man Elihu who observed that if the old are not always wise, neither can the
teacher's way be ordered by the young whom he would teach.

For example, I once received an unexpected lesson from a spider.

It happened far away on a rainy morning in the West. I had come up a
long gulch looking for fossils, and there, just at eye level, lurked a huge
yellow-and-black orb spider, whose web was moored to the tall spear of
buffalo grass at the edge of the arroyo. It was her universe, and her senses
did not extend beyond the lines and spokes of the great wheel she inhabited.
Her extended claws could feel every vibration throughout that delicate structure. She knew the tug of wind, the fall of a raindrop, the flutter of a trapped
moth's wing. Down one spoke of the web ran a stout ribbon of gossamer
on which she could hurry out to investigate her prey.

Curious, I took a pencil from my pocket and touched a strand of the
web. Immediately there was a response. The web, plucked by its menacing
occupant, began to vibrate until it was a blur. Anything that had brushed
claw or wing against that amazing snare would be thoroughly entrapped.

5

As the vibrations slowed, I could see the owner fingering her guidelines for signs of struggle. A pencil point was an intrusion into this universe for which no precedent existed. Spider was circumscribed by spider ideas; its universe was spider universe. All outside was irrational, extraneous, at best raw material for spider. As I proceeded on my way along the gully, like a vast impossible shadow, I realized that in the world of spider I did not exist.

Moreover, I considered, as I tramped along, that to the phagocytes, the white blood cells, clambering even now with some kind of elementary intelligence amid the thin pipes and tubing of my body — creatures without whose ministrations I could not exist — the conscious "I" of which I was aware had no significance to these amoeboid beings. I was, instead, a kind of chemical web that brought meaningful messages to them, a natural environment seemingly immortal if they could have thought about it, since generations of them had lived and perished, and would continue to so live and die, in that odd fabric which contained my intelligence — a misty light that was beginning to seem floating and tenuous even to me.

I began to see that, among the many universes in which the world of living creatures existed, some were large, some small, but that all, including man's, were in some way limited or finite. We were creatures of many different dimensions passing through each other's lives like ghosts through doors.

In the years since, my mind has many times returned to that far moment of my encounter with the orb spider. A message has arisen only now from the misty shreds of that webbed universe. What was it that had so troubled me about the incident? Was it that spidery indifference to the human triumph?

If so, that triumph was very real and could not be denied. I saw, had   10
many times seen, both mentally and in the seams of exposed strata, the long backward stretch of time whose recovery is one of the great feats of modern science. I saw the drifting cells of the early seas from which all life, including our own, has arisen. The salt of those ancient seas is in our blood, its lime is in our bones. Every time we walk along a beach some ancient urge disturbs us so that we find ourselves shedding shoes and garments or scavenging among seaweed and whitened timbers like the homesick refugees of a long war.

And war it has been indeed — the long war of life against its inhospitable environment, a war that has lasted for perhaps three billion years. It began with strange chemicals seething under a sky lacking in oxygen: it was waged through long ages until the first green plants learned to harness the light of the nearest star, our sun. The human brain, so frail, so perishable, so full of inexhaustible dreams and hungers, burns by the power of the leaf.

The hurrying blood cells charged with oxygen carry more of that element to the human brain than to any other part of the body. A few moments' loss of vital air and the phenomenon we know as consciousness goes down into the black night of inorganic things. The human body is a magical vessel, but its life is linked with an element it cannot produce. Only the green plant knows the secret of transforming the light that comes to us across the far reaches of space. There is no better illustration of the intricacy of man's relationship with other living things.

The student of fossil life would be forced to tell us that if we take the past into consideration the vast majority of earth's creatures — perhaps over 90 percent — have vanished. Forms that flourished for a far longer time than man has existed upon earth have become either extinct or so transformed that their descendants are scarcely recognizable. The specialized perish with the environment that created them, the tooth of the tiger fails at last, the lances of men strike down the last mammoth.

In three billion years of slow change and groping effort only one living creature has succeeded in escaping the trap of specialization that has led in time to so much death and wasted endeavor. It is man, but the word should be uttered softly, for his story is not yet done.

With the rise of the human brain, with the appearance of a creature   15
whose upright body enabled two limbs to be freed for the exploration and manipulation of his environment, there had at last emerged a creature with a specialization — the brain — that, paradoxically, offered escape from specialization. Many animals driven into the nooks and crannies of nature have achieved momentary survival only at the cost of later extinction.

Was it this that troubled me and brought my mind back to a tiny universe among the grass blades, a spider's universe concerned with spider thought?

Perhaps.

The mind that once visualized animals on a cave wall is now engaged in a vast ramification of itself through time and space. Man has broken through the boundaries that control all other life. I saw, at last, the reason for my recollection of that great spider on the arroyo's rim, fingering its universe against the sky.

The spider was a symbol of man in miniature. The wheel of the web brought the analogy home clearly. Man, too, lies at the heart of a web, a web extending through the starry reaches of sidereal space, as well as backward into the dark realm of prehistory. His great eye upon Mount Palomar looks into a distance of millions of light-years, his radio ear hears the whisper of even more remote galaxies, he peers through the electron microscope upon the minute particles of his own being. It is a web no creature of earth has ever spun before. Like the orb spider, man lies at the heart of it, listening. Knowledge has given him the memory of earth's history beyond the time of his emergence. Like the spider's claw, a part of him touches a world he will never enter in the flesh. Even now, one can see him reaching forward into time with new machines, computing, analyzing, until elements of the shadowy future will also compose part of the invisible web he fingers.

Yet still my spider lingers in memory against the sunset sky. Spider   20
thoughts in a spider universe — senstive to raindrop and moth flutter, nothing beyond, nothing allowed for the unexpected, the inserted pencil from
the world outside.

Is man at heart any different from the spider, I wonder: man thoughts,
as limited as spider thoughts, contemplating now the nearest star with the
threat of bringing with him the fungus rot from earth, wars, violence, the
burden of a population he refuses to control, cherishing again his dream of
the Adamic Eden he had pursued and lost in the green forests of America.
Now it beckons again like a mirage from beyond the moon. Let man spin
his web, I thought further; it is his nature. But I considered also the work of
the phagocytes swarming in the rivers of my body, the unresting cells in
their mortal universe. What is it we are a part of that we do not see, as the
spider was not gifted to discern my face, or my little probe into her world?

We are too content with our sensory extensions, with the fulfillment
of that Ice Age mind that began its journey amidst the cold of vast
tundras and that pauses only briefly before its leap into space. It is no longer
enough to see as a man sees — even to the ends of the universe. It is not
enough to hold nuclear energy in one's hand like a spear, as a man would
hold it, or to see the lightning, or times past, or time to come, as a man
would see it. If we continue to do this, the great brain — the human brain —
will be only a new version of the old trap, and nature is full of traps for the
beast that cannot learn.

It is not sufficient any longer to listen at the end of a wire to the
rustlings of galaxies; it is not enough even to examine the great coil of DNA
in which is coded the very alphabet of life. These are our extended perceptions. But beyond lies the great darkness of the ultimate Dreamer, who
dreamed the light and the galaxies. Before act was, or substance existed,
imagination grew in the dark. Man partakes of that ultimate wonder and
creativeness. As we turn from the galaxies to the swarming cells of our own
being, which toil for something, some entity beyond their grasp, let us
remember man, the self-fabricator who came across an ice age to look into
the mirrors and the magic of science. Surely he did not come to see himself
or his wild visage only. He came because he is at heart a listener and a
searcher for some transcendent realm beyond himself. This he has worshiped
by many names, even in the dismal caves of his beginning. Man, the self-
fabricator, is so by reason of gifts he had no part in devising — and so he
searches as the single living cell in the beginning must have sought the
ghostly creature it was to serve.

II

The young man Elihu, Job's counselor and critic, spoke simply of the
"Teacher," and it is of this teacher I speak when I refer to gifts man had no
part in devising. Perhaps — though it is purely a matter of emotional reac-

tions to words — it is easier for us today to speak of this teacher as "nature," that omnipresent all which contained both the spider and my invisible intrusion into her carefully planned universe. But nature does not simply represent reality. In the shapes of life, it prepares the future; it offers alternatives. Nature teaches, though what it teaches is often hidden and obscure, just as the voice from the spinning dust cloud belittled Job's thought but gave back no answers to its own formidable interrogation.

A few months ago I encountered an amazing little creature on a windy   25 corner of my local shopping center. It seemed, at first glance, some long-limbed, feathery spider teetering rapidly down the edge of a store front. Then it swung into the air and, as hesitantly as a spider on a thread, blew away into the parking lot. It returned in a moment on a gust of wind and ran toward me once more on its spindly legs with amazing rapidity.

With great difficulty I discovered the creature was actually a filamentous seed, seeking a hiding place and scurrying about with the uncanny surety of a conscious animal. In fact, it *did* escape me before I could secure it. Its flexible limbs were stiffer than milkweed down, and, propelled by the wind, it ran rapidly and evasively over the pavement. It was like a gnome scampering somewhere with a hidden packet — for all that I could tell, a totally new one: one of the jumbled alphabets of life.

A new one? So stable seem the years and all green leaves, a botanist might smile at my imaginings. Yet bear with me a moment. I would like to tell a tale, a genuine tale of childhood. Moreover, I was just old enough to know the average of my kind and to marvel at what I saw. And what I saw was straight from the hidden Teacher, whatever be his name.

It is told in the Orient of the Hindu god Krishna that his mother, wiping his mouth when he was a child, inadvertently peered in and beheld the universe, though the sight was mercifully and immediately veiled from her. In a sense, this is what happened to me. One day there arrived at our school a newcomer, who entered the grade above me. After some days this lad, whose look of sleepy-eyed arrogance is still before me as I write, was led into my mathematics classroom by the principal. Our class was informed severely that we should learn to work harder.

With this preliminary exhortation, great rows of figures were chalked upon the blackboard, such difficult mathematical problems as could be devised by adults. The class watched in helpless wonder. When the preparations had been completed, the young pupil sauntered forward and, with a glance of infinite boredom that swept from us to his fawning teachers, wrote the answers, as instantaneously as a modern computer, in their proper place upon the board. Then he strolled out with a carelessly exaggerated yawn.

Like some heavy-browed child at the wood's edge, clutching the last   30 stone hand ax, I was witnessing the birth of a new type of humanity — one so beyond its teachers that it was being used for mean purposes while the intangible web of the universe in all its shimmering mathematical perfection glistened untaught in the mind of a chance little boy. The boy, by then grown self-centered and contemptuous, was being dragged from room to room to encourage us, the paleanthropes, to duplicate what, in reality, our teachers could not duplicate. He was too precious an object to be released upon the playground among us, and with reason. In a few months his parents took him away.

Long after, looking back from maturity, I realized that I had been exposed on that occasion, not to human teaching, but to the Teacher, toying with some sixteen billion nerve cells interlocked in ways past understanding. Or, if we do not like the anthropomorphism implied in the word teacher, then nature, the old voice from the whirlwind fumbling for the light. At all events, I had been the fortunate witness to life's unbounded creativity — a creativity seemingly still as unbalanced and chance-filled as in that far era when a black-scaled creature had broken from an egg and the age of the giant reptiles, the creatures of the prime, had tentatively begun.

Because form cannot be long sustained in the living, we collapse inward with age. We die. Our bodies, which were the product of a kind of hidden teaching by an alphabet we are only beginning dimly to discern, are dismissed into their elements. What is carried onward, assuming we have descendants, is the little capsule of instructions such as I encountered hastening by me in the shape of a running seed. We have learned the first biological lesson: that in each generation life passes through the eye of a needle. It exists for a time molecularly and in no recognizable semblance to its adult condition. It *instructs* its way again into man or reptile. As the ages pass, so do variants of the code. Occasionally, a species vanishes on a wind as unreturning as that which took the pterodactyls.

Or the code changes by subtle degrees through the statistical altering of individuals; until I, as the fading Neanderthals must once have done, have looked with still-living eyes upon the creature whose genotype was quite possibly to replace me. The genetic alphabets, like genuine languages, ramify and evolve along unreturning pathways.

If nature's instructions are carried through the eye of a needle, through the molecular darkness of a minute world below the field of human vision and of time's decay, the same, it might be said, is true of those monumental structures known as civilizations. They are transmitted from one generation to another in invisible puffs of air known as words — words that can also be symbolically incised on clay. As the delicate printing on the mud at the water's edge retraces a visit of autumn birds long since departed, so the little scrabbled tablets in perished cities carry the seeds of human thought across the deserts of millennia. In this instance the teacher is the social brain, but it, too, must be compressed into minute hieroglyphs, and the minds that wrought the miracle efface themselves amidst the jostling torrent of messages, which, like the genetic code, are shuffled and reshuffled as they hurry through eternity. Like a mutation, an idea may be recorded in the wrong time, to lie latent like a recessive gene and spring once more to life in an auspicious era.

Occasionally, in the moments when an archaeologist lifts the slab over   35
a tomb that houses a great secret, a few men gain a unique glimpse through
that dark portal out of which all men living have emerged, and through
which messages again must pass. Here the Mexican archaeologist Ruz Lhuil-
lier speaks of his first penetration of the great tomb hidden beneath dripping
stalactites at the pyramid of Palenque: "Out of the dark shadows, rose a
fairy-tale vision, a weird ethereal spectacle from another world. It was like a
magician's cave carved out of ice, with walls glittering and sparkling like
snow crystals." After shining his torch over hieroglyphs and sculptured
figures, the explorer remarked wonderingly: "We were the first people for
more than a thousand years to look at it."

Or again, one may read the tale of an unknown pharaoh who had
secretly arranged that a beloved woman of his household should be buried
in the tomb of the god-king — an act of compassion carrying a personal
message across the millennia in defiance of all precedent.

Up to this point we have been talking of the single hidden teacher, the
taunting voice out of that old Biblical whirlwind which symbolizes nature.
We have seen incredible organic remembrance passed through the needle's
eye of a microcosmic world hidden completely beneath the observational
powers of creatures preoccupied and ensorcelled by dissolution and decay.
We have seen the human mind unconsciously seize upon the principles of
that very code to pass its own societal memory forward into time. The
individual, the momentary living cell of the society, vanishes, but the insti-
tutional structures stand, or if they change, do so in an invisible flux not too
dissimilar from that persisting in the stream of genetic continuity.

Upon this world, life is still young, not truly old as stars are measured.
Therefore it comes about that we minimize the role of the synapsid reptiles,
our remote forerunners, and correspondingly exalt our own intellectual
achievements. We refuse to consider that in the old eye of the hurricane we
may be, and doubtless are, in aggregate, a slightly more diffuse and dangerous dragon of the primal morning that still enfolds us.

Note that I say "in aggregate." For it is just here, among men, that the
role of messages, and, therefore, the role of the individual teacher — or, I
should say now, the hidden teachers — begin to be more plainly apparent and
their instructions become more diverse. The dead pharaoh, though uninten-
tionally, by a revealing act, had succeeded in conveying an impression of
human tenderness that has outlasted the trappings of a vanished religion.

Like most modern educators I have listened to student demands to   40
grade their teachers. I have heard the words repeated until they have become
a slogan, that no man over thirty can teach the young of this generation.
How would one grade a dead pharaoh, millennia gone, I wonder, one who
did not intend to teach, but who, to a few perceptive minds, succeeded by
the simple nobility of an act.

Many years ago, a student who was destined to become an interna-
tionally known anthropologist sat in a course in linguistics and heard his

instructor, a man of no inconsiderable wisdom, describe some linguistic peculiarities of Hebrew words. At the time, the young student, at the urging of his family, was contemplating a career in theology. As the teacher warmed to his subject, the student, in the back row, ventured excitedly, "I believe I can understand that, sir. It is very similar to what exists in Mohegan."

The linguist paused and adjusted his glasses. "Young man," he said, "Mohegan is a dead language. Nothing has been recorded of it since the eighteenth century. Don't bluff."

"But sir," the young student countered hopefully, "It can't be dead so long as an old woman I know still speaks it. She is Pequot-Mohegan. I learned a bit of vocabulary from her and could speak with her myself. She took care of me when I was a child."

"Young man," said the austere, old-fashioned scholar, "be at my house for dinner at six this evening. You and I are going to look into this matter."

A few months later, under careful guidance, the young student published a paper upon Mohegan linguistics, the first of a long series of studies upon the forgotten languages and ethnology of the Indians of the northeastern forests. He had changed his vocation and turned to anthropology because of the attraction of a hidden teacher. But just who was the teacher? The young man himself, his instructor, or that solitary speaker of a dying tongue who had so yearned to hear her people's voice that she had softly babbled it to a child?

Later, this man was to become one of my professors. I absorbed much from him, though I hasten to make the reluctant confession that he was considerably beyond thirty. Most of what I learned was gathered over cups of coffee in a dingy campus restaurant. What we talked about were things some centuries older than either of us. Our common interest lay in snakes, scapulimancy, and other forgotten rites of benighted forest hunters.

I have always regarded this man as an extraordinary individual, in fact, a hidden teacher. But alas, it is all now so old-fashioned. We never protested the impracticality of his quaint subjects. We were all too ready to participate in them. He was an excellent canoeman, but he took me to places where I fully expected to drown before securing my degree. To this day, fragments of his unused wisdom remain stuffed in some back attic of my mind. Much of it I have never found the opportunity to employ, yet it has somehow colored my whole adult existence. I belong to that elderly professor in somewhat the same way that he, in turn, had become the wood child of a hidden forest mother.

There are, however, other teachers. For example, among the hunting peoples there were the animal counselors who appeared in prophetic dreams. Or, among the Greeks, the daemonic supernaturals who stood at the headboard while a man lay stark and listened — sometimes to dreadful things. "You are asleep," the messengers proclaimed over and over again, as though the man lay in a spell to hear his doom pronounced. "You, Achilles, you, son of Atreus. You are asleep, asleep," the hidden ones pronounced and vanished.

We of this modern time know other things of dreams, but we know also that they can be interior teachers and healers as well as the anticipators of disaster. It has been said that great art is the night thought of man. It may emerge without warning from the soundless depths of the unconscious, just as supernovas may blaze up suddenly in the farther reaches of void space. The critics, like astronomers, can afterward triangulate such worlds but not account for them.

A writer friend of mine with bitter memories of his youth, and es-   50 tranged from his family, who, in the interim, had died, gave me this account of the matter in his middle years. He had been working, with an unusual degree of reluctance, upon a novel that contained certain autobiographical episodes. One night he dreamed; it was a very vivid and stunning dream in its detailed reality.

He found himself hurrying over creaking snow through the blackness of a winter night. He was ascending a familiar path through a long-vanished orchard. The path led to his childhood home. The house, as he drew near, appeared dark and uninhabited, but, impelled by the power of the dream, he stepped upon the porch and tried to peer through a dark window into his own old room.

"Suddenly," he told me, "I was drawn by a strange mixture of repulsion and desire to press my face against the glass. I knew intuitively they were all there waiting for me within, if I could but see them. My mother and my father. Those I had loved and those I hated. But the window was black to my gaze. I hesitated a moment and struck a match. For an instant in that freezing silence I saw my father's face glimmer wan and remote behind the glass. My mother's face was there, with the hard, distorted lines that marked her later years.

"A surge of fury overcame my cowardice. I cupped the match before me and stepped closer, closer toward that dreadful confrontation. As the match guttered down, my face was pressed almost to the glass. In some quick transformation, such as only a dream can effect, I saw that it was my own face into which I stared, just as it was reflected in the black glass. My father's haunted face was but my own. The hard lines upon my mother's aging countenance were slowly reshaping themselves upon my living face. The light burned out. I awoke sweating from the terrible psychological tension of that nightmare. I was in a far port in a distant land. It was dawn. I could hear the waves breaking on the reef."

"And how do you interpret the dream?" I asked, concealing a sympathetic shudder and sinking deeper into my chair.

"It taught me something," he said slowly, and with equal slowness a   55 kind of beautiful transfiguration passed over his features. All the tired lines I had known so well seemed faintly to be subsiding.

"Did you ever dream it again?" I asked out of a comparable experience of my own.

"No, never," he said, and hesitated. "You see, I had learned it was just I, but more, much more, I had learned that I was they. It makes a difference. And at the last, late — much too late — it was all right. I understood. My line was dying, but I understood. I hope they understood, too." His voice trailed into silence.

"It is a thing to learn," I said. "You were seeking something and it came." He nodded, wordless. "Out of a tomb," he added after a silent moment, "my kind of tomb — the mind."

On the dark street, walking homeward, I considered my friend's experience. Man, I concluded, may have come to the end of that wild being who had mastered the fire and the lightning. He can create the web but not hold it together, nor save himself except by transcending his own image. For at last, before the ultimate mystery, it is himself he shapes. Perhaps it is for this that the listening web lies open: that by knowledge we may grow beyond our past, our follies, and ever closer to what the Dreamer in the dark intended before the dust arose and walked. In the pages of an old book it has been written that we are in the hands of a Teacher, nor does it yet appear what man shall be.

Considerations

1. Summarize Eiseley's encounter with the spider. What questions does the encounter raise? What does he learn from the encounter?
2. After explaining the encounter between the young student and the linguistics instructor, Eiseley asks: "But just who was the teacher? The young man himself, his instructor, or that solitary speaker of a dying tongue who had so yearned to hear her people's voice that she had softly babbled it to a child?" How would you respond to this question?
3. In describing a professor who touched his life, Eiseley says "He was an excellent canoeman, but he took me to places where I fully expected to drown before securing my degree." What does this metaphor suggest to you about the professor and about Eiseley's philosophy of learning?
4. What do you think Eiseley's friend learned from the dream he described? In what way was the dream a hidden teacher?
5. Consider the hidden teachers in your own life. Who and what are they? Explain one particularly important lesson you have learned from a hidden teacher.

FREDERICK DOUGLASS (1817?–1895)

Learning to Read and Write

I lived in Master Hugh's family about seven years. During this time, I succeeded in learning to read and write. In accomplishing this, I was compelled to resort to various stratagems. I had no regular teacher. My mistress, who had kindly commenced to instruct me, had, in compliance with the advice and direction of her husband, not only ceased to instruct, but had set her face against my being instructed by any one else. It is due, however, to my mistress to say of her, that she did not adopt this course of treatment immediately. She at first lacked the depravity indispensable to shutting me up in mental darkness. It was at least necessary for her to have some training in the exercise of irresponsible power, to make her equal to the task of treating me as though I were a brute.

My mistress was, as I have said, a kind and tender-hearted woman; and in the simplicity of her soul she commenced, when I first went to live with her, to treat me as she supposed one human being ought to treat another. In entering upon the duties of a slaveholder, she did not seem to perceive that I sustained to her the relation of a mere chattel, and that for her to treat me as a human being was not only wrong, but dangerously so. Slavery proved as injurious to her as it did to me. When I went there, she was a pious, warm, and tender-hearted woman. There was no sorrow or suffering for which she had not a tear. She had bread for the hungry, clothes for the naked, and comfort for every mourner that came within her reach. Slavery soon proved its ability to divest her of these heavenly qualities. Under its influence, the tender heart became stone, and the lamblike disposition gave way to one of tiger-like fierceness. The first step in her downward course was in her ceasing to instruct me. She now commenced to practise her husband's precepts. She finally became even more violent in her opposition than her husband himself. She was not satisfied with simply doing as well as he had commanded; she seemed anxious to do better. Nothing seemed to make her more angry than to see me with a newspaper. She seemed to think that here lay the danger. I have had her rush at me with a face made all up of fury, and snatch from me a newspaper, in a manner that fully revealed her apprehension. She was an apt woman; and a little experience soon demonstrated, to her satisfaction, that education and slavery were incompatible with each other.

From this time I was most narrowly watched. If I was in a separate room any considerable length of time, I was sure to be suspected of having a book, and was at once called to give an account of myself. All this, however, was too late. The first step had been taken. Mistress, in teaching me the alphabet, had given me the *inch,* and no precaution could prevent me from taking the *ell.*

The plan which I adopted, and the one by which I was most successful, was that of making friends of all the little white boys whom I met in the street. As many of these as I could, I converted into teachers. With their kindly aid, obtained at different times and in different places, I finally succeeded in learning to read. When I was sent on errands, I always took my book with me, and by going one part of my errand quickly, I found time to get a lesson before my return. I used also to carry bread with me, enough of which was always in the house, and to which I was always welcome; for I was much better off in this regard than many of the poor white children in our neighborhood. This bread I used to bestow upon the hungry little urchins, who, in return, would give me that more valuable bread of knowledge. I am strongly tempted to give the names of two or three of those little boys, as a testimonial of the gratitude and affection I bear them; but prudence forbids; — not that it would injure me, but it might embarrass them; for it is almost an unpardonable offence to teach slaves to read in this Christian country. It is enough to say of the dear little fellows, that they lived on Philpot Street, very near Durgin and Bailey's ship-yard. I used to talk this matter of slavery over with them. I would sometimes say to them, I wished I could be as free as they would be when they got to be men. "You will be free as soon as you are twenty-one, *but I am a slave for life!* Have not I as good a right to be free as you have?" These words used to trouble them; they would express for me the liveliest sympathy, and console me with the hope that something would occur by which I might be free.

I was now about twelve years old, and the thought of being *a slave for life* began to bear heavily upon my heart. Just about this time, I got hold of a book entitled "The Columbian Orator." Every opportunity I got, I used to read this book. Among much of other interesting matter, I found in it a dialogue between a master and his slave. The slave was represented as having run away from his master three times. The dialogue represented the conversation which took place between them, when the slave was retaken the third time. In this dialogue, the whole argument in behalf of slavery was brought forward by the master, all of which was disposed of by the slave. The slave was made to say some very smart as well as impressive things in reply to his master — things which had the desired though unexpected effect; for the conversation resulted in the voluntary emancipation of the slave on the part of the master.

In the same book, I met with one of Sheridan's mighty speeches on and in behalf of Catholic emancipation. These were choice documents to me. I read them over and over again with unabated interest. They gave tongue to interesting thoughts of my own soul, which had frequently flashed through my mind, and died away for want of utterance. The moral which I gained from the dialogue was the power of truth over the conscience of even a slaveholder. What I got from Sheridan was a bold denunciation of slavery, and a powerful vindication of human rights. The reading of these documents enabled me to utter my thoughts, and to meet the arguments

5

brought forward to sustain slavery; but while they relieved me of one difficulty, they brought on another even more painful than the one of which I was relieved. The more I read, the more I was led to abhor and detest my enslavers. I could regard them in no other light than a band of successful robbers, who had left their homes, and gone to Africa, and stolen us from our homes, and in a strange land reduced us to slavery. I loathed them as being the meanest as well as the most wicked of men. As I read and contemplated the subject, behold! that very discontentment which Master Hugh had predicted would follow my learning to read had already come, to torment and sting my soul to unutterable anguish. As I writhed under it, I would at times feel that learning to read had been a curse rather than a blessing. It had given me a view of my wretched condition, without the remedy. It opened my eyes to the horrible pit, but to no ladder upon which to get out. In moments of agony, I envied my fellow-slaves for their stupidity. I have often wished myself a beast. I preferred the condition of the meanest reptile to my own. Any thing, no matter what, to get rid of thinking! It was this everlasting thinking of my condition that tormented me. There was no getting rid of it. It was pressed upon me by every object within sight or hearing, animate or inanimate. The silver trump of freedom had roused my soul to eternal wakefulness. Freedom now appeared, to disappear no more forever. It was heard in every sound, and seen in every thing. It was ever present to torment me with a sense of my wretched condition. I saw nothing without seeing it, I heard nothing without hearing it, and felt nothing without feeling it. It looked from every star, it smiled in every calm, breathed in every wind, and moved in every storm.

I often found myself regretting my own existence, and wishing myself dead; and but for the hope of being free, I have no doubt but that I should have killed myself, or done something for which I should have been killed. While in this state of mind, I was eager to hear any one speak of slavery. I was a ready listener. Every little while, I could hear something about the abolitionists. It was some time before I found what the word meant. It was always used in such connections as to make it an interesting word to me. If a slave ran away and succeeded in getting clear, or if a slave killed his master, set fire to a barn, or did any thing very wrong in the mind of a slaveholder, it was spoken of as the fruit of *abolition*. Hearing the word in this connection very often, I set about learning what it meant. The dictionary afforded me little or no help. I found it was "the act of abolishing"; but then I did not know what was to be abolished. Here I was perplexed. I did not dare to ask any one about its meaning, for I was satisfied that it was something they wanted me to know very little about. After a patient waiting, I got one of our city papers, containing an account of the number of petitions from the north, praying for the abolition of slavery in the District of Columbia, and of the slave trade between the States. From this time I understood the words *abolition* and *abolitionist,* and always drew near when that word was spoken, expecting to hear something of importance to myself and fellow-slaves. The light broke in upon me by degrees. I went one day down on the wharf of Mr. Waters; and seeing two Irishmen unloading a scow of stone, I went, unasked, and helped them. When we had finished, one of them came to me and asked me if I were a slave. I told him I was. He asked, "Are ye a slave for life?" I told him that I was. The good Irishman seemed to be deeply affected by the statement. He said to the other that it was a pity so fine a little fellow as myself should be a slave for life. He said it was a shame to hold me. They both advised me to run away to the north; that I should find friends there, and that I should be free. I pretended not to be interested in what they said, and treated them as if I did not understand them; for I feared they might be treacherous. White men have been known to encourage slaves to escape, and then, to get the reward, catch them and return them to their masters. I was afraid that these seemingly good men might use me so; but I nevertheless remembered their advice, and from that time I resolved to run away. I looked forward to a time at which it would be safe for me to escape. I was too young to think of doing so immediately; besides, I wished to learn how to write, as I might have occasion to write my own pass. I consoled myself with the hope that I should one day find a good chance. Meanwhile, I would learn to write.

The idea as to how I might learn to write was suggested to me by being in Durgin and Bailey's ship-yard, and frequently seeing the ship carpenters, after hewing, and getting a piece of timber ready to use, write on the timber the name of that part of the ship for which it was intended. When a piece of timber was intended for the larboard side, it would be marked thus — "L." When a piece was for the starboard side, it would be marked thus — "S." A piece for the larboard side forward, would be marked thus — "L. F." When a piece was for starboard side forward, it would be marked thus — "S. F." For larboard aft, it would be marked thus — "L. A." For starboard aft, it would be marked thus — "S. A." I soon learned the names of these letters, and for what they were intended when placed upon a piece of timber in the ship-yard. I immediately commenced copying them, and in a short time was able to make the four letters named. After that, when I met with any boy who I knew could write, I would tell him I could write as well as he. The next word would be, "I don't believe you. Let me see you try it." I would then make the letters which I had been so fortunate as to learn, and ask him to beat that. In this way I got a good many lessons in writing, which it is quite possible I should never have gotten in any other way. During this time, my copy-book was the board fence, brick wall, and pavement; my pen and ink was a lump of chalk. With these, I learned mainly how to write. I then commenced and continued copying the Italics in Webster's Spelling Book, until I could make them all without looking on the book. By this time, my little Master Thomas had gone to school, and learned how to write, and had written over a number of copy-books. These had been brought home, and shown to some of our near neighbors, and then laid aside. My mistress used to go to class meeting at the Wilk Street meetinghouse every Monday afternoon, and leave me to take care of the house. When left thus, I used to spend the time in writing in the spaces left in Master Thomas's copy-book, copying what he had written. I continued to do this until I could write a hand very similar to that of Master Thomas. Thus, after a long, tedious effort for years, I finally succeeded in learning how to write.

Considerations

1. Douglass chooses to report certain incidents in his process of learning to read and write and to show other incidents by dramatizing them. Summarize one of these dramatized incidents and discuss why you think this episode might have been particularly significant to Douglass.

2. Although this selection, a chapter from Douglass's book, *The Narrative of the Life of Frederick Douglass: An American Slave* (1841), is primarily told in story form, it also makes a profound argument against slavery. Explain how Douglass develops this argument and evaluate the evidence he uses to support his contentions.

3. Douglass compares the circumstances of slaves to the circumstances of Irish Catholics. Locate and list every mention of the Irish or of Catholicism in this selection and explain how Douglass uses this comparison to argue his case persuasively.

4. Discuss the role of Master Hugh's wife. What might her motives have been as she first sets out to educate Douglass and then becomes almost fanatic in her attempts to keep him away from books?

5. Put yourself in the place of one of the people who chooses to help Douglass. Describe the circumstances of your decision from that person's point of view. Keep in mind that it was against the law to educate slaves.

CONNECTIONS: LEARNING AND TEACHING

1. Compare and contrast the problems, hopes, and possibilities faced by minority children as they become educated, both now and in the past. Consider the following works: "The Lesson," "The Loudest Voice," "Battle Royale," and "Learning to Read and Write."

2. Consider the role teachers play in our lives. Use examples from any or all of the following works: "Why I Love Country Music," "The Lesson," "Sister Imelda," "Naming of Parts," "The Hidden Teacher."

3. Discuss how we can learn — and the importance of what we learn — outside of school. Consider any of the following works: "The Lesson," "Battle Royal," "There Was a Child Went Forth," "The Hidden Teacher," "Learning to Read and Write."

4. Define "education." Refer to any of the works in this section as you develop and explain your definition.

5. Mark Twain once said, "Never let school get in the way of your education." Respond to this quotation, referring to any of the following works: "The Loudest Voice," "Sister Imelda," "The Scholars," "The School Children," "The Hidden Teacher," "Learning to Read and Write."

Death

KATHERINE ANNE PORTER (1890–1980)

The Jilting of Granny Weatherall

She flicked her wrist neatly out of Doctor Harry's pudgy careful fingers and pulled the sheet up to her chin. The brat ought to be in knee breeches. Doctoring around the country with spectacles on his nose! "Get along now, take your schoolbooks and go. There's nothing wrong with me."

Doctor Harry spread a warm paw like a cushion on her forehead where the forked green vein danced and made her eyelids twitch. "Now, now, be a good girl, and we'll have you up in no time."

"That's no way to speak to a woman nearly eighty years old just because she's down. I'd have you respect your elders, young man."

"Well, Missy, excuse me." Doctor Harry patted her cheek. "But I've got to warn you, haven't I? You're a marvel, but you must be careful or you're going to be good and sorry."

"Don't tell me what I'm going to be. I'm on my feet now, morally   5
speaking. It's Cornelia. I had to go to bed to get rid of her."

Her bones felt loose, and floated around in her skin, and Doctor Harry floated like a balloon around the foot of the bed. He floated and pulled down his waistcoat and swung his glasses on a cord. "Well, stay where you are, it certainly can't hurt you."

"Get along and doctor your sick," said Granny Weatherall. "Leave a well woman alone. I'll call for you when I want you. . . . Where were you forty years ago when I pulled through milk-leg and double pneumonia? You weren't even born. Don't let Cornelia lead you on," she shouted, because Doctor Harry appeared to float up to the ceiling and out. "I pay my own bills, and I don't throw my money away on nonsense!"

She meant to wave good-by, but it was too much trouble. Her eyes closed of themselves, it was like a dark curtain drawn around the bed. The pillow rose and floated under her, pleasant as a hammock in a light wind. She listened to the leaves rustling outside the window. No, somebody was swishing newspapers: no, Cornelia and Doctor Harry were whispering together. She leaped broad awake, thinking they whispered in her ear.

"She was never like this, *never* like this!" "Well, what can we expect?" "Yes, eighty years old. . . ."

Well, and what if she was? She still had ears. It was like Cornelia to   10
whisper around doors. She always kept things secret in such a public way. She was always being tactful and kind. Cornelia was dutiful; that was the trouble with her. Dutiful and good: "So good and dutiful," said Granny, "that I'd like to spank her." She saw herself spanking Cornelia and making a fine job of it.

"What'd you say, Mother?"

Granny felt her face tying up in hard knots.

"Can't a body think, I'd like to know?"

"I thought you might want something."

"I do. I want a lot of things. First off, go away and don't whisper."   15

She lay and drowsed, hoping in her sleep that the children would keep out and let her rest a minute. It had been a long day. Not that she was tired. It was always pleasant to snatch a minute now and then. There was always so much to be done, let me see: tomorrow.

Tomorrow was far away and there was nothing to trouble about. Things were finished somehow when the time came; thank God there was always a little margin over for peace: then a person could spread out the plan of life and tuck in the edges orderly. It was good to have everything clean and folded away, with the hair brushes and tonic bottles sitting straight on the white embroidered linen: the day started without fuss and the pantry shelves laid out with rows of jelly glasses and brown jugs and white stone-china jars with blue whirligigs and words painted on them: coffee, tea, sugar, ginger, cinnamon, allspice: and the bronze clock with the lion on top nicely dusted off. The dust that lion could collect in twenty-four hours! The box in the attic with all those letters tied up, well she'd have to go through that tomorrow. All those letters—George's letters and John's letters and her letters to them both—lying around for the children to find afterwards made her uneasy. Yes, that would be tomorrow's business. No use to let them know how silly she had been once.

While she was rummaging around she found death in her mind and it felt clammy and unfamiliar. She had spent so much time preparing for death there was no need for bringing it up again. Let it care of itself now. When she was sixty she had felt very old, finished, and went around making farewell trips to see her children and grandchildren, with a secret in her mind: This is the very last of your mother, children! Then she made her will and came down with a long fever. That was all just a notion like a lot of other things, but it was lucky too, for she had once for all got over the idea of dying for a long time. Now she couldn't be worried. She hoped she had better sense now. Her father had lived to be one hundred and two years old and had drunk a noggin of strong hot toddy on his last birthday. He told the reporters it was his daily habit, and he owed his long life to that. He had made quite a scandal and was very pleased about it. She believed she'd just plague Cornelia a little.

"Cornelia! Cornelia!" No footsteps, but a sudden hand on her cheek. "Bless you, where have you been?"

"Here, mother."   20

"Well, Cornelia, I want a noggin of hot toddy."

"Are you cold, darling?"

"I'm chilly, Cornelia. Lying in bed stops the circulation. I must have told you that a thousand times."

Well, she could just hear Cornelia telling her husband that Mother was getting childish and they'd have to humor her. The thing that most annoyed her was that Cornelia thought she was deaf, dumb, and blind. Little hasty glances and tiny gestures tossed around her and over her head saying, "Don't cross her, let her have her way, she's eighty years old," and she sitting there as if she lived in a thin glass cage. Sometimes Granny almost made up her mind to pack up and move back to her own house where nobody could remind her every minute that she was old. Wait, wait, Cornelia, till your own children whisper behind your back!

In her day she had kept a better house and had got more work done. She wasn't too old yet for Lydia to be driving eighty miles for advice when one of the children jumped the track, and Jimmy still dropped in and talked things over: "Now, Mammy, you've a good business head, I want to know what you think of this? . . ." Old Cornelia couldn't change the furniture around without asking. Little things, little things! They had been so sweet when they were little. Granny wished the old days were back again with the children young and everything to be done over. It had been a hard pull, but not too much for her. When she thought of all the food she had cooked, and all the clothes she had cut and sewed, and all the gardens she had made — well, the children showed it. There they were, made out of her, and they couldn't get away from that. Sometimes she wanted to see John again and point to them and say, Well, I didn't do so badly, did I? But that would have to wait. That was for tomorrow. She used to think of him as a man, but now all the children were older than their father, and he would be a child beside her if she saw him now. It seemed strange and there was something wrong in the idea. Why, he couldn't possibly recognize her. She had fenced in a hundred acres once, digging the post holes herself and clamping the wires with just a negro boy to help. That changed a woman. John would be looking for a young woman with the peaked Spanish comb in her hair and the painted fan. Digging post holes changed a woman. Riding country roads in the winter when women had their babies was another thing: sitting up nights with sick horses and sick negroes and sick children and hardly ever losing one. John, I hardly ever lost one of them! John would see that in a minute, that would be something he could understand, she wouldn't have to explain anything!

It made her feel like rolling up her sleeves and putting the whole place to rights again. No matter if Cornelia was determined to be everywhere at once, there were a great many things left undone on this place. She would start tomorrow and do them. It was good to be strong enough for everything, even if all you made melted and changed and slipped under your hands, so that by the time you finished you almost forgot what you were working for. What was it I set out to do? she asked herself intently, but she could not remember. A fog rose over the valley, she saw it marching across the creek swallowing the trees and moving up the hill like an army of ghosts. Soon it would be at the near edge of the orchard, and then it was time to go in and light the lamps. Come in, children, don't stay out in the night air.

Lighting the lamps had been beautiful. The children huddled up to her and breathed like little calves waiting at the bars in the twilight. Their eyes followed the match and watched the flame rise and settle in a blue curve,

25

then they moved away from her. The lamp was lit, they didn't have to be scared and hang on to mother any more. Never, never, never more. God, for all my life I thank Thee. Without Thee, my God, I could never have done it. Hail, Mary, full of grace.

I want you to pick all the fruit this year and see that nothing is wasted. There's always someone who can use it. Don't let good things rot for want of using. You waste life when you waste good food. Don't let things get lost. It's bitter to lose things. Now, don't let me get to thinking, not when I am tired and taking a little nap before supper. . . .

The pillow rose about her shoulders and pressed against her heart and the memory was being squeezed out of it: oh, push down the pillow, somebody: it would smother her if she tried to hold it. Such a fresh breeze blowing and such a green day with no threats in it. But he had not come, just the same. What does a woman do when she has put on the white veil and set out the white cake for a man and he doesn't come? She tried to remember. No, I swear he never harmed me but in that. He never harmed me but in that . . . and what if he did? There was the day, the day, but a whirl of dark smoke rose and covered it, crept up and over into the bright field where everything was planted so carefully in orderly rows. That was hell, she knew hell when she saw it. For sixty years she had prayed against remembering him and against losing her soul in the deep pit of hell, and now the two things were mingled in one and the thought of him was a smoky cloud from hell that moved and crept in her head when she had just got rid of Doctor Harry and was trying to rest a minute. Wounded vanity, Ellen, said a sharp voice in the top of her mind. Don't let your wounded vanity get the upper hand of you. Plenty of girls get jilted. You were jilted, weren't you? Then stand up to it. Her eyelids wavered and let in streamers of blue-gray light like tissue paper over her eyes. She must get up and pull the shades down or she'd never sleep. She was in bed again and the shades were not down. How could that happen? Better turn over, hide from the light, sleeping in the light gave you nightmares. "Mother, how do you feel now?" and a stinging wetness on her forehead. But I don't like having my face washed in cold water!

Hapsy? George? Lydia? Jimmy? No, Cornelia, and her features were swollen and full of little puddles. "They're coming, darling, they'll all be here soon." Go wash your face, child, you look funny.

Instead of obeying, Cornelia knelt down and put her head on the pillow. She seemed to be talking but there was no sound. "Well, are you tongue-tied? Whose birthday is it? Are you going to give a party?"

Cornelia's mouth moved urgently in strange shapes. "Don't do that, you bother me, daughter."

"Oh, no, Mother, Oh, no. . . ."

Nonsense. It was strange about children. They disputed your every word. "No what, Cornelia?"

"Here's Doctor Harry."

"I won't see that boy again. He just left five minutes ago."

"That was this morning, Mother. It's night now. Here's the nurse."

"This is Doctor Harry, Mrs. Weatherall. I never saw you look so young and happy!"

"Ah, I'll never be young again—but I'd be happy if they'd let me lie in peace and get rested."

She thought she spoke up loudly, but no one answered. A warm weight on her forehead, a warm bracelet on her wrist, and a breeze went on whispering, trying to tell her something. A shuffle of leaves in the everlasting hand of God. He blew on them and they danced and rattled. "Mother, don't mind, we're going to give you a little hypodermic." "Look here, daughter, how do ants get in this bed? I saw sugar ants yesterday." Did you send for Hapsy too?

It was Hapsy she really wanted. She had to go a long way back through a great many rooms to find Hapsy standing with a baby on her arm. She seemed to herself to be Hapsy also, and the baby on Hapsy's arm was Hapsy and himself and herself, all at once, and there was no surprise in the meeting. Then Hapsy melted from within and turned flimsy as gray gauze and the baby was a gauzy shadow, and Hapsy came up close and said, "I thought you'd never come," and looked at her very searchingly and said, "You haven't changed a bit!" They leaned forward to kiss, when Cornelia began whispering from a long way off, "Oh, is there anything you want to tell me? Is there anything I can do for you?"

Yes, she had changed her mind after sixty years and she would like to see George. I want you to find George. Find him and be sure to tell him I forgot him. I want him to know I had my husband just the same and my children and my house like any other woman. A good house too and a good husband that I loved and fine children out of him. Better than I hoped for even. Tell him I was given back everything he took away and more. Oh, no, oh, God, no, there was something else besides the house and the man and the children. Oh, surely they were not all? What was it? Something not given back. . . . Her breath crowded down under her ribs and grew into a monstrous frightening shape with cutting edges; it bored up into her head, and the agony was unbelievable: Yes, John, get the doctor now, no more talk, my time has come.

When this one was born it should be the last. The last. It should have been born first, for it was the one she had truly wanted. Everthing came in good time. Nothing left out, left over. She was strong, in three days she would be as well as ever. Better. A woman needed milk in her to have her full health.

"Mother, do you hear me?"

"I've been telling you—"

"Mother, Father Connolly's here."

"I went to Holy Communion only last week. Tell him I'm not so sinful as all that."

"Father just wants to speak to you."

He could speak as much as he pleased. It was like him to drop in and inquire about her soul as if it were a teething baby, and then stay on for a cup of tea and a round of cards and gossip. He always had a funny story of some sort, usually about an Irishman who made his little mistakes and confessed them, and the point lay in some absurd thing he would blurt out in the confessional showing his struggles between native piety and original sin. Granny felt easy about her soul. Cornelia, where are your manners? Give Father Connolly a chair. She had her secret comfortable understanding with a few favorite saints who cleared a straight road to God for her. All as surely signed and sealed as the papers for the new Forty Acres. Forever . . . heirs and assigns forever. Since the day the wedding cake was not cut, but thrown out and wasted. The whole bottom dropped out of the world, and there she was blind and sweating with nothing under her feet and the walls falling away. His hand had caught her under the breast, she had not fallen, there was the freshly polished floor with the green rug on it, just as before. He had cursed like a sailor's parrot and said, "I'll kill him for you." Don't lay a hand on him, for my sake leave something to God. "Now, Ellen, you must believe what I tell you. . . ."

So there was nothing, nothing to worry about any more, except some-   50
times in the night one of the children screamed in a nightmare, and they both hustled out shaking and hunting for the matches and calling, "There, wait a minute, here we are!" John, get the doctor now, Hapsy's time has come. But there was Hapsy standing by the bed in a white cap. "Cornelia, tell Hapsy to take off her cap. I can't see her plain."

Her eyes opened very wide and the room stood out like a picture she had seen somewhere. Dark colors with the shadows rising towards the ceiling in long angles. The tall black dresser gleamed with nothing on it but John's picture, enlarged from a little one, with John's eyes very black when they should have been blue. You never saw him, so how do you know how he looked? But the man insisted the copy was perfect, it was very rich and handsome. For a picture, yes, but it's not my husband. The table by the bed had a linen cover and a candle and a crucifix. The light was blue from Cornelia's silk lampshades. No sort of light at all, just frippery. You had to live forty years with kerosene lamps to appreciate honest electricity. She felt very strong and she saw Doctor Harry with a rosy nimbus around him.

"You look like a saint, Doctor Harry, and I vow that's as near as you'll ever come to it."

"She's saying something."

"I heard you, Cornelia. What's all this carrying-on?"

"Father Connolly's saying —"   55

Cornelia's voice staggered and bumped like a cart in a bad road. It rounded corners and turned back again and arrived nowhere. Granny stepped up in the cart very lightly and reached for the reins, but a man sat beside her and she knew him by his hands, driving the cart. She did not look in his face, for she knew without seeing, but looked instead down the road where the trees leaned over and bowed to each other and a thousand birds were singing a Mass. She felt like singing too, but she put her hand in the bosom of her dress and pulled out a rosary, and Father Connolly murmured Latin in a very solemn voice and tickled her feet. My God, will you stop that nonsense? I'm a married woman. What if he did run away and leave me to face the priest by myself? I found another a whole world better. I wouldn't have exchanged my husband for anybody except St. Michael himself, and you may tell him that for me with a thank you in the bargain.

Light flashed on her closed eyelids, and a deep roaring shook her. Cornelia, is that lightning? I hear thunder. There's going to be a storm. Close all the windows. Call the children in. . . . "Mother, here we are, all of us." "Is that you, Hapsy?" "Oh, no, I'm Lydia. We drove as fast as we could." Their faces drifted above her, drifted away. The rosary fell out of her hands and Lydia put it back. Jimmy tried to help, their hands fumbled together, and Granny closed two fingers around Jimmy's thumb. Beads wouldn't do, it must be something alive. She was so amazed her thoughts ran round and round. So, my dear Lord, this is my death and I wasn't even thinking about it. My children have come to see me die. But I can't, it's not time. Oh, I always hated surprises. I wanted to give Cornelia the amethyst set — Cornelia, you're to have the amethyst set, but Hapsy's to wear it when she wants, and, Doctor Harry, do shut up. Nobody sent for you. Oh, my dear Lord, do wait a minute. I meant to do something about the Forty Acres, Jimmy doesn't need it and Lydia will later on, with that worthless husband of hers. I meant to finish the altar cloth and send six bottles of wine to Sister Borgia for her dyspepsia. I want to send six bottles of wine to Sister Borgia, Father Connolly, now don't let me forget.

Cornelia's voice made short turns and tilted over and crashed. "Oh, Mother, oh, Mother, oh, Mother. . . ."

"I'm not going, Cornelia. I'm taken by surprise. I can't go."

You'll see Hapsy again. What about her? "I thought you'd never come." Granny made a long journey outward, looking for Hapsy. What if I don't find her? What then? Her heart sank down and down, there was no bottom to death, she couldn't come to the end of it. The blue light from Cornelia's lampshade drew into a tiny point in the center of her brain, it flickered and winked like an eye, quietly it fluttered and dwindled. Granny lay curled down within herself, amazed and watchful, staring at the point of light that was herself; her body was now only a deeper mass of shadow in an endless darkness and this darkness would curl around the light and swallow it up. God, give a sign!

For the second time there was no sign. Again no bridegroom and the priest in the house. She could not remember any other sorrow because this grief wiped them all away. Oh, no, there's nothing more cruel than this — I'll never forgive it. She stretched herself with a deep breath and blew out the light.

Considerations

1. How appropriate is the title? Would you argue that it is more appropriate than, say, "The Death of Granny Weatherall"? Explain.
2. Compare the words Granny uses to describe her state of health to Doctor Harry with the words the author/narrator uses to describe Granny's physical and emotional feelings. Discuss the tone established by the contrast between the two descriptions. What does the discrepancy suggest about Granny's character?
3. Describe Granny's attitude toward death. In what ways does this attitude parallel (or contrast to) her approach to life?
4. Describe the relationships between Granny and her children. What significance do you see in the ways the children respond to their mother's old age and dying?
5. Describe Granny's response to the priest, then consider that response in relation to the final paragraph of the story.

LEO TOLSTOY (1828–1910)

The Death of Iván Ilých

Chapter 1

During an interval in the Melvínski trial in the large building of the Law Courts the members and the public prosecutor met in Iván Egorovich Shébek's private room, where the conversation turned on the celebrated Krasóvski case. Fëdor Vasílievich warmly maintained that it was not subject to their jurisdiction, Iván Egórovich maintained the contrary, while Peter Ivánovich, not having entered into the discussion at the start, took no part in it but looked through the *Gazette* which had just been handed in.

"Gentlemen," he said, "Iván Ilých has died!"

"You don't say so!"

"Here, read it yourself," replied Peter Ivánovich, handing Fëdor Vasílievich the paper still damp from the press. Surrounded by a black border were the words: "Praskóvya Fëdorovna Goloviná, with profound sorrow, informs relatives and friends of the demise of her beloved husband Iván Ilých Golovín, Member of the Court of Justice, which occurred on February the 4th of this year 1882. The funeral will take place on Friday at one o'clock in the afternoon."

Iván Ilých had been a colleague of the gentlemen present and was liked by them all. He had been ill for some weeks with an illness said to be incurable. His post had been kept open for him, but there had been conjectures that in case of his death Alexéev might receive his appointment, and that either Vínnikov or Shtábel would succeed Alexéev. So on receiving the news of Iván Ilých's death the first thought of each of the gentlemen in that private room was of the changes and promotions it might occasion among themselves or their acquaintances.

"I shall be sure to get Shtábel's place or Vínnikov's," thought Fëdor Vasílievich. "I was promised that long ago, and the promotion means an extra eight hundred rubles a year for me besides the allowance."

"Now I must apply for my brother-in-law's transfer from Kalúga," thought Peter Ivánovich. "My wife will be very glad, and then she won't be able to say that I never do anything for her relations."

"I thought he would never leave his bed again," said Peter Ivánovich aloud. "It's very sad."

"But what really was the matter with him?"

"The doctors couldn't say—at least they could, but each of them said something different. When last I saw him I thought he was getting better."

"And I haven't been to see him since the holidays. I always meant to go."

"Had he any property?"

"I think his wife had a little — but something quite trifling."

"We shall have to go to see her, but they live so terribly far away."

"Far away from you, you mean. Everything's far away from your place."   15

"You see, he never can forgive my living on the other side of the river," said Peter Ivánovich, smiling at Shébek. Then, still talking of the distances between different parts of the city, they returned to the Court.

Besides considerations as to the possible transfers and promotions likely to result from Iván Ilých's death, the mere fact of the death of a near acquaintance aroused, as usual, in all who heard of it the complacent feeling that "it is he who is dead and not I."

Each one thought or felt, "Well, he's dead but I'm alive!" But the more intimate of Iván Ilých's acquaintances, his so-called friends, could not help thinking also that they would now have to fulfill the very tiresome demands of propriety by attending the funeral service and paying a visit of condolence to the widow.

Fëdor Vasílievich and Peter Ivánovich had been his nearest acquaintances. Peter Ivánovich had studied law with Iván Ilých and had considered himself to be under obligations to him.

Having told his wife at dinner-time of Iván Ilých's death, and of his   20 conjecture that it might be possible to get her brother transferred to their circuit, Peter Ivánovich sacrificed his usual nap, put on his evening clothes, and drove to Iván Ilých's house.

At the entrance stood a carriage and two cabs. Leaning against the wall in the hall downstairs near the cloak-stand was a coffin-lid covered with cloth of gold, ornamented with gold cord and tassles, that had been polished up with metal powder. Two ladies in black were taking off their fur cloaks. Peter Ivánovich recognized one of them as Iván Ilých's sister, but the other was a stranger to him. His colleague Schwartz was just coming downstairs, but on seeing Peter Ivánovich enter he stopped and winked at him, as if to say: "Iván Ilých has made a mess of things — not like you and me."

Schwartz's face with his Piccadilly whiskers, and his slim figure in evening dress, had as usual an air of elegant solemnity which contrasted with the playfulness of his character and had a special piquancy here, or so it seemed to Peter Ivánovich.

Peter Ivánovich allowed the ladies to precede him and slowly followed them upstairs. Schwartz did not come down but remained where he was, and Peter Ivánovich understood that he wanted to arrange where they should play bridge that evening. The ladies went upstairs to the widow's room, and Schwartz with seriously compressed lips but a playful look in his eyes, indicated by a twist of his eye-brows the room to the right where the body lay.

Peter Ivánovich, like everyone else on such occasions, entered feeling uncertain what he would have to do. All he knew was that at such times it is always safe to cross oneself. But he was not quite sure whether one should make obeisances while doing so. He therefore adopted a middle course. On entering the room he began crossing himself and made a slight movement resembling a bow. At the same time, as far as the motion of his head and arm allowed, he surveyed the room. Two young men — apparently nephews, one of whom was a high school pupil — were leaving the room, crossing themselves as they did so. An old woman was standing motionless, and a lady with strangely arched eyebrows was saying something to her in a whisper. A vigorous, resolute Church Reader, in a frock-coat, was reading something in a loud voice with an expression that precluded any contradiction. The butler's assistant, Gerásim, stepping lightly in front of Peter Ivánovich, was strewing something on the floor. Noticing this, Peter Ivánovich was immediately aware of a faint odour of a decomposing body.

The last time he had called on Iván Ilých, Peter Ivánovich had seen   25
Gerásim in the study. Iván Ilých had been particularly fond of him and he was performing the duty of a sick nurse.

Peter Ivánovich continued to make the sign of the cross slightly inclining his head in an intermediate direction between the coffin, the Reader, and the icons on the table in a corner of the room. Afterwards, when it seemed to him that this movement of his arm in crossing himself had gone on too long, he stopped and began to look at the corpse.

The dead man lay, as dead men always lie, in a specially heavy way, his rigid limbs sunk in the soft cushions of the coffin, with the head forever bowed on the pillow. His yellow waxen brow with bald patches over his sunken temples was thrust up in the way peculiar to the dead, the protruding ·
nose seeming to press on the upper lip. He was much changed and had grown even thinner since Peter Ivánovich had last seen him, but, as is always the case with the dead, his face was handsomer and above all more dignified than when he was alive. The expression on the face said that what was necessary had been accomplished, and accomplished rightly. Besides this there was in that expression a reproach and a warning to the living. This warning seemed to Peter Ivánovich out of place, or at least not applicable to him. He felt a certain discomfort and so he hurriedly crossed himself once more and turned and went out of the door — too hurriedly and too regardless of propriety, as he himself was aware.

Schwartz was waiting for him in the adjoining room with legs spread wide apart and both hands toying with his top-hat behind his back. The mere sight of that playful, well-groomed, and elegant figure refreshed Peter Ivánovich. He felt that Schwartz was above all these happenings and would not surrender to any depressing influences. His very look said that this incident of a church service for Iván Ilých could not be a sufficient reason for infringing the order of the session — in other words, that it would certainly not prevent his unwrapping a new pack of cards and shuffling them that evening while a footman placed four fresh candles on the table: in fact, there was no reason for supposing that this incident would hinder their spending the evening agreeably. Indeed he said this in a whisper as Peter Ivánovich passed him, proposing that they should meet for a game at Fëdor Vasílievich's. But apparently Peter Ivánovich was not destined to play bridge that evening. Praskóvya Fëdorovna (a short, fat woman who despite all efforts to the contrary had continued to broaden steadily from her shoulders downwards and who had the same extraordinarily arched eyebrows as the lady who had been standing by the coffin), dressed all in black, her head covered with lace, came out of her own room with some other ladies, conducted them to the room where the dead body lay, and said: "The service will begin immediately. Please go in."

Schwartz, making an indefinite bow, stood still, evidently neither accepting nor declining this invitation. Praskóvya Fëdorovna recognizing Peter Ivánovich, sighed, went close up to him, took his hand, and said: "I know you were a true friend to Iván Ilých . . ." and looked at him awaiting some suitable response. And Peter Ivánovich knew that, just as it had been the right thing to cross himself in that room, so what he had to do here was to press her hand, sigh, and say, "Believe me . . ." So he did all this and as he did it felt that the desired result had been achieved; that both he and she were touched.

"Come with me. I want to speak to you before it begins," said the widow. "Give me your arm."

30

Peter Ivánovich gave her his arm and they went to the inner rooms, passing Schwartz who winked at Peter Ivánovich compassionately.

"That does for our bridge! Don't object if we find another player. Perhaps you can cut in when you do escape," said his playful look.

Peter Ivánovich sighed still more deeply and despondently, and Praskóvya Fëdorovna pressed his arm gratefully. When they reached the drawing-room, upholstered in pink cretonne and lighted by a dim lamp, they sat down at the table — she on a sofa and Peter Ivánovich on a low pouffe, the springs of which yielded spasmodically under his weight. Praskóvya Fëdorovna had been on the point of warning him to take another seat, but felt that such a warning was out of keeping with her present condition and so changed her mind. As he sat down on the pouffe Peter Ivánovich recalled how Iván Ilých had arranged this room and had consulted him regarding this pink cretonne with green leaves. The whole room was full of furniture and knick-knacks, and on her way to the sofa the lace of the widow's black shawl caught on the carved edge of the table. Peter Ivánovich rose to detach it, and the springs of the pouffe, relieved of his weight, rose also and gave him a push. The widow began detaching her shawl herself, and Peter Ivánovich again sat down, suppressing the rebellious springs of the pouffe under him. But the widow had not quite freed herself and Peter Ivánovich got up again, and again the pouffe rebelled and even creaked. When this was all over she took out a clean cambric handkerchief and began to weep. The

episode with the shawl and the struggle with the pouffe had cooled Peter
Ivánovich's emotions and he sat there with a sullen look on his face. This
awkward situation was interrupted by Sokolóv, Iván Ilých's butler, who
came to report that the plot in the cemetery that Praskóvya Fëdorovna had
chosen would cost two hundred rubles. She stopped weeping and, looking
at Peter Ivánovich with the air of a victim, remarked in French that it was
very hard for her. Peter Ivánovich made a silent gesture signifying his full
conviction that it must indeed be so.

"Please smoke," she said in a magnanimous yet crushed voice, and
turned to discuss with Sokolóv the price of the plot for the grave.

Peter Ivánovich while lighting his cigarette heard her inquiring very   35
circumstantially into the price of different plots in the cemetery and finally
decide which she would take. When that was done she gave instructions
about engaging the choir. Sokolóv then left the room.

"I look after everything myself," she told Peter Ivánovich, shifting the
albums that lay on the table; and noticing that the table was endangered by
his cigarette-ash, she immediately passed him an ashtray, saying as she did
so: "I consider it an affectation to say that my grief prevents my attending
to practical affairs. On the contrary, if anything can — I won't say console
me, but — distract me, it is seeing to everything concerning him." She again
took out her handkerchief as if preparing to cry, but suddenly, as if master-
ing her feeling, she shook herself and began to speak calmly. "But there is
something I want to talk to you about."

Peter Ivánovich bowed, keeping control of the springs of the pouffe,
which immediately began quivering under him.

"He suffered terribly the last few days."

"Did he?" said Peter Ivánovich.

"Oh, terribly! He screamed unceasingly, not for minutes but for hours.   40
For the last three days he screamed incessantly. It was unendurable. I cannot
understand how I bore it; you could hear him three rooms off. Oh, what I
have suffered!"

"Is it possible that he was conscious all that time?" asked Peter
Ivánovich.

"Yes," she whispered. "To the last moment. He took leave of us a
quarter of an hour before he died, and asked us to take Volódya away."

The thought of the sufferings of this man he had known so intimately,
first as a merry little boy, then as a school-mate, and later as a grown-up
colleague, suddenly struck Peter Ivánovich with horror, despite an unpleasant consciousness of his own and this woman's dissimulation. He again saw
that brow, and that nose pressing down on the lip, and felt afraid for himself.

"Three days of frightful suffering and then death! Why, that might
suddenly, at any time, happen to me," he thought, and for a moment felt
terrified. But — he did not himself know how — the customary reflection at
once occurred to him that this had happened to Iván Ilých and not to him,

and that it should not and could not happen to him, and that to think that it could would be yielding to depression which he ought not to do, as Schwartz's expression plainly showed. After which reflection Peter Ivánovich felt reassured, and began to ask with interest about the details of Iván Ilých's death, as though death was an accident natural to Iván Ilých but certainly not to himself.

After many details of the really dreadful physical sufferings Iván Ilých   45
had endured (which details he learnt only from the effect those sufferings had produced on Praskóvya Fëdorovna's nerves) the widow apparently found it necessary to get to business.

"Oh, Peter Ivánovich, how hard it is! How terribly, terribly hard!" and she again began to weep.

Peter Ivánovich sighed and waited for her to finish blowing her nose. When she had done so he said, "Believe me . . ." and she again began talking and brought out what was evidently her chief concern with him — namely, to question him as to how she could obtain a grant of money from the government on the occasion of her husband's death. She made it appear that she was asking Peter Ivánovich's advice about her pension, but he soon saw that she already knew about that to the minutest detail, more even than he did himself. She knew how much could be got out of the government in consequence of her husband's death, but wanted to find out whether she could not possibly extract something more. Peter Ivánovich tried to think of some means of doing so, but after reflecting for a while and, out of propriety, condemning the government for its niggardliness, he said he thought that nothing more could be got. Then she sighed and evidently began to devise means of getting rid of her visitor. Noticing this, he put out his cigarette, rose, pressed her hand, and went out into the anteroom.

In the dining-room where the clock stood that Iván Ilých had liked so much and had bought at an antique shop, Peter Ivánovich met a priest and a few acquaintances who had come to attend the service, and he recognized Iván Ilých's daughter, a handsome young woman. She was in black and her slim figure appeared slimmer than ever. She had a gloomy, determined, almost angry expression, and bowed to Peter Ivánovich as though he were in some way to blame. Behind her, with the same offended look, stood a wealthy young man, an examining magistrate, whom Peter Ivánovich also knew and who was her fiancé, as he had heard. He bowed mournfully to them and was about to pass into the death-chamber, when from under the stairs appeared the figure of Iván Ilých's schoolboy son, who was extremely like his father. He seemed a little Iván Ilých, such as Peter Ivánovich remembered when they studied law together. His tear-stained eyes had in them the look that is seen in the eyes of boys of thirteen or fourteen who are not pure-minded. When he saw Peter Ivánovich he scowled morosely and shame-facedly. Peter Ivánovich nodded to him and entered the death-chamber. The service began: candles, groans, incense, tears, and sobs. Peter Ivánovich stood looking gloomily down at his feet. He did not look once at the dead man, did not yield to any depressing influence, and was one of the first to leave the room. There was no one in the anteroom, but Gerásim darted out of the dead man's room, rummaged with his strong hands among the fur coats to find Peter Ivánovich's and helped him on with it.

"Well, friend Gerásim," said Peter Ivánovich, so as to say something. "It's a sad affair, isn't it?"

"It's God's will. We shall all come to it some day," said Gerásim,   50 displaying his teeth — the even, white teeth of a healthy peasant — and, like a man in the thick of urgent work, he briskly opened the front door, called the coachman, helped Peter Ivánovich into the sledge, and sprang back to the porch as if in readiness for what he had to do next.

Peter Ivánovich found the fresh air particularly pleasant after the smell of incense, the dead body, and carbolic acid.

"Where to, sir?" asked the coachman.

"It's not too late even now. . . . I'll call around on Fëdor Vasílievich."

He accordingly drove there and found them just finishing the first rubber, so that it was quite convenient for him to cut in.

Chapter II

Iván Ilých's life had been most simple and most ordinary and therefore most terrible.

He had been a member of the Court of Justice, and died at the age of forty-five. His father had been an official who after serving in various ministries and departments of Petersburg had made the sort of career which brings men to positions from which by reason of their long service they cannot be dismissed, though they are obviously unfit to hold any responsible position, and for whom therefore posts are specially created, which though fictitious carry salaries of from six to ten thousand rubles that are not fictitious, and in receipt of which they live on to a great age.

Such was the Privy Councillor and superfluous member of various superfluous institutions, Ilyá Epímovich Golovín.

He had three sons, of whom Iván Ilých was second. The eldest son was following in his father's footsteps only in another department, and was already approaching that stage in the service at which a similar sinecure would be reached. The third son was a failure. He had ruined his prospects in a number of positions and was now serving in the railway department. His father and brothers, and still more their wives, not merely disliked meeting him, but avoided remembering his existence unless compelled to do so. His sister had married Baron Greff, a Petersburg official of her father's type. Iván Ilých was *le phénix de la famille* as people said. He was neither as cold and formal as his elder brother nor as wild as the younger, but was a happy mean between them — an intelligent, polished, lively, and agreeable man. He had studied with his younger brother at the School of Law, but the latter had failed to complete the course and was expelled when he was in the fifth class. Iván Ilých finished the course well. Even when he was at the School of Law he was just what he remained for the rest of his life: a capable, cheerful, good-natured, and sociable man, though strict in the fulfilment of what he considered to be his duty: and he considered his duty to be what was so considered by those in authority. Neither as a boy nor as a man was he a toady, but from early youth was by nature attracted to people of high station as a fly is drawn to the light, assimilating their ways and views of life and establishing friendly relations with them. All the enthusiasms of childhood and youth passed without leaving much trace on him; he succumbed to sensuality, to vanity, and latterly among the highest classes to liberalism, but always within limits which his instinct unfailingly indicated to him as correct.

At school he had done things which had formerly seemed to him very   5
horrid and made him feel disgusted with himself when he did them; but when later on he saw that such actions were done by people of good position and that they did not regard them as wrong, he was able not exactly to regard them as right, but to forget about them entirely or not be at all troubled at remembering them.

Having graduated from the School of Law and qualified for the tenth rank of the civil service, and having received money from his father for his equipment, Iván Ilých ordered himself clothes at Scharmer's, the fashionable tailor, hung a medallion inscribed *respice finen* on his watch-chain, took leave of his professor and the prince who was patron of the school, had a farewell dinner with his comrades at Donon's first-class restaurant, and with his new and fashionable portmanteau, linen, clothes, shaving and other toilet appliances, and a travelling rug, all purchased at the best shops, he set off for one of the provinces where, through his father's influence, he had been attached to the Governor as an official for special service.

In the province Iván Ilých soon arranged as easy and agreeable a position for himself as he had had at the School of Law. He performed his official tasks, made his career, and at the same time amused himself pleasantly and decorously. Occasionally he paid official visits to country districts, where he behaved with dignity both to his superiors and inferiors, and performed the duties entrusted to him, which related chiefly to the sectarians, with an exactness and incorruptible honesty of which he could not but feel proud.

In official matters, despite his youth and taste for frivolous gaiety, he was exceedingly reserved, punctilious, and even severe; but in society he was often amusing and witty, and always good-natured, correct in his manner, and *bon enfant,* as the governor and his wife — with whom he was like one of the family — used to say of him.

In the provinces he had an affair with a lady who made advances to the elegant young lawyer, and there was also a milliner; and there were

carousals with aides-de-camp who visited the district, and after-supper visits to a certain outlying street of doubtful reputation; and there was too some
obsequiousness to his chief and even to his chief's wife, but all this was done
with such a tone of good breeding that no hard names could be applied to
it. It all came under the heading of the French saying: "Il faut que jeunesse
se passe." It was all done with clean hands, in clean linen, with French
phrases, and above all among people of the best society and consequently
with the approval of people of rank.

So Iván Ilých served for five years and then came a change in his   10
official life. The new and reformed judicial institutions were introduced, and
new men were needed. Iván Ilých became such a new man. He was offered
the post of Examining Magistrate, and he accepted it though the post was
in another province and obliged him to give up the connexions he had
formed and to make new ones. His friends met to give him a send-off; they
had a group-photograph taken and presented him with a silver cigarette-
case, and he set off to his new post.

As examining magistrate Iván Ilých was just as *comme il faut* and decorous a man, inspiring general respect and capable of separating his official
duties from his private life, as he had been when acting as an official on
special service. His duties now as examining magistrate were far more interesting and attractive than before. In his former position it had been pleasant
to wear an undress uniform made by Scharmer, and to pass through the
crowd of petitioners and officials who were timorously awaiting an audience
with the governor, and who envied him as with free and easy gait he went
straight into his chief's private room to have a cup of tea and a cigarette with
him. But not many people had then been directly dependent on him — only
police officials and the sectarians when he went on special missions — and he
liked to treat them politely, almost as comrades, as if he were letting them
feel that he who had the power to crush them was treating them in this
simple, friendly way. There were then but few such people. But now, as an
examining magistrate, Iván Ilých felt that everyone without exception, even
the most important and self-satisfied, was in his power, and that he need
only write a few words on a sheet of paper with a certain heading, and this
or that important, self-satisfied person would be brought before him in the
role of an accused person or a witness, and if he did not choose to allow him
to sit down, would have to stand before him and answer his questions. Iván
Ilých never abused his power; he tried on the contrary to soften its expression, but the consciousness of it and of the possibility of softening its effect,
supplied the chief interest and attraction of his office. In his work itself,
especially in his examinations, he very soon acquired a method of eliminat-
ing all considerations irrelevant to the legal aspect of the case, and reducing
even the most complicated case to a form in which it would be presented on
paper only in its externals, completely excluding his personal opinion of the
matter, while above all observing every prescribed formality. The work was

new and Iván Ilých was one of the first men to apply the new Code of 1864.

On taking up the post of examining magistrate in a new town, he made new acquaintances and connexions, placed himself on a new footing, and assumed a somewhat different tone. He took up an attitude of rather dignified aloofness towards the provincial authorities, but picked out the best circle of legal gentlemen and wealthy gentry living in the town and assumed a tone of slight dissatisfaction with the government, of moderate liberalism, and of enlightened citizenship. At the same time, without at all altering the elegance of his toilet, he ceased shaving his chin and allowed his beard to grow as it pleased.

Iván Ilých settled down very pleasantly in this new town. The society there, which inclined towards opposition to the Governor, was friendly, his salary was larger, and he began to play *vint,* which he found added not a little to the pleasure of life, for he had a capacity for cards, played good-humouredly, and calculated rapidly and astutely, so that he usually won.

After living there for two years he met his future wife, Praskóvya Fëdorovna Míkhel, who was the most attractive, clever, and brilliant girl of the set in which he moved, and among other amusements and relaxations from his labours as examining magistrate, Iván Ilých established light and playful relations with her.

While he had been an official on special service he had been accus- 15
tomed to dance, but now as an examining magistrate it was exceptional for him to do so. If he danced now, he did it as if to show that though he served under the reformed order of things, and had reached the fifth official rank, yet when it came to dancing he could do it better than most people. So at the end of an evening he sometimes danced with Praskóvya Fëdorovna, and it was chiefly during these dances that he captivated her. She fell in love with him. Iván Ilých had at first no definite intention of marrying, but when the girl fell in love with him he said to himself: "Really, why shouldn't I marry?"

Praskóvya Fëdorovna came of a good family, was not bad looking and had some little property. Iván Ilých might have aspired to a more brilliant match, but even this was good. He had his salary, and she, he hoped, would have an equal income. She was well connected, and was a sweet, pretty, and thoroughly correct young woman. To say that Iván Ilých married because he fell in love with Praskóvya Fëdorovna and found that she sympathized with his views of life would be as incorrect as to say that he married because his social circle approved of the match. He was swayed by both these considerations: the marriage gave him personal satisfaction, and at the same time it was considered the right thing by the most highly placed of his associates.

So Iván Ilých got married.

The preparations for marriage and the beginning of married life, with its conjugal caresses, the new furniture, new crockery, and new linen, were very pleasant until his wife became pregnant — so that Iván Ilých had begun to think that marriage would not impair the easy, agreeable, gay and always decorous character of his life, approved of by society and regarded by himself as natural, but would even improve it. But from the first months of his wife's pregnancy, something new, unpleasant, depressing, and unseemly, and from which there was no way of escape, unexpectedly showed itself.

His wife, without any reason — *de gaieté de coeur* as Iván Ilých expressed it to himself — began to disturb the pleasure and propriety of their life. She began to be jealous without any cause, expected him to devote his whole attention to her, found fault with everything, and made coarse and ill-mannered scenes.

At first Iván Ilých hoped to escape from the unpleasantness of this state of affairs by the same easy and decorous relation to life that had served him heretofore: he tried to ignore his wife's disagreeable moods, continued to live in his usual easy and pleasant way, invited friends to his house for a game of cards, and also tried going out to his club or spending his evenings with friends. But one day his wife began upbraiding him so vigorously, using such coarse words, and continued to abuse him every time he did not fulfil her demands, so resolutely and with such evident determination not to give way till he submitted — that is, till he stayed at home and was bored just as she was — that he became alarmed. He now realized that matrimony — at any rate with Praskóvya Fëdorovna — was not always conducive to the pleasures and amenities of life but on the contrary often infringed both comfort and propriety, and that he must therefore entrench himself against such infringement. And Iván Ilých began to seek for means of doing so. His official duties were the one thing that imposed upon Praskóvya Fëdorovna, and by means of his official work and the duties attached to it he began struggling with his wife to secure his own independence.

With the birth of their child, the attempts to feed it and the various failures in doing so, and with the real and imaginary illnesses of mother and child, in which Iván Ilých's sympathy was demanded but about which he understood nothing, the need of securing for himself an existence outside his family life became still more imperative.

As his wife grew more irritable and exacting and Iván Ilých transferred the centre of gravity of his life more and more to his official work, so did he grow to like his work better and became more ambitious than before.

Very soon, within a year of his wedding, Iván Ilých had realized that marriage, though it may add some comforts to life, is in fact a very intricate and difficult affair towards which in order to perform one's duty, that is, to lead a decorous life approved of by society, one must adopt a definite attitude just as towards one's official duties.

And Iván Ilých evolved such an attitude towards married life. He only required of it those conveniences — dinner at home, housewife, and bed — which it could give him, and above all that propriety of external forms required by public opinion. For the rest he looked for light-hearted pleasure and propriety, and was very thankful when he found them, but if he met with antagonism and querulousness he at once retired into his separate fenced-off world of official duties, where he found satisfaction.

Iván Ilých was esteemed a good official, and after three years was made Assistant Public Prosecutor. His new duties, their importance, the possibility of indicting and imprisoning anyone he chose, the publicity his speeches received, and the success he had in all these things, made his work still more attractive.

More children came. His wife became more and more querulous and ill-tempered, but the attitude Iván Ilých had adopted towards his home life rendered him almost impervious to her grumbling.

After seven years' service in that town he was transferred to another province as Public Prosecutor. They moved, but were short of money and his wife did not like the place they moved to. Though the salary was higher the cost of living was greater, besides which two of their children died and family life became still more unpleasant for him.

Praskóvya Fëdorovna blamed her husband for every inconvenience they encountered in their new home. Most of the conversations between husband and wife, especially as to the children's education, led to topics which recalled former disputes, and those disputes were apt to flare up again at any moment. There remained only those rare periods of amorousness which still came to them at times but did not last long. These were islets at which they anchored for a while and then again set out upon that ocean of veiled hostility which showed itself in their aloofness from one another. This aloofness might have grieved Iván Ilých had he considered that it ought not to exist, but he now regarded the position as normal, and even made it the goal at which he aimed in family life. His aim was to free himself more and more from those unpleasantnesses and to give them a semblance of harmlessness and propriety. He attained this by spending less and less time with his family, and when obliged to be at home he tried to safeguard his position by the presence of outsiders. The chief thing however was that he had his official duties. The whole interest of his life now centered in the official world and that interest absorbed him. The consciousness of his power, being able to ruin anybody he wished to ruin, the importance, even the external dignity of his entry into court, or meetings with his subordinates, his success with superiors and inferiors, and above all his masterly handling of cases, of which he was conscious—all this gave him pleasure and filled his life, together with chats with his colleagues, dinners, and bridge. So that on the whole Iván Ilých's life continued to flow as he considered it should do—pleasantly and properly.

So things continued for another seven years. His eldest daughter was already sixteen, another child had died, and only one son was left, a schoolboy and a subject of dissension. Iván Ilých wanted to put him in the School

of Law, but to spite him Praskóvya Fëdorovna entered him at the High
School. The daughter had been educated at home and had turned out well:
the boy did not learn badly either.

Chapter III

So Iván Ilých lived for seventeen years after his marraige. He was
already a Public Prosecutor of long standing, and had declined several proposed transfers while awaiting a more desirable post, when an unanticipated
and unpleasant occurrence quite upset the peaceful course of his life. He was
expecting to be offered the post of presiding judge in a University town,
but Happe somehow came to the front and obtained the appointment instead. Iván Ilých became irritable, reproached Happe, and quarrelled both
with him and with his immediate superiors — who became colder to him
and again passed him over when other appointments were made.

This was in 1880, the hardest year of Iván Ilých's life. It was then that
it became evident on the one hand that his salary was insufficient for them
to live on, and on the other that he had been forgotten, and not only this,
but that what was for him the greatest and most cruel injustice appeared to
others a quite ordinary occurrence. Even his father did not consider it his
duty to help him. Iván Ilých felt himself abandoned by everyone, and that
they regarded his position with a salary of 3,500 rubles as quite normal and
even fortunate. He alone knew that with the consciousness of the injustices
done him, with his wife's incessant nagging, and with the debts he had
contracted by living beyond his means, his position was far from normal.

In order to save money that summer he obtained a leave of absence and
went with his wife to live in the country at her brother's place.

In the country, without his work, he experienced *ennui* for the first
time in his life, and not only *ennui* but intolerable depression, and he decided
that it was impossible to go on living like that, and that it was necessary to
take energetic measures.

Having passed a sleepless night pacing up and down the veranda, he
decided to go to Petersburg and bestir himself, in order to punish those who
had failed to appreciate him and to get transferred to another ministry.

Next day, despite many protests from his wife and her brother, he
started for Petersburg with the sole object of obtaining a post with a salary
of five thousand rubles a year. He was no longer bent on any particular
department, or tendency, or kind of activity. All he now wanted was an
appointment to another post with a salary of five thousand rubles, either in
the administration, in the banks, with the railways, in one of the Empress
Márya's Institutions, or even in the customs — but it had to carry with it a
salary of five thousand rubles and be in a ministry other than that in which
they had failed to appreciate him.

And this quest of Iván Ilých's was crowned with remarkable and unexpected success. At Kursk an acquaintance of his, F. I. Ilýin, got into the

first-class carriage, sat down beside Iván Ilých, and told him of a telegram just received by the Governor of Kursk announcing that a change was about to take place in the ministry: Peter Ivánovich was to be superseded by Iván Semënovich.

The proposed change, apart from its significance for Russia, had a special significance for Iván Ilých, because by bringing forward a new man, Peter Petróvich, and consequently his friend Zachár Ivánovich, it was highly favourable for Iván Ilých, since Zachár Ivánovich was a friend and colleague of his.

In Moscow this news was confirmed, and on reaching Petersburg Iván Ilých found Zachár Ivánovich and received a definite promise of an appointment in his former Department of Justice.

A week later he telegraphed to his wife: "Zachár in Miller's place. I   10 shall receive appointment on presentation of report."

Thanks to this change of personnel, Iván Ilých had unexpectedly obtained an appointment in his former ministry which placed him two stages above his former colleagues besides giving him five thousand rubles salary and three thousand five hundred rubles for expenses connected with his removal. All his ill humour towards his former enemies and the whole department vanished, and Iván Ilých was completely happy.

He returned to the country more cheerful and contented than he had been for a long time. Praskóvya Fëdorovna also cheered up and a truce was arranged between them. Iván Ilých told of how he had been fêted by everybody in Petersburg, how all those who had been his enemies were put to shame and now fawned on him, how envious they were of his appointment, and how much everybody in Petersburg had liked him.

Praskóvya Fëdorovna listened to all this and appeared to believe it. She did not contradict anything, but only made plans for their life in the town to which they were going. Iván Ilých saw with delight that these plans were his plans, that he and his wife agreed, and that, after a stumble, his life was regaining its due and natural character of pleasant lightheartedness and decorum.

Iván Ilých had come back for a short time only, for he had to take up his new duties on the 10th of September. Moreover, he needed time to settle into the new place, to move all his belongings from the province, and to buy and order many additional things: in a word, to make such arrangements as he had resolved on, which were almost exactly what Praskóvya Fëdorovna too had decided on.

Now that everything had happened so fortunately, and that he and his   15 wife were at one in their aims and moreover saw so little of one another, they got on together better than they had done since the first years of marriage. Iván Ilých had thought of taking his family away with him at once, but the insistence of his wife's brother and her sister-in-law, who had suddenly become particularly amiable and friendly to him and his family, induced him to depart alone.

So he departed, and the cheerful state of mind induced by his success and by the harmony between his wife and himself, the one intensifying the other, did not leave him. He found a delightful house, just the thing both he and his wife had dreamt of. Spacious, lofty reception rooms in the old style, a convenient and dignified study, rooms for his wife and daughter, a study for his son — it might have been specially built for them. Iván Ilých himself superintended the arrangements, chose the wall-papers, supplemented the furniture (preferably with antiques which he considered particularly *comme il faut*), and supervised the upholstering. Everything progressed and progressed and approached the ideal he had set himself: even when things were only half completed they exceeded his expectations. He saw what a refined and elegant character, free from vulgarity, it would all have when it was ready. On falling asleep he pictured to himself how the reception-room would look. Looking at the yet unfinished drawing-room he could see the fireplace, the screen, the what-not, the little chairs dotted here and there, the dishes and plates on the walls, and the bronzes, as they would be when everything was in place. He was pleased by the thought of how his wife and daughter, who shared his taste in this matter, would be impressed by it. They were certainly not expecting as much. He had been particularly successful in finding, and buying cheaply, antiques which gave a particularly aristocratic character to the whole place. But in his letters he intentionally understated everything in order to be able to surprise them. All this so absorbed him that his new duties — though he liked his official work — interested him less than he had expected. Sometimes he even had moments of absent-mindedness during the Court Sessions, and would consider whether he should have straight or curved cornices for his curtains. He was so interested in it all that he often did things himself, rearranging the furniture, or rehanging the curtains. Once when mounting a step-ladder to show the upholsterer, who did not understand, how he wanted the hangings draped, he made a false step and slipped, but being a strong and agile man he clung on and only knocked his side against the knob of the window frame. The bruised place was painful but the pain soon passed, and he felt particularly bright and well just then. He wrote: "I feel fifteen years younger." He thought he would have everything ready by September, but it dragged on till mid-October. But the result was charming not only in his eyes but to everyone who saw it.

In reality it was just what is usually seen in the houses of people of moderate means who want to appear rich, and therefore succeed only in resembling others like themselves: there were damasks, dark wood, plants, rugs, and dull and polished bronzes — all the things people of a certain class have in order to resemble other people of that class. His house was so like the others that it would never have been noticed, but to him it all seemed to be quite exceptional. He was very happy when he met his family at the station and brought them to the newly furnished house all lit up, where a footman in a white tie opened the door into the hall decorated with plants,

and when they went on into the drawing-room and the study uttering
exclamations of delight. He conducted them everywhere, drank in their
praises eagerly, and beamed with pleasure. At tea that evening, when Praskóvya Fëdorovna among other things asked him about his fall, he laughed,
and showed them how he had gone flying and had frightened the upholsterer.

"It's a good thing I'm a bit of an athlete. Another man might have
been killed, but I merely knocked myself, just here; it hurts when it's
touched, but it's passing off already—it's only a bruise."

So they began living in their new home—in which, as always happens,
when they got thoroughly settled in they found they were just one room
short—and with the increased income, which as always was just a little
(some five hundred rubles) too little, but it was all very nice.

Things went particularly well at first, before everything was finally   20
arranged and while something had still to be done: this thing bought, that
thing ordered, another thing moved, and something else adjusted. Though
there were some disputes between husband and wife, they were both so well
satisfied and had so much to do that it all passed off without any serious
quarrels. When nothing was left to arrange it became rather dull and something seemed to be lacking, but they were then making acquaintances,
forming habits, and life was growing fuller.

Iván Ilých spent his mornings at the law court and came home to
dinner, and at first he was generally in a good humour, though he occasionally became irritable just on account of his house. (Every spot on the table-
cloth or the upholstery, and every broken window-blind string, irritated
him. He had devoted so much trouble to arranging it all that every disturbance of it distressed him.) But on the whole his life ran its course as he
believed life should do: easily, pleasantly, and decorously.

He got up at nine, drank his coffee, read the paper, and then put on his
undress uniform and went to the law courts. There the harness in which he
worked had already been stretched to fit him and he donned it without a
hitch: petitioners, inquiries at the chancery, the chancery itself, and the sit-
tings public and administrative. In all this the thing was to exclude everything fresh and vital, which always disturbs the regular course of official
business, and to admit only official relations with people, and then only on
official grounds. A man would come, for instance, wanting some information. Iván Ilých, as one in whose sphere the matter did not lie, would have
nothing to do with him: but if the man had some business with him in his
official capacity, something that could be expressed on officially stamped
paper, he would do everything, positively everything he could within the
limits of such relations, and in doing so would maintain the semblance of
friendly human relations, that is, would observe the courtesies of life. As
soon as the official relations ended, so did everything else. Iván Ilých possessed this capacity to separate his real life from the official side of affairs
and not mix the two, in the highest degree, and by long practice and natural
aptitude had brought it to such a pitch that sometimes, in the manner of a

virtuoso, he would even allow himself to let the human and official relations mingle. He let himself do this just because he felt that he could at any time he chose resume the strictly official attitude again and drop the human relation. And he did it all easily, pleasantly, correctly, and even artistically. In the intervals between the sessions he smoked, drank tea, chatted a little about politics, a little about general topics, a little about cards, but most of all about official appointments. Tired, but with the feelings of a virtuoso — one of the first violins who has played his part in an orchestra with precision — he would return home to find that his wife and daughter had been out paying calls, or had a visitor, and that his son had been to school, had done his homework with his tutor, and was duly learning what is taught at High Schools. Everything was as it should be. After dinner, if they had no visitors, Iván Ilých sometimes read a book that was being much discussed at the time, and in the evening settled down to work, that is, read official papers, compared the depositions of witnesses, and noted paragraphs of the Code applying to them. This was neither dull nor amusing. It was dull when he might have been playing bridge, but if no bridge was available it was at any rate better than doing nothing or sitting with his wife. Iván Ilých's chief pleasure was giving little dinners to which he invited men and women of good social position, and just as his drawing-room resembled all other drawing-rooms so did his enjoyable little parties resemble all other such parties.

Once they even gave a dance. Iván Ilých enjoyed it and everything went off well, except that it led to a violent quarrel with his wife about the cakes and sweets. Praskóvya Fёdorovna had made her own plans, but Iván Ilých insisted on getting everything from an expensive confectioner and ordered too many cakes, and the quarrel occurred because some of those cakes were left over and the confectioner's bill came to forty-five rubles. It was a great and disagreeable quarrel. Praskóvya Fёdorovna called him "a fool and an imbecile," and he clutched at his head and made angry allusions to divorce.

But the dance itself had been enjoyable. The best people were there, and Iván Ilých had danced with Princess Trúfonova, a sister of the distinguished founder of the Society "Bear my Burden."

The pleasures connected with his work were pleasures of ambition; his social pleasures were those of vanity; but Iván Ilých's greatest pleasure was playing bridge. He acknowledged that whatever disagreeable incident happened in his life, the pleasure that beamed like a ray of light above everything else was to sit down to bridge with good players, not noisy partners, and of course to four-handed bridge (with five players it was annoying to have to stand out, though one pretended not to mind), to play a clever and serious game (when the cards allowed it) and then to have supper and drink a glass of wine. After a game of bridge, especially if he had won a little (to win a large sum was unpleasant), Iván Ilých went to bed in specially good humour.

So they lived. They formed a circle of acquaintances among the best people and were visited by people of importance and by young folk. In their views as to their acquaintances, husband, wife and daughter were entirely agreed, and tacitly and unanimously kept at arm's length and shook off the various shabby friends and relations who, with much show of affection, gushed into the drawing-room with its Japanese plates on the walls. Soon these shabby friends ceased to obtrude themselves and only the best people remained in the Golovíns' set.

Young men made up to Lisa, and Petríshchev, an examining magistrate and Dmítri Ivanovich Petríshchev's son and sole heir, began to be so attentive to her that Iván Ilých had already spoken to Praskóvya Fëdorovna about it, and considered whether they should not arrange a party for them or get up some private theatricals.

So they lived, and all went well, without change, and life flowed pleasantly.

Chapter IV

They were all in good health. It could not be called ill health if Iván Ilých sometimes said that he had a queer taste in his mouth and felt some discomfort in his left side.

But this discomfort increased and, though not exactly painful, grew into a sense of pressure in his side accompanied by ill humour. And his irritability became worse and worse and began to mar the agreeable, easy, and correct life that had established itself in the Golovín family. Quarrels between husband and wife became more and more frequent, and soon the ease and amenity disappeared and even the decorum was barely maintained. Scenes again became frequent, and very few of those islets remained on which husband and wife could meet without an explosion. Praskóvya Fëdorovna now had good reason to say that her husband's temper was trying. With characteristic exaggeration she said he had always had a dreadful temper, and that it had needed all her good nature to put up with it for twenty years. It was true that now the quarrels were started by him. His bursts of temper always came just before dinner, often just as he began to eat his soup. Sometimes he noticed that a plate or dish was chipped, or the food was not right, or his son put his elbow on the table, or his daughter's hair was not done as he liked it, and for all this he blamed Praskóvya Fëdorovna. At first she retorted and said disagreeable things to him, but once or twice he fell into such a rage at the beginning of dinner that she realized it was due to some physical derangement brought on by taking food, and so she restrained herself and did not answer, but only hurried to get the dinner over. She regarded this self-restraint as highly praiseworthy. Having come to the conclusion that her husband had a dreadful temper and made her life miserable, she began to feel sorry for herself, and the more she pitied herself the more she hated her husband. She began to wish he would die; yet she did not want him to die because then his salary would cease. And this irritated her against him still more. She considered herself dreadfully unhappy just because not even his death could save her, and though she concealed her exasperation, that hidden exasperation of hers increased his irritation also.

After one scene in which Iván Ilých had been particularly unfair and after which he had said in explanation that he certainly was irritable but that it was due to his not being well, she said that if he was ill it should be attended to, and insisted on his going to see a celebrated doctor.

He went. Everything took place as he had expected and as it always does. There was the usual waiting and the important air assumed by the doctor, with which he was so familiar (resembling that which he himself assumed in court), and the sounding and listening, and the questions which called for answers that were foregone conclusions and were evidently unnecessary, and the look of importance which implied that "if only you put yourself in our hands we will arrange everything — we know indubitably how it has to be done, always in the same way for everybody alike." It was all just as it was in the law courts. The doctor put on just the same air towards him as he himself put on towards an accused person.

The doctor said that so-and-so indicated that there was so-and-so inside the patient, but if the investigation of so-and-so did not confirm this, then he must assume that and that. If he assumed that and that, then . . . and so on. To Iván Ilých only one question was important: was his case serious or not? But the doctor ignored that inappropriate question. From his point of view it was not the one under consideration, the real question was to decide between a floating kidney, chronic catarrh, or appendicitis. It was not a question of Iván Ilých's life or death, but one between a floating kidney and appendicitis. And that question the doctor solved brilliantly, as it seemed to Iván Ilých, in favour of the appendix, with the reservation that should an examination of the urine give fresh indications the matter would be reconsidered. All this was just what Iván Ilých had himself brilliantly accomplished a thousand times in dealing with men on trial. The doctor summed up just as brilliantly, looking over his spectacles triumphantly and even gaily at the accused. From the doctor's summing up Iván Ilých concluded that things were bad, but that for the doctor, and perhaps for everybody else, it was a matter of indifference, though for him it was bad. And this conclusion struck him painfully, arousing in him a great feeling of pity for himself and of bitterness towards the doctor's indifference to a matter of such importance.

He said nothing of this, but rose, placed the doctor's fee on the table, and remarked with a sigh: "We sick people probably often put inappropriate questions. But tell me, in general, is this complaint dangerous, or not? . . ."

The doctor looked at him sternly over his spectacles with one eye, as if to say: "Prisoner, if you will not keep to the questions put to you, I shall be obliged to have you removed from the court."

"I have already told you what I consider necessary and proper. The analysis may show something more." And the doctor bowed.

Iván Ilých went out slowly, seated himself disconsolately in his sledge, and drove home. All the way home he was going over what the doctor had said, trying to translate those complicated, obscure, scientific phrases into plain language and find in them an answer to the question: "Is my condition bad? Is it very bad? Or is there as yet nothing much wrong?" And it seemed to him that the meaning of what the doctor had said was that it was very bad. Everything in the streets seemed depressing. The cabmen, the houses, the passers-by, and the shops, were dismal. His ache, this dull gnawing ache that never ceased for a moment, seemed to have acquired a new and more serious significance from the doctor's dubious remarks. Iván Ilých now watched it with a new and oppressive feeling.

He reached home and began to tell his wife about it. She listened, but in the middle of his account his daughter came in with her hat on, ready to go out with her mother. She sat down reluctantly to listen to this tedious story, but could not stand it long, and her mother too did not hear him to the end.

"Well, I am very glad," she said. "Mind now to take your medicine regularly. Give me the prescription and I'll send Gerásim to the chemist's." And she went to get ready to go out.

While she was in the room Iván Ilých had hardly taken time to breathe, but he sighed deeply when she left it.

"Well," he thought, "perhaps it isn't so bad after all."

He began taking his medicine and following the doctor's directions, which had been altered after the examination of the urine. But then it happened that there was a contradiction between the indications drawn from the examination of the urine and the symptoms that showed themselves. It turned out that what was happening differed from what the doctor had told him, and that he had either forgotten, or blundered, or hidden something from him. He could not, however, be blamed for that, and Iván Ilých still obeyed his orders implicitly and at first derived some comfort from doing so.

From the time of his visit to the doctor, Iván Ilých's chief occupation was the exact fulfilment of the doctor's instructions regarding hygiene and the taking of medicine, and the observation of his pain and his excretions. His chief interests came to be people's ailments and people's health. When sickness, deaths, or recoveries were mentioned in his presence, especially when the illness resembled his own, he listened with agitation which he tried to hide, asked questions, and applied what he heard to his own case.

The pain did not grow less, but Iván Ilých made efforts to force himself to think that he was better. And he could do this so long as nothing agitated him. But as soon as he had any unpleasantness with his wife, any lack of success in his official work, or held bad cards at bridge, he was at once acutely sensible of his disease. He had formerly borne such mischances, hoping soon to adjust what was wrong, to master it and attain success, or make a grand slam. But now every mischance upset him and plunged him into despair. He would say to himself: "There now, just as I was beginning to get better and the medicine had begun to take effect, comes this accursed misfortune, or unpleasantness . . ." And he was furious with the mishap, or with the people who were causing the unpleasantness and killing him, for he felt that this fury was killing him but could not restrain it. One would have thought that it should have been clear to him that this exasperation with circumstances and people aggravated his illness, and that he ought therefore to ignore unpleasant occurrences. But he drew the very opposite conclusion: he said that he needed peace, and he watched for everything that might disturb it and became irritable at the slightest infringement of it. His condition was rendered worse by the fact that he read medical books and consulted doctors. The progress of his disease was so gradual that he could deceive himself when comparing one day with another — the difference was so slight. But when he consulted the doctors it seemed to him that he was getting worse, and even very rapidly. Yet despite this he was continually consulting them.

That month he went to see another celebrity, who told him almost the same as the first had done but put his questions rather differently, and the interview with this celebrity only increased Iván Ilých's doubts and fears. A friend of a friend of his, a very good doctor, diagnosed his illness again quite differently from the others, and though he predicted recovery, his questions and suppositions bewildered Iván Ilých still more and increased his doubts. A homoeopathist diagnosed the disease in yet another way, and prescribed medicine which Iván Ilých took secretly for a week. But after a week, not feeling any improvement and having lost confidence both in the former doctor's treatment and in this one's, he became still more despondent. One day a lady acquaintance mentioned a cure effected by a wonder-working icon. Iván Ilých caught himself listening attentively and beginning to believe that it had occurred. This incident alarmed him. "Has my mind really weakened to such an extent?" he asked himself. "Nonsense! It's all rubbish. I mustn't give way to nervous fears but having chosen a doctor must keep strictly to his treatment. That is what I will do. Now it's all settled. I won't think about it, but will follow the treatment seriously till summer, and then we shall see. From now there must be no more of this wavering!" This was easy to say but impossible to carry out. The pain in his side oppressed him and seemed to grow worse and more incessant, while the taste in his mouth grew stranger and stranger. It seemed to him that his breath had a disgusting smell, and he was conscious of a loss of appetite and strength. There was no deceiving himself: something terrible, new, and more important than anything before in his life, was taking place within him of which he alone was aware. Those about him did not understand or would not understand it, but thought everything in the world was going on as usual. That tormented Iván Ilých more than anything. He saw that his household, especially his wife and daughter who were in a perfect whirl of visiting, did not understand anything of it and were annoyed that he was so depressed and so exacting, as if he were to blame for it. Though they tried to disguise it he saw that he was an obstacle in their path, and that his wife had adopted a definite line in regard to his illness and kept to it regardless of anything he said or did. Her attitude was this: "You know," she would say to her friends, "Iván Ilých can't do as other people do, and keep to the treatment prescribed for him. One day he'll take his drops and keep strictly to his diet and go to bed in good time, but the next day unless I watch him he'll suddenly forget his medicine, eat sturgeon—which is forbidden—and sit up playing cards till one o'clock in the morning."

"Oh, come, when was that?" Iván Ilých would ask in vexation. "Only once at Peter Ivánovich's."

"And yesterday with Shébek."

"Well, even if I hadn't stayed up, this pain would have kept me awake."   20

"Be that as it may you'll never get well like that, but will always make us wretched."

Praskóvya Fëdorovna's attitude to Iván Ilých's illness, as she expressed it both to others and to him, was that it was his own fault and was another of the annoyances he caused her. Iván Ilých felt that this opinion escaped her involuntarily—but that did not make it easier for him.

At the law courts too, Iván Ilých noticed, or thought he noticed, a strange attitude towards himself. It sometimes seemed to him that people were watching him inquisitively as a man whose place might soon be vacant. Then again, his friends would suddenly begin to chaff him in a friendly way about his low spirits, as if the awful, horrible, and unheard-of thing that was going on within him, incessantly gnawing at him and irresistibly drawing him away, was a very agreeable subject for jests. Schwartz in particular irritated him by his jocularity, vivacity, and *savoir-faire,* which reminded him of what he himself had been ten years ago.

Friends came to make up a set and they sat down to cards. They dealt, bending the new cards to soften them, and he sorted the diamonds in his hand and found he had seven. His partner said "No trumps" and supported him with two diamonds. What more could be wished for? It ought to be jolly and lively. They would make a grand slam. But suddenly Iván Ilých was conscious of that gnawing pain, that taste in his mouth, and it seemed ridiculous that in such circumstances he should be pleased to make a grand slam.

He looked at his partner Mikháil Mikháylovich, who rapped the table   25
with his strong hand and instead of snatching up the tricks pushed the cards courteously and indulgently towards Iván Ilých that he might have the pleasure of gathering them up without the trouble of stretching out his hand for them. "Does he think I am too weak to stretch out my arm?" thought Iván Ilých, and forgetting what he was doing he over-trumped his partner, missing the grand slam by three tricks. And what was most awful of all was that he saw how upset Mikháil Mikháylovich was about it but did not himself care. And it was dreadful to realize why he did not care.

They all saw that he was suffering, and said: "We can stop if you are tired. Take a rest." Lie down? No, he was not at all tired, and he finished the rubber. All were gloomy and silent. Iván Ilých felt that he diffused this gloom over them and could not dispel it. They had supper and went away, and Iván Ilých was left alone with the consciousness that his life was poisoned and was poisoning the lives of others, and that this poison did not weaken but penetrated more and more deeply into his whole being.

With this consciousness, and with physical pain besides the terror, he must go to bed, often to lie awake the greater part of the night. Next morning he had to get up again, dress, go to the law courts, speak, and write; or if he did not go out, spend at home those twenty-four hours a day each of which was a torture. And he had to live thus all alone on the brink of an abyss, with no one who understood or pitied him.

Chapter V

So one month passed and then another. Just before the New Year his brother-in-law came to town and stayed at their house. Iván Ilých was at the law courts and Praskóvya Fëdorovna had gone shopping. When Iván Ilých came home and entered his study he found his brother-in-law there—a healthy, florid man—unpacking his portmanteau himself. He raised his head on hearing Iván Ilých's footsteps and looked up at him for a moment without a word. That stare told Iván Ilých everything. His brother-in-law opened his mouth to utter an exclamation of surprise but checked himself, and that action confirmed it all.

"I have changed, eh?"

"Yes, there is a change."

And after that, try as he would to get his brother-in-law to return to the subject of his looks, the latter would say nothing about it. Praskóvya Fëdorovna came home and her brother went out to her. Iván Ilých locked the door and began to examine himself in the glass, first full face, then in profile. He took up a portrait of himself taken with his wife, and compared it with what he saw in the glass. The change in him was immense. Then he bared his arms to the elbow, looked at them, drew the sleeves down again, sat down on an ottoman, and grew blacker than night.

"No, no, this won't do!" he said to himself, and jumped up, went to the table, took up some law papers and began to read them, but could not continue. He unlocked the door and went into the reception-room. The door leading to the drawing-room was shut. He approached it on tiptoe and listened.

"No, you are exaggerating!" Praskóvya Fëdorovna was saying.

"Exaggerating! Don't you see it? Why, he's a dead man! Look at his eyes—there's no light in them. But what is it that is wrong with him?"

"No one knows. Nikoláevich (that was another doctor) said something, but I don't know what. And Leshchetítsky (this was the celebrated specialist) said quite the contrary . . ."

Iván Ilých walked away, went to his own room, lay down, and began musing: "The kidney, a floating kidney." He recalled all the doctors had told him of how it detached itself and swayed about. And by an effort of imagination he tried to catch that kidney and arrest it and support it. So little was needed for this, it seemed to him. "No, I'll go to see Peter Ivánovich again." (That was the friend whose friend was a doctor.) He rang, ordered the carriage, and got ready to go.

"Where are you going, Jean?" asked his wife, with a specially sad and exceptionally kind look.

This exceptionally kind look irritated him. He looked morosely at her.

"I must go see Peter Ivánovich."

He went to see Peter Ivánovich, and together they went to see his friend, the doctor. He was in, and Iván Ilých had a long talk with him.

Reviewing the anatomical and physiological details of what in the doctor's opinion was going on inside him, he understood it all.

There was something, a small thing, in the vermiform appendix. It might all come right. Only stimulate the energy of one organ and check the activity of another, then absorption would take place and everything would come right. He got home rather late for dinner, ate his dinner, and conversed cheerfully, but could not for a long time bring himself to go back to work in his room. At last, however, he went to his study and did what was necessary, but the consciousness that he had put something aside — an important, intimate matter which he would revert to when his work was done — never left him. When he had finished his work he remembered that this intimate matter was the thought of his vermiform appendix. But he did not give himself up to it, and went to the drawing-room for tea. There were callers there, including the examining magistrate who was a desirable match for his daughter, and they were conversing, playing the piano and singing. Iván Ilých, as Praskóvya Fëdorovna remarked, spent that evening more cheerfully than usual, but he never for a moment forgot that he had postponed the important matter of the appendix. At eleven o'clock he said goodnight and went to his bedroom. Since his illness he had slept alone in a small room next to his study. He undressed and took up a novel by Zola, but instead of reading it he fell into thought, and in his imagination that desired improvement in the vermiform appendix occurred. There was the absorption and evacuation and the reestablishment of normal activity. "Yes, that's it!" he said to himself. "One need only assist nature, that's all." He remembered his medicine, rose, took it, and lay down on his back watching for the beneficent action of the medicine and for it to lessen the pain. "I need only take it regularly and avoid all injurious influences. I am already feeling better, much better." He began touching his side: it was not painful to the touch. "There, I really don't feel it. It's much better already." He put out the light and turned on his side . . . "The appendix is getting better, absorption is occurring." Suddenly he felt the old, familiar, dull, gnawing pain, stubborn and serious. There was the same familiar loathsome taste in his mouth. His heart sank and he felt dazed. "My God! My God!" he muttered. "Again, again! And it will never cease." And suddenly the matter presented itself in a quite different aspect. "Vermiform appendix! Kidney!" he said to himself. "It's not a question of appendix or kidney, but of life and . . . death. Yes, life was there and now it is going, going and I cannot stop it. Yes. Why deceive myself? Isn't it obvious to everyone but me that I'm dying, and that it's only a question of weeks, days . . . it may happen this moment. There was light and now there is darkness. I was here and now I'm going there! Where?" A chill came over him, his breathing ceased, and he felt only the throbbing of his heart.

"When I am not, what will there be? There will be nothing. Then where shall I be when I am no more? Can this be dying? No, I don't want to!" He jumped up and tried to light the candle, felt for it with trembling hands, dropped candle and candlestick on the floor, and fell back on his pillow.

"What's the use? It makes no difference," he said to himself, staring with wide-open eyes into the darkness. "Death. Yes, death. And none of them know or wish to know it, and they have no pity for me. Now they are playing." (He heard through the door the distant sound of a song and its accompaniment.) "It's all the same to them, but they will die too! Fools! I first, and they later, but it will be the same for them. And now they are merry . . . the beasts!"

Anger choked him and he was agonizingly, unbearably miserable. "It is impossible that all men have been doomed to suffer this awful horror!" He raised himself.

"Something must be wrong. I must calm myself—must think it all over from the beginning." And he again began thinking. "Yes, the beginning of my illness: I knocked my side, but I was still quite well that day and the next. It hurt a little, then rather more. I saw the doctors, then followed despondency and anguish, more doctors, and I drew nearer to the abyss. My strength grew less and I kept coming nearer and nearer, and now I have wasted away and there is no light in my eyes. I think of the appendix—but this is death! I think of mending the appendix, and all the while here is death! Can it really be death?" Again terror seized him and he gasped for breath. He leant down and began feeling for the matches, pressing with his elbow on the stand beside the bed. It was in his way and hurt him, he grew furious with it, pressed on it still harder, and upset it. Breathless and in despair he fell on his back, expecting death to come immediately.

Meanwhile the visitors were leaving. Praskóvya Fëdorovna was seeing them off. She heard something fall and came in.

"What has happened?"

20

"Nothing. I knocked it over accidentally."

She went out and returned with a candle. He lay there panting heavily, like a man who has run a thousand yards, and stared upwards at her with a fixed look.

"What is it, Jean?"

"No . . . o . . . thing. I upset it." ("Why speak of it? She won't understand," he thought.)

And in truth she did not understand. She picked up the stand, lit his candle, and hurried away to see another visitor off. When she came back he still lay on his back, looking upwards.

"What is it? Do you feel worse?"

"Yes."

She shook her head and sat down.

"Do you know, Jean, I think we must ask Leshchetítsky to come and see you here."

This meant calling in the famous specialist, regardless of expense. He smiled malignantly and said "No." She remained a little longer and then went up to him and kissed his forehead.

While she was kissing him he hated her from the bottom of his soul and with difficulty refrained from pushing her away.

"Good-night. Please God you'll sleep."

"Yes."

Chapter VI

Iván Ilých saw that he was dying, and he was in continual despair.

In the depth of his heart he knew he was dying, but not only was he not accustomed to the thought, he simply did not and could not grasp it.

The syllogism he had learnt from Kiezewetter's Logic: "Caius is a man, men are mortal, therefore Caius is mortal," had always seemed to him correct as applied to Caius, but certainly not as applied to himself. That Caius—man in the abstract—was mortal, was perfectly correct, but he was not Caius, not an abstract man, but a creature quite, quite separate from all others. He had been little Ványa, with a mamma and a papa; with Mitya and Volódya, and the toys, a coachman and a nurse, afterwards with Kátenka and with all the joys, griefs, and delights of childhood, boyhood, and youth. What did Caius know of the smell of that striped leather ball Ványa had been so fond of? Had Caius kissed his mother's hand like that, and did the silk of her dress rustle so for Caius? Had he rioted like that at school when the pastry was bad? Had Caius been in love like that? Could Caius preside at a session as he did? "Caius really was mortal, and it was right for him to die; but for me, little Ványa, Iván Ilých, with all my thoughts and emotions, it's altogether a different matter. It cannot be that I ought to die. That would be too terrible."

Such was his feeling.

"If I had to die like Caius I should have known it was so. An inner   5
voice would have told me so, but there was nothing of the sort in me and I
and all my friends felt that our case was quite different from that of Caius.
And now here it is!" he said to himself. "It can't be. It's impossible! But here
it is. How is this? How is one to understand it?"

He could not understand it, and tried to drive this false, incorrect,
morbid thought away and to replace it by other proper and healthy thoughts.
But that thought and not the thought only but the reality itself, seemed to
come and confront him.

And to replace that thought he called up a succession of others, hoping
to find in them some support. He tried to get back into the former current
of thoughts that had once screened the thought of death from him. But
strange to say, all that had formerly shut off, hidden, and destroyed, his
consciousness of death, no longer had that effect. Iván Ilých now spent most
of his time in attempting to re-establish that old current. He would say to
himself: "I will take up my duties again — after all I used to live by them."
And banishing all doubts he would go to the law courts, enter into conversation with his colleagues, and sit carelessly as was his wont, scanning the
crowd with a thoughtful look and leaning both his emaciated arms on the
arms of his oak chair; bending over as usual to a colleague and drawing his
papers nearer he would interchange whispers with him, and then suddenly
raising his eyes and sitting erect would pronounce certain words and open
the proceedings. But suddenly in the midst of those proceedings the pain in
his side, regardless of the stage the proceedings had reached, would begin
its own gnawing work. Iván Ilých would turn his attention to it and try to
drive the thought of it away, but without success. *It* would come and stand
before him and look at him, and he would be petrified and the light would
die out of his eyes, and he would again begin asking himself whether *It*
alone was true. And his colleagues and subordinates would see with surprise
and distress that he, the brilliant and subtle judge, was becoming confused
and making mistakes. He would shake himself, try to pull himself together,
manage somehow to bring the sitting to a close, and return home with the
sorrowful consciousness that his judicial labours could not as formerly hide
from him what he wanted them to hide, and could not deliver him from
It. And what was worst of all was that *It* drew his attention to itself not
in order to make him take some action but only that he should look at *It,*
look it straight in the face: look at it and without doing anything, suffer
inexpressibly.

And to save himself from this condition Iván Ilých looked for consola-
tions — new screens — and new screens were found and for a while seemed to
save him, but then they immediately fell to pieces or rather became transparent, as if *It* penetrated them and nothing could veil *It*.

In these latter days he would go into the drawing-room he had arranged — that drawing-room where he had fallen and for the sake of which

(how bitterly ridiculous it seemed) he had sacrificed his life — for he knew that his illness originated with that knock. He would enter and see that something had scratched the polished table. He would look for the cause of this and find that it was the bronze ornamentation of an album, that had got bent. He would take up the expensive album which he had lovingly arranged, and feel vexed with his daughter and her friends for their untidiness — for the album was torn here and there and some of the photographs turned upside down. He would put it carefully in order and bend the ornamentation back into position. Then it would occur to him to place all those things in another corner of the room, near the plants. He could call the footman, but his daughter or wife would come to help him. They would not agree, and his wife would contradict him, and he would dispute and grow angry. But that was all right, for then he did not think about *It*. *It* was invisible.

But then, when he was moving something himself, his wife would   10
say: "Let the servants do it. You will hurt yourself again." And suddenly *It* would flash through the screen and he would see it. It was just a flash, and he hoped it would disappear, but he would involuntarily pay attention to his side. "It sits there as before, gnawing just the same!" And he could no longer forget *It,* but could distinctly see it looking at him from behind the flowers. "What is it all for?"

"It really is so! I lost my life over that curtain as I might have done when storming a fort. Is that possible? How terrible and how stupid. It can't be true! It can't, but it is!"

He would go to his study, lie down, and again be alone with *It:* face to face with *It*. And nothing could be done with *It* except to look at it and shudder.

Chapter VII

How it happened it is impossible to say because it came about step by step, unnoticed, but in the third month of Iván Ilých's illness, his wife, his daughter, his son, his acquaintances, the doctors, the servants, and above all he himself, were aware that the whole interest he had for other people was whether he would soon vacate his place, and at last release the living from the discomfort caused by his presence and be himself released from his sufferings.

He slept less and less. He was given opium and hypodermic injections of morphine, but this did not relieve him. The dull depression he experienced in a somnolent condition at first gave him a little relief, but only as something new, afterwards it became as distressing as the pain itself or even more so.

Special foods were prepared for him by the doctors' orders, but all those foods became increasingly distasteful and disgusting to him.

For his excretions also special arrangements had to be made, and this was a torment to him every time — a torment from the uncleanliness, the unseemliness, and the smell, and from knowing that another person had to take part in it.

But just through this most unpleasant matter Iván Ilých obtained comfort. Gerásim, the butler's young assistant, always came in to carry the things out. Gerásim was a clean, fresh peasant lad, grown stout on town food and always cheerful and bright. At first the sight of him, in his clean Russian peasant costume, engaged on that disgusting task embarrassed Iván Ilých.

Once when he got up from the commode too weak to draw up his trousers, he dropped into a soft armchair and looked with horror at his bare, enfeebled thighs with the muscles so sharply marked on them.

Gerásim with a firm light tread, his heavy boots emitting a pleasant smell of tar and fresh winter air, came in wearing a clean Hessian apron, the sleeves of his print shirt tucked up over his strong bare young arms; and refraining from looking at his sick master out of consideration for his feelings, and restraining the joy of life that beamed from his face, went up to the commode.

"Gerásim!" said Iván Ilých in a weak voice.

Gerásim started, evidently afraid he might have committed some blunder, and with a rapid movement turned his fresh, kind, simple young face which just showed the first downy signs of a beard.

"Yes, sir?"

"That must be very unpleasant for you. You must forgive me. I am helpless."

"Oh, why, sir," and Gerásim's eyes beamed and he showed his glistening white teeth, "what's a little trouble? It's a case of illness with you, sir."

And his deft strong hands did their accustomed task, and he went out of the room stepping lightly. Five minutes later he as lightly returned.

Iván Ilých was still sitting in the same position in the armchair.

"Gerásim," he said when the latter had replaced the freshly-washed utensil. "Please come here and help me." Gerásim went up to him. "Lift me up. It is hard for me to get up, and I have sent Dmítri away."

Gerásim went up to him, grasped his master with his strong arms deftly but gently, in the same way that he stepped — lifted him, supported him with one hand, and with the other drew up his trousers and would have set him down again, but Iván Ilých asked to be led to the sofa. Gerásim, without an effort and without apparent pressure, led him, almost lifting him, to the sofa and placed him on it.

"Thank you. How easily and well you do it all!"

Gerásim smiled again and turned to leave the room. But Iván Ilých felt his presence such a comfort that he did not want to let him go.

"One thing more, please move up that chair. No, the other one — under my feet. It is easier for me when my feet are raised."

Gerásim brought the chair, set it down gently in place, and raised Iván   20
Ilých's legs on to it. It seemed to Iván Ilých that he felt better while Gerásim
was holding up his legs.

"It's better when my legs are higher," he said. "Place that cushion
under them."

Gerásim did so. He again lifted the legs and placed them, and again
Iván Ilých felt better while Gerásim held his legs. When he set them down
Iván Ilých fancied he felt worse.

"Gerásim," he said. "Are you busy now?"

"Not at all, sir," said Gerásim, who had learnt from the townsfolk
how to speak to gentlefolk.

"What have you still to do?"   25

"What have I to do? I've done everything except chopping the logs for
tomorrow."

"Then hold my legs up a bit higher, can you?"

"Of course I can. Why not?" And Gerásim raised his master's legs
higher and Iván Ilých thought that in that position he did not feel any pain
at all.

"And how about the logs?"

"Don't trouble about that, sir. There's plenty of time."   30

Iván Ilých told Gerásim to sit down and hold his legs, and began to
talk to him. And strange to say it seemed to him that he felt better while
Gerásim held his legs up.

After that Iván Ilých would sometimes call Gerásim and get him to
hold his legs on his shoulders, and he liked talking to him. Gerásim did it
all easily, willingly, simply, and with a good nature that touched Iván Ilých.
Health, strength, and vitality in other people were offensive to him, but
Gerásim's strength and vitality did not mortify but soothed him.

What tormented Iván Ilých most was the deception, the lie, which for
some reason they all accepted, that he was not dying but was simply ill, and
that he only need keep quiet and undergo a treatment and then something
very good would result. He however knew that do what they would nothing
would come of it, only still more agonizing suffering and death. This deception tortured him — their not wishing to admit what they all knew and what
he knew, but wanting to lie to him concerning his terrible condition, and
wishing and forcing him to participate in that lie. Those lies — lies enacted
over him on the eve of his death and destined to degrade this awful, solemn
act to the level of their visitings, their curtains, their sturgeon for dinner —
were a terrible agony for Iván Ilých. And strangely enough, many times
when they were going through their antics over him he had been within a
hairbreadth of calling out to them: "Stop lying! You know and I know
that I am dying. Then at least stop lying about it!" But he had never
had the spirit to do it. The awful, terrible act of his dying was, he could see,
reduced by those about him to the level of a casual, unpleasant, and almost
indecorous incident (as if someone entered a drawing-room diffusing an

unpleasant odour) and this was done by that very decorum which he had served all his life long. He saw that no one felt for him, because no one even wished to grasp his position. Only Gerásim recognized it and pitied him. And so Iván Ilých felt at ease only with him. He felt comforted when Gerásim supported his legs (sometimes all night long) and refused to go to bed, saying: "Don't you worry, Iván Ilých. I'll get sleep enough later on," or when he suddenly became familiar and exclaimed: "If you weren't sick it would be another matter, but as it is, why should I grudge a little trouble?" Gerásim alone did not lie; everything showed that he alone understood the facts of the case and did not consider it necessary to disguise them, but simply felt sorry for his emaciated and enfeebled master. Once when Iván Ilých was sending him away he even said straight out: "We shall all of us die, so why should I grudge a little trouble?"—expressing the fact that he did not think his work burdensome, because he was doing it for a dying man and hoped someone would do the same for him when his time came.

Apart from this lying, or because of it, what most tormented Iván Ilých was that no one pitied him as he wished to be pitied. At certain moments after prolonged suffering he wished most of all (though he would have been ashamed to confess it) for someone to pity him as a sick child is pitied. He longed to be petted and comforted. He knew he was an important functionary, that he had a beard turning grey, and that therefore what he longed for was impossible, but still he longed for it. And in Gerásim's attitude towards him there was something akin to what he wished for, and so that attitude comforted him. Iván Ilých wanted to weep, wanted to be petted and cried over, and then his colleague Shébek would come, and instead of weeping and being petted, Iván Ilých would assume a serious, severe, and profound air, and by force of habit would express his opinion on a decision of the Court of Cassation and would stubbornly insist on that view. This falsity around him and within him did more than anything else to poison his last days.

Chapter VIII

It was morning. He knew it was morning because Gerásim had gone, and Peter the footman had come and put out the candles, drawn back one of the curtains, and begun quietly to tidy up. Whether it was morning or evening, Friday or Sunday, made no difference, it was all just the same: the gnawing, unmitigated, agonizing pain, never ceasing for an instant, the consciousness of life inexorably waning but not yet extinguished, that approach of that ever dreaded and hateful Death which was the only reality, and always the same falsity. What were days, weeks, hours, in such a case?

"Will you have some tea, sir?"

"He wants things to be regular, and wishes the gentlefolk to drink tea in the morning," thought Iván Ilých, and only said "No."

"Wouldn't you like to move onto the sofa, sir?"

"He wants to tidy up the room, and I'm in the way. I am uncleanliness   5
and disorder," he thought, and said only:

"No, leave me alone."

The man went on bustling about. Iván Ilých stretched out his hand.
Peter came up, ready to help.

"What is it, sir?"

"My watch."

Peter took the watch which was close at hand and gave it to his master.   10

"Half-past eight. Are they up?"

"No sir, except Vladímir Ivánich" (the son) "who has gone to school.
Praskóvya Fĕdorovna ordered me to wake her if you asked for her. Shall I
do so?"

"No, there's no need to." "Perhaps I'd better have some tea," he
thought, and added aloud: "Yes, bring me some tea."

Peter went to the door but Iván Ilých dreaded being left alone. "How
can I keep him here? Oh yes, my medicine." "Peter, give me my medicine."
"Why not? Perhaps it may still do me some good." He took a spoonful and
swallowed it. "No, it won't help. It's all tomfoolery, all deception," he
decided as soon as he became aware of the familiar, sickly, hopeless taste.
"No, I can't believe in it any longer. But the pain, why this pain? If it would
only cease just for a moment!" And he moaned. Peter turned towards him.
"It's all right. Go and fetch me some tea."

Peter went out. Left alone Iván Ilých groaned not so much with pain,   15
terrible though that was, as from mental anguish. Always and for ever the
same, always these endless days and nights. If only it would come quicker!
If only *what* would come quicker? Death, darkness? . . . No, no! Anything
rather than death!

When Peter returned with the tea on a tray, Iván Ilých stared at him
for a time in perplexity, not realizing who and what he was. Peter was
disconcerted by that look and his embarrassment brought Iván Ilých to
himself.

"Oh, tea! All right, put it down. Only help me to wash and put on a
clean shirt."

And Iván Ilých began to wash. With pauses for rest, he washed his
hands and then his face, cleaned his teeth, brushed his hair, and looked in
the glass. He was terrified by what he saw, especially by the limp way in
which his hair clung to his pallid forehead.

While his shirt was being changed he knew that he would be still more
frightened at the sight of his body, so he avoided looking at it. Finally he
was ready. He drew on a dressing-gown, wrapped himself in a plaid, and
sat down in the armchair to take his tea. For a moment he felt refreshed, but
as soon as he began to drink the tea he was again aware of the same taste,
and the pain also returned. He finished it with an effort, and then lay down
stretching out his legs, and dismissed Peter.

Always the same. Now a spark of hope flashes up, then a sea of despair   20
rages, and always pain; always pain, always despair, and always the same.
When alone he had a dreadful and distressing desire to call someone, but he
knew beforehand that with others present it would be still worse. "Another
dose of morphine — to lose consciousness. I will tell him, the doctor, that he
must think of something else. It's impossible, impossible, to go on like this."

An hour and another pass like that. But now there is a ring at the door
bell. Perhaps it's the doctor? It is. He comes in fresh, hearty, plump, and
cheerful, with that look on his face that seems to say: "There now, you're in
a panic about something, but we'll arrange it all for you directly!" The
doctor knows this expression is out of place here, but he has put it on once
for all and can't take it off — like a man who has put on a frock-coat in the
morning to pay a round of calls.

The doctor rubs his hands vigorously and reassuringly.

"Brr! How cold it is! There's such a sharp frost; just let me warm
myself!" he says, as if it were only a matter of waiting till he was warm,
and then he would put everything right.

"Well now, how are you?"

Iván Ilých feels that the doctor would like to say: "Well, how are our   25
affairs?" but that even he feels that this would not do, and says instead:
"What sort of a night have you had?"

Iván Ilých looks at him as much as to say: "Are you really never
ashamed of lying?" But the doctor does not wish to understand this question, and Iván Ilých says: "Just as terrible as ever. The pain never leaves me
and never subsides. If only something . . ."

"Yes, you sick people are always like that. . . . There, now I think I
am warm enough. Even Praskóvya Fëdorovna, who is so particular, could
find no fault with my temperature. Well, now I can say good-morning,"
and the doctor presses his patient's hand.

Then, dropping his former playfulness, he begins with a most serious
face to examine the patient, feeling his pulse and taking his temperature,
and then begins the sounding and ausculation.

Iván Ilých knows quite well and definitely that all this is nonsense and
pure deception, but when the doctor, getting down on his knee, leans over
him, putting his ear first higher then lower, and performs various gymnastic
movements over him with a significant expression on his face, Iván Ilých
submits to it all as he used to submit to the speeches of the lawyers, though
he knew very well that they were all lying and why they were lying.

The doctor, kneeling on the sofa, is still sounding him when Praskóvya   30
Fëdorovna's silk dress rustles at the door and she is heard scolding Peter for
not having let her know of the doctor's arrival.

She comes in, kisses her husband, and at once proceeds to prove that
she has been up a long time already, and only owing to a misunderstanding
failed to be there when the doctor arrived.

Iván Ilých looks at her, scans her all over, sets against her the whiteness and plumpness and cleanness of her hands and neck, the gloss of her hair, and the sparkle of her vivacious eyes. He hates her with his whole soul. And the thrill of hatred he feels for her makes him suffer from her touch.

Her attitude towards him and his disease is still the same. Just as the doctor had adopted a certain relation to his patient which he could not abandon, so had she formed one towards him — that he was not doing something he ought to do and was himself to blame, and that she reproached him lovingly for this — and she could not now change that attitude.

"You see he doesn't listen to me and doesn't take his medicine at the proper time. And above all he lies in a position that is no doubt bad for him — with his legs up."

She described how he made Gerásim hold his legs up.   35

The doctor smiled with a contemptuous affability that said: "What's to be done? These sick people do have foolish fancies of that kind, but we must forgive them."

When the examination was over the doctor looked at his watch, and then Praskóvya Fëdorovna announced to Iván Ilých that it was of course as he pleased, but she had sent to-day for a celebrated specialist who would examine him and have a consultation with Michael Danílovich (their regular doctor).

"Please don't raise any objections. I am doing this for my own sake," she said ironically, letting it be felt that she was doing it all for his sake and only said that to leave him no right to refuse. He remained silent, knitting his brows. He felt that he was so surrounded and involved in a mesh of falsity that it was hard to unravel anything.

Everything she did for him was entirely for her own sake, and she told him she was doing for herself what she actually was doing for herself, as if that was so incredible that he must understand the opposite.

At half-past eleven the celebrated specialist arrived. Again the sound-   40 ing began and the significant conversations in his presence and in another room, about the kidneys and the appendix, and the questions and answers, with such an air of importance that again, instead of the real question of life and death which now alone confronted him, the question arose of the kidney and appendix which were not behaving as they ought to and would now be attacked by Michael Danílovich and the specialist and forced to amend their ways.

The celebrated specialist took leave of him with a serious though not hopeless look, and in reply to the timid question Iván Ilých, with eyes glistening with fear and hope, put to him as to whether there was a chance of recovery, said that he could not vouch for it but there was a possibility. The look of hope with which Iván Ilých watched the doctor out was so pathetic that Praskóvya Fëdorovna, seeing it, even wept as she left the room to hand the doctor his fee.

The gleam of hope kindled by the doctor's encouragement did not last long. The same room, the same pictures, curtains, wall-paper, medicine bottles, were all there, and the same aching suffering body, and Iván Ilých began to moan. They gave him a subcutaneous injection and he sank into oblivion.

It was twilight when he came to. They brought him his dinner and he swallowed some beef tea with difficulty, and then everything was the same again and night was coming on.

After dinner, at seven o'clock, Praskóvya Fëdorovna came into the room in evening dress, her full bosom pushed up by her corset, and with traces of powder on her face. She had reminded him in the morning that they were going to the theatre. Sarah Bernhardt was visiting the town and they had a box, which he had insisted on their taking. Now he had forgotten about it and her toilet offended him, but he concealed his vexation when he remembered that he had himself insisted on their securing a box and going because it would be an instructive and aesthetic pleasure for the children.

Praskóvya Fëdorovna came in, self-satisfied but yet with a rather   45
guilty air. She sat down and asked how he was but, as he saw, only for the sake of asking and not in order to learn about it, knowing that there was nothing to learn — and then went on to what she really wanted to say: that she would not on any account have gone but that the box had been taken and Helen and their daugther were going, as well as Petríshchev (the examining magistrate, their daughter's fiancé) and that it was out of the question to let them go alone; but that she would have much preferred to sit with him for a while; and he must be sure to follow the doctor's orders while she was away.

"Oh, and Fëdor Petróvich" (the fiancé) "would like to come in. May he? And Lisa?"

"All right."

Their daughter came in in full evening dress, her fresh young flesh exposed (making a show of that very flesh which in his own case caused so much suffering), strong, healthy, evidently in love, and impatient with illness, suffering, and death, because they interfered with her happiness.

Fëdor Petróvich came in too, in evening dress, his hair curled á la Capoul, a tight stiff collar round his long sinewy neck, an enormous white shirt-front and narrow black trousers tighly stretched over his strong thighs. He had one white glove tightly drawn on, and was holding his opera hat in his hand.

Following him the schoolboy crept in unnoticed, in a new uniform,   50
poor little fellow, and wearing gloves. Terribly dark shadows showed under his eyes, the meaning of which Iván Ilých knew well.

His son had always seemed pathetic to him, and now it was dreadful to see the boy's frightened look of pity. It seemed to Iván Ilých that Vásya was the only one besides Gerásim who understood and pitied him.

They all sat down and again asked how he was. A silence followed. Lisa asked her mother about the opera-glasses, and there was an altercation between mother and daughter as to who had taken them and where they had been put. This occasioned some unpleasantness.

Fëdor Petróvich inquired of Iván Ilých whether he had ever seen Sarah Bernhardt. Iván Ilých did not at first catch the question, but then replied: "No, have you seen her before?"

"Yes, in *Adrienne Lecouvreur.*"

Praskóvya Fëdorovna mentioned some roles in which Sarah Bernhardt   55 was particularly good. Her daughter disagreed. Conversation sprang up as to the elegance and realism of her acting — the sort of conversation that is always repeated and is always the same.

In the midst of the conversation Fëdor Petróvich glanced at Iván Ilých and became silent. The others also looked at him and grew silent. Iván Ilých was staring with glittering eyes straight before him, evidently indignant with them. This had to be rectified, but it was impossible to do so. The silence had to be broken, but for a time no one dared to break it and they all became afraid that the conventional deception would suddenly become obvious and the truth become plain to all. Lisa was the first to pluck up courage and break that silence, but by trying to hide what everybody was feeling, she betrayed it.

"Well, if we are going it's time to start," she said, looking at her watch, a present from her father, and with a faint and significant smile at Fëdor Petróvich relating to something known only to them. She got up with a rustle of her dress.

They all rose, said good-night, and went away.

When they had gone it seemed to Iván Ilých that he felt better; the falsity had gone with them. But the pain remained — that same pain and that same fear that made everything monotonously alike, nothing harder and nothing easier. Everything was worse.

Again minute followed minute and hour followed hour. Everything   60 remained the same and there was no cessation. And the inevitable end of it all became more and more terrible.

"Yes, send Gerásim here," he replied to a question Peter asked.

Chapter IX

His wife returned late at night. She came in on tiptoe, but he heard her, opened his eyes, and made haste to close them again. She wished to send Gerásim away and to sit with him herself, but he opened his eyes and said: "No, go away."

"Are you in great pain?"

"Always the same."

"Take some opium."

He agreed and took some. She went away.   5

Till about three in the morning he was in a state of stupefied misery. It seemed to him that he and his pain were being thrust into a narrow, deep black sack, but though they were pushed further and further in they could not be pushed to the bottom. And this, terrible enough in itself, was accompanied by suffering. He was frightened yet wanted to fall through the sack, he struggled but yet co-operated. And suddenly he broke through, fell, and regained consciousness. Gerásim was sitting at the foot of the bed dozing quietly and patiently, while he himself lay with his emaciated stockinged legs resting on Gerásim's shoulders; the same shaded candle was there and the same unceasing pain.

"Go away, Gerásim," he whispered.

"It's all right, sir. I'll stay a while."

"No. Go away."

He removed his legs from Gerásim's shoulders, turned sideways onto   10 his arm, and felt sorry for himself. He only waited till Gerásim had gone into the next room and then restrained himself no longer but wept like a child. He wept on account of his helplessness, his terrible loneliness, the cruelty of man, the cruelty of God, and the absence of God.

"Why hast Thou done all this? Why hast Thou brought me here? Why, why dost Thou torment me so terribly?"

He did not expect an answer and yet wept because there was no answer and could be none. The pain again grew more acute, but he did not stir and did not call. He said to himself: "Go on! Strike me! But what is it for? What have I done to Thee? What is it for?"

Then he grew quiet and not only ceased weeping but even held his breath and became all attention. It was as though he were listening not to an audible voice but to the voice of his soul, to the current of thoughts arising within him.

"What is it you want?" was the first clear conception capable of expression in words, that he heard.

"What do you want? What do you want?" he repeated to himself.   15

"What do I want? To live and not to suffer," he answered.

And again he listened with such concentrated attention that even his pain did not distract him.

"To live? How?" asked his inner voice.

"Why, to live as I used to — well and pleasantly."

"As you lived before, well and pleasantly?" the voice repeated.   20

And in imagination he began to recall the best moments of his pleasant life. But strange to say none of these best moments of his pleasant life now seemed at all what they had then seemed — none of them except the first recollections of childhood. There, in childhood, there had been something really pleasant with which it would be possible to live if it could return. But the child who had experienced that happiness existed no longer, it was like a reminiscence of somebody else.

As soon as the period began which had produced the present Iván Ilých, all that had then seemed joys now melted before his sight and turned into something trivial and often nasty.

And the further he departed from childhood and the nearer he came to the present the more worthless and doubtful were the joys. This began with the School of Law. A little that was really good was still found there — there was light-heartedness, friendship, and hope. But in the upper classes there had already been fewer of such good moments. Then during the first years of his official career, when he was in the service of the Governor, some pleasant moments again occurred: they were the memories of love for a woman. Then all became confused and there was still less of what was good; later on again there was still less that was good, and the further he went the less there was. His marriage, a mere accident, then the disenchantment that followed it, his wife's bad breath and the sensuality and hypocrisy: then that deadly official life and those preoccupations about money, a year of it, and two, and ten, and twenty, and always the same thing. And the longer it lasted the more deadly it became. "It is as if I had been going downhill while I imagined I was going up. And that is really what it was. I was going up in public opinion, but to the same extent life was ebbing away from me. And now it is all done and there is only death."

"Then what does it mean? Why? It can't be that life is so senseless and horrible. But if it really has been so horrible and senseless, why must I die and die in agony? There is something wrong!"

"Maybe I did not live as I ought to have done," it suddenly occurred   25
to him. "But how could that be, when I did everything properly?" he replied, and immediately dismissed from his mind this, the sole solution of all the riddles of life and death, as something quite impossible.

"Then what do you want now? To live? Live how? Live as you lived in the law courts when the usher proclaimed 'The judge is coming!'" "The judge is coming, the judge!" he repeated to himself. "Here he is, the judge. But I am not guilty!" he exclaimed angrily. "What is it for?" And he ceased crying, but turning his face to the wall continued to ponder on the same question: Why, and for what purpose, is there all this horror? But however much he pondered he found no answer. And whenever the thought occurred to him, as it often did, that it all resulted from his not having lived as he ought to have done, he at once recalled the correctness of his whole life and dismissed so strange an idea.

Chapter X

Another fortnight passed. Iván Ilých now no longer left his sofa. He would not lie in bed but lay on the sofa, facing the wall nearly all the time. He suffered ever the same unceasing agonies and in his loneliness pondered always on the same insoluble question: "What is this? Can it be that it is Death?" And the inner voice answered: "Yes, it is Death."

"Why these sufferings?" And the voice answered, "For no reason—
they just are so." Beyond and besides this there was nothing.

From the very beginning of his illness, ever since he had first been to
see the doctor, Iván Ilých's life had been divided between two contrary and
alternating moods: now it was despair and the expectation of this uncompre-
hended and terrible death, and now hope and an intently interested observation of the functioning of his organs. Now before his eyes there was only
a kidney or an intestine that temporarily evaded its duty, and now only that
incomprehensible and dreadful death from which it was impossible to
escape.

These two states of mind had alternated from the very beginning of
his illness, but the further it progressed the more doubtful and fantastic
became the conception of the kidney, and the more real the sense of impending death.

He had but to call to mind what he had been three months before and   5
what he was now, to call to mind with what regularity he had been going
downhill, for every possibility of hope to be shattered.

Latterly during that loneliness in which he found himself as he lay
facing the back of the sofa, a loneliness in the midst of a populous town and
surrounded by numerous acquaintances and relations but that yet could not
have been more complete anywhere—either at the bottom of the sea or
under the earth—during that terrible loneliness Iván Ilých had lived only in
memories of the past. Pictures of his past rose before him one after another.
They always began with what was nearest in time and then went back to
what was most remote—to his childhood—and rested there. If he thought
of the stewed prunes that had been offered him that day, his mind went back
to the raw shrivelled French plums of his childhood, their peculiar flavour
and the flow of saliva when he sucked their stones, and along with the
memory of that taste came a whole series of memories of those days: his
nurse, his brother, and their toys. "No, I mustn't think of that. . . . It is too
painful," Iván Ilých said to himself, and brought himself back to the present—to the button on the back of the sofa and the creases in its morocco.
"Morocco is expensive, but it does not wear well: There had been a quarrel
about it. It was a different kind of quarrel and a different kind of morocco
that time when we tore father's portfolio and were punished, and mamma
brought us some tarts. . . ." And again his thoughts dwelt on his childhood,
and again it was painful and he tried to banish them and fix his mind on
something else.

Then again together with that chain of memories another series passed
through his mind—of how his illness had progressed and grown worse.
There also the further back he looked the more life there had been. There
had been more of what was good in life and more of life itself. The two
merged together. "Just as the pain went on getting worse and worse so my
life grew worse and worse," he thought. "There is one bright spot there at

the back, at the beginning of life, and afterwards all becomes blacker and blacker and proceeds more and more rapidly—in inverse ratio to the square of the distance from death," thought Iván Ilých. And the example of a stone falling downwards with increasing velocity entered his mind. Life, a series of increasing sufferings, flies, further and further towards its end—the most terrible suffering. "I am flying. . . ." He shuddered, shifted himself, and tried to resist, but was already aware that resistance was impossible, and again with eyes weary of gazing but unable to cease seeing what was before them, he stared at the back of the sofa and waited—awaiting that dreadful fall and shock and destruction.

"Resistance is impossible!" he said to himself. "If I could only understand what it is all for! But that too is impossible. An explanation would be possible if it could be said that I have not lived as I ought to. But it is impossible to say that," and he remembered all the legality, correctitude, and propriety of his life. "That at any rate can certainly not be admitted," he thought, and his lips smiled ironically as if someone could see that smile and be taken in by it. "There is no explanation! Agony, death. . . . What for?"

Chapter XI

Another two weeks went by in this way and during that fortnight an event occurred that Iván Ilých and his wife had desired. Petríshchev formally proposed. It happened in the evening. The next day Praskóvya Fēdorovna came into her husband's room considering how best to inform him of it, but that very night there had been a fresh change for the worse in his condition. She found him still lying on the sofa but in a different position. He lay on his back, groaning and staring fixedly straight in front of him.

She began to remind him of his medicines, but he turned his eyes towards her with such a look that she did not finish what she was saying; so great an animosity, to her in particular, did that look express.

"For Christ's sake, let me die in peace!" he said.

She would have gone away, but just then their daughter came in and went up to say good morning. He looked at her as he had done at his wife, and in reply to her inquiry about his health said dryly that he would soon free them all of himself. They were both silent and after sitting with him for a while went away.

"Is it our fault?" Lisa said to her mother. "It's as if we were to blame! I am sorry for papa, but why should we be tortured?"

The doctor came at his usual time. Iván Ilých answered "Yes" and "No," never taking his angry eyes from him, and at last said: "You know you can do nothing for me, so leave me alone."

"We can ease your sufferings."

"You can't even do that. Let me be."

The doctor went into the drawing-room and told Praskóvya Fëdorovna that the case was very serious and that the only resource left was
opium to allay her husband's sufferings, which must be terrible.

It was true, as the doctor said, that Iván Ilých's physical sufferings   10
were terrible, but worse than the physical sufferings were his mental sufferings which were his chief torture.

His mental sufferings were due to the fact that that night, as he looked
at Gerásim's sleepy, good-natured face with its prominent cheek-bones, the
question suddenly occurred to him: "What if my whole life has really been
wrong?"

It occurred to him that what had appeared perfectly impossible before,
namely that he had not spent his life as he should have done, might after all
be true. It occurred to him that his scarcely perceptible attempts to struggle
against what was considered good by the most highly placed people, those
scarcely noticeable impulses which he had immediately suppressed, might
have been the real thing, and all the rest false. And his professional duties
and the whole arrangement of his life and of his family, and all his social and
official interests, might all have been false. He tried to defend all those things
to himself and suddenly felt the weakness of what he was defending. There
was nothing to defend.

"But if that is so," he said to himself, "and I am leaving this life with
the consciousness that I have lost all that was given me and it is impossible
to rectify it — what then?"

He lay on his back and began to pass his life in review in quite a new
way. In the morning when he saw first his footman, then his wife, then his
daughter, and then the doctor, their every word and movement confirmed
to him the awful truth that had been revealed to him during the night. In
them he saw himself — all that for which he had lived — and saw clearly that
it was not real at all, but a terrible and huge deception which had hidden
both life and death. This consciousness intensified his physical suffering
tenfold. He groaned and tossed about, and pulled at his clothing which
choked and stifled him. And he hated them on that account.

He was given a large dose of opium and became unconscious, but at   15
noon his sufferings began again. He drove everybody away and tossed from
side to side.

His wife came to him and said:

"Jean my dear, do this for me. It can't do any harm and often helps.
Healthy people often do it."

He opened his eyes wide.

"What? Take communion? Why? It's unnecessary! However. . . ."

She began to cry.   20

"Yes, do, my dear. I'll send for our priest. He is such a nice man."

"All right. Very well," he muttered.

When the priest came and heard his confession, Iván Ilých was softened
and seemed to feel a relief from his doubts and consequently from his suf-

ferings, and for a moment there came a ray of hope. He again began to think of the vermiform appendix and the possibility of correcting it. He received the sacrament with tears in his eyes.

When they laid him down again afterwards he felt a moment's ease, and the hope that he might live awoke in him again. He began to think of the operation that had been suggested to him. "To live! I want to live!" he said to himself.

His wife came in to congratulate him after his communion, and when uttering the usual conventional words she added:

"You feel better, don't you?"

Without looking at her he said "Yes."

Her dress, her figure, the expression of her face, the tone of her voice, all revealed the same thing. "This is wrong, it is not as it should be. All you have lived for and still live for is falsehood and deception, hiding life and death from you." And as soon as he admitted that thought, his hatred and his agonizing physical suffering again sprang up, and with that suffering a consciousness of the unavoidable, approaching end. And to this was added a new sensation of grinding shooting pain and a feeling of suffocation.

The expression of his face when he uttered that "yes" was dreadful. Having uttered it, he looked her straight in the eyes, turned on his face with a rapidity extraordinary in his weak state and shouted:

"Go away! Go away and leave me alone!"

Chapter XII

From that moment the screaming began that continued for three days, and was so terrible that one could not hear it through two closed doors without horror. At the moment he answered his wife he realized that he was lost, that there was no return, that the end had come, the very end, and his doubts were still unsolved and remained doubts.

"Oh! Oh! Oh!" he cried in various intonations. He had begun by screaming "I won't!" and continued screaming on the letter "o."

For three whole days, during which time did not exist for him, he struggled in that black sack into which he was being thrust by an invisible, resistless force. He struggled as a man condemned to death struggles in the hands of the executioner, knowing that he cannot save himself. And every moment he felt that despite all his efforts he was drawing nearer and nearer to what terrified him. He felt that his agony was due to his being thrust into that black hole and still more to his not being able to get right into it. He was hindered from getting into it by his conviction that his life had been a good one. That very justification of his life held him fast and prevented his moving forward, and it caused him most torment of all.

Suddenly some force struck him in the chest and side, making it still harder to breathe, and he fell through the hole and there at the bottom was a light. What had happened to him was like the sensation one sometimes experiences in a railway carriage when one thinks one is going backwards while one is really going forwards and suddenly becomes aware of the real direction.

"Yes, it was all not the right thing," he said to himself, "but that's no matter. It can be done. But what *is* the right thing?" he asked himself, and suddenly grew quiet.

This occurred at the end of the third day, two hours before his death. Just then his schoolboy son had crept softly in and gone up to the bedside. The dying man was still screaming desperately and waving his arms. His hand fell on the boy's head, and the boy caught it, pressed it to his lips, and began to cry.

At that very moment Iván Ilých fell through and caught sight of the light, and it was revealed to him that though his life had not been what it should have been, this could still be rectified. He asked himself, "What *is* the right thing?" and grew still, listening. Then he felt that someone was kissing his hand. He opened his eyes, looked at his son, and felt sorry for him. His wife came up to him and he glanced at her. She was gazing at him open-mouthed, with undried tears on her nose and cheek and a despairing look on her face. He felt sorry for her too.

"Yes, I am making them wretched," he thought. "They are sorry, but it will be better for them when I die." He wished to say this but had not the strength to utter it. "Besides, why speak? I must act," he thought. With a look at his wife he indicated his son and said: "Take him away . . . sorry for him . . . sorry for you too. . . ." He tried to add, "forgive me," but said "forego" and waved his hand, knowing that He whose understanding mattered would understand.

And suddenly it grew clear to him that what had been oppressing him and would not leave him was all dropping away at once from two sides, from ten sides, and from all sides. He was sorry for them, he must act so as not to hurt them: release them and free himself from these sufferings. "How good and how simple!" he thought. "And the pain?" he asked himself. "What has become of it? Where are you, pain?"

He turned his attention to it.

"Yes, here it is. Well, what of it? Let the pain be."

"And death . . . where is it?"

He sought his former accustomed fear of death and did not find it. "Where is it? What death?" There was no fear because there was no death.

In place of death there was light.

"So that's what it is!" he suddenly exclaimed aloud. "What joy!"

To him all this happened in a single instant, and the meaning of that instant did not change. For those present his agony continued for another two hours. Something rattled in his throat, his emaciated body twitched, then the gasping and rattle became less and less frequent.

"It is finished!" said someone near him.

He heard these words and repeated them in his soul.

"Death is finished," he said to himself. "It is no more!"

He drew in a breath, stopped in the midst of a sigh, stretched out,   20
and died.

Considerations

1. Write a brief summary of each section of the story. Then place these summaries in chronological order and consider how the story would be changed for you if Tolstoy had selected this arrangement rather than beginning with the scene that shows Iván Ilých already dead.
2. List several significant details from Iván Ilých's life prior to the onset of his illness. What values were important to him? Cite specific incidents to support your evaluation.
3. Describe Iván Ilých's relationship with his wife and children, explaining and analyzing how and why that relationship changes at various points during the story.
4. How do the scenes between the doctor and Iván Ilých and the scenes between Gerásim and Iván Ilých suggest his changing values? Explain your response to these changes.
5. Analyze the view of death suggested by this story. To what extent do the final scenes, in particular, suggest horror, defeat, and/or triumph?

ALICE WALKER (1944–   )

To Hell with Dying

"To hell with dying," my father would say. "These children want Mr. Sweet!"

Mr. Sweet was a diabetic and an alcoholic and a guitar player and lived down the road from us on a neglected cotton farm. My older brothers and sisters got the most benefit from Mr. Sweet, for when they were growing up he had quite a few years ahead of him and so was capable of being called back from the brink of death any number of times — whenever the voice of my father reached him as he lay expiring. "To hell with dying, man," my father would say, pushing the wife away from the bedside (in tears although she knew the death was not necessarily the last one unless Mr. Sweet really wanted it to be). "These children want Mr. Sweet!" And they did want him, for at a signal from Father they would come crowding around the bed and throw themselves on the covers, and whoever was the smallest at the time would kiss him all over his wrinkled brown face and tickle him so that he would laugh all down in his stomach, and his mustache, which was long and sort of straggly, would shake like Spanish moss and was also that color.

Mr. Sweet had been ambitious as a boy, wanted to be a doctor or lawyer or sailor, only to find that black men fare better if they are not. Since he could become none of these things he turned to fishing as his only earnest career and playing the guitar as his only claim to doing anything extraordinarily well. His son, the only one that he and his wife, Miss Mary, had, was shiftless as the day is long and spent money as if he were trying to see the bottom of the mint, which Mr. Sweet would tell him was the clean brown palm of his hand. Miss Mary loved her "baby," however, and worked hard to get him the "li'l necessaries" of life, which turned out mostly to be women.

Mr. Sweet was a tall, thinnish man with thick kinky hair going dead white. He was dark brown, his eyes were squinty and sort of bluish, and he chewed Brown Mule tobacco. He was constantly on the verge of being blind drunk, for he brewed his own liquor and was not in the least a stingy sort of man, and was always very melancholy and sad, though frequently when he was "feelin' good" he'd dance around the yard with us, usually keeling over just as my mother came to see what the commotion was.

Toward all of us children he was very kind, and had the grace to be shy with us, which is unusual in grown-ups. He had great respect for my mother for she never held his drunkenness against him and would let us play with him even when he was about to fall in the fireplace from drink. Although Mr. Sweet would sometimes lose complete or nearly complete control of his head and neck so that he would loll in his chair, his mind remained strangely acute and his speech not too affected. His ability to be drunk and sober at the same time made him an ideal playmate, for he was as weak as we were and we could usually best him in wrestling, all the while keeping a fairly coherent conversation going.

We never felt anything of Mr. Sweet's age when we played with him. We loved his wrinkles and would draw some on our brows to be like him, and his white hair was my special treasure and he knew it and would never come to visit us just after he had had his hair cut off at the barbershop. Once he came to our house for something, probably to see my father about fertilizer for his crops because, although he never paid the slightest attention to his crops, he liked to know what things would be best to use on them if he ever did. Anyhow, he had not come with his hair since he had just had it shaved off at the barbershop. He wore a huge straw hat to keep off the sun and also to keep his head away from me. But as soon as I saw him I ran up and demanded that he take me up and kiss me with his funny beard which smelled so strongly of tobacco. Looking forward to burying my small fingers into his woolly hair I threw away his hat only to find he had done something to his hair, that it was no longer there! I let out a squall which made my mother think that Mr. Sweet had finally dropped me in the well or something and from that day I've been wary of men in hats. However, not long after, Mr. Sweet showed up with his hair grown out and just as white and kinky and impenetrable as it ever was.

Mr. Sweet used to call me his princess, and I believed it. He made me feel pretty at five and six, and simply outrageously devastating at the blazing age of eight and a half. When he came to our house with his guitar the whole family would stop whatever they were doing to sit around him and listen to him play. He liked to play "Sweet Georgia Brown," that was what he called me sometimes, and also he liked to play "Caldonia" and all sorts of sweet, sad, wonderful songs which he sometimes made up. It was from one of these songs that I heard that he had had to marry Miss Mary when he had in fact loved somebody else (now living in Chi-ca-go, or De-stroy, Michigan). He was not sure that Joe Lee, her "baby," was also his baby. Sometimes he would cry and that was an indication that he was about to die again. And so we would all get prepared, for we were sure to be called upon.

I was seven the first time I remember actually participating in one of Mr. Sweet's "revivals" — my parents told me I had participated before, I had been the one chosen to kiss him and tickle him long before I knew the rite of Mr. Sweet's rehabilitation. He had come to our house, it was a few years after his wife's death, and was very sad, and also, typically, very drunk. He sat on the floor next to me and my older brother, the rest of the children were grown up and lived elsewhere, and began to play his guitar and cry. I held his woolly head in my arms and wished I could have been old enough to have been the woman he loved so much and that I had not been lost years and years ago.

When he was leaving, my mother said to us that we'd better sleep light that night for we'd probably have to go over to Mr. Sweet's before daylight. And we did. For soon after we had gone to bed one of the neighbors knocked on our door and called my father and said that Mr. Sweet was sinking fast and if he wanted to get in a word before the crossover he'd better shake a leg and get over to Mr. Sweet's house. All the neighbors knew to come to our house if something was wrong with Mr. Sweet, but they did not know how we always managed to make him well, or at least stop him from dying, when he was so often near death. As soon as we heard the cry we got up, my brother and I and my mother and father, and put on our clothes. We hurried out of the house and down the road for we were always afraid that we might someday be too late and Mr. Sweet would get tired of dallying.

When we got to the house, a very poor shack really, we found the front room full of neighbors and relatives and someone met us at the door and said it was all very sad that old Mr. Sweet Little (for Little was his family name, although we mostly ignored it) was about to kick the bucket. My parents were advised not to take my brother and me into the "death room," seeing we were so young and all, but we were so much more accustomed to the death room than he that we ignored him and dashed in without giving his warning a second thought. I was almost in tears, for these deaths upset me fearfully, and the thought of how much depended on me and my brother (who was such a ham most of the time) made me very nervous.

The doctor was bending over the bed and turned back to tell us for at least the tenth time in the history of my family that, alas, old Mr. Sweet Little was dying and that the children had best not see the face of implacable death (I didn't know what "implacable" was, but whatever it was, Mr. Sweet was not!). My father pushed him rather abruptly out of the way saying, as he always did and very loudly for he was saying it to Mr. Sweet, "To hell with dying, man, these children want Mr. Sweet" — which was my cue to throw myself upon the bed and kiss Mr. Sweet all around the whiskers and under the eyes and around the collar of his nightshirt where he smelled so strongly of all sorts of things, mostly liniment.

I was very good at bringing him around, for as soon as I saw that he was struggling to open his eyes I knew he was going to be all right, and so could finish my revival sure of success. As soon as his eyes were open he would begin to smile and that way I knew that I had surely won. Once, though, I got a tremendous scare, for he could not open his eyes and later I learned that he had had a stroke and that one side of his face was stiff and hard to get into motion. When he began to smile I could tickle him in earnest because I was sure that nothing would get in the way of his laughter, although once he began to cough so hard that he almost threw me off his stomach, but that was when I was very small, little more than a baby, and my bushy hair had gotten in his nose.

When we were sure he would listen to us we would ask him why he was in bed and when he was coming to see us again and could we play his guitar, which more than likely would be leaning against the bed. His eyes

10

would get all misty and he would sometimes cry out loud, but we never let it embarrass us, for he knew that we loved him and that we sometimes cried too for no reason. My parents would leave the room to just the three of us; Mr. Sweet, by that time, would be propped up in bed with a number of pillows behind his head and with me sitting and lying on his shoulder and along his chest. Even when he had trouble breathing he would not ask me to get down. Looking into my eyes he would shake his white head and run a scratchy old finger all around my hairline, which was rather low down, nearly to my eyebrows, and made some people say I looked like a baby monkey.

My brother was very generous in all this, he let me do all the revival-ing — he had done it for years before I was born and so was glad to be able to pass it on to someone new. What he would do while I talked to Mr. Sweet was pretend to play the guitar, in fact pretend that he was a young version of Mr. Sweet, and it always made Mr. Sweet glad to think that someone wanted to be like him — of course, we did not know this then, we played the thing by ear, and whatever he seemed to like, we did. We were desperately afraid that he was just going to take off one day and leave us.

It did not occur to us that we were doing anything special; we had not learned that death was final when it did come. We thought nothing of triumphing over it so many times, and in fact became a trifle contemptuous of people who let themselves be carried away. It did not occur to us that if our father had been dying we could not have stopped it, that Mr. Sweet was the only person over whom we had power. 15

When Mr. Sweet was in his eighties I was studying in the university many miles from home. I saw him whenever I went home, but he was never on the verge of dying that I could tell and I began to feel that my anxiety for his health and psychological well-being was unnecessary. By this time he not only had a mustache but a long flowing snow-white beard, which I loved and combed and braided for hours. He was very peaceful, fragile, gentle, and the only jarring note about him was his old steel guitar, which he still played in the old sad, sweet, down-home blues way.

On Mr. Sweet's ninetieth birthday I was finishing my doctorate in Massachusetts and had been making arrangements to go home for several weeks' rest. That morning I got a telegram telling me that Mr. Sweet was dying again and could I please drop everything and come home. Of course I could. My dissertation could wait and my teachers would understand when I explained to them when I got back. I ran to the phone, called the airport, and within four hours I was speeding along the dusty road to Mr. Sweet's.

The house was more dilapidated than when I was last there, barely a shack, but it was overgrown with yellow roses which my family had planted many years ago. The air was heavy and sweet and very peaceful. I felt strange walking through the gate and up the old rickety steps. But the strangeness left me as I caught sight of the long white beard I loved so well flowing down the thin body over the familiar quilt coverlet. Mr. Sweet!

His eyes were closed tight and his hands, crossed over his stomach, were thin and delicate, no longer scratchy. I remembered how always before I had run and jumped up on him just anywhere; now I knew he would not be able to support my weight. I looked around at my parents, and was surprised to see that my father and mother also looked old and frail. My father, his own hair very gray, leaned over the quietly sleeping old man, who, incidentally, smelled still of wine and tobacco, and said, as he'd done so many times, "To hell with dying, man! My daughter is home to see Mr. Sweet!" My brother had not been able to come as he was in the war in Asia. I bent down and gently stroked the closed eyes and gradually they began to open. The closed, wine-stained lips twitched a little, then parted in a warm, slightly embarrassed smile. Mr. Sweet could see me and he recognized me and his eyes looked very spry and twinkly for a moment. I put my head down on the pillow next to his and we just looked at each other for a long time. Then he began to trace my peculiar hairline with a thin, smooth finger. I closed my eyes when his finger halted above my ear (he used to rejoice at the dirt in my ears when I was little), his hand stayed cupped around my cheek. When I opened my eyes, sure that I had reached him in time, his were closed.

Even at twenty-four how could I believe that I had failed? that Mr.   20
Sweet was really gone? He had never gone before. But when I looked at my parents I saw that they were holding back tears. They had loved him dearly. He was like a piece of rare and delicate china which was always being saved from breaking and which finally fell. I looked long at the old face, the wrinkled forehead, the red lips, the hands that still reached out to me. Soon I felt my father pushing something cool into my hands. It was Mr. Sweet's guitar. He had asked them months before to give it to me; he had known that even if I came next time he would not be able to respond in the old way. He did not want me to feel that my trip had been for nothing.

The old guitar! I plucked the strings, hummed "Sweet Georgia Brown." The magic of Mr. Sweet lingered still in the cool steel box. Through the window I could catch the fragrant delicate scent of tender yellow roses. The man on the high old-fashioned bed with the quilt coverlet and the flowing white beard had been my first love.

Considerations

1. What is your response to Mr. Sweet? The mother and father in the story see him as a fine companion to accompany the growing years of their children. Do you agree? Explain.
2. What reasons does the narrator suggest for Mr. Sweet's life choices (including his many "deaths")? What is your response to these reasons?
3. What do the narrator and her brother learn from the many "rescues" they perform? Do you see these lessons as negative? Positive? A combination? Explain.

4. The narrator leaves her dissertation and her classes behind—assuming that her teachers will understand—to rush to the bedside of Mr. Sweet. If you were one of her professors, listening to her explanation, how would you respond? Explain your reasons.

5. What does the narrator learn from her final encounter with Mr. Sweet? Consider the way she sees her parents as well as the way she sees herself. What insights does she seem to have about the relationship between life and death?

YUKIO MISHIMA (1925–1970)

Patriotism

In the twenty-eighth of February, 1936 (on the third day, that is, of the February Incident°) Lieutenant Shinji Takeyama of the Konoe Transport Battalion — profoundly disturbed by the knowledge that his closest colleagues had been with the mutineers from the beginning, and indignant at the imminent prospect of Imperial troops attacking Imperial troops — took his officer's sword and ceremonially disemboweled himself in the eight-mat room of his private residence in the sixth block of Aoba-chō, in Yotsuya Ward. His wife, Reiko, followed him, stabbing herself to death. The lieutenant's farewell note consisted of one sentence: "Long live the Imperial Forces." His wife's, after apologies for her unfilial conduct in thus preceding her parents to the grave, concluded: "The day which, for a soldier's wife, had to come, has come. . . ." The last moments of this heroic and dedicated couple were such as to make the gods themselves weep. The lieutenant's age, it should be noted, was thirty-one, his wife's twenty-three; and it was not half a year since the celebration of their marriage.

2

Those who saw the bride and bridegroom in the commemorative photograph — perhaps no less than those actually present at the lieutenant's wedding — had exclaimed in wonder at the bearing of this handsome couple. The lieutenant, majestic in military uniform, stood protectively beside his bride, his right hand resting upon his sword, his officer's cap held at his left side. His expression was severe, and his dark brows and wide-gazing eyes well conveyed the clear integrity of youth. For the beauty of the bride in her white over-robe no comparisons were adequate. In the eyes, round beneath soft brows, in the slender, finely shaped nose, and in the full lips, there was both sensuousness and refinement. One hand, emerging shyly from a sleeve of the over-robe, held a fan, and the tips of the fingers, clustering delicately, were like the bud of a moonflower.

After the suicide, people would take out this photograph and examine it, and sadly reflect that too often there was a curse on these seemingly flawless unions. Perhaps it was no more than imagination, but looking at the picture after the tragedy it almost seemed as if the two young people before the gold-lacquered screen were gazing, each with equal clarity, at the deaths which lay before them.

Thanks to the good offices of their go-between, Lieutenant General Ozeki, they had been able to set themselves up in a new home at Aoba-chō

February Incident: On February 26, 1936, a group of young officers of the Imperial troops of Japan led an attempted coup. For several days, the rebels occupied government offices in Tokyo and executed several government officials. The coup attempt ultimately failed, and its leaders were executed.

in Yotsuya. "New home" is perhaps misleading. It was an old three-room rented house backing onto a small garden. As neither the six- nor the four-and-a-half-mat room downstairs was favored by the sun, they used the upstairs eight-mat room as both bedroom and guest room. There was no maid, so Reiko was left alone to guard the house in her husband's absence.

The honeymoon trip was dispensed with on the grounds that these   5 were times of national emergency. The two of them had spent the first night of their marriage at this house. Before going to bed, Shinji, sitting erect on the floor with his sword laid before him, had bestowed upon his wife a soldierly lecture. A woman who had become the wife of a soldier should know and resolutely accept that her husband's death might come at any moment. It could be tomorrow. It could be the day after. But, no matter when it came — he asked — was she steadfast in her resolve to accept it? Reiko rose to her feet, pulled open a drawer of the cabinet, and took out what was the most prized of her new possessions, the dagger her mother had given her. Returning to her place, she laid the dagger without a word on the mat before her, just as her husband had laid his sword. A silent understanding was achieved at once and the lieutenant never again sought to test his wife's resolve.

In the first few months of her marriage Reiko's beauty grew daily more radiant, shining serene like the moon after rain.

As both were possessed of young, vigorous bodies, their relationship was passionate. Nor was this merely a matter of the night. On more than one occasion, returning home straight from maneuvers, and begrudging even the time it took to remove his mud-splashed uniform, the lieutenant had pushed his wife to the floor almost as soon as he had entered the house. Reiko was equally ardent in her response. For a little more or a little less than a month, from the first night of their marriage Reiko knew happiness, and the lieutenant, seeing this, was happy too.

Reiko's body was white and pure, and her swelling breasts conveyed a firm and chaste refusal; but, upon consent, those breasts were lavish with their intimate, welcoming warmth. Even in bed these two were frighteningly and awesomely serious. In the very midst of wild, intoxicating passions, their hearts were sober and serious.

By day the lieutenant would think of his wife in the brief rest periods between training; and all day long, at home, Reiko would recall the image of her husband. Even when apart, however, they had only to look at the wedding photograph for their happiness to be once more confirmed. Reiko felt not the slightest surprise that a man who had been a complete stranger until a few months ago should now have become the sun about which her whole world revolved.

All these things had a moral basis, and were in accordance with   10 the Education Rescript's° injunction that "husband and wife should be

Education Rescript: A code of behavior first instituted during the reign of Emperor Mutsuhito (1867–1912).

harmonious." Not once did Reiko contradict her husband, nor did the lieutenant ever find reason to scold his wife. On the god shelf below the stairway, alongside the tablet from the Great Ise Shrine,° were set photographs
of their Imperial Majesties, and regularly every morning, before leaving for
duty, the lieutenant would stand with his wife at this hallowed place and together they would bow their heads low. The offering water was renewed each
morning, and the sacred sprig of *sasaki* was always green and fresh. Their
lives were lived beneath the solemn protection of the gods and were filled
with an intense happiness which set every fiber in their bodies trembling.

3

Although Lord Privy Seal Saitō's house was in their neighborhood,
neither of them heard any noise of gunfire on the morning of February 26.
It was a bugle, sounding muster in the dim, snowy dawn, when the ten-
minute tragedy had already ended, which first disrupted the lieutenant's
slumbers. Leaping at once from his bed, and without speaking a word, the
lieutenant donned his uniform, buckled on the sword held ready for him by
his wife, and hurried swiftly out into the snow-covered streets of the still
darkened morning. He did not return until the evening of the twenty-eighth.

Later, from the radio news, Reiko learned the full extent of this sudden
eruption of violence. Her life throughout the subsequent two days was lived
alone, in complete tranquility, and behind locked doors.

In the lieutenant's face, as he hurried silently out into the snowy morning, Reiko had read the determination to die. If her husband did not return,
her own decision was made: she too would die. Quietly she attended to the
disposition of her personal possessions. She chose her sets of visiting kimonos as keepsakes for friends of her schooldays, and she wrote a name and
address on the stiff paper wrapping in which each was folded. Constantly
admonished by her husband never to think of the morrow, Reiko had not
even kept a diary and was now denied the pleasure of assiduously rereading
her record of the happiness of the past few months and consigning each page
to the fire as she did so. Ranged across the top of the radio were a small
china dog, a rabbit, a squirrel, a bear, and a fox. There were also a small
vase and a water pitcher. These comprised Reiko's one and only collection.
But it would hardly do, she imagined, to give such things as keepsakes. Nor
again would it be quite proper to ask specifically for them to be included in
the coffin. It seemed to Reiko, as these thoughts passed through her mind,
that the expressions on the small animals' faces grew even more lost and
forlorn.

Reiko took the squirrel in her hand and looked at it. And then, her
thoughts turning to a realm far beyond these childlike affections, she gazed
up into the distance at the great sunlike principle which her husband embod-

---

Great Ise Shrine: The emperor's ancestors are buried in this shrine, giving it special significance.

ied. She was ready, and happy, to be hurtled along to her destruction in that gleaming sun chariot—but now, for these few moments of solitude, she allowed herself to luxuriate in this innocent attachment to trifles. The time when she had genuinely loved these things, however, was long past. Now she merely loved the memory of having once loved them, and their place in her heart had been filled by more intense passions, by a more frenzied happiness. . . . For Reiko had never, even to herself, thought of those soaring joys of the flesh as a mere pleasure. The February cold, and the icy touch of the china squirrel, had numbed Reiko's slender fingers; yet, even so, in her lower limbs, beneath the ordered repetition of the pattern which crossed the skirt of her trim *meisen* kimono, she could feel now, as she thought of the lieutenant's powerful arms reaching out toward her, a hot moistness of the flesh which defied the snows.

She was not in the least afraid of the death hovering in her mind. Waiting alone at home, Reiko firmly believed that everything her husband was feeling or thinking now, his anguish and distress, was leading her—just as surely as the power in his flesh—to a welcome death. She felt as if her body could melt away with ease and be transformed to the merest fraction of her husband's thought. 15

Listening to the frequent announcements on the radio, she heard the names of several of her husband's colleagues mentioned among those of the insurgents. This was news of death. She followed the developments closely, wondering anxiously, as the situation became daily more irrevocable, why no Imperial ordinance was sent down, and watching what had at first been taken as a movement to restore the nation's honor come gradually to be branded with the infamous name of mutiny. There was no communication from the regiment. At any moment, it seemed, fighting might commence in the city streets where the remains of the snow still lay.

Toward sundown on the twenty-eighth Reiko was startled by a furious pounding on the front door. She hurried downstairs. As she pulled with fumbling fingers at the bolt, the shape dimly outlined beyond the frosted-glass panel made no sound, but she knew it was her husband. Reiko had never known the bolt on the sliding door to be so stiff. Still it resisted. The door just would not open.

In a moment, almost before she knew she had succeeded, the lieutenant was standing before her on the cement floor inside the porch, muffled in a khaki greatcoat, his top boots heavy with slush from the street. Closing the door behind him, he returned the bolt once more to its socket. With what significance, Reiko did not understand.

"Welcome home."

Reiko bowed deeply, but her husband made no response. As he had already unfastened his sword and was about to remove his greatcoat, Reiko moved around behind to assist. The coat, which was cold and damp and had lost the odor of horse dung it normally exuded when exposed to the sun, weighed heavily upon her arm. Draping it across a hanger, and cradling the 20 sword and leather belt in her sleeves, she waited while her husband removed his top boots and then followed behind him into the "living room." This was the six-mat room downstairs.

Seen in the clear light from the lamp, her husband's face, covered with a heavy growth of bristle, was almost unrecognizably wasted and thin. The cheeks were hollow, their luster and resilience gone. In his normal good spirits he would have changed into old clothes as soon as he was home and have pressed her to get supper at once, but now he sat before the table still in his uniform, his head dropping dejectedly. Reiko refrained from asking whether she should prepare the supper.

After an interval the lieutenant spoke.

"I knew nothing. They hadn't asked me to join. Perhaps out of consideration, because I was newly married. Kano, and Homma too, and Yamaguchi."

Reiko recalled momentarily the faces of high-spirited young officers, friends of her husband, who had come to the house occasionally as guests.

"There may be an Imperial ordinance sent down tomorrow. They'll be posted as rebels, I imagine. I shall be in command of a unit with orders to attack them. . . . I can't do it. It's impossible to do a thing like that."

He spoke again.

"They've taken me off guard duty, and I have permission to return home for one night. Tomorrow morning, without question, I must leave to join the attack. I can't do it, Reiko."

Reiko sat erect with lowered eyes. She understood clearly that her husband had spoken of his death. The lieutenant was resolved. Each word, being rooted in death, emerged sharply and with powerful significance against this dark, unmovable background. Although the lieutenant was speaking of his dilemma, already there was no room in his mind for vacillation.

However, there was a clarity, like the clarity of a stream fed from melting snows, in the silence which rested between them. Sitting in his own home after the long two-day ordeal, and looking across at the face of his beautiful wife, the lieutenant was for the first time experiencing true peace of mind. For he had at once known, though she said nothing, that his wife divined the resolve which lay beneath his words.

"Well, then . . ." The lieutenant's eyes opened wide. Despite his exhaustion they were strong and clear, and now for the first time they looked straight into the eyes of his wife. "Tonight I shall cut my stomach."

Reiko did not flinch.

Her round eyes showed tension, as taut as the clang of a bell.

"I am ready," she said. "I ask permission to accompany you."

The lieutenant felt almost mesmerized by the strength in those eyes. His words flowed swiftly and easily, like the utterances of a man in delirium, and it was beyond his understanding how permission in a matter of such weight could be expressed so casually.

"Good. We'll go together. But I want you as a witness, first, for my   35
own suicide. Agreed?"

When this was said a sudden release of abundant happiness welled up
in both their hearts. Reiko was deeply affected by the greatness of her
husband's trust in her. It was vital for the lieutenant, whatever else might
happen, that there should be no irregularity in his death. For that reason
there had to be a witness. The fact that he had chosen his wife for this was
the first mark of his trust. The second, and even greater mark, was that
though he had pledged that they should die together he did not intend to kill
his wife first — he had deferred her death to a time when he would no longer
be there to verify it. If the lieutenant had been a suspicious husband, he
would doubtless, as in the usual suicide pact, have chosen to kill his wife
first.

When Reiko said, "I ask permission to accompany you," the lieutenant
felt these words to be the final fruit of the education which he had himself
given his wife, starting on the first night of their marriage, and which had
schooled her, when the moment came, to say what had to be said without a
shadow of hesitation. This flattered the lieutenant's opinion of himself as a
self-reliant man. He was not so romantic or conceited as to imagine that the
words were spoken spontaneously, out of love for her husband.

With happiness welling almost too abundantly in their hearts, they
could not help smiling at each other. Reiko felt as if she had returned to her
wedding night.

Before her eyes was neither pain nor death. She seemed to see only a
free and limitless expanse opening out into vast distances.

"The water is hot. Will you take your bath now?"   40

"Ah yes, of course."

"And supper . . . ?"

The words were delivered in such level, domestic tones that the lieutenant came near to thinking, for the fraction of a second, that everything
had been a hallucination.

"I don't think we'll need supper. But perhaps you could warm some
sake?"

"As you wish."   45

As Reiko rose and took a *tanzen* gown from the cabinet for after the
bath, she purposely directed her husband's attention to the opened drawer.
The lieutenant rose, crossed to the cabinet, and looked inside. From the
ordered array of paper wrappings he read, one by one, the addresses of the
keepsakes. There was no grief in the lieutenant's response to this demonstration of heroic resolve. His heart was filled with tenderness. Like a husband
who is proudly shown the childish purchases of a young wife, the lieutenant,
overwhelmed by affection, lovingly embraced his wife from behind and
implanted a kiss upon her neck.

Reiko felt the roughness of the lieutenant's unshaven skin against her
neck. This sensation, more than being just a thing of this world, was for

Reiko almost the world itself, but now—with the feeling that it was soon to be lost forever—it had freshness beyond all her experience. Each moment had its own vital strength, and the senses in every corner of her body were reawakened. Accepting her husband's caresses from behind, Reiko raised herself on the tips of her toes, letting the vitality seep through her entire body.

"First the bath, and then, after some sake . . . lay out the bedding upstairs, will you?"

The lieutenant whispered the words into his wife's ear. Reiko silently nodded.

Flinging off his uniform, the lieutenant went to the bath. To faint background noises of slopping water Reiko tended the charcoal brazier in the living room and began preparations for warming the sake. 50

Taking the *tanzen,* a sash, and some underclothes, she went to the bathroom to ask how the water was. In the midst of a coiling cloud of steam the lieutenant was sitting cross-legged on the floor, shaving, and she could dimly discern the rippling movements of the muscles on his damp, powerful back as they responded to the movement of his arms.

There was nothing to suggest a time of any special significance. Reiko, going busily about her tasks, was preparing side dishes from odds and ends in stock. Her hands did not tremble. If anything, she managed even more efficiently and smoothly than usual. From time to time, it is true, there was a strange throbbing deep within her breast. Like distant lightning, it had a moment of sharp intensity and then vanished without trace. Apart from that, nothing was in any way out of the ordinary.

The lieutenant, shaving in the bathroom, felt his warmed body miraculously healed at last of the desperate tiredness of the days of indecision and filled—in spite of the death which lay ahead—with pleasurable anticipation. The sound of his wife going about her work came to him faintly. A healthy physical craving, submerged for two days, reasserted itself.

The lieutenant was confident there had been no impurity in that joy they had experienced when resolving upon death. They had both sensed at that moment—though not, of course, in any clear and conscious way—that those permissible pleasures which they shared in private were once more beneath the protection of Righteousness and Divine Power, and of a complete and unassailable morality. On looking into each other's eyes and discovering there an honorable death, they had felt themselves safe once more behind steel walls which none could destroy, encased in an impenetrable armor of Beauty and Truth. Thus, so far from seeing any inconsistency or conflict between the urges of his flesh and the sincerity of his patriotism, the lieutenant was even able to regard the two as parts of the same thing.

Thrusting his face close to the dark, cracked, misted wall mirror, the lieutenant shaved himself with great care. This would be his death face. There must be no unsightly blemishes. The clean-shaven face gleamed once more with a youthful luster, seeming to brighten the darkness of the mirror. 55

There was a certain elegance, he even felt, in the association of death with this radiantly healthy face.

Just as it looked now, this would become his death face! Already, in fact, it had half departed from the lieutenant's personal possession and had become the bust above a dead soldier's memorial. As an experiment he closed his eyes tight. Everything was wrapped in blackness, and he was no longer a living, seeing creature.

Returning from the bath, the traces of the shave glowing faintly blue beneath his smooth cheeks, he seated himself beside the now well-kindled charcoal brazier. Busy though Reiko was, he noticed, she had found time lightly to touch up her face. Her cheeks were gay and her lips moist. There was no shadow of sadness to be seen. Truly, the lieutenant felt, as he saw this mark of his young wife's passionate nature, he had chosen the wife he ought to have chosen.

As soon as the lieutenant had drained his sake cup he offered it to Reiko. Reiko had never before tasted sake, but she accepted without hesitation and sipped timidly.

"Come here," the lieutenant said.

Reiko moved to her husband's side and was embraced as she leaned   60
backward across his lap. Her breast was in violent commotion, as if sadness, joy, and the potent sake were mingling and reacting within her. The lieutenant looked down into his wife's face. It was the last face he would see in this world, the last face he would see of his wife. The lieutenant scrutinized the face minutely, with the eyes of a traveler bidding farewell to splendid vistas which he will never revisit. It was a face he could not tire of looking at — the features regular yet not cold, the lips lightly closed with a soft strength. The lieutenant kissed those lips, unthinkingly. And suddenly, though there was not the slightest distortion of the face into the unsightliness of sobbing, he noticed that tears were welling slowly from beneath the long lashes of the closed eyes and brimming over into a glistening stream.

When, a little later, the lieutenant urged that they should move to the upstairs bedroom, his wife replied that she would follow after taking a bath. Climbing the stairs alone to the bedroom, where the air was already warmed by the gas heater, the lieutenant lay down on the bedding with arms outstretched and legs apart. Even the time at which he lay waiting for his wife to join him was no later and no earlier than usual.

He folded his hands beneath his head and gazed at the dark boards of the ceiling in the dimness beyond the range of the standard lamp. Was it death he was now waiting for? Or a wild ecstasy of the senses? The two seemed to overlap, almost as if the object of this bodily desire was death itself. But, however that might be, it was certain that never before had the lieutenant tasted such total freedom.

There was the sound of a car outside the window. He could hear the screech of its tires skidding in the snow piled at the side of the street. The sound of its horn re-echoed from near-by walls. . . . Listening to these noises he had the feeling that this house rose like a solitary island in the ocean of a society going as restlessly about its business as ever. All around, vastly and untidily, stretched the country for which he grieved. He was to give his life for it. But would that great country, with which he was prepared to remonstrate to the extent of destroying himself, take the slightest heed of his death? He did not know; and it did not matter. His was a battlefield without glory, a battlefield where none could display deeds of valor: it was the front line of the spirit.

Reiko's footsteps sounded on the stairway. The steep stairs in this old house creaked badly. There were fond memories in that creaking, and many a time, while waiting in bed, the lieutenant had listened to its welcome sound. At the thought that he would hear it no more he listened with intense concentration, striving for every corner of every moment of this precious time to be filled with the sound of those soft footfalls on the creaking stairway. The moments seemed transformed to jewels, sparkling with inner light.

Reiko wore a Nagoya sash about the waist of her *yukata,* but as the   65
lieutenant reached toward it, its redness sobered by the dimness of the light, Reiko's hand moved to his assistance and the sash fell away, slithering swiftly to the floor. As she stood before him, still in her *yukata,* the lieutenant inserted his hands through the side slits beneath each sleeve, intending to embrace her as she was; but at the touch of his finger tips upon the warm naked flesh, and as the armpits closed gently about his hands, his whole body was suddenly aflame.

In a few moments the two lay naked before the glowing gas heater.

Neither spoke the thought, but their hearts, their bodies, and their pounding breasts blazed with the knowledge that this was the very last time. It was as if the words "The Last Time" were spelled out, in invisible brush-strokes, across every inch of their bodies.

The lieutenant drew his wife close and kissed her vehemently. As their tongues explored each other's mouths, reaching out into the smooth, moist interior, they felt as if the still unknown agonies of death had tempered their senses to the keenness of red-hot steel. The agonies they could not yet feel, the distant pains of death, had refined their awareness of pleasure.

"This is the last time I shall see your body," said the lieutenant. "Let me look at it closely." And, tilting the shade on the lampstand to one side, he directed the rays along the full length of Reiko's outstretched form.

Reiko lay still with her eyes closed. The light from the low lamp   70
clearly revealed the majestic sweep of her white flesh. The lieutenant, not without a touch of egocentricity, rejoiced that he would never see this beauty crumble in death.

At his leisure, the lieutenant allowed the unforgettable spectacle to engrave itself upon his mind. With one hand he fondled the hair, with the other he softly stroked the magnificent face, implanting kisses here and there where his eyes lingered. The quiet coldness of the high, tapering forehead, the closed eyes with their long lashes beneath faintly etched brows, the set of the finely shaped nose, the gleam of teeth glimpsed between full, regular lips, the soft cheeks and the small, wise chin . . . these things conjured up in the lieutenant's mind the vision of a truly radiant death face, and again and again he pressed his lips tight against the white throat — where Reiko's own hand was soon to strike — and the throat reddened faintly beneath his kisses. Returning to the mouth he laid his lips against it with the gentlest of pressures, and moved them rhythmically over Reiko's with the light rolling motion of a small boat. If he closed his eyes, the world became a rocking cradle.

Wherever the lieutenant's eyes moved his lips faithfully followed. The high, swelling breasts, surmounted by nipples like the buds of a wild cherry, hardened as the lieutenant's lips closed about them. The arms flowed smoothly downward from each side of the breast, tapering toward the wrists, yet losing nothing of their roundness or symmetry, and at their tips were those delicate fingers which had held the fan at the wedding ceremony. One by one, as the lieutenant kissed them, the fingers withdrew behind their neighbor as if in shame. . . . The natural hollow curving between the bosom and the stomach carried in its lines a suggestion not only of softness but of resilient strength, and while it gave forewarning of the rich curves spreading outward from here to the hips it had, in itself, an appearance only of restraint and proper discipline. The whiteness and richness of the stomach and hips was like milk brimming in a great bowl, and the sharply shadowed dip of the navel could have been the fresh impress of a raindrop, fallen there that very moment. Where the shadows gathered more thickly, hair clustered, gentle and sensitive, and as the agitation mounted in the now no longer passive body there hung over this region a scent like the smoldering of fragrant blossoms, growing steadily more pervasive.

At length, in a tremulous voice, Reiko spoke.

"Show me. . . . Let me look too, for the last time."

Never before had he heard from his wife's lips so strong and unequiv- 75 ocal a request. It was as if something which her modesty had wished to keep hidden to the end had suddenly burst its bonds of constraint. The lieutenant obediently lay back and surrendered himself to his wife. Lithely she raised her white, trembling body, and — burning with an innocent desire to return to her husband what he had done for her — placed two white fingers on the lieutenant's eyes, which gazed fixedly up at her, and gently stroked them shut.

Suddenly overwhelmed by tenderness, her cheeks flushed by a dizzying uprush of emotion, Reiko threw her arms about the lieutenant's close-cropped head. The bristly hairs rubbed painfully against her breast, the prominent nose was cold as it dug into her flesh, and his breath was hot. Relaxing her embrace, she gazed down at her husband's masculine face. The severe brows, the closed eyes, the splendid bridge of the nose, the shapely lips drawn firmly together . . . the blue, cleanshaven cheeks reflecting the light and gleaming smoothly. Reiko kissed each of these. She kissed the broad nape of the neck, the strong, erect shoulders, the powerful chest with its twin circles like shields and its russet nipples. In the armpits, deeply shadowed by the ample flesh of the shoulders and chest, a sweet and melancholy odor emanated from the growth of hair, and in the sweetness of this odor was contained, somehow, the essence of young death. The lieutenant's naked skin glowed like a field of barley, and everywhere the muscles showed in sharp relief, converging on the lower abdomen about the small, unassuming navel. Gazing at the youthful, firm stomach, modestly covered by a vigorous growth of hair, Reiko thought of it as it was soon to be, cruelly cut by the sword, and she laid her head upon it, sobbing in pity, and bathed it with kisses.

At the touch of his wife's tears upon his stomach the lieutenant felt ready to endure with courage the cruelest agonies of his suicide.

What ecstasies they experienced after these tender exchanges may well be imagined. The lieutenant raised himself and enfolded his wife in a powerful embrace, her body now limp with exhaustion after her grief and tears. Passionately they held their faces close, rubbing cheek against cheek. Reiko's body was trembling. Their breasts, moist with sweat, were tightly joined, and every inch of the young and beautiful bodies had become so much one with the other that it seemed impossible there should ever again be a separation. Reiko cried out. From the heights they plunged into the abyss, and from the abyss they took wing and soared once more to dizzying heights. The lieutenant panted like the regimental standard-bearer on a route march. . . . As one cycle ended, almost immediately a new wave of passion would be generated, and together—with no trace of fatigue—they would climb again in a single breathless movement to the very summit.

4

When the lieutenant at last turned away, it was not from weariness. For one thing, he was anxious not to undermine the considerable strength he would need in carrying out his suicide. For another, he would have been sorry to mar the sweetness of these last memories by overindulgence.

Since the lieutenant had clearly desisted, Reiko too, with her usual compliance, followed his example. The two lay naked on their backs, with fingers interlaced, staring fixedly at the dark ceiling. The room was warm from the heater, and even when the sweat had ceased to pour from their bodies they felt no cold. Outside, in the hushed night, the sounds of passing traffic had ceased. Even the noises of the trains and streetcars around Yotsuya station did not penetrate this far. After echoing through the region bounded by the moat, they were lost in the heavily wooded park fronting the broad

driveway before Akasaka Palace. It was hard to believe in the tension gripping this whole quarter, where the two factions of the bitterly divided
Imperial Army now confronted each other, poised for battle.

Savoring the warmth glowing within themselves, they lay still and
recalled the ecstasies they had just known. Each moment of the experience
was relived. They remembered the taste of kisses which had never wearied,
the touch of naked flesh, episode after episode of dizzying bliss. But already,
from the dark boards of the ceiling, the face of death was peering down.
These joys had been final, and their bodies would never know them again.
Not that joy of this intensity — and the same thought had occurred to them
both — was ever likely to be reexperienced, even if they should live on to
old age.

The feel of their fingers intertwined — this too would soon be lost.
Even the wood-grain patterns they now gazed at on the dark ceiling boards
would be taken from them. They could feel death edging in, nearer and
nearer. There could be no hesitation now. They must have the courage to
reach out to death themselves, and to seize it.

"Well, let's make our preparations," said the lieutenant. The note of
determination in the words was unmistakable, but at the same time Reiko
had never heard her husband's voice so warm and tender.

After they had risen, a variety of tasks awaited them.

The lieutenant, who had never once before helped with the bedding, 85
now cheerfully slid back the door of the closet, lifted the mattress across the
room by himself, and stowed it away inside.

Reiko turned off the gas heater and put away the lamp standard. During the lieutenant's absence she had arranged this room carefully, sweeping
and dusting it to a fresh cleanness, and now — if one overlooked the rose-
wood table drawn into one corner — the eight-mat room gave all the appearance of a reception room ready to welcome an important guest.

"We've seen some drinking here, haven't we? With Kanō and Homma
and Noguchi. . . ."

"Yes, they were great drinkers, all of them."

"We'll be meeting them before long, in the other world. They'll tease
us, I imagine, when they find I've brought you with me."

Descending the stairs, the lieutenant turned to look back into this calm 90
clean room, now brightly illuminated by the ceiling lamp. There floated
across his mind the faces of the young officers who had drunk there, and
laughed, and innocently bragged. He had never dreamed then that he would
one day cut open his stomach in this room.

In the two rooms downstairs husband and wife busied themselves
smoothly and serenely with their respective preparations. The lieutenant
went to the toilet, and then to the bathroom to wash. Meanwhile Reiko
folded away her husband's padded robe, placed his uniform tunic, his trousers, and a newly cut bleached loincloth in the bathroom, and set out sheets

of paper on the living-room table for the farewell notes. Then she removed the lid from the writing box and began rubbing ink from the ink tablet. She had already decided upon the wording of her own note.

Reiko's fingers pressed hard upon the cold gilt letters of the ink tablet, and the water in the shallow well at once darkened, as if a black cloud had spread across it. She stopped thinking that this repeated action, this pressure from her fingers, this rise and fall of faint sound, was all and solely for death. It was a routine domestic task, a simple paring away of time until death should finally stand before her. But somehow, in the increasingly smooth motion of the tablet rubbing on the stone, and in the scent from the thickening ink, there was unspeakable darkness.

Neat in his uniform, which he now wore next to his skin, the lieutenant emerged from the bathroom. Without a word he seated himself at the table, bolt upright, took a brush in his hand, and stared undecidedly at the paper before him.

Reiko took a white silk kimono with her and entered the bathroom. When she reappeared in the living room, clad in the white kimono and with her face lightly made up, the farewell note lay completed on the table beneath the lamp. The thick black brushstrokes said simply:

"Long Live the Imperial Forces—Army Lieutenant Takeyama Shinji."   95

While Reiko sat opposite him writing her own note, the lieutenant gazed in silence, intensely serious, at the controlled movement of his wife's pale fingers as they manipulated the brush.

With their respective notes in their hands—the lieutenant's sword strapped to his side, Reiko's small dagger thrust into the sash of her white kimono—the two of them stood before the god shelf and silently prayed. Then they put out all the downstairs lights. As he mounted the stairs the lieutenant turned his head and gazed back at the striking, white-clad figure of his wife, climbing behind him, with lowered eyes, from the darkness beneath.

The farewell notes were laid side by side in the alcove of the upstairs room. They wondered whether they ought not to remove the hanging scroll, but since it had been written by their go-between, Lieutenant General Ozeki, and consisted, moreover, of two Chinese characters signifying "Sincerity," they left it where it was. Even if it were to become stained with splashes of blood, they felt that the lieutenant general would understand.

The lieutenant sitting erect with his back to the alcove, laid his sword on the floor before him.

Reiko sat facing him, a mat's width away. With the rest of her so   100
severely white the touch of rouge on her lips seemed remarkably seductive.

Across the dividing mat they gazed intently into each other's eyes. The lieutenant's sword lay before his knees. Seeing it, Reiko recalled their first night and was overwhelmed with sadness. The lieutenant spoke, in a hoarse voice:

"As I have no second to help me I shall cut deep. It may look un,
ant, but please do not panic. Death of any sort is a fearful thing to w.
You must not be discouraged by what you see. Is that all right?"

"Yes."

Reiko nodded deeply.

Looking at the slender white figure of his wife the lieutenant experienced a bizarre excitement. What he was about to perform was an act in his
public capacity as a soldier, something he had never previously shown his
wife. It called for a resolution equal to the courage to enter battle; it was a
death of no less degree and quality than death in the front line. It was his
conduct on the battlefield that he was now to display.

Momentarily the thought led the lieutenant to a strange fantasy. A
lonely death on the battlefield, a death beneath the eyes of his beautiful wife
. . . in the sensation that he was now to die in these two dimensions, realizing an impossible union of them both, there was sweetness beyond words.
This must be the very pinnacle of good fortune, he thought. To have every
moment of his death observed by those beautiful eyes — it was like being
borne to death on a gentle, fragrant breeze. There was some special favor
here. He did not understand precisely what it was, but it was a domain
unknown to others: a dispensation granted to no one else had been permitted
to himself. In the radiant, bridelike figure of his white-robed wife the lieutenant seemed to see a vision of all those things he had loved and for which
he was to lay down his life — the Imperial Household, the Nation, the Army
Flag. All these, no less than the wife who sat before him, were presences
observing him closely with clear and never-faltering eyes.

Reiko too was gazing intently at her husband, so soon to die, and she
thought that never in this world had she seen anything so beautiful. The
lieutenant always looked well in uniform, but now, as he contemplated death
with severe brows and firmly closed lips, he revealed what was perhaps
masculine beauty at its most superb.

"It's time to go," the lieutenant said at last.

Reiko bent her body low to the mat in a deep bow. She could not raise
her face. She did not wish to spoil her make-up with tears, but the tears
could not be held back.

When at length she looked up she saw hazily through the tears that her
husband had wound a white bandage around the blade of his now unsheathed sword, leaving five or six inches of naked steel showing at the
point.

Resting the sword in its cloth wrapping on the mat before him, the
lieutenant rose from his knees, resettled himself cross-legged, and unfastened the hooks of his uniform collar. His eyes no longer saw his wife.
Slowly, one by one, he undid the flat brass buttons. The dusky brown chest
was revealed, and then the stomach. He unclasped his belt and undid the
buttons of his trousers. The pure whiteness of the thickly coiled loincloth

showed itself. The lieutenant pushed the cloth down with both hands, further to ease his stomach, and then reached for the white-bandaged blade of his sword. With his left hand he massaged his abdomen, glancing downward as he did so.

To reassure himself on the sharpness of his sword's cutting edge the lieutenant folded back the left trouser flap, exposing a little of his thigh, and lightly drew the blade across the skin. Blood welled up in the wound at once, and several streaks of red trickled downward, glistening in the strong light.

It was the first time Reiko had ever seen her husband's blood, and she felt a violent throbbing in her chest. She looked at her husband's face. The lieutenant was looking at the blood with calm appraisal. For a moment — though thinking at the same time that it was hollow comfort — Reiko experienced a sense of relief.

The lieutenant's eyes fixed his wife with an intense, hawk-like stare. Moving the sword around to his front, he raised himself slightly on his hips and let the upper half of his body lean over the sword point. That he was mustering his whole strength was apparent from the angry tension of the uniform at his shoulders. The lieutenant aimed to strike deep into the left of his stomach. His sharp cry pierced the silence of the room.

Despite the effort he had himself put into the blow, the lieutenant had the impression that someone else had struck the side of his stomach agonizingly with a thick rod of iron. For a second or so his head reeled and he had no idea what had happened. The five or six inches of naked point had vanished completely into his flesh, and the white bandage, gripped in his clenched fist, pressed directly against his stomach. 115

He returned to consciousness. The blade had certainly pierced the wall of the stomach, he thought. His breathing was difficult, his chest thumped violently, and in some far deep region, which he could hardly believe was a part of himself, a fearful and excruciating pain came welling up as if the ground had split open to disgorge a boiling stream of molten rock. The pain came suddenly nearer, with terrifying speed. The lieutenant bit his lower lip and stifled an instinctive moan.

Was this *seppuku?* — he was thinking. It was a sensation of utter chaos, as if the sky had fallen on his head and the world was reeling drunkenly. His will power and courage, which had seemed so robust before he made the incision, had now dwindled to something like a single hairlike thread of steel, and he was assailed by the uneasy feeling that he must advance along this thread, clinging to it with desperation. His clenched fist had grown moist. Looking down, he saw that both his hand and the cloth were drenched in blood. His loincloth too was dyed a deep red. It struck him as incredible that, amidst this terrible agony, things which could be seen could still be seen, and existing things existed still.

The moment the lieutenant thrust the sword into his left side and she saw the deathly pallor fall across his face, like an abruptly lowered curtain,

Reiko had to struggle to prevent herself from rushing to his side. Whatever happened, she must watch. She must be a witness. That was the duty her husband had lain upon her. Opposite her, a mat's space away, she could clearly see her husband biting his lip to stifle the pain. The pain was there, with absolute certainty, before her eyes. And Reiko had no means of rescuing him from it.

The sweat glistened on her husband's forehead. The lieutenant closed his eyes, and then opened them again, as if experimenting. The eyes had lost their luster, and seemed innocent and empty like the eyes of a small animal.

The agony before Reiko's eyes burned as strong as the summer sun, utterly remote from the grief which seemed to be tearing herself apart within. The pain grew steadily in stature, stretching upward. Reiko felt that her husband had already become a man in a separate world, a man whose whole being had been resolved into pain, a prisoner in a cage of pain where no hand could reach out to him. But Reiko felt no pain at all. Her grief was not pain. As she thought about this, Reiko began to feel as if someone had raised a cruel wall of glass high between herself and her husband.

Ever since her marriage her husband's existence had been her own existence, and every breath of his had been a breath drawn by herself. But now, while her husband's existence in pain was a vivid reality, Reiko could find in this grief of hers no certain proof at all of her own existence.

With only his right hand on the sword the lieutenant began to cut sideways across his stomach. But as the blade became entangled with the entrails it was pushed constantly outward by their soft resilience; and the lieutenant realized that it would be necessary, as he cut, to use both hands to keep the point pressed deep into his stomach. He pulled the blade across. It did not cut as easily as he had expected. He directed the strength of his whole body into his right hand and pulled again. There was a cut of three or four inches.

The pain spread slowly outward from the inner depths until the whole stomach reverberated. It was like the wild clanging of a bell. Or like a thousand bells which jangled simultaneously at every breath he breathed and every throb of his pulse, rocking his whole being. The lieutenant could no longer stop himself from moaning. But by now the blade had cut its way through to below the navel, and when he noticed this he felt a sense of satisfaction, and a renewal of courage.

The volume of blood had steadily increased, and now it spurted from the wound as if propelled by the beat of the pulse. The mat before the lieutenant was drenched red with splattered blood, and more blood overflowed onto it from pools which gathered in folds of the lieutenant's khaki trousers. A spot, like a bird, came flying across to Reiko and settled on the lap of her white silk kimono.

By the time the lieutenant had at last drawn the sword across to the right side of his stomach, the blade was already cutting shallow and had revealed its naked tip, slippery with blood and grease. But, suddenly stricken by a fit of vomiting, the lieutenant cried out hoarsely. The vomiting made the fierce pain fiercer still, and the stomach, which had thus far remained firm and compact, now abruptly heaved, opening wide its wound, and the entrails burst through, as if the wound too were vomiting. Seemingly ignorant of their master's suffering, the entrails gave an impression of robust health and almost disagreeable vitality as they slipped smoothly out and spilled over into the crotch. The lieutenant's head dropped, his shoulders heaved, his eyes opened to narrow slits, and a thin trickle of saliva dribbled from his mouth. The gold markings on his epaulettes caught the light and glinted.

Blood was scattered everywhere. The lieutenant was soaked in it to his knees, and he sat now in a crumpled and listless posture, one hand on the floor. A raw smell filled the room. The lieutenant, his head drooping, retched repeatedly, and the movement showed vividly in his shoulders. The blade of the sword, now pushed back by the entrails and exposed to its tip, was still in the lieutenant's right hand.

It would be difficult to imagine a more heroic sight than that of the lieutenant at this moment, as he mustered his strength and flung back his head. The movement was performed with sudden violence, and the back of his head struck with a sharp crack against the alcove pillar. Reiko had been sitting until now with her face lowered, gazing in fascination at the tide of blood advancing toward her knees, but the sound took her by surprise and she looked up.

The lieutenant's face was not the face of a living man. The eyes were hollow, the skin parched, the once so lustrous cheeks and lips the color of dried mud. The right hand alone was moving. Laboriously gripping the sword, it hovered shakily in the air like the hand of a marionette and strove to direct the point at the base of the lieutenant's throat. Reiko watched her husband make this last, most heart-rending, futile exertion. Glistening with blood and grease, the point was thrust at the throat again and again. And each time it missed its aim. The strength to guide it was no longer there. The straying point struck the collar and the collar badges. Although its hooks had been unfastened, the stiff military collar had closed together again and was protecting the throat.

Reiko could bear the sight no longer. She tried to go to her husband's help, but she could not stand. She moved through the blood on her knees, and her white skirts grew deep red. Moving to the rear of her husband, she helped no more than by loosening the collar. The quivering blade at last contacted the naked flesh of the throat. At that moment Reiko's impression was that she herself had propelled her husband forward; but that was not the case. It was a movement planned by the lieutenant himself, his last exertion of strength. Abruptly he threw his body at the blade, and the blade pierced his neck, emerging at the nape. There was a tremendous spurt of blood and the lieutenant lay still, cold blue-tinged steel protruding from his neck at the back.

5

Slowly, her socks slippery with blood, Reiko descended the stairway. 130 The upstairs room was now completely still.

Switching on the ground-floor lights, she checked the gas jet and the main gas plug and poured water over the smoldering, half-buried charcoal in the brazier. She stood before the upright mirror in the four-and-a-half-mat room and held up her skirts. The bloodstains made it seem as if a bold, vivid pattern was printed across the lower half of her white kimono. When she sat down before the mirror, she was conscious of the dampness and coldness of her husband's blood in the region of her thighs, and she shivered. Then, for a long while, she lingered over her toilet preparations. She applied the rouge generously to her cheeks, and her lips too she painted heavily. This was no longer make-up to please her husband. It was make-up for the world which she would leave behind, and there was a touch of the magnificent and the spectacular in her brushwork. When she rose, the mat before the mirror was wet with blood. Reiko was not concerned about this.

Returning from the toilet, Reiko stood finally on the cement floor of the porchway. When her husband had bolted the door here last night it had been in preparation for death. For a while she stood immersed in the consideration of a simple problem. Should she now leave the bolt drawn? If she were to lock the door, it could be that the neighbors might not notice their suicide for several days. Reiko did not relish the thought of their two corpses putrifying before discovery. After all, it seemed, it would be best to leave it open. . . . She released the bolt, and also drew open the frosted-glass door a fraction. . . . At once a chill wind blew in. There was no sign of anyone in the midnight streets and stars glittered ice-cold through the trees in the large house opposite.

Leaving the door as it was, Reiko mounted the stairs. She had walked here and there for some time and her socks were no longer slippery. About halfway up, her nostrils were already assailed by a peculiar smell.

The lieutenant was lying on his face in a sea of blood. The point protruding from his neck seemed to have grown even more prominent than before. Reiko walked heedlessly across the blood. Sitting beside the lieutenant's corpse, she stared intently at the face, which lay on one cheek on the mat. The eyes were opened wide, as if the lieutenant's attention had been attracted by something. She raised the head, folding it in her sleeve, wiped the blood from the lips, and bestowed a last kiss.

Then she rose and took from the closet a new white blanket and a 135 waist cord. To prevent any derangement of her skirts, she wrapped the blanket about her waist and bound it firmly with the cord.

Reiko sat herself on a spot about one foot distant from the lieutenant's body. Drawing the dagger from her sash, she examined its dully gleaming blade intently, and held it to her tongue. The taste of the polished steel was slightly sweet.

Reiko did not linger. When she thought how the pain which had previously opened such a gulf between herself and her dying husband was now to become a part of her own experience, she saw before her only the joy of herself entering a realm her husband had already made his own. In her husband's agonized face there had been something inexplicable which she was seeing for the first time. Now she would solve that riddle. Reiko sensed that at last she too would be able to taste the true bitterness and sweetness of that great moral principle in which her husband believed. What had until now been tasted only faintly through her husband's example she was about to savor directly with her own tongue.

Reiko rested the point of the blade against the base of her throat. She thrust hard. The wound was only shallow. Her head blazed, and her hands shook uncontrollably. She gave the blade a strong pull sideways. A warm substance flooded into her mouth, and everything before her eyes reddened, in a vision of spouting blood. She gathered her strength and plunged the point of the blade deep into her throat.

Considerations

1. Why do you think the author chooses to begin the story by stating the facts of the suicide and then retracing the events leading up to it? How would the story be changed if the events were, instead, presented chronologically?

2. Why is the story called "Patriotism"? How does patriotism relate to Lieutenant Takeyama's death? To Reiko's death?

3. Evaluate the relationship between the husband and wife. Cite specific incidents to support the points you make.

4. What does the story suggest about the relationship between love and death for Lieutenant Takeyama and Reiko?

5. Both Lieutenant Takeyama and Reiko regard their actions as courageous and honorable. Their expectations indicate that members of their community share these values. How do your own responses to Lieutenant Takeyama's and Reiko's motives and actions compare and contrast with their responses and with the anticipated responses of their community?

MIGUEL DE UNAMUNO (1864–1936)

Juan Manso: A Dead Man's Tale

And now for a story.

While he was on this wicked earth Juan Manso was a simple soul, a harmless fellow who during his whole life had never hurt a fly. As a child, when he played donkey with his friends, he was always the donkey. Later, his comrades confided in him about their love affairs, and when he grew to full manhood his acquaintances still used to greet him with an affectionate "Hello, little Johnny!"

His favorite maxim was from the Chinese: "Never commit yourself, and stick to the person who can help you the most."

He loathed politics, hated business, and avoided everything that might upset the even tenor of his ways.

He lived on a small income which he spent in its entirety without ever touching the capital. He was quite devout, would never contradict anyone, and as he had a bad opinion of everybody he spoke well of them.

If you mentioned politics to him he would say: "I'm nothing — neither one side nor the other: I don't care which party runs the government. I'm just a poor sinner who wants to live at peace with everyone."

His meekness, however, was of no avail against the finality of death. It was the only definite thing he ever did in his life.

An angel armed with a great flaming sword was sorting out souls according to the sign made upon them as they went by an enrollment desk which they had to pass as they departed from this world and went through a kind of immigration control where angels and devils were sitting side by side in friendly fashion examining documents to see if they were all in order.

The entrance to the registration room looked like the scene outside the box office on the day of a big bullfight. There were so many people milling around, pushing and shoving, with everyone in such a hurry to learn his fate, and such was the hubbub raised by the curses, entreaties, insults and excuses in the thousands of languages, dialects and jargons of this world, that Juan Manso said to himself:

"Who says I have to get mixed up in all this? There must be some very rough characters around here."

He said this *sotto voce,* so no one could hear him. The fact is that the angel with the great flaming sword paid not the slightest attention to him, so he was able to slip past and start on his way to Heaven.

He walked along very quietly all by himself. From time to time happy groups would pass by, chanting litanies; some were dancing wildly, which seemed to him not quite a proper thing for the blessed to be doing on their way up to Heaven. When he reached the heights he found a long line of people standing beside the walls of Paradise, and a few angels keeping order like policemen on earth. Juan Manso got on the very end of the line.

Shortly a humble Franciscan friar came along, and he was so clever in advancing pathetic arguments as to why he was in such a hurry to get inside right away that Juan Manso gave him his place in line, saying to himself:

"It's a good idea to make friends for yourself even in Heaven."

The next man to come along, though not a Franciscan, wanted the same privilege, and the same thing happened. In short, there wasn't a pious soul who did not trick Juan Manso out of his place; his reputation for meekness ran along the whole line, and was handed down as a continuing tradition among the constantly-changing crowd there. And Juan Manso stayed where he was, the prisoner of his own good reputation.

Centuries went by — or so it seemed to Juan Manso, for it took that much time for the meek little lamb to begin to lose his patience. Finally one day he happened to meet a wise and saintly bishop who turned out to be the great-great grandson of one of Manso's brothers. Juan voiced his complaints to his great-great-grandnephew, and the wise and saintly bishop offered to intercede for him when he came before the Eternal Father. On the strength of this, Juan yielded his place to the wise and saintly bishop who, when he entered Heaven, quite properly went straight to the Eternal Father to pay Him his respects. He concluded his little talk with The Almighty, who listened absent-mindedly and said:

"Wasn't there something else you wanted to say?"

And with His glance He searched the depths of the bishop's heart.

"Lord, permit me to intercede for one of Thy servants who is out there at the very tip end of the line. . . ."

"Don't beat about the bush," thundered The Lord. "You mean Juan Manso."

"Yes, Lord, he is the one; Juan Manso, who. . . ."

"All right! All right! Let him look out for himself, and don't you get mixed up again in other people's affairs!" And turning to the angel who was introducing souls, He added: "Let the next one in!"

If anything is capable of marring the eternal happiness of a soul in everlasting bliss, we could say that the soul of the wise and saintly bishop was troubled. But at least, moved by pity, he went to Heaven's walls, next to which the long line was standing. He climbed up, and calling to Juan Manso he said:

"Great-great-uncle, how sad I am about this — how very sad, my dear man! The Lord told me that you should look out for yourself, and that I shouldn't get mixed up in other people's affairs again. But . . . are you still at the end of the line? Come now, my dear man! Summon up some courage and don't yield your place again."

"Now he tells me!" exclaimed Juan Manso, shedding tears as big as chick-peas. But it was too late, for the tragic tradition was now attached to him: people no longer even asked him for his place, they just took it.

Crestfallen, he abandoned the line and began to wander about the lonely wastelands beyond the grave until he came upon many people, all downcast, walking along a road. He followed their footsteps and found himself at the gates of Purgatory.

"It will be easier to get in here," he said to himself, "and once inside they will send me directly to Heaven after I have been purified."

"Hey! Where are you going, my friend?"

Juan Manso turned around and found himself face to face with an angel who was wearing an academic mortarboard and had a pen behind his ear. He looked at Juan over the top of his glasses, had him turn around, and after examining him from head to foot frowned and said:

"H-m-m! *Malorum causa* — the root of all ills! You are completely grey, and I'm afraid to put you through our procedures for fear you'll melt. You would do better to go to Limbo." 30

"To Limbo!"

Upon hearing this, Juan Manso became indignant for the first time, for no man is so patient and long-suffering that he will stand for having an angel treat him like a complete idiot.

In desperation, he set out for Hell. Here there was no waiting line, nor anything like one. It had a broad entrance, from which came puffs of thick smoke and an infernal din. At the door a poor devil was playing a hand-organ and shrieking at the top of his voice:

"Come inside, gentlemen, step inside . . . Here you will see the human comedy . . . Anyone may enter. . . ."

Juan Manso closed his eyes. 35

"Hey, young man! Stop!" the poor devil said to him.

"Didn't you say that anyone might enter?"

"Yes, but . . . Look," said the poor devil earnestly, as he stroked his tail, "we still have some slight spark of conscience . . . and, after all . . . you?"

"All right, all right!" said Juan Manso, turning away because he could not stand the smoke.

And he heard the devil mutter to himself, "Poor fellow!" 40

"Poor fellow? Even the devil pities me!"

Desperate now to the point of madness, he began to bob around like a cork in mid-ocean as he crossed the vast spaces beyond the grave. From time to time he would meet other legendary lost souls.

One day, attracted by the appetizing odor that was coming from Heaven, he approached its walls to see what they were cooking inside. It was about time for sunset, and he saw that The Lord was coming out to enjoy the cool air in the gardens of Paradise. Juan Manso waited for Him near the wall, and when he saw His noble head he opened his arms wide in supplication and said in a rather indignant tone:

"Lord, Lord, didst Thou not promise the Kingdom of Heaven to the meek?"

"Yes, but to the enterprising, not to the weak-kneed." 45

And He turned His back on Juan.

An old legend recounts that The Lord, taking pity on Juan Manso, let him return to this wicked world, and that when he got here again he began to push people around right and left. When he died a second time, he shoved his way right past the famous line and slipped boldly into Paradise.

Now inside, he keeps repeating:

"Man has to fight his way through life on earth!"

Considerations

1. In Spanish, *manso* means "meek" or "tame." Do you think Juan Manso's name suits him? Could it be considered ironic in any way? Explain.
2. How are Juan Manso's earthly values reflected by his thoughts, actions, and words in the afterlife?
3. What does Unamuno's tale suggest about his view of the afterlife? In what ways is it different from earthly life? In what ways is it the same? What significance do you see in these comparisons and contrasts?
4. Check the definition of "limbo" in any good dictionary. Why is Manso particularly insulted when the angel guarding purgatory tells him to apply to limbo?
5. What views of traditional religion does this tale suggest? To what extent are we meant to take the final sentence of the story seriously? To what extent does it seem ironic? Explain your response.

JOHN DONNE (1572–1631)

Death, be not proud

Death, be not proud, though some have called thee
Mighty and dreadful, for thou are not so;
For those whom thou think'st thou dost overthrow
Die not, poor Death, nor yet canst thou kill me.
From rest and sleep, which but thy pictures be,   5
Much pleasure; then from thee much more must flow,
And soonest our best men with thee do go,
Rest of their bones, and soul's delivery.
Thou art slave to fate, chance, kings, and desperate men,
And dost with poison, war, and sickness dwell,   10
And poppy or charms can make us sleep as well
And better than thy stroke; why swell'st thou then?
One short sleep past, we wake eternally
And death shall be no more; Death, thou shalt die.

Considerations

1. In this poem, the speaker directly addresses death. Death becomes personified, rather than remaining an abstract concept. Give a brief description of the character Death as pictured by the speaker.
2. Discuss the paradox (apparent contradiction) in the final line: "Death, thou shalt die." How can death die? What value system is implied by this statement?
3. Using the approach suggested here, plan a speech addressing an abstract concept: Love, Anger, Hope, Envy, Pride (or a concept of your choice).

EMILY DICKINSON (1830–1886)

Apparently with no surprise

Apparently with no surprise
To any happy Flower
The Frost beheads it at its play —
In accidental power —
The blonde Assassin passes on —   5
The Sun proceeds unmoved
To measure off another Day
For an Approving God.

Considerations

1. Who or what might be represented by the "blonde Assassin"?
2. What is implied by the phrase "an Approving God"? Why not "the Approving God" or "our Approving God"? To what and why does this God give approval?
3. What view of death does the poem suggest?

e. e. cummings (1894–1962)

[Buffalo Bill's]

Buffalo Bill's
defunct
        who used to
        ride a watersmooth-silver
                        stallion   5

and break onetwothreefourfive   pigeons justlikethat
                                              Jesus
he was a handsome man
                        and what i want to know is
how do you like your blueeyed boy   10
Mister Death

Considerations

1. Consider the effect of the word "defunct" as opposed to these words: "dead," "deceased," "passed on," "gone to his just reward."
2. How would the poem be changed if the lines were printed as traditional sentences rather than in the arrangement cummings chose?
3. Three names are capitalized in this poem: Buffalo Bill; Jesus; Mister Death. Consider the possible significance of this choice. For example, what relationship among the three might be implied?

RUTH WHITMAN (1922–   )

Castoff Skin

She lay in her girlish sleep at ninety-six,
small as a twig.
Pretty good figure

for an old lady, she said to me once.
Then she crawled away, leaving   5
a tiny stretched transparence

behind her. When I kissed her paper cheek
I thought of the snake,
of his quick motion.

Considerations

1. What is the central metaphor of the poem? What does this metaphor suggest about the speaker's view of death?
2. What can you tell about the woman who is described by the poem?
3. What does the speaker imply about her view of the woman she describes?

JANE COOPER (1924–   )

In the House of the Dying

So once again, hearing the tired aunts
whisper together under the kitchen globe,
I turn away; I am not one of them.

At the sink I watch the water cover my hands
in a sheath of light. Upstairs she lies alone   5
dreaming of autumn nights when her children were born.

On the steps between us grows in a hush of waiting
the impossible silence between two generations.
The aunts buzz on like flies around a bulb.

I am dressed like them. Standing with my back turned   10
I wash the dishes in the same easy way.
Only at birth and death do I utterly fail.

For death is my old friend who waits on the stairs.
Whenever I pass I nod to him like the newsman
who is there every day; for them he is the priest.   15

While the birth of love is so terrible to me
I feel unworthy of the commonest marriage.
Upstairs she lies, washed through by the two miracles.

Considerations

1. What are the "two miracles" the speaker mentions in the final line of the poem? How does she see these "miracles" as related?
2. What can you infer about the relationship between the speaker and the woman who lies upstairs dying?
3. What view of death is suggested by this poem? Note particularly the contrast between the speaker's view and the view she ascribes to the aunts.

ROBERT BROWNING (1812–1889)

The Bishop Orders His Tomb at Saint Praxed's Church
Rome, 15 —

Vanity, saith the preacher, vanity!
Draw round my bed: is Anselm keeping back?
Nephews — sons mine . . . ah God, I know not! Well —
She, men would have to be your mother once,
Old Gandolf envied me, so fair she was!   5
What's done is done, and she is dead beside,
Dead long ago, and I am Bishop since,
And as she died so must we die ourselves,
And thence ye may perceive the world's a dream.
Life, how and what is it? As here I lie   10
In this state chamber, dying by degrees,
Hours and long hours in the dead night, I ask
"Do I live, am I dead?" Peace, peace seems all.
Saint Praxed's ever was the church for peace;
And so, about this tomb of mine. I fought   15
With tooth and nail to save my niche, ye know:
— Old Gandolf cozened me, despite my care;
Shrewd was that snatch from out the corner south
He graced his carrion with, God curse the same!
Yet still my niche is not so cramped but thence   20
One sees the pulpit o' the epistle side,
And somewhat of the choir, those silent seats,
And up into the aery dome where live
The angels, and a sunbeam's sure to lurk:
And I shall fill my slab of basalt there,   25
And 'neath my tabernacle take my rest,
With those nine columns round me, two and two,
The odd one at my feet where Anselm stands:
Peach-blossom marble all, the rare, the ripe
As fresh-poured red wine of a mighty pulse.   30
— Old Gandolf with his paltry onion-stone,
Put me where I may look at him! True peach,
Rosy and flawless: how I earned the prize!
Draw close: that conflagration of my church
— What then? So much was saved if aught were missed!   35
My sons, ye would not be my death? Go dig
The white-grape vineyard where the oil-press stood,
Drop water gently till the surface sink,
And if ye find . . . Ah God, I know not, I! . . .

Bedded in store of rotten fig leaves soft,   40
And corded up in a tight olive-frail,
Some lump, ah God, of *lapis lazuli,*
Big as a jew's head cut off at the nape,
Blue as a vein o'er the Madonna's breast . . .
Sons, all have I bequeathed you, villas, all,   45
That brave Frascati villa with its bath,
So, let the blue lump poise between my knees,
Like God the Father's globe on both his hands
Ye worship in the Jesu Church so gay,
For Gandolf shall not choose but see and burst!   50
Swift as a weaver's shuttle fleet our years:
Man goeth to the grave, and where is he?
Did I say basalt for my slab, sons? Black —
'Twas ever antique-black I meant! How else
Shall ye contrast my frieze to come beneath?   55
The bas-relief in bronze ye promised me,
Those Pans and Nymphs ye wot of, and perchance
Some tripod, thyrsus, with a vase or so,
The Saviour at his sermon on the mount,
Saint Praxed in a glory, and one Pan   60
Ready to twitch the Nymph's last garment off,
And Moses with the tables . . . but I know
Ye mark me not! What do they whisper thee,
Child of my bowels, Anselm? Ah, ye hope
To revel down my villas while I gasp   65
Bricked o'er with beggar's moldy travertine
Which Gandolf from his tomb-top chuckles at!
Nay, boys, ye love me — all of jasper, then!
'Tis jasper ye stand pledged to, lest I grieve
My bath must needs be left behind, alas!   70
One block, pure green as a pistachio nut,
There's plenty jasper somewhere in the world —
And have I not Saint Praxed's ear to pray
Horses for ye, and brown Greek manuscripts,
And mistresses with great smooth marbly limbs?   75
— That's if ye carve my epitaph aright,
Choice Latin, picked phrase, Tully's every word,
No gaudy ware like Gandolf's second line —
Tully, my masters? Ulpian serves his need!
And then how I shall lie through centuries,   80
And hear the blessed mutter of the mass,
And see God made and eaten all day long,
And feel the steady candle flame, and taste

Good strong thick stupefying incense-smoke!
For as I lie here, hours of the dead night,   85
Dying in state and by such slow degrees,
I fold my arms as if they clasped a crook,
And stretch my feet forth straight as stone can point,
And let the bedclothes, for a mortcloth, drop
Into great laps and folds of sculptor's-work: 90
And as yon tapers dwindle, and strange thoughts
Grow, with a certain humming in my ears,
About the life before I lived this life,
And this life too, popes, cardinals, and priests,
Saint Praxed at his sermon on the mount,   95
Your tall pale mother with her talking eyes,
And new-found agate urns as fresh as day,
And marble's language, Latin pure, discreet
—Aha, ELUCESCEBAT quoth our friend?
No Tully, said I, Ulpian at the best!   100
Evil and brief hath been my pilgrimage.
All *lapis,* all, sons! Else I give the Pope
My villas! Will ye ever eat my heart?
Ever your eyes were as a lizard's quick,
They glitter like your mother's for my soul,   105
Or ye would heighten my impoverished frieze,
Pierce out its starved design, and fill my vase
With grapes, and add a vizor and a Term,
And to the tripod ye would tie a lynx
That in his struggle throws the thyrsus down,   110
To comfort me on my entablature
Whereon I am to lie till I must ask
"Do I live, am I dead?" There, leave me, there!
For ye have stabbed me with ingratitude
To death—ye wish it—God, ye wish it! Stone—   115
Gritstone, a-crumble! Clammy squares which sweat
As if the corpse they keep were oozing through—
And no more *lapis* to delight the world!
Well go! I bless ye. Fewer tapers there,
But in a row: and, going, turn your backs   120
—Aye, like departing altar-ministrants,
And leave me in my church, the church for peace,
That I may watch at leisure if he leers—
Old Gandolf, at me, from his onion-stone,
As still he envied me, so fair she was!   125

EMILY DICKINSON (1830–1886)

I heard a Fly buzz — when I died —

I heard a Fly buzz — when I died —
The Stillness in the Room
Was like the Stillness in the Air —
Between the Heaves of Storm —

The Eyes around — had wrung them dry —   5
And Breaths were gathering firm
For the last Onset — when the King
Be witnessed — in the Room —

I willed my Keepsakes — Signed away
What portion of me be   10
Assignable — and then it was
There interposed a Fly —

With Blue — uncertain stumbling Buzz —
Between the light — and me —
And then the Windows failed — and then   15
I could not see to see —

EMILY DICKINSON (1830–1886)

The Bustle in a House

The Bustle in a House
The Morning after Death
Is solemnest of industries
Enacted upon Earth —

The Sweeping up the Heart   5
And putting Love away
We shall not want to use again
Until Eternity.

A. E. HOUSMAN (1859–1936)

To an Athlete Dying Young

The time you won your town the race
We chaired you through the market-place;
Man and boy stood cheering by,
And home we brought you shoulder-high.

To-day, the road all runners come,   5
Shoulder-high we bring you home,
And set you at your threshold down,
Townsman of a stiller town.

Smart lad, to slip betimes away
From fields where glory does not stay   10
And early though the laurel grows
It withers quicker than the rose.

Eyes the shady night has shut
Cannot see the record cut,
And silence sounds no worse than cheers   15
After earth has stopped the ears:

Now you will not swell the rout
Of lads that wore their honours out,
Runners whom renown outran
And the name died before the man.   20

So set, before its echoes fade,
The fleet foot on the sill of shade,
And hold to the low lintel up
The still-defended challenge-cup.

And round early-laurelled head   25
Will flock to gaze the strengthless dead,
And find unwithered on its curls
The garland briefer than a girl's.

EDWIN ARLINGTON ROBINSON (1869–1935)

Richard Cory

Whenever Richard Cory went downtown,
We people on the pavement looked at him;
He was a gentleman from sole to crown,
Clean favored, and imperially slim.

And he was always quietly arrayed,   5
And he was always human when he talked;
But still he fluttered pulses when he said,
"Good-morning," and he glittered when he walked.

And he was rich — yes, richer than a king —
And admirably schooled in every grace: 10
In fine, we thought that he was everything
To make us wish that we were in his place.

So on we worked, and waited for the light,
And went without the meat, and cursed the bread;
And Richard Cory, one calm summer night,   15
Went home and put a bullet through his head.

ROBERT FROST (1874–1963)

"Out, Out — "

The buzz saw snarled and rattled in the yard
And made dust and dropped stove-length sticks of wood,
Sweet-scented stuff when the breeze drew across it.
And from there those that lifted eyes could count
Five mountain ranges one behind the other   5
Under the sunset far into Vermont.
And the saw snarled and rattled, snarled and rattled,
As it ran light, or had to bear a load.
And nothing happened: day was all but done.
Call it a day, I wish they might have said   10
To please the boy by giving him the half hour
That a boy counts so much when saved from work.
His sister stood beside them in her apron
To tell them "Supper." At the word, the saw,
As if to prove saws knew what supper meant,   15

Leaped out at the boy's hand, or seemed to leap—
He must have given the hand. However it was,
Neither refused the meeting. But the hand!
The boy's first outcry was a rueful laugh,
As he swung toward them holding up the hand,   20
Half in appeal, but half as if to keep
The life from spilling. Then the boy saw all—
Since he was old enough to know, big boy
Doing a man's work, though a child at heart—
He saw all spoiled. "Don't let him cut my hand off—   25
The doctor, when he comes. Don't let him, sister!"
So. But the hand was gone already.
The doctor put him in the dark of ether.
He lay and puffed his lips out with his breath.
And then—the watcher at his pulse took fright.   30
No one believed. They listened at his heart.
Little—less—nothing!—and that ended it.
No more to build on there. And they, since they
Were not the one dead, turned to their affairs.

THEODORE ROETHKE (1908–1963)

Elegy for Jane
My Student, Thrown by a Horse

I remember the neckcurls, limp and damp as tendrils;
And her quick look, a sidelong pickerel smile;
And how, once startled into talk, the light syllables leaped for her,
And she balanced in the delight of her thought,
A wren, happy, tail into the wind,   5
Her song trembling the twigs and small branches.
The shade sang with her;
The leaves, their whispers turned to kissing;
And the mold sang in the bleached valleys under the rose.

Oh, when she was sad, she cast herself down into such a pure depth,   10
Even a father could not find her:
Scraping her cheek against straw;
Stirring the clearest water.

My sparrow, you are not here,
Waiting like a fern, making a spiny shadow.   15
The sides of wet stones cannot console me,
Nor the moss, wound with the last light.

If only I could nudge you from this sleep,
My maimed darling, my skittery pigeon.
Over this damp grave I speak the words of my love: 20
I, with no rights in this matter,
Neither father nor lover.

WILLIAM STAFFORD (1914–   )

Traveling through the dark

Traveling through the dark I found a deer
dead on the edge of the Wilson River road.
It is usually best to roll them into the canyon:
that road is narrow; to swerve might make more dead.

By glow of the tail-light I stumbled back of the car   5
and stood by the heap, a doe, a recent killing;
she had stiffened already, almost cold.
I dragged her off; she was large in the belly.

My fingers touching her side brought me the reason—
her side was warm; her fawn lay there waiting,   10
alive, still, never to be born.
Beside that mountain road I hesitated.

The car aimed ahead its lowered parking lights;
under the hood purred the steady engine.
I stood in the glare of the warm exhaust turning red;   15
around our group I could hear the wilderness listen.

I thought hard for us all—my only swerving—,
then pushed her over the edge into the river.

SEAMUS HEANEY (1939–   )

Mid-Term Break

I sat all morning in the college sick bay
Counting bells knelling classes to a close.
At two o'clock our neighbors drove me home.

In the porch I met my father crying—
He had always taken funerals in his stride—   5
And Big Jim Evans saying it was a hard blow.

The baby cooed and laughed and rocked the pram
When I came in, and I was embarrassed
By old men standing up to shake my hand

And tell me they were "sorry for my trouble,"   10
Whispers informed strangers I was the eldest,
Away at school, as my mother held my hand

In hers and coughed out angry tearless sighs.
At ten o'clock the ambulance arrived
With the corpse, stanched and bandaged by the nurses.   15

Next morning I went up into the room. Snowdrops
And candles soothed the bedside; I saw him
For the first time in six weeks. Paler now,

Wearing a poppy bruise on his left temple,
He lay in the four foot box as in his cot.   20
No gaudy scars, the bumper knocked him clear.

A four foot box, a foot for every year.

HARVEY FIERSTEIN (1954–   )

On Tidy Endings

The curtain rises on a deserted, modern Upper West Side apartment. In the bright daylight that pours in through the windows we can see the living room of the apartment. Far Stage Right is the galley kitchen, next to it the multilocked front door with intercom. Stage Left reveals a hallway that leads to the two bedrooms and baths.

Though the room is still fully furnished (couch, coffee table, etc.), there are boxes stacked against the wall and several photographs and paintings are on the floor leaving shadows on the wall where they once hung. Obviously someone is moving out. From the way the boxes are neatly labeled and stacked, we know that this is an organized person.

From the hallway just outside the door we hear the rattling of keys and two arguing voices:

JIM *(Offstage)*: I've got to be home by four. I've got practice.

MARION *(Offstage)*: I'll get you to practice, don't worry.

JIM *(Offstage)*: I don't want to go in there.

MARION *(Offstage)*: Jimmy, don't make Mommy crazy, alright? We'll go inside, I'll call Aunt Helen and see if you can go down and play with Robbie.

(The door opens. MARION is a handsome woman of forty. Dressed in a business suit, her hair conservatively combed, SHE appears to be going to a business meeting. JIM is a boy of eleven. His playclothes are typical, but someone has obviously just combed his hair. MARION recovers the key from the lock.)

JIM: Why can't I just go down and ring the bell?

MARION: Because I said so.

(As MARION steps into the room SHE is struck by some unexpected emotion. SHE freezes in her path and stares at the empty apartment. JIM lingers by the door.)

JIM: I'm going downstairs.

MARION: Jimmy, please.

JIM: This place gives me the creeps.

MARION: This was your father's apartment. There's nothing creepy about it.

JIM: Says you.

MARION: You want to close the door, please?

(JIM reluctantly obeys.)

MARION: Now, why don't you go check your room and make sure you didn't leave anything.

JIM: It's empty.

MARION: Go look.

JIM: I looked last time.

MARION *(Trying to be patient)*: Honey, we sold the apartment. You're never going to be here again. Go make sure you have everything you want.

JIM: But Uncle Arthur packed everything.

MARION *(Less patiently)*: Go make sure.

JIM: There's nothing in there.

MARION *(Exploding)*: I said make sure!

(JIM *jumps, then realizing that* SHE'S *not kidding, obeys.*)

MARION: Everything's an argument with that one. (SHE *looks around the room and breathes deeply. There is sadness here. Under her breath:*) I can still smell you. *(Suddenly not wanting to be alone)* Jimmy? Are you okay?

JIM *(Returning)*: Nothing. Told you so.

MARION: Uncle Arthur must have worked very hard. Make sure you thank him.

JIM: What for? Robbie says, *(Fey mannerisms)* "They love to clean up things!"

MARION: Sometimes you can be a real joy.

JIM: Did you call Aunt Helen?

MARION: Do I get a break here? *(Approaching the* BOY *understandingly)* Wouldn't you like to say good-bye?

JIM: To who?

MARION: To the apartment. You and your daddy spent a lot of time here together. Don't you want to take one last look around?

JIM: Ma, get a real life.

MARION: "Get a real life." *(Going for the phone)* Nice. Very nice.

JIM: Could you call already?

MARION *(Dialing)*: Jimmy, what does this look like I'm doing?

(JIM *kicks at the floor impatiently. Someone answers the phone at the other end.*)

MARION *(Into the phone)*: Helen? Hi, we're upstairs. . . . No, we just walked in the door. Jimmy wants to know if he can come down. . . . Oh, thanks.

(Hearing that, JIM *breaks for the door.)*

MARION *(Yelling after him)*: Don't run in the halls! And don't play with the elevator buttons!

(The door slams shut behind him.)

MARION *(Back to the phone)*: Hi. . . . No, I'm okay. It's a little weird being here. . . . No. Not since the funeral, and then there were so many people. Jimmy told me to get "a real life." I don't think I could handle anything realer. . . . No, please. Stay where you are. I'm fine. The doorman said Arthur would be right back and my lawyer should have been here already. . . . Well, we've got the papers to sign and a few other odds and ends to clean up. Shouldn't take long.

(The intercom buzzer rings.)

MARION: Hang on, that must be her.

(MARION goes to the intercom and speaks) Yes? . . . Thank you.

(Back to the phone) Helen? Yeah, it's the lawyer. I'd better go. . . . Well, I could use a stiff drink, but I drove down. Listen, I'll stop by on my way out. Okay? Okay. 'Bye.

(SHE hangs up the phone, looks around the room. That uncomfortable feeling returns to her quickly. SHE gets up and goes to the front door, opens it and looks out. No one there yet. SHE closes the door, shakes her head knowing that SHE's being silly and starts back into the room. SHE looks around, can't make it and retreats to the door. SHE opens it, looks out, closes it, but stays right there, her hand on the doorknob. The bell rings. SHE throws open the door.)

MARION: That was quick.

(JUNE LOWELL still has her finger on the bell. Her arms are loaded with contracts. MARION's contemporary, JUNE is less formal in appearance and more hyper in her manner.)

JUNE: *That* was quicker. What, were you waiting by the door?
MARION *(Embarrassed)*: No. I was just passing it. Come on in.
JUNE: Have you got your notary seal?
MARION: I think so.
JUNE: Great. Then you can witness. I left mine at the office and thanks to gentrification I'm double-parked downstairs. *(Looking for a place to dump her load)* Where?
MARION *(Definitely pointing to the coffee table)*: Anywhere. You mean you're not staying?
JUNE: If you really think you need me I can go down and find a parking lot. I think there's one over on Columbus. So, I can go down, park the car in the lot and take a cab back if you really think you need me.
MARION: Well . . . ?
JUNE: But you shouldn't have any problems. The papers are about as straightforward as papers get. Arthur is giving you power of attorney to sell the apartment and you're giving him a check for half the purchase price. Everything else is just signing papers that state that you know that you signed the other papers. Anyway, he knows the deal, his lawyers have been over it all with him, it's just a matter of signatures.

MARION *(Not fine)*: Oh, fine.

JUNE: Unless you just don't want to be alone with him . . . ?

MARION: With Arthur? Don't be silly.

JUNE *(Laying out the papers)*: Then you'll handle it solo? Great. My car thanks you, the parking lot thanks you, and the cab driver that wouldn't have gotten a tip thanks you. Come have a quick look-see.

MARION *(Joining her on the couch)*: There are a lot of papers here.

JUNE: Copies. Not to worry. Start here.

(MARION *starts to read*)

JUNE: I ran into Jimmy playing Elevator Operator.

(MARION *jumps*)

JUNE: I got him off at the sixth floor. Read on.

MARION: This is definitely not my day for dealing with him.

(JUNE *gets up and has a look around*)

JUNE: I don't believe what's happening to this neighborhood. You made quite an investment when you bought this place.

MARION: Collin was always very good at figuring out those things.

JUNE: Well, he sure figured this place right. What, have you tripled your money in ten years?

MARION: More.

JUNE: It's a shame to let it go.

MARION: We're not ready to be a two-dwelling family.

JUNE: So, sublet it again.

MARION: Arthur needs the money from the sale.

JUNE: Arthur got plenty already. I'm not crying for Arthur.

MARION: I don't hear you starting in again, do I?

JUNE: Your interests and your wishes are my only concern.

MARION: Fine.

JUNE: I still say we should contest Collin's will.

MARION: June! . . .

JUNE: You've got a child to support.

MARION: And a great job, and a husband with a great job. Tell me what Arthur's got.

JUNE: To my thinking, half of everything that should have gone to you. And more. All of Collin's personal effects, his record collection . . .

MARION: And I suppose their three years together meant nothing.

JUNE: When you compare them to your sixteen-year marriage? Not nothing, but not half of everything.

MARION *(Trying to change the subject)*: June, who gets which copies?

JUNE: Two of each to Arthur. One you keep. The originals and anything else come back to me. *(Looking around)* I still say you should've sublet the apartment for a year and then sold it. You would've gotten an even better price. Who wants to buy an apartment when they know someone died in it. No one. And certainly no one wants to buy an apartment when they know the person died of AIDS.

MARION *(Snapping)*: June. Enough!

JUNE *(Catching herself)*: Sorry. That was out of line. Sometimes my mouth does that to me. Hey, that's why I'm a lawyer. If my brain worked as fast as my mouth I would have gotten a real job.

MARION *(Holding out a stray paper)*: What's this?

JUNE: I forgot. Arthur's lawyer sent that over yesterday. He found it in Collin's safety-deposit box. It's an insurance policy that came along with some consulting job he did in Japan. He either forgot about it when he made out his will or else he wanted you to get the full payment. Either way, it's yours.

MARION: Are you sure we don't split this?

JUNE: Positive.

MARION: But everything else . . . ?

JUNE: Hey, Arthur found it, his lawyer sent it to me. Relax, it's all yours. Minus my commission, of course. Go out and buy yourself something. Anything else before I have to use my cut to pay the towing bill?

MARION: I guess not.

JUNE *(Starting to leave)*: Great. Call me when you get home. *(Stopping at the door and looking back)* Look, I know that I'm attacking this a little coldly. I am aware that someone you loved has just died. But there's a time and place for everything. This is about tidying up loose ends, not holding hands. I hope you'll remember that when Arthur gets here. Call me.

(And SHE'S *gone.)*

*(*MARION *looks ill at ease to be alone again.* SHE *nervously straightens the papers into neat little piles, looks at them and then remembers:)*

MARION: Pens. We're going to need pens.

(At last a chore to be done. SHE *looks in her purse and finds only one.* SHE *goes to the kitchen and opens a drawer where* SHE *finds two more.* SHE *starts back to the table with them but suddenly remembers something else.* SHE *returns to the kitchen and begins going through the cabinets until* SHE *finds what* SHE'S *looking for: a blue Art Deco teapot. Excited to find it,* SHE *takes it back to the couch.*

Guilt strikes. SHE *stops, considers putting it back, wavers, then:)*

MARION *(To herself)*: Oh, he won't care. One less thing to pack.

*(*SHE *takes the teapot and places it on the couch next to her purse.* SHE *is happier. Now* SHE *searches the room with her eyes for any other treasures* SHE *may have overlooked. Nothing here.* SHE *wanders off into the bedroom.*

We hear keys outside the front door. ARTHUR *lets himself into the apartment carrying a load of empty cartons and a large shopping bag.*

ARTHUR *is in his mid-thirties, pleasant looking though sloppily dressed in work clothes and slightly overweight.*

ARTHUR *enters the apartment just as* MARION *comes out of the bedroom carrying a framed watercolor painting.* THEY *jump at the sight of each other.)*

MARION: Oh, hi, Arthur. I didn't hear the door.

ARTHUR *(Staring at the painting)*: Well hello, Marion.

MARION *(Guiltily)*: I was going to ask you if you were thinking of taking this painting because if you're not going to then I'll take it. Unless, of course, you want it.

ARTHUR: No. You can have it.

MARION: I never really liked it, actually. I hate cats. I didn't even like the show. I needed something for my college dorm room. I was never the rock star poster type. I kept it in the back of a closet for years until Collin moved in here and took it. He said he liked it.

ARTHUR: I do too.

MARION: Well, then you keep it.

ARTHUR: No. Take it.

MARION: We've really got no room for it. You keep it.

ARTHUR: I don't want it.

MARION: Well, if you're sure.

ARTHUR *(Seeing the teapot)*: You want the teapot?

MARION: If you don't mind.

ARTHUR: One less thing to pack.

MARION: Funny, but that's exactly what I thought. One less thing to pack. You know, my mother gave it to Collin and me when we moved in to our first apartment. Silly sentimental piece of junk, but you know.

ARTHUR: That's not the one.

MARION: Sure it is. Hall used to make them for Westinghouse back in the thirties. I see them all the time at antiques shows and I always wanted to buy another, but they ask such a fortune for them.

ARTHUR: We broke the one your mother gave you a couple of years ago. That's a reproduction. You can get them almost anywhere in the Village for eighteen bucks.

MARION: Really? I'll have to pick one up.

ARTHUR: Take this one. I'll get another.

MARION: No, it's yours. You bought it.

ARTHUR: One less thing to pack.

MARION: Don't be silly. I didn't come here to raid the place.

ARTHUR: Well, was there anything else of Collin's that you thought you might like to have?

MARION: Now I feel so stupid, but actually I made a list. Not for me. But I started thinking about different people; friends, relatives, you know, that might want to have something of Collin's to remember him by. I wasn't sure just what you were taking and what you were throwing out. Anyway, I brought the list. *(Gets it from her purse)* Of course these are only suggestions. You probably thought of a few of these people yourself. But I figured it couldn't hurt to write it all down. Like I said, I don't know what you are planning on keeping.

ARTHUR *(Taking the list)*: I was planning on keeping it all.

MARION: Oh, I know. But most of these things are silly. Like his high school yearbooks. What would you want with them?

ARTHUR: Sure. I'm only interested in his Gay period.

MARION: I didn't mean it that way. Anyway, you look it over. They're only suggestions. Whatever you decide to do is fine with me.

ARTHUR *(Folding the list)*: It would have to be, wouldn't it. I mean, it's all mine now. He did leave this all to me.

(MARION is becoming increasingly nervous, but tries to keep a light approach as SHE takes a small bundle of papers from her bag.)

MARION: While we're on the subject of what's yours. I brought a batch of condolence cards that were sent to you care of me. Relatives mostly.

ARTHUR *(Taking them)*: More cards? I'm going to have to have another printing of thank-you notes done.

MARION: I answered these last week, so you don't have to bother. Unless you want to.

ARTHUR: Forge my signature?

MARION: Of course not. They were addressed to both of us and they're mostly distant relatives or friends we haven't seen in years. No one important.

ARTHUR: If they've got my name on them, then I'll answer them myself.

MARION: I wasn't telling you not to, I was only saying that you don't have to.

ARTHUR: I understand.

(MARION picks up the teapot and brings it to the kitchen.)

MARION: Let me put this back.

ARTHUR: I ran into Jimmy in the lobby.

MARION: Tell me you're joking.

ARTHUR: I got him to Helen's.

MARION: He's really racking up the points today.

ARTHUR: You know, he still can't look me in the face.

MARION: He's reacting to all of this in strange ways. Give him time. He'll come around. He's really very fond of you.

ARTHUR: I know. But he's at that awkward age: under thirty. I'm sure in twenty years we'll be the best of friends.

MARION: It's not what you think.

ARTHUR: What do you mean?

MARION: Well, you know.

ARTHUR: No I don't know. Tell me.

MARION: I thought that you were intimating something about his blaming you for Collin's illness and I was just letting you know that it's not true. *(Foot in mouth,* SHE *braves on)* We discussed it a lot and . . . uh . . . he understands that his father was sick before you two ever met.

ARTHUR: I don't believe this.

MARION: I'm just trying to say that he doesn't blame you.

ARTHUR: First of all, who asked you? Second of all, that's between him and me. And third and most importantly, of course he blames me. Marion, he's eleven years old. You can discuss all you want, but the fact is that his father died of a "fag" disease and I'm the only fag around to finger.

MARION: My son doesn't use that kind of language.

ARTHUR: Forget the language. I'm talking about what he's been through. Can you imagine the kind of crap he's taken from his friends? That poor kid's been chased and chastised from one end of town to the other. He's got to have someone to blame just to survive. He can't blame you, you're all he's got. He can't blame his father; he's dead. So, Uncle Arthur gets the shaft. Fine, I can handle it.

MARION: You are so wrong, Arthur. I know my son and that is not the way his mind works.

ARTHUR: I don't know what you know. I only know what I know. And all I know is what I hear and see. The snide remarks, the little smirks . . . And it's not just the illness. He's been looking for a scapegoat since the day you and Collin first split up. Finally he has one.

MARION *(Getting very angry now)*: Wait. Are you saying that if he's going to blame someone it should be me?

ARTHUR: I think you should try to see things from his point of view.

MARION: Where do you get off thinking you're privy to my son's point of view?

ARTHUR: It's not that hard to imagine. Life's rolling right along, he's having a happy little childhood, when suddenly one day his father's moving out. No explanations, no reasons, none of the fights that usually accompany such things. Divorce is hard enough for a kid to understand when he's listened to years of battles, but yours?

MARION: So what should we have done? Faked a few months' worth of fights before Collin moved out?

ARTHUR: You could have told him the truth, plain and simple.

MARION: He was seven years old at the time. How the hell do you tell a seven-year-old that his father is leaving his mother to go sleep with other men?

ARTHUR: Well, not like that.

MARION: You know, Arthur, I'm going to say this as nicely as I can: Butt out. You're not his mother and you're not his father.

ARTHUR: Thank you. I wasn't acutely aware of that fact. I will certainly keep that in mind from now on.

MARION: There's only so much information a child that age can handle.

ARTHUR: So it's best that he reach his capacity on the street.

MARION: He knew about the two of you. We talked about it.

ARTHUR: Believe me, he knew before you talked about it. He's young, not stupid.

MARION: It's very easy for you to stand here and criticize, but there are aspects that you will just never be able to understand. You weren't there. You have no idea what it was like for me. You're talking to someone who thought that a girl went to college to meet a husband. I went to protest rallies because I liked the music. I bought a guitar because I thought it looked good on the bed! This lifestyle, this knowledge that you take for granted, was all a little out of left field for me.

ARTHUR: I can imagine.

MARION: No. I don't think you can. I met Collin in college, married him right after graduation and settled down for a nice quiet life of Kids and Careers. You think I had any idea about this? Talk about life's little surprises. You live with someone for sixteen years, you share your life, your bed, you have a child together, and then you wake up one day and he tells you that to him it's all been a lie. A lie. Try that on for size. Here you are the happiest couple you know, fulfilling your every life fantasy and he tells you he's living a lie.

ARTHUR: I'm sure he never said that.

MARION: Don't be so sure. There was a lot of new ground being broken back then and plenty of it was muddy.

ARTHUR: You know that he loved you.

MARION: What's that supposed to do, make things easier? It doesn't. I was brought up to believe, among other things, that if you had love that was enough. So what if I wasn't everything he wanted. Maybe he wasn't exactly everything I wanted either. So, you know what? You count your blessings and you settle.

ARTHUR: No one has to settle. Not him. Not you.

MARION: Of course not. You can say, "Up yours!" to everything and everyone who depends and needs you, and go off to make yourself happy.

ARTHUR: It's not that simple.

MARION: No. This is simpler. Death is simpler. *(Yelling out)* Happy now?

(THEY stare at each other. MARION calms the rage and catches her breath. ARTHUR holds his emotions in check.)

ARTHUR: How about a nice hot cup of coffee? Tea with lemon? Hot cocoa with a marshmallow floating in it?

MARION *(Laughs)*: I was wrong. You *are* a mother.

(ARTHUR *goes into the kitchen and starts preparing things.* MARION *loafs by the doorway.*)

MARION: I lied before. He *was* everything I ever wanted.

(ARTHUR *stops, looks at her, and then changes the subject as* HE *goes on with his work.*)

ARTHUR: When I came into the building and saw Jimmy in the lobby I absolutely freaked for a second. It's amazing how much they look alike. It was like seeing a little miniature Collin standing there.

MARION: I know. He's like Collin's clone. There's nothing of me in him.

ARTHUR: I always kinda hoped that when he grew up he'd take after me. Not much chance, I guess.

MARION: Don't do anything fancy in there.

ARTHUR: Please. Anything we can consume is one less thing to pack.

MARION: So you've said.

ARTHUR: So *we've* said.

MARION: I want to keep seeing you and I want you to see Jim. You're still part of this family. No one's looking to cut you out.

ARTHUR: Ah, who'd want a kid to grow up looking like me anyway. I had enough trouble looking like this. Why pass on the misery?

MARION: You're adorable.

ARTHUR: Is that like saying I have a good personality?

MARION: I think you are one of the most naturally handsome men I know.

ARTHUR: Natural is right, and the bloom is fading.

MARION: All you need is a few good nights' sleep to kill those rings under your eyes.

ARTHUR: Forget the rings under my eyes, (*Grabbing his middle*) . . . how about the rings around my moon?

MARION: I like you like this.

ARTHUR: From the time that Collin started using the wheelchair until he died, about six months, I lost twenty-three pounds. No gym, no diet. In the last seven weeks I've gained close to fifty.

MARION: You're exaggerating.

ARTHUR: I'd prove it on the bathroom scale, but I sold it in working order.

MARION: You'd never know.

ARTHUR: Marion, *you'd* never know, but ask my belt. Ask my pants. Ask my underwear. Even my stretch socks have stretch marks. I called the ambulance at five A.M., he was gone at nine and by nine-thirty, I was on a first-name basis with Sara Lee. I can quote the business hours of every ice-cream parlor, pizzeria and bakery on the island of Manhattan. I know the location of every twenty-four-hour grocery in the greater New York area, and I have memorized the phone numbers of every Mandarin, Szechuan and Hunan restaurant with free delivery.

MARION: At least you haven't wasted your time on useless hobbies.

ARTHUR: Are you kidding? I'm opening my own Overeater's Hotline. We'll have to start small, but expansion is guaranteed.

MARION: You're the best, you know that? If I couldn't be everything that Collin wanted then I'm grateful that he found someone like you.

ARTHUR *(Turning on her without missing a beat)*: Keep your goddamned gratitude to yourself. I didn't go through any of this for you. So your thanks are out of line. And he didn't find "someone like" me. It was me.

MARION *(Frightened)*: I didn't mean . . .

ARTHUR: And I wish you'd remember one thing more: He died in my arms, not yours.

(MARION is totally caught off guard. SHE stares disbelieving, openmouthed. ARTHUR walks past her as HE leaves the kitchen with place mats. HE puts them on the coffee table. As HE arranges the papers and place mats HE speaks, never looking at her.)

ARTHUR: Look, I know you were trying to say something supportive. Don't waste your breath. There's nothing you can say that will make any of this easier for me. There's no way for you to help me get through this. And that's your fault. After three years you still have no idea or understanding of who I am. Or maybe you do know but refuse to accept it. I don't know and I don't care. But at least understand, from my point of view, who you are: You are my husband's *ex*-wife. If you like, the mother of *my* stepson. Don't flatter yourself into thinking you're any more than that. And whatever you are, you're certainly not my friend.

(HE stops, looks up at her, then passes her again as HE goes back to the kitchen.

MARION is shaken, working hard to control herself. SHE moves toward the couch.)

MARION: Why don't we just sign these papers and I'll be out of your way.

ARTHUR: Shouldn't you say *I'll* be out of *your* way? After all, I'm not just signing papers, I'm signing away my home.

MARION *(Resolved not to fight, SHE gets her purse)*: I'll leave the papers here. Please have them notarized and returned to my lawyer.

ARTHUR: Don't forget my painting.

MARION *(Exploding)*: What do you want from me, Arthur?

ARTHUR *(Yelling back)*: I want you the hell out of my apartment! I want you out of my life! And I want you to leave Collin alone!

MARION: The man's dead. I don't know how much more alone I can leave him.

(ARTHUR laughs at the irony, but behind the laughter is something much more desperate.)

ARTHUR: Lots more, Marion. You've got to let him go.

MARION: For the life of me, I don't know what I did, or what you think I did, for you to treat me like this. But you're not going to get away with it. You will not take your anger out on me. I will not stand here and be badgered and insulted by you. I know you've been hurt and I know you're hurting but you're not the only one who lost someone here.

ARTHUR *(Topping her)*: Yes I am! You didn't just lose him. I did! You lost him five years ago when he divorced you. This is not your moment of grief and loss, it's mine! *(Picking up the bundle of cards and throwing it toward her)* These condolences do not belong to you, they're mine. *(Tossing her list back to her)* His things are not yours to give away, they're mine! This death does not belong to you, it's mine! Bought and paid for outright. I suffered for it, I bled for it. I was the one who cooked his meals. I was the one who spoon-fed them. I pushed his wheelchair. I carried and bathed him. I wiped his backside and changed his diapers. I breathed life into and wrestled fear out of his heart. I kept him alive for two years longer than any doctor thought possible and when it was time I was the one who prepared him for death.

I paid in full for my place in his life and I will *not* share it with you. We are not the two widows of Collin Redding. Your life was not here. Your husband didn't just die. You've got a son and a life somewhere else. Your husband's sitting, waiting for you at home, wondering, as I am, what the hell you're doing here and why you can't let go.

(MARION leans back against the couch. SHE'S blown away. ARTHUR stands staring at her.)

ARTHUR *(Quietly)*: Let him go, Marion. He's mine. Dead or alive; mine.

(The teakettle whistles. ARTHUR leaves the room, goes to the kitchen and pours the water as MARION pulls herself together.
ARTHUR carries the loaded tray back into the living room and sets it down on the coffee table. HE sits and pours a cup.)

ARTHUR: One marshmallow or two?

(MARION stares, unsure as to whether the attack is really over or not.)

ARTHUR *(Placing them in her cup)*: Take three, they're small.

(MARION smiles and takes the offered cup)

ARTHUR *(Campily)*: Now let me tell you how I *really* feel.

(MARION jumps slightly, then THEY share a small laugh. Silence as THEY each gather themselves and sip their refreshments.)

MARION *(Calmly)*: Do you think that I sold the apartment just to throw you out?

ARTHUR: I don't care about the apartment . . .

MARION: . . . Because I really didn't. Believe me.

ARTHUR: I know.

MARION: I knew the expenses here were too much for you, and I knew you couldn't afford to buy out my half . . . I figured if we sold it, that you'd at least have a nice chunk of money to start over with.

ARTHUR: You could've given me a little more time.

MARION: Maybe. But I thought the sooner you were out of here, the sooner you could go on with your life.

ARTHUR: Or the sooner you could go on with yours.

MARION: Maybe. *(Pause to gather her thoughts)* Anyway, I'm not going to tell you that I have no idea what you're talking about. I'd have to be worse than deaf and blind not to have seen the way you've been treated. Or mistreated. When I read Collin's obituary in the newspaper and saw my name and Jimmy's name and no mention of you . . . *(Shakes her head, not knowing what to say)* You know that his secretary was the one who wrote that up and sent it in. Not me. But I should have done something about it and I didn't. I know.

ARTHUR: Wouldn't have made a difference. I wrote my own obituary for him and sent it to the smaller papers. They edited me out.

MARION: I'm sorry. I remember, at the funeral, I was surrounded by all of Collin's family and business associates while you were left with your friends. I knew it was wrong. I knew I should have said something but it felt good to have them around me and you looked like you were holding up . . . Wrong. But saying that it's all my fault for not letting go? . . . There were other people involved.

ARTHUR: Who took their cue from you.

MARION: Arthur, you don't understand. Most people that we knew as a couple had no idea that Collin was Gay right up to his death. And even those that did know only found out when he got sick and the word leaked out that it was AIDS. I don't think I have to tell you how stupid and ill-informed most people are about homosexuality. And AIDS . . . ? The kinds of insane behavior that word inspires? . . .

Those people at the funeral, how many times did they call to see how he was doing over these years? How many of them ever went to see him in the hospital? Did any of them even come here? So, why would you expect them to act any differently after his death?

So, maybe that helps to explain their behavior, but what about mine, right? Well, maybe there is no explanation. Only excuses. And excuse number one is that you're right, I have never really let go of him. And I am jealous of you. Hell, I was jealous of anyone that Collin ever talked to, let alone slept with . . . let alone loved.

The first year, after he moved out, we talked all the time about the different men he was seeing. And I always listened and advised. It was kind of fun. It kept us close. It kept me a part of his intimate life.

And the bottom line was always that he wasn't happy with the men he was meeting. So, I was always allowed to hang on to the hope that one day he'd give it all up and come home. Then he got sick.

He called me, told me he was in the hospital and asked if I'd come see him. I ran. When I got to his door there was a sign, IN-STRUCTIONS FOR VISITORS OF AN AIDS PATIENT. I nearly died.

ARTHUR: He hadn't told you?

MARION: No. And believe me, a sign is not the way to find these things out. I was so angry . . . And he was so sick . . . I was sure that he'd die right then. If not from the illness then from the hospital staff's neglect. No one wanted to go near him and I didn't bother fighting with them because I understood that they were scared. I was scared. That whole month in the hospital I didn't let Jimmy visit him once.

You learn.

Well, as you know, he didn't die. And he asked if he could come stay with me until he was well. And I said yes. Of course, yes. Now, here's something I never thought I'd ever admit to anyone: had he asked to stay with me for a few weeks I would have said no. But he asked to stay with me until he was well and knowing there was no cure I said yes. In my craziness I said yes because to me that meant forever. That he was coming back to me forever. Not that I wanted him to die, but I assumed from everything I'd read . . . And we'd be back together for whatever time he had left. Can you understand that?

(ARTHUR nods)

MARION *(Gathers her thoughts again)*: Two weeks later he left. He moved in here. Into this apartment that we had bought as an investment. Never to live in. Certainly never to live apart in. Next thing I knew, the name Arthur starts appearing in every phone call, every dinner conversation.

"Did you see the doctor?"

"Yes. Arthur made sure I kept the appointment."

"Are you going to your folks for Thanksgiving?"

"No. Arthur and I are having some friends over."

I don't know which one of us was more of a coward, he for not telling or me for not asking about you. But eventually you became a given. Then, of course, we met and became what I had always thought of as friends.

(ARTHUR winces in guilt)

MARION: I don't care what you say, how could we not be friends with something so great in common: love for one of the most special human beings there ever was. And don't try and tell me there weren't times when you enjoyed my being around as an ally. I can think of a dozen occasions when we ganged up on him, teasing him with our intimate knowledge of his personal habits.

(ARTHUR *has to laugh*)

MARION: Blanket stealing? Snoring? Excess gas, no less? *(Takes a moment to enjoy this truce)* I don't think that my loving him threatened your relationship. Maybe I'm not being truthful with myself. But I don't. I never tried to step between you. Not that I ever had the opportunity. Talk about being joined at the hip! And that's not to say I wasn't jealous. I was. Terribly. Hatefully. But always lovingly. I was happy for Collin because there was no way to deny that he was happy. With everything he was facing, he was happy. Love did that. You did that.

He lit up with you. He came to life. I envied that and all the time you spent together, but more, I watched you care for him (sometimes *overcare* for him), and I was in awe. I could never have done what you did. I never would have survived. I really don't know how you did.

ARTHUR: Who said I survived?

MARION: Don't tease. You did an absolutely incredible thing. It's not as if you met him before he got sick. You entered a relationship that you knew in all probability would end this way and you never wavered.

ARTHUR: Of course I did. Don't have me sainted, Marion. But sometimes you have no choice. Believe me, if I could've gotten away from him I would've. But I was a prisoner of love.

(HE *makes a campy gesture and pose.*)

MARION: Stop.

ARTHUR: And there were lots of pluses. I got to quit a job I hated, stay home all day and watch game shows. I met a lot of doctors and learned a lot of big words. (ARTHUR *jumps up and goes to the pile of boxes where* HE *extracts one and brings it back to the couch*) And then there was all the exciting traveling I got to do. This box has a souvenir from each one of our trips. Wanna see?

(MARION *nods.* HE *opens the box and pulls things out one by one.*)

ARTHUR *(Continued)* *(Holding up an old bottle)*: This is from the house we rented in Reno when we went to clear out his lungs. *(Holding handmade potholders)* This is from the hospital in Reno. Collin made them. They had a great arts and crafts program. *(Copper bracelets)* These are from a faith healer in Philly. They don't do much for a fever, but they look great with a green sweater. *(Glass ashtrays)* These are from our first visit to the clinic in France. Such lovely people. *(A Bible)* This is from our second visit to the clinic in France. *(A bead necklace)* A Voodoo doctor in New Orleans. Next time we'll have to get there earlier in the year. I think he sold all the pretty ones at Mardi Gras. *(A tiny piñata)*

Then there was Mexico. Black market drugs and empty wallets. *(Now pulling things out at random)* L.A., San Francisco, Houston, Boston . . . We traveled everywhere they offered hope for sale and came home with souvenirs. *(ARTHUR quietly pulls a few more things out and then begins to put them all back into the box slowly. Softly as HE works:)*

Marion, I would have done anything, traveled anywhere to avoid . . . or delay . . . Not just because I loved him so desperately, but when you've lived the way we did for three years . . . the battle becomes your life. *(HE looks at her and then away)*

His last few hours were beyond any scenario I had imagined. He hadn't walked in nearly six months. He was totally incontinent. If he spoke two words in a week I was thankful. Days went by without his eyes ever focusing on me. He just stared out at I don't know what. Not the meals as I fed him. Not the TV I played constantly for company. Just out. Or maybe in.

It was the middle of the night when I heard his breathing become labored. His lungs were filling with fluid again. I knew the sound. I'd heard it a hundred times before. So, I called the ambulance and got him to the hospital. They hooked him up to the machines, the oxygen, shot him with morphine and told me that they would do what they could to keep him alive.

But, Marion, it wasn't the machines that kept him breathing. He did it himself. It was that incredible will and strength inside him. Whether it came from his love of life or fear of death, who knows. But he'd been counted out a hundred times and a hundred times he fought his way back.

I got a magazine to read him, pulled a chair up to the side of his bed and holding his hand, I wondered whether I should call Helen to let the cleaning lady in or if he'd fall asleep and I could sneak home for an hour. I looked up from the page and he was looking at me. Really looking right into my eyes. I patted his cheek and said, "Don't worry, honey, you're going to be fine."

But there was something else in his eyes. He wasn't satisfied with that. And I don't know why, I have no idea where it came from, I just heard the words coming out of my mouth, "Collin, do you want to die?" His eyes filled and closed, he nodded his head.

I can't tell you what I was thinking, I'm not sure I was. I slipped off my shoes, lifted his blanket and climbed into bed next to him. I helped him to put his arms around me, and mine around him, and whispered as gently as I could into his ear, "It's alright to let go now. It's time to go on." And he did.

Marion, you've got your life and his son. All I have is an intangible place in a man's history. Leave me that. Respect that.

MARION: I understand.

(ARTHUR suddenly comes to life, running to get the shopping bag that
HE'D *left at the front door.)*

ARTHUR: Jeez! With all the screamin' and sad storytelling I forget something. *(HE extracts a bouquet of flowers from the bag)* I brung you flowers
and everything.

MARION: You brought *me* flowers?

ARTHUR: Well, I knew you'd never think to bring me flowers and I felt
that on an occasion such as this somebody oughta get flowers from
somebody.

MARION: You know, Arthur, you're really making me feel like a worthless
piece of garbage.

ARTHUR: So what else is new? *(HE presents the flowers)* Just promise me
one thing: Don't press one in a book. Just stick them in a vase and
when they fade just toss them out. No more memorabilia.

MARION: Arthur, I want to do something for you and I don't know what.
Tell me what you want.

ARTHUR: I want little things. Not much. I want to be remembered. If you
get a Christmas card from Collin's mother, make sure she sent me one
too. If his friends call to see how you are, ask if they've called me.
Have me to dinner so I can see Jimmy. Let me take him out now and
then. Invite me to his wedding.

(THEY BOTH laugh.)

MARION: You've got it.

ARTHUR *(Clearing the table)*: Let me get all this cold cocoa out of the way.
We still have the deed to do.

MARION *(Checking her watch)*: And I've got to get Jimmy home in time for
practice.

ARTHUR: Band practice?

MARION: Baseball. *(Picking her list off the floor)* About this list, you do
what you want.

ARTHUR: Believe me, I will. But I promise to consider your suggestions.
Just don't rush me. I'm not ready to give it all away. *(ARTHUR is off
to the kitchen with his tray and the phone rings.* HE *answers it in the kitchen)*
Hello? . . . Just a minute. *(Calling out)* It's your eager Little Leaguer.

*(MARION picks up the living room extension and ARTHUR hangs
his up.)*

MARION *(Into phone)*: Hello, honey. . . . I'll be down in five minutes. No.
You know what? You come up here and get me. . . . No, I said you
should come up here. . . . I said I want to come up here. . . . Because
I said so. . . . Thank you.

(SHE hangs the receiver.)

ARTHUR *(Rushing to the papers)*: Alright, where do we start on these?

MARION *(Getting out her seal)*: I guess you should just start signing everything and I'll stamp along with you. Keep one of everything on the
side for yourself.

ARTHUR: Now I feel so rushed. What am I signing?

MARION: You want to do this another time?

ARTHUR: No. Let's get it over with. I wouldn't survive another session
like this.

(HE starts to sign and SHE starts her job.)

MARION: I keep meaning to ask you; how are you?

ARTHUR *(At first puzzled and then)*: Oh, you mean my health? Fine. No,
I'm fine. I've been tested, and nothing. We were very careful. We took
many precautions. Collin used to make jokes about how we should
invest in rubber futures.

MARION: I'll bet.

ARTHUR *(Stops what HE's doing)*: It never occurred to me until now. How
about you?

MARION *(Not stopping)*: Well, we never had sex after he got sick.

ARTHUR: But before?

MARION *(Stopping but not looking up)*: I have the antibodies in my blood.
No signs that it will ever develop into anything else. And it's been five
years so my chances are pretty good that I'm just a carrier.

ARTHUR: I'm so sorry. Collin never told me.

MARION: He didn't know. In fact, other than my husband and the doctors,
you're the only one I've told.

ARTHUR: You and your husband . . . ?

MARION: Have invested in rubber futures. There'd only be a problem if
we wanted to have a child. Which we do. But we'll wait. Miracles
happen every day.

ARTHUR: I don't know what to say.

MARION: Tell me you'll be there if I ever need you.

*(ARTHUR gets up, goes to her and puts his arms around her. THEY hold
each other. HE gently pushes her away to make a joke.)*

ARTHUR: Sure! Take something else that should have been mine.

MARION: Don't even joke about things like that.

(The doorbell rings. THEY pull themselves together.)

ARTHUR: You know we'll never get these done today.

MARION: So, tomorrow.

*(ARTHUR goes to open the door as MARION gathers her things. HE
opens the door and JIMMY is standing in the hall.)*

JIM: C'mon, Ma. I'm gonna be late.

ARTHUR: Would you like to come inside?

JIM: We've gotta go.

MARION: Jimmy, come on.

JIM: Ma!

(SHE *glares.* HE *comes in.* ARTHUR *closes the door.*)

MARION (*Holding out the flowers*): Take these for Mommy.

JIM (*Taking them*): Can we go?

MARION (*Picking up the painting*): Say good-bye to your Uncle Arthur.

JIM: 'Bye, Arthur. Come on.

MARION: Give him a kiss.

ARTHUR: Marion, don't.

MARION: Give your uncle a kiss good-bye.

JIM: He's not my uncle.

MARION: No. He's a hell of a lot more than your uncle.

ARTHUR (*Offering his hand*): A handshake will do.

MARION: Tell Uncle Arthur what your daddy told you.

JIM: About what?

MARION: Stop playing dumb. You know.

ARTHUR: Don't embarrass him.

MARION: Jimmy, please.

JIM (HE *regards his* MOTHER'S *softer tone and then speaks*): He said that after me and Mommy he loved you the most.

MARION (*Standing behind him*): Go on.

JIM: And that I should love you too. And make sure that you're not lonely or very sad.

ARTHUR: Thank you.

(ARTHUR *reaches down to the* BOY *and* THEY *hug.* JIM *gives him a little peck on the cheek and then breaks away.*)

MARION (*Going to open the door*): Alright, kid, you done good. Now let's blow this joint before you muck it up.

(JIM *rushes out the door.* MARION *turns to* ARTHUR.)

MARION: A child's kiss is magic. Why else would they be so stingy with them. I'll call you.

(ARTHUR *nods understanding.* MARION *pulls the door closed behind her.* ARTHUR *stands quietly as the lights fade to black.*)

THE END

NOTE: *If being performed on film, the final image should be of* ARTHUR *leaning his back against the closed door on the inside of the apartment and* MARION *leaning on the outside of the door. A moment of thought and then* THEY BOTH *move on.*

Considerations

1. Describe the relationship between Jim and Marion. Evaluate the way each responds to Collin's death and to the other's response to Collin's death.
2. June says, "Arthur got plenty already. I'm not crying for Arthur." What does she mean by this? What is your evaluation of Arthur's losses — and gains — from his relationship with Collin and from Collin's death?
3. Think about the title of the play. June warns Marion to "[tidy] up loose ends . . . when Arthur gets here." What is implied by a "tidy" ending or by "tidying up loose ends"? To what extent is the ending described "tidy"? How might the play's title be considered ironic?
4. Describe the relationship between Arthur and Marion. For whom do you have more sympathy? Explain.
5. What do the three main characters in the play (Arthur, Marion, and Jimmy) learn about themselves, about each other, about Collin, and — especially — about facing death (either their own or the death of others)?

JESSICA MITFORD (1917–   )

The American Way of Death

The drama begins to unfold with the arrival of the corpse at the mortuary.

Alas, poor Yorick!° How surprised he would be to see how his counterpart of today is whisked off to a funeral parlor and is in short order sprayed, sliced, pierced, pickled, trussed, trimmed, creamed, waxed, painted, rouged, and neatly dressed — transformed from a common corpse into a Beautiful Memory Picture. This process is known in the trade as embalming and restorative art, and is so universally employed in the United States and Canada that the funeral director does it routinely, without consulting corpse or kin. He regards as eccentric those few who are hardy enough to suggest that it might be dispensed with. Yet no law requires embalming, no religious doctrine commends it, nor is it dictated by considerations of health, sanitation, or even of personal daintiness. In no part of the world but in Northern America is it widely used. The purpose of embalming is to make the corpse presentable for viewing in a suitably costly container; and here too the funeral director routinely, without first consulting the family, prepares the body for public display.

Is all this legal? The processes to which a dead body may be subjected are after all to some extent circumscribed by law. In most states, for instance, the signature of next of kin must be obtained before an autopsy may be performed, before the deceased may be cremated, before the body may be turned over to a medical school for research purposes; or such provision must be made in the decedent's will. In the case of embalming, no such permission is required nor is it ever sought. A textbook, *The Principles and Practices of Embalming,* comments on this: "There is some question regarding the legality of much that is done within the preparation room." The author points out that it would be most unusual for a responsible member of a bereaved family to instruct the mortician, in so many words, to *"embalm"* the body of a deceased relative. The very term "embalming" is so seldom used that the mortician must rely upon custom in the matter. The author concludes that unless the family specifies otherwise, the act of entrusting the body to the care of a funeral establishment carries with it an implied permission to go ahead and embalm.

Embalming is indeed a most extraordinary procedure, and one must wonder at the docility of Americans who each year pay hundreds of millions of dollars for its perpetuation, blissfully ignorant of what it is all about, what is done, how it is done. Not one in ten thousand has any idea of what actually

---

Alas, poor Yorick: A reference to Shakespeare's *Hamlet;* in a comic scene, two gravediggers discover the skull of a man they knew, and Hamlet addresses his remains with these words.

takes place. Books on the subject are extremely hard to come by. They are not to be found in most libraries or bookshops.

In an era when huge television audiences watch surgical operations in   5
the comfort of their living rooms, when, thanks to the animated cartoon, the geography of the digestive system has become familiar territory even to the nursery school set, in a land where the satisfaction of curiosity about almost all matters is a national pastime, the secrecy surrounding embalming can, surely, hardly be attributed to the inherent gruesomeness of the subject. Custom in this regard has within this century suffered a complete reversal. In the early days of American embalming, when it was performed in the home of the deceased, it was almost mandatory for some relative to stay by the embalmer's side and witness the procedure. Today, family members who might wish to be in attendance would certainly be dissuaded by the funeral director. All others, except apprentices, are excluded by law from the preparation room.

A close look at what does actually take place may explain in large measure the undertaker's intractable reticence concerning a procedure that has become his major *raison d'être.°* It is possible he fears the public information about embalming might lead patrons to wonder if they really want this service? If the funeral men are loath to discuss the subject outside the trade, the reader may, understandably, be equally loath to go on reading at this point. For those who have the stomach for it, let us part the formaldehyde curtain. . . .

The body is first laid out in the undertaker's morgue — or rather, Mr. Jones is reposing in the preparation room — to be readied to bid the world farewell.

The preparation room in any of the better funeral establishments has the tiled and sterile look of a surgery, and indeed the embalmer-restorative artist who does his chores there is beginning to adopt the term "dermasurgeon" (appropriately corrupted by some mortician-writers as "demi-surgeon") to describe his calling. His equipment, consisting of scalpels, scissors, augurs, forceps, clamps, needles, pumps, tubes, bowls and basins, is crudely imitative of the surgeon's, as is his technique, acquired in a nine- or twelve-month post-high-school course in an embalming school. He is supplied by an advanced chemical industry with a bewildering array of fluids, sprays, pastes, oils, powders, creams, to fix or soften tissue, shrink or distend it as needed, dry it here, restore the moisture there. There are cosmetics, waxes and paints to fill and cover features, even plaster of Paris to replace entire limbs. There are ingenious aids to prop and stabilize the cadaver: a Vari-Pose Head Rest, the Edwards Arm and Hand Positioner, the Repose Block (to support the shoulders during the embalming), and the Throop Foot Positioner, which resembles an old-fashioned stocks.

Mr. John H. Eckels, president of the Eckels College of Mortuary Science, thus describes the first part of the embalming procedure: "In the hands

raison d'être: French; reason for being.

of a skilled practitioner, this work may be done in a comparatively short time and without mutilating the body other than by slight incision — so slight that it scarcely would cause serious inconvenience if made upon a living person. It is necessary to remove the blood, and doing this not only helps in the disinfecting, but removes the principal cause of disfigurements due to discoloration."

Another textbook discusses the all-important time element: "The ear-   10 lier this is done, the better, for every hour that elapses between death and embalming will add to the problems and complications encountered. . . ." Just how soon should one get going on the embalming? The author tells us, "On the basis of such scanty information made available to this profession through its rudimentary and haphazard system of technical research, we must conclude that the best results are to be obtained if the subject is embalmed before life is completely extinct — that is, before cellular death has occurred. In the average case, this would mean within an hour after somatic death." For those who feel that there is something a little rudimentary, not to say haphazard, about this advice, a comforting thought is offered by another writer. Speaking of fears entertained in early days of premature burial, he points out, "One of the effects of embalming by chemical injection, however, has been to dispel fears of live burial." How true; once blood is removed, chances of live burial are indeed remote.

To return to Mr. Jones, the blood is drained out through the veins and replaced by embalming fluid pumped in through the arteries. As noted in *The Principles and Practices of Embalming,* "every operator has a favorite injection and drainage point — a fact which becomes a handicap only if he fails or refuses to forsake his favorites when conditions demand it." Typical favorites are the carotid artery, femoral artery, jugular vein, subclavian vein. There are various choices of embalming fluid. If Flextone is used, it will produce a "mild, flexible rigidity. The skin retains a velvety softness, the tissues are rubbery and pliable. Ideal for women and children." It may be blended with B. and G. Products Company's Lyf-Lyk tint, which is guaranteed to reproduce "nature's own skin texture . . . the velvety appearance of living tissue." Suntone comes in three separate tints: Suntan; Special Cosmetic Tint, a pink shade "especially indicated for young female subjects"; and Regular Cosmetic Tint, moderately pink.

About three to six gallons of a dyed and perfumed solution of formaldehyde, glycerin, borax, phenol, alcohol, and water is soon circulating through Mr. Jones, whose mouth has been sewn together with a "needle directed upward between the upper lip and gum and brought out through the left nostril," with the corners raised slightly "for a more pleasant expression." If he should be bucktoothed, his teeth are cleaned with Bon Ami and coated with colorless nail polish. His eyes, meanwhile, are closed with flesh-tinted eye caps and eye cement.

The next step is to have at Mr. Jones with a thing called a trocar. This is a long, hollow needle attached to a tube. It is jabbed into the abdomen, poked around the entrails and chest cavity, the contents of which are pumped out and replaced with "cavity fluid." This done, and the hole in the abdomen sewn up, Mr. Jones's face is heavily creamed (to protect the skin from burns which may be caused by leakage of the chemicals), and he is covered with a sheet and left unmolested for a while. But not for long—there is more, much more, in store for him. He has been embalmed, but not yet restored, and the best time to start the restorative work is eight to ten hours after embalming, when the tissues have become firm and dry.

The object of all this attention to the corpse, it must be remembered, is to make it presentable for viewing in an attitude of healthy repose. "Our customs require the presentation of our dead in the semblance of normality . . . unmarred by the ravages of illness, disease or mutilation," says Mr. J. Sheridan Mayer in his *Restorative Art*. This is rather a large order since few people die in the full bloom of health, unravaged by illness and unmarked by some disfigurement. The funeral industry is equal to the challenge: "In some cases the gruesome appearance of a mutilated or disease-ridden subject may be quite discouraging. The task of restoration may seem impossible and shake the confidence of the embalmer. This is the time for intestinal fortitude and determination. Once the formative work is begun and affected tissues are cleaned or removed, all doubts of success vanish. It is surprising and gratifying to discover the results which may be obtained."

The embalmer, having allowed an appropriate interval to elapse, re-   15
turns to the attack, but now he brings into play the skill and equipment of sculptor and cosmetician. Is a hand missing? Casting one in plaster of Paris is a simple matter. "For replacement purposes, only a cast of the back of the hand is necessary; this is within the ability of the average operator and is quite adequate." If a lip or two, a nose or an ear should be missing, the embalmer has at hand a variety of restorative waxes with which to model replacements. Pores and skin texture are simulated by stipping with a little brush, and over this cosmetics are laid on. Head off? Decapitation cases are rather routinely handled. Ragged edges are trimmed, and head joined to torso with a series of splints, wires and sutures. It is a good idea to have a little something at the neck—a scarf or high collar—when time for viewing comes. Swollen mouth? Cut out tissue as needed from inside the lips. If too much is removed, the surface contour can easily be restored by padding with cotton. Swollen necks and cheeks are reduced by removing tissue through vertical incisions made down each side of the neck. "When the deceased is casketed, the pillow will hide the suture incisions . . . as an extra precaution against leakage, the suture may be painted with liquid sealer."

The opposite condition is more likely to present itself—that of emaciation. His hypodermic syringe now loaded with massage cream, the embalmer seeks out and fills the hollowed and sunken areas by injection. In this procedure the backs of the hands and fingers and the under-chin area should not be neglected.

Positioning the lips is a problem that recurrently challenges the ingenuity of the embalmer. Closed too tightly they tend to give a stern, even disapproving expression. Ideally, embalmers feel, the lips should give the impression of being ever so slightly parted, the upper lip protruding slightly for a more youthful appearance. This takes some engineering, however, as the lips tend to drift apart. Lip drift can sometimes be remedied by pushing one or two straight pins through the inner margin of the lower lip and then inserting them between the two front upper teeth. If Mr. Jones happens to have no teeth, the pins can just as easily be anchored in his Armstrong Face Former and Denture Replacer. Another method to maintain lip closure is to dislocate the lower jaw, which is then held in its new position by a wire run through holes which have been drilled through the upper and lower jaws at the midline. As the French are fond of saying, *il faut souffrir pour être belle.*°

If Mr. Jones has died of jaundice, the embalming fluid will very likely turn him green. Does this deter the embalmer? Not if he has intestinal fortitude. Masking pastes and cosmetics are heavily laid on, burial garments and casket interiors are color-correlated with particular care, and Jones is displayed beneath rose-colored lights. Friends will say, "How *well* he looks." Death by carbon monoxide, on the other hand, can be rather a good thing from the embalmer's viewpoint: "One advantage is the fact that this type of discoloration is an exaggerated form of a natural pink coloration." This is nice because the healthy glow is already present and needs but little attention.

The patching and filling completed, Mr. Jones is now shaved, washed and dressed. Cream-based cosmetic, available in pink, flesh, suntan, brunette, and blond, is applied to his hands and face, his hair is shampooed and combed (and, in the case of Mrs. Jones, set), his hands manicured. For the horny-handed son of toil special care must be taken; cream should be applied to remove ingrained grime, and the nails cleaned. "If he were not in the habit of having them manicured in life, trimming and shaping is advised for better appearance — never questioned by kin."

Jones is now ready for casketing (this is the present participle of the verb "to casket"). In this operation his right shoulder should be depressed slightly "to turn the body a bit to the right and soften the appearance of lying flat on the back." Positioning the hands is a matter of importance, and special rubber positioning blocks may be used. The hands should be cupped slightly for a more lifelike, relaxed appearance. Proper placement of the body requires a delicate sense of balance. It should lie as high as possible in the casket, yet not so high that the lid, when lowered, will hit the nose. On the other hand, we are cautioned, placing the body too low "creates the impression that the body is in a box."

Jones is next wheeled into the appointed slumber room where a few last touches may be added — his favorite pipe placed in his hand or, if he was a great reader, a book propped into position. (In the case of little Master Jones a Teddy bear may be clutched.) Here he will hold open house for a few days, visiting hours 10 A.M. to 9 P.M.

20

Il faut souffrir pour être belle: French; one must suffer to be beautiful.

Considerations

1. Although her topic in this essay is certainly serious, Mitford often uses humor. List several comments or observations you consider humorous and analyze the effect of humor on the tone of the essay. In addition, consider how Mitford's use of humor suggests her theme(s).
2. What are the benefits and disadvantages of embalming and restoration, according to Mitford? In her view, what values have caused these practices to be nearly universally adopted throughout the United States (as well as some other parts of the world)?
3. Note that Mitford frequently includes quotations from the professional journals and textbooks used by funeral directors. Why might she use this strategy? Analyze the effect of this strategy on your response to her essay.
4. What is the effect of Mitford's naming the corpse "Mr. Jones" rather than simply referring to "the body"?
5. Analyze Mitford's attitude toward American funeral practices. Then explain why you agree or disagree with the views she supports.

ELIZABETH KÜBLER-ROSS (1926–   )

On the Fear of Death

*Let me not pray to be sheltered from
dangers but to be fearless in facing
them.
Let me not beg for the stilling of
my pain but for the heart to conquer it.
Let me not look for allies in life's
battlefield but to my own strength.
Let me not crave in anxious fear to
be saved but hope for the patience to
win my freedom.
Grant me that I may not be a
coward, feeling your mercy in my
success alone; but let me find the grasp
of your hand in my failure.*

Rabindranath Tagore, *Fruit-Gathering*

Epidemics have taken a great toll of lives in past generations. Death in infancy and early childhood was frequent and there were few families who didn't lose a member of the family at an early age. Medicine has changed greatly in the last decades. Widespread vaccinations have practically eradicated many illnesses, at least in western Europe and the United States. The use of chemotherapy, especially the antibiotics, has contributed to an ever-decreasing number of fatalities in infectious diseases. Better child care and education has effected a low morbidity and mortality among children. The many diseases that have taken an impressive toll among the young and middle-aged have been conquered. The number of old people is on the rise, and with this fact come the number of people with malignancies and chronic diseases associated more with old age.

Pediatricians have less work with acute and life-threatening situations as they have an ever-increasing number of patients with psychosomatic disturbances and adjustment and behavior problems. Physicians have more people in their waiting rooms with emotional problems than they have ever had before, but they also have more elderly patients who not only try to live with their decreased physical abilities and limitations but who also face loneliness and isolation with all its pains and anguish. The majority of these people are not seen by a psychiatrist. Their needs have to be elicited and gratified by other professional people, for instance, chaplains and social workers. It is for them that I am trying to outline the changes that have taken place in the last few decades, changes that are ultimately responsible for the increased fear of death, the rising number of emotional problems, and the greater need for understanding of and coping with the problems of death and dying.

When we look back in time and study old cultures and people, we are impressed that death has always been distasteful to man and will probably always be. From a psychiatrist's point of view this is very understandable and can perhaps best be explained by our basic knowledge that, in our unconscious, death is never possible in regard to ourselves. It is inconceivable for our unconscious to imagine an actual ending of our own life here on earth, and if this life of ours has to end, the ending is always attributed to a malicious intervention from the outside by someone else. In simple terms, in our unconscious mind we can only be killed; it is inconceivable to die of a natural cause or of old age. Therefore death in itself is associated with a bad act, a frightening happening, something that in itself calls for retribution and punishment.

One is wise to remember these fundamental facts as they are essential in understanding some of the most important, otherwise unintelligible communications of our patients.

The second fact that we have to comprehend is that in our unconscious mind we cannot distinguish between a wish and a deed. We are all aware of some of our illogical dreams in which two completely opposite statements can exist side by side — very acceptable in our dreams but unthinkable and illogical in our wakening state. Just as our unconscious mind cannot differentiate between the wish to kill somebody in anger and the act of having done so, the young child is unable to make this distinction. The child who angrily wishes his mother to drop dead for not having gratified his needs will be traumatized greatly by the actual death of his mother — even if this event is not linked closely in time with his destructive wishes. He will always take part or the whole blame for the loss of his mother. He will always say to himself — rarely to others — "I did it, I am responsible, I was bad, therefore Mommy left me." It is well to remember that the child will react in the same manner if he loses a parent by divorce, separation, or desertion. Death is often seen by a child as an impermanent thing and has therefore little distinction from a divorce in which he may have an opportunity to see a parent again.

Many a parent will remember remarks of their children such as, "I will bury my doggy now and next spring when the flowers come up again, he will get up." Maybe it was the same wish that motivated the ancient Egyptians to supply their dead with food and goods to keep them happy and the old Amerian Indians to bury their relatives with their belongings.

When we grow older and begin to realize that our omnipotence is really not so omnipotent, that our strongest wishes are not powerful enough to make the impossible possible, the fear that we have contributed to the death of a loved one diminishes — and with it the guilt. The fear remains diminished, however, only so long as it is not challenged too strongly. Its

5

vestiges can be seen daily in hospital corridors and in people associated with the bereaved.

A husband and wife may have been fighting for years, but when the partner dies, the survivor will pull his hair, whine and cry louder and beat his chest in regret, fear and anguish, and will hence fear his own death more than before, still believing in the law of talion—an eye for an eye, a tooth for a tooth—"I am responsible for her death, I will have to die a pitiful death in retribution."

Maybe this knowledge will help us understand many of the old customs and rituals which have lasted over the centuries and whose purpose is to diminish the anger of the gods or the people as the case may be, thus decreasing the anticipated punishment. I am thinking of the ashes, the torn clothes, the veil, the *Klage Weiber*° of the old days—they are all means to ask you to take pity on them, the mourners, and are expressions of sorrow, grief, and shame. If someone grieves, beats his chest, tears his hair, or refuses to eat, it is an attempt at self-punishment to avoid or reduce the anticipated punishment for the blame that he takes on the death of a loved one.

This grief, shame, and guilt are not very far removed from feelings of   10
anger and rage. The process of grief always includes some qualities of anger. Since none of us likes to admit anger at a deceased person, these emotions are often disguised or repressed and prolong the period of grief or show up in other ways. It is well to remember that it is not up to us to judge such feelings as bad or shameful but to understand their true meaning and origin as something very human. In order to illustrate this I will again use the example of the child—and the child in us. The five-year-old who loses his mother is both blaming himself for her disappearance and being angry at her for having deserted him and for no longer gratifying his needs. The dead person then turns into something the child loves and wants very much but also hates with equal intensity for this severe deprivation.

The ancient Hebrews regarded the body of a dead person as something unclean and not to be touched. The early American Indians talked about the evil spirits and shot arrows in the air to drive the spirits away. Many other cultures have rituals to take care of the "bad" dead person, and they all originate in this feeling of anger which still exists in all of us, though we dislike admitting it. The tradition of the tombstone may originate in the wish to keep the bad spirits deep down in the ground, and the pebbles that many mourners put on the grave are leftover symbols of the same wish. Though we call the firing of guns at military funerals a last salute, it is the same symbolic ritual as the Indian used when he shot his spears and arrows into the skies.

I give these examples to emphasize that man has not basically changed. Death is still a fearful, frightening happening, and the fear of death is a universal fear even if we think we have mastered it on many levels.

Klage Weiber: Lamenting widows.

What has changed is our way of coping and dealing with death and dying and our dying patients.

Having been raised in a country in Europe where science is not so advanced, where modern techniques have just started to find their way into medicine, and where people still live as they did in this country half a century ago, I may have had an opportunity to study a part of the evolution of mankind in a shorter period.

I remember as a child the death of a farmer. He fell from a tree and 15 was not expected to live. He asked simply to die at home, a wish that was granted without question. He called his daughters into the bedroom and spoke with each one of them alone for a few moments. He arranged his affairs quietly, though he was in great pain, and distributed his belongings and his land, none of which was to be split until his wife should follow him in death. He also asked each of his children to share in the work, duties, and tasks that he had carried on until the time of the accident. He asked his friends to visit him once more, to bid goodbye to them. Although I was a small child at the time, he did not exclude me or my siblings. We were allowed to share in the preparations of the family just as we were permitted to grieve with them until he died. When he did die, he was left at home, in his own beloved home which he had built, and among his friends and neighbors who went to take a last look at him where he lay in the midst of flowers in the place he had lived in and loved so much. In that country today there is still no make-believe slumber room, no embalming, no false makeup to pretend sleep. Only the signs of very disfiguring illnesses are covered up with bandages and only infectious cases are removed from the home prior to the burial.

Why do I describe such "old-fashioned" customs? I think they are an indication of our acceptance of a fatal outcome, and they help the dying patient as well as his family to accept the loss of a loved one. If a patient is allowed to terminate his life in the familiar and beloved environment, it requires less adjustment for him. His own family knows him well enough to replace a sedative with a glass of his favorite wine; or the smell of a home-cooked soup may give him the appetite to sip a few spoons of fluid which, I think, is still more enjoyable than an infusion. I will not minimize the need for sedatives and infusions and realize full well from my own experience as a country doctor that they are sometimes life-saving and often unavoidable. But I also know that patience and familiar people and foods could replace many a bottle of intravenous fluids given for the simple reason that it fulfills the physiological need without involving too many people and/or individual nursing care.

The fact that children are allowed to stay at home where a fatality has struck and are included in the talk, discussions, and fears gives them the feeling that they are not alone in their grief and gives them the comfort of shared responsibility and shared mourning. It prepares them gradually and helps them view death as part of life, an experience which may help them grow and mature.

This is in great contrast to a society in which death is viewed as taboo, discussion of it is regarded as morbid, and children are excluded with the presumption and pretext that it would be "too much" for them. They are then sent off to relatives, often accompanied by some unconvincing lies of "Mother has gone on a long trip" or other unbelievable stories. The child senses that something is wrong, and his distrust in adults will only multiply if other relatives add new variations of the story, avoid his questions or suspicions, shower him with gifts as a meager substitute for a loss he is not permitted to deal with. Sooner or later the child will become aware of the changed family situation and, depending on the age and personality of the child, will have an unresolved grief and regard this incident as a frightening, mysterious, in any case very traumatic experience with untrustworthy grownups, which he has no way to cope with.

It is equally unwise to tell a little child who lost her brother that God loved little boys so much that he took little Johnny to heaven. When this little girl grew up to be a woman she never solved her anger at God, which resulted in a psychotic depression when she lost her own little son three decades later.

We would think that our great emancipation, our knowledge of science and of man, has given us better ways and means to prepare ourselves and our families for this inevitable happening. Instead the days are gone when a man was allowed to die in peace and dignity in his own home.

The more we are making advancements in science, the more we seem to fear and deny the reality of death. How is this possible?

We use euphemisms, we make the dead look as if they were asleep, we ship the children off to protect them from the anxiety and turmoil around the house if the patient is fortunate enough to die at home, we don't allow children to visit their dying parents in the hospitals, we have long and controversial discussions about whether patients should be told the truth — a question that rarely arises when the dying person is tended by the family physician who has known him from delivery to death and who knows the weaknesses and strengths of each member of the family.

I think there are many reasons for this flight away from facing death calmly. One of the most important facts is that dying nowadays is more gruesome in many ways, namely, more lonely, mechanical, and dehumanized; at times it is even difficult to determine technically when the time of death has occurred.

Dying becomes lonely and impersonal because the patient is often taken out of his familiar environment and rushed to an emergency room. Whoever has been very sick and has required rest and comfort especially may recall his experience of being put on a stretcher and enduring the noise of the ambulance siren and hectic rush until the hospital gates open. Only those who have lived through this may appreciate the discomfort and cold necessity of such transportation which is only the beginning of a long ordeal — hard to endure when you are well, difficult to express in words when noise, light, pumps, and voices are all too much to put up with. It may well be that we might consider more the patient under the sheets and blankets and perhaps stop our well-meant efficiency and rush in order to hold the patient's hand, to smile, or to listen to a question. I include the trip to the hospital as the first episode in dying, as it is for many. I am putting it exaggeratedly in contrast to the sick man who is left at home — not to say that lives should not be saved if they can be saved by a hospitalization but to keep the focus on the patient's experience, his needs and his reactions.

When a patient is severely ill, he is often treated like a person with no   25 right to an opinion. It is often someone else who makes the decision if and when and where a patient should be hospitalized. It would take so little to remember that the sick person too has feelings, has wishes and opinions, and has — most important of all — the right to be heard.

Well, our presumed patient has now reached the emergency room. He will be surrounded by busy nurses, orderlies, interns, residents, a lab technician perhaps who will take some blood, an electrocardiogram technician who takes the cardiogram. He may be moved to X-ray and he will overhear opinions of his condition and discussions and questions to members of the family. He slowly but surely is beginning to be treated like a thing. He is no longer a person. Decisions are made often without his opinion. If he tries to rebel he will be sedated and after hours of waiting and wondering whether he has the strength, he will be wheeled into the operating room or intensive treatment unit and become an object of great concern and great financial investment.

He may cry for rest, peace, and dignity, but he will get infusions, transfusions, a heart machine, or tracheotomy if necessary. He may want one single person to stop for one single minute so that he can ask one single question — but he will get a dozen people around the clock, all busily preoccupied with his heart rate, pulse, electrocardiogram or pulmonary functions, his secretions or excretions but not with him as a human being. He may wish to fight it all but it is going to be a useless fight since all this is done in the fight for his life, and if they can save his life they can consider the person afterwards. Those who consider the person first may lose precious time to save his life! At least this seems to be the rationale or justification behind all this — or is it? Is the reason for this increasingly mechanical, depersonalized approach our own defensiveness? Is this approach our own way to cope with and repress the anxieties that a terminally or critically ill patient evokes in us? Is our concentration on equipment, on blood pressure, our desperate attempt to deny the impending death which is so frightening and discomforting to us that we displace all our knowledge onto machines, since they are less close to us than the suffering face of another human being which would remind us once more of our lack of omnipotence, our own limits and failures, and last but not least perhaps our own mortality?

Maybe the question has to be raised: Are we becoming less human or more human? . . . it is clear that whatever the answer may be, the patient is suffering more—not physically, perhaps, but emotionally. And his needs have not changed over the centuries, only our ability to gratify them.

Considerations

1. What relationship do you see between the poem that serves as the introduction and the essay itself?
2. Consider the various examples and explanations the essay provides of children's reactions to death and then give your responses to the points Kübler-Ross makes.
3. Summarize briefly the story of the farmer's death. Evaluate the values and the attitudes toward death suggested by this story.
4. According to Kübler-Ross, why do humans find facing death or talking about death (particularly their own death) so difficult? Do you agree with her observations? Explain.
5. In paragraph 2, Kübler-Ross suggests particular readers she hopes to reach. Evaluate the essay, keeping these readers in mind. How successfully do you think she communicates to them? Cite specific passages from the essay to support your analysis.

CONNECTIONS: DEATH

1. Several works in this section depict death as an enemy to be faced and fought; others view death as a natural part of the life cycle, to be accepted and even welcomed. Respond to these opposing views of death, considering any or all of the following works: "The Jilting of Granny Weatherall," "The Death of Iván Ilých," "To Hell with Dying," "Death be not proud," "In the House of the Dying," "The American Way of Death," and "On the Fear of Death."

2. Compare the use of humor to address the serious subject of death as demonstrated in the following works: "To Hell with Dying," "Juan Manso: A Dead Man's Tale," *On Tidy Endings,* "The American Way of Death."

3. Discuss the responses of—and the roles played by—those who are well and living as they face the dying and death of people close to them. Consider any or all these works: "The Jilting of Granny Weatherall," "The Death of Iván Ilých," "Patriotism," *On Tidy Endings,* "In the House of the Dying," and "On the Fear of Death."

4. Consider the relationships suggested between love and death by any or all of the following works: "The Jilting of Granny Weatherall," "Patriotism," *On Tidy Endings*.

5. Explain the advice you think Elizabeth Kübler-Ross would give the following people: (1) The parents in "To Hell with Dying" during the time their young children were called on to act as resurrecting angels, (2) the family and doctor of Iván Ilých during his illness, (3) the family, doctor, and priest who wait at Granny Weatherall's bedside.

Additional Readings

An Introduction to Short Fiction

Cave paintings showing the outcome of a hunting expedition or imagining the exploits of a fantastic beast testify to the ancient roots of the human love for stories. From the time when people first discovered how to communicate through spoken words or written symbols, they have instructed, amazed, warned, and entertained each other with tales — both true and fictional.

EARLY FORMS OF FICTION

Allegory

Allegories are stories in which each character, action, and setting stands for one specific meaning. For example, in John Bunyan's allegory, *A Pilgrim's Progress,* a character named Christian represents the virtues associated with the ideal member of that faith. In the allegory, Christian passes through a landscape of temptations and dangers with areas symbolically named the "Slough of Despond," the "City of Destruction," and the "Valley of Humiliation" before he reaches the "Celestial City." Allegories, which are intended to teach moral lessons, may also be written as poetry and drama.

Myth

Myths often tell the stories of ancient deities, sometimes describing their exploits, sometimes explaining how a particular god or goddess came into being. Other myths address the mysteries of nature, including the creation of the universe and its diverse inhabitants. Ancient people probably invented myths as a way to make sense of the world in which they lived. For instance, gods and goddesses were described as experiencing human emotions — hate, jealousy, love, passion, despair — and as facing the human conflicts these feelings create.

Legend

Legends recount the amazing achievements of fictional characters or exaggerate the exploits of people who actually lived. For example, the story of Paul Bunyan is apparently based on a real man, but his size, his blue ox (Babe), and his astounding feats are inventions of those who told and retold tales of the resourceful lumberjack. Legends — which often include the entertaining tall tale — frequently praise and confirm traits that a society particularly values. For instance, Paul Bunyan works hard, never backs down from a fight, and knows how to enjoy a party — all qualities that were greatly admired during the early years of the American westward expansion.

Fairy Tale

Like myths, fairy tales focus on supernatural beings and events. They are not peopled by gods and goddesses, however, but by giants, trolls, fairy godmothers, and talking animals who happily coexist with humans — both royalty and common folk. Fairy tales do not attempt to explain the natural world or to affirm national values but instead focus on the struggle between clearly defined good and evil. In fairy tales, good always prevails over evil, although — in those that have not been censored to suit modern sensibilities — the "good" is often achieved by rather terrifying means. Figures of evil drop into pots of boiling oil, are flayed alive, or are cooked into (evidently tasty) pies.

Fable

The best-known fables are those told by the Greek slave Aesop. Fables usually feature animals who can talk and, in general, act just as rationally (and just as irrationally) as humans. Unlike myths, legends, and fairy tales — but like allegories — fables state an explicit lesson. For instance, nearly everyone knows the story of the race between the boastful Hare who runs quickly ahead of the plodding Tortoise, stops for a rest, and is beaten to the finish line by his slow yet determined rival. "Slow but steady wins the race," Aesop told his listeners, stating specifically the moral he wished to teach.

Parable

Like fables, parables teach a lesson or explain a complex spiritual concept. Unlike a fable, which tells a story that demonstrates the stated moral, a parable is a narrative that serves as an analogy for the principle being taught. For example, the New Testament contains many parables that suggest the relationship between God and humans. In one parable, God is depicted as a Good Shepherd who looks for one lost sheep in a flock of one hundred. In another parable, God is compared to a father who rejoices at the return of a son who has strayed.

MODERN SHORT FICTION

All of these early forms of short fiction still exist today. In the nineteenth century, however, a new form evolved. It was exemplified by the work of writers such as Guy De Maupassant in France; Anton Chekhov in Russia; George Eliot and Thomas Hardy in Great Britain; and Edgar Allan Poe, Nathaniel Hawthorne, Herman Melville, Mary Wilkins Freeman, and Sarah Orne Jewett in the United States.

The Realistic Short Story

The nineteenth-century **realistic short story** differed from early forms of fiction in many ways. Nineteenth-century realistic short stories focused on scenes and events of everyday life. Ordinary men, women, and children — not fabulous gods, powerful giants, and talking animals — inhabited these stories. Characters were developed more fully; rather than representing one primary trait, the central figures of short stories exhibited the complexities and contradictions of real people. Plots became more intricate to suggest the workings of characters' souls and minds and to depict their external actions. Settings became more than briefly sketched backdrops; times and places were described in vivid detail. Most importantly, realistic short stories moved away from teaching one particular moral or lesson. Although the theme of a short story often suggested certain values, readers were expected to find meaning for themselves. The author no longer served up a moral or a lesson in a direct and obvious way.

The realistic short story, as it evolved from the nineteenth century to the twentieth, usually focuses on a conflict experienced by a character or group of characters. Often, by facing that conflict, the characters come to know themselves (and other people) more fully. A short story that shows a young person moving from innocence to experience is called a **story of initiation.** A related form is the **story of epiphany,** in which a character experiences a conflict that leads to a sudden insight or profound understanding. (The word "epiphany" comes from the name of the Christian feast day celebrating the revelation of the infant Jesus to the Magi. These wise men, who had traveled from the East, returned to their own countries deeply moved and changed by what they had seen in Bethlehem.)

The Nonrealistic Short Story

The nineteenth century also saw the development of the **nonrealistic short story.** For example, many of Edgar Allan Poe's and Nathaniel Hawthorne's stories introduced supernatural beings, strange settings, or plot events that could not be explained by the traditional laws of nature. (See, for example, Poe's "The Black Cat" page 903.) Although these nonrealistic stories often incorporated elements of earlier forms of short fiction (for instance, characters—human or animal—with unusual powers) they shared certain qualities with the realistic short story. Their characters were more fully developed and had spiritual and psychological depth; their plots were more complex; and their settings were more fully described. Most importantly, their themes often led the reader to speculate, wonder, and question rather than to accept a directly stated moral or lesson.

In the twentieth century, writers such as Donald Barthelme ("The Balloon," page 1086) and Gabriel García Márquez ("The Handsomest Drowned Man in the World," page 1032) continue the tradition of the nonrealistic short story. Unbound by realistic dimensions of time and space, unfettered by the laws of physics or even by the conventions of human psychology, these writers push their own imaginations—and the imaginations of their readers—in new, and sometimes unsettling, directions. Reading nonrealistic fiction requires what the nineteenth-century poet Samuel Taylor Coleridge called "the willing suspension of disbelief"—the willingness to read, enjoy, and ponder settings, plots, and characters that seem strange and unconventional. Even more so than realistic fiction, nonrealistic stories lead in many diverse directions rather than toward a single theme.

A WORD ABOUT FICTION AND TRUTH

What distinguishes true stories from fiction? An easy answer is that true stories tell about events that actually happened to people who actually lived, whereas fiction tells about events and people who are imaginary. It's often difficult, however, to make such neat distinctions clearly. For example, consider a short story set during a recent time in a familiar city. As you read, you may recognize the names of streets and remember some of the events of the era. Although most of the characters who inhabit this familiar city are imagined, occasionally one of those fictional characters meets—or refers to—a person who was alive at the time the story takes place. To what extent, then, is this story true? Are only the parts that can be verified by your own observation (street names, for example) or through historical reports (assassinations, wars, economic upheavals) true? Or are the created characters—their actions, their conflicts, their emotions—also true in some sense? And what about stories that take place entirely outside the realm of what we currently recognize as reality—for example, stories set in the future or in an imagined country with no familiar patterns or rules? In what ways might such stories tell the "truth"? Consider such possibilities as human emotions, conflicts, and interactions that the story portrays.

As you read the short stories that follow, think about the people you meet, the places they live, the conflicts they face. Sort out for yourself what truths these people, places, and conflicts have to offer. Consider how those truths fit—or do not fit—with your life, your hopes, your fears, your values.

Guidelines: Short Fiction

These considerations provide guidelines for reading, thinking about, and writing about short fiction. Although not every consideration applies to every story, these guidelines can help you read more deeply and experience the story more fully.

1. Read the opening paragraphs carefully several times. Jot down questions, predictions, and expectations for the rest of the story. After you finish reading the story, look back at your early responses. To what extent were your questions answered and your predictions and expectations fulfilled?

2. As you read, list the conflicts in the story (consider major as well as minor characters). Note how the characters face and resolve (or do not resolve) those conflicts. Then discuss the implications of the characters' actions (or inaction).

3. To continue thinking about conflict, identify a character who faces a difficult choice, perhaps a moral decision. What would you do under the same or similar circumstances? Compare your imagined response to the character's response.

4. Describe the setting of the story in detail. Remember to consider the following: (a) large elements of place (city, state, section of country, nation); (b) small elements of place (a bedroom, a business office, a battlefield); (c) large elements of time (century, part of century); (d) small elements of time (day, night, season of the year, holiday). How important is setting to the meaning you find in the story? How would the story be changed if any (or several) of the elements of setting were changed?

5. Consider the viewpoint from which the story is told. How would the story change if that viewpoint were different? Try retelling any part of the story through the eyes of a different character or through the eyes of an objective observer.

6. Read the story once quickly, then jot down your responses, impressions, and questions. Wait several days, then reread the story slowly and carefully. Return to your original responses, impressions, and questions to consider what you now have to add or to change. Note the reasons for making these changes and additions.

7. Note any objects, animals, gestures, or aspects of nature that are mentioned repeatedly or receive unusual emphasis. What do these elements contribute to your experience of the story? In what ways might they ... meaning(s) you see?

8. Think about the comparisons and contrasts you see in the story. For example, are there two characters who face the same situation yet act very differently? Consider also comparisons you can make between the characters, setting, conflicts, and action in two different stories. What significance can you see in the differences and similarities you've discovered?

9. Compare any situation, character, choice, or decision in the story to some aspect of your own life. Explain how the story is different from or similar to your own experience.

10. Write a continuation of the story. For example, imagine what will happen immediately after the ending scene. Or project what one — or more — of the characters might be like in five or ten years. Explain the thinking that led you to your speculations.

NATHANIEL HAWTHORNE (1804–1864)

The Wives of the Dead

The following story, the simple and domestic incidents of which may be deemed scarcely worth relating, after such a lapse of time, awakened some degree of interest, a hundred years ago, in a principal seaport of the Bay Province. The rainy twilight of an autumn day; a parlor on the second floor of a small house, plainly furnished, as beseemed the middling circumstances of its inhabitants, yet decorated with little curiosities from beyond the sea, and a few delicate specimens of Indian Manufacture, — these are the only particulars to be premised in regard to scene and season. Two young and comely women sat together by the fireside, nursing their mutual and peculiar sorrows. They were the recent brides of two brothers, a sailor and a landsman, and two successive days had brought tidings of the death of each, by the chances of Canadian warfare, and the tempestuous Atlantic. The universal sympathy excited by this bereavement, drew numerous condoling guests to the habitation of the widowed sisters. Several, among whom was the minister, had remained till the verge of evening; when one by one, whispering many comfortable passages of Scripture, that were answered by more abundant tears, they took their leave and departed to their own happier homes. The mourners, though not insensible to the kindness of their friends, had yearned to be left alone. United, as they had been, by the relationship of the living, and now more closely so by that of the dead, each felt as if whatever consolation her grief admitted, were to be found in the bosom of the other. They joined their hearts, and wept together silently. But after an hour of such indulgence, one of the sisters, all of whose emotions were influenced by her mild, quiet, yet not feeble character, began to recollect the precepts of resignation and endurance, which piety had taught her, when she did not think to need them. Her misfortune, besides, as earliest known, should earliest cease to interfere with her regular course of duties; accordingly, having placed the table before the fire, and arranged a frugal meal, she took the hand of her companion.

"Come, dearest sister; you have eaten not a morsel to-day," she said. "Arise, I pray you, and let us ask a blessing on that which is provided for us."

Her sister-in-law was of a lively and irritable temperament, and the first pangs of her sorrow had been expressed by shrieks and passionate lamentation. She now shrunk from Mary's words, like a wounded sufferer from a hand that revives the throb.

"There is no blessing left for me, neither will I ask it," cried Margaret, with a fresh burst of tears. "Would it were His will that I might never taste food more."

Yet she trembled at these rebellious expressions, almost as soon as they were uttered, and, by degrees, Mary succeeded in bringing her sister's mind 5 nearer to the situation of her own. Time went on, and their usual hour of repose arrived. The brothers and their brides, entering the married state with no more than the slender means which then sanctioned such a step, had confederated themselves in one household, with equal rights to the parlor, and claiming exclusive privileges in two sleeping rooms contiguous to it. Thither the widowed ones retired, after heaping ashes upon the dying embers of their fire, and placing a lighted lamp upon the hearth. The doors of both chambers were left open, so that a part of the interior of each, and the beds with their unclosed curtains, were reciprocally visible. Sleep did not steal upon the sisters at one and the same time. Mary experienced the effect often consequent upon grief quietly borne, and soon sunk into temporary forgetfulness, while Margaret became more disturbed and feverish, in proportion as the night advanced with its deepest and stillest hours. She lay listening to the drops of rain, that came down in monotonous succession, unswayed by a breath of wind; and a nervous impulse continually caused her to lift her head from the pillow, and gaze into Mary's chamber and the intermediate apartment. The cold light of the lamp threw the shadows of the furniture up against the wall, stamping them immoveably there, except when they were shaken by a sudden flicker of the flame. Two vacant armchairs were in their old positions on opposite sides of the hearth, where the brothers had been wont to sit in young and laughing dignity, as heads of families; two humbler seats were near them, the true thrones of that little empire, where Mary and herself had exercised in love, a power that love had won. The cheerful radiance of the fire had shot upon the happy circle, and the dead glimmer of the lamp might have befitted their reunion now. While Margaret groaned in bitterness, she heard a knock at the street-door.

"How would my heart have leapt at that sound but yesterday!" thought she, remembering the anxiety with which she had long awaited tidings from her husband. "I care not for it now; let them begone, for I will not arise."

But even while a sort of childish fretfulness made her thus resolve, she was breathing hurriedly, and straining her ears to catch a repetition of the summons. It is difficult to be convinced of the death of one whom we have deemed another self. The knocking was now renewed in slow and regular strokes, apparently given with the soft end of a doubled fist, and was accompanied by words, faintly heard through several thicknesses of wall. Margaret looked to her sister's chamber, and beheld her still lying in the depths of sleep. She arose, placed her foot upon the floor, and slightly arrayed herself, trembling between fear and eagerness as she did so.

"Heaven help me!" sighed she. "I have nothing left to fear, and methinks I am ten times more a coward than ever."

Seizing the lamp from the hearth, she hastened to the window that overlooked the street-door. It was a lattice, turning upon hinges; and having thrown it back, she stretched her head a little way into the moist atmosphere. A lantern was reddening the front of the house, and melting its light in the neighboring puddles, while a deluge of darkness overwhelmed every other object. As the window grated on its hinges, a man in a broad brimmed hat and blanket-coat, stepped from under the shelter of the projecting story, and looked upward to discover whom his application had aroused. Margaret knew him as a friendly innkeeper of the town.

"What would you have, Goodman Parker?" cried the widow.   10

"Lack-a-day, is it you, Mistress Margaret?" replied the innkeeper. "I was afraid it might be your sister Mary; for I hate to see a young woman in trouble, when I haven't a word of comfort to whisper her."

"For Heaven's sake, what news do you bring?" screamed Margaret.

"Why, there has been an express through the town within this half hour," said Goodman Parker, "travelling from the eastern jurisdiction with letters from the governor and council. He tarried at my house to refresh himself with a drop and a morsel, and I asked him what tidings on the frontiers. He tells me we had the better in the skirmish you wot of, and that thirteen men reported slain are well and sound, and your husband among them. Besides, he is appointed of the escort to bring the captivated Frenchers and Indians home to the province jail. I judged you wouldn't mind being broke of your rest, and so I stepped over to tell you. Good night."

So saying, the honest man departed; and his lantern gleamed along the street, bringing to view indistinct shapes of things, and the fragments of a world, like order glimmering through the chaos, or memory roaming over the past. But Margaret stayed not to watch these picturesque effects. Joy flashed into her heart, and lighted it up at once, and breathless, and with winged steps, she flew to the bedside of her sister. She paused, however, at the door of the chamber, while a thought of pain broke in upon her.

"Poor Mary!" said she to herself. "Shall I waken her, to feel her sorrow   15
sharpened by my happiness? No; I will keep it within my own bosom till the morrow."

She approached the bed to discover if Mary's sleep were peaceful. Her face was turned partly inward to the pillow, and had been hidden there to weep; but a look of motionless contentment was now visible upon it, as if her heart, like a deep lake, had grown calm because its dead had sunk down so far within. Happy is it, and strange, that the lighter sorrows are those from which dreams are chiefly fabricated. Margaret shrunk from disturbing her sister-in-law, and felt as if her own better fortune, had rendered her involuntarily unfaithful, and as if altered and diminished affection must be the consequence of the disclosure she had to make. With a sudden step, she turned away. But joy could not long be repressed, even by circumstances that would have excited heavy grief at another moment. Her mind was thronged with delightful thoughts, till sleep stole on and transformed them to visions, more delightful and more wild, like the breath of winter, (but what a cold comparison!) working fantastic tracery upon a window.

When the night was far advanced, Mary awoke with a sudden start. A vivid dream had latterly involved her in its unreal life, of which, however, she could only remember that it had been broken in upon at the most interesting point. For a little time, slumber hung about her like a morning mist, hindering her from perceiving the distinct outline of her situation. She listened with imperfect consciousness to two or three volleys of a rapid and eager knocking; and first she deemed the noise a matter of course, like the breath she drew; next, it appeared a thing in which she had no concern; and lastly, she became aware that it was a summons necessary to be obeyed. At the same moment, the pang of recollection darted into her mind; the pall of sleep was thrown back from the face of grief; the dim light of the chamber, and the objects therein revealed, had retained all her suspended ideas, and restored them as soon as she unclosed her eyes. Again, there was a quick peal upon the street-door. Fearing that her sister would also be disturbed, Mary wrapped herself in a cloak and hood, took the lamp from the hearth, and hastened to the window. By some accident, it had been left unhasped, and yielded easily to her hand.

"Who's there?" asked Mary, trembling as she looked forth.

The storm was over, and the moon was up; it shone upon broken clouds above, and below upon houses black with moisture, and upon little lakes of the fallen rain, curling into silver beneath the quick enchantment of a breeze. A young man in a sailor's dress, wet as if he had come out of the depths of the sea, stood alone under the window. Mary recognized him as one whose livelihood was gained by short voyages along the coast; nor did she forget, that, previous to her marriage, he had been an unsuccessful wooer of her own.

"What do you seek here, Stephen?" said she.   20

"Cheer up, Mary, for I seek to comfort you," answered the rejected lover. "You must know I got home not ten minutes ago, and the first thing my good mother told me was the news about your husband. So, without saying a word to the old woman, I clapped on my hat, and ran out of the house. I couldn't have slept a wink before speaking to you, Mary, for the sake of old times."

"Stephen, I thought better of you!" exclaimed the widow, with gushing tears, and preparing to close the lattice; for she was no whit inclined to imitate the first wife of Zadig.

"But stop, and hear my story out," cried the young sailor. "I tell you we spoke a brig yesterday afternoon, bound in from Old England. And who do you think I saw standing on deck well and hearty, only a bit thinner than he was five months ago?"

Mary leaned from the window, but could not speak.

"Why, it was your husband himself," continued the generous seaman.   25
"He and three others saved themselves on a spar, when the *Blessing* turned bottom upwards. The brig will beat into the bay by daylight with this wind, and you'll see him here tomorrow. There's the comfort I bring you, Mary, and so good night."

He hurried away, while Mary watched him with a doubt of waking reality, that seemed stronger or weaker as he alternately entered the shade of the houses, or emerged into the broad streaks of moonlight. Gradually, however, a blessed flood of conviction swelled into her heart, in strength enough to overwhelm her, had its increase been more abrupt. Her first impulse was to rouse her sister-in-law, and communicate the new-born gladness. She opened the chamber-door, which had been closed in the course of the night, though not latched, advanced to the bedside, and was about to lay her hand upon the slumberer's shoulder. But then she remembered that Margaret would awake to thoughts of death and woe, rendered not the less bitter by their contrast with her own felicity. She suffered the rays of the lamp to fall upon the unconscious form of the bereaved one. Margaret lay in unquiet sleep, and the drapery was displaced around her; her young cheek was rosy-tinted, and her lips half opened in a vivid smile; an expression of joy, debarred its passage by her sealed eyelids, struggled forth like incense from the whole countenance.

"My poor sister! you will waken too soon from that happy dream," thought Mary.

Before retiring, she set down the lamp and endeavored to arrange the bed-clothes, so that the chill air might not do harm to the feverish slumberer. But her hand trembled against Margaret's neck, a tear also fell upon her cheek, and she suddenly awoke.

EDGAR ALLAN POE (1809–1849)

The Black Cat

For the most wild yet most homely narrative which I am about to pen, I neither expect nor solicit belief. Mad indeed would I be to expect it, in a case where my very senses reject their own evidence. Yet, mad am I not — and very surely do I not dream. But to-morrow I die, and to-day I would unburden my soul. My immediate purpose is to place before the world, plainly, succinctly, and without comment, a series of mere household events. In their consequences, these events have terrified — have tortured — have destroyed me. Yet I will not attempt to expound them. To me, they have presented little but horror — to many they will seem less terrible than *baroques*. Hereafter, perhaps, some intellect may be found which will reduce my phantasm to the commonplace — some intellect more calm, more logical, and far less excitable than my own, which will perceive, in the circumstances I detail with awe, nothing more than an ordinary succession of very natural causes and effects.

From my infancy I was noted for the docility and humanity of my disposition. My tenderness of heart was even so conspicuous as to make me the jest of my companions. I was especially fond of animals, and was indulged by my parents with a great variety of pets. With these I spent most of my time, and never was so happy as when feeding and caressing them. This peculiarity of character grew with my growth, and, in my manhood, I derived from it one of my principal sources of pleasure. To those who have cherished an affection for a faithful and sagacious dog, I need hardly be at the trouble of explaining the nature or the intensity of the gratification thus derivable. There is something in the unselfish and self-sacrificing love of a brute, which goes directly to the heart of him who has had frequent occasion to test the paltry friendship and gossamer fidelity of mere *Man*.

I married early, and was happy to find in my wife a disposition not uncongenial with my own. Observing my partiality for domestic pets, she lost no opportunity of procuring those of the most agreeable kind. We had birds, gold-fish, a fine dog, rabbits, a small monkey, and a *cat*.

This latter was a remarkably large and beautiful animal, entirely black, and sagacious to an astonishing degree. In speaking of his intelligence, my wife, who at heart was not a little tinctured with superstition, made frequent allusion to the ancient popular notion, which regarded all black cats as witches in disguise. Not that she was ever *serious* upon this point — and I mention the matter at all for no better reason than that it happens, just now, to be remembered.

Pluto — this was the cat's name — was my favorite pet and playmate. I alone fed him, and he attended me wherever I went about the house. It was even with difficulty that I could prevent him from following me through the streets.

5

Our friendship lasted, in this manner, for several years, during which my general temperament and character — through the instrumentality of the Fiend Intemperance — had (I blush to confess it) experienced a radical alteration for the worse. I grew, day by day, more moody, more irritable, more regardless of the feelings of others. I suffered myself to use intemperate language to my wife. At length, I even offered her personal violence. My pets, of course, were made to feel the change in my disposition. I not only neglected, but ill-used them. For Pluto, however, I still retained sufficient regard to restrain me from maltreating him, as I made no scruple of maltreating the rabbits, the monkey, or even the dog, when, by accident, or through affection, they came in my way. But my disease grew upon me — for what disease is like Alcohol! — and at length even Pluto, who was now becoming old, and consequently somewhat peevish — even Pluto began to experience the effects of my ill temper.

One night, returning home, much intoxicated, from one of my haunts about town, I fancied that the cat avoided my presence. I seized him; when, in his fright at my violence, he inflicted a slight wound upon my hand with his teeth. The fury of a demon instantly possessed me. I knew myself no longer. My original soul seemed, at once, to take its flight from my body; and a more than fiendish malevolence, gin-nurtured, thrilled every fibre of my frame. I took from my waistcoat-pocket a penknife, opened it, grasped the poor beast by the throat, and deliberately cut one of its eyes from the socket! I blush, I burn, I shudder, while I pen the damnable atrocity.

When reason returned with the morning — when I had slept off the fumes of the night's debauch — I experienced a sentiment half of horror, half of remorse, for the crime of which I had been guilty; but it was, at best, a feeble and equivocal feeling, and the soul remained untouched. I again plunged into excess, and soon drowned in wine all memory of the deed.

In the meantime the cat slowly recovered. The socket of the lost eye presented, it is true, a frightful appearance, but he no longer appeared to suffer any pain. He went about the house as usual, but, as might be expected, fled in extreme terror at my approach. I had so much of my old heart left, as to be at first grieved by this evident dislike on the part of a creature which had once so loved me. But this feeling soon gave place to irritation. And then came, as if to my final and irrevocable overthrow, the spirit of PERVERSENESS. Of this spirit philosophy takes no account. Yet I am not more sure that my soul lives, than I am that perverseness is one of the primitive impulses of the human heart — one of the indivisible primary faculties, or sentiments, which give direction to the character of Man. Who has not, a hundred times, found himself committing a vile or stupid action, for no other reason than because he knows he should *not*? Have we not a perpetual inclination, in the teeth of our best judgment, to violate that which is *Law*, merely because we understand it to be such? This spirit of perverseness, I say, came to my final overthrow. It was this unfathomable longing of the soul *to vex itself* — to offer violence to its own nature — to do wrong for

the wrong's sake only—that urged me to continue and finally to consummate the injury I had inflicted upon the unoffending brute. One morning,
in cold blood, I slipped a noose about its neck and hung it to the limb of a
tree;—hung it with the tears streaming from my eyes, and with the bitterest
remorse at my heart;—hung it *because* I knew that it had loved me, and
because I felt it had given me no reason of offence;—hung it *because* I knew
that in so doing I was committing a sin—a deadly sin that would so jeopardize my immortal soul as to place it—if such a thing were possible—even
beyond the reach of the infinite mercy of the Most Merciful and Most
Terrible God.

On the night of the day on which this most cruel deed was done, I
was aroused from sleep by the cry of fire. The curtains of my bed were in
flames. The whole house was blazing. It was with great difficulty that my
wife, a servant, and myself, made our escape from the conflagration. The
destruction was complete. My entire worldly wealth was swallowed up, and
I resigned myself thenceforward to despair.

I am above the weakness of seeking to establish a sequence of cause
and effect, between the disaster and the atrocity. But I am detailing a chain
of facts—and wish not to leave even a possible link imperfect. On the day
succeeding the fire, I visited the ruins. The walls, with one exception, had
fallen in. This exception was found in a compartment wall, not very thick,
which stood about the middle of the house, and against which had rested
the head of my bed. The plastering had here, in great measure, resisted the
action of the fire—a fact which I attributed to its having been recently
spread. About this wall a dense crowd were collected, and many persons
seemed to be examining a particular portion of it with very minute and
eager attention. The words "strange!" "singular!" and other similar expressions, excited my curiosity. I approached and saw, as if graven in *bas-relief*
upon the white surface, the figure of a gigantic *cat*. The impression was
given with an accuracy truly marvelous. There was a rope about the animal's
neck.

When I first beheld this apparition—for I could scarcely regard it as
less—my wonder and my terror were extreme. But at length reflection came
to my aid. The cat, I remembered, had been hung in a garden adjacent to
the house. Upon the alarm of fire, this garden had been immediately filled
by the crowd—by some one of whom the animal must have been cut from
the tree and thrown, through an open window, into my chamber. This had
probably been done with the view of arousing me from sleep. The falling of
other walls had compressed the victim of my cruelty into the substance of
the freshly-spread plaster, the lime of which, with the flames, and the *ammonia* from the carcass, had then accomplished the portraiture as I saw it.

Although I thus readily accounted to my reason, if not altogether to
my conscience, for the startling fact just detailed, it did not the less fail to
make a deep impression upon my fancy. For months I could not rid myself
of the phantasm of the cat; and, during this period, there came back into my

10

spirit a half-sentiment that seemed, but was not, remorse. I went so far as to regret the loss of the animal, and to look about me, among the vile haunts which I now habitually frequented, for another pet of the same species, and of somewhat similar appearance, with which to supply its place.

One night as I sat, half stupefied, in a den of more than infamy, my attention was suddenly drawn to some black object, reposing upon the head of one of the immense hogsheads of gin, or of rum, which constituted the chief furniture of the apartment. I had been looking steadily at the top of this hogshead for some minutes, and what now caused me surprise was the fact that I had not sooner perceived the object thereupon. I approached it, and touched it with my hand. It was a black cat — a very large one — fully as large as Pluto, and closely resembling him in every respect but one. Pluto had not a white hair upon any portion of his body; but this cat had a large, although indefinite splotch of white, covering nearly the whole region of the breast.

Upon my touching him, he immediately arose, purred loudly, rubbed   15
against my hand, and appeared delighted with my notice. This, then, was the very creature of which I was in search. I at once offered to purchase it of the landlord; but this person made no claim to it — knew nothing of it — had never seen it before.

I continued my caresses, and when I prepared to go home, the animal evinced a disposition to accompany me. I permitted it to do so; occasionally stooping and patting it as I proceeded. When it reached the house it domesticated itself at once, and became immediately a great favorite with my wife.

For my own part, I soon found a dislike to it arising within me. This was just the reverse of what I had anticipated; but — I know not how or why it was — its evident fondness for myself rather disgusted and annoyed me. By slow degrees these feelings of disgust and annoyance rose into the bitterness of hatred. I avoided the creature; a certain sense of shame, and the remembrance of my former deed of cruelty, preventing me from physically abusing it. I did not, for some weeks, strike, or otherwise violently ill use it; but gradually — very gradually — I came to look upon it with unutterable loathing, and to flee silently from its odious presence, as from the breath of a pestilence.

What added, no doubt, to my hatred of the beast, was the discovery on the morning after I brought it home, that, like Pluto, it also had been deprived of one of its eyes. This circumstance, however, only endeared it to my wife, who, as I have already said, possessed, in a high degree, that humanity of feeling which had once been my distinguishing trait, and the source of many of my simplest and purest pleasures.

With my aversion to this cat, however, its partiality for myself seemed to increase. It followed my footsteps with a pertinacity which it would be difficult to make the reader comprehend. Whenever I sat, it would crouch beneath my chair, or spring upon my knees, covering me with its loathsome caresses. If I arose to walk it would get between my feet and thus nearly throw me down, or, fastening its long and sharp claws in my dress, clamber, in this manner, to my breast. At such times, although I longed to destroy it with a blow, I was yet withheld from so doing, partly by a memory of my former crime, but chiefly — let me confess it at once — by absolute dread of the beast.

This dread was not exactly a dread of physical evil — and yet I should be at a loss how otherwise to define it. I am almost ashamed to own — yes, even in this felon's cell, I am almost ashamed to own — that the terror and horror with which the animal inspired me, had been heightened by one of the merest chimeras it would be possible to conceive. My wife had called my attention, more than once, to the character of the mark of white hair, of which I have spoken, and which constituted the sole visible difference between the strange beast and the one I had destroyed. The reader will remember that this mark, although large, had been originally very indefinite; but, by slow degrees — degrees nearly imperceptible, and which for a long time my reason struggled to reject as fanciful — it had, at length, assumed a rigorous distinctness of outline. It was now the representation of an object that I shudder to name — and for this, above all, I loathed, and dreaded, and would have rid myself of the monster *had I dared* — it was now, I say, the image of a hideous — of a ghastly thing — of the GALLOWS! — oh, mournful and terrible engine of Horror and of Crime — of Agony and of Death!

And now was I indeed wretched beyond the wretchedness of mere Humanity. And *a brute beast* — whose fellow I had contemptuously destroyed — *a brute beast* to work out for *me* — for me, a man fashioned in the image of the High God — so much of insufferable woe! Alas! neither by day nor by night knew I the blessing of rest any more! During the former the creature left me no moment alone, and in the latter I started hourly from dreams of unutterable fear to find the hot breath of *the thing* upon my face, and its vast weight — an incarnate nightmare that I had not power to shake off — incumbent eternally upon my *heart!*

Beneath the pressure of torments such as these the feeble remnant of the good within me succumbed. Evil thoughts became my sole intimates — the darkest and most evil of thoughts. The moodiness of my usual temper increased to hatred of all things and of all mankind; while from the sudden, frequent, and ungovernable outbursts of a fury to which I now blindly abandoned myself, my uncomplaining wife, alas, was the most usual and the most patient of sufferers.

One day she accompanied me, upon some household errand, into the cellar of the old building which our poverty compelled us to inhabit. The cat followed me down the steep stairs, and, nearly throwing me headlong, exasperated me to madness. Uplifting an axe, and forgetting in my wrath the childish dread which had hitherto stayed my hand, I aimed a blow at the animal, which, of course, would have proved instantly fatal had it descended as I wished. But this blow was arrested by the hand of my wife. Goaded by the interference into a rage more than demoniacal, I withdrew my arm from her grasp and buried the axe in her brain. She fell dead upon the spot without a groan.

This hideous murder accomplished, I set myself forthwith, and with entire deliberation, to the task of concealing the body. I knew that I could not remove it from the house, either by day or by night, without the risk of being observed by the neighbors. Many projects entered my mind. At one period I thought of cutting the corpse into minute fragments, and destroying them by fire. At another, I resolved to dig a grave for it in the floor of the cellar. Again, I deliberated about casting it in the well in the yard—about packing it in a box, as if merchandise, with the usual arrangements, and so getting a porter to take it from the house. Finally I hit upon what I considered a far better expedient than either of these. I determined to wall it up in the cellar, as the monks of the Middle Ages are recorded to have walled up their victims.

For a purpose such as this the cellar was well adapted. Its walls were   25 loosely constructed, and had lately been plastered throughout with a rough plaster, which the dampness of the atmosphere had prevented from hardening. Moreover, in one of the walls was a projection, caused by a false chimney, or fireplace, that had been filled up and made to resemble the rest of the cellar. I made no doubt that I could readily displace the bricks at this point, insert the corpse, and wall the whole up as before, so that no eye could detect anything suspicious.

And in this calculation I was not deceived. By means of a crowbar I easily dislodged the bricks, and, having carefully deposited the body against the inner wall, I propped it in that position, while with little trouble I relaid the whole structure as it originally stood. Having procured mortar, sand, and hair, with every possible precaution, I prepared a plaster which could not be distinguished from the old, and with this, I very carefully went over the new brick-work. When I had finished, I felt satisfied that all was right. The wall did not present the slightest appearance of having been disturbed. The rubbish on the floor was picked up with the minutest care. I looked around triumphantly, and said to myself: "Here at least, then, my labor has not been in vain."

My next step was to look for the beast which had been the cause of so much wretchedness; for I had, at length, firmly resolved to put it to death. Had I been able to meet with it at the moment, there could have been no doubt of its fate; but it appeared that the crafty animal had been alarmed at the violence of my previous anger, and forbore to present itself in my present mood. It is impossible to describe or to imagine the deep, blissful sense of relief which the absence of the detested creature occasioned in my bosom. It did not make its appearance during the night; and thus for one night, at least, since its introduction into the house, I soundly and tranquilly slept; aye, slept even with the burden of murder upon my soul.

The second and the third day passed, and still my tormentor came not. Once again I breathed as a freeman. The monster, in terror, had fled the premises for ever! I should behold it no more! My happiness was supreme! The guilt of my dark deed disturbed me but little. Some few inquiries had been made, but these had been readily answered. Even a search had been instituted—but of course nothing was to be discovered. I looked upon my future felicity as secured.

Upon the fourth day of the assassination, a party of the police came, very unexpectedly, into the house, and proceeded again to make a rigorous investigation of the premises. Secure, however, in the inscrutability of my place of concealment, I felt no embarrassment whatever. The officers bade me accompany them in their search. They left no nook or corner unexplored. At length, for the third or fourth time, they descended into the cellar. I quivered not in a muscle. My heart beat calmly as that of one who slumbers in innocence. I walked the cellar from end to end. I folded my arms upon my bosom, and roamed easily to and fro. The police were thoroughly satisified and prepared to depart. The glee at my heart was too strong to be restrained. I burned to say if but one word, by way of triumph, and to render doubly sure their assurance of my guiltlessness.

"Gentlemen," I said at last, as the party ascended the steps, "I delight to have allayed your suspicions. I wish you all health and a little more courtesy. By the bye, gentlemen, this—this is a very well-constructed house," (in the rabid desire to say something easily, I scarcely knew what I uttered at all), —"I may say an excellently well-constructed house. These walls—are you going, gentlemen?—these walls are solidly put together"; and here, through the mere frenzy of bravado, I rapped heavily with a cane which I held in my hand, upon that very portion of the brick-work behind which stood the corpse of the wife of my bosom.

But may God shield and deliver me from the fangs of the Arch-Fiend! No sooner had the reverberation of my blows sunk into silence, than I was answered by a voice from within the tomb!—by a cry, at first muffled and broken, like the sobbing of a child, and then quickly swelling into one long, loud, and continuous scream, utterly anomalous and inhuman—a howl—a wailing shriek, half of horror and half of triumph, such as might have arisen only out of hell, conjointly from the throats of the damned in their agony and of the demons that exult in the damnation.

Of my own thoughts it is folly to speak. Swooning, I staggered to the opposite wall. For one instant the party on the stairs remained motionless, through extremity of terror and awe. In the next a dozen stout arms were toiling at the wall. It fell bodily. The corpse, already greatly decayed and clotted with gore, stood erect before the eyes of the spectators. Upon its head, with red extended mouth and solitary eye of fire, sat the hideous beast whose craft had seduced me into murder, and whose informing voice had consigned me to the hangman. I had walled the monster up within the tomb.

ANTON CHEKHOV (1860–1904)

The Lady with the Pet Dog

I

A new person, it was said, had appeared on the esplanade: a lady with a pet dog. Dmitry Dmitrich Gurov, who had spent a fortnight at Yalta and had got used to the place, had also begun to take an interest in new arrivals. As he sat in Vernet's confectionery shop, he saw, walking on the esplanade, a fair-haired young woman of medium height, wearing a beret; a white Pomeranian was trotting behind her.

And afterwards he met her in the public garden and in the square several times a day. She walked alone, always wearing the same beret and always with the white dog; no one knew who she was and everyone called her simply "the lady with the pet dog."

"If she is here alone without husband or friends," Gurov reflected, "it wouldn't be a bad thing to make her acquaintance."

He was under forty, but he already had a daughter twelve years old, and two sons at school. They had found a wife for him when he was very young, a student in his second year, and by now she seemed half as old again as he. She was a tall, erect woman with dark eyebrows, stately and dignified and, as she said of herself, intellectual. She read a great deal, used simplified spelling in her letters, called her husband, not Dmitry, but Dimitry, while he privately considered her of limited intelligence, narrowminded, dowdy, was afraid of her, and did not like to be at home. He had begun being unfaithful to her long ago — had been unfaithful to her often and, probably for that reason, almost always spoke ill of women, and when they were talked of in his presence used to call them "the inferior race."

It seemed to him that he had been sufficiently tutored by bitter experience to call them what he pleased, and yet he could not have lived without "the inferior race" for two days together. In the company of men he was bored and ill at ease, he was chilly and uncommunicative with them; but when he was among women he felt free, and knew what to speak to them about and how to comport himself; and even to be silent with them was no strain on him. In his appearance, in his character, in his whole make-up there was something attractive and elusive that disposed women in his favor and allured them. He knew that, and some force seemed to draw him to them, too. 5

Oft-repeated and really bitter experience had taught him long ago that with decent people — particularly Moscow people — who are irresolute and slow to move, every affair which at first seems a light and charming adventure inevitably grows into a whole problem of extreme complexity, and in the end a painful situation is created. But at every new meeting with an interesting woman this lesson of experience seemed to slip from his memory, and he was eager for life, and everything seemed so simple and diverting.

One evening while he was dining in the public garden the lady in the beret walked up without haste to take the next table. Her expression, her gait, her dress, and the way she did her hair told him that she belonged to the upper class, that she was married, that she was in Yalta for the first time and alone, and that she was bored there. The stories told of the immorality in Yalta are to a great extent untrue; he despised them, and knew that such stories were made up for the most part by persons who would have been glad to sin themselves if they had had the chance; but when the lady sat down at the next table three paces from him, he recalled these stories of easy conquests, of trips to the mountains, and the tempting thought of a swift, fleeting liaison, a romance with an unknown woman of whose very name he was ignorant suddenly took hold of him.

He beckoned invitingly to the Pomeranian, and when the dog approached him, shook his finger at it. The Pomeranian growled; Gurov threatened it again.

The lady glanced at him and at once dropped her eyes.

"He doesn't bite," she said and blushed.   10

"May I give him a bone?" he asked; and when she nodded he inquired affably, "Have you been in Yalta long?"

"About five days."

"And I am dragging out the second week here."

There was a short silence.

"Time passes quickly, and yet it is so dull here!" she said, not looking   15
at him.

"It's only the fashion to say it's dull here. A provincial will live in Belyov or Zhizdra and not be bored, but when he comes here it's 'Oh, the dullness! Oh, the dust!' One would think he came from Granada."

She laughed. Then both continued eating in silence, like strangers, but after dinner they walked together and there sprang up between them the light banter of people who are free and contented, to whom it does not matter where they go or what they talk about. They walked and talked of the strange light on the sea: the water was a soft, warm, lilac color, and there was a golden band of moonlight upon it. They talked of how sultry it was after a hot day. Gurov told her that he was a native of Moscow, that he had studied languages and literature at the university, but had a post in a bank; that at one time he had trained to become an opera singer but had given it up, that he owned two houses in Moscow. And he learned from her that she had grown up in Petersburg, but had lived in S—— since her marriage two years previously, that she was going to stay in Yalta for about another month, and that her husband, who needed a rest, too, might perhaps come to fetch her. She was not certain whether her husband was a member of a Government Board or served on a Zemstvo Council, and this amused her. And Gurov learned too that her name was Anna Sergeyevna.

Afterwards in his room at the hotel he thought about her—and was certain that he would meet her the next day. It was bound to happen. Getting into bed he recalled that she had been a schoolgirl only recently, doing lessons like his own daughter; he thought how much timidity and angularity there was still in her laugh and her manner of talking with a stranger. It must have been the first time in her life that she was alone in a setting in which she was followed, looked at, and spoken to for one secret purpose alone, which she could hardly fail to guess. He thought of her slim, delicate throat, her lovely gray eyes.

"There's something pathetic about her, though," he thought, and dropped off.

II

A week had passed since they had struck up an acquaintance. It was a holiday. It was close indoors, while in the street the wind whirled the dust about and blew people's hats off. One was thirsty all day, and Gurov often went into the restaurant and offered Anna Sergeyevna a soft drink or ice cream. One did not know what to do with oneself.

In the evening when the wind had abated they went out on the pier to watch the steamer come in. There were a great many people walking about the dock; they had come to welcome someone and they were carrying bunches of flowers. And two peculiarities of a festive Yalta crowd stood out: the elderly ladies were dressed like young ones and there were many generals.

Owing to the choppy sea, the steamer arrived late, after sunset, and it was a long time tacking about before it put in at the pier. Anna Sergeyevna peered at the steamer and the passengers through her lorgnette as though looking for acquaintances, and whenever she turned to Gurov her eyes were shining. She talked a great deal and asked questions jerkily, forgetting the next moment what she had asked; then she lost her lorgnette in the crush.

The festive crowd began to disperse; it was now too dark to see people's faces; there was no wind any more, but Gurov and Anna Sergeyevna still stood as though waiting to see someone else come off the steamer. Anna Sergeyevna was silent now, and sniffed her flowers without looking at Gurov.

"The weather has improved this evening," he said. "Where shall we go now? Shall we drive somewhere?"

She did not reply.

Then he looked at her intently, and suddenly embraced her and kissed her on the lips, and the moist fragrance of her flowers enveloped him; and at once he looked round him anxiously, wondering if anyone had seen them.

"Let us go to your place," he said softly. And they walked off together rapidly.

The air in her room was close and there was the smell of the perfume she had bought at the Japanese shop. Looking at her, Gurov thought: "What

20

25

encounters life offers!" From the past he preserved the memory of carefree, good-natured women whom love made gay and who were grateful to him for the happiness he gave them, however brief it might be; and of women like his wife who loved without sincerity, with too many words, affectedly, hysterically, with an expression that it was not love or passion that engaged them but something more significant; and of two or three others, very beautiful, frigid women, across whose faces would suddenly flit a rapacious expression—an obstinate desire to take from life more than it could give, and these were women no longer young, capricious, unreflecting, domineering, unintelligent, and when Gurov grew cold to them their beauty aroused his hatred, and the lace on their lingerie seemed to him to resemble scales.

But here there was the timidity, the angularity of inexperienced youth, a feeling of awkwardness; and there was a sense of embarrassment, as though someone had suddenly knocked at the door. Anna Sergeyevna, "the lady with the pet dog," treated what had happened in a peculiar way, very seriously, as though it were her fall—so it seemed, and this was odd and inappropriate. Her features drooped and faded, and her long hair hung down sadly on either side of her face; she grew pensive and her dejected pose was that of a Magdalene in a picture by an old master.

"It's not right," she said. "You don't respect me now, you first of all."   30

There was a watermelon on the table. Gurov cut himself a slice and began eating it without haste. They were silent for at least half an hour.

There was something touching about Anna Sergeyevna; she had the purity of a well-bred, naive woman who has seen little of life. The single candle burning on the table barely illumined her face, yet it was clear that she was unhappy.

"Why should I stop respecting you, darling?" asked Gurov. "You don't know what you're saying."

"God forgive me," she said, and her eyes filled with tears. "It's terrible."

"It's as though you were trying to exonerate yourself."   35

"How can I exonerate myself? No. I am a bad, low woman; I despise myself and I have no thought of exonerating myself. It's not my husband but myself I have deceived. And not only just now; I have been deceiving myself for a long time. My husband may be a good, honest man, but he is a flunkey! I don't know what he does, what his work is, but I know he is a flunkey! I was twenty when I married him. I was tormented by curiosity; I wanted something better. 'There must be a different sort of life,' I said to myself. I wanted to live! To live, to live! Curiosity kept eating at me—you don't understand it, but I swear to God I could no longer control myself; something was going on in me; I could not be held back. I told my husband I was ill, and came here. And here I have been walking about as though in a daze, as though I were mad; and now I have become a vulgar, vile woman whom anyone may despise."

Gurov was already bored with her; he was irritated by her naive tone, by her repentance, so unexpected and so out of place, but for the tears in her eyes he might have thought she was joking or play-acting.

"I don't understand, my dear," he said softly. "What do you want?"

She hid her face on his breast and pressed close to him.

"Believe me, believe me, I beg you," she said, "I love honesty and 40 purity, and sin is loathsome to me; I don't know what I'm doing. Simple people say, 'The Evil One has led me astray.' And I may say of myself now that the Evil One has led me astray."

"Quiet, quiet," he murmured.

He looked into her fixed, frightened eyes, kissed her, spoke to her softly and affectionately, and by degrees she calmed down, and her gaiety returned; both began laughing.

Afterwards when they went out there was not a soul on the esplanade. The town with its cypresses looked quite dead, but the sea was still sounding as it broke upon the beach; a single launch was rocking on the waves and on it a lantern was blinking sleepily.

They found a cab and drove to Oreanda.

"I found out your surname in the hall just now: it was written on the 45 board — von Dideritz," said Gurov. "Is your husband German?"

"No; I believe his grandfather was German, but he is Greek Orthodox himself."

At Oreanda they sat on a bench not far from the church, looked down at the sea, and were silent. Yalta was barely visible through the morning mist; white clouds rested motionlessly on the mountaintops. The leaves did not stir on the trees, cicadas twanged, and the monotonous muffled sound of the sea that rose from below spoke of the peace, the eternal sleep awaiting us. So it rumbled below when there was no Yalta, no Oreanda here; so it rumbles now, and it will rumble as indifferently and as hollowly when we are no more. And in this constancy, in this complete indifference to the life and death of each of us, there lies, perhaps, a pledge of our eternal salvation, of the unceasing advance of life upon earth, of unceasing movement towards perfection. Sitting beside a young woman who in the dawn seemed so lovely, Gurov, soothed and spellbound by these magical surroundings — the sea, the mountains, the clouds, the wide sky — thought how everything is really beautiful in this world when one reflects: everything except what we think or do ourselves when we forget the higher aims of life and our own human dignity.

A man strolled up to them — probably a guard — looked at them and walked away. And this detail, too, seemed so mysterious and beautiful. They saw a steamer arrive from Feodosia, its lights extinguished in the glow of dawn.

"There is dew on the grass," said Anna Sergeyevna, after a silence.

"Yes, it's time to go home." 50

They returned to the city.

Then they met every day at twelve o'clock on the esplanade, lunched and dined together, took walks, admired the sea. She complained that she slept badly, that she had palpitations, asked the same questions, troubled now by jealousy and now by the fear that he did not respect her sufficiently. And often in the square or the public garden, when there was no one near them, he suddenly drew her to him and kissed her passionately. Complete idleness, these kisses in broad daylight exchanged furtively in dread of someone's seeing them, the heat, the smell of the sea, and the continual flitting before his eyes of idle, well-dressed, well-fed people, worked a complete change in him; he kept telling Anna Sergeyevna how beautiful she was, how seductive, was urgently passionate; he would not move a step away from her, while she was often pensive and continually pressed him to confess that he did not respect her, did not love her in the least, and saw in her nothing but a common woman. Almost every evening rather late they drove somewhere out of town, to Oreanda or to the waterfall; and the excursion was always a success, the scenery invariably impressed them as beautiful and magnificent.

They were expecting her husband, but a letter came from him saying that he had eye-trouble, and begging his wife to return home as soon as possible. Anna Sergeyevna made haste to go.

"It's a good thing I am leaving," she said to Gurov. "It's the hand of Fate!"

She took a carriage to the railway station, and he went with her. They were driving the whole day. When she had taken her place in the express, and when the second bell had rung, she said, "Let me look at you once more — let me look at you again. Like this." 55

She was not crying but was so sad that she seemed ill and her face was quivering.

"I shall be thinking of you — remembering you," she said. "God bless you; be happy. Don't remember evil against me. We are parting forever — it has to be, for we ought never to have met. Well, God bless you."

The train moved off rapidly, its lights soon vanished, and a minute later there was no sound of it, as though everything had conspired to end as quickly as possible that sweet trance, that madness. Left alone on the platform, and gazing into the dark distance, Gurov listened to the twang of the grasshoppers and the hum of the telegraph wires, feeling as though he had just waked up. And he reflected, musing, that there had now been another episode or adventure in his life, and it, too, was at an end, and nothing was left of it but a memory. He was moved, sad, and slightly remorseful: this young woman whom he would never meet again had not been happy with him; he had been warm and affectionate with her, but yet in his manner, his tone, and his caresses there had been a shade of light irony, the slightly coarse arrogance of a happy male who was, besides, almost twice her age.

She had constantly called him kind, exceptional, high-minded; obviously he had seemed to her different from what he really was, so he had involuntarily deceived her.

Here at the station there was already a scent of autumn in the air; it was a chilly evening.

"It is time for me to go north, too," thought Gurov as he left the   60 platform. "High time!"

III

At home in Moscow the winter routine was already established; the stoves were heated, and in the morning it was still dark when the children were having breakfast and getting ready for school, and the nurse would light the lamp for a short time. There were frosts already. When the first snow falls, on the first day the sleighs are out, it is pleasant to see the white earth, the white roofs; one draws easy, delicious breaths, and the season brings back the days of one's youth. The old limes and birches, white with hoar-frost, have a good-natured look; they are closer to one's heart than cypresses and palms, and near them one no longer wants to think of mountains and the sea.

Gurov, a native of Moscow, arrived there on a fine frosty day, and when he put on his fur coat and warm gloves and took a walk along Petrovka, and when on Saturday night he heard the bells ringing, his recent trip and the places he had visited lost all charm for him. Little by little he became immersed in Moscow life, greedily read three newspapers a day, and declared that he did not read the Moscow papers on principle. He already felt a longing for restaurants, clubs, formal dinners, anniversary celebrations, and it flattered him to entertain distinguished lawyers and actors, and to play cards with a professor at the physicians' club. He could eat a whole portion of meat stewed with pickled cabbage and served in a pan, Moscow style.

A month or so would pass and the image of Anna Sergeyevna, it seemed to him, would become misty in his memory, and only from time to time he would dream of her with her touching smile as he dreamed of others. But more than a month went by, winter came into its own, and everything was still clear in his memory as though he had parted from Anna Sergeyevna only yesterday. And his memories glowed more and more vividly. When in the evening stillness the voices of his children preparing their lessons reached his study, or when he listened to a song or to an organ playing in a restaurant, or when the storm howled in the chimney, suddenly everything would rise up in his memory; what had happened on the pier and the early morning with the mist on the mountains, and the steamer coming from Feodosia, and the kisses. He would pace about his room a long time, remembering and smiling; then his memories passed into reveries, and in his imagination the past would mingle with what was to come. He did not dream of Anna Sergeyevna, but she followed him about everywhere and watched him. When he shut his eyes he saw her before him as though she were there in the flesh, and she seemed to him lovelier, younger, tenderer than she had been, and he imagined himself a finer man than he had been in Yalta. Of evenings she peered out at him from the bookcase, from the fireplace, from the corner—he heard her breathing, the caressing rustle of her clothes. In the street he followed the women with his eyes, looking for someone who resembled her.

Already he was tormented by a strong desire to share his memories with someone. But in his home it was impossible to talk of his love, and he had no one to talk to outside; certainly he could not confide in his tenants or in anyone at the bank. And what was there to talk about? He hadn't loved her then, had he? Had there been anything beautiful, poetical, edifying, or simply interesting in his relations with Anna Sergeyevna? And he was forced to talk vaguely of love, of women, and no one guessed what he meant; only his wife would twitch her black eyebrows and say, "The part of a philanderer does not suit you at all, Dimitry."

One evening, coming out of the physicians' club with an official with   65
whom he had been playing cards, he could not resist saying:

"If you only knew what a fascinating woman I became acquainted with at Yalta!"

The official got into his sledge and was driving away, but turned suddenly and shouted:

"Dmitry Dmitrich!"

"What is it?"

"You were right this evening: the sturgeon was a bit high."   70

These words, so commonplace, for some reason moved Gurov to indignation, and struck him as degrading and unclean. What savage manners, what mugs! What stupid nights, what dull, humdrum days! Frenzied gambling, gluttony, drunkenness, continual talk always about the same thing! Futile pursuits and conversations always about the same topics take up the better part of one's time, the better part of one's strength, and in the end there is left a life clipped and wingless, an absurd mess, and there is no escaping or getting away from it—just as though one were in a madhouse or a prison.

Gurov, boiling with indignation, did not sleep all night. And he had a headache all the next day. And the following nights too he slept badly; he sat up in bed, thinking, or paced up and down his room. He was fed up with his children, fed up with the bank; he had no desire to go anywhere or to talk of anything.

In December during the holidays he prepared to take a trip and told his wife he was going to Petersburg to do what he could for a young friend—and he set off for S——. What for? He did not know, himself. He wanted to see Anna Sergeyevna and talk with her, to arrange a rendezvous if possible.

He arrived at S——in the morning, and at the hotel took the best room, in which the floor was covered with gray army cloth, and on the table there was an inkstand, gray with dust and topped by a figure on horseback, its hat in its raised hand and its head broken off. The porter gave him the necessary information: von Dideritz lived in a house of his own on Staro-Goncharnaya Street, not far from the hotel: he was rich and lived well and kept his own horses; everyone in the town knew him. The porter pronounced the name: "Dridiritz."

Without haste Gurov made his way to Staro-Goncharnaya Street and   75
found the house. Directly opposite the house stretched a long gray fence studded with nails.

"A fence like that would make one run away," thought Gurov, looking now at the fence, now at the windows of the house.

He reflected: this was a holiday, and the husband was apt to be at home. And in any case, it would be tactless to go into the house and disturb her. If he were to send her a note, it might fall into her husband's hands, and that might spoil everything. The best thing was to rely on chance. And he kept walking up and down the street and along the fence, waiting for the chance. He saw a beggar go in at the gate and heard the dogs attack him; then an hour later he heard a piano, and the sound came to him faintly and indistinctly. Probably it was Anna Sergeyevna playing. The front door opened suddenly, and an old woman came out, followed by the familiar white Pomeranian. Gurov was on the point of calling to the dog, but his heart began beating violently, and in his excitement he could not remember the Pomeranian's name.

He kept walking up and down, and hated the gray fence more and more, and by now he thought irritably that Anna Sergeyevna had forgotten him, and was perhaps already diverting herself with another man, and that that was very natural in a young woman who from morning till night had to look at that damn fence. He went back to his hotel room and sat on the couch for a long while, not knowing what to do, then he had dinner and a long nap.

"How stupid and annoying all this is!" he thought when he woke and looked at the dark windows: it was already evening. "Here I've had a good sleep for some reason. What am I going to do at night?"

He sat on the bed, which was covered with a cheap gray blanket of the   80
kind seen in hospitals, and he twitted himself in his vexation:

"So there's your lady with the pet dog. There's your adventure. A nice place to cool your heels in."

That morning at the station a playbill in large letters had caught his eye. *The Geisha* was to be given for the first time. He thought of this and drove to the theater.

"It's quite possible that she goes to first nights," he thought.

The theater was full. As in all provincial theaters, there was a haze above the chandelier, the gallery was noisy and restless; in the front row, before the beginning of the performance the local dandies were standing with their hands clasped behind their backs; in the Governor's box the Governor's daughter, wearing a boa, occupied the front seat, while the Governor himself hid modestly behind the portiere and only his hands were visible; the curtain swayed; the orchestra was a long time tuning up. While the audience was coming in and taking their seats, Gurov scanned the faces eagerly.

Anna Sergeyevna, too, came in. She sat down in the third row, and when Gurov looked at her his heart contracted, and he understood clearly that in the whole world there was no human being so near, so precious, and so important to him; she, this little, undistinguished woman, lost in a provincial crowd, with a vulgar lorgnette in her hand, filled his whole life now, was his sorrow and his joy, the only happiness that he now desired for himself, and to the sounds of the bad orchestra, of the miserable local violins, he thought how lovely she was. He thought and dreamed.

A young man with small side-whiskers, very tall and stooped, came in with Anna Sergeyevna and sat down beside her; he nodded his head at every step and seemed to be bowing continually. Probably this was the husband whom at Yalta, in an access of bitter feeling, she had called a flunkey. And there really was in his lanky figure, his side-whiskers, his small bald patch, something of a flunkey's retiring manner; his smile was mawkish, and in his buttonhole there was an academic badge like a waiter's number.

During the first intermission the husband went out to have a smoke; she remained in her seat. Gurov, who was also sitting in the orchestra, went up to her and said in a shaky voice, with a forced smile:

"Good evening!"

She glanced at him and turned pale, then looked at him again in horror, unable to believe her eyes, and gripped the fan and the lorgnette tightly together in her hands, evidently trying to keep herself from fainting. Both were silent. She was sitting, he was standing, frightened by her distress and not daring to take a seat beside her. The violins and the flute that were being tuned up sang out. He suddenly felt frightened: it seemed as if all the people in the boxes were looking at them. She got up and went hurriedly to the exit; he followed her, and both of them walked blindly along the corridors and up and down stairs, and figures in the uniforms prescribed for magistrates, teachers, and officials of the Department of Crown Lands, all wearing badges, flitted before their eyes, as did also ladies, and fur coats on hangers; they were conscious of drafts and the smell of stale tobacco. And Gurov, whose heart was beating violently, thought:

"Oh, Lord! Why are these people here and this orchestra!"

And at that instant he suddenly recalled how when he had seen Anna Sergeyevna off at the station he had said to himself that all was over between them and that they would never meet again. But how distant the end still was!

On the narrow, gloomy staircase over which it said "To the Amphitheatre," she stopped.

"How you frightened me!" she said, breathing hard, still pale and stunned. "Oh, how you frightened me! I am barely alive. Why did you come? Why?"

"But do understand, Anna, do understand — " he said hurriedly, under his breath. "I implore you, do understand — "

She looked at him with fear, with entreaty, with love; she looked at   95
him intently, to keep his features more distinctly in her memory.

"I suffer so," she went on, not listening to him. "All this time I have been thinking of nothing but you; I live only by the thought of you. And I wanted to forget, to forget; but why, oh, why have you come?"

On the landing above them two high school boys were looking down and smoking, but it was all the same to Gurov; he drew Anna Sergeyevna to him and began kissing her face and hands.

"What are you doing, what are you doing!" she was saying in horror, pushing him away. "We have lost our senses. Go away today; go away at once — I conjure you by all that is sacred, I implore you — People are coming this way!"

Someone was walking up the stairs.

"You must leave," Anna Sergeyevna went on in a whisper. "Do you   100
hear, Dmitry Dmitrich? I will come and see you in Moscow. I have never been happy; I am unhappy now, and I never, never shall be happy, never! So don't make me suffer still more! I swear I'll come to Moscow. But now let us part. My dear, good, precious one, let us part!"

She pressed his hand and walked rapidly downstairs, turning to look round at him, and from her eyes he could see that she really was unhappy. Gurov stood for a while, listening, then when all grew quiet, he found his coat and left the theater.

IV

And Anna Sergeyevna began coming to see him in Moscow. Once every two or three months she left S—— telling her husband that she was going to consult a doctor about a woman's ailment from which she was suffering — and her husband did and did not believe her. When she arrived in Moscow she would stop at the Slavyansky Bazar Hotel, and at once send a man in a red cap to Gurov. Gurov came to see her, and no one in Moscow knew of it.

Once he was going to see her in this way on a winter morning (the messenger had come the evening before and not found him in). With him walked his daughter, whom he wanted to take to school; it was on the way. Snow was coming down in big wet flakes.

"It's three degrees above zero,° and yet it's snowing," Gurov was saying to his daughter. "But this temperature prevails only on the surface of

---

three degrees above zero: About 37 degrees Fahrenheit.

the earth; in the upper layers of the atmosphere there is quite a different temperature."

"And why doesn't it thunder in winter, papa?" 105

He explained that, too. He talked, thinking all the while that he was on his way to a rendezvous, and no living soul knew of it, and probably no one would ever know. He had two lives, an open one, seen and known by all who needed to know it, full of conventional truth and conventional falsehood, exactly like the lives of his friends and acquaintances; and another life that went on in secret. And through some strange, perhaps accidental, combination of circumstances, everything that was of interest and importance to him, everything that was essential to him, everything about which he felt sincerely and did not deceive himself, everything that constituted the core of his life, was going on concealed from others; while all that was false, the shell in which he hid to cover the truth—his work at the bank, for instance, his discussions at the club, his references to the "inferior race," his appearances at anniversary celebrations with his wife—all that went on in the open. Judging others by himself, he did not believe what he saw, and always fancied that every man led his real, most interesting life under cover of secrecy as under cover of night. The personal life of every individual is based on secrecy, and perhaps it is partly for that reason that civilized man is so nervously anxious that personal privacy should be respected.

Having taken his daughter to school, Gurov went on to the Slavyansky Bazar Hotel. He took off his fur coat in the lobby, went upstairs, and knocked gently at the door. Anna Sergeyevna, wearing his favorite gray dress, exhausted by the journey and by waiting, had been expecting him since the previous evening. She was pale, and looked at him without a smile, and he had hardly entered when she flung herself on his breast. That kiss was a long, lingering one, as though they had not seen one another for two years.

"Well, darling, how are you getting on there?" he asked. "What news?"

"Wait; I'll tell you in a moment—I can't speak."

She could not speak; she was crying. She turned away from him, and 110 pressed her handkerchief to her eyes.

"Let her have her cry; meanwhile I'll sit down," he thought, and he seated himself in an armchair.

Then he rang and ordered tea, and while he was having his tea she remained standing at the window with her back to him. She was crying out of sheer agitation, in the sorrowful consciousness that their life was so sad; that they could only see each other in secret and had to hide from people like thieves! Was it not a broken life?

"Come, stop now, dear!" he said.

It was plain to him that this love of theirs would not be over soon, that the end of it was not in sight. Anna Sergeyevna was growing more and more attached to him. She adored him, and it was unthinkable to tell her that their love was bound to come to an end some day; besides, she would not have believed it!

He went up to her and took her by the shoulders, to fondle her and say something diverting, and at that moment he caught sight of himself in the mirror. 115

His hair was already beginning to turn gray. And it seemed odd to him that he had grown so much older in the last few years, and lost his looks. The shoulders on which his hands rested were warm and heaving. He felt compassion for this life, still so warm and lovely, but probably already about to begin to fade and wither like his own. Why did she love him so much? He always seemed to women different from what he was, and they loved in him not himself, but the man whom their imagination created and whom they had been eagerly seeking all their lives; and afterwards, when they saw their mistake, they loved him nevertheless. And not one of them had been happy with him. In the past he had met women, come together with them, parted from them, but he had never once loved; it was anything you please, but not love. And only now when his head was gray he had fallen in love, really, truly — for the first time in his life.

Anna Sergeyevna and he loved each other as people do who are very close and intimate, like man and wife, like tender friends; it seemed to them that Fate itself had meant them for one another, and they could not understand why he had a wife and she a husband; and it was as though they were a pair of migratory birds, male and female, caught and forced to live in different cages. They forgave each other what they were ashamed of in their past, they forgave everything in the present, and felt that this love of theirs had altered them both.

Formerly in moments of sadness he had soothed himself with whatever logical arguments came into his head, but now he no longer cared for logic; he felt profound compassion, he wanted to be sincere and tender.

"Give it up now, my darling," he said. "You've had your cry; that's enough. Let us have a talk now, we'll think up something."

Then they spent a long time taking counsel together, they talked of how to avoid the necessity for secrecy, for deception, for living in different cities, and not seeing one another for long stretches of time. How could they free themselves from these intolerable fetters? 120

"How? How?" he asked, clutching his head. "How?"

And it seemed as though in a little while the solution would be found, and then a new and glorious life would begin; and it was clear to both of them that the end was still far off, and that what was to be most complicated and difficult for them was only just beginning.

MARY E. WILKINS FREEMAN (1852–1930)

The Revolt of "Mother"

"Father!"

"What is it?"

"What are them men diggin' over there in the field for?"

There was a sudden dropping and enlarging of the lower part of the old man's face, as if some heavy weight had settled therein; he shut his mouth tight, and went on harnessing the great bay mare. He hustled the collar on to her neck with a jerk.

"Father!"   5

The old man slapped the saddle upon the mare's back.

"Look here, father, I want to know what them men are diggin' over in the field for, an' I'm goin' to know."

"I wish you'd go into the house, mother, an' 'tend to your own affairs," the old man said then. He ran his words together, and his speech was almost as inarticulate as a growl.

But the woman understood; it was her most native tongue. "I ain't goin' into the house till you tell me what them men are doin' over there in the field," said she.

Then she stood waiting. She was a small woman, short and straight-   10
waisted like a child in her brown cotton gown. Her forehead was mild and benevolent between the smooth curves of gray hair; there were meek downward lines about her nose and mouth; but her eyes, fixed upon the old man, looked as if the meekness had been the result of her own will, never of the will of another.

They were in the barn, standing before the wide open doors. The spring air, full of the smell of growing grass and unseen blossoms, came in their faces. The deep yard in front was littered with farm wagons and piles of wood; on the edges, close to the fence and the house, the grass was a vivid green, and there were some dandelions.

The old man glanced doggedly at his wife as he tightened the last buckles on the harness. She looked as immovable to him as one of the rocks in his pasture-land, bound to the earth with generations of blackberry vines. He slapped the reins over the horse, and started forth from the barn.

"Father!" said she.

The old man pulled up. "What is it?"

"I want to know what them men are diggin' over there in that field   15
for."

"They're diggin' a cellar, I s'pose, if you've got to know."

"A cellar for what?"

"A barn."

"A barn? You ain't goin' to build a barn over there where we was goin' to have a house, father?"

The old man said not another word. He hurried the horse into the   20 farm wagon, and clattered out of the yard, jouncing as sturdily on his seat as a boy.

The woman stood a moment looking after him, then she went out of the barn across a corner of the yard to the house. The house, standing at right angles with the great barn and a long reach of sheds and out-buildings, was infinitesimal compared with them. It was scarcely as commodious for people as the little boxes under the barn eaves were for doves.

A pretty girl's face, pink and delicate as a flower, was looking out of one of the house windows. She was watching three men who were digging over in the field which bounded the yard near the road line. She turned quietly when the woman entered.

"What are they digging for, mother?" said she. "Did he tell you?"

"They're diggin' for — a cellar for a new barn."

"Oh, mother, he ain't going to build another barn?" 25

"That's what he says."

A boy stood before the kitchen glass combing his hair. He combed slowly and painstakingly, arranging his brown hair in a smooth hillock over his forehead. He did not seem to pay any attention to the conversation.

"Sammy, did you know father was going to build a new barn?" asked the girl.

The boy combed assiduously.

"Sammy!" 30

He turned, and showed a face like his father's under his smooth crest of hair. "Yes, I s'pose I did," he said, reluctantly.

"How long have you known it?" asked his mother.

"'Bout three months, I guess."

"Why didn't you tell of it?"

"Didn't think 'twould do no good." 35

"I don't see what father wants another barn for," said the girl, in her sweet, slow voice. She turned again to the window, and stared out at the digging men in the field. Her tender, sweet face was full of a gentle distress. Her forehead was as bald and innocent as a baby's, with the light hair strained back from it in a row of curl-papers. She was quite large, but her soft curves did not look as if they covered muscles.

Her mother looked sternly at the boy. "Is he goin' to buy more cows?" said she.

The boy did not reply; he was tying his shoes.

"Sammy, I want you to tell me if he's goin' to buy more cows."

"I s'pose he is." 40

"How many?"

"Four, I guess."

His mother said nothing more. She went into the pantry, and there was a clatter of dishes. The boy got his cap from a nail behind the door, took an old arithmetic from the shelf, and started for school. He was lightly built, but clumsy. He went out of the yard with a curious spring in his hips, that made his loose home-made jacket tilt up in the rear.

The girl went to the sink, and began to wash the dishes that were piled up there. Her mother came promptly out of the pantry, and shoved her aside. "You wipe 'em," said she; "I'll wash. There's a good many this mornin'."

The mother plunged her hands vigorously into the water, the girl   45
wiped the plates slowly and dreamily. "Mother," said she, "don't you think it's too bad father's going to build that new barn, much as we need a decent house to live in?"

Her mother scrubbed a dish fiercely. "You ain't found out yet we're women-folks, Nanny Penn," said she. "You ain't seen enough of men-folks yet to. One of these days you'll find it out, an' then you'll know that we know only what men-folks think we do, so far as any use of it goes, an' how we'd ought to reckon men-folks in with Providence, an' not complain of what they do any more than we do of the weather."

"I don't care; I don't believe George is anything like that, anyhow," said Nanny. Her delicate face flushed pink, her lips pouted softly, as if she were going to cry.

"You wait an' see. I guess George Eastman ain't no better than other men. You hadn't ought to judge father, though. He can't help it, 'cause he don't look at things jest the way we do. An' we've been pretty comfortable here, after all. The roof don't leak — ain't never but once — that's one thing. Father's kept it shingled right up."

"I do wish we had a parlor."

"I guess it won't hurt George Eastman any to come to see you in a   50
nice clean kitchen. I guess a good many girls don't have as good a place as this. Nobody's ever heard me complain."

"I ain't complained either, mother."

"Well, I don't think you'd better, a good father an' a good home as you've got. S'pose your father made you go out an' work for your livin'? Lots of girls have to that ain't no stronger an' better able to than you be."

Sarah Penn washed the frying pan with a conclusive air. She scrubbed the outside of it as faithfully as the inside. She was a masterly keeper of her box of a house. Her one living room never seemed to have in it any of the dust which the friction of life with inanimate matter produces. She swept, and there seemed to be no dirt to go before the broom; she cleaned, and one could see no difference. She was like an artist so perfect that he has apparently no art. To-day she got out a mixing bowl and a board, and rolled some pies, and there was no more flour upon her than upon her daughter who was doing finer work. Nanny was to be married in the fall, and she was sewing on some white cambric and embroidery. She sewed industriously while her mother cooked, her soft milk-white hands and wrists showed whiter than her delicate work.

"We must have the stove moved out in the shed before long," said Mrs. Penn. "Talk about not havin' things, it's been a real blessin' to be able to put a stove up in that shed in hot weather. Father did one good thing when he fixed that stove-pipe out there."

Sarah Penn's face as she rolled her pies had that expression of meek   55
vigor which might have characterized one of the New Testament saints. She
was making mince-pies. Her husband, Adoniram Penn, liked them better
than any other kind. She baked twice a week. Adoniram often liked a piece
of pie between meals. She hurried this morning. It had been later than usual
when she began, and she wanted to have a pie baked for dinner. However
deep a resentment she might be forced to hold against her husband, she
would never fail in sedulous attention to his wants.

Nobility of character manifests itself at loop-holes when it is not provided with large doors. Sarah Penn's showed itself to-day in flaky dishes of
pastry. So she made the pies faithfully, while across the table she could see,
when she glanced up from her work, the sight that rankled in her patient
and steadfast soul — the digging of the cellar of the new barn in the place
where Adoniram forty years ago had promised her their new house should
stand.

The pies were done for dinner. Adoniram and Sammy were home a
few minutes after twelve o'clock. The dinner was eaten with serious haste.
There was never much conversation at the table in the Penn family. Adoniram asked a blessing, and they ate promptly, then rose up and went about
their work.

Sammy went back to school, taking soft sly lopes out of the yard like
a rabbit. He wanted a game of marbles before school, and feared his father
would give him some chores to do. Adoniram hastened to the door and
called after him, but he was out of sight.

"I don't see what you let him go for, mother," said he. "I wanted him
to help me unload that wood."

Adoniram went to work out in the yard unloading wood from the   60
wagon. Sarah put away the dinner dishes, while Nanny took down her curl-
papers and changed her dress. She was going down to the store to buy some
more embroidery and thread.

When Nanny was gone, Mrs. Penn went to the door. "Father!" she
called.

"Well, what is it!"

"I want to see you jest a minute, father."

"I can't leave this wood nohow. I've got to git it unloaded an' go for a
load of gravel afore two o'clock. Sammy had ought to helped me. You
hadn't ought to let him go to school so early."

"I want to see you jest a minute."   65

"I tell ye I can't, nohow, mother."

"Father, you come here." Sarah Penn stood in the door like a queen;
she held her head as if it bore a crown; there was that patience which makes
authority royal in her voice. Adoniram went.

Mrs. Penn led the way into the kitchen, and pointed to a chair. "Sit
down, father," said she: "I've got somethin' I want to say to you."

He sat down heavily; his face was quite stolid, but he looked at her
with restive eyes. "Well, what is it, mother?"

"I want to know what you're buildin' that new barn for, father?"   70
"I ain't got nothin' to say about it."
"It can't be you think you need another barn?"
"I tell ye I ain't got nothin' to say about it, mother; an' I ain't goin' to say nothin'."
"Be you goin' to buy more cows?"
Adoniram did not reply; he shut his mouth tight.   75
"I know you be, as well as I want to. Now, father, look here" — Sarah Penn had not sat down; she stood before her husband in the humble fashion of a Scripture woman — "I'm goin' to talk real plain to you; I never have sence I married you, but I'm goin' to now. I ain't never complained, an' I ain't goin' to complain now, but I'm goin' to talk plain. You see this room here, father; you look at it well. You see there ain't no carpet on the floor, an' you see the paper is all dirty, an' droppin' off the walls. We ain't had no new paper on it for ten year, an' then I put it on myself, an' it didn't cost but ninepence a roll. You see this room, father; it's all the one I've had to work in an' eat in an' sit in sence we was married. There ain't another woman in the whole town whose husband ain't got half the means you have but what's got better. It's all the room Nanny's got to have her company in; an' there ain't one of her mates but what's got better, an' their fathers not so able as hers is. It's all the room she'll have to be married in. What would you have thought, father, if we had had our weddin' in a room no better than this? I was married in my mother's parlor, with a carpet on the floor, an' stuffed furniture, an' a mahogany card-table. An' this is all the room my daughter will have to be married in. Look here, father!"

Sarah Penn went across the room as though it were a tragic stage. She flung open a door and disclosed a tiny bedroom, only large enough for a bed and bureau, with a path between. "There, father," said she — "there's all the room I've had to sleep in forty year. All my children were born there — the two that died, an' the two that's livin'. I was sick with a fever there."

She stepped to another door and opened it. It led into the small, ill-lighted pantry. "Here," said she, "is all the buttery I've got — every place I've got for my dishes, to set away my victuals in, an' to keep my milk-pans in. Father, I've been takin' care of the milk of six cows in this place, an' now you're goin' to build a new barn, an' keep more cows, an' give me more to do in it."

She threw open another door. A narrow crooked flight of stairs wound upward from it. "There, father," said she, "I want you to look at the stairs that go up to them two unfinished chambers that are all the places our son an' daughter have had to sleep in all their lives. There ain't a prettier girl in town nor a more ladylike one than Nanny, an' that's the place she has to sleep in. It ain't so good as your horse's stall; it ain't so warm an' tight."

Sarah Penn went back and stood before her husband. "Now, father,"   80
said she, "I want to know if you think you're doin' right an' accordin' to what you profess. Here, when we was married, forty year ago, you promised me faithful that we should have a new house built in that lot over in the

field before the year was out. You said you had money enough, an' you wouldn't ask me to live in no such place as this. It is forty year now, an' you've been makin' more money, an' I've been savin' of it for you ever since, an' you ain't built no house yet. You've built sheds an' cowhouses an' one new barn, an' now you're goin' to build another. Father, I want to know if you think it's right. You're lodgin' your dumb beasts better than you are your own flesh an' blood. I want to know if you think it's right."

"I ain't got nothin' to say."

"You can't say nothin' without ownin' it ain't right, father. An' there's another thing — I ain't complained; I've got along forty year, an' I s'pose I should forty more, if it wa'n't for that — if we don't have another house. Nanny she can't live with us after she's married. She'll have to go somewheres else to live away from us, an' it don't seem as if I could have it so, noways, father. She wa'n't ever strong. She's got considerable color, but there wa'n't ever any backbone to her. I've always took the heft of everything off her, an' she ain't fit to keep house an' do everything herself. She'll be all worn out inside of a year. Think of her doin' all the washin' an' ironin' an' bakin' with them soft white hands an' arms, an' sweepin'! I can't have it so, noways, father."

Mrs. Penn's face was burning; her mild eyes gleamed. She had pleaded her little cause like a Webster; she had ranged from severity to pathos; but her opponent employed that obstinate silence which makes eloquence futile with mocking echoes. Adoniram arose clumsily.

"Father, ain't you got nothin' to say?" said Mrs. Penn.

"I've got to go off after that load of gravel. I can't stan' here talkin' all   85
day."

"Father, won't you think it over, an' have a house built there instead of a barn?"

"I ain't got nothin' to say."

Adoniram shuffled out. Mrs. Penn went into her bedroom. When she came out, her eyes were red. She had a roll of unbleached cotton cloth. She spread it out on the kitchen table, and began cutting out some shirts for her husband. The men over in the field had a team to help them this afternoon; she could hear their halloos. She had a scanty pattern for the shirts; she had to plan and piece the sleeves.

Nanny came home with her embroidery, and sat down with her needlework. She had taken down her curl-papers, and there was a soft roll of fair hair like an aucrole over her forehead; her face was as delicately fine and clear as porcelain. Suddenly she looked up, and the tender red flamed all over her face and neck. "Mother," said she.

"What say?"   90

"I've been thinking — I don't see how we're goin' to have any — wedding in this room. I'd be ashamed to have his folks come if we didn't have anybody else."

"Mebbe we can have some new paper before then; I can put it on. I guess you won't have no call to be ashamed of your belongin's."

"We might have the wedding in the new barn," said Nanny, with gentle pettishness. "Why, mother, what makes you look so?"

Mrs. Penn had started, and was staring at her with a curious expression. She turned again to her work, and spread out a pattern carefully on the cloth. "Nothin'," said she.

Presently Adoniram clattered out of the yard in his two-wheeled dump cart, standing as proudly upright as a Roman charioteer. Mrs. Penn opened the door and stood there a minute looking out; the halloos of the men sounded louder.

It seemed to her all through the spring months that she heard nothing but the halloos and the noises of saws and hammers. The new barn grew fast. It was a fine edifice for this little village. Men came on pleasant Sundays, in their meeting suits and clean shirt bosoms, and stood around it admiringly. Mrs. Penn did not speak of it, and Adoniram did not mention it to her, although sometimes, upon a return from inspecting it, he bore himself with injured dignity.

"It's a strange thing how your mother feels about the new barn," he said, confidentially, to Sammy one day.

Sammy only grunted after an odd fashion for a boy; he had learned it from his father.

The barn was all completed ready for use by the third week in July. Adoniram had planned to move his stock in on Wednesday; on Tuesday he received a letter which changed his plans. He came in with it early in the morning. "Sammy's been to the post-office," said he, "an' I've got a letter from Hiram." Hiram was Mrs. Penn's brother, who lived in Vermont.

"Well," said Mrs. Penn, "what does he say about the folks?"

"I guess they're all right. He says he thinks if I come up country right off there's a chance to buy jest the kind of a horse I want." He stared reflectively out of the window at the new barn.

Mrs. Penn was making pies. She went on clapping the rolling-pin into the crust, although she was very pale, and her heart beat loudly.

"I dun' know but what I'd better go," said Adoniram. "I hate to go off just now, right in the midst of hayin', but the ten-acre lot's cut, an' I guess Rufus an' the others can git along without me three or four days. I can't get a horse round here to suit me, nohow, an' I've got to have another for all that wood-haulin' in the fall. I told Hiram to watch out, an' if he got wind of a good horse to let me know. I guess I'd better go."

"I'll get out your clean shirt an' collar," said Mrs. Penn calmly.

She laid out Adoniram's Sunday suit and his clean clothes on the bed in the little bedroom. She got his shaving-water and razor ready. At last she buttoned on his collar and fastened his black cravat.

Adoniram never wore his collar and cravat except on extra occasions. He held his head high, with a rasped dignity. When he was all ready, with his coat and hat brushed, and a lunch of pie and cheese in a paper bag, he hesitated on the threshold of the door. He looked at his wife, and his manner was defiantly apologetic. "*If* them cows come to-day, Sammy can drive

95

100

105

'em into the new barn," said he; "an' when they bring the hay up, they can pitch it in there."

"Well," replied Mrs. Penn.

Adoniram set his shaven face ahead and started. When he had cleared the door-step, he turned and looked back with a kind of nervous solemnity. "I shall be back by Saturday if nothin' happens," said he.

"Do be careful, father," returned his wife.

She stood in the door with Nanny at her elbow and watched him out of sight. Her eyes had a strange, doubtful expression in them; her peaceful forehead was contracted. She went in, and about her baking again. Nanny sat sewing. Her wedding-day was drawing nearer, and she was getting pale and thin with her steady sewing. Her mother kept glancing at her. 110

"Have you got that pain in your side this mornin'?" she asked.

"A little."

Mrs. Penn's face, as she worked, changed, her perplexed forehead smoothed, her eyes were steady, her lips firmly set. She formed a maxim for herself, although incoherently with her unlettered thoughts. "Unsolicited opportunities are the guide-posts of the Lord to the new roads of life," she repeated in effect and she made up her mind to her course of action.

"S'posin' I had wrote to Hiram," she muttered once, when she was in the pantry — "s'posin' I had wrote, an' asked him if he knew of any horse? But I didn't, an' father's goin' wa'n't none of my doin'. It looks like a providence." Her voice rang out quite loud at the last.

"What you talkin' about, mother?" called Nanny. 115

"Nothin'."

Mrs. Penn hurried her baking; at eleven o'clock it was all done. The load of hay from the west field came slowly down the cart track, and drew up at the new barn. Mrs. Penn ran out. "Stop!" she screamed — "stop!"

The men stopped and looked; Sammy upreared from the top of the load, and stared at his mother.

"Stop!" she cried out again. "Don't you put the hay in that barn; put it in the old one."

"Why, he said to put it in here," returned one of the hay-makers, wonderingly. He was a young man, a neighbor's son, whom Adoniram hired by the year to help on the farm. 120

"Don't you put the hay in the new barn; there's room enough in the old one, ain't there?" said Mrs. Penn.

"Room enough," returned the hired man, in his thick, rustic tones. "Didn't need the new barn, nohow, far as room's concerned. Well, I s'pose he changed his mind." He took hold of the horses' bridles.

Mrs. Penn went back to the house. Soon the kitchen windows were darkened, and a fragrance like warm honey came into the room.

Nanny laid down her work. "I thought father wanted them to put the hay into the new barn?" she said, wonderingly.

"It's all right," replied her mother. 125

Sammy slid down from the load of hay, and came in to see if dinner was ready.

"I ain't goin' to get a regular dinner to-day, as long as father's gone," said his mother. "I've let the fire go out. You can have some bread an' milk an' pie. I thought we could get along." She set out some bowls of milk, some bread and a pie on the kitchen table. "You'd better eat your dinner now," said she. "You might jest as well get through with it. I want you to help me afterward."

Nanny and Sammy stared at each other. There was something strange in their mother's manner. Mrs. Penn did not eat anything herself. She went into the pantry, and they heard her moving dishes while they ate. Presently she came out with a pile of plates. She got the clothes-basket out of the shed, and packed them in it. Nanny and Sammy watched. She brought out cups and saucers, and put them in with the plates.

"What you goin' to do, mother?" inquired Nanny, in a timid voice. A sense of something unusual made her tremble, as if it were a ghost. Sammy rolled his eyes over his pie.

"You'll see what I'm goin' to do," replied Mrs. Penn. "If you're   130 through Nanny, I want you to go up-stairs an' pack up your things; an' I want you, Sammy, to help me take down the bed in the bedroom."

"Oh, mother, what for?" gasped Nanny.

"You'll see."

During the next few hours a feat was performed by this simple, pious New England mother which was equal in its way to Wolfe's° storming of the Heights of Abraham. It took no more genius and audacity of bravery for Wolfe to cheer his wondering soldiers up those steep precipices, under the sleeping eyes of the enemy, than for Sarah Penn, at the head of her children, to move all their little household goods into the new barn while her husband was away.

Nanny and Sammy followed their mother's instructions without a murmur; indeed, they were overawed. There is a certain uncannny and superhuman quality about all such purely original undertakings as their mother's was to them. Nanny went back and forth with her light loads, and Sammy tugged with sober energy.

At five o'clock in the afternoon the little house in which the Penns had   135 lived for forty years had emptied itself into the new barn.

Every builder builds somewhat for unknown purposes, and is in a measure a prophet. The architect of Adoniram Penn's barn, while he designed it for the comfort of four-footed animals, had planned better than he knew for the comfort of humans. Sarah Penn saw at a glance its possibilities.

Wolfe: James Wolfe, a British general, and his troops climbed the steep bluffs called the Heights of Abraham to win an important battle against Quebec during the Seven Years War (1756–1763).

These great box-stalls, with quilts hung before them, would make better bedrooms than the one she had occupied for forty years, and there was a tight carriage-room. The harness-room, with its chimney and shelves, would make a kitchen of her dreams. The great middle space would make a parlor, by-and-by, fit for a palace. Up-stairs there was as much room as down. With partitions and windows, what a house would there be! Sarah looked at the row of stanchions before the allotted space for cows, and reflected that she would have her front entry there.

At six o'clock the stove was up in the harness-room, the kettle was boiling, and the table set for tea. It looked almost as home-like as the abandoned house across the yard had ever done. The young hired man milked, and Sarah directed him calmly to bring the milk to the new barn. He came gaping, dropping little blots of foam from the brimming pails on the grass. Before the next morning he had spread the story of Adoniram Penn's wife moving into the new barn all over the little village. Men assembled in the store and talked it over, women with shawls over their heads scuttled into each other's houses before their work was done. Any deviation from the ordinary course of life in this quiet town was enough to stop all progress in it. Everybody paused to look at the staid, independent figure on the side track. There was a difference of opinion with regard to her. Some held her to be insane; some, of a lawless and rebellious spirit.

Friday the minister went to see her. It was in the forenoon, and she was at the barn door shelling pease for dinner. She looked up and returned his salutation with dignity, then she went on with her work. She did not invite him in. The saintly expression of her face remained fixed, but there was an angry flush over it.

The minister stood awkwardly before her, and talked. She handled the pease as if they were bullets. At last she looked up, and her eyes showed the spirit that her meek front had covered for a lifetime.

"There ain't no use talkin', Mr. Hersey," said she. "I've thought it all 140
over an' over, an' I believe I'm doin' what's right. I've made it the subject of prayer, an' it's betwixt me an' the Lord an' Adoniram. There ain't no call for nobody else to worry about it."

"Well, of course, if you have brought it to the Lord in prayer, and feel satisfied that you are doing right, Mrs. Penn," said the minister, helplessly. His thin gray-bearded face was pathetic. He was a sickly man; his youthful confidence had cooled; he had to scourge himself up to some of his pastoral duties as relentlessly as a Catholic ascetic, and then he was prostrated by the smart.

"I think it's right jest as much as I think it was right for our forefathers to come over from the old country 'cause they didn't have what belonged to 'em," said Mrs. Penn. She arose. The barn threshold might have been Plymouth Rock from her bearing. "I don't doubt you mean well, Mr. Hersey," said she, "but there are things people hadn't ought to interfere with. I've been a member of the church for over forty year. I've got my own mind an' my own feet, an' I'm goin' to think my own thoughts an' go my own ways, an' nobody but the Lord is goin' to dictate to me unless I've a mind to have him. Won't you come in an' set down? How is Mis' Hersey?"

"She is well, I thank you," replied the minister. He added some more perplexed apologetic remarks; then he retreated.

He could expound the intricacies of every character study in the Scriptures, he was competent to grasp the Pilgrim Fathers and all historical innovators, but Sarah Penn was beyond him. He could deal with primal cases, but parallel ones worsted him. But, after all, although it was aside from his province, he wondered more how Adoniram Penn would deal with his wife than how the Lord would. Everybody shared the wonder. When Adoniram's four new cows arrived, Sarah ordered three to be put in the old barn, the other in the house shed where the cooking-stove had stood. That added to the excitement. It was whispered that all four cows were domiciled in the house.

Towards sunset on Saturday, when Adoniram was expected home, there was a knot of men in the road near the new barn. The hired man had milked, but he still hung around the premises. Sarah Penn had supper all ready. There were brown bread and baked beans and a custard pie; it was the supper Adoniram loved on a Saturday night. She had a clean calico, and she bore herself imperturbably. Nanny and Sammy kept close at her heels. Their eyes were large, and Nanny was full of nervous tremors. Still there was to them more pleasant excitement than anything else. An inborn confidence in their mother over their father asserted itself.

Sammy looked out of the harness-room window. "There he is," he announced, in an awed whisper. He and Nanny peeped around the casing. Mrs. Penn kept on about her work. The children watched Adoniram leave the new horse standing in the drive while he went to the house door. It was fastened. Then he went around to the shed. That door was seldom locked, even when the family was away. The thought how her father would be confronted by the cow flashed upon Nanny. There was a hysterical sob in her throat. Adoniram emerged from the shed and stood looking about in a dazed fashion. His lips moved; he was saying something, but they could not hear what it was. The hired man was peeping around a corner of the old barn, but nobody saw him.

Adoniram took the new horse by the bridle and led him across the yard to the new barn. Nanny and Sammy slunk close to their mother. The barn doors rolled back, and there stood Adoniram, with the long mild face of the great Canadian farm horse looking over his shoulder.

Nanny kept behind her mother, but Sammy stepped suddenly forward, and stood in front of her.

Adoniram stared at the group. "What on airth you all down here for?" said he. "What's the matter over to the house?"

"We've come here to live, father," said Sammy. His shrill voice qua- 150
vered out bravely.

"What" — Adoniram sniffed — "what is it smells like cookin'?" said he.
He stepped forward and looked in the open door of the harness-room. Then
he turned to his wife. His old bristling face was pale and frightened. "What
on airth does this mean, mother?" he gasped.

"You come in here, father," said Sarah. She led the way into the harness-room and shut the door. "Now, father," said she, "you needn't be
scared. I ain't crazy. There ain't nothin' to be upset over. But we've come
here to live, an' we're goin' to live here. We've got jest as good a right here
as new horses an' cows. The house wa'n't fit for us to live in any longer, an'
I made up my mind I wa'n't goin' to stay there. I've done my duty by you
forty year, an' I'm goin' to do it now; but I'm goin' to live here. You've got
to put in some windows and partitions; an' you'll have to buy some
furniture."

"Why, mother!" the old man gasped.

"You'd better take your coat off an' get washed — there's the wash-
basin — an' then we'll have supper."

"Why, mother!" 155

Sammy went past the window, leading the new horse to the old barn.
The old man saw him, and shook his head speechlessly. He tried to take off
his coat, but his arms seemed to lack the power. His wife helped him. She
poured some water into the tin basin, and put in a piece of soap. She got the
comb and brush, and smoothed his thin gray hair after he had washed. Then
she put the beans, hot bread, and tea on the table. Sammy came in, and the
family drew up. Adoniram sat looking dazedly at his plate, and they waited.

"Ain't you goin' to ask a blessin', father?" said Sarah.

And the old man bent his head and mumbled.

All through the meal he stopped eating at intervals, and stared furtively at his wife; but he ate well. The home food tasted good to him, and
his old frame was too sturdily healthy to be affected by his mind. But after
supper he went out, and sat down on the step of the smaller door at the
right of the barn, through which he had meant his Jerseys to pass in stately
file, but which Sarah designed for her front house door, and he leaned his
head on his hands.

After the supper dishes were cleared away and the milk-pans washed, 160
Sarah went out to him. The twilight was deepening. There was a clear green
glow in the sky. Before them stretched the smooth level of field; in the
distance was a cluster of hay-stacks like the huts of a village; the air was very
cool and calm and sweet. The landscape might have been an ideal one of
peace.

Sarah bent over and touched her husband on one of his thin, sinewy
shoulders. "Father!"

The old man's shoulders heaved: he was weeping.

"Why, don't do so, father," said Sarah.

"I'll — put up the — partitions, an' — everything you — want, mother."

Sarah put her apron up to her face; she was overcome by her own 165
triumph.

Adoniram was like a fortress whose walls had no active resistance, and
went down the instant the right besieging tools were used. "Why, mother,"
he said, hoarsely, "I hadn't no idee you was so set on't as all this comes to."

GUY DE MAUPASSANT (1850–1893)

Moonlight

His warlike name well suited the Abbé Marignan. He was a tall thin priest, full of zeal, his soul always exalted but just. All his beliefs were fixed; they never wavered. He sincerely believed that he understood his God, entered into His plans, His wishes, His intentions.

As he strode down the aisle of his little country church, sometimes a question would take shape in his mind: "Now why has God done that?" He would seek the answer stubbornly, putting himself in God's place, and he nearly always found it. He was not one of those who murmur with an air of pious humility, "O Lord, your designs are impenetrable!" He would say to himself: "I am the servant of God, I should know His purposes, and if I don't know them I should divine them."

Everything in nature seemed to him created with an absolute and admirable logic. The "why" and the "because" always balanced out. Dawns existed to make waking up a pleasure, days to ripen the crops, rain to water them, evening to prepare for slumber, and the night was dark for sleeping.

The four seasons were perfectly fitted to all the needs of agriculture; and it would never have occurred to the priest to suspect that nature has no intentions at all, and that, on the contrary, every living thing has bowed to the hard necessities of times, climates, and matter itself.

But he hated women, he hated them unconsciously and despised them   5 by instinct. He often repeated the words of Christ: "Woman, what have I to do with thee?" and he added, "You'd think that not even God himself was happy with that particular piece of work." Woman for him was precisely that child twelve times unclean of whom the poet speaks. She was the temptress who had ensnared the first man and who still continued her damnable work — a weak creature, dangerous, curiously disturbing. And even more than her devilish body he hated her loving soul.

He had often felt the yearning affection of women, and, even though he knew himself invulnerable, he was exasperated by this need to love which always trembled in them.

God, in his opinion, had made woman only to tempt man and test him. Thus man should approach her with great care, ever fearful of traps. She was, in fact, even shaped like a trap, with her arms extended and her lips parted for a man.

He was indulgent only of nuns, made inoffensive by their vows; and he treated even them severely, because he felt stirring in the depths of their fettered hearts — those hearts so humbled — that eternal yearning which still sought him out, even though he was a priest.

He felt it in their gaze — more steeped in piety than that of monks — in their religious ecstasy tainted with sex, in their transports of love for Christ, which infuriated him because it was woman's love, fleshly love. He felt it —

this wicked yearning — even in their docility, in the sweetness of their voices in talking to him, in their lowered eyes, and in their submissive tears when he rebuffed them rudely.

And he shook out his soutane on leaving the gates of a convent and   10 strode quickly away as though fleeing from danger.

He had a niece who lived with her mother in a little house nearby. He was determined to make her a Sister of Charity.

She was pretty, light-headed, and impish. When the Abbé preached, she laughed; and when he got angry at her she kissed him eagerly, clasping him to her heart while he tried instinctively to escape this embrace which nevertheless gave him a taste of sweet happiness, waking deep within him those paternal impulses which slumber in every man.

Often he spoke to her of God — of his God — while walking beside her along country lanes. She scarcely listened but looked at the sky, the grass, the flowers, with a lively joy which showed in her eyes. Sometimes she leaped to catch some flying thing and brought it back to him, crying: "Look, uncle, how pretty it is. I want to pet it." And this impulse to "pet bugs" or nuzzle lilac blossoms disturbed, annoyed, sickened the priest, who discerned in it that ineradicable yearning which always springs up in the female heart.

Then, it happened that one day the sacristan's wife, who kept house for the Abbé Marignan, cautiously told him that his niece had a lover. The news shocked him terribly and he stopped, choking, with his face full of soap, for he was busy shaving.

When he recovered so that he could think and speak, he shouted: "It is   15 not true, you are lying, Mélanie!"

But the good woman put her hand on her heart: "May the Good Lord strike me dead if I'm lying, M. le Curé. She goes out there every night, I tell you, as soon as your sister's in bed. They meet down by the river. You've only to go and watch there between ten and midnight."

He stopped scraping his chin and started walking up and down violently, as he always did in his hours of solemn meditation. When he tried to finish shaving he cut himself three times between the nose and the ear.

All day he was silenced, swollen with indignation and rage. To his fury as a priest, confronted by love, the invincible, was added the exasperation of a strict father, of a guardian, of a confessor fooled, cheated, tricked by a child. He shared that self-centered feeling of suffocation experienced by parents whose daughter tells them she has — without them and despite them — chosen a husband.

After dinner he tried to read a bit, but he could not get into it. He got more and more exasperated. When ten o'clock struck he took down his walking stick, a formidable oaken cudgel he always used when making his evening rounds to visit the sick. And he smiled as he looked at this big club, whirling it about fiercely in his great countryman's fist. Then, suddenly, he raised it and, gritting his teeth brought it down on a chair, knocking its splintered back to the floor.

He opened the door to go out, but stopped on the sill, surprised by a   20
splendor of moonlight such as he had rarely seen.

And, endowed as he was with an exalted spirit — such as those poetical
dreamers the Fathers of the Church might have had — he was immediately
distracted, moved by the glorious and serene beauty of the pale night.

In his little garden, all bathed in soft light, the ordered ranks of his
fruit trees traced on the path the shadows of their slender limbs lightly veiled
with foliage, while the giant honeysuckle, clinging to the wall of the house,
exhaled a delicious, sugary breath that floated through the calm clear air like
a ghostly perfume.

He began to breathe deeply, drinking the air as a drunkard drinks
wine, and he took a few slow, dreaming, wondering steps, almost forgetting
his niece.

When he reached the open country, he stopped to contemplate the
fields all flooded with tender light, bathed in the delicate and languid charm
that calm nights have. Incessantly the frogs gave out their short metallic
note, and distant nightingales, inspiring dream not thought, blended their
unstrung tune — a rapid throbbing music made for kisses — with the enchantment of the moonlight.

The Abbé pressed on, losing heart, though he could not tell why. He   25
felt feeble, suddenly drained; he wanted to sit down, to stay there, to contemplate, to admire God in His handiwork.

Below, following the undulations of the little river, a tall line of poplars
wound like a snake. A fine mist, a white vapor which the moonbeams
pierced and turned to glowing silver, hung around and above the banks
wrapping the whole tortuous watercourse in a sort of delicate and transparent gauze.

The priest halted again, struck to the depths of his soul by an irresistible wave of yearning.

And a doubt, a vague disturbance, came over him. He sensed within
himself another of those questions he sometimes posed.

Why had God done this? Since the night is intended for sleep, for
unconsciousness, for repose, for oblivion, why make it more charming than
the day, sweeter than dawn or evening? And why this slow and seductive
moon, which is more poetic than the sun and seems intended by its very
delicacy to illumine things too fragile and mysterious for daylight, why
should it come to make the shadows so transparent?

Why should the loveliest of songbirds not go to sleep with the others   30
but linger on to sing in the disturbing shade?

Why this half-veil thrown over the world? Why this thrill in the heart,
this stirring of the soul, this languor of the flesh?

Why this display of delights that men never see, since they are deep in
their beds? For whom was it intended, this sublime spectacle, this flood of
poetry poured from the sky over the earth?

And the Abbé found no answer.

But then, down below, on the edge of the fields, under the vault of trees drenched with glowing mist, two shadows appeared, walking side by side.

The man was taller and held the neck of his lover and sometimes kissed   35 her forehead. Their sudden appearance brought the still countryside to life, and it enfolded the young lovers like a setting divinely made for them. They seemed, the pair, a single being, the being for whom this calm and silent night was intended, and they moved toward the priest like a living answer, the answer to his question, flung back by his Master.

He stood still, his heart pounding in confusion, and he felt as if he were looking at a biblical scene, like the love of Ruth and Boaz, like the accomplishment of the will of God as presented in one of the great scenes of holy scripture. In his head echoed verses of the Song of Songs: the passionate cries, the calls of the flesh, all the ardent poetry of this poem that seethes with passionate yearning.

And he said to himself: "Perhaps God has made such nights to veil the loves of men with ideal beauty."

He recoiled before the couple who kept walking arm in arm. It was certainly his niece. But he asked himself now if he was not on the verge of disobeying God. Must not God permit love since He lavished upon it such visible splendor?

And he fled, distraught, almost ashamed, as if he had entered a temple where he had no right to be.

STEPHEN CRANE (1871–1900)

The Bride Comes to Yellow Sky

I

The great Pullman° was whirling onward with such dignity of motion that a glance from the window seemed simply to prove that the plains of Texas were pouring eastward. Vast flats of green grass, dull-hued spaces of mesquit and cactus, little groups of frame houses, woods of light and tender trees, all were sweeping into the east, sweeping over the horizon, a precipice.

A newly married pair had boarded this coach at San Antonio. The man's face was reddened from many days in the wind and sun, and a direct result of his new black clothes was that his brick-colored hands were constantly performing in a most conscious fashion. From time to time he looked down respectfully at his attire. He sat with a hand on each knee, like a man waiting in a barber's shop. The glances he devoted to other passengers were furtive and shy.

The bride was not pretty, nor was she very young. She wore a dress of blue cashmere, with small reservations of velvet here and there, and with steel buttons abounding. She continually twisted her head to regard her puff sleeves, very stiff, straight, and high. They embarrassed her. It was quite apparent that she had cooked, and that she expected to cook, dutifully. The blushes caused by the careless scrutiny of some passengers as she had entered the car were strange to see upon this plain, under-class countenance, which was drawn in placid, almost emotionless lines.

They were evidently very happy. "Ever been in a parlor-car before?" he asked, smiling with delight.

"No," she answered: "I never was. It's fine, ain't it?"   5

"Great! And then after a while we'll go forward to the diner, and get a big lay-out. Finest meal in the world. Charge a dollar."

"Oh, do they?" cried the bride. "Charge a dollar? Why, that's too much — for us — ain't it, Jack?"

"Not this trip, anyhow," he answered bravely. "We're going to go the whole thing."

Later he explained to her about the trains. "You see, it's a thousand miles from one end of Texas to the other; and this train runs right across it, and never stops but four times." He had the pride of an owner. He pointed out to her the dazzling fittings of the coach; and in truth her eyes opened wider as she contemplated the sea-green figured velvet, the shining brass, silver, and glass, the wood that gleamed as darkly brilliant as the surface of a pool of oil. At one end a bronze figure sturdily held a support for a

---

Pullman: A railroad car with sleeping compartments.

separated chamber, and at convenient places on the ceiling were frescos in olive and silver.

To the minds of the pair, their surroundings reflected the glory of their   10 marriage that morning in San Antonio; this was the environment of their new estate; and the man's face in particular beamed with an elation that made him appear ridiculous to the negro porter. This individual at times surveyed them from afar with an amused and superior grin. On other occasions he bullied them with skill in ways that did not make it exactly plain to them that they were being bullied. He subtly used all the manners of the most unconquerable kind of snobbery. He oppressed them; but of this oppression they had small knowledge, and they speedily forgot that infrequently a number of travellers covered them with stares of derisive enjoyment. Historically there was supposed to be something infinitely humorous in their situation.

"We are due in Yellow Sky at 3:42," he said, looking tenderly into her eyes.

"Oh, are we?" she said, as if she had not been aware of it. To evince surprise at her husband's statement was part of her wifely amiability. She took from a pocket a little silver watch; and as she held it before her, and stared at it with a frown of attention, the new husband's face shone.

"I bought it in San Anton' from a friend of mine," he told her gleefully.

"It's seventeen minutes past twelve," she said, looking up at him with a kind of shy and clumsy coquetry. A passenger, noting this play, grew excessively sardonic, and winked at himself in one of the numerous mirrors.

At last they went to the dining-car. Two rows of negro waiters, in   15 glowing white suits, surveyed their entrance with the interest, and also the equanimity, of men who had been forewarned. The pair fell to the lot of a waiter who happened to feel pleasure in steering them through their meal. He viewed them with the manner of a fatherly pilot, his countenance radiant with benevolence. The patronage, entwined with the ordinary deference, was not plain to them. And yet, as they returned to their coach, they showed in their faces a sense of escape.

To the left, miles down a long purple slope, was a little ribbon of mist where moved the keening Rio Grande. The train was approaching it at an angle, and the apex was Yellow Sky. Presently it was apparent that, as the distance from Yellow Sky grew shorter, the husband became commensurately restless. His brick-red hands were more insistent in their prominence. Occasionally he was even rather absent-minded and far-away when the bride leaned forward and addressed him.

As a matter of truth, Jack Potter was beginning to find the shadow of a deed weigh upon him like a leaden slab. He, the town marshal of Yellow Sky, a man known, liked, and feared in his corner, a prominent person, had gone to San Antonio to meet a girl he believed he loved, and there, after the usual prayers, had actually induced her to marry him, without consulting

Yellow Sky for any part of the transaction. He was now bringing his bride before an innocent and unsuspecting community.

Of course people in Yellow Sky married as it pleased them in accordance with a general custom; but such was Potter's thought of his duty to his friends, or of their idea of his duty, or of an unspoken form which does not control men in these matters, that he felt he was heinous. He had committed an extraordinary crime. Face to face with this girl in San Antonio, and spurred by his sharp impulse, he had gone headlong over all the social hedges. At San Antonio he was like a man hidden in the dark. A knife to sever any friendly duty, any form, was easy to his hand in that remote city. But the hour of Yellow Sky — the hour of daylight — was approaching.

He knew full well that his marriage was an important thing to his town. It could only be exceeded by the burning of the new hotel. His friends could not forgive him. Frequently he had reflected on the advisability of telling them by telegraph, but a new cowardice had been upon him. He feared to do it. And now the train was hurrying him toward a scene of amazement, glee, and reproach. He glanced out of the window at the line of haze swinging slowly in toward the train.

Yellow Sky had a kind of brass band, which played painfully, to the   20
delight of the populace. He laughed without heart as he thought of it. If the citizens could dream of his prospective arrival with his bride, they would parade the band at the station and escort them, amid cheers and laughing congratulations, to his adobe home.

He resolved that he would use all the devices of speed and plainscraft in making the journey from the station to his house. Once within that safe citadel, he could issue some sort of vocal bulletin, and then not go among the citizens until they had time to wear off a little of their enthusiasm.

The bride looked anxiously at him. "What's worrying you, Jack?"

He laughed again. "I'm not worrying, girl; I'm only thinking of Yellow Sky."

She flushed in comprehension.

A sense of mutual guilt invaded their minds and developed a finer   25
tenderness. They looked at each other with eyes softly aglow. But Potter often laughed the same nervous laugh; the flush upon the bride's face seemed quite permanent.

The traitor to the feelings of Yellow Sky narrowly watched the speeding landscape. "We're nearly there," he said.

Presently the porter came and announced the proximity of Potter's home. He held a brush in his hand, and, with all his airy superiority gone, he brushed Potter's new clothes as the latter slowly turned this way and that way. Potter fumbled out a coin and gave it to the porter, as he had seen others do. It was a heavy and muscle-bound business, as that of a man shoeing his first horse.

The porter took their bag, and as the train began to slow they moved forward to the hooded platform of the car. Presently the two engines and their long string of coaches rushed into the station of Yellow Sky.

"They have to take water here," said Potter, from a constricted throat and in mournful cadence, as one announcing death. Before the train stopped his eye had swept the length of the platform, and he was glad and astonished to see there was none upon it but the station-agent, who, with a slightly hurried and anxious air, was walking toward the water-tanks. When the train had halted, the porter alighted first, and placed in position a little temporary step.

"Come on, girl," said Potter, hoarsely. As he helped her down they each laughed on a false note. He took the bag from the negro, and bade his wife cling to his arm. As they slunk rapidly away, his hang-dog glance perceived that they were unloading the two trunks, and also that the station-agent, far ahead near the baggage-car, had turned and was running toward him, making gestures. He laughed, and groaned as he laughed, when he noted the first effect of his marital bliss upon Yellow Sky. He gripped his wife's arm firmly to his side, and they fled. Behind them the porter stood, chuckling fatuously.

II

The California express on the Southern Railway was due at Yellow Sky in twenty-one minutes. There were six men at the bar of the Weary Gentleman saloon. One was a drummer who talked a great deal and rapidly; three were Texans who did not care to talk at that time; and two were Mexican sheepherders, who did not talk as a general practice in the Weary Gentleman saloon. The barkeeper's dog lay on the board walk that crossed in front of the door. His head was on his paws, and he glanced drowsily here and there with the constant vigilance of a dog that is kicked on occasion. Across the sandy street were some vivid green grass-plots, so wonderful in appearance, amid the sands that burned near them in a blazing sun, that they caused a doubt in the mind. They exactly resembled the grass mats used to represent lawns on the stage. At the cooler end of the railway station, a man without a coat sat in a tilted chair and smoked his pipe. The fresh-cut bank of the Rio Grande circled near the town, and there could be seen beyond it a great plum-colored plain of mesquit.

Save for the busy drummer and his companions in the saloon, Yellow Sky was dozing. The new-comer leaned gracefully upon the bar, and recited many tales with the confidence of a bard who has come upon a new field.

" — and at the moment that the old man fell downstairs with the bureau in his arms, the old woman was coming up with two scuttles of coal, and of course — "

The drummer's tale was interrupted by a young man who suddenly appeared in the open door. He cried: "Scratchy Wilson's drunk, and has turned loose with both hands." The two Mexicans at once set down their glasses and faded out of the rear entrance of the saloon.

The drummer, innocent and jocular, answered: "All right, old man. S'pose he has? Come in and have a drink, anyhow."

But the information had made such an obvious cleft in every skull in the room that the drummer was obliged to see its importance. All had become instantly solemn. "Say," said he, mystified, "what is this?" His three companions made the introductory gesture of eloquent speech; but the young man at the door forestalled them.

"It means, my friend," he answered, as he came into the saloon, "that for the next two hours this town won't be a health resort."

The barkeeper went to the door, and locked and barred it; reaching out of the window, he pulled in heavy wooden shutters, and barred them. Immediately a solemn, chapel-like gloom was upon the place. The drummer was looking from one to another.

"But, say," he cried, "what is this, anyhow? You don't mean there is going to be a gun-fight?"

"Don't know whether there'll be a fight or not," answered one man,   40
grimly; "but there'll be some shootin' — some good shootin'."

The young man who had warned them waved his hand. "Oh, there'll be a fight fast enough, if any one wants it. Anybody can get a fight out there in the street. There's a fight just waiting."

The drummer seemed to be swayed between the interest of a foreigner and a perception of personal danger.

"What did you say his name was?" he asked.

"Scratchy Wilson," they answered in chorus.

"And will he kill anybody? What are you going to do? Does this   45
happen often? Does he rampage around like this once a week or so? Can he break in that door?"

"No; he can't break down that door," replied the barkeeper. "He's tried it three times. But when he comes you'd better lay down on the floor, stranger. He's dead sure to shoot at it, and a bullet may come through."

Thereafter the drummer kept a strict eye upon the door. The time had not yet called for him to hug the floor, but, as a minor precaution, he sidled near the wall. "Will he kill anybody?" he said again.

The men laughed low and scornfully at the question.

"He's out to shoot, and he's out for trouble. Don't see any good in experimentin' with him."

"But what do you do in a case like this? What do you do?"   50

A man responded: "Why, he and Jack Potter — "

"But," in chorus the other men interrupted, "Jack Potter's in San Anton'."

"Well, who is he? What's he got to do with it?"

"Oh, he's the town marshal. He goes out and fights Scratchy when he gets on one of these tears."

"Wow!" said the drummer, mopping his brow. "Nice job he's got."   55

The voices had toned away to mere whisperings. The drummer wished to ask further questions, which were born of an increasing anxiety and bewilderment; but when he attempted them, the men merely looked at him in irritation and motioned him to remain silent. A tense waiting hush was upon them. In the deep shadows of the room their eyes shone as they listened for sounds from the street. One man made three gestures at the barkeeper; and the latter, moving like a ghost, handed him a glass and a bottle. The man poured a full glass of whisky, and set down the bottle noiselessly. He gulped the whisky in a swallow, and turned again toward the door in immovable silence. The drummer saw that the barkeeper, without a sound, had taken a Winchester from beneath the bar. Later he saw this individual beckoning to him, so he tiptoed across the room.

"You better come with me back of the bar."

"No thanks," said the drummer, perspiring; "I'd rather be where I can make a break for the back door."

Whereupon the man of bottles made a kindly but peremptory gesture. The drummer obeyed it, and, finding himself seated on a box with his head below the level of the bar, balm was laid upon his soul at sight of various zinc and copper fittings that bore a resemblance to armor-plate. The barkeeper took a seat comfortably upon an adjacent box.

"You see," he whispered, "this here Scratchy Wilson is a wonder with a gun — a perfect wonder; and when he goes on the war-trail, we hunt our holes — naturally. He's about the last one of the old gang that used to hang out along the river here. He's a terror when he's drunk. When he's sober he's all right — kind of simple — wouldn't hurt a fly — nicest fellow in town. But when he's drunk — whoo!" 60

There were periods of stillness. "I wish Jack Potter was back from San Anton'," said the barkeeper. "He shot Wilson up once — in the leg — and he would sail in and pull out the kinks in this thing."

Presently they heard from a distance the sound of a shot, followed by three wild yowls. It instantly removed a bond from the men in the darkened saloon. There was a shuffling of feet. They looked at each other. "Here he comes," they said.

III

A man in a maroon-colored flannel shirt, which had been purchased for purposes of decoration, and made principally by some Jewish women on the East Side of New York, rounded a corner and walked into the middle of the main street of Yellow Sky. In either hand the man held a long, heavy, blue-black revolver. Often he yelled, and these cries rang through a semblance of a deserted village, shrilly flying over the roofs in a volume that seemed to have no relation to the ordinary vocal strength of a man. It was as if the surrounding stillness formed the arch of a tomb over him. These cries of ferocious challenge rang against walls of silence. And his boots had red tops with gilded imprints, of the kind beloved in winter by little sledding boys on the hillsides of New England.

The man's face flamed in a rage begot of whisky. His eyes, rolling, and yet keen for ambush, hunted the still doorways and windows. He walked with the creeping movement of the midnight cat. As it occurred to

946 AN ANTHOLOGY OF SHORT FICTION

him, he roared menacing information. The long revolvers in his hands were as easy as straws; they were removed with an electric swiftness. The little fingers of each hand played sometimes in a musician's way. Plain from the low collar of the shirt, the cords of his neck straightened and sank, straightened and sank, as passion moved him. The only sounds were his terrible invitations. The calm adobes preserved their demeanor at the passing of this small thing in the middle of the street.

There was no offer of fight — no offer of fight. The man called to the sky. There were no attractions. He bellowed and fumed and swayed his revolvers here and everywhere.

The dog of the barkeeper of the Weary Gentleman saloon had not appreciated the advance of events. He yet lay dozing in front of his master's door. At sight of the dog, the man paused and raised his revolver humorously. At sight of the man, the dog sprang up and walked diagonally away, with a sullen head, and growling. The man yelled, and the dog broke into a gallop. As it was about to enter the alley, there was a loud noise, a whistling, and something spat the ground directly before it. The dog screamed, and, wheeling in terror, galloped headlong in a new direction. Again there was a noise, a whistling, and sand was kicked viciously before it. Fear-stricken, the dog turned and flurried like an animal in a pen. The man stood laughing, his weapons at his hips.

Ultimately the man was attracted by the closed door of the Weary Gentleman saloon. He went to it and, hammering with a revolver, demanded drink.

The door remaining imperturbable, he picked a bit of paper from the walk, and nailed it to the framework with a knife. He then turned his back contemptuously upon this popular resort and, walking to the opposite side of the street and spinning there on his heel quickly and lithely, fired at the bit of paper. He missed it by a half inch. He swore at himself, and went away. Later he comfortably fusilladed the windows of his most intimate friend. The man was playing with this town; it was a toy for him.

But still there was no offer of fight. The name of Jack Potter, his ancient antagonist, entered his mind, and he concluded that it would be a glad thing if he should go to Potter's house, and by bombardment induce him to come out and fight. He moved in the direction of his desire, chanting Apache scalp-music.

When he arrived at it, Potter's house presented the same still front as had the other adobes. Taking up a strategic position, the man howled a challenge. But this house regarded him as might a great stone god. It gave no sign. After a decent wait, the man howled further challenges, mingling with them wonderful epithets.

Presently there came the spectacle of a man churning himself into deepest rage over the immobility of a house. He fumed at it as the winter wind attacks a prairie cabin in the North. To the distance there should have gone the sound of a tumult like the fighting of two hundred Mexicans. As necessity bade him, he paused for breath or to reload his revolvers.

65

70

IV

Potter and his bride walked sheepishly and with speed. Sometimes they laughed together shamefacedly and low.

"Next corner, dear," he said finally.

They put forth the efforts of a pair walking bowed against a strong wind. Potter was about to raise a finger to point the first appearance of the new home when, as they circled the corner, they came face to face with a man in a maroon-colored shirt, who was feverishly pushing cartridges into a large revolver. Upon the instant the man dropped his revolver to the ground and, like lightning, whipped another from its holster. The second weapon was aimed at the bridegroom's chest.

There was a silence. Potter's mouth seemed to be merely a grave for   75
his tongue. He exhibited an instinct to at once loosen his arm from the woman's grip, and he dropped the bag to the sand. As for the bride, her face had gone as yellow as old cloth. She was a slave to hideous rites, gazing at the apparitional snake.

The two men faced each other at a distance of three paces. He of the revolver smiled with a new and quiet ferocity.

"Tried to sneak up on me," he said. "Tried to sneak up on me!" His eyes grew more baleful. As Potter made a slight movement, the man thrust his revolver venomously forward. "No, don't you do it, Jack Potter. Don't you move a finger toward a gun just yet. Don't you move an eyelash. The time has come for me to settle with you and I'm goin' to do it my own way, and loaf along with no interferin'. So if you don't want a gun bent on you, just mind what I tell you."

Potter looked at his enemy. "I ain't got a gun on me, Scratchy," he said. "Honest, I ain't." He was stiffening and steadying, but yet somewhere at the back of his mind a vision of the Pullman floated: the sea-green figured velvet, the shining brass, silver, and glass, the wood that gleamed as darkly brilliant as the surface of a pool of oil — all the glory of marriage, the environment of the new estate. "You know I fight when it comes to fighting, Scratchy Wilson; but I ain't got a gun on me. You'll have to do all the shootin' yourself."

His enemy's face went livid. He stepped forward, and lashed his weapon to and fro before Potter's chest. "Don't you tell me you ain't got no gun on you, you whelp. Don't tell me no lie like that. There ain't a man in Texas ever seen you without no gun. Don't take me for no kid." His eyes blazed with light, and his throat worked like a pump.

"I ain't takin' you for no kid," answered Potter. His heels had not   80
moved an inch backward. "I'm takin' you for a damn fool. I tell you I ain't got a gun, and I ain't. If you're goin' to shoot me up, you better begin now; you'll never get a chance like this again."

So much enforced reasoning had told on Wilson's rage; he was calmer. "If you ain't got a gun, why ain't you got a gun?" he sneered. "Been to Sunday-school?"

"I ain't got a gun because I've just come from San Anton' with my wife. I'm married," said Potter. "And if I'd thought there was going to be any galoots like you prowling around when I brought my wife home, I'd had a gun, and don't you forget it."

"Married!" said Scratchy, not at all comprehending.

"Yes, married. I'm married," said Potter, distinctly.

"Married?" said Scratchy. Seemingly for the first time, he saw the   85
drooping, drowning woman at the other man's side. "No!" he said. He was like a creature allowed a glimpse of another world. He moved a pace backward, and his arm, with the revolver, dropped to his side. "Is this the lady?" he asked.

"Yes; this is the lady," answered Potter.

There was another period of silence.

"Well," said Wilson at last, slowly, "I s'pose it's all off now."

"It's all off if you say so, Scratchy. You know I didn't make the trouble." Potter lifted his valise.

"Well, I 'low it's off, Jack," said Wilson. He was looking at the ground.   90
"Married!" He was not a student of chivalry; it was merely that in the presence of this foreign condition he was a simple child of the earlier plains. He picked up his starboard revolver, and, placing both weapons in their holsters, he went away. His feet made funnel-shaped tracks in the heavy sand.

SHERWOOD ANDERSON (1876–1941)

Death in the Woods

I

She was an old woman and lived on a farm near the town in which I lived. All country and small-town people have seen such old women, but no one knows much about them. Such an old woman comes into town driving an old worn-out horse or she comes afoot carrying a basket. She may own a few hens and have eggs to sell. She brings them in a basket and takes them to a grocer. There she trades them in. She gets some salt pork and some beans. Then she gets a pound or two of sugar and some flour.

Afterwards she goes to the butcher's and asks for some dog-meat. She may spend ten or fifteen cents, but when she does she asks for something. Formerly the butchers gave liver to any one who wanted to carry it away. In our family we were always having it. Once one of my brothers got a whole cow's liver at the slaughter-house near the fairgrounds in our town. We had it until we were sick of it. It never cost a cent. I have hated the thought of it ever since.

The old farm woman got some liver and a soup-bone. She never visited with any one, and as soon as she got what she wanted she lit out for home. It made quite a load for such an old body. No one gave her a lift. People drive right down a road and never notice an old woman like that.

There was such an old woman who used to come into town past our house one Summer and Fall when I was a young boy and was sick with what was called inflammatory rheumatism. She went home later carrying a heavy pack on her back. Two or three large gaunt-looking dogs followed at her heels.

The old woman was nothing special. She was one of the nameless ones that hardly anyone knows, but she got into my thoughts. I have just suddenly now, after all these years, remembered her and what happened. It is a story. Her name was Grimes, and she lived with her husband and son in a small unpainted house on the bank of a small creek four miles from town.

The husband and son were a tough lot. Although the son was but twenty-one, he had already served a term in jail. It was whispered about that the woman's husband stole horses and ran them off to some other county. Now and then, when a horse turned up missing, the man had also disappeared. No one ever caught him. Once, when I was loafing at Tom Whitehead's livery-barn, the man came there and sat on the bench in front. Two or three other men were there, but no one spoke to him. He sat for a few minutes and then got up and went away. When he was leaving he turned around and stared at the men. There was a look of defiance in his eyes. "Well, I have tried to be friendly. You don't want to talk to me. It has been so wherever I have gone in this town. If, some day, one of your fine horses turns up missing, well, then what?" He did not say anything actually. "I'd like to bust one of you on the jaw," was about what his eyes said. I remember how the look in his eyes made me shiver.

The old man belonged to a family that had had money once. His name was Jake Grimes. It all comes back clearly now. His father, John Grimes, had owned a sawmill when the country was new, and had made money. Then he got to drinking and running after women. When he died there wasn't much left.

Jake blew in the rest. Pretty soon there wasn't any more lumber to cut and his land was nearly all gone.

He got his wife off a German farmer, for whom he went to work one June day in the wheat harvest. She was a young thing then and scared to death. You see, the farmer was up to something with the girl — she was, I think, a bound girl and his wife had her suspicions. She took it out on the girl when the man wasn't around. Then, when the wife had to go off to town for supplies, the farmer got after her. She told young Jake that nothing really ever happened, but he didn't know whether to believe it or not.

He got her pretty easy himself, the first time he was out with her. He wouldn't have married her if the German farmer hadn't tried to tell him where to get off. He got her to go riding with him in his buggy one night when he was threshing on the place, and then he came for her the next Sunday night.

She managed to get out of the house without her employer's seeing, but when she was getting into the buggy he showed up. It was almost dark, and he just popped up suddenly at the horse's head. He grabbed the horse by the bridle and Jake got out his buggy-whip.

They had it out all right! The German was a tough one. Maybe he didn't care whether his wife knew or not. Jake hit him over the face and shoulders with the buggy-whip, but the horse got to acting up and he had to get out.

Then the two men went for it. The girl didn't see it. The horse started to run away and went nearly a mile down the road before the girl got him stopped. Then she managed to tie him to a tree beside the road. (I wonder how I know all this. It must have stuck in my mind from small-town tales when I was a boy.) Jake found her there after he got through with the German. She was huddled up in the buggy seat, crying, scared to death. She told Jake a lot of stuff, how the German had tried to get her, how he chased her once into the barn, how another time, when they happened to be alone in the house together, he tore her dress open clear down the front. The German, she said, might have got her that time if he hadn't heard his old woman drive in at the gate. She had been off to town for supplies. Well, she would be putting the horse in the barn. The German managed to sneak off to the fields without his wife seeing. He told the girl he would kill her if she told. What could she do? She told a lie about ripping her dress in the barn when she was feeding the stock. I remember now that she was a bound girl and did not know where her father and mother were. Maybe she did not have any father. You know what I mean.

Such bound children were often enough cruelly treated. They were children who had no parents, slaves really. There were very few orphan homes then. They were legally bound into some home. It was a matter of pure luck how it came out.

II

She married Jake and had a son and daughter, but the daughter died.   15

Then she settled down to feed stock. That was her job. At the German's place she had cooked the food for the German and his wife. The wife was a strong woman with big hips and worked most of the time in the fields with her husband. She fed them and fed the cows in the barn, fed the pigs, the horses and the chickens. Every moment of every day, as a young girl, she spent feeding something.

Then she married Jake Grimes and he had to be fed. She was a slight thing, and when she had been married for three or four years, and after the two children were born, her slender shoulders became stooped.

Jake always had a lot of big dogs around the house, that stood near the unused sawmill near the creek. He was always trading horses when he wasn't stealing something and had a lot of poor bony ones about. Also he kept three or four pigs and a cow. They were all pastured in the few acres left of the Grimes place and Jake did little enough work.

He went into debt for a threshing outfit and ran it for several years, but it did not pay. People did not trust him. They were afraid he would steal the grain at night. He had to go a long way off to get work and it cost too much to get there. In the Winter he hunted and cut a little firewood, to be sold in some nearby town. When the son grew up he was just like the father. They got drunk together. If there wasn't anything to eat in the house when they came home the old man gave his old woman a cut over the head. She had a few chickens of her own and had to kill one of them in a hurry. When they were all killed she wouldn't have any eggs to sell when she went to town, and then what would she do?

She had to scheme all her life about getting things fed, getting the pigs   20
fed so they would grow fat and could be butchered in the Fall. When they were butchered her husband took most of the meat off to town and sold it. If he did not do it first the boy did. They fought sometimes and when they fought the old woman stood aside trembling.

She had got the habit of silence anyway — that was fixed. Sometimes, when she began to look old — she wasn't forty yet — and when the husband and son were both off, trading horses or drinking or hunting or stealing, she went around the house and the barnyard muttering to herself.

How was she going to get everything fed? — that was her problem. The dogs had to be fed. There wasn't enough hay in the barn for the horses and the cow. If she didn't feed the chickens how could they lay eggs? Without eggs to sell how could she get things in town, things she had to have to keep the life of the farm going? Thank heaven, she did not have to feed her husband—in a certain way. That hadn't lasted long after their marriage and after the babies came. Where he went on his long trips she did not know. Sometimes he was gone from home for weeks, and after the boy grew up they went off together.

They left everything at home for her to manage and she had no money. She knew no one. No one ever talked to her in town. When it was Winter she had to gather sticks of wood for her fire, had to try to keep the stock fed with very little grain.

The stock in the barn cried to her hungrily, the dogs followed her about. In the Winter the hens laid few enough eggs. They huddled in the corners of the barn and she kept watching them. If a hen lays an egg in the barn in the Winter and you do not find it, it freezes and breaks.

One day in Winter the old woman went off to town with a few eggs   25
and the dogs followed her. She did not get started until nearly three o'clock and the snow was heavy. She hadn't been feeling very well for several days and so she went muttering along, scantily clad, her shoulders stooped. She had an old grain bag in which she carried her eggs, tucked away down in the bottom. There weren't many of them, but in Winter the price of eggs is up. She would get a little meat in exchange for the eggs, some salt pork, a little sugar, and some coffee perhaps. It might be the butcher would give her a piece of liver.

When she had got to town and was trading in her eggs the dogs lay by the door outside. She did pretty well, got the things she needed, more than she had hoped. Then she went to the butcher and he gave her some liver and some dog-meat.

It was the first time any one had spoken to her in a friendly way for a long time. The butcher was alone in his shop when she came in and was annoyed by the thought of such a sick-looking old woman out on such a day. It was bitter cold and the snow, that had let up during the afternoon, was falling again. The butcher said something about her husband and her son, swore at them, and the old woman stared at him, a look of mild surprise in her eyes as he talked. He said that if either the husband or the son were going to get any of the liver or the heavy bones with scraps of meat hanging to them that he had put into the grain bag, he'd see them starve first.

Starve, eh? Well, things had to be fed. Men had to be fed, and horses that weren't any good but maybe could be traded off, and the poor thin cow that hadn't given any milk for three months.

Horses, cows, pigs, dogs, men.

III

The old woman had to get back before darkness came if she could.   30
The dogs followed at her heels, sniffing at the heavy grain bag she had fastened on her back. When she got to the edge of town she stopped by a fence and tied the bag on her back with a piece of rope she had carried in

her dress-pocket for just that purpose. It was hard when she had to crawl over fences and once she fell over and landed in the snow. The dogs went frisking about. She had to struggle to get to her feet again, but she made it. The point of climbing over the fences was that there was a short cut over a hill and through a woods. She might have gone around by the road, but it was a mile farther that way. She was afraid she couldn't make it. And then, besides, the stock had to be fed. There was a little hay left and a little corn. Perhaps her husband and son would bring some home when they came. They had driven off in the only buggy the Grimes family had, a rickety thing, a rickety horse hitched to the buggy, two other rickety horses led by halters. They were going to trade horses, get a little money if they could. They might come home drunk. It would be well to have something in the house when they came back.

The son had an affair on with a woman at the county seat, fifteen miles away. She was a rough enough woman, a tough one. Once, in the Summer, the son had brought her to the house. Both she and the son had been drinking. Jake Grimes was away and the son and his woman ordered the old woman about like a servant. She didn't mind much; she was used to it. Whatever happened she never said anything. That was her way of getting along. She had managed that way when she was a young girl at the German's and ever since she had married Jake. That time her son brought his woman to the house they stayed all night, sleeping together just as though they were married. It hadn't shocked the old woman, not much. She had got past being shocked early in life.

With the pack on her back she went painfully along across an open field, wading in the deep snow, and got into the woods.

There was a path, but it was hard to follow. Just beyond the top of the hill, where the woods was thickest, there was a small clearing. Had some one once thought of building a house there? The clearing was as large as a building lot in town, large enough for a house and a garden. The path ran along the side of the clearing, and when she got there the old woman sat down to rest at the foot of a tree.

It was a foolish thing to do. When she got herself placed, the pack against the tree's trunk, it was nice, but what about getting up again? She worried about that for a moment and then quietly closed her eyes.

She must have slept for a time. When you are about so cold you can't get any colder. The afternoon grew a little warmer and the snow came thicker than ever. Then after a time the weather cleared. The moon even came out.

There were four Grimes dogs that had followed Mrs. Grimes into town, all tall gaunt fellows. Such men as Jake Grimes and his son always keep just such dogs. They kick and abuse them, but they stay. The Grimes dogs, in order to keep from starving, had to do a lot of foraging for themselves, and they had been at it while the old woman slept with her back to the tree at the side of the clearing. They had been chasing rabbits in the

35

woods and in adjoining fields and in their ranging had picked up three other farm dogs.

After a time all the dogs came back to the clearing. They were excited about something. Such nights, cold and clear and with a moon, do things to dogs. It may be that some old instinct, come down from the time when they were wolves, and ranged the woods in packs on Winter nights, comes back to them.

The dogs in the clearing, before the old woman, had caught two or three rabbits and their immediate hunger had been satisfied. They began to play, running in circles in the clearing. Round and round they ran, each dog's nose at the tail of the next dog. In the clearing, under the snow-laden trees and under the wintry moon they made a strange picture, running thus silently, in a circle their running had beaten in the soft snow. The dogs made no sound. They ran around and around in the circle.

It may have been that the old woman saw them doing that before she died. She may have awakened once or twice and looked at the strange sight with dim old eyes.

She wouldn't be very cold now, just drowsy. Life hangs on a long 40
time. Perhaps the old woman was out of her head. She may have dreamed of her girlhood at the German's, and before that, when she was a child and before her mother lit out and left her.

Her dreams couldn't have been very pleasant. Not many pleasant things had happened to her. Now and then one of the Grimes dogs left the running circle and came to stand before her. The dog thrust his face to her face. His red tongue was hanging out.

The running of the dogs may have been a kind of death ceremony. It may have been that the primitive instinct of the wolf, having been aroused in the dogs by the night and the running, made them somehow, afraid.

"Now we are no longer wolves. We are dogs, the servants of men. Keep alive, man! When man dies we become wolves again." When one of the dogs came to where the old woman sat with her back against the tree and thrust his nose close to her face he seemed satisfied and went back to run with the pack. All the Grimes dogs did it at some time during the evening, before she died. I knew all about it afterward, when I grew to be a man, because once in a woods in Illinois, on another Winter night, I saw a pack of dogs act just like that. The dogs were waiting for me to die as they had waited for the old woman that night when I was a child, but when it happened to me I was a young man and had no intention whatever of dying.

The old woman died softly and quietly. When she was dead and when one of the Grimes dogs had come to her and had found her dead all the dogs stopped running.

They gathered about her.

Well, she was dead now. She had fed the Grimes dogs when she was 45
alive, what about now?

There was the pack on her back, the grain bag containing the piece of salt pork, the liver the butcher had given her, the dog-meat, the soup bones.

The butcher in town, having been suddenly overcome with a feeling of pity, had loaded her grain bag heavily. It had been a big haul for the old woman.

It was a big haul for the dogs now.

IV

One of the Grimes dogs sprang suddenly out from among the others and began worrying the pack on the old woman's back. Had the dogs really been wolves that one would have been the leader of the pack. What he did, all the others did.

All of them sank their teeth into the grain bag the old woman had   50 fastened with ropes to her back.

They dragged the old woman's body out into the open clearing. The worn-out dress was quickly torn from her shoulders. When she was found, a day or two later, the dress had been torn from her body clear to the hips, but the dogs had not touched her body. They had got the meat out of the grain bag, that was all. Her body was frozen stiff when it was found, and the shoulders were so narrow and the body so slight that in death it looked like the body of some charming young girl.

Such things happened in towns of the Middle West, on farms near town, when I was a boy. A hunter out after rabbits found the old woman's body and did not touch it. Something, the beaten round path in the little snow-covered clearing, the silence of the place, the place where the dogs had worried the body trying to pull the grain bag away or tear it open — something startled the man and he hurried off to town.

I was in Main Street with one of my brothers who was town newsboy and who was taking the afternoon papers to the stores. It was almost night.

The hunter came into a grocery and told his story. Then he went into a hardware-shop and into a drugstore. Men began to gather on the sidewalks. Then they started out along the road to the place in the woods.

My brother should have gone on about his business of distributing   55 papers but he didn't. Every one was going to the woods. The undertaker went and the town marshal. Several men got on a dray and rode out to where the path left the road and went into the woods, but the horses weren't very sharply shod and slid about on the slippery roads. They made no better time than those of us who walked.

The town marshal was a large man whose leg had been injured in the Civil War. He carried a heavy cane and limped rapidly along the road. My brother and I followed at his heels, and as we went other men and boys joined the crowd.

It had grown dark by the time we got to where the old woman had left the road but the moon had come out. The marshal was thinking there might have been a murder. He kept asking the hunter questions. The hunter went along with his gun across his shoulders, a dog following at his heels. It isn't often a rabbit hunter has a chance to be so conspicuous. He was taking full advantage of it, leading the procession with the town marshal. "I didn't see any wounds. She was a beautiful young girl. Her face was buried in the snow. No, I didn't know her." As a matter of fact, the hunter had not looked closely at the body. He had been frightened. She might have been murdered and some one might spring out from behind a tree and murder him. In a woods, in the late afternoon, when the trees are all bare and there is white snow on the ground, when all is silent, something creepy steals over the mind and body. If something strange or uncanny has happened in the neighborhood all you think about is getting away from there as fast as you can.

The crowd of men and boys had got to where the old woman had crossed the field and went, following the marshal and the hunter, up the slight incline and into the woods.

My brother and I were silent. He had his bundle of papers in a bag slung across his shoulder. When he got back to town he would have to go on distributing his papers before he went home to supper. If I went along, as he had no doubt already determined I should, we would both be late. Either mother or our older sister would have to warm our supper.

Well, we would have something to tell. A boy did not get such a chance very often. It was lucky we just happened to go into the grocery when the hunter came in. The hunter was a country fellow. Neither of us had ever seen him before. 60

Now the crowd of men and boys had got to the clearing. Darkness comes quickly on such Winter nights, but the full moon made everything clear. My brother and I stood near the tree, beneath which the old woman had died.

She did not look old, lying there in that light, frozen and still. One of the men turned her over in the snow and I saw everything. My body trembled with some strange mystical feeling and so did my brother's. It might have been the cold.

Neither of us had ever seen a woman's body before. It may have been the snow, clinging to the frozen flesh, that made it look so white and lovely, so like marble. No woman had come with the party from town; but one of the men, he was the town blacksmith, took off his overcoat and spread it over her. Then he gathered her into his arms and started off to town, all the others following silently. At that time no one knew who she was.

V

I had seen everything, had seen the oval in the snow, like a miniature race-track, where the dogs had run, had seen how the men were mystified, had seen the white bare young-looking shoulders, had heard the whispered comments of the men.

The men were simply mystified. They took the body to the undertaker's, and when the blacksmith, the hunter, the marshal and several others had got inside they closed the door. If father had been there perhaps he could have got in, but we boys couldn't. 65

I went with my brother to distribute the rest of his papers and when we got home it was my brother who told the story.

I kept silent and went to bed early. It may have been I was not satisfied with the way he told it.

Later, in the town, I must have heard other fragments of the old woman's story. She was recognized the next day and there was an investigation.

The husband and son were found somewhere and brought to town and there was an attempt to connect them with the woman's death, but it did not work. They had perfect enough alibis.

However, the town was against them. They had to get out. Where   70
they went I never heard.

I remember only the picture there in the forest, the men standing about, the naked girlish-looking figure, face down in the snow, the tracks made by the running dogs and the clear cold Winter sky above. White fragments of clouds were drifting across the sky. They went racing across the little open space among the trees.

The scene in the forest had become for me, without my knowing it, the foundation for the real story I am now trying to tell. The fragments, you see, had to be picked up slowly, long afterwards.

Things happened. When I was a young man I worked on the farm of a German. The hired-girl was afraid of her employer. The farmer's wife hated her.

I saw things at that place. Once later, I had a half-uncanny, mystical adventure with dogs in an Illinois forest on a clear, moon-lit Winter night. When I was a schoolboy, and on a Summer day, I went with a boy friend out along a creek some miles from town and came to the house where the old woman had lived. No one had lived in the house since her death. The doors were broken from the hinges; the window lights were all broken. As the boy and I stood in the road outside, two dogs, just roving farm dogs no doubt, came running around the corner of the house. The dogs were tall, gaunt fellows and came down to the fence and glared through at us, standing in the road.

The whole thing, the story of the old woman's death, was to me as I   75
grew older like music heard from far off. The notes had to be picked up slowly one at a time. Something had to be understood.

The woman who died was one destined to feed animal life. Anyway, that is all she ever did. She was feeding animal life before she was born, as a child, as a young woman working on the farm of the German, after she married, when she grew old and when she died. She fed animal life in cows, in chickens, in pigs, in horses, in dogs, in men. Her daughter had died in childhood and with her one son she had no articulate relations. On the night when she died she was hurrying homeward, bearing on her body food for animal life.

She died in the clearing in the woods and even after her death continued feeding animal life.

You see it is likely that, when my brother told the story, that night when we got home and my mother and sister sat listening, I did not think he got the point. He was too young and so was I. A thing so complete has its own beauty.

I shall not try to emphasize the point. I am only explaining why I was dissatisifed then and have been ever since. I speak of that only that you may understand why I have been impelled to try to tell the simple story over again.

FRANZ KAFKA (1883–1924)

A Hunger Artist

During these last decades the interest in professional fasting has markedly diminished. It used to pay very well to stage such great performances under one's own management, but today that is quite impossible. We live in a different world now. At one time the whole town took a lively interest in the hunger artist; from day to day of his fast the excitement mounted; everybody wanted to see him at least once a day; there were people who bought season tickets for the last few days and sat from morning till night in front of his small barred cage; even in the nighttime there were visiting hours, when the whole effect was heightened by torch flares; on fine days the cage was set out in the open air, and then it was the children's special treat to see the hunger artist; for their elders he was often just a joke that happened to be in fashion, but the children stood open-mouthed, holding each other's hands for greater security, marveling at him as he sat there pallid in black tights, with his ribs sticking out so prominently, not even on a seat but down among straw on the ground, sometimes giving a courteous nod, answering questions with a constrained smile, or perhaps stretching an arm through the bars so that one might feel how thin it was, and then again withdrawing deep into himself, paying no attention to anyone or anything, not even to the all-important striking of the clock that was the only piece of furniture in his cage, but merely staring into vacancy with half shut eyes, now and then taking a sip from a tiny glass of water to moisten his lips.

Beside casual onlookers there were also relays of permanent watchers selected by the public, usually butchers, strangely enough, and it was their task to watch the hunger artist day and night, three of them at a time, in case he should have some secret recourse to nourishment. This was nothing but a formality, instituted to reassure the masses, for the initiates knew well enough that during his fast the artist would never in any circumstances, not even under forcible compulsion, swallow the smallest morsel of food; the honor of his profession forbade it. Not every watcher, of course, was capable of understanding this; there were often groups of night watchers who were very lax in carrying out their duties and deliberately huddled together in a retired corner to play cards with great absorption, obviously intending to give the hunger artist the chance of a little refreshment, which they supposed he could draw from some private hoard. Nothing annoyed the artist more than such watchers; they made him miserable; they made his fast seem unendurable; sometimes he mastered his feebleness sufficiently to sing during their watch for as long as he could keep going, to show them how unjust their suspicions were. But that was of little use; they only wondered at his cleverness in being able to fill his mouth even while singing. Much more to his taste were the watchers who sat close up to the bars, who were not content with the dim night lighting of the hall but focused him in the full glare of the electric pocket torch given them by the impresario. The harsh light did not trouble him at all, in any case he could never sleep properly, and he could always drowse a little, whatever the light, at any hour, even when the hall was thronged with noisy onlookers. He was quite happy at the prospect of spending a sleepless night with such watchers; he was ready to exchange jokes with them, to tell them stories out of his nomadic life, anything at all to keep them awake and demonstrate to them again that he had no eatables in his cage and that he was fasting as not one of them could fast. But his happiest moment was when the morning came and an enormous breakfast was brought them, at his expense, on which they flung themselves with the keen appetite of healthy men after a weary night of wakefulness. Of course there were people who argued that this breakfast was an unfair attempt to bribe the watchers, but that was going rather too far, and when they were invited to take on a night's vigil without a breakfast, merely for the sake of the cause, they made themselves scarce, although they stuck stubbornly to their suspicions.

Such suspicions, anyhow, were a necessary accompaniment to the profession of fasting. No one could possibly watch the hunger artist continuously, day and night, and so no one could produce first-hand evidence that the fast had really been rigorous and continuous; only the artist himself could know that, he was therefore bound to be the sole completely satisfied spectator of his own fast. Yet for other reasons he was never satisfied; it was not perhaps mere fasting that had brought him to such skeleton thinness that many people had regretfully to keep away from his exhibitions, because the sight of him was too much for them, perhaps it was dissatisfaction with himself that had worn him down. For he alone knew, what no other initiate knew, how easy it was to fast. It was the easiest thing in the world. He made no secret of this, yet people did not believe him, at the best they set him down as modest; most of them, however, thought he was out for publicity or else was some kind of cheat who found it easy to fast because he had discovered a way of making it easy, and then had the impudence to admit the fact, more or less. He had to put up with all that, and in the course of time had got used to it, but his inner dissatisfaction always rankled, and never yet, after any term of fasting — this must be granted to his credit — had he left the cage of his own free will. The longest period of fasting was fixed by his impresario at forty days, beyond that term he was not allowed to go, not even in great cities, and there was good reason for it, too. Experience had proved that for about forty days the interest of the public could be stimulated by a steadily increasing pressure of advertisement, but after that the town began to lose interest, sympathetic support began notably to fall off; there were of course local variations as between one town and another or one country and another, but as a general rule forty days marked the limit. So on the fortieth day the flower bedecked cage was opened, enthusiastic spectators filled the hall, a military band played, two doctors entered the cage to measure the results of the fast, which were announced

through a megaphone, and finally two young ladies appeared, blissful at having been selected for the honor, to help the hunger artist down the few steps leading to a small table on which was spread a carefully chosen invalid repast. And at this very moment the artist always turned stubborn. True, he would entrust his bony arms to the outstretched helping hands of the ladies bending over him, but stand up he would not. Why stop fasting at this particular moment, after forty days of it? He had held out for a long time, an illimitably long time; why stop now, when he was in his best fasting form, or rather, not yet quite in his best fasting form? Why should he be cheated of the fame he would get for fasting longer, for being not only the record hunger artist of all time, which presumably he was already, but for beating his own record by a performance beyond human imagination, since he felt that there were no limits to his capacity for fasting? His public pretended to admire him so much, why should it have so little patience with him; if he could endure fasting longer, why shouldn't the public endure it? Besides, he was tired, he was comfortable sitting in the straw, and now he was supposed to lift himself to his full height and go down to a meal the very thought of which gave him a nausea that only the presence of the ladies kept him from betraying, and even that with an effort. And he looked up into the eyes of the ladies who were apparently so friendly and in reality so cruel, and shook his head, which felt too heavy on its strengthless neck. But then there happened yet again what always happened. The impresario came forward, without a word — for the band made speech impossible — lifted his arms in the air above the artist, as if inviting Heaven to look down upon its creature here in the straw, this suffering martyr, which indeed he was, although in quite another sense; grasped him round the emaciated waist, with exaggerated caution, so that the frail condition he was in might be appreciated; and committed him to the care of the blenching ladies, not without secretly giving him a shaking so that his legs and body tottered and swayed. The artist now submitted completely; his head lolled on his breast as if it had landed there by chance; his body was hollowed out; his legs in a spasm of self-preservation clung close to each other at the knees, yet scraped on the ground as if it were not really solid ground, as if they were only trying to find solid ground; and the whole weight of his body, a featherweight after all, relapsed onto one of the ladies, who, looking round for help and panting a little — this post of honor was not at all what she had expected it to be — first stretched her neck as far as she could to keep her face at least free from contact with the artist, when finding this impossible, and her more fortunate companion not coming to her aid but merely holding extended on her own trembling hand the little bunch of knucklebones that was the artist's, to the great delight of the spectators burst into tears and had to be replaced by an attendant who had long been stationed in readiness. Then came the food, a little of which the impresario managed to get between the artist's lips, while he sat in a kind of half-fainting trance, to the accompaniment of cheerful patter designed to distract the public's attention

from the artist's condition; after that, a toast was drunk to the public, supposedly prompted by a whisper from the artist in the impresario's ear; the
band confirmed it with a mighty flourish, the spectators melted away, and
no one had any cause to be dissatisfied with the proceedings, no one except
the hunger artist himself, he only, as always.

So he lived for many years, with small regular intervals of recupera-
tion, in visible glory, honored by the world, yet in spite of that troubled in
spirit, and all the more troubled because no one would take his trouble
seriously. What comfort could he possibly need? What more could he possibly wish for? And if some good-natured person, feeling sorry for him,
tried to console him by pointing out that his melancholy was probably
caused by fasting; it could happen, especially when he had been fasting for
some time, that he reacted with an outburst of fury and to the general alarm
began to shake the bars of his cage like a wild animal. Yet the impresario
had a way of punishing these outbreaks which he rather enjoyed putting
into operation. He would apologize publicly for the artist's behavior, which
was only to be excused, he admitted, because of the irritability caused by
fasting; a condition hardly to be understood by well-fed people; then by
natural transition he went on to mention the artist's equally incomprehensible boast that he could fast for much longer than he was doing; he praised
the high ambition, the good will, the great self-denial undoubtedly implicit
in such a statement; and then quite simply countered it by bringing out
photographs, which were also on sale to the public, showing the artist on
the fortieth day of a fast lying in bed almost dead from exhaustion. This
perversion of the truth, familiar to the artist though it was, always unnerved
him afresh and proved too much for him. What was a consequence of
the premature ending of his fast was here presented as the cause of it! To
fight against this lack of understanding, against a whole world of non-
understanding, was impossible. Time and again in good faith he stood by
the bars listening to the impresario, but as soon as the photographs appeared
he always let go and sank with a groan back on to his straw, and the
reassured public could once more come close and gaze at him.

A few years later when the witnesses of such scenes called them to
mind, they often failed to understand themselves at all. For meanwhile the
aforementioned change in public interest had set in; it seemed to happen
almost overnight; there may have been profound causes for it, but who was
going to bother about that; at any rate the pampered hunger artist suddenly
found himself deserted one fine day by the amusement seekers, who went
streaming past him to other more favored attractions. For the last time the
impresario hurried him over half Europe to discover whether the old interest
might still survive here and there; all in vain; everywhere, as if by secret
agreement, a positive revulsion from professional fasting was in evidence.
Of course it could not really have sprung up so suddenly as all that, and
many premonitory symptoms which had not been sufficiently remarked or
suppressed during the rush and glitter of success now came retrospectively

5

to mind, but it was now too late to take any countermeasures. Fasting would surely come into fashion again at some future date, yet that was no comfort for those living in the present. What, then, was the hunger artist to do? He had been applauded by thousands in his time and could hardly come down to showing himself in a street booth at village fairs, and as for adopting another profession, he was not only too old for that but too frantically devoted to fasting. So he took leave of the impresario, his partner in an unparalleled career, and hired himself to a large circus; in order to spare his own feelings he avoided reading the conditions of his contract.

A large circus with its enormous traffic in replacing and recruiting men, animals and apparatus can always find a use for people at any time, even for a hunger artist, provided of course that he does not ask too much, and in this particular case anyhow it was not only the artist who was taken on but his famous and long-known name as well, indeed considering the peculiar nature of his performance, which was not impaired by advancing age, it could not be objected that there was an artist past his prime, no longer at the height of his professional skill, seeking a refuge in some quiet corner of a circus; on the contrary, the hunger artist averred that he could fast as well as ever, which was entirely credible; he even alleged that if he were allowed to fast as he liked, and this was at once promised him without more ado, he could astound the world by establishing a record never yet achieved, a statement which certainly provoked a smile among the other professionals, since it left out of account the change in public opinion, which the hunger artist in his zeal conveniently forgot.

He had not, however, actually lost his sense of the real situation and took it as a matter of course that he and his cage should be stationed, not in the middle of the ring as a main attraction, but outside, near the animal cages, on a site that was after all easily accessible. Large and gaily painted placards made a frame for the cage and announced what was to be seen inside it. When the public came thronging out in the intervals to see the animals, they could hardly avoid passing the hunger artist's cage and stopping there for a moment; perhaps they might even have stayed longer had not those pressing behind them in the narrow gangway, who did not understand why they should be held up on their way toward the excitements of the menagerie, made it impossible for anyone to stand gazing quietly for any length of time. And that was the reason why the hunger artist, who had of course been looking forward to these visiting hours as the main achievement of his life, began instead to shrink from them. At first he could hardly wait for the intervals; it was exhilarating to watch the crowds come streaming his way, until only too soon—not even the most obstinate self-deception, clung to almost consciously, could hold out against the fact—the conviction was borne in upon him that these people, most of them, to judge from their actions, again and again, without exception, were all on their way to the menagerie. And the first sight of them from the distance remained the best. For when they reached his cage he was at once deafened by the storm of shouting and abuse that arose from the two contending factions, which renewed themselves continuously, of those who wanted to stop and stare at him — he soon began to dislike them more than the others — not out of real interest but only out of obstinate self-assertiveness, and those who wanted to go straight on to the animals. When the first great rush was past, the stragglers came along, and these, whom nothing could have prevented from stopping to look at him as long as they had breath, raced past with long strides, hardly even glancing at him, in their haste to get to the menagerie in time. And all too rarely did it happen that he had a stroke of luck, when some father of a family fetched up before him with his children, pointed a finger at the hunger artist and explained at length what the phenomenon meant, telling stories of earlier years when he himself had watched similar but much more thrilling performances, and the children, still rather uncomprehending, since neither inside nor outside school had they been sufficiently prepared for this lesson — what did they care about fasting? — yet showed by the brightness of their intent eyes that new and better times might be coming. Perhaps, said the hunger artist to himself many a time, things would be a little better if his cage were set not quite so near the menagerie. That made it too easy for people to make their choice, to say nothing of what he suffered from the stench of the menagerie, the animals' restlessness by night, the carrying past of raw lumps of flesh for the beasts of prey, the roaring at feeding times, which depressed him continually. But he did not dare to lodge a complaint with the management; after all, he had the animals to thank for the troops of people who passed his cage, among whom there might always be one here and there to take an interest in him, and who could tell where they might seclude him if he called attention to his existence and thereby to the fact that, strictly speaking, he was only an impediment on the way to the menagerie.

A small impediment, to be sure, one that grew steadily less. People grew familiar with the strange idea that they could be expected, in times like these, to take an interest in a hunger artist, and with this familiarity the verdict went out against him. He might fast as much as he could, and he did so; but nothing could save him now, people passed him by. Just try to explain to anyone the art of fasting! Anyone who has no feeling for it cannot be made to understand it. The fine placards grew dirty and illegible, they were torn down; the little notice board telling the number of fast days achieved, which at first was changed carefully every day, had long stayed at the same figure, for after the first few weeks even this small task seemed pointless to the staff; and so the artist simply fasted on and on, as he had once dreamed of doing, and it was no trouble to him, just as he had always foretold, but no one counted the days, no one, not even the artist himself, knew what records he was already breaking, and his heart grew heavy. And when once in a time some leisurely passer-by stopped, made merry over the old figure on the board and spoke of swindling, that was in its way the stupidest lie ever invented by indifference and inborn malice, since it was not the hunger artist who was cheating; he was working honestly, but the world was cheating him of his reward.

Many more days went by, however, and that too came to an end. An overseer's eye fell on the cage one day and asked the attendants why this perfectly good cage should be left standing there unused with dirty straw inside it; nobody knew, until one man, helped out by the notice board, remembered about the hunger artist. They poked into the straw with sticks and found him in it. "Are you still fasting?" asked the overseer. "When on earth do you mean to stop?" "Forgive me, everybody," whispered the hunger artist; only the overseer, who had his ear to the bars, understood him. "Of course," said the overseer, and tapped his forehead with a finger to let the attendants know what state the man was in, "we forgive you." "I always wanted you to admire my fasting," said the hunger artist. "We do admire it," said the overseer, affably. "But you shouldn't admire it," said the hunger artist. "Well, then we don't admire it," said the overseer, "but why shouldn't we admire it?" "Because I have to fast, I can't help it," said the hunger artist. "What a fellow you are," said the overseer, "and why can't you help it?" "Because," said the hunger artist, lifting his head a little and speaking, with his lips pursed, as if for a kiss, right into the overseer's ear, so that no syllable might be lost, "because I couldn't find the food I liked. If I had found it, believe me, I should have made no fuss and stuffed myself like you or anyone else." These were his last words, but in his dimming eyes remained the firm though no longer proud persuasion that he was still continuing to fast.

"Well, clear this out now!" said the overseer, and they buried the   10
hunger artist, straw and all. Into the cage they put a young panther. Even the most insensitive felt it refreshing to see this wild creature leaping around the cage that had so long been dreary. The panther was all right. The food he liked was brought him without hesitation by the attendants; he seemed not even to miss his freedom; his noble body, furnished almost to the bursting point with all that it needed, seemed to carry freedom around with it too; somewhere in his jaws it seemed to lurk; and the joy of life streamed with such ardent passion from his throat that for the onlookers it was not easy to stand the shock of it. But they braced themselves, crowded round the cage, and did not want ever to move away.

KATHERINE MANSFIELD (1888–1923)

The Garden Party

And after all the weather was ideal. They could not have had a more perfect day for a garden-party if they had ordered it. Windless, warm, the sky without a cloud. Only the blue was veiled with a haze of light gold, as it is sometimes in early summer. The gardener had been up since dawn, mowing the lawns and sweeping them, until the grass and the dark flat rosettes where the daisy plants had been seemed to shine. As for the roses, you could not help feeling they understood that roses are the only flowers that impress people at garden-parties; the only flowers that everybody is certain of knowing. Hundreds, yes, literally hundreds, had come out in a single night; the green bushes bowed down as though they had been visited by archangels.

Breakfast was not yet over before the men came to put up the marquee.

"Where do you want the marquee put, mother?"

"My dear child, it's no use asking me. I'm determined to leave everything to you children this year. Forget I am your mother. Treat me as an honored guest."

But Meg could not possibly go and supervise the men. She had washed   5
her hair before breakfast, and she sat drinking her coffee in a green turban, with a dark wet curl stamped on each cheek. Jose, the butterfly, always came down in a silk petticoat and a kimono jacket.

"You'll have to go, Laura; you're the artistic one."

Away Laura flew, still holding her piece of bread-and-butter. It's so delicious to have an excuse for eating out of doors, and besides, she loved having to arrange things; she always felt she could do it so much better than anybody else.

Four men in their shirt-sleeves stood grouped together on the garden path. They carried staves covered with rolls of canvas, and they had big tool-bags slung on their backs. They looked impressive. Laura wished now that she had not got the bread-and-butter, but there was nowhere to put it, and she couldn't possibly throw it away. She blushed and tried to look severe and even a little bit short-sighted as she came up to them.

"Good morning," she said, copying her mother's voice. But that sounded so fearfully affected that she was ashamed, and stammered like a little girl, "Oh — er — have you come — is it about the marquee?"

"That's right, miss," said the tallest of the men, a lanky, freckled   10
fellow, and he shifted his tool-bag, knocked back his straw hat and smiled down at her. "That's about it."

His smile was so easy, so friendly that Laura recovered. What nice eyes he had, small, but such a dark blue! And now she looked at the others, they were smiling too. "Cheer up, we won't bite," their smile seemed to say. How very nice workmen were! And what a beautiful morning! She mustn't mention the morning; she must be businesslike. The marquee.

"Well, what about the lily-lawn? Would that do?"

And she pointed to the lily-lawn with the hand that didn't hold the bread-and-butter. They turned, they stared in the direction. A little fat chap thrust out his under-lip, and the tall fellow frowned.

"I don't fancy it," said he. "Not conspicuous enough. You see, with a thing like a marquee," and he turned to Laura in his easy way, "you want to put it somewhere where it'll give you a bang slap in the eye, if you follow me."

Laura's upbringing made her wonder for a moment whether it was quite respectful of a workman to talk to her of bangs slap in the eye. But she did quite follow him.

"A corner of the tennis-court," she suggested. "But the band's going to be in one corner."

"H'm, going to have a band, are you?" said another of the workmen. He was pale. He had a haggard look as his dark eyes scanned the tennis-court. What was he thinking?

"Only a very small band," said Laura gently. Perhaps he wouldn't mind so much if the band was quite small. But the tall fellow interrupted.

"Look here, miss, that's the place. Against those trees. Over there. That'll do fine."

Against the karakas. Then the karaka-trees would be hidden. And they were so lovely, with their broad, gleaming leaves, and their clusters of yellow fruit. They were like trees you imagined growing on a desert island, proud, solitary, lifting their leaves and fruits to the sun in a kind of silent splendor. Must they be hidden by a marquee?

They must. Already the men had shouldered their staves and were making for the place. Only the tall fellow was left. He bent down, pinched a sprig of lavender, put his thumb and forefinger to his nose and snuffed up the smell. When Laura saw that gesture she forgot all about the karakas in her wonder at him caring for things like that—caring for the smell of lavender. How many men that she knew would have done such a thing? Oh, how extraordinarily nice workmen were, she thought. Why couldn't she have workmen for friends rather than the silly boys she danced with and who came to Sunday night supper? She would get on much better with men like these.

It's all the fault, she decided, as the tall fellow drew something on the back of an envelope, something that was to be looped up or left to hang, of these absurd class distinctions. Well, for her part, she didn't feel them. Not a bit, not an atom. . . . And now there came the chock-chock of wooden hammers. Some one whistled, some one sang out, "Are you right there, matey?" "Matey!" The friendliness of it, the—the—Just to prove how happy she was, just to show the tall fellow how at home she felt, and how she despised stupid conventions, Laura took a big bite of her bread-and-butter as she stared at the little drawing. She felt just like a work-girl.

"Laura, Laura, where are you? Telephone, Laura!" a voice cried from the house.

"Coming!" Away she skimmed, over the lawn, up the path, up the steps, across the veranda, and into the porch. In the hall her father and Laurie were brushing their hats ready to go to the office.

"I say, Laura," said Laurie very fast, "you might just give a squiz at my coat before this afternoon. See if it wants pressing."

"I will," said she. Suddenly she couldn't stop herself. She ran at Laurie and gave him a small, quick squeeze. "Oh, I do love parties, don't you?" gasped Laura.

"Ra-ther," said Laurie's warm, boyish voice, and he squeezed his sister too, and gave her a gentle push. "Dash off to the telephone, old girl."

The telephone. "Yes, yes; oh yes. Kitty? Good morning, dear. Come to lunch? Do, dear. Delighted of course. It will only be a very scratch meal — just the sandwich crusts and broken meringue-shells and what's left over. Yes, isn't it a perfect morning? Your white? Oh, I certainly should. One moment — hold the line. Mother's calling." And Laura sat back. "What, mother? Can't hear."

Mrs. Sheridan's voice floated down the stairs. "Tell her to wear that sweet hat she had on last Sunday."

"Mother says you're to wear that *sweet* hat you had on last Sunday. Good. One o'clock. Bye-bye."

Laura put back the receiver, flung her arms over her head, took a deep breath, stretched and let them fall. "Huh," she sighed, and the moment after the sigh she sat up quickly. She was still, listening. All the doors in the house seemed to be open. The house was alive with soft, quick steps and running voices. The green baize door that led to the kitchen regions swung open and shut with a muffled thud. And now there came a long, chuckling absurd sound. It was the heavy piano being moved on its stiff castors. But the air! If you stopped to notice, was the air always like this? Little faint winds were playing chase, in at the tops of the windows, out at the doors. And there were two tiny spots of sun, one on the inkpot, one on a silver photograph frame, playing too. Darling little spots. Especially the one on the inkpot lid. It was quite warm. A warm little silver star. She could have kissed it.

The front door bell pealed, and there sounded the rustle of Sadie's print skirt on the stairs. A man's voice murmured; Sadie answered, careless, "I'm sure I don't know. Wait. I'll ask Mrs. Sheridan."

"What is it, Sadie?" Laura came into the hall.

"It's the florist, Miss Laura."

It was, indeed. There, just inside the door, stood a wide, shallow tray full of pots of pink lilies. No other kind. Nothing but lilies — canna lilies, big pink flowers, wide open, radiant, almost frighteningly alive on bright crimson stems.

"O-oh, Sadie!" said Laura, and the sound was like a little moan. She crouched down as if to warm herself at that blaze of lilies; she felt they were in her fingers, on her lips, growing in her breast.

"It's some mistake," she said faintly. "Nobody ever ordered so many. Sadie, go and find mother."

But at that moment Mrs. Sheridan joined them.

"It's quite right," she said calmly. "Yes, I ordered them. Aren't they lovely?" She pressed Laura's arm. "I was passing the shop yesterday, and I saw them in the window. And I suddenly thought for once in my life I shall have enough canna lilies. The garden-party will be a good excuse."

"But I thought you said you didn't mean to interfere," said   40 Laura. Sadie had gone. The florist's man was still outside at his van. She put her arm round her mother's neck and gently, very gently, she bit her mother's ear.

"My darling child, you wouldn't like a logical mother, would you? Don't do that. Here's the man."

He carried more lilies still, another whole tray.

"Bank them up, just inside the door, on both sides of the porch, please," said Mrs. Sheridan. "Don't you agree, Laura?"

"Oh, I *do,* mother."

In the drawing-room Meg, Jose and good little Hans had at last suc-   45 ceeded in moving the piano.

"Now, if we put this chesterfield against the wall and move everything out of the room except the chairs, don't you think?"

"Quite."

"Hans, move these tables into the smoking-room, and bring a sweeper to take these marks off the carpet and — one moment, Hans — " Jose loved giving orders to the servants, and they loved obeying her. She always made them feel they were taking part in some drama. "Tell mother and Miss Laura to come here at once."

"Very good, Miss Jose."

She turned to Meg. "I want to hear what the piano sounds like, just in   50 case I'm asked to sing this afternoon. Let's try over 'This Life is Weary.' "

Pom! Ta-ta-ta *Tee*-ta! The piano burst out so passionately that Jose's face changed. She clasped her hands. She looked mournfully and enigmatically at her mother and Laura as they came in.

This Life is *Wee*-ary,
A Tear — a Sigh.
A Love that *Chan*-ges,
    This Life is *Wee*-ary,
A Tear — a Sigh.
A Love that *Chan*-ges,
And then . . . Goodbye!

But at the word "Goodbye," and although the piano sounded more desperate than ever, her face broke into a brilliant, dreadfully unsympathetic smile.

"Aren't I in good voice, mummy?" she beamed.

This Life is *Wee*-ary,
Hope comes to Die.
A Dream — A *Wa*-kening.

But now Sadie interrupted them. "What is it, Sadie?"

"If you please, m'm, cook says have you got the flags for the   55
sandwiches?"

"The flags for the sandwiches, Sadie?" echoed Mrs. Sheridan dreamily.
And the children knew by her face that she hadn't got them. "Let me see."
And she said to Sadie firmly, "Tell cook I'll let her have them in ten
minutes."

Sadie went.

"Now, Laura," said her mother quickly. "Come with me into the
smoking-room. I've got the names somewhere on the back of an envelope.
You'll have to write them out for me. Meg, go upstairs this minute and take
that wet thing off your head. Jose, run and finish dressing this instant. Do
you hear me, children, or shall I have to tell your father when he comes
home to-night? And—and, Jose, pacify cook if you do go into the kitchen,
will you? I'm terrified of her this morning."

The envelope was found at last behind the dining-room clock, though
how it had got there Mrs. Sheridan could not imagine.

"One of you children must have stolen it out of my bag, because I   60
remember vividly—cream cheese and lemon-curd. Have you done that?"

"Yes."

"Egg and—" Mrs. Sheridan held the envelope away from her. "It looks
like mice. It can't be mice, can it?"

"Olive, pet," said Laura, looking over her shoulder.

"Yes, of course, olive. What a horrible combination it sounds. Egg
and olive."

They were finished at last, and Laura took them off to the kitchen. She   65
found Jose there pacifying the cook, who did not look at all terrifying.

"I have never seen such exquisite sandwiches," said Jose's rapturous
voice. "How many kinds did you say there were, cook? Fifteen?"

"Fifteen, Miss Jose."

"Well, cook, I congratulate you."

Cook swept up crusts with the long sandwich knife, and smiled
broadly.

"Godber's has come," announced Sadie, issuing out of the pantry. She   70
had seen the man pass the window.

That meant the cream puffs had come. Godber's were famous for their
cream puffs. Nobody ever thought of making them at home.

"Bring them in and put them on the table, my girl," ordered cook.

Sadie brought them in and went back to the door. Of course Laura
and Jose were far too grown-up to really care about such things. All the
same, they couldn't help agreeing that the puffs looked very attractive. Very.
Cook began arranging them, shaking off the extra icing sugar.

"Don't they carry one back to all one's parties?" said Laura.

"I suppose they do," said practical Jose, who never liked to be carried   75
back. "They look beautifully light and feathery, I must say."

"Have one each, my dears," said cook in her comfortable voice. "Yer ma won't know."

Oh, impossible. Fancy cream puffs so soon after breakfast. The very idea made one shudder. All the same, two minutes later Jose and Laura were licking their fingers with that absorbed inward look that only comes from whipped cream.

"Let's go into the garden, out by the back way," suggested Laura. "I want to see how the men are getting on with the marquee. They're such awfully nice men."

But the back door was blocked by cook, Sadie, Godber's man and Hans.

Something had happened.

"Tuk-tuk-tuk," clucked cook like an agitated hen. Sadie had her hand clapped to her cheek as though she had toothache. Hans's face was screwed up in the effort to understand. Only Godber's man seemed to be enjoying himself; it was his story.

"What's the matter? What's happened?"

"There's been a horrible accident," said Cook. "A man killed."

"A man killed! Where? How? When?"

But Godber's man wasn't going to have his story snatched from under his very nose.

"Know those little cottages just below here, miss?" Know them? Of course, she knew them. "Well, there's a young chap living there, name of Scott, a carter. His horse shied at a traction-engine, corner of Hawke Street this morning, and he was thrown out on the back of his head. Killed."

"Dead!" Laura stared at Godber's man.

"Dead when they picked him up," said Godber's man with relish. "They were taking the body home as I come up here." And he said to the cook, "He's left a wife and five little ones."

"Jose, come here." Laura caught hold of her sister's sleeve and dragged her through the kitchen to the other side of the green baize door. There she paused and leaned against it. "Jose!" she said, horrified, "however are we going to stop everything?"

"Stop everything, Laura!" cried Jose in astonishment. "What do you mean?"

"Stop the garden-party, of course." Why did Jose pretend?

But Jose was still more amazed. "Stop the garden-party? My dear Laura, don't be so absurd. Of course we can't do anything of the kind. Nobody expects us to. Don't be so extravagant."

"But we can't possibly have a garden-party with a man dead just outside the front gate."

That really was extravagant, for the little cottages were in a lane to themselves at the very bottom of a steep rise that led up to the house. A broad road ran between. True, they were far too near. They were the greatest possible eyesore, and they had no right to be in that neighborhood at all.

They were little mean dwellings painted a chocolate brown. In the garden patches there was nothing but cabbage stalks, sick hens and tomato cans. The very smoke coming out of their chimneys was poverty-stricken. Little rags and shreds of smoke, so unlike the great silvery plumes that uncurled from the Sheridans' chimneys. Washerwomen lived in the lane and sweeps and a cobbler, and a man whose house-front was studded all over with minute bird-cages. Children swarmed. When the Sheridans were little they were forbidden to set foot there because of the revolting language and of what they might catch. But since they were grown up, Laura and Laurie on their prowls sometimes walked through. It was disgusting and sordid. They came out with a shudder. But still one must go everywhere; one must see everything. So through they went.

"And just think of what the band would sound like to that poor   95
woman," said Laura.

"Oh, Laura!" Jose began to be seriously annoyed. "If you're going to stop a band playing every time some one has an accident, you'll lead a very strenuous life. I'm every bit as sorry about it as you. I feel just as sympathetic." Her eyes hardened. She looked at her sister just as she used to when they were little and fighting together. "You won't bring a drunken workman back to life by being sentimental," she said softly.

"Drunk! Who said he was drunk?" Laura turned furiously on Jose. She said, just as they had used to say on those occasions, "I'm going straight up to tell mother."

"Do, dear," cooed Jose.

"Mother, can I come into your room?" Laura turned the big glass doorknob.

"Of course, child. Why, what's the matter? What's given you such a   100
color?" And Mrs. Sheridan turned round from her dressing-table. She was trying on a new hat.

"Mother, a man's been killed," began Laura.

"*Not* in the garden?" interrupted her mother.

"No, no!"

"Oh, what a fright you gave me!" Mrs. Sheridan sighed with relief, and took off the big hat and held it on her knees.

"But listen, mother," said Laura. Breathless, half-choking, she told the   105
dreadful story. "Of course, we can't have our party, can we?" she pleaded. "The band and everybody arriving. They'd hear us, mother; they're nearly neighbors!"

To Laura's astonishment her mother behaved just like Jose; it was harder to bear because she seemed amused. She refused to take Laura seriously.

"But, my dear child, use your common sense. It's only by accident we've heard of it. If some one had died there normally — and I can't understand how they keep alive in those poky little holes — we should still be having our party, shouldn't we?"

Laura had to say "yes" to that, but she felt it was all wrong. She sat down on her mother's sofa and pinched the cushion frill.

"Mother, isn't it really terribly heartless of us?" she asked.

"Darling!" Mrs. Sheridan got up and came over to her, carrying the   110 hat. Before Laura could stop her she had popped it on. "My child!" said her mother, "the hat is yours. It's made for you. It's much too young for me. I have never seen you look such a picture. Look at yourself!" And she held up her hand-mirror.

"But, mother," Laura began again. She couldn't look at herself; she turned aside.

This time Mrs. Sheridan lost patience just as Jose had done.

"You are being very absurd, Laura," she said coldly. "People like that don't expect sacrifices from us. And it's not very sympathetic to spoil everybody's enjoyment as you're doing now."

"I don't understand," said Laura, and she walked quickly out of the room into her own bedroom. There, quite by chance, the first thing she saw was this charming girl in the mirror, in her black hat trimmed with gold daisies, and a long black velvet ribbon. Never had she imagined she could look like that. Is mother right? she thought. And now she hoped her mother was right. Am I being extravagant? Perhaps it was extravagant. Just for a moment she had another glimpse of that poor woman and those little children, and the body being carried into the house. But it all seemed blurred, unreal, like a picture in the newspaper. I'll remember it again after the party's over, she decided. And somehow that seemed quite the best plan. . . .

Lunch was over by half-past one. By half-past two they were all ready   115 for the fray. The green-coated band had arrived and was established in a corner of the tennis-court.

"My dear!" trilled Kitty Maitland, "aren't they too like frogs for words? You ought to have arranged them round the pond with the conductor in the middle on a leaf."

Laurie arrived and hailed them on his way to dress. At the sight of him Laura remembered the accident again. She wanted to tell him. If Laurie agreed with the others, then it was bound to be all right. And she followed him into the hall.

"Laurie!"

"Hallo!" He was half-way upstairs, but when he turned round and saw Laura he suddenly puffed out his cheeks and goggled his eyes at her. "My word, Laura! You do look stunning," said Laurie, "What an absolutely topping hat!"

Laura said faintly "Is it?" and smiled up at Laurie, and didn't tell him   120 after all.

Soon after that people began coming in streams. The band struck up; the hired waiters ran from the house to the marquee. Wherever you looked there were couples strolling, bending to the flowers, greeting, moving on over the lawn. They were like bright birds that had alighted in the Sheridans' garden for this one afternoon, on their way to — where? Ah, what happiness it is to be with people who all are happy, to press hands, press cheeks, smile into eyes.

"Darling Laura, how well you look!"

"What a becoming hat, child!"

"Laura, you look quite Spanish. I've never seen you look so striking."

And Laura, glowing, answered softly, "Have you had tea? Won't you have an ice? The passion-fruit ices really are rather special." She ran to her father and begged him. "Daddy darling, can't the band have something to drink?" 125

And the perfect afternoon slowly ripened, slowly faded, slowly its petals closed.

"Never a more delightful garden-party . . . " "The greatest success . . . " "Quite the most . . . "

Laura helped her mother with the good-byes. They stood side by side in the porch till it was all over.

"All over, all over, thank heaven," said Mr. Sheridan. "Round up the others, Laura. Let's go and have some fresh coffee. I'm exhausted. Yes, it's been very successful. But oh, these parties, these parties! Why will you children insist on giving parties!" And they all of them sat down in the deserted marquee.

"Have a sandwich, daddy dear. I wrote the flag." 130

"Thanks." Mr. Sheridan took a bite and the sandwich was gone. He took another. "I suppose you didn't hear of a beastly accident that happened today?" he said.

"My dear," said Mrs. Sheridan, holding up her hand, "we did. It nearly ruined the party. Laura insisted we should put it off."

"Oh, mother!" Laura didn't want to be teased about it.

"It was a horrible affair all the same," said Mr. Sheridan. "The chap was married too. Lived just below in the lane, and leaves a wife and half a dozen kiddies, so they say."

An awkward little silence fell. Mrs. Sheridan fidgeted with her cup. 135 Really, it was very tactless of father . . .

Suddenly she looked up. There on the table were all those sandwiches, cakes, puffs, all uneaten, all going to be wasted. She had one of her brilliant ideas.

"I know," she said. "Let's make up a basket. Let's send that poor creature some of this perfectly good food. At any rate, it will be the greatest treat for the children. Don't you agree? And she's sure to have neighbors calling in and so on. What a point to have it all ready prepared. Laura!" She jumped up. "Get me the big basket out of the stairs cupboard."

"But, mother, do you really think it's a good idea?" said Laura.

Again, how curious, she seemed to be different from them all. To take scraps from their party. Would the poor woman really like that?

"Of course! What's the matter with you today? An hour or two ago 140 you were insisting on us being sympathetic, and now — "

Oh, well! Laura ran for the basket. It was filled, it was heaped by her mother.

"Take it yourself, darling," said she. "Run down just as you are. No, wait, take the arum lilies too. People of that class are so impressed by arum lilies."

"The stems will ruin her lace frock," said practical Jose.

So they would. Just in time. "Only the basket, then. And, Laura!" — her mother followed her out of the marquee — "don't on any account — "

"What, mother?"   145

No, better not put such ideas into the child's head! "Nothing! Run along."

It was just growing dusky as Laura shut their garden gates. A big dog ran by like a shadow. The road gleamed white, and down below in the hollow the little cottages were in deep shade. How quiet it seemed after the afternoon. Here she was going down the hill to somewhere where a man lay dead, and she couldn't realize it. Why couldn't she? She stopped a minute. And it seemed to her that kisses, voices, tinkling spoons, laughter, the smell of crushed grass were somehow inside her. She had no room for anything else. How strange! She looked up at the pale sky, and all she thought was, "Yes, it was the most successful party."

Now the broad road was crossed. The lane began, smoky and dark. Women in shawls and men's tweed caps hurried by. Men hung over the palings; the children played in the doorways. A low hum came from the mean little cottages. In some of them there was a flicker of light, and a shadow, crab-like, moved across the window. Laura bent her head and hurried on. She wished now she had put on a coat. How her frock shone! And the big hat with the velvet streamer — if only it was another hat! Were the people looking at her? They must be. It was a mistake to have come; she knew all along it was a mistake. Should she go back even now?

No, too late. This was the house. It must be. A dark knot of people stood outside. Beside the gate an old, old woman with a crutch sat in a chair, watching. She had her feet on a newspaper. The voices stopped as Laura drew near. The group parted. It was as though she was expected, as though they had known she was coming here.

Laura was terribly nervous. Tossing the velvet ribbon over her shoul-   150
der, she said to a woman standing by, "Is this Mrs. Scott's house?" and the woman, smiling queerly, said, "It is, my lass."

Oh, to be away from this! She actually said, "Help me, God," as she walked up the tiny path and knocked. To be away from those staring eyes, or to be covered up in anything, one of those women's shawls even. I'll just leave the basket and go, she decided. I shan't even wait for it to be emptied.

Then the door opened. A little woman in black showed in the gloom.

Laura said, "Are you Mrs. Scott?" But to her horror the woman answered, "Walk in please, miss," and she was shut in the passage.

"No," said Laura, "I don't want to come in. I only want to leave this basket. Mother sent — "

The little woman in the gloomy passage seemed not to have heard   155
her. "Step this way, please, miss," she said in an oily voice, and Laura
followed her.

She found herself in a wretched little low kitchen, lighted by a smoky
lamp. There was a woman sitting before the fire.

"Em," said the little creature who had let her in. "Em! It's a young
lady." She turned to Laura. She said meaningly, "I'm 'er sister, Miss. You'll
excuse 'er, won't you?"

"Oh, but of course!" said Laura. "Please, please don't disturb her. I—
I only want to leave—"

But at that moment the woman at the fire turned round. Her face,
puffed up, red, with swollen eyes and swollen lips, looked terrible. She
seemed as though she couldn't understand why Laura was there. What did
it mean? Why was this stranger standing in the kitchen with a basket? What
was it all about? And the poor face puckered up again.

"All right, my dear," said the other. "I'll thank the young lady."   160

And again she began, "You'll excuse her, miss, I'm sure," and her face,
swollen too, tried an oily smile.

Laura only wanted to get out, to get away. She was back in the passage.
The door opened. She walked straight through into the bedroom, where the
dead man was lying.

"You'd like a look at 'im, wouldn't you?" said Em's sister, and she
brushed past Laura over to the bed. "Don't be afraid, my lass—" and now
her voice sounded fond and sly, and fondly she drew down the sheet—"'e
looks a picture. There's nothing to show. Come along, my dear."

Laura came.

There lay a young man, fast asleep—sleeping so soundly, so deeply,   165
that he was far, far away from them both. Oh, so remote, so peaceful. He
was dreaming. Never wake him up again. His head was sunk in the pillow,
his eyes were closed; they were blind under the closed eyelids. He was given
up to his dream. What did garden-parties and baskets and lace frocks matter
to him? He was far from all those things. He was wonderful, beautiful.
While they were laughing and while the band was playing, this marvel had
come to the lane. Happy . . . happy. . . . All is well, said that sleeping face.
This is just as it should be. I am content.

But all the same you had to cry, and she couldn't go out of the room
without saying something to him. Laura gave a loud childish sob.

"Forgive my hat," she said.

And this time she didn't wait for Em's sister. She found her way out
of the door, down the path, past all those dark people. At the corner of the
lane she met Laurie.

He stepped out of the shadow. "Is that you, Laura?"

"Yes."   170

"Mother was getting anxious. Was it all right?"

"Yes, quite. Oh, Laurie!" She took his arm, she pressed up against
him.

"I say, you're not crying, are you?" asked her brother.

Laura shook her head. She was.

Laurie put his arm round her shoulder. "Don't cry," he said in his 175 warm, loving voice. "Was it awful?"

"No," sobbed Laura. "It was simply marvelous. But, Laurie—" She stopped, she looked at her brother. "Isn't life," she stammered, "isn't life—" But what life was she couldn't explain. No matter. He quite understood.

"*Isn't* it, darling?" said Laurie.

WILLIAM FAULKNER (1897–1962)

A Rose for Emily

I

When Miss Emily Grierson died, our whole town went to her funeral: the men through a sort of respectful affection for a fallen monument, the women mostly out of curiosity to see the inside of her house, which no one save an old manservant—a combined gardener and cook—had seen in at least ten years.

It was a big, squarish frame house that had once been white, decorated with cupolas and spires and scrolled balconies in the heavily lightsome style of the seventies, set on what had once been our most select street. But garages and cotton gins had encroached and obliterated even the august names of that neighborhood; only Miss Emily's house was left, lifting its stubborn and coquettish decay above the cotton wagons and the gasoline pumps—an eyesore among eyesores. And now Miss Emily had gone to join the representatives of those august names where they lay in the cedar-bemused cemetery among the ranked and anonymous graves of Union and Confederate soldiers who fell at the battle of Jefferson.

Alive, Miss Emily had been a tradition, a duty, and a care; a sort of hereditary obligation upon the town, dating from that day in 1894 when Colonel Sartoris, the mayor—he who fathered the edict that no Negro woman should appear on the streets without an apron—remitted her taxes, the dispensation dating from the death of her father on into perpetuity. Not that Miss Emily would have accepted charity. Colonel Sartoris invented an involved tale to the effect that Miss Emily's father had loaned money to the town, which the town, as a matter of business, preferred this way of repaying. Only a man of Colonel Sartoris' generation and thought could have invented it, and only a woman could have believed it.

When the next generation, with its more modern ideas, became mayors and aldermen, this arrangement created some little dissatisfaction. On the first of the year they mailed her a tax notice. February came, and there was no reply. They wrote her a formal letter, asking her to call at the sheriff's office at her convenience. A week later the mayor wrote her himself, offering to call or to send his car for her, and received in reply a note on paper of an archaic shape, in a thin, flowing calligraphy in faded ink, to the effect that she no longer went out at all. The tax notice was also enclosed, without comment.

They called a special meeting of the Board of Aldermen. A deputation waited upon her, knocked at the door through which no visitor had passed since she ceased giving china-painting lessons eight or ten years earlier. They were admitted by the old Negro into a dim hall from which a stairway mounted into still more shadow. It smelled of dust and disuse—a close, dank smell. The Negro led them into the parlor. It was furnished in heavy, 5 leather-covered furniture. When the Negro opened the blinds of one window, they could see that the leather was cracked; and when they sat down, a faint dust rose sluggishly about their thighs, spinning with slow motes in the single sun-ray. On a tarnished gilt easel before the fireplace stood a crayon portrait of Miss Emily's father.

They rose when she entered — a small, fat woman in black, with a thin gold chain descending to her waist and vanishing into her belt, leaning on an ebony cane with a tarnished gold head. Her skeleton was small and spare; perhaps that was why what would have been merely plumpness in another was obesity in her. She looked bloated, like a body long submerged in motionless water, and of that pallid hue. Her eyes, lost in the fatty ridges of her face, looked like two small pieces of coal pressed into a lump of dough as they moved from one face to another while the visitors stated their errand.

She did not ask them to sit. She just stood in the door and listened quietly until the spokesman came to a stumbling halt. Then they could hear the invisible watch ticking at the end of the gold chain.

Her voice was dry and cold. "I have no taxes in Jefferson. Colonel Sartoris explained it to me. Perhaps one of you can gain access to the city records and satisfy yourselves."

"But we have. We are the city authorities, Miss Emily. Didn't you get a notice from the sheriff, signed by him?"

"I received a paper, yes," Miss Emily said. "Perhaps he considers   10 himself the sheriff . . . I have no taxes in Jefferson."

"But there is nothing on the books to show that, you see. We must go by the—"

"See Colonel Sartoris. I have no taxes in Jefferson."

"But, Miss Emily—"

"See Colonel Sartoris." (Colonel Sartoris had been dead almost ten years.) "I have no taxes in Jefferson. Tobe!" The Negro appeared. "Show these gentlemen out."

II

So she vanquished them, horse and foot, just as she had vanquished   15 their fathers thirty years before about the smell. That was two years after her father's death and a short time after her sweetheart–the one we believed would marry her — had deserted her. After her father's death she went out very little; after her sweetheart went away, people hardly saw her at all. A few of the ladies had the temerity to call, but were not received, and the only sign of life about the place was the Negro man — a young man then — going in and out with a market basket.

"Just as if a man — any man — could keep a kitchen properly," the ladies said; so they were not surprised when the smell developed. It was another link between the gross, teeming world and the high and mighty Griersons.

A neighbor, a woman, complained to the mayor, Judge Stevens, eighty years old.

"But what will you have me do about it, madam?" he said.

"Why, send her word to stop it," the woman said. "Isn't there a law?"

"I'm sure that won't be necessary," Judge Stevens said. "It's probably   20
just a snake or a rat that nigger of hers killed in the yard. I'll speak to him
about it."

The next day he received two more complaints, one from a man who
came in diffident deprecation. "We really must do something about it,
Judge. I'd be the last one in the world to bother Miss Emily, but we've got
to do something." That night the Board of Aldermen met — three gray-
beards and one younger man, a member of the rising generation.

"It's simple enough," he said. "Send her word to have her place cleaned
up. Give her a certain time to do it in, and if she don't . . . "

"Dammit, sir," Judge Stevens said, "will you accuse a lady to her face
of smelling bad?"

So the next night, after midnight, four men crossed Miss Emily's lawn
and slunk about the house like burglars, sniffing along the base of the
brickwork and at the cellar openings while one of them performed a regular
sowing motion with his hand out of a sack slung from his shoulder. They
broke open the cellar door and sprinkled lime there, and in all the outbuildings. As they recrossed the lawn, a window that had been dark was lighted
and Miss Emily sat in it, the light behind her, and her upright torso motionless as that of an idol. They crept quietly across the lawn and into the shadow
of the locusts that lined the street. After a week or two the smell went away.

That was when people had begun to feel really sorry for her. People in   25
our town, remembering how old lady Wyatt, her great-aunt, had gone
completely crazy at last, believed that the Griersons held themselves a little
too high for what they really were. None of the young men were quite good
enough for Miss Emily and such. We had long thought of them as a tableau,
Miss Emily a slender figure in white in the background, her father a sprad-
dled silhouette in the foreground, his back to her and clutching a horsewhip,
the two of them framed by the back-flung front door. So when she got to
be thirty and was still single, we were not pleased exactly, but vindicated;
even with insanity in the family she wouldn't have turned down all of her
chances if they had really materialized.

When her father died, it got about that the house was all that was left
to her; and in a way, people were glad. At last they could pity Miss Emily.
Being left alone, and a pauper, she had become humanized. Now she too
would know the old thrill and the old despair of a penny more or less.

The day after his death all the ladies prepared to call at the house and
offer condolence and aid, as is our custom. Miss Emily met them at the
door, dressed as usual and with no trace of grief on her face. She told them
that her father was not dead. She did that for three days, with the ministers
calling on her, and the doctors, trying to persuade her to let them dispose of
the body. Just as they were about to resort to law and force, she broke down,
and they buried her father quickly.

We did not say she was crazy then. We believed she had to do that. We remembered all the young men her father had driven away, and we knew that with nothing left, she would have to cling to that which had robbed her, as people will.

III

She was sick for a long time. When we saw her again, her hair was cut short, making her look like a girl, with a vague resemblance to those angels in colored church windows — sort of tragic and serene.

The town had just let the contracts for paving the sidewalks, and in the summer after her father's death they began the work. The construction company came with niggers and mules and machinery, and a foreman named Homer Barron, a Yankee — a big, dark, ready man, with a big voice and eyes lighter than his face. The little boys would follow in groups to hear him cuss the niggers, and the niggers singing in time to the rise and fall of picks. Pretty soon he knew everybody in town. Whenever you heard a lot of laughing anywhere about the square, Homer Barron would be in the center of the group. Presently we began to see him and Miss Emily on Sunday afternoons driving in the yellow-wheeled buggy and the matched team of bays from the livery stable.

At first we were glad that Miss Emily would have an interest, because the ladies all said, "Of course a Grierson would not think seriously of a Northerner, a day laborer." But there were still others, older people, who said that even grief could not cause a real lady to forget *noblesse oblige*° — without calling it *noblesse oblige.* They just said, "Poor Emily. Her kinsfolk should come to her." She had some kin in Alabama; but years ago her father had fallen out with them over the estate of old lady Wyatt, the crazy woman, and there was no communication between the two families. They had not even been represented at the funeral.

And as soon as the old people said, "Poor Emily," the whispering began. "Do you suppose it's really so?" they said to one another. "Of course it is. What else could . . . " This behind their hands; rustling of craned silk and satin behind jalousies closed upon the sun of Sunday afternoon as the thin, swift clop-clop-clop of the matched team passed: "Poor Emily."

She carried her head high enough — even when we believed that she was fallen. It was as if she demanded more than ever the recognition of her dignity as the last Grierson; as if it had wanted that touch of earthiness to reaffirm her imperviousness. Like when she bought the rat poison, the arsenic. That was over a year after they had begun to say "Poor Emily," and while the two female cousins were visiting her.

"I want some poison," she said to the druggist. She was over thirty then, still a slight woman, though thinner than usual, with cold, haughty

30

noblesse oblige: the obligation of those holding high rank or social position to behave generously and courteously toward others.

black eyes in a face the flesh of which was strained across the temples and about the eye-sockets as you imagine a lighthouse-keeper's face ought to look. "I want some poison," she said.

"Yes, Miss Emily. What kind? For rats and such? I'd recom — "   35

"I want the best you have. I don't care what kind."

The druggist named several. "They'll kill anything up to an elephant. But what you want is — "

"Arsenic," Miss Emily said. "Is that a good one?"

"Is . . . arsenic? Yes, ma'am. But what you want — "

"I want arsenic."   40

The druggist looked down at her. She looked back at him, erect, her face like a strained flag. "Why, of course," the druggist said. "If that's what you want. But the law requires you to tell what you are going to use it for."

Miss Emily just stared at him, her head tilted back in order to look him eye for eye, until he looked away and went and got the arsenic and wrapped it up. The Negro delivery boy brought her the package; the druggist didn't come back. When she opened the package at home there was written on the box, under the skull and bones: "For rats."

IV

So the next day we all said, "She will kill herself"; and we said it would be the best thing. When she had first begun to be seen with Homer Barron, we had said, "She will marry him." Then we said, "She will persuade him yet," because Homer himself had remarked — he liked men, and it was known that he drank with the younger men in the Elks' Club — that he was not a marrying man. Later we said, "Poor Emily" behind the jalousies as they passed on Sunday afternoon in the glittering buggy, Miss Emily with her head high and Homer Barron with his hat cocked and a cigar in his teeth, reins and whip in a yellow glove.

Then some of the ladies began to say that it was a disgrace to the town and a bad example to the young people. The men did not want to interfere, but at last the ladies forced the Baptist minister — Miss Emily's people were Episcopal — to call upon her. He would never divulge what happened during that interview, but he refused to go back again. The next Sunday they again drove about the streets, and the following day the minister's wife wrote to Miss Emily's relations in Alabama.

So she had blood-kin under her roof again and we sat back to watch   45
developments. At first nothing happened. Then we were sure that they were to be married. We learned that Miss Emily had been to the jeweler's and ordered a man's toilet set in silver, with the letters H. B. on each piece. Two days later we learned that she had bought a complete outfit of men's clothing, including a nightshirt, and we said, "They are married." We were really glad. We were glad because the two female cousins were even more Grierson than Miss Emily had ever been.

So we were not surprised when Homer Barron—the streets had been finished some time since—was gone. We were a little disappointed that there was not a public blowing-off, but we believed that he had gone on to prepare for Miss Emily's coming, or to give her a chance to get rid of the cousins. (By that time it was a cabal, and we were all Miss Emily's allies to help circumvent the cousins.) Sure enough, after another week they departed. And, as we had expected all along, within three days Homer Barron was back in town. A neighbor saw the Negro man admit him at the kitchen door at dusk one evening.

And that was the last we saw of Homer Barron. And of Miss Emily for some time. The Negro man went in and out with the market basket, but the front door remained closed. Now and then we would see her at a window for a moment, as the men did that night when they sprinkled the lime, but for almost six months she did not appear on the streets. Then we knew that this was to be expected too; as if that quality of her father which had thwarted her woman's life so many times had been too virulent and too furious to die.

When we next saw Miss Emily, she had grown fat and her hair was turning gray. During the next few years it grew grayer and grayer until it attained an even pepper-and-salt iron-gray, when it ceased turning. Up to the day of her death at seventy-four it was still that vigorous iron-gray, like the hair of an active man.

From that time on her front door remained closed, save for a period of six or seven years, when she was about forty, during which she gave lessons in china-painting. She fitted up a studio in one of the downstairs rooms, where the daughters and granddaughters of Colonel Sartoris' contemporaries were sent to her with the same regularity and in the same spirit that they were sent to church on Sundays with a twenty-five-cent piece for the collection plate. Meanwhile her taxes had been remitted.

Then the newer generation became the backbone and the spirit of the town, and the painting pupils grew up and fell away and did not send their children to her with boxes of color and tedious brushes and pictures cut from the ladies' magazines. The front door closed upon the last one and remained closed for good. When the town got free postal delivery, Miss Emily alone refused to let them fasten the metal numbers above her door and attach a mailbox to it. She would not listen to them.

Daily, monthly, yearly we watched the Negro grow grayer and more stooped, going in and out with the market basket. Each December we sent her a tax notice, which would be returned by the post office a week later, unclaimed. Now and then we would see her in one of the downstairs windows—she had evidently shut up the top floor of the house—like the carven torso of an idol in a niche, looking or not looking at us, we could never tell which. Thus she passed from generation to generation—dear, inescapable, impervious, tranquil, and perverse.

And so she died. Fell ill in the house filled with dust and shadows, with only a doddering Negro man to wait on her. We did not even know she was sick; we had long since given up trying to get any information from the Negro. He talked to no one, probably not even to her, for his voice had grown harsh and rusty, as if from disuse.

She died in one of the downstairs rooms, in a heavy walnut bed with a curtain, her gray head propped on a pillow yellow and moldy with age and lack of sunlight.

V

The Negro met the first of the ladies at the front door and let them in, with their hushed, sibilant voices and their quick, curious glances, and then he disappeared. He walked right through the house and out the back and was not seen again.

The two female cousins came at once. They held the funeral on the second day, with the town coming to look at Miss Emily beneath a mass of bought flowers, with the crayon face of her father musing profoundly above the bier and the ladies sibilant and macabre; and the very old men — some in their brushed Confederate uniforms — on the porch and the lawn, talking of Miss Emily as if she had been a contemporary of theirs, believing that they had danced with her and courted her perhaps, confusing time with its mathematical progression, as the old do, to whom all the past is not a diminishing road but, instead, a huge meadow which no winter ever quite touches, divided from them now by the narrow bottle-neck of the most recent decade of years.

Already we knew that there was one room in that region above stairs which no one had seen in forty years, and which would have to be forced. They waited until Miss Emily was decently in the ground before they opened it.

The violence of breaking down the door seemed to fill this room with pervading dust. A thin, acrid pall as of the tomb seemed to lie everywhere upon this room decked and furnished as for a bridal: upon the valance curtains of faded rose color, upon the rose-shaded lights, upon the dressing table, upon the delicate array of crystal and the man's toilet things backed with tarnished silver, silver so tarnished that the monogram was obscured. Among them lay collar and tie, as if they had just been removed, which, lifted, left upon the surface a pale crescent in the dust. Upon a chair hung the suit, carefully folded; beneath it the two mute shoes and the discarded socks.

The man himself lay in the bed.

For a long while we just stood there, looking down at the profound and fleshless grin. The body had apparently once lain in the attitude of an embrace, but now the long sleep that outlasts love, that conquers even the grimace of love, had cuckolded him. What was left of him, rotted beneath what was left of the nightshirt, had become inextricable from the bed in which he lay; and upon him and upon the pillow beside him lay that even coating of the patient and biding dust.

Then we noticed that in the second pillow was the indentation of a   60
head. One of us lifted something from it, and leaning forward, that faint and invisible dust dry and acrid in the nostrils, we saw a long strand of iron-gray hair.

ERNEST HEMINGWAY (1898–1961)

Hills Like White Elephants

The hills across the valley of the Ebro were long and white. On this side there was no shade and no trees and the station was between two lines of rails in the sun. Close against the side of the station there was the warm shadow of the building and a curtain, made of strings of bamboo beads, hung across the open door into the bar, to keep out flies. The American and the girl with him sat at a table in the shade, outside the building. It was very hot and the express from Barcelona would come in forty minutes. It stopped at this junction for two minutes and went on to Madrid.

"What should we drink?" the girl asked. She had taken off her hat and put it on the table.

"It's pretty hot," the man said.

"Let's drink beer."

"Dos cervezas," the man said into the curtain. 5

"Big ones?" a woman asked from the doorway.

"Yes. Two big ones."

The woman brought two glasses of beer and two felt pads. She put the felt pads and the beer glasses on the table and looked at the man and the girl. The girl was looking off at the line of hills. They were white in the sun and the country was brown and dry.

"They look like white elephants," she said.

"I've never seen one," the man drank his beer. 10

"No, you wouldn't have."

"I might have," the man said. "Just because you say I wouldn't have doesn't prove anything."

The girl looked at the bead curtain. "They've painted something on it," she said. "What does it say?"

"Anis del Toro. It's a drink."

"Could we try it?" 15

The man called "Listen" through the curtain. The woman came out from the bar.

"Four reales."

"We want two Anis del Toro."

"With water?"

"Do you want it with water?" 20

"I don't know," the girl said. "Is it good with water?"

"It's all right."

"You want them with water?" asked the woman.

"Yes, with water."

"It tastes like licorice," the girl said and put the glass down. 25

"That's the way with everything."

"Yes," said the girl. "Everything tastes of licorice. Especially all the things you've waited so long for, like absinthe."

"Oh, cut it out."

"You started it," the girl said. "I was being amused. I was having a fine time."

"Well, let's try and have a fine time."   30

"All right. I was trying. I said the mountains looked like white elephants. Wasn't that bright?"

"That was bright."

"I wanted to try this new drink. That's all we do, isn't it—look at things and try new drinks?"

"I guess so."

The girl looked across at the hills.   35

"They're lovely hills," she said. "They don't really look like white elephants. I just meant the coloring of their skin through the trees."

"Should we have another drink?"

"All right."

The warm wind blew the bead curtain against the table.

"The beer's nice and cool," the man said.   40

"It's lovely," the girl said.

"It's really an awfully simple operation, Jig," the man said. "It's not really an operation at all."

The girl looked at the ground the table legs rested on.

"I know you wouldn't mind it, Jig. It's really not anything. It's just to let the air in."

The girl did not say anything.   45

"I'll go with you and I'll stay with you all the time. They just let the air in and then it's all perfectly natural."

"Then what will we do afterward?"

"We'll be fine afterward. Just like we were before."

"What makes you think so?"

"That's the only thing that bothers us. It's the only thing that's made   50
us unhappy."

The girl looked at the bead curtain, put her hand out and took hold of two of the strings of beads.

"And you think then we'll be all right and be happy."

"I know we will. You don't have to be afraid. I've known lots of people that have done it."

"So have I," said the girl. "And afterward they were all so happy."

"Well," the man said, "if you don't want to you don't have to. I   55
wouldn't have you do it if you didn't want to. But I know it's perfectly simple."

"And you really want to?"

"I think it's the best thing to do. But I don't want you to do it if you don't really want to."

"And if I do it you'll be happy and things will be like they were and you'll love me?"

"I love you now. You know I love you."

"I know. But if I do it, then it will be nice again if I say things are like   60
white elephants, and you'll like it?"

"I'll love it. I love it now but I just can't think about it. You know how
I get when I worry."

"If I do it you won't ever worry?"

"I won't worry about that because it's perfectly simple."

"Then I'll do it. Because I don't care about me."

"What do you mean?"   65

"I don't care about me."

"Well, I care about you."

"Oh, yes. But I don't care about me. And I'll do it and then everything
will be fine."

"I don't want you to do it if you feel that way."

The girl stood up and walked to the end of the station. Across, on the   70
other side, were fields of grain and trees along the banks of the Ebro. Far
away, beyond the river, were mountains. The shadow of a cloud moved
across the field of grain and she saw the river through the trees.

"And we could have all this," she said. "And we could have everything
and every day we make it more impossible."

"What did you say?"

"I said we could have everything."

"We can have everything."

"No, we can't."   75

"We could have the whole world."

"No, we can't."

"We can go everywhere."

"No, we can't. It isn't ours any more."

"It's ours."   80

"No, it isn't. And once they take it away, you never get it back."

"But they haven't taken it away."

"We'll wait and see."

"Come on back in the shade," he said. "You mustn't feel that way."

"I don't feel any way," the girl said. "I just know things."   85

"I don't want you to do anything that you don't want to do —"

"Not that isn't good for me," she said. "I know. Could we have another beer?"

"All right. But you've got to realize —"

"I realize," the girl said. "Can't we maybe stop talking?"

They sat down at the table and the girl looked across at the hills on the   90
dry side of the valley and the man looked at her and at the table.

"You've got to realize," he said, "that I don't want you to do it if you
don't want to. I'm perfectly willing to go through with it if it means
anything to you."

"Doesn't it mean anything to you? We could get along."

"Of course it does. But I don't want anybody but you. I don't want
any one else. And I know it's perfectly simple."

"Yes, you know it's perfectly simple."

"It's all right for you to say that, but I do know it."   95

"Would you do something for me now?"

"I'd do anything for you."

"Would you please please please please please please please stop talking?"

He did not say anything but looked at the bags against the wall of the station. There were labels on them from all the hotels where they had spent nights.

"But I don't want you to," he said, "I don't care anything about it."   100

"I'll scream," the girl said.

The woman came out through the curtains with two glasses of beer and put them down on the damp felt pads. "The train comes in five minutes," she said.

"What did she say?" asked the girl.

"That the train is coming in five minutes."

The girl smiled brightly at the woman, to thank her.   105

"I'd better take the bags over to the other side of the station," the man said. She smiled at him.

"All right. Then come back and we'll finish the beer."

He picked up the two heavy bags and carried them around the station to the other tracks. He looked up the tracks but could not see the train. Coming back, he walked through the barroom, where people waiting for the train were drinking. He drank an Anis at the bar and looked at the people. They were all waiting reasonably for the train. He went out through the bead curtain. She was sitting at the table and smiled at him.

"Do you feel better?" he asked.

"I feel fine," she said. "There's nothing wrong with me. I feel fine."   110

EUDORA WELTY (1909–   )

A Worn Path

It was December — a bright frozen day in the early morning. Far out in the country there was an old Negro woman with her head tied in a red rag, coming along a path through the pinewoods. Her name was Phoenix Jackson. She was very old and small and she walked slowly in the dark pine shadows, moving a little from side to side in her steps, with the balanced heaviness and lightness of a pendulum in a grandfather clock. She carried a thin, small cane made from an umbrella, and with this she kept tapping the frozen earth in front of her. This made a grave and persistent noise in the still air, that seemed meditative like the chirping of a solitary little bird.

She wore a dark striped dress reaching down to her shoetops, and an equally long apron of bleached sugar sacks, with a full pocket; all neat and tidy, but every time she took a step she might have fallen over her shoe-laces, which dragged from her unlaced shoes. She looked straight ahead. Her eyes were blue with age. Her skin had a pattern all its own of number-less branching wrinkles and as though a whole little tree stood in the middle of her forehead, but a golden color ran underneath, and the two knobs of her cheeks were illuminated by a yellow burning under the dark. Under the red rag her hair came down on her neck in the frailest of ringlets, still black, and with an odor like copper.

Now and then there was a quivering in the thicket. Old Phoenix said, "Out of my way, all you foxes, owls, beetles, jack rabbits, coons, and wild animals! . . . Keep out from under these feet, little bobwhites. . . . Keep the big wild hogs out of my path. Don't let none of those come running my direction. I got a long way." Under her small black-freckled hand her cane, limber as a buggy whip, would switch at the brush as if to rouse up any hiding things.

On she went. The woods were deep and still. The sun made the pine needles almost too bright to look at, up where the wind rocked. The cones dropped as light as feathers. Down in the hollow was the mourning dove — it was not too late for him.

The path ran up a hill. "Seems like there is chains about my feet, time   5
I get this far," she said, in the voice of argument old people keep to use with themselves. "Something always take a hold on this hill — pleads I should stay."

After she got to the top she turned and gave a full, severe look behind her where she had come. "Up through pines," she said at length. "Now down through oaks."

Her eyes opened their widest and she started down gently. But before she got to the bottom of the hill a bush caught her dress.

Her fingers were busy and intent, but her skirts were full and long, so that before she could pull them free in one place they were caught in another. It was not possible to allow the dress to tear. "I in the thorny bush," she said. "Thorns, you doing your appointed work. Never want to let folks pass—no sir. Old eyes thought you was a pretty little green bush."

Finally, trembling all over, she stood free, and after a moment dared to stoop for her cane.

"Sun so high!" she cried, leaning back and looking, while the thick   10
tears went over her eyes. "The time getting all gone here."

At the foot of this hill was a place where a log was laid across the creek.

"Now comes the trial," said Phoenix.

Putting her right foot out, she mounted the log and shut her eyes. Lifting her skirt, levelling her cane fiercely before her, like a festival figure in some parade, she began to march across. Then she opened her eyes and she was safe on the other side.

"I wasn't as old as I thought," she said.

But she sat down to rest. She spread her skirts on the bank around her   15
and folded her hands over her knees. Up above her was a tree in a pearly cloud of mistletoe. She did not dare to close her eyes, and when a little boy brought her a little plate with a slice of marble-cake on it she spoke to him. "That would be acceptable," she said. But when she went to take it there was just her own hand in the air.

So she left that tree, and had to go through a barbed-wire fence. There she had to creep and crawl, spreading her knees and stretching her fingers like a baby trying to climb the steps. But she talked loudly to herself: she could not let her dress be torn now, so late in the day, and she could not pay for having her arm or her leg sawed off if she got caught fast where she was.

At last she was safe through the fence and risen up out in the clearing. Big dead trees, like black men with one arm, were standing in the purple stalks of the withered cotton field. There sat a buzzard.

"Who you watching?"

In the burrow she made her way along.

"Glad this not the season for bulls," she said, looking sideways, "and   20
the good Lord made his snakes to curl up and sleep in the winter. A pleasure I don't see no two-headed snake coming around that tree, where it come once. It took a while to get by him, back in the summer."

She passed through the old cotton and went into a field of dead corn. It whispered and shook, and was taller than her head. "Through the maze now," she said, for there was no path.

Then there was something tall, black, and skinny there, moving before her.

At first she took it for a man. It could have been a man dancing in the field. But she stood still and listened, and it did not make a sound. It was as silent as a ghost.

"Ghost," she said sharply, "who be you the ghost of? For I have heard of nary death close by."

But there was no answer, only the ragged dancing in the wind.   25

She shut her eyes, reached out her hand, and touched a sleeve. She found a coat and inside that an emptiness, cold as ice.

"You scarecrow," she said. Her face lighted. "I ought to be shut up for good," she said with laughter. "My senses is gone. I too old. I the oldest people I ever know. Dance, old scarecrow," she said, "while I dancing with you."

She kicked her foot over the furrow, and with mouth drawn down shook her head once or twice in a little strutting way. Some husks blew down and whirled in streamers about her skirts.

Then she went on, parting her way from side to side with the cane, through the whispering field. At last she came to the end, to a wagon track, where the silver grass blew between the red ruts. The quail were walking around like pullets, seeming all dainty and unseen.

"Walk pretty," she said. "This the easy place. This the easy going."   30

She followed the track, swaying through the quiet bare fields, through the little strings of trees silver in their dead leaves, past cabins silver from weather, with the doors and windows boarded shut, all like old women under a spell sitting there. "I walking in their sleep," she said, nodding her head vigorously.

In a ravine she went where a spring was silently flowing through a hollow log. Old Phoenix bent and drank. "Sweetgum makes the water sweet," she said, and drank more. "Nobody knows who made this well, for it was here when I was born."

The track crossed a swampy part where the moss hung as white as lace from every limb. "Sleep on, alligators, and blow your bubbles." Then the track went into the road.

Deep, deep the road went down between the high green-colored banks. Overhead the live-oaks met, and it was as dark as a cave.

A black dog with a lolling tongue came up out of the weeds by the   35 ditch. She was meditating, and not ready, and when he came at her she only hit him a little with her cane. Over she went in the ditch, like a little puff of milk-weed.

Down there, her senses drifted away. A dream visited her, and she reached her hand up, but nothing reached down and gave her a pull. So she lay there and presently went to talking. "Old woman," she said to herself, "that black dog came up out of the weeds to stall you off, and now there he sitting on his fine tail, smiling at you."

A white man finally came along and found her—a hunter, a young man, with his dog on a chain.

"Well, Granny!" he laughed. "What are you doing there?"

"Lying on my back like a June-bug waiting to be turned over, mister," she said, reaching up her hand.

He lifted her up, gave her a swing in the air, and set her down, "Any- ⁴⁰ thing broken, Granny?"

"No sir, them old dead weeds is springy enough," said Phoenix, when she had got her breath. "I thank you for your trouble."

"Where do you live, Granny?" he asked, while the two dogs were growling at each other.

"Away back yonder, sir, behind the ridge. You can't even see it from here."

"On your way home?"

"No, sir, I going to town." ⁴⁵

"Why, that's too far! That's as far as I walk when I come out myself, and I get something for my trouble." He patted the stuffed bag he carried, and there hung down a little closed claw. It was one of the bobwhites, with its beak hooked bitterly to show it was dead. "Now you go on home, Granny!"

"I bound to go to town, mister," said Phoenix. "The time come around."

He gave another laugh, filling the whole landscape. "I know you colored people! Wouldn't miss going to town to see Santa Claus!"

But something held Old Phoenix very still. The deep lines in her face went into a fierce and different radiation. Without warning she had seen with her own eyes a flashing nickel fall out of the man's pocket on to the ground.

"How old are you, Granny?" he was saying. ⁵⁰

"There is no telling, mister," she said, "no telling."

Then she gave a little cry and clapped her hands, and said, "Git on away from here, dog! Look at that dog!" She laughed as if in admiration. "He ain't scared of nobody. He a big black dog." She whispered, "Sick him!"

"Watch me get rid of that cur," said the man. "Sick him, Pete! Sick him!"

Phoenix heard the dogs fighting and heard the man running and throwing sticks. She even heard a gunshot. But she was slowly bending forward by that time, further and further forward, the lids stretched down over her eyes, as if she were doing this in her sleep. Her chin was lowered almost to her knees. The yellow palm of her hand came out from the fold of her apron. Her fingers slid down and along the ground under the piece of money with the grace and care they would have in lifting an egg from under a sitting hen. Then she slowly straightened up, she stood erect, and the nickel was in her apron pocket. A bird flew by. Her lips moved. "God watching me the whole time. I come to stealing."

The man came back, and his own dog panted about them. "Well, I ⁵⁵ scared him off that time," he said, and then he laughed and lifted his gun and pointed it at Phoenix.

She stood straight and faced him.

"Doesn't the gun scare you?" he said, still pointing it.

"No, sir, I seen plenty go off closer by, in my day, and for less than what I done," she said, holding utterly still.

He smiled, and shouldered the gun. "Well, Granny," he said, "you must be a hundred years old and scared of nothing. I'd give you a dime if I had any money with me. But you take my advice and stay home, and nothing will happen to you."

"I bound to go on my way, mister," said Phoenix. She inclined her   60 head in the red rag. Then they went in different directions, but she could hear the gun shooting again and again over the hill.

She walked on. The shadows hung from the oak trees to the road like curtains. Then she smelled wood-smoke, and smelled the river, and she saw a steeple and the cabins on their steep steps. Dozens of little black children whirled around her. There ahead was Natchez shining. Bells were ringing. She walked on.

In the paved city it was Christmas time. There were red and green electric lights strung and crisscrossed everywhere, and all turned on in the daytime. Old Phoenix would have been lost if she had not distrusted her eyesight and depended on her feet to know where to take her.

She paused quietly on the sidewalk, where people were passing by. A lady came along in the crowd, carrying an armful of red-, green-, and silver-wrapped presents; she gave off perfume like the red roses in hot summer, and Phoenix stopped her.

"Please, missy, will you lace up my shoe?" She held up her foot.

"What do you want, Grandma?"   65

"See my shoe," said Phoenix. "Do all right for out in the country, but wouldn't look right to go in a big building."

"Stand still then, Grandma," said the lady. She put her packages down carefully on the sidewalk beside her and laced and tied both shoes tightly.

"Can't lace 'em with a cane," said Phoenix. "Thank you, missy. I doesn't mind asking a nice lady to tie up my shoe when I gets out on the street."

Moving slowly and from side to side, she went into the stone building and into a tower of steps, where she walked up and around and around until her feet knew to stop.

She entered a door, and there she saw nailed up on the wall the docu-   70 ment that had been stamped with the gold seal and framed in the gold frame which matched the dream that was hung up in her head.

"Here I be," she said. There was a fixed and ceremonial stiffness over her body.

"A charity case, I suppose," said an attendant who sat at the desk before her.

But Phoenix only looked above her head. There was sweat on her face; the wrinkles shone like a bright net.

"Speak up, Grandma," the woman said. "What's your name? We must have your history, you know. Have you been here before? What seems to be the trouble with you?"

Old Phoenix only gave a twitch to her face as if a fly were bother-   75
ing her.

"Are you deaf?" cried the attendant.

But then the nurse came in.

"Oh, that's just old Aunt Phoenix," she said. "She doesn't come for herself—she has a little grandson. She makes these trips just as regular as clockwork. She lives away back off the Old Natchez Trace." She bent down. "Well, Aunt Phoenix, why don't you just take a seat? We won't keep you standing after your long trip." She pointed.

The old woman sat down, bolt upright in the chair.

"Now, how is the boy?" asked the nurse.   80

Old Phoenix did not speak.

"I said, how is the boy?"

But Phoenix only waited and stared straight ahead, her face very solemn and withdrawn into rigidity.

"Is his throat any better?" asked the nurse. "Aunt Phoenix, don't you hear me? Is your grandson's throat any better since the last time you came for the medicine?"

With her hand on her knees, the old woman waited, silent, erect and   85
motionless, just as if she were in armor.

"You mustn't take up our time this way, Aunt Phoenix," the nurse said. "Tell us quickly about your grandson, and get it over. He isn't dead, is he?"

At last there came a flicker and then a flame of comprehension across her face, and she spoke.

"My grandson. It was my memory had left me. There I sat and forgot why I made my long trip."

"Forgot?" The nurse frowned. "After you came so far?"

Then Phoenix was like an old woman begging a dignified forgiveness   90
for waking up frightened in the night. "I never did go to school—I was too old at the Surrender," she said in a soft voice. "I'm an old woman without an education. It was my memory fail me. My little grandson, he is just the same, and I forgot it in the coming."

"Throat never heals, does it?" said the nurse, speaking in a loud, sure voice to Old Phoenix. By now she had a card with something written on it, a little list. "Yes. Swallowed lye. When was it—January—two—three years ago—"

Phoenix spoke unasked now. "No, missy, he not dead, he just the same. Every little while his throat begin to close up again, and he not able to swallow. He not get his breath. He not able to help himself. So the time come around, and I go on another trip for the soothing-medicine."

"All right. The doctor said as long as you came to get it you could have it," said the nurse. "But it's an obstinate case."

"My little grandson, he sit up there in the house all wrapped up, waiting by himself," Phoenix went on. "We is the only two left in the world. He suffer and it don't seem to put him back at all. He got a sweet look. He going to last. He wear a little patch quilt and peep out, holding his mouth open like a little bird. I remembers so plain now. I not going to forget him again, no, the whole enduring time. I could tell him from all the others in creation."

"All right." The nurse was trying to hush her now. She brought her a   95
bottle of medicine. "Charity," she said, making a check mark in a book.

Old Phoenix held the bottle close to her eyes and then carefully put it into her pocket.

"I thank you," she said.

"It's Christmas time, Grandma," said the attendant. "Could I give you a few pennies out of my purse?"

"Five pennies is a nickel," said Phoenix stiffly.

"Here's a nickel," said the attendant.   100

Phoenix rose carefully and held out her hand. She received the nickel and then fished the other nickel out of her pocket and laid it beside the new one. She stared at her palm closely, with her head on one side.

Then she gave a tap with her cane on the floor.

"This is what come to me to do," she said. "I going to the store and buy my child a little windmill they sells, made out of paper. He going to find it hard to believe there such a thing in the world. I'll march myself back where he waiting, holding it straight up in this hand."

She lifted her free hand, gave a little nod, turned round, and walked out of the doctor's office. Then her slow step began on the stairs, going down.

JAMES BALDWIN (1924–1989)

Sonny's Blues

I read about it in the paper, in the subway, on my way to work. I read it, and I couldn't believe it, and I read it again. Then perhaps I just stared at it, at the newsprint spelling out his name, spelling out the story. I stared at it in the swinging lights of the subway car, and in the faces and bodies of the people, and in my own face, trapped in the darkness which roared outside.

It was not to be believed and I kept telling myself that, as I walked from the subway station to the high school. And at the same time I couldn't doubt it. I was scared, scared for Sonny. He became real to me again. A great block of ice got settled in my belly and kept melting there slowly all day long, while I taught my classes algebra. It was a special kind of ice. It kept melting, sending trickles of ice water all up and down my veins, but it never got less. Sometimes it hardened and seemed to expand until I felt my guts were going to come spilling out or that I was going to choke or scream. This would always be at a moment when I was remembering some specific thing Sonny had once said or done.

When he was about as old as the boys in my class his face had been bright and open, there was a lot of copper in it; and he'd had wonderfully direct brown eyes, and great gentleness and privacy. I wondered what he looked like now. He had been picked up, the evening before, in a raid on an apartment downtown, for peddling and using heroin.

I couldn't believe it: but what I mean by that is that I couldn't find any room for it anywhere inside me. I had kept it outside me for a long time. I hadn't wanted to know. I had had suspicions, but I didn't name them, I kept putting them away. I told myself that Sonny was wild, but he wasn't crazy. And he'd always been a good boy, he hadn't ever turned hard or evil or disrespectful, the way kids can, so quick, so quick, especially in Harlem. I didn't want to believe that I'd ever see my brother going down, coming to nothing, all that light in his face gone out, in the condition I'd already seen so many others. Yet it had happened and here I was, talking about algebra to a lot of boys who might, every one of them for all I knew, be popping off needles every time they went to the head. Maybe it did more for them than algebra could.

I was sure that the first time Sonny had ever had horse, he couldn't have been much older than these boys were now. These boys, now, were living as we'd been living then, they were growing up with a rush and their heads bumped abruptly against the low ceiling of their actual possibilities. They were filled with rage. All they really knew were two darknesses, the darkness of their lives, which was now closing in on them, and the darkness of the movies, which had blinded them to that other darkness, and in which they now, vindictively, dreamed, at once more together than they were at any other time, and more alone.

When the last bell rang, the last class ended, I let out my breath. It seemed I'd been holding it for all that time. My clothes were wet—I may have looked as though I'd been sitting in a steam bath, all dressed up, all afternoon. I sat alone in the classroom a long time. I listened to the boys outside, downstairs, shouting and cursing and laughing. Their laughter struck me for perhaps the first time. It was not the joyous laughter which—God knows why—one associates with children. It was mocking and insular, its intent was to denigrate. It was disenchanted, and in this, also, lay the authority of their curses. Perhaps I was listening to them because I was thinking about my brother and in them I heard my brother. And myself.

One boy was whistling a tune, at once very complicated and very simple, it seemed to be pouring out of him as though he were a bird, and it sounded very cool and moving through all that harsh, bright air, only just holding its own through all those other sounds.

I stood up and walked over to the window and looked down into the courtyard. It was the beginning of the spring and the sap was rising in the boys. A teacher passed through them every now and again, quickly, as though he or she couldn't wait to get out of that courtyard, to get those boys out of their sight and off their minds. I started collecting my stuff. I thought I'd better get home and talk to Isabel.

The courtyard was almost deserted by the time I got downstairs. I saw this boy standing in the shadow of a doorway, looking just like Sonny. I almost called his name. Then I saw that it wasn't Sonny, but somebody we used to know, a boy from around our block. He'd been Sonny's friend. He'd never been mine, having been too young for me, and, anyway, I'd never liked him. And now, even though he was a grown-up man, he still hung around that block, still spent hours on the street corners, was always high and raggy. I used to run into him from time to time and he'd often work around to asking me for a quarter or fifty cents. He always had some real good excuse, too, and I always gave it to him, I don't know why.

But now, abruptly, I hated him. I couldn't stand the way he looked at   10
me, partly like a dog, partly like a cunning child. I wanted to ask him what the hell he was doing in the school courtyard.

He sort of shuffled over to me, and he said, "I see you got the papers. So you already know about it."

"You mean about Sonny? Yes, I already know about it. How come they didn't get you?"

He grinned. It made him repulsive and it also brought to mind what he'd looked like as a kid. "I wasn't there. I stay away from them people."

"Good for you." I offered him a cigarette and I watched him through the smoke. "You come all the way down here just to tell me about Sonny?"

"That's right." He was sort of shaking his head and his eyes looked   15
strange, as though they were about to cross. The bright sun deadened his damp dark brown skin and it made his eyes look yellow and showed up the dirt in his kinked hair. He smelled funky. I moved a little away from

him and I said, "Well, thanks. But I already know about it and I got to get home."

"I'll walk you a little ways," he said. We started walking. There were a couple of kids still loitering in the courtyard and one of them said good-night to me and looked strangely at the boy beside me.

"What're you going to do?" he asked me. "I mean, about Sonny?"

"Look. I haven't seen Sonny for over a year, I'm not sure I'm going to do anything. Anyway, what the hell *can* I do?"

"That's right," he said quickly, "ain't nothing you can do. Can't much help old Sonny no more, I guess."

It was what I was thinking and so it seemed to me he had no right to say it.   20

"I'm surprised at Sonny, though," he went on — he had a funny way of talking, he looked straight ahead as though he were talking to himself — "I thought Sonny was a smart boy, I thought he was too smart to get hung."

"I guess he thought so too," I said sharply, "and that's how he got hung. And how about you? You're pretty goddamn smart, I bet."

Then he looked directly at me, just for a minute. "I ain't smart," he said. "If I was smart, I'd have reached for a pistol a long time ago."

"Look. Don't tell *me* your sad story, if it was up to me, I'd give you one." Then I felt guilty — guilty, probably, for never having supposed that the poor bastard *had* a story of his own, much less a sad one, and I asked, quickly, "What's going to happen to him now?"

He didn't answer this. He was off by himself some place. "Funny   25
thing," he said, and from his tone we might have been discussing the quick-est way to get to Brooklyn, "when I saw the papers this morning, the first thing I asked myself was if I had anything to do with it. I felt sort of responsible."

I began to listen more carefully. The subway station was on the corner, just before us, and I stopped. He stopped, too. We were in front of a bar and he ducked slightly, peering in, but whoever he was looking for didn't seem to be there. The juke box was blasting away with something black and bouncy and I half watched the barmaid as she danced her way from the juke box to her place behind the bar. And I watched her face as she laughingly responded to something someone said to her, still keeping time to the music. When she smiled one saw the little girl, one sensed the doomed, still-strug-gling woman beneath the battered face of the semi-whore.

"I never *give* Sonny nothing," the boy said finally, "but a long time ago I come to school high and Sonny asked me how it felt." He paused, I couldn't bear to watch him, I watched the barmaid, and I listened to the music which seemed to be causing the pavement to shake. "I told him it felt great." The music stopped, the barmaid paused and watched the juke box until the music began again. "It did."

All this was carrying me some place I didn't want to go. I certainly didn't want to know how it felt. It filled everything, the people, the houses, the music, the dark, quicksilver barmaid, with menace; and this menace was their reality.

"What's going to happen to him now?" I asked again.

"They'll send him away some place and they'll try to cure him." 30
He shook his head. "Maybe he'll even think he's kicked the habit. Then they'll let him loose" — he gestured, throwing his cigarette into the gutter. "That's all."

"What do you mean, that's *all?*"

But I knew what he meant.

"I *mean,* that's *all*." He turned his head and looked at me, pulling down the corners of his mouth. "Don't you know what I mean?" he asked, softly.

"How the hell *would* I know what you mean?" I almost whispered it, I don't know why.

"That's right," he said to the air, "how would *he* know what I mean?" 35
He turned toward me again, patient and calm, and yet I somehow felt him shaking, shaking as though he were going to fall apart. I felt that ice in my guts again, the dread I'd felt all afternoon; and again I watched the barmaid, moving about the bar, washing glasses, and singing. "Listen. They'll let him out and then it'll just start all over again. That's what I mean."

"You mean — they'll let him out. And then he'll just start working his way back in again. You mean he'll never kick the habit. Is that what you mean?"

"That's right," he said, cheerfully. "*You* see what I mean."

"Tell me," I said at last, "why does he want to die? He must want to die, he's killing himself, why does he want to die?"

He looked at me in surprise. He licked his lips. "He don't want to die. He wants to live. Don't nobody want to die, ever."

Then I wanted to ask him — too many things. He could not have 40
answered, or if he had, I could not have borne the answers. I started walking. "Well, I guess it's none of my business."

"It's going to be rough on old Sonny," he said. We reached the subway station. "This is your station?" he asked. I nodded. I took one step down. "Damn!" he said, suddenly. I looked up at him. He grinned again. "Damn it if I didn't leave all my money home. You ain't got a dollar on you, have you? Just for a couple of days, is all."

All at once something inside gave and threatened to come pouring out of me. I didn't hate him any more. I felt that in another moment I'd start crying like a child.

"Sure," I said. "Don't swear." I looked in my wallet and didn't have a dollar, I only had a five. "Here," I said. "That hold you?"

He didn't look at it — he didn't want to look at it. A terrible, closed look came over his face, as though he were keeping the number on the bill a secret from him and me. "Thanks," he said, and now he was dying to see me go. "Don't worry about Sonny. Maybe I'll write him or something."

"Sure," I said. "You do that. So long." 45

"Be seeing you," he said. I went down the steps.

And I didn't write Sonny or send him anything for a long time. When I finally did, it was just after my little girl died, he wrote me back a letter which made me feel like a bastard.

Here's what he said:

Dear Brother,

You don't know how much I needed to hear from you. I wanted to write you many a time but I dug how much I must have hurt you and so I didn't write. But now I feel like a man who's been trying to climb up out of some deep, real deep and funky hole and just saw the sun up there, outside. I got to get outside.

I can't tell you much about how I got here. I mean I don't know how to tell you. I guess I was afraid of something or I was trying to escape from something and you know I have never been very strong in the head (smile). I'm glad Mama and Daddy are dead and can't see what's happened to their son and I swear if I'd known what I was doing I would never have hurt you so, you and a lot of other fine people who were nice to me and who believed in me.

I don't want you to think it had anything to do with me being a musician. It's more than that. Or maybe less than that. I can't get anything straight in my head down here and I try not to think about what's going to happen to me when I get outside again. Sometime I think I'm going to flip and *never* get outside and sometime I think I'll come straight back. I tell you one thing, though, I'd rather blow my brains out than go through this again. But that's what they all say, so they tell me. If I tell you when I'm coming to New York and if you could meet me, I sure would appreciate it. Give my love to Isabel and the kids and I was sure sorry to hear about little Gracie. I wish I could be like Mama and say the Lord's will be done, but I don't know it seems to me that trouble is the one thing that never does get stopped and I don't know what good it does to blame it on the Lord. But maybe it does some good if you believe it.

Your brother,
Sonny

50

Then I kept in constant touch with him and I sent him whatever I could and I went to meet him when he came back to New York. When I saw him many things I thought I had forgotten came flooding back to me. This was because I had begun, finally, to wonder about Sonny, about the life that Sonny lived inside. This life, whatever it was, had made him older and thinner and it had deepened the distant stillness in which he had always moved. He looked very unlike my baby brother. Yet, when he smiled, when we shook hands, the baby brother I'd never known looked out from the depths of his private life, like an animal waiting to be coaxed into the light.

"How you been keeping?" he asked me.

"All right. And you?"

"Just fine." He was smiling all over his face. "It's good to see you again."

"It's good to see you."   55

The seven years' difference in our ages lay between us like a chasm: I wondered if these years would ever operate between us as a bridge. I was remembering, and it made it hard to catch my breath, that I had been there when he was born; and I had heard the first words he had ever spoken. When he started to walk, he walked from our mother straight to me. I caught him just before he fell when he took the first steps he ever took in this world.

"How's Isabel?"

"Just fine. She's dying to see you."

"And the boys?"

"They're fine, too. They're anxious to see their uncle."   60

"Oh, come on. You know they don't remember me."

"Are you kidding? Of course they remember you."

He grinned again. We got into a taxi. We had a lot to say to each other, far too much to know how to begin.

As the taxi began to move, I asked, "You still want to go to India?"

He laughed. "You still remember that. Hell, no. This place is Indian   65
enough for me."

"It used to belong to them," I said.

And he laughed again. "They damn sure knew what they were doing when they got rid of it."

Years ago, when he was around fourteen, he'd been all hipped on the idea of going to India. He read books about people sitting on rocks, naked, in all kinds of weather, but mostly bad, naturally, and walking barefoot through hot coals and arriving at wisdom. I used to say that it sounded to me as though they were getting away from wisdom as fast as they could. I think he sort of looked down on me for that.

"Do you mind," he asked, "if we have the driver drive alongside the park? On the west side—I haven't seen the city in so long."

"Of course not," I said. I was afraid that I might sound as though I   70
were humoring him, but I hoped he wouldn't take it that way.

So we drove along, between the green of the park and the stony, lifeless elegance of hotels and apartment buildings, toward the vivid, killing streets of our childhood. These streets hadn't changed, though housing projects jutted up out of them now like rocks in the middle of a boiling sea. Most of the houses in which we had grown up had vanished, as had the stores from which we had stolen, the basements in which we had first tried sex, the rooftops from which we had hurled tin cans and bricks. But houses exactly like the houses of our past yet dominated the landscape, boys exactly like the boys we once had been found themselves smothering in these houses, came down into the streets for light and air and found themselves encircled by disaster. Some escaped the trap, most didn't. Those who got out always left something of themselves behind, as some animals amputate a leg and leave it in the trap. It might be said, perhaps, that I had escaped, after all, I was a school teacher; or that Sonny had, he hadn't lived in Harlem for years. Yet, as the cab moved uptown through streets which seemed, with a rush, to darken with dark people, and as I covertly studied Sonny's face, it came to me that what we were both seeking through our separate cab windows was that part of ourselves which had been left behind. It's always at the hour of trouble and confrontation that the missing member aches.

We hit 110th Street and started rolling up Lenox Avenue. And I'd known this avenue all my life, but it seemed to me again, as it had seemed on the day I'd first heard about Sonny's trouble, filled with a hidden menace which was its very breath of life.

"We almost there," said Sonny.

"Almost." We were both too nervous to say anything more.

We lived in a housing project. It hasn't been up long. A few days after it was up it seemed uninhabitably new, now, of course, it's already rundown. It looks like a parody of the good, clean, faceless life—God knows the people who live in it do their best to make it a parody. The beat-looking grass lying around isn't enough to make their lives green, the hedges will never hold out the streets, and they know it. The big windows fool no one, they aren't big enough to make space out of no space. They don't bother with the windows, they watch the TV screen instead. The playground is most popular with the children who don't play at jacks, or skip rope, or roller skate, or swing, and they can be found in it after dark. We moved in partly because it's not too far from where I teach, and partly for the kids; but it's really just like the houses in which Sonny and I grew up. The same things happen, they'll have the same things to remember. The moment Sonny and I started into the house I had the feeling that I was simply bringing him back into the danger he had almost died trying to escape.

Sonny has never been talkative. So I don't know why I was sure he'd be dying to talk to me when supper was over the first night. Everything went fine, the oldest boy remembered him, and the youngest boy liked him, and Sonny had remembered to bring something for each of them; and Isabel, who is really much nicer than I am, more open and giving, had gone to a lot of trouble about dinner and was genuinely glad to see him. And she's always been able to tease Sonny in a way that I haven't. It was nice to see her face so vivid again and to hear her laugh and watch her make Sonny laugh. She wasn't, or, anyway, she didn't seem to be, at all uneasy or embarrassed. She chatted as though there were no subject which had to be avoided and she got Sonny past his first, faint stiffness. And thank God she was there, for I was filled with that icy dread again. Everything I did seemed awkward to me, and everything I said sounded freighted with hidden meaning. I was trying to remember everything I'd heard about dope addiction

75

and I couldn't help watching Sonny for signs. I wasn't doing it out of malice. I was trying to find out something about my brother. I was dying to hear him tell me he was safe.

"Safe!" my father grunted, whenever Mama suggested trying to move to a neighborhood which might be safer for children. "Safe, hell! Ain't no place safe for kids, nor nobody."

He always went on like this, but he wasn't, ever, really as bad as he sounded, not even on weekends, when he got drunk. As a matter of fact, he was always on the lookout for "something a little better," but he died before he found it. He died suddenly, during a drunken weekend in the middle of the war, when Sonny was fifteen. He and Sonny hadn't ever got on too well. And this was partly because Sonny was the apple of his father's eye. It was because he loved Sonny so much and was frightened for him, that he was always fighting with him. It doesn't do any good to fight with Sonny. Sonny just moves back, inside himself, where he can't be reached. But the principal reason that they never hit it off is that they were so much alike. Daddy was big and rough and loud-talking, just the opposite of Sonny, but they both had — that same privacy.

Mama tried to tell me something about this, just after Daddy died. I was home on leave from the army.

This was the last time I ever saw my mother alive. Just the same, this   80
picture gets all mixed up in my mind with pictures I had of her when she was younger. The way I always see her is the way she used to be on a Sunday afternoon, say, when the old folks were talking after the big Sunday dinner. I always see her wearing pale blue. She'd be sitting on the sofa. And my father would be sitting in the easy chair, not far from her. And the living room would be full of church folks and relatives. There they sit, in chairs all around the living room, and the night is creeping up outside, but nobody knows it yet. You can see the darkness growing against the windowpanes and you hear the street noises every now and again, or maybe the jangling beat of a tambourine from one of the churches close by, but it's real quiet in the room. For a moment nobody's talking, but every face looks darkening, like the sky outside. And my mother rocks a little from the waist, and my father's eyes are closed. Everyone is looking at something a child can't see. For a minute they've forgotten the children. Maybe a kid is lying on the rug, half asleep. Maybe somebody's got a kid in his lap and is absent-mindedly stroking the kid's head. Maybe there's a kid, quiet and big-eyed, curled up in a big chair in the corner. The silence, the darkness coming, and the darkness in the faces frightens the child obscurely. He hopes that the hand which strokes his forehead will never stop — will never die. He hopes that there will never come a time when the old folks won't be sitting around the living room, talking about where they've come from, and what they've seen, and what's happening to them and their kinfolk.

But something deep and watchful in the child knows that this is bound to end, is already ending. In a moment someone will get up and turn on the light. Then the old folks will remember the children and they won't talk any more that day. And when light fills the room, the child is filled with darkness. He knows that every time this happens he's moved just a little closer to that darkness outside. The darkness outside is what the old folks have been talking about. It's what they've come from. It's what they endure. The child knows that they won't talk any more because if he knows too much about what's happened to *them,* he'll know too much too soon, about what's going to happen to *him.*

The last time I talked to my mother, I remember I was restless. I wanted to get out and see Isabel. We weren't married then and we had a lot to straighten out between us.

There Mama sat, in black, by the window. She was humming an old church song, *Lord, you brought me from a long ways off.* Sonny was out somewhere. Mama kept watching the streets.

"I don't know," she said, "if I'll ever see you again, after you go off from here. But I hope you'll remember the things I tried to teach you."

"Don't talk like that," I said, and smiled. "You'll be here a long   85
time yet."

She smiled, too, but she said nothing. She was quiet for a long time. And I said, "Mama, don't you worry about nothing. I'll be writing all the time, and you be getting the checks. . . ."

"I want to talk to you about your brother," she said, suddenly. "If anything happens to me he ain't going to have nobody to look out for him."

"Mama," I said, "ain't nothing going to happen to you *or* Sonny. Sonny's all right. He's a good boy and he's got good sense."

"It ain't a question of his being a good boy," Mama said, "nor of his having good sense. It ain't only the bad ones, nor yet the dumb ones that gets sucked under." She stopped, looking at me. "Your Daddy once had a brother," she said, and she smiled in a way that made me feel she was in pain. "You didn't never know that, did you?"

"No," I said, "I never knew that," and I watched her face.   90

"Oh, yes," she said, "your Daddy had a brother." She looked out of the window again. "I know you never saw your Daddy cry. But I did — many a time, through all these years."

I asked her, "What happened to his brother? How come nobody's ever talked about him?"

This was the first time I ever saw my mother look old.

"His brother got killed," she said, "when he was just a little younger than you are now. I knew him. He was a fine boy. He was maybe a little full of the devil, but he didn't mean nobody no harm."

Then she stopped and the room was silent, exactly as it had sometimes   95
been on those Sunday afternoons. Mama kept looking out into the streets.

"He used to have a job in the mill," she said, "and, like all young folks, he just liked to perform on Saturday nights. Saturday nights, him and your father would drift around to different places, go to dances and things like that, or just sit around with people they knew, and your father's brother would sing, he had a fine voice, and play along with himself on his guitar. Well, this particular Saturday night, him and your father was coming home from some place, and they were both a little drunk and there was a moon that night, it was bright like day. Your father's brother was feeling kind of good, and he was whistling to himself, and he had his guitar slung over his shoulder. They was coming down a hill and beneath them was a road that turned off from the highway. Well, your father's brother, being always kind of frisky, decided to run down this hill, and he did, with that guitar banging and clanging behind him, and he ran across the road, and he was making water behind a tree. And your father was sort of amused at him and he was still coming down the hill, kind of slow. Then he heard a car motor and that same minute his brother stepped from behind the tree, into the road, in the moonlight. And he started to cross the road. And your father started to run down the hill, he says he don't know why. This car was full of white men. They was all drunk, and when they seen your father's brother they let out a great whoop and holler and they aimed the car straight at him. They was having fun, they just wanted to scare him, the way they do sometimes, you know. But they was drunk. And I guess the boy, being drunk, too, and scared, kind of lost his head. By the time he jumped it was too late. Your father says he heard his brother scream when the car rolled over him, and he heard the wood of that guitar when it give, and he heard them strings go flying, and he heard them white men shouting, and the car kept on a-going and it ain't stopped till this day. And, time your father got down the hill, his brother weren't nothing but blood and pulp."

Tears were gleaming on my mother's face. There wasn't anything I could say.

"He never mentioned it," she said, "because I never let him mention it before you children. Your Daddy was like a crazy man that night and for many a night thereafter. He says he never in his life seen anything as dark as that road after the lights of that car had gone away. Weren't nothing; weren't nobody on that road, just your Daddy and his brother and that busted guitar. Oh, yes. Your Daddy never did really get right again. Till the day he died he wasn't sure but that every white man he saw was the man that killed his brother."

She stopped and took out a handkerchief and dried her eyes and looked at me.

"I ain't telling you all this," she said, "to make you scared or bitter or 100 to make you hate nobody. I'm telling you this because you got a brother. And the world ain't changed."

I guess I didn't want to believe this. I guess she saw this in my face. She turned away from me, toward the window again, searching those streets.

"But I praise my Redeemer," she said at last, "that He called your Daddy home before me. I ain't saying it to throw no flowers at myself, but,

I declare, it keeps me from feeling too cast down to know I helped your father get safely through this world. Your father always acted like he was the roughest, strongest man on earth. And everybody took him to be like that. But if he hadn't had *me* there — to see his tears!"

She was crying again. Still, I couldn't move. I said, "Lord, Lord, Mama, I didn't know it was like that."

"Oh, honey," she said, "There's a lot that you don't know. But you are going to find out." She stood up from the window and came over to me. "You got to hold on to your brother," she said, "and don't let him fall, no matter what it looks like is happening to him and no matter how evil you gets with him. You going to be evil with him many a time. But don't you forget what I told you, you hear?"

"I won't forget," I said. "Don't you worry, I won't forget. I won't let 105
nothing happen to Sonny."

My mother smiled as though she were amused at something she saw in my face. Then, "You may not be able to stop nothing from happening. But you got to let him know you's *there*."

Two days later I was married, and then I was gone. And I had a lot of things on my mind and I pretty well forgot my promise to Mama until I got shipped home on a special furlough for her funeral.

And, after the funeral, with just Sonny and me alone in the empty kitchen, I tried to find out something about him.

"What do you want to do?" I asked him.

"I'm going to be a musician," he said. 110

For he had graduated, in the time I had been away, from dancing to the juke box to finding out who was playing what, and what they were doing with it, and he had bought himself a set of drums.

"You mean, you want to be a drummer?" I somehow had the feeling that being a drummer might be all right for other people but not for my brother Sonny.

"I don't think," he said, looking at me very gravely, "that I'll ever be a good drummer. But I think I can play a piano."

I frowned. I'd never played the role of the older brother quite so seriously before, had scarcely ever, in fact, *asked* Sonny a damn thing. I sensed myself in the presence of something I didn't really know how to handle, didn't understand. So I made my frown a little deeper as I asked: "What kind of musician do you want to be?"

He grinned. "How many kinds do you think there are?" 115

"Be *serious*," I said.

He laughed, throwing his head back, and looked at me. "I *am* serious."

"Well, then, for Christ's sake, stop kidding around and answer a serious question. I mean, do you want to be a concert pianist, you want to play classical music and all that, or — or what?" Long before I finished he was laughing again. "For Christ's *sake*, Sonny!"

He sobered, but with difficulty. "I'm sorry. But you sound so—
scared!" and he was off again.

"Well, you may think it's funny now, baby, but it's not going to be so   120
funny when you have to make your living at it, let me tell you *that*." I was
furious because I knew he was laughing at me and I didn't know why.

"No," he said, very sober now, and afraid, perhaps, that he'd hurt me,
"I don't want to be a classical pianist. That isn't what interests me. I
mean"—he paused, looking hard at me, as though his eyes would help me
to understand, and then gestured helplessly, as though perhaps his hand
would help—"I mean, I'll have a lot of studying to do, and I'll have to study
everything, but, I mean, I want to play *with*—jazz musicians." He stopped.
"I want to play jazz," he said.

Well, the word had never before sounded as heavy, as real, as it sounded
that afternoon in Sonny's mouth. I just looked at him and I was probably
frowning a real frown by this time. I simply couldn't see why on earth he'd
want to spend his time hanging around nightclubs, clowning around on
bandstands, while people pushed each other around a dance floor. It
seemed—beneath him, somehow. I had never thought about it before, had
never been forced to, but I suppose I had always put jazz musicians in a class
with what Daddy called "goodtime people."

"Are you *serious?*"

"Hell, *yes,* I'm serious."

He looked more helpless than ever, and annoyed, and deeply hurt.   125

I suggested, helpfully: "You mean—like Louis Armstrong?"

His face closed as though I'd struck him. "No. I'm not talking about
none of that old-time, down home crap."

"Well, look, Sonny, I'm sorry, don't get mad. I just don't altogether
get it, that's all. Name somebody—you know, a jazz musician you admire."

"Bird."

"Who?"   130

"Bird! Charlie Parker! Don't they teach you nothing in the goddamn
army?"

I lit a cigarette. I was surprised and then a little amused to discover
that I was trembling. "I've been out of touch," I said. "You'll have to be
patient with me. Now. Who's this Parker character?"

"He's just one of the greatest jazz musicians alive," said Sonny, sullenly, his hands in his pockets, his back to me. "Maybe *the* greatest," he
added, bitterly, "that's probably why *you* never heard of him."

"All right," I said, "I'm ignorant. I'm sorry. I'll go out and buy all the
cat's records right away, all right?"

"It don't," said Sonny, with dignity, "make any difference to me. I   135
don't care what you listen to. Don't do me no favors."

I was beginning to realize that I'd never seen him so upset before. With
another part of my mind I was thinking that this would probably turn out
to be one of those things kids go through and that I shouldn't make it seem

important by pushing it too hard. Still, I didn't think it would do any harm to ask: "Doesn't all this take a lot of time? Can you make a living at it?"

He turned back to me and half leaned, half sat, on the kitchen table. "Everything takes time," he said, "and — well, yes, sure, I can make a living at it. But what I don't seem to be able to make you understand is that it's the only thing I want to do."

"Well, Sonny," I said, gently, "you know people can't always do exactly what they *want* to do — "

"*No,* I don't know that," said Sonny, surprising me. "I think people *ought* to do what they want to do, what else are they alive for?"

"You getting to be a big boy," I said desperately, "it's time you started   140 thinking about your future."

"I'm thinking about my future," said Sonny, grimly. "I think about it all the time."

I gave up. I decided, if he didn't change his mind, that we could always talk about it later. "In the meantime," I said, "you got to finish school." We had already decided that he'd have to move in with Isabel and her folks. I knew this wasn't the ideal arrangement because Isabel's folks are inclined to be dicty and they hadn't especially wanted Isabel to marry me. But I didn't know what else to do. "And we have to get you fixed up at Isabel's."

There was a long silence. He moved from the kitchen table to the window. "That's a terrible idea. You know it yourself."

"Do you have a *better* idea?"

He just walked up and down the kitchen for a minute. He was as tall   145 as I was. He had started to shave. I suddenly had the feeling that I didn't know him at all.

He stopped at the kitchen table and picked up my cigarettes. Looking at me with a kind of mocking, amused defiance, he put one between his lips. "You mind?"

"You smoking already?"

He lit the cigarette and nodded, watching me through the smoke. "I just wanted to see if I'd have the courage to smoke in front of you." He grinned and blew a great cloud of smoke to the ceiling. "It was easy." He looked at my face. "Come on, now. I bet you was smoking at my age, tell the truth."

I didn't say anything but the truth was on my face, and he laughed. But now there was something very strained in his laugh. "Sure. And I bet that ain't all you was doing."

He was frightening me a little. "Cut the crap," I said. "We already   150 decided that you was going to go and live at Isabel's. Now what's got into you all of a sudden?"

"*You* decided it," he pointed out. "*I* didn't decide nothing." He stopped in front of me, leaning against the stove, arms loosely folded. "Look, brother. I don't want to stay in Harlem no more, I really don't." He was very earnest. He looked at me, then over toward the kitchen window.

There was something in his eyes I'd never seen before, some thoughtfulness, some worry all his own. He rubbed the muscle of one arm. "It's time I was getting out of here."

"Where do you want to go, Sonny?"

"I want to join the army. Or the navy, I don't care. If I say I'm old enough, they'll believe me."

Then I got mad. It was because I was so scared. "You must be crazy. You god-damn fool, what the hell do you want to go and join the *army* for?"

"I just told you. To get out of Harlem."   155

"Sonny, you haven't even finished *school*. And if you really want to be a musician, how do you expect to study if you're in the *army?*"

He looked at me, trapped, and in anguish. "There's ways. I might be able to work out some kind of deal. Anyway, I'll have the G.I. Bill when I come out."

"*If* you come out." We stared at each other. "Sonny, please. Be reasonable. I know the setup is far from perfect. But we got to do the best we can."

"I ain't learning nothing in school," he said. "Even when I go." He turned away from me and opened the window and threw his cigarette out into the narrow alley. I watched his back. "At least, I ain't learning nothing you'd want me to learn." He slammed the window so hard I thought the glass would fly out, and turned back to me. "And I'm sick of the stink of these garbage cans!"

"Sonny," I said, "I know how you feel. But if you don't finish school 160 now, you're going to be sorry later that you didn't." I grabbed him by the shoulders. "And you only got another year. It ain't so bad. And I'll come back and I swear I'll help you do *whatever* you want to do. Just try to put up with it till I come back. Will you please do that? For me?"

He didn't answer and he wouldn't look at me.

"Sonny. You hear me?"

He pulled away. "I hear you. But you never hear anything I say."

I didn't know what to say to that. He looked out of the window and then back at me. "OK," he said, and sighed. "I'll try."

Then I said, trying to cheer him up a little, "They got a piano at 165 Isabel's. You can practice on it."

And as a matter of fact, it did cheer him up for a minute. "That's right," he said to himself. "I forgot that." His face relaxed a little. But the worry, the thoughtfulness, played on it still, the way shadows play on a face which is staring into the fire.

But I thought I'd never hear the end of that piano. At first, Isabel would write me, saying how nice it was that Sonny was so serious about his music and how, as soon as he came in from school, or wherever he had been when he was supposed to be at school, he went straight to that piano and stayed there until suppertime. And, after supper, he went back to that piano and stayed there until everybody went to bed. He was at the piano all day

Saturday and all day Sunday. Then he bought a record player and started playing records. He'd play one record over and over again, all day long sometimes, and he'd improvise along with it on the piano. Or he'd play one section of the record, one chord, one change, one progression, then he'd do it on the piano. Then back to the record. Then back to the piano.

Well, I really don't know how they stood it. Isabel finally confessed that it wasn't like living with a person at all, it was like living with sound. And the sound didn't make any sense to her, didn't make any sense to any of them — naturally. They began, in a way, to be afflicted by this presence that was living in their home. It was as though Sonny were some sort of god, or monster. He moved in an atmosphere which wasn't like theirs at all. They fed him and he ate, he washed himself, he walked in and out of their door; he certainly wasn't nasty or unpleasant or rude, Sonny isn't any of those things; but it was as though he were all wrapped up in some cloud, some fire, some vision all his own; and there wasn't any way to reach him.

At the same time, he wasn't really a man yet, he was still a child, and they had to watch out for him in all kinds of ways. They certainly couldn't throw him out. Neither did they dare to make a great scene about that piano because even they dimly sensed, as I sensed, from so many thousands of miles away, that Sonny was at that piano playing for his life.

But he hadn't been going to school. One day a letter came from the   170 school board and Isabel's mother got it — there had, apparently, been other letters but Sonny had torn them up. This day, when Sonny came in, Isabel's mother showed him the letter and asked where he'd been spending his time. And she finally got it out of him that he'd been down in Greenwich Village, with musicians and other characters, in a white girl's apartment. And this scared her and she started to scream at him and what came up, once she began — though she denies it to this day — was what sacrifices they were making to give Sonny a decent home and how little he appreciated it.

Sonny didn't play the piano that day. By evening, Isabel's mother had calmed down but then there was the old man to deal with, and Isabel herself. Isabel says she did her best to be calm but she broke down and started crying. She says she just watched Sonny's face. She could tell, by watching him, what was happening with him. And what was happening was that they penetrated his cloud, they had reached him. Even if their fingers had been a thousand times more gentle than human fingers ever are, he could hardly help feeling that they had stripped him naked and were spitting on that nakedness. For he also had to see that his presence, that music, which was life or death to him, had been torture for them and that they had endured it, not at all for his sake, but only for mine. And Sonny couldn't take that. He can take it a little better today than he could then but he's still not very good at it and, frankly, I don't know anybody who is.

The silence of the next few days must have been louder than the sound of all the music ever played since time began. One morning, before she went to work, Isabel was in his room for something and she suddenly realized that all of his records were gone. And she knew for certain that he was gone.

And he was. He went as far as the navy would carry him. He finally sent me a postcard from some place in Greece and that was the first I knew that Sonny was still alive. I didn't see him any more until we were both back in New York and the war had long been over.

He was a man by then, of course, but I wasn't willing to see it. He came by the house from time to time, but we fought almost every time we met. I didn't like the way he carried himself, loose and dreamlike all the time, and I didn't like his friends, and his music seemed to be merely an excuse for the life he led. It sounded just that weird and disordered.

Then we had a fight, a pretty awful fight, and I didn't see him for months. By and by I looked him up, where he was living, in a furnished room in the Village, and I tried to make it up. But there were lots of other people in the room and Sonny just lay on his bed, and he wouldn't come downstairs with me, and he treated these other people as though they were his family and I weren't. So I got mad and then he got mad, and then I told him that he might just as well be dead as live the way he was living. Then he stood up and he told me not to worry about him any more in life, that he *was* dead as far as I was concerned. Then he pushed me to the door and the other people looked on as though nothing were happening, and he slammed the door behind me. I stood in the hallway, staring at the door. I heard somebody laugh in the room and then the tears came to my eyes. I started down the steps, whistling to keep from crying, I kept whistling to myself, *You going to need me, baby, one of these cold, rainy days.*

I read about Sonny's trouble in the spring. Little Grace died in the fall. 175 She was a beautiful little girl. But she only lived a little over two years. She died of polio and she suffered. She had a slight fever for a couple of days, but it didn't seem like anything and we just kept her in bed. And we would certainly have called the doctor, but the fever dropped, she seemed to be all right. So we thought it had just been a cold. Then, one day, she was up, playing, Isabel was in the kitchen fixing lunch for the two boys when they'd come in from school, and she heard Grace fall down in the living room. When you have a lot of children you don't always start running when one of them falls, unless they start screaming or something. And, this time, Grace was quiet. Yet, Isabel says that when she heard that *thump* and then that silence, something happened in her to make her afraid. And she ran to the living room and there was little Grace on the floor, all twisted up, and the reason she hadn't screamed was that she couldn't get her breath. And when she did scream, it was the worst sound, Isabel says, that she'd ever heard in all her life, and she still hears it sometimes in her dreams. Isabel will sometimes wake me up with a low, moaning, strangled sound and I have to be quick to awaken her and hold her to me and where Isabel is weeping against me seems a mortal wound.

I think I may have written Sonny the very day that little Grace was buried. I was sitting in the living room in the dark, by myself, and I suddenly thought of Sonny. My trouble made his real.

One Saturday afternoon, when Sonny had been living with us, or, anyway, been in our house, for nearly two weeks, I found myself wandering aimlessly about the living room, drinking from a can of beer, and trying to work up the courage to search Sonny's room. He was out, he was usually out whenever I was home, and Isabel had taken the children to see their grandparents. Suddenly I was standing still in front of the living room window, watching Seventh Avenue. The idea of searching Sonny's room made me still. I scarcely dared to admit to myself what I'd be searching for. I didn't know what I'd do if I found it. Or if I didn't.

On the sidewalk across from me, near the entrance to a barbecue joint, some people were holding an old-fashioned revival meeting. The barbecue cook, wearing a dirty white apron, his conked hair reddish and metallic in the pale sun, and a cigarette between his lips, stood in the doorway, watching them. Kids and older people paused in their errands and stood there, along with some older men and a couple of very tough-looking women who watched everything that happened on the avenue, as though they owned it, or were maybe owned by it. Well, they were watching this, too. The revival was being carried on by three sisters in black, and a brother. All they had were their voices and their Bibles and a tambourine. The brother was testifying and while he testified two of the sisters stood together, seeming to say, amen, and the third sister walked around with the tambourine outstretched and a couple of people dropped coins into it. Then the brother's testimony ended and the sister who had been taking up the collection dumped the coins into her palm and transferred them to the pocket of her long black robe. Then she raised both hands, striking the tambourine against the air, and then against one hand, and she started to sing. And the two other sisters and the brother joined in.

It was strange, suddenly, to watch, though I had been seeing these street meetings all my life. So, of course, had everybody else down there. Yet, they paused and watched and listened and I stood still at the window. *"Tis the old ship of Zion,"* they sang, and the sister with the tambourine kept a steady, jangling beat, *"it has rescued many a thousand!"* Not a soul under the sound of their voices was hearing this song for the first time, not one of them had been rescued. Nor had they seen much in the way of rescue work being done around them. Neither did they especially believe in the holiness of the three sisters and the brother, they knew too much about them, knew where they lived, and how. The woman with the tambourine, whose voice dominated the air, whose face was bright with joy, was divided by very little from the woman who stood watching her, a cigarette between her heavy, chapped lips, her hair a cuckoo's nest, her face scarred and swollen from many beatings, and her black eyes glittering like coal. Perhaps they both knew this, which was why, when, as rarely, they addressed each other, they addressed each other as Sister. As the singing filled the air the watching, listening faces underwent a change, the eyes focusing on something within; the music seemed to soothe a poison out of them; and time seemed, nearly, to fall away from the sullen, belligerent, battered faces, as though they were

fleeing back to their first condition, while dreaming of their last. The barbecue cook half shook his head and smiled, and dropped his cigarette and
disappeared into his joint. A man fumbled in his pockets for change and
stood holding it in his hand impatiently, as though he had just remembered
a pressing appointment further up the avenue. He looked furious. Then I
saw Sonny, standing on the edge of the crowd. He was carrying a wide, flat
notebook with a green cover, and it make him look, from where I was
standing, almost like a schoolboy. The coppery sun brought out the copper
in his skin, he was very faintly smiling, standing very still. Then the singing
stopped, the tambourine turned into a collection plate again. The furious
man dropped in his coins and vanished, so did a couple of the women, and
Sonny dropped some change in the plate, looking directly at the woman
with a little smile. He started across the avenue, toward the house. He has a
slow, loping walk, something like the way Harlem hipsters walk, only he's
imposed on this his own half-beat. I had never really noticed it before.

I stayed at the window, both relieved and apprehensive. As Sonny   180
disappeared from my sight, they began singing again. And they were still
singing when his key turned in the lock.

"Hey," he said.

"Hey, yourself. You want some beer?"

"No. Well, maybe." But he came up to the window and stood beside
me, looking out. "What a warm voice," he said.

They were singing *If I could only hear my mother pray again!*

"Yes," I said, "and she can sure beat that tambourine."   185

"But what a terrible song," he said, and laughed. He dropped his
notebook on the sofa and disappeared into the kitchen. "Where's Isabel and
the kids?"

"I think they went to see their grandparents. You hungry?"

"No." He came back into the living room with his can of beer. "You
want to come some place with me tonight?"

I sensed, I don't know how, that I couldn't possibly say no. "Sure.
Where?"

He sat down on the sofa and picked up his notebook and started leafing   190
through it. "I'm going to sit in with some fellows in a joint in the Village."

"You mean, you're going to play, tonight?"

"That's right." He took a swallow of his beer and moved back to the
window. He gave me a sidelong look. "If you can stand it."

"I'll try," I said.

He smiled to himself and we both watched as the meeting across the
way broke up. The three sisters and the brother, heads bowed, were singing
God be with you till we meet again. The faces around them were very quiet.
Then the song ended. The small crowd dispersed. We watched the three
women and the lone man walk slowly up the avenue.

"When she was singing before," said Sonny, abruptly, "her voice re-   195
minded me for a minute of what heroin feels like sometimes — when it's in

your veins. It makes you feel sort of warm and cool at the same time. And distant. And — and sure." He sipped his beer, very deliberately not looking at me. I watched his face. "It makes you feel — in control. Sometimes you've got to have that feeling."

"Do you?" I sat down slowly in the easy chair.

"Sometimes." He went to the sofa and picked up his notebook again. "Some people do."

"In order," I asked, "to play?" And my voice was very ugly, full of contempt and anger.

"Well" — he looked at me with great, troubled eyes, as though, in fact, he hoped his eyes would tell me things he could never otherwise say — "they *think* so. And *if* they think so — !"

"And what do *you* think?" I asked.   200

He sat on the sofa and put his can of beer on the floor. "I don't know," he said, and I couldn't be sure if he were answering my question or pursuing his thoughts. His face didn't tell me. "It's not so much to *play*. It's to *stand* it, to be able to make it at all. On any level." He frowned and smiled: "In order to keep from shaking to pieces."

"But these friends of yours," I said, "they seem to shake themselves to pieces pretty goddamn fast."

"Maybe." He played with his notebook. And something told me that I should curb my tongue, that Sonny was doing his best to talk, that I should listen. "But of course you only know the ones that've gone to pieces. Some don't — or at least they haven't *yet* and that's just about all *any* of us can say." He paused. "And then there are some who just live, really, in hell, and they know it and they see what's happening and they go right on. I don't know." He sighed, dropped the notebook, folded his arms. "Some guys, you can tell from the way they play, they on something *all* the time. And you can see that, well, it makes something real for them. But of course," he picked up his beer from the floor and sipped it and put the can down again, "they *want* to, too, you've got to see that. Even some of them that say they don't — *some, not all.*"

"And what about you?" I asked — I couldn't help it. "What about you? Do *you* want to?"

He stood up and walked to the window and remained silent for a long   205 time. Then he sighed. "Me," he said. Then: "While I was downstairs before, on my way here, listening to that woman sing, it struck me all of a sudden how much suffering she must have had to go through — to sing like that. It's *repulsive* to think that you have to suffer that much."

I said: "But there's no way not to suffer — is there, Sonny?"

"I believe not," he said and smiled, "but that's never stopped anyone from trying." He looked at me. "Has it?" I realized, with this mocking look, that there stood between us, forever, beyond the power of time or forgiveness, the fact that I had held silence — so long! — when he had needed human speech to help him. He turned back to the window. "No, there's no way not to suffer. But you try all kinds of ways to keep from drowning in it, to keep on top of it, and to make it seem—well, like *you.* Like you did something, all right, and now you're suffering for it. You know?" I said nothing. "Well you know," he said, impatiently, "Why *do* people suffer? Maybe it's better to do something to give it a reason, *any* reason."

"But we just agreed," I said, "that there's no way not to suffer. Isn't it better, then, just to—take it?"

"But nobody just takes it," Sonny cried, "that's what I'm telling you! *Everybody* tries not to. You're just hung up on the *way* some people try—it's not *your* way!"

The hair on my face began to itch, my face felt wet. "That's not true," I said, "that's not true. I don't give a damn what other people do, I don't even care how they suffer. I just care how *you* suffer." And he looked at me. "Please believe me," I said, "I don't want to see you—die—trying not to suffer."

"I won't," he said, flatly, "die trying not to suffer. At least, not any faster than anybody else."

"But there's no need," I said, trying to laugh, "is there? in killing yourself."

I wanted to say more, but I couldn't. I wanted to talk about will power and how life could be—well, beautiful. I wanted to say that it was all within; but was it? or, rather, wasn't that exactly the trouble? And I wanted to promise that I would never fail him again. But it would all have sounded—empty words and lies.

So I made the promise to myself and prayed that I would keep it.

"It's terrible sometimes, inside," he said, "that's what's the trouble. You walk these streets, black and funky and cold, and there's not really a living ass to talk to, and there's nothing shaking, and there's no way of getting it out—that storm inside. You can't talk it and you can't make love with it, and when you finally try to get with it and play it, you realize *nobody's* listening. So *you've* got to listen. You got to find a way to listen."

And then he walked away from the window and sat on the sofa again, as though all the wind had suddenly been knocked out of him. "Sometimes you'll do *anything* to play, even cut your mother's throat." He laughed and looked at me. "Or your brother's." Then he sobered. "Or your own." Then: "Don't worry. I'm all right now and I think I'll *be* all right. But I can't forget—where I've been. I don't mean just the physical place I've been, I mean where I've *been*. And *what* I've been."

"What have you been, Sonny?" I asked.

He smiled—but sat sideways on the sofa, his elbow resting on the back, his fingers playing with his mouth and chin, not looking at me. "I've been something I didn't recognize, didn't know I could be. Didn't know anybody could be." He stopped, looking inward, looking helplessly young, looking old. "I'm not talking about it now because I feel *guilty* or anything like that—maybe it would be better if I did, I don't know. Anyway, I can't really talk about it. Not to you, not to anybody," and now he turned and faced me. "Sometimes, you know, and it was actually when I was most *out* of the world, I felt that I was in it, that I was *with* it, really, and I could play or I didn't really have to *play*, it just came out of me, it was there. And I don't know how I played, thinking about it now, but I know I did awful things, those times, sometimes, to people. Or it wasn't that I *did* anything to them — it was that they weren't real." He picked up the beer can; it was empty; he rolled it between his palms: "And other times — well, I needed a fix, I needed to find a place to lean, I needed to clear a space to *listen* — and I couldn't find it, and I — went crazy, I did terrible things to *me*, I was terrible *for* me." He began pressing the beer can between his hands, I watched the metal begin to give. It glittered, as he played with it, like a knife, and I was afraid he would cut himself, but I said nothing. "Oh well. I can never tell you. I was all by myself at the bottom of something, stinking and sweating and crying and shaking, and I smelled it, you know? *my* stink, and I thought I'd die if I couldn't get away from it and yet, all the same, I knew that everything I was doing was just locking me in with it. And I didn't know," he paused, still flattening the beer can, "I didn't know, I still *don't* know, something kept telling me that maybe it was good to smell your own stink, but I didn't think that *that* was what I'd been trying to do — and — who can stand it?" and he abruptly dropped the ruined beer can, looking at me with a small, still smile, and then rose, walking to the window as though it were the lodestone rock. I watched his face, he watched the avenue. "I couldn't tell you when Mama died — but the reason I wanted to leave Harlem so bad was to get away from drugs. And then, when I ran away, that's what I was running from — really. When I came back, nothing had changed, I hadn't changed, I was just — older." And he stopped, drumming with his fingers on the windowpane. The sun had vanished, soon darkness would fall. I watched his face. "It can come again," he said, almost as though speaking to himself. Then he turned to me. "It can come again," he repeated. "I just want you to know that."

"All right," I said, at last. "So it can come again. All right."

He smiled, but the smile was sorrowful. "I had to try to tell you,"   220
he said.

"Yes," I said. "I understand that."

"You're my brother," he said, looking straight at me, and not smiling at all.

"Yes," I repeated, "yes. I understand that."

He turned back to the window, looking out. "All that hatred down there," he said, "all that hatred and misery and love. It's a wonder it doesn't blow the avenue apart."

We went to the only nightclub on a short, dark street, downtown. We   225
squeezed through the narrow, chattering, jam-packed bar to the entrance of the big room, where the bandstand was. And we stood there for a moment,

for the lights were very dim in this room and we couldn't see. Then, "Hello, boy," said a voice and an enormous black man, much older than Sonny or myself, erupted out of all that atmospheric lighting and put an arm around Sonny's shoulder. "I been sitting right here," he said, "waiting for you."

He had a big voice, too, and heads in the darkness turned toward us.

Sonny grinned and pulled a little away, and said, "Creole, this is my brother. I told you about him."

Creole shook my hand. "I'm glad to meet you, son," he said, and it was clear that he was glad to meet me *there* for Sonny's sake. And he smiled, "You got a real musician in *your* family," and he took his arm from Sonny's shoulder and slapped him, lightly, affectionately, with the back of his hand.

"Well. Now I've heard it all," said a voice behind us. This was another musician, and a friend of Sonny's, a coal-black, cheerful-looking man, built close to the ground. He immediately began confiding to me, at the top of his lungs, the most terrible things about Sonny, his teeth gleaming like a lighthouse and his laugh coming up out of him like the beginning of an earthquake. And it turned out that everyone at the bar knew Sonny, or almost everyone; some were musicians, working there, or nearby, or not working, some were simply hangers-on, and some were there to hear Sonny play. I was introduced to all of them and they were all very polite to me. Yet, it was clear that, for them, I was only Sonny's brother. Here, I was in Sonny's world. Or, rather: his kingdom. Here, it was not even a question that his veins bore royal blood.

They were going to play soon and Creole installed me, by myself, at a   230 table in a dark corner. Then I watched them, Creole, and the little black man, and Sonny, and the others, while they horsed around, standing just below the bandstand. The light from the bandstand spilled just a little short of them and, watching them laughing and gesturing and moving about, I had the feeling that they, nevertheless, were being most careful not to step into that circle of light too suddenly: that if they moved into the light too suddenly, without thinking, they would perish in flame. Then, while I watched, one of them, the small, black man, moved into the light and crossed the bandstand and started fooling around with his drums. Then — being funny and being, also, extremely ceremonious — Creole took Sonny by the arm and led him to the piano. A woman's voice called Sonny's name and a few hands started clapping. And Sonny, also being funny and being ceremonious, and so touched, I think, that he could have cried, but neither hiding it nor showing it, riding it like a man, grinned, and put both hands to his heart and bowed from the waist.

Creole then went to the bass fiddle and a lean, very bright-skinned brown man jumped up on the bandstand and picked up his horn. So there they were, and the atmosphere on the bandstand and in the room began to change and tighten. Someone stepped up to the microphone and announced them. Then there were all kinds of murmurs. Some people at the bar shushed others. The waitress ran around, frantically getting in the last orders, guys and chicks got closer to each other, and the lights on the bandstand, on the quartet, turned to a kind of indigo. Then they all looked different there. Creole looked about him for the last time, as though he were making certain that all his chickens were in the coop, and then he—jumped and struck the fiddle. And there they were.

All I know about music is that not many people ever really hear it. And even then, on the rare occasions when something opens within, and the music enters, what we mainly hear, or hear corroborated, are personal, private, vanishing evocations. But the man who creates the music is hearing something else, is dealing with the roar rising from the void and imposing order on it as it hits the air. What is evoked in him, then, is of another order, more terrible because it has no words, and triumphant, too, for that same reason. And his triumph, when he triumphs, is ours. I just watched Sonny's face. His face was troubled, he was working hard, but he wasn't with it. And I had the feeling that, in a way, everyone on the bandstand was waiting for him, both waiting for him and pushing him along. But as I began to watch Creole, I realized that it was Creole who held them all back. He had them on a short rein. Up there, keeping the beat with his whole body, wailing on the fiddle, with his eyes half closed, he was listening to everything, but he was listening to Sonny. He was having a dialogue with Sonny. He wanted Sonny to leave the shoreline and strike out for the deep water. He was Sonny's witness that deep water and drowning were not the same thing—he had been there, and he knew. And he wanted Sonny to know. He was waiting for Sonny to do the things on the keys which would let Creole know that Sonny was in the water.

And, while Creole listened, Sonny moved, deep within, exactly like someone in torment. I had never before thought of how awful the relationship must be between the musician and his instrument. He has to fill it, this instrument, with the breath of life, his own. He has to make it do what he wants it to do. And a piano is just a piano. It's made out of so much wood and wires and little hammers and big ones, and ivory. While there's only so much you can do with it, the only way to find this out is to try; to try and make it do everything.

And Sonny hadn't been near a piano for over a year. And he wasn't on much better terms with his life, not the life that stretched before him now. He and the piano stammered, started one way, got scared, stopped; started another way, panicked, marked time, started again; then seemed to have found a direction, panicked again, got stuck. And the face I saw on Sonny I'd never seen before. Everything had been burned out of it, and, at the same time, things usually hidden were being burned in, by the fire and fury of the battle which was occurring in him up there.

Yet, watching Creole's face as they neared the end of the first set, I had the feeling that something had happened, something I hadn't heard. Then they finished, there was scattered applause, and then, without an instant's warning, Creole started into something else, it was almost sardonic, it was

235

Am I Blue. And, as though he commanded, Sonny began to play. Something began to happen. And Creole let out the reins. The dry, low, black man said something awful on the drums, Creole answered, and the drums talked back. Then the horn insisted, sweet and high, slightly detached perhaps, and Creole listened, commenting now and then, dry, and driving, beautiful and calm and old. Then they all came together again, and Sonny was part of the family again. I could tell this from his face. He seemed to have found, right there beneath his fingers, a damn brand-new piano. It seemed that he couldn't get over it. Then, for awhile, just being happy with Sonny, they seemed to be agreeing with him that brand-new pianos certainly were a gas.

Then Creole stepped forward to remind them that what they were playing was the blues. He hit something in all of them, he hit something in me, myself, and the music tightened and deepened, apprehension began to beat the air. Creole began to tell us what the blues were all about. They were not about anything very new. He and his boys up there were keeping it new, at the risk of ruin, destruction, madness, and death, in order to find new ways to make us listen. For, while the tale of how we suffer, and how we are delighted, and how we may triumph is never new, it always must be heard. There isn't any other tale to tell, it's the only light we've got in all this darkness.

And this tale, according to that face, that body, those strong hands on those strings, has another aspect in every country, and a new depth in every generation. Listen, Creole seemed to be saying, listen. Now these are Sonny's blues. He made the little black man on the drums know it, and the bright, brown man on the horn. Creole wasn't trying any longer to get Sonny in the water. He was wishing him Godspeed. Then he stepped back, very slowly, filling the air with the immense suggestion that Sonny speak for himself.

Then they all gathered around Sonny and Sonny played. Every now and again one of them seemed to say, amen. Sonny's fingers filled the air with life, his life. But that life contained so many others. And Sonny went all the way back, he really began with the spare, flat statement of the opening phrase of the song. Then he began to make it his. It was very beautiful because it wasn't hurried and it was no longer a lament. I seemed to hear with what burning he had made it his, with what burning we had yet to make it ours, how we could cease lamenting. Freedom lurked around us and I understood, at last, that he could help us to be free if we would listen, that he would never be free until we did. Yet, there was no battle in his face now. I heard what he had gone through, and would continue to go through until he came to rest in earth. He had made it his: that long line, of which we knew only Mama and Daddy. And he was giving it back, as everything must be given back, so that, passing through death, it can live forever. I saw my mother's face again, and felt, for the first time, how the stones of the road she had walked on must have bruised her feet. I saw the moonlit road where my father's brother died. And it brought something else back to me, and carried me past it, I saw my little girl again and felt Isabel's tears again, and I felt my own tears begin to rise. And I was yet aware that this was only a moment, that the world waited outside, as hungry as a tiger, and that trouble stretched above us, longer than the sky.

Then it was over. Creole and Sonny let out their breath, both soaking wet, and grinning. There was a lot of applause and some of it was real. In the dark, the girl came by and I asked her to take drinks to the bandstand. There was a long pause, while they talked up there in the indigo light and after awhile I saw the girl put a Scotch and milk on top of the piano for Sonny. He didn't seem to notice it, but just before they started playing again, he sipped from it and looked toward me, and nodded. Then he put it back on top of the piano. For me, then, as they began to play again, it glowed and shook above my brother's head like the very cup of trembling.

FLANNERY O'CONNOR (1925–1964)

A Temple of the Holy Ghost

All weekend the two girls were calling each other Temple One and Temple Two, shaking with laughter and getting so red and hot that they were positively ugly, particularly Joanne who had spots on her face anyway. They came in the brown convent uniforms they had to wear to Mount St. Scholastica but as soon as they opened their suitcases, they took off the uniforms and put on red skirts and loud blouses. They put on lipstick and their Sunday shoes and walked around in the high heels all over the house, always passing the long mirror in the hall slowly to get a look at their legs. None of their ways were lost on the child. If only one of them had come, that one would have played with her, but since there were two of them, she was out of it and watched them suspiciously from a distance.

They were fourteen — two years older than she was — but neither of them was bright, which was why they had been sent to the convent. If they had gone to a regular school, they wouldn't have done anything but think about boys; at the convent the sisters, her mother said, would keep a grip on their necks. The child decided, after observing them for a few hours, that they were practically morons and she was glad to think that they were only second cousins and she couldn't have inherited any of their stupidity. Susan called herself Su-zan. She was very skinny but she had a pretty pointed face and red hair. Joanne had yellow hair that was naturally curly but she talked through her nose and when she laughed, she turned purple in patches. Neither one of them could say an intelligent thing and all their sentences began, "You know this boy I know well one time he . . ."

They were to stay all weekend and her mother said she didn't see how she would entertain them since she didn't know any boys their age. At this, the child, struck suddenly with genius, shouted, "There's Cheat! Get Cheat to come! Ask Miss Kirby to get Cheat to come show them around!" and she nearly choked on the food she had in her mouth. She doubled over laughing and hit the table with her fist and looked at the two bewildered girls while water started in her eyes and rolled down her fat cheeks and the braces she had in her mouth glared like tin. She had never thought of anything so funny before.

Her mother laughed in a guarded way and Miss Kirby blushed and carried her fork delicately to her mouth with one pea on it. She was a long-faced blonde schoolteacher who boarded with them and Mr. Cheatam was her admirer, a rich old farmer who arrived every Saturday afternoon in a fifteen-year-old baby-blue Pontiac powdered with red clay dust and black inside with Negroes that he charged ten cents apiece to bring into town on Saturday afternoons. After he dumped them he came to see Miss Kirby, always bringing a little gift — a bag of boiled peanuts or a watermelon or a stalk of sugar cane and once a wholesale box of Baby Ruth candy bars. He was bald-headed except for a little fringe of rust-colored hair and his face was nearly the same color as the unpaved roads and washed like them with ruts and gulleys. He wore a pale green shirt with a thin black stripe in it and blue galluses and his trousers cut across a protruding stomach that he pressed tenderly from time to time with his big flat thumb. All his teeth were backed with gold and he would roll his eyes at Miss Kirby in an impish way and say, "Haw haw," sitting in their porch swing with his legs spread apart and his hightopped shoes pointing in opposite directions on the floor.

"I don't think Cheat is going to be in town this weekend," Miss Kirby   5
said, not in the least understanding that this was a joke, and the child was convulsed afresh, threw herself backward in her chair, fell out of it, rolled on the floor, and lay there heaving. Her mother told her if she didn't stop this foolishness she would have to leave the table.

Yesterday her mother had arranged with Alonzo Myers to drive them the forty-five miles to Mayville, where the convent was, to get the girls for the weekend and Sunday afternoon he was hired to drive them back again. He was an eighteen-year-old boy who weighed two hundred and fifty pounds and worked for the taxi company and he was all you could get to drive you anywhere. He smoked or rather chewed a short black cigar and he had a round sweaty chest that showed through the yellow nylon shirt he wore. When he drove all the windows of the car had to be open.

"Well there's Alonzo!" the child roared from the floor. "Get Alonzo to show em around! Get Alonzo!"

The two girls, who had seen Alonzo, began to scream their indignation.

Her mother thought this was funny too but she said, "That'll be about enough out of you," and changed the subject. She asked them why they called each other Temple One and Temple Two and this sent them off into gales of giggles. Finally they managed to explain. Sister Perpetua, the oldest nun at the Sisters of Mercy in Mayville, had given them a lecture on what to do if a young man should — here they laughed so hard they were not able to go on without going back to the beginning — on what to do if a young man should — they put their heads in their laps — on what to do if — they finally managed to shout it out — if he should "behave in an ungentlemanly manner with them in the back of an automobile." Sister Perpetua said they were to say, "Stop sir! I am a Temple of the Holy Ghost!" and that would put an end to it. The child sat up off the floor with a blank face. She didn't see anything so funny in this. What was really funny was the idea of Mr. Cheatam or Alonzo Myers beauing them around. That killed her.

Her mother didn't laugh at what they had said. "I think you girls are   10
pretty silly," she said. "After all, that's what you are — Temples of the Holy Ghost."

The two of them looked up at her, politely concealing their giggles, but with astonished faces as if they were beginning to realize that she was made of the same stuff as Sister Perpetua.

Miss Kirby preserved her set expression and the child thought, it's all over her head anyhow. I am a Temple of the Holy Ghost, she said to herself, and was pleased with the phrase. It made her feel as if somebody had given her a present.

After dinner, her mother collapsed on the bed and said, "Those girls are going to drive me crazy if I don't get some entertainment for them. They're awful."

"I bet I know who you could get," the child started.

"Now listen. I don't want to hear any more about Mr. Cheatam," her   15
mother said. "You embarrass Miss Kirby. He's her only friend. Oh my Lord," and she sat up and looked mournfully out the window, "that poor soul is so lonesome she'll even ride in that car that smells like the last circle in hell."

And she's a Temple of the Holy Ghost too, the child reflected. "I wasn't thinking of him," she said. "I was thinking of those two Wilkinses, Wendell and Cory, that visit old lady Buchell out on her farm. They're her grandsons. They work for her."

"Now that's an idea," her mother murmured and gave her an appreciative look. But then she slumped again. "They're only farm boys. These girls would turn up their noses at them."

"Huh," the child said. "They wear pants. They're sixteen and they got a car. Somebody said they were both going to be Church of God preachers because you don't have to know nothing to be one."

"They would be perfectly safe with those boys all right," her mother said and in a minute she got up and called their grandmother on the telephone and after she had talked to the old woman a half an hour, it was arranged that Wendell and Cory would come to supper and afterwards take the girls to the fair.

Susan and Joanne were so pleased that they washed their hair and rolled   20
it up on aluminum curlers. Hah, thought the child, sitting crosslegged on the bed to watch them undo the curlers, wait'll you get a load of Wendell and Cory! "You'll like these boys," she said. "Wendell is six feet tall ands got red hair. Cory is six feet six inches talls got black hair and wears a sport jacket and they gottem this car with a squirrel tail on the front."

"How does a child like you know so much about these men?" Susan asked and pushed her face up close to the mirror to watch the pupils in her eyes dilate.

The child lay back on the bed and began to count the narrow boards in the ceiling until she lost her place. I know them all right, she said to someone. We fought in the world war together. They were under me and I saved them five times from Japanese suicide divers and Wendell said I am going to marry that kid and the other said oh no you ain't I am and I said neither one of you is because I will court marshall you all before you can bat an eye. "I've seen them around is all," she said.

When they came the girls stared at them a second and then began to giggle and talk to each other about the convent. They sat in the swing together and Wendell and Cory sat on the banisters together. They sat like monkeys, their knees on a level with their shoulders and their arms hanging down between. They were short thin boys with red faces and high cheek-bones and pale seed-like eyes. They had brought a harmonica and a guitar. One of them began to blow softly on the mouth organ, watching the girls over it, and the other started strumming the guitar and then began to sing, not watching them but keeping his head tilted upward as if he were only interested in hearing himself. He was singing a hillbilly song that sounded half like a love song and half like a hymn.

The child was standing on a barrel pushed into some bushes at the side of the house, her face on a level with the porch floor. The sun was going down and the sky was turning a bruised violet color that seemed to be connected with the sweet mournful sound of the music. Wendell began to smile as he sang and to look at the girls. He looked at Susan with a dog-like loving look and sang,

> I've found a friend in Jesus,
> He's everything to me,
> He's the lily of the valley,
> He's the One who's set me free!

Then he turned the same look on Joanne and sang,

25

> A wall of fire about me,
> I've nothing now to fear,
> He's the lily of the valley,
> And I'll always have Him near!

The girls looked at each other and held their lips stiff so as not to giggle but Susan let out one anyway and clapped her hand on her mouth. The singer frowned and for a few seconds only strummed the guitar. Then he began "The Old Rugged Cross" and they listened politely but when he had finished they said, "Let us sing one!" and before he could start another, they began to sing with their convent-trained voices,

> Tantum ergo Sacramentum
>   Veneremur Cernui:
> Et antiquum documentum
>   Novo cedat ritui:

The child watched the boys' solemn faces turn with perplexed frowning stares at each other as if they were uncertain whether they were being made fun of.

> Praestet fides supplementum
>   Sensuum defectui.
> Genitori, Genitoque
>   Laus et jubilatio

> Salus, honor, virtus quoque . . .

The boys' faces were dark red in the gray-purple light. They looked fierce and startled.

Sit et benedictio;
Procedenti ab utroque
Compar sit laudatio.
Amen.

The girls dragged out the Amen and then there was a silence.

"That must be Jew singing," Wendell said and began to tune the guitar.   30

The girls giggled idiotically but the child stamped her foot on the barrel. "You big dumb ox!" she shouted. "You big dumb Church of God ox!" she roared and fell off the barrel and scrambled up and shot around the corner of the house as they jumped from the banister to see who was shouting.

Her mother had arranged for them to have supper in the back yard and she had a table laid out there under some Japanese lanterns that she pulled out for garden parties. "I ain't eating with them," the child said and snatched her plate off the table and carried it to the kitchen and sat down with the thin blue-gummed cook and ate her supper.

"Howcome you be so ugly sometime?" the cook asked.

"Those stupid idiots," the child said.

The lanterns gilded the leaves of the trees orange on the level where   35 they hung and above them was black-green and below them were different dim muted colors that made the girls sitting at the table look prettier than they were. From time to time, the child turned her head and glared out the kitchen window at the scene below.

"God could strike you deaf dumb and blind," the cook said, "and then you wouldn't be as smart as you is."

"I would still be smarter than some," the child said.

After supper they left for the fair. She wanted to go to the fair but not with them so even if they had asked her she wouldn't have gone. She went upstairs and paced the long bedroom with her hands locked together behind her back and her head thrust forward and an expression, fierce and dreamy both, on her face. She didn't turn on the electric light but let the darkness collect and make the room smaller and more private. At regular intervals a light crossed the open window and threw shadows on the wall. She stopped and stood looking out over the dark slopes, past where the pond glinted silver, past the wall of woods to the speckled sky where a long finger of light was revolving up and around and away, searching the air as if it were hunting for the lost sun. It was the beacon light from the fair.

She could hear the distant sound of the calliope and she saw in her head all the tents raised up in a kind of gold sawdust light and the diamond ring of the ferris wheel going around and around up in the air and down again and the screeking merry-go-round going around and around on the ground. A fair lasted five or six days and there was a special afternoon for school children and a special night for niggers. She had gone last year on the afternoon for school children and had seen the monkeys and the fat man and had ridden on the ferris wheel. Certain tents were closed then because they contained things that would be known only to grown people but she had looked with interest at the advertising on the closed tents, at the faded-looking pictures on the canvas of people in tights, with stiff stretched composed faces like the faces of the martyrs waiting to have their tongues cut out by the Roman soldier. She had imagined that what was inside these tents concerned medicine and she had made up her mind to be a doctor when she grew up.

She had since changed and decided to be an engineer but as she looked out the window and followed the revolving searchlight as it widened and shortened and wheeled in its arc, she felt that she would have to be much more than just a doctor or an engineer. She would have to be a saint because that was the occupation that included everything you could know; and yet she knew she would never be a saint. She did not steal or murder but she was a born liar and slothful and she sassed her mother and was deliberately ugly to almost everybody. She was eaten up also with the sin of Pride, the worst one. She made fun of the Baptist preacher who came to the school at commencement to give the devotional. She would pull down her mouth and hold her forehead as if she were in agony and groan, "Fawther, we thank Thee," exactly the way he did and she had been told many times not to do it. She could never be a saint, but she thought she could be a martyr if they killed her quick. 40

She could stand to be shot but not to be burned in oil. She didn't know if she could stand to be torn to pieces by lions or not. She began to prepare her martyrdom, seeing herself in a pair of tights in a great arena, lit by the early Christians hanging in cages of fire, making a gold dusty light that fell on her and the lions. The first lion charged forward and fell at her feet, converted. A whole series of lions did the same. The lions liked her so much she even slept with them and finally the Romans were obliged to burn her but to their astonishment she would not burn down and finding she was so hard to kill, they finally cut off her head very quickly with a sword and she went immediately to heaven. She rehearsed this several times, returning each time at the entrance of Paradise to the lions.

Finally she got up from the window and got ready for bed and got in without saying her prayers. There were two heavy double beds in the room. The girls were occupying the other one and she tried to think of something cold and clammy that she could hide in their bed but her thought was fruitless. She didn't have anything she could think of, like a chicken carcass or a piece of beef liver. The sound of the calliope coming through the window kept her awake and she remembered that she hadn't said her prayers and got up and knelt down and began them. She took a running start and went through to the other side of the Apostle's Creed and then hung by her chin on the side of the bed, empty-minded. Her prayers, when she remembered to say them, were usually perfunctory but sometimes when she had done something wrong or heard music or lost something, or sometimes for no reason at all, she would be moved to fervor and would think of Christ on the long journey to Calvary, crushed three times on the rough cross. Her mind would stay on this a while and then get empty and when something roused her, she would find that she was thinking of a different thing entirely, of some dog or some girl or something she was going to do some day. Tonight, remembering Wendell and Cory, she was filled with thanksgiving and almost weeping with delight, she said, "Lord, Lord, thank You that I'm not in the Church of God, thank You Lord, thank You!" and got back in bed and kept repeating it until she went to sleep.

The girls came in at a quarter to twelve and waked her up with their giggling. They turned on the small blue-shaded lamp to see to get undressed by and their skinny shadows climbed up the wall and broke and continued moving about softly on the ceiling. The child sat up to hear what all they had seen at the fair. Susan had a plastic pistol full of cheap candy and Joanne a pasteboard cat with red polka dots on it. "Did you see the monkeys dance?" the child asked. "Did you see that fat man and those midgets?"

"All kinds of freaks," Joanne said. And then she said to Susan, "I enjoyed it all but the you-know-what," and her face assumed a peculiar expression as if she had bit into something that she didn't know if she liked or not.

The other stood still and shook her head once and nodded slightly at   45 the child. "Little pitchers," she said in a low voice but the child heard it and her heart began to beat very fast.

She got out of bed and climbed onto the footboard of theirs. They turned off the light and got in but she didn't move. She sat there, looking hard at them until their faces were well defined in the dark. "I'm not as old as you all," she said, "but I'm about a million times smarter."

"There are some things," Susan said, "that a child of your age doesn't know," and they both began to giggle.

"Go back to your own bed," Joanne said.

The child didn't move. "One time," she said, her voice hollow-sounding in the dark, "I saw this rabbit have rabbits."

There was a silence. Then Susan said, "How?" in an indifferent tone   50 and she knew that she had them. She said she wouldn't tell until they told about the you-know-what. Actually she had never seen a rabbit have rabbits but she forgot this as they began to tell what they had seen in the tent.

It had been a freak with a particular name but they couldn't remember the name. The tent where it was had been divided into two parts by a black curtain, one side for men and one for women. The freak went from one side to the other, talking first to the men and then to the women, but everyone could hear. The stage ran all the way across the front. The girls heard the freak say to the men, "I'm going to show you this and if you laugh, God may strike you the same way." The freak had a country voice, slow and nasal and neither high nor low, just flat. "God made me thisaway and if you laugh He may strike you the same way. This is the way He wanted me to be and I ain't disputing His way. I'm showing you because I got to make the best of it. I expect you to act like ladies and gentlemen. I never done it to myself nor had a thing to do with it but I'm making the best of it. I don't dispute hit." Then there was a long silence on the other side of the tent and finally the freak left the men and came over onto the women's side and said the same thing.

The child felt every muscle strained as if she were hearing the answer to a riddle that was more puzzling than the riddle itself. "You mean it had two heads?" she said.

"No," Susan said, "it was a man and woman both. It pulled up its dress and showed us. It had on a blue dress."

The child wanted to ask how it could be a man and woman both without two heads but she did not. She wanted to get back into her own bed and think it out and she began to climb down off the footboard.

"What about the rabbit?" Joanne asked.   55

The child stopped and only her face appeared over the footboard, abstracted, absent. "It spit them out of its mouth," she said, "six of them."

She lay in bed trying to picture the tent with the freak walking from side to side but she was too sleepy to figure it out. She was better able to see the faces of the country people watching, the men more solemn than they were in church, and the women stern and polite, with painted-looking eyes, standing as if they were waiting for the first note of the piano to begin the hymn. She could hear the freak saying, "God made me thisaway and I don't dispute hit," and the people saying, "Amen. Amen."

"God done this to me and I praise Him."

"Amen. Amen."

"He could strike you thisaway."   60

"Amen. Amen."

"But He has not."

"Amen."

"Raise yourself up. A temple of the Holy Ghost. You! You are God's temple, don't you know? Don't you know? God's Spirit has a dwelling in you, don't you know?"

"Amen. Amen."   65

"If anybody desecrates the temple of God, God will bring him to ruin and if you laugh, He may strike you thisaway. A temple of God is a holy thing. Amen. Amen."

"I am a temple of the Holy Ghost."

"Amen."

The people began to slap their hands without making a loud noise and with a regular beat between the Amens, more and more softly, as if they knew there was a child near, half asleep.

The next afternoon the girls put on their brown convent uniforms   70
again and the child and her mother took them back to Mount St. Scholastica.

"Oh glory, oh Pete!" they said. "Back to the salt mines." Alonzo Myers drove them and the child sat in front with him and her mother sat in back between the two girls, telling them such things as how pleased she was to have had them and how they must come back again and then about the good times she and their mothers had had when they were girls at the convent. The child didn't listen to any of this twaddle but kept as close to the locked door as she could get and held her head out the window. They had thought Alonzo would smell better on Sunday but he did not. With her hair blowing over her face she could look directly into the ivory sun which was framed in the middle of the blue afternoon but when she pulled it away from her eyes she had to squint.

Mount St. Scholastica was a red brick house set back in a garden in the center of town. There was a filling station on one side of it and a firehouse on the other. It had a high black grillework fence around it and narrow bricked walks between old trees and japonica bushes that were heavy with blooms. A big moon-faced nun came bustling to the door to let them in and embraced her mother and would have done the same to her but she stuck out her hand and preserved a frigid frown, looking just past the sister's shoes at the wainscoting. They had a tendency to kiss even homely children, but the nun shook her hand vigorously and even cracked her knuckles a little and said they must come to the chapel, that benediction was just beginning. You put your foot in their door and they got you praying, the child thought as they hurried down the polished corridor.

You'd think she had to catch a train, she continued in the same ugly vein as they entered the chapel where the sisters were kneeling on one side and the girls, all in brown uniforms, on the other. The chapel smelled of incense. It was light green and gold, a series of springing arches that ended with the one over the altar where the priest was kneeling in front of the monstrance, bowed low. A small boy in a surplice was standing behind him, swinging the censer. The child knelt down between her mother and the nun and they were well into the *"Tantum Ergo"* before her ugly thoughts stopped and she began to realize that she was in the presence of God. Hep me not to be so mean, she began mechanically. Hep me not to give her so much sass. Hep me not to talk like I do. Her mind began to get quiet and then empty but when the priest raised the monstrance with the Host shining ivory-colored in the center of it, she was thinking of the tent at the fair that had the freak in it. The freak was saying, "I don't dispute hit. This is the way He wanted me to be."

As they were leaving the convent door, the big nun swooped down on her mischievously and nearly smothered her in the black habit, mashing the side of her face into the crucifix hitched onto her belt and then holding her off and looking at her with little periwinkle eyes.

On the way home she and her mother sat in the back and Alonzo drove by himself in the front. The child observed three folds of fat in the back of his neck and noted that his ears were pointed almost like a pig's. Her mother, making conversation, asked him if he had gone to the fair.

"Gone," he said, "and never missed a thing and it was good I gone   75 when I did because they ain't going to have it next week like they said they was."

"Why?" asked her mother.

"They shut it on down," he said. "Some of the preachers from town gone out and inspected it and got the police to shut it on down."

Her mother let the conversation drop and the child's round face was lost in thought. She turned it toward the window and looked out over a stretch of pasture land that rose and fell with a gathering greenness until it touched the dark woods. The sun was a huge red ball like an elevated Host drenched in blood and when it sank out of sight, it left a line in the sky like a red clay road hanging over the trees.

GABRIEL GARCÍA MÁRQUEZ (1928–   )

The Handsomest Drowned Man in the World
A Tale for Children

The first children who saw the dark and slinky bulge approaching through the sea let themselves think it was an enemy ship. Then they saw it had no flags or masts and they thought it was a whale. But when it washed up on the beach, they removed the clumps of seaweed, the jellyfish tentacles, and the remains of fish and flotsam, and only then did they see that it was a drowned man.

They had been playing with him all afternoon, burying him in the sand and digging him up again, when someone chanced to see them and spread the alarm in the village. The men who carried him to the nearest house noticed that he weighed more than any dead man they had ever known, almost as much as a horse, and they said to each other that maybe he'd been floating too long and the water had got into his bones. When they laid him on the floor they said he'd been taller than all other men because there was barely enough room for him in the house, but they thought that maybe the ability to keep on growing after death was part of the nature of certain drowned men. He had the smell of the sea about him and only his shape gave one to suppose that it was the corpse of a human being, because the skin was covered with a crust of mud and scales.

They did not even have to clean off his face to know that the dead man was a stranger. The village was made up of only twenty-odd wooden houses that had stone courtyards with no flowers and which were spread about on the end of a desertlike cape. There was so little land that mothers always went about with the fear that the wind would carry off their children and the few dead that the years had caused among them had to be thrown off the cliffs. But the sea was calm and bountiful and all the men fit into seven boats. So when they found the drowned man they simply had to look at one another to see that they were all there.

That night they did not go out to work at sea. While the men went to find out if anyone was missing in neighboring villages, the women stayed behind to care for the drowned man. They took the mud off with grass swabs, they removed the underwater stones entangled in his hair, and they scraped the crust off with tools used for scaling fish. As they were doing that they noticed that the vegetation on him came from faraway oceans and deep water and that his clothes were in tatters, as if he had sailed through labyrinths of coral. They noticed too that he bore his death with pride, for he did not have the lonely look of other drowned men who came out of the sea or that haggard, needy look of men who drowned in rivers. But only when they finished cleaning him off did they become aware of the kind of man he was and it left them breathless. Not only was he the tallest, strongest, most virile, and best built man they had ever seen, but even though they were looking at him there was no room for him in their imagination.

They could not find a bed in the village large enough to lay him on   5 nor was there a table solid enough to use for his wake. The tallest men's holiday pants would not fit him, nor the fattest ones' Sunday shirts, nor the shoes of the one with the biggest feet. Fascinated by his huge size and his beauty, the women then decided to make him some pants from a large piece of sail and a shirt from some bridal brabant linen so that he could continue through his death with dignity. As they sewed, sitting in a circle and gazing at the corpse between stitches, it seemed to them that the wind had never been so steady nor the sea so restless as on that night and they supposed that the change had something to do with the dead man. They thought that if that magnificent man had lived in the village, his house would have had the widest doors, the highest ceiling, and the strongest floor, his bedstead would have been made from a midship frame held together by iron bolts, and his wife would have been the happiest woman. They thought that he would have had so much authority that he could have drawn fish out of the sea simply by calling their names and that he would have put so much work into his land that springs would have burst forth from among the rocks so that he would have been able to plant flowers on the cliffs. They secretly compared him to their own men, thinking that for all their lives theirs were incapable of doing what he could do in one night, and they ended up dismissing them deep in their hearts as the weakest, meanest, and most useless creatures on earth. They were wandering through that maze of fantasy when the oldest woman, who as the oldest had looked upon the drowned man with more compassion than passion, sighed:

"He has the face of someone called Esteban."

It was true. Most of them had only to take another look at him to see that he could not have any other name. The more stubborn among them, who were the youngest, still lived for a few hours with the illusion that when they put his clothes on and he lay among the flowers in patent leather shoes his name might be Lautaro. But it was a vain illusion. There had not been enough canvas, the poorly cut and worse sewn pants were too tight, and the hidden strength of his heart popped the buttons on his shirt. After midnight the whistling of the wind died down and the sea fell into its Wednesday drowsiness. The silence put an end to any last doubts: he was Esteban. The women who had dressed him, who had combed his hair, had cut his nails and shaved him were unable to hold back a shudder of pity when they had to resign themselves to his being dragged along the ground. It was then that they understood how unhappy he must have been with that huge body since it bothered him even after death. They could see him in life, condemned to going through doors sideways, cracking his head on crossbeams, remaining on his feet during visits, not knowing what to do with his soft, pink, sea lion hands while the lady of the house looked for her most resistant chair and begged him, frightened to death, sit here, Esteban, please, and he, leaning against the wall, smiling, don't bother, ma'am, I'm fine where I am, his heels raw and his back roasted from having done the same thing so many times whenever he paid a visit, don't bother, ma'am, I'm fine where I am, just to avoid the embarrassment of breaking up the chair, and never knowing perhaps that the ones who said don't go, Esteban, at least wait till the coffee's ready, were the ones who later on would whisper the big boob finally left, how nice, the handsome fool has gone. That was what the women were thinking beside the body a little before dawn. Later, when they covered his face with a handkerchief so that the light would not bother him, he looked so forever dead, so defenseless, so much like their men that the first furrows of tears opened in their hearts. It was one of the younger ones who began the weeping. The others coming to, went from sighs to wails, and the more they sobbed the more they felt like weeping, because the drowned man was becoming all the more Esteban for them, and so they wept so much, for he was the most destitute, most peaceful, and most obliging man on earth, poor Esteban. So when the men returned with the news that the drowned man was not from the neighboring villages either, the women felt an opening of jubilation in the midst of their tears.

"Praise the Lord," they sighed, "he's ours!"

The men thought the fuss was only womanish frivolity. Fatigued because of the difficult nighttime inquiries, all they wanted was to get rid of the bother of the newcomer once and for all before the sun grew strong on that arid, windless day. They improvised a litter with the remains of foremasts and gaffs, tying it together with rigging so that it would bear the weight of the body until they reached the cliffs. They wanted to tie the anchor from a cargo ship to him so that he would sink easily into the deepest waves, where fish are blind and divers die of nostalgia, and bad currents would not bring him back to shore, as had happened with other bodies. But the more they hurried, the more the women thought of ways to waste time. They walked about like startled hens, pecking with the sea charms on their breasts, some interfering on one side to put a scapular of the good wind on the drowned man, some on the other side to put a wrist compass on him, and after a great deal of *get away from there, woman, stay out of the way, look, you almost made me fall on top of the dead man,* the men began to feel mistrust in their livers and started grumbling about why so many main-altar decorations for a stranger, because no matter how many nails and holy-water jars he had on him, the sharks would chew him all the same, but the women kept piling on their junk relics, running back and forth, stumbling, while they released in sighs what they did not in tears, so that the men finally exploded with *since when has there ever been such a fuss over a drifting corpse, a drowned nobody, a piece of cold Wednesday meat.* One of the women, mortified by so much lack of care, then removed the handkerchief from the dead man's face and the men were left breathless too.

He was Esteban. It was not necessary to repeat it for them to recognize   10
him. If they had been told Sir Walter Raleigh, even they might have been
impressed with his gringo accent, the macaw on his shoulder, his cannibal-
killing blunderbuss, but there could be only one Esteban in the world and
there he was, stretched out like a sperm whale, shoeless, wearing the pants
of an undersized child, and with those stony nails that had to be cut with a
knife. They only had to take the handkerchief off his face to see that he was
ashamed, that it was not his fault that he was so big or so heavy or so
handsome, and if he had known that this was going to happen, he would
have looked for a more discreet place to drown in, seriously, I even would
have tied the anchor off a galleon around my neck and staggered off a cliff
like someone who doesn't like things in order not to be upsetting people
now with this Wednesday dead body, as you people say, in order not to be
bothering anyone with this filthy piece of cold meat that doesn't have anything to do with me. There was so much truth in his manner that even the
most mistrustful men, the ones who felt the bitterness of endless nights at
sea fearing that their women would tire of dreaming about them and begin
to dream of drowned men, even they and others who were harder still
shuddered in the marrow of their bones at Esteban's sincerity.

That was how they came to hold the most splendid funeral they could
conceive of for an abandoned drowned man. Some women who had gone to
get flowers in the neighboring villages returned with other women who
could not believe what they had been told, and those women went back for
more flowers when they saw the dead man, and they brought more and
more until there were so many flowers and so many people that it was hard
to walk about. At the final moment it pained them to return him to the
waters as an orphan and they chose a father and mother from among the
best people, and aunts and uncles and cousins, so that through him all the inhabitants of the village became kinsmen. Some sailors who heard the
weeping from a distance went off course and people heard of one who had
himself tied to the mainmast, remembering ancient fables about sirens.
While they fought for the privilege of carrying him on their shoulders along
the steep escarpment by the cliffs, men and women became aware for the
first time of the desolation of their streets, the dryness of their courtyards,
the narrowness of their dreams as they faced the splendor and beauty of their
drowned man. They let him go without an anchor so that he could come
back if he wished and whenever he wished, and they all held their breath for
the fraction of centuries the body took to fall into the abyss. They did not
need to look at one another to realize that they were no longer all present,
that they would never be. But they also knew that everything would be
different from then on, that their houses would have wider doors, higher
ceilings, and stronger floors so that Esteban's memory could go everywhere
without bumping into beams and so that no one in the future would dare
whisper the big boob finally died, too bad, the handsome fool has finally

died, because they were going to paint their house fronts gay colors to make Esteban's memory eternal and they were going to break their backs digging for springs among the stones and planting flowers on the cliffs so that in future years at dawn the passengers on great liners would awaken, suffocated by the smell of gardens on the high seas, and the captain would have to come down from the bridge in his dress uniform, with his astrolabe, his pole star, and his row of war medals and, pointing to the promontory of roses on the horizon, he would say in fourteen languages, look there, where the wind is so peaceful now that it's gone to sleep beneath the beds, over there, where the sun's so bright that the sunflowers don't know which way to turn, yes, over there, that's Esteban's village.

CHINUA ACHEBE (1930–   )

Marriage Is a Private Affair

"Have you written to your dad yet?" asked Nene one afternoon as she sat with Nnaemeka in her room at 16 Kasanga Street, Lagos.

"No. I've been thinking about it. I think it's better to tell him when I get home on leave!"

"But why? Your leave is such a long way off yet — six whole weeks. He should be let into our happiness now."

Nnaemeka was silent for a while, and then began very slowly as if he groped for his words: "I wish I were sure it would be happiness to him."

"Of course it must," replied Nene, a little surprised. "Why shouldn't it?"   5

"You have lived in Lagos all your life, and you know very little about people in remote parts of the country."

"That's what you always say. But I don't believe anybody will be so unlike other people that they will be unhappy when their sons are engaged to marry."

"Yes. They are most unhappy if the engagement is not arranged by them. In our case it's worse — you are not even an Ibo."

This was said so seriously and so bluntly that Nene could not find speech immediately. In the cosmopolitan atmosphere of the city it had always seemed to her something of a joke that a person's tribe could determine whom he married.

At last she said, "You don't really mean that he will object to your   10 marrying me simply on that account? I had always thought you Ibos were kindly disposed to other people."

"So we are. But when it comes to marriage, well, its not quite so simple. And this," he added, "is not peculiar to the Ibos. If your father were alive and lived in the heart of Ibibio-land he would be exactly like my father."

"I don't know. But anyway, as your father is so fond of you, I'm sure he will forgive you soon enough. Come on then, be a good boy and send him a nice lovely letter . . ."

"It would not be wise to break the news to him by writing. A letter will bring it upon him with a shock. I'm quite sure about that."

"All right, honey, suit yourself. You know your father."

As Nnaemeka walked home that evening he turned over in his mind   15 the different ways of overcoming his father's opposition, especially now that he had gone and found a girl for him. He had thought of showing his letter to Nene but decided on second thoughts not to, at least for the moment. He read it again when he got home and couldn't help smiling to himself. He remembered Ugoye quite well, an Amazon of a girl who used to beat up all the boys, himself included, on the way to the stream, a complete dunce at school.

> I have found a girl who will suit you admirably — Ugoye Nweke, the eldest daughter of our neighbour, Jacob Nweke. She has a proper Christian upbringing. When she stopped schooling some years ago her father (a man of sound judgment) sent her to live in the house of a pastor where she has received all the training a wife could need. Her Sunday School teacher has told me that she reads her Bible very fluently. I hope we shall begin negotiations when you come home in December.

On the second evening of his return from Lagos Nnaemeka sat with his father under a cassia tree. This was the old man's retreat where he went to read his Bible when the parching December sun had set and a fresh, reviving wind blew on the leaves.

"Father," began Nnaemeka suddenly, "I have come to ask forgiveness."

"Forgiveness? For what, my son?" he asked in amazement.

"It's about this marriage question!"

"Which marriage question." 20

"I can't — we must — I mean it is impossible for me to marry Nweke's daughter."

"Impossible? Why?" asked his father.

"I don't love her."

"Nobody said you did. Why should you?" he asked.

"Marriage today is different . . ." 25

"Look here, my son," interrupted his father, "nothing is different. What one looks for in a wife are a good character and a Christian background."

Nnaemeka saw there was no hope along the present line of argument.

"Moreover," he said, "I am engaged to marry another girl who has all of Ugoye's good qualities, and who . . ."

His father did not believe his ears. "What did you say?" he asked slowly and disconcertingly.

"She is a good Christian," his son went on, "and a teacher in a Girls' 30 School in Lagos."

"Teacher, did you say? If you consider that a qualification for a good wife I should like to point out to you, Emeka, that no Christian woman should teach. St. Paul in his letter to the Corinthians says that women should keep silence." He rose slowly from his seat and paced forwards and backwards. This was his pet subject, and he condemned vehemently those church leaders who encouraged women to teach in their schools. After he had spent his emotion on a long homily he at last came back to his son's engagement, in a seemingly milder tone.

"Whose daughter is she, anyway?"

"She is Nene Atang."

"What!" All the mildness was gone again. "Did you say Neneataga, what does that mean?"

"Nene Atang from Calabar. She is the only girl I can marry." This was   35
a very rash reply and Nnaemeka expected the storm to burst. But it did not. His father merely walked away into his room. This was most unexpected and perplexed Nnaemeka. His father's silence was infinitely more menacing than a flood of threatening speech. That night the old man did not eat.

When he sent for Nnaemeka a day later he applied all possible ways of dissuasion. But the young man's heart was hardened, and his father eventually gave him up as lost.

"I owe it to you, my son, as a duty to show you what is right and what is wrong. Whoever put this idea into your head might as well have cut your throat. It is Satan's work." He waved his son away.

"You will change your mind, Father, when you know Nene."

"I shall never see her," was the reply. From that night the father scarcely spoke to his son. He did not, however, cease hoping that he would realize how serious was the danger he was heading for. Day and night he put him in his prayers.

Nnaemeka, for his own part, was very deeply affected by his father's   40
grief. But he kept hoping that it would pass away. If it had occurred to him that never in the history of his people had a man married a woman who spoke a different tongue, he might have been less optimistic. "It has never been heard," was the verdict of an old man speaking a few weeks later. In that short sentence he spoke for all of his people. This man had come with others to commiserate with Okeke when news went round about his son's behaviour. By that time the son had gone back to Lagos.

"It has never been heard," said the old man again with a sad shake of his head.

"What did Our Lord say?" asked another gentleman. "Sons shall rise against their Fathers; it is there in the Holy Book."

"It is the beginning of the end," said another.

The discussion thus tending to become theological, Madubogwu, a highly practical man, brought it down once more to the ordinary level.

"Have you thought of consulting a native doctor about your son?" he   45
asked Nnaemeka's father.

"He isn't sick," was the reply.

"What is he then? The boy's mind is diseased and only a good herbalist can bring him back to his right senses. The medicine he requires is *Amalile,* the same that women apply with success to recapture their husbands' straying affection."

"Madubogwu is right," said another gentleman. "This thing calls for medicine."

"I shall not call in a native doctor." Nnaemeka's father was known to be obstinately ahead of his more superstitious neighbours in these matters.

"I will not be another Mrs. Ochuba. If my son wants to kill himself let him do it with his own hands. It is not for me to help him."

"But it was her fault," said Madubogwu. "She ought to have gone to an honest herbalist. She was a clever woman, nevertheless." 50

"She was a wicked murderess," said Jonathan who rarely argued with his neighbours because, he often said, they were incapable of reasoning. "The medicine was prepared for her husband, it was his name they called in its preparation and I am sure it would have been perfectly beneficial to him. It was wicked to put it into the herbalist's food, and say you were only trying it out."

Six months later, Nnaemeka was showing his young wife a short letter from his father:

> It amazes me that you could be so unfeeling as to send me your wedding picture. I would have sent it back. But on further thought I decided just to cut off your wife and sent it back to you because I have nothing to do with her. How I wish that I had nothing to do with you either.

When Nene read through this letter and looked at the mutilated picture her eyes filled with tears, and she began to sob.

"Don't cry, my darling," said her husband. "He is essentially good-natured and will one day look more kindly on our marriage." But years passed and that one day did not come.

For eight years, Okeke would have nothing to do with his son, Nnae- 55 meka. Only three times (when Nnaemeka asked to come home and spend his leave) did he write to him.

"I can't have you in my house," he replied on one occasion. "It can be of no interest to me where or how you spend your leave—or your life, for that matter."

The prejudice against Nnaemeka's marriage was not confined to his little village. In Lagos, especially among his people who worked there, it showed itself in a different way. Their women, when they met at their village meeting were not hostile to Nene. Rather, they paid her such excessive deference as to make her feel she was not one of them. But as time went on, Nene gradually broke through some of this prejudice and even began to make friends among them. Slowly and grudgingly they began to admit that she kept her home much better than most of them.

The story eventually got to the little village in the heart of the Ibo country that Nnaemeka and his young wife were a most happy couple. But his father was one of the few people who knew nothing about this. He always displayed so much temper whenever his son's name was mentioned that everyone avoided it in his presence. By a tremendous effort of will he had succeeded in pushing his son to the back of his mind. The strain had nearly killed him but he had persevered, and won.

Then one day he received a letter from Nene, and in spite of himself he began to glance through it perfunctorily until all of a sudden the expression on his face changed and he began to read more carefully.

> . . . Our two sons, from the day they learnt that they have a grandfather, have insisted on being taken to him. I find it impossible to tell them that you will not see them. I implore you to allow Nnaemeka to bring them home for a short time during his leave next month. I shall remain here in Lagos . . .

The old man at once felt the resolution he had built up over so many   60
years falling in. He was telling himself that he must not give in. He tried to steel his heart against all emotional appeals. It was a reenactment of that other struggle. He leaned against a window and looked out. The sky was overcast with heavy black clouds and a high wind began to blow filling the air with dust and dry leaves. It was one of those rare occasions when even Nature takes a hand in a human fight. Very soon it began to rain, the first rain in the year. It came down in large sharp drops and was accompanied by the lightning and thunder which mark a change of season. Okeke was trying hard not to think of his two grandsons. But he knew he was now fighting a losing battle. He tried to hum a favourite hymn but the pattering of large rain drops on the roof broke up the tune. His mind immediately returned to the children. How could he shut his door against them? By a curious mental process he imagined them standing, sad and forsaken, under the harsh angry weather — shut out from his house.

That night he hardly slept, from remorse — and a vague fear that he might die without making it up to them.

JOYCE CAROL OATES (1938–   )

The Lady with the Pet Dog

I

Strangers parted as if to make way for him.

There he stood. He was there in the aisle, a few yards away, watching her.

She leaned forward at once in her seat, her hand jerked up to her face as if to ward off a blow—but then the crowd in the aisle hid him, he was gone. She pressed both hands against her cheeks. He was not there, she had imagined him.

"My God," she whispered.

She was alone. Her husband had gone out to the foyer to make a   5
telephone call; it was intermission at the concert, a Thursday evening.

Now she saw him again, clearly. He was standing there. He was staring at her. Her blood rocked in her body, draining out of her head . . . she was going to faint. . . . They stared at each other. They gave no sign of recognition. Only when he took a step forward did she shake her head *no—no—keep away.* It was not possible.

When her husband returned, she was staring at the place in the aisle where her lover had been standing. Her husband leaned forward to interrupt that stare.

"What's wrong?" he said. "Are you sick?"

Panic rose in her in long shuddering waves. She tried to get to her feet, panicked at the thought of fainting here, and her husband took hold of her. She stood like an aged woman, clutching the seat before her.

At home he helped her up the stairs and she lay down. Her head was   10
like a large piece of crockery that had to be held still, it was so heavy. She was still panicked. She felt it in the shallows of her face, behind her knees, in the pit of her stomach. It sickened her, it made her think of mucus, of something thick and gray congested inside her, stuck to her, that was herself and yet not herself—a poison.

She lay with her knees drawn up toward her chest, her eyes hotly open, while her husband spoke to her. She imagined that other man saying, *Why did you run away from me?* Her husband was saying other words. She tried to listen to them. He was going to call the doctor, he said, and she tried to sit up. "No, I'm all right now," she said quickly. The panic was like lead inside her, so thickly congested. How slow love was to drain out of her, how fluid and sticky it was inside her head!

Her husband believed her. No doctor. No threat. Grateful, she drew her husband down to her. They embraced, not comfortably. For years now they had not been comfortable together, in their intimacy and at a distance, and now they struggled gently as if the paces of this dance were too rigorous for them. It was something they might have known once, but had now outgrown. The panic in her thickened at this double betrayal: she drew her husband to her, she caressed him wildly, she shut her eyes to think about that other man.

A crowd of men and women parting, unexpectedly, and there he stood — there he stood — she kept seeing him, and yet her vision blotched at the memory. It has been finished between them, six months before, but he had come out here . . . and she had escaped him, now she was lying in her husband's arms, in his embrace, her face pressed against his. It was a kind of sleep, this love-making. She felt herself falling asleep, her body falling from her. Her eyes shut.

"I love you," her husband said fiercely, angrily.

She shut her eyes and thought of that other man, as if betraying him   15
would give her life a center.

"Did I hurt you? Are you — ?" her husband whispered.

Always this hot flashing of shame between them, the shame of her husband's near failure, the clumsiness of his love —

"You didn't hurt me," she said.

II

They had said good-by six months before. He drove her from Nantucket, where they had met, to Albany, New York, where she visited her sister. The hours of intimacy in the car had sealed something between them, a vow of silence and impersonality: she recalled the movement of the highways, the passing of other cars, the natural rhythms of the day hypnotizing her toward sleep while he drove. She trusted him, she could sleep in his presence. Yet she could not really fall asleep in spite of her exhaustion, and she kept jerking awake, frightened, to discover that nothing had changed — still the stranger who was driving her to Albany, still the highway, the sky, the antiseptic odor of the rented car, the sense of a rhythm behind the rhythm of the air that might unleash itself at any second. Everywhere on this highway, at this moment, there were men and women driving together, bonded together — what did that mean, to be together? What did it mean to enter into a bond with another person?

No, she did not really trust him; she did not really trust men. He   20
would glance at her with his small cautious smile and she felt a declaration of shame between them.

Shame.

In her head she rehearsed conversations. She said bitterly, "You'll be relieved when we get to Albany. Relieved to get rid of me." They had spent so many days talking, confessing too much, driven to a pitch of childish excitement, laughing together on the beach, breaking into that pose of laughter that seems to eradicate the soul, so many days of this that the silence of the trip was like the silence of a hospital — all these surface noises, these rattles and hums, but an interior silence, a befuddlement. She said to him in her imagination, "One of us should die." Then she leaned over to touch him. She caressed the back of his neck. She said, aloud, "Would you like me to drive for a while?"

They stopped at a picnic area where other cars were stopped — couples, families — and walked together, smiling at their good luck. He put his arm around her shoulders and she sensed how they were in a posture together, a man and a woman forming a posture, a figure, that someone might sketch and show to them. She said slowly, "I don't want to go back. . . ."

Silence. She looked up at him. His face was heavy with her words, as if she had pulled at his skin with her fingers. Children ran nearby and distracted him — yes, he was a father too, his children ran like that, they tugged at his skin with their light, busy fingers.

"Are you so unhappy?" he said.   25

"I'm not unhappy, back there. I'm nothing. There's nothing to me," she said.

They stared at each other. The sensation between them was intense, exhausting. She thought that this man was her savior, that he had come to her at a time in her life when her life demanded completion, an end, a permanent fixing of all that was troubled and shifting and deadly. And yet it was absurd to think this. No person could save another. So she drew back from him and released him.

A few hours later they stopped at a gas station in a small city. She went to the women's rest room, having to ask the attendant for a key, and when she came back her eye jumped nervously onto the rented car — why? did she think he might have driven off without her? — onto the man, her friend, standing in conversation with the young attendant. Her friend was as old as her husband, over forty, with lanky, sloping shoulders, a full body, his hair thick, a dark, burnished brown, a festive color that made her eye twitch a little — and his hands were always moving, always those rapid conversational circles, going nowhere, gestures that were at once a little aggressive and apologetic.

She put her hand on his arm, a claim. He turned to her and smiled and she felt that she loved him, that everything in her life had forced her to this moment and that she had no choice about it.

They sat in the car for two hours, in Albany, in the parking lot of a   30
Howard Johnson's restaurant, talking, trying to figure out their past. There was no future. They concentrated on the past, the several days behind them, lit up with a hot, dazzling August sun, like explosions that already belonged to other people, to strangers. Her face was faintly reflected in the green-tinted curve of the windshield, but she could not have recognized that face. She began to cry; she told herself: *I am not here, this will pass, this is nothing.* Still, she could not stop crying. The muscles of her face were springy, like a child's, unpredictable muscles. He stroked her arms, her shoulders, trying to comfort her. "This is so hard . . . this is impossible . . ." he said. She felt panic for the world outside this car, all that was not herself and this man, and at the same time she understood that she was free of him, as people are

free of other people, she would leave him soon, safely, and within a few days he would have fallen into the past, the impersonal past. . . .

"I'm so ashamed of myself!" she said finally.

She returned to her husband and saw that another woman, a shadow-woman, had taken her place — noiseless and convincing, like a dancer performing certain difficult steps. Her husband folded her in his arms and talked to her of his own loneliness, his worries about his business, his health, his mother, kept tranquillized and mute in a nursing home, and her spirit detached itself from her and drifted about the rooms of the large house she lived in with her husband, a shadow-woman delicate and imprecise. There was no boundary to her, no edge. Alone, she took hot baths and sat exhausted in the steaming water, wondering at her perpetual exhaustion. All that winter she noticed the limp, languid weight of her arms, her veins bulging slightly with the pressure of her extreme weariness. *This is fate,* she thought, to be here and not there, to be one person and not another, a certain man's wife and not the wife of another man. The long, slow pain of this certainty rose in her, but it never became clear, it was baffling and imprecise. She could not be serious about it; she kept congratulating herself on her own good luck, to have escaped so easily, to have freed herself. So much love had gone into the first several years of her marriage that there wasn't much left, now, for another man. . . . She was certain of that. But the bath water made her dizzy, all that perpetual heat, and one day in January she drew a razor blade lightly across the inside of her arm, near the elbow, to see what would happen.

Afterward she wrapped a small towel around it, to stop the bleeding. The towel soaked through. She wrapped a bath towel around that and walked through the empty rooms of her home, lightheaded, hardly aware of the stubborn seeping of blood. There was no boundary to her in this house, no precise limit. She could flow out like her own blood and come to no end.

She sat for a while on a blue love seat, her mind empty. Her husband telephoned her when he would be staying late at the plant. He talked to her always about his plans, his problems, his business friends, his future. It was obvious that he had a future. As he spoke she nodded to encourage him, and her heartbeat quickened with the memory of her own, personal shame, the shame of this man's particular, private wife. One evening at dinner he leaned forward and put his head in his arms and fell asleep, like a child. She sat at the table with him for a while watching him. His hair had gone gray, almost white, at the temples — no one would guess that he was so quick, so careful a man, still fairly young about the eyes. She put her hand on his head, lightly, as if to prove to herself that he was real. He slept, exhausted.

One evening they went to a concert and she looked up to see her lover there, in the crowded aisle, in this city, watching her. He was standing there, with his overcoat on, watching her. She went cold. That morning the telephone had rung while her husband was still home, and she had heard him

35

answer it, heard him hang up—it must have been a wrong number—and when the telephone rang again, at 9:30, she had been afraid to answer it. She had left home to be out of the range of that ringing, but now, in this public place, in this busy auditorium, she found herself staring at that man, unable to make any sign to him, any gesture of recognition. . . .

He would have come to her but she shook her head. *No. Stay away.*

Her husband helped her out of the row of seats, saying, "Excuse us, please. Excuse us," so that strangers got to their feet, quickly, alarmed, to let them pass. Was that woman about to faint? What was wrong?

At home she felt the blood drain slowly back into her head. Her husband embraced her hips, pressing his face against her, in that silence that belonged to the earliest days of their marriage. She thought, *He will drive it out of me.* He made love to her and she was back in the auditorium again, sitting alone, now that the concert was over. The stage was empty; the heavy velvet curtains had not been drawn; the musicians' chairs were empty, everything was silent and expectant; in the aisle her lover stood and smiled at her—Her husband was impatient. He was apart from her, working on her, operating on her; and then, stricken, he whispered, "Did I hurt you?"

The telephone rang the next morning. Dully, sluggishly, she answered it. She recognized his voice at once—that "Anna?" with its lifting of the second syllable, questioning and apologetic and making its claim—"Yes, what do you want?" she said.

"Just to see you. Please—"   40

"I can't."

"Anna, I'm sorry, I didn't mean to upset you—"

"I can't see you."

"Just for a few minutes—I have to talk to you—"

"But why, why now? Why now?" she said.   45

She heard her voice rising, but she could not stop it. He began to talk again, drowning her out. She remembered his rapid conversation. She remembered his gestures, the witty energetic circling of his hands.

"Please don't hang up!" he cried.

"I can't—I don't want to go through it again—"

"I'm not going to hurt you. Just tell me how you are."

"Everything is the same."   50

"Everything is the same with me."

She looked up at the ceiling, shyly. "Your wife? Your children?"

"The same."

"Your son?"

"He's fine—"   55

"I'm glad to hear that. I—"

"Is it still the same with you, your marriage? Tell me what you feel. What are you thinking?"

"I don't know. . . ."

She remembered his intense, eager words, the movement of his hands, that impatient precise fixing of the air by his hands, the jabbing of his fingers.

"Do you love me?" he said.   60

She could not answer.

"I'll come over to see you," he said.

"No," she said.

What will come next, what will happen?

Flesh hardening on his body, aging. Shrinking. He will grow old, but   65 not soft like her husband. They are two different types: he is nervous, lean, energetic, wise. She will grow thinner, as the tension radiates out from her backbone, wearing down her flesh. Her collarbones will jut out of her skin. Her husband, caressing her in their bed, will discover that she is another woman — she is not there with him — instead she is rising in an elevator in a downtown hotel, carrying a book as a prop, or walking quickly away from that hotel, her head bent and filled with secrets. Love, what to do with it? . . . Useless as moths' wings, as moths' fluttering. . . . She feels the flutterings of silky, crazy wings in her chest.

He flew out to visit her every several weeks, staying at a different hotel each time. He telephoned her, and she drove down to park in an underground garage at the very center of the city.

She lay in his arms while her husband talked to her, miles away, one body fading into another. He will grow old, his body will change, she thought, pressing her cheek against the back of one of these men. If it was her lover, they were in a hotel room: always the propped-up little booklet describing the hotel's many services, with color photographs of its cocktail lounge and dining room and coffee shop. Grow old, leave me, die, go back to your neurotic wife and your sad, ordinary children, she thought, but still her eyes closed gratefully against his skin and she felt how complete their silence was, how they had come to rest in each other.

"Tell me about your life here. The people who love you," he said, as he always did.

One afternoon they lay together for four hours. It was her birthday and she was intoxicated with her good fortune, this prize of the afternoon, this man in her arms! She was a little giddy, she talked too much. She told him about her parents, about her husband. . . . "They were all people I believed in, but it turned out wrong. Now, I believe in you. . . ." He laughed as if shocked by her words. She did not understand. Then she understood. "But I believe truly in you. I can't think of myself without you," she said. . . . He spoke of his wife, her ambitions, her intelligence, her use of the children against him, her use of his younger son's blindness, all of his words gentle and hypnotic and convincing in the late afternoon peace of this hotel room . . . and she felt the terror of laughter, threatening laughter. Their words, like their bodies, were aging.

She dressed quickly in the bathroom, drawing her long hair up around   70 the back of her head, fixing it as always, anxious that everything be the same. Her face was slightly raw, from his face. The rubbing of his skin. Her eyes were too bright, wearily bright. Her hair was blond but not so blond as it had been that summer in the white Nantucket air.

She ran water and splashed it on her face. She blinked at the water. Blind. Drowning. She thought with satisfaction that soon, soon, he would be back home, in that house on Long Island she had never seen, with that woman she had never seen, sitting on the edge of another bed, putting on his shoes. She wanted nothing except to be free of him. Why not be free? *Oh,* she thought suddenly, *I will follow you back and kill you. You and her and the little boy. What is there to stop me?*

She left him. Everyone on the street pitied her, that look of absolute zero.

III

A man and a child, approaching her. The sharp acrid smell of fish. The crashing of waves. Anna pretended not to notice the father with his son — there was something strange about them. That frank, silent intimacy, too gentle, the man's bare feet in the water and the boy a few feet away, leaning away from his father. He was about nine years old and still his father held his hand.

A small yipping dog, a golden dog, bounded near them.

Anna turned shyly back to her reading; she did not want to have to   75
speak to these neighbors. She saw the man's shadow falling over her legs, then over the pages of her book, and she had the idea that he wanted to see what she was reading. The dog nuzzled her; the man called him away.

She watched them walk down the beach. She was relieved that the man had not spoken to her.

She saw them in town later that day, the two of them brown–haired and patient, now wearing sandals, walking with that same look of care. The man's white shorts were soiled and a little baggy. His pullover shirt was a faded green. His face was broad, the cheekbones wide, spaced widely apart, the eyes stark in their sockets, as if they fastened onto objects for no reason, ponderous and edgy. The little boy's face was pale and sharp; his lips were perpetually parted.

Anna realized that the child was blind.

The next morning, early, she caught sight of them again. For some reason she went to the back door of her cottage. She faced the sea breeze eagerly. Her heart hammered. . . . She had been here, in her family's old house, for three days, alone, bitterly satisfied at being alone, and now it was a puzzle to her how her soul strained to fly outward, to meet with another person. She watched the man with his son, his cautious, rather stooped shoulders above the child's small shoulders.

The man was carrying something, it looked like a notebook. He sat   80
on the sand, not far from Anna's spot of the day before, and the dog rushed up to them. The child approached the edge of the ocean, timidly. He moved

in short jerky steps, his legs stiff. The dog ran around him. Anna heard the
child crying out a word that sounded like "Ty" — it must have been the dog's
name — and the man joined in, his voice heavy and firm.

"Ty — "

Anna tied her hair back with a yellow scarf and went down to the
beach.

The man glanced around at her. He smiled. She stared past him at the
waves. To talk to him or not to talk — she had the freedom of that choice.
For a moment she felt that she had made a mistake, that the child and the
dog would not protect her, that behind this man's ordinary, friendly face
there was a certain arrogant maleness — then she relented, she smiled shyly.

"A nice house you've got there," the man said.

She nodded her thanks.   85

The man pushed his sunglasses up on his forehead. Yes, she recognized
the eyes of the day before — intelligent and nervous, the sockets pale,
untanned.

"Is that your telephone ringing?" he said.

She did not bother to listen. "It's a wrong number," she said.

Her husband calling: she had left home for a few days, to be alone.

But the man, settling himself on the sand, seemed to misinterpret this.   90
He smiled in surprise, one corner of his mouth higher than the other. He
said nothing. Anna wondered: *What is he thinking?* The dog was leaping
about her, panting against her legs, and she laughed in embarrassment. She
bent to pet it, grateful for its busyness. "Don't let him jump up on you,"
the man said. "He's a nuisance."

The dog was a small golden retriever, a young dog. The blind child,
standing now in the water, turned to call the dog to him. His voice was
shrill and impatient.

"Our house is the third one down — the white one," the man said.

She turned, startled. "Oh, did you buy it from Dr. Patrick? Did he
die?"

"Yes, finally. . . ."

Her eyes wandered nervously over the child and the dog. She felt the   95
nervous beat of her heart out to the very tips of her fingers, the fleshy tips
of her fingers: little hearts were there, pulsing. *What is he thinking?* The man
had opened his notebook. He had a piece of charcoal and he began to sketch
something.

Anna looked down at him. She saw the top of his head, his thick
brown hair, the freckles on his shoulders, the quick, deft movement of his
hand. Upside down, Anna herself being drawn. She smiled in surprise.

"Let me draw you. Sit down," he said.

She knelt awkwardly a few yards away. He turned the page of the
sketch pad. The dog ran to her and she sat, straightening out her skirt
beneath her, flinching from the dog's tongue. "Ty!" cried the child. Anna
sat, and slowly the pleasure of the moment began to glow in her; her skin
flushed with gratitude.

She sat there for nearly an hour. The man did not talk much. Back and
forth the dog bounded, shaking itself. The child came to sit near them, in
silence. Anna felt that she was drifting into a kind of trance while the man
sketched her, half a dozen rapid sketches, the surface of her face given up to
him. "Where are you from?" the man asked.

"Ohio. My husband lives in Ohio."   100

She wore no wedding band.

"Your wife — " Anna began.

"Yes?"

"Is she here?"

"Not right now."   105

She was silent, ashamed. She had asked an improper question. But the
man did not seem to notice. He continued drawing her, bent over the sketch
pad. When Anna said she had to go, he showed her the drawings — one after
another of her, Anna, recognizably Anna, a woman in her early thirties,
her hair smooth and flat across the top of her head, tied behind by a scarf.
"Take the one you like best," he said, and she picked one of her with the
dog in her lap, sitting very straight, her brows and eyes clearly defined,
her lips girlishly pursed, the dog and her dress suggested by a few quick
irregular lines.

"Lady with pet dog," the man said.

She spent the rest of the day reading, nearer her cottage. It was not
really a cottage — it was a two-story house, large and ungainly and weathered. It was mixed up in her mind with her family, her own childhood, and
she glanced up from her book, perplexed, as if waiting for one of her parents
or her sister to come up to her. Then she thought of the man, the man with
the blind child, the man with the dog, and she could not concentrate on her
reading. Someone — probably her father — had marked a passage that must
be important, but she kept reading and rereading it: *We try to discover in things,
endeared to us on that account, the spiritual glamour which we ourselves have
cast upon them; we are disillusioned, and learn that they are in themselves barren
and devoid of the charm that they owed, in our minds, to the association of certain
ideas. . . .*

She thought again of the man on the beach. She lay the book aside and
thought of him: his eyes, his aloneness, his drawings of her.

They began seeing each other after that. He came to her front door in   110
the evening, without the child; he drove her into town for dinner. She was
shy and extremely pleased. The darkness of the expensive restaurant released
her; she heard herself chatter; she leaned forward and seemed to be offering
her face up to him, listening to him. He talked about his work on a Long
Island newspaper and she seemed to be listening to him, as she stared at his
face, arranging her own face into the expression she had seen in that charcoal
drawing. Did he see her like that, then? — girlish and withdrawn and patrician? She felt the weight of his interest in her, a force that fell upon her like
a blow. A repeated blow. Of course he was married, he had children — of

course she was married, permanently married. This flight from her husband was not important. She had left him before, to be alone, it was not important. Everything in her was slender and delicate and not important.

They walked for hours after dinner, looking at the other strollers, the weekend visitors, the tourists, the couples like themselves. Surely they were mistaken for a couple, a married couple. *This is the hour in which everything is decided,* Anna thought. They both had several drinks and they talked a great deal. Anna found herself saying too much, stopping and starting giddily. She put her hand to her forehead, feeling faint.

"It's from the sun — you've had too much sun — " he said.

At the door to her cottage, on the front porch, she heard herself asking him if he would like to come in. She allowed him to lead her inside, to close the door. *This is not important,* she thought clearly, *he doesn't mean it, he doesn't love me, nothing will come of it.* She was frightened, yet it seemed to her necessary to give in; she had to leave Nantucket with that act completed, an act of adultery, an accomplishment she would take back to Ohio and to her marriage.

Later, incredibly, she heard herself asking: "Do you . . . do you love me?"

"You're so beautiful!" he said, amazed.

She felt this beauty, shy and glowing and centered in her eyes. He stared at her. In this large, drafty house, alone together, they were like accomplices, conspirators. She could not think: how old was she? which year was this? They had done something unforgivable together, and the knowledge of it was tugging at their faces. A cloud seemed to pass over her. She felt herself smiling shrilly.

Afterward, a peculiar raspiness, a dryness of breath. He was silent. She felt a strange, idle fear, a sense of the danger outside this room and this old, comfortable bed — a danger that would not recognize her as the lady in that drawing, the lady with the pet dog. There was nothing to say to this man, this stranger. She felt the beauty draining out of her face, her eyes fading.

"I've got to be alone," she told him.

He left, and she understood that she would not see him again. She stood by the window of the room, watching the ocean. A sense of shame overpowered her: it was smeared everywhere on her body, the smell of it, the richness of it. She tried to recall him, and his face was confused in her memory: she would have to shout to him across a jumbled space, she would have to wave her arms wildly. *You love me! You must love me!* But she knew he did not love her, and she did not love him; he was a man who drew everything up into himself, like all men, walking away, free to walk away, free to have his own thoughts, free to envision her body, all the secrets of her body. . . . And she lay down again in the bed, feeling how heavy this body had become, her insides heavy with shame, the very backs of her eyelids coated with shame.

"This is the end of one part of my life," she thought.

But in the morning the telephone rang. She answered it. It was her lover: they talked brightly and happily. She could hear the eagerness in his voice, the love in his voice, that same still, sad amazement — she understood how simple life was, there were no problems.

They spent most of their time on the beach, with the child and the dog. He joked and was serious at the same time. He said, once, "You have defined my soul for me," and she laughed to hide her alarm. In a few days it was time for her to leave. He got a sitter for the boy and took the ferry with her to the mainland, then rented a car to drive her up to Albany. She kept thinking: *Now something will happen. It will come to an end.* But most of the drive was silent and hypnotic. She wanted him to joke with her, to say again that she had defined his soul for him, but he drove fast, he was serious, she distrusted the hawkish look of his profile — she did not know him at all. At a gas station she splashed her face with cold water. Alone in the grubby little rest room, shaky and very much alone. In such places are women totally alone with their bodies. The body grows heavier, more evil, in such silence. . . . On the beach everything had been noisy with sunlight and gulls and waves; here, as if run to earth, everything was cramped and silent and dead.

She went outside, squinting. There he was, talking with the station attendant. She could not think as she returned to him whether she wanted to live or not.

She stayed in Albany for a few days, then flew home to her husband. He met her at the airport, near the luggage counter, where her three pieces of pale-brown luggage were brought to him on a conveyer belt, to be claimed by him. He kissed her on the cheek. They shook hands, a little embarrassed. She had come home again.

"How will I live out the rest of my life?" she wondered.   125

In January her lover spied on her: she glanced up and saw him, in a public place, in the DeRoy Symphony Hall. She was paralyzed with fear. She nearly fainted. In this faint she felt her husband's body, loving her, working its love upon her, and she shut her eyes harder to keep out the certainty of his love — sometimes he failed at loving her, sometimes he succeeded, it had nothing to do with her or her pity or her ten years of love for him, it had nothing to do with a woman at all. It was a private act accomplished by a man, a husband or a lover, in communion with his own soul, his manhood.

Her husband was forty-two years old now, growing slowly into middle age, getting heavier, softer. Her lover was about the same age, narrower in the shoulders, with a full, solid chest, yet lean, nervous. She thought, in her paralysis, of men and how they love freely and eagerly so long as their bodies are capable of love, love for a woman; and then, as love fades in their bodies, it fades from their souls and they become immune and immortal and ready to die.

Her husband was a little rough with her, as if impatient with himself. "I love you," he said fiercely, angrily. And then, ashamed, he said, "Did I hurt you? . . ."

"You didn't hurt me," she said.

Her voice was too shrill for their embrace.   130

While he was in the bathroom she went to her closet and took out that drawing of the summer before. There she was, on the beach at Nantucket, a lady with a pet dog, her eyes large and defined, the dog in her lap hardly more than a few snarls, a few coarse soft lines of charcoal . . . her dress smeared, her arms oddly limp . . . her hands not well drawn at all. . . . She tried to think: did she love the man who had drawn this? did he love her? The fever in her husband's body had touched her and driven her temperature up, and now she stared at the drawing with a kind of lust, fearful of seeing an ugly soul in that woman's face, fearful of seeing the face suddenly through her lover's eyes. She breathed quickly and harshly, staring at the drawing.

And so, the next day, she went to him at his hotel. She wept, pressing against him, demanding of him, "What do you want? Why are you here? Why don't you let me alone?" He told her that he wanted nothing. He expected nothing. He would not cause trouble.

"I want to talk about last August," he said.

"Don't—" she said.

She was hypnotized by his gesturing hands, his nervousness, his   135
obvious agitation. He kept saying, "I understand. I'm making no claims upon you."

They became lovers again.

He called room service for something to drink and they sat side by side on his bed, looking through a copy of *The New Yorker*, laughing at the cartoons. It was so peaceful in this room, so complete. They were on a holiday. It was a secret holiday. Four-thirty in the afternoon, on a Friday, an ordinary Friday: a secret holiday.

"I won't bother you again," he said.

He flew back to see her again in March, and in late April. He telephoned her from his hotel—a different hotel each time—and she came down to him at once. She rose to him in various elevators, she knocked on the doors of various rooms, she stepped into his embrace, breathless and guilty and already angry with him, pleading with him. One morning in May, when he telephoned, she pressed her forehead against the doorframe and could not speak. He kept saying, "What's wrong? Can't you talk? Aren't you alone?" She felt that she was going insane. Her head would burst. Why, why did he love her, why did he pursue her? Why did he want her to die?

She went to him in the hotel room. A familiar room: had they been   140
here before? "Everything is repeating itself. Everything is stuck," she said. He framed her face in his hands and said that she looked thinner—was she sick?—what was wrong? She shook herself free. He, her lover, looked about the same. There was a small, angry pimple on his neck. He stared at her, eagerly and suspiciously. Did she bring bad news?

"So you love me? You love me?" she asked.

"Why are you so angry?"

"I want to be free of you. The two of us free of each other."

"That isn't true—you don't want that—"

He embraced her. She was wild with that old, familiar passion for him,   145
her body clinging to his, her arms not strong enough to hold him. Ah, what
despair!—what bitter hatred she felt!—she needed this man for her salvation,
he was all she had to live for, and yet she could not believe in him. He
embraced her thighs, her hips, kissing her, pressing his warm face against
her, and yet she could not believe in him, not really. She needed him in order
to live, but he was not worth her love, he was not worth her dying. . . . She
promised herself this: when she got back home, when she was alone, she
would draw the razor more deeply across her arm.

The telephone rang and he answered it: a wrong number.

"Jesus," he said.

They lay together, still. She imagined their posture like this, the two
of them one figure, one substance; and outside this room and this bed there
was a universe of disjointed, separate things, blank things, that had nothing
to do with them. She would not be Anna out there, the lady in the drawing.
He would not be her lover.

"I love you so much. . . ." she whispered.

"Please don't cry! We have only a few hours, please. . . ."   150

It was absurd, their clinging together like this. She saw them as a
single figure in a drawing, their arms and legs entwined, their heads pressing
mutely together. Helpless substance, so heavy and warm and doomed. It
was absurd that any human being should be so important to another human
being. She wanted to laugh: a laugh might free them both.

She could not laugh.

Sometime later he said, as if they had been arguing, "Look. It's you.
You're the one who doesn't want to get married. You lie to me—"

"Lie to you?"

"You love me but you won't marry me, because you want something   155
left over—Something not finished—All your life you can attribute your
misery to me, to our not being married—you are using me—"

"Stop it! You'll make me hate you!" she cried.

"You can say to yourself that you're miserable because of *me*. We will
never be married, you will never be happy, neither one of us will ever be
happy—"

"I don't want to hear this!" she said.

She pressed her hands flatly against her face.

She went to the bathroom to get dressed. She washed her face and part   160
of her body, quickly. The fever was in her, in the pit of her belly. She would
rush home and strike a razor across the inside of her arm and free that
pressure, that fever.

The impatient bulging of the veins: an ordeal over.

The demand of the telephone's ringing: that ordeal over.

The nuisance of getting the car and driving home in all that five
o'clock traffic: an ordeal too much for a woman.

The movements of this stranger's body in hers: over, finished.

Now, dressed, a little calmer, they held hands and talked. They had to 165 talk swiftly, to get all their news in: he did not trust the people who worked for him, he had faith in no one, his wife had moved to a textbook publishing company and was doing well, she had inherited a Ben Shahn painting from her father and wanted to "touch it up a little"—she was crazy!—his blind son was at another school, doing fairly well, in fact his children were all doing fairly well in spite of the stupid mistake of their parents' marriage— and what about her? what about her life? She told him in a rush the one thing he wanted to hear: that she lived with her husband lovelessly, the two of them polite strangers, sharing a bed, lying side by side in the night in that bed, bodies out of which souls had fled. There was no longer even any shame between them.

"And what about me? Do you feel shame with me still?" he asked.

She did not answer. She moved away from him and prepared to leave.

Then, a minute later, she happened to catch sight of his reflection in the bureau mirror—he was glancing down at himself, checking himself mechanically, impersonally, preparing also to leave. He too would leave this room: he too was headed somewhere else.

She stared at him. It seemed to her that in this instant he was breaking from her, the image of her lover fell free of her, breaking from her . . . and she realized that he existed in a dimension quite apart from her, a mysterious being. And suddenly, joyfully, she felt a miraculous calm. This man was her husband, truly—they were truly married, here in this room—they had been married haphazardly and accidentally for a long time. In another part of the city she had another husband, a "husband," but she had not betrayed that man, not really. This man, whom she loved above any other person in the world, above even her own self-pitying sorrow and her own life, was her truest lover, her destiny. And she did not hate him, she did not hate herself any longer; she did not wish to die; she was flooded with a strange certainty, a sense of gratitude, of pure selfless energy. It was obvious to her that she had, all along, been behaving correctly; out of instinct.

What triumph, to love like this in any room, anywhere, risking even 170 the craziest of accidents!

"Why are you so happy? What's wrong?" he asked, startled. He stared at her. She felt the abrupt concentration in him, the focusing of his vision on her, almost a bitterness in his face, as if he feared her. What, was it beginning all over again? Their love beginning again, in spite of them? "How can you look so happy?" he asked. "We don't have any right to it. Is it because . . . ?"

"Yes," she said.

RAYMOND CARVER (1939–1988)

Cathedral

This blind man, an old friend of my wife's, he was on his way to spend the night. His wife had died. So he was visiting the dead wife's relatives in Connecticut. He called my wife from his in-laws'. Arrangements were made. He would come by train, a five-hour trip, and my wife would meet him at the station. She hadn't seen him since she worked for him one summer in Seattle ten years ago. But she and the blind man had kept in touch. They made tapes and mailed them back and forth. I wasn't enthusiastic about his visit. He was no one I knew. And his being blind bothered me. My idea of blindness came from the movies. In the movies, the blind moved slowly and never laughed. Sometimes they were led by seeing-eye dogs. A blind man in my house was not something I looked forward to.

That summer in Seattle she had needed a job. She didn't have any money. The man she was going to marry at the end of the summer was in officers' training school. He didn't have any money, either. But she was in love with the guy, and he was in love with her, etc. She'd seen something in the paper: HELP WANTED — *Reading to Blind Man,* and a telephone number. She phoned and went over, was hired on the spot. She'd worked with this blind man all summer. She read stuff to him, case studies, reports, that sort of thing. She helped him organize his little office in the county social-service department. They'd become good friends, my wife and the blind man. How do I know these things? She told me. And she told me something else. On her last day in the office, the blind man asked if he could touch her face. She agreed to this. She told me he touched his fingers to every part of her face, her nose — even her neck! She never forgot it. She even tried to write a poem about it. She was always trying to write a poem. She wrote a poem or two every year, usually after something really important had happened to her.

When we first started going out together, she showed me the poem. In the poem, she recalled his fingers and the way they had moved around over her face. In the poem, she talked about what she had felt at the time, about what went through her mind when the blind man touched her nose and lips. I can remember I didn't think much of the poem. Of course, I didn't tell her that. Maybe I just don't understand poetry. I admit it's not the first thing I reach for when I pick up something to read.

Anyway, this man who'd first enjoyed her favors, the officer-to-be, he'd been her childhood sweetheart. So okay. I'm saying that at the end of the summer she let the blind man run his hands over her face, said goodbye to him, married her childhood etc., who was now a commissioned officer, and she moved away from Seattle. But they'd kept in touch, she and the blind man. She made the first contact after a year or so. She called him up one night from an Air Force base in Alabama. She wanted to talk. They talked. He asked her to send him a tape and tell him about her life. She did this. She sent the tape. On the tape, she told the blind man about her husband and about their life together in the military. She told the blind man she loved her husband but she didn't like it where they lived and she didn't like it that he was part of the military-industrial thing. She told the blind man she'd written a poem and he was in it. She told him that she was writing a poem about what it was like to be an Air Force officer's wife. The poem wasn't finished yet. She was still writing it. The blind man made a tape. He sent her the tape. She made a tape. This went on for years. My wife's officer was posted to one base and then another. She sent tapes from Moody AFB, McGuire, McConnell, and finally Travis, near Sacramento, where one night she got to feeling lonely and cut off from people she kept losing in that moving-around life. She got to feeling she couldn't go it another step. She went in and swallowed all the pills and capsules in the medicine chest and washed them down with a bottle of gin. Then she got into a hot bath and passed out.

But instead of dying, she got sick. She threw up. Her officer — why should he have a name? he was the childhood sweetheart, and what more does he want? — came home from somewhere, found her, and called the ambulance. In time, she put it all on a tape and sent the tape to the blind man. Over the years, she put all kinds of stuff on tapes and sent the tapes off lickety-split. Next to writing a poem every year, I think it was her chief means of recreation. On one tape, she told the blind man she'd decided to live away from her officer for a time. On another tape, she told him about her divorce. She and I began going out, and of course she told her blind man about it. She told him everything, or so it seemed to me. Once she asked me if I'd like to hear the latest tape from the blind man. This was a year ago. I was on the tape, she said. So I said okay, I'd listen to it. I got us drinks and we settled down in the living room. We made ready to listen. First she inserted the tape into the player and adjusted a couple of dials. Then she pushed a lever. The tape squeaked and someone began to talk in this loud voice. She lowered the volume. After a few minutes of harmless chitchat, I heard my own name in the mouth of this stranger, this blind man I didn't even know! And then this: "From all you've said about him, I can only conclude — " But we were interrupted, a knock at the door, something, and we didn't ever get back to the tape. Maybe it was just as well. I'd heard all I wanted to. 5

Now this same blind man was coming to sleep in my house.

"Maybe I could take him bowling," I said to my wife. She was at the draining board doing scalloped potatoes. She put down the knife she was using and turned around.

"If you love me," she said, "you can do this for me. If you don't love me, okay. But if you had a friend, any friend, and the friend came to visit, I'm make him feel comfortable." She wiped her hands with the dish towel.

"I don't have any blind friends," I said.

"You don't have *any* friends," she said. "Period. Besides," she said, "goddamn it, his wife's just died! Don't you understand that? The man's lost his wife!" 10

I didn't answer. She'd told me a little about the blind man's wife. Her name was Beulah. Beulah! That's a name for a colored woman.

"Was his wife a Negro?" I asked.

"Are you crazy?" my wife said. "Have you just flipped or something?" She picked up a potato. I saw it hit the floor, then roll under the stove. "What's wrong with you?" she said. "Are you drunk?"

"I'm just asking," I said.

Right then my wife filled me in with more detail than I cared to know.   15
I made a drink and sat at the kitchen table to listen. Pieces of the story began to fall into place.

Beulah had gone to work for the blind man the summer after my wife had stopped working for him. Pretty soon Beulah and the blind had themselves a church wedding. It was a little wedding—who'd want to go to such a wedding in the first place?—just the two of them, plus the minister and the minister's wife. But it was a church wedding just the same. It was what Beulah had wanted, he'd said. But even then Beulah must have been carrying the cancer in her glands. After they had been inseparable for eight years—my wife's word, *inseparable*—Beulah's health went into rapid decline. She died in a Seattle hospital room, the blind man sitting beside the bed and holding on to her hand. They'd married, lived and worked together, slept together—had sex, sure—and then the blind man had to bury her. All this without his having ever seen what the goddamned woman looked like. It was beyond my understanding. Hearing this, I felt sorry for the blind man for a little bit. And then I found myself thinking what a pitiful life this woman must have led. Imagine a woman who could never see herself as she was seen in the eyes of her loved one. A woman who could go on day after day and never receive the smallest compliment from her beloved. A woman whose husband could never read the expression on her face, be it misery or something better. Someone who could wear makeup or not—what difference to him? She could, if she wanted, wear green eye-shadow around one eye, a straight pin in her nostril, yellow slacks and purple shoes, no matter. And then to slip off into death, the blind man's hand on her hand, his blind eyes streaming tears—I'm imagining now—her last thought maybe this: that he never even knew what she looked like, and she on an express to the grave. Robert was left with a small insurance policy and half of a twenty-peso Mexican coin. The other half of the coin went into the box with her. Pathetic.

So when the time rolled around, my wife went to the depot to pick him up. With nothing to do but wait—sure, I blamed him for that—I was having a drink and watching the TV when I heard the car pull into the drive. I got up from the sofa with my drink and went to the window to have a look.

I saw my wife laughing as she parked the car. I saw her get out of the car and shut the door. She was still wearing a smile. Just amazing. She went around to the other side of the car to where the blind man was already starting to get out. This blind man, feature this, he was wearing a full beard! A beard on a blind man! Too much, I say. The blind man reached into the back seat and dragged out a suitcase. My wife took his arm, shut the car door, and, talking all the way, moved him down the drive and then up the steps to the front porch. I turned off the TV. I finished my drink, rinsed the glass, dried my hands. Then I went to the door.

My wife said, "I want you to meet Robert. Robert, this is my husband. I've told you all about him." She was beaming. She had this blind man by his coat sleeve.

The blind man let go of his suitcase and up came his hand.   20

I took it. He squeezed hard, held my hand, and then he let it go.

"I feel like we've already met," he boomed.

"Likewise," I said. I didn't know what else to say. Then I said, "Welcome. I've heard a lot about you." We began to move then, a little group, from the porch into the living room, my wife guiding him by the arm. The blind man was carrying his suitcase in his other hand. My wife said things like, "To your left here, Robert. That's right. Now watch it, there's a chair. That's it. Sit down right here. This is the sofa. We just bought this sofa two weeks ago."

I started to say something about the old sofa. I'd liked that old sofa. But I didn't say anything. Then I wanted to say something else, small-talk, about the scenic ride along the Hudson. How going *to* New York, you should sit on the right-hand side of the train, and coming *from* New York, the left-hand side.

"Did you have a good train ride?" I said. "Which side of the train did   25
you sit on, by the way?"

"What a question, which side!" my wife said. "What's it matter which side?" she said.

"I just asked," I said.

"Right side," the blind man said. "I hadn't been on a train in nearly forty years. Not since I was a kid. With my folks. That's been a long time. I'd nearly forgotten the sensation. I have winter in my beard now," he said. "So I've been told, anyway. Do I look distinguished, my dear?" the blind man said to my wife.

"You look distinguished, Robert," she said. "Robert," she said. "Robert, it's just so good to see you."

My wife finally took her eyes off the blind man and looked at me. I   30
had the feeling she didn't like what she saw. I shrugged.

I've never met, or personally known, anyone who was blind. This blind man was late forties, a heavy-set, balding man with stooped shoulders, as if he carried a great weight there. He wore brown slacks, brown shoes, a light-brown shirt, a tie, a sports coat. Spiffy. He also had this full beard. But he didn't use a cane and he didn't wear dark glasses. I'd always thought dark glasses were a must for the blind. Fact was, I wished he had a pair. At first glance, his eyes looked like anyone else's eyes. But if you looked close, there was something different about them. Too much white in the iris, for one thing, and the pupils seemed to move around in the sockets without his knowing it or being able to stop it. Creepy. As I stared at his face, I saw the left pupil turn in toward his nose while the other made an effort to keep in one place. But it was only an effort, for that eye was on the roam without his knowing it or wanting it to be.

I said, "Let me get you a drink. What's your pleasure? We have a little of everything. It's one of our pastimes."

"Bub, I'm a Scotch man myself," he said fast enough in this big voice.

"Right," I said. Bub! "Sure you are. I knew it."

He let his fingers touch his suitcase, which was sitting alongside the   35
sofa. He was taking his bearings. I didn't blame him for that.

"I'll move that up to your room," my wife said.

"No, that's fine," the blind man said loudly. "It can go up when I go up."

"A little water with the Scotch?" I said.

"Very little," he said.

"I knew it," I said.   40

He said, "Just a tad. The Irish actor, Barry Fitzgerald? I'm like that fellow. When I drink water, Fitzgerald said, I drink water. When I drink whiskey, I drink whiskey." My wife laughed. The blind man brought his hand up under his beard. He lifted his beard slowly and let it drop.

I did the drinks, three big glasses of Scotch with a splash of water in each. Then we made ourselves comfortable and talked about Robert's travels. First the long flight from the West Coast to Connecticut, we covered that. Then from Connecticut up here by train. We had another drink concerning that leg of the trip.

I remembered having read somewhere that the blind didn't smoke because, as speculation had it, they couldn't see the smoke they exhaled. I thought I knew that much and that much only about blind people. But this blind man smoked his cigarette down to the nubbin and then lit another one. This blind man filled his ashtray and my wife emptied it.

When we sat down at the table for dinner, we had another drink. My wife heaped Robert's plate with cube steak, scalloped potatoes, green beans. I buttered him up two slices of bread. I said, "Here's bread and butter for you." I swallowed some of my drink. "Now let us pray," I said, and the blind man lowered his head. My wife looked at me, her mouth agape. "Pray the phone won't ring and the food doesn't get cold," I said.

We dug in. We ate everything there was to eat on the table. We ate like   45
there was no tomorrow. We didn't talk. We ate. We scarfed. We grazed that table. We were into serious eating. The blind man had right away located his foods, he knew just where everything was on his plate. I watched with admiration as he used his knife and fork on the meat. He'd cut two pieces of meat, fork the meat into his mouth, and then go all out for the scalloped

potatoes, the beans next, and then he'd tear off a hunk of buttered bread and eat that. He'd follow this up with a big drink of milk. It didn't seem to bother him to use his fingers once in a while, either.

We finished everything, including half a strawberry pie. For a few moments, we sat as if stunned. Sweat beaded on our faces. Finally, we got up from the table and left the dirty plates. We didn't look back. We took ourselves into the living room and sank into our places again. Robert and my wife sat on the sofa. I took the big chair. We had us two or three more drinks while they talked about the major things that had come to pass for them in the past ten years. For the most part, I just listened. Now and then I joined in. I didn't want him to think I'd left the room, and I didn't want her to think I was feeling left out. They talked of things that had happened to them — to them — these past ten years. I waited in vain to hear my name on my wife's sweet lips: "And then my dear husband came into my life" — something like that. But I heard nothing of the sort. More talk of Robert. Robert had done a little of everything, it seemed, a regular blind jack-of-all-trades. But most recently he and his wife had had an Amway distributorship, from which, I gathered, they'd earned their living, such as it was. The blind man was also a ham radio operator. He talked in his loud voice about conversations he'd had with fellow operators in Guam, in the Philippines, in Alaska, and even in Tahiti. He said he'd have a lot of friends there if he ever wanted to go visit those places. From time to time, he'd turn his blind face toward me, put his hand under his beard, ask me something. How long had I been in my present position? (Three years.) Did I like my work? (I didn't.) Was I going to stay with it? (What were the options?) Finally, when I thought he was beginning to run down, I got up and turned on the TV.

My wife looked at me with irritation. She was heading toward a boil. Then she looked at the blind man and said, "Robert, do you have a TV?"

The blind man said, "My dear, I have two TVs. I have a color set and a black-and-white thing, an old relic. It's funny, but if I turn the TV on, and I'm always turning it on, I turn on the color set. It's funny, don't you think?"

I didn't know what to say to that. I had absolutely nothing to say to that. No opinion. So I watched the news program and tried to listen to what the announcer was saying.

"This is a color TV," the blind man said. "Don't ask me how, but I can tell." 50

"We traded up a while ago," I said.

The blind man had another taste of his drink. He lifted his beard, sniffed it, and let it fall. He leaned forward on the sofa. He positioned his ashtray on the coffee table, then put the lighter to his cigarette. He leaned back on the sofa and crossed his legs at the ankles.

My wife covered her mouth, and then she yawned. She stretched. She said, "I think I'll go upstairs and put on my robe. I think I'll change into something else. Robert, you make yourself comfortable," she said.

"I'm comfortable," the blind man said.

"I want you to feel comfortable in this house," she said. 55

"I am comfortable," the blind man said.

After she'd left the room, he and I listened to the weather report and then to the sports roundup. By that time, she'd been gone so long I didn't know if she was going to come back. I thought she might have gone to bed. I wished she'd come back downstairs. I didn't want to be left alone with a blind man. I asked him if he wanted another drink, and he said sure. Then I asked if he wanted to smoke some dope with me. I said I'd just rolled a number. I hadn't, but I planned to do so in about two shakes. "I'll try some with you," he said.

"Damn right," I said. "That's the stuff."

I got our drinks and sat down on the sofa with him. Then I roll us two fat numbers. I lit one and passed it. I brought it to his fingers. He took it and inhaled.

"Hold it as long as you can," I said. I could tell he didn't know the 60
first thing.

My wife came back downstairs wearing her pink robe and her pink slippers.

"What do I smell?" she said.

"We thought we'd have us some cannabis," I said.

My wife gave me a savage look. Then she looked at the blind man and said, "Robert, I didn't know you smoked."

He said, "I do now, my dear. There's a first time for everything. But I 65
don't feel anything yet."

"This stuff is pretty mellow," I said. "This stuff is mild. It's dope you can reason with," I said. "It doesn't mess you up."

"Not much it doesn't, bub," he said, and laughed.

My wife sat on the sofa between the blind man and me. I passed her the number. She took it and toked and then passed it back to me. "Which way is this going?" she said. Then she said, "I shouldn't be smoking this. I can hardly keep my eyes open as it is. That dinner did me in. I shouldn't have eaten so much."

"It was the strawberry pie," the blind man said. "That's what did it," he said, and he laughed his big laugh. Then he shook his head.

"There's more strawberry pie," I said. 70

"Do you want some more, Robert?" my wife said.

"Maybe in a little while," he said.

We gave our attention to the TV. My wife yawned again. She said, "Your bed is made up when you feel like going to bed, Robert. I know you must have had a long day. When you're ready to go to bed, say so." She pulled his arm. "Robert?"

He came to and said, "I've had a real nice time. This beats tapes, doesn't it?"

I said, "Coming at you," and I put the number between his fingers. 75
He inhaled, held the smoke, and then let it go. It was like he'd been doing
it since he was nine years old.

"Thanks, bub," he said. "But I think this is all for me. I think I'm
beginning to feel it," he said. He held the burning roach out for my wife.

"Same here," she said. "Ditto. Me, too." She took the roach and
passed it to me. "I may just sit here for a while between you two guys with
my eyes closed. But don't let me bother you, okay? Either one of you. If it
bothers you, say so. Otherwise, I may just sit here with my eyes closed
until you're ready to go to bed," she said. "You bed's made up, Robert,
when you're ready. It's right next to our room at the top of the stairs. We'll
show you up when you're ready. You wake me up now, you guys, if I fall
asleep." She said that and then she closed her eyes and went to sleep.

The news program ended. I got up and changed the channel. I sat back
down on the sofa. I wished my wife hadn't pooped out. Her head lay across
the back of the sofa, her mouth open. She'd turned so that her robe had
slipped away from her legs, exposing a juicy thigh. I reached to draw her
robe back over her, and it was then that I glanced at the blind man. What
the hell! I flipped the robe open again.

"You say when you want some strawberry pie," I said.

"I will," he said. 80

I said, "Are you tired? Do you want me to take you up to your bed?
Are you ready to hit the hay?"

"Not yet," he said. "No, I'll stay up with you bub. If that's all right.
I'll stay up until you're ready to turn in. We haven't had a chance to talk.
Know what I mean? I feel like me and her monopolized the evening." He
lifted his beard and he let it fall. He picked up his cigarettes and his lighter.

"That's all right," I said. Then I said, "I'm glad for the company."

And I guess I was. Every night I smoked dope and stayed up as long
as I could before I fell asleep. My wife and I hardly ever went to bed at the
same time. When I did go to sleep, I had these dreams. Sometimes I'd wake
up from one of them, my heart going crazy.

Something about the church and the Middle Ages was on the TV. Not 85
your run-of-the-mill TV fare. I wanted to watch something else. I turned to
the other channels. But there was nothing on them, either. So I turned back
to the first channel and apologized.

"Bub, it's all right," the blind man said. "It's fine with me. Whatever
you want to watch is okay. I'm always learning something. Learning never
ends. It won't hurt me to learn something tonight. I got ears," he said.

We didn't say anything for a time. He was leaning forward with his
head turned at me, his right ear aimed in the direction of the set. Very
disconcerting. Now and then his eyelids drooped and then they snapped
open again. Now and then he put his fingers into his beard and tugged, like
he was thinking about something he was hearing on the television.

On the screen, a group of men wearing cowls was being set upon and tormented by men dressed in skeleton costumes and men dressed as devils. The men dressed as devils wore devil masks, horns, and long tails. This pageant was part of a procession. The Englishman who was narrating the thing said it took place in Spain once a year. I tried to explain to the blind man what was happening.

"Skeletons," he said. "I know about skeletons," he said, and he nodded.

The TV showed this one cathedral. Then there was a long, slow look   90
at another one. Finally, the picture switched to the famous one in Paris, with its flying buttresses and its spires reaching up to the clouds. The camera pulled away to show the whole of the cathedral rising above the skyline.

There were times when the Englishman who was telling the thing would shut up, would simply let the camera move around over the cathedrals. Or else the camera would tour the countryside, men in fields walking behind oxen. I waited as long as I could. Then I felt I had to say something. I said, "They're showing the outside of this cathedral now. Gargoyles. Little statues carved to look like monsters. Now I guess they're in Italy. Yeah, they're in Italy. There's paintings on the walls of this one church."

"Are those fresco paintings, bub?" he asked, and he sipped from his drink.

I reached for my glass. But it was empty. I tried to remember what I could remember. "You're asking me are those frescoes?" I said. "That's a good question. I don't know."

The camera moved to a cathedral outside Lisbon. The differences in the Portuguese cathedral compared with the French and Italian were not that great. But they were there. Mostly the interior stuff. Then something occurred to me, and I said, "Something has occurred to me. Do you have any idea what a cathedral is? What they look like, that is? Do you follow me? If somebody says cathedral to you, do you have any notion what they're talking about? Do you know the difference between that and a Baptist church, say?"

He let the smoke dribble from his mouth. "I know they took hundreds   95
of workers fifty or a thousand years to build," he said. "I just heard the man say that, of course. I know generations of the same families worked on a cathedral. I heard him say that, too. The men who began their life's work on them, they never lived to see the completion of their work. In that wise, bub, they're no different from the rest of us, right?" He laughed. Then his eyelids drooped again. His head nodded. He seemed to be snoozing. Maybe he was imagining himself in Portugal. The TV was showing another cathedral now. This one was in Germany. The Englishman's voice droned on. "Cathedrals," the blind man said. He sat up and rolled his head back and forth. "If you want the truth, bub, that's about all I know. What I just said. What I heard him say. But maybe you could describe one to me? I wish you'd do it. I'd like that. If you want to know, I really don't have a good idea."

I stared hard at the shot of the cathedral on the TV. How could I even begin to describe it? But say my life depended on it. Say my life was being threatened by an insane guy who said I had to do it or else.

I stared some more at the cathedral before the picture flipped off into the countryside. There was no use. I turned to the blind man and said, "To begin with, they're very tall." I was looking around the room for clues. "They reach way up. Up and up. Toward the sky. They're so big, some of them, they have to have these supports. To help hold them up, so to speak. These supports are called buttresses. They remind me of viaducts, for some reason. But maybe you don't know viaducts, either? Sometimes the cathedrals have devils and such carved into the front. Sometimes lords and ladies. Don't ask me why this is," I said.

He was nodding. The whole upper part of his body seemed to be moving back and forth.

"I'm not doing so good, am I?" I said.

He stopped nodding and leaned forward on the edge of the sofa. As he   100 listened to me, he was running his fingers through his beard. I wasn't getting through to him, I could see that. But he waited for me to go on just the same. He nodded, like he was trying to encourage me. I tried to think what else to say. "They're really big," I said. "They're massive. They're built of stone. Marble, too, sometimes. In those olden days, when they built cathedrals, men wanted to be close to God. In those olden days, God was an important part of everyone's life. You could tell this from their cathedral-building. I'm sorry," I said, "but it looks like that's the best I can do for you. I'm just no good at it."

"That's all right, bub," the blind man said. "Hey, listen. I hope you don't mind my asking you. Can I ask you something? Let me ask you a simple question, yes or no. I'm just curious and there's no offense. You're my host. But let me ask if you are in any way religious? You don't mind my asking?"

I shook my head. He couldn't see that, though. A wink is the same as a nod to a blind man. "I guess I don't believe in it. In anything. Sometimes it's hard. You know what I'm saying?"

"Sure, I do," he said.

"Right," I said.

The Englishman was still holding forth. My wife sighed in her sleep.   105 She drew a long breath and went on with her sleeping.

"You'll have to forgive me," I said. "But I can't tell you what a cathedral looks like. It just isn't in me to do it. I can't do any more than I've done."

The blind man sat very still, his head down, as he listened to me.

I said, "The truth is, cathedrals don't mean anything special to me. Nothing. Cathedrals. They're something to look at on late-night TV. That's all they are."

It was then that the blind man cleared his throat. He brought something up. He took a handkerchief from his back pocket. Then he said, "I get it, bub. It's okay. It happens. Don't worry about it," he said. "Hey, listen to me. Will you do me a favor? I got an idea. Why don't you find us some heavy paper? And a pen. We'll do something. We'll draw one together. Get us a pen and some heavy paper. Go on, bub, get the stuff," he said.

So I went upstairs. My legs felt like they didn't have any strength in them. They felt like they did after I'd done some running. In my wife's room, I looked around. I found some ballpoints in a little basket on her table. And then I tried to think where to look for the kind of paper he was talking about.

Downstairs, in the kitchen, I found a shopping bag with onion skins in the bottom of the bag. I emptied the bag and shook it. I brought it into the living room and sat down with it near his legs. I moved some things, smoothed the wrinkles from the bag, spread it out on the coffee table.

The blind man got down from the sofa and sat next to me on the carpet.

He ran his fingers over the paper. He went up and down the sides of the paper. The edges, even the edges. He fingered the corners.

"All right," he said. "All right, let's do her."

He found my hand, the hand with the pen. He closed his hand over my hand. "Go ahead, bub, draw," he said. "Draw. You'll see. I'll follow along with you. It'll be okay. Just begin now like I'm telling you. You'll see. Draw," the blind man said.

So I began. First I drew a box that looked like a house. It could have been the house I lived in. Then I put a roof on it. At either end of the roof, I drew spires. Crazy.

"Swell," he said. "Terrific. You're doing fine," he said. "Never thought anything like this could happen in your lifetime, did you, bub? Well, it's a strange life, we all know that. Go on now. Keep it up."

I put in windows with arches. I drew flying buttresses. I hung great doors. I couldn't stop. The TV station went off the air. I put down the pen and closed and opened my fingers. The blind man felt around over the paper. He moved the tips of his fingers over the paper, all over what I had drawn, and he nodded.

"Doing fine," the blind man said.

I took up the pen again, and he found my hand. I kept at it. I'm no artist. But I kept drawing just the same.

My wife opened her eyes and gazed at us. She sat up on the sofa, her robe hanging open. She said, "What are you doing? Tell me, I want to know."

I didn't answer her.

The blind man said, "We're drawing a cathedral. Me and him are working on it. Press hard," he said to me. "That's right. That's good," he said. "Sure, you got it, bub. I can tell. You didn't think you could. But you can, can't you? You're cooking with gas now. You know what I'm saying? We're going to really have us something here in a minute. How's the old arm?" he said. "Put some people in there now. What's a cathedral without people?"

My wife said, "What's going on? Robert, what are you doing? What's going on?"

"It's all right," he said to her. "Close your eyes now," the blind man   125
said to me.

I did it. I closed them just like he said.

"Are they closed?" he said. "Don't fudge."

"They're closed," I said.

"Keep them that way," he said, "Don't stop now. Draw."

So we kept on with it. His fingers rode my fingers as my hand went   130
over the paper. It was like nothing else in my life up to now.

Then he said, "I think that's it. I think you got it," he said. "Take a look. What do you think?"

But I had my eyes closed. I thought I'd keep them that way for a little longer. I thought it was something I ought to do.

"Well?" he said. "Are you looking?"

My eyes were still closed. I was in my house. I knew that. But I didn't feel like I was inside anything.

"It's really something," I said.   135

ALICE WALKER (1944–   )

Everyday Use
For Your Grandmama

I will wait for her in the yard that Maggie and I made so clean and wavy yesterday afternoon. A yard like this is more comfortable than most people know. It is not just a yard. It is like an extended living room. When the hard clay is swept clean as a floor and the fine sand around the edges lined with tiny, irregular grooves anyone can come and sit and look up into the elm tree and wait for the breezes that never come inside the house.

Maggie will be nervous until after her sister goes: she will stand hopelessly in corners homely and ashamed of the burn scars down her arms and legs, eyeing her sister with a mixture of envy and awe. She thinks her sister has held life always in the palm of one hand, that "no" is a word the world never learned to say to her.

You've no doubt seen those TV shows where the child who has "made it" is confronted, as a surprise, by her own mother and father, tottering in weakly from backstage. (A pleasant surprise, of course: What would they do if parent and child came on the show only to curse out and insult each other?) On TV mother and child embrace and smile into each other's faces. Sometimes the mother and father weep, the child wraps them in her arms and leans across the table to tell how she would not have made it without their help. I have seen these programs.

Sometimes I dream a dream in which Dee and I are suddenly brought together on a TV program of this sort. Out of a dark and soft-seated limousine I am ushered into a bright room filled with many people. There I meet a smiling, gray, sporty man like Johnny Carson who shakes my hand and tells me what a fine girl I have. Then we are on the stage and Dee is embracing me with tears in her eyes. She pins on my dress a large orchid, even though she has told me once that she thinks orchids are tacky flowers.

In real life I am a large, big-boned woman with rough, man-working   5
hands. In the winter I wear flannel nightgowns to bed and overalls during the day. I can kill and clean a hog as mercilessly as a man. My fat keeps me hot in zero weather. I can work outside all day, breaking ice to get water for washing; I can eat pork liver cooked over the open fire minutes after it comes steaming from the hog. One winter I knocked a bull calf straight in the brain between the eyes with a sledge hammer and had the meat hung up to chill before nightfall. But of course all this does not show on television. I am the way my daughter would want me to be: a hundred pounds lighter, my skin like an uncooked barley pancake. My hair glistens in the hot bright lights. Johnny Carson has much to do to keep up with my quick and witty tongue.

But that is a mistake. I know even before I wake up. Who ever knew a

Johnson with a quick tongue? Who can even imagine me looking a strange white man in the eye? It seems to me I have talked to them always with one foot raised in flight, with my head turned in whichever way is farthest from them. Dee, though. She would always look anyone in the eye. Hesitation was no part of her nature.

"How do I look, Mama?" Maggie says, showing just enough of her thin body enveloped in pink skirt and red blouse for me to know she's there, almost hidden by the door.

"Come out into the yard," I say.

Have you ever seen a lame animal, perhaps a dog run over by some careless person rich enough to own a car, sidle up to someone who is ignorant enough to be kind to him? That is the way my Maggie walks. She has been like this, chin on chest, eyes on ground, feet in shuffle, ever since the fire that burned the other house to the ground.

Dee is lighter than Maggie, with nicer hair and a fuller figure. She's a 10 woman now, though sometimes I forget. How long ago was it that the other house burned? Ten, twelve years? Sometimes I can still hear the flames and feel Maggie's arms sticking to me, her hair smoking and her dress falling off her in little black papery flakes. Her eyes seemed stretched open, blazed open by the flames reflected in them. And Dee. I see her standing off under the sweet gum tree she used to dig gum out of; a look of concentration on her face as she watched the last dingy gray board of the house fall in toward the red-hot brick chimney. Why don't you do a dance around the ashes? I'd wanted to ask her. She had hated the house that much.

I used to think she hated Maggie, too. But that was before we raised the money, the church and me, to send her to Augusta to school. She used to read to us without pity; forcing words, lies, other folks' habits, whole lives upon us two, sitting trapped and ignorant underneath her voice. She washed us in a river of make-believe, burned us with a lot of knowledge we didn't necessarily need to know. Pressed us to her with the serious way she read, to shove us away at just the moment, like dimwits, we seemed about to understand.

Dee wanted nice things. A yellow organdy dress to wear to her graduation from high school; black pumps to match a green suit she'd made from an old suit somebody gave me. She was determined to stare down any disaster in her efforts. Her eyelids would not flicker for minutes at a time. Often I fought off the temptation to shake her. At sixteen she had a style of her own: and knew what style was.

I never had an education myself. After second grade the school was closed down. Don't ask me why: in 1927 colored asked fewer questions than they do now. Sometimes Maggie reads to me. She stumbles along good-naturedly but can't see well. She knows she is not bright. Like good looks and money, quickness passed her by. She will marry John Thomas (who has mossy teeth in an earnest face) and then I'll be free to sit here and I guess just sing church songs to myself. Although I never was a good singer. Never could carry a tune. I was always better at a man's job. I used to love to milk till I was hooked in the side in '49. Cows are soothing and slow and don't bother you, unless you try to milk them the wrong way.

I have deliberately turned my back on the house. It is three rooms, just like the one that burned, except the roof is tin; they don't make shingle roofs any more. There are no real windows, just some holes cut in the sides, like the portholes in a ship, but not round and not square, with rawhide holding the shutters up on the outside. This house is in a pasture, too, like the other one. No doubt when Dee sees it she will want to tear it down. She wrote me once that no matter where we "choose" to live, she will manage to come see us. But she will never bring her friends. Maggie and I thought about this and Maggie asked me, "Mama, when did Dee ever *have* any friends?"

She had a few. Furtive boys in pink shirts hanging about on washday   15
after school. Nervous girls who never laughed. Impressed with her they worshiped the well-turned phrase, the cute shape, the scalding humor that erupted like bubbles in lye. She read to them.

When she was courting Jimmy T she didn't have much time to pay to us, but turned all her faultfinding power on him. He *flew* to marry a cheap gal from a family of ignorant flashy people. She hardly had time to recompose herself.

When she comes I will meet — but there they are!

Maggie attempts to make a dash for the house, in her shuffling way, but I stay her with my hand. "Come back here," I say. And she stops and tries to dig a well in the sand with her toe.

It is hard to see them clearly through the strong sun. But even the first glimpse of leg out of the car tells me it is Dee. Her feet were always neat-looking, as if God himself had shaped them with a certain style. From the other side of the car comes a short, stocky man. Hair is all over his head a foot long and hanging from his chin like a kinky mule tail. I hear Maggie suck in her breath. "Uhnnnh," is what it sounds like. Like when you see the wriggling end of a snake just in front of your foot on the road. "Uhnnnh."

Dee next. A dress down to the ground, in this hot weather. A dress so   20
loud it hurts my eyes. There are yellows and oranges enough to throw back the light of the sun. I feel my whole face warming from the heat waves it throws out. Earrings gold, too, and hanging down to her shoulders. Bracelets dangling and making noises when she moves her arm up to shake the folds of the dress out of her armpits. The dress is loose and flows, and as she walks closer, I like it. I hear Maggie go "Uhnnnh" again. It is her sister's hair. It stands straight up like the wool on a sheep. It is black as night and around the edges are two long pigtails that rope about like small lizards disappearing behind her ears.

"Wa-su-zo-Tean-o!" she says, coming on in that gliding way the dress makes her move. The short stocky fellow with the hair to his navel is all grinning and he follows up with "Asalamalakim, my mother and sister!" He moves to hug Maggie but she falls back, right up against the back of my chair. I feel her trembling there and when I look up I see the perspiration falling off her chin.

"Don't get up," says Dee. Since I am stout it takes something of a push. You can see me trying to move a second or two before I make it. She turns, showing white heels through her sandals, and goes back to the car. Out she peeks next with a Polaroid. She stoops down quickly and lines up picture after picture of me sitting there in front of the house with Maggie cowering behind me. She never takes a shot without making sure the house is included. When a cow comes nibbling around the edge of the yard she snaps it and me and Maggie *and* the house. Then she puts the Polaroid in the back seat of the car, and comes up and kisses me on the forehead.

Meanwhile Asalamalakim is going through the motions with Maggie's hand. Maggie's hand is as limp as a fish, and probably as cold, despite the sweat, and she keeps trying to pull it back. It looks like Asalamalakim wants to shake hands but wants to do it fancy. Or maybe he don't know how people shake hands. Anyhow, he soon gives up on Maggie.

"Well," I say. "Dee."

"No, Mama," she says. "Not 'Dee,' Wangero Leewanika Kemanjo!"   25

"What happened to 'Dee'?" I wanted to know.

"She's dead," Wangero said. "I couldn't bear it any longer being named after the people who oppress me."

"You know as well as me you was named after your aunt Dicie," I said. Dicie is my sister. She named Dee. We called her "Big Dee" after Dee was born.

"But who was *she* named after?" asked Wangero.

"I guess after Grandma Dee," I said.   30

"And who was she named after?" asked Wangero.

"Her mother," I said, and saw Wangero was getting tired. "That's about as far back as I can trace it," I said. Though, in fact, I probably could have carried it back beyond the Civil War through the branches.

"Well," said Asalamalakim, "there you are."

"Uhnnnh," I heard Maggie say.

"There I was not," I said, "before 'Dicie' cropped up in our family, so   35 why should I try to trace it that far back?"

He just stood there grinning, looking down on me like somebody inspecting a Model A car. Every once in a while he and Wangero sent eye signals over my head.

"How do you pronounce this name?" I asked.

"You don't have to call me by it if you don't want to," said Wangero.

"Why shouldn't I?" I asked. "If that's what you want us to call you, we'll call you."

"I know it might sound awkward at first," said Wangero.   40

"I'll get used to it," I said. "Ream it out again."

Well, soon we got the name out of the way. Asalamalakim had a name twice as long and three times as hard. After I tripped over it two or three times he told me to just call him Hakim-a-barber. I wanted to ask him was he a barber, but I didn't really think he was, so I didn't ask.

"You must belong to those beef-cattle peoples down the road," I said. They said "Asalamalakim" when they met you, too, but they didn't shake hands. Always too busy: feeding the cattle, fixing the fences, putting up salt-lick shelters, throwing down hay. When the white folks poisoned some of the herd the men stayed up all night with rifles in their hands. I walked a mile and a half just to see the sight.

Hakim-a-barber said, "I accept some of their doctrines, but farming and raising cattle is not my style." (They didn't tell me, and I didn't ask, whether Wangero [Dee] had really gone and married him.)

We sat down to eat and right away he said he didn't eat collards and 45 pork was unclean. Wangero, though, went on through the chitlins and corn bread, the greens and everything else. She talked a blue streak over the sweet potatoes. Everything delighted her. Even the fact that we still used the benches her daddy made for the table when we couldn't afford to buy chairs.

"Oh, Mama!" she cried. Then turned to Hakim-a-barber. "I never knew how lovely these benches are. You can feel the rump prints," she said, running her hands underneath her and along the bench. Then she gave a sigh and her hand closed over Grandma Dee's butter dish. "That's it!" she said. "I knew there was something I wanted to ask you if I could have." She jumped up from the table and went over in the corner where the churn stood, the milk in it clabber by now. She looked at the churn and looked at it.

"This churn top is what I need," she said. "Didn't Uncle Buddy whittle it out of a tree you all used to have?"

"Yes," I said.

"Uh huh," she said happily. "And I want the dasher, too."

"Uncle Buddy whittle that, too?" asked the barber. 50

Dee (Wangero) looked up at me.

"Aunt Dee's first husband whittled the dash," said Maggie so low you almost couldn't hear her. "His name was Henry, but they called him Stash."

"Maggie's brain is like an elephant's," Wangero said, laughing. "I can use the churn top as a centerpiece for the alcove table," she said, sliding a plate over the churn, "and I'll think of something artistic to do with the dasher."

When she finished wrapping the dasher the handle stuck out. I took it for a moment in my hands. You didn't even have to look close to see where hands pushing the dasher up and down to make butter had left a kind of sink in the wood. In fact, there were a lot of small sinks; you could see where thumbs and fingers had sunk into the wood. It was beautiful light yellow wood, from a tree that grew in the yard where Big Dee and Stash had lived.

After dinner Dee (Wangero) went to the trunk at the foot of my bed 55
and started rifling through it. Maggie hung back in the kitchen over the
dishpan. Out came Wangero with two quilts. They had been pieced by
Grandma Dee and then Big Dee and me had hung them on the quilt frames
on the front porch and quilted them. One was in the Lone Star pattern. The
other was Walk Around the Mountain. In both of them were scraps of
dresses Grandma Dee had worn fifty and more years ago. Bits and pieces of
Grandpa Jarrell's paisley shirts. And one teeny faded blue piece, about the
size of a penny matchbox, that was from Great Grandpa Ezra's uniform that
he wore in the Civil War.

"Mama," Wangero said sweet as a bird. "Can I have these old quilts?"

I heard something fall in the kitchen, and a minute later the kitchen
door slammed.

"Why don't you take one or two of the others?" I asked. "These old
things was just done by me and Big Dee from some tops your grandma
pieced before she died."

"No," said Wangero. "I don't want those. They are stitched around
the borders by machine."

"That'll make them last better," I said. 60

"That's not the point," said Wangero. "These are all pieces of dresses
Grandma used to wear. She did all this stitching by hand. Imagine!" She
held the quilts securely in her arms, stroking them.

"Some of the pieces, like those lavender ones, come from old clothes
her mother handed down to her," I said, moving up to touch the quilts. Dee
(Wangero) moved back just enough so that I couldn't reach the quilts. They
already belonged to her.

"Imagine!" she breathed again, clutching them closely to her bosom.

"The truth is," I said, "I promised to give them quilts to Maggie, for
when she marries John Thomas."

She gasped like a bee had stung her. 65

"Maggie can't appreciate these quilts!" she said. "She'd probably be
backward enough to put them to everyday use."

"I reckon she would," I said. "God knows I been saving 'em for long
enough with nobody using 'em. I hope she will!" I didn't want to bring up
how I had offered Dee (Wangero) a quilt when she went away to college.
Then she had told me they were old-fashioned, out of style.

"But they're *priceless!*" she was saying now, furiously; for she has a
temper. "Maggie would put them on the bed and in five years they'd be in
rags. Less than that!"

"She can always make some more," I said. "Maggie knows how to
quilt."

Dee (Wangero) looked at me with hatred. "You just will not under- 70
stand. The point is these quilts, *these* quilts!"

"Well," I said, stumped. "What would *you* do with them?"

"Hang them," she said. As if that was the only thing you *could* do
with quilts.

Maggie by now was standing in the door. I could almost hear the sound her feet made as they scraped over each other.

"She can have them, Mama," she said, like somebody used to never winning anything, or having anything reserved for her. "I can 'member Grandma Dee without the quilts."

I looked at her hard. She had filled her bottom lip with checkerberry   75
snuff and it gave her face a kind of dopey, hangdog look. It was Grandma Dee and Big Dee who taught her how to quilt herself. She stood there with her scarred hands hidden in the folds of her skirt. She looked at her sister with something like fear but she wasn't mad at her. This was Maggie's portion. This was the way she knew God to work.

When I looked at her like that something hit me in the top of my head and ran down to the soles of my feet. Just like when I'm in church and the spirit of God touches me and I get happy and shout. I did something I never had done before: hugged Maggie to me, then dragged her on into the room, snatched the quilts out of Miss Wangero's hands and dumped them into Maggie's lap. Maggie just sat there on my bed with her mouth open.

"Take one or two of the others," I said to Dee.

But she turned without a word and went out to Hakim-a-barber.

"You just don't understand," she said, as Maggie and I came out to the car.

"What don't I understand?" I wanted to know.   80

"Your heritage," she said. And then she turned to Maggie, kissed her, and said, "You ought to try to make something of yourself, too, Maggie. It's really a new day for us. But from the way you and Mama still live you'd never know it."

She put on some sunglasses that hid everything above the tip of her nose and her chin.

Maggie smiled; maybe at the sunglasses. But a real smile, not scared. After we watched the car dust settle I asked Maggie to bring me a dip of snuff. And then the two of us sat there just enjoying, until it was time to go in the house and go to bed.

ALICE MUNRO (1931–   )

Spelling

In the store, in the old days, Flo used to say she could tell when some woman was going off the track. Special headgear or footwear were often the first giveaways. Galoshes flopping open on a summer day. Rubber boots they slopped around in, or men's workboots. They might say it was on account of corns, but Flo knew better. It was deliberate, it was meant to tell. Next might come the old felt hat, the torn raincoat worn in all weathers, the trousers held up at the waist with twine, the dim shredded scarves, the layers of ravelling sweaters.

Mothers and daughters often the same way. It was always in them. Waves of craziness, always rising, irresistible as giggles, from some place deep inside, gradually getting the better of them.

They used to come telling Flo their stories. Flo would string them along. "Is that so?" she would say. "Isn't that a shame?"

My vegetable grater is gone and I know who took it.

There is a man comes and looks at me when I take my clothes off at night. I   5
pull the blind down and he looks through the crack.

Two hills of new potatoes stolen. A jar of whole peaches. Some nice ducks' eggs.

One of those women they took to the County Home at last. The first thing they did, Flo said, was give her a bath. The next thing they did was cut off her hair, which had grown out like a haystack. They expected to find anything in it, a dead bird or maybe a nest of baby mouse skeletons. They did find burrs and leaves and a bee that must have got caught and buzzed itself to death. When they had cut down far enough they found a cloth hat. It had rotted on her head and the hair had just pushed up through it, like grass through wire.

Flo had got into the habit of keeping the table set for the next meal, to save trouble. The plastic cloth was gummy, the outline of the plate and saucer plain on it as the outline of pictures on a greasy wall. The refrigerator was full of sulfurous scraps, dark crusts, furry oddments. Rose got to work cleaning, scraping, scalding. Sometimes Flo came lumbering through on her two canes. She might ignore Rose's presence altogether, she might tip the jug of maple syrup up against her mouth and drink it like wine. She loved sweet things now, craved them. Brown sugar by the spoonful, maple syrup, tinned puddings, jelly, globs of sweetness to slide down her throat. She had given up smoking, probably for fear of fire.

Another time she said, "What are you doing in there behind the counter? You ask me what you want, and I'll get it." She thought the kitchen was the store.

"I'm *Rose,*" Rose said in a loud, slow voice. "We're in the *kitchen.* I'm   10
cleaning up the *kitchen.*"

The old arrangement of the kitchen: mysterious, personal, eccentric. Big pan in the oven, medium-sized pan under the potato pot on the corner shelf, little pan hanging on the nail by the sink. Colander under the sink. Dishrags, newspaper clippings, scissors, muffin tins, hanging on various nails. Piles of bills and letters on the sewing machine, on the telephone shelf. You would think someone had set them down a day or two ago, but they were years old. Rose had come across some letters written by herself, in a forced and spritely style. False messengers; false connections, with a lost period of her life.

"Rose is away," Flo said. She had a habit now of sticking her bottom lip out, when she was displeased or perplexed. "Rose got married."

The second morning Rose got up and found that a gigantic stirring-up had occurred in the kitchen, as if someone had wielded a big shaky spoon. The big pan was lodged behind the refrigerator; the egg lifter was in with the towels, the bread knife was in the flour bin and the roasting pan wedged in the pipes under the sink. Rose made Flo's breakfast porridge and Flo said, "You're that woman they were sending to look after me."

"Yes."

"You aren't from around here?"   15

"No."

"I haven't got money to pay you. They sent you, they can pay you."

Flo spread brown sugar over her porridge until the porridge was entirely covered, then patted the sugar smooth with her spoon.

After breakfast she spied the cutting board, which Rose had been using when she cut bread for her own toast. "What is this thing doing here getting in our road?" said Flo authoritatively, picking it up and marching off—as well as anybody with two canes could march—to hide it somewhere, in the piano bench or under the back steps.

Years ago, Flo had had a little glassed-in side porch built on to the   20
house. From there she could watch the road just as she used to watch from behind the counter of the store (the store window was now boarded up, the old advertising signs painted over). The road wasn't the main road out of Hanratty through West Hanratty to the Lake anymore; there was a highway bypass. And it was paved, now, with wide gutters, new mercury vapor street lights. The old bridge was gone and a new, wide bridge, much less emphatic, had taken its place. The change from Hanratty to West Hanratty was hardly noticeable. West Hanratty had got itself spruced up with paint and aluminum siding; Flo's place was about the only eyesore left.

What were the things Flo put up to look at, in her little porch, where she had been sitting for years now with her joints and arteries hardening?

A calendar with a picture of a puppy and a kitten on it. Faces turned toward each other so that the noses touched, and the space between the two bodies made a heart.

A photograph, in color, of Princess Anne as a child.

A Blue Mountain pottery vase, gift from Brian and Phoebe, with three yellow plastic roses in it, vase and roses bearing several seasons' sifting of dust.

Six shells from the Pacific coast, sent home by Rose but not gathered by her, as Flo believed, or had once believed. Bought on a vacation in the state of Washington. They were an impulse item in a plastic bag by the cashier's desk in a tourist restaurant.

THE LORD IS MY SHEPHERD, in black cutout scroll with a sprinkling of glitter. Free gift from a dairy.

Newspaper photograph of seven coffins in a row. Two large and five small. Parents and children, all shot by the father in the middle of the night, for reasons nobody knew, in a farmhouse out in the country. That house was not easy to find but Flo had seen it. Neighbors took her, on a Sunday drive, in the days when she was using only one cane. They had to ask directions at a gas station on the highway, and again at a crossroads store. They were told that many people had asked the same questions, had been equally determined. Though Flo had to admit there was nothing much to see. A house like any other. The chimney, the windows, the shingles, the door. Something that could have been a dish towel, or a diaper, that nobody had felt like taking in, left to rot on the line.

Rose had not been back to see Flo for nearly two years. She had been busy, she had been traveling with small companies, financed by grants, putting on plays or scenes from plays, or giving readings, in high school auditoriums and community halls, all over the country. It was part of her job to go on local television chatting about these productions, trying to drum up interest, telling amusing stories about things that had happened during the tour. There was nothing shameful about any of this, but sometimes Rose was deeply, unaccountably ashamed. She did not let her confusion show. When she talked in public she was frank and charming; she had a puzzled, diffident way of leading into her anecdotes, as if she were just now remembering, had not told them a hundred times already. Back in her hotel room, she often shivered and moaned, as if she were having an attack of fever. She blamed it on exhaustion, or her approaching menopause. She couldn't remember any of the people she had met, the charming, interesting people who had invited her to dinner and to whom, over drinks in various cities, she had told intimate things about her life.

Neglect in Flo's house had turned a final corner, since Rose saw it last. The rooms were plugged up with rags and papers and dirt. Pull a blind to let some light in, and the blind comes apart in your hand. Shake a curtain and the curtain falls to rags, letting loose a choking dust. Put a hand into a drawer and it sinks into something soft and dark and rubbishy.

We hate to write bad news but it looks like she has got past where she can look after herself. We try to look in on her but we are not so young ourselves anymore so it looks like maybe the time has come.

The same letter, more or less, had been written to Rose and to her half brother, Brian, who was an engineer, living in Toronto. Rose had just come back from her tour. She had assumed that Brian and his wife, Phoebe, whom she saw seldom, were keeping in touch with Flo. After all, Flo was Brian's mother, Rose's stepmother. And it turned out that they had been keeping in touch, or so they thought. Brian had recently been in South America but Phoebe had been phoning Flo every Sunday night. Flo had little to say but she had never talked to Phoebe anyway; she had said she was fine, everything was fine, she had offered some information about the weather. Rose had observed Flo on the telephone, since she came home, and she saw how Phoebe could have been deceived. Flo spoke normally, she said hello, fine, that was a big storm we had last night, yes, the lights were out here for hours. If you didn't live in the neighborhood you wouldn't realize there hadn't been any storm.

It wasn't that Rose had entirely forgotten Flo in those two years. She had fits of worry about her. It was just that for some time now she had been between fits. One time the fit had come over her in the middle of a January storm, she had driven two hundred miles through blizzards, past ditched cars, and when she finally parked on Flo's street, finally tramped up the walk Flo had not been able to shovel, she was full of relief for herself and concern for Flo, a general turmoil of feelings both anxious and pleasurable. Flo opened the door and gave a bark of warning.

"You can't park there!"

"What?"

"Can't park there!"   35

Flo said there was a new bylaw; no parking on the streets during the winter months.

"You'll have to shovel out a place."

Of course Rose had an explosion.

"If you say one more word right now I'll get in the car and drive back."

"Well you can't park —"   40

"One more word!"

"Why do you have to stand here and argue with the cold blasting into the house?"

Rose stepped inside. Home.

That was one of the stories she told about Flo. She did it well; her own exhaustion and sense of virtue; Flo's bark, her waving cane, her fierce unwillingness to be the object of anybody's rescue.

After she read the letter Rose had phoned Phoebe, and Phoebe had   45
asked her to come to dinner, so they could talk. Rose resolved to behave well. She had an idea that Brian and Phoebe moved in a permanent cloud of disapproval of her. She thought that they disapproved of her success, limited and precarious and provincial though it might be, and that they disapproved of her even more when she failed. She also knew it was not likely they would have her on their minds so much, or feel anything so definite.

She put on a plain skirt and an old blouse, but at the last minute changed into a long dress, made of thin red and gold cotton from India, the very thing that would justify their saying that Rose was always so theatrical.

Nevertheless she made up her mind as she usually did that she would speak in a low voice, stick to facts, not get into any stale and silly arguments with Brian. And as usual most of the sense seemed to fly out of her head as soon as she entered their house, was subjected to their calm routines, felt the flow of satisfaction, self-satisfaction, perfectly justified self-satisfaction, that emanated from the very bowls and draperies. She was nervous, when Phoebe asked her about her tour, and Phoebe was a bit nervous too, because Brian sat silent, not exactly frowning but indicating that the frivolity of the subject did not please him. In Rose's presence Brian had said more than once that he had no use for people in her line of work. But he had no use for a good many people. Actors, artists, journalists, rich people (he would never admit to being one himself), the entire Arts faculty of universities. Whole classes and categories, down the drain. Convicted of woolly-mindedness, and showy behavior; inaccurate talk, many excesses. Rose did not know if he spoke the truth or if this was something he had to say in front of her. He offered the bait of his low-voiced contempt; she rose to it; they had fights, she had left his house in tears. And underneath all this, Rose felt, they loved each other. But they could never stop the old, old competition; who is the better person, who has chosen the better work? What were they looking for? Each other's good opinion, which perhaps they meant to grant, in full, but not yet. Phoebe, who was a calm and dutiful woman with a great talent for normalizing things (the very opposite of their family talent for blowing things up) would serve food and pour coffee and regard them with a polite puzzlement; their contest, their vulnerability, their hurt, perhaps seemed as odd to her as the antics of comic-strip characters who stick their fingers into light sockets.

"I always wished Flo could have come back for another visit with us," Phoebe said. Flo had come once, and asked to be taken home after three days. But afterward it seemed to be a pleasure to her, to sit and list the things Brian and Phoebe owned, the features of their house. Brian and Phoebe lived quite unostentatiously, in Don Mills, and the things Flo dwelt on — the door chimes, the automatic garage doors, the swimming pool — were among the ordinary suburban acquisitions. Rose had said as much to Flo who believed that she, Rose, was jealous.

"You wouldn't turn them down if you was offered."

"Yes I would."   50

That was true, Rose believed it was true, but how could she ever explain it to Flo or anybody in Hanratty? If you stay in Hanratty and do not get rich it is all right because you are living out your life as was intended, but if you go away and do not get rich, or, like Rose, do not remain rich, then what was the point?

After dinner Rose and Brian and Phoebe sat in the backyard beside the pool, where the youngest of Brian and Phoebe's four daughters was riding

an inflated dragon. Everything had gone amicably, so far. It had been decided that Rose would go to Hanratty, that she would make arrangements
to get Flo into the Wawanash County Home. Brian had already made inquiries about it, or his secretary had, and he said that it seemed not only
cheaper but better run, with more facilities, than any private nursing home.

"She'll probably meet old friends there," Phoebe said.

Rose's docility, her good behavior, was partly based on a vision she
had been building up all evening, and would never reveal to Brian and
Phoebe. She pictured herself going to Hanratty and looking after Flo, living
with her, taking care of her for as long as was necessary. She thought how
she would clean and paint Flo's kitchen, patch the shingles over the leaky
spots (that was one of the things the letter had mentioned), plant flowers in
the pots, and make nourishing soup. She wasn't so far gone as to imagine
Flo fitting comfortably into this picture, settling down to a life of gratitude.
But the crankier Flo got, the milder and more patient Rose would become,
and who, then, could accuse her of egotism and frivolity?

This vision did not survive the first two days of being home.   55

"Would you like a pudding?" Rose said.

"Oh, I don't care."

The elaborate carelessness some people will show, the gleam of hope,
on being offered a drink.

Rose made a trifle. Berries, peaches, custard, cake, whipped cream and
sweet sherry.

Flo ate half the bowlful. She dipped in greedily, not bothering to   60
transfer a portion to a smaller bowl.

"That was lovely," she said. Rose had never heard such an admission
of grateful pleasure from her. "Lovely," said Flo and sat remembering, appreciating, belching a little. The suave dreamy custard, the nipping berries,
robust peaches, luxury of sherry-soaked cake, munificence of whipped
cream.

Rose thought that she had never done anything in her life that came as
near pleasing Flo as this did.

"I'll make another soon."

Flo recovered herself. "Oh well. You do what you like."

Rose drove out to the County Home. She was conducted through it.   65
She tried to tell Flo about it when she came back.

"Whose home?" said Flo.

"No, the *County* Home."

Rose mentioned some people she had seen there. Flo would not admit
to knowing any of them. Rose spoke of the view and the pleasant rooms.
Flo looked angry; her face darkened and she stuck out her lip. Rose handed
her a mobile she had bought for fifty cents in the County Home Crafts

Center. Cutout birds of blue and yellow paper were bobbing and dancing, on undetectable currents of air.

"Stick it up your arse," said Flo.

Rose put the mobile up in the porch and said she had seen the trays   70
coming up, with supper on them.

"They go to the dining room if they're able, and if they're not they have trays in their rooms. I saw what they were having.

"Roast beef, well done, mashed potatoes and green beans, the frozen not the canned kind. Or an omelette. You could have a mushroom omelette or a chicken omelette or a plain omelette, if you liked."

"What was for dessert?"

"Ice cream. You could have sauce on it."

"What kind of sauce was there?"   75

"Chocolate. Butterscotch. Walnut."

"I can't eat walnuts."

"There was marshmallow too."

Out at the Home the old people were arranged in tiers. On the first floor were the bright and tidy ones. They walked around, usually with the help of canes. They visited each other, played cards. They had singsongs and hobbies. In the Crafts Center they painted pictures, hooked rugs, made quilts. If they were not able to do things like that they could make rag dolls, mobiles like the one Rose bought, poodles and snowmen which were constructed of Styrofoam balls, with sequins for eyes; they also made silhouette pictures by placing thumbtacks on traced outlines: knights on horseback, battleships, airplanes, castles.

They organized concerts; they held dances; they had checker tour-   80
naments.

"Some of them say they are the happiest here they have ever been in their lives."

Up one floor there was more television watching, there were more wheelchairs. There were those whose heads drooped, whose tongues lolled, whose limbs shook uncontrollably. Nevertheless sociability was still flourishing, also rationality, with occasional blanks and absences.

On the third floor you might get some surprises.

Some of them up there had given up speaking.

Some had given up moving, except for odd jerks and tosses of the   85
head, flailing of the arms, that seemed to be without purpose or control.

Nearly all had given up worrying about whether they were wet or dry.

Bodies were fed and wiped, taken up and tied in chairs, untied and put to bed. Taking in oxygen, giving out carbon dioxide, they continued to participate in the life of the world.

Crouched in her crib, diapered, dark as a nut, with three tufts of hair like dandelion floss sprouting from her head, an old woman was making loud shaky noises.

"Hello Aunty," the nurse said. "You're spelling today. It's lovely weather outside." She bent to the old woman's ear. "Can you spell weather?"

This nurse showed her gums when she smiled, which was all the time; she had an air of nearly demented hilarity. 90

"Weather," said the old woman. She strained forward, grunting, to get the word. Rose thought she might be going to have a bowel movement. "W-E-A-T-H-E-R."

That reminded her.

"Whether. W-H-E-T-H-E-R."

So far so good.

"Now you say something to her," the nurse said to Rose. 95

The words in Rose's mind were for a moment all obscene or despairing.

But without prompting came another.

"Forest. F-O-R-E-S-T."

"Celebrate," said Rose suddenly.

"C-E-L-E-B-R-A-T-E." 100

You had to listen very hard to make out what the old woman was saying, because she had lost much of the power to shape sounds. What she said seemed to come not from her mouth or her throat, but from deep in her lungs and belly.

"Isn't she a wonder," the nurse said. "She can't see and that's the only way we can tell she can hear. Like if you say, 'Here's your dinner,' she won't pay any attention to it, but she might start spelling *dinner.*"

"Dinner," she said, to illustrate, and the old woman picked it up. "D-I-N-N . . ." Sometimes a long wait, a long wait between letters. It seemed she had only the thinnest thread to follow, meandering through that emptiness or confusion that nobody on this side can do more than guess at. But she didn't lose it, she followed it through to the end, however tricky the word might be, or cumbersome. Finished. Then she was sitting waiting; waiting, in the middle of her sightless eventless day, till up from somewhere popped another word. She would encompass it, bend all her energy to master it. Rose wondered what the words were like, when she held them in her mind. Did they carry their usual meaning, or any meaning at all? Were they like words in dreams or in the minds of young children, each one marvelous and distinct and alive as a new animal? This one limp and clear, like a jellyfish, that one hard and mean and secretive, like a horned snail. They could be austere and comical as top hats, or smooth and lively and flattering as ribbons. A parade of private visitors, not over yet.

Something woke Rose early the next morning. She was sleeping in the little porch, the only place in Flo's house where the smell was bearable. The sky was milky and brightening. The trees across the river — due to be cut down soon, to make room for a trailer park — were hunched against the dawn sky like shaggy dark animals, like buffalo. Rose had been dreaming.

She had been having a dream obviously connected with her tour of the Home the day before.

Someone was taking her through a large building where there were 105 people in cages. Everything was dim and cobwebby at first, and Rose was protesting that this seemed a poor arrangement. But as she went on the cages got larger and more elaborate, they were like enormous wicker bird-cages, Victorian birdcages, fancifully shaped and decorated. Food was being offered to the people in the cages and Rose examined it, saw that it was choice; chocolate mousse, trifle, Black Forest cake. Then in one of the cages Rose spotted Flo, who was handsomely seated on a thronelike chair, spelling out words in a clear authoritative voice (what the words were, Rose, wakening, could not remember) and looking pleased with herself, for showing powers she had kept secret till now.

Rose listened to hear Flo breathing, stirring, in her rubble-lined room. She heard nothing. What if Flo had died? Suppose she had died at the very moment she was making her radiant, satisfied appearance in Rose's dream? Rose hurried out of bed, ran barefoot to Flo's room. The bed there was empty. She went into the kitchen and found Flo sitting at the table, dressed to go out, wearing the navy blue summer coat and matching turban hat she had worn to Brian's and Phoebe's wedding. The coat was rumpled and in need of cleaning, the turban was crooked.

"Now I'm ready for to go," Flo said.

"Go where?"

"Out there," said Flo, jerking her head. "Out to the whattayacallit. The Poorhouse."

"The Home," said Rose. "You don't have to go today." 110

"They hired you to take me, now you get a move on and take me," Flo said.

"I'm not hired. I'm Rose. I'll make you a cup of tea."

"You can make it. I won't drink it."

She made Rose think of a woman who had started in labor. Such was her concentration, her determination, her urgency. Rose thought Flo felt her death moving in her like a child, getting ready to tear her. So she gave up arguing, she got dressed, hastily packed a bag for Flo, got her to the car and drove her out to the Home, but in the matter of Flo's quickly tearing and relieving death she was mistaken.

Some time before this, Rose had been in a play, on national television. 115 *The Trojan Women.* She had no lines, and in fact she was in the play simply to do a favor for a friend, who had got a better part elsewhere. The director thought to liven all the weeping and mourning by having the Trojan women go bare-breasted. One breast apiece, they showed, the right in the case of royal personages such as Hecuba and Helen; the left, in the case of ordinary virgins or wives, such as Rose. Rose didn't think herself enhanced by this exposure — she was getting on, after all, her bosom tended to flop — but she got used to the idea. She didn't count on the sensation they would create. She didn't think many people would be watching. She forgot about those parts of the country where people can't exercise their preference for quiz shows, police-car chases, American situation comedies, and are compelled to put up with talks on public affairs and tours of art galleries and ambitious offerings of drama. She did not think they would be so amazed, either, now that every magazine rack in every town was serving up slices and cutlets of bare flesh. How could such outrage fasten on the Trojan ladies' sad-eyed collection, puckered with cold then running with sweat under the lights, badly and chalkily made-up, all looking rather foolish without their mates, rather pitiful and unnatural, like tumors?

Flo took to pen and paper over that, forced her still swollen fingers, crippled almost out of use with arthritis, to write the word *Shame*. She wrote that if Rose's father had not been dead long ago he would now wish that he was. That was true. Rose read the letter, or part of it, out loud to some friends she was having for dinner. She read it for comic effect, and dramatic effect, to show the gulf that lay behind her, though she did realize, if she thought about it, that such a gulf was nothing special. Most of her friends, who seemed to her ordinarily hardworking, anxious, and hopeful people, could lay claim to being disowned or prayed for, in some disappointed home.

Halfway through she had to stop reading. It wasn't that she thought how shabby it was, to be exposing and making fun of Flo this way. She had done it often enough before; it was no news to her that it was shabby. What stopped her was, in fact, that gulf; she had a fresh and overwhelming realization of it, and it was nothing to laugh about. These reproaches of Flo's made as much sense as a protest about raising umbrellas, a warning against eating raisins. But they were painfully, truly, meant; they were all a hard life had to offer. Shame on a bare breast.

Another time, Rose was getting an award. So were several other people. A reception was being held, in a Toronto hotel. Flo had been sent an invitation, but Rose had never thought that she would come. She had thought she should give someone's name, when the organizers asked about relatives, and she could hardly name Brian and Phoebe. Of course it was possible that she did, secretly, want Flo to come, wanted to show Flo, intimidate her, finally remove herself from Flo's shade. That would be a natural thing to want to do.

Flo came down on the train, unannounced. She got to the hotel. She was arthritic then, but still moving without a cane. She had always been decently, soberly, cheaply, dressed, but now it seemed she had spent money and asked advice. She was wearing a mauve and purple checked pants suit, and beads like strings of white and yellow popcorn. Her hair was covered by a thick gray-blue wig, pulled low on her forehead like a woollen cap. From the vee of the jacket, and its too-short sleeves, her neck and wrists stuck out brown and warty as if covered with bark. When she saw Rose she stood still. She seemed to be waiting—not just for Rose to go over to her but for her feelings about the scene in front of her to crystallize.

Soon they did.

"Look at the nigger!" said Flo in a loud voice, before Rose was anywhere near her. Her tone was one of simple, gratified astonishment, as if she had been peering down the Grand Canyon or seen oranges growing on a tree.

She meant George, who was getting one of the awards. He turned around, to see if someone was feeding him a comic line. And Flo did look like a comic character, except that her bewilderment, her authenticity, were quite daunting. Did she note the stir she had caused? Possibly. After that one outburst she clammed up, would not speak again except in the most grudging monosyllables, would not eat any food or drink any drink offered her, would not sit down, but stood astonished and unflinching in the middle of that gathering of the bearded and beaded, the unisexual and the unashamedly un-Anglo-Saxon, until it was time for her to be taken to her train and sent home.

Rose found that wig under the bed, during the horrifying cleanup that followed Flo's removal. She took it out to the Home, along with some clothes she had washed or had dry-cleaned, and some stockings, talcum powder, cologne, that she had bought. Sometimes Flo seemed to think Rose was a doctor, and she said, "I don't want no woman doctor, you can just clear out." But when she saw Rose carrying the wig she said, "Rose! What is that you got in your hands, is it a dead gray squirrel?"

"No," said Rose, "it's a wig."

"What?"

"A wig," said Rose, and Flo began to laugh. Rose laughed too. The wig did look like a dead cat or squirrel, even though she had washed and brushed it; it was a disturbing-looking object.

"My God, Rose, I thought what is she doing bringing me a dead squirrel! If I put it on somebody'd be sure to take a shot at me."

Rose stuck it on her own head, to continue the comedy, and Flo laughed so that she rocked back and forth in her crib.

When she got her breath Flo said, "What am I doing with these damn sides up on my bed? Are you and Brian behaving yourselves? Don't fight, it gets on your father's nerves. Do you know how many gallstones they took out of me? Fifteen! One as big as a pullet's egg. I got them somewhere. I'm going to take them home." She pulled at the sheets searching. "They were in a bottle."

"I've got them already," said Rose. "I took them home."

"Did you? Did you show your father?"

"Yes."

"Oh, well, that's where they are then," said Flo, and she lay down and closed her eyes.

DONALD BARTHELME (1931–1989)

The Balloon

The balloon, beginning at a point on Fourteenth Street, the exact location of which I cannot reveal, expanded northward all one night, while people were sleeping, until it reached the Park. There, I stopped it; at dawn the northernmost edges lay over the Plaza; the free-hanging motion was frivolous and gentle. But experiencing a faint irritation at stopping, even to protect the trees, and seeing no reason the balloon should not be allowed to expand upward, over the parts of the city it was already covering, into the "air space" to be found there, I asked the engineers to see to it. This expansion took place throughout the morning, soft imperceptible sighing of gas through the valves. The balloon then covered forty-five blocks north-south and an irregular area east-west, as many as six crosstown blocks on either side of the Avenue in some places. That was the situation, then.

But it is wrong to speak of "situations," implying sets of circumstances leading to some resolution, some escape of tension; there were no situations, simply the balloon hanging there — muted heavy grays and browns for the most part, contrasting with walnut and soft yellows. A deliberate lack of finish, enhanced by skillful installation, gave the surface a rough, forgotten quality; sliding weights on the inside, carefully adjusted, anchored the great, vari-shaped mass at a number of points. Now we have had a flood of original ideas in all media, works of singular beauty as well as significant milestones in the history of inflation, but at that moment there was only *this balloon,* concrete particular, hanging there.

There were reactions. Some people found the balloon "interesting." As a response this seemed inadequate to the immensity of the balloon, the suddenness of its appearance over the city; on the other hand, in the absence of hysteria or other societally-induced anxiety, it must be judged a calm, "mature" one. There was a certain amount of initial argumentation about the "meaning" of the balloon; this subsided, because we have learned not to insist on meanings, and they are rarely even looked for now, except in cases involving the simplest, safest phenomena. It was agreed that since the meaning of the balloon could never be known absolutely, extended discussion was pointless, or at least less purposeful than the activities of those who, for example, hung green and blue paper lanterns from the warm gray underside, in certain streets, or seized the occasion to write messages on the surface, announcing their availability for the performance of unnatural acts, or the availability of acquaintances.

Daring children jumped, especially at those points where the balloon hovered close to a building, so that the gap between balloon and building was a matter of a few inches, or points where the balloon actually made contact, exerting an ever-so-slight pressure against the side of a building, so that balloon and building seemed a unity. The upper surface was so structured that a "landscape" was presented, small valleys as well as slight knolls, or mounds; once atop the balloon, a stroll was possible, or even a trip, from one place to another. There was pleasure in being able to run down an incline, then up the opposing slope, both gently graded, or in making a leap from one side to the other. Bouncing was possible, because of the pneumaticity of the surface, and even falling, if that was your wish. That all these varied motions, as well as others, were within one's possibilities, in experiencing the "up" side of the balloon, was extremely exciting for children, accustomed to the city's flat, hard skin. But the purpose of the balloon was not to amuse children.

Too, the number of people, children and adults, who took advantage   5
of the opportunities described was not so large as it might have been: a certain timidity, lack of trust in the balloon, was seen. There was, furthermore, some hostility. Because we had hidden the pumps, which fed helium to the interior, and because the surface was so vast that the authorities could not determine the point of entry — that is, the point at which the gas was injected — a degree of frustration was evidenced by those city officers into whose province such manifestations normally fell. The apparent purposelessness of the balloon was vexing (as was the fact that it was "there" at all). Had we painted, in great letters, "LABORATORY TESTS PROVE" or "18% MORE EFFECTIVE" on the sides of the balloon, this difficulty would have been circumvented. But I could not bear to do so. On the whole, these officers were remarkably tolerant, considering the dimensions of the anomaly, this tolerance being the result of, first, secret tests conducted by night that convinced them that little or nothing could be done in the way of removing or destroying the balloon, and, secondly, a public warmth that arose (not uncolored by touches of the aforementioned hostility) toward the balloon, from ordinary citizens.

As a single balloon must stand for a lifetime of thinking about balloons, so each citizen expressed, in the attitude he chose, a complex of attitudes. One man might consider that the balloon had to do with the notion *sullied,* as in the sentence *The big balloon sullied the otherwise clear and radiant Manhattan sky.* That is, the balloon was, in this man's view, an imposture, something inferior to the sky that had formerly been there, something interposed between the people and their "sky." But in fact it was January, the sky was dark and ugly; it was not a sky you could look up into, lying on your back in the street, with pleasure, unless pleasure, for you, proceeded from having been threatened, from having been misused. And the underside of the balloon was a pleasure to look up into, we had seen to that, muted grays and browns for the most part, contrasted with walnut and soft, forgotten yellows. And so, while this man was thinking *sullied,* still there was an admixture of pleasurable cognition in his thinking, struggling with the original perception.

Another man, on the other hand, might view the balloon as if it were part of a system of unanticipated rewards, as when one's employer walks in and says, "Here, Henry, take this package of money I have wrapped for you, because we have been doing so well in the business here, and I admire the way you bruise the tulips, without which bruising your department would not be a success, or at least not the success that it is." For this man the balloon might be a brilliantly heroic "muscle and pluck" experience, even if an experience poorly understood.

Another man might say, "Without the example of ———, it is doubtful that ——— would exist today in its present form," and find many to agree with him, or to argue with him. Ideas of "bloat" and "float" were introduced, as well as concepts of dream and responsibility. Others engaged in remarkably detailed fantasies having to do with a wish either to lose themselves in the balloon, or to engorge it. The private character of these wishes, of their origins, deeply buried and unknown, was such that they were not much spoken of; yet there is evidence that they were widespread. It was also argued that what was important was what you felt when you stood under the balloon; some people claimed that they felt sheltered, warmed, as never before, while enemies of the balloon felt, or reported feeling, constrained, a "heavy" feeling.

Critical opinion was divided:

"monstrous pourings"

"harp"

XXXXXXX "certain contrasts with darker portions"

"inner joy"

"large, square corners"

"conservative eclecticism that has so far governed
modern balloon design"

::::::: "abnormal vigor"

"warm, soft, lazy passages"

"Has unity been sacrificed for a sprawling quality?"

"*Quelle catastrophe!*"

"munching"

People began, in a curious way, to locate themselves in relation to 10 aspects of the balloon: "I'll be at that place where it dips down into Forty-seventh Street almost to the sidewalk, near the Alamo Chile House," or,

"Why don't we go stand on top, and take the air, and maybe walk about a bit, where it forms a tight, curving line with the façade of the Gallery of Modern Art — " Marginal intersections offered entrances within a given time duration, as well as "warm, soft, lazy passages" in which . . . But it is wrong to speak of "marginal intersections," each intersection was crucial, none could be ignored (as if, walking there, you might not find someone capable of turning your attention, in a flash, from old exercises to new exercises, risks and escalations). Each intersection was crucial, meeting of balloon and building, meeting of balloon and man, meeting of balloon and balloon.

It was suggested that what was admired about the balloon was finally this: that it was not limited, or defined. Sometimes a bulge, blister, or sub-section would carry all the way east to the river on its own initiative, in the manner of an army's movements on a map, as seen in a headquarters remote from the fighting. Then that part would be, as it were, thrown back again, or would withdraw into new dispositions; the next morning, that part would have made another sortie, or disappeared altogether. This ability of the balloon to shift its shape, to change, was very pleasing, especially to people whose lives were rather rigidly patterned, persons to whom change, al-though desired, was not available. The balloon, for the twenty-two days of its existence, offered the possibility, in its randomness, of mislocation of the self, in contradistinction to the grid of precise, rectangular pathways under our feet. The amount of specialized training currently needed, and the con-sequent desirability of longterm commitments, has been occasioned by the steadily growing importance of complex machinery, in virtually all kinds of operations; as this tendency increases, more and more people will turn, in bewildered inadequacy, to solutions for which the balloon may stand as a prototype, or "rough draft."

I met you under the balloon, on the occasion of your return from Norway; you asked if it was mine; I said it was. The balloon, I said, is a spontaneous autobiographical disclosure, having to do with the unease I felt at your absence, and with sexual deprivation, but now that your visit to Bergen has been terminated, it is no longer necessary or appropriate. Re-moval of the balloon was easy; trailer trucks carried away the depleted fabric, which is now stored in West Virginia, awaiting some other time of unhap-piness, sometime, perhaps, when we are angry with one another.

An Introduction to Poetry

Long before humans could read or write, they created, understood, and valued poetry. Historic events, natural catastrophes, and dramatic predictions were remembered and embellished in the verses of song-makers, court poets, and minstrels, who also invented ballads recording the universal emotions evoked by lovers' quarrels, forbidden romance, and family fights.

The works of early poets were recited or sung; the audience gathered in groups and listened. These ancient settings suggest the important connection between the sound of a poem and the meaning it creates. More than any other qualities, rhythm and structural patterns distinguish poetry from prose. Today, most poetry is read silently and alone. To bring poetry to life, however, we must reach back into the past to revive its music.

SUGGESTIONS FOR READING POETRY

When you first approach a poem, try reading it aloud. Stay alert to the ways the words sound as you pronounce them. You may notice rhyme or alliteration (see page 44), although not every poem uses these sound devices. devices.

Enjambment

Listen carefully to how the lines flow together. Be aware of **enjambment**: the carrying over of meaning and sound from one line to the next, with no pause between lines. Consider this example from Sappho's "To me he seems like a god."

> To me he seems like a god
> as he sits facing you and
> hears you near as you speak
> softly and laugh
> in a sweet echo that jolts
> the heart in my ribs.

Although there are six lines, there is only one sentence. If you come to a full stop at the end of each line as you read, the poem will sound disjointed and the meaning will be obscured. Do *not* read these lines like this:

> To me he seems like a god *(long pause)*
> as he sits facing you and *(long pause)*
> hears you near as you speak *(long pause)*

Rather, read them like this:

> To me he seems like a god *(very brief pause)* as he sits facing you and *(very brief pause)* hears you near as you speak *(very brief pause)* softly and laugh *(very brief pause)* in a sweet echo that jolts *(very brief pause)* the heart in my ribs.

Notice that when you pay attention to the enjambment, the lines flow together and become more coherent. The sound and meaning work together rather than against each other.

At this point you may well wonder why poets bother to write lines rather than standard sentences and paragraphs. Often, poets use enjambed lines because they want the reader to pause (but only for an instant) so that the next words (those that begin the next line) will be particularly noticed.

Enjambment, then, lets the poet emphasize a phrase or idea or (sometimes) surprise the reader with the thought on the next line. Look at enjambed lines with aroused curiosity and read them with a sense of discovery. Try to discover why the poet chose to end the line at this particular point rather than at another.

Once you understand how enjambment works, you'll be able to read poetry aloud smoothly and with enjoyment. Try, also, to keep it in mind as you read poetry silently. Learn to "hear" with your mind so that every experience with poetry, whether actually voiced or not, combines sound and meaning.

Syntax

The **syntax** (the arrangement of words in a sentence) of poetry is sometimes different from the syntax of prose. Consider, for example, these lines from W. H. Auden's "Unknown Citizen":

Except for the War till the day he retired
He worked in a factory and never got fired

Most speakers would use this word order:

Except for the War, he worked in a factory till the day he retired
and never got fired.

The poet inverts the expected order of the phrases and clauses within the sentence to focus our attention both on the length of the citizen's working time ("till the day he retired") and on his steadiness ("never got fired"). In addition, the inversion allows for the rhyme of "retired" and "fired," which further emphasizes the length of the citizen's work life.

Pay attention to the syntax as you read, especially if you are pondering the meaning of some lines. Often, experimenting with ways to rearrange the words and phrases will lead you to see meanings you had not noticed before.

Structure

Although poetry was originally a strictly oral art form, for centuries it has also been a visual form. When asked how they differentiate prose from poetry, many readers say, "The way it looks on the page" or "The way the lines are arranged."

CLOSED FORM In many traditional forms of poetry, the lines and stanzas must be arranged according to established patterns. Japanese haiku is one example. Each haiku must have seventeen syllables (in the original Japanese), generally divided into three lines. Here is a haiku:

The piercing chill I feel:
my dead wife's comb, in our bedroom,
under my heel . . .

Taniguchi Buscon
(translated by Harold G. Henderson)

Other examples of traditional poetic forms are the ode and the sonnet (see pages 1093–94). When you read closed form poetry, ask yourself why the poet chose this form and how the form contributes to the meaning the work conveys to you.

OPEN FORM Many readers think of closed form as an inherent part of poetry. And, indeed, for centuries poems from all cultures and in all languages conformed to set rules of line, stanza, and/or syllable length and often had set rhyme patterns. In the nineteenth century, however, poets began to experiment, resisting the limitations they believed were imposed by traditional poetic forms.

These poets determined the length of their own lines and stanzas, used unexpected rhythms and rhymes, and frequently did away with rhyme entirely. For examples of open form poetry, read e.e. cummings's "if everything happens that can't be done" (page 1156), Lawrence Ferlinghetti's "I Am Waiting" (page 1168), and Marge Piercy's "Unlearning to Not Speak" (page 1179).

When you read such a poem, ask yourself why the poet chose not to use a traditional form. How would the meaning of the poem be changed if the same images and themes were set in a carefully rhymed sonnet, for example, rather than an unrhymed series of lines that are uniquely arranged?

TYPES OF POETRY

Although not all poems fit neatly into categories, the two major types of poems are **narrative** and **lyric**. Narrative poems tell stories. They often present a significant episode or series of episodes in the life of one primary character (or, sometimes, two primary characters). Lyric poems express the feelings, musings, or emotions of a single character (the speaker).

Narrative Poetry

Examples of narrative poems include long **epics** (such as Homer's *Iliad* or Milton's *Paradise Lost*) as well as short **ballads** (such as "Lord Randal," page 474). Nearly all narrative poems stress action and suggest a conflict. Many focus on a moral choice or difficult decision. For examples of modern narrative poems, see William Stafford's "Traveling through the dark" (page 855), Seamus Heaney's "Mid-Term Break" (page 855), or Kristine Batey's "Lot's Wife" (page 409).

Lyric Poetry

The word "lyric" comes from the "lyre," the Greek instrument used for musical accompaniment of poetry, which was often sung or chanted. Although a lyric poem may depict an outward action, it generally focuses on inward reactions, insights, or responses. Lyric poems are written in many forms, including the following:

ODE An **ode** is a relatively long lyric poem with many stanzas that may vary in form and length. Examples are Percy Bysshe Shelley's "Ode to the West Wind" (page 1113) and John Keats's "Ode on a Grecian Urn" (page 1115).

ITALIAN (OR PETRARCHAN) SONNET The **Italian sonnet** is divided into two parts, an **octave** (eight lines) with the rhyme scheme *abbaabba* and a **sestet** (six lines) with the rhyme scheme *cdecde* (or some variation). The octave usually develops an idea or image, and the sestet comments on this idea or image. For an example, see John Milton's "When I consider how my light is spent" (page 1100).

ENGLISH (OR SHAKESPEAREAN) SONNET The **English sonnet** falls into three **quatrains** (four lines) and a concluding **couplet** (two lines). The rhyme scheme is *abab cdcd efef gg*. The first three quatrains usually develop an idea or image, and the closing couplet comments on this idea or image. For an example, see any of Shakespeare's sonnets (pages 1096–1097).

OPEN FORM Open form lyric poems do not follow any particular pattern or structure.

Guidelines: Poetry

These considerations provide guidelines for reading, thinking about, and writing about poetry. Although not every consideration applies to every poem, these guidelines can help you read more deeply and experience the poem more fully.

1. After reading and thinking about a poem, read it aloud several times to an audience (at least two or three people). With each reading, use a different tone of voice and emphasize different lines and words. Discuss with your audience how the different readings changed the poem for them. Explain your discoveries about the possible ways to read this poem.

2. Write a brief character sketch of the speaker in the poem. What values do you think the speaker holds? What is your response to these values? Refer to specific details in the poem to support your evaluation.

3. Using Christopher Marlowe's "The Passionate Shepherd to His Love" (page 403) and Sir Walter Raleigh's "The Nymph's Reply to the Shepherd" (page 403) as models, write your own "reply" to any of the poems in this anthology. Reply in poetry or in prose.

4. Consider two or three poems that treat the same theme (perhaps in one of the thematic anthology sections, pages 109–889). Compare and explain the significant differences and similarities you see in your responses to these poems.

5. Consider a poem in which the speaker describes or addresses another person. Imagine how that person might respond to the poem. For example, consider how the man described in Sappho's "To me he seems like a god" (page 402) might react to his deification or how Lucasta might answer her lover's farewell, "To Lucasta, Going to the Wars" (page 605).

6. Find a poem with figures of speech (metaphors, similes, personifications) you find particularly intriguing, puzzling, moving, affirming (or whatever) and explain your response. As you write, focus specifically on one or two figures of speech. Explain the meanings they suggest as well as the emotions they evoke.

7. Read a poem whose title caught your attention. Discuss the connection you see between the poem and its title. Were you disappointed, surprised, pleased by the relationship between the poem and its title? Explain whether and why your expectations were fulfilled, disappointed, or exceeded.

8. Consider the final stanza or lines of a poem carefully. Then suggest an alternative ending. Explain why you would make the changes you have indicated.
9. Discover a poem that describes a character, place, action, conflict, or decision that relates in some way to a person, place, action, conflict, or decision in your own life. Compare your experience to the experience described in the poem.
10. After reading the works of several poets, choose one you would like to know more about. Read biographical information as well as more of the poet's works. Then choose *one* aspect of the poet's life that particularly intrigues you and that you see reflected in the poet's work. Write a paper explaining what you have discovered.

ANONYMOUS

Western Wind

Westron wynde when wyll thow blow
the smalle rayne downe can rayne
Chryst yf my love were in my armys
and I yn my bed agayne

Western wind, when will thou blow,   5
    The small rain down can rain?
Christ, if my love were in my arms
    And I in my bed again!

THOMAS WYATT (1503–1542)

They flee from me, that sometime did me seek

They flee from me, that sometime did me seek,
With naked foot stalking in my chamber.
I have seen them, gentle, tame, and meek,
That now are wild, and do not remember
That sometime they put themselves in danger   5
To take bread at my hand; and now they range,
Busily seeking with a continual change.

Thanked be Fortune it hath been otherwise,
Twenty times better; but once in special,
In thin array, after a pleasant guise,   10
When her loose gown from her shoulders did fall,

And she me caught in her arms long and small,
And therewith all sweetly did me kiss
And softly said, "Dear heart, how like you this?"

It was no dream, I lay broad waking.   15
But all is turned, thorough my gentleness,
Into a strange fashion of forsaking;
And I have leave to go, of her goodness.
And she also to use newfangleness.
But since that I so kindely am served,   20
I fain would know what she hath deserved.

QUEEN ELIZABETH I (1533–1603)

On Monsieur's Departure

I grieve and dare not show my discontent,
I love and yet am forced to seem to hate,
I do, yet dare not say I ever meant,
I seem stark mute but inwardly do prate.
    I am and not, I freeze and yet am burned,   5
    Since from myself another self I turned.

My care is like my shadow in the sun,
Follows me flying, flies when I pursue it,
Stands and lies by me, doth what I have done.
His too familiar care doth make me rue it.   10
    No means I find to rid him from my breast,
    Till by the end of things it be suppressed.

Some gentler passion slide into my mind,
For I am soft and made of melting snow;
Or be more cruel, love, and so be kind.
Let me or float or sink, be high or low.   15
    Or let me live with some more sweet content,
    Or die and so forget what love ere meant.

WILLIAM SHAKESPEARE (1564–1616)

Let me not to the marriage of true minds

Let me not to the marriage of true minds
Admit impediments. Love is not love
Which alters when it alteration finds,
Or bends with the remover to remove:

Oh, no! it is an ever-fixéd mark,   5
That looks on tempests and is never shaken;
It is the star to every wandering bark,
Whose worth's unknown, although his height be taken.
Love's not Time's fool, though rosy lips and cheeks
Within his bending sickle's compass come;   10
Love alters not with his brief hours and weeks,
But bears it out even to the edge of doom.
   If this be error and upon me proved,
   I never writ, nor no man ever loved.

WILLIAM SHAKESPEARE (1564–1616)

Shall I compare thee to a summer's day?

Shall I compare thee to a summer's day?
Thou art more lovely and more temperate:
Rough winds do shake the darling buds of May,
And summer's lease hath all too short a date;
Sometime too hot the eye of heaven shines,   5
And often is his gold complexion dimm'd;
And every fair from fair sometime declines,
By chance or nature's changing course untrimm'd:
But thy eternal summer shall not fade
Nor lose possession of that fair thou ow'st;   10
Nor shall Death brag thou wand'rest in his shade,
When in eternal lines to time thou grow'st;
   So long as men can breathe or eyes can see,
   So long lives this, and this gives life to thee.

WILLIAM SHAKESPEARE (1564–1616)

That time of year thou mayst in me behold

That time of year thou mayst in me behold
When yellow leaves, or none, or few, do hang
Upon those boughs which shake against the cold,
Bare [ruin'd] choirs where late the sweet birds sang.
In me thou see'st the twilight of such day   5
As after sunset fadeth in the west,
Which by and by black night doth take away,
Death's second self, that seals up all in rest.
In me thou see'st the glowing of such fire
That on the ashes of his youth doth lie,   10
As the death-bed whereon it must expire,

Consum'd with that which it was nourish'd by.
   This thou perceiv'st, which makes thy love more strong,
   To love that well which thou must leave ere long.

JOHN DONNE (1572–1631)

The Flea

Mark but this flea, and mark in this
How little that which thou deny'st me is;
It sucked me first, and now sucks thee,
And in this flea our two bloods mingled be;
Thou know'st that this cannot be said   5
A sin, nor shame, nor loss of maidenhead;
   Yet this enjoys before it woo,
   And pampered swells with one blood made of two,
   And this, alas, is more than we would do.

Oh stay, three lives in one flea spare,   10
Where we almost, yea, more than married are.
This flea is you and I, and this
Our marriage bed and marriage temple is;
Though parents grudge, and you, we are met
And cloistered in these living walls of jet.   15
   Though use make you apt to kill me,
   Let not to that, self-murder added be,
   And sacrilege, three sins in killing three.

Cruel and sudden, hast thou since
Purpled thy nail in blood of innocence?   20
Wherein could this flea guilty be,
Except in that drop which it sucked from thee?
Yet thou triumph'st and say'st that thou
Find'st not thyself, nor me the weaker now.
   'Tis true. Then learn how false fears be: 25
   Just so much honor, when thou yield'st to me,
   Will waste, as this flea's death took life from thee.

JOHN DONNE (1572–1631)

Batter my heart, three-personed God

Batter my heart, three-personed God; for You
As yet but knock, breathe, shine, and seek to mend;
That I may rise and stand, o'erthrow me, and bend

Your force to break, blow, burn, and make me new.
I, like an usurped town, to another due,   5
Labor to admit You, but O, to no end;
Reason, Your viceroy in me, me should defend,
But is captived, and proves weak or untrue.
Yet dearly I love You, and would be loved fain,
But am betrothed unto Your enemy,   10
Divorce me, untie or break that knot again;
Take me to You, imprison me, for I,
   Except You enthrall me, never shall be free,
   Nor ever chaste, except You ravish me.

JOHN DONNE (1572–1631)

The Canonization

For God's sake hold your tongue, and let me love,
   Or chide my palsy, or my gout,
My five gray hairs, or ruined fortune, flout,
   With wealth your state, your mind with arts improve,
     Take you a course,° get you a place,°   *direction/appointment* 5
     Observe His Honor, or His Grace,
Or the King's real, or his stampéd face°   *image on a coin*
   Contémplate; what you will, approve,°   *try*
   So you will let me love.

Alas, alas, who's injured by my love?   10
   What merchant's ships have my sighs drowned?
Who says my tears have overflowed his ground?
   When did my colds a forward spring remove?
     When did the heats which my veins fill
     Add one more to the plague bill?°   *list of plague victims* 15
Soldiers find wars, and lawyers find out still
   Litigious men, which quarrels move,
   Though she and I do love.

Call us what you will, we're made such by love;
   Call her one, me another fly,   20
We're tapers too, and at our own cost die,°
   And we in us find th' eagle and the dove
     The phoenix riddle° hath more wit
     By us: we two being one, are it.

21 *at our own cost die:* "Die" was used as a metaphor for sexual climax; also, each sexual experience was believed to shorten one's life by a day. 23 *phoenix riddle:* The phoenix, a mythological bird, is destroyed by fire but always rises from its own ashes to begin a new life.

So, to one neutral thing both sexes fit.   25
  We die and rise the same, and prove
  Mysterious by this love.

We can die by it, if not live by love,
  And if unfit for tombs and hearse
Our legend be, it will be fit for verse;   30
  And if no piece of chronicle we prove,
    We'll build in sonnets pretty rooms;
    As well a well-wrought urn becomes
The greatest ashes, as half-acre tombs;
    And by these hymns, all shall approve   35
    Us canonized for love:

And thus invoke us: You whom reverend love
  Made one another's hermitage;
You, to whom love was peace, that now is rage;
  Who did the whole world's soul contract, and drove   40
    Into the glasses of your eyes
    (So made such mirrors, and such spies,
That they did all to you epitomize)
    Countries, towns, courts: Beg from above
    A pattern of your love!   45

JOHN MILTON (1608–1674)

When I consider how my light is spent

When I consider how my light is spent
Ere half my days, in this dark world and wide,
And that one talent which is death to hide
Lodged with me useless, though my soul more bent
To serve therewith my Maker and present   5
My true account, lest he returning chide;
"Doth God exact day-labor, light denied?"
I fondly ask; but Patience to prevent
That murmur, soon replies, "God doth not need
Either man's work or his own gifts; who best   10
Bear his mild yoke, they serve him best. His state
Is kingly. Thousands at his bidding speed
And post o'er land and ocean without rest:
They also serve who only stand and wait."

GEORGE HERBERT (1593–1633)

Easter Wings

Lord, who createdst man in wealth and store,
    Though foolishly he lost the same,
        Decaying more and more
           Till he became
             Most poor: 5
             With thee
           O let me rise
        As larks, harmoniously,
    And sing this day thy victories:
Then shall the fall further the flight in me.   10

My tender age in sorrow did begin;
    And still with sicknesses and shame
        Thou didst so punish sin,
           That I became
             Most thin.   15
             With thee
           Let me combine,
        And feel this day thy victory;
    For, if I imp my wing on thine,
Affliction shall advance the flight in me.   20

JONATHAN SWIFT (1667–1745)

A Description of the Morning

Now hardly here and there a hackney-coach
Appearing, showed the ruddy morn's approach.
Now Betty from her master's bed had flown,
And softly stole to discompose her own;
The slip-shod 'prentice from his master's door   5
Had pared the dirt and sprinkled round the floor.
Now Moll had whirled her mop with dext'rous airs,
Prepared to scrub the entry and the stairs.
The youth with broomy stumps began to trace
The kennel-edge, where wheels had worn the place.   10
The small-coal man was heard with cadence deep,
Till drowned in shriller notes of chimney-sweep:
Duns at his lordship's gate began to meet;
And brickdust Moll had screamed through half the street.

The turnkey now his flock returning sees,   15
Duly let out a-nights to steal for fees:
The watchful bailiffs take their silent stands,
And schoolboys lag with satchels in their hands.

ALEXANDER POPE (1688–1744)

From Part II of **An Essay on Criticism**

. . . Thus Critics, of less judgment than caprice,   85
Curious not knowing, not exact but nice,
Form short Ideas; and offend in arts
(As most in manners) by a love to parts.
    Some to *Conceit*° alone their taste confine,
And glittering thoughts struck out at every line;   90
Pleased with a work where nothing's just or fit;
One glaring Chaos and wild heap of wit.
Poets like painters, thus, unskilled to trace
The naked nature and the living grace,
With gold and jewels cover every part,   95
And hide with ornaments their want of art.
True Wit is Nature to advantage dressed,
What oft was thought, but ne'er so well expressed;
Something, whose truth convinced at sight we find,
That gives us back the image of our mind.   100
As shades more sweetly recommend the light,
So modest plainness sets off sprightly wit.
For works may have more wit than does 'em good,
As bodies perish through excess of blood.
    Others for *Language* all their care express,   105
And value books, as women men, for Dress:
Their praise is still, — the Style is excellent:
The Sense, they humbly take upon content.
Words are like leaves; and where they most abound,
Much fruit of sense beneath is rarely found.   110
False Eloquence, like the prismatic glass,
Its gaudy colours spreads on every place;
The face of Nature we no more survey,
All glares alike, without distinction gay:
But true Expression, like th' unchanging Sun,   115
Clears, and improves whate'er it shines upon,
It gilds all objects, but it alters none.

89 Conceit: A complex, extended metaphor.

Expression is the dress of thought, and still
Appears more decent, as more suitable;
A vile conceit in pompous words expressed,   120
Is like a clown in regal purple dressed:
For different styles with different subjects sort,
As several garbs with country, town, and court.
Some by old words to fame have made pretence,
Ancients in phrase, mere moderns in their sense;   125
Such laboured nothings, in so strange a style,
Amaze th' unlearned, and make the learnéd smile.
Unlucky, as Fungoso in the Play,°
These sparks with awkward vanity display
What the fine gentleman wore yesterday;   130
And but so mimic ancient wits at best,
As apes our grandsires, in their doublets drest.
In words, as fashions, the same rule will hold;
Alike fantastic, if too new, or old:
Be not the first by whom the new are tried,   135
Nor yet the last to lay the old aside.
    But most by Numbers judge a Poet's song;
And smooth or rough, with them is right or wrong:
In the bright Muse though thousand charms conspire,
Her voice is all these tuneful fools admire;   140
Who haunt Parnassus° but to please their ear,
Not mend their minds; as some to Church repair,
Not for the doctrine, but the music there.
These equal syllables alone require,
Though oft the ear the open vowels tire;   145
While expletives their feeble aid do join;
And ten low words oft creep in one dull line:
While they ring round the same unvaried chimes,
With sure returns of still expected rhymes;
Where'er you find "the cooling western breeze,"   150
In the next line, it "whispers through the trees:"
If crystal streams "with pleasing murmurs creep,"
The reader's threatened (not in vain) with "sleep:"
Then, at the last and only couplet, fraught
With some unmeaning thing they call a thought,   155
A needless Alexandrine ends the song,
That, like a wounded snake, drags its slow length along.
Leave such to tune their own dull rhymes, and know
What's roundly smooth, or languishingly slow;

128 *Play: Every Man Out of His Humor* by Ben Johnson.   141 *Parnassus:* Mountain where the
muses, the nine goddesses who preside over literature and the arts, live.

And praise the easy vigour of a line,   160
Where Denham's° strength, and Waller's° sweetness join.
True ease in writing comes from art, not chance,
As those move easiest who have learned to dance.
'Tis not enough no harshness gives offence,
The sound must seem an Echo to the sense: 165
Soft is the strain when Zephyr° gently blows,
And the smooth stream in smoother numbers flows;
But when loud surges lash the sounding shore,
The hoarse, rough verse should like the torrent roar:
When Ajax° strives some rock's vast weight to throw,   170
The line too labours, and the words move slow;
Not so, when swift Camilla° scours the plain,
Flies o'er th' unbending corn, and skims along the main.
Hear how Timotheus'° varied lays surprise,
And bid alternate passions fall and rise!   175
While, at each change, the son of Libyan Jove°
Now burns with glory, and then melts with love;
Now his fierce eyes with sparkling fury glow,
Now sighs steal out, and tears begin to flow:
Persians and Greeks like turns of nature found,   180
And the World's victor stood subdued by Sound!
The power of Music all our hearts allow,
And what Timotheus was, is DRYDEN now.
    Avoid Extremes; and shun the fault of such,
Who still are pleased too little or too much.   185
At every trifle scorn to take offence,
That always shows great pride, or little sense;
Those heads, as stomachs, are not sure the best;
Which nauseate all, and nothing can digest.
Yet let not each gay Turn thy rapture move;   190
For fools admire, but men of sense approve:
As things seem large which we through mists descry,
Dulness is ever apt to magnify.
    Some foreign writers, some our own despise;
The Ancients only, or the Moderns prize.   195
Thus Wit, like Faith, by each man is applied
To one small sect, and all are damned beside.
Meanly they seek the blessing to confine,

---

161 *Denham:* Sir John Denham (1615–1669); poet admired by Pope; *Waller:* Edmund Waller (1606–1687); poet admired by Pope.   166 *Zephyr:* The West wind.   170 *Ajax:* A mighty warrior in Homer's *Iliad.*   172 *Camilla:* A brave woman who is a warrior in Vergil's *Aeneid.*   174 *Timotheus:* A Greek musician.   176 *son of Libyan Jove:* Refers to "Alexander's Feast," John Dryden's poem praising music.

And force that sun but on a part to shine,
Which not alone the southern wit sublimes, 200
But ripens spirits in cold northern climes;
Which from the first has shone on ages past,
Enlights the present, and shall warm the last;
Though each may feel increases and decays,
And see now clearer and now darker days. 205
Regard not then if Wit be old or new,
But blame the false, and value still the true.
    Some ne'er advance a Judgment of their own,
But catch the spreading notion of the Town;
They reason and conclude by precedent, 210
And own stale nonsense which they ne'er invent.
Some judge of authors' names, not works, and then
Nor praise nor blame the writings, but the men.
Of all this servile herd, the worst is he
That in proud dulness joins with Quality. 215
A constant Critic at the great man's board,
To fetch and carry nonsense for my Lord.
What woeful stuff this madrigal would be,
In some starved hackney sonneteer, or me?
But let a Lord once own the happy lines, 220
How the wit brightens! how the style refines!
Before his sacred name flies every fault,
And each exalted stanza teems with thought!
    The Vulgar thus through Imitation err;
As oft the Learned by being singular; 225
So much they scorn the crowd, that if the throng
By chance go right, they purposely go wrong:
So Schismatics the plain believers quit,
And are but damned for having too much wit.
Some praise at morning what they blame at night; 230
But always think the last opinion right.
A Muse by these is like a mistress used,
This hour she's idolized, the next abused;
While their weak heads like towns unfortified,
Twixt sense and nonsense daily change their side. 235
Ask them the cause; they're wiser still, they say;
And still tomorrow's wiser than today.
We think our fathers fools, so wise we grow;
Our wiser sons, no doubt, will think us so.
Once School divines this zealous isle o'erspread; 240
Who knew most Sentences, was deepest read;
Faith, Gospel, all, seemed made to be disputed,
And none had sense enough to be confuted:

Scotists° and Thomists,° now, in peace remain,
Amidst their kindred cobwebs in Duck Lane.   245
If Faith itself has different dresses worn,
What wonder modes in Wit should take their turn?
Oft, leaving what is natural and fit,
The current folly proves the ready wit;
And authors think their reputation safe,   250
Which lives as long as fools are pleased to laugh.
     Some valuing those of their own side or mind,
Still make themselves the measure of mankind:
Fondly we think we honour merit then,
When we but praise ourselves in other men.   255
Parties in Wit attend on those of State,
And public faction doubles private hate.
Pride, Malice, Folly, against Dryden rose,
In various shapes of Parsons, Critics, Beaus;
But sense survived, when merry jests were past;   260
For rising merit will buoy up at last.
Might he return, and bless once more our eyes,
New Blackmores° and new Milbourns° must arise:
Nay should great Homer lift his awful head,
Zoilus° again would start up from the dead.   265
Envy will merit, as its shade, pursue;
But like a shadow, proves the substance true;
For envied Wit, like Sol eclipsed, makes known
Th' opposing body's grossness, not its own.
When first that sun too powerful beams displays,   270
It draws up vapours which obscure its rays;
But even those clouds at last adorn its way,
Reflect new glories, and augment the day.
     Be thou the first true merit to befriend;
His praise is lost, who stays till all commend.   275
Short is the date, alas, of modern rhymes,
And 'tis but just to let them live betimes.
No longer now that golden age appears,
When Patriarch wits survived a thousand years:
Now length of Fame (our second life) is lost,   280

---

244 *Scotists:* Followers of John Duns Scotus (ca. 1266–1308); opposing the Thomists, Duns Scotus argued that God's existence must be demonstrated by experiences of the senses, *Thomists:* Followers of St. Thomas Aquinas (1225–1274); Italian philosopher who believed that faith and science constitute two separate, but harmonious, realms. These two realms neither prove nor disprove each other.   263 *Blackmore* and *Milbourn:* Richard Blackmore (1652–1729) and Luke Milbourn (1649–1720), critics of Dryden.   265 *Zoilus:* ca. 4th century B.C.; critic of Homer.

And bare threescore is all even that can boast;
Our sons their fathers' failing language see,
And such as Chaucer is, shall Dryden be.
So when the faithful pencil has designed
Some bright Idea of the master's mind,   285
Where a new world leaps out at his command,
And ready Nature waits upon his hand;
When the ripe colours soften and unite,
And sweetly melt into just shade and light;
When mellowing years their full perfection give,   290
And each bold figure just begins to live,
The treacherous colours the fair art betray,
And all the bright creation fades away!
   Unhappy Wit, like most mistaken things,
Atones not for that envy which it brings.   295
In youth alone its empty praise we boast,
But soon the short-lived vanity is lost:
Like some fair flower the early spring supplies,
That gaily blooms, but even in blooming dies.
What is this Wit, which must our cares employ?   300
The owner's wife, that other men enjoy;
Then most our trouble still when most admired,
And still the more we give, the more required;
Whose fame with pains we guard, but lose with ease,
Sure some to vex, but never all to please;   305
'Tis what the vicious fear, the virtuous shun,
By fools 'tis hated, and by knaves undone!
   If Wit so much from Ignorance undergo,
Ah let not Learning too commence its foe!
Of old, those met rewards who could excel,   310
And such were praised who but endeavoured well:
Though triumphs were to generals only due,
Crowns were reserved to grace the soldiers too.
Now, they who reach Parnassus' lofty crown,
Employ their pains to spurn some others down;   315
And while self-love each jealous writer rules,
Contending wits become the sport of fools:
But still the worst with most regret commend,
For each ill Author is as bad a Friend.
To what base ends, and by what abject ways,   320
Are mortals urged through sacred lust of praise!
Ah ne'er so dire a thirst of glory boast,
Nor in the Critic let the Man be lost.
Good nature and good sense must ever join;
To err is human, to forgive, divine.   325

But if in noble minds some dregs remain
Not yet purged off, of spleen and sour disdain;
Discharge that rage on more provoking crimes,
Nor fear a dearth in these flagitious times.
No pardon vile Obscenity should find, 330
Though wit and art conspire to move your mind;
But Dulness with Obscenity must prove
As shameful sure as Impotence in love.
In the fat age of pleasure, wealth and ease,
Sprung the rank weed, and thrived with large increase: 335
When love was all an easy Monarch's care;
Seldom at council, never in a war:
Jilts ruled the state, and statesmen farces writ;
Nay wits had pensions, and young Lords had wit:
The Fair sat panting at a Courtier's play, 340
And not a Mask went unimproved away:
The modest fan was lifted up no more,
And Virgins smiled at what they blushed before.
The following license of a Foreign reign
Did all the dregs of bold Socinus° drain; 345
Then unbelieving Priests reformed the nation,
And taught more pleasant methods of salvation:
Where Heaven's free subjects might their rights dispute,
Lest God himself should seem too absolute:
Pulpits their sacred satire learned to spare, 350
And Vice admired to find a flatterer there!
Encouraged thus, Wit's Titans braved the skies,
And the press groaned with licensed blasphemies.
These monsters, Critics! with your darts engage,
Here point your thunder, and exhaust your rage! 355
Yet shun their fault, who, scandalously nice,
Will needs mistake an author into vice;
All seems infected that th' infected spy,
As all looks yellow to the jaundiced eye.

345 *Socinus:* Condemned by the Inquisition for writings judged to be heretical.

WILLIAM BLAKE (1757–1827)

The Lamb

Little Lamb, who made thee?
  Dost thou know who made thee?
Gave thee life & bid thee feed,

By the stream & o'er the mead;
Gave thee clothing of delight, 5
Softest clothing wooly bright;
Gave thee such a tender voice,
Making all the vales rejoice!
   Little Lamb who made thee?
   Dost thou know who made thee? 10

   Little Lamb I'll tell thee,
   Little Lamb I'll tell thee!
He is callèd by thy name,
For he calls himself a Lamb:
He is meek & he is mild, 15
He became a little child:
I a child & thou a lamb,
We are callèd by his name.
   Little Lamb God bless thee.
   Little Lamb God bless thee. 20

WILLIAM BLAKE (1757–1827)

The Tyger

Tyger! Tyger! burning bright
In the forests of the night,
What immortal hand or eye
Could frame thy fearful symmetry?

In what distant deeps or skies 5
Burnt the fire of thine eyes?
On what wings dare he aspire?
What the hand, dare seize the fire?

And what shoulder, & what art,
Could twist the sinews of thy heart? 10
And when thy heart began to beat,
What dread hand? & what dread feet?

What the hammer? what the chain?
In what furnace was thy brain?
What the anvil? what dread grasp 15
Dare its deadly terrors clasp?

WILLIAM WORDSWORTH (1770–1850)

My heart leaps up

My heart leaps up when I behold
   A rainbow in the sky:
So was it when my life began;
So is it now I am a man;
So be it when I shall grow old,   5
   Or let me die!
The Child is father of the Man;
And I could wish my days to be
Bound each to each by natural piety.

WILLIAM WORDSWORTH (1770–1850)

The world is too much with us

The world is too much with us; late and soon,
Getting and spending, we lay waste our powers;
Little we see in Nature that is ours;
We have given our hearts away, a sordid boon!
This Sea that bares her bosom to the moon,   5
The winds that will be howling at all hours,
And are up-gathered now like sleeping flowers,
For this, for everything, we are out of tune;
It moves us not. — Great God! I'd rather be
A Pagan suckled in a creed outworn;   10
So might I, standing on this pleasant lea,
Have glimpses that would make me less forlorn;
Have sight of Proteus° rising from the sea;
Or hear old Triton° blow his wreathéd horn.

13 *Proteus:* Sea god who could change his appearance.   14 *Triton:* Sea god with the upper body of a man and the lower body of a fish. He used a conch shell as a horn.

SAMUEL TAYLOR COLERIDGE (1772–1834)

Kubla Khan

Or a Vision in a Dream. A Fragment

In Xanadu did Kubla Khan
A stately pleasure dome decree:
Where Alph, the sacred river, ran

Through caverns measureless to man
   Down to a sunless sea. 5
So twice five miles of fertile ground
With walls and towers were girdled round:
And there were gardens bright with sinuous rills,
Where blossomed many an incense-bearing tree;
And here were forests ancient as the hills, 10
Enfolding sunny spots of greenery.

But oh! that deep romantic chasm which slanted
Down the green hill athwart a cedarn cover!
A savage place! as holy and enchanted
As e'er beneath a waning moon was haunted 15
By woman wailing for her demon lover!
And from this chasm, with ceaseless turmoil seething,
As if this earth in fast thick pants were breathing,
A mighty fountain momently was forced:
Amid whose swift half-intermitted burst 20
Huge fragments vaulted like rebounding hail,
Or chaffy grain beneath the thresher's flail:
And 'mid these dancing rocks at once and ever
It flung up momently the sacred river.
Five miles meandering with a mazy motion 25
Through wood and dale the sacred river ran,
Then reached the caverns measureless to man,
And sank in tumult to a lifeless ocean:
And 'mid this tumult Kubla heard from far
Ancestral voices prophesying war! 30
   The shadow of the dome of pleasure
   Floated midway on the waves;
   Where was heard the mingled measure
   From the fountain and the caves.
It was a miracle of rare device, 35
A sunny pleasure dome with caves of ice!

   A damsel with a dulcimer
   In a vision once I saw:
   It was an Abyssinian maid,
   And on her dulcimer she played, 40
   Singing of Mount Abora.
   Could I revive within me
   Her symphony and song,
   To such a deep delight 'twould win me,
That with music loud and long, 45
I would build that dome in air,
That sunny dome! those caves of ice!
And all who heard should see them there,

And all should cry, Beware! Beware!
His flashing eyes, his floating hair!   50
Weave a circle round him thrice,
And close your eyes with holy dread,
For he on honey-dew hath fed,
And drunk the milk of Paradise.

GEORGE GORDON, LORD BYRON (1788—1824)

She walks in beauty

I

She walks in beauty, like the night
    Of cloudless climes and starry skies;
And all that's best of dark and bright
    Meet in her aspect and her eyes:
Thus mellowed to that tender light   5
    Which heaven to gaudy day denies.

II

One shade the more, one ray the less,
    Had half impaired the nameless grace
Which waves in every raven tress,
    Or softly lightens o'er her face;   10
Where thoughts serenely sweet express
    How pure, how dear their dwelling place.

III

And on that cheek, and o'er that brow,
    So soft, so calm, yet eloquent,
The smiles that win, the tints that glow,   15
    But tell of days in goodness spent,
A mind at peace with all below,
    A heart whose love is innocent!

PERCY BYSSHE SHELLEY (1792–1822)

Ozymandias

I met a traveler from an antique land
Who said: Two vast and trunkless legs of stone
Stand in the desert . . . Near them, on the sand,

Half sunk, a shattered visage lies, whose frown,
And wrinkled lip, and sneer of cold command, 5
Tell that its sculptor well those passions read
Which yet survive, stamped on these lifeless things,
The hand that mocked them, and the heart that fed:
And on the pedestal these words appear:
"My name is Ozymandias, king of kings: 10
Look on my works, ye Mighty, and despair!"
Nothing beside remains. Round the decay
Of that colossal wreck, boundless and bare
The lone and level sands stretch far away.

PERCY BYSSHE SHELLEY (1792–1822)

Ode to the West Wind

I

O wild West Wind, thou breath of Autumn's being,
Thou, from whose unseen presence the leaves dead
Are driven, like ghosts from an enchanter fleeing,

Yellow, and black, and pale, and hectic red,
Pestilence-stricken multitudes: O thou, 5
Who chariotest to their dark wintry bed

The wingéd seeds, where they lie cold and low,
Each like a corpse within its grave, until
Thine azure sister of the Spring shall blow

Her clarion o'er the dreaming earth, and fill 10
(Driving sweet buds like flocks to feed in air)
With living hues and odors plain and hill:

Wild Spirit, which art moving everywhere;
Destroyer and preserver; hear, oh, hear!

II

Thou on whose stream, mid the steep sky's commotion, 15
Loose clouds like earth's decaying leaves are shed,
Shook from the tangled boughs of Heaven and Ocean,

Angels of rain and lightning: there are spread
On the blue surface of thine aery surge,
Like the bright hair uplifted from the head 20

Of some fierce Maenad,° even from the dim verge
Of the horizon to the zenith's height,
The locks of the approaching storm. Thou dirge

Of the dying year, to which this closing night
Will be the dome of a vast sepulcher,   25
Vaulted with all thy congregated might

Of vapors, from whose solid atmosphere
Black rain, and fire, and hail will burst: oh, hear!

III

Thou who didst waken from his summer dreams
The blue Mediterranean, where he lay,   30
Lulled by the coil of his crystálline streams,

Beside a pumice isle in Baiae's bay
And saw in sleep old palaces and towers
Quivering within the wave's intenser day,

All overgrown with azure moss and flowers   35
So sweet, the sense faints picturing them! Thou
For whose path the Atlantic's level powers

Cleave themselves into chasms, while far below
The sea-blooms and the oozy woods which wear
The sapless foliage of the ocean, know   40

Thy voice, and suddenly grow gray with fear,
And tremble and despoil themselves; oh, hear!

IV

If I were a dead leaf thou mightest bear;
If I were a swift cloud to fly with thee;
A wave to pant beneath thy power, and share   45

The impulse of thy strength, only less free
Than thou, O uncontrollable! If even
I were as in my boyhood, and could be

The comrade of thy wanderings over Heaven,
As then, when to outstrip thy skyey speed   50
Scarce seemed a vision; I would ne'er have striven

---

21 *Maenad:* Female follower of Dionysus. Maenads worshipped this god of wine and fertility
in frenzied rites.

As thus with thee in prayer in my sore need.
Oh, lift me as a wave, a leaf, a cloud!
I fall upon the thorns of life! I bleed!

A heavy weight of hours has chained and bowed   55
One too like thee: tameless, and swift, and proud.

V

Make me thy lyre, even as the forest is:
What if my leaves are falling like its own!
The tumult of thy mighty harmonies

Will take from both a deep, autumnal tone,   60
Sweet though in sadness. Be thou, Spirit fierce,
My spirit! Be thou me, impetuous one!

Drive my dead thoughts over the universe
Like withered leaves to quicken a new birth!
And, by the incantation of this verse,   65

Scatter, as from an unextinguished hearth
Ashes and sparks, my words among mankind!
Be through my lips to unawakened earth

The trumpet of a prophecy! O Wind,
If Winter comes, can Spring be far behind?   70

JOHN KEATS (1795–1821)

Ode on a Grecian Urn

I

Thou still unravish'd bride of quietness,
   Thou foster-child of silence and slow time,
Sylvan° historian, who canst thus express
   A flowery tale more sweetly than our rhyme:
What leaf-fring'd legend haunts about thy shape   5
   Of deities or mortals, or of both,
      In Tempe or the dales of Arcady?°
   What men or gods are these? What maidens loath?
What mad pursuit? What struggle to escape?
      What pipes and timbrels? What wild ecstasy?   10

3 *Sylvan:* From a forest or woodland.   7 *Tempe . . . Arcady:* Peaceful country regions in Greece.

II

Heard melodies are sweet, but those unheard
   Are sweeter; therefore, ye soft pipes, play on;
Not to the sensual ear, but, more endear'd,
   Pipe to the spirit ditties of no tone:
Fair youth, beneath the trees, thou canst not leave   15
   Thy song, nor ever can those trees be bare;
      Bold Lover, never, never canst thou kiss,
Though winning near the goal — yet, do not grieve;
   She cannot fade, though thou hast not thy bliss,
Forever wilt thou love, and she be fair!   20

III

Ah, happy, happy boughs! that cannot shed
   Your leaves, nor ever bid the Spring adieu;
And, happy melodist, unwearied,
   Forever piping songs forever new;
More happy love! more happy, happy love!   25
   Forever warm and still to be enjoy'd,
      Forever panting, and forever young;
All breathing human passion far above,
   That leaves a heart high-sorrowful and cloy'd,
      A burning forehead, and a parching tongue.   30

IV

Who are these coming to the sacrifice?
   To what green altar, O mysterious priest,
Lead'st thou that heifer lowing at the skies,
   And all her silken flanks with garlands drest?
What little town by river or sea shore,   35
   Or mountain-built with peaceful citadel,
      Is emptied of this folk, this pious morn?
And, little town, thy streets forevermore
   Will silent be; and not a soul to tell
      Why thou art desolate, can e'er return.   40

V

O Attic° shape! Fair attitude! with brede°
   Of marble men and maidens overwrought,
With forest branches and the trodden weed;
   Thou, silent form, dost tease us out of thought

41 *Attic:* From the Greek province of Attica; *brede:* Braided or embroidered pattern.

As doth eternity: Cold Pastoral!   45
   When old age shall this generation waste,
      Thou shalt remain, in midst of other woe
    Than ours, a friend to man, to whom thou say'st,
"Beauty is truth, truth beauty,"—that is all
   Ye know on earth, and all ye need to know.   50

JOHN KEATS (1795–1821)

La Belle Dame sans Merci°

O what can ail thee, Knight at arms,
   Alone and palely loitering?
The sedge has withered from the Lake
   And no birds sing!

O what can ail thee, Knight at arms,   5
   So haggard, and so woebegone?
The squirrel's granary is full
   And the harvest's done.

I see a lily on thy brow
   With anguish moist and fever dew,   10
And on thy cheeks a fading rose
   Fast withereth too.

"I met a Lady in the Meads,°   *meadows*
   Full beautiful, a faery's child,
Her hair was long, her foot was light   15
   And her eyes were wild.

"I made a Garland for her head,
   And bracelets too, and fragrant Zone;°   *belt*
She looked at me as she did love
   And made sweet moan.   20

"I set her on my pacing steed
   And nothing else saw all day long,
For sidelong would she bend and sing
   A faery's song.

"She found me roots of relish sweet,   25
   And honey wild, and manna dew,
And sure in language strange she said
   'I love thee true.'

La Belle Dame sans Merci: The beautiful lady without mercy.

"She took me to her elfin grot
   And there she wept and sighed full sore,   30
And there I shut her wild wild eyes
   With kisses four.

"And there she lulléd me asleep,
   And there I dreamed, Ah Woe betide!
The latest dream I ever dreamt   35
   On the cold hill side.

"I saw pale Kings, and Princes too,
   Pale warriors, death-pale were they all;
They cried, 'La belle dame sans merci
   Hath thee in thrall!'   40

"I saw their starved lips in the gloam
   With horrid warming gapéd wide,
And I awoke, and found me here
   On the cold hill's side.

"And this is why I sojourn here,   45
   Alone and palely loitering;
Though the sedge is withered from the Lake
   And no birds sing."

EDGAR ALLAN POE (1809–1849)

The Raven

Once upon a midnight dreary, while I pondered, weak and weary,
Over many a quaint and curious volume of forgotten lore —
While I nodded, nearly napping, suddenly there came a tapping,
As of some one gently rapping, rapping at my chamber door.
"'T is some visiter," I muttered, "tapping at my chamber door —   5
                       Only this and nothing more."

Ah, distinctly I remember it was in the bleak December;
And each separate dying ember wrought its ghost upon the floor.
Eagerly I wished the morrow; — vainly I had sought to borrow
From my books surcease of sorrow — sorrow for the lost Lenore —   10
For the rare and radiant maiden whom the angels name Lenore —
                    Nameless *here* for evermore.

And the silken, sad, uncertain rustling of each purple curtain
Thrilled me — filled me with fantastic terrors never felt before;
So that now, to still the beating of my heart, I stood repeating   15

"'T is some visiter entreating entrance at my chamber door —
Some late visiter entreating entrance at my chamber door; —
          This it is and nothing more."

Presently my soul grew stronger; hesitating then no longer,
"Sir," said I, "or Madam, truly your forgiveness I implore;   20
But the fact is I was napping, and so gently you came rapping,
And so faintly you came tapping, tapping at my chamber door,
That I scarce was sure I heard you" — here I opened wide the door; —
          Darkness there and nothing more.

Deep into that darkness peering, long I stood there wondering, fearing,   25
Doubting, dreaming dreams no mortal ever dared to dream before;
But the silence was unbroken, and the stillness gave no token,
And the only word there spoken was the whispered word, "Lenore!"
This I whispered, and an echo murmured back the word "Lenore!"
          Merely this and nothing more.   30

Back into the chamber turning, all my soul within me burning,
Soon again I heard a tapping somewhat louder than before.
"Surely," said I, "surely that is something at my window lattice;
Let me see, then, what thereat is, and this mystery explore —
Let my heart be still a moment and this mystery explore; —   35
          'T is the wind and nothing more!"

Open here I flung the shutter, when, with many a flirt and flutter
In there stepped a stately Raven of the saintly days of yore.
Not the least obeisance made he; not a minute stopped or stayed he;
But, with mien of lord or lady, perched above my chamber door —   40
Perched upon a bust of Pallas just above my chamber door —
          Perched, and sat, and nothing more.

Then this ebony bird beguiling my sad fancy into smiling,
By the grave and stern decorum of the countenance it wore,
"Though thy crest be shorn and shaven, thou," I said, "art sure no craven,   45
Ghastly grim and ancient Raven wandering from the Nightly shore
Tell me what thy lordly name is on the Night's Plutonian shore!"
          Quoth the Raven, "Nevermore."

Much I marvelled this ungainly fowl to hear discourse so plainly,
Though its answer little meaning — little relevancy bore;   50
For we cannot help agreeing that no living human being
Ever yet was blessed with seeing bird above his chamber door —
Bird or beast upon the sculptured bust above his chamber door
          With such a name as "Nevermore."

But the Raven, sitting lonely on the placid bust, spoke only   55
That one word, as if his soul in that one word he did outpour
Nothing farther then he uttered — not a feather then he fluttered —

Till I scarcely more than muttered "Other friends have flown before —
On the morrow *he* will leave me, as my hopes have flown before."
                              Then the bird said "Nevermore."   60

Startled at the stillness broken by reply so aptly spoken,
"Doubtless," said I, "what it utters is its only stock and store
Caught from some unhappy master whom unmerciful Disaster
Followed fast and followed faster till his songs one burden bore
Till the dirges of his Hope that melancholy burden bore   65
                              Of 'Never — nevermore.'"

But the Raven still beguiling all my fancy into smiling,
Straight I wheeled a cushioned seat in front of bird, and bust and door;
Then, upon the velvet sinking, I betook myself to linking
Fancy unto fancy, thinking what this ominous bird of yore —   70
What this grim, ungainly, ghastly, gaunt, and ominous bird of yore
                              Meant in croaking "Nevermore."

This I sat engaged in guessing, but no syllable expressing
To the fowl whose fiery eyes now burned into my bosom's core;
This and more I sat divining, with my head at ease reclining   75
On the cushion's velvet lining that the lamp-light gloated o'er,
But whose velvet violet lining with the lamp-light gloating o'er,
                              She shall press, ah, nevermore!

Then, methought, the air grew denser, perfumed from an unseen censer
Swung by Seraphim whose foot-falls tinkled on the tufted floor.   80
"Wretch," I cried, "thy God hath lent thee — by these angels he hath
    sent thee
Respite — respite and nepenthe° from thy memories of Lenore;
Quaff, oh quaff this kind nepenthe and forget this lost Lenore!"
                              Quoth the Raven "Nevermore."

"Prophet!" said I, "thing of evil! prophet still, if bird or devil! — 85
Whether Tempter sent, or whether tempest tossed thee here ashore,
Desolate yet all undaunted, on this desert land enchanted —
On this home by Horror haunted — tell me truly, I implore —
Is there — *is* there balm in Gilead?° — tell me — tell me, I implore!"
                              Quoth the Raven "Nevermore."   90

"Prophet!" said I, "thing of evil! — prophet still, if bird or devil!
By that Heaven that bends above us — by that God we both adore —
Tell this soul with sorrow laden if, within the distant Aidenn,
It shall clasp a sainted maiden whom the angels name Lenore —
Clasp a rare and radiant maiden whom the angels name Lenore."   95
                              Quoth the Raven "Nevermore."

---

82 *nepenthe:* A drink believed by the ancient Greeks to make one forget sorrow.   89 *balm in
Gilead:* Biblical reference meaning "Is there respite in the afterlife for those who suffer on
earth?"

"Be that word our sign of parting, bird or fiend!" I shrieked, upstarting —
"Get thee back into the tempest and the Night's Plutonian shore!
Leave no black plume as a token of that lie thy soul hath spoken!
Leave my loneliness unbroken! — quit the bust above my door!   100
Take thy beak from out my heart, and take thy form from off my door!"
                                  Quoth the Raven "Nevermore."

And the Raven, never flitting, still is sitting, *still* is sitting
On the pallid bust of Pallas just above my chamber door;
And his eyes have all the seeming of a demon's that is dreaming,   105
And the lamp-light o'er him streaming throws his shadow on the floor;
And my soul from out that shadow that lies floating on the floor
                                  Shall be lifted — nevermore!

ALFRED, LORD TENNYSON (1809–1892)

Ulysses°

It little profits that an idle king,
By this still hearth, among these barren crags,
Matched with an aged wife, I mete and dole
Unequal laws unto a savage race,
That hoard, and sleep, and feed, and know not me.   5
I cannot rest from travel; I will drink
Life to the lees. All times I have enjoyed
Greatly, have suffered greatly, both with those
That loved me, and alone; on shore, and when
Through scudding drifts the rainy Hyades°   10
Vext the dim sea. I am become a name;
For always roaming with a hungry heart
Much have I seen and known — cities of men
And manners, climates, councils, governments,
Myself not least, but honored of them all, —   15
And drunk delight of battle with my peers,
Far on the ringing plains of windy Troy.
I am a part of all that I have met;
Yet all experience is an arch wherethrough
Gleams that untraveled world whose margin fades   20
For ever and for ever when I move.
How dull it is to pause, to make an end,
To rust unburnished, not to shine in use!
As though to breathe were life! Life piled on life

Ulysses: In *The Inferno,* Dante depicts Ulysses as returning to Ithaca, his island kingdom, after
have been away fighting the Trojan War for ten years. Because he can find no peace at home,
he convinces a band of his warriors to set out with him on another journey.   10 *Hyades:* The
rising of this constellation with the sun forecasts rain.

Were all too little, and of one to me   25
Little remains; but every hour is saved
From that eternal silence, something more,
A bringer of new things; and vile it were
For some three suns to store and hoard myself,
And this gray spirit yearning in desire   30
To follow knowledge like a sinking star,
Beyond the utmost bound of human thought.
    This is my son, mine own Telemachus,
To whom I leave the scepter and the isle,
Well-loved of me, discerning to fulfill   35
This labor, by slow prudence to make mild
A rugged people, and through soft degrees
Subdue them to the useful and the good.
Most blameless is he, centered in the sphere
Of common duties, decent not to fail   40
In offices of tenderness, and pay
Meet adoration to my household gods,
When I am gone. He works his work, I mine.
    There lies the port; the vessel puffs her sail;
There gloom the dark, broad seas. My mariners,   45
Souls that have toiled, and wrought, and thought with me,
That ever with a frolic welcome took
The thunder and the sunshine, and opposed
Free hearts, free foreheads — you and I are old;
Old age hath yet his honor and his toil.   50
Death closes all; but something ere the end,
Some work of noble note, may yet be done,
Not unbecoming men that strove with gods.
The lights begin to twinkle from the rocks;
The long day wanes; the slow moon climbs; the deep   55
Moans round with many voices. Come, my friends,
'Tis not too late to seek a newer world.
Push off, and sitting well in order smite
The sounding furrows; for my purpose holds
To sail beyond the sunset, and the baths   60
Of all the western stars, until I die.
It may be that the gulfs will wash us down;
It may be we shall touch the Happy Isles,
And see the great Achilles, whom we knew.
Though much is taken, much abides; and though   65
We are not now that strength which in old days
Moved earth and heaven, that which we are, we are,
One equal temper of heroic hearts,
Made weak by time and fate, but strong in will
To strive, to seek, to find, and not to yield.   70

ALFRED, LORD TENNYSON (1809–1892)

The Lady of Shalott

Part 1

On either side the river lie
Long fields of barley and of rye,
That clothe the wold° and meet the sky;   *plain*
And through the field the road runs by
   To many-towered Camelot;   5
And up and down the people go,
Gazing where the lilies blow
Round an island there below,
   The island of Shalott.

Willows whiten, aspens quiver,   10
Little breezes dusk and shiver
Through the wave that runs forever
By the island in the river
   Flowing down to Camelot.
Four gray walls, and four gray towers,   15
Overlook a space of flowers,
And the silent isle imbowers
   The Lady of Shalott.

By the margin, willow-veiled,
Slide the heavy barges trailed   20
By slow horses; and unhailed
The shallop° flitteth silken-sailed   *small, open boat*
   Skimming down to Camelot:
But who hath seen her wave her hand?
Or at the casement seen her stand?   25
Or is she known in all the land,
   The Lady of Shalott?

Only reapers, reaping early
In among the bearded barley,
Hear a song that echoes cheerly   30
From the river winding clearly,
   Down to towered Camelot;
And by the moon the reaper weary,
Piling sheaves in uplands airy,
Listening, whispers " 'Tis the fairy   35
   Lady of Shalott."

Part 2

There she weaves by night and day
A magic web with colors gay.
She has heard a whisper say,
A curse is on her if she stay   40
      To look down to Camelot.
She knows not what the curse may be,
And so she weaveth steadily,
And little other care hath she,
      The Lady of Shalott.   45

And moving through a mirror clear°
That hangs before her all the year,
Shadows of the world appear.
There she sees the highway near
      Winding down to Camelot;   50
There the river eddy whirls,
And there the surly village churls,
And the red cloaks of market girls,
      Pass onward from Shalott.

Sometimes a troop of damsels glad,   55
An abbot on an ambling pad,°   *gentle horse*
Sometimes a curly shepherd lad,
Or long-haired page in crimson clad,
      Goes by to towered Camelot;
And sometimes through the mirror blue   60
The knights come riding two and two:
She hath no loyal knight and true,
      The Lady of Shalott.

But in her web she still delights
To weave the mirror's magic sights,   65
For often through the silent nights
A funeral, with plumes and lights
      And music, went to Camelot;
Or when the moon was overhead,
Came two young lovers lately wed: 70
"I am half sick of shadows," said
      The Lady of Shalott.

46 *mirror clear:* Weavers worked with mirrors opposite their looms so that they could see the
patterns they were weaving.

Part 3

A bowshot from her bower eaves,
He rode between the barley sheaves,
The sun came dazzling through the leaves,   75
And flamed upon the brazen greaves°
      Of bold Sir Lancelot.
A red-cross knight forever kneeled
To a lady in his shield,
That sparkled on the yellow field,   80
      Beside remote Shalott.

The gemmy bridle glittered free,
Like to some branch of stars we see
Hung in the golden Galaxy.
The bridle bells rang merrily   85
      As he rode down to Camelot;
And from his blazoned baldric° slung   *embroidered sash*
A mighty silver bugle hung,
And as he rode his armor rung,
      Beside remote Shalott.   90

All in the blue unclouded weather
Thick-jeweled shone the saddle leather,
The helmet and the helmet-feather
Burned like one burning flame together,
      As he rode down to Camelot;   95
As often through the purple night,
Below the starry clusters bright,
Some bearded meteor, trailing light,
      Moves over still Shalott.

His broad clear brow in sunlight glowed;   100
On burnished hooves his war horse trode;
From underneath his helmet flowed
His coal-black curls as on he rode,
      As he rode down to Camelot.
From the bank and from the river   105
He flashed into the crystal mirror,
"Tirra lirra," by the river
      Sang Sir Lancelot.

She left the web, she left the loom,
She made three paces through the room,   110
She saw the water lily bloom,

---

76 *greaves:* The part of a knight's armor that protects the bottom of the leg.

She saw the helmet and the plume,
        She looked down to Camelot.
Out flew the web and floated wide;
The mirror cracked from side to side;   115
"The curse is come upon me," cried
        The Lady of Shalott.

Part 4

In the stormy east wind straining,
The pale yellow woods were waning,
The broad stream in his banks complaining,   120
Heavily the low sky raining
        Over towered Camelot;
Down she came and found a boat
Beneath a willow left afloat,
And round about the prow she wrote   125
        The Lady of Shalott.

And down the river's dim expanse
Like some bold seër in a trance,
Seeing all his own mischance —
With a glassy countenance   130
        Did she look to Camelot.
And at the closing of the day
She loosed the chain, and down she lay;
The broad steam bore her far away,
        The Lady of Shalott.   135

Lying, robed in snowy white
That loosely flew to left and right —
The leaves upon her falling light —
Through the noises of the night
        She floated down to Camelot;   140
And as the boat-head wound along
The willowy hills and fields among,
They heard her singing her last song,
        The Lady of Shalott.

Heard a carol, mournful, holy,   145
Chanted loudly, chanted lowly,
Till her blood was frozen slowly,
And her eyes were darkened wholly,
        Turned to towered Camelot.
For ere she reached upon the tide   150

The first house by the waterside,
Singing in her song she died,
      The Lady of Shalott.

Under tower and balcony
By garden wall and gallery,   155
A gleaming shape she floated by,
Dead-pale between the houses high,
      Silent into Camelot.
Out upon the wharfs they came,
Knight and burgher, lord and dame,   160
And round the prow they read her name
      The Lady of Shalott.

Who is this? and what is here?
And in the lighted palace near
Died the sound of royal cheer;   165
And they crossed themselves for fear,
      All the knights at Camelot:
But Lancelot mused a little space;
He said, "She has a lovely face;
God in his mercy lend her grace,   170
      The Lady of Shalott."

WALT WHITMAN (1819–1892)

Beat! beat! drums!

Beat! beat! drums! blow! bugles! blow!
Through the windows — through doors — burst like a ruthless force,
Into the solemn church, and scatter the congregation,
Into the school where the scholar is studying;
Leave not the bridegroom quiet — no happiness must he have now   5
   with his bride,
Nor the peaceful farmer any peace, ploughing his field or gathering
   his grain,
So fierce you whirr and pound you drums — so shrill you bugles blow.

Beat! beat! drums! — blow! bugles! blow!
Over the traffic of cities — over the rumble of wheels in the streets;
Are beds prepared for sleepers at night in the houses? no sleepers must sleep   10
   in those beds,
No bargainers' bargains by day — no brokers or speculators — would
   they continue?

Would the talkers be talking? would the singer attempt to sing?
Would the lawyer rise in the court to state his case before the judge?
Then rattle quicker, heavier drums — you bugles wilder blow.

Beat! beat! drums! — blow! bugles! blow!   15
Make no parley — stop for no expostulation,
Mind not the timid — mind not the weeper or prayer,
Mind not the old man beseeching the young man,
Let not the child's voice be heard, nor the mother's entreaties,
Make even the trestles to shake the dead where they lie awaiting the hearses,   20
So strong you thump O terrible drums — so loud you bugles blow.

WALT WHITMAN (1819–1892)

A noiseless patient spider

A noiseless patient spider,
I mark'd where on a little promontory it stood isolated,
Mark'd how to explore the vacant vast surrounding,
It launch'd forth filament, filament, filament, out of itself,
Ever unreeling them, ever tirelessly speeding them.   5
And you O my soul where you stand,
Surrounded, detached, in measureless oceans of space,
Ceaselessly musing, venturing, throwing, seeking the spheres
    to connect them,
Till the bridge you will need be form'd, till the ductile anchor hold,
Till the gossamer thread you fling catch somewhere, O my soul.   10

MATTHEW ARNOLD (1822–1888)

Dover Beach

The sea is calm tonight.
The tide is full, the moon lies fair
Upon the straits; on the French coast the light
Gleams and is gone; the cliffs of England stand,
Glimmering and vast, out in the tranquil bay.   5
Come to the window, sweet is the night-air!
Only, from the long line of spray
Where the sea meets the moon-blanched land,
Listen! you hear the grating roar
Of pebbles which the waves draw back, and fling,   10

At their return, up the high strand,
Begin, and cease, and then again begin,
With tremulous cadence slow, and bring
The eternal note of sadness in.

Sophocles° long ago   15
Heard it on the Aegean, and it brought
Into his mind the turbid ebb and flow
Of human misery; we
Find also in the sound a thought,
Hearing it by this distant northern sea.   20
The Sea of Faith°
Was once, too, at the full, and round earth's shore
Lay like the folds of a bright girdle furled.
But now I only hear
Its melancholy, long, withdrawing roar,   25
Retreating, to the breath
Of the night-wind, down the vast edges drear
And naked shingles° of the world.

Ah, love, let us be true
To one another! for the world, which seems   30
To lie before us like a land of dreams,
So various, so beautiful, so new,
Hath really neither joy, nor love, nor light,
Nor certitude, nor peace, nor help for pain;
And we are here as on a darkling plain   35
Swept with confused alarms of struggle and flight,
Where ignorant armies clash by night.

---

15 *Sophocles:* (496?—406 B.C.) Greek writer of tragic drama.   21 *Sea of Faith:* Unquestioning belief in religious doctrine.   28 *shingles:* Gravel-covered beaches.

EMILY DICKINSON (1830–1886)

Success is counted sweetest

Success is counted sweetest
By those who ne'er succeed.
To comprehend a nectar
Requires sorest need.

Not one of all the purple Host   5
Who took the Flag today

Can tell the definition
So clear of Victory

As he defeated — dying —
On whose forbidden ear   10
The distant strains of triumph
Burst agonized and clear!

EMILY DICKINSON (1830–1886)

I like a look of Agony

I like a look of Agony,
Because I know it's true —
Men do not sham Convulsion,
Nor simulate, a Throe —

The Eyes glaze once — and that is Death —   5
Impossible to feign
The Beads upon the Forehead
By homely Anguish strung.

EMILY DICKINSON (1830–1886)

There's a certain Slant of light

There's a certain Slant of light,
Winter Afternoons —
That oppresses, like the Heft
Of Cathedral Tunes —

Heavenly Hurt, it gives us —   5
We can find no scar,
But internal difference,
Where the Meanings, are —

None may teach it — Any —
'Tis the Sea Despair —   10
An imperial affliction
Sent us of the Air —

When it comes, the Landscape listens —
Shadows — hold their breath —
When it goes, 'tis like the Distance   15
On the look of Death —

EMILY DICKINSON (1830–1886)

I felt a Funeral, in my Brain

I felt a Funeral, in my Brain,
And Mourners to and fro
Kept treading — treading — till it seemed
That Sense was breaking through —

And when they all were seated,   5
A Service, like a Drum —
Kept beating — beating — till I thought
My Mind was going numb —

And I heard them lift a Box
And creak across my Soul   10
With those same Boots of Lead, again,
The Space — began to toll,

As all the Heavens were a Bell,
And Being, but an Ear,
And I, and Silence, some strange Race   15
Wrecked, solitary, here —

And then a Plank in Reason, broke,
And I dropped down, and down —
And hit a World, at every plunge,
And Finished knowing — then —   20

EMILY DICKINSON (1830–1886)

I died for Beauty — but was scarce

I died for Beauty — but was scarce
Adjusted in the Tomb
When One who died for Truth, was lain
In an adjoining Room —

He questioned softly "Why I failed"?   5
"For Beauty", I replied —
"And I — for Truth — Themself are One —
We Brethren, are", He said —

And so, as Kinsmen, met a Night —
We talked between the Rooms —   10
Until the Moss had reached our lips —
And covered up — our names —

EMILY DICKINSON (1830–1886)

One Sister have I in our house

One Sister have I in our house,
And one, a hedge away.
There's only one recorded,
But both belong to me.

One came the road that I came —   5
And wore my last year's gown —
The other, as a bird her nest,
Builded our hearts among.

She did not sing as we did —
It was a different tune —   10
Herself to her a music
As Bumble bee of June.

Today is far from Childhood —
But up and down the hills
I held her hand the tighter —   15
Which shortened all the miles —

And still her hum
The years among,
Deceives the Butterfly;
Still in her Eye   20
The Violets lie
Mouldered this many May.

I spilt the dew —
But took the morn —
I chose this single star   25
From out the wide night's numbers —
Sue — forevermore!

EMILY DICKINSON (1830–1886)

She sweeps with many-colored Brooms

She sweeps with many-colored Brooms —
And leaves the Shreds behind —
Oh Housewife in the Evening West —
Come back, and dust the Pond!

You dropped a Purple Ravelling in —   5
You dropped an Amber thread —
And now you've littered all the East
With Duds of Emerald!

And still, she plies her spotted Brooms,
And still the Aprons fly,   10
Till Brooms fade softly into stars —
And then I come away —

EMILY DICKINSON (1830–1886)

The Soul selects her own Society

The Soul selects her own Society —
Then — shuts the Door —
To her divine Majority —
Present no more —

Unmoved — she notes the Chariots — pausing —   5
At her low Gate —
Unmoved — an Emperor be kneeling
Upon her Mat —

I've known her — from an ample nation —
Choose One —   10
Then — close the Valves of her attention —
Like Stone —

EMILY DICKINSON (1830–1886)

Some keep the Sabbath going to Church

Some keep the Sabbath going to Church —
I keep it, staying at Home —
With a Bobolink for a Chorister —
And an Orchard, for a Dome —

Some keep the Sabbath in Surplice —   5
I just wear my Wings —
And instead of tolling the Bell, for Church,
Our little Sexton — sings.

God preaches, a noted Clergyman —
And the sermon is never long,   10
So instead of getting to Heaven, at last —
I'm going, all along.

EMILY DICKINSON (1830–1886)

After great pain, a formal feeling comes

After great pain, a formal feeling comes —
The Nerves sit ceremonious, like Tombs —
The stiff Heart questions was it He, that bore,
And Yesterday, or Centuries before?

The Feet, mechanical, go round —   5
Of Ground, or Air, or Ought —
A Wooden way
Regardless grown,
A Quartz contentment, like a stone —

This is the Hour of Lead —   10
Remembered, if outlived,
As Freezing persons, recollect the Snow —
First — Chill — then Stupor — then the letting go —

EMILY DICKINSON (1830–1886)

I dreaded that first Robin

I dreaded that first Robin, so,
But He is mastered, now,
I'm some accustomed to Him grown,
He hurts a little, though —

I thought if I could only live   5
Till that first Shout got by —
Not all Pianos in the Woods
Had power to mangle me —

I dared not meet the Daffodils —
For fear their Yellow Gown   10
Would pierce me with a fashion
So foreign to my own —

I wished the Grass would hurry —
So — when 'twas time to see —
He'd be too tall, the tallest one   15
Could stretch — to look at me —

I could not bear the Bees should come,
I wished they'd stay away

In those dim countries where they go,
What word had they, for me? 20

They're here, though; not a creature failed —
No Blossom stayed away
In gentle deference to me —
The Queen of Calvary —

Each one salutes me, as he goes, 25
And I, my childish Plumes,
Life, in bereaved acknowledgement
Of their unthinking Drums —

EMILY DICKINSON (1830–1886)

Witchcraft was hung, in History

Witchcraft was hung, in History,
But History and I
Find all the Witchcraft that we need
Around us, every Day —

EMILY DICKINSON (1830–1886)

Rearrange a "Wife's" affection!

Rearrange a "Wife's" affection!
When they dislocate my Brain!
Amputate my freckled Bosom!
Make me bearded like a man!

Blush, my spirit, in thy Fastness — 5
Blush, my unacknowledged clay —
Seven years of troth have taught thee
More than Wifehood ever may!

Love that never leaped its socket —
Trust entrenched in narrow pain — 10
Constancy thro' fire — awarded —
Anguish — bare of anodyne!

Burden — borne so far triumphant —
None suspect me of the crown,
For I wear the "Thorns" till *Sunset* — 15
Then — my Diadem put on.

Big my Secret but it's *bandaged* —
It will never get away
Till the Day its Weary Keeper
Leads it through the Grave to thee.   20

EMILY DICKINSON (1830–1886)

Wild Nights — Wild Nights

Wild Nights — Wild Nights!
Were I with thee
Wild Nights should be
Our luxury!

Futile — the Winds —   5
To a Heart in port —
Done with the Compass —
Done with the Chart!

Rowing in Eden —
Ah, the Sea!   10
Might I but moor — Tonight —
In Thee!

EMILY DICKINSON (1830–1886)

Much Madness is divinest Sense

Much Madness is divinest Sense —
To a discerning Eye —
Much Sense — the starkest Madness —
'Tis the Majority
In this, as All, prevail —   5
Assent — and you are sane —
Demur — you're straightway dangerous —
And handled with a Chain —

THOMAS HARDY (1840–1928)

The Darkling Thrush

I leant upon a coppice gate
        When Frost was specter-gray,
And Winter's dregs made desolate

The weakening eye of day.
The tangled bine-stems scored the sky   5
    Like strings of broken lyres,
And all mankind that haunted nigh
    Had sought their household fires.

The land's sharp features seemed to be
    The Century's corpse outleant,   10
His crypt the cloudy canopy,
    The wind his death-lament.
The ancient pulse of germ and birth
    Was shrunken hard and dry,
And every spirit upon earth   15
    Seemed fervorless as I.

At once a voice arose among
    The bleak twigs overhead
In a full-hearted evensong
    Of joy illimited;   20
An aged thrush, frail, gaunt, and small,
    In blast-beruffled plume,
Had chosen thus to fling his soul
    Upon the growing gloom.

So little cause for carolings   25
    Of such ecstatic sound
Was written on terrestrial things
    Afar or night around,
That I could think there trembled through
    His happy good-night air   30
Some blessed Hope, whereof he knew
    And I was unaware.

GERARD MANLEY HOPKINS (1844–1889)

God's Grandeur

The world is charged with the grandeur of God.
    It will flame out, like shining from shook foil;
    It gathers to a greatness, like the ooze of oil
Crushed. Why do men then now not reck his rod?
Generations have trod, have trod, have trod;   5
    And all is seared with trade; bleared, smeared with toil;
    And wears man's smudge and shares man's smell: the soil
Is bare now, nor can foot feel, being shod.

And for all this, nature is never spent;
    There lives the dearest freshness deep down things;   10
And though the last lights off the black West went
    Oh, morning, at the brown brink eastward, springs —
Because the Holy Ghost over the bent
    World broods with warm breast and with ah! bright wings.

GERARD MANLEY HOPKINS (1844–1889)

Pied Beauty

Glory be to God for dappled things —
    For skies of couple-colour as a brinded cow;
        For rose-moles all in stipple upon trout that swim;
Fresh-firecoal chestnut-falls; finches' wings;
    Landscape plotted and pieced — fold, fallow, and plough;   5
        And all trades, their gear and tackle and trim.

All things counter, original, spare, strange;
    Whatever is fickle, freckled (who know how?)
        With swift, slow; sweet, sour; adazzle, dim;
He fathers-forth whose beauty is past change: 10
                    Praise Him.

WILLIAM BUTLER YEATS (1865–1939)

The Lake Isle of Innisfree

I will arise and go now, and go to Innisfree,
And a small cabin build there, of clay and wattles made:
Nine bean-rows will I have there, a hive for the honey-bee.
And live alone in the bee-loud glade.

And I shall have some peace there, for peace comes dropping slow   5
Dropping from the veils of the morning to where the cricket sings;
There midnight's all a glimmer, and noon a purple glow,
And evening full of the linnet's wings.

I will arise and go now, for always night and day
I hear lake water lapping with low sounds by the shore;   10
While I stand on the roadway, or on the pavements grey,
I hear it in the deep heart's core.

WILLIAM BUTLER YEATS (1865–1939)

Crazy Jane Talks with the Bishop

I met the Bishop on the road
And much said he and I.
'Those breasts are flat and fallen now,
Those veins must soon be dry;
Live in a heavenly mansion,   5
Not in some foul sty.'

'Fair and foul are near of kin,
And fair needs foul,' I cried.
'My friends are gone, but that's a truth
Nor grave nor bed denied,   10
Learned in bodily lowliness
And in the heart's pride.

'A woman can be proud and stiff
When on love intent;
But Love has pitched his mansion in   15
The place of excrement;
For nothing can be sole or whole
That has not been rent.'

WILLIAM BUTLER YEATS (1865–1939)

The Second Coming

Turning and turning in the widening gyre
The falcon cannot hear the falconer;
Things fall apart; the center cannot hold;
Mere anarchy is loosed upon the world,
The blood-dimmed tide is loosed, and everywhere   5
The ceremony of innocence is drowned;
The best lack all conviction, while the worst
Are full of passionate intensity.

Surely some revelation is at hand;
Surely the Second Coming is at hand;   10
The Second Coming! Hardly are those words out
When a vast image out of *Spiritus Mundi*°
Troubles my sight: somewhere in sands of the desert

12 Spiritus Mundi: The soul of the world. Yeats believed in the existence of a body of shared human memory.

A shape with lion body and the head of a man,
A gaze blank and pitiless as the sun,   15
Is moving its slow thighs, while all about it
Reel shadows of the indignant desert birds.
The darkness drops again; but now I know
That twenty centuries of stony sleep
Were vexed to nightmare by a rocking cradle,   20
And what rough beast, its hour come round at last,
Slouches toward Bethlehem to be born?

JAMES WELDON JOHNSON (1871–1938)

O Black and Unknown Bards

O black and unknown bards of long ago,
How came your lips to touch the sacred fire?
How, in your darkness, did you come to know
The power and beauty of the minstrel's lyre?
Who first from midst his bonds lifted his eyes?   5
Who first from out the still watch, lone and long,
Feeling the ancient faith of prophets rise
Within his dark-kept soul, burst into song?

Heart of what slave poured out such melody
As "Steal Away to Jesus"? On its strains   10
His spirit must have nightly floated free,
Though still about his hands he felt his chains.
Who heard great "Jordan roll"? Whose starward eye
Saw chariot "swing low"? And who was he
That breathed that comforting, melodic sigh,   15
"Nobody Knows de Trouble I See"?

What merely living clod, what captive thing,
Could up toward God through all its darkness grope,
And find within its deadened heart to sing
These songs of sorrow, love, and faith, and hope?   20
How did it catch that subtle undertone,
That note in music heard not with the ears?
How sound the elusive reed so seldom blown,
Which stirs the soul or melts the heart to tears?

Not that great German master in his dream   25
Of harmonies that thundered amongst the stars
At the creation, ever heard a theme
Nobler than "Go Down, Moses." Mark its bars,

How like a mighty trumpet-call they stir
The blood. Such are the notes that men have sung   30
Going to valorous deeds; such tones there were
That helped make history when Time was young.

There is a wide, wide wonder in it all,
That from degraded rest servile toil
The fiery spirit of the seer should call   35
These simple children of the sun and soil.
O black slave singers, gone, forgot, unfamed,
You — you alone, of all the long, long line
Of those who've sung untaught, unknown, unnamed,
Have stretched out upward, seeking the divine.   40

You sang not deeds of heroes or of kings;
No chant of bloody war, no exulting paean
Of arms-won triumphs; but your humble strings
You touched in chord with music empyrean.
You sang far better than you knew; the songs   45
That for your listeners' hungry hearts sufficed
Still live — but more than this to you belongs;
You sang a race from wood and stone to Christ.

PAUL LAURENCE DUNBAR (1872–1906)

We wear the mask

We wear the mask that grins and lies,
It hides our cheeks and shades our eyes —
This debt we pay to human guile;
With torn and bleeding hearts we smile,
And mouth with myriad subtleties.   5

Why should the world be over-wise,
In counting all our tears and sighs?
Nay, let them only see us, while
　　We wear the mask.

We smile, but, O great Christ, our cries   10
To thee from tortured souls arise.
We sing, but oh the clay is vile
Beneath our feet, and long the mile;
But let the world dream otherwise,
　　We wear the mask!   15

ROBERT FROST (1874–1963)

An Old Man's Winter Night

All out-of-doors looked darkly in at him
Through the thin frost, almost in separate stars,
That gathers on the pane in empty rooms.
What kept his eyes from giving back the gaze
Was the lamp tilted near them in his hand. 5
What kept him from remembering what it was
That brought him to that creaking room was age.
He stood with barrels round him — at a loss.
And having scared the cellar under him
In clomping here, he scared it once again 10
In clomping off; — and scared the outer night,
Which has its sounds, familiar, like the roar
Of trees and crack of branches, common things,
But nothing so like beating on a box.
A light he was to no one but himself 15
Where now he sat, concerned with he knew what,
A quiet light, and then not even that.
He consigned to the moon, such as she was,
So late-arising, to the broken moon
As better than the sun in any case 20
For such a charge, his snow upon the roof,
His icicles along the wall to keep;
And slept. The log that shifted with a jolt
Once in the stove, disturbed him and he shifted,
And eased his heavy breathing, but still slept. 25
One aged man — one man — can't keep a house,
A farm, a countryside, or if he can,
It's thus he does it of a winter night.

ROBERT FROST (1874–1963)

Mending Wall

Something there is that doesn't love a wall,
That sends the frozen-ground-swell under it,
And spills the upper boulders in the sun;
And makes gaps even two can pass abreast.
The work of hunters is another thing: 5
I have come after them and made repair
Where they have left not one stone on a stone,
But they would have the rabbit out of hiding,
To please the yelping dogs. The gaps I mean,

No one has seen them made or heard them made,   10
But at spring mending-time we find them there.
I let my neighbor know beyond the hill;
And on a day we meet to walk the line
And set the wall between us once again.
We keep the wall between us as we go.   15
To each the boulders that have fallen to each.
And some are loaves and some so nearly balls
We have to use a spell to make them balance:
'Stay where you are until our backs are turned!'
We wear our fingers rough with handling them.   20
Oh, just another kind of outdoor game,
One on a side. It comes to little more:
There where it is we do not need the wall:
He is all pine and I am apple orchard.
My apple trees will never get across   25
And eat the cones under his pines, I tell him.
He only says, 'Good fences make good neighbors.'
Spring is the mischief in me, and I wonder
If I could put a notion in his head:
'*Why* do they make good neighbors? Isn't it   30
Where there are cows? But here there are no cows.
Before I built a wall I'd ask to know
What I was walling in or walling out,
And to whom I was like to give offense.
Something there is that doesn't love a wall,   35
That wants it down.' I could say 'Elves' to him,
But it's not elves exactly, and I'd rather
He said it for himself. I see him there
Bringing a stone grasped firmly by the top
In each hand, like an old-stone savage armed.   40
He moves in darkness as it seems to me,
Not of woods only and the shade of trees.
He will not go behind his father's saying,
And he likes having thought of it so well
He says again, 'Good fences make good neighbors.'   45

ROBERT FROST (1874–1963)

The Gift Outright

The land was ours before we were the land's.
She was our land more than a hundred years
Before we were her people. She was ours
In Massachusetts, in Virginia,
But we were England's, still colonials,   5

Possessing what we still were unpossessed by,
Possessed by what we now no more possessed.
Something we were withholding made us weak
Until we found out that it was ourselves
We were withholding from our land of living,   10
And forthwith found salvation in surrender.
Such as we were we gave ourselves outright
(The deed of gift was many deeds of war)
To the land vaguely realizing westward,
But still unstoried, artless, unenhanced,   15
Such as she was, such as she would become.

ROBERT FROST (1874–1963)

Stopping by Woods on a Snowy Evening

Whose woods these are I think I know.
His house is in the village, though;
He will not see me stopping here
To watch his woods fill up with snow.

My little horse must think it queer   5
To stop without a farmhouse near
Between the woods and frozen lake
The darkest evening of the year.

He gives his harness bells a shake
To ask if there is some mistake.   10
The only other sound's the sweep
Of easy wind and downy flake.

The woods are lovely, dark and deep,
But I have promises to keep,
And miles to go before I sleep,   15
And miles to go before I sleep.

ROBERT FROST (1874–1963)

After Apple-Picking

My long two-pointed ladder's sticking through a tree
Toward heaven still,
And there's a barrel that I didn't fill
Beside it, and there may be two or three
Apples I didn't pick upon some bough.   5
But I am done with apple-picking now.

Essence of winter sleep is on the night,
The scent of apples: I am drowsing off.
I cannot rub the strangeness from my sight
I got from looking through a pane of glass   10
I skimmed this morning from the drinking trough
And held against the world of hoary grass.
It melted, and I let it fall and break.
But I was well
Upon my way to sleep before it fell,   15
And I could tell
What form my dreaming was about to take.
Magnified apples appear and disappear,
Stem end and blossom end,
And every fleck of russet showing clear.   20
My instep arch not only keeps the ache,
It keeps the pressure of a ladder-round.
I feel the ladder sway as the boughs bend.
And I keep hearing from the cellar bin
The rumbling sound   25
Of load on load of apples coming in.
For I have had too much
Of apple-picking: I am overtired
Of the great harvest I myself desired.
There were ten thousand thousand fruit to touch, 30
Cherish in hand, lift down, and not let fall.
For all
That struck the earth,
No matter if not bruised or spiked with stubble,
Went surely to the cider-apple heap   35
As of no worth.
One can see what will trouble
This sleep of mine, whatever sleep it is.
Were he not gone,
The woodchuck could say whether it's like his   40
Long sleep, as I describe its coming on,
Or just some human sleep.

ROBERT FROST (1874–1963)

Fire and Ice

Some say the world will end in fire,
Some say in ice.
From what I've tasted of desire
I hold with those who favor fire.

But if it had to perish twice,   5
I think I know enough of hate
To say that for destruction ice
Is also great
And would suffice.

ROBERT FROST (1874–1963)

Design

I found a dimpled spider, fat and white,
On a white heal-all, holding up a moth
Like a white piece of rigid satin cloth —
Assorted characters of death and blight
Mixed ready to begin the morning right,   5
Like the ingredients of a witches' broth —
A snow-drop spider, a flower like a froth,
And dead wings carried like a paper kite.

What had that flower to do with being white,
The wayside blue and innocent heal-all?   10
What brought the kindred spider to that height,
Then steered the white moth thither in the night?
What but design of darkness to appall? —
If design govern in a thing so small.

ROBERT FROST (1874–1963)

Acquainted with the Night

I have been one acquainted with the night.
I have walked out in rain — and back in rain.
I have outwalked the furthest city light.

I have looked down the saddest city lane.
I have passed by the watchman on his beat   5
And dropped my eyes, unwilling to explain.

I have stood still and stopped the sound of feet
When far away an interrupted cry
Came over houses from another street,

But not to call me back or say good-by;   10
And further still at an unearthly height
One luminary clock against the sky

Proclaimed the time was neither wrong nor right.
I have been one acquainted with the night.

ROBERT FROST (1874–1963)
Nothing Gold Can Stay

Nature's first green is gold,
Her hardest hue to hold.
Her early leaf's a flower;
But only so an hour.
Then leaf subsides to leaf.   5
So Eden sank to grief,
So dawn goes down to day.
Nothing gold can stay.

EZRA POUND (1885–1972)
In a Station of the Metro

The apparition of these faces in the crowd;
Petals on a wet, black bough.

H. D. (HILDA DOOLITTLE) (1886–1961)
Helen

All Greece hates
the still eyes in the white face,
the lustre as of olives
where she stands,
and the white hands.   5

All Greece reviles
the wan face when she smiles,
hating it deeper still
when it grows wan and white,
remembering past enchantments   10
and past ills.

Greece sees unmoved,
God's daughter, born of love,
the beauty of cool feet

and slenderest knees,
could love indeed the maid,
only if she were laid,
white ash amid funereal cypresses.

15

MARIANNE MOORE (1887–1972)

The Mind Is an Enchanting Thing

is an enchanted thing
 like the glaze on a
katydid-wing
  subdivided by sun
  till the nettings are legion.
Like Gieseking playing Scarlatti;°

5

like the apteryx-awl°
 as a beak, or the
kiwi's rain-shawl
  of haired feathers, the mind
  feeling its way as though blind,
walks along with its eyes on the ground.

10

It has memory's ear
 that can hear without
having to hear.
  Like the gyroscope's fall,
  truly unequivocal
because trued by regnant certainty,

15

it is a power of
 strong enchantment. It
is like the dove-
  neck animated by
  sun; it is memory's eye;
it's conscientious inconsistency.

20

It tears off the veil; tears
 the temptation, the
mist the heart wears,

25

---

6 *Gieseking . . . Scarlatti:* German pianist Walter Gieseking (1895–1956) was acclaimed for his
performance of Italian composer Domenico Scarlatti's (1685–1757) complex sonatas.   7 *apteryx-
awl:* The apteryx is a bird that is here described as having a beak that is sharp and pointed
like an awl, a pointed tool used to puncture leather and wood.

from its eyes, — if the heart
has a face; it takes apart
   dejection. It's fire in the dove-neck's   30

iridescence; in the
   inconsistencies
of Scarlatti.
      Unconfusion submits
        its confusion to proof; it's   35
not a Herod's oath° that cannot change.

---

36 *Herod's oath:* See Matthew 2:1–16; King Herod orders the death of all male infants in Bethlehem.

MARIANNE MOORE (1887–1972)

The Fish

wade
through black jade.
   Of the crow-blue mussel shells, one keeps
   adjusting the ash heaps;
      opening and shutting itself like   5

an
injured fan.
   The barnacles which encrust the side
   of the wave, cannot hide
      there for the submerged shafts of the   10

sun.
split like spun
   glass, move themselves with spotlight swiftness
   into the crevices —
      in and out, illuminating   15

the
turquoise sea
   of bodies. The water drives a wedge
   of iron through the iron edge
      of the cliff; whereupon the stars,   20

pink
rice-grains, ink-
   bespattered jellyfish, crabs like green
   lilies, and submarine
      toadstools, slide each on the other.   25

all
external
   marks of abuse are present on this
   defiant edifice —
      all the physical features of   30

ac-
cident — lack
   of cornice, dynamite grooves, burns, and
   hatchet strokes, these things stand
      out on it; the chasm side is   35

dead.
Repeated
   evidence has proved that it can live
   on what can not revive
      its youth. The sea grows old in it.   40

ROBINSON JEFFERS (1887–1962)

Hurt Hawks

1

The broken pillar of the wing jags from the clotted shoulder,
The wing trails like a banner in defeat,
No more to use the sky forever but live with famine
And pain a few days: cat nor coyote
Will shorten the week of waiting for death, there is game without talons.   5
He stands under the oak-bush and waits
The lame feet of salvation; at night he remembers freedom
And flies in a dream, the dawns ruin it.
He is strong and pain is worse to the strong, incapacity is worse.
The curs of the day come and torment him   10
At distance, no one but death the redeemer will humble that head,
The intrepid readiness, the terrible eyes.
The wild God of the world is sometimes merciful to those
That ask mercy, not often to the arrogant.

You do not know him, you communal people, or you have forgotten him;   15
Intemperate and savage, the hawk remembers him;
Beautiful and wild, the hawks, and men that are dying, remember him.

2

I'd sooner, except the penalties, kill a man than a hawk; but the great redtail
Had nothing left but unable misery
From the bone too shattered for mending, the wing that trailed under his   20
    talons when he moved.
We had fed him six weeks, I gave him freedom,
He wandered over the foreland hill and returned in the evening, asking
    for death,
Not like a beggar, still eyed with the old
Implacable arrogance. I gave him the lead gift in the twilight. What fell was
    relaxed,
Owl-downy, soft feminine feathers; but what   25
Soared: the fierce rush: the night-herons by the flooded river cried fear at
    its rising
Before it was quite unsheathed from reality.

T. S. ELIOT (1888–1965)

Journey of the Magi

'A cold coming we had of it,
Just the worst time of the year
For a journey, and such a long journey:
The ways deep and the weather sharp,
The very dead of winter.'   5
And the camels galled, sore-footed, refractory,
Lying down in the melting snow.
There were times we regretted
The summer palaces on slopes, the terraces,
And the silken girls bringing sherbet.   10
Then the camel men cursing and grumbling
And running away, and wanting their liquor and women,
And the night-fires going out, and the lack of shelters,
And the cities hostile and the towns unfriendly
And the villages dirty and charging high prices: 15
A hard time we had of it.
At the end we preferred to travel all night,
Sleeping in snatches,
With the voices singing in our ears, saying
That this was all folly.   20

Then at dawn we came down to a temperate valley,
Wet, below the snow line, smelling of vegetation;
With a running stream and a water-mill beating the darkness,
And three trees on the low sky,
And an old white horse galloped away in the meadow.   25
Then we came to a tavern with vine-leaves over the lintel,
Six hands at an open door dicing for pieces of silver,
And feet kicking the empty wine-skins.
But there was no information, and so we continued
And arrived at evening, not a moment too soon   30
Finding the place; it was (you may say) satisfactory.

All this was a long time ago, I remember,
And I would do it again, but set down
This set down
This: were we led all that way for   35
Birth or Death? There was a Birth, certainly,
We had evidence and no doubt. I had seen birth and death,
But had thought they were different; this Birth was
Hard and bitter agony for us, like Death, our death.
We returned to our places, these Kingdoms,   40
But no longer at ease here, in the old dispensation,
With an alien people clutching their gods.
I should be glad of another death.

T. S. ELIOT (1888–1965)

The Love Song of J. Alfred Prufrock

> *S'io credesse che mia risposta fosse*
> *A persona che mai tornasse al mondo,*
> *Questa fiamma staria senza più scosse.*
> *Ma per ciò che giammai di questo fondo*
> *Non tornò vivo alcun, s'i'odo il vero,*
> *Senza tema d'infamia ti rispondo.°*

Let us go then, you and I,
When the evening is spread out against the sky
Like a patient etherized upon a table;

Epigraph from Dante's *Inferno*, canto XXVII, 61–66: "If I thought my answer were given to anyone who could ever return to the world, this flame would shake no more; but since none ever did return above from this depth, if what I hear is true, without fear of infamy, I answer thee." This response is given by Guido da Montelfetro when he is asked who he is.

Let us go, through certain half-deserted streets,
The muttering retreats   5
Of restless nights in one-night cheap hotels
And sawdust restaurants with oyster-shells:
Streets that follow like a tedious argument
Of insidious intent
To lead you to an overwhelming question . . .   10
Oh, do not ask, "What is it?"
Let us go and make our visit.

In the room the women come and go
Talking of Michelangelo.

The yellow fog that rubs its back upon the window-panes   15
The yellow smoke that rubs its muzzle on the window-panes
Licked its tongue into the corners of the evening,
Lingered upon the pools that stand in drains,
Let fall upon its back the soot that falls from chimneys,
Slipped by the terrace, made a sudden leap,   20
And seeing that it was a soft October night,
Curled once about the house, and fell asleep.

And indeed there will be time
For the yellow smoke that slides along the street,
Rubbing its back upon the window-panes;   25
There will be time, there will be time
To prepare a face to meet the faces that you meet;
There will be time to murder and create,
And time for all the works and days of hands
That lift and drop a question on your plate;   30
Time for you and time for me,
And time yet for a hundred indecisions,
And for a hundred visions and revisions,
Before the taking of a toast and tea.

In the room the women come and go   35
Talking of Michelangelo.

And indeed there will be time
To wonder, "Do I dare?" and, "Do I dare?"
Time to turn back and descend the stair,
With a bald spot in the middle of my hair —   40
[They will say: "How his hair is growing thin!"]
My morning coat, my collar mounting firmly to the chin,

My necktie rich and modest, but asserted by a simple pin —
[They will say: "But how his arms and legs are thin!"]
Do I dare   45
Disturb the universe?
In a minute there is time
For decisions and revisions which a minute will reverse.

For I have known them all already, known them all:
Have known the evenings, mornings, afternoons,   50
I have measured out my life with coffee spoons;
I know the voices dying with a dying fall
Beneath the music from a farther room.
      So how should I presume?

And I have known the eyes already, known them all —   55
The eyes that fix you in a formulated phrase,
And when I am formulated, sprawling on a pin,
When I am pinned and wriggling on the wall,
Then how should I begin
To spit out all the butt-ends of my days and ways?   60
      And how should I presume?

And I have known the arms already, known them all —
Arms that are braceleted and white and bare
[But in the lamplight, downed with light brown hair!]
Is it perfume from a dress   65
That makes me so digress?
Arms that lie along a table, or wrap about a shawl.
      And should I then presume?
      And how should I begin?
      . . . . .
Shall I say, I have gone at dusk through narrow streets   70
And watched the smoke that rises from the pipes
Of lonely men in shirt-sleeves, leaning out of windows? . . .

I should have been a pair of ragged claws
Scuttling across the floors of silent seas.
      . . . . .
And the afternoon, the evening, sleeps so peacefully!   75
Smoothed by long fingers,
Asleep . . . tired . . . or it malingers,
Stretched on the floor, here beside you and me.
Should I, after tea and cakes and ices,
Have the strength to force the moment to its crisis?   80

But though I have wept and fasted, wept and prayed,
Though I have seen my head [grown slightly bald] brought in upon a
    platter,°
I am no prophet — and here's no great matter;
I have seen the moment of my greatness flicker,
And I have seen the eternal Footman hold my coat, and snicker,   85
And in short, I was afraid.

And would it have been worth it, after all,
After the cups, the marmalade, the tea,
Among the porcelain, among some talk of you and me,
Would it have been worth while,   90
To have bitten off the matter with a smile,
To have squeezed the universe into a ball
To roll it toward some overwhelming question,
To say: "I am Lazarus,° come from the dead,
Come back to tell you all, I shall tell you all" —   95
If one, settling a pillow by her head,
    Should say: "That is not what I meant at all.
    That is not it, at all."

And would it have been worth it, after all,
Would it have been worth while,   100
After the sunsets and the dooryards and the sprinkled streets,
After the novels, after the teacups, after the skirts that trail
    along the floor —
And this, and so much more? —
It is impossible to say just what I mean!
But as if a magic lantern threw the nerves in patterns on a screen: 105
Would it have been worth while
If one, settling a pillow or throwing off a shawl,
And turning toward the window, should say:
    "That is not it at all,
    That is not what I meant, at all."   110

   . . . . .
No! I am not Prince Hamlet, nor was meant to be;
Am an attendant lord, one that will do
To swell a progress, start a scene or two,
Advise the prince; no doubt, an easy tool,
Deferential, glad to be of use,   115

---

82 *head . . . platter:* See Matthew 14:1–11. King Herod ordered John the Baptist beheaded and
presented his wife and daughter with the head on a platter.   94 *Lazarus:* See John 11:1–44.
Jesus raised Lazarus from the dead.

Politic, cautious, and meticulous;
Full of high sentence, but a bit obtuse;
At times, indeed, almost ridiculous —
Almost, at times, the Fool.

I grow old . . . I grow old . . .   120
I shall wear the bottoms of my trousers rolled.

Shall I part my hair behind? Do I dare to eat a peach?
I shall wear white flannel trousers, and walk upon the beach.
I have heard the mermaids singing, each to each.

I do not think that they will sing to me.   125

I have seen them riding seaward on the waves
Combing the white hair of the waves blown back
When the wind blows the water white and black.

We have lingered in the chambers of the sea
By sea-girls wreathed with seaweed red and brown   130
Till human voices wake us, and we drown.

e. e. cummings (1894–1962)

if everything happens that can't be done

if everything happens that can't be done
(and anything's righter
than books
could plan)
the stupidest teacher will almost guess   5
(with a run
skip
around we go yes)
there's nothing as something as one

one hasn't a why or because or although   10
(and buds know better
than books
don't grow)
one's anything old being everything new
(with a what   15

which
around we come who)
one's everyanything so

so world is a leaf so tree is a bough
(and birds sing sweeter   20
than books
tell how)
so here is away and so your is a my
(with a down
up   25
around again fly)
forever was never till now

now i love you and you love me
(and books are shuter
than books   30
can be)
and deep in the high that does nothing but fall
(with a shout
each
around we go all)   35
there's somebody calling who's we

we're anything brighter than even the sun
(we're everything greater
than books
might mean)   40
we're everyanything more than believe
(with a spin
leap
alive we're alive)
we're wonderful one times one   45

e. e. cummings (1894–1962)

in Just-

in Just-
spring   when the world is mud-
luscious the little
lame balloonman

whistles   far   and wee   5

and eddieandbill come
running from marbles and
piracies and it's
spring

when the world is puddle-wonderful   10

the queer
old balloonman whistles
far   and   wee
and bettyandisbel come dancing

from hop-scotch and jump-rope and   15

it's
spring
and
        the

            goat-footed   20
balloonMan   whistles
far
and
wee

e. e. cummings (1894–1962)

[1(a]

1(a

le
af
fa

ll   5

s)
one
l

iness

JORGE LUIS BORGES (1899–   )

The Blind Man

1

He is divested of the diverse world,
of faces, which still stay as once they were,
of the adjoining streets, now far away,
and of the concave sky, once infinite.
Of books, he keeps no more than what is left him   5
by memory, that brother of forgetting,
which keeps the formula but not the feeling
and which reflects no more than tag and name.
Traps lie in wait for me. My every step
might be a fall. I am a prisoner   10
shuffling through a time which feels like dream,
taking no note of mornings or of sunsets.
It is night. I am alone. In verse like this,
I must create my insipid universe.

2

Since I was born, in 1899,   15
beside the concave vine and the deep cistern,
frittering time, so brief in memory,
kept taking from me all my eye-shaped world.
Both days and nights would wear away the profiles
of human letters and of well-loved faces.   20
My wasted eyes would ask their useless questions
of pointless libraries and lecterns.
Blue and vermilion both are now a fog,
both useless sounds. The mirror I look into
is gray. I breathe a rose across the garden,   25
a wistful rose, my friends, out of the twilight.
Only the shades of yellow stay with me
and I can see only to look on nightmares.

LANGSTON HUGHES (1902–1967)

Harlem

What happens to a dream deferred?

  Does it dry up
  like a raisin in the sun?
  Or fester like a sore —

And then run?   5
Does it stink like rotten meat?
Or crust and sugar over —
like a syrupy sweet?

Maybe it just sags
like a heavy load.   10

Or does it explode?

PABLO NERUDA (1904–1973)

The Word

The word
was born in the blood,
grew in the dark body, beating,
and took flight through the lips and the mouth.

Farther away and nearer   5
still, still it came
from dead fathers and from wandering races,
from lands which had turned to stone,
lands weary of their poor tribes,
for when grief took to the roads   10
the people set out and arrived
and married new land and water
to grow their words again.
And so this is the inheritance;
this is the wavelength which connects us   15
with dead men and the dawning
of new beings not yet come to light.

Still the atmosphere quivers
with the first word uttered
dressed up   20
in terror and sighing.
It emerged
from the darkness
and until now there is no thunder
that ever rumbles with the iron voice   25
of that word,
the first

word uttered —
perhaps it was only a ripple, a single drop,
and yet its great cataract falls and falls.   30

Later on, the word fills with meaning.
Always with child, it filled up with lives.
Everything was births and sounds —
affirmation, clarity, strength,
negation, destruction, death —   35
the verb took over all the power
and blended existence with essence
in the electricity of its grace.

Human word, syllable, flank
of extending light and solid silverwork,   40
hereditary goblet which receives
the communications of the blood —
here is where silence came together with
the wholeness of the human word,
and, for human beings, not to speak is to die —   45
language extends even to the hair,
the mouth speaks without the lips moving,
all of a sudden, the eyes are words.

I take the word and pass it through my senses
as though it were no more than a human shape;   50
its arrangements awe me and I find my way
through each resonance of the spoken word —
I utter and I am and, speechless, I approach
across the edge of words silence itself.

I drink to the word, raising   55
a word or a shining cup;
in it I drink

the pure wine of language
or inexhaustible water,
maternal source of words,   60
and cup and water and wine
give rise to my song
because the verb is the source
and vivid life — it is blood,
blood which expresses its substance   65
and so ordains its own unwinding.
Words give glass quality to glass, blood to blood,
and life to life itself.

ELIZABETH BISHOP (1911–1978)

In the Waiting Room

In Worcester, Massachusetts,
I went with Aunt Consuelo
to keep her dentist's appointment
and sat and waited for her
in the dentist's waiting room.   5
It was winter. It got dark
early. The waiting room
was full of grown-up people,
arctics and overcoats,
lamps and magazines.   10
My aunt was inside
what seemed like a long time
and while I waited I read
the *National Geographic*
(I could read) and carefully   15
studied the photographs:
the inside of a volcano,
black, and full of ashes;
then it was spilling over
in rivulets of fire.   20
Osa and Martin Johnson
dressed in riding breeches,
laced boots, and pith helmets.
A dead man slung on a pole
— "Long Pig," the caption said.   25
Babies with pointed heads
wound round and round with string;
black, naked women with necks
wound round and round with wire
like the necks of light bulbs.   30
Their breasts were horrifying.
I read it right straight through.
I was too shy to stop.
And then I looked at the cover:
the yellow margins, the date.   35

Suddenly, from inside,
came an *oh!* of pain
— Aunt Consuelo's voice·
not very loud or long.

I wasn't at all surprised;   40
even then I knew she was
a foolish, timid woman.
I might have been embarrassed,
but wasn't. What took me
completely by surprise   45
was that it was *me:*
my voice, in my mouth.
Without thinking at all
I was my foolish aunt,
I — we — were falling, falling,   50
our eyes glued to the cover
of the *National Geographic,*
February, 1918.

I said to myself: three days
and you'll be seven years old.   55
I was saying it to stop
the sensation of falling off
the round, turning world
into cold, blue-black space.
But I felt: you are an *I,*   60
you are an *Elizabeth,*
you are one of *them.*
Why should you be one, too?
I scarcely dared to look
to see what it was I was.   65
I gave a sidelong glance
— I couldn't look any higher —
at shadowy gray knees,
trousers and skirts and boots
and different pairs of hands   70
lying under the lamps.
I knew that nothing stranger
had ever happened, that nothing
stranger could ever happen.

Why should I be my aunt,   75
or me, or anyone?
What similarities —
boots, hands, the family voice
I felt in my throat, or even
the *National Geographic*   80
and those awful hanging breasts —

held us all together
or made us all just one?
How—I didn't know any
word for it—how "unlikely" . . .   85
How had I come to be here,
like them, and overhear
a cry of pain that could have
got loud and worse but hadn't?

The waiting room was bright   90
and too hot. It was sliding
beneath a big black wave,
another, and another.

Then I was back in it.
The War was on. Outside,   95
in Worcester, Massachusetts,
were night and slush and cold,
and it was still the fifth
of February, 1918.

ROBERT HAYDEN (1913–1980)

Those Winter Sundays

Sundays too my father got up early
and put his clothes on in the blueblack cold,
then with cracked hands that ached
from labor in the weekday weather made
banked fires blaze. No one ever thanked him.   5

I'd wake and hear the cold splintering, breaking.
When the rooms were warm, he'd call,
and slowly I would rise and dress,
fearing the chronic angers of that house,

Speaking indifferently to him,   10
who had driven out the cold
and polished my good shoes as well.
What did I know, what did I know
of love's austere and lonely offices?

ROBERT LOWELL (1917–1977)

The Drinker

The man is killing time — there's nothing else.
No help now from the fifth of Bourbon
chucked helter-skelter into the river,
even its cork sucked under.

Stubbed before-breakfast cigarettes   5
burn bull's-eyes on the bedside table;
a plastic tumbler of alka seltzer
champagnes in the bathroom.

No help from his body, the whale's
warm-hearted blubber, foundering down   10
leagues of ocean, gasping whiteness.
The barbed hooks fester. The lines snap tight.

When he looks for neighbors, their names blur in the window,
his distracted eye sees only glass sky.
His despair has the galvanized color   15
of the mop and water in the galvanized bucket.

Once she was close to him
as water to the dead metal.

He looks at her engagements inked on her calendar.
A list of indictments.   20
At the numbers in her thumbed black telephone book.
A quiver full of arrows.

PHILIP LARKIN (1922–1985)

The Whitsun Weddings

That Whitsun,° I was late getting away:
    Not till about
One-twenty on the sunlit Saturday
Did my three-quarters-empty train pull out,

1 *Whitsun*: Whitsunday, the seventh Sunday after Easter, is a legal holiday in England.

All windows down, all cushions hot, all sense   5
Of being in a hurry gone. We ran
Behind the backs of houses, crossed a street
Of blinding windscreens, smelt the fish-dock; thence
The river's level drifting breadth began,
Where sky and Lincolnshire and water meet.   10

All afternoon, through the tall heat that slept
   For miles inland,
A slow and stopping curve southwards we kept.
Wide farms went by, short-shadowed cattle, and
Canals with floatings of industrial froth;   15
A hothouse flashed uniquely: hedges dipped
And rose: and now and then a smell of grass
Displaced the reek of buttoned carriage-cloth
Until the next town, new and nondescript,
Approached with acres of dismantled cars.   20

At first, I didn't notice what a noise
   The weddings made
Each station that we stopped at: sun destroys
The interest of what's happening in the shade,
And down the long cool platforms whoops and skirls   25
I took for porters larking with the mails,
And went on reading. Once we started, though,
We passed them, grinning and pomaded, girls
In parodies of fashion, heels and veils,
All posed irresolutely, watching us go,   30

As if out on the end of an event
   Waving goodbye
To something that survived it. Struck, I leant
More promptly out next time, more curiously,
And saw it all again in different terms: 35
The fathers with broad belts under their suits
And seamy foreheads; mothers loud and fat;
An uncle shouting smut; and then the perms,
The nylon gloves and jewellery-substitutes,
The lemons, mauves, and olive-ochres that   40

Marked off the girls unreally from the rest.
   Yes, from cafés
And banquet-halls up yards, and bunting-dressed

Coach-party annexes, the wedding-days
Were coming to an end. All down the line   45
Fresh couples climbed aboard: the rest stood round;
The last confetti and advice were thrown,
And, as we moved, each face seemed to define
Just what it saw departing: children frowned
At something dull; fathers had never known   50

Success so huge and wholly farcical;
      The women shared
The secret like a happy funeral;
While girls, gripping their handbags tighter, stared
At a religious wounding. Free at last,   55
And loaded with the sum of all they saw,
We hurried towards London, shuffling gouts of steam.
Now fields were building-plots, and poplars cast
Long shadows over major roads, and for
Some fifty minutes, that in time would seem   60

Just long enough to settle hats and say
      I nearly died,
A dozen marriages got under way.
They watched the landscape, sitting side by side
—An Odeon went past, a cooling tower,   65
And someone running up to bowl—and none
Thought of the others they would never meet
Or how their lives would all contain this hour.
I thought of London spread out in the sun,
Its postal districts packed like squares of wheat: 70

There we were aimed. And as we raced across
      Bright knots of rail
Past standing Pullmans, walls of blackened moss
Came close, and it was nearly done, this frail
Travelling coincidence; and what it held   75
Stood ready to be loosed with all the power
That being changed can give. We slowed again,
And as the tightened brakes took hold, there swelled
A sense of falling, like an arrow-shower
Sent out of sight, somewhere becoming rain.   80

LAWRENCE FERLINGHETTI (1919–   )

I Am Waiting°

I am waiting for my case to come up
and I am waiting
for a rebirth of wonder
and I am waiting for someone
to really discover America   5
and wail
and I am waiting
for the discovery
of a new symbolic western frontier
and I am waiting   10
for the American Eagle
to really spread its wings
and straighten up and fly right
and I am waiting
for the Age of Anxiety   15
to drop dead
amd I am waiting
for the war to be fought
which will make the world safe
for anarchy   20
and I am waiting
for the final withering away
of all governments
and I am perpetually awaiting
a rebirth of wonder   25

I am waiting for the Second Coming
and I am waiting
for a religious revival
to sweep thru the state of Arizona
and I am waiting   30
for the Grapes of Wrath to be stored
and I am waiting
for them to prove
that God is really American

In this poem, the speaker refers to many other literary works, for example, in line 26, Yeats's "The Second Coming" (page 1139), "The Battle Hymn of the Republic" and John Steinbeck's novel *The Grapes of Wrath* (line 31), Mark Twain's novel *Tom Sawyer* (line 87), Lewis Carroll's *Alice in Wonderland* (line 93), Robert Browning's poem "Childe Roland to the Dark Tower Came" (line 97), William Wordsworth's poem "Intimations of Immortality" (lines 105 and 106), and, in line 119, Keats's "Ode on a Grecian Urn" (page 1115).

and I am waiting   35
to see God on television
piped onto church altars
if only they can find
the right channel
to tune in on   40
and I am waiting
for the Last Supper to be served again
with a strange new appetizer
and I am perpetually awaiting
a rebirth of wonder   45

I am waiting for my number to be called
and I am waiting
for the Salvation Army to take over
and I am waiting
for the meek to be blessed   50
and inherit the earth
without taxes
and I am waiting
for forests and animals
to reclaim the earth as theirs   55
and I am waiting
for a way to be devised
to destroy all nationalisms
without killing anybody
and I am waiting   60
for linnets and planets to fall like rain
and I am waiting for lovers and weepers
to lie down together again
in a new rebirth of wonder

I am waiting for the Great Divide to be crossed   65
and I am anxiously waiting
for the secret of eternal life to be discovered
by an obscure general practitioner
and I am waiting
for the storms of life   70
to be over
and I am waiting
to set sail for happiness
and I am waiting
for a reconstructed Mayflower   75
to reach America

with its picture story and tv rights
sold in advance to the natives
and I am waiting
for the lost music to sound again   80
in the Lost Continent
in a new rebirth of wonder

I am waiting for the day
that maketh all things clear
and I am awaiting retribution   85
for what America did
to Tom Sawyer
and I am waiting
for the American Boy
to take off Beauty's clothes   90
and get on top of her
and I am waiting
for Alice in Wonderland
to retransmit to me
her total dream of innocence   95
and I am waiting
for Childe Roland to come
to the final darkest tower
and I am waiting
for Aphrodite   100
to grow live arms
at a final disarmament conference
in a new rebirth of wonder

I am waiting
to get some intimations   105
of immortality
by recollecting my early childhood
and I am waiting
for the green mornings to come again
youth's dumb green fields come back again   110
and I am waiting
for some strains of unpremeditated art
to shake my typewriter
and I am waiting to write
the great indelible poem   115
and I am waiting
for the last long careless rapture
and I am perpetually waiting

for the fleeing lovers on the Grecian Urn
to catch each other up at last   120
and embrace
and I am awaiting
perpetually and forever
a renaissance of wonder

JAMES DICKEY (1923–   )

The Heaven of Animals

Here they are. The soft eyes open.
If they have lived in a wood
It is a wood.
If they have lived on plains
It is grass rolling   5
Under their feet forever.

Having no souls, they have come,
Anyway, beyond their knowing.
Their instincts wholly bloom
And they rise.   10
The soft eyes open.

To match them, the landscape flowers,
Outdoing, desperately
Outdoing what is required:
The richest wood,   15
The deepest field.

For some of these,
It could not be the place
It is, without blood.
These hunt, as they have done,   20
But with claws and teeth grown perfect,

More deadly than they can believe.
They stalk more silently,
And crouch on the limbs of trees,
And their descent   25
Upon the bright backs of their prey

May take years
In a sovereign floating of joy.
And those that are hunted
Know this as their life,   30
Their reward: to walk

Under such trees in full knowledge
Of what is in glory above them,
And to feel no fear,
But acceptance, compliance.   35
Fulfilling themselves without pain

At the cycle's center,
They tremble, they walk
Under the tree,
They fall, they are torn,   40
They rise, they walk again.

MARI EVANS (1923–   )

I Am a Black Woman

I am a black woman
the music of my song
some sweet arpeggio of tears
is written in a minor key
and I   5
can be heard hun   ig in the night
Can be heard
                    humming
in the night

I saw my mate leap screaming to the sea   10
and I/with these hands/cupped the lifebreath
from my issue in the canebrake
I lost Nat's swinging body in a rain of tears
and heard my son scream all the way from Anzio
for Peace he never knew. . . . I   15
learned Da Nang and Pork Chop Hill
in anguish

Now my nostrils know the gas
and these trigger tire/d fingers
seek the softness in my warrior's beard   20

I
am a black woman
tall as a cypress
strong
beyond all definition still   25
defying place
and time
and circumstance
  assailed
    impervious   30
      indestructible
Look
  on me and be
renewed

DENISE LEVERTOV (1923–   )

In Mind

There's in my mind a woman
of innocence, unadorned but

fair-featured, and smelling of
apples or grass. She wears

a utopian smock or shift, her hair   5
is light brown and smooth, and she

is kind and very clean without
ostentation —
      but she has
no imagination.   10
      And there's a
turbulent moon-ridden girl
or old woman, or both,
dressed in opals and rags, feathers

and torn taffeta,   15
who knows strange songs —

but she is not kind.

ALLEN GINSBERG (1926–   )

A Supermarket in California

What thoughts I have of you tonight, Walt Whitman, for I walked down the sidestreets under the trees with a headache self-conscious looking at the full moon.

In my hungry fatigue, and shopping for images, I went into the neon fruit supermarket, dreaming of your enumerations!

What peaches and what penumbras! Whole families shopping at night! Aisles full of husbands! Wives in the avocados, babies in the tomatoes! — and you, Garcia Lorca, what were you doing down by the watermelons?

I saw you, Walt Whitman, childless, lonely old grubber, poking among the meats in the refrigerator and eyeing the grocery boys.

I heard you asking questions of each: Who killed the pork chops? What   5
price bananas? Are you my Angel?

I wandered in and out of the brilliant stacks of cans following you, and followed in my imagination by the store detective.

We strode down the open corridors together in our solitary fancy tasting artichokes, possessing every frozen delicacy, and never passing the cashier.

Where are we going, Walt Whitman? The doors close in an hour. Which way does your beard point tonight?

(I touch your book and dream of our odyssey in the supermarket and feel absurd.)

Will we walk all night through solitary streets? The trees add shade to   10
shade, lights out in the houses, we'll both be lonely.

Will we stroll dreaming of the lost America of love past blue automobiles in driveways, home to our silent cottage?

Ah, dear father, graybeard, lonely old courage-teacher, what America did you have when Charon° quit poling his ferry and you got out on a smoking bank and stood watching the boat disappear on the black waters of Lethe?°

12 *Charon:* Boatman who ferried souls across the river Styx, in the mythological Greek underworld; *Lethe:* Another river in the Greek underworld (Hades); drinking from its waters brings forgetfulness.

JAMES WRIGHT (1927–   )

A Blessing

Just off the highway to Rochester, Minnesota,
Twilight bounds softly forth on the grass.
And the eyes of those two Indian ponies

Darken with kindness.
They have come gladly out of the willows   5
To welcome my friend and me.
We step over the barbed wire into the pasture
Where they have been grazing all day, alone.
They ripple tensely, they can hardly contain their happiness
That we have come.   10
They bow shyly as wet swans. They love each other.
There is no loneliness like theirs.
At home once more,

They begin munching the young tufts of spring in the darkness.
I would like to hold the slenderer one in my arms,   15
For she has walked over to me
And nuzzled my left hand.
She is black and white,
Her mane falls wild on her forehead,
And the light breeze moves me to caress her long ear   20
That is delicate as the skin over a girl's wrist.
Suddenly I realize
That if I stepped out of my body I would break
Into blossom.

ADRIENNE RICH (1929–   )

Planetarium

(Thinking of Caroline Herschel, 1750–1848,
Astronomer, Sister of William; and Others)°

A woman in the shape of a monster
a monster in the shape of a woman
the skies are full of them

a woman   "in the snow
among the Clocks and instruments   5
or measuring the ground with poles"

in her 98 years to discover
8 comets
she whom the moon ruled
like us   10

Caroline Herschel was an astronomer who worked with her brother, William, also an astronomer. She is now believed to have made many discoveries formerly attributed to him.

levitating into the night sky
riding the polished lenses

Galaxies of women, there
doing penance for impetuousness
ribs chilled   15
in those spaces   of the mind

An eye,
        "virile, precise and absolutely certain"
        from the mad webs of Uranisborg°
                                    encountering the NOVA   20

every impulse of light exploding
from the core
as life flies out of us
        Tycho whispering at last
        "Let me not seem to have lived in vain"   25

What we see, we see
and seeing is changing

the light that shrivels a mountain
and leaves a man alive

Heartbeat of the pulsar   30
heart sweating through my body

The radio impulse
pouring in from Taurus

        I am bombarded yet   I stand

I have been standing all my life in the   35
direct path of a battery of signals
the most accurately transmitted most
untranslateable language in the universe
I am a galactic cloud so deep   so invo-
luted that a light wave could take 15   40
years to travel through me   And has
taken   I am an instrument in the shape
of a woman trying to translate pulsations
into images   for the relief of the body
and the reconstruction of the mind.   45

19 *Uranisborg:* Observatory built by Danish astronomer Tycho Brahe (1546–1601).

ROBERT BLY (1926–   )

Words Rising

I open my journal, write a few
sounds with green ink, and suddenly
fierceness enters me, stars
begin to revolve, and pick up
alligator dust from under the ocean.   5
The music comes, I feel the bushy
tail of the Great Bear
reach down and brush the seafloor.

All those lives we lived in the sunlit
shelves of the Dordogne, the thousand   10
tunes we sang to the skeletons
of Papua, the many times
we died — wounded — under the cloak
of an animal's sniffling, all of these
return, and the grassy nights   15
we ran for hours in the moonlight.

Watery syllables come welling up.
Anger that barked and howled in the cave,
the luminous head of barley
the priest holds up, growls   20
from under fur, none of that is lost.
The old earth fragrance remains
in the word "and." We experience
"the" in its lonely suffering.

We are bees then; our honey is language.   25
Now the honey lies stored in caves
beneath us, and the sound of words
carries what we do not.
When a man or woman feeds a few words
with private grief, the shames we knew   30
before we could invent the wheel,
then words grow. We slip out

into farmyards, where rabbits lie
stretched out on the ground for buyers.
Wicker baskets and hanged men   35
come to us as stanzas and vowels.
We see a crowd with dusty
palms turned up inside each
verb. There are eternal vows
held inside the word "Jericho."   40

Blessings then on the man who labors
in his tiny room, writing stanzas on the lamb;
blessings on the woman who picks the brown
seeds of solitude in afternoon light
out of the black seeds of loneliness.   45
And blessings on the dictionary maker, huddled among
his bearded words, and on the setter of songs
who sleeps at night inside his violin case.

GARY SNYDER (1930–   )

Riprap

Lay down these words
Before your mind like rocks.
          placed solid, by hands
In choice of place, set
Before the body of the mind   5
          in space and time:
Solidity of bark, leaf, or wall
          riprap of things:
Cobble of milky way,
          straying planets,   10
These poems, people,
          lost ponies with
Dragging saddles—
          and rocky sure-foot trails.
The worlds like an endless   15
          four-dimensional
Game of *Go*.
          ants and pebbles
In the thin loam, each rock a word
          a creek-washed stone   20
Granite: ingrained
          with torment of fire and weight
Crystal and sediment linked hot
          all change, in thoughts,
As well as things.   25

NATALIE SAFIR (1935–   )

And She Did

I confess to my love
for Little Red Hen —
the quick pluck of her strut
level-headed squawks
her hard-boiled litany   5
the crackle of her resolve

We're not talking about winging it
We are talking about bread
about making it

This was no chicken — no   10
hysterical adolescent
issuing red alerts about the sky
No dumb cluck at the mercy
of barnyard poachers

This was a hard-working chick   15
who did and she did, and she did!

MARGE PIERCY (1936–   )

Unlearning to Not Speak

Blizzards of paper
in slow motion
sift through her.
In nightmares she suddenly recalls
a class she signed up for   5
but forgot to attend.
Now it is too late.
Now it is time for finals:
losers will be shot.
Phrases of men who lectured her   10
drift and rustle in piles:
Why don't you speak up?
Why are you shouting?
You have the wrong answer,
wrong line, wrong face.   15
They tell her she is womb-man,

babymachine, mirror image, toy,
earth mother and penis-poor,
a dish of synthetic strawberry icecream
rapidly melting.   20
She grunts to a halt.
She must learn again to speak
starting with I
starting with We
starting as the infant does   25
with her own true hunger
and pleasure
and rage.

MARGARET ATWOOD (1939–   )

you fit into me

you fit into me
like a hook into an eye

a fish hook
an open eye

JANICE MIRIKITANI (1942–   )

For My Father

He came over the ocean
carrying Mt. Fuji
on his back/Tule Lake on his chest
hacked through the brush
of deserts   5
and made them grow
strawberries

    we stole berries
    from the stem
    we could not afford them   10
    for breakfast

his eyes held
nothing
as he whipped us
for stealing.   15

the desert had dried
his soul.

wordless
he sold
the rich,   20
full berries
to hakujines
whose children
pointed at our eyes

    they ate fresh   25
    strawberries
    with cream.

Father,
I wanted to scream
at your silence.   30
Your strength
was a stranger
I could never touch.
iron
in your eyes   35
to shield
the pain
to shield desert-like wind
from patches
of strawberries   40
grown
from
tears.

WENDY ROSE (1948–   )

Loo-wit°

The way they do
this old woman
no longer cares
what others think
but spits her black tobacco   5
any which way
stretching full length

Loo-wit: Native American name for the volcanic Mt. St. Helens; literally "lady of fire."

from her bumpy bed.
Finally up
she sprinkles ash on the snow,   10
cold and rocky buttes
that promise nothing
but winter is going at last.
Centuries of cedar
have bound her to earth,   15
huckleberry ropes
lay prickly about her neck.
Her children play games
(no sense of tomorrow);
her eyes are covered   20
with bark and she wakes
at night, fears
she is blind.
Nothing but tricks
left in this world,   25
nothing to keep
an old woman home.
Around her
machinery growls,
snarls and ploughs   30
great patches of her skin.
She crouches
in the north,
the source
of her trembling—   35
dawn appearing
with the shudder
of her slopes.
Blackberries unravel,
stones dislodge;   40
it's not as if
they weren't warned.

She was sleeping
but she heard the boot scrape,
the creaking floor;   45
felt the pull of the blanket
from her thin shoulder.
With one free hand
she finds her weapons
and raises them high;   50
clearing the twigs from her throat

she sings, she sings,
shaking the sky like a blanket about her
Loo-wit sings and sings and sings!

WOLE SOYINKA (1934–   )

Telephone Conversation

The price seemed reasonable, location
Indifferent. The landlady swore she lived
Off premises. Nothing remained
But self-confession. 'Madam,' I warned,
'I hate a wasted journey — I am African.'   5
Silence. Silenced transmission of
Pressurized good-breeding. Voice, when it came,
Lipstick coated, long gold-rolled
Cigarette-holder pipped. Caught I was, foully.
'HOW DARK?' . . . I had not misheard. . . . 'ARE YOU LIGHT   10
OR VERY DARK?' Button B. Button A. Stench
Of rancid breath of public hide-and-speak.
Red booth. Red pillar-box. Red double-tiered
Omnibus squelching tar. It *was* real! Shamed
By ill-mannered silence, surrender   15
Pushed dumbfoundment to beg simplification.
Considerate she was, varying the emphasis —
'ARE YOU DARK? OR VERY LIGHT?' Revelation came.
'You mean — like plain or milk chocolate?'
Her assent was clinical, crushing in its light   20
Impersonality. Rapidly, wave-length adjusted.
I chose. 'West African sepia' — and as afterthought,
'Down in my passport.' Silence for spectroscopic
Flight of fancy, till truthfulness clanged her accent
Hard on the mouthpiece. 'WHAT'S THAT?' conceding   25
'DON'T KNOW WHAT THAT IS.' 'Like brunette.'
'THAT'S DARK, ISN'T IT?' 'Not altogether.
Facially, I am brunette, but madam, you should see
The rest of me. Palm of my hand, soles of my feet
Are a peroxide blonde. Friction, caused —   30
Foolishly madam — by sitting down, has turned
My bottom raven black — One moment madam!' — sensing
Her receiver rearing on the thunderclap
About my ears — 'Madam,' I pleaded, 'wouldn't you rather
See for yourself?'   35

VICTOR HERNANDEZ CRUZ (1949–   )

urban dream

1

there was fire & the people were yelling.   running crazing.
screaming & falling.   moving up side down.   there was fire.
fires.   & more fires.   & walls caving to the ground.   & mercy
mercy.   death.   bodies falling down.   under bottles flying in the
air. garbage cans going up against windows.   a car singing   5
brightly a blue flame.   a snatch. a snag.   sounds of bombs.   &
other things blowing up.
times square
electrified.   burned.   smashed. stomped
hey over here   10
hey you.   where you going.
no walking.   no running.   no standing.
STOP
you crazy.   running.   stick
this stick up your eyes.   pull your heart out.   15
hey.

2

after noise.   comes silence.   after brightness (or great big flames)
comes darkness.   goes with whispering.   (even soft music can be heard)
even lips smacking.   foots stepping all over bones & ashes, all over
blood & broken lips that left their head somewhere else, all over   20
livers, & bright white skulls with hair on them.   standing over a river
watching hamburgers floating by.   steak with teeth in them.
flags.   & chairs.   & beds.   & golf sets.   & mickeymouse broken
        in
half.   25
governors & mayors step out the show.   they split.

3

dancing arrives.

RITA DOVE (1952–   )

Geometry

I prove a theorem and the house expands:
the windows jerk free to hover near the ceiling,
the ceiling floats away with a sigh.

As the walls clear themselves of everything
but transparency, the scent of carnations   5
leaves with them. I am out in the open

and above the windows have hinged into butterflies,
sunlight glinting where they've intersected.
They are going to some point true and unproven.

CATHY SONG (1955–   )

The Youngest Daughter

The sky has been dark
for many years.
My skin has become as damp
and pale as rice paper
and feels the way   5
mother's used to before the drying sun
parched it out there in the fields.

    Lately, when I touch my eyelids,
my hands react as if
I had just touched something   10
hot enough to burn.
My skin, aspirin colored,
tingles with migraine. Mother
has been massaging the left side of my face
especially in the evenings   15
when the pain flares up.

This morning
her breathing was graveled,
her voice gruff with affection
when I wheeled her into the bath.   20
She was in a good humor,
making jokes about her great breasts,
floating in the milky water
like two walruses,
flaccid and whiskered around the nipples.   25
I scrubbed them with a sour taste
in my mouth, thinking:
six children and an old man
have sucked from these brown nipples.

I was almost tender   30
when I came to the blue bruises
that freckle her body,

places where she has been injecting insulin
for thirty years. I soaped her slowly,
she sighed deeply, her eyes closed.   35
It seems it has always
been like this: the two of us
in this sunless room,
the splashing of the bathwater.

In the afternoons   40
when she has rested,
she prepares our ritual of tea and rice,
garnished with a shred of gingered fish,
a slice of pickled turnip,
a token for my white body.   45
We eat in the familiar silence.
She knows I am not to be trusted,
even now planning my escape.
As I toast to her health
with the tea she has poured,   50
a thousand cranes curtain the window,
fly up in a sudden breeze.

An Introduction to Drama

Since the days of ancient Greece, people have created, watched, and participated in drama. Drama makes events and emotions — whether realistic or fantastic — come to life before the eyes of the audience. More than any other literary form, drama is a visual experience. Whether we read it or see it on stage, a play leaves pictures in our minds. These pictures, along with the echoes of the characters' (and, of course, the playwright's) words, create the emotions and ideas that together make up that play's themes.

SUGGESTIONS FOR READING DRAMA

Reading drama, of course, is not exactly the same as seeing a play performed. Some qualities are lost — yet others are gained — when you read the playwright's descriptions and dialogue without the intervening interpretation of directors and actors.

Dialogue

For some people, reading plays is difficult because they find the structure of the dialogue (the characters' conversations with others, with themselves, or with the audience) hard to follow. Although it may seem artificial to have the character's name at the beginning of each speech, it is obviously essential to know who is talking.

With a little practice, you can adjust to this distraction by training yourself to "read through" the characters' names. Try simply to note the name, rather than actually reading it as part of the speech. Consider the name almost as you would a mark of punctuation. It's there to guide you, but you don't consciously think about it any more than you consciously note a period, apostrophe, or comma when you come across those guides to meaning.

If you find this strategy unworkable, try providing your own transitional words to link the name to the speech. For instance, consider these speeches from *Antigone:*

> ISMENE: Why do you speak so strangely?
> ANTIGONE: Listen, Ismene:
> Kreon buried our brother Eteocles
> With military honors.

To get rid of the artificial introductory names, read the speeches this way:

> Ismene *says,* "Why do you speak so strangely?"
> Antigone *answers,* "Listen, Ismene . . ."

Using this strategy, you create a bridge from the name of the character to the words the character says.

Stage Directions

Playwrights provide stage directions that explain details of setting and give information about the way characters speak and move. For some readers, stage directions divert attention from the dialogue, causing them to lose their train of thought. Yet it is necessary to be aware of stage directions to understand fully how the playwright envisioned both setting and action.

Some people read a play at least twice, once paying close attention to the stage directions and once simply noting the stage directions as brief guides but not stopping to read them in detail. They try to hold the information in their minds from the first reading, and, during the second reading, they use the stage directions to start "creating" or "directing" their own version of the play.

Some students read the play in short sections — by scenes or parts of scenes. They read the stage directions for a scene first (without paying much attention to the dialogue). Then they return to read the dialogue, this time integrating what they learned about setting and action from their reading of the stage directions.

List of Characters

At the beginning of most plays, the playwright gives a list of characters and often a brief description of each. Read this list before you start reading the play; you'll get a head start on understanding the relationships and dynamics between characters. Reading the list of characters also alerts you to watch for the entrance of each individual and helps you become aware of the role — however important or minor — each plays in the drama.

TRADITIONAL FORMS OF DRAMA

Traditional forms of drama are still performed and enjoyed. In addition, modern playwrights often adapt, incorporate, or rebel against elements of traditional drama as they write today's plays.

Greek Drama

Formal competitions among Greek playwrights began in approximately 530 B.C. These competitions continued to be held for several centuries, always in connection with religious celebrations dedicated to Dionysus, the god of wine who symbolized life-giving power. Greek plays were performed in large, outdoor, semicircular amphitheaters that held as many as 15,000 people.

These audiences, of course, understood the conventions of Greek theater. For example, the **chorus** (usually representing the voice of the community) danced and sang in the **orchestra** (a round area at the foot of the amphitheater). On an elevated stage behind the orchestra, the actors — wearing masks that symbolized their primary characteristics and, in addition, amplified their voices — performed their roles. Although Greek theaters did not have elaborate sets, they did have one rather spectacular stage device, the **deus ex machina** (god from the machine). By means of elaborate mechanisms, actors were lowered from above to the stage to play the role of gods meting out punishments or rewards to the human characters.

Scenes end with the dances and songs of the chorus (the **ode**), which sometimes comment on the action of the scene or provide background information clarifying the action of the scene. As the chorus sang one part of their observation (the **strophe**), they moved from right to left on the stage; as they sang another part (the **antistrophe**), they moved to the right.

Greek plays are short in comparison to five-act Shakespearean plays or modern three-act plays. Because the audience was familiar with the myths and legends on which most of the plays are based, the playwrights did not have to spend time explaining many of the background circumstances. Most Greek plays can be acted in about an hour and a half.

For an example of a Greek tragedy, read Sophocles' *Antigone* (page 1195); for a comedy, read Aristophanes' *Lysistrata* (page 609).

Elizabethan Drama

William Shakespeare's plays exemplify the drama written during the reign of Queen Elizabeth I of England (1558–1603). Shakespeare wrote tragedy, comedy, and history; he captures the large, spectacular actions of kings, queens, and other highborn characters (and the people who serve them) as well as the romances and intrigues that are part of their lives.

Elizabethans followed Greek tradition by barring women from the stage. Adolescent boys played the parts of young heroines such as Juliet, and male character actors eagerly sought the parts of older women.

Although currently there is much speculation about the design of Elizabethan theaters, most scholars agree that early Elizabethan plays were performed in makeshift locations such as inn yards or open spaces between buildings such as the Inns at Court, which was a London Law College. When theaters were built, they were usually octagonal on the outside. Inside, they were circular. The audience sat on both sides as well as in front of the raised stage. As in the Greek theater, there was little scenery or stage setting, except for the booms and machinery used to lower actors who came as messengers or agents of supernatural forces. Unlike Greek theaters, however, Elizabethan theaters had a second-level balcony, doors at the back for entrances and exits, a curtained alcove, and a trap door in the stage floor for surprise entrances of ghosts and spirits. Although the huge Greek amphitheaters could accommodate many thousands of theater-goers, most Elizabethan theaters could house no more than about 1000 to 2000, including 500 to 800 **groundlings** (common folk who could not afford seats and thus stood at the foot of the stage). The composition of the Elizabethan audiences — ranging from the illiterate groundlings to the highly educated nobility — presented a challenge to the playwright. Successful plays usually melded action, humor, and violence with philosophical insights and evocative poetry. For an example of such a play, read *Othello* (page 1226).

MODERN FORMS OF DRAMA

Following the flourishing drama during the Elizabethan period, playwrights — particularly in England and in France — focused on comedy. These eighteenth- and nineteenth-century playwrights frequently satirized the failings and foibles of society in witty dramas depicting romantic intrigues and entanglements. For an example of such a play, see Molière's *The Doctor in Spite of Himself,* page 1315. During this same time in the United States, playwrights developed the tradition of **melodrama,** plays with stereotyped villains and heroes representing extremes of good and evil.

Realistic Drama

Reacting against both stylized comedy and exaggerated melodrama, some late nineteenth- and early twentieth-century dramatists began to develop a new form: the **realistic drama.** These dramatists worked to present everyday life — crises, conflicts, and emotional responses to which ordinary people could relate.

Dramatists writing in the realistic tradition depict problems with work, with family relationships, with community politics. Ghosts do not pop up from the floor of the realistic stage to introduce problems into the characters' lives, nor do gods descend from above to solve those problems. Instead, the difficulties the characters face seem to follow logically from events and decisions with which most members of the audience can identify. Most can also relate to — if not agree with — the responses characters have to the conflicts in their lives.

Settings and props in the realistic theater are more important than in earlier forms of drama, because the dramatist seeks to create the illusion of real life. Often the stage is like a room with the fourth wall removed. The audience is invited to watch ordinary people and listen to them conversing in ordinary language rather than in polished poetry, stylized witty exchanges, or highly dramatic pronouncements.

Examples of realistic drama in this anthology include Ibsen's *An Enemy of the People* (page 1341), Glaspell's *Trifles* (page 319), and Hansberry's *A Raisin in the Sun* (page 1414).

Theater of the Absurd

In the second half of the twentieth century, a number of playwrights rejected the conventions of realistic drama. Instead of a sequence of logically connected events, absurdist drama offers actions that lead in no predictable direction. The motivations of characters are contradictory or absent altogether. Conversations and speeches ramble disjointedly, leaping first one way and then another for no apparent reason.

Rather than suggesting coherent themes, absurdist dramas invite the audience to ask questions about the world in which we live Martin Esslin, who first called these dramas "theater of the absurd," offers the following insights:

> The Theater of the Absurd shows the world as an incomprehensible place. The spectators see the happenings on the stage entirely from the outside, without ever understanding the full meaning of these strange patterns of events, as newly arrived visitors might watch life in a country of which they have not yet mastered the language.
> (*The Theater of the Absurd,* New York: Doubleday, 1969)

In this anthology, Ionesco's *The Lesson* (page 722) provides a fine example of absurdist drama.

TYPES OF DRAMA

Whether ancient or modern, plays represent a wide range of emotions and views of the world. Although most plays contain both serious and comic elements, they usually fit into one of two major dramatic categories: **tragedy,** which focuses on life's sorrows and serious problems, and **comedy,** which focuses on life's joys and humorous absurdities.

Tragedy

Traditionally, the tragic play looks at the life of a royal figure or highly respected official. During the course of the drama, this character's fortunes change drastically from good to bad. Having enjoyed high status in society, the **tragic hero** meets his or her downfall for one (or a combination) of these three reasons: fate or coincidence beyond the control of the character, a flaw in character, or a mistake in judgment.

Because the traditional tragic hero is a noble character, his or her fall has been regarded as particularly moving to the audience. After all, if someone as brave, stalwart, wise (and so on) as the tragic hero can fall prey to random accidents, character flaws, or poor judgment, how much more vulnerable must we ordinary mortals be. In the *Poetics,* Aristotle suggested that watching the tragic hero's downfall (the **catastrophe,** which generally involves the death not only of the hero but also of other, often innocent, individuals) inspires in us the emotions of pity and terror. By watching the tragic hero move steadily toward disaster, and by seeing the drama's **resolution** (the conclusion, in which order is generally restored to the society at large), we viewers may experience **catharsis** (profound relief from the tension of the play and a sense that we have gained insight and enlightenment, rather than simply entertainment, from the drama). For classic examples of traditional tragic heroes, consider the title characters in Sophocles' *Antigone* or Shakespeare's *Othello.*

Modern plays that are sometimes termed tragedies do not always follow the conventions of traditional tragedy strictly. For instance, the main character may not be highborn but may instead be a rather ordinary person like Dr. Stockmann in Ibsen's *An Enemy of the People.* Also, like *An Enemy of the People,* a modern tragedy may not end with the main character's physical death but rather with the death of a way of life. Some scholars argue that these modern plays are not true tragedies and that their main characters are not true tragic heroes. Such plays as *An Enemy of the People* (page 1341) or Miller's *All My Sons* (page 478) provide ample opportunity to consider the nature of modern tragic drama and modern tragic characters.

Comedy

Unlike traditional tragic drama, which focuses on the lives of noble, highborn characters, comic drama shows us the lives of ordinary people. Like the characters in tragedies, these people encounter conflicts, challenges, and difficulties. Yet their problems are seldom deeply serious — or if they are serious, they are treated in a lighthearted way. Consider, for instance, the Greek comedy *Lysistrata* whose title character urges the women of her community to deny their men sexual relations until the men agree to give up war. Certainly war is a serious issue, yet here the treatment is clearly comic.

The humor in comic plots has many sources. **Satiric comedy** exposes the foibles and shortcomings of humanity, inviting us not only to laugh at the often-exaggerated stage examples but also to pay attention to our own idiosyncrasies and follies. Satiric comedy may be light and witty, but often its humor is rather dark and biting. Consider, for instance, Molière's *The Doctor in Spite of Himself.* We laugh at the characters, yet we cannot help but see the selfishness and egotism in their plights. The source of satiric humor is often both verbal and visual. Writers of satiric comedy use sharp words and cutting phrases as well as pratfalls and fisticuffs to inspire laughter in their audience.

In **romantic comedy,** by contrast, the source of humor is frequently mistaken identity and unexpected discoveries as well as romping stage chases, mock fistfights, and other physical actions. Unlike satiric comedy, romantic comedy does not aim at chastising and improving human behavior but rather at inviting the gentle laughter of self-recognition. Romantic comedy seeks to delight the audience rather than to teach a lesson. Shakespeare's comedies, such as *As You Like It,* typify romantic comedy.

Whether the comic drama is satiric or romantic, it differs in major ways from tragedy. Whereas tragedy moves toward the main characters' downfall, comedy moves toward the improvement of the main characters' fortunes. Tragedy usually ends with death and then with restoration of order; comedy concludes with reconciliation, often through the marriage of the main characters as well as the marriage of minor or supporting characters.

Tragicomedy

More common among modern dramas than the comedy is the **tragicomedy:** a play that mixes elements of comedy and tragedy. For instance, Glaspell's *Trifles* (page 319) focuses on a tragedy, a woman's murder of her husband. Yet the bumbling sheriff and his male cohorts become darkly comic figures as they make fun of the two women who manage to solve the crime that stumps all the men. Other plays in this anthology that combine comedy and tragedy include Hansberry's *A Raisin in the Sun* (page 1414) and Ibsen's *An Enemy of the People* (page 1341).

Tragicomedy takes many forms. Sometimes, as with *Trifles,* the play is primarily tragic yet is relieved by moments of humor. Sometimes humor dominates the play, yet serious themes lie behind the comic words and actions. Consider, for example, Fierstein's *On Tidy Endings* (page 857) with its witty exchanges between the characters yet with underlying themes relating to loss and death.

Guidelines: Drama

1. Find one scene (or part of one scene) that you find particularly strange, intriguing, puzzling, powerful, or moving. Briefly summarize the scene and explain your response. As you explain, indicate the relationship between the scene you are discussing and the rest of the play.
2. Compare the primary qualities of two characters in the play. Explain why you find their similarities and differences significant.
3. Describe your initial response to one of the play's main characters (after reading the first act or scene); then explain your response after you finished reading (and rereading) the entire play. Evaluate the events, actions, and speeches in the play that either confirmed your first response or caused you to change it.

4. List all the conflicts you see in the play, whether they are experienced by major or minor characters. Then consider how these conflicts might be related. How are they similar? How are they different? How does the characters' resolution of conflicts contribute to the play's resolution?

5. Rewrite a significant scene (or part of a scene) from the play in short story form. Provide detailed descriptions of the characters' inner feelings and thoughts as well as the setting in which the action takes place.

6. Watch a live or filmed performance of one of the plays (or a film based on the play). Compare your responses to the play as you read it to your responses as you viewed the stage or film version. Notice particularly aspects the stage or film directors have chosen to change. For example, are any characters eliminated? Added? Are scenes omitted? Added? Evaluate the effect of these decisions.

7. Explicate the opening dialogue of any of the plays. Consider each line — and the language within each line — very carefully. What tone does this dialogue establish? What expectations do these lines raise concerning the play's conflicts and themes?

8. Consider the conflicts and choices of any character. Explain your response to the way the character deals with conflict. Draw on your own experiences and observations as you evaluate this character's decisions and actions (or failure to make decisions or to act).

9. Write either an alternative ending for one of the plays or an additional scene to take place at a specified time after the current final scene. Explain the reasons for your changes or for your speculations concerning the futures of the characters. Refer to specific details in the play as you make this explanation.

10. Read either biographical background on the playwright, reviews of performances of the play, or critical essays analyzing and evaluating the play. Choose one or two new insights about the play that you have gained from your reading and explain those insights. How has your research changed, challenged, affirmed, or enriched your initial reading of the play?

SOPHOCLES (c. 496–c. 406 B.C.)

Antigone

Characters

ANTIGONE ⎫ *daughters of Oedipus*
ISMENE ⎭
EURYDICE, *wife of Kreon*
KREON, *King of Thebes*
HAIMON, *son of Kreon*
TEIRESIAS, *a blind seer*
A SENTRY
A MESSENGER
CHORUS

Scene *Before the palace of* KREON, *King of Thebes. A central double door, and two lateral doors. A platform extends the length of the facade, and from this platform three steps lead down into the orchestra, or chorus-ground.*

Time *Dawn of the day after the repulse of the Argive army from the assault on Thebes.*

Prologue° *(*ANTIGONE *and* ISMENE *enter from the central door of the palace.)*

ANTIGONE: Ismene, dear sister,
    You would think that we had already suffered enough
    For the curse on Oedipus.°
    I cannot imagine any grief
    That you and I have not gone through. And now —   5
    Have they told you of the new decree of our King Kreon?
ISMENE: I have heard nothing: I know
    That two sisters lost two brothers, a double death
    In a single hour; and I know that the Argive army
    Fled in the night; but beyond this, nothing.   10
ANTIGONE: I thought so. And that is why I wanted you
    To come out here with me. There is something we must do.
ISMENE: Why do you speak so strangely?

Prologue: Section of the play that explains the background and current action. 3 *curse on Oedipus:* Ismene's and Antigone's father, Oedipus, was formerly King of Thebes. As an infant, Oedipus was ordered to be killed when an Oracle predicted that he would one day kill his father and marry his mother. Rescued and raised by a shepherd and his wife, Oedipus later returns to Thebes, where, unaware, he fulfills the prophecy by killing King Laios (his father) and marrying Jocasta (his mother). When Oedipus and Jocasta discover the truth, Jocasta kills herself and Oedipus blinds himself and leaves Thebes. His sons, Eteocles and Polyneices, later kill each other in battle. Kreon, Oedipus' uncle and now King of Thebes, orders Eteocles to be buried but commands that Polyneices, who has attacked Thebes, remain unburied.

ANTIGONE: Listen, Ismene:

    Kreon buried our brother Eteocles   15

    With military honors, gave him a soldier's funeral,

    And it was right that he should; but Polyneices,

    Who fought as bravely and died as miserably, —

    They say that Kreon has sworn

    No one shall bury him, no one mourn for him,   20

    But his body must lie in the fields, a sweet treasure

    For carrion birds to find as they search for food.

    That is what they say, and our good Kreon is coming here

    To announce it publicly; and the penalty —

    Stoning to death in the public square!

                            There it is,   25

    And now you can prove what you are:

    A true sister, or a traitor to your family.

ISMENE: Antigone, you are mad! What could I possibly do?

ANTIGONE: You must decide whether you will help me or not.

ISMENE: I do not understand you. Help you in what?   30

ANTIGONE: Ismene, I am going to bury him. Will you come?

ISMENE: Bury him! You have just said the new law forbids it.

ANTIGONE: He is my brother. And he is your brother, too.

ISMENE: But think of the danger! Think what Kreon will do!

ANTIGONE: Kreon is not strong enough to stand in my way.   35

ISMENE: Ah sister!

    Oedipus died, everyone hating him

    For what his own search brought to light, his eyes

    Ripped out by his own hand; and Iocaste died,

    His mother and wife at once: she twisted the cords   40

    That strangled her life; and our two brothers died,

    Each killed by the other's sword. And we are left:

    But oh, Antigone,

    Think how much more terrible than these

    Our own death would be if we should go against Kreon   45

    And do what he has forbidden! We are only women,

    We cannot fight with men, Antigone!

    The law is strong, we must give in to the law

    In this thing, and in worse. I beg the Dead

    To forgive me, but I am helpless: I must yield   50

    To those in authority. And I think it is dangerous business

    To be always meddling.

ANTIGONE: If that is what you think,

    I should not want you, even if you asked to come.

    You have made your choice, you can be what you want to be.

    But I will bury him; and if I must die,   55

    I say that this crime is holy: I shall lie down

With him in death, and I shall be as dear
To him as he is to me.
                              It is the dead,
Not the living, who make the longest demands:
We die for ever . . .
                              You may do as you like,   60
Since apparently the laws of the gods mean nothing to you.
ISMENE: They mean a great deal to me; but I have no strength
To break laws that were made for the public good.
ANTIGONE: That must be your excuse, I suppose. But as for me,
I will bury the brother I love.
ISMENE: Antigone,   65
I am so afraid for you!
ANTIGONE: You need not be:
You have yourself to consider, after all.
ISMENE: But no one must hear of this, you must tell no one!
I will keep it a secret, I promise!
ANTIGONE: O tell it! Tell everyone!
Think how they'll hate you when it all comes out   70
If they learn that you knew about it all the time!
ISMENE: So fiery! You should be cold with fear.
ANTIGONE: Perhaps. But I am doing only what I must.
ISMENE: But can you do it? I say that you cannot.
ANTIGONE: Very well: when my strength gives out,   75
I shall do no more.
ISMENE: Impossible things should not be tried at all.
ANTIGONE: Go away, Ismene:
I shall be hating you soon, and the dead will too,
For your words are hateful. Leave me my foolish plan: 80
I am not afraid of the danger; if it means death,
It will not be the worst of deaths—death without honor.
ISMENE: Go then, if you feel that you must.
You are unwise,
But a loyal friend indeed to those who love you.

(Exit into the palace. ANTIGONE *goes off, left. Enter the* CHORUS.*)*

PARODOS° • Strophe° 1

CHORUS: Now the long blade of the sun, lying
Level east to west, touches with glory
Thebes of the Seven Gates. Open, unlidded
Eye of golden day! O marching light
Across the eddy and rush of Dirce's stream,°   5

Parodos: Chant sung by Chorus as they enter; *Strophe:* Chant sung by Chorus as they move
from stage right to stage left.   5 *Dirce's stream:* River near Thebes.

Striking the white shields of the enemy
Thrown headlong backward from the blaze of morning!
CHORAGOS:° Polyneices their commander
    Roused them with windy phrases,
    He the wild eagle screaming   10
    Insults above our land,
    His wings their shields of snow,
    His crest their marshalled helms.

Antistrophe° 1

CHORUS: Against our seven gates in a yawning ring
    The famished spears came onward in the night;   15
    But before his jaws were sated with our blood,
    Or pinefire took the garland of our towers,
    He was thrown back, and as he turned, great Thebes —
    No tender victim for his noisy power —
    Rose like a dragon behind him, shouting war.   20
CHORAGOS: For God hates utterly
    The bray of bragging tongues;
    And when he beheld their smiling,
    Their swagger of golden helms,
    The frown of his thunder blasted   25
    Their first man from our walls.

Strophe 2

CHORUS: We heard his shout of triumph high in the air
    Turn to a scream; far out in a flaming arc
    He fell with his windy torch, and the earth struck him.
    And others storming in fury no less than his   30
    Found shock of death in the dusty joy of battle.
CHORAGOS: Seven captains at seven gates
    Yielded their clanging arms to the god
    That bends the battle-line and breaks it.
    These two only, brothers in blood,   35
    Face to face in matchless rage,
    Mirroring each the other's death,
    Clashed in long combat.

Antistrophe 2

CHORUS: But now in the beautiful morning of victory
    Let Thebes of the many chariots sing for joy!   40

---

8 *Choragos:* Leader of chorus.   *Antistrophe:* Chant sung by Chorus as they move from stage
left to stage right.

With hearts for dancing we'll take leave of war:
Our temples shall be sweet with hymns of praise,
And the long nights shall echo with our chorus.

SCENE 1

CHORAGOS: But now at last our new King is coming:
    Kreon of Thebes, Menoikeus' son.
    In this auspicious dawn of his reign
    What are the new complexities
    That shifting Fate has woven for him?   5
    What is his counsel? Why has he summoned
    The old men to hear him?

(Enter KREON *from the palace, center. He addresses the* CHORUS *from the top step.)*

KREON: Gentlemen: I have the honor to inform you that our Ship of State, which recent storms have threatened to destroy, has come safely to harbor at last, guided by the merciful wisdom of Heaven. I have sum- 10 moned you here this morning because I know that I can depend upon you: your devotion to King Laios was absolute; you never hesitated in your duty to our late ruler Oedipus; and when Oedipus died, your loyalty was transferred to his children. Unfortunately, as you know, his two sons, the princes Eteocles and Polyneices, have killed each 15 other in battle; and I, as the next in blood, have succeeded to the full power of the throne.

    I am aware, of course, that no Ruler can expect complete loyalty from his subjects until he has been tested in office. Nevertheless, I say to you at the very outset that I have nothing but contempt for the kind 20 of Governor who is afraid, for whatever reason, to follow the course that he knows is best for the State; and as for the man who sets private friendship above the public welfare, —I have no use for him, either. I call God to witness that if I saw my country headed for ruin, I should not be afraid to speak out plainly; and I need hardly remind you that I 25 would never have any dealings with an enemy of the people. No one values friendship more highly than I; but we must remember that friends made at the risk of wrecking our Ship are not real friends at all.

    These are my principles, at any rate, and that is why I have made the following decision concerning the sons of Oedipus: Eteocles, who 30 died as a man should die, fighting for his country, is to be buried with full military honors, with all the ceremony that is usual when the greatest heroes die; but his brother Polyneices, who broke his exile to come back with fire and sword against his native city and the shrines of his fathers' gods, whose one idea was to spill the blood of his blood 35 and sell his own people into slavery —Polyneices, I say, is to have no burial: no man is to touch him or say the least prayer for him; he shall

lie on the plain, unburied; and the birds and the scavenging dogs can
do with him whatever they like.

> This is my command, and you can see the wisdom behind it. As   40
long as I am King, no traitor is going to be honored with the loyal
man. But whoever shows by word and deed that he is on the side of
the State, —he shall have my respect while he is living and my reverence when he is dead.

CHORAGOS: If that is your will, Kreon son of Menoikeus,   45
> You have the right to enforce it: we are yours.

KREON: That is my will. Take care that you do your part.

CHORAGOS: We are old men: let the younger ones carry it out.

KREON: I do not mean that: the sentries have been appointed.

CHORAGOS: Then what is it that you would have us do?   50

KREON: You will give no support to whoever breaks this law.

CHORAGOS: Only a crazy man is in love with death!

KREON: And death it is; yet money talks, and the wisest
> Have sometimes been known to count a few coins too many.

(Enter SENTRY *from left.)*

SENTRY: I'll not say that I'm out of breath from running, King, because   55
> every time I stopped to think about what I have to tell you, I felt like
> going back. And all the time a voice kept saying, "You fool, don't you
> know you're walking straight into trouble?"; and then another voice:
> "Yes, but if you let somebody else get the news to Kreon first, it will
> be even worse than that for you!" But good sense won out, at least I   60
> hope it was good sense, and here I am with a story that makes no sense
> at all; but I'll tell it anyhow, because, as they say, what's going to
> happen's going to happen and—

KREON: Come to the point. What have you to say?

SENTRY: I did not do it. I did not see who did it. You must not punish me   65
> for what someone else has done.

KREON: A comprehensive defense! More effective, perhaps,
> If I knew its purpose. Come: what is it?

SENTRY: A dreadful thing . . . I don't know how to put it—

KREON: Out with it!

SENTRY: Well, then;   70
> The dead man—
>   Polyneices—

(Pause. The SENTRY *is overcome, fumbles for words.* KREON *waits
impassively.)*

>   out there—
>   someone, —
> New dust on the slimy flesh!

(Pause. No sign from KREON.*)*

Someone has given it burial that way, and
Gone . . .

(Long pause. KREON *finally speaks with deadly control.)*

KREON: And the man who dared do this?
SENTRY: I swear I   75
Do not know! You must believe me!
                                            Listen:
The ground was dry, not a sign of digging, no,
Not a wheeltrack in the dust, no trace of anyone.
It was when they relieved us this morning: and one of them,
The corporal, pointed to it.
                                    There it was,   80
The strangest —
                    Look:
The body, just mounded over with light dust: you see?
Not buried really, but as if they'd covered it
Just enough for the ghost's peace. And no sign
Of dogs or any wild animal that had been there.   85

And then what a scene there was! Every man of us
Accusing the other: we all proved the other man did it.
We all had proof that we could not have done it.
We were ready to take hot iron in our hands,
Walk through fire, swear by all the gods,   90
It was not I!
I do not know who it was, but it was not I!

*(*KREON*'s rage has been mounting steadily, but the* SENTRY *is too intent
upon his story to notice it.)*

And then, when this came to nothing, someone said
A thing that silenced us and made us stare
Down at the ground: you had to be told the news,   95
And one of us had to do it! We threw the dice,
And the bad luck fell to me. So here I am,
No happier to be here than you are to have me:
Nobody likes the man who brings bad news.
CHORAGOS: I have been wondering, King: can it be that the gods have
      done this?   100
KREON *(furiously)*: Stop!
      Must you doddering wrecks
      Go out of your heads entirely? "The gods"!

Intolerable!

The gods favor this corpse? Why? How had he served them?   105

Tried to loot their temples, burn their images,

Yes, and the whole State, and its laws with it!

Is it your senile opinion that the gods love to honor bad men?

A pious thought! —

                        No, from the very beginning

There have been those who have whispered together,   110

Stiff-necked anarchists, putting their heads together,

Scheming against me in alleys. These are the men,

And they have bribed my own guard to do this thing.

(Sententiously.) Money!

There's nothing in the world so demoralizing as money.   115

Down go your cities,

Homes gone, men gone, honest hearts corrupted,

Crookedness of all kinds, and all for money!

(To SENTRY.*)*   But you—

I swear by God and by the throne of God,

The man who has done this thing shall pay for it!   120

Find that man, bring him here to me, or your death

Will be the least of your problems: I'll string you up

Alive, and there will be certain ways to make you

Discover your employer before you die;

And the process may teach you a lesson you seem to have missed: 125

The dearest profit is sometimes all too dear:

That depends on the source. Do you understand me?

A fortune won is often misfortune.

SENTRY: King, may I speak?

KREON: Your very voice distresses me.

SENTRY: Are you sure that it is my voice, and not your conscience?   130

KREON: By God, he wants to analyze me now!

SENTRY: It is not what I say, but what has been done, that hurts you.

KREON: You talk too much.

SENTRY: Maybe; but I've done nothing.

KREON: Sold your soul for some silver: that's all you've done.

SENTRY: How dreadful it is when the right judge judges wrong!   135

KREON: Your figures of speech

    May entertain you now; but unless you bring me the man,

    You will get little profit from them in the end.

                      (Exit KREON *into the palace.)*

SENTRY: "Bring me the man"—!

    I'd like nothing better than bringing him the man!   140

    But bring him or not, you have seen the last of me here.

    At any rate, I am safe!   *(Exit* SENTRY.*)*

ODE° 1 • Strophe 1

CHORUS: Numberless are the world's wonders, but none
    More wonderful than man; the stormgray sea
    Yields to his prows, the huge crests bear him high;
    Earth, holy and inexhaustible, is graven
    With shining furrows where his plows have gone   5
    Year after year, the timeless labor of stallions.

Antistrophe 1

    The lightboned birds and beasts that cling to cover,
    The lithe fish lighting their reaches of dim water,
    All are taken, tamed in the net of his mind;
    The lion on the hill, the wild horse windy-maned,   10
    Resign to him; and his blunt yoke has broken
    The sultry shoulders of the mountain bull.

Strophe 2

    Words also, and thought as rapid as air,
    He fashions to his good use; statecraft is his,
    And his the skill that deflects the arrows of snow,   15
    The spears of winter rain: from every wind
    He has made himself secure—from all but one:
    In the late wind of death he cannot stand.

Antistrophe 2

    O clear intelligence, force beyond all measure!
    O fate of man, working both good and evil!   20
    When the laws are kept, how proudly his city stands!
    When the laws are broken, what of his city then?
    Never may the anarchic man find rest at my hearth,
    Never be it said that my thoughts are his thoughts.

SCENE 2

    (Reenter SENTRY *leading* ANTIGONE.*)*

CHORAGOS: What does this mean? Surely this captive woman
    Is the Princess, Antigone. Why should she be taken?
SENTRY: Here is the one who did it! We caught her
    In the very act of burying him. — Where is Kreon?
CHORAGOS: Just coming from the house.

    (Enter KREON, *center.)*

Ode: Chant sung by the Chorus.

KREON: What has happened?   5
   Why have you come back so soon?
SENTRY *(expansively)*:   O King,
   A man should never be too sure of anything:
   I would have sworn
   That you'd not see me here again: your anger
   Frightened me so, and the things you threatened me with;   10
   But how could I tell then
   That I'd be able to solve the case so soon?
   No dice-throwing this time: I was only too glad to come!
   Here is this woman. She is the guilty one:
   We found her trying to bury him.   15
   Take her, then; question her; judge her as you will.
   I am through with the whole thing now, and glad of it.
KREON: But this is Antigone! Why have you brought her here?
SENTRY: She was burying him, I tell you!
KREON *(severely)*:   Is this the truth?
SENTRY: I saw her with my own eyes. Can I say more?   20
KREON: The details: come, tell me quickly!
SENTRY: It was like this:
   After those terrible threats of yours, King,
   We went back and brushed the dust away from the body.
   The flesh was soft by now, and stinking,
   So we sat on a hill to windward and kept guard.   25
   No napping this time! We kept each other awake.
   But nothing happened until the white round sun
   Whirled in the center of the round sky over us:
   Then, suddenly,
   A storm of dust roared up from the earth, and the sky   30
   Went out, the plain vanished with all its trees
   In the stinging dark. We closed our eyes and endured it.
   The whirlwind lasted a long time, but it passed;
   And then we looked, and there was Antigone!
   I have seen   35
   A mother bird come back to a stripped nest, heard
   Her crying bitterly a broken note or two
   For the young ones stolen. Just so, when this girl
   Found the bare corpse, and all her love's work wasted,
   She wept, and cried on heaven to damn the hands   40
   That had done this thing.
               And then she brought more dust
   And sprinkled wine three times for her brother's ghost.

   We ran and took her at once. She was not afraid,
   Not even when we charged her with what she had done.

She denied nothing.
          And this was a comfort to me,   45
And some uneasiness: for it is a good thing
To escape from death, but it is no great pleasure
To bring death to a friend.
              Yet I always say
There is nothing so comfortable as your own safe skin!
KREON *(slowly, dangerously):* And you, Antigone,   50
You with your head hanging, — do you confess this thing?
ANTIGONE: I do. I deny nothing.
KREON *(to* SENTRY*):*   You may go.
                    (Exit SENTRY.*)*

(To ANTIGONE.*)* Tell me, tell me briefly:
Had you heard my proclamation touching this matter?
ANTIGONE: It was public. Could I help hearing it?   55
KREON: And yet you dared defy the law.
ANTIGONE: I dared.
It was not God's proclamation. That final Justice
That rules the world below makes no such laws.

Your edict, King, was strong,
But all your strength is weakness itself against   60
The immortal unrecorded laws of God.
They are not merely now: they were, and shall be,
Operative for ever, beyond man utterly.

I knew I must die, even without your decree:
I am only mortal. And if I must die   65
Now, before it is my time to die,
Surely this is no hardship: can anyone
Living, as I live, with evil all about me,
Think Death less than a friend? This death of mine
Is of no importance; but if I had left my brother   70
Lying in death unburied, I should have suffered.
Now I do not.
           You smile at me. Ah Kreon,
Think me a fool, if you like; but it may well be
That a fool convicts me of folly.
CHORAGOS: Like father, like daughter: both headstrong, deaf to reason!   75
She has never learned to yield:
KREON: She has much to learn.
The inflexible heart breaks first, the toughest iron
Cracks first, and the wildest horses bend their necks
At the pull of the smallest curb.
               Pride? In a slave?

This girl is guilty of a double insolence,   80
Breaking the given laws and boasting of it.
Who is the man here,
She or I, if this crime goes unpunished?
Sister's child, or more than sister's child,
Or closer yet in blood — she and her sister   85
Win bitter death for this!
(To Servants.)   Go, some of you,
Arrest Ismene. I accuse her equally.
Bring her: you will find her sniffling in the house there.

Her mind's a traitor: crimes kept in the dark
Cry for light, and the guardian brain shudders;   90
But how much worse than this
Is brazen boasting of barefaced anarchy!
ANTIGONE: Kreon, what more do you want than my death?
KREON: Nothing.
That gives me everything.
ANTIGONE: Then I beg you: kill me.
This talking is a great weariness: your words   95
Are distasteful to me, and I am sure that mine
Seem so to you. And yet they should not seem so:
I should have praise and honor for what I have done.
All these men here would praise me
Were their lips not frozen shut with fear of you.   100
(Bitterly.) Ah the good fortune of kings,
Licensed to say and do whatever they please!
KREON: You are alone here in that opinion.
ANTIGONE: No, they are with me. But they keep their tongues in leash.
KREON: Maybe. But you are guilty, and they are not.   105
ANTIGONE: There is no guilt in reverence for the dead.
KREON: But Eteocles — was he not your brother too?
ANTIGONE: My brother too.
KREON: And you insult his memory?
ANTIGONE *(softly)*: The dead man would not say that I insult it.
KREON: He would: for you honor a traitor as much as him.   110
ANTIGONE: His own brother, traitor or not, and equal in blood.
KREON: He made war on his country. Eteocles defended it.
ANTIGONE: Nevertheless, there are honors due all the dead.
KREON: But not the same for the wicked as for the just.
ANTIGONE: Ah Kreon, Kreon,   115
Which of us can say what the gods hold wicked?
KREON: An enemy is an enemy, even dead.
ANTIGONE: It is my nature to join in love, not hate.

KREON *(finally losing patience)*: Go join them then; if you must have
>   your love,
> Find it in hell!   120
CHORAGOS: But see, Ismene comes:

(Enter ISMENE, *guarded.)*

> Those tears are sisterly, the cloud
> That shadows her eyes rains down gentle sorrow.
KREON: You too, Ismene,
>   Snake in my ordered house, sucking my blood   125
>   Stealthily — and all the time I never knew
>   That these two sisters were aiming at my throne!

>   Ismene,
>   Do you confess your share in this crime, or deny it?
>   Answer me.
ISMENE: Yes, if she will let me say so. I am guilty.   130
ANTIGONE *(coldly)*: No, Ismene. You have no right to say so.
>   You would not help me, and I will not have you help me.
ISMENE: But now I know what you meant: and I am here
>   To join you, to take my share of punishment.
ANTIGONE: The dead man and the gods who rule the dead   135
>   Know whose act this was. Words are not friends.
ISMENE: Do you refuse me, Antigone? I want to die with you:
>   I too have a duty that I must discharge to the dead.
ANTIGONE: You shall not lessen my death by sharing it.
ISMENE: What do I care for life when you are dead?   140
ANTIGONE: Ask Kreon. You're always hanging on his opinions.
ISMENE: You are laughing at me. Why, Antigone?
ANTIGONE: It's a joyless laughter, Ismene.
ISMENE: But can I do nothing?
ANTIGONE: Yes. Save yourself. I shall not envy you.
>   There are those who will praise you; I shall have honor, too.   145
ISMENE: But we are equally guilty!
ANTIGONE: No more, Ismene.
>   You are alive, but I belong to Death.
KREON *(to the* CHORUS): Gentlemen, I beg you to observe these girls:
>   One has just now lost her mind; the other,
>   It seems, has never had a mind at all.   150
ISMENE: Grief teaches the steadiest minds to waver, King.
KREON: Yours certainly did, when you assumed guilt with the guilty!
ISMENE: But how could I go on living without her?
KREON: You are.
>   She is already dead.
ISMENE: But your own son's bride!

KREON: There are places enough for him to push his plow.   155
    I want no wicked women for my sons!
ISMENE: O dearest Haimon, how your father wrongs you!
KREON: I've had enough of your childish talk of marriage!
CHORAGOS: Do you really intend to steal this girl from your son?
KREON: No; Death will do that for me.
CHORAGOS: Then she must die?   160
KREON (*ironically*): You dazzle me.

                           —But enough of this talk!
    (*To Guards.*) You, there, take them away and guard them well:
    For they are but women, and even brave men run
    When they see Death coming.
                     (*Exeunt*° ISMENE, ANTIGONE, *and Guards.*)

ODE 2 • Strophe 1

CHORUS: Fortunate is the man who has never tasted God's vengeance!
    Where once the anger of heaven has struck, that house is shaken
    For ever: damnation rises behind each child
    Like a wave cresting out of the black northeast,
    When the long darkness under sea roars up   5
    And bursts drumming death upon the windwhipped sand.

Antistrophe 1

    I have seen this gathering sorrow from time long past
    Loom upon Oedipus' children: generation from generation
    Takes the compulsive rage of the enemy god.
    So lately this last flower of Oedipus' line   10
    Drank the sunlight! but now a passionate word
    And a handful of dust have closed up all its beauty.

Strophe 2

    What mortal arrogance
    Transcends the wrath of Zeus?
    Sleep cannot lull him nor the effortless long months   15
    Of the timeless gods: but he is young for ever,
    And his house is the shining day of high Olympos.
    All that is and shall be,
    And all the past, is his.
    No pride on earth is free of the curse of heaven.   20

Antistrophe 2

    The straying dreams of men
    May bring them ghosts of joy:

Exeunt: Latin for "they exit."

But as they drowse, the waking embers burn them;
Or they walk with fixed eyes, as blind men walk.
But the ancient wisdom speaks for our own time: 25
Fate works most for woe
With Folly's fairest show.
Man's little pleasure is the spring of sorrow.

SCENE 3

CHORAGOS: But here is Haimon, King, the last of all your sons.
        Is it grief for Antigone that brings him here,
        And bitterness at being robbed of his bride?

(Enter HAIMON.*)*

KREON: We shall soon see, and no need of diviners.
                                                    —Son,
        You have heard my final judgment on that girl: 5
        Have you come here hating me, or have you come
        With deference and with love, whatever I do?
HAIMON: I am your son, father. You are my guide.
        You make things clear for me, and I obey you.
        No marriage means more to me than your continuing wisdom.   10
KREON: Good. That is the way to behave: subordinate
        Everything else, my son, to your father's will.
        This is what a man prays for, that he may get
        Sons attentive and dutiful in his house,
        Each one hating his father's enemies,   15
        Honoring his father's friends. But if his sons
        Fail him, if they turn out unprofitably,
        What has he fathered but trouble for himself
        And amusement for the malicious?
                                        So you are right
        Not to lose your head over this woman.   20
        Your pleasure with her would soon grow cold, Haimon,
        And then you'd have a hellcat in bed and elsewhere.
        Let her find her husband in Hell!
        Of all the people in this city, only she
        Has had contempt for my law and broken it.   25

        Do you want me to show myself weak before the people?
        Or to break my sworn word? No, and I will not.
        The woman dies.
        I suppose she'll plead "family ties." Well, let her.
        If I permit my own family to rebel,   30
        How shall I earn the world's obedience?

Show me the man who keeps his house in hand,
He's fit for public authority.
                              I'll have no dealings
With lawbreakers, critics of the government:
Whoever is chosen to govern should be obeyed —   35
Must be obeyed, in all things, great and small,
Just and unjust! O Haimon,
The man who knows how to obey, and that man only,
Knows how to give commands when the time comes.
You can depend on him, no matter how fast   40
The spears come: he's a good soldier, he'll stick it out.
Anarchy, anarchy! Show me a greater evil!
This is why cities tumble and the great houses rain down,
This is what scatters armies!
No, no: good lives are made so by discipline.   45
We keep the laws then, and the lawmakers,
And no woman shall seduce us. If we must lose,
Let's lose to a man, at least! Is a woman stronger than we?
CHORAGOS: Unless time has rusted my wits,
What you say, King, is said with point and dignity.   50
HAIMON (boyishly earnest): Father:
Reason is God's crowning gift to man, and you are right
To warn me against losing mine. I cannot say —
I hope that I shall never want to say! — that you
Have reasoned badly. Yet there are other men   55
Who can reason, too; and their opinions might be helpful.
You are not in a position to know everything
That people say or do, or what they feel:
Your temper terrifies — everyone
Will tell you only what you like to hear.   60
But I, at any rate, can listen; and I have heard them
Muttering and whispering in the dark about this girl.
They say no woman has ever, so unreasonably,
Died so shameful a death for a generous act:
"She covered her brother's body. Is this indecent?   65
She kept him from dogs and vultures. Is this a crime?
Death? — She should have all the honor that we can give her!"

This is the way they talk out there in the city.

You must believe me:
Nothing is closer to me than your happiness.   70
What could be closer? Must not any son
Value his father's fortune as his father does his?

I beg you, do not be unchangeable:
Do not believe that you alone can be right.
The man who thinks that,   75
The man who maintains that only he has the power
To reason correctly, the gift to speak, the soul —
A man like that, when you know him, turns out empty.
It is not reason never to yield to reason!

In flood time you can see how some trees bend,   80
And because they bend, even their twigs are safe,
While stubborn trees are torn up, roots and all.
And the same thing happens in sailing:
Make your sheet fast, never slacken, — and over you go,
Head over heels and under: and there's your voyage.   85
Forget you are angry! Let yourself be moved!
I know I am young; but please let me say this:
The ideal condition
Would be, I admit, that men should be right by instinct;
But since we are all too likely to go astray,   90
The reasonable thing is to learn from those who can teach.
CHORAGOS: You will do well to listen to him, King,
    If what he says is sensible. And you, Haimon,
    Must listen to your father. — Both speak well.
KREON: You consider it right for a man of my years and experience   95
    To go to school to a boy?
HAIMON: It is not right
    If I am wrong. But if I am young, and right,
    What does my age matter?
KREON: You think it is right to stand up for an anarchist?
HAIMON: Not at all. I pay no respect to criminals.   100
KREON: Then she is not a criminal?
HAIMON: The City would deny it, to a man.
KREON: And the City proposes to teach me how to rule?
HAIMON: Ah. Who is it that's talking like a boy now?
KREON: My voice is the one voice giving orders in this City!   105
HAIMON: It is no City if it takes orders from one voice.
KREON: The State is the King!
HAIMON: Yes, if the State is a desert.

    (Pause.)

KREON: This boy, it seems, has sold out to a woman.
HAIMON: If you are a woman: my concern is only for you.
KREON: So? Your "concern"! In a public brawl with your father!   110
HAIMON: How about you, in a public brawl with justice?

KREON: With justice, when all that I do is within my rights?

HAIMON: You have no right to trample on God's right.

KREON (*completely out of control*): Fool, adolescent fool! Taken in by a woman!

HAIMON: You'll never see me taken in by anything vile.   115

KREON: Every word you say is for her!

HAIMON (*quietly, darkly*):   And for you.
     And for me. And for the gods under the earth.

KREON: You'll never marry her while she lives.

HAIMON: Then she must die. — But her death will cause another.

KREON: Another?   120
     Have you lost your senses? Is this an open threat?

HAIMON: There is no threat in speaking to emptiness.

KREON: I swear you'll regret this superior tone of yours!
     You are the empty one!

HAIMON: If you were not my father,
     I'd say you were perverse.   125

KREON: You girl-struck fool, don't play at words with me!

HAIMON: I am sorry. You prefer silence.

KREON: Now, by God —
     I swear, by all the gods in heaven above us,
     You'll watch it, I swear you shall!
     (*To the Servants.*)   Bring her out!
     Bring the woman out! Let her die before his eyes!   130
     Here, this instant, with her bridegroom beside her!

HAIMON: Not here, no; she will not die here, King.
     And you will never see my face again.
     Go on raving as long as you've a friend to endure you. (*Exit*
     HAIMON.)

CHORAGOS: Gone, gone.   135
     Kreon, a young man in a rage is dangerous!

KREON: Let him do, or dream to do, more than a man can.
     He shall not save these girls from death.

CHORAGOS: These girls?
     You have sentenced them both?

KREON: No, you are right.
     I will not kill the one whose hands are clean.   140

CHORAGOS: But Antigone?

KREON (*somberly*):   I will carry her far away
     Out there in the wilderness, and lock her
     Living in a vault of stone. She shall have food,
     As the custom is, to absolve the State of her death.
     And there let her pray to the gods of hell: 145
     They are her only gods:
     Perhaps they will show her an escape from death,

Or she may learn,
            though late,
That piety shown the dead is pity in vain.

                        (Exit KREON.*)*

ODE 3 • Strophe

CHORUS: Love, unconquerable
    Waster of rich men, keeper
    Of warm lights and all-night vigil
    In the soft face of a girl:
    Sea-wanderer, forest-visitor!   5
    Even the pure Immortals cannot escape you,
    And mortal man, in his one day's dusk,
    Trembles before your glory.

Antistrophe

    Surely you swerve upon ruin
    The just man's consenting heart,   10
    As here you have made bright anger
    Strike between father and son —
    And none has conquered but Love!
    A girl's glance working the will of heaven:
    Pleasure to her alone who mocks us,   15
    Merciless Aphrodite.°

SCENE 4

CHORAGOS *(as* ANTIGONE *enters guarded)*: But I can no longer stand in awe
        of this,
    Nor, seeing what I see, keep back my tears.
    Here is Antigone, passing to that chamber
    Where all find sleep at last.

Strophe 1

ANTIGONE: Look upon me, friends, and pity me   5
    Turning back at the night's edge to say
    Good-by to the sun that shines for me no longer;
    Now sleepy Death
    Summons me down to Acheron,° that cold shore:
    There is no bridesong there, nor any music.   10

16 *Aphrodite:* Goddess of beauty and love.   9 *Acheron:* River in the underworld, the domain of the dead.

CHORUS: Yet not unpraised, not without a kind of honor,
    You walk at last into the underworld;
    Untouched by sickness, broken by no sword.
    What woman has ever found your way to death?

Antistrophe 1

ANTIGONE: How often I have heard the story of Niobe,°   15
    Tantalos' wretched daughter, how the stone
    Clung fast about her, ivy-close: and they say
    The rain falls endlessly
    And sifting soft snow; her tears are never done.
    I feel the loneliness of her death in mine.   20
CHORUS: But she was born of heaven, and you
    Are woman, woman-born. If her death is yours,
    A mortal woman's, is this not for you
    Glory in our world and in the world beyond?

Strophe 2

ANTIGONE: You laugh at me. Ah, friends, friends,   25
    Can you not wait until I am dead? O Thebes,
    O men many-charioted, in love with Fortune,
    Dear springs of Dirce, sacred Theban grove,
    Be witnesses for me, denied all pity,
    Unjustly judged! and think a word of love   30
    For her whose path turns
    Under dark earth, where there are no more tears.
CHORUS: You have passed beyond human daring and come at last
    Into a place of stone where Justice sits.
    I cannot tell   35
           pe of your father's guilt appears in this.

An   phe 2

ANT   hed it at last: that bridal bed
      ble, horror of son and mother mingling:
      me, infection of all our family!
      ous, father and brother!   40
    You   arriage strikes from the grave to murder mine.
    I have been a stranger here in my own land:
    All my life
    The blasphemy of my birth has followed me.

---

15 *Niobe:* Mythological figure whose children were killed as punishment for her boastfulness. She was turned into a stone, and her tears became rushing streams that coursed down the mountainside.

CHORUS: Reverence is a virtue, but strength   45
 Lives in established law: that must prevail.
 You have made your choice,
 Your death is the doing of your conscious hand.

Epode°

ANTIGONE: Then let me go, since all your words are bitter,
 And the very light of the sun is cold to me.   50
 Lead me to my vigil, where I must have
 Neither love nor lamentation; no song, but silence.

 (KREON interrupts impatiently.)

KREON: If dirges and planned lamentations could put off death,
 Men would be singing for ever.
 (To the Servants.)   Take her, go!
 You know your orders: take her to the vault   55
 And leave her alone there. And if she lives or dies,
 That's her affair, not ours: our hands are clean.
ANTIGONE: O tomb, vaulted bride-bed in eternal rock,
 Soon I shall be with my own again
 Where Persephone° welcomes the thin ghosts underground: 60
 And I shall see my father again, and you, mother,
 And dearest Polyneices —
      dearest indeed
 To me, since it was my hand
 That washed him clean and poured the ritual wine:
 And my reward is death before my time!   65

 And yet, as men's hearts know, I have done no wrong,
 I have not sinned before God. Or if I have,
 I shall know the truth in death. But if the guilt
 Lies upon Kreon who judged me, then, I pray,
 May his punishment equal my own.
CHORAGOS: O passionate heart,   70
 Unyielding, tormented still by the same winds!
KREON: Her guards shall have good cause to regret their delay.
ANTIGONE: Ah! That voice is like the voice of death!
KREON: I can give you no reason to think you are mistaken.
ANTIGONE: Thebes, and you my fathers' gods,   75
 And rulers of Thebes, you see me now, the last
 Unhappy daughter of a line of kings,
 Your kings, led away to death. You will remember
 What things I suffer, and at what men's hands,

Epode: Chant sung by the chorus following the strophe and antistrophe. *60 Persephone:* Kidnapped by Pluto, god of the underworld, to be his wife and queen.

Because I would not transgress the laws of heaven.   80
(To the Guards, simply.) Come: let us wait no longer. *(Exit* ANTIGONE,
   left, guarded.)

ODE 4 • Strophe 1

CHORUS: All Danae's° beauty was locked away
      In a brazen cell where the sunlight could not come:
      A small room still as any grave, enclosed her.
      Yet she was a princess too,
      And Zeus in a rain of gold poured love upon her.   5
      O child, child,
      No power in wealth or war
      Or tough sea-blackened ships
      Can prevail against untiring Destiny!

Antistrophe 1

      And Dryas' son° also, that furious king,   10
      Bore the god's prisoning anger for his pride:
      Sealed up by Dionysos in deaf stone,
      His madness died among echoes.
      So at the last he learned what dreadful power
      His tongue had mocked: 15
      For he had profaned the revels,
      And fired the wrath of the nine
      Implacable Sisters° that love the sound of the flute.

Strophe 2

      And old men tell a half-remembered tale
      Of horror where a dark ledge splits the sea   20
      And a double surf beats on the gray shores:
      How a king's new woman,° sick
      With hatred for the queen he had imprisoned,
      Ripped out his two sons' eyes with her bloody hands
      While grinning Ares° watched the shuttle plunge   25
      Four times: four blind wounds crying for revenge.

Antistrophe 2

      Crying, tears and blood mingled. — Piteously born,
      Those sons whose mother was of heavenly birth!

---

1 *Danae:* She was hidden away because of a prophecy that she would bear a son who would kill
her father. In spite of this precaution, she became pregnant when Zeus came to her in a shower
of gold. Her son later killed her father.   10 *Dryas' son:* King Lycurgas of Thrace, who had been
made insane by the god of wine and revelry, Dionysius.   18 *Implacable Sisters:* The muses.
22 *king's new woman:* Eidothea, the second wife of King Phineas, who blinded his sons after he
had imprisoned their mother, Cleopatra, in a cave.   25 *Ares:* God of war.

Her father was the god of the North Wind
And she was cradled by gales,   30
She raced with young colts on the glittering hills
And walked untrammeled in the open light:
But in her marriage deathless Fate found means
To build a tomb like yours for all her joy.

SCENE 5

(Enter blind TEIRESIAS, *led by a boy. The opening speeches of*
TEIRESIAS *should be in singsong contrast to the realistic lines of* KREON.*)*

TEIRESIAS: This is the way the blind man comes, Princes, Princes,
    Lockstep, two heads lit by the eyes of one.
KREON: What new thing have you to tell us, old Teiresias?
TEIRESIAS: I have much to tell you: listen to the prophet, Kreon.
KREON: I am not aware that I have ever failed to listen.   5
TEIRESIAS: Then you have done wisely, King, and ruled well.
KREON: I admit my debt to you. But what have you to say?
TEIRESIAS: This, Kreon: you stand once more on the edge of fate.
KREON: What do you mean? Your words are a kind of dread.
TEIRESIAS: Listen, Kreon: 10
    I was sitting in my chair of augury, at the place
    Where the birds gather about me. They were all a-chatter,
    As is their habit, when suddenly I heard
    A strange note in their jangling, a scream, a
    Whirring fury; I knew that they were fighting,   15
    Tearing each other, dying
    In a whirlwind of wings clashing. And I was afraid.
    I began the rites of burnt-offering at the altar,
    But Hephaistos° failed me: instead of bright flame,
    There was only the sputtering slime of the fat thigh-flesh   20
    Melting: the entrails dissolved in gray smoke,
    The bare bone burst from the welter. And no blaze!

    This was a sign from heaven. My boy described it,
    Seeing for me as I see for others.
    I tell you, Kreon, you yourself have brought   25
    This new calamity upon us. Our hearths and altars
    Are stained with the corruption of dogs and carrion birds
    That glut themselves on the corpse of Oedipus' son.
    The gods are deaf when we pray to them, their fire
    Recoils from our offering, their birds of omen   30
    Have no cry of comfort, for they are gorged
    With the thick blood of the dead.
                O my son,

19 *Hephaistos:* God of fire.

These are no trifles! Think: all men make mistakes,
But a good man yields when he knows his course is wrong,
And repairs the evil. The only crime is pride. 35

Give in to the dead man, then: do not fight with a corpse—
What glory is it to kill a man who is dead?
Think, I beg you:
It is for your own good that I speak as I do.
You should be able to yield for your own good. 40
KREON: It seems that prophets have made me their especial province.
All my life long
I have been a kind of butt for the dull arrows
Of doddering fortune-tellers!
            No, Teiresias:
If your birds—if the great eagles of God himself 45
Should carry him stinking bit by bit to heaven,
I would not yield. I am not afraid of pollution:
No man can defile the gods.
            Do what you will,
Go into business, make money, speculate
In India gold or that synthetic gold from Sardis, 50
Get rich otherwise than by my consent to bury him.
Teiresias, it is a sorry thing when a wise man
Sells his wisdom, lets out his words for hire!
TEIRESIAS: Ah Kreon! Is there no man left in the world—
KREON: To do what?—Come, let's have the aphorism! 55
TEIRESIAS: No man who knows that wisdom outweighs any wealth?
KREON: As surely as bribes are baser than any baseness.
TEIRESIAS: You are sick, Kreon! You are deathly sick!
KREON: As you say: it is not my pl.... ....allenge a prophet.
TEIRESIAS: Yet you have said my prophecy is for sale. 60
KREON: .ne generation of prophets has always loved gold.
TEIRESIAS: The generation of kings has always loved brass.
KREON: You forget yourself! You are speaking to your King.
TEIRESIAS: I know it. You are a king because of me.
KREON: You have a certain skill; but you have sold out. 65
TEIRESIAS: King, you will drive me to words that—
KREON: Say them, say them!
    Only remember: I will not pay you for them.
TEIRESIAS: No, you will find them too costly.
KREON: No doubt. Speak:
    Whatever you say, you will not change my will.
TEIRESIAS: Then take this, and take it to heart! 70
    The time is not far off when you shall pay back
    Corpse for corpse, flesh of your own flesh.

You have thrust the child of this world into living night,
You have kept from the gods below the child that is theirs:
The one in a grave before her death, the other,   75
Dead, denied the grave. This is your crime:
And the Furies° and the dark gods of Hell
Are swift with terrible punishment for you.

Do you want to buy me now, Kreon?

                                        Not many days,
And your house will be full of men and women weeping,   80
And curses will be hurled at you from far
Cities grieving for sons unburied, left to rot
Before the walls of Thebes.

These are my arrows, Kreon: they are all for you.

(To Boy.) But come, child: lead me home.   85
Let him waste his fine anger upon younger men.
Maybe he will learn at last
To control a wiser tongue in a better head.
                                (Exit TEIRESIAS.*)*
CHORAGOS: The old man has gone, King, but his words
    Remain to plague us. I am old, too,   90
    But I cannot remember that he was ever false.
KREON: That is true. . . . It troubles me.
    Oh it is hard to give in! but it is worse
    To risk everything for stubborn pride.
CHORAGOS: Kreon: take my advice.
KREON: do of the What shall I do?   95
CHORAGOS: Go quickly: free Antigone from her vault   of
    And build a tomb for the body of Polyneices.   and I
KREON: You would have me do this!
CHORAGOS: Kreon, yes!
    And it must be done at once: God moves
    Swiftly to cancel the folly of stubborn men.   100
KREON: It is hard to deny the heart! But I
    Will do it: I will not fight with destiny.
CHORAGOS: You must go yourself, you cannot leave it to others.
KREON: I will go.
            — Bring axes, servants:
    Come with me to the tomb. I buried her, I   105

---

77 *Furies:* Supernatural beings called upon to avenge crimes, especially those against relatives.

Will set her free.

Oh, quickly!

My mind misgives —
The laws of the gods are mighty, and a man must serve them
To the last day of his life!   *(Exit* KREON.*)*

PAEAN° • Strophe 1

CHORAGOS: God of many names
CHORUS: O Iacchos°

                          son

    of Kadmeian Semele°
               O born of the Thunder!
    Guardian of the West
             Regent
    of Eleusis' plain
           O Prince of maenad° Thebes
    and the Dragon Field by rippling Ismenos:°   5

Antistrophe 1

CHORAGOS: God of many names
CHORUS: the flame of torches
    flares on our hills
             the nymphs of Iacchos
    dance at the spring of Castalia:°
    from the vine-close mountain
               come ah come in ivy:
    Evohe evohe!° sings through the streets of Thebes.   10

Strophe 2

CHORAGOS: God of many names
CHORUS: Iacchos of Thebes
    heavenly Child
           of Semele bride of the Thunderer!
    The shadow of plague is upon us:
                come
    with clement feet
            oh come from Parnasos
    down the long slopes
            across the lamenting water   15

Paean: A prayer, hymn, or song of praise.   1 *Iacchos:* Bacchus or Dionysius, god of wine.
2 *Semele:* Iacchos's mother; consort of Zeus.   3 *maenad:* Woman who worshipped Iacchos.
5 *Ismenos:* River near Thebes, where dragon's teeth were planted and the original residents
of Thebes sprang forth.   8 *Castalia:* Spring on Mount Parnassus, used by priestesses of Dionysius in purification rites.   10 *Evohe, evohe!:* "Come forth, come forth!" The maenads' call to
Dionysius.

Antistrophe 2

CHORAGOS: Io° Fire! Chorister of the throbbing stars!
  O purest among the voices of the night!
  Thou son of God, blaze for us!
CHORUS: Come with choric rapture of circling Maenads
  Who cry *Io Iacche!*
      God of many names!   20

EXODOS°

(Enter MESSENGER *from left.)*

MESSENGER: Men of the line of Kadmos,° you who live
  Near Amphion's citadel,°
        I cannot say
  Of any condition of human life "This is fixed,
  This is clearly good, or bad." Fate raises up,
  And Fate casts down the happy and unhappy alike: 5
  No man can foretell his Fate.
        Take the case of Kreon:
  Kreon was happy once, as I count happiness:
  Victorious in battle, sole governor of the land,
  Fortunate father of children nobly born.
  And now it has all gone from him! Who can say   10
  That a man is still alive when his life's joy fails?
  He is a walking dead man. Grant him rich,
  Let him live like a king in his great house:
  If his pleasure is gone, I would not give
  So much as the shadow of smoke for all he owns.   15
CHORAGOS: Your words hint at sorrow: what is your news for us?
MESSENGER: They are dead. The living are guilty of their death.
CHORAGOS: Who is guilty? Who is dead? Speak!
MESSENGER: Haimon.
  Haimon is dead; and the hand that killed him
  Is his own hand.
CHORAGOS: His father's? or his own?   20
MESSENGER: His own, driven mad by the murder his father had done.
CHORAGOS: Teiresias, Teiresias, how clearly you saw it all!
MESSENGER: This is my news: you must draw what conclusions you can
  from it.
CHORAGOS: But look: Eurydice, our Queen:
  Has she overheard us?   25

(Enter EURYDICE *from the palace, center.)*

---

16 *Io:* "Hail!" *Exodos:* Concluding scene. 1 *Kadmos:* Planted dragon's teeth from which grew
the founders of Thebes. 2 *Amphion's citadel:* Thebes.

EURYDICE: I have heard something, friends:
　　　　As I was unlocking the gate of Pallas'° shrine,
　　　　For I needed her help today, I heard a voice
　　　　Telling of some new sorrow. And I fainted
　　　　There at the temple with all my maidens about me.　　　　　　30
　　　　But speak again: whatever it is, I can bear it:
　　　　Grief and I are no strangers.
MESSENGER:　　　　　　　　　　　　Dearest Lady,
　　　　I will tell you plainly all that I have seen.
　　　　I shall not try to comfort you: what is the use,
　　　　Since comfort could lie only in what is not true?　　　　　　35
　　　　The truth is always best.
　　　　　　　　　　　　I went with Kreon
　　　　To the outer plain where Polyneices was lying,
　　　　No friend to pity him, his body shredded by dogs.
　　　　We made our prayers in that place to Hecate
　　　　And Pluto,° that they would be merciful. And we bathed　　　40
　　　　The corpse with holy water, and we brought
　　　　Fresh-broken branches to burn what was left of it,
　　　　And upon the urn we heaped up a towering barrow
　　　　Of the earth of his own land.
　　　　　　　　　　　　When we were done, we ran
　　　　To the vault where Antigone lay on her couch of stone.　　　45
　　　　One of the servants had gone ahead,
　　　　And while he was yet far off he heard a voice
　　　　Grieving within the chamber, and he came back
　　　　And told Kreon. And as the King went closer,
　　　　The air was full of wailing, the words lost,　　　　　　　　50
　　　　And he begged us to make all haste. "Am I a prophet?"
　　　　He said, weeping, "And must I walk this road,
　　　　The saddest of all that I have gone before?
　　　　My son's voice calls me on. Oh quickly, quickly!
　　　　Look through the crevice there, and tell me　　　　　　　55
　　　　If it is Haimon, or some deception of the gods!"

　　　　We obeyed; and in the cavern's farthest corner
　　　　We saw her lying:
　　　　She had made a noose of her fine linen veil
　　　　And hanged herself. Haimon lay beside her,　　　　　　　60
　　　　His arms about her waist, lamenting her,
　　　　His love lost under ground, crying out
　　　　That his father had stolen her away from him.

---

27 *Pallas:* Pallas Athene, goddess of wisdom.　39–40 *Hecate and Pluto:* Goddess of witchcraft and sorcery and King of Hades, the underworld, realm of the dead.

When Kreon saw him the tears rushed to his eyes
And he called to him: "What have you done, child? speak to me.   65
What are you thinking that makes your eyes so strange?
O my son, my son, I come to you on my knees!"
But Haimon spat in his face. He said not a word,
Staring —
          And suddenly drew his sword
And lunged. Kreon shrank back, the blade missed; and the boy,   70
Desperate against himself, drove it half its length
Into his own side, and fell. And as he died
He gathered Antigone close in his arms again,
Choking, his blood bright red on her white cheek.
And now he lies dead with the dead, and she is his   75
At last, his bride in the house of the dead.
                              (*Exit* EURYDICE *into the palace.*)
CHORAGOS: She has left us without a word. What can this mean?
MESSENGER: It troubles me, too; yet she knows what is best,
     Her grief is too great for public lamentation,
     And doubtless she has gone to her chamber to weep   80
     For her dead son, leading her maidens in his dirge.

     (*Pause*)

CHORAGOS: It may be so: but I fear this deep silence.
MESSENGER: I will see what she is doing. I will go in.
                              (*Exit* MESSENGER *into the palace.*)

     (*Enter* KREON *with attendants, bearing* HAIMON'S *body.*)

CHORAGOS: But here is the king himself: oh look at him,
     Bearing his own damnation in his arms.   85
KREON: Nothing you say can touch me any more.
     My own blind heart has brought me
     From darkness to final darkness. Here you see
     The father murdering, the murdered son —
     And all my civic wisdom!   90

     Haimon my son, so young, so young to die,
     I was the fool, not you; and you died for me.
CHORAGOS: That is the truth; but you were late in learning it.
KREON: This truth is hard to bear. Surely a god
     Has crushed me beneath the hugest weight of heaven,   95
     And driven me headlong a barbaric way
     To trample out the thing I held most dear.

     The pains that men will take to come to pain!

     (*Enter* MESSENGER *from the palace.*)

MESSENGER: The burden you carry in your hands is heavy,
    But it is not all: you will find more in your house.   100
KREON: What burden worse than this shall I find there?
MESSENGER: The Queen is dead.
KREON: O port of death, deaf world,
    Is there no pity for me? And you, Angel of evil,
    I was dead, and your words are death again.   105
    Is it true, boy? Can it be true?
    Is my wife dead? Has death bred death?
MESSENGER: You can see for yourself.

(The doors are opened and the body of EURYDICE *is disclosed within.)*

KREON: Oh pity!
    All true, all true, and more than I can bear!   110
    O my wife, my son!
MESSENGER: She stood before the altar, and her heart
    Welcomed the knife her own hand guided,
    And a great cry burst from her lips for Megareus° dead,
    And for Haimon dead, her sons; and her last breath   115
    Was a curse for their father, the murderer of her sons.
    And she fell, and the dark flowed in through her closing eyes.
KREON: O God, I am sick with fear.
    Are there no swords here? Has no one a blow for me?
MESSENGER: Her curse is upon you for the deaths of both.   120
KREON: It is right that it should be. I alone am guilty.
    I know it, and I say it. Lead me in,
    Quickly, friends.
    I have neither life nor substance. Lead me in.
CHORAGOS: You are right, if there can be right in so much wrong.   125
    The briefest way is best in a world of sorrow.
KREON: Let it come,
    Let death come quickly, and be kind to me.
    I would not ever see the sun again.
CHORAGOS: All that will come when it will; but we, meanwhile,   130
    Have much to do. Leave the future to itself.
KREON: All my heart was in that prayer!
CHORAGOS: Then do not pray any more: the sky is deaf.
KREON: Lead me away. I have been rash and foolish.
    I have killed my son and my wife.   135
    I look for comfort; my comfort lies here dead.
    Whatever my hands have touched has come to nothing.
    Fate has brought all my pride to a thought of dust.

---

114 *Megareus:* Haimon's brother, son of Kreon. He believed his death would save Thebes and
so sacrificed himself in the unsuccessful attack on the city.

(As KREON *is being led into the house, the* CHORAGOS *advances and speaks directly to the audience.)*

CHORAGOS: There is no happiness where there is no wisdom;
    No wisdom but in submission to the gods.   140
    Big words are always punished,
    And proud men in old age learn to be wise.

WILLIAM SHAKESPEARE (1564–1616)

The Tragedy of Othello
The Moor of Venice

Characters

OTHELLO, *the Moor*
BRABANTIO, *father to Desdemona*
CASSIO, *an honorable lieutenant*
IAGO, *a villain*
RODERIGO, *a gulled gentleman*
DUKE OF VENICE
SENATORS
MONTANO, *Governor of Cyprus*
GENTLEMEN OF CYPRUS
LODOVICO AND GRATIANO, *two noble Venetians*
SAILORS
CLOWN
DESDEMONA, *wife to Othello*
EMILIA, *wife to Iago*
BIANCA, *a courtesan*
(MESSENGER, HERALD, OFFICERS, GENTLEMEN, MUSICIANS,
   ATTENDANTS)

Scene *Venice and Cyprus.*

ACT I

Scene I *[Venice. A street.]*
RODERIGO: Tush! Never tell me? I take it much unkindly
   That thou, Iago, who hast had my purse
   As if the strings were thine, shouldst know of this.
IAGO: 'Sblood,° but you'll not hear me! If ever I did dream
Of such a matter, abhor me.
RODERIGO: Thou told'st me   5
   Thou didst hold him in thy hate.
IAGO: Despise me
   If I do not. Three great ones of the city,
   In personal suit to make me his lieutenant,
   Off-capped° to him; and, by the faith of man,
   I know my price; I am worth no worse a place.   10

ACT I, SCENE I. 4 *'Sblood:* By God's blood.   9 *Off-capped:* Doffed their caps—as a mark of
respect.

But he, as loving his own pride and purposes,
Evades them with a bombast circumstance,°
Horribly stuffed with epithets of war;
Nonsuits° my mediators. For, "Certes," says he,
"I have already chose my officer." And what was he?   15
Forsooth, a great arithmetician,°
One Michael Cassio, a Florentine,
(A fellow almost damned in a fair wife)°
That never set a squadron in the field,
Nor the division of a battle knows   20
More than a spinster; unless the bookish theoric,
Wherein the tonguèd° consuls can propose
As masterly as he. Mere prattle without practice
Is all his soldiership. But he, sir, had th' election;
And I, of whom his eyes had seen the proof   25
At Rhodes, at Cyprus, and on other grounds
Christian and heathen, must be belee'd and calmed
By debitor and creditor. This counter-caster,°
He, in good time, must his lieutenant be,
And I—God bless the mark!—his Moorship's ancient.°   30

RODERIGO: By heaven, I rather would have been his hangman.
IAGO: Why, there's no remedy. 'Tis the curse of service:
Preferment goes by letter and affection,°
And not by old gradation,° where each second
Stood heir to th' first. Now, sir, be judge yourself,   35
Whether I in any just term am affined°
To love the Moor.
RODERIGO: I would not follow him then.
IAGO: O, sir, content you.   ¶
I follow him to serve my turn upon him.
We cannot all be masters, nor all masters   40
Cannot be truly followed. You shall mark
Many a duteous and knee-crooking° knave
That, doting on his own obsequious bondage,
Wears out his time, much like his master's ass,
For naught but provender; and when he's old, cashiered.   45

---

12 *bombast circumstance:* Stuffed, roundabout speech.   14 *Nonsuits:* Rejects.   16 *arithmetician:* Theorist (rather than practical).   18 *A . . . wife:* (A much-disputed passage, probably best taken as a general sneer at Cassio as a dandy and a ladies' man. But in the story from which Shakespeare took his plot the counterpart of Cassio is married, and it may be that at the beginning of the play Shakespeare had decided to keep him married but later changed his mind.)   22 *tonguèd:* Eloquent.   28 *counter-caster:* i.e., a bookkeeper who casts (reckons up) figures on a counter (abacus).   30 *ancient:* Standard-bearer; an under-officer.   33 *letter and affection:* Recommendations (from men of power) and personal preference.   34 *old gradation:* Seniority.   36 *affined:* Bound.   42 *knee-crooking:* Bowing.

Whip me such honest knaves! Others there are
Who, trimmed in forms and visages of duty,
Keep yet their hearts attending on themselves,
And, throwing but shows of service on their lords,
Do well thrive by them, and when they have lined their coats,   50
Do themselves homage. These fellows have some soul;
And such a one do I profess myself. For, sir,
It is as sure as you are Roderigo,
Were I the Moor, I would not be Iago.
In following him, I follow but myself.   55
Heaven is my judge, not I for love and duty,
But seeming so, for my peculiar° end;
For when my outward action doth demonstrate
The native° act and figure of my heart
In complement extern,° 'tis not long after   60
But I will wear my heart upon my sleeve
For daws to peck at; I am not what I am.
RODERIGO: What a full fortune does the thick-lips owe°
    If he can carry't thus!
IAGO: Call up her father,
    Rouse him. Make after him, poison his delight,   65
    Proclaim him in the streets, incense her kinsmen,
    And though he in a fertile climate dwell,
    Plague him with flies; though that his joy be joy,
    Yet throw such chances of vexation on't
    As it may lose some color.   70
RODERIGO: Here is her father's house. I'll call aloud.
IAGO: Do, with like timorous° accent and dire yell
    As when, by night and negligence, the fire
    Is spied in populous cities.
RODERIGO: What, ho, Brabantio! Signior Brabantio, ho!   75
IAGO: Awake! What, ho, Brabantio! Thieves! Thieves!
    Look to your house, your daughter, and your bags!
    Thieves! Thieves!

    BRABANTIO *above° [at a window].*

BRABANTIO: What is the reason of this terrible summons?
    What is the matter there?   80
RODERIGO: Signior, is all your family within?
IAGO: Are your doors locked?
BRABANTIO: Why, wherefore ask you this?

---

57 *peculiar:* Personal.   59 *native:* Natural, innate.   60 *complement extern:* Outward appearance.   63 *owe:* Own.   72 *timorous:* Frightening.   78 *s.d. above:* (i.e., on the small upper stage
above and to the rear of the main platform stage, which resembled the projecting upper story
of an Elizabethan house.)

IAGO: Zounds, sir, y'are robbed! For shame. Put on your gown!
 Your heart is burst, you have lost half your soul.
 Even now, now, very now, an old black ram   85
 Is tupping your white ewe. Arise, arise!
 Awake the snorting citizens with the bell,
 Or else the devil will make a grandsire of you.
 Arise, I say!
BRABANTIO: What, have you lost your wits?
RODERIGO: Most reverend signior, do you know my voice? 90
BRABANTIO: Not I. What are you?
RODERIGO: My name is Roderigo.
BRABANTIO: The worser welcome!
 I have charged thee not to haunt about my doors.
 In honest plainness thou hast heard me say
 My daughter is not for thee; and now, in madness,   95
 Being full of supper and distemp'ring draughts,°
 Upon malicious knavery dost thou come
 To start° my quiet.
RODERIGO: Sir, sir, sir —
BRABANTIO: But thou must needs be sure
 My spirits and my place° have in their power   100
 To make this bitter to thee.
RODERIGO: Patience, good sir.
BRABANTIO: What tell'st thou me of robbing? This is Venice,
 My house is not a grange.°
RODERIGO: Most grave Brabantio,
 In simple and pure soul I come to you.
IAGO: Zounds, sir, you are one of those that will not serve God if the devil 105
 bid you. Because we come to do you service and you think we are
 ruffians, you'll have your daughter covered with a Barbary° horse,
 you'll have your nephews° neigh to you, you'll have coursers for cous-
 ins,° and gennets for germans.°
BRABANTIO: What profane wretch art thou?   110
IAGO: I am one, sir, that comes to tell you your daughter and the Moor are
 making the beast with two backs.
BRABANTIO: Thou art a villain.
IAGO: You are — a senator.
BRABANTIO: This thou shalt answer. I know thee, Roderigo.
RODERIGO: Sir, I will answer anything. But I beseech you,   115
 If't be your pleasure and most wise consent,
 As partly I find it is, that your fair daughter,

---

96 *distemp'ring draughts:* Unsettling drinks. 98 *start:* Disrupt. 100 *place:* Rank, i.e., of senator. 103 *grange:* Isolated house. 107 *Barbary:* Arabian, i.e., Moorish. 108 *nephews:* i.e.,
grandsons. 109 *cousins:* Relations; *gennets for germans:* Spanish horses for blood relatives.

At this odd-even° and dull watch o' th' night,
Transported, with no worse nor better guard
But with a knave of common hire, a gondolier,   120
To the gross clasps of a lascivious Moor —
If this be known to you, and your allowance,
We then have done you bold and saucy wrongs;
But if you know not this, my manners tell me
We have your wrong rebuke. Do not believe   125
That from the sense of all civility°
I thus would play and trifle with your reverence.
Your daughter, if you have not given her leave,
I say again, hath made a gross revolt,
Tying her duty, beauty, wit, and fortunes   130
In an extravagant° and wheeling stranger
Of here and everywhere. Straight satisfy yourself.
If she be in her chamber, or your house,
Let loose on me the justice of the state
For thus deluding you.
BRABANTIO: Strike on the tinder, ho!   135
    Give me a taper! Call up all my people!
    This accident° is not unlike my dream.
    Belief of it oppresses me already.
    Light, I say! Light!   *Exit [above].*
IAGO: Farewell, for I must leave you.
    It seems not meet, nor wholesome to my place,   140
    To be produced — as, if I stay, I shall —
    Against the Moor. For I do know the State,
    However this may gall him with some check,°
    Cannot with safety cast° him; for he's embarked
    With such loud reason to the Cyprus wars,   145
    Which even now stands in act,° that for their souls
    Another of his fathom° they have none
    To lead their business; in which regard,
    Though I do hate him as I do hell-pains,
    Yet, for necessity of present life,   150
    I must show out a flag and sign of love,
    Which is indeed but sign. That you shall surely find him,
    Lead to the Sagittary° that raisèd search:
    And there will I be with him. So farewell.   *[Exit.]*

Enter BRABANTIO *[in his nightgown], with* SERVANTS *and torches.*

---

118 *odd-even:* Between night and morning.   126 *sense of all civility:* Feeling of what is
proper.   131 *extravagant:* Vagrant, wandering (Othello is not Venetian and thus may be considered a wandering soldier of fortune).   137 *accident:* Happening.   143 *check:* Restraint.   144 *cast:*
Dismiss.   146 *stands in act:* Takes place.   147 *fathom:* Ability.   153 *Sagittary:* (Probably the
name of an inn.)

BRABANTIO: It is too true an evil. Gone she is;
　　And what's to come of my despisèd time
　　Is naught but bitterness. Now, Roderigo,
　　Where didst thou see her? — O unhappy girl! —
　　With the Moor, say'st thou? — Who would be a father? —
　　How didst thou know 'twas she? — O, she deceives me　　　　　160
　　Past thought! — What said she to you? Get moe° tapers!
　　Raise all my kindred! — Are they married, think you?
RODERIGO: Truly I think they are.
BRABANTIO: O heaven! How got she out? O treason of the blood!
　　Fathers, from hence trust not your daughters' minds　　　　　165
　　By what you see them act.° Is there not charms
　　By which the property° of youth and maidhood
　　May be abused? Have you not read, Roderigo,
　　Of some such thing?
RODERIGO:　　　　　　　　Yes, sir, I have indeed.
BRABANTIO: Call up my brother. — O, would you had had her! —　　　　　170
　　Some one way, some another. — Do you know
　　Where we may apprehend her and the Moor?
RODERIGO: I think I can discover him, if you please
　　To get good guard and go along with me.
BRABANTIO: Pray you lead on. At every house I'll call;　　　　　175
　　I may command at most. — Get weapons, ho!
　　And raise some special officers of night. —
　　On, good Roderigo; I will deserve your pains.°　　　　　*(Exeunt.)*

Scene II *[A street.]*

Enter OTHELLO, IAGO, ATTENDANTS *with torches.*

IAGO: Though in the trade of war I have slain men,
　　Yet do I hold it very stuff° o' th' conscience
　　To do no contrived murder. I lack iniquity
　　Sometime to do me service. Nine or ten times
　　I had thought t' have yerked° him here, under the ribs.　　　　　5
OTHELLO: 'Tis better as it is.
IAGO:　　　　　　　　Nay, but he prated,
　　And spoke such scurvy and provoking terms
　　Against your honor, that with the little godliness I have
　　I did full hard forbear him. But I pray you, sir,
　　Are you fast married? Be assured of this,　　　　　10
　　That the magnifico° is much beloved,
　　And hath in his effect a voice potential
　　As double as the Duke's.° He will divorce you,

---

161 *moe:* More.　166 *act:* Do.　167 *property:* True nature.　178 *deserve your pains:* Be worthy of (and reward) your efforts.　SCENE II. 2 *stuff:* Essence.　5 *yerked:* Stabbed.　11 *magnifico:* Nobleman.　12–13 *hath . . . Duke's:* i.e., can be as effective as the Duke.

Or put upon you what restraint or grievance
The law, with all his might to enforce it on,   15
Will give him cable.°
OTHELLO: Let him do his spite.
My services which I have done the Signiory°
Shall out-tongue his complaints. 'Tis yet to know°—
Which when I know that boasting is an honor
I shall promulgate—I fetch my life and being   20
From men of royal siege,° and my demerits°
May speak unbonneted to as proud a fortune
As this that I have reached.° For know, Iago,
But that I love the gentle Desdemona,
I would not my unhousèd° free condition   25
Put into circumscription and confine
For the seas' worth. But look, what lights come yond?

Enter CASSIO, *with [*OFFICERS *and] torches.*

IAGO: Those are the raisèd father and his friends.
You were best go in.
OTHELLO: Not I. I must be found.
My parts, my title, and my perfect soul°   30
Shall manifest me rightly. Is it they?
IAGO: By Janus, I think no.
OTHELLO: The servants of the Duke? And my lieutenant?
The goodness of the night upon you, friends.
What is the news?
CASSIO: The Duke does greet you, general;   35
And he requires your haste-posthaste appearance
Even on the instant.
OTHELLO: What is the matter, think you?
CASSIO: Something from Cyprus, as I may divine.
It is a business of some heat. The galleys
Have sent a dozen sequent° messengers   40
This very night at one another's heels,
And many of the consuls, raised and met,
Are at the Duke's already. You have been hotly called for.
When, being not at your lodging to be found,
The Senate hath sent about three several° quests   45
To search you out.
OTHELLO: 'Tis well I am found by you.
I will but spend a word here in the house,
And go with you.   [*Exit.*]

---

16 *cable:* Range, scope.   17 *Signiory:* The rulers of Venice.   18 *yet to know:* Unknown as
yet.   21 *siege:* Rank; *demerits:* Deserts.   22–23 *May . . . reached:* i.e., are the equal of the family
I have married into.   25 *unhousèd:* Unconfined.   30 *perfect soul:* Clear, unflawed conscience.   40 *sequent:* Successive.   45 *several:* Separate.

CASSIO: Ancient, what makes he here?
IAGO: Faith, he tonight hath boarded a land carack.°
    If it prove lawful prize, he's made forever. 50
CASSIO: I do not understand.
IAGO: He's married.
CASSIO: To who?

    [Enter OTHELLO.]

IAGO: Marry,° to—Come captain, will you go?
OTHELLO: Have with you.
CASSIO: Here comes another troop to seek for you.

    Enter BRABANTIO, RODERIGO, *with* OFFICERS *and torches.*

IAGO: It is Brabantio. General, be advised.
    He comes to bad intent.
OTHELLO: Holla! Stand there! 55
RODERIGO: Signior, it is the Moor.
BRABANTIO: Down with him, thief! *[They draw swords.]*
IAGO: You, Roderigo? Come, sir, I am for you.
OTHELLO: Keep up your bright swords, for the dew will rust them.
    Good signior, you shall more command with years
    Than with your weapons. 60
BRABANTIO: Oh thou foul thief, where hast thou stowed my daughter?
    Damned as thou art, thou hast enchanted her!
    For I'll refer me to all things of sense,°
    If she in chains of magic were not bound,
    Whether a maid so tender, fair, and happy, 65
    So opposite to marriage that she shunned
    The wealthy, curlèd darlings of our nation,
    Would ever have, t'incur a general mock,°
    Run from her guardage to the sooty bosom
    Of such a thing as thou—to fear, not to delight. 70
    Judge me the world if 'tis not gross in sense°
    That thou hast practiced° on her with foul charms,
    Abused her delicate youth with drugs or minerals
    That weaken motion.° I'll have't disputed on;
    'Tis probable, and palpable to thinking. 75
    I therefore apprehend and do attach° thee
    For an abuser of the world, a practicer
    Of arts inhibited and out of warrant.°
    Lay hold upon him. If he do resist,
    Subdue him at his peril.

---

49 *carack:* Treasure ship. 52 *Marry:* By Mary (an interjection). 63 *refer . . . sense:* i.e., base (my argument) on all ordinary understanding of nature. 68 *general mock:* Public shame. 71 *gross in sense:* Obvious. 72 *practiced:* Used tricks. 74 *motion:* Thought, i.e., reason. 76 *attach:* Arrest. 78 *inhibited . . . warrant:* Prohibited and illegal (black magic).

OTHELLO: Hold your hands,   80
  Both you of my inclining and the rest.
  Were it my cue to fight, I should have known it
  Without a prompter. Whither will you that I go
  To answer this your charge?
BRABANTIO: To prison, till fit time
  Of law and course of direct session   85
  Call thee to answer.
OTHELLO: What if I do obey?
  How may the Duke be therewith satisfied,
  Whose messengers are here about my side
  Upon some present° business of the state
  To bring me to him?
OFFICER: 'Tis true, most worthy signior.   90
  The Duke's in council, and your noble self
  I am sure is sent for.
BRABANTIO: How? The Duke in council?
  In this time of the night? Bring him away.
  Mine's not an idle cause. The Duke himself,
  Or any of my brothers° of the state,   95
  Cannot but feel this wrong as 'twere their own;
  For if such actions may have passage free,
  Bondslaves and pagans shall our statesmen be.   *Exeunt.*

Scene III *[A council chamber.]*

Enter DUKE, SENATORS, *and* OFFICERS *[set at a table, with lights and* ATTENDANTS].

DUKE: There's no composition° in this news
  That gives them credit.°
FIRST SENATOR: Indeed, they are disproportioned.
  My letters say a hundred and seven galleys.
DUKE: And mine a hundred forty.
SECOND SENATOR: And mine two hundred.
  But though they jump° not on a just accompt° —   5
  As in these cases where the aim° reports
  'Tis oft with difference — yet do they all confirm
  A Turkish fleet, and bearing up to Cyprus.
DUKE: Nay, it is possible enough to judgment.°
  I do not so secure me in the error,   10
  But the main article I do approve
  In fearful sense.°

---

89 *present:* Immediate.   95 *brothers:* i.e., the other senators.   SCENE III. 1 *composition:* Agreement.   2 *gives them credit:* Makes them believable.   5 *jump:* Agree; *just accompt:* Exact counting.   6 *aim:* Approximation.   9 *to judgment:* When carefully considered.   10–12 *I do . . . sense:* i.e., just because the numbers disagree in the reports, I do not doubt that the principal information (that the Turkish fleet is out) is fearfully true.

SAILOR [*Within*]:   What, ho! What, ho! What, ho!

Enter SAILOR.

OFFICER: A messenger from the galleys.

DUKE: Now? What's the business?

SAILOR: The Turkish preparation makes for Rhodes.
　So was I bid report here to the State   15
　By Signior Angelo.

DUKE: How say you by this change?

FIRST SENATOR: This cannot be
　By no assay of reason. 'Tis a pageant°
　To keep us in false gaze.° When we consider
　Th' importancy of Cyprus to the Turk,   20
　And let ourselves again but understand
　That, as it more concerns the Turk than Rhodes,
　So may he with more facile question° bear it,
　For that it stands not in such warlike brace,°
　But altogether lacks th' abilities   25
　That Rhodes is dressed in. If we make thought of this,
　We must not think the Turk is so unskillful
　To leave that latest which concerns him first,
　Neglecting an attempt of ease and gain
　To wake and wage a danger profitless.   30

DUKE: Nay, in all confidence he's not for Rhodes.

OFFICER: Here is more news.

Enter a MESSENGER.

MESSENGER: The Ottomites, reverend and gracious,
　Steering with due course toward the isle of Rhodes,
　Have there injointed them with an after° fleet.   35

FIRST SENATOR: Ay, so I thought. How many, as you guess?

MESSENGER: Of thirty sail; and now they do restem
　Their backward course, bearing with frank appearance
　Their purposes toward Cyprus. Signior Montano,
　Your trusty and most valiant servitor,   40
　With his free duty° recommends° you thus,
　And prays you to believe him.

DUKE: 'Tis certain then for Cyprus.
　Marcus Luccicos, is not he in town?

FIRST SENATOR: He's now in Florence.   45

DUKE: Write from us to him; post-posthaste dispatch.

FIRST SENATOR: Here comes Brabantio and the valiant Moor.

---

18 *pageant:* Show, pretense.   19 *in false gaze:* Looking the wrong way.   23 *facile question:* Easy
struggle.   24 *warlike brace:* "Military posture."   35 *after:* Following.   41 *free duty:* Unlimited
respect; *recommends:* Informs.

Enter BRABANTIO, OTHELLO, CASSIO, IAGO, RODERIGO, *and* OFFICERS.

DUKE: Valiant Othello, we must straight° employ you
    Against the general° enemy Ottoman.
    [To BRABANTIO*]* I did not see you. Welcome, gentle signior.   50
    We lacked your counsel and your help tonight.
BRABANTIO: So did I yours. Good your grace, pardon me.
    Neither my place, nor aught I heard of business,
    Hath raised me from my bed; nor doth the general care
    Take hold on me; for my particular grief   55
    Is of so floodgate and o'erbearing nature
    That it engluts and swallows other sorrows,
    And it is still itself.
DUKE: Why, what's the matter?
BRABANTIO: My daughter! O, my daughter!
SENATORS: Dead?
BRABANTIO: Ay, to me.
    She is abused, stol'n from me, and corrupted   60
    By spells and medicines bought of mountebanks;
    For nature so prepost'rously to err,
    Being not deficient, blind, or lame of sense,
    Sans° witchcraft could not.
DUKE: Whoe'er he be that in this foul proceeding   65
    Hath thus beguiled your daughter of herself,
    And you of her, the bloody book of law
    You shall yourself read in the bitter letter
    After your own sense; yea, though our proper° son
    Stood in your action.°
BRABANTIO: Humbly I thank your Grace.   70
    Here is the man — this Moor, whom now, it seems,
    Your special mandate for the state affairs
    Hath hither brought.
ALL: We are very sorry for't.
DUKE *[To* OTHELLO*]*: What in your own part can you say to this?
BRABANTIO: Nothing, but this is so.   75
OTHELLO: Most potent, grave, and reverend signiors,
    My very noble and approved° good masters,
    That I have ta'en away this old man's daughter,
    It is most true; true I have married her.
    The very head and front° of my offending   80
    Hath this extent, no more. Rude am I in my speech,
    And little blessed with the soft phrase of peace.

---

48 *straight:* At once. 49 *general:* Universal. 64 *Sans:* Without. 69 *proper:* Own. 70 *Stood in your action:* Were the accused in your suit. 77 *approved:* Tested, proven by past performance. 80 *head and front:* Extreme form (front = forehead).

For since these arms of mine had seven years' pith°
Till now some nine moons wasted,° they have used
Their dearest° action in the tented field;   85
And little of this great world can I speak
More than pertains to feats of broils and battle;
And therefore little shall I grace my cause
In speaking for myself. Yet, by your gracious patience,
I will a round° unvarnished tale deliver   90
Of my whole course of love — what drugs, what charms,
What conjuration, and what mighty magic,
For such proceeding I am charged withal,
I won his daughter —
BRABANTIO: A maiden never bold,
Of spirit so still and quiet that her motion   95
Blushed at herself,° and she, in spite of nature,
Of years, of country, credit, everything,
To fall in love with what she feared to look on!
It is a judgment maimed and most imperfect
That will confess perfection so could err   100
Against all rules of nature, and must be driven
To find out practices of cunning hell
Why this should be. I therefore vouch again
That with some mixtures pow'rful o'er the blood,
Or with some dram, conjured to this effect,   105
He wrought upon her.
DUKE: To vouch this is no proof,
Without more wider and more overt test
Than these thin habits° and poor likelihoods
Of modern° seeming do prefer against him.
FIRST SENATOR: But, Othello, speak.   110
Did you by indirect and forcèd courses
Subdue and poison this young maid's affections?
Or came it by request, and such fair question°
As soul to soul affordeth?
OTHELLO: I do beseech you,
Send for the lady to the Sagittary   115
And let her speak of me before her father.
If you do find me foul in her report,
The trust, the office, I do hold of you
Not only take away, but let your sentence
Even fall upon my life.
DUKE: Fetch Desdemona hither.   120

---

83 *pith:* Strength.   84 *wasted:* Past.   85 *dearest:* Most important.   90 *round:* Blunt.   95–96 *her motion/Blushed at herself:* i.e., she was so modest that she blushed at every thought (and movement).   108 *habits:* Clothing.   109 *modern:* Trivial.   113 *question:* Discussion.

OTHELLO: Ancient, conduct them; you best know the place.

[Exit IAGO, *with two or three* ATTENDANTS.*]*

And till she come, as truly as to heaven
I do confess the vices of my blood,
So justly to your grave ears I'll present
How I did thrive in this fair lady's love,   125
And she in mine.
DUKE: Say it, Othello.
OTHELLO: Her father loved me; oft invited me;
Still° questioned me the story of my life
From year to year, the battle, sieges, fortune
That I have passed.   130
I ran it through, even from my boyish days
To th' very moment that he bade me tell it.
Wherein I spoke of most disastrous chances,
Of moving accidents by flood and field,
Of hairbreadth scapes i' th' imminent° deadly breach,   135
Of being taken by the insolent foe
And sold to slavery, of my redemption thence
And portance° in my travel's history,
Wherein of anters° vast and deserts idle,°
Rough quarries, rocks, and hills whose heads touch heaven,   140
It was my hint to speak. Such was my process.
And of the Cannibals that each other eat,
The Anthropophagi,° and men whose heads
Grew beneath their shoulders. These things to hear
Would Desdemona seriously incline;   145
But still the house affairs would draw her thence;
Which ever as she could with haste dispatch,
She'd come again, and with a greedy ear
Devour up my discourse. Which I observing,
Took once a pliant hour, and found good means   150
To draw from her a prayer of earnest heart
That I would all my pilgrimage dilate,°
Whereof by parcels she had something heard,
But not intentively.° I did consent,
And often did beguile her of her tears   155
When I did speak of some distressful stroke
That my youth suffered. My story being done,
She gave me for my pains a world of kisses.
She swore in faith 'twas strange, 'twas passing° strange;
'Twas pitiful, 'twas wondrous pitiful.   160

128 *Still:* Regularly.   135 *imminent:* Threatening.   138 *portance:* Manner of acting.   139 *anters:*
Caves; *idle:* Empty, sterile.   143 *Anthropophagi:* Maneaters.   152 *dilate:* Relate in full. 154
intentively: At length and in sequence.   159 *passing:* Surpassing.

She wished she had not heard it; yet she wished
That heaven had made her such a man. She thanked me,
And bade me, if I had a friend that loved her,
I should but teach him how to tell my story,
And that would woo her. Upon this hint I spake.   165
She loved me for the dangers I had passed,
And I loved her that she did pity them.
This only is the witchcraft I have used.
Here comes the lady. Let her witness it.

Enter DESDEMONA, IAGO, ATTENDANTS.

DUKE: I think this tale would win my daughter too.   170
   Good Brabantio, take up this mangled matter at the best.°
   Men do their broken weapons rather use
   Than their bare hands.
BRABANTIO: I pray you hear her speak.
   If she confess that she was half the wooer,
   Destruction on my head if my bad blame   175
   Light on the man. Come hither, gentle mistress.
   Do you perceive in all this noble company
   Where most you owe obedience?
DESDEMONA: My noble father,
   I do perceive here a divided duty.
   To you I am bound for life and education;   180
   My life and education both do learn me
   How to respect you. You are the lord of duty,
   I am hitherto your daughter. But here's my husband,
   And so much duty as my mother showed
   To you, preferring you before her father,   185
   So much I challenge° that I may profess
   Due to the Moor my lord.
BRABANTIO: God be with you. I have done.
   Please it your Grace, on to the state affairs.
   I had rather to adopt a child than get° it.
   Come hither, Moor.   190
   I here do give thee that with all my heart
   Which, but thou hast already, with all my heart
   I would keep from thee. For your sake,° jewel,
   I am glad at soul I have no other child,
   For thy escape would teach me tyranny,   195
   To hang clogs on them. I have done, my lord.
DUKE: Let me speak like yourself and lay a sentence°
   Which, as a grise° or step, may help these lovers.

---

171 *take . . . best:* i.e., make the best of this disaster.   186 *challenge:* Claim as right.   189 *get:* Beget.   193 *For your sake:* Because of you.   197 *lay a sentence:* Provide a maxim.   198 *grise:* Step.

When remedies are past, the griefs are ended
By seeing the worst, which late on hopes depended.° 200
To mourn a mischief that is past and gone
Is the next° way to draw new mischief on.
What cannot be preserved when fortune takes,
Patience her injury a mock'ry makes.
The robbed that smiles, steals something from the thief; 205
He robs himself that spends a bootless° grief.
BRABANTIO: So let the Turk of Cyprus us beguile:
We lose it not so long as we can smile.
He bears the sentence well that nothing bears
But the free comfort which from thence he hears; 210
But he bears both the sentence and the sorrow
That to pay grief must of poor patience borrow.
These sentences, to sugar, or to gall,
Being strong on both sides, are equivocal.
But words are words. I never yet did hear 215
That the bruisèd heart was piercèd° through the ear.
I humbly beseech you, proceed to th' affairs of state.
DUKE: The Turk with a most mighty preparation makes for Cyprus.
Othello, the fortitude° of the place is best known to you; and though
we have there a substitute° of most allowed sufficiency,° yet opinion, 220
a more sovereign mistress of effects, throws a more safer voice on
you.° You must therefore be content to slubber° the gloss of your new
fortunes with this more stubborn and boisterous° expedition.
OTHELLO: The tyrant Custom, most grave senators,
Hath made the flinty and steel couch of war 225
My thrice-driven° bed of down. I do agnize°
A natural and prompt alacrity
I find in hardness and do undertake
These present wars against the Ottomites.
Most humbly, therefore, bending to your state, 230
I crave fit disposition for my wife,
Due reference of place, and exhibition,°
With such accommodation and besort

200 *late on hopes depended:* Was supported by hope (of a better outcome) until lately. 202 *next:* Closest, surest. 206 *bootless:* Valueless.
216 *piercèd:* (Some editors emend to *piecèd,* i.e., "healed." But *piercèd* makes good sense: Brabantio is saying in effect that his heart cannot be further hurt [pierced] by the indignity of the useless, conventional advice the Duke offers him. *Piercèd* can also mean, however, "lanced" in the medical sense, and would then mean "treated"). 219 *fortitude:* Fortification. 220 *substitute:* Viceroy; *most allowed sufficiency:* Generally acknowledged capability. 220–222 *opinion . . . you:* i.e., the general opinion, which finally controls affairs, is that you would be the best man in this situation. 222 *slubber:* Besmear. 223 *stubborn and boisterous:* Rough and violent. 226 *thrice-driven:* i.e., softest; *agnize:* Know in myself. 232 *exhibition:* Grant of funds.

As levels with° her breeding.

DUKE: Why, at her father's.

BRABANTIO: I will not have it so.

OTHELLO: Nor I.   235

DESDEMONA: Nor would I there reside,
    To put my father in impatient thoughts
    By being in his eye. Most gracious Duke,
    To my unfolding° lend your prosperous° ear,
    And let me find a charter° in your voice,   240
    T' assist my simpleness.

DUKE: What would you, Desdemona?

DESDEMONA: That I love the Moor to live with him,
    My downright violence, and storm of fortunes,
    May trumpet to the world. My heart's subdued
    Even to the very quality of my lord.°   245
    I saw Othello's visage in his mind,
    And to his honors and his valiant parts
    Did I my soul and fortunes consecrate.
    So that, dear lords, if I be left behind,
    A moth of peace, and he go to the war,   250
    The rites° for why I love him are bereft me,
    And I a heavy interim shall support
    By his dear absence. Let me go with him.

OTHELLO: Let her have your voice.°
    Vouch with me, heaven, I therefore beg it not   255
    To please the palate of my appetite,
    Nor to comply with heat° — the young affects°
    In me defunct — and proper satisfaction;°
    But to be free and bounteous to her mind;
    And heaven defend° your good souls that you think   260
    I will your serious and great business scant
    When she is with me. No, when light-winged toys
    Of feathered Cupid seel° with wanton° dullness
    My speculative and officed instrument,°
    That my disports corrupt and taint my business,   265
    Let housewives make a skillet of my helm,
    And all indign° and base adversities
    Make head° against my estimation!° —

---

234 *levels with:* Is suitable to.   239 *unfolding:* Explanation; *prosperous:* Favoring.   240 *charter:* Permission.   244–245 *My . . . lord:* i.e., I have become one in nature and being with the man I married (therefore, I too would go to the wars like a soldier).   251 *rites:* (May refer either to the marriage rites or to the rites, formalities, of war.)   254 *voice:* Consent.   257 *heat:* Lust; *affects:* Passions.   258 *proper satisfaction:* i.e., consummation of the marriage.   260 *defend:* Forbid.   263 *seel:* Sew up; *wanton:* Lascivious.   264 *speculative . . . instrument:* i.e., sight (and, by extension, the mind).   267 *indign:* Unworthy.   268 *Make head:* Form an army, i.e., attack; *estimation:* Reputation.

DUKE: Be it as you shall privately determine,
    Either for her stay or going. Th' affair cries haste,   270
    And speed must answer it.
FIRST SENATOR: You must away tonight.
OTHELLO: With all my heart.
DUKE: At nine i' th' morning here we'll meet again.
    Othello, leave some officer behind,
    And he shall our commission bring to you,   275
    And such things else of quality and respect
    As doth import you.
OTHELLO: So please your grace, my ancient;
    A man he is of honesty and trust.
    To his conveyance I assign my wife,
    With what else needful your good grace shall think   280
    to be sent after me.
DUKE: Let it be so.
    Good night to every one. *[To* BRABANTIO*]* And, noble signior,
    If virtue no delighted° beauty lack,
    Your son-in-law is far more fair than black.
FIRST SENATOR: Adieu, brave Moor. Use Desdemona well.   285
BRABANTIO: Look to her, Moor, if thou hast eyes to see:
    She has deceived her father, and may thee.

    [Exeunt DUKE, SENATORS, OFFICERS, *& c.]*

OTHELLO: My life upon her faith! Honest Iago,
    My Desdemona must I leave to thee.
    I prithee let thy wife attend on her,   290
    And bring them after in the best advantage.°
    Come, Desdemona. I have but an hour
    Of love, of worldly matter, and direction
    To spend with thee. We must obey the time.

    *Exit [*MOOR *with* DESDEMONA*].*

RODERIGO: Iago?   295
IAGO: What say'st thou, noble heart?
RODERIGO: What will I do, think'st thou?
IAGO: Why, go to bed and sleep.
RODERIGO: I will incontinently° drown myself.
IAGO: If thou dost, I shall never love thee after. Why, thou silly gentleman? 300
RODERIGO: It is silliness to live when to live is torment; and then have
    we a prescription to die when death is our physician.
IAGO: O villainous! I have looked upon the world for four times seven
    years, and since I could distinguish betwixt a benefit and an injury, I

---

283 *delighted:* Delightful.   291 *advantage:* Opportunity.   299 *incontinently:* At once.

never found man that knew how to love himself. Ere I would say I 305
would drown myself for the love of a guinea hen, I would change my
humanity with a baboon.

RODERIGO: What should I do? I confess it is my shame to be so fond, but
it is not in my virtue° to amend it.

IAGO: Virtue? A fig! 'Tis in ourselves that we are thus, or thus. Our bodies 310
are our gardens, to the which our wills are gardeners; so that if we
will plant nettles or sow lettuce, set hyssop and weed up thyme, supply
it with one gender of herbs or distract° it with many — either to have
it sterile with idleness or manured with industry — why, the power and
corrigible° authority of this lies in our wills. If the balance of our lives 315
had not one scale of reason to poise another of sensuality, the blood
and baseness of our natures would conduct us to most prepost'rous
conclusions.° But we have reason to cool our raging motions, our
carnal sting or unbitted° lusts, whereof I take this that you call love to
be a sect or scion.° 320

RODERIGO: It cannot be.

IAGO: It is merely a lust of the blood and a permission of the will. Come,
be a man! Drown thyself? Drown cats and blind puppies! I have professed me thy friend, and I confess me knit to thy deserving with
cables of perdurable toughness. I could never better stead° thee than 325
now. Put money in thy purse. Follow thou the wars; defeat thy favor°
with an usurped° beard. I say, put money in thy purse. It cannot be
long that Desdemona should continue her love to the Moor. Put money
in thy purse. Nor he his to her. It was a violent commencement in her
and thou shalt see an answerable° sequestration — put but money in thy 330
purse. These Moors are changeable in their wills — fill thy purse with
money. The food that to him now is as luscious as locusts° shall be to
him shortly as bitter as coloquintida.° She must change for youth;
when she is sated with his body, she will find the errors of her choice.
Therefore, put money in thy purse. If thou wilt needs damn thyself, 335
do it a more delicate way than drowning. Make all the money thou
canst. If sanctimony° and a frail vow betwixt an erring° barbarian and
supersubtle Venetian be not too hard for my wits, and all the tribe of
hell, thou shalt enjoy her. Therefore, make money. A pox of drowning
thyself, it is clean out of the way. Seek thou rather to be hanged in 340
compassing° thy joy than to be drowned and go without her.

RODERIGO: Wilt thou be fast to my hopes, if I depend on the issue?

IAGO: Thou art sure of me. Go, make money. I have told thee often, and I
retell thee again and again, I hate the Moor. My cause is hearted;° thine

---

309 *virtue:* Strength (Roderigo is saying that his nature controls him). 313 *distract:* Vary.
315 *corrigible:* Corrective. 318 *conclusions:* Ends. 319 *unbitted:* i.e., uncontrolled. 320 *sect
or scion:* Off-shoot. 325 *stead:* Serve. 326 *defeat thy favor:* Disguise your face. 327 *usurped:*
Assumed. 330 *answerable:* Similar. 332 *locusts:* (A sweet fruit). 333 *coloquintida:* A purgative derived from a bitter apple. 337 *sanctimony:* Sacred bond (of marriage); *erring:* Wandering. 341 *compassing:* Encompassing, achieving. 344 *hearted:* Deepseated in the heart.

hath no less reason. Let us be conjunctive° in our revenge against him.   345
If thou canst cuckold him, thou dost thyself a pleasure, me a sport.
There are many events in the womb of time, which will be delivered.
Traverse, go, provide thy money! We will have more of this tomorrow.
Adieu.

RODERIGO: Where shall we meet i' th' morning?   350
IAGO: At my lodging.
RODERIGO: I'll be with thee betimes.
IAGO: Go to, farewell. Do you hear, Roderigo?
RODERIGO: I'll sell all my land.   *Exit.*
IAGO: Thus do I ever make my fool my purse;   355
  For I mine own gained knowledge° should profane
  If I would time expend with such snipe
  But for my sport and profit. I hate the Moor,
  And it is thought abroad that 'twixt my sheets
  H'as done my office. I know not if 't be true,   360
  But I, for mere suspicion in that kind,
  Will do, as if for surety.° He holds me well;
  The better shall my purpose work on him.
  Cassio's a proper° man. Let me see now:
  To get his place, and to plume up my will°   365
  In double knavery. How? How? Let's see.
  After some time, to abuse Othello's ears
  That he is too familiar with his wife.
  He hath a person and a smooth dispose°
  To be suspected — framed° to make women false.   370
  The Moor is of a free and open nature
  That thinks men honest that but seem to be so;
  And will as tenderly be led by th' nose
  As asses are.
  I have 't! It is engendered! Hell and night   375
  Must bring this monstrous birth to the world's light.   *(Exit.)*

ACT II

Scene I *[Cyprus.]*

Enter MONTANO *and two* GENTLEMEN *[one above].*°

MONTANO: What from the cape can you discern at sea?

---

345 *conjunctive:* Joined. 356 *gained knowledge:* i.e., practical, worldly wisdom. 362 *surety:* Certainty. 364 *proper:* Handsome. 365 *plume up my will:* (Many explanations have been offered for this crucial line, which in Q₁ reads "make up my will." The general sense is something like "to make more proud and gratify my ego".) 369 *dispose:* Manner. 370 *framed:* Designed. ACT II, SCENE I. *s.d.:* (The Folio arrangement of this scene requires that the First Gentleman stand above — on the upper stage — and act as a lookout reporting sights which cannot be seen by Montano standing below on the main stage.)

FIRST GENTLEMAN: Nothing at all, it is a high-wrought flood.
 I cannot 'twixt the heaven and the main
 Descry a sail.
MONTANO: Methinks the wind hath spoke aloud at land;   5
 A fuller blast ne'er shook our battlements.
 If it hath ruffianed so upon the sea,
 What ribs of oak, when mountains melt on them,
 Can hold the mortise? What shall we hear of this?
SECOND GENTLEMEN: A segregation° of the Turkish fleet.   10
 For do but stand upon the foaming shore,
 The chidden billow seems to pelt the clouds;
 The wind-shaked surge, with high and monstrous main,°
 Seems to cast water on the burning Bear
 And quench the guards of th' ever-fixèd pole.°   15
 I never did like molestation view
 On the enchafèd flood.
MONTANO: If that the Turkish fleet
 Be not ensheltered and embayed, they are drowned;
 It is impossible to bear it out.

 Enter a [third] GENTLEMAN.

THIRD GENTLEMAN: News, lads! Our wars are done.   20
 The desperate tempest hath so banged the Turks
 That their designment halts. A noble ship of Venice
 Hath seen a grievous wrack and sufferance°
 On most part of their fleet.
MONTANO: How? Is this true?
THIRD GENTLEMAN: The ship is here put in,   25
 A Veronesa; Michael Cassio,
 Lieutenant to the warlike Moor Othello,
 Is come on shore; the Moor himself at sea,
 And is in full commission here for Cyprus.
MONTANO: I am glad on't. 'Tis a worthy governor.   30
THIRD GENTLEMAN: But this same Cassio, though he speak of comfort
 Touching the Turkish loss, yet he looks sadly
 And prays the Moor be safe, for they were parted
 With foul and violent tempest.
MONTANO: Pray heavens he be;
 For I have served him, and the man commands   35
 Like a full soldier. Let's to the seaside, ho!
 As well to see the vessel that's come in
 As to throw out our eyes for brave Othello,

---

10 *segregation:* Separation. 13 *main:* (Both "ocean" and "strength".) 14–15 *Seems . . . pole:*
(The constellation Ursa Minor contains two stars which are the guards, or companions, of the
pole, or North Star.) 23 *sufferance:* Damage.

Even till we make the main and th' aerial blue
An indistinct regard.°
THIRD GENTLEMAN: Come, let's do so;   40
For every minute is expectancy
Of more arrivancie.°

Enter CASSIO.

CASSIO: Thanks, you the valiant of the warlike isle,
That so approve° the Moor. O, let the heavens
Give him defense against the elements,   45
For I have lost him on a dangerous sea.
MONTANO: Is he well shipped?
CASSIO: His bark is stoutly timbered, and his pilot
Of very expert and approved allowance;°
Therefore my hopes, not surfeited to death,°   50
Stand in bold cure.° *(Within:* A sail, a sail, a sail!*)*
CASSIO: What noise?
FIRST GENTLEMAN: The town is empty; on the brow o' th' sea
Stand ranks of people, and they cry, "A sail!"
CASSIO: My hopes do shape him for the governor.   *[A shot.]*   55
SECOND GENTLEMAN: They do discharge their shot of courtesy:
Our friends at least.
CASSIO: I pray you, sir, go forth
And give us truth who 'tis that is arrived.
SECOND GENTLEMAN: I shall.   *[Exit.]*
MONTANO: But, good lieutenant, is your general wived?   60
CASSIO: Most fortunately. He hath achieved a maid
That paragons° description and wild fame;°
One that excels the quirks of blazoning pens,°
And in th' essential vesture of creation°
Does tire the ingener.°

Enter [Second] GENTLEMAN.

                     How now? Who has put in?   65
SECOND GENTLEMAN: 'Tis one Iago, ancient to the general.
CASSIO: H'as had most favorable and happy speed:
Tempests themselves, high seas, and howling winds,
The guttered° rocks and congregated° sands,

39–40 *the main . . . regard:* i.e., the sea and sky become indistinguishable.   42 *arrivancie:*
Arrivals.   44 *approve:* ("Honor" or, perhaps, "are as warlike and valiant as your governor".)
49 *approved allowance:* Known and tested.   50 *not surfeited to death:* i.e., not so great as to be
in danger.   51 *Stand in bold cure:* i.e., are likely to be restored.   62 *paragons:* Exceeds; *wild
fame:* Extravagant report.   63 *quirks of blazoning pens:* Ingenuities of praising pens.   64 *essential
vesture of creation:* Essential human nature as given by the Creator.   65 *tire the ingener:* A difficult
line that probably means something like "outdo the human ability to imagine and picture."
69 *guttered:* Jagged; *congregated:* Gathered.

Traitors ensteeped° to enclog the guiltless keel,   70
As having sense° of beauty, do omit
Their mortal° natures, letting go safely by
The divine Desdemona.

MONTANO: What is she?

CASSIO: She that I spake of, our great captain's captain,
Left in the conduct of the bold Iago,   75
Whose footing° here anticipates our thoughts
A se'nnight's° speed. Great Jove, Othello guard,
And swell his sail with thine own pow'rful breath,
That he may bless this bay with his tall° ship,
Make love's quick pants in Desdemona's arms,   80
Give renewed fire to our extincted spirits.

Enter DESDEMONA, IAGO, RODERIGO, *and* EMILIA.

O, behold! The riches of the ship is come on shore!
You men of Cyprus, let her have your knees.   *[Kneeling.]*
Hail to thee, lady! and the grace of heaven,
Before, behind thee, and on every hand,   85
Enwheel thee round.

DESDEMONA: I thank you, valiant Cassio.
What tidings can you tell of my lord?

CASSIO: He is not yet arrived, nor know I aught
But that he's well and will be shortly here.

DESDEMONA: O but I fear. How lost you company?   90

CASSIO: The great contention of sea and skies
Parted our fellowship. *(Within:* A sail, a sail!*)*   *[A shot.]*
But hark. A sail!

SECOND GENTLEMAN: They give this greeting to the citadel;
This likewise is a friend.

CASSIO: See for the news.   *[Exit* GENTLEMAN.*]*   95
Good ancient, you are welcome. *[To* EMILIA*]* Welcome, mistress.
Let it not gall your patience, good Iago,
That I extend° my manners. 'Tis my breeding°
That gives me this bold show of courtesy.   *[Kisses* EMILIA.*]*

IAGO: Sir, would she give you so much of her lips   100
As of her tongue she oft bestows on me,
You would have enough.

DESDEMONA: Alas, she has no speech.

IAGO: In faith, too much.
I find it still when I have leave to sleep.°

---

70 *ensteeped:* Submerged.   71 *sense:* Awareness.   72 *mortal:* Deadly.   76 *footing:* Landing.   77 *se'n-night's:* Week's.   79 *tall:* Brave.   98 *extend:* Stretch; *breeding:* Careful training in manners (Cassio is considerably more the polished gentleman than Iago, and aware of it).   104 *still . . . sleep:* i.e., even when she allows me to sleep she continues to scold.

Marry, before your ladyship,° I grant,   105
    She puts her tongue a little in her heart
    And chides with thinking.
EMILIA: You have little cause to say so.
IAGO: Come on, come on! You are pictures° out of door,
    Bells in your parlors, wildcats in your kitchens,
    Saints in your injuries,° devils being offended,   110
    Players in your housewifery,° and housewives in your beds.
DESDEMONA: O, fie upon thee, slanderer!
IAGO: Nay, it is true, or else I am a Turk:
    You rise to play, and go to bed to work.
EMILIA: You shall not write my praise.
IAGO: No, let me not.   115
DESDEMONA: What wouldst write of me, if thou shouldst praise me?
IAGO: O gentle lady, do not put me to 't.
    For I am nothing if not critical.
DESDEMONA: Come on, assay. There's one gone to the harbor?
IAGO: Ay, madam.
DESDEMONA *[Aside]*: I am not merry; but I do beguile   120
    The thing I am by seeming otherwise. —
    Come, how wouldst thou praise me?
IAGO: I am about it; but indeed my invention
    Comes from my pate as birdlime° does from frieze° —
    It plucks out brains and all. But my Muse labors,   125
    And thus she is delivered:
    If she be fair° and wise: fairness and wit,
    The one's for use, the other useth it.
DESDEMONA: Well praised. How if she be black° and witty?
IAGO: If she be black, and thereto have a wit,   130
    She'll find a white that shall her blackness fit.
DESDEMONA: Worse and worse!
EMILIA: How if fair and foolish?
IAGO: She never yet was foolish that was fair,
    For even her folly helped her to an heir.   135
DESDEMONA: Those are old fond° paradoxes to make fools laugh i' th'
    alehouse. What miserable praise hast thou for her that's foul and
    foolish?
IAGO: There's none so foul, and foolish thereunto,
    But does foul pranks which fair and wise ones do.   140

---

105 *before your ladyship:* In your presence.   108 *pictures:* Models (of virtue).   110 *in your injuries:* When you injure others.   111 *housewifery:* This word can mean "careful, economical household management," and Iago would then be accusing women of only pretending to be good housekeepers, while in bed they are either (1) economical of their favors, or more likely (2) serious and dedicated workers.   124 *birdlime:* A sticky substance put on branches to catch birds; *frieze:* Rough cloth.   127 *fair:* Light-complexioned.   129 *black:* Brunette.   136 *fond:* Foolish.

DESDEMONA: O heavy ignorance. Thou praisest the wcrst best. But what praise couldst thou bestow on a deserving woman indeed — one that in the authority of her merit did justly put on the vouch of very malice itself?°

IAGO: She that was ever fair, and never proud;   145
    Had tongue at will, and yet was never loud;
    Never lacked gold, and yet went never gay;
    Fled from her wish, and yet said "Now I may";
    She that being angered, her revenge being nigh,
    Bade her wrong stay, and her displeasure fly;   150
    She that in wisdom never was so frail
    To change the cod's head for the salmon's tail;°
    She that could think, and nev'r disclose her mind;
    See suitors following, and not look behind:
    She was a wight° (if ever such wights were) —   155

DESDEMONA: To do what?

IAGO: To suckle fools and chronicle small beer.°

DESDEMONA: O most lame and impotent conclusion. Do not learn of him, Emilia, though he be thy husband. How say you, Cassio? Is he not a most profane and liberal° counselor?   160

CASSIO: He speaks home,° madam. You may relish him more in° the soldier than in the scholar. *[Takes DESDEMONA's hand.]*

IAGO *[Aside]*: He takes her by the palm. Ay, well said, whisper! With as little a web as this will I ensnare as great a fly as Cassio. Ay, smile upon her, do! I will gyve° thee in thine own courtship. — You say true; 165
'tis so, indeed! — If such tricks as these strip you out cf your lieutenantry, it had been better you had not kissed your three fingers so oft — which now again you are most apt to play the sir° in. Very good! Well kissed! An excellent curtsy!° 'Tis so, indeed. Yet again your fingers to your lips? Would they were clyster pipes° for your sake! *[Trumpets* 170
within.] The Moor! I know his trumpet.°

CASSIO: 'Tis truly so.

DESDEMONA: Let's meet him and receive him.

CASSIO: Lo, where he comes.

Enter OTHELLO *and* ATTENDANTS.

OTHELLO: O my fair warrior!

DESDEMONA: My dear Othello.   175

142–144 *one . . . itself:* i.e., a woman so honest and deserving that even malice would be forced to approve of her.   152 *To . . . tail:* i.e., to exchange something valuable for something useless.   155 *wight:* Person.   157 *chronicle small beer:* i.e., keep household accounts (the most trivial of occupations in Iago's opinion).   160 *liberal:* Licentious.   161 *speaks home:* Thrusts deeply with his speech; *relish him more in:* enjoy him more as.   165 *gyve:* Bind. 168 *the sir:* The fashionable gentleman.   169 *curtsy:* Courtesy, i.e., bow.   170 *clyster pipes:* Enema tubes.   171 *his trumpet:* (Great men had their own distinctive calls).

OTHELLO: It gives me wonder great as my content
　　To see you here before me. O my soul's joy!
　　If after every tempest come such calms,
　　May the winds blow till they have wakened death.
　　And let the laboring bark climb hills of seas　　　　　　　　　180
　　Olympus-high, and duck again as low
　　As hell's from heaven. If it were now to die,
　　'Twere now to be most happy; for I fear
　　My soul hath her content so absolute
　　That not another comfort like to this　　　　　　　　　　　185
　　Succeeds in unknown fate.
DESDEMONA:　　　　　　　　The heavens forbid
　　But that our loves and comforts should increase
　　Even as our days do grow.
OTHELLO:　　　　　　　　Amen to that, sweet powers!
　　I cannot speak enough of this content:
　　It stops me here [touches his heart]; it is too much of joy.　　　190
　　And this, and this, the greatest discords be　　　　　[They kiss.]
　　That e'er our hearts shall make!
IAGO [Aside]:　　　　　　　O, you are well tuned now!
　　But I'll set down the pegs° that make this music,
　　As honest as I am.
OTHELLO:　　　　　　Come, let us to the castle.
　　News, friends! Our wars are done; the Turks are drowned.　　　195
　　How does my old acquaintance of this isle?
　　Honey, you shall be well desired in Cyprus;
　　I have found great love amongst them. O my sweet,
　　I prattle out of fashion, and I dote
　　In mine own comforts. I prithee, good Iago,　　　　　　　200
　　Go to the bay and disembark my coffers.
　　Bring thou the master to the citadel;
　　He is a good one and his worthiness
　　Does challenge° much respect. Come, Desdemona,
　　Once more well met at Cyprus.　　　　　　　　　　205

　　Exit OTHELLO *and* DESDEMONA *[and all but* IAGO *and*
　　RODERIGO].

IAGO [To an Attendant]: Do thou meet me presently at the harbor. [To
　　RODERIGO] Come hither. If thou be'st valiant (as they say base men
　　being in love have then a nobility in their natures more than is native
　　to them), list me. The lieutenant tonight watches on the court of
　　guard.° First, I must tell thee this: Desdemona is directly in love with　210
　　him.

---

193 *set down the pegs:* Loosen the strings (to produce discord).　204 *challenge:* Require, exact.　210 *court of guard:* Guardhouse.

RODERIGO: With him? Why, 'tis not possible.

IAGO: Lay thy finger thus *[puts his finger to his lips],* and let thy soul be instructed. Mark me with what violence she first loved the Moor but for bragging and telling her fantastical lies. To love him still for prat- 215 ing? Let not thy discreet heart think it. Her eye must be fed. And what delight shall she have to look on the devil? When the blood is made dull with the act of sport, there should be a game° to inflame it and to give satiety a fresh appetite, loveliness in favor,° sympathy in years,° manners, and beauties; all which the Moor is defective in. Now for 220 want of these required conveniences,° her delicate tenderness will find itself abused, begin to heave the gorge,° disrelish and abhor the Moor. Very nature will instruct her in it and compel her to some second choice. Now sir, this granted—as it is a most pregnant° and unforced position—who stands so eminent in the degree of this fortune as Cas- 225 sio does? A knave very voluble; no further conscionable° than in put- ting on the mere form of civil and humane° seeming for the better compass of his salt° and most hidden loose° affection. Why, none! Why, none! A slipper° and subtle knave, a finder of occasion, that has an eye can stamp and counterfeit advantages, though true advantage 230 never present itself. A devilish knave. Besides, the knave is handsome, young, and hath all those requisites in him that folly and green minds look after. A pestilent complete knave, and the woman hath found him already.

RODERIGO: I cannot believe that in her; she's full of most blessed 235 condition.

IAGO: Blessed fig's-end! The wine she drinks is made of grapes. If she had been blessed, she would never have loved the Moor. Blessed pudding! Didst thou not see her paddle with the palm of his hand? Didst not mark that? 240

RODERIGO: Yes, that I did; but that was but courtesy.

IAGO: Lechery, by this hand! *[Extends his index finger.]* An index° and ob- scure prologue to the history of lust and foul thoughts. They met so near with their lips that their breaths embraced together. Villainous thoughts, Roderigo. When these mutualities so marshal the way, hard 245 at hand comes the master and main exercise, th' incorporate° conclu- sion: Pish! But, sir, be you ruled by me. I have brought you from Venice. Watch you tonight; for the command, I'll lay't upon you. Cassio knows you not. I'll not be far from you. Do you find some occasion to anger Cassio, either by speaking too loud, or tainting° his 250 discipline, or from what other course you please which the time shall more favorably minister.

---

218 *game:* Sport (with the added sense of "gamey," "rank"). 219 *favor:* Countenance, appear- ance; *sympathy in years:* Sameness of age. 221 *conveniences:* Advantages. 222 *heave the gorge:* Vomit. 224 *pregnant:* Likely. 226 *no further conscionable:* Having no more conscience. 227 *humane:* Polite. 228 *salt:* Lecherous; *loose:* Immoral. 229 *slipper:* Slippery. 242 *index:* Pointer. 246 *incorporate:* Carnal. 250 *tainting:* Discrediting.

RODERIGO: Well.

IAGO: Sir, he's rash and very sudden in choler,° and haply may strike at
      you. Provoke him that he may; for even out of that will I cause these   255
      of Cyprus to mutiny, whose qualification shall come into no true taste°
      again but by the displanting of Cassio. So shall you have a shorter
      journey to your desires by the means I shall then have to prefer them;
      and the impediment most profitably removed without the which there
      were no expectation of our prosperity.   260

RODERIGO: I will do this if you can bring it to any opportunity.

IAGO: I warrant thee. Meet me by and by at the citadel. I must fetch his
      necessaries ashore. Farewell.

RODERIGO: Adieu.   *Exit.*

IAGO: That Cassio loves her, I do well believe't;   265
      That she loves him, 'tis apt and of great credit.
      The Moor, howbeit that I endure him not,
      Is of a constant, loving, noble nature,
      And I dare think he'll prove to Desdemona
      A most dear° husband. Now I do love her too;   270
      Not out of absolute° lust, though peradventure°
      I stand accountant for as great a sin,
      But partly led to diet° my revenge,
      For that I do suspect the lusty Moor
      Hath leaped into my seat; the thought whereof   275
      Doth, like a poisonous mineral, gnaw my inwards;
      And nothing can or shall content my soul
      Till I am evened with him, wife for wife.
      Or failing so, yet that I put the Moor
      At least into a jealousy so strong   280
      That judgment cannot cure. Which thing to do,
      If this poor trash of Venice, whom I trace°
      For his quick hunting, stand the putting on,
      I'll have our Michael Cassio on the hip,
      Abuse him to the Moor in the right garb°   285
      (For I fear Cassio with my nightcap too),
      Make the Moor thank me, love me, and reward me
      For making him egregiously an ass
      And practicing upon° his peace and quiet,
      Even to madness. 'Tis here, but yet confused: 290
      Knavery's plain face is never seen till used.   *Exit.*

---

254 *choler:* Anger.   256 *qualification . . . taste:* i.e., appeasement will not be brought about (wine
was "qualified" by adding water).   270 *dear:* Expensive.   271 *out of absolute:* Absolutely out
of; *peradventure:* Perchance.   273 *diet:* Feed.   282 *trace:* (Most editors emend to "trash," meaning to hang weights on a dog to slow his hunting: but "trace" clearly means something like
"put on the trace" or "set on the track".)   285 *right garb:* i.e., "proper fashion."   289 *practicing
upon:* Scheming to destroy.

Scene II *[A street.]*

Enter OTHELLO'S HERALD, *with a proclamation.*

HERALD: It is Othello's pleasure, our noble and valiant general, that upon
certain tidings now arrived importing the mere perdition° of the Turkish fleet, every man put himself into triumph. Some to dance, some to
make bonfires, each man to what sport and revels his addition° leads
him. For, besides these beneficial news, it is the celebration of his   5
nuptial. So much was his pleasure should be proclaimed. All offices°
are open, and there is full liberty of feasting from this present hour of
five till the bell have told eleven. Bless the isle of Cyprus and our noble
general Othello!   *Exit.*

Scene III *[The citadel of Cyprus.]*

Enter OTHELLO, DESDEMONA, CASSIO, *and* ATTENDANTS.

OTHELLO: Good Michael, look you to the guard tonight.
　　Let's teach ourselves that honorable stop,
　　Not to outsport direction.
CASSIO: Iago hath discretion what to do;
　　But notwithstanding, with my personal eye   5
　　Will I look to't.
OTHELLO:　　　　　Iago is most honest.
　　Michael, good night. Tomorrow with your earliest
　　Let me have speech with you. *[To* DESDEMONA*]* Come, my dear
　　　love,
　　The purchase made, the fruits are to ensue.
　　That profit's yet to come 'tween me and you.   10
　　Good night.
　　　　　　*Exit [*OTHELLO *with* DESDEMONA *and* ATTENDANTS*].*

Enter IAGO.

CASSIO: Welcome, Iago. We must to the watch.
IAGO: Not this hour, lieutenant; 'tis not yet ten o' th' clock. Our general
cast° us thus early for the love of his Desdemona; who let us not
therefore blame. He hath not yet made wanton the night with her, and   15
she is sport for Jove.
CASSIO: She's a most exquisite lady.
IAGO: And, I'll warrant her, full of game.
CASSIO: Indeed, she's a most fresh and delicate creature.
IAGO: What an eye she has! Methinks it sounds a parley to provocation.   20
CASSIO: An inviting eye; and yet methinks right modest.
IAGO: And when she speaks, is it not an alarum° to love?

SCENE II. 2 *mere perdition:* Absolute destruction.　4 *addition:* Rank.　6 *offices:* Kitchens and
storerooms of food.　SCENE III. 14 *cast:* Dismissed.　22 *alarum:* The call to action, "general
quarters."

CASSIO: She is indeed perfection.

IAGO: Well, happiness to their sheets! Come, lieutenant, I have a stoup° of
wine, and here without are a brace of Cyprus gallants that would fain   25
have a measure to the health of black Othello.

CASSIO: Not tonight, good Iago. I have very poor and unhappy brains for
drinking; I could well wish courtesy would invent some other custom
of entertainment.

IAGO: O, they are our friends. But one cup! I'll drink for you.   30

CASSIO: I have drunk but one tonight, and that was craftily qualified° too;
and behold what innovation it makes here. I am unfortunate in the
infirmity and dare not task my weakness with any more.

IAGO: What, man! 'Tis a night of revels, the gallants desire it.

CASSIO: Where are they?   35

IAGO: Here, at the door. I pray you call them in.

CASSIO: I'll do't, but it dislikes me.   *Exit.*

IAGO: If I can fasten but one cup upon him
With that which he hath drunk tonight already,
He'll be as full of quarrel and offense   40
As my young mistress' dog. Now, my sick fool Roderigo,
Whom love hath turned almost the wrong side out,
To Desdemona hath tonight caroused
Potations pottle-deep;° and he's to watch.
Three else° of Cyprus, noblé swelling spirits,   45
That hold their honors in a wary distance,°
The very elements of this warlike isle,
Have I tonight flustered with flowing cups,
And they watch too. Now, 'mongst this flock of drunkards
Am I to put our Cassio in some action   50
That may offend the isle. But here they come.

Enter CASSIO, MONTANO, *and* GENTLEMEN.

If consequence do but approve my dream,
My boats sails freely, both with wind and stream.

CASSIO: 'Fore God, they have given me a rouse° already.

MONTANO: Good faith, a little one; not past a pint, as I am a soldier.   55

IAGO: Some wine, ho!
[Sings] And let me the canakin clink, clink;
And let me the canakin clink.
A soldier's a man;
O man's life's but a span.   60
Why then, let a soldier drink.
Some wine, boys!

CASSIO: 'Fore God, an excellent song!

---

24 *stoup:* Two-quart tankard. 31 *qualified:* Diluted. 44 *pottle-deep:* To the bottom of
the cup. 45 *else:* Others. 46 *hold . . . distance:* Are scrupulous in maintaining their honor.
54 *rouse:* Drink.

IAGO: I learned it in England, where indeed they are most potent in pot-
   ting. Your Dane, your German, and your swag-bellied° Hollander —   65
   Drink, ho! — are nothing to your English.

CASSIO: Is your Englishman so exquisite° in his drinking?

IAGO: Why, he drinks you with facility your Dane dead drunk; he sweats
   not to overthrow your Almain; he gives your Hollander a vomit ere
   the next pottle can be filled.   70

CASSIO: To the health of our general!

MONTANO: I am for it, lieutenant, and I'll do you justice.

IAGO: O sweet England!

   [Sings] King Stephen was and a worthy peer;
         His breeches cost him but a crown;   75
         He held them sixpence all too dear,
         With that he called the tailor lown.°
         He was a wight of high renown,
         And thou art but of low degree:
         'Tis pride that pulls the country down;   80
         And take thine auld cloak about thee.
   Some wine, ho!

CASSIO: 'Fore God, this is a more exquisite song than the other.

IAGO: Will you hear't again?

CASSIO: No, for I hold him to be unworthy of his place that does those   85
   things. Well, God's above all; and there be souls must be saved, and
   there be souls must not be saved.

IAGO: It's true, good lieutenant.

CASSIO: For mine own part — no offense to the general, nor any man of
   quality — I hope to be saved.   90

IAGO: And so do I too, lieutenant.

CASSIO: Ay, but, by your leave, not before me. The lieutenant is to be
   saved before the ancient. Let's have no more of this; let's to our affairs. — God forgive us our sins! — Gentlemen, let's look to our business. Do not think, gentlemen, I am drunk. This is my ancient; this is   95
   my right hand, and this is my left. I am not drunk now. I can stand
   well enough, and I speak well enough.

GENTLEMEN: Excellent well!

CASSIO: Why, very well then. You must not think then that I am drunk.

Exit.

MONTANO: To th' platform, masters. Come, let's set the watch.   100

IAGO: You see this fellow that is gone before.
   He's a soldier fit to stand by Caesar
   And give direction; and do but see his vice.
   'Tis to his virtue a just equinox,°
   The one as long as th' other. 'Tis pity of him.   105

65 *swag-bellied:* Pendulous-bellied.   67 *exquisite:* Superb.   77 *lown:* Lout.   104 *just equinox:*
Exact balance (of dark and light).

I fear the trust Othello puts him in,
On some odd time of his infirmity,
Will shake this island.
MONTANO: But is he often thus?
IAGO: 'Tis evermore his prologue to his sleep:
    He'll watch the horologe a double set°   110
    If drink rock not his cradle.
MONTANO: It were well
    The general were put in mind of it.
    Perhaps he sees it not, or his good nature
    Prizes the virtue that appears in Cassio
    And looks not on his evils. Is not this true?   115

    Enter RODERIGO.

IAGO *(Aside)*: How now, Roderigo?
    I pray you after the lieutenant, go!   *[Exit* RODERIGO.*]*
MONTANO: And 'tis great pity that the noble Moor
    Should hazard such a place as his own second
    With one of an ingraft° infirmity.   120
    It were an honest action to say so
    To the Moor.
IAGO: Not I, for this fair island!
    I do love Cassio well and would do much
    To cure him of this evil.   *[Help! Help! Within.]*
    But hark! What noise?   125

    Enter CASSIO, *pursuing* RODERIGO.

CASSIO: Zounds, you rogue! You rascal!
MONTANO: What's the matter, lieutenant?
CASSIO: A knave teach me my duty? I'll beat the knave into a twiggen°
    bottle.
RODERIGO: Beat me?   130
CASSIO: Dost thou prate, rogue?   *[Strikes him.]*
MONTANO: Nay, good lieutenant! I pray you, sir, hold your hand.

    [Stays him.]

CASSIO: Let me go, sir, or I'll knock you o'er the mazzard.°
MONTANO: Come, come, you're drunk!
CASSIO: Drunk?   *[They fight.]* 135
IAGO *(Aside to* RODERIGO): Away, I say! Go out and cry a mutiny!
                                                [Exit RODERIGO.*]*
    Nay, good lieutenant. God's will, gentlemen!
    Help, ho! Lieutenant. Sir. Montano.
    Help, masters! Here's a goodly watch indeed!   *[A bell rung.]*

110 *watch . . . set:* Stay awake twice around the clock.   120 *ingraft:* Ingrained.   128 *twiggen:*
Wicker-covered.   133 *mazzard:* Head.

Who's that which rings the bell? Diablo, ho!   140
The two will rise. God's will, lieutenant,
You'll be ashamed forever.

Enter OTHELLO *and* ATTENDANTS.

OTHELLO: What is the matter here?
MONTANO: Zounds, I bleed still. I am hurt to the death.
    He dies.   *[He and* CASSIO *fight again.]*
OTHELLO: Hold for your lives!   145
IAGO: Hold, ho! Lieutenant. Sir. Montano. Gentlemen!
    Have you forgot all place of sense and duty?
    Hold! The general speaks to you. Hold, for shame!
OTHELLO: Why, how now, ho? From whence ariseth this?
    Are we turned Turks, and to ourselves do that   150
    Which heaven hath forbid the Ottomites?°
    For Christian shame put by this barbarous brawl!
    He that stirs next to carve for his own rage
    Holds his soul light;° he dies upon his motion.
    Silence that dreadful bell! It frights the isle   155
    From her propriety.° What is the matter, masters?
    Honest Iago, that looks dead with grieving,
    Speak. Who began this? On thy love, I charge thee.
IAGO: I do not know. Friends all, but now, even now,
    In quarter° and in terms like bride and groom   160
    Devesting them for bed; and then, but now —
    As if some planet had unwitted men —
    Swords out, and tilting one at other's breasts
    In opposition bloody. I cannot speak
    Any beginning to this peevish odds,°   165
    And would in action glorious I had lost
    Those legs that brought me to a part of it!
OTHELLO: How comes it, Michael, you are thus forgot?
CASSIO: I pray you pardon me; I cannot speak.
OTHELLO: Worthy Montano, you were wont to be civil;   170
    Thy gravity and stillness of your youth
    The world hath noted, and your name is great
    In mouths of wisest censure.° What's the matter
    That you unlace° your reputation thus
    And spend your rich opinion° for the name   175
    Of a night-brawler? Give me answer to it.
MONTANO: Worthy Othello, I am hurt to danger.
    Your officer, Iago, can inform you.

---

151 *heaven . . . Ottomites:* i.e., by sending the storm which dispersed the Turks.   154 *Holds his soul light:* Values his soul lightly.   156 *propriety:* Proper order.   160 *In quarter:* On duty.   165 *odds:* Quarrel.   173 *censure:* Judgment.   174 *unlace:* Undo (the term refers specifically to the dressing of a wild boar killed in the hunt).   175 *opinion:* Reputation.

While I spare speech, which something now offends° me,
Of all that I do know; nor know I aught   180
By me that's said or done amiss this night,
Unless self-charity be sometimes a vice,
And to defend ourselves it be a sin
When violence assails us.

OTHELLO: Now, by heaven,
My blood begins my safer guides to rule,   185
And passion, having my best judgment collied,°
Assays to lead the way. If I once stir
Or do but lift this arm, the best of you
Shall sink in my rebuke. Give me to know
How this foul rout began, who set it on;   190
And he that is approved in this offense,
Though he had twinned with me, both at a birth,
Shall lose me. What? In a town of war
Yet wild, the people's hearts brimful of fear,
To manage° private and domestic quarrel?   195
In night, and on the court and guard of safety?
'Tis monstrous. Iago, who began't?

MONTANO: If partially affined, or leagued in office,°
Thou dost deliver more or less than truth,
Thou art no soldier.

IAGO: Touch me not so near.   200
I had rather have this tongue cut from my mouth
Than it should do offense to Michael Cassio.
Yet I persuade myself to speak the truth
Shall nothing wrong him. This it is, general.
Montano and myself being in speech,   205
There comes a fellow crying out for help,
And Cassio following him with determined sword
To execute upon him. Sir, this gentleman
Steps in to Cassio and entreats his pause.
Myself the crying fellow did pursue,   210
Lest by his clamor—as it so fell out—
The town might fall in fright. He, swift of foot,
Outran my purpose; and I returned then rather
For that I heard the clink and fall of swords,
And Cassio high in oath; which till tonight   215
I ne'er might say before. When I came back—
For this was brief—I found them close together
At blow and thrust, even as again they were

179 *offends:* Harms, hurts.   186 *collied:* Darkened.   195 *manage:* Conduct.   198 *If . . . office:*
If you are partial because you are related ("affined") or the brother officer (of Cassio).

When you yourself did part them.
More of this matter cannot I report;   220
But men are men; the best sometimes forget.
Though Cassio did some little wrong to him,
As men in rage strike those that wish them best,
Yet surely Cassio I believe received
From him that fled some strange indignity,   225
Which patience could not pass.°

OTHELLO: I know, Iago,
Thy honesty and love doth mince° this matter,
Making it light to Cassio. Cassio, I love thee;
But never more be officer of mine.

Enter DESDEMONA, *attended.*

Look if my gentle love be not raised up.   230
I'll make thee an example.

DESDEMONA: What is the matter, dear?

OTHELLO: All's well, sweeting; come away to bed.
    (To MONTANO) Sir, for your hurts, myself will be your surgeon.
Lead him off.   [MONTANO *led off.*]
Iago, look with care about the town   235
And silence those whom this vile brawl distracted.
Come, Desdemona: 'tis the soldiers' life
To have their balmy slumbers waked with strife.

Exit [with all but IAGO *and* CASSIO].

IAGO: What, are you hurt, lieutenant?

CASSIO: Ay, past all surgery.   240

IAGO: Marry, God forbid!

CASSIO: Reputation, reputation, reputation! O, I have lost my reputation!
    I have lost the immortal part of myself, and what remains is bestial.
    My reputation, Iago, my reputation.

IAGO: As I am an honest man, I had thought you had received some bodily   245
    wound. There is more sense° in that than in reputation. Reputation is
    an idle and most false imposition,° oft got without merit and lost
    without deserving. You have lost no reputation at all unless you repute
    yourself such a loser. What, man, there are more ways to recover the
    general again. You are but now cast in his mood°—a punishment more   250
    in policy° than in malice—even so as one would beat his offenseless
    dog to affright an imperious lion. Sue to him again, and he's yours.

CASSIO: I will rather sue to be despised than to deceive so good a com-
    mander with so slight, so drunken, and so indiscreet an officer. Drunk!

---

226 *pass:* Allow to pass.   227 *mince:* Cut up (i.e., tell only part of).   246 *sense:* Physical
feeling.   247 *imposition:* External thing.   250 *cast in his mood:* Dismissed because of his anger.   251 *in policy:* Politically necessary.

And speak parrot!° And squabble! Swagger! Swear! and discourse fus- 255
tian° with one's own shadow! O thou invisible spirit of wine, if thou
hast no name to be known by, let us call thee devil!

IAGO: What was he that you followed with your sword?
What had he done to you?

CASSIO: I know not. 260

IAGO: Is't possible?

CASSIO: I remember a mass of things, but nothing distinctly: a quarrel,
but nothing wherefore. O God, that men should put an enemy in their
mouths to steal away their brains! that we should with joy, pleasance,
revel, and applause transform ourselves into beasts! 265

IAGO: Why, but you are now well enough. How came you thus recovered?

CASSIO: It hath pleased the devil drunkenness to give place to the devil
wrath. One unperfectness shows me another, to make me frankly despise myself.

IAGO: Come, you are too severe a moraler. As the time, the place, and the 270
condition of this country stands, I could heartily wish this had not
befall'n; but since it is as it is, mend it for your own good.

CASSIO: I will ask him for my place again: he shall tell me I am a drunkard. Had I as many mouths as Hydra, such an answer would stop
them all. To be now a sensible man, by and by a fool, and presently a 275
beast! O strange! Every inordinate cup is unblest, and the ingredient is a
devil.

IAGO: Come, come, good wine is a good familiar creature if it be well
used. Exclaim no more against it. And, good lieutenant, I think you
think I love you. 280

CASSIO: I have well approved it, sir. I drunk?

IAGO: You or any man living may be drunk at a time, man. I tell you what
you shall do. Our general's wife is now the general. I may say so in
this respect, for all he hath devoted and given up himself to the con-
templation, mark, and devotement of her parts° and graces. Confess 285
yourself freely to her; importune her help to put you in your place
again. She is of so free, so kind, so apt, so blessed a disposition she
holds it a vice in her goodness not to do more than she is requested.
This broken joint between you and her husband entreat her to splinter;° and my fortunes against any lay° worth naming, this crack of 290
your love shall grow stronger than it was before.

CASSIO: You advise me well.

IAGO: I protest, in the sincerity of love and honest kindness.

CASSIO: I think it freely; and betimes in the morning I will beseech the
virtuous Desdemona to undertake for me. I am desperate of my for- 295
tunes if they check° me.

---

255 *speak parrot:* Gabble without sense.   256 *discourse fustian:* Speak non-sense ("fustian" was a
coarse cloth used for stuffing).   285 *devotement of her parts:* Devotion to her qualities.   290
splinter: Splint; *lay:* Wager.   296 *check:* Repulse.

IAGO: You are in the right. Good night, lieutenant; I must to the watch.
CASSIO: Good night, honest Iago.   *Exit* CASSIO.
IAGO: And what's he then that says I play the villain,
     When this advice is free° I give, and honest,   300
     Probal to° thinking, and indeed the course
     To win the Moor again? For 'tis most easy
     Th' inclining° Desdemona to subdue
     In any honest suit; she's framed as fruitful°
     As the free elements.° And then for her   305
     To win the Moor — were't to renounce his baptism,
     All seals and symbols of redeemèd sin —
     His soul is so enfettered to her love
     That she may make, unmake, do what she list,
     Even as her appetite° shall play the god   310
     With his weak function.° How am I then a villain
     To counsel Cassio to this parallel course,
     Directly to his good? Divinity of hell!
     When devils will the blackest sins put on,°
     They do suggest at first with heavenly shows,°   315
     As I do now. For whiles this honest fool
     Plies Desdemona to repair his fortune,
     And she for him pleads strongly to the Moor,
     I'll pour this pestilence into his ear:
     That she repeals him° for her body's lust;   320
     And by how much she strives to do him good,
     She shall undo her credit with the Moor.
     So will I turn her virtue into pitch,
     And out of her own goodness make the net
     That shall enmesh them all. How now, Roderigo?   325

    Enter RODERIGO.

RODERIGO: I do not follow here in the chase, not like a hound that hunts,
    but one that fills up the cry.° My money is almost spent; I have been
    tonight exceedingly well cudgeled; and I think the issue will be, I shall
    have so much experience for my pains; and so, with no money at all,
    and a little more wit, return again to Venice.   330
IAGO: How poor are they that have not patience!
     What wound did ever heal but by degrees?
     Thou know'st we work by wit, and not by witchcraft;
     And wit depends on dilatory time.

---

300 *free:* Generous and open.   301 *Probal to:* Provable by.   303 *inclining:* Inclined (to be helpful).   304 *framed as fruitful:* Made as generous.   305 *elements:* i.e., basic nature.   310 *appetite:*
Liking.   311 *function:* Thought.   314 *put on:* Advance, further.   315 *shows:* Appearances.   320 *repeals him:* Asks for (Cassio's reinstatement).   327 *fills up the cry:* Makes up one
of the hunting pack, adding to the noise but not actually tracking.

Does't not go well? Cassio hath beaten thee,   335
And thou by that small hurt hath cashiered Cassio.
Though other things grow fair against the sun,
Yet fruits that blossom first will first be ripe.
Content thyself awhile. By the mass, 'tis morning!
Pleasure and action make the hours seem short.   340
Retire thee, go where thou art billeted.
Away, I say! Thou shalt know more hereafter.
Nay, get thee gone!   *Exit* RODERIGO.
              Two things are to be done:
My wife must move° for Cassio to her mistress;
I'll set her on;   345
Myself awhile° to draw the Moor apart
And bring him jump° when he may Cassio find
Soliciting his wife. Ay, that's the way!
Dull not device by coldness and delay.   *Exit.*

ACT III

Scene I *[A street.]*

   Enter CASSIO *[and]* MUSICIANS.

CASSIO: Masters, play here. I will content your pains.°
   Something that's brief; and bid "Good morrow, general." *[They play.]*

   [Enter CLOWN.°*]*

CLOWN: Why, masters, have your instruments been in Naples° that they
   speak i' th' nose thus?
MUSICIAN: How, sir, how?   5
CLOWN: Are these, I pray you, wind instruments?
MUSICIAN: Ay, marry, are they, sir.
CLOWN: O, thereby hangs a tale.
MUSICIAN: Whereby hangs a tale, sir?
CLOWN: Marry, sir, by many a wind instrument that I know. But, mas-   10
   ters, here's money for you; and the general so likes your music that he
   desires you, for love's sake, to make no more noise with it.
MUSICIAN: Well, sir, we will not.
CLOWN: If you have any music that may not be heard, to't again. But, as
   they say, to hear music the general does not greatly care.   15
MUSICIAN: We have none such, sir.

344 *move:* Petition. 346 *awhile:* At the same time. 347 *jump:* At the precise moment
and place. ACT III, SCENE I. 1 *content your pains:* Reward your efforts. *s.d. Clown:* Fool.
3 *Naples:* This may refer either to the Neopolitan nasal tone, or to syphilis — rife in Naples —
which breaks down the nose.

CLOWN: Then put up your pipes in your bag, for I'll away. Go, vanish
    into air, away!   *Exit* MUSICIANS.

CASSIO: Does thou hear me, mine honest friend?

CLOWN: No. I hear not your honest friend. I hear you.   20

CASSIO: Prithee keep up thy quillets.° There's a poor piece of gold for
    thee. If the gentlewoman that attends the general's wife be stirring, tell
    her there's one Cassio entreats her a little favor of speech. Wilt thou
    do this?

CLOWN: She is stirring, sir. If she will stir hither, I shall seem to notify   25
    unto her.°   *Exit* CLOWN.

CASSIO: In happy time, Iago.

IAGO: You have not been abed then?

CASSIO: Why no, the day had broke before we parted.
    I have made bold, Iago, to send in to your wife;
    My suit to her is that she will to virtuous Desdemona   30
    Procure me some access.

IAGO: I'll send her to you presently,
    And I'll devise a mean to draw the Moor
    Out of the way, that your converse and business
    May be more free.

CASSIO: I humbly thank you for't.   *Exit* [IAGO].
                            I never knew   35
    A Florentine° more kind and honest.

    Enter EMILIA.

EMILIA: Good morrow, good lieutenant. I am sorry
    For your displeasure;° but all will sure be well.
    The general and his wife are talking of it,
    And she speaks for you stoutly. The Moor replies   40
    That he you hurt is of great fame in Cyprus
    And great affinity,° and that in wholesome wisdom
    He might not but refuse you. But he protests he loves you.
    And needs no other suitor but his likings
    To bring you in again.

CASSIO: Yet I beseech you,   45
    If you think fit, or that it may be done,
    Give me advantage of some brief discourse
    With Desdemona alone.

EMILIA: Pray you come in.
    I will bestow you where you shall have time
    To speak your bosom° freely.   50

---

21 *quillets:* Puns.   25–26 *seem . . . her:* (The Clown is mocking Cassio's overly elegant manner
of speaking).   36 *Florentine:* i.e., Iago is as kind as if he were from Cassio's home town,
Florence.   38 *displeasure:* Discomforting.   42 *affinity:* Family.   50 *bosom:* Inmost thoughts.

CASSIO: I am much bound to you.   *[Exeunt.]*

Scene II *[The citadel.]*

   Enter OTHELLO, IAGO, *and* GENTLEMEN.

OTHELLO: These letters give, Iago, to the pilot
   And by him do my duties to the Senate.
   That done, I will be walking on the works;
   Repair° there to me.
IAGO: Well, my good lord, I'll do't.
OTHELLO: This fortification, gentlemen, shall we see't?   5
GENTLEMEN: We'll wait upon your lordship.   *Exeunt.*

Scene III *[The citadel.]*

   Enter DESDEMONA, CASSIO, *and* EMILIA.

DESDEMONA: Be thou assured, good Cassio, I will do
   All my abilities in thy behalf.
EMILIA: Good madam, do. I warrant it grieves my husband
   As if the cause were his.
DESDEMONA: O, that's an honest fellow. Do not doubt, Cassio,   5
   But I will have my lord and you again
   As friendly as you were.
CASSIO: Bounteous madam,
   Whatever shall become of Michael Cassio,
   He's never anything but your true servant.
DESDEMONA: I know't; I thank you. You do love my lord.   10
   You have known him long, and be you well assured
   He shall in strangeness stand no farther off
   Than in a politic distance.°
CASSIO: Ay, but, lady,
   That policy may either last so long,
   Or feed upon such nice° and waterish diet,   15
   Or breed itself so out of circumstances,°
   That, I being absent, and my place supplied,°
   My general will forget my love and service.
DESDEMONA: Do not doubt° that; before Emilia here
   I give thee warrant of thy place. Assure thee,   20
   If I do vow a friendship, I'll perform it
   To the last article. My lord shall never rest;
   I'll watch him tame° and talk him out of patience;

SCENE II. 4 *Repair:* Go.   Scene III. 12–13 *He . . . distance:* i.e., he shall act no more distant
to you than is necessary for political reasons.   15 *nice:* Trivial.   16 *Or . . . circumstances:* i.e.,
or grow so on the basis of accidental happenings and political needs.   17 *supplied:* Filled.
19 *doubt:* Imagine.   23 *watch him tame:* (Animals were tamed by being kept awake.)

His bed shall seem a school, his board a shrift;°
I'll intermingle everything he does   25
With Cassio's suit. Therefore be merry, Cassio,
For thy solicitor shall rather die
Than give thy cause away.

Enter OTHELLO *and* IAGO *[at a distance].*

EMILIA: Madam, here comes my lord.
CASSIO: Madam, I'll take my leave.   30
DESDEMONA: Why, stay, and hear me speak.
CASSIO: Madam, not now. I am very ill at ease,
    Unfit for mine own purposes.
DESDEMONA: Well, do your discretion.   *Exit* CASSIO.
IAGO: Ha! I like not that.
OTHELLO: What dost thou say?   35
IAGO: Nothing, my lord; or if—I know not what.
OTHELLO: Was not that Cassio parted from my wife?
IAGO: Cassio, my lord? No, sure, I cannot think it
    That he would steal away so guilty-like,
    Seeing you coming.
OTHELLO: I do believe 'twas he.   40
DESDEMONA *(Coming to them)*: How now, my lord?
    I have been talking with a suitor here,
    A man that languishes in your displeasure.
OTHELLO: Who is't you mean?
DESDEMONA: Why, your lieutenant, Cassio. Good my lord,   45
    If I have any grace or power to move you,
    His present° reconciliation take.
    For if he be not one that truly loves you,
    That errs in ignorance, and not in cunning,
    I have no judgment in an honest face.   50
    I prithee call him back.
OTHELLO: Went he hence now?
DESDEMONA: I' sooth so humbled
    That he hath left part of his grief with me
    To suffer with him. Good love, call him back.
OTHELLO: Not now, sweet Desdemon; some other time.   55
DESDEMONA: But shall't be shortly?
OTHELLO: The sooner, sweet, for you.
DESDEMONA: Shall't be tonight at supper?
OTHELLO: No, not tonight.
DESDEMONA: Tomorrow dinner then?

---

24 *board a shrift:* Table (seem) a confessional.   47 *present:* Immediate.

OTHELLO: I shall not dine at home;
    I meet the captains at the citadel.
DESDEMONA: Why then, tomorrow night, on Tuesday morn,   60
    On Tuesday noon, or night, on Wednesday morn.
    I prithee name the time, but let it not
    Exceed three days. In faith, he's penitent;
    And yet his trespass, in our common reason
    (Save that, they say, the wars must make example   65
    Out of her best), is not almost a fault
    T' incur a private check.° When shall he come?
    Tell me, Othello. I wonder in my soul
    What you would ask me that I should deny
    Or stand so mamm'ring° on. What? Michael Cassio,   70
    That came awooing with you, and so many a time,
    When I have spoke of you dispraisingly,
    Hath ta'en your part — to have so much to do
    To bring him in? By'r Lady, I could do much —
OTHELLO: Prithee no more. Let him come when he will!   75
    I will deny thee nothing.
DESDEMONA: Why, this is not a boon;
    'Tis as I should entreat you wear your gloves,
    Or feed on nourishing dishes, or keep you warm,
    Or sue to you to do a peculiar profit°
    To your own person. Nay, when I have a suit   80
    Wherein I mean to touch your love indeed,
    It shall be full of poise° and difficult weight,
    And fearful to be granted.
OTHELLO: I will deny thee nothing!
    Whereon I do beseech thee grant me this,
    To leave me but a little to myself.   85
DESDEMONA: Shall I deny you? No. Farewell, my lord.
OTHELLO: Farewell, my Desdemona: I'll come to thee straight.°
DESDEMONA: Emilia, come. Be as your fancies teach you;
    Whate'er you be, I am obedient.   *Exit [with* EMILIA*].*
OTHELLO: Excellent wretch! Perdition catch my soul   90
    But I do love thee! And when I love thee not,
    Chaos is come again.
IAGO: My noble lord —
OTHELLO: What dost thou say, Iago?
IAGO: Did Michael Cassio, when you wooed my lady,
    Know of your love?   95

66–67 *is . . . check:* Is almost not serious enough for a private rebuke (let alone a public
disgrace).   70 *mamm'ring:* Hesitating.   79 *peculiar profit:* Particularly personal good.   82 *poise:*
Weight.   87 *straight:* At once.

OTHELLO: He did, from first to last. Why dost thou ask?

IAGO: But for a satisfaction of my thought,
No further harm.

OTHELLO: Why of thy thought, Iago?

IAGO: I did not think he had been acquainted with her.

OTHELLO: O, yes, and went between us° very oft.   100

IAGO: Indeed?

OTHELLO: Indeed? Ay, indeed! Discern'st thou aught in that?
Is he not honest?

IAGO: Honest, my lord?

OTHELLO: Honest? Ay, honest.

IAGO: My lord, for aught I know.

OTHELLO: What dost thou think?

IAGO: Think, my lord?

OTHELLO: Think, my lord?   105
By heaven, thou echoest me,
As if there were some monster in thy thought
Too hideous to be shown. Thou dost mean something.
I heard thee say even now, thou lik'st not that,
When Cassio left my wife. What didst not like?   110
And when I told thee he was of my counsel°
Of my whole course of wooing, thou cried'st "Indeed?"
And didst contract and purse thy brow together,
As if thou then hadst shut up in thy brain
Some horrible conceit.° If thou dost love me,   115
Show me thy thought.

IAGO: My lord, you know I love you.

OTHELLO: I think thou dost;
And, for I know thou'rt full of love and honesty
And weigh'st thy words before thou giv'st them breath,
Therefore these stops° of thine fright me the more;   120
For such things in a false disloyal knave
Are tricks of custom;° but in a man that's just
They're close dilations,° working from the heart
That passion cannot rule.

IAGO: For Michael Cassio,
I dare be sworn, I think that he is honest.   125

OTHELLO: I think so too.

IAGO: Men should be what they seem;
Or those that be not, would they might seem none!

OTHELLO: Certain, men should be what they seem.

---

100 *between us:* i.e., as messenger.   111 *of my counsel:* In my confidence.   115 *conceit:* Thought.   120 *stops:* Interruptions.   122 *of custom:* Customary.   123 *close dilations:* Expressions of hidden thoughts.

IAGO: Why then, I think Cassio's an honest man.

OTHELLO: Nay, yet there's more in this?   130
    I prithee speak to me as to thy thinkings,
    As thou dost ruminate, and give thy worst of thoughts
    The worst of words.

IAGO: Good my lord, pardon me:
    Though I am bound to every act of duty,
    I am not bound to that all slaves are free to.   135
    Utter my thoughts? Why, say they are vile and false,
    As where's that palace whereinto foul things
    Sometimes intrude not? Who has that breast so pure
    But some uncleanly apprehensions
    Keep leets and law days,° and in sessions sit   140
    With meditations lawful?

OTHELLO: Thou dost conspire against thy friend, Iago,
    If thou but think'st him wronged, and mak'st his ear
    A stranger to thy thoughts.

IAGO: I do beseech you —
    Though I perchance am vicious in my guess   145
    (As I confess it is my nature's plague
    To spy into abuses, and of my jealousy
    Shape faults that are not), that your wisdom
    From one that so imperfectly conceits
    Would take no notice, nor build yourself a trouble   150
    Out of his scattering and unsure observance.
    It were not for your quiet nor your good,
    Nor for my manhood, honesty, and wisdom,
    To let you know my thoughts.

OTHELLO: What dost thou mean?

IAGO: Good name in man and woman, dear my lord,   155
    Is the immediate jewel of their souls.
    Who steals my purse steals trash; 'tis something, nothing;
    'Twas mine, 'tis his, and has been slave to thousands;
    But he that filches from me my good name
    Robs me of that which not enriches him   160
    And makes me poor indeed.

OTHELLO: By heaven, I'll know thy thoughts!

IAGO: You cannot, if my heart were in your hand;
    Nor shall not whilst 'tis in my custody.

OTHELLO: Ha!

IAGO: O, beware, my lord, of jealousy!   165
    It is the green-eyed monster, which doth mock

---

140 *leets and law days:* Meetings of local courts.

The meat it feeds on. That cuckold lives in bliss
Who, certain of his fate, loves not his wronger;
But O, what damnèd minutes tells° he o'er
Who dotes, yet doubts — suspects, yet fondly° loves!   170
OTHELLO: O misery.
IAGO: Poor and content is rich, and rich enough;
      But riches fineless° is as poor as winter
      To him that ever fears he shall be poor.
      Good God the souls of all my tribe defend   175
      From jealousy!
OTHELLO: Why? Why is this?
      Think'st thou I'd make a life of jealousy,
      To follow still° the changes of the moon
      With fresh suspicions? No! To be once in doubt
      Is to be resolved. Exchange me for a goat   180
      When I shall turn the business of my soul
      To such exsufflicate and blown° surmises,
      Matching thy inference. 'Tis not to make me jealous
      To say my wife is fair, feeds well, loves company,
      Is free of speech, sings, plays, and dances;   185
      Where virtue is, these are more virtuous.
      Nor from mine own weak merits will I draw
      The smallest fear or doubt of her revolt,
      For she had eyes, and chose me. No, Iago;
      I'll see before I doubt; when I doubt, prove;   190
      And on the proof there is no more but this:
      Away at once with love or jealousy!
IAGO: I am glad of this; for now I shall have reason
      To show the love and duty that I bear you
      With franker spirit. Therefore, as I am bound,   195
      Receive it from me. I speak not yet of proof.
      Look to your wife; observe her well with Cassio;
      Wear your eyes thus: not jealous nor secure.
      I would not have your free and noble nature
      Out of self-bounty° be abused. Look to't.   200
      I know our country disposition well:
      In Venice they do let heaven see the pranks
      They dare not show their husbands; their best conscience
      Is not to leave't undone, but kept unknown.°
OTHELLO: Dost thou say so?   205

---

169 *tells:* Counts.   170 *fondly:* Foolishly.   173 *fineless:* Infinite.   178 *To follow still:* To change always (as the phases of the moon).   182 *exsufflicate and blown:* Inflated and flyblown. 200 *self-bounty:* Innate kindness (which attributes his own motives to others).   203–204 *their . . . unknown:* i.e., their morality does not forbid adultery, but it does forbid being found out.

IAGO: She did deceive her father, marrying you;
    And when she seemed to shake and fear your looks,
    She loved them most.
OTHELLO: And so she did.
IAGO: Why, go to then!
    She that so young could give out such a seeming
    To seel° her father's eyes up close as oak° —   210
    He thought 'twas witchcraft. But I am much to blame.
    I humbly do beseech you of your pardon
    For too much loving you.
OTHELLO: I am bound to thee forever.
IAGO: I see this hath a little dashed your spirits.
OTHELLO: Not a jot, not a jot.
IAGO: Trust me, I fear it has.   215
    I hope you will consider what is spoke
    Comes from my love. But I do see y' are moved.
    I am to pray you not to strain° my speech
    To grosser issues nor to larger reach°
    Than to suspicion.   220
OTHELLO: I will not.
IAGO: Should you do so, my lord,
    My speech should fall into such vile success
    Which my thoughts aimed not. Cassio's my worthy friend —
    My lord, I see y' are moved.
OTHELLO: No, not much moved.
    I do not think but Desdemona's honest.   225
IAGO: Long live she so. And long live you to think so.
OTHELLO: And yet, how nature erring from itself —
IAGO: Ay, there's the point, as (to be bold with you)
    Not to affect many proposèd matches
    Of her own clime, complexion, and degree,°   230
    Whereto we see in all things nature tends° —
    Foh! one may smell in such a will most rank,
    Foul disproportions, thoughts unnatural.
    But, pardon me, I do not in position°
    Distinctly° speak of her; though I may fear   235
    Her will, recoiling to her better judgment,
    May fall to match° you with her country forms,°
    And happily° repent.
OTHELLO: Farewell, farewell!

---

210 *seel:* Hoodwink; *oak:* (A close-grained wood).   218 *strain:* Enlarge the meaning.   219 *reach:* Meaning.   230 *degree:* Social station.   231 *in . . . tends:* i.e., all things in nature seek out their own kind.   234 *position:* General argument.   235 *Distinctly:* Specifically.   237 *fall to match:* Happen to compare; *country forms:* i.e., the familiar appearance of her countrymen.   238 *happily:* By chance.

If more thou dost perceive, let me know more.
Set on thy wife to observe. Leave me, Iago.   240
IAGO: My lord, I take my leave.   *[Going.]*
OTHELLO: Why did I marry? This honest creature doubtless
　　Sees and knows more, much more, than he unfolds.
IAGO *(Returns)*: My lord, I would I might entreat your honor
　　To scan this thing no farther. Leave it to time.   245
　　Although 'tis fit that Cassio have his place,
　　For sure he fills it up with great ability,
　　Yet, if you please to hold him off awhile,
　　You shall by that perceive him and his means.
　　Note if your lady strains his entertainment°   250
　　With any strong or vehement importunity;
　　Much will be seen in that. In the meantime
　　Let me be thought too busy in my fears
　　(As worthy cause I have to fear I am)
　　And hold her free, I do beseech your honor.   255
OTHELLO: Fear not my government.°
IAGO:　　　　　　　　　　　　　　　I once more take my leave.　　*Exit.*
OTHELLO: This fellow's of exceeding honesty,
　　And knows all qualities,° with a learnèd spirit
　　Of human dealings. If I do prove her haggard,°
　　Though that her jesses° were my dear heartstrings,   260
　　I'd whistle her off and let her down the wind°
　　To prey at fortune. Haply for° I am black
　　And have not those soft parts° of conversation
　　That chamberers° have, or for I am declined
　　Into the vale of years—yet that's not much—   265
　　She's gone. I am abused, and my relief
　　Must be to loathe her. O curse of marriage,
　　That we can call these delicate creatures ours,
　　And not their appetites! I had rather be a toad
　　And live upon the vapor of a dungeon   270
　　Than keep a corner in the thing I love
　　For others' uses. Yet 'tis the plague to great ones;
　　Prerogatived are they less than the base.
　　'Tis destiny unshunnable, like death.
　　Even then this forkèd° plague is fated to us   275
　　When we do quicken.° Look where she comes.

---

250 *strains his entertainment:* Urge strongly that he be reinstated.   256 *government:* Self-control.   258 *qualities:* Natures, types of people.   259 *haggard:* A partly trained hawk which has gone wild again.   260 *jesses:* Straps which held the hawk's legs to the trainer's wrist. 261 *I'd . . . wind:* I would release her (like an untamable hawk) and let her fly free.   262 *Haply for:* It may be because.   263 *soft parts:* Gentle qualities and manners.   264 *chamberers:* Courtiers—or, perhaps, accomplished seducers.   275 *forkèd:* Horned (the sign of the cuckold was horns).   276 *do quicken:* Are born.

Enter DESDEMONA *and* EMILIA.

If she be false, heaven mocked itself!
I'll not believe't.
DESDEMONA: How now, my dear Othello?
    Your dinner, and the generous islanders
    By you invited, do attend° your presence.   280
OTHELLO: I am to blame.
DESDEMONA: Why do you speak so faintly?
    Are you not well?
OTHELLO: I have a pain upon my forehead, here.°
DESDEMONA: Why, that's with watching; 'twill away again,
    Let me but bind it hard, within this hour   285
    It will be well.
OTHELLO: Your napkin° is too little;

[He pushes the handerchief away, and it falls.]

    Let it° alone. Come, I'll go in with you.
DESDEMONA: I am very sorry that you are not well.

                                          Exit [with OTHELLO*]*.

EMILIA: I am glad I have found this napkin;
    This was her first remembrance from the Moor.   290
    My wayward husband hath a hundred times
    Wooed me to steal it; but she so loves the token
    (For he conjured her she should ever keep it)
    That she reserves it evermore about her
    To kiss and talk to. I'll have the work ta'en out°   295
    And give't Iago. What he will do with it,
    Heaven knows, not I; I nothing° but to please his fantasy.°

Enter IAGO.

IAGO: How now? What do you here alone?
EMILIA: Do not you chide; I have a thing for you.
IAGO: You have a thing for me? It is a common thing —   300
EMILIA: Ha?
IAGO: To have a foolish wife.
EMILIA: O, is that all? What will you give me now
    For that same handkerchief?
IAGO: What handkerchief?

---

280 *attend:* Wait.   283 *here:* (He points to his imaginary horns).   286 *napkin:* Elaborately worked handkerchief.   287 *it:* (It makes a considerable difference in the interpretation of later events whether this "it" refers to Othello's forehead or to the handkerchief; nothing in the text makes the reference clear).   295 *work ta'en out:* Needlework copied.   297 *I nothing:* I wish nothing; *fantasy:* Fancy, whim.

EMILIA: What handkerchief!   305
    Why, that the Moor first gave to Desdemona,
    That which so often you did bid me steal.
IAGO: Hast stol'n it from her?
EMILIA: No, but she let it drop by negligence,
    And to th' advantage,° I, being here, took't up.   310
    Look, here 't is.
IAGO: A good wench. Give it me.
EMILIA: What will you do with't, that you have been so earnest
    To have me filch it?
IAGO: Why, what is that to you?   *[Takes it.]*
EMILIA: If it be not for some purpose of import,°
    Give't me again. Poor lady, she'll run mad   315
    When she shall lack° it.
IAGO: Be not acknown on't.°
    I have use for it. Go, leave me.   *Exit* EMILIA.
    I will in Cassio's lodging lose this napkin
    And let him find it. Trifles light as air
    Are to the jealous confirmations strong   320
    As proofs of Holy Writ. This may do something.
    The Moor already changes with my poison:
    Dangerous conceits are in their natures poisons,
    Which at the first are scarce found to distaste,°
    But with a little,° act upon the blood,   325
    Burn like the mines of sulfur. I did say so.

Enter OTHELLO.

    Look where he comes! Not poppy nor mandragora,°
    Nor all the drowsy syrups of the world,
    Shall ever medicine thee to that sweet sleep
    Which thou owedst° yesterday.
OTHELLO: Ha! ha! False to me?   330
IAGO: Why, how now, general? No more of that.
OTHELLO: Avaunt! be gone! Thou hast set me on the rack.
    I swear 'tis better to be much abused
    Than but to know't a little.
IAGO: How now, my lord?
OTHELLO: What sense had I of her stol'n hours of lust?   335
    I saw't not, thought it not, it harmed not me;
    I slept the next night well, fed well, was free and merry;
    I found not Cassio's kisses on her lips.

310 *to th' advantage:* Being lucky.   314 *import:* Importance.   316 *lack:* Miss. *Be not acknown on't:*
Forget you ever saw it.   324 *are scarce found to distaste:* Scarcely can be tasted.   325 *with a little:*
In a short time.   327 *poppy nor mandragora:* Soporifics.   330 *owedst:* Possessed.

He that is robbed, not wanting° what is stol'n,
Let him not know't, and he's not robbed at all.   340
IAGO: I am sorry to hear this.
OTHELLO: I had been happy if the general camp,
    Pioners° and all, had tasted her sweet body,
    So I had nothing known. O now, forever
    Farewell the tranquil mind! Farewell content!   345
    Farewell the plumèd troops, and the big wars
    That make ambition virtue! O, farewell!
    Farewell the neighing steed and the shrill trump,
    The spirit-stirring drum, th' ear-piercing fife,
    The royal banner, and all quality,   350
    Pride, pomp, and circumstance° of glorious war!
    And O you mortal engines° whose rude throats
    Th' immortal Jove's dread clamors° counterfeit,
    Farewell! Othello's occupation's gone!
IAGO: Is't possible, my lord?   355
OTHELLO: Villain, be sure thou prove my love a whore!
    Be sure of it; give me the ocular proof;
    Or, by the worth of mine eternal soul,
    Thou hadst been better have been born a dog
    Than answer my waked wrath!
IAGO: Is't come to this?   360
OTHELLO: Make me to see't; or at the least so prove it
    That the probation° bear no hinge nor loop
    To hang a doubt on — or woe upon thy life!
IAGO: My noble lord —
OTHELLO: If thou dost slander her and torture me,   365
    Never pray more; abandon all remorse;
    On horror's head horrors accumulate;
    Do deeds to make heaven weep, all earth amazed;
    For nothing canst thou to damnation add
    Greater than that.
IAGO: O grace! O heaven forgive me!   370
    Are you a man? Have you a soul or sense?
    God b' wi' you! Take mine office. O wretched fool,
    That lov'st to make thine honesty a vice!
    O monstrous world! Take note, take note, O world,
    To be direct and honest is not safe.   375
    I thank you for this profit, and from hence
    I'll love no friend, sith° love breeds such offense.
OTHELLO: Nay, stay. Thou shouldst be honest.

---

339 *wanting:* Missing.   343 *Pioners:* The basest manual laborers in the army, who dug trenches
and mines.   351 *circumstance:* Pageantry.   352 *mortal engines:* Lethal weapons, i.e., cannon.
353 *clamors:* i.e., thunder.   362 *probation:* Proof.   377 *sith:* Since.

IAGO: I should be wise; for honesty's a fool
    And loses that it works for.
OTHELLO: By the world,   380
    I think my wife be honest, and think she is not;
    I think that thou art just, and think thou are not.
    I'll have some proof. My name, that was as fresh
    As Dian's° visage, is now begrimed and black
    As mine own face. If there be cords, or knives,   385
    Poison, or fire, or suffocating streams,
    I'll not endure it. Would I were satisfied!
IAGO: I see you are eaten up with passion.
    I do repent me that I put it to you.
    You would be satisfied?
OTHELLO: Would? Nay, and I will.   390
IAGO: And may; but how? How satisfied, my lord?
    Would you, the supervisor,° grossly gape on?
    Behold her topped?
OTHELLO: Death and damnation! O!
IAGO: It were a tedious° difficulty, I think,
    To bring them to that prospect.° Damn them then,   395
    If ever mortal eyes do see them bolster°
    More than their own! What then? How then?
    What shall I say? Where's satisfaction?
    It is impossible you should see this,
    Were they as prime° as goats, as hot as monkeys,   400
    As salt as wolves in pride,° and fools as gross
    As ignorance made drunk. But yet, I say,
    If imputation and strong circumstances
    Which lead directly to the door of truth
    Will give you satisfaction, you might hav't.   405
OTHELLO: Give me a living reason she's disloyal.
IAGO: I do not like the office.°
    But sith I am entered in this cause so far,
    Pricked° to't by foolish honesty and love,
    I will go on. I lay with Cassio lately,   410
    And being troubled with a raging tooth,
    I could not sleep.
    There are a kind of men so loose of soul
    That in their sleeps will mutter their affairs.
    One of this kind is Cassio.   415
    In sleep I heard him say, "Sweet Desdemona,

384 *Dian's:* Diana's (goddess of the moon and of chastity).   392 *supervisor:* On-looker.
394 *tedious:* Hard to arrange.   395 *prospect:* Sight (where they can be seen).   396 *bolster:* Go to
bed with.   400–401 *prime, salt:* Lustful.   401 *pride:* Heat.   407 *office:* Duty.   409 *Pricked:*
Spurred.

Let us be wary, let us hide our loves!"
And then, sir, would he gripe° and wring my hand,
Cry "O sweet creature!" Then kiss me hard,
As if he plucked up kisses by the roots   420
That grew upon my lips; laid his leg o'er my thigh,
And sigh, and kiss, and then cry, "Cursèd fate
That gave thee to the Moor!"
OTHELLO: O monstrous! monstrous!
IAGO: Nay, this was but his dream.
OTHELLO: But this denoted a foregone conclusion,°   425
'Tis a shrewd doubt,° though it be but a dream.
IAGO: And this may help to thicken other proofs
That do demonstrate° thinly.
OTHELLO: I'll tear her all to pieces!
IAGO: Nay, yet be wise. Yet we see nothing done;
She may be honest yet. Tell me but this: 430
Have you not sometimes seen a handkerchief
Spotted with strawberries in your wife's hand?
OTHELLO: I gave her such a one; 'twas my first gift.
IAGO: I know not that; but such a handkerchief —
I am sure it was your wife's — did I today   435
See Cassio wipe his beard with.
OTHELLO: If it be that —
IAGO: If it be that or any that was hers,
It speaks against her with the other proofs.
OTHELLO: O, that the slave had forty thousand lives!
One is too poor, too weak for my revenge.   440
Now do I see 'tis true. Look here, Iago:
All my fond love thus do I blow to heaven.
'Tis gone.
Arise, black vengeance, from the hollow hell!
Yield up, O love, thy crown and hearted° throne
To tyrannous hate! Swell, bosom, with thy fraught,°   445
For 'tis of aspics'° tongues.
IAGO: Yet be content.°
OTHELLO: O, blood, blood, blood!
IAGO: Patience, I say. Your mind may change.
OTHELLO: Never, Iago. Like to the Pontic Sea,°   450
Whose icy current and compulsive course
Nev'r keeps retiring ebb, but keeps due on
To the Propontic and the Hellespont,

---

418 *gripe*: Seize.   425 *foregone conclusion*: Consummated fact.   426 *shrewd doubt*: Penetrating guess.   428 *demonstrate*: Show, appear.   445 *hearted*: Seated in the heart.   446 *fraught*: Burden.   447 *aspics'*: Asps'; *content*: Patient, quiet.   450 *Pontic Sea*: The Black Sea (famous for the strong and constant current with which it flows through the Bosporus into the Mediterranean, where the water level is lower).

Even so my bloody thoughts, with violent pace,   455
Shall nev'r look back, nev'r ebb to humble love,
Till that a capable and wide° revenge
Swallow them up. *(He kneels.)* Now, by yond marble heaven,
In the due reverence of a sacred vow
I here engage my words.
IAGO: Do not rise yet.   *[IAGO kneels.]*
   Witness, you ever-burning lights above,   460
   You elements that clip° us round about,
   Witness that here Iago doth give up
   The execution° of his wit, hands, heart
   To wronged Othello's service! Let him command,
   And to obey shall be in me remorse,°   465
   What bloody business ever.°   *[They rise.]*
OTHELLO: I greet thy love,
   Not with vain thanks but with acceptance bounteous,°
   And will upon the instant put thee to 't°
   Within these three days let me hear thee say
   That Cassio's not alive.   470
IAGO: My friend is dead. 'Tis done at your request.
   But let her live.
OTHELLO: Damn her, lewd minx! O, damn her! Damn her!
   Come, go with me apart. I will withdraw
   To furnish me with some swift means of death
   For the fair devil. Now art thou my lieutenant.   475
IAGO: I am your own forever.   *Exeunt.*

Scene IV *[A street.]*

   Enter DESDEMONA, EMILIA, *and* CLOWN.

DESDEMONA: Do you know, sirrah, where Lieutenant Cassio lies?°
CLOWN: I dare not say he lies anywhere.
DESDEMONA: Why, man?
CLOWN: He's a soldier, and for me to say a soldier lies, 'tis stabbing.
DESDEMONA: Go to. Where lodges he?   5
CLOWN: To tell you where he lodges is to tell you where I lie.
DESDEMONA: Can anything be made of this?
CLOWN: I know not where he lodges, and for me to devise a lodging, and
   say he lies here or he lies there, were to lie in mine own throat.°
DESDEMONA: Can you enquire him out, and be edified° by report?   10

---

456 *capable and wide:* Sufficient and far-reaching.   461 *clip:* Enfold.   463 *execution:* Workings,
action.   465 *remorse:* Pity.   466 *ever:* Soever.   467 *bounteous:* Absolute.   468 *to't:* i.e., to the
work you have said you are prepared to do.   SCENE IV. 1 *lies:* Lodges.   9 *lie in mine own throat:*
(To lie in the throat is to lie absolutely and completely).   10 *edified:* Enlightened (Desdemona
mocks the Clown's overly elaborate diction).

CLOWN: I will catechize the world for him; that is, make questions, and
    by them answer.
DESDEMONA: Seek him, bid him come hither. Tell him I have moved°
    my lord on his behalf and hope all will be well.
CLOWN: To do this is within the compass° of man's wit, and therefore I   15
    will attempt the doing it.   *Exit* CLOWN.
DESDEMONA: Where should° I lose the handkerchief, Emilia?
EMILIA: I know not, madam.
DESDEMONA: Believe me, I had rather have lost my purse
    Full of crusadoes.° And but my noble Moor   20
    Is true of mind, and made of no such baseness
    As jealous creatures are, it were enough
    To put him to ill thinking.
EMILIA: Is he not jealous?
DESDEMONA: Who? He? I think the sun where he was born
    Drew all such humors° from him.
EMILIA: Look where he comes.   25

    Enter OTHELLO.

DESDEMONA: I will not leave him now till Cassio
    Be called to him. How is't with you, my lord?
OTHELLO: Well, my good lady. *[Aside]* O, hardness to dissemble!° —
    How do you, Desdemona?
DESDEMONA: Well, my good lord.
OTHELLO: Give me your hand. This hand is moist,° my lady.   30
DESDEMONA: It hath felt no age nor known no sorrow.
OTHELLO: This argues° fruitfulness and liberal° heart.
    Hot, hot, and moist. This hand of yours requires
    A sequester° from liberty; fasting and prayer;
    Much castigation; exercise devout;   35
    For here's a young and sweating devil here
    That commonly rebels. 'Tis a good hand,
    A frank one.
DESDEMONA: You may, indeed, say so;
    For 'twas that hand that gave away my heart.
OTHELLO: A liberal hand! The hearts of old gave hands,   40
    But our new heraldry° is hands, not hearts.
DESDEMONA: I cannot speak of this. Come now, your promise!

13 *moved:* Pleaded with.   15 *compass:* Reach.   17 *should:* Might.   20 *crusadoes:* Portuguese gold
coins.   24 *humors:* Characteristics.   28 *hardness to dissemble:* (Othello may refer here either to
the difficulty he has in maintaining his appearance of composure, or to what he believes to be
Desdemona's hardened hypocrisy).   30 *moist:* (A moist, hot hand was taken as a sign of a
lustful nature).   32 *argues:* Suggests; *liberal:* Free, open (but also with a suggestion of "licentious"; from here on in this scene Othello's words bear a double meaning, seeming to be
normal but accusing Desdemona of being unfaithful).   34 *sequester:* Separation.   41 *heraldry:*
Heraldic symbolism.

OTHELLO: What promise, chuck?

DESDEMONA: I have sent to bid Cassio come speak with you.

OTHELLO: I have a salt and sorry rheum° offends me.   45
    Lend me thy handkerchief.

DESDEMONA: Here, my lord.

OTHELLO: That which I gave you.

DESDEMONA: I have it not about me.

OTHELLO: Not?

DESDEMONA: No, indeed, my lord.

OTHELLO: That's a fault.
    That handkerchief
    Did an Egyptian to my mother give.   50
    She was a charmer,° and could almost read
    The thoughts of people. She told her, while she kept it
    'Twould make her amiable° and subdue my father
    Entirely to her love; but if she lost it
    Or made a gift of it, my father's eye   55
    Should hold her loathèd, and his spirits should hunt
    After new fancies. She, dying, gave it me,
    And bid me, when my fate would have me wived,
    To give it her. I did so; and take heed on't;
    Make it a darling like your precious eye.   60
    To lose't or give't away were such perdition
    As nothing else could match.

DESDEMONA: Is't possible?

OTHELLO: 'Tis true. There's magic in the web° of it.
    A sibyl that had numbered in the world
    The sun to course two hundred compasses,   65
    In her prophetic fury° sewed the work;
    The worms were hallowed that did breed the silk,
    And it was dyed in mummy° which the skillful
    Conserved of maidens' hearts.

DESDEMONA: Indeed? Is't true?

OTHELLO: Most veritable. Therefore look to't well.   70

DESDEMONA: Then would to God that I had never seen't!

OTHELLO: Ha! Wherefore?

DESDEMONA: Why do you speak so startingly and rash?

OTHELLO: Is't lost? Is't gone? Speak, is it out o' th' way?

DESDEMONA: Heaven bless us!   75

OTHELLO: Say you?

DESDEMONA: It is not lost. But what an if it were?

OTHELLO: How?

DESDEMONA: I say it is not lost.

---

45 *a salt and sorry rheum:* A heavy, running head cold.   51 *charmer:* Magician.   53 *amiable:* Desirable.   63 *web:* Weaving.   66 *prophetic fury:* Seized by the spirit and able to prophesy. 68 *mummy:* Liquid drained from embalmed bodies.

OTHELLO: Fetch't, let me see't!   80
DESDEMONA: Why, so I can; but I will not now.
    This is a trick to put me from my suit:
    Pray you let Cassio be received again.
OTHELLO: Fetch me the handkerchief! My mind misgives.
DESDEMONA: Come, come!   85
    You'll never meet a more sufficient° man —
OTHELLO: The handkerchief!
DESDEMONA: A man that all his time
    Hath founded his good fortunes on your love,
    Shared dangers with you —
OTHELLO: The handkerchief!   90
DESDEMONA: I'faith, you are to blame.
OTHELLO: Away!   *Exit* OTHELLO.
EMILIA: Is not this man jealous?
DESDEMONA: I nev'r saw this before.
    Sure there's some wonder in this handkerchief;   95
    I am most unhappy in the loss of it.
EMILIA: 'Tis not a year or two shows us a man.
    They are all but stomachs, and we all but food;
    They eat us hungerly, and when they are full,
    They belch us.

    Enter IAGO *and* CASSIO.

            Look you, Cassio and my husband.   100
IAGO: There is no other way; 'tis she must do't.
    And lo the happiness! Go and importune her.
DESDEMONA: How now, good Cassio? What's the news with you?
CASSIO: Madam, my former suit. I do beseech you
    That by your virtuous means I may again   105
    Exist, and be a member of his love
    Whom I with all the office° of my heart
    Entirely honor. I would not be delayed.
    If my offense be of such mortal kind
    That nor my service past, nor present sorrows,   110
    Nor purposed merit in futurity,
    Can ransom me into his love again,
    But to know so must be my benefit.°
    So shall I clothe me in a forced content,
    And shut myself up in some other course   115
    To fortune's alms.
DESDEMONA: Alas, thrice-gentle Cassio,
    My advocation° is not now in tune.

---

86 *sufficient:* Complete, with all proper qualities.   107 *office:* Duty.   113 *benefit:* Good.   117 *advo-cation:* Advocacy.

My lord is not my lord; nor should I know him
Were he in favor° as in humor altered.
So help me every spirit sanctified   120
As I have spoken for you all my best
And stood within the blank° of his displeasure
For my free speech. You must awhile be patient.
What I can do I will; and more I will
Than for myself I dare. Let that suffice you.   125

IAGO: Is my lord angry?

EMILIA: He went hence but now,
And certainly in strange unquietness.

IAGO: Can he be angry? I have seen the cannon
When it hath blown his ranks into the air
And, like the devil, from his very arm   130
Puffed his own brother. And is he angry?
Something of moment° then. I will go meet him.
There's matter in't indeed if he be angry.

DESDEMONA: I prithee do so.   *Exit [IAGO.]*
                          Something sure of state,°
Either from Venice or some unhatched practice°   135
Made demonstrable here in Cyprus to him,
Hath puddled° his clear spirit; and in such cases
Men's natures wrangle with inferior things,
Though great ones are their object. 'Tis even so.
For let our finger ache, and it endues°   140
Our other, healthful members even to a sense
Of pain. Nay, we must think men are not gods,
Nor of them look for such observancy
As fits the bridal. Beshrew me much, Emilia,
I was, unhandsome warrier as I am,   145
Arraigning his unkindness with my soul;
But now I find I had suborned the witness,
And he's indicted falsely.

EMILIA: Pray heaven it be
State matters, as you think, and no conception
Nor no jealous toy° concerning you.   150

DESDEMONA: Alas the day! I never gave him cause.

EMILIA: But jealous souls will not be answered so;
They are not ever jealous for the cause,
But jealous for they're jealous. It is a monster
Begot upon itself, born on itself.   155

DESDEMONA: Heaven keep the monster from Othello's mind!

---

119 *favor:* Countenance.   122 *blank:* Bull's-eye of a target.   132 *moment:* Importance.
134 *of state:* State affairs.   135 *unhatched practice:* Undisclosed plot.   137 *puddled:* Muddied.
140 *endues:* Leads.   150 *toy:* Trifle.

EMILIA: Lady, amen.

DESDEMONA: I will go seek him. Cassio, walk here about.
 If I do find him fit,° I'll move your suit
 And seek to effect it to my uttermost.   160

CASSIO: I humbly thank your ladyship.

*Exit [*DESDEMONA *with* EMILIA*].*

Enter BIANCA.

BIANCA: Save you, friend Cassio!

CASSIO: What make you from home?
 How is't with you, my most fair Bianca?
 I' faith, sweet love, I was coming to your house.

BIANCA: And I was going to your lodging, Cassio.   165
 What, keep a week away? Seven days and nights?
 Eightscore eight hours? And lovers' absent hours
 More tedious than the dial eightscore times?
 O weary reck'ning.°

CASSIO: Pardon me, Bianca.
 I have this while with leaden thoughts been pressed,   170
 But I shall in a more continuate° time
 Strike off this score° of absence. Sweet Bianca,

[Gives her DESDEMONA*'s handkerchief.]*

Take me this work out.

BIANCA: O Cassio, whence came this?
 This is some token from a newer friend.
 To the felt absence now I feel a cause.   175
 Is't come to this? Well, well.

CASSIO: Go to, woman!
 Throw your vile guesses in the devil's teeth,
 From whence you have them. You are jealous now
 That this is from some mistress, some remembrance.
 No, by my faith, Bianca.

BIANCA: Why, whose is it?   180

CASSIO: I know not neither; I found it in my chamber.
 I like the work well; ere it be demanded,°
 As like enough it will, I would have it copied.
 Take it and do't, and leave me for this time.

BIANCA: Leave you? Wherefore?   185

CASSIO: I do attend here on the general
 And think it no addition, nor my wish,
 To have him see me womaned.

---

159 *fit:* Receptive. 169 *reck'ning:* Addition. 171 *continuate:* Uninterrupted. 172 *Strike off this score:* i.e., pay this bill (the *score* being the account of drinks kept in a tavern). 182 *demanded:* Asked for (by the person who lost it).

BIANCA: Why, I pray you?
CASSIO: Not that I love you not.
BIANCA: But that you do not love me!
 I pray you bring° me on the way a little,   190
 And say if I shall see you soon at night.
CASSIO: 'Tis but a little way that I can bring you,
 For I attend here; but I'll see you soon.
BIANCA: 'Tis very good. I must be circumstanced.° *Exeunt omnes.*

ACT IV

Scene I *[A street.]*

 Enter OTHELLO *and* IAGO.

IAGO: Will you think so?
OTHELLO: Think so, Iago?
IAGO: What,
 To kiss in private?
OTHELLO: An unauthorized° kiss?
IAGO: Or to be naked with her friend in bed
 An hour or more, not meaning any harm?
OTHELLO: Naked in bed, Iago, and not mean harm?   5
 It is hypocrisy against the devil.
 They that mean virtuously, and yet do so,
 The devil their virtue tempts, and they tempt heaven.
IAGO: If they do nothing, 'tis a venial slip.
 But if I give my wife a handkerchief—   10
OTHELLO: What then?
IAGO: Why, then 'tis hers, my lord; and being hers,
 She may, I think, bestow't on any man.
OTHELLO: She is protectress of her honor too.
 May she give that?   15
IAGO: Her honor is an essence that's not seen;
 They have it very oft that have it not.
 But for the handkerchief—
OTHELLO: By heaven, I would most gladly have forgot it!
 Thou said'st—O, it comes o'er my memory   20
 As doth the raven° o'er the infected house,
 Boding to all—he had my handkerchief.
IAGO: Ay, what of that?
OTHELLO: That's not so good now.
IAGO: What if I had said I had seen him do you wrong?
 Or heard him say—as knaves be such abroad°   25

190 *bring:* Accompany. 194 *be circumstanced:* Accept things as they are ACT IV, SCENE I.
2 *unauthorized:* Illicit. 21 *raven:* (A harbinger of death). 25 *abroad:* i.e., in the world.

Who having, by their own importunate suit,
Or voluntary dotage° of some mistress,
Convincèd or supplied° them, cannot choose
But they must blab —

OTHELLO: Hath he said anything?

IAGO: He hath, my lord: but be you well assured,   30
No more than he'll unswear.

OTHELLO: What hath he said?

IAGO: Why, that he did — I know not what he did.

OTHELLO: What? what?

IAGO: Lie —

OTHELLO: With her?

IAGO: With her, on her; what you will.   35

OTHELLO: Lie with her? Lie on her? — We say lie on her when they belie
her. — Lie with her! Zounds, that's fulsome.° — Handkerchief — confessions — handkerchief! — To confess, and be hanged for his labor — first
to be hanged, and then to confess! I tremble at it. Nature would not
invest herself in such shadowing passion without some instruction.° It   40
is not words that shakes me thus. — Pish! Noses, ears, and lips? Is't
possible? — Confess? — Handkerchief? — O devil!   *Falls in a trance.*

IAGO: Work on.
My med'cine works! Thus credulous fools are caught,
And many worthy and chaste dames even thus,   45
All guiltless, meet reproach.° What, ho! My lord!
My lord, I say! Othello!

Enter CASSIO.
                         How now, Cassio?

CASSIO: What's the matter?

IAGO: My lord is fall'n into an epilepsy.
This is his second fit; he had one yesterday.   50

CASSIO: Rub him about the temples.

IAGO: The lethargy° must have his quiet course.
If not, he foams at mouth, and by and by
Breaks out to savage madness. Look, he stirs.
Do you withdraw yourself a little while.   55
He will recover straight. When he is gone,
I would on great occasion° speak with you.   *[Exit* CASSIO.*]*
How is it, general? Have you not hurt your head?

OTHELLO: Dost thou mock° me?

---

27 *voluntary dotage:* Weakness of the will.   28 *Convincèd or supplied:* Persuaded or gratified (the
mistress).   37 *fulsome:* Foul, repulsive.   39–40 *Nature . . . instruction:* i.e., my mind would not
become so darkened (with anger) unless there were something in this (accusation); (it should
be remembered that Othello believes in the workings of magic and supernatural forces).
46 *reproach:* Shame.   52 *lethargy:* Coma.   57 *great occasion:* Very important matter.   59 *mock:*
(Othello takes Iago's comment as a reference to his horns — which it is).

IAGO: I mock you not, by heaven.
    Would you would bear your fortune like a man.   60
OTHELLO: A hornèd man's a monster and a beast.
IAGO: There's many a beast then in a populous city,
    And many a civil° monster.
OTHELLO: Did he confess it?
IAGO: Good, sir, be a man.
    Think every bearded fellow that's but yoked   65
    May draw° with you. There's millions now alive
    That nightly lie in those unproper° beds
    Which they dare swear peculiar.° Your case is better.
    O, 'tis the spite of hell, the fiend's arch-mock,
    To lip a wanton in a secure couch,   70
    And to suppose her chaste. No, let me know;
    And knowing what I am, I know what she shall be.
OTHELLO: O, thou art wise! 'Tis certain.
IAGO: Stand you awhile apart;
    Confine yourself but in a patient list.°
    Whilst you were here, o'erwhelmèd with your grief—   75
    A passion most unsuiting such a man—
    Cassio came hither. I shifted him away°
    And laid good 'scuses upon your ecstasy,°
    Bade him anon return, and here speak with me;
    The which he promised. Do but encave° yourself   80
    And mark the fleers°, the gibes, and notable° scorns
    That dwell in every region of his face.
    For I will make him tell the tale anew:
    Where, how, how oft, how long ago, and when
    He hath, and is again to cope your wife.   85
    I say, but mark his gesture. Marry patience,
    Or I shall say you're all in all in spleen,°
    And nothing of a man.
OTHELLO: Dost thou hear, Iago?
    I will be found most cunning in my patience;
    But—dost thou hear?—most bloody.
IAGO: That's not amiss;   90
    But yet keep time in all. Will you withdraw?

*[OTHELLO moves to one side, where his remarks are not audible to
CASSIO and IAGO.]*

---

63 *civil:* City-dwelling.   66 *draw:* i.e., like the horned ox.   67 *unproper.* i.e., not exclusively
the husband's.   68 *peculiar:* Their own alone.   74 *a patient list:* The bounds of patience.
77 *shifted him away:* Got rid of him by a strategem.   78 *ecstasy:* Trance (the literal meaning,
"outside oneself," bears on the meaning of the change Othello is undergoing).   80 *encave:*
Hide.   81 *fleers:* Mocking looks or speeches; *notable:* Obvious.   87 *spleen.* Passion, particularly
anger.

Now will I question Cassio of Bianca,
A huswife° that by selling her desires
Buys herself bread and cloth. It is a creature
That dotes on Cassio, as 'tis the strumpet's plague   95
To beguile many and be beguiled by one.
He, when he hears of her, cannot restrain
From the excess of laughter. Here he comes.

Enter CASSIO.

As he shall smile, Othello shall go mad:
And his unbookish° jealousy must conster°   100
Poor Cassio's smiles, gestures, and light behaviors
Quite in the wrong. How do you, lieutenant?
CASSIO: The worser that you give me the addition°
  Whose want even kills me.
IAGO: Ply Desdemona well, and you are sure on't.   105
  Now, if this suit lay in Bianca's power,
  How quickly should you speed!
CASSIO: Alas, poor caitiff!°
OTHELLO: Look how he laughs already!
IAGO: I never knew woman love man so.
CASSIO: Alas, poor rogue! I think, i' faith, she loves me.   110
OTHELLO: Now he denies it faintly, and laughs it out.
IAGO: Do you hear, Cassio?
OTHELLO: Now he importunes him
  To tell it o'er. Go to! Well said, well said!
IAGO: She gives it out that you shall marry her.
  Do you intend it?   115
CASSIO: Ha, ha, ha!
OTHELLO: Do ye triumph, Roman? Do you triumph?
CASSIO: I marry? What, a customer?° Prithee bear some charity to my
  wit; do not think it so unwholesome. Ha, ha, ha!
OTHELLO: So, so, so, so. They laugh that win.   120
IAGO: Why, the cry goes that you marry her.
CASSIO: Prithee, say true.
IAGO: I am a very villain else.
OTHELLO: Have you scored° me? Well.
CASSIO: This is the monkey's own giving out. She is persuaded I will 125
  marry her out of her own love and flattery, not out of my promise.
OTHELLO: Iago beckons me; now he begins the story.

  *[*OTHELLO *moves close enough to hear.]*

---

93 *huswife:* Housewife (but with the special meaning here of "prostitute"). 100 *unbookish:*
Ignorant; *conster:* Construe. 103 *addition:* Title. 107 *caitiff:* Wretch. 118 *customer:* One who
sells, a merchant (here, a prostitute). 124 *scored:* Marked, defaced.

CASSIO: She was here even now; she haunts me in every place. I was the other day talking on the sea bank with certain Venetians, and thither comes the bauble,° and falls me thus about my neck — 130
OTHELLO: Crying "O dear Cassio!" as it were. His gesture imports it.
CASSIO: So hangs, and lolls, and weeps upon me; so shakes and pulls me! Ha, ha, ha!
OTHELLO: Now he tells how she plucked him to my chamber. O, I see that nose of yours, but not that dog I shall throw it to. 135
CASSIO: Well, I must leave her company.
IAGO: Before me!° Look where she comes.

Enter BIANCA.

CASSIO: 'Tis such another fitchew!° Marry a perfumed one? What do you mean by this haunting of me?
BIANCA: Let the devil and his dam haunt you! What did you mean by 140 that same handkerchief you gave me even now? I was a fine fool to take it. I must take out the work? A likely piece of work that you should find it in your chamber and know not who left it there! This is some minx's token, and I must take out the work? There! *[She throws down the handkerchief.]* Give it your hobbyhorse.° Wheresoever you had 145 it, I'll take out no work on't.
CASSIO: How now, my sweet Bianca? How now? how now?
OTHELLO: By heaven, that should be my handkerchief!
BIANCA: If you'll come to supper tonight, you may; if you will not, come when you are next prepared for.°   *Exit.* 150
IAGO: After her, after her!
CASSIO: Faith, I must; she'll rail in the streets else.
IAGO: Will you sup there?
CASSIO: Yes, I intend so.
IAGO: Well, I may chance to see you, for I would very fain speak with 155 you.
CASSIO: Prithee come. Will you?
IAGO: Go to, say no more.   *[Exit* CASSIO.*]*
OTHELLO: *[Comes forward]*: How shall I murder him, Iago?
IAGO: Did you perceive how he laughed at his vice? 160
OTHELLO: O Iago!
IAGO: And did you see the handkerchief?
OTHELLO: Was that mine?
IAGO: Yours, by this hand! And to see how he prizes the foolish woman your wife! She gave it him, and he hath giv'n it his whore. 165
OTHELLO: I would have him nine years a-killing! — A fine woman, a fair woman, a sweet woman?

---

130 *bauble:* Plaything.   137 *Before me!:* (An exclamation of surprise).   133 *fitchew:* Polecat, i.e., strong-smelling creature.   145 *hobbyhorse:* Prostitute.   150 *next prepared for:* Next expected — i.e., never.

IAGO: Nay, you must forget that.

OTHELLO: Ay, let her rot, and perish, and be damned tonight; for she shall not live. No, my heart is turned to stone; I strike it, and it hurts my hand. O, the world hath not a sweeter creature! She might lie by an emperor's side and command him tasks. 170

IAGO: Nay, that's not your way.°

OTHELLO: Hang her! I do but say what she is. So delicate with her needle. An admirable musician. O, she will sing the savageness out of a bear! Of so high and plenteous wit and invention°— 175

IAGO: She's the worse for all this.

OTHELLO: O, a thousand, a thousand times. And then, of so gentle a condition?°

IAGO: Ay, too gentle. 180

OTHELLO: Nay, that's certain. But yet the pity of it, Iago. O Iago, the pity of it, Iago.

IAGO: If you are so fond over her iniquity, give her patent to offend; for if it touch° not you, it comes near nobody.

OTHELLO: I will chop her into messes!° Cuckold me! 185

IAGO: O, 'tis foul in her.

OTHELLO: With mine officer!

IAGO: That's fouler.

OTHELLO: Get me some poison, Iago, this night. I'll not expostulate with her, lest her body and beauty unprovide my mind° again. This night, Iago! 190

IAGO: Do it not with poison. Strangle her in her bed, even the bed she hath contaminated.

OTHELLO: Good, good! The justice of it pleases. Very good!

IAGO: And for Cassio, let me be his undertaker.° You shall hear more by midnight. 195

OTHELLO: Excellent good!   [*A trumpet.*]
                    What trumpet is that same?

IAGO: I warrant something from Venice.

Enter LODOVICO, DESDEMONA, *and* ATTENDANTS.

                    'Tis Lodovico.
        This comes from the Duke. See, your wife's with him.

LODOVICO: God save you, worthy general.

OTHELLO: With° all my heart, sir. 200

LODOVICO: The Duke and the senators of Venice greet you.

                    [*Gives him a letter.*]

---

173 *way:* Proper course.   176 *invention:* Imagination.   178–179 *gentle a condition:* (1) Well born (2) of a gentle nature.   184 *touch:* Affects.   185 *messes:* Bits.   190 *unprovide my mind:* Undo my resolution.   195 *undertaker:* (Not "burier" but "one who undertakes to do something").   200 *With:* i.e., I greet you with.

OTHELLO: I kiss the instrument of their pleasures.

[Opens the letter and reads.]

DESDEMONA: And what's the news, good cousin Lodovico?
IAGO: I am very glad to see you, signior.
 Welcome to Cyprus.   205
LODOVICO: I thank you. How does Lieutenant Cassio?
IAGO: Lives, sir.
DESDEMONA: Cousin, there's fall'n between him and my lord
 An unkind° breach; but you shall make all well.
OTHELLO: Are you sure of that?
DESDEMONA: My lord?   210
OTHELLO *[Reads]*: "This fail you not to do, as you will —"
LODOVICO: He did not call; he's busy in the paper.
 Is there division 'twixt my lord and Cassio?
DESDEMONA: A most unhappy one. I would do much
 T' atone° them, for the love I bear to Cassio. 215
OTHELLO: Fire and brimstone!
DESDEMONA: My lord?
OTHELLO: Are you wise?
DESDEMONA: What, is he angry?
LODOVICO: May be th' letter moved him;
 For, as I think, they do command him home,
 Deputing Cassio in his government.°
DESDEMONA: Trust me, I am glad on't.
OTHELLO: Indeed?
DESDEMONA: My lord?   220
OTHELLO: I am glad to see you mad.
DESDEMONA: Why, sweet Othello —
OTHELLO: Devil!   *[Strikes her.]*
DESDEMONA: I have not deserved this.
LODOVICO: My lord, this would not be believed in Venice,
 Though I should swear I saw't. 'Tis very much.
 Make her amends; she weeps.
OTHELLO: O devil, devil!   225
 If that the earth could teem° with woman's tears,
 Each drop she falls° would prove a crocodile.°
 Out of my sight!
DESDEMONA: I will not stay to offend you. *[Going.]*
LODOVICO: Truly, an obedient lady.
 I do beseech your lordship call her back.   230
OTHELLO: Mistress!

---

208 *unkind:* Unnatural. 215 *atone:* Reconcile. 219 *government:* Office. 226 *teem:* Conceive. 227 *falls:* Drops; *crocodile:* (The crocodile was supposed to shed false tears to lure its victims.)

DESDEMONA: My lord?

OTHELLO: What would you with her, sir?

LODOVICO: Who? I, my lord?

OTHELLO: Ay! You did wish that I would make her turn.
    Sir, she can turn, and turn, and yet go on
    And turn again; and she can weep, sir, weep;   235
    And she's obedient; as you say, obedient.
    Very obedient. Proceed you in your tears.
    Concerning this, sir — O well-painted passion!
    I am commanded home. — Get you away;
    I'll send for you anon. — Sir, I obey the mandate   240
    And will return to Venice. — Hence, avaunt!   *[Exit* DESDEMONA.*]*
    Cassio shall have my place. And, sir, tonight
    I do entreat that we may sup together.
    You are welcome, sir, to Cyprus. — Goats and monkeys!   *Exit.*

LODOVICO: Is this the noble Moor whom our full Senate   245
    Call all in all sufficient? Is this the nature
    Whom passion could not shake? whose solid virtue
    The shot of accident nor dart of chance
    Could neither raze nor pierce?

IAGO: He is much changed.

LODOVICO: Are his wits safe? Is he not light of brain?   250

IAGO: He's that he is; I may not breathe my censure.
    What he might be (if, what he might, he is not)
    I would to heaven he were!

LODOVICO: What, strike his wife?

IAGO: Faith, that was not so well; yet would I knew
    That stroke would prove the worst.

LODOVICO: Is it his use?°   255
    Or did the letters work upon his blood°
    And new-create his fault?

IAGO: Alas, alas!
    It is not honesty in me to speak
    What I have seen and known. You shall observe him,
    And his own courses° will denote him so   260
    That I may save my speech. Do but go after
    And mark how he continues.

LODOVICO: I am sorry that I am deceived in him.   *Exeunt.*

Scene II *[The citadel.]*

Enter OTHELLO *and* EMILIA.

OTHELLO: You have seen nothing then?

---

255 *use:* Habit.   256 *blood:* Passion.   260 *courses:* Actions.

EMILIA: Nor ever heard, nor ever did suspect.
OTHELLO: Yes, you have seen Cassio and she together.
EMILIA: But then I saw no harm, and then I heard
    Each syllable that breath made up° between them.   5
OTHELLO: What, did they never whisper?
EMILIA: Never, my lord.
OTHELLO: Nor send you out o' th' way?
EMILIA: Never.
OTHELLO: To fetch her fan, her gloves, her mask, nor nothing?
EMILIA: Never, my lord.   10
OTHELLO: That's strange.
EMILIA: I durst, my lord, to wager she is honest,
    Lay down my soul at stake.° If you think other,
    Remove your thought. It doth abuse your bosom.
    If any wretch have put this in your head,   15
    Let heaven requite it with the serpent's curse,°
    For if she be not honest,° chaste, and true,
    There's no man happy. The purest of their wives
    Is foul as slander.
OTHELLO: Bid her come hither. Go.   *Exit* EMILIA.
    She says enough; yet she's a simple bawd°   20
    That cannot say as much. This is a subtle whore,
    A closet lock and key of villainous secrets,
    And yet she'll kneel and pray; I have seen her do't.

    Enter DESDEMONA *and* EMILIA.

DESDEMONA: My lord, what is your will?
OTHELLO: Pray you, chuck, come hither.
DESDEMONA: What is your pleasure?
OTHELLO: Let me see your eyes.   25
    Look in my face.
DESDEMONA: What horrible fancy's this?
OTHELLO *[To* EMILIA*]*: Some of your function,° mistress:
    Leave procreants alone and shut the door;
    Cough or cry hem if anybody come.
    Your mystery,° your mystery! Nay, dispatch!   *Exit* EMILIA. 30
DESDEMONA: Upon my knee, what doth your speech import?
    I understand a fury in your words.°
OTHELLO: Why, what art thou?
DESDEMONA: Your wife, my lord; your true
    And loyal wife.

SCENE II. 5 *that breath made up:* Spoken.   13 *at stake:* As the wager.   15 *serpent's curse:* (God's curse on the serpent after the fall in Eden.)   17 *honest:* Chaste.   20 *bawd:* Procuress.   27 *Some of your function:* Do your proper work (as the operator of a brothel).   30 *mystery:* Trade. 32 *words:* (Q1 adds to this line, "But not the words".)

OTHELLO: Come, swear it, damn thyself;
    Lest, being like one of heaven, the devils themselves   35
    Should fear to seize thee. Therefore be doubledamned:
    Swear thou art honest.
DESDEMONA: Heaven doth truly know it.
OTHELLO: Heaven truly knows that thou art false as hell.
DESDEMONA: To whom, my lord? With whom? How am I false?
OTHELLO: Ah, Desdemon! Away! Away! Away!   40
DESDEMONA: Alas the heavy day! Why do you weep?
    Am I the motive° of these tears, my lord?
    If haply° you my father do suspect
    An instrument of this your calling back,
    Lay not your blame on me. If you have lost him,   45
    I have lost him too.
OTHELLO: Had it pleased heaven
    To try me with affliction, had they rained
    All kinds of sores and shames on my bare head,
    Steeped° me in poverty to the very lips,
    Given to captivity me and my utmost hopes,   50
    I should have found in some place of my soul
    A drop of patience. But alas, to make me
    The fixèd figure for the time of scorn°
    To point his slow and moving finger at.
    Yet could I bear that too, well, very well.   55
    But there where I have garnered up my heart,
    Where either I must live or bear no life,
    The fountain from the which my current runs
    Or else dries up—to be discarded thence,
    Or keep it as a cistern for foul toads   60
    To knot and gender° in—turn thy complexion there,
    Patience, thou young and rose-lipped cherubin!
    I here look grim as hell!°
DESDEMONA: I hope my noble lord esteems me honest.
OTHELLO: O, ay, as summer flies are in the shambles,°   65
    That quicken even with blowing.° O thou weed,
    Who art so lovely fair, and smell'st so sweet,
    That the sense aches at thee, would thou hadst never been born!
DESDEMONA: Alas, what ignorant° sin have I committed?

---

42 *motive:* Cause. 43 *haply:* By chance. 49 *Steeped:* Submerged. 53 *The . . . scorn:*
The very image of scorn in our time. 61 *knot and gender:* Twist in bunches and procreate.
61–63 *turn . . . hell:* (The rough sense would seem to be "even Patience would grow pale, turn
complexion, at Desdemona's perfidy, but that Othello looks grimly on".) 65 *shambles:* Abat-
oirs. 66 *quicken even with blowing:* Become impregnated as soon as they lay their eggs.
69 *ignorant:* Unknowing.

OTHELLO: Was this fair paper, this most goodly book, 70
 Made to write "whore" upon? What committed?
 Committed? O thou public commoner,°
 I should make very forges of my cheeks
 That would to cinders burn up modesty,
 Did I but speak thy deeds. What committed? 75
 Heaven stops the nose at it, and the moon winks;°
 The bawdy wind that kisses all it meets
 Is hushed within the hollow mine of earth
 And will not hear't. What committed?
DESDEMONA: By heaven, you do me wrong! 80
OTHELLO: Are not you a strumpet?
DESDEMONA: No, as I am a Christian!
 If to preserve this vessel for my lord
 From any other foul unlawful touch
 Be not to be a strumpet, I am none.
OTHELLO: What, not a whore?
DESDEMONA: No, as I shall be saved! 85
OTHELLO: Is't possible?
DESDEMONA: O, heaven forgive us!
OTHELLO: I cry you mercy° then.
 I took you for that cunning whore of Venice
 That married with Othello. *[Calling]* You, mistress,

Enter EMILIA.

 That have the office opposite to Saint Peter 90
 And keep the gate of hell! You, you, ay, you!
 We have done our course; there's money for your pains.

[Throws her some coins.]

 I pray you turn the key and keep our counsel.   *Exit.*
EMILIA: Alas, what does this gentleman conceive?
 How do you, madam? How do you, my good lady? 95
DESDEMONA: Faith, half asleep.
EMILIA: Good madam, what's the matter with my lord?
DESDEMONA: With who?
EMILIA: Why, with my lord, madam.
DESDEMONA: Who is thy lord?
EMILIA: He that is yours, sweet lady. 100
DESDEMONA: I have none. Do not talk to me, Emilia.
 I cannot weep, nor answers have I none
 But what should go by water.° Prithee tonight

---

72 *commoner:* Prostitute. 76 *winks:* Closes its eyes (the moon was the symbol of chastity).
87 *cry you mercy:* Ask your pardon. 103 *water:* Tears.

Lay on my bed my wedding sheets, remember;
And call thy husband hither.

EMILIA: Here's a change indeed!   *Exit.*   105

DESDEMONA: 'Tis meet I should be used so, very meet.
How have I been behaved, that he might stick
The small'st opinion on my least misuse?°

Enter IAGO *and* EMILIA.

IAGO: What is your pleasure, madam? How is't with you?

DESDEMONA: I cannot tell. Those that do teach young babes   110
Do it with gentle means and easy tasks.
He might have chid me so; for, in good faith,
I am a child to chiding.

IAGO: What is the matter, lady?

EMILIA: Alas, Iago, my lord hath so bewhored her,
Thrown such despite° and heavy terms upon her   115
That true hearts cannot bear it.

DESDEMONA: Am I that name, Iago?

IAGO: What name, fair lady?

DESDEMONA: Such as she said my lord did say I was.

EMILIA: He called her whore. A beggar in his drink
Could not have laid such terms upon his callet.°   120

IAGO: Why did he so?

DESDEMONA: I do not know; I am sure I am none such.

IAGO: Do not weep, do not weep. Alas the day.

EMILIA: Hath she forsook so many noble matches,
Her father and her country, and her friends,   125
To be called whore? Would it not make one weep?

DESDEMONA: It is my wretched fortune.

IAGO: Beshrew° him for't!
How comes this trick upon him?

DESDEMONA: Nay, heaven doth know.

EMILIA: I will be hanged if some eternal villain,
Some busy and insinuating rogue,   130
Some cogging,° cozening slave, to get some office,
Have not devised this slander. I will be hanged else.

IAGO: Fie, there is no such man! It is impossible.

DESDEMONA: If any such there be, heaven pardon him.

EMILIA: A halter pardon him! And hell gnaw his bones!   135
Why should he call her whore? Who keeps her company?
What place? What time? What form? What likelihood?
The Moor's abused by some most villainous knave,

107–108 *stick . . . misuse:* Base any doubt on my smallest fault.   115 *despite:* Abuse.   120
callet: Slut.   127 *Beshrew:* Curse.   131 *cogging:* Cheating.

Some base notorious knave, some scurvy fellow.
O heavens, that such companions° thou'dst unfold,°   140
And put in every honest hand a whip
To lash the rascals naked through the world
Even from the east to th' west!

IAGO: Speak within door.°

EMILIA: O, fie upon them! Some such squire° he was
That turned your wit the seamy side without   145
And made you to suspect me with the Moor.

IAGO: You are a fool. Go to.

DESDEMONA: Alas, Iago,
What shall I do to win my lord again?
Good friend, go to him, for, by this light of heaven,
I know not how I lost him. Here I kneel: 150
If e'er my will did trespass 'gainst his love
Either in discourse of thought° or actual deed,
Or that mine eyes, mine ears, or any sense
Delighted them in any other form;
Or that I do not yet, and ever did,   155
And ever will (though he do shake me off
To beggarly divorcement) love him dearly,
Comfort forswear me. Unkindness may do much,
And his unkindness may defeat° my life,
But never taint my love. I cannot say "whore."   160
It does abhor me now I speak the word;
To do the act that might the addition earn
Not the world's mass of vanity could make me.

IAGO: I pray you be content. 'Tis but his humor.°
The business of the state does him offense.   165

DESDEMONA: If 'twere no other.

IAGO: It is but so, I warrant. *[Trumpets within.]*
Hark how these instruments summon to supper.
The messengers of Venice stay the meat.°
Go in, and weep not. All things shall be well.

[Exeunt DESDEMONA *and* EMILIA. *Enter* RODERIGO.*]*

How now, Roderigo?   170

RODERIGO: I do not find that thou deal'st justly with me.

IAGO: What in the contrary?

RODERIGO: Every day thou daff'st° me with some device,° Iago, and
rather, as it seems to me now, keep'st from me all conveniency° than

---

140 *companions:* Fellows, rogues; *unfold:* Disclose.   143 *within door:* More quietly and
moderately.   144 *squire:* (A term of contempt.)   152 *discourse of thought:* Thinking.   159 *defeat:*
Destroy.   164 *humor:* Mood.   168 *stay the meat:* Await the meal.   173 *daff'st:* Put off; *device:*
Scheme.   174 *conveniency:* What is needful.

suppliest me with the least advantage of hope. I will indeed no longer   175
endure it; nor am I yet persuaded to put up° in peace what already I
have foolishly suffered.

IAGO: Will you hear me, Roderigo?

RODERIGO: I have heard too much, and your words and performances
are no kin together.   180

IAGO: You charge me most unjustly.

RODERIGO: With naught but truth. I have wasted myself out of my
means. The jewels you have had from me to deliver Desdemona would
half have corrupted a votarist.° You have told me she hath received
them, and returned me expectations and comforts of sudden respect°   185
and acquaintance; but I find none.

IAGO: Well, go to; very well.

RODERIGO: Very well? Go to? I cannot go to, man; nor 'tis not very
well. Nay, I think it is scurvy, and begin to find myself fopped° in it.

IAGO: Very well.   190

RODERIGO: I tell you 'tis not very well. I will make myself known to
Desdemona. If she will return me my jewels, I will give over my suit
and repent my unlawful solicitation. If not, assure yourself I will seek
satisfaction of you.

IAGO: You have said now?   195

RODERIGO: Ay, and said nothing but what I protest° intendment of
doing.

IAGO: Why, now I see there's mettle° in thee, and even from this instant
do build on thee a better opinion than ever before. Give me thy hand,
Roderigo. Thou hast taken against me a most just exception,° but yet   200
I protest I have dealt most directly° in thy affair.

RODERIGO: It hath not appeared.

IAGO: I grant indeed it hath not appeared, and your suspicion is not
without wit and judgment. But, Roderigo, if thou hast that in thee
indeed which I have greater reason to believe now than ever — I mean   205
purpose, courage, and valor — this night show it. If thou the next night
following enjoy not Desdemona, take me from this world with treachery and devise engines for° my life.

RODERIGO: Well, what is it? Is it within reason and compass?°

IAGO: Sir, there is especial commission come from Venice to depute Cas-   210
sio in Othello's place.

RODERIGO: Is that true? Why, then Othello and Desdemona return again
to Venice.

IAGO: O, no; he goes into Mauritania and taketh away with him the fair
Desdemona, unless his abode be lingered here by some accident;   215
wherein none can be so determinate° as the removing of Cassio.

---

176 *put up:* Accept.   184 *votarist:* Nun.   185 *sudden respect:* Immediate consideration.
189 *fopped:* Duped.   196 *protest:* Aver.   198 *mettle:* Spirit.   200 *exception:* Objection.
201 *directly:* Straightforwardly.   208 *engines for:* Schemes against.   209 *compass:* Possibility.   216 *determinate:* Effective.

RODERIGO: How do you mean, removing him?

IAGO: Why, by making him uncapable of Othello's place — knocking out his brains.

RODERIGO: And that you would have me to do? 220

IAGO: Ay, if you dare do yourself a profit and a right. He sups tonight with a harlotry,° and thither will I go to him. He knows not yet of his honorable fortune. If you will watch his going thence, which I will fashion to fall out° between twelve and one, you may take him at your pleasure. I will be near to second° your attempt, and he shall fall 225 between us. Come, stand not amazed at it, but go along with me. I will show you such a necessity in his death that you shall think yourself bound to put it on him. It is now high supper time, and the night grows to waste. About it.

RODERIGO: I will hear further reason for this. 230

IAGO: And you shall be satisfied. *Exeunt.*

Scene III *[The citadel.]*

Enter OTHELLO, LODOVICO, DESDEMONA, EMILIA, *and* ATTENDANTS.

LODOVICO: I do beseech you, sir, trouble yourself no further.

OTHELLO: O, pardon me; 'twill do me good to walk.

LODOVICO: Madam, good night. I humbly thank your ladyship.

DESDEMONA: Your honor is most welcome.

OTHELLO: Will you walk, sir? O, Desdemona. 5

DESDEMONA: My lord?

OTHELLO: Get you to bed on th' instant; I will be returned forthwith. Dismiss your attendant there. Look't be done.

DESDEMONA: I will, my lord. *Exit [*OTHELLO, *with* LODOVICO *and* ATTENDANTS.]

EMILIA: How goes it now? He looks gentler than he did. 10

DESDEMONA: He says he will return incontinent,°
And hath commanded me to go to bed.
And bade me to dismiss you.

EMILIA: Dismiss me?

DESDEMONA: It was his bidding; therefore, good Emilia,
Give me my nightly wearing, and adieu. 15
We must not now displease him.

EMILIA: I would you had never seen him!

DESDEMONA: So would not I. My love doth so approve him
That even his stubbornness, his checks,° his frowns —
Prithee unpin me — have grace and favor. 20

---

222 *harlotry:* Female.   224 *fall out:* Occur.   225 *second:* Support.   SCENE III. 11 *incontinent:* At once.   19 *checks:* Rebukes.

EMILIA: I have laid these sheets you bade me on the bed.

DESDEMONA: All's one.° Good Father, how foolish are our minds!
  If I do die before, prithee shroud me
  In one of these same sheets.

EMILIA: Come, come! You talk.

DESDEMONA: My mother had a maid called Barbary.   25
  She was in love; and he she loved proved mad
  And did forsake her. She had a song of "Willow";
  An old thing 'twas, but it expressed her fortune,
  And she died singing it. That song tonight
  Will not go from my mind; I have much to do   30
  But to go hang my head all at one side
  And sing it like poor Barbary. Prithee dispatch.

EMILIA: Shall I go fetch your nightgown?

DESDEMONA: No, unpin me here.
  This Lodovico is a proper man.   35

EMILIA: A very handsome man.

DESDEMONA: He speaks well.

EMILIA: I know a lady in Venice would have walked barefoot to Palestine
  for a touch of his nether lip.

DESDEMONA *[Sings]*:
  "The poor soul sat singing by a sycamore tree,   40
    Sing all a green willow;
  Her hand on her bosom, her head on her knee,
    Sing willow, willow, willow.
  The fresh streams ran by her and murmured her moans;
    Sing willow, willow, willow;   45
  Her salt tears fell from her, and soft'ned the stones —
    Sing willow, willow, willow — "
  Lay by these.   *[Gives* EMILIA *her clothes.]*
  "Willow, Willow" —
  Prithee hie° thee; he'll come anon.°   50
  "Sing all a green willow must be my garland
  Let nobody blame him; his scorn I approve" —
  Nay, that's not next. Hark! Who is't that knocks?

EMILIA: It is the wind.

DESDEMONA *[Sings]*:
  "I called my love false love; but what said he then?   55
    Sing willow, willow, willow:
  If I court moe° women, you'll couch with moe men."
  So, get thee gone; good night. Mine eyes do itch.
  Doth that bode weeping?

---

22 *All's one:* No matter.   50 *hie:* Hurry; *anon:* At once.   57 *moe:* More.

EMILIA: 'Tis neither here nor there.

DESDEMONA: I have heard it said so. O, these men, these men.   60
    Dost thou in conscience think, tell me, Emilia,
    That there be women do abuse their husbands
    In such gross kind?

EMILIA: There be some such, no question.

DESDEMONA: Wouldst thou do such a deed for all the world?

EMILIA: Why, would not you?

DESDEMONA: No, by this heavenly light!   65

EMILIA: Nor I neither by this heavenly light.
    I might do't as well i' th' dark.

DESDEMONA: Wouldst thou do such a deed for all the world?

EMILIA: The world's a huge thing; it is a great price for a small vice.

DESDEMONA: In troth, I think thou wouldst not.   70

EMILIA: In troth, I think I should; and undo't when I had done. Marry, I
    would not do such a thing for a joint-ring,° nor for measures of lawn,°
    nor for gowns, petticoats, nor caps, nor any petty exhibition,° but for
    all the whole world? Why, who would not make her husband a cuckold
    to make him a monarch? I should venture purgatory for't.   75

DESDEMONA: Beshrew me if I would do such a wrong for the whole
    world.

EMILIA: Why, the wrong is but a wrong i' th' world; and having the world
    for your labor, 'tis a wrong in your own world, and you might quickly
    make it right.   80

DESDEMONA: I do not think there is any such woman.

EMILIA: Yes, a dozen; and as many to th' vantage as would store° the
    world
       they played for.
    But I do think it is their husbands' faults
    If wives do fall. Say that they slack their duties   85
    And pour our treasures into foreign° laps;
    Or else break out in peevish jealousies,
    Throwing restraint upon us; or say they strike us,
    Or scant our former having in despite° —
    Why, we have galls; and though we have some grace.   90
    Yet have we some revenge. Let husbands know
    Their wives have sense like them. They see, and smell,
    And have their palates both for sweet and sour,
    As husbands have. What is it that they do
    When they change° us for others? Is is sport?   95
    I think it is. And doth affection° breed it?

---

72 *joint-ring:* (A ring with two interlocking halves); *lawn:* Fine linen.   73 *exhibition:* Payment.   82 *to . . . store:* In addition as would fill.   86 *foreign:* Alien, i.e., other than the
wife.   89 *scant . . . despite:* Reduce, in spite, our household allowance (?).   95 *change:* Exchange.   96 *affection:* Strong feeling, desire.

I think it doth. Is't frailty that thus errs?
It is so too. And have not we affections?
Desires for sport? and frailty? as men have?
Then let them use us well; else let them know,   100
The ills we do, their ills instruct us so.°
DESDEMONA: Good night, good night. Heaven me such uses° send,
Not to pick bad from bad, but by bad mend.   *Exeunt.*

ACT V

Scene I *(A street.)*

Enter IAGO *and* RODERIGO.

IAGO: Here, stand behind this bulk;° straight will he come.
Wear thy good rapier bare, and put it home.
Quick, quick! Fear nothing; I'll be at thy elbow.
It makes us, or it mars us, think on that,
And fix most firm thy resolution.   5
RODERIGO: Be near at hand; I may miscarry in't.
IAGO: Here, at thy hand. Be bold, and take thy stand.   *[Moves to one side.]*
RODERIGO: I have no great devotion to the deed,
And yet he hath given me satisfying reasons.
'Tis but a man gone. Forth my sword! He dies!   10
IAGO: I have rubbed this young quat° almost to the sense,°
And he grows angry. Now, whether he kill Cassio,
Or Cassio him, or each do kill the other,
Every way makes my gain. Live Roderigo,
He calls me to a restitution large   15
Of gold and jewels that I bobbed° from him
As gifts to Desdemona.
It must not be. If Cassio do remain,
He hath a daily beauty in his life
That makes me ugly; and besides, the Moor   20
May unfold me to him; there stand I in much peril.
No, he must die. But so, I hear him coming.

Enter CASSIO.

RODERIGO: I know his gait. 'Tis he. Villain, thou diest!
                    [Thrusts at CASSIO.*]*
CASSIO: That thrust had been mine enemy indeed
But that my coat° is better than thou know'st.   25
I will make proof of thine.   *[Fights with* RODERIGO.*]*

---

101 *instruct us so:* Teach us to do likewise.   102 *uses:* Practices.   ACT V, SCENE I.   1 *bulk:*
Projecting stall of a shop.   11 *quat:* Pimple; *to the sense:* Raw.   16 *bobbed:* Swindled.   25 *coat:*
i.e., a mail shirt or bulletproof vest.

RODERIGO: O, I am slain!°
CASSIO: I am maimed forever. Help, ho! Murder! Murder!

Enter OTHELLO *[to one side].*

OTHELLO: The voice of Cassio. Iago keeps his word.
RODERIGO: O, villain that I am!
OTHELLO: It is even so.
CASSIO: O help, ho! Light! A surgeon!   30
OTHELLO: 'Tis he. O brave Iago, honest and just,
    That hast such noble sense of thy friend's wrong!
    Thou teachest me. Minion,° your dear lies dead,
    And your unblest° fate hies.° Strumpet, I come.
    Forth of my heart those charms, thine eyes, are blotted.   35
    Thy bed, lust-stained, shall with lust's blood be spotted.

Exit OTHELLO. *Enter* LODOVICO *and* GRATIANO.

CASSIO: What, ho? No watch? No passage?° Murder! Murder!
GRATIANO: 'Tis some mischance. The voice is very direful.
CASSIO: O, help!
LODOVICO: Hark!   40
RODERIGO: O wretched villain!
LODOVICO: Two or three groan. 'Tis heavy night.
    These may be counterfeits. Let's think't unsafe
    To come into the cry without more help.
RODERIGO: Nobody come? Then shall I bleed to death.   45
LODOVICO: Hark!

Enter IAGO *[with a light].*

GRATIANO: Here's one comes in his shirt, with light and weapons.
IAGO: Who's there? Whose noise is this that cries on murder?
LODOVICO: We do not know.
IAGO: Do not you hear a cry?
CASSIO: Here, here! For heaven's sake, help me!
IAGO: What's the matter?   50
GRATIANO: This is Othello's ancient, as I take it.
LODOVICO: The same indeed, a very valiant fellow.
IAGO: What are you here that cry so grievously?
CASSIO: Iago? O, I am spoiled, undone by villains.
    Give me some help.   55

---

26 *slain:* Most editors add here a stage direction that has Iago wounding Cassio in the leg from behind, but remaining unseen. However, nothing in the text requires this, and Cassio's wound can be given him in the fight with Roderigo, for presumably when Cassio attacks Roderigo the latter would not simply accept the thrust but would parry. Since Iago enters again at line 46, he must exit at some point after line 22.   33 *Minion:* Hussy, i.e., Desdemona.   34 *unblest:* Unsanctified; *hies:* Approaches swiftly.   37 *passage:* Passers-by.

IAGO: O me, lieutenant! What villains have done this?
CASSIO: I think that one of them is hereabout
    And cannot make away.
IAGO: O treacherous villains!
    [To LODOVICO *and* GRATIANO*]* What are you there?
    Come in, and give some help.   60
RODERIGO: O, help me here!
CASSIO: That's one of them.
IAGO: O murd'rous slave! O villain!
                                    [Stabs RODERIGO.*]*
RODERIGO: O damned Iago! O inhuman dog!
IAGO: Kill men i' th' dark? — Where be these bloody thieves? —
    How silent is this town! — Ho! Murder! Murder! —   65
    What may you be? Are you of good or evil?
LODOVICO: As you shall prove us, praise us.
IAGO: Signior Lodovico?
LODOVICO: He, sir.
IAGO: I cry you mercy. Here's Cassio hurt by villains.   70
GRATIANO: Cassio?
IAGO: How is't, brother?
CASSIO: My leg is cut in two.
IAGO: Marry, heaven forbid!
    Light, gentlemen. I'll bind it with my shirt.

    Enter BIANCA.

BIANCA: What is the matter, ho? Who is't that cried?   75
IAGO: Who is't that cried?
BIANCA: O my dear Cassio! My sweet Cassio!
    O Cassio, Cassio, Cassio!
IAGO: O notable strumpet! — Cassio, may you suspect
    Who they should be that have thus mangled you?   80
CASSIO: No.
GRATIANO: I am sorry to find you thus. I have been to seek you.
IAGO: Lend me a garter. So. O for a chair
    To bear him easily hence.
BIANCA: Alas, he faints! O Cassio, Cassio, Cassio!   85
IAGO: Gentlemen all, I do suspect this trash
    To be a party in this injury. —
    Patience awhile, good Cassio. — Come, come.
    Lend me a light. Know we this face or no?
    Alas, my friend and my dear countryman   90
    Roderigo? No. — Yes, sure. — Yes, 'tis Roderigo!
GRATIANO: What, of Venice?
IAGO: Even he, sir. Did you know him?
GRATIANO: Know him? Ay.

IAGO: Signior Gratiano? I cry your gentle pardon.
 These bloody accidents must excuse my manners   95
 That so neglected you.
GRATIANO: I am glad to see you.
IAGO: How do you, Cassio?—O, a chair, a chair!
GRATIANO: Roderigo?
IAGO: He, he, 'tis he! *[A chair brought in.]* O, that's well said;° the chair.
 Some good man bear him carefully from hence.   100
 I'll fetch the general's surgeon. *[To* BIANCA*]* For you, mistress,
 Save you your labor. *[To* CASSIO*]* He that lies slain here, Cassio,
 Was my dear friend. What malice was between you?
CASSIO: None in the world; nor do I know the man.
IAGO: What, look you pale?—O, bear him out o' th' air.   105

*[*CASSIO *is carried off.]*

 Stay you, good gentlemen.—Look you pale, mistress?
 Do you perceive the gastness° of her eye?
 Nay, if you stare, we shall hear more anon.
 Behold her well; I pray you look upon her.
 Do you see, gentlemen? Nay, guiltiness will speak,   110
 Though tongues were out of use.°

[Enter EMILIA.*]*

EMILIA: Alas, what is the matter? What is the matter, husband?
IAGO: Cassio hath here been set on in the dark
 By Roderigo and fellows that are scaped.
 He's almost slain, and Roderigo quite dead.   115
EMILIA: Alas, good gentleman! Alas, good Cassio!
IAGO: This is the fruits of whoring. Prithee, Emilia,
 Go know of Cassio where he supped tonight.
 (To BIANCA*)* What, do you shake at that?
BIANCA: He supped at my house; but I therefore shake not.   120
IAGO: O, did he so? I charge° you go with me.
EMILIA: Oh fie upon thee, strumpet!
BIANCA: I am no strumpet, but of life as honest
 As you that thus abuse me.
EMILIA: As I? Fie upon thee!
IAGO: Kind gentlemen, let's go see poor Cassio dressed,°   125
 [To BIANCA*]* Come, mistress, you must tell's another tale.
 Emilia, run you to the citadel
 And tell my lord and lady what hath happed   *[Exit* EMILIA.*]*

99 *well said:* Well done. 107 *gastness:* Terror. 111 *tongues were out of use:* Men no longer
spoke. 121 *charge:* Command. 125 *dressed:* Bandaged.

Will you go on afore?   *Exeunt [all but* IAGO.*]*
                This is the night
That either makes me or fordoes me quite.°   [Exit.]   130

Scene II *[*DESDEMONA*'s chamber.]*

Enter OTHELLO *[with a light], and* DESDEMONA *in her bed.*

OTHELLO: It is the cause, it is the cause, my soul.
    Let me not name it to you, you chaste stars.
    It is the cause. Yet I'll not shed her blood,
    Nor scar that whiter skin of hers than snow
    And smooth as monumental alabaster.   5
    Yet she must die, else she'll betray more men.
    Put out the light, and then put out the light.
    If I quench thee, thou flaming minister,°
    I can again thy former light restore,
    Should I repent me; but once put out thy light,   10
    Thou cunning'st° pattern of excelling nature,
    I know not where is that Promethean heat°
    That can thy light relume.° When I have plucked the rose,
    I cannot give it vital° growth again;
    It needs must wither. I'll smell thee on the tree.   *[He kisses her.]*   15
    O balmy breath, that dost almost persuade
    Justice to break her sword. One more, one more!
    Be thus when thou art dead, and I will kill thee,
    And love thee after. One more, and that's the last!
    So sweet was ne'er so fatal. I must weep,   20
    But they are cruel tears. This sorrow's heavenly;
    It strikes where it doth love. She wakes.
DESDEMONA: Who's there? Othello?
OTHELLO: Ay, Desdemona.
DESDEMONA: Will you come to bed, my lord?
OTHELLO: Have you prayed tonight, Desdemon?
DESDEMONA: Ay, my lord.   25
OTHELLO: If you bethink yourself of any crime
    Unreconciled as yet to heaven and grace,
    Solicit for it straight.
DESDEMONA: Alack, my lord, what may you mean by that?
OTHELLO: Well, do it, and be brief; I will walk by.°   30
    I would not kill thy unprepared spirit.
    No, heavens forfend! I would not kill thy soul.

---

130 *fordoes me quite:* Completely ruins me.   SCENE II. 8 *minister:* Worker, servant.   11 *cunning'st:* Most intricate and skillfully wrought (by nature excelling itself).   12 *Promethean heat:* Divine fire (Prometheus is the Titan who stole fire from heaven and gave it to man).   13 *relume:* Relight.   14 *vital:* Living.   30 *by:* Nearby.

DESDEMONA: Talk you of killing?
OTHELLO: Ay, I do.
DESDEMONA: Then heaven
    Have mercy on me!
OTHELLO: Amen, with all my heart.
DESDEMONA: If you say so, I hope you will not kill me.   35
OTHELLO: Humh.
DESDEMONA: And yet I fear you; for you're fatal then
    When your eyes roll so. Why I should fear I know not,
    Since guiltiness I know not; but yet I feel I fear.
OTHELLO: Think on thy sins.
DESDEMONA: They are loves I bear to you.   40
OTHELLO: Ay, and for that thou diest.
DESDEMONA: That death's unnatural that kills for loving.
    Alas, why gnaw you so your nether lip?
    Some bloody passion shakes your very frame.
    These are portents; but yet I hope, I hope,   45
    They do not point on me.
OTHELLO: Peace and be still.
DESDEMONA: I will so. What's the matter?
OTHELLO: That handkerchief which I so loved and gave thee,
    Thou gav'st to Cassio.
DESDEMONA: No, by my life and soul!
    Send for the man and ask him.
OTHELLO: Sweet soul, take heed,   50
    Take heed of perjury; thou art on thy deathbed.
DESDEMONA: Ay, but not yet to die.
OTHELLO: Presently.°
    Therefore confess thee freely of thy sin,
    For to deny each article° with oath
    Cannot remove nor choke the strong conception   55
    That I do groan withal. Thou art to die.
DESDEMONA: Then Lord have mercy on me.
OTHELLO: I say, amen.
DESDEMONA: And have you mercy too. I never did
    Offend you in my life; never loved Cassio
    But with such general warranty° of heaven   60
    As I might love. I never gave him token.
OTHELLO: By heaven, I saw my handkerchief in's hand!
    O perjured woman! thou dost stone° my heart,
    And mak'st me call what I intend to do
    A murder, which I thought a sacrifice.   65
    I saw the handkerchief.

52 *Presently:* Immediately.   54 *article:* Item (of the charge of adultery. Othello makes heavy use of legal terms in this scene).   60 *warranty:* Allowance.   63 *stone:* Turn to stone.

DESDEMONA: He found it then.
    I never gave it him. Send for him hither.
    Let him confess a truth.
OTHELLO: He hath confessed.
DESDEMONA: What, my lord?
OTHELLO: That he hath used thee.
DESDEMONA: How? Unlawfully?
OTHELLO: Ay.   70
DESDEMONA: He will not say so.
OTHELLO: No, his mouth is stopped.
    Honest Iago hath ta'en order for't.°
DESDEMONA: O, my fear interprets. What, is he dead?
OTHELLO: Had all his hairs been lives, my great revenge
    Had stomach° for them all.   75
DESDEMONA: Alas, he is betrayed, and I undone!
OTHELLO: Out, strumpet! Weep'st thou for him to my face?
DESDEMONA: O, banish me, my lord, but kill me not!
OTHELLO: Down, strumpet!
DESDEMONA: Kill me tomorrow; let me live tonight!   80
OTHELLO: Nay, if you strive—
DESDEMONA: But half an hour!
OTHELLO: Being done, there is no pause.
DESDEMONA: But while I say one prayer!
OTHELLO: It is too late.   *Smothers her.*

    EMILIA *at the door.*

EMILIA *[Calls within]*: My lord, my lord! What, ho, my lord, my lord!
OTHELLO: What noise is this? Not dead? Not yet quite dead?   85
    I that am cruel am yet merciful;
    I would not have thee linger in thy pain.
EMILIA *[Within]*: What, ho! My lord, my lord!
OTHELLO: So, so. Who's there?
EMILIA *[Within]*: O, good my lord, I would speak a word with you.
OTHELLO: Yes, 'tis Emilia. — By and by. — She's dead. —   90
    'Tis like she comes to speak of Cassio's death.
    The noise was high.° Ha! No more moving?
    Still as the grave. — Shall she come in? Were't good? —
    I think she stirs again. No. — What's best to do?
    If she come in, she'll sure speak to my wife.   95
    My wife! My wife! What wife? I have no wife.
    O, insupportable! O heavy hour!
    Methinks it should be now a huge eclipse

---

72 *ta'en order for't:* Made sure of it.   75 *stomach:* Appetite.   92 *high:* Loud (Q1 reads
"here").   98–100 *Methinks . . . alteration:* (The Elizabethans believed that great changes in human affairs were reflected by disorders in nature.)

Of sun and moon, and that th' affrighted globe
Should yawn° at alteration.

EMILIA *[Within]:*   I do beseech you   100
    That I may speak with you, O good my lord!

OTHELLO: I had forgot thee. O, come in, Emilia.
    Soft, by and by. — Let me the curtains draw. —

[Draws the bed hangings and then opens the door.]

Where art thou?

Enter EMILIA.

                    What's the matter with thee now?

EMILIA: O my good lord, yonder's foul murders done!   105

OTHELLO: What? Now?

EMILIA: But now, my lord.

OTHELLO: It is the very error° of the moon.
    She comes more nearer earth than she was wont
    And makes men mad.   110

EMILIA: Cassio, my lord, hath killed a young Venetian
    Called Roderigo.

OTHELLO: Roderigo killed?
    And Cassio killed?

EMILIA: No, Cassio is not killed.

OTHELLO: Not Cassio killed? Then murder's out of tune,
    And sweet revenge grows harsh.   115

DESDEMONA: O, falsely, falsely murdered!

EMILIA: O Lord! What cry is that?

OTHELLO: That? What?

EMILIA: Out and alas! that was my lady's voice.
    Help! Help, ho! Help! O lady, speak again!
    Sweet Desdemona! O sweet mistress, speak!   120

DESDEMONA: A guiltless death I die.

EMILIA: O, who hath done this deed?

DESDEMONA: Nobody — I myself. Farewell.
    Commend me to my kind lord. O, farewell!   *[She dies.]*

OTHELLO: Why, how should she be murd'red?

EMILIA: Alas, who knows?   125

OTHELLO: You heard her say herself, it was not I.

EMILIA: She said so. I must needs report the truth.

OTHELLO: She's like a liar gone to burning hell!
    'Twas I that killed her.

EMILIA: O, the more angel she,
    And you the blacker devil!   130

---

100 *yawn:* Gape open (as in an earthquake). 108 *error:* Wandering out of regular course (disorders in the heavens were believed by some to cause disorders on earth, as well as vice versa).

OTHELLO: She turned to folly, and she was a whore.

EMILIA: Thou dost belie her, and thou art a devil.

OTHELLO: She was false as water.

EMILIA: Thou art rash as fire to say
That she was false. O, she was heavenly true!

OTHELLO: Cassio did top her. Ask thy husband else.   135
O, I were damned beneath all depth in hell
But that I did proceed upon just grounds
To this extremity. Thy husband knew it all.

EMILIA: My husband?

OTHELLO: Thy husband.

EMILIA: That she was false to wedlock?

OTHELLO: Ay, with Cassio. Had she been true,   140
If heaven would make me such another world
Of one entire and perfect chrysolite,°
I'd not have sold her for it.

EMILIA: My husband?

OTHELLO: Ay, 'twas he that told me on her first.
An honest man he is, and hates the slime   145
That sticks on filthy deeds.

EMILIA: My husband?

OTHELLO: What needs this iterance? Woman, I say thy husband.

EMILIA: O mistress, villainy hath made mocks with love!
My husband say she was false?

OTHELLO: He, woman.
I say, thy husband. Dost understand the word?   150
My friend, thy husband; honest, honest Iago.

EMILIA: If he say so, may his pernicious soul
Rot half a grain a day! He lies to th' heart.
She was too fond of her most filthy bargain.

OTHELLO: Hah?   155

EMILIA: Do thy worst.
This deed of thine is no more worthy heaven
Than thou wast worthy her.

OTHELLO: Peace, you were best.°

EMILIA: Thou hast not half that pow'r to do me harm
As I have to be hurt. O gull! O dolt!   160
As ignorant as dirt! Thou hast done a deed —

[OTHELLO moves to draw his sword.]

I care not for thy sword; I'll make thee known,
Though I lost twenty lives. Help! Help! Ho! Help!
The Moor hath killed my mistress! Murder! murder!

142 *chrysolite:* Topaz.   158 *Peace, you were best:* i.e., you had better be silent.

Enter MONTANO, GRATIANO, *and* IAGO *[and Others].*

MONTANO: What is the matter? How now, general?   165
EMILIA: O, are you come, Iago? You have done well,
    That men must lay their murders on your neck.
GRATIANO: What is the matter?
EMILIA: Disprove this villain, if thou be'st a man.
    He says thou told'st him that his wife was false.   170
    I know thou didst not; thou'rt not such a villain.
    Speak, for my heart is full.
IAGO: I told him what I thought, and told no more
    Than what he found himself was apt and true.
EMILIA: But did you ever tell him she was false?   175
IAGO: I did.
EMILIA: You told a lie, an odious damnèd lie!
    Upon my soul, a lie! A wicked lie!
    She false with Cassio? Did you say with Cassio?
IAGO: With Cassio, mistress. Go to, charm° your tongue.   180
EMILIA: I will not charm my tongue; I am bound to speak:
    My mistress here lies murdered in her bed.
ALL: O heavens forfend!
EMILIA: And your reports have set the murder on.
OTHELLO: Nay, stare not, masters. It is true indeed.   185
GRATIANO: 'Tis a strange truth.
MONTANO: O monstrous act!
EMILIA: Villainy, villainy, villainy!
    I think upon't — I think I smell't! — O villainy!
    I thought so then. — I'll kill myself for grief. —
    O villainy, villainy!   190
IAGO: What, are you mad? I charge you get you home.
EMILIA: Good gentlemen, let me have leave to speak.
    'Tis proper I obey him, but not now.
    Perchance, Iago, I will ne'er go home.
OTHELLO: O! O! O!   *[Falls on the bed.]*
EMILIA: Nay, lay thee down and roar,   195
    For thou hast killed the sweetest innocent
    That e'er did lift up eye.
OTHELLO: O, she was foul!   *[Rises.]*
    I scarce did know you, uncle. There lies your niece,
    Whose breath, indeed, these hands have newly stopped.
    I know this act shows horrible and grim.   200
GRATIANO: Poor Desdemona! I am glad thy father's dead.
    Thy match was mortal to him, and pure grief
    Shore his old thread in twain. Did he live now,

180 *charm:* Control.

This sight would make him do a desperate turn;
Yea, curse his better angel from his side,   205
And fall to reprobation.°
OTHELLO: 'Tis pitiful; but yet Iago knows
That she with Cassio hath the act of shame
A thousand times committed. Cassio confessed it;
And she did gratify his amorous works   210
With that recognizance and pledge of love,
Which I first gave her. I saw it in his hand.
It was a handkerchief, an antique token
My father gave my mother.
EMILIA: O God! O heavenly God!   215
IAGO: Zounds, hold your peace!
EMILIA: 'Twill out, 'twill out! I peace?
No, I will speak as liberal as the north.°
Let heaven and men and devils, let them all,
All, all, cry shame against me, yet I'll speak.
IAGO: Be wise, and get you home.
EMILIA: I will not.   220

[IAGO *draws and threatens* EMILIA.]

GRATIANO: Fie! Your sword upon a woman?
EMILIA: O thou dull Moor, that handkerchief thou speak'st of
I found by fortune, and did give my husband;
For often with a solemn earnestness —
More than indeed belonged to such a trifle —   · 225
He begged of me to steal't.
IAGO: Villainous whore!
EMILIA: She give it Cassio? No, alas, I found it,
And I did give't my husband.
IAGO: Filth, thou liest!
EMILIA: By heaven, I do not, I do not, gentlemen.
O murd'rous coxcomb! What should such a fool   230
Do with so good a wife?
OTHELLO: Are there no stones° in heaven
But what serves for the thunder? Precious villain!

[The MOOR *runs at* IAGO, *but is disarmed by* MONTANO. IAGO
kills his wife.]

GRATIANO: The woman falls. Sure he hath killed his wife.
EMILIA: Ay, ay. O, lay me by my mistress' side.   [Exit IAGO.]
GRATIANO: He's gone, but his wife's killed.   235

---

206 *reprobation:* Damnation.   217 *liberal as the north:* Freely (and bitingly) the north wind
blows.   231 *stones:* Thunderbolts.

MONTANO: 'Tis a notorious° villain. Take you this weapon,
    Which I have recovered from the Moor.
    Come, guard the door without. Let him not pass,
    But kill him rather. I'll after that same villain,
    For 'tis a damnèd slave.   *Exit [with all but* OTHELLO *and* EMILIA*]*.
OTHELLO: I am not valiant neither;   240
    But every puny whipster° gets my sword.
    But why should honor outlive honesty?
    Let it go all.
EMILIA: What did thy song bode, lady?
    Hark, canst thou hear me? I will play the swan,
    And die in music. *[Sings]* "Willow, willow, willow."   245
    Moor, she was chaste. She loved thee, cruel Moor,
    So come my soul to bliss as I speak true.
    So speaking as I think, alas, I die.   *[She dies.]*
OTHELLO: I have another weapon in this chamber;
    It was a sword of Spain, the ice-brook's temper.   250
    O, here it is. — Uncle, I must come forth.
GRATIANO *[Within]:* If thou attempt it, it will cost thee dear.
    Thou hast no weapon, and perforce must suffer.
OTHELLO: Look in upon me then and speak with me,
    Or, naked as I am, I will assault thee.   255

    [Enter GRATIANO.*]*

GRATIANO: What is the matter?
OTHELLO: Behold, I have a weapon;
    A better never did itself sustain
    Upon a soldier's thigh. I have seen the day
    That with this little arm and this good sword
    I have made my way through more impediments   260
    Than twenty times your stop. But O vain boast!
    Who can control his fate? 'Tis not so now.
    Be not afraid, though you do see me weaponed.
    Here is my journey's end, here is my butt,°
    And very seamark of my utmost sail.°   265
    Do you go back dismayed? 'Tis a lost fear.
    Man but a rush° against Othello's breast.
    And he retires. Where should Othello go?
    Now, how dost thou look now? O ill-starred wench!
    Pale as thy smock! When we shall meet at compt,°   270
    This look of thine will hurl my soul from heaven,

---

236 *notorious:* Out-and-out.   241 *puny whipster:* Small top-whipping boy (?).   264 *butt:* Target,
stopping place.   265 *seamark of my utmost sail:* Maker of my furthest journey.   267 *Man but a
rush:* Attack with only a reed.   270 *compt:* Judgment Day.

And fiends will snatch at it. Cold, cold, my girl?
Even like thy chastity.
O cursèd, cursèd slave! Whip me, ye devils,
From the possession of° this heavenly sight!   275
Blow me about in winds! roast me in sulfur!
Wash me in steep-down gulfs of liquid fire!
O Desdemon! Dead Desdemon; dead. O! O!

Enter LODOVICO, CASSIO, MONTANO, *and* IAGO *[as prisoner,]*
with Officers.

LODOVICO: Where is this rash and most unfortunate man?
OTHELLO: That's he that was Othello? Here I am.   280
LODOVICO: Where is that viper? Bring the villain forth.
OTHELLO: I look down towards his feet° — but that's a fable.
    If that thou be'st a devil, I cannot kill thee.   *[Wounds* IAGO.*]*
LODOVICO: Wrench his sword from him.   *[*OTHELLO *is disarmed.]*
IAGO: I bleed, sir, but not killed.
OTHELLO: I am not sorry neither. I'd have thee live;   285
    For in my sense, 'tis happiness to die.
LODOVICO: O thou Othello that was once so good,
    Fall'n in the practice° of a cursèd slave,
    What shall be said to thee?
OTHELLO: Why, anything:
    An honorable murder, if you will;   290
    For naught I did in hate, but all in honor.
LODOVICO: This wretch hath part confessed his villainy.
    Did you and he consent in Cassio's death?
OTHELLO: Ay.
CASSIO: Dear general, I never gave you cause.   295
OTHELLO: I do believe it, and I ask your pardon.
    Will you, I pray, demand that demi-devil
    Why he hath thus ensnared my soul and body?
IAGO: Demand me nothing. What you know, you know.
    From this time forth I never will speak word.   300
LODOVICO: What, not to pray?
GRATIANO: Torments will ope your lips.
OTHELLO: Well, thou dost best.
LODOVICO: Sir, you shall understand what hath befall'n,
    Which, as I think, you know not. Here is a letter
    Found in the pocket of the slain Roderigo;   305
    And here another. The one of them imports
    The death of Cassio to be undertook
    By Roderigo.

275 *the possession of:* Being possessed by.   282 *towards . . . feet* i.e., for his cloven hoofs.   288 *prac-*
tice: Plotting.

OTHELLO: O villain!

CASSIO: Most heathenish and most gross!

LODOVICO: Now here's another discontented paper   310
    Found in his pocket too; and this, it seems,
    Roderigo meant t' have sent this damnèd villain;
    But that, belike, Iago in the interim
    Came in and satisfied him.

OTHELLO: O thou pernicious caitiff!
    How came you, Cassio, by that handkerchief   315
    That was my wife's?

CASSIO: I found it in my chamber;
    And he himself confessed it but even now
    That there he dropped it for a special purpose
    Which wrought to his desire.

OTHELLO: O fool! Fool! Fool!

CASSIO: There is besides in Roderigo's letter,   320
    How he upbraids Iago that he made him
    Brave me upon the watch; whereon it came
    That I was cast; and even but now he spake,
    After long seeming dead — Iago hurt him,
    Iago set him on.   325

LODOVICO: You must forsake this room and go with us.
    Your power and your command is taken off,
    And Cassio rules in Cyprus. For this slave,
    If there be any cunning cruelty
    That can torment him much and hold him long,   330
    It shall be his. You shall close prisoner rest
    Till that the nature of your fault be known
    To the Venetian state. Come, bring away.

OTHELLO: Soft you, a word or two before you go.
    I have done the state some service and they know't.   335
    No more of that. I pray you, in your letters,
    When you shall these unlucky deeds relate,
    Speak of me as I am. Nothing extenuate,
    Nor set down aught in malice. Then must you speak
    Of one that loved not wisely, but too well;   340
    Of one not easily jealous, but, being wrought,
    Perplexed in the extreme; of one whose hand,
    Like the base Judean,° threw a pearl away
    Richer than all his tribe; of one whose subdued eyes,
    Albeit unusèd to the melting mood,   345
    Drops tears as fast as the Arabian trees
    Their med'cinable gum. Set you down this.

343 *Judean:* (Most editors use the Q1 reading, "Indian," here, but F is clear: both readings point toward the infidel, the unbeliever.)

    And say besides that in Aleppo once,
    Where a malignant and a turbaned Turk
    Beat a Venetian and traduced the state,   350
    I took by th' throat the circumcisèd dog
    And smote him — thus.   *[He stabs himself.]*
LODOVICO: O bloody period!°
GRATIANO: All that is spoke is marred.
OTHELLO: I kissed thee ere I killed thee. No way but this,
    Killing myself, to die upon a kiss.   355
                    [He falls over DESDEMONA *and dies.]*
CASSIO: This did I fear, but thought he had no weapon;
    For he was great of heart.
LODOVICO *[To* IAGO*]*:   O Spartan dog,
    More fell° than anguish, hunger, or the sea!
    Look on the tragic loading of this bed.
    This is thy work. The object poisons sight;   360
    Let it be hid.   *[Bed curtains drawn.]*
                    Gratiano, keep° the house,
    And seize upon the fortunes of the Moor,
    For they succeed on you. To you, lord governor,
    Remains the censure of this hellish villain,
    The time, the place, the torture. O, enforce it!   365
    Myself will straight aboard, and to the state
    This heavy act with heavy heart relate.   *Exeunt.*

353 *period:* End.   358 *fell:* Cruel.   361 *keep:* Remain in.

MOLIÈRE (1622–1673)

The Doctor in Spite of Himself

Characters

SGANARELLE, *husband of* MARTINE
MARTINE, *wife of* SGANARELLE
MONSIEUR ROBERT, *neighbor of* SGANARELLE
VALÈRE, *servant of* GÉRONTE
LUCAS, *husband of* JACQUELINE
GÉRONTE, *father of* LUCINDE
JACQUELINE, *wet-nurse at Géronte's and wife of* LUCAS
LUCINDE, *daughter of* GÉRONTE
LÉANDRE, *in love with* LUCINDE
THIBAUT, *a peasant, father of* PERRIN
PERRIN, *a peasant, son of* THIBAUT

ACT I

A clearing. The houses of SGANARELLE *and* MONSIEUR ROBERT *may be seen through the trees.*

Scene I SGANARELLE, MARTINE *(who enter quarreling)*

SGANARELLE: No, I tell you I won't do anything of the sort, and I'm the one to say and be the master.

MARTINE: And *I* tell *you* that I want you to live to suit me, and I didn't marry you to put up with your carryings-on.

SGANARELLE: Oh, what a weary business it is to have a wife, and how right Aristotle is when he says a wife is worse than a demon!

MARTINE: Just listen to that smart fellow with his half-wit Aristotle!

SGANARELLE: Yes, a smart fellow. Just find me a woodcutter who knows how to reason about things, like me, who served a famous doctor for six years, and who as a youngster knew his elementary Latin book by heart.

MARTINE: A plague on the crazy fool!

SGANARELLE: A plague on the slut!

MARTINE: Cursed be the day when I went and said yes!

SGANARELLE: Cursed be the hornified notary who had me sign my own ruin!

MARTINE: Really, it's a fine thing for you to complain of that affair! Should you let a single moment go by without thanking Heaven for having me for your wife? And did you deserve to marry a person like me?

SGANARELLE: Oh, yes, you did me too much honor, and I had reason to congratulate myself on our wedding night! Oh, my Lord! Don't get me started on that! I'd have a few things to say . . .

MARTINE: What? What would you say?

SGANARELLE: Let it go at that; let's drop that subject. Enough that we know what we know, and that you were very lucky to find me.

MARTINE: What do you mean, lucky to find you? A man who drags me down to the poorhouse, a debauchee, a traitor, who eats up everything I own?

SGANARELLE: That's a lie: I drink part of it.

MARTINE: Who sells, piece by piece, everything in the house.

SGANARELLE: That's living on our means.

MARTINE: Who's taken even my bed from under me.

SGANARELLE: You'll get up all the earlier in the morning.

MARTINE: In short, who doesn't leave a stick of furniture in the whole house.

SGANARELLE: All the easier to move out.

MARTINE: And who does nothing but gamble and drink from morning to night.

SGANARELLE: That's so I won't get bored.

MARTINE: And what do you expect me to do with my family in the meantime?

SGANARELLE: Whatever you like.

MARTINE: I have four poor little children on my hands.

SGANARELLE: Set them on the floor.

MARTINE: Who are constantly asking me for bread.

SGANARELLE: Give them the whip. When I've had plenty to eat and drink, I want everyone in my house to have his fill.

MARTINE: And you, you drunkard, do you expect things to go on forever like this?

SGANARELLE: My good wife, let's go easy, if you please.

MARTINE: And me to endure your insolence and debauchery to all eternity?

SGANARELLE: Let's not get excited, my good wife.

MARTINE: And that I can't find a way to make you do your duty?

SGANARELLE: My good wife, you know that my soul isn't very patient and my arm is pretty good.

MARTINE: You make me laugh with your threats.

SGANARELLE: My good little wife, my love, you're itching for trouble, as usual.

MARTINE: I'll show you I'm not afraid of you.

SGANARELLE: My dear better half, you're asking for something.

MARTINE: Do you think your words frighten me?

SGANARELLE: Sweet object of my eternal vows, I'll box your ears.

MARTINE: Drunkard that you are!

SGANARELLE: I'll beat you.

MARTINE: Wine-sack!

SGANARELLE: I'll wallop you.

MARTINE: Wretch!

SGANARELLE: I'll tan your hide.

MARTINE: Traitor, wiseacre, deceiver, coward, scoundrel, gallowsbird, beggar, good-for-nothing, rascal, villain, thief . . .

SGANARELLE: *(takes a stick and beats her)*: Ah! So you want it, eh?

MARTINE: Oh, oh, oh, oh!

SGANARELLE: That's the right way to pacify you.

Scene II MONSIEUR ROBERT, SGANARELLE, MARTINE

MONSIEUR ROBERT: Hey there, hey there, hey there! Fie! What's this? What infamy! Confound the rascal for beating his wife that way!

MARTINE *(arms akimbo, forces* MONSIEUR ROBERT *back as she talks, and finally gives him a slap)*: And as for me, I want him to beat me.

MONSIEUR ROBERT: Oh! Then with all my heart, I consent.

MARTINE: What are you meddling for?

MONSIEUR ROBERT: I'm wrong.

MARTINE: Is it any business of yours?

MONSIEUR ROBERT: You're right.

MARTINE: Just look at this meddler, trying to keep husbands from beating their wives.

MONSIEUR ROBERT: I take it all back.

MARTINE: What have you got to do with it?

MONSIEUR ROBERT: Nothing.

MARTINE: Have you any right to poke your nose in?

MONSIEUR ROBERT: No.

MARTINE: Mind your own business.

MONSIEUR ROBERT: I won't say another word.

MARTINE: I like to be beaten.

MONSIEUR ROBERT: All right.

MARTINE: It's no skin off your nose.

MONSIEUR ROBERT: That's true.

MARTINE: And you're a fool to come butting in where it's none of your business. *(Slaps* MONSIEUR ROBERT. *He turns toward* SGANARELLE, *who likewise forces him back as he talks, threatening him with the same stick and finally beating and routing him with it.)*

MONSIEUR ROBERT: Neighbor, I beg your pardon with all my heart. Go on, beat your wife and thrash her to your heart's content; I'll help you if you want.

SGANARELLE: Me, I don't want to.

MONSIEUR ROBERT: Oh well, that's another matter.

SGANARELLE: I want to beat her if I want to; and I don't want to beat her if I don't want to.

MONSIEUR ROBERT: Very well.

SGANARELLE: She's my wife, not yours.

MONSIEUR ROBERT: Undoubtedly.

SGANARELLE: I don't take orders from you.

MONSIEUR ROBERT: Agreed.

SGANARELLE: I don't need any help from you.

MONSIEUR ROBERT: That's fine with me.

SGANARELLE: And you're a meddler to interfere in other people's affairs. Learn that Cicero says that you mustn't put the bark between the tree and your finger. *(Beats* MONSIEUR ROBERT *and drives him offstage, then returns to his wife and clasps her hand.)* Well now, let's us two make peace. Shake on it.

MARTINE: Oh yes! After beating me that way!

SGANARELLE: That's nothing. Shake.

MARTINE: I will not.

SGANARELLE: Eh?

MARTINE: No.

SGANARELLE: My little wife!

MARTINE: No sir.

SGANARELLE: Come on, I say.

MARTINE: I won't do anything of the kind.

SGANARELLE: Come, come, come.

MARTINE: No, I want to be angry.

SGANARELLE: Fie! It's nothing. Come on, come on.

MARTINE: Let me be.

SGANARELLE: Shake, I say.

MARTINE: You've treated me too badly.

SGANARELLE: All right then, I ask your pardon: give me your hand.

MARTINE: I forgive you; *(aside)* but you'll pay for it.

SGANARELLE: You're crazy to pay any attention to that: those little things are necessary from time to time for a good friendship; and five or six cudgel-blows between people in love only whet their affection. There now, I'm off to the woods, and I promise you more than a hundred bundles of kindling wood today.

Scene III MARTINE *(alone)*

MARTINE: All right, whatever face I put on, I'm not forgetting my resentment; and I'm burning inside to find ways to punish you for the beatings you give me. I know very well that a wife always has in hand means of taking revenge on a husband; but that's too delicate a punishment for my gallowsbird. I want a vengeance that he'll feel a bit more; and that would be no satisfaction for the offense I've received.

Scene IV VALÈRE, LUCAS, MARTINE

LUCAS: Doggone it! We sure both tooken on one heck of a job; and me, I don't know what I'm gonna come up with.

VALÈRE: Well, what do you expect as the wet-nurse's husband? We have to obey our master; and then we both have an interest in the health of the mistress, his daughter; and no doubt her marriage, put off by her illness, would be worth some kind of present to us. Horace, who is generous, has the best chances of anyone to win her hand; and although she has shown a fondness for a certain Léandre, you know very well that her father has never consented to accept him as a son-in-law.

MARTINE *(musing, aside)*: Can't I think up some scheme to get revenge?

LUCAS: But what kind of wild idea has the master tooken into his head, now that the doctors have used up all their Latin?

VALÈRE: You sometimes find, by looking hard, what you don't find at first; and often in simple places . . .

MARTINE: Yes, I must get revenge, whatever the price; that beating sticks in my crop, I can't swallow it, and . . . *(She says all this still musing, not noticing the two men, so that when she turns around she bumps into them.)* Oh! Gentlemen, I beg your pardon; I didn't see you, and I was trying to think of something that's bothering me.

VALÈRE: Everyone has his problems in this world, and we too are looking for something we would very much like to find.

MARTINE: Would it be anything I might help you with?

VALÈRE: It just might. We're trying to find some able man, some special doctor, who might give some relief to our master's daughter, ill with a disease that has suddenly taken away the use of her tongue. Several doctors have already exhausted all their learning on her; but you sometimes find people with wonderful secrets, with certain special remedies, who can very often do what the others couldn't; and that's what we're looking for.

MARTINE *(aside)*: Oh! What a wonderful scheme Heaven inspires me with to get revenge on my gallowsbird! *(Aloud)* You couldn't have come to a better place to find what you're looking for; and we have a man here, the most marvelous man in the world for hopeless illnesses.

VALÈRE: And, pray, where can we find him?

MARTINE: You'll find him right now in that little clearing over there, spending his time cutting wood.

LUCAS: A doctor cutting wood?

VALÈRE: Spending his time gathering herbs, do you mean?

MARTINE: No, he's an extraordinary man who enjoys that — strange, fantastic, crotchety — you'd never take him for what he is. He goes around dressed in an eccentric way, sometimes affects ignorance, keeps his knowledge hidden, and every day avoids nothing so much as exercising the marvelous talents Heaven has given him for medicine.

VALÈRE: It's an amazing thing that all great men always have some caprice, some little grain of folly mingled with their learning.

MARTINE: This one's mania is beyond all belief, for it sometimes goes to the point of his wanting to be beaten before he'll acknowledge his capacity; and I'm telling you you'll never get the better of him, he'll never admit he's a doctor, if he's in that mood, unless you each take a stick and beat him into confessing in the end what he'll hide from you at first. That's what *we* do when we need him.

VALÈRE: That's a strange mania!

MARTINE: That's true; but afterward, you'll see he does wonders.

VALÈRE: What's his name?

MARTINE: His name is Sganarelle, but he's easy to recognize. He's a man with a big black beard, wearing a ruff and a green and yellow coat.

LUCAS: A green and yaller coat?° So he's a parrot doctor?

VALÈRE: But is it really true that he's as skillful as you say?

MARTINE: What? He's a man who works miracles. Six months ago a woman was abandoned by all the other doctors. They thought she'd been dead for a good six hours, and were getting ready to bury her, when they forced the man we're talking about to come. After he'd looked her over, he put a little drop of something or other in her mouth, and that very moment she got up out of bed and right away started walking around her room as if nothing had happened.

LUCAS: Ah!

VALÈRE: It must have been a drop of elixir of gold.

MARTINE: That might well be. Then again, not three weeks ago a young-ster twelve years old fell down from the top of the steeple and broke his head, arms, and legs on the pavement. They had no sooner brought our man in than he rubbed the boy's whole body with a certain oint-ment he knows how to make; and right away the boy got up on his feet and ran off to play marbles.

LUCAS: Ah!

VALÈRE: That man must have a universal cure.

MARTINE: Who doubts it?

LUCAS: By jingo, that's sure the man we need. Let's go get him quick.

VALÈRE: We thank you for the favor you're doing us.

MARTINE: But anyway, be sure to remember what I warned you about.

LUCAS: Tarnation! Leave it to us. If a beating is all it takes, she's our cow.

VALÈRE: That certainly was a lucky encounter for us; and for my part, I'm very hopeful about it.

Scene V   SGANARELLE, VALÈRE, LUCAS

SGANARELLE *(enters singing, bottle in hand)*: La, la, la!

VALÈRE: I hear someone singing and cutting wood.

SGANARELLE: La, la, la . . . ! My word, that's enough work for a while. Let's take a little breather. *(Drinks)* That wood is salty as the devil. *(Sings)*

Sweet glug-glug,
How I love thee!

---

green and yaller coat: In Molière's time, doctors always wore black robes.

Sweet glug-glug
Of my little jug!
But everybody would think me too smug
If you were as full as you can be.
Just never be empty, that's my plea.
Come, sweet, let me give you a hug.

(Speaks again) Come on, good Lord, we mustn't breed melancholy.

VALÈRE: There's the man himself.

LUCAS: I think you're right, and we done stumbled right onto him.

VALÈRE: Let's get a closer look.

SGANARELLE *(seeing them, looks at them, turning first toward one then toward the other, and lowers his voice)*: Ah! my little hussy! How I love you, my little jug!

But everybody . . . would think . . . me . . . too smug,
If . . .

What the devil! What do these people want?

VALÈRE: That's the one, no doubt about it.

LUCAS: That's him, his spit an' image, just like they prescribed him to us.

SGANARELLE *(aside)*: They're looking at me and consulting. What can they have in mind? *(He puts his bottle on the ground. As* VALÈRE *bows to greet him,* SGANARELLE *thinks he is reaching down to take his bottle away, and so puts it on the other side of him. When* LUCAS *bows in turn, he picks it up again and clutches it to his belly, with much other byplay.)*

VALÈRE: Sir, isn't your name Sganarelle?

SGANARELLE: How's that?

VALÈRE: I'm asking you if you're not the man named Sganarelle?

SGANARELLE *(turning toward* VALÈRE, *then toward* LUCAS*)*: Yes and no, depending on what you want with him.

VALÈRE: All we want is to pay him all the civilities we can.

SGANARELLE: In that case, my name *is* Sganarelle.

VALÈRE: Sir, we are delighted to see you. We have been addressed to you for something we're looking for; and we come to implore your aid, which we need.

SGANARELLE: If it's something, sirs, connected with my little line of business, I am all ready to serve you.

VALÈRE: Sir, you are too kind. But sir, put on your hat, please; the sun might give you trouble.

LUCAS: Slap it on, sir.

SGANARELLE *(aside)*: These are very ceremonious people.

VALÈRE: Sir, you must not find it strange that we should come to you. Able men are always sought out, and we are well informed about your capability.

SGANARELLE: It is true, gentlemen, that I'm the best man in the world for cutting kindling wood.

VALÈRE: Ah, sir . . . !

SGANARELLE: I spare no pains, and cut it in such a way that it's above criticism.

VALÈRE: Sir, that's not the point.

SGANARELLE: But also I sell it at a hundred and ten sous for a hundred bundles.

VALÈRE: Let's not talk about that, if you please.

SGANARELLE: I promise you I can't let it go for less.

VALÈRE: Sir, we know how things stand.

SGANARELLE: If you know how things stand, you know that that's what I sell them for.

VALÈRE: Sir, you're joking when . . .

SGANARELLE: I'm not joking, I can't take anything off for it.

VALÈRE: Let's talk in other terms, please.

SGANARELLE: You can find it for less elsewhere: there's kindling and kindling; but as for what I cut . . .

VALÈRE: What? Sir, let's drop this subject.

SGANARELLE: I swear you couldn't get it for a penny less.

VALÈRE: Fie now!

SGANARELLE: No, on my conscience, that's what you'll pay. I'm speaking sincerely, and I'm not the man to overcharge.

VALÈRE: Sir, must a person like you waste his time on these crude pretenses and stoop to speaking like this? Must such a learned man, a famous doctor like yourself, try to disguise himself in the eyes of the world and keep his fine talents buried?

SGANARELLE *(aside)*: He's crazy.

VALÈRE: Please, sir, don't dissimulate with us.

SGANARELLE: What?

LUCAS: All this here fiddle-faddle don't do no good; we knows what we knows.

SGANARELLE: What about it? What are you trying to tell me? Whom do you take me for?

VALÈRE: For what you are: for a great doctor.

SGANARELLE: Doctor yourself: I'm not one and I've never been one.

VALÈRE *(aside)*: That's his madness gripping him. *(Aloud)* Sir, please don't deny things any longer; and pray let's not come to regrettable extremes.

SGANARELLE: To what?

VALÈRE: To certain things that we would be sorry for.

SGANARELLE: Good Lord! Come to whatever you like. I'm no doctor, and I don't know what you're trying to tell me.

VALÈRE *(aside)*: I can certainly see we'll have to use the remedy. *(Aloud)* Once more, sir, I beg you to admit what you are.

LUCAS: Dad bust it! No more messin' around; confess franklike that you're a doctor.

SGANARELLE: I'm getting mad.

VALÈRE: Why deny what everyone knows?

LUCAS: Why all this fuss and feathers? And what good does that done you?

SGANARELLE: Gentlemen, I tell you in one word as well as in two thousand: *I'm not a doctor.*

VALÈRE: You're not a doctor?

SGANARELLE: No.

LUCAS: You ain't no doc?

SGANARELLE: No, I tell you.

VALÈRE: Since you insist, we'll have to go ahead.

They each take a stick and beat him.

SGANARELLE: Oh, oh, oh! Gentlemen, I'm whatever you like.

VALÈRE: Why, sir, do you force us to this violence?

LUCAS: Why do you give us the botherment of beating you?

VALÈRE: I assure you that I could not regret it more.

LUCAS: By jeepers, I'm sorry about it, honest.

SGANARELLE: What the devil is this, gentlemen? I ask you, is it a joke, or are you both crazy, to insist I'm a doctor?

VALÈRE: What? You still won't give in, and you deny you're a doctor?

SGANARELLE: Devil take me if I am!

LUCAS: It ain't true that you're a doc?

SGANARELLE: No, plague take me! *(They start beating him again.)* Oh, oh! Well, gentlemen, since you insist, I'm a doctor, I'm a doctor; an apothecary too, if you see fit. I'd rather consent to anything than get myself beaten to death.

VALÈRE: Ah! That's fine, sir; I'm delighted to find you in a reasonable mood.

LUCAS: You fair cram my heart with joy when I see you talk thataway.

VALÈRE: I beg your pardon with all my heart.

LUCAS: I begs your excuse for the liberty I done tooken.

SGANARELLE *(aside)*: Well now! Suppose I'm the one that's mistaken? Could I have become a doctor without noticing it?

VALÈRE: Sir, you won't regret showing us what you are; and you'll certainly be satisfied with your treatment.

SGANARELLE: But, gentlemen, aren't you making a mistake yourselves? Is it quite certain that I'm a doctor?

LUCAS: Yup, by jiminy!

SGANARELLE: Honestly?

VALÈRE: Beyond a doubt.

SGANARELLE: Devil take me if I knew it!

VALÈRE: What? You're the ablest doctor in the world.

SGANARELLE: Aha!

LUCAS: A doc which has cureded I don't know how many maladies.

SGANARELLE: My Lord!

VALÈRE: A woman had been taken for dead six hours before; she was ready to be buried, when, with a drop of something or other, you brought her back to life and set her walking around the room right away.

SGANARELLE: I'll be darned!

LUCAS: A little boy twelve years old left himself fall from the top of a steeple, from which he got his head, legs, and arms busted; and you, with some kind of ointment or other, you fixed him so he gets right up on his feet and goes off to play marbles.

SGANARELLE: The devil you say!

VALÈRE: In short, sir, you will have every satisfaction with us; and you'll earn whatever you like if you'll let us take you where we mean to.

SGANARELLE: I'll earn whatever I like?

VALÈRE: Yes.

SGANARELLE: Oh! I'm a doctor, there's no denying it. I'd forgotten, but now I remember. What's the problem? Where do we have to go?

VALÈRE: We'll take you. The problem is to go see a girl who's lost her speech.

SGANARELLE: My word! I haven't found it.

VALÈRE: He likes his little joke. Let's go, sir.

SGANARELLE: Without a doctor's gown?

VALÈRE: We'll get one.

SGANARELLE (*presenting his bottle to* VALÈRE): Hold that, you, that's where I put my potions. (*Turning toward* LUCAS *and spitting on the ground.*) You, step on that; doctor's orders.

LUCAS: Land's sakes! That's a doctor I like. I reckon he'll do all right, 'cause he's a real comic.°

ACT II

A room in Géronte's house

Scene I GÉRONTE, VALÈRE, LUCAS, JACQUELINE

VALÈRE: Yes, sir, I think you'll be satisfied; and we've brought you the greatest doctor in the world.

LUCAS: Oh, gee whillikins! You gotta pull up the ladder after that one, and all the rest ain't good enough to take off his shoon.

VALÈRE: He's a man who has performed wonderful cures.

LUCAS: As has cureded some folk as were dead.

VALÈRE: He's a bit capricious, as I've told you; and sometimes he has moments when his mind wanders and he doesn't seem what he really is.

---

a real comic: Some have taken this remark as Molière's own disgruntled comment on the mediocre success of *The Misanthrope*.

LUCAS: Yup, he likes to clown; and sometimes you'd say, with no offense, that he'd been hit on the head with an axe.

VALÈRE: But underneath it, he's all learning, and very often he says quite lofty things.

LUCAS: When he gets to it, he talks right straight out just like he was reading out of a book.

VALÈRE: His reputation has already spread hereabouts, and everybody is coming to see him.

GÉRONTE: I'm dying to meet him. Bring him to me quick.

VALÈRE: I'll go and get him.

JACQUELINE: Land's sakes, sir, this'un'll do just what the others done. I reckon it'll be just the same old stuff; and the bestest med'cine anyone could slip your daughter, if you're asking me, would be a good handsome husband she had a hankering for.

GÉRONTE: Well now! My good wet-nurse, you certainly meddle in lots of things.

LUCAS: Be quiet, Jacqueline, keep to your housework: you ain't the one to stick your nose in there.

JACQUELINE: I told you before and I'll tell you some more that all these here doctors won't do nothing more for her than plain branch water, that your daughter needs something mighty different from rhubarb and senna, and that a husband is the kind of poultice that'll cure all a girl's troubles.

GÉRONTE: Is she in condition now for anyone to want to take her on, with the infirmity she has? And when I was minded to have her married, didn't she oppose my will?

JACQUELINE: I should think she did: you was wanting to pass her a man she don't love. Why didn't you take that Monsieur Léandre that she had a soft spot for? She would've been real obedient; and I'm gonna bet you he'd take her just like she is, if you'd give her to him.

GÉRONTE: That Léandre is not what she needs; he's not well off like the other.

JACQUELINE: He's got such a rich uncle, and he's his heir.

GÉRONTE: All this property to come is just so much nonsense to me. There's nothing like what you've got; and you run a big risk of fooling yourself when you count on what someone else is keeping for you. Death doesn't always keep her ears open to the wishes and prayers of their honors the heirs; and you can grow a long set of teeth when you're waiting for someone's death so as to have a livelihood.

JACQUELINE: Anyway I've always heard that in marriage, as elsewhere, happiness counts more than riches. The pas and mas, they have that goldarned custom of always asking "How much has he got?" and "How much has she got?" and neighbor Peter married off his daughter Simonette to fat Thomas 'cause he had a quarter vineyard more than young Robin, which she'd set her heart on; and now, poor critter, it's turned her yellow as a quince, and she hasn't got her property in all the time since. That's a fine example for *you,* sir. All we got in this world is our pleasure; and I'd rather give my daughter a good husband which she liked than all the revenues in Beauce.

GÉRONTE: Plague take it, Madame Nurse, how you do spit it out! Be quiet, please; you're getting too involved and you're heating up your milk.

LUCAS *(by mistake, tapping* GÉRONTE *on the chest instead of* JACQUE-LINE*)*: Gosh darn it! Shut up, you're just a meddler. The master don't have no use for your speeches, and he knows what he's got to do. You see to nursing the child you're nurse to, and don't give us none of your big ideas. The master is his daughter's father, and he's good enough and wise enough to see what she needs.

GÉRONTE: Easy! Oh! Easy!

LUCAS: Sir, I want to mortify her a bit, and teach her the *re*spect she owes you.

GÉRONTE: Yes, but those gestures aren't necessary.

Scene II   VALÈRE, SGANARELLE, GÉRONTE, LUCAS, JACQUELINE

VALÈRE: Sir, prepare yourself. Here comes our doctor.

GÉRONTE: Sir, I'm delighted to have you in my house, and we need you badly.

SGANARELLE *(in a doctor's gown, with a sharply pointed hat)*:   Hippocrates says . . . that we should both put our hats on.

GÉRONTE: Hippocrates says that?

SGANARELLE: Yes.

GÉRONTE: In what chapter, if you please?

SGANARELLE: In his chapter on hats.

GÉRONTE: Since Hippocrates says it, we must do it.

SGANARELLE: Sir Doctor, since I have heard the wonderful things . . .

GÉRONTE: Whom are you speaking to, pray?

SGANARELLE: You.

GÉRONTE: I'm not a doctor.

SGANARELLE: You're not a doctor?

GÉRONTE: No, really.

SGANARELLE *(takes a stick and beats him just as he himself was beaten)*: You really mean it?

GÉRONTE: I really mean it. Oh, oh, oh!

SGANARELLE: You're a doctor now. I never got any other license.

GÉRONTE: What the devil kind of a man have you brought me?

VALÈRE: I told you he was a joker of a doctor.

GÉRONTE: Yes, but I'd send him packing with his jokes.

LUCAS: Don't pay no attention to that, sir: that's just for a laugh.

GÉRONTE: I don't like that kind of a laugh.

SGANARELLE: Sir, I ask your pardon for the liberty I took.

GÉRONTE: Your servant, sir.

SGANARELLE: I'm sorry . . .

GÉRONTE: That's nothing.

SGANARELLE: For the cudgeling . . .

GÉRONTE: No harm done.

SGANARELLE: That I had the honor of giving you.

GÉRONTE: Let's say no more about it. Sir, I have a daughter who has caught a strange disease.

SGANARELLE: Sir, I'm delighted that your daughter needs me; and I wish with all my heart that you and your whole family needed me too, just to show you how much I want to serve you.

GÉRONTE: I am obliged to you for those sentiments.

SGANARELLE: I assure you that I'm speaking straight from the heart.

GÉRONTE: You do me too much honor.

SGANARELLE: What's your daughter's name?

GÉRONTE: Lucinde.

SGANARELLE: Lucinde! Oh, what a fine name to prescribe for! Lucinde!°

GÉRONTE: I'll just go and have a look to see what she's doing.

SGANARELLE: Who's that big buxom woman?

GÉRONTE: She's the wet-nurse of a little baby of mine.

SGANARELLE: Plague take it! That's a pretty piece of goods! Ah, nurse, charming nurse, my medicine is the very humble slave of your nurse-ship, and I'd certainly like to be the lucky little doll who sucked the milk *(puts his hand on her breast)* of your good graces. All my remedies, all my learning, all my capacity is at your service, and . . .

LUCAS: With your pummission, Mister Doctor, leave my wife be, I beg you.

SGANARELLE: What? Is she your wife?

LUCAS: Yes.

SGANARELLE *(makes as if to embrace* LUCAS, *then, turning toward the nurse, embraces her)*: Oh! really! I didn't know that, and I'm delighted for the sake of you both.

LUCAS *(pulling him away)*: Easy now, please.

SGANARELLE: I assure you I'm delighted that you're united. I congratulate her *(he again makes as if to embrace* LUCAS, *and passing under his arms, throws himself on* JACQUELINE's *neck)* on having a husband like you; and you, I congratulate you on having a wife as beautiful, modest, and well-built as she is.

LUCAS *(pulling him away again)*: Hey! Goldarn it! Not so much compliment, I ask you now.

SGANARELLE: Don't you want me to rejoice with you at such a fine assembly?

Lucinde: Here a theatrical tradition has Sganarelle decline the name: Lucindus, Lucinda, Lucindum.

LUCAS: With me, all you like; but with my wife, let's skip these kind of formalities.

SGANARELLE: I take part in the happiness of you both alike; and *(same business as before)* if I embrace you to attest my joy to you, I embrace her as well to attest my joy to her too.

LUCAS *(pulling him away once more)*: Oh! Dad blast it, Mister Doctor, what a lot of fiddle-faddle!

Scene III SGANARELLE, GÉRONTE, LUCAS, JACQUELINE

GÉRONTE: Sir, they're going to bring my daughter to you. She'll be here right away.

SGANARELLE: I await her sir, and all medicine with me.

GÉRONTE: Where is it?

SGANARELLE *(tapping his forehead)*: In there.

GÉRONTE: Very good.

SGANARELLE *(trying to touch the nurse's breasts)*: But since I am interested in your whole family, I must take a small sample of your nurse's milk, and inspect her bosom.

LUCAS *(pulling him away and spinning him around)*: Nah, nah, I don't want no truck with that.

SGANARELLE: It's the doctor's job to examine nurses' breasts.

LUCAS: Job nor no job, I'm your servant.

SGANARELLE: Do you really have the audacity to set yourself up against the doctor? Begone!

LUCAS: The heck with that!

SGANARELLE *(looking at him askance)*: I'll give you the fever.

JACQUELINE *(taking LUCAS by the arm and spinning him around)*: That's right, get out of there. Ain't I big enough to defend myself if he does something to me as a person hadn't ought?

LUCAS: Well, me, I don't want him a-feeling you.

SGANARELLE: Fie! The peasant! He's jealous of his wife!

GÉRONTE: Here is my daughter.

Scene IV LUCINDE, VALÈRE, GÉRONTE, LUCAS, SGANARELLE, JACQUELINE

SGANARELLE: Is this the patient?

GÉRONTE: Yes, she's the only daughter I have, and I'd be heartbroken if she were to die.

SGANARELLE: She'd better not! She musn't die except on doctor's orders.

GÉRONTE: Come, come, a chair!°

SGANARELLE: That's not such a bad-looking patient, and I maintain that a really healthy man would make out all right with her.

---

chair: Chairs were relatively rare luxuries in Molière's France. By ordering a regular chair, not a folding stool, Géronte shows his respect for the learned doctor.

GÉRONTE: You've made her laugh, sir.

SGANARELLE: That's fine. When the doctor makes the patient laugh, that's the best possible sign. Well! What's the problem? What's wrong with you? Where does it hurt?

LUCINDE *(answers in sign language, putting her hand to her mouth, her head, and under her chin)*: Hah, heeh, hoh, hah.

SGANARELLE: Eh? What's that you say?

LUCINDE *(same gestures as before)*: Hah, heeh, hoh, hah, hah, heeh, hoh.

SGANARELLE: What?

LUCINDE: Hah, heeh, hoh.

SGANARELLE *(imitating her)*: Hah, heeh, hoh, hah, hah: I don't understand you. What the devil kind of language is that?

GÉRONTE: Sir, that's her illness. She's been struck dumb, and up to now no one has been able to learn the reason why; and it's an accident that has put off her marriage.

SGANARELLE: And why so?

GÉRONTE: The man she is to marry wants to wait until she's cured to make things final.

SGANARELLE: And who is the fool that doesn't want his wife to be dumb? Would God mine had that disease! I'd be the last one to want to cure her.

GÉRONTE: Anyway, sir, we beg you to make every effort to relieve her of her trouble.

SGANARELLE: Oh! Don't worry. Tell me now, does this trouble bother her a lot?

GÉRONTE: Yes, sir.

SGANARELLE: Very good. Does she feel great pains?

GÉRONTE: Very great.

SGANARELLE: That's just fine. Does she go — you know where?

GÉRONTE: Yes.

SGANARELLE: Copiously?

GÉRONTE: I don't know anything about that.

SGANARELLE: Does she achieve laudable results?

GÉRONTE: I'm no expert in those matters.

SGANARELLE *(turning to the patient)*: Give me your arm. That pulse shows your daughter is dumb.

GÉRONTE: Why yes, sir, that's her trouble! You found it the very first thing.

SGANARELLE: Aha!

JACQUELINE: Just lookit how he guessed her illness!

SGANARELLE: We great doctors, we know things right away. An ignorant one would have been embarrassed and would have gone and told you "It's this" or "It's that"; but *I* hit the mark on the first shot, and I inform you that your daughter is dumb.

GÉRONTE: Yes; but I wish you could tell me what it comes from.

SGANARELLE: Nothing easier: it comes from the fact that she has lost her speech.

GÉRONTE: Very good; but the reason, please, why she has lost her speech?

SGANARELLE: All our best authors will tell you that it's the stoppage of the action of her tongue.

GÉRONTE: But still, what are your views about this stoppage of the action of her tongue?

SGANARELLE: Aristotle, on that subject, says . . . some very fine things.

GÉRONTE: I believe it.

SGANARELLE: Oh! He was a great man!

GÉRONTE: No doubt.

SGANARELLE (raising his forearm): An utterly great man: a man who was greater than I by all of that! So, to get back to our reasoning, I hold that this stoppage of the action of her tongue is caused by certain humors, which among us scholars we call peccant humors: peccant, that is to say . . . peccant humors; because the vapors formed by the exhalations of the influences arising in the region where the maladies lie, when they come . . . so to speak . . . to . . . Do you understand Latin?

GÉRONTE: Not in the least.

SGANARELLE (getting up in astonishment): You don't understand Latin?

GÉRONTE: No.

SGANARELLE (assuming various comical poses): Cabricias arci thuram, catalamus, singulariter, nominativo haec Musa, "the Muse," bonus, bona, bonum, Deus sanctus, estne oratio latinas? Etiam, "yes." Quare, "why?" Quia substantivo et adjectivum concordat in generi, numerum, et casus.°

GÉRONTE: Oh! Why did I never study?

JACQUELINE: Land! That's an able man!

LUCAS: Yup, that's so purty I can't make out a word of it.

SGANARELLE: Now when these vapors I'm speaking of come to pass from the left side, where the liver is, to the right side, where the heart is, it happens that the lungs, which in Latin we call armyan, having communication with the brain, which in Greek we call nasmus, by means of the vena cava, which in Hebrew we call cubile,° on its way encounters the said vapors, which the ventricles of the omoplate; and because the said vapors — follow this reasoning closely, I beg you — and because the said vapors have a certain malignity . . . Listen to this carefully, I conjure you.

GÉRONTE: Yes.

SGANARELLE: Have a certain malignity, which is caused . . . Be attentive, please.

Cabricias . . . casus: Traditionally, as Sganarelle winds up this hodge-podge of gibberish and elementary Latin phrases with the word *casus* ("case," or "fall"), he throws himself back in his chair too hard, and falls over in it on his back. He remains in this position during the next two remarks.

armyan; nasmus; cubile: These are all invented names, except that *cubile* is Latin for *bed.*

GÉRONTE: I am.

SGANARELLE: Which is caused by the acridity of the humors engendered in the concavity of the diaphragm, it happens that these vapors . . . *Ossabandus, nequeys, nequer, potarinum, quipsa milus.* That's exactly what is making your daughter dumb.

JACQUELINE: Oh! That man of ourn! Ain't that well said?

LUCAS: Why ain't *my* tongue that slick?

GÉRONTE: No one could reason any better, no doubt about it. There's just one thing that surprised me: the location of the liver and the heart. It seems to me that you place them otherwise than they are; that the heart is on the left side and the liver on the right side.

SGANARELLE: Yes, it used to be that way; but we have changed all that, and now we practice medicine in a completely new way.

GÉRONTE: That's something I didn't know, and I beg your pardon for my ignorance.

SGANARELLE: No harm done, and you're not obliged to be as able as we are.

GÉRONTE: To be sure. But, sir, what do you think needs to be done for this illness?

SGANARELLE: What I think needs to be done?

GÉRONTE: Yes.

SGANARELLE: My advice is to put her back in bed and have her take, as a remedy, a lot of bread steeped in wine.

GÉRONTE: And why that, sir?

SGANARELLE: Because in bread and wine mixed together there is a sympathetic virtue that makes people speak. Haven't you noticed that they don't give anything else to parrots, and that they learn to speak by eating that?

GÉRONTE: That's true. Oh, what a great man! Quick, lots of bread and wine!

SGANARELLE: I'll come back toward evening and see how she is. *(To the nurse)* Hold on, you. Sir, here is a nurse to whom I must administer a few little remedies.

JACQUELINE: Who? Me? I couldn't be in better health.

SGANARELLE: Too bad, nurse, too bad. Such good health is alarming, and it won't be a bad thing to give you a friendly little bloodletting, a little dulcifying enema.

GÉRONTE: But, sir, that's a fashion I don't understand. Why should we go and be bled when we haven't any illness?

SGANARELLE: No matter, it's a salutary fashion; and just as we drink on account of the thirst to come, so we must have ourselves bled on account of the illness to come.

JACQUELINE *(starting to go off)*: My Lord! The heck with that, and I don't want to make my body into a drugstore.

SGANARELLE: You are resistant to remedies, but we'll manage to bring you to reason.

Exit JACQUELINE.

(To GÉRONTE*)* I bid you good day.

GÉRONTE: Wait a bit, please.

SGANARELLE: What do you want to do?

GÉRONTE: Give you some money, sir.

SGANARELLE *(holding out his hand behind, beneath his gown, while* GÉRONTE *opens his purse)*: I won't take any, sir.

GÉRONTE: Sir . . .

SGANARELLE: Not at all.

GÉRONTE: Just a moment.

SGANARELLE: By no means.

GÉRONTE: Please!

SGANARELLE: You're joking.

GÉRONTE: That's that.

SGANARELLE: I'll do nothing of the sort.

GÉRONTE: Eh?

SGANARELLE: Money is no motive to me.

GÉRONTE: I believe it.

SGANARELLE *(after taking the money)*: Is this good weight?

GÉRONTE: Yes, sir.

SGANARELLE: I'm not a mercenary doctor.

GÉRONTE: I'm well aware of it.

SGANARELLE: I'm not ruled by self-interest.

GÉRONTE: I have no such idea.

Scene V   SGANARELLE, LÉANDRE

SGANARELLE *(looking at his money)*: My word! That's not too bad; and if only . . .

LÉANDRE: Sir, I've been waiting for you a long time, and I come to implore your assistance.

SGANARELLE *(taking his wrist)*: That's a very bad pulse.

LÉANDRE: I'm not sick, sir, and that's not why I've come to see you.

SGANARELLE: If you're not sick, why the devil don't you say so?

LÉANDRE: No. To put the whole thing in a word, my name is Léandre, and I'm in love with Lucinde, whom you've just examined; and since, because of her father's bad disposition, I'm denied all access to her, I'm venturing to beg you to serve my love, and give me a chance to carry out a scheme I've thought up to say a word or two to her on which my happiness and my life depend absolutely.

SGANARELLE *(feigning anger)*: Whom do you take me for? How can you dare come up and ask me to serve you in your love, and try to degrade the dignity of a doctor to this type of employment?

LÉANDRE: Sir, don't make so much noise.

SGANARELLE: *I* want to make noise. You're an impertinent young man.

LÉANDRE: Ah! Gently, sir.

SGANARELLE: A dunderhead.

LÉANDRE: Please!

SGANARELLE: I'll teach you that I'm not the kind of man for that, and that it's the height of insolence . . .

LÉANDRE (*pulling out a purse and giving it to him*): Sir . . .

SGANARELLE: To want to use me . . . I'm not speaking about you, for you're a gentleman, and I would be delighted to do you a service; but there are some impertinent people in the world who come and take people for what they're not; and I admit that makes me angry.

LÉANDRE: I ask your pardon, sir, for the liberty that . . .

SGANARELLE: Don't be silly. What's the problem?

LÉANDRE: You shall know, then, sir, that this illness that you want to cure is make-believe. The doctors have reasoned in due form about it, and have not failed to say that it came, some say from the brain, some from the intestines, some from the spleen, some from the liver; but it is certain that love is the real cause of it, and that Lucinde hit upon this illness only to deliver herself from a threatened marriage. But, for fear we may be seen together, let's get out of here, and as we walk I'll tell you what I would like from you.

SGANARELLE: Let's go, sir: you've given me an inconceivable fondness for your love; and unless I'm no doctor, either the patient will die or else she'll be yours.

ACT III

Géronte's garden

Scene I SGANARELLE, LÉANDRE

LÉANDRE: It seems to me I don't look bad this way as an apothecary; and since the father has scarcely ever seen me, this change of costume and wig may well succeed, I think, in disguising me to his eyes.

SGANARELLE: No doubt about it.

LÉANDRE: All I could wish would be to know five or six big medical terms to adorn my speech and make me seem like a learned man.

SGANARELLE: Come, come, all that is unnecessary: the costume is enough, and I know no more about it than you.

LÉANDRE: What?

SGANARELLE: Devil take me if I know anything about medicine! You're a good sort, and I'm willing to confide in you, just as you are confiding in me.

LÉANDRE: What? You're not really . . . ?

SGANARELLE: No, I tell you: they made me a doctor in spite of me. I had never bothered my head about being that learned; and all my studies went only up to seventh grade. I don't know what put this idea into their heads; but when I saw that they absolutely insisted on my being a doctor, I decided to be one, at the expense of whom it may concern. However, you'd never believe how the mistaken idea has gotten around, and how everybody is hell-bent on thinking me a learned man. They come looking for me from all directions; and if things keep on this way, I believe I'll stick to medicine all my life. I think it's the best trade of all; for whether you do well or badly, you're always paid just the same. Bad work never comes back onto our backs, and we cut the material we work on as we please. A cobbler making shoes could never botch a piece of leather without paying for the broken crockery; but in this work we can botch a man without its costing us anything. The blunders are never ours, and it's always the fault of the person who dies. In short, the best part of this profession is that there's a decency, an unparalleled discretion, among the dead; and you never see one of them complaining of the doctor who killed him.

LÉANDRE: It's true that dead men are very decent folk on that score.

SGANARELLE (*seeing some men coming toward him*): There are some people who look as though they were coming to consult me. Go ahead and wait for me near your sweetheart's house.

Scene II THIBAUT, PERRIN, SGANARELLE

THIBAUT: Sir, we done come to see you, my son Perrin and me.

SGANARELLE: What's the matter?

THIBAUT: His poor mother, her name is Perrette, is sick in bed these six months now.

SGANARELLE (*holding out his hand to receive money*): And what do you expect me to do about it?

THIBAUT: We'd like, sir, for you to slip us some kind of funny business for to cure her.

SGANARELLE: I'll have to see what she's sick of.

THIBAUT: She's sick of a proxy, sir.

SGANARELLE: Of a proxy?

THIBAUT: Yes, that is to say she's all swelled up all over; and they say it's a whole lot of seriosities she's got inside her, and that her liver, her belly, or her spleen, whatever you want to call it, 'stead of making blood don't make nothing but water. Every other day she has a quotigian fever, with pains and lassitules in the muskles of her legs. You can hear in her throat phleg-ums like to choke her; and sometimes she gets tooken with syncopations and compulsions till I think she done passed away. In our village we got a 'pothecary, all respect to him, who's given her I don't know how many kinds of stuff; and it costs me more'n a dozen good crowns in enemas, no offense, and beverages he had her take, in jacinth confusions and cordial portions. But all that stuff, like the feller said, was just a kind of salve that didn't make her no better nor no worse. He wanted to slip her one certain drug that they call hermetic wine; but me, frankly, I got scared that would send her to join her ancestors; and they do say those big doctors are killing off I don't know how many people with that there invention.°

SGANARELLE *(still holding out his hand and signaling with it for money)*: Let's get to the point, my friend, let's get to the point.

THIBAUT: The fact is, sir, that we done come to ask you to tell us what we should do.

SGANARELLE: I don't understand you at all.

PERRIN: Sir, my mother is sick; and here be two crowns that we've brung you so you'll give us some cure.

SGANARELLE: Oh! Now *you*, I understand you. Here's a lad who speaks clearly and explains himself properly. You say that your mother is ill with dropsy, that her whole body is swollen, that she has a fever and pains in her legs, and that she is sometimes seized with syncopes and convulsions, that is to say, fainting spells?

PERRIN: Oh, yes, sir, that's exactly it.

SGANARELLE: I understood you right away. You have a father who doesn't know what he's talking about. Now you're asking me for a remedy?

PERRIN: Yes, sir.

SGANARELLE: A remedy to cure her?

PERRIN: That's what we got in mind.

SGANARELLE: Look, here's a piece of cheese that you must have her take.

PERRIN: Cheese, sir?

SGANARELLE: Yes, it's a specially prepared cheese containing gold, coral, pearls, and lots of other precious things.

PERRIN: Sir, we be much obliged to you; and we'll have her take this right away.

SGANARELLE: Go ahead. If she dies, don't fail to give her the best burial you can.

Scene III   JACQUELINE, SGANARELLE; LUCAS *(backstage)*

SGANARELLE: Here's that beautiful nurse. Ah, nurse of my heart, I'm delighted that we meet again, and the sight of you is the rhubarb, cassia, and senna that purge my soul of all its melancholy!

JACQUELINE: Well I swan, Mister Doctor, you say that too purty for me, and I don't understand none of your Latin.

SGANARELLE: Fall ill, nurse, I beg you; fall ill for my sake: it would give me all the pleasure in the world to cure you.

JACQUELINE: I'm your servant, sir: I'd much rather not have no one cure me.

---

invention: A big medical controversy of the time concerned the value of emetic wine, which contained antimony.

SGANARELLE: How sorry I am for you, fair nurse, for having a jealous, troublesome husband like the one you have!

JACQUELINE: What would you have me do, sir? It's a penance for my sins. Where the goat is tied, that's where she's got to graze.

SGANARELLE: What? A clod like that! A man who's always watching you, and won't let anyone talk to you!

JACQUELINE: Mercy me, you ain't seen nothin' yet, and that's only a little sample of his bad humor.

SGANARELLE: Is it possible? And can a man have a soul so base as to mistreat a person like you? Ah, lovely nurse, I know people, and not far from here either, who would think themselves happy just to kiss the little tips of your footsies! Why must so lovely a person have fallen into such hands, and must a mere animal, a brute, a lout, a fool . . . ? Pardon me, nurse, if I speak in this way of your husband.

JACQUELINE: Oh, sir, I know good and well he deserves all them names.

SGANARELLE: Yes, nurse, he certainly does deserve them; and he would also deserve to have you plant a certain decoration on his head, to punish him for his suspicions.

JACQUELINE: It's quite true that if I was only thinking about him, he might drive me to some strange carryings-on.

SGANARELLE: My word! It wouldn't be a bad idea for you to take vengeance on him with someone else. He's a man, I tell you, who really deserves that; and if I were fortunate enough, beautiful nurse, to be chosen to . . . (*At this point they both notice* LUCAS, *who was in back of them all the time listening to their talk. They go off in opposite directions, the doctor with comical byplay.*)

Scene IV GÉRONTE, LUCAS

GÉRONTE: Hey there, Lucas! Haven't you seen our doctor around?

LUCAS: Yup, tarnation take it! I seen him, and my wife too.

GÉRONTE: Then where can he be?

LUCAS: I dunno, but I wish he'd go to the devil in hell.

GÉRONTE: Go take a look and see what my daughter is doing.

Scene V SGANARELLE, LÉANDRE, GÉRONTE

GÉRONTE: Ah, sir! I was just asking where you were.

SGANARELLE: I was busy in your courtyard—expelling the superfluity of my potations. How is the patient?

GÉRONTE: A little worse since taking your prescription.

SGANARELLE: Very good: that's a sign that it's working.

GÉRONTE: Yes; but as it works, I'm afraid it will choke her.

SGANARELLE: Don't worry; I have remedies that make light of everything, and I'll wait for her in her death agony.

GÉRONTE: Who's this man you're bringing with you?

SGANARELLE *(gesturing like an apothecary giving an enema)*: He's . . .

GÉRONTE: What?

SGANARELLE: The one . . .

GÉRONTE: Eh?

SGANARELLE: Who . . .

GÉRONTE: I understand.

SGANARELLE: Your daughter will need him.

Scene VI JACQUELINE, LUCINDE, GÉRONTE, LÉANDRE, SGANARELLE

JACQUELINE: Sir, here's your daughter as wants to take a little walk.

SGANARELLE: That will do her good. Mister Apothecary, go along and take her pulse a bit so that I can discuss her illness with you presently. *(At this point he draws GÉRONTE to one side of the stage, and, passing one arm over his shoulders, puts his hand under his chin and turns him back toward himself whenever GÉRONTE tries to watch what his daughter and the apothecary are doing together.)* Sir, it's a great and subtle question among the learned whether women are easier to cure than men. I beg you to listen to this, if you please. Some say no, others say yes; and *I* say yes and no: inasmuch as the incongruity of the opaque humors that are found in the natural temperament of women, is the reason why the brutish part always tries to gain power over the sensitive part, we see that the inequality of their opinions depends on the oblique movement of the moon's circle; and since the sun, which darts its rays over the concavity of the earth, finds . . .

LUCINDE: No, I'm utterly incapable of changing my feelings.

GÉRONTE: That's my daughter speaking! Oh, what wonderful virtue in that remedy! Oh, what an admirable doctor! How obliged I am to you for this marvelous cure! And what can I do for you after such a service?

SGANARELLE *(walking around the stage and wiping his brow)*: That's an illness that gave me a lot of trouble!

LUCINDE: Yes, father, I've recovered my speech; but I've recovered it to tell you that I shall never have any other husband than Léandre, and that there's no use your trying to give me Horace.

GÉRONTE: But . . .

LUCINDE: Nothing can shake my resolution.

GÉRONTE: What . . . ?

LUCINDE: All your fine objections will be in vain.

GÉRONTE: If . . .

LUCINDE: All your arguments will be no use.

GÉRONTE: I . . .

LUCINDE: It's a thing I'm determined on.

GÉRONTE: But . . .

LUCINDE: There is no paternal authority that can force me to marry in spite of myself.

GÉRONTE: I've . . .

LUCINDE: All your efforts will not avail.

GÉRONTE: He . . .

LUCINDE: My heart could never submit to this tyranny.

GÉRONTE: There . . .

LUCINDE: And I'll cast myself into a convent rather than marry a man I don't love.

GÉRONTE: But . . .

LUCINDE *(in a deafening voice)*: No. By no means. Nothing doing. You're wasting your time. I won't do anything of the sort. That's settled.

GÉRONTE: Oh! What a rush of words! There's no way to resist it. Sir, I beg you to make her dumb again.

SGANARELLE: That's impossible for me. All I can do for your service is to make you deaf, if you want.

GÉRONTE: Many thanks! *(To* LUCINDE*)* Then do you think . . . ?

LUCINDE: No. All your reasons will make no impression on my soul.

GÉRONTE: You shall marry Horace this very evening.

LUCINDE: I'll sooner marry death.

SGANARELLE: Good Lord! Stop, let me medicate this affair. Her illness still grips her, and I know the remedy we must apply.

GÉRONTE: Is it possible, sir, that you can also cure this illness of the mind?

SGANARELLE: Yes. Leave it to me, I have remedies for everything, and our apothecary will serve us for this cure. *(Calls the apothecary.)* One word. You see that ardor she has for this Léandre is completely contrary to her father's will, that there is no time to lose, that the humors are very inflamed, and that it is necessary to find a remedy promptly for this ailment, which could get worse with delay. For my part, I see only one, which is a dose of purgative flight, which you will combine properly with two drams of matrimonium in pill form. She may make some difficulty about taking this remedy; but since you are an able man at your trade, it's up to you to persuade her and make her swallow the dose as best you can. Go along and get her to take a little turn around the garden, so as to prepare the humors, while I talk to her father here; but above all don't waste time. The remedy, quickly, the one specific remedy!

Scene VII   GÉRONTE, SGANARELLE

GÉRONTE: What are those drugs, sir, that you just mentioned? It seems to me I've never heard of them.

SGANARELLE: They are drugs used in great emergencies.

GÉRONTE: Did you ever see such insolence as hers?

SGANARELLE: Daughters are sometimes a little headstrong.

GÉRONTE: You wouldn't believe how crazy she is about this Léandre.

SGANARELLE: The heat of the blood does this to young minds.

GÉRONTE: For my part, ever since I discovered the violence of this love, I've managed to keep my daughter always locked up.

SGANARELLE: You've done wisely.

GÉRONTE: And I've kept them from having any communication together.

SGANARELLE: Very good.

GÉRONTE: Some folly would have resulted if I'd allowed them to see each other.

SGANARELLE: No doubt.

GÉRONTE: And I think she'd have been just the girl to run off with him.

SGANARELLE: That's prudent reasoning.

GÉRONTE: I've been warned that he's making every effort to speak to her.

SGANARELLE: What a clown!

GÉRONTE: But he'll be wasting his time.

SGANARELLE: Ha, ha!

GÉRONTE: And I'll keep him from seeing her, all right.

SGANARELLE: He's not dealing with a dolt, and you know tricks of the game that he doesn't. Smarter than you is no fool.

Scene VIII   LUCAS, GÉRONTE, SGANARELLE

LUCAS: Dad blast it, sir, here's a lot of ruckus: your daughter's done run off with her Léandre. The 'pothecary, that was him; and Mister Doctor here's the one as pufformed that fine operation.

GÉRONTE: What? Assassinate me in that way! Here, get a policeman! Don't let him get out. Ah, traitor! I'll have the law on you.

LUCAS: Hah! By jingo, Mister Doctor, you'll be hung: just don't move outa there.

Scene IX   MARTINE, SGANARELLE, LUCAS

MARTINE: Oh, Good Lord! What a time I've had finding this house! Tell me, what's the news of the doctor I provided for you?

LUCAS: Here he be. Gonna be hung.

MARTINE: What? My husband hanged? Alas! What's he done?

LUCAS: He fixed it for our master's daughter to get run away with.

MARTINE: Alas! My dear husband, is it really true they're going to hang you?

SGANARELLE: As you see. Oh!

MARTINE: Must you let yourself die in the presence of all these people?

SGANARELLE: What do you expect me to do about it?

MARTINE: At least if you'd finished cutting our wood, I'd have some consolation.

SGANARELLE: Get out of here, you're breaking my heart.

MARTINE: No, I mean to stay to give you courage in the face of death, and I won't leave you until I see you hanged.

SGANARELLE: Oh!

Scene X GÉRONTE, SGANARELLE, MARTINE, LUCAS

GÉRONTE: The constable will be here soon, and they'll put you in a place where they'll be answerable for you to me.

SGANARELLE *(hat in hand)*: Alas! Can't this be changed to a modest cudgeling?

GÉRONTE: No, no, justice will take its course . . . But what's this I see?

Scene XI LÉANDRE, LUCINDE, JACQUELINE, LUCAS, GÉRONTE, SGANARELLE, MARTINE

LÉANDRE: Sir, I come to reveal Léandre to you and restore Lucinde to your power. We both intended to run away and get married; but this plan has given way to a more honorable procedure. I do not aim to steal your daughter from you, and it is only from your hands that I wish to receive her. I will tell you this, sir: I have just received letters informing me that my uncle has died and that I am heir to all his property.

GÉRONTE: Sir, I have the highest consideration for your virtues, and I give you my daughter with the greatest pleasure in the world.

SGANARELLE: That was a close shave for medicine!

MARTINE: Since you're not going to be hanged, you can thank me for being a doctor; for I'm the one who procured you that honor.

SGANARELLE: Yes, you're the one who procured me quite a beating.

LÉANDRE: The result is too fine for you to harbor resentment.

SGANARELLE: All right: I forgive you for the beatings in consideration of the dignity you've raised me to; but prepare henceforth to live in the greatest respect with a man of my consequence, and bear in mind that the wrath of a doctor is more to be feared than anyone can ever believe.

HENRIK IBSEN (1828–1906)

An Enemy of the People

Characters

DR. THOMAS STOCKMANN, *staff physician at the municipal baths*
MRS. STOCKMANN, *his wife*
PETRA , *their daughter, a teacher*
EILIF
MORTEN } *their sons, aged 12 and 10*
PETER STOCKMANN, *the doctor's older brother, mayor, police chief, chairman of the board of the municipal baths, etc.*
MORTEN KIIL, *master tanner;* MRS. STOCKMANN's *foster-father*
HOVSTAD, *editor of the* People's Courier
BILLING, *his assistant on the paper*
CAPTAIN HORSTER
ASLAKSEN, *a printer*
PARTICIPANTS IN A PUBLIC MEETING: *men of all social ranks, several women, and a gang of schoolboys*

Scene   *The action takes place in a coastal town in southern Norway.*

ACT I

Evening. DR. STOCKMANN's *living room, simply but attractively furnished and decorated. In the side wall to the right are two doors, the farther one leading out to the hall, and the nearer into the* DOCTOR's *study. In the facing wall, directly opposite the hall door, is a door to the family's living quarters. At the middle of this wall stands the stove; closer in the foreground, a sofa with a mirror above it, and in front of these, an oval table covered by a cloth. On the table a lamp, shaded and lit. In the back wall, an open door to the dining room. The table is set for dinner within, with a lit lamp on it.*

BILLING, napkin under his chin, sits at the table inside. MRS. STOCKMANN *is standing by the table, passing him a plate with a large slice of roast beef. The other places at the table are empty; the settings are in disorder, as after a meal.*

MRS. STOCKMANN: Well, if you come an hour late, Mr. Billing, then you have to accept cold food.
BILLING *(eating)*: It tastes simply marvelous—just perfect.
MRS. STOCKMANN: Because you know how precise my husband is about keeping his regular mealtime—
BILLING: Doesn't bother me in the least. In fact, I really think food tastes best to me when I can eat like this, alone and undisturbed.

MRS. STOCKMANN: Yes, well—just so you enjoy it— *(Turns, listening, toward the hall door.)* Now that must be Hovstad coming.

BILLING: Probably.

PETER STOCKMANN *enters, wearing an overcoat and the official hat of his mayor's office. He carries a walking stick.*

MAYOR STOCKMANN: A most pleasant good evening, my dear Katherine.

MRS. STOCKMANN *(comes into the living room)*: Why, good evening! So it's you? How nice that you stopped up to see us.

MAYOR STOCKMANN: I was just passing by, so— *(With a glance toward the dining room.)* Ah, but it seems you have company already.

MRS. STOCKMANN *(somewhat embarrassed)*: No, no—he was quite unexpected. *(Hurriedly.)* Won't you step in and join him for a bite?

MAYOR STOCKMANN: I? No, thank you. Good heavens, hot food at night! Not with *my* digestion.

MRS. STOCKMANN: Oh, but just this once—

MAYOR STOCKMANN: No, really, that's kind of you; but I'll stick to my bread and butter and tea. It's healthier in the long run—and a bit more economical, too.

MRS. STOCKMANN *(smiling)*: Now you mustn't think that Thomas and I live so lavishly, either.

MAYOR STOCKMANN: Not *you*, Katherine. *That* never crossed my mind. *(Points toward the* DOCTOR's *study.)* I suppose he isn't home?

MRS. STOCKMANN: No, he went for a little walk after dinner—he and the boys.

MAYOR STOCKMANN: How healthy is that, I wonder? *(Listening.)* That ought to be him.

MRS. STOCKMANN: No, I don't think it is. *(A knock at the door.)* Come in!

HOVSTAD *enters from the hall.*

MRS. STOCKMANN: Ah, so it's Mr. Hovstad—

HOVSTAD: Yes, you'll have to excuse me, but I got held up at the printer's. Good evening, Mr. Mayor.

MAYOR STOCKMANN *(bowing rather stiffly)*: Mr. Hovstad. Here on business, I suppose?

HOVSTAD: Partly. It's about something going in the paper.

MAYOR STOCKMANN: I'm not surprised. I hear my brother's become a very active contributor to the *People's Courier*.

HOVSTAD: Yes, he deigns to write for the *Courier* whenever he has a little plain speaking to do about this and that.

MRS. STOCKMANN *(to* HOVSTAD*)*: But won't you—? *(Points toward the dining room.)*

MAYOR STOCKMANN: Oh, well now, I can hardly blame him for writing for the sort of readers who'd give him the best reception. And of course, personally, you know, I haven't the least cause for any ill will toward your paper, Mr. Hovstad.

HOVSTAD: No, I wouldn't think so.

MAYOR STOCKMANN: On the whole, there's a fine spirit of tolerance in this town of ours—a remarkable public spirit. And that stems, of course, from our having a great common concern that binds us all together—a concern that involves to the same high degree every right-minded citizen—

HOVSTAD: The spa, yes.

MAYOR STOCKMANN: Exactly. We have our great, new, magnificent installation, the spa. Mark my words, Mr. Hovstad—these baths will become the very life-principle of our town. Unquestionably!

MRS. STOCKMANN: That's what Thomas says, too.

MAYOR STOCKMANN: Why, it's simply extraordinary the way this place has revived in the past two years! People here have some money again. There's life, excitement! Land and property values are rising every day.

HOVSTAD: And unemployment's down.

MAYOR STOCKMANN: Yes, that too. The taxes for public welfare have been cut by a comfortable margin for the propertied classes, and will be still more if we can only have a really good summer this year—hordes of visitors—masses of invalids who can give the baths a reputation.

HOVSTAD: And that's the prospect, I hear.

MAYOR STOCKMANN: The outlook is very auspicious. Every day, inquiries coming in about accommodations and the like.

HOVSTAD: Well, then the doctor's article ought to be quite timely.

MAYOR STOCKMANN: Has he been writing something again?

HOVSTAD: This is something he wrote last winter: a recommendation of the baths, and a report on the health-promoting character of the life here. But I held the article back at the time.

MAYOR STOCKMANN: There was a flaw in it somewhere, I suppose?

HOVSTAD: No, that's not it. I thought it was better to wait till now, in the spring, when people start planning their summer vacations—

MAYOR STOCKMANN: Quite right. Absolutely right, Mr. Hovstad.

MRS. STOCKMANN: Yes, Thomas spares nothing when the baths are involved.

MAYOR STOCKMANN: Well, he *is* on the staff, after all.

HOVSTAD: Yes, and then he's the one, too, who really originated the idea.

MAYOR STOCKMANN: He *did?* Really? Yes, I do occasionally hear that certain people hold that opinion. But I still had an impression that *I* also played some modest part in this enterprise.

MRS. STOCKMANN: Yes, Thomas says that always.

HOVSTAD: No one denies that, Mr. Mayor. You got the thing moving and put it into practical reality—we all know that. I only meant that the idea came from the doctor first.

MAYOR STOCKMANN: Yes, my brother's had more than enough ideas in his time, I'm afraid. But when there's something to be done, it's another sort of man that's called for, Mr. Hovstad. And I really had thought that, at least here, in this house—

MRS. STOCKMANN: But, my dear Peter—

HOVSTAD: Sir, how can you possibly think—?

MRS. STOCKMANN: Mr. Hovstad, do go in and take some refreshment. My husband's sure to be back any moment.

HOVSTAD: Thank you; just a bite, maybe. (He goes into the dining room.)

MAYOR STOCKMANN (dropping his voice): It's curious with these people of peasant stock: they never can learn any tact.

MRS. STOCKMANN: But why let that bother you? It's not worth it. Can't you and Thomas share the honor, like brothers?

MAYOR STOCKMANN: Yes, it would seem so; but it isn't everyone who can be satisfied with his share, apparently.

MRS. STOCKMANN: Oh, nonsense! You and Thomas get along splendidly together. (Listening.) There, now I think we have him. (Goes over and opens the hall door.)

DR. STOCKMANN (laughing and raising commotion outside): Look, Katherine—you've got another guest here. Isn't this a treat, eh? There we are, Captain Horster; hang your coat up on the peg. Oh, that's right—you don't wear a coat. Imagine, Katherine, I met him on the street, and he almost didn't want to come up.

CAPTAIN HORSTER enters and greets MRS. STOCKMANN.
DR. STOCKMANN appears in the doorway.

In you go, boys. They're ravenous all over again! Come on, Captain Horster; now you're going to have some roast beef—

He propels HORSTER into the dining room; EILIF and MORTEN follow after.

MRS. STOCKMANN: But, Thomas, don't you see—?

DR. STOCKMANN (turning by the door): Oh, it's you, Peter! (Goes over to shake hands.) Well, this is a pleasure.

MAYOR STOCKMANN: I'm afraid I have to be going in just a moment—

DR. STOCKMANN: Rubbish! There's hot toddy on the table now, any minute. You haven't forgotten the toddy, Katherine?

MRS. STOCKMANN: Of course not. The water's boiling. (She goes into the dining room.)

MAYOR STOCKMANN: Toddy, too—!

DR. STOCKMANN: Yes, have a seat, so we can get comfortable.

MAYOR STOCKMANN: Thank you, I never take part in toddy parties.

DR. STOCKMANN: But this isn't a party.

MAYOR STOCKMANN: Well, it looks to me— *(Glancing toward the dining room.)* It's astonishing how they put all that food away.

DR. STOCKMANN *(rubbing his hands)*: Yes, isn't it wonderful to watch young people eat? Endless appetites—just as it ought to be! They've got to have food—for strength! They're the ones who'll put a kick in the future, Peter.

MAYOR STOCKMANN: May I ask what, here, needs a "kick put in it," in your manner of speaking?

DR. STOCKMANN: Well, you better ask the young ones that—when the time comes. We don't see it, of course. Naturally. A pair of old fogies like you and me—

MAYOR STOCKMANN: Now really! That's a very peculiar term—

DR. STOCKMANN: Oh, you mustn't take things so literally with me, Peter. Because you know, I've been feeling so buoyant and happy. I can't tell you how lucky I feel to be part of this life that's budding and bursting out everywhere. What an amazing age we live in! It's as if a whole new world were rising around us.

MAYOR STOCKMANN: You really believe that?

DR. STOCKMANN: Of course you can't see it as well as I can. You've lived in the midst of it all your life, and that dulls the impression. But I, who've been stuck all these many years in my little limbo up north, hardly ever seeing a stranger with a fresh idea to share—to me, it's as if I'd been plunked down in the middle of a swarming metropolis.

MAYOR STOCKMANN: Hm—metropolis—

DR. STOCKMANN: Oh, I'm well aware this is small scale compared with a lot of other places. But there's life here—a promise, an immensity of things to work and fight for; and *that's* what's important. *(Calls.)* Katherine, didn't the mailman come?

MRS. STOCKMANN *(from the dining room)*: No, not today.

DR. STOCKMANN: And then to make a good living, Peter! That's something you learn to appreciate when you've been getting along, as we have, on starvation wages—

MAYOR STOCKMANN: Oh, come—

DR. STOCKMANN: You can just imagine how tight things were for us up there, yes, many times. And now we can live like kings! Today, for instance, we had roast beef for dinner, and we had some more for supper. Don't you want a piece? Or, anyway, let me show it to you. Come here—

MAYOR STOCKMANN: No, definitely not—

DR. STOCKMANN: Well, then come over here. Look, we bought a new tablecloth.

MAYOR STOCKMANN: Yes, so I noticed.

DR. STOCKMANN: And we got a lampshade. See? It's all out of Katherine's savings. And it makes the room so cozy, don't you think? Just stand right here — no, no, no, not there. Just — so! Look, how the light concentrates there where it falls. Really, I find that quite elegant. Don't you?

MAYOR STOCKMANN: Yes, if you can allow yourself luxuries like that —

DR. STOCKMANN: Oh yes. I can allow myself that. Katherine says I'm now earning almost as much as we spend.

MAYOR STOCKMANN: Almost — !

DR. STOCKMANN: But a man of science ought to live with a little style. I'm sure the average district judge spends more in a year than I do.

MAYOR STOCKMANN: Yes, I expect so! A district judge, a superior magistrate —

DR. STOCKMANN: Well, an ordinary businessman then. That kind of man spends a lot more —

MAYOR STOCKMANN: It's a matter of circumstances.

DR. STOCKMANN: In any case, I honestly don't waste anything on luxuries, Peter. But I don't feel I can deny myself the gratification of having people in. You see, I need that. Having been shut out for so long — for me it's a necessity of life to spend time with high-spirited, bold young people, with adventurous minds and a wealth of energy — and that's what they are, all of them sitting and savoring their food in there. I wish you knew Hovstad a bit better —

MAYOR STOCKMANN: Yes, come to think of it, Hovstad told me he'll be printing another of your articles.

DR. STOCKMANN: Of *my* articles?

MAYOR STOCKMANN: Yes, about the baths. Something you wrote last winter.

DR. STOCKMANN: Oh yes, that! No, I don't want that in right now.

MAYOR STOCKMANN: No? It strikes me this is just the opportune time.

DR. STOCKMANN: Yes, you might be right — under ordinary circumstances — *(He paces about the room.)*

MAYOR STOCKMANN *(following him with his eyes)*: What's extraordinary about the circumstances now?

DR. STOCKMANN *(stops)*: Peter, I swear, at this moment I can't tell you — anyway, not this evening. There could be something quite extraordinary about the circumstances — or it might be nothing at all. It could well be that it's just imagination.

MAYOR STOCKMANN: I have to confess, it sounds very mysterious. Is anything wrong? Something I'm excluded from? I would assume that I, as chairman of the board of the municipal baths —

DR. STOCKMANN: And I would assume that — oh, come on, Peter, let's not fly at each other like this.

MAYOR STOCKMANN: Heaven forbid! I'm not in the habit of flying at people, as you put it. But I most definitely must insist that all necessary steps be taken and carried out in a businesslike manner by the legally constituted authorities. I can't condone any sly or underhanded activities.

DR. STOCKMANN: When have I ever been sly or underhanded?

MAYOR STOCKMANN: You have an inveterate tendency to go your own way, in any case. And in a well-ordered society, that's nearly as inexcusable. The individual has to learn to subordinate himself to the whole — or, I should say, to those authorities charged with the common good.

DR. STOCKMANN: Possibly. But what in thunder does that have to do with me?

MAYOR STOCKMANN: Because, my dear Thomas, it's this you seem never to want to learn. But watch out; someday you're going to pay for it — sooner or later. Now I've told you. Good-bye.

DR. STOCKMANN: Are you stark, raving mad? You're completely on the wrong track —

MAYOR STOCKMANN: That's not my custom. And now, if I may excuse myself — *(With a bow toward the dining room.)* Good night, Katherine. Good night, gentlemen. *(Goes out.)*

MRS. STOCKMANN *(coming into the living room)*: He's gone?

DR. STOCKMANN: Yes, and in a foul humor.

MRS. STOCKMANN: Oh, Thomas dear, what did you do to him this time?

DR. STOCKMANN: Nothing at all. He can't demand that I settle accounts with him before the time comes.

MRS. STOCKMANN: What accounts do you have to settle with him?

DR. STOCKMANN: Hm, don't ask me, Katherine. It's odd that the mailman hasn't come.

HOVSTAD, BILLING, *and* HORSTER *have risen from the table and come into the living room.* EILIF *and* MORTEN *follow after a moment.*

BILLING *(stretching his arms)*: Ah, a meal like that and, aye gods, you feel like a new man!

HOVSTAD: The mayor wasn't in his best spirits tonight.

DR. STOCKMANN: It's his stomach; he has bad digestion.

HOVSTAD: I'm sure it was mainly us from the *Courier* he couldn't digest.

MRS. STOCKMANN: You were getting on rather well with him, I thought.

HOVSTAD: Oh yes, but it's nothing more than an armistice.

BILLING: That's it! That's the word for it.

DR. STOCKMANN: We have to remember, Peter's a lonely man. Poor fellow, he has no home to give him comfort — just business, business. And all that damn weak tea he's always sloshing down. Well, now, pull up your chairs to the table, boys! Katherine, don't we get any toddy?

MRS. STOCKMANN (*going toward the dining room*): I'm just bringing it.

DR. STOCKMANN: And you sit here on the sofa by me, Captain Horster. A rare guest like you — please, sit down, everyone.

The men seat themselves at the table. MRS. STOCKMANN *comes back with a tray, holding a hotplate, glasses, decanters, and the like.*

MRS. STOCKMANN: There now. This is arrack, and here's rum, and cognac. So just help yourselves.

DR. STOCKMANN (*taking a glass*): Oh, I think we'll manage! (*While the toddy is mixed.*) And let's have the cigars. Eilif, I'm sure you know where the box is. And, Morten, you can fetch my pipe. (*The boys go into the room on the right.*) I have a suspicion that Eilif sneaks a cigar now and then — but I play innocent. (*Calls.*) And my smoking cap too, Morten! Katherine, can't you tell him where I left it? Ah, he's got it! (*The boys bring in the various items.*) Help yourselves, everybody. I'll stick to my pipe. This one's taken me through a lot of dirty weather on my rounds up north. (*Clinking glasses.*) Skoal! Ah, it's a lot better sitting here, snug and warm.

MRS. STOCKMANN (*sits and starts knitting*): Are you sailing soon, Captain Horster?

HORSTER: I think we'll be ready by next week.

MRS. STOCKMANN: And you'll be going to America then?

HORSTER: That's the intention, yes.

BILLING: But then you can't vote in the new town election.

HORSTER: There's an election coming up?

BILLING: Didn't you know?

HORSTER: No, I don't bother with such things.

BILLING: But you *are* concerned about public affairs, aren't you?

HORSTER: No, I don't understand them.

BILLING: Even so, a person at least ought to vote.

HORSTER: People who don't understand, too?

BILLING: Understand? What do you mean by that? Society's like a ship: all hands have to stand to the wheel.

HORSTER: Maybe on land; but at sea it wouldn't work too well.

HOVSTAD: It's remarkable how most sailors are so little concerned with what happens on land.

BILLING: Very strange.

DR. STOCKMANN: Sailors are like birds of passage: north, south, wherever they are is home. But it's why the rest of us have to be all the more effective, Mr. Hovstad. Anything of general interest in tomorrow's *Courier*?

HOVSTAD: No local items. But I was thinking of running your article the day after tomorrow —

DR. STOCKMANN: Hell's bells, that article! No, listen, you'll have to wait on that.

HOVSTAD: Oh? We have so much space right now, and it seems like the opportune moment —

DR. STOCKMANN: Yes, yes, you're probably right; but you'll have to wait all the same —

PETRA, wearing a hat and coat, comes in from the hall, with a stack of exercise books under her arm.

PETRA: Good evening.

DR. STOCKMANN: That's you, Petra? Good evening.

Greetings all around. PETRA *takes off her hat and coat and leaves them, with the books, on a chair by the door.*

PETRA: And here you all sit partying while I'm out slaving away.

DR. STOCKMANN: Well, now it's your party, too.

BILLING: Can I fix you a little drink?

PETRA *(coming to the table)*: Thanks, I'll do it myself. You always make it too strong. Oh, Father, by the way, I have a letter for you. *(Goes over to the chair where her things are.)*

DR. STOCKMANN: A letter! Who from?

PETRA *(searching in her coat pocket)*: I got it from the mailman as I was just going out —

DR. STOCKMANN *(gets up and goes toward her)*: And you don't bring it till now!

PETRA: I really hadn't the time to run up again. Here it is.

DR. STOCKMANN *(seizing the letter)*: Let me see, let me see, child. *(Looks at the envelope.)* Yes, that's it —!

MRS. STOCKMANN: Is *this* the one you've been so impatient for?

DR. STOCKMANN: Exactly. I must take it straight in and — where can I find a light, Katherine? Is there no lamp in my room again?

MRS. STOCKMANN: The lamp is lit and standing on your desk.

DR. STOCKMANN: Good, good. Excuse me a minute — *(Goes into his study to the right.)*

PETRA: Mother, what do you suppose that is?

MRS. STOCKMANN: I don't know. These last days he's been asking constantly about the mailman.

BILLING: Most likely some patient out of town —

PETRA: Poor Father, he's taking on too much work. *(Mixing a drink.)* Ooh, this'll be good!

HOVSTAD: Were you teaching night school again today?

PETRA *(sipping her glass)*: Two hours.

BILLING: And four hours mornings at the Institute —

PETRA *(sitting by the door)*: Five hours.

MRS. STOCKMANN: And papers to correct in the evening, I see.

PETRA: A whole batch, yes.

HORSTER: It looks like you take on your own full share.

PETRA: Yes, but that's fine. You feel so delectably tired afterward.

BILLING: You like that?

PETRA: Yes. Then you sleep so well.

MORTEN: You must be horribly wicked, Petra.

PETRA: Wicked?

MORTEN: Yes, when you work so hard. Mr. Rørland says that work is a punishment for our sins.

EILIF *(snorts)*: Pah, how stupid you are, to believe that stuff.

MRS. STOCKMANN: Now, now, Eilif!

BILLING *(laughing)*: Oh, marvelous!

HOVSTAD: You'd rather not work so hard, Morten?

MORTEN: No, I wouldn't.

HOVSTAD: Yes, but what do you want to be in life?

MORTEN: Best of all, I want to be a Viking.

EILIF: But then you'd have to be a pagan.

MORTEN: Well, so then I'll be a pagan!

BILLING: I'm with you, Morten! Exactly what I say!

MRS. STOCKMANN *(making signals)*: No, you don't really, Mr. Billing.

BILLING: Ye gods, yes—! I *am* a pagan, and proud of it. Just wait, we'll all be pagans soon.

MORTEN: And can we then do anything we want?

BILLING: Well, you see, Morten—

MRS. STOCKMANN: Now, in you go, boys, both of you. I'm sure you've got homework for tomorrow.

EILIF: *I* could stay a little longer—

MRS. STOCKMANN: Oh no, you can't. The two of you, out!

The boys say good night and go into the room to the left.

HOVSTAD: Do you really think it could hurt the boys to hear these things?

MRS. STOCKMANN: Well, I don't know. But I don't like it.

PETRA: Oh, Mother, I think you're just being silly.

MRS. STOCKMANN: Yes, that's possible; but I don't like it—not here at home.

PETRA: Oh, there's so much hypocrisy, both at home and in school. At home we have to keep quiet, and in school we have to stand there and lie to the children.

HORSTER: You have to lie?

PETRA: Yes, don't you know, we have to teach them all kinds of things we don't believe in ourselves?

BILLING: Yes, that's for certain.

PETRA: If I only had the means, then I'd start a school myself, and things would be different there.

BILLING: Pah, the means—!

HORSTER: Well, if that's your idea, Miss Stockmann, I'll gladly provide you the facilities. My father's old place has been standing nearly empty; there's a huge dining room on the ground floor—

PETRA *(laughing)*: Oh, thank you! But nothing'll come of it, I'm sure.

HOVSTAD: No, I think Miss Petra's more apt to go in for journalism. Incidentally, have you had time to look over that English story you promised to translate for us?

PETRA: No, not yet. But I'll get it to you in time.

DR. STOCKMANN *comes in from his study, the open letter in his hand.*

DR. STOCKMANN *(waving the letter)*: Well, let me tell you, here's news for the town!

BILLING: News?

MRS. STOCKMANN: What sort of news?

DR. STOCKMANN: A great discovery, Katherine!

HOVSTAD: Really?

MRS. STOCKMANN: That you've made?

DR. STOCKMANN: My own, yes. *(Pacing back and forth.)* Now let them come around the way they do, saying it's just whims and wild fantasies. But they better watch out! *(With a laugh.)* They're going to watch out, I think!

PETRA: But, Father, tell what it is!

DR. STOCKMANN: Yes, all right, just give me time, and you'll learn everything. If I only had Peter here now! There you see how we human beings can go around, passing judgments as blind as moles —

HOVSTAD: What do you mean by that, Doctor?

DR. STOCKMANN *(stops by the table)*: It's the general opinion, isn't it, that our town is a healthy place?

HOVSTAD: Why, of course.

DR. STOCKMANN: A most outstandingly healthy place, as a matter of fact — a place to be glowingly recommended to sick and well alike —

MRS. STOCKMANN: But, Thomas, dear —

DR. STOCKMANN: And recommend it we have, and praised it to the skies. I've written endlessly in the *Courier* and in pamphlets —

HOVSTAD: All right, so?

DR. STOCKMANN: This establishment, the baths, that's been called the "main artery" of the town, and its "nerve center," and — who the hell knows what else —

BILLING: "The pulsating heart of our town" I once, in a moment of exuberance, went so far as to —

DR. STOCKMANN: Oh yes, that too. But do you know what they are in reality, these great, splendid, celebrated baths that have cost such a lot of money — you know what they are?

HOVSTAD: No, what are they?

MRS. STOCKMANN: What?

DR. STOCKMANN: The whole setup's a pesthole.

PETRA: The baths, Father!

MRS. STOCKMANN *(simultaneously)*: Our baths!

HOVSTAD *(likewise)*: But, Doctor—

BILLING: Simply incredible!

DR. STOCKMANN: It's a whited sepulcher, the whole establishment—poisoned, you hear me! A health hazard in the worst way. All that pollution up at Mølledal—all that reeking waste from the mill—it's seeped into the pipes feeding the pump-room; and the same damn poisonous slop's been draining out on the beach as well.

HORSTER: You mean in the bathing area?

DR. STOCKMANN: Exactly.

HOVSTAD: How can you be so certain of all this, Doctor?

DR. STOCKMANN: I've investigated the facts as scrupulously as possible. Oh, I've had suspicions for quite a while. Last year there were a number of unusual cases among the visitors here—typhoid and gastritis—

MRS. STOCKMANN: That's right, there were.

DR. STOCKMANN: At the time we assumed the visitors had brought their maladies with them. But later, over the past winter, I began having second thoughts; so I set out to analyze the water with the best means available.

MRS. STOCKMANN: So *that's* what you've been so involved in!

DR. STOCKMANN: Yes, involved—you can well say that, Katherine. But here, of course, I lacked the necessary scientific equipment, so I sent samples of both the drinking water and the seawater to the university for a strict laboratory analysis.

HOVSTAD: And this you've just gotten?

DR. STOCKMANN *(showing the letter)*: This is it! There's irrefutable proof of the presence of decayed organic matter in the water—millions of bacteria. It's positively injurious to health, for either internal or external use.

MRS. STOCKMANN: What a godsend that you found out in time!

DR. STOCKMANN: You can say that again.

HOVSTAD: And what do you plan to do now, Doctor?

DR. STOCKMANN: To see things set to rights, of course.

HOVSTAD: Can that be done?

DR. STOCKMANN: It's got to be. Otherwise, the baths are totally useless—ruined. But there's no need for that. I'm quite clear about what actions have to be taken.

MRS. STOCKMANN: But, Thomas dear, why have you made such a secret of all this?

DR. STOCKMANN: Maybe I should have run out in the streets, blabbering about it before I had sure proof. No thanks, I'm not that crazy.

PETRA: But to us at home—

DR. STOCKMANN: Not to one living soul! But tomorrow you can run over to the Badger—

MRS. STOCKMANN: Really, Thomas!

DR. STOCKMANN: All right then, your grandfather. Yes, this'll stand the old boy on his ear. He's always thought I'm a bit unhinged—oh yes, and a lot more think the same, I'm aware. But now these good people are going to find out—! *(Walks about, rubbing his hands.)* What a stir this'll make in town, Katherine! You can't imagine. The whole water system has to be relaid.

HOVSTAD *(rising)*: The whole water system—?

DR. STOCKMANN: Well, obviously. The intake's too low; it's got to be placed much higher up.

PETRA: So you were right, after all.

DR. STOCKMANN: Ah, you remember that, Petra? I wrote a protest when they were just starting construction. But nobody would listen to me then. Well, now you can bet I'll pour on the heat—yes, because naturally I've written a report for the board of directors. It's been lying in my drawer a whole week; I've just been waiting for this. *(Waving the letter.)* But now it'll be sent right off. *(Goes into his study and returns with a sheaf of papers.)* See here! Four closely written pages! And a covering letter. A newspaper, Katherine—something to wrap this in! Good, that's it. Give it to—to— *(Stamps his foot.)*—what the hell's her name? The maid! Well, give it to her and tell her to take it straight to the mayor.

MRS. STOCKMANN *takes the packet and goes out through the dining room.*

PETRA: What do you think Uncle Peter will say, Father?

DR. STOCKMANN: What should he say? Undoubtedly he has to be glad that a fact of such importance is brought to light.

HOVSTAD: May I have permission to run a little item on your discovery in the *Courier?*

DR. STOCKMANN: I'd be most gratified if you would.

HOVSTAD: The public should hear about this, and the sooner the better.

DR. STOCKMANN: Absolutely.

MRS. STOCKMANN *(returning)*: She's gone with it.

BILLING: So help me, Doctor, you're the foremost citizen of this town!

DR. STOCKMANN *(walks about, looking pleased)*: Oh, come on—really, I haven't done anything more than my duty. I've been a lucky treasure-hunter, and that's it. All the same—

BILLING: Hovstad, don't you think this town owes Doctor Stockmann a parade?

HOVSTAD: I'll come out for it, in any case.

BILLING: And I'll put it up to Aslaksen.

DR. STOCKMANN: No, my dear friends, please—forget all this nonsense. I don't want any ceremonies. And if the board tries to vote me a raise in salary, I won't take it. Katherine, I'm telling you this—I won't take it.

MRS. STOCKMANN: That's only right, Thomas.

PETRA *(raising her glass)*: Skoal, Father!

HOVSTAD *and* BILLING: Skoal, skoal, Doctor!

HORSTER *(clinking glasses with him)*: May this bring you nothing but joy.

DR. STOCKMANN: Thank you. Dear friends, thank you! My heart is so full of happiness—! Ah, what a blessing it is to feel that you've done some service for your own home town and your fellow citizens. Hurrah, Katherine!

He wraps both hands around her neck and whirls about the room with her; she screams and struggles against him. Laughter, applause, and cheers for the DOCTOR. *The* BOYS *poke their heads in at the door.*

ACT II

The DOCTOR's *living room. The dining-room door is closed. It is morning.* MRS. STOCKMANN, *with a sealed letter in her hand, enters from the dining room, goes across to the door of the* DOCTOR's *study, and peers inside.*

MRS. STOCKMANN: Are you in, Thomas?

DR. STOCKMANN *(from within)*: Yes, I just got back. *(Entering)* Is there something?

MRS. STOCKMANN: Letter from your brother. *(Hands it to him.)*

DR. STOCKMANN: Ah, let's see. *(Opens the envelope and reads.)* "The enclosed manuscript is returned herewith—" *(Reads on in an undertone.)* Hm—

MRS. STOCKMANN: What does he say?

DR. STOCKMANN *(slips the papers in his pocket)*: Only that he'll be stopping up around noon sometime.

MRS. STOCKMANN: You *must* remember not to go out, then.

DR. STOCKMANN: Oh, that's no problem. I've finished my calls for the morning.

MRS. STOCKMANN: I'm terribly curious to know how he takes it.

DR. STOCKMANN: You'll see, he's not going to like it that I made the discovery, and he didn't.

MRS. STOCKMANN: Yes, doesn't that worry you?

DR. STOCKMANN: Oh, basically he'll be pleased, you can imagine. All the same—Peter's so damned nervous that somebody besides himself might do this town a little good.

MRS. STOCKMANN: But, you know what, Thomas—that's why you ought to be nice and share the honors with him. Couldn't it get around that he was the one who put you on the track—?

DR. STOCKMANN: Fine, as far as I'm concerned. If I can just get this thing cleared up—

Old MORTEN KIIL *sticks in his head at the hall door, looks about inquisitively, and shakes with silent laughter.*

MORTEN KIIL *(slyly)*: Is is—is it true?

MRS. STOCKMANN *(moving toward him)*: Father—it's you!

DR. STOCKMANN: Why, Father-in-law, good morning, good morning!

MRS. STOCKMANN: Oh, but aren't you coming in?

MORTEN KIIL: Yes, if it's true — if not, I'm leaving —

DR. STOCKMANN: If what's true?

MORTEN KIIL: This wild story about the waterworks. Is that true?

DR. STOCKMANN: Of course it's true. But how did *you* hear about it?

MORTEN KIIL *(entering)*: Petra flew in on her way to school —

DR. STOCKMANN: Oh, did she?

MORTEN KIIL: Oh yes, and she told me. I thought she was just making a fool of me; but that isn't like Petra, either.

DR. STOCKMANN: You don't mean that!

MORTEN KIIL: Oh, you can't trust anybody. You can be made a fool of before you know it. It really is true, though?

DR. STOCKMANN: Yes, irrefutably. Now, please, have a seat, Father. *(Pressing him down onto the sofa.)* Isn't this a real piece of luck for the town?

MORTEN KIIL *(stifling his laughter)*: Luck for the town?

DR. STOCKMANN: Yes, that I made this discovery in the nick of time —

MORTEN KIIL *(as before)*: Yes, yes, yes! But I'd never have dreamed that you'd play your monkeyshines on your own brother.

DR. STOCKMANN: Monkeyshines!

MRS. STOCKMANN: But, Father —

MORTEN KIIL *(rests his hands and chin on the handle of his cane and winks slyly at the DOCTOR)*: How was it now? You're saying that some animals got loose in the waterpipes?

DR. STOCKMANN: Yes, bacteria.

MORTEN KIIL: And there are lots of those animals in there, Petra said. A huge crowd of them.

DR. STOCKMANN: Up in the millions, most likely.

MORTEN KIIL: But no one can see them — wasn't that it?

DR. STOCKMANN: You can't *see* them, of course not.

MORTEN KIIL *(chuckling to himself)*: Damned if this isn't the best one you've pulled off yet.

DR. STOCKMANN: What do you mean?

MORTEN KIIL: But you'll never get the mayor believing anything like that.

DR. STOCKMANN: Well, we'll see.

MORTEN KIIL: You think he's that crazy?

DR. STOCKMANN: I hope the whole town will be that crazy.

MORTEN KIIL: The whole town! Yes, that's not impossible. It'd serve them right — and show them up. They think they're so much smarter than us old boys. They hounded me out of the town council. That's right, I'm telling you, like a dog they hounded me out, they did. But now they're going to get it. You just go on and lay your monkeyshines on them, Stockmann.

DR. STOCKMANN: Yes, but—

MORTEN KIIL: Make monkeys out of them, I say. *(Getting up.)* If you can work it so the mayor and his cronies get their ears pinned back, right then and there I'll donate a hundred crowns to the poor.

DR. STOCKMANN: You're very generous.

MORTEN KIIL: Yes, of course I've got little enough to spare, you understand. But if you can do that, I'll remember the poor next Christmas with a good fifty crowns.

HOVSTAD *comes in from the hall.*

HOVSTAD: Good morning! *(Stopping.)* Oh, excuse me—

DR. STOCKMANN: No, come in, come in.

MORTEN KIIL *(chuckling again)*: Him! Is he in on this too?

HOVSTAD: What do you mean?

DR. STOCKMANN: Why, of course he is.

MORTEN KIIL: I might have guessed it. It's going into the paper. You're really the limit, Stockmann. Well, now you two get together; I'm leaving.

DR. STOCKMANN: No, stay a while, Father.

MORTEN KIIL: No, I'm leaving. And scheme up all the monkeyshines you can. You damn well aren't going to lose by it!

He goes, accompanied by MRS. STOCKMANN.

DR. STOCKMANN *(laughing)*: What do you think—the old man doesn't believe a word of this about the water system.

HOVSTAD: Oh, was it *that*—?

DR. STOCKMANN: Yes, that's what we were talking about. And I suppose you're here for the same.

HOVSTAD: That's right. Do you have just a moment, Doctor?

DR. STOCKMANN: As long as you like.

HOVSTAD: Have you heard anything from the mayor?

DR. STOCKMANN: Not yet. He's stopping by later.

HOVSTAD: I've been thinking a good deal about this business since last evening.

DR. STOCKMANN: Oh?

HOVSTAD: For you, as a doctor and a scientist, this condition in the water system is something all to itself. I mean, it hasn't occurred to you that it's interrelated with a lot of other things.

DR. STOCKMANN: How so? Here, let's sit down. No, on the sofa there.

HOVSTAD *sits on the sofa, and* STOCKMANN *in an armchair on the other side of the table.*

DR. STOCKMANN: Well? You were thinking—?

HOVSTAD: You said yesterday that the polluted water came from impurities in the soil.

DR. STOCKMANN: Yes, beyond any doubt it comes from that poisoned swamp up at Mølledal.

HOVSTAD: If you'll pardon me, Doctor, I think it comes from another swamp altogether.

DR. STOCKMANN: What sort?

HOVSTAD: The swamp where our whole community lies rotting.

DR. STOCKMANN: What the deuce is that supposed to mean, Mr. Hovstad?

HOVSTAD: Little by little every activity in this town has passed into the hands of a little clique of politicians —

DR. STOCKMANN: Come on now, they're not all of them politicians.

HOVSTAD: No, but those who aren't politicians are their friends and camp followers. All the rich in town, and the old established names — they're the powers that rule our lives.

DR. STOCKMANN: Yes, but then those people have a great deal of competence and vision.

HOVSTAD: Did they show competence and vision when they laid the water mains where they are now?

DR. STOCKMANN: No, of course that was an enormous piece of stupidity. But that'll be straightened out now.

HOVSTAD: You think it'll go so smoothly?

DR. STOCKMANN: Smoothly or not — it's going to go through.

HOVSTAD: Yes, if the press steps in.

DR. STOCKMANN: That won't be necessary, really. I'm positive that my brother —

HOVSTAD: Excuse me, Doctor; but I'm telling you that I plan to take this matter up.

DR. STOCKMANN: In the paper?

HOVSTAD: Yes. When I took over the *Courier,* it was my intention to break up that ring of pig-headed reactionaries who hold all the power.

DR. STOCKMANN: But you've told me yourself what the outcome was: you nearly wrecked the paper over them.

HOVSTAD: Yes, that time we had to back down, it's true. There was some risk that the baths might never have been constructed if those men had fallen. But now we have the baths, and the high and mighty are expendable now.

DR. STOCKMANN: Expendable, yes; but we still owe them a great debt.

HOVSTAD: And we'll acknowledge that, in all fairness. But a journalist of my radical leanings can't let an opportunity like this go by. The myth of the infallibility of the ruling class has to be shattered. It has to be rooted out, like any other superstition.

DR. STOCKMANN: I fully agree with you there, Mr. Hovstad. If it's a superstition, then out with it!

HOVSTAD: Of course I'm rather loath to involve the mayor, since he *is* your brother. But certainly you believe as I do, that the truth comes before anything else.

DR. STOCKMANN: No question of that. *(In an outburst.)* Yes, but — but —!

HOVSTAD: You mustn't think badly of me. I'm no more self-seeking or power-hungry than most people.

DR. STOCKMANN: But — whoever said you were?

HOVSTAD: I come from a poor family, as you know; and I've had ample opportunity to observe what the most pressing need is among the lower classes. Doctor, it's to play some part in directing our public life. That's the thing that develops skills and knowledge and self-respect —

DR. STOCKMANN: I understand absolutely —

HOVSTAD: Yes — and so I think a journalist is terribly remiss if he neglects the least opportunity for the liberation of the powerless, oppressed masses. Oh, I know — those on top are going to label this agitation, among other things; but they can say what they please. So long as my conscience is clear, then —

DR. STOCKMANN: That's it, yes! That's it, Mr. Hovstad. But all the same — damn it —! *(A knock at the door.)* Come in!

ASLAKSEN, the printer, appears at the hall door. He is plainly but respectably dressed in black, with a white, somewhat wrinkled cravat; he holds gloves and a high silk hat in his hand.

ASLAKSEN *(bowing)*: Pardon me, Doctor, for intruding like this —

DR. STOCKMANN *(rises)*: Well, now — it's Mr. Aslaksen!

ASLAKSEN: That's right, Doctor.

HOVSTAD *(getting up)*: Were you looking for me, Aslaksen?

ASLAKSEN: No, I didn't think to meet you here. No, it was the doctor himself —

DR. STOCKMANN: Well, what can I do for you?

ASLAKSEN: Is it true, what I heard from Mr. Billing, that you're of a mind to get us a better water system?

DR. STOCKMANN: Yes, for the baths.

ASLAKSEN: Of course; I understand. Well, then I'm here to say, I'm throwing my full support behind you in this.

HOVSTAD *(to the DOCTOR)*: You see!

ASLAKSEN: Because it might just come in handy to have us small businessmen in back of you. We make up pretty much of a solid majority in this town — that is, when we *choose* to. And it's always good to have the majority with you, Doctor.

DR. STOCKMANN: That's undoubtedly true. But I can hardly believe that any special measures are going to be needed here. With something as clear-cut as this, it would seem to me —

ASLAKSEN: Oh, it could be a good thing all the same. Because I know these local authorities. The ones that run things don't take too kindly to propositions coming from the outside. And so I was thinking it wouldn't be out of the way if we staged a little demonstration.

HOVSTAD: That's the idea.

DR. STOCKMANN: You say, a demonstration? Just how would you plan to demonstrate?

ASLAKSEN: Naturally with great moderation, Doctor. I always make every effort for moderation. Because moderation is a citizen's chief virtue — in *my* opinion, anyway.

DR. STOCKMANN: You're certainly well known for it, Mr. Aslaksen.

ASLAKSEN: Yes, I think that's not too much to say. And this question of the water system, it's immensely important to us little businessmen. The baths show every sign of becoming like a miniature gold mine for this town. It's the baths that'll give us all a living, and especially us home owners. That's why we want to support this operation in every possible way. And since I'm now chairman of the Home Owners Council —

DR. STOCKMANN: Yes —?

ASLAKSEN: And since, moreover, I'm a representative of the Temperance Union — you knew, Doctor, did you not, that I am a temperance worker?

DR. STOCKMANN: Yes, that follows.

ASLAKSEN: Well — so it's quite obvious that I come in contact with a wide variety of people. And since I'm known for being a sober, law-abiding citizen, as you yourself said, Doctor, I've acquired a certain influence in this town — just a little position of power — if I may say so myself.

DR. STOCKMANN: I'm well aware of that, Mr. Aslaksen.

ASLAKSEN: So you see — it would be a small matter for me to work up a tribute, in a pinch.

DR. STOCKMANN: A tribute?

ASLAKSEN: Yes, a kind of tribute of thanks from the townspeople to you, for having advanced such a vital interest for the community. It goes without saying that it's got to be phrased with all due moderation, so it doesn't offend the authorities, or anyone else in power. And if we just watch ourselves *there,* then I don't think anyone will object, do you?

HOVSTAD: So, even if they didn't like it too well —

ASLAKSEN: No, no, no! No affronts to the authorities, Mr. Hovstad. No collisions with people so much involved in our lives. I've had enough of that in my time; and no good ever comes of it, either. But a citizen's sober and honest opinions are not to be scorned by any man.

DR. STOCKMANN (*shaking his hand*): My dear Mr. Aslaksen, I can't tell you how deeply it pleases me to find so much sympathy among my fellow citizens. It makes me so happy — so happy! Listen, why not a little glass of sherry, what?

ASLAKSEN: Many thanks, but no. I never indulge in spirits.

DR. STOCKMANN: Well, then a glass of beer — what do you say to that?

ASLAKSEN: Thanks again, Doctor, but I never partake so early in the day. Just now I want to get around town and talk to some of the home owners and prepare their reactions.

DR. STOCKMANN: That's exceptionally kind of you, Mr. Aslaksen. But I simply can't get it through my head that all these measures are going to be necessary. I think the matter could very well take care of itself.

ASLAKSEN: Authorities tend to need goading, Doctor Stockmann — though, on my soul, I don't mean to be critical of them —!

HOVSTAD: We'll go after them in the paper tomorrow, Aslaksen.

ASLAKSEN: But without violence, Mr. Hovstad. Proceed in moderation, or you'll never get anywhere. You can trust my word on that, because I've gleaned my experience in the school of life. Well, then — I'll say good-bye to you, Doctor. Now you know that, in any event, we small businessmen stand behind you, like a wall. You've got the solid majority on your side, Doctor.

DR. STOCKMANN: Thank you for that, Mr. Aslaksen. *(Shaking his hand.)* Good-bye, good-bye!

ASLAKSEN: Will you be coming along to the pressroom, Mr. Hovstad?

HOVSTAD: I'll be in later. I still have a bit more to do.

ASLAKSEN: Very good.

He bows and leaves. DR. STOCKMANN *accompanies him into the hall.*

HOVSTAD *(as the* DOCTOR *re-enters)*: Well, what do you say now, Doctor? Don't you think it's about time to stir up and air out all the stale, spineless inertia in this town?

DR. STOCKMANN: You're referring to Aslaksen?

HOVSTAD: Yes, I am. He's one of them who's sunk in the swamp — good a man as he is in some other ways. He's what most of them are around here: they go along tacking and trimming from this side to that. With all their scruples and second thoughts, they never dare strike out for anything.

DR. STOCKMANN: But to me Aslaksen seemed so thoroughly well-intentioned.

HOVSTAD: There's something I value more — and that's standing your ground as a strong, self-reliant man.

DR. STOCKMANN: I agree with you there entirely.

HOVSTAD: That's why I want to take this opportunity now and see if I can't force some of these models of intention to make men of themselves for once. The worship of authority in this town has to be uprooted. This inexcusable lapse of judgment about the water system has to be driven home to every eligible voter.

DR. STOCKMANN: All right. If you think it's best for the community, then go ahead. But not before I've talked with my brother.

HOVSTAD: Meanwhile, I'm writing an editorial to have on hand. And if the mayor doesn't get after this thing —

DR. STOCKMANN: Oh, but how can you think he wouldn't?

HOVSTAD: It's quite thinkable. And, if so — ?

DR. STOCKMANN: Well, then I promise you — listen — then you can print my report — complete and uncut.

HOVSTAD: May I? Your word on that?

DR. STOCKMANN *(hands him the manuscript)*: Here it is. Take it along. It can't hurt if you read it through; and you can give it back to me later.

HOVSTAD: Very good; I'll do that. Good-bye then, Doctor.

DR. STOCKMANN: Good-bye, good-bye. Yes, you'll see now, it'll all go smoothly, Mr. Hovstad. Very smoothly.

HOVSTAD: Hm — we'll see. *(He bows and goes out by the hall door.)*

DR. STOCKMANN *(goes over to the dining room and looks in)*: Katherine — ! Oh, are you back, Petra?

PETRA *(entering)*: Yes, I just came from school.

MRS. STOCKMANN *(entering)*: He's still not been in?

DR. STOCKMANN: Peter? No. But I had a long talk with Hovstad. He's very much excited by the discovery I've made. Its repercussions go a lot further, apparently, than I thought at first. So he's put his paper at my disposal, if it comes to that.

MRS. STOCKMANN: Do you think it will come to that?

DR. STOCKMANN: Oh, of course not. But all the same, it's a heady feeling to know you've got the independent liberal press on your side. Yes, and guess what? I also had a visit from the chairman of the Home Owners Council.

MRS. STOCKMANN: Oh? And what did he want?

DR. STOCKMANN: To support me, as well. They'll all support me, if things get rough. Katherine — do you know what I have backing me up?

MRS. STOCKMANN: Backing you up? No, what do you have?

DR. STOCKMANN: The solid majority.

MRS. STOCKMANN: Really. And that's a good thing, is it, Thomas?

DR. STOCKMANN: Well, I should hope it's a good thing! *(Paces up and down, rubbing his hands together.)* My Lord, how gratifying it is to stand like this, joined together in brotherhood with your fellow citizens.

PETRA: And then to accomplish so much that's fine and useful, Father!

DR. STOCKMANN: And for one's own birthplace in the bargain.

MRS. STOCKMANN: There's the bell.

DR. STOCKMANN: That's got to be him. *(A knock at the door.)* Come in!

MAYOR STOCKMANN *(entering from the hall)*: Good morning.

DR. STOCKMANN: Good to see you, Peter!

MRS. STOCKMANN: Morning, Peter. How's everything with you?

MAYOR STOCKMANN: Just so-so, thank you. *(To the DOCTOR.)* Yesterday, after office hours, I received a report from you, discussing the condition of the water at the baths.

DR. STOCKMANN: Yes. Have you read it?

MAYOR STOCKMANN: I have.

DR. STOCKMANN: What have you got to say about it?

MAYOR STOCKMANN (*glancing at the others*): Hm —
MRS. STOCKMANN: Come along, Petra.

She and PETRA *go into the room on the left.*

MAYOR STOCKMANN (*after a moment*): Was it necessary to press all these investigations behind my back?
DR. STOCKMANN: Well, as long as I didn't have absolute proof, then —
MAYOR STOCKMANN: And now you think you do?
DR. STOCKMANN: You must be convinced of that yourself.
MAYOR STOCKMANN: Is it your object to put this document before the board of directors by way of an official recommendation?
DR. STOCKMANN: Of course. Something has to be done about this. And fast.
MAYOR STOCKMANN: As usual, in your report you let your language get out of hand. You say, among other things, that what we're offering our summer visitors is guaranteed poison.
DR. STOCKMANN: But, Peter, how else can you describe it? You've got to realize — this water *is* poison for internal *or* external use! And it's foisted on poor, suffering creatures who turn to us in good faith and pay us exorbitant fees to gain their health back again!
MAYOR STOCKMANN: And then you arrive at the conclusion, by your line of reasoning, that we have to build a sewer to drain off these so-called impurities from Mølledal, and that all the water mains have to be relaid.
DR. STOCKMANN: Well, do you see any other way out? I don't.
MAYOR STOCKMANN: I invented a little business this morning down at the town engineer's office. And in a half-joking way, I brought up these proposals as something we perhaps ought to take under advisement at some time in the future.
DR. STOCKMANN: Some time in the future!
MAYOR STOCKMANN: He smiled at my whimsical extravagance — naturally. Have you gone to the trouble of estimating just what these proposed changes would cost? From the information I received, the expenditure would probably run up into several hundred thousand crowns.
DR. STOCKMANN: As high as that?
MAYOR STOCKMANN: Yes. But that's not the worst. The work would extend over at least two years.
DR. STOCKMANN: Two years? Two full years?
MAYOR STOCKMANN: At the least. And meanwhile what do we do with the baths? Shut them down? Yes, we'll have to. Do you really think anyone would make the effort to come all the distance here if the rumor got out that the water was contaminated?
DR. STOCKMANN: Yes, but Peter, that's what it is.

MAYOR STOCKMANN: And then all this happens now—just now, when the baths were being recognized. Other towns in this area have the same resources for development as health resorts. Don't you think they'll leap at the chance to attract the whole flow of tourists to them? No question of it. And there we are, left stranded. We'll most likely have to abandon the whole costly enterprise; and then you'll have ruined the town you were born in.

DR. STOCKMANN: I—ruined—!

MAYOR STOCKMANN: It's through the baths alone that this town has any future to speak of. You can see that just as plain as I can.

DR. STOCKMANN: But then what do you think ought to be done?

MAYOR STOCKMANN: From your report I'm unable to persuade myself that the condition of the baths is as critical as you claim.

DR. STOCKMANN: Look, if anything, it's worse! Or it'll be that by summer, when the warm weather comes.

MAYOR STOCKMANN: Once again. I think you're exaggerating considerably. A capable doctor must know the right steps to take—he should be able to control toxic elements, and to treat them if they make their presence too obvious.

DR. STOCKMANN: And then—? What else—?

MAYOR STOCKMANN: The water system for the baths as it now stands is simply a fact and clearly has to be accepted as such. But in time the directors will more than likely agree to take under consideration to what extent—depending on the funds available—they can institute certain improvements.

DR. STOCKMANN: And you can think I'd play along with that kind of trickery?

MAYOR STOCKMANN: Trickery?

DR. STOCKMANN: Yes, it's a trick—a deception, a lie, an out-and-out crime against the public and society at large!

MAYOR STOCKMANN: As I've already observed, I've not yet persuaded myself that there's any real impending danger here.

DR. STOCKMANN: Yes, you have! There's no alternative. My report is perfectly accurate, I know that! And you're very much aware of it, Peter, but you won't admit it. You're the one who got the baths and the water system laid out where they are today; and it's *this*—it's this hellish miscalculation that you won't concede. Pah! You don't think I can see right through you?

MAYOR STOCKMANN: And even if it were true? Even if I seem a bit overanxious about my reputation, it's all for the good of the town. Without moral authority I could hardly guide and direct affairs in the way I believe serves the general welfare. For this reason—among many others—it strikes me as imperative that your report not be submitted to the board of directors. It has to be withheld for the common good.

Then, later, I'll bring the matter up for discussion, and we'll do the very best we can, as quietly as possible. But nothing — not the slightest word of this catastrophe must leak out to the public.

DR. STOCKMANN: My dear Peter, there's no stopping it now.

MAYOR STOCKMANN: It must and it will be stopped.

DR. STOCKMANN: I'm telling you, it's no use. Too many people know already.

MAYOR STOCKMANN: Know already! Who? Not those fellows from the *Courier* — ?

DR. STOCKMANN: Why, of course they know. The independent liberal press is going to see that you do your duty.

MAYOR STOCKMANN *(after a short pause)*: You're an exceptionally thoughtless man, Thomas. Haven't you considered the consequences that can follow for you?

DR. STOCKMANN: Consequences? For me?

MAYOR STOCKMANN: For you and your family as well.

DR. STOCKMANN: What the devil does *that* mean?

MAYOR STOCKMANN: I think, over the years, I've proved a helpful and accommodating brother to you.

DR. STOCKMANN: Yes, you have, and I'm thankful to you for that.

MAYOR STOCKMANN: I'm not after thanks. Because, in part, I was forced into it — for my own sake. I always hoped I could keep you in check somewhat if I helped better your economic status.

DR. STOCKMANN: What? Just for your own sake — !

MAYOR STOCKMANN: In part, I said. It's embarrassing for a public servant when his closest relative goes and compromises himself again and again.

DR. STOCKMANN: And that's what you think I do?

MAYOR STOCKMANN: Yes, unfortunately you do, without your knowing it. You have a restless, unruly, combative nature. And then this unhappy knack of bursting into print on all kinds of likely and unlikely subjects. You're no sooner struck by an idea than right away you have to scribble a newspaper article on it, or a whole pamphlet even.

DR. STOCKMANN: Well, but isn't it a citizen's duty to inform the public if he comes on a new idea?

MAYOR STOCKMANN: Oh, the public doesn't need new ideas. The public is served best by the good, old, time-tested ideas it's always had.

DR. STOCKMANN: That's putting it plainly!

MAYOR STOCKMANN: I have to talk to you plainly for once. Up till now I've always tried to avoid that because I know how irritable you are; but now I'm telling you the truth, Thomas. You have no conception how much you injure yourself with your impetuosity. You complain about the authorities and, yes, the government; you rail against them — and insist you're being passed over and persecuted. But what can you expect — someone as troublesome as you.

DR. STOCKMANN: Ah—so I'm troublesome, too?

MAYOR STOCKMANN: Yes, Thomas, you're a very troublesome man to work with. I know from experience. You show no consideration at all. You seem to forget completely that I'm the one you can thank for your post here as staff physician at the baths—

DR. STOCKMANN: I was the inevitable choice—I and nobody else! I was the first to see that this town could become a flourishing spa; and I was the *only* one who could see it then. I stood alone fighting for that idea for years; and I wrote and wrote—

MAYOR STOCKMANN: Unquestionably. But the right moment hadn't arrived yet. Of course you couldn't judge that from up there in the wilds. But when the opportune time came, and I—and a few others— took the matter in hand—

DR. STOCKMANN: Yes, and bungled the whole magnificent plan. Oh yes, it's really coming out now what a brilliant crew you've been!

MAYOR STOCKMANN: All that's coming out, to my mind, is your usual hunger for a good fight. You want to attack your superiors—it's your old pattern. You can't stand any authority over you; you resent anyone in a higher position and regard him as a personal enemy—and then one weapon's as good as another to use. But now I've acquainted you with the vital interests at stake here for this whole town—and, natu- rally, for me as well. And so I'm warning you, Thomas, I'll be ada- mant about the demand I am going to make of you.

DR. STOCKMANN: What demand?

MAYOR STOCKMANN: Since you've been so indiscreet as to discuss this delicate issue with outsiders, even though it should have been kept secret among the directors, it of course can't be hushed up now. All kinds of rumors will go flying around, and the maliciously inclined will dress them up with trimmings of their own. It'll therefore be necessary that you publicly deny these rumors.

DR. STOCKMANN: I! How? I don't understand.

MAYOR STOCKMANN: We can expect that, after further investigation, you'll arrive at the conclusion that things are far from being as critical or dangerous as you'd first imagined.

DR. STOCKMANN: Ah—you expect that!

MAYOR STOCKMANN: Moreover, we expect that you'll support and publicly affirm your confidence in the present directors to take thor- ough and conscientious measures, as necessary, to remedy any possible defects.

DR. STOCKMANN: But that's utterly out of the question for me, as long as they try to get by with patchwork. I'm telling you that, Peter; and it's my unqualified opinion—!

MAYOR STOCKMANN: As a member of the staff, you're not entitled to any personal opinions.

DR. STOCKMANN *(stunned)*: Not entitled—!

MAYOR STOCKMANN: As a staff member, I said. As a private person—why, that's another matter. But as a subordinate official at the baths, you're not entitled to express any opinions that contradict your superiors.

DR. STOCKMANN: That's going too far! I, as a doctor, a man of science, aren't entitled to—!

MAYOR STOCKMANN: What's involved here isn't a purely scientific problem. It's a mixture of both technical and economic considerations.

DR. STOCKMANN: I don't care what the hell it is! I want the freedom to express myself on any problem under the sun!

MAYOR STOCKMANN: Anything you like—except for the baths. We forbid you that.

DR. STOCKMANN (shouting): You forbid—! You! A crowd of—!

MAYOR STOCKMANN: I forbid it—I, your supervisor. And when I forbid you, then you obey.

DR. STOCKMANN (controls himself): Peter—if you weren't my brother—

PETRA (flinging the door open): You don't have to take this, Father!

MRS. STOCKMANN (following her): Petra, Petra!

MAYOR STOCKMANN: Ah, an ear to the keyhole.

MRS. STOCKMANN: You were so loud, we couldn't avoid—

PETRA: Oh, but I was there, listening.

MAYOR STOCKMANN: Well, I'm just as glad, really—

DR. STOCKMANN (approaching him): You were talking to me about forbidding and obeying—?

MAYOR STOCKMANN: You forced me to adopt that tone.

DR. STOCKMANN: So you want me to stand up in public and confess I'm a liar?

MAYOR STOCKMANN: We find it absolutely essential that you make a public statement along the lines I've indicated.

DR. STOCKMANN: And what if I don't—obey?

MAYOR STOCKMANN: Then we ourselves will issue a statement to soothe the public.

DR. STOCKMANN: Very well. But then I'll attack you in print. I'll stand my ground. I'll prove that I'm right, and you're wrong. And then what will you do?

MAYOR STOCKMANN: Then I won't be able to prevent your dismissal.

DR. STOCKMANN: What—!

PETRA: Father—dismissal!

MRS. STOCKMANN: Dismissal!

MAYOR STOCKMANN: You'll be dismissed from the staff. I'll find myself obliged to see you put on immediate notice and suspended from all activities involving the baths.

DR. STOCKMANN: And you'll dare that!

MAYOR STOCKMANN: You're the one playing the daredevil.

PETRA: Uncle, this is a shameful way to treat a man like Father!

MRS. STOCKMANN: Will you please be quiet, Petra!

MAYOR STOCKMANN *(regarding* PETRA*)*: Ah, so we've already learned to voice opinions. Yes, naturally. *(To* MRS. STOCKMANN.*)* Katherine, I expect you're the most sensible member of this household. Use whatever influence you have over your husband, and make him understand what effect this will have on both his family —

DR. STOCKMANN: My family concerns no one else but me.

MAYOR STOCKMANN: As I was saying, on both his family and the town he lives in.

DR. STOCKMANN: I'm the one who really wants the best for the town! I want to expose failings that'll come to light sooner or later anyway. That ought to show that I love this town.

MAYOR STOCKMANN: Yes, by setting out in blind spite to cut off our major source of revenue.

DR. STOCKMANN: That source is poisoned, man! Are you crazy! We live by marketing filth and corruption. The whole affluence of this community has its roots in a lie!

MAYOR STOCKMANN: Sheer fantasy — or something worse. Any man who could hurl such nauseating charges at his own home town must be an enemy of society.

DR. STOCKMANN *(going for him)*: You dare —!

MRS. STOCKMANN *(throws herself between them)*: Thomas!

PETRA *(seizing her father by the arm)*: Easy, Father!

MAYOR STOCKMANN: I don't have to subject myself to violence. Now you've been warned. Just consider what you owe yourself and your family. Good-bye. *(He leaves.)*

DR. STOCKMANN *(pacing up and down)*: And I have to take this treatment! In my own house, Katherine! What do you say to that!

MRS. STOCKMANN: Of course it's humiliating, Thomas —

PETRA: Oh, what I could do to Uncle —!

DR. STOCKMANN: It's my own fault. I should have faced them down long ago — shown my teeth — and bit back! Call *me* an enemy of society! So help me God, I'm not going to swallow that!

MRS. STOCKMANN: But, Thomas dear, your brother does have the power —

DR. STOCKMANN: Yes, but I'm in the right!

MRS. STOCKMANN: The right? Ah, what does it help to be in the right if you don't have any power?

PETRA: Mother, no — why do you talk like that?

DR. STOCKMANN: You mean it doesn't help in a free society to be on the side of right? Don't be absurd, Katherine. And besides — don't I have the independent liberal press to lead the way — and the solid majority behind me? There's power enough in them, I'd say!

MRS. STOCKMANN: But Thomas, for heaven's sake — surely you're not thinking of—

DR. STOCKMANN: Thinking of what?

MRS. STOCKMANN: Of setting yourself up against your brother.

DR. STOCKMANN: What in hell do you want me to do? Abandon everything that's true and right?

PETRA: Yes, I'd ask the same.

MRS. STOCKMANN: But it won't do you the least bit of good. If they won't, they won't.

DR. STOCKMANN: Oh ho, Katherine, just give me time! You'll see, I'll push this fight through to the end.

MRS. STOCKMANN: Yes, maybe you'll just push yourself out of your job—that's what you'll do.

DR. STOCKMANN: Then anyway I'll have done my duty to the people— to society. Though they call me its enemy!

MRS. STOCKMANN: And to your family, Thomas? To us at home? You think that's doing your duty to those who depend on you?

PETRA: Oh, stop always thinking of us first of all, Mother.

MRS. STOCKMAN: Yes, it's easy for *you* to talk. If need be, you can stand on your own feet. But remember the boys, Thomas. And think of yourself a little, and of me—

DR. STOCKMANN: You must be utterly mad, Katherine! If I had to crawl like an abject coward to Peter and his damned cohorts—do you think I'd ever know one moment's happiness for the rest of my life?

MRS. STOCKMANN: I don't know about that. But God preserve us from the kind of happiness we'll share if you press your defiance. You'll be back again where you started—no position, no assured income. I thought we'd had enough of that in the old days. Remember that, Thomas; and think of what lies ahead.

DR. STOCKMANN (*clenching his fists and writhing in inner conflict*): And this is how these bureaucrats can clamp down on a plain, honest man! It's despicable, Katherine, isn't it?

MRS. STOCKMANN: Yes, they've acted shamefully toward you, of course. But, my Lord, there's so much injustice that people have to bear with in this world—There are the boys, Thomas! Look at them! What'll become of them? No, no, you wouldn't have the heart—

As she speaks, EILIF *and* MORTEN *come in, carrying their schoolbooks.*

DR. STOCKMANN: The boys—! (*Suddenly resolved.*) I don't care if all the world caves in, I'm not going to lick the dust. (*He heads for his study.*)

MRS. STOCKMANN (*following him*): Thomas—what are you doing?

DR. STOCKMANN (*at the door*): I want the chance to look my boys straight in the eyes when they've grown up to be free men. (*He goes within.*)

MRS. STOCKMANN (*bursting into tears*): Oh, God help us all!

PETRA: Father—he's wonderful! He's not giving in.

The boys, in bewilderment, ask what has happened; PETRA *signals them to be quiet.*

ACT III

The editorial office of the People's Courier. *At the back, left, is the entrance door; to the right in the same wall is another door, through which one can see the pressroom. In the wall to the right, a third door. At the center of the room is a large table covered with papers, newspapers, and books. In the foreground at the left a window and, next to it, a writing desk with a high stool. A couple of armchairs are drawn up by the table; several other chairs along the walls. The room is barren and cheerless, the furnishings old, the armchairs grimy and torn. In the pressroom two typesetters can be seen at work, and, beyond them, a handpress in operation.*

HOVSTAD is seated at the desk, writing. After a moment BILLING *enters from the right, the* DOCTOR's *manuscript in his hand.*

BILLING: Well, that's really something—!

HOVSTAD *(writing)*: Did you read it all?

BILLING *(lays the manuscript on the desk)*: I'll say I did.

HOVSTAD: He makes a pretty sharp statement, doesn't he?

BILLING: Sharp? Ye gods, it's pulverizing? Every word hits home like a sledgehammer.

HOVSTAD: Yes, but that crowd isn't going to come down at one blow.

BILLING: That's true. But then we'll keep on hitting them—blow upon blow, till their whole leadership crumbles. When I sat in there reading this, it was exactly as if I could see the revolution breaking like the dawn.

HOVSTAD *(turning)*: Shh! Don't say that so Aslaksen hears.

BILLING *(dropping his voice)*: Aslaksen's a chicken-livered coward; there's no spine in the man. But this time you'll carry your own will through, uh? Right? You'll run the doctor's article?

HOVSTAD: Yes, if only the mayor doesn't give in—

BILLING: That'd be boring as hell.

HOVSTAD: Well, fortunately, no matter what happens, we can make something out of the situation. If the mayor won't buy the doctor's proposal, then he gets the small businessmen down on his neck—the Home Owners Council and that sort. And if he does buy it, he'll fall out with a whole host of the big stockholders in the baths, the ones who've been his best supporters up to now—

BILLING: Yes, that's right; they'll have to kick in a lot of new capital—

HOVSTAD: You bet they will! And then the ring is broken, see. And day after day in the paper we'll keep drumming it into the public that the mayor's incompetent on one score after another, and that all the elective offices in town — the whole administration — ought to be placed in the hands of the liberals.

BILLING: Ye gods, that's the living truth! I see it — I can see it! We're right on the verge of a revolution!

A knock at the door.

HOVSTAD: Shh! *(Calls out.)* Come in!

DR. STOCKMANN *enters by the door at the back, left.*

HOVSTAD *(goes to meet him)*: Ah, here's the doctor. Well?

DR. STOCKMANN: Roll your presses, Mr. Hovstad!

HOVSTAD: Then it's come to that?

BILLING: Hurray!

DR. STOCKMANN: I said, roll your presses. Yes, it's come to that. But now they'll get what they're asking for. Now it's war in this town, Mr. Billing!

BILLING: War to the knife, I hope! Lay into them, Doctor!

DR. STOCKMANN: This article's only the beginning. My head's already brimming with ideas for four or five more pieces. Where do I find Aslaksen?

BILLING *(shouting into the pressroom)*: Aslaksen, come here a minute!

HOVSTAD: Four or five more pieces, you say? On the same subject?

DR. STOCKMANN: No, not by a long shot. No, they're on totally different topics. But they all originate from the water system and the sewers. One thing leads to another, you know. It's the way it is when you start patching up an old building. Precisely like that.

BILLING: Ye gods, but that's the truth. You find out you'll never be done with it till you've torn down the whole rotten structure.

ASLAKSEN *(comes in from the pressroom)*: Torn down! You don't plan to tear down the baths, Doctor?

HOVSTAD: Not at all. Don't get frightened.

DR. STOCKMANN: No, that was something else entirely. Well, what do you say about my article, Mr. Hovstad?

HOVSTAD: I think it's a pure masterpiece —

DR. STOCKMANN: Yes, isn't it — ? Well, I'm most gratified, most gratified.

HOVSTAD: It's so clear and readable; you don't have to be a specialist at all to follow the argument. I daresay you'll have every reasonable man on your side.

ASLAKSEN: And all the moderates, too?

BILLING: Moderates and immoderates both — well, I mean, practically the entire town.

ASLAKSEN: Then we might take a chance on running it.

DR. STOCKMANN: Yes, I should think so!

HOVSTAD: It'll go in tomorrow morning.

DR. STOCKMANN: Good grief, it better; we can't waste a single day. Look, Mr. Aslaksen, I know what I wanted to ask you: would you give the manuscript your personal attention?

ASLAKSEN: I certainly will.

DR. STOCKMANN: Handle it like gold. No misprints; every word is vital. I'll stop back in again later; maybe I could glance over the proofs. Oh, I can't tell you how I'm dying to see this thing in print — delivered —

BILLING: Delivered — like a lightning-bolt!

DR. STOCKMANN: —addressed to the judgment of every thinking man. Ah, you can't imagine what I've been subjected to today. They've threatened me from all sides; they've tried to deprive me of my most fundamental human rights —

HOVSTAD: Of your rights!

DR. STOCKMANN: They've tried to humiliate me, and turn me into a jellyfish, and make me deny my deepest and holiest convictions for private profit.

BILLING: Ye gods, that's unforgivable.

HOVSTAD: Oh well, you have to expect anything from that crowd.

DR. STOCKMANN: But with me it's not going to work: they're going to get it, spelled out in black and white. I'm going to drop anchor right here at the *Courier* and rake them with broadsides: a fresh article every day —

ASLAKSEN: Yes, but now listen —

BILLING: Hurray! It's war — war!

DR. STOCKMANN: I'll smash them into the ground and shatter them! I'll wreck their defenses in the eyes of every fair-minded man! That's what I'll do!

ASLAKSEN: But do it temperately, Doctor. War, yes — in moderation.

BILLING: No, no! Don't spare the dynamite!

DR. STOCKMANN: *(continues, unruffled)*: Because now, you see, this isn't simply a matter of sewers and water mains anymore. No, it's the whole society that has to be purged and disinfected —

BILLING: That's the remedy!

DR. STOCKMANN: All these lunkheads in the old generation have to be dumped. And that means: no matter *who* they are! I've had such endless vistas opening up for me today. I haven't quite clarified it yet, but I'm working it out. My friends, we have to go forth and search out fresh, young standard-bearers; we have to have new commanders for all our outposts.

BILLING: Hear, hear!

DR. STOCKMANN: And if we only can stick together, everything will go off smoothly. The entire revolution will be launched as trim as a ship down the ways. Don't you think so?

HOVSTAD: For my part, I think we now have every prospect of seeing community control put right where it belongs.

ASLAKSEN: And if we just move ahead in moderation, I can't believe there's likely to be any danger.

DR. STOCKMANN: Who the hell cares about danger! Whatever I do will be done in the name of truth, for the sake of my conscience.

HOVSTAD: You're a man who deserves support, Doctor.

ASLAKSEN: Yes, that's a fact: the doctor's a true friend to the town, and a real friend to society.

BILLING: Ye gods, Aslaksen; Doctor Stockmann is the people's friend!

ASLAKSEN: I can imagine the Home Owners Council may pick that up as a slogan.

DR. STOCKMANN (moved, pressing their hands): Thank you, thank you, my dear, unfailing friends — it's so heartening to hear you say these things — my esteemed brother called me something quite different. Well, I swear he's going to get it back, with interest! But now I've got to look in on a patient, poor devil. I'll stop by again, as I said. Don't forget to look out for my manuscript, Mr. Aslaksen — and, whatever you do, don't cut any exclamation points. If anything, put a few more in! Fine, fine! Good-bye till later, good-bye, good-bye!

Amid mutual farewells, he is escorted to the door and departs.

HOVSTAD: He can be an exceptionally useful man for us.

ASLAKSEN: As long as he limits himself to the baths. But if he goes further, then it wouldn't be politic to join forces with him.

HOVSTAD: Hm, that all depends —

BILLING: You're always so damn fearful, Aslaksen.

ASLAKSEN: Fearful? Yes, as far as the local authorities go, I'm fearful, Mr. Billing. Let me tell you, it's something I've learned in the school of experience. But put me in the arena of national politics, opposed to the government itself, and then you'll see if I'm fearful.

BILLING: No, you're certainly not. But that's exactly where you're so inconsistent.

ASLAKSEN: I'm a man of conscience, that's the thing. As long as you attack the government, you can't do any real damage to society. You see, the men on that level, they aren't affected — they just ride it out. But the *local* authorities, *they* can be ousted; and then you might wind up with a lot of bunglers in power, who could do enormous damage to the property owners, among others.

HOVSTAD: But how about self-government as part of a citizen's education — don't you care about that?

ASLAKSEN: When a man has material assets at stake, he can't go thinking of everything.

HOVSTAD: Then I hope I'm never burdened with material assets.

BILLING: Hear, hear!

ASLAKSEN *(smiles)*: Hm. *(Pointing at the desk.)* In that editor's chair, right there, your predecessor, Councilman Stengaard, used to sit.

BILLING *(spits)*: Pah! That renegade.

HOVSTAD: I'm no double-dealer — and I never well be.

ASLAKSEN: A politician has to keep all possibilities open, Mr. Hovstad. And you, Mr. Billing — I think you better take a reef or two in your sails, now that you've put in for a job in the town clerk's office.

BILLING: I—!

HOVSTAD: *You* have, Billing?

BILLING: Yes, uh — you can damn well imagine I only did it to needle the establishment.

ASLAKSEN: Well, it's no business of mine, of course. But when I get labeled fearful and inconsistent in my stand, there's one thing I want to emphasize: my political record is available to all comers. I've never changed my position, except that I've become more moderate. My heart belongs to the people, always; but I can't deny that my reason disposes me toward the authorities — I mean, only the local ones, that is.

He goes into the pressroom.

BILLING: Shouldn't we call it quits with him, Hovstad?

HOVSTAD: You know any other printer who'll extend us credit for paper and labor costs?

BILLING: It's damnable that we don't have any capital.

HOVSTAD *(sitting at the desk)*: Yes, if we only had that—

BILLING: How about approaching Stockmann?

HOVSTAD *(leafing through some papers)*: What use would there be in that? He has nothing.

BILLING: No, but he's got a good man backing him: old Morten Kiil — the one they call the Badger.

HOVSTAD *(writing)*: How can you know for sure *he* has anything?

BILLING: Ye gods, of course he does! And some part of it has to come to the Stockmanns. He's got to make provision — at least for the children.

HOVSTAD *(half turning)*: Are you figuring on *that?*

BILLING: Figuring? I never figure on anything.

HOVSTAD: That's wise. And you'd better not figure on that job with the town, because I can promise you — you won't get it.

BILLING: Don't you think I've known that all along? There's nothing I'd welcome more than not getting it. A rejection like that really kindles your fighting spirit — it's almost like an infusion of fresh gall, and that's exactly what you need in an anthill like this, where hardly anything ever happens to really stir you up.

HOVSTAD *(continues writing)*: How true, how true.

BILLING: Well—they'll soon be hearing from *me!* Now I'll go in and write that appeal to the Home Owners Council. *(He goes into the room to the right.)*

HOVSTAD *(sits at the desk, chews the end of his pen and says slowly)*: Hm—so that's how it is. *(A knock at the door.)* Come in!

PETRA *enters by the door at the back, left.*

HOVSTAD *(getting up)*: Oh, it's you? What are you doing here?

PETRA: You'll have to excuse me—

HOVSTAD *(pulls an armchair forward)*: Won't you sit?

PETRA: No, thanks—I can't stay.

HOVSTAD: Is it something from your father that—?

PETRA: No, it's something from me. *(Takes a book out of her coat pocket.)* Here's that English story.

HOVSTAD: Why are you giving it back?

PETRA: Because I don't want to translate it.

HOVSTAD: But you promised me, definitely—

PETRA: Well, I hadn't read it then. And of course you haven't read it either.

HOVSTAD: No. You know I don't understand English; but—

PETRA: All right, that's why I wanted to tell you that you'll have to find somebody else. *(Lays the book on the table.)* This could never be used in the *Courier.*

HOVSTAD: Why not?

PETRA: It's totally opposed to everything you stand for.

HOVSTAD: Well, actually—

PETRA: You still don't understand me. It shows how a supernatural power, watching over the so-called good people of this world, arranges everything for the best in their lives—and how all the so-called wicked get their punishment.

HOVSTAD: But that's fair enough. It's exactly what the public wants.

PETRA: And do you want to be the one who feeds the public that sort of thing? You don't believe a word of it yourself. You know perfectly well things don't happen like that in reality.

HOVSTAD: You're perfectly right; but then an editor can't always do what he might prefer. You often have to bow to public opinions in lesser matters. After all, politics is the main thing in life—for a newspaper, in any event. And if I want to lead people toward greater liberation and progress, then I mustn't scare them away. When they find a moral story like this in the back pages, they're more willing to accept what we print up front—they feel more secure.

PETRA: Oh, come! You wouldn't be so tricky and lay snares for your readers. You're not a spider.

HOVSTAD *(smiles)*: Thank you for thinking so well of me. No, it really was Billing's scheme, and not mine.

PETRA: Billing's!

HOVSTAD: Yes. At any rate, he was speaking of it just the other day. It's Billing who's been so hot about getting that story in; I don't know the book.

PETRA: But how could Billing, with his liberal attitude—?

HOVSTAD: Oh, Billing is a many-sided man. Now I hear he's out for a job in the town clerk's office.

PETRA: I don't believe it, Hovstad. How could he ever conform himself to that?

HOVSTAD: That's something you'll have to ask him.

PETRA: I never would have thought it of Billing.

HOVSTAD *(looks more sharply at her)*: You wouldn't? Does it surprise you so?

PETRA: Yes. Or maybe not, really. Oh, honestly, I don't know—

HOVSTAD: We journalists don't amount to much, Miss Stockmann.

PETRA: You actually mean that?

HOVSTAD: It's what I think sometimes.

PETRA: Yes, in your normal day-to-day existence—I can understand that well enough. But now that you're lending a hand in a great cause—

HOVSTAD: This matter of your father, you mean?

PETRA: Exactly. Now I think you must feel like a man who's more valuable than most.

HOVSTAD: Yes, I feel something of that today.

PETRA: Yes, you do, don't you? Oh, it's a glorious calling you've chosen! To pioneer the way for embattled truths and daring new insights—or simply to stand up fearlessly for a man who's been wronged—

HOVSTAD: Especially when that man who's been wronged is—hm—I don't quite know how to put it—

PETRA: When he's so direct and honest, you mean?

HOVSTAD *(in a softer voice)*: No, I meant—especially when he's your father.

PETRA *(startled)*: It's *that!*

HOVSTAD: Yes, Petra—Miss Petra.

PETRA: Is *that* the main thing for you? Not the issue itself? Not the truth? Not my father's compassion for life?

HOVSTAD: Why, yes—of course, that too.

PETRA: No, thanks, Mr. Hovstad; you betrayed yourself. And now I'll never trust you again, in anything.

HOVSTAD: How can you be so hard on me, when it's mostly for your own sake—?

PETRA: What I'm mad at you about is you haven't played fair with Father. You've talked to him as if the truth and the good of the community lay closest to your heart. You've made fools of both him and me. You're not the man you pretend to be. And for that I'll never forgive you—never!

HOVSTAD: You shouldn't be so bitter, Miss Petra—particularly right now.

PETRA: Why not now?

HOVSTAD: Because your father can't dispense with my help.

PETRA *(scanning him)*: And you're that kind, too? So!

HOVSTAD: No, no, I'm not. I don't know what brought that on. You have to believe me.

PETRA: I know what I have to believe. Good-bye.

ASLAKSEN *(entering from the pressroom, brusquely and cryptically)*: God Almighty, Hovstad—*(Sees* PETRA.*)* Oh, what a mess—

PETRA: There's the book; you can give it to somebody else. *(Goes toward the entrance door.)*

HOVSTAD *(following her)*: But, Miss Petra—

PETRA: Good-bye. *(She leaves.)*

ASLAKSEN: Mr. Hovstad, listen!

HOVSTAD: Yes, all right, what is it?

ASLAKSEN: The mayor's out there in the pressroom.

HOVSTAD: You say, the mayor?

ASLAKSEN: Yes, he wants to talk to you. He came in the back entrance— didn't want to be seen, I guess.

HOVSTAD: What's this all about? No, wait, I'll go—

He crosses to the door of the pressroom, opens it, and beckons the MAYOR *in.*

HOVSTAD: Keep an eye out, Aslaksen, so nobody—

ASLAKSEN: I understand— *(Goes into the pressroom.)*

MAYOR STOCKMANN: I imagine you hardly expected to see me here, Mr. Hovstad.

HOVSTAD: No, I really hadn't.

MAYOR STOCKMANN *(looking about)*: You've certainly made yourself quite comfortable here. Very nice.

HOVSTAD: Oh—

MAYOR STOCKMANN: And now I come along unceremoniously and monopolize your time.

HOVSTAD: By all means, Mr. Mayor; I'm at your service. But please, let me take your things— *(Sets the* MAYOR*'s hat and stick on a chair.)* Won't you have a seat?

MAYOR STOCKMANN *(sitting at the table)*: Thank you.

HOVSTAD *likewise sits at the table.*

MAYOR STOCKMANN: I've gone through—really a most troublesome episode today, Mr. Hovstad.

HOVSTAD: Yes? Oh well, with all the cares that the mayor has—

MAYOR STOCKMANN: It involves the staff physician at the baths.

HOVSTAD: You mean, the doctor?

MAYOR STOCKMANN: He's penned a kind of report to the board of directors, alleging that the baths have certain deficiencies.

HOVSTAD: He has?

MAYOR STOCKMANN: Yes, didn't he tell you—? I thought he said—

HOVSTAD: Oh yes, that's true. He made some mention of it—

ASLAKSEN *(entering from the pressroom)*: I need to have that manuscript—

HOVSTAD *(vexed)*: Hm, it's there on the desk.

ASLAKSEN *(locating it)*: Good.

MAYOR STOCKMANN: But look—that's *it,* exactly—

ASLAKSEN: Yes, that's the doctor's article, Mr. Mayor.

HOVSTAD: Oh, is *that* what you were talking about?

MAYOR STOCKMANN: None other. What do you think of it?

HOVSTAD: I'm really no expert, and I've barely skimmed through it.

MAYOR STOCKMANN: Still, you're going to print it.

HOVSTAD: A man of his reputation I can hardly refuse—

ASLAKSEN: I have no say at all in this paper, Mr. Mayor.

MAYOR STOCKMANN: Naturally.

ASLAKSEN: I only print what's put in my hands.

MAYOR STOCKMANN: Quite properly.

ASLAKSEN: So, if you'll pardon me— *(Goes toward the pressroom.)*

MAYOR STOCKMANN: No, just a minute, Mr. Aslaksen. With your permission, Mr. Hovstad—

HOVSTAD: My pleasure.

MAYOR STOCKMANN: You're a sober-minded and thoughtful man, Mr. Aslaksen.

ASLAKSEN: I'm glad Your Honor holds that opinion.

MAYOR STOCKMANN: And a man of influence in many circles.

ASLAKSEN: That's mostly among the little people.

MAYOR STOCKMANN: The small taxpayers are the great majority—here, as elsewhere.

ASLAKSEN: That's the truth.

MAYOR STOCKMANN: And I don't doubt that you know the general sentiment among most of them. Am I right?

ASLAKSEN: Yes, I daresay I do Mr. Mayor.

MAYOR STOCKMANN: Well—if there's such a worthy spirit of self-sacrifice prevailing among the town's less affluent citizens, then—

ASLAKSEN: How's that?

HOVSTAD: Self-sacrifice?

MAYOR STOCKMANN: It's a beautiful token of community spirit, an exceptionally beautiful token. I was close to saying that I wouldn't have expected it. But you know the feelings of these people far better than I.

ASLAKSEN: Yes, but, Your Honor—

MAYOR STOCKMANN: And as a matter of fact, it's no small sacrifice this town will be asked to bear.

HOVSTAD: The town?

ASLAKSEN: But I don't follow—It's the baths—!

MAYOR STOCKMANN: At a tentative estimate, the changes that our staff physician finds desirable run up to a couple of hundred thousand crowns.

ASLAKSEN: That's a lot of money, but—

MAYOR STOCKMANN: Of course it'll be necessary for us to take out a municipal loan.

HOVSTAD *(rises)*: It can't be your intention for the town to—

ASLAKSEN: Not out of property taxes! Out of the empty pockets of the home owners!

MAYOR STOCKMANN: Well, my dear Mr. Aslaksen, where else would the capital come from?

ASLAKSEN: The men who own the baths can raise it.

MAYOR STOCKMANN: The owners find themselves in no position to extend themselves further than they are already.

ASLAKSEN: Is that quite definite, Mr. Mayor?

MAYOR STOCKMANN: I've ascertained it for a fact. So if one wants all these elaborate changes, the town itself will have to pay for them.

ASLAKSEN: But hell and damnation—excuse me, sir!—but this is a totally different picture, Mr. Hovstad.

HOVSTAD: It certainly is.

MAYOR STOCKMANN: The worst part of it is that we'll be forced to shut down the baths for a two-year period.

HOVSTAD: Shut down? Completely?

ASLAKSEN: For two years!

MAYOR STOCKMANN: Yes, the work has to take that long—at the least.

ASLAKSEN: But, God Almighty, we'll never last that out, Mr. Mayor! What'll we home owners live on in the meantime?

MAYOR STOCKMANN: Unhappily, it's extremely difficult to answer that, Mr. Aslaksen. But what do you want us to do? You think we'll get a single summer visitor here if anyone goes around posing suppositions that the water is polluted, that we're living in a pesthole, that the whole town—

ASLAKSEN: And it's all just supposition?

MAYOR STOCKMANN: With the best will in the world, I haven't been able to persuade myself otherwise.

ASLAKSEN: Yes, but then its absolutely indefensible of Dr. Stockmann— begging your pardon, Mayor, but—

MAYOR STOCKMANN: It's distressingly true, what you imply, Mr. Aslaksen. I'm afraid my brother's always been a reckless man.

ASLAKSEN: And in spite of this, you want to go on supporting him, Mr. Hovstad!

HOVSTAD: But how could anyone have suspected—?

MAYOR STOCKMANN: I've drawn up a brief statement of the relevant facts, as they might appear to a disinterested observer; and I've suggested therein how any possible deficiencies might well be covered without exceeding the current budget for the baths.

HOVSTAD: Do you have this statement with you, Mr. Mayor?

MAYOR STOCKMANN *(groping in his pocket)*: Yes, I took it along just in case —

ASLAKSEN *(abruptly)*: Oh, my God, there he is!

MAYOR STOCKMANN: Who? My brother?

HOVSTAD: Where — where!

ASLAKSEN: Coming through the pressroom.

MAYOR STOCKMANN: How embarrassing! I don't want to run up against him here, and I still have things to talk to you about.

HOVSTAD *(pointing toward the door at the right)*: Step in there for a moment.

MAYOR STOCKMANN: But — ?

HOVSTAD: It's just Billing in there.

ASLAKSEN: Quick, Your Honor! He's coming!

MAYOR STOCKMANN: Yes, all right, but try to get rid of him fast.

He goes out the door, right, as ASLAKSEN *opens and closes it for him.*

HOVSTAD: Look like you're doing something, Aslaksen.

He sits and starts to write. ASLAKSEN *rummages in a pile of papers on a chair to the right.*

DR. STOCKMANN *(entering from the pressroom)*: Here I am again. *(Puts down his hat and stick.)*

HOVSTAD *(writing)*: Already, Doctor? Get going on what we were talking about, Aslaksen. We can't waste time today.

DR. STOCKMANN *(to* ASLAKSEN*)*: I gather, no proofs as yet.

ASLAKSEN *(without turning)*: How could you expect that, Doctor?

DR. STOCKMANN: No, no, I'm just impatient — you have to understand. I won't have a moment's peace till I see it in print.

HOVSTAD: Hm — it's bound to be a good hour still. Don't you think so, Aslaksen?

ASLAKSEN: Yes, I'm afraid so.

DR. STOCKMANN: My dear friends, that's quite all right; I'll come back. I'll gladly come back twice, if necessary. With anything so important — the welfare of this whole town — it's no time to take it easy. *(Starts to go, then pauses and returns.)* Oh, listen — there's still something I want to mention to you.

HOVSTAD: Sorry, but couldn't we some other time — ?

DR. STOCKMANN: I can say it in two seconds. It's simply this — when people read my article in the paper tomorrow and find out as well that

I've spent the whole winter in seclusion, working for the good of the town —

HOVSTAD: Yes, but Doctor —

DR. STOCKMANN: I know what you'll say. You don't think it was any more than my blasted duty — ordinary civic responsibility. Well, of course; I know that just as well as you do. But my fellow townspeople, you see — bless their souls, they hold such a high regard for me —

ASLAKSEN: Yes, the people have held you in the highest regard — up till now, Doctor.

DR. STOCKMANN: Yes, and it's just the reason I'm afraid that — What I'm trying to say is this: my article, if it affects the people — especially the deprived classes — as an incitement to take the future affairs of the town into their own hands —

HOVSTAD *(getting up)*: Hm, Doctor, I don't want to mislead you —

DR. STOCKMANN: Aha — I thought there was something brewing! But I won't hear of it. So if they go preparing anything —

HOVSTAD: Such as?

DR. STOCKMANN: Oh, anything of the kind — a parade or a banquet or a testimonial award or whatever, then you promise me by all that's holy to get it quashed. And you too, Mr. Aslaksen; you hear me!

HOVSTAD: Pardon me, Doctor, but we'd better tell you the unvarnished truth right now —

MRS. STOCKMANN, *in hat and coat, comes in by the entrance door, back left.*

MRS. STOCKMANN *(seeing the DOCTOR)*: I thought so!

HOVSTAD *(going toward her)*: Mrs. Stockmann, you too?

DR. STOCKMANN: Katherine, what the deuce are you doing here?

MRS. STOCKMANN: You know very well what I want.

HOVSTAD: Won't you have a seat? Or perhaps —

MRS. STOCKMANN: Thanks, but don't bother. And please, don't be offended that I'm here to fetch Stockmann; because I'm the mother of three children, I want you to know.

DR. STOCKMANN: Oh, bosh! We know all that.

MRS. STOCKMANN: Well, it really doesn't seem as if you're thinking much of your wife and children these days, or else you wouldn't have gone on this way, hurling us all into perdition.

DR. STOCKMANN: Are you utterly insane, Katherine? Does a man with a wife and children have no right to proclaim the truth — no right to be an effective citizen — or to serve the town he lives in?

MRS. STOCKMANN: All those things — in moderation, Thomas!

ASLAKSEN: I agree. Moderation in all things.

MRS. STOCKMANN: That's why you wrong us terribly, Mr. Hovstad, when you inveigle my husband out of house and home and down here to make a fool of himself in this.

HOVSTAD: I don't make fools of people —

DR. STOCKMANN: Fools! Nobody fools *me!*

MRS. STOCKMANN: Oh yes, they do. I know you're the smartest man in town, but you're so very easy to fool, Thomas. *(To* HOVSTAD.*)* And just consider that he'll lose his job at the baths if you print what he's written —

ASLAKSEN: What!

HOVSTAD: Yes, but you know, Doctor —

DR. STOCKMANN *(laughing):* Just let them try! Oh, no — they won't dare. Because, you see, I've got the solid majority behind me.

MRS. STOCKMANN: Yes, that's the trouble, exactly. An ugly lot like that behind you.

DR. STOCKMANN: Balderdash, Katherine! Go home and take care of your house and let me take care of society. How can you be so scared, when I'm so secure and happy? *(Walks up and down, rubbing his hands.)* Truth and the people will win the battle, you can count on that. Oh, I can see all the liberal-minded citizens everywhere gathering into a victorious army —! *(Stops by a chair.)* What — what the hell is *this?*

ASLAKSEN *(looking over):* Ow-ah!

HOVSTAD *(likewise):* Hm —!

DR. STOCKMANN: Here we see the summit of authority.

He takes the MAYOR's *hat delicately between his fingertips and holds it high.*

MRS. STOCKMANN: The mayor's hat!

DR. STOCKMANN: And here's the scepter of command, too. How in blazes —?

HOVSTAD: Well, uh —

DR. STOCKMANN: Ah, I get it! He's been here to coax you over. Ho ho, he knew right where to come. And then he caught sight of me in the pressroom. *(Explodes with laughter.)* Did he run, Mr. Aslaksen?

ASLAKSEN *(hurriedly):* Oh yes, Doctor, he ran off.

DR. STOCKMANN: Ran away from his stick and his— My eye! Peter never runs from anything. But where the devil have you put him? Ah — inside, of course. Now you watch this, Katherine!

MRS. STOCKMANN: Thomas — please —!

ASLAKSEN: Watch yourself, Doctor!

DR. STOCKMANN *sets the* MAYOR's *hat on his head and takes his stick; he then goes over, throws open the door, and raises his hand in salute. The* MAYOR *comes in, red with anger.* BILLING *enters behind him.*

MAYOR STOCKMANN: What's the meaning of this rowdyism?

DR. STOCKMANN: Some respect, if you will, Peter. I'm the authority in town now. *(He parades up and down.)*

MRS. STOCKMANN *(nearly in tears)*: Thomas, no!

MAYOR STOCKMANN *(following him)*: Give me my hat and my stick!

DR. STOCKMANN: If you're the police chief, then I'm the mayor. I'm in charge of the whole town, see!

MAYOR STOCKMANN: I'm telling you, take off that hat. Remember, that's an insignia of office!

DR. STOCKMANN: Pah! Do you think the waking lion of the people's strength is going to be scared of a hat? Yes, because you better know: tomorrow we're making a revolution in town. You threatened me with my dismissal, but now I'm dismissing you—from all your public offices. You don't think I can? Oh yes, you'll see. I've got the ascendant forces of society on my side. Hovstad and Billing will thunder in the *People's Courier;* and Aslaksen will take the field, leading the whole Home Owners Council—

ASLAKSEN: I won't do it, Doctor.

DR. STOCKMANN: Why, of course you will—

MAYOR STOCKMANN: Ah, but perhaps, even so, Mr. Hovstad will be joining this rebellion?

HOVSTAD: No, Mr. Mayor.

ASLAKSEN: No, Mr. Hovstad isn't so crazy that he'd go and wreck both himself and the paper for the sake of a mere surmise.

DR. STOCKMANN *(looking about)*: What's going on here?

HOVSTAD: You've presented your case in a false light, Doctor; and that's why I can't support it.

BILLING: No, after what the mayor was good enough to tell me in there—

DR. STOCKMANN: False! You can leave that to me. Just print my article. I can take care of defending it.

HOVSTAD: I'm not printing it. I cannot and will not and dare not print it.

DR. STOCKMANN: You dare not? What kind of rot is that? You're the editor, aren't you? And it's the editors who run the press, I hope!

ASLAKSEN: No, it's the readers, Doctor.

MAYOR STOCKMANN: Thankfully, yes.

ASLAKSEN: It's public opinion, the informed citizens, the home owners, and all the rest—they're the ones that run the press.

DR. STOCKMANN *(comprehending)*: And all these powers I have against me?

ASLAKSEN: That's right. If your article is printed, it'll mean absolute ruin for this town.

DR. STOCKMANN: I see.

MAYOR STOCKMANN: My hat and my stick!

DR. STOCKMANN *removes the hat and sets it, along with the stick, on the table.*

MAYOR STOCKMANN *(reclaiming them both)*: That was a sudden end to your first term in office.

DR. STOCKMANN: It's not the end yet. *(To* HOVSTAD.*)* Then there's
no possibility of getting my article in the *Courier?*

HOVSTAD: None whatever. Partly out of regard for your family.

MRS. STOCKMANN: Oh, never mind about this family, Mr. Hovstad.

MAYOR STOCKMANN *(takes a sheet of paper from his pocket)*: For the protection of the public, it will be sufficient if this goes in. It's an authorized statement. If you will.

HOVSTAD *(taking the sheet)*: Good. We'll insert it right away.

DR. STOCKMANN: But not mine! People think they can stifle me and
choke off the truth! But it won't go as smooth as you think. Mr.
Aslaksen, would you take my manuscript and issue it at once as a
pamphlet—at my expense—under my own imprint. I'll want four
hundred copies; no, five—six hundred I'll need.

ASLAKSEN: Even if you gave me its weight in gold, I couldn't put my
plant to that use, Doctor. I wouldn't dare, in view of public opinion.
You won't get that printed anywhere in this town.

DR. STOCKMANN: Then give it back.

HOVSTAD *(hands him the manuscript)*: There.

DR. STOCKMANN *(picks up his hat and stick)*: It's coming out, no matter
what. I'll hold a mass meeting and read it aloud. All my fellow townspeople are going to hear the voice of truth.

MAYOR STOCKMANN: There's not an organization in town that'll rent
you a hall for such a purpose.

ASLAKSEN: Not one. I'm positive of that.

BILLING: Ye gods, no!

MRS. STOCKMANN: But this is shameful. Why do they all turn against
you, these men?

DR. STOCKMANN *(furiously)*: I'll tell you why! It's because all the so-
called men in this town are old women—like you. They all just think
of their families and never the common good.

MRS. STOCKMANN *(taking his arm)*: Then I'll show them a—an old
woman who can be a man for once. I'm standing with you, Thomas!

DR. STOCKMANN: That was well said, Katherine. And, by God, I'll get
this out! If I can't rent a hall, then I'll hire a drummer to walk the town
with me, and I'll cry out the truth on every street corner.

MAYOR STOCKMANN: You're not going to act like a raving maniac!

DR. STOCKMANN: Yes, I am!

ASLAKSEN: In this whole town, you won't get one solitary man to go
with you.

BILLING: Ye gods, I'll say you won't!

MRS. STOCKMANN: Don't give in, Thomas. I'll ask the boys to go with
you.

DR. STOCKMANN: That's a marvelous idea!

MRS. STOCKMANN: Morten would love to do it; and Eilif—he'll go
along.

DR. STOCKMANN: Yes, and Petra too! And you yourself, Katherine!

MRS. STOCKMANN: No, no, that's not for me. But I'll stand at the window and watch you; that I'll do.

DR. STOCKMANN *(throws his arms about her and kisses her)*: Thanks for that! And now, gentlemen, let's try our steel. I'd just like to see if conniving hypocrisy can gag the mouth of a patriot who's out to clean up society!

He and MRS. STOCKMANN *leave by the entrance door, back left.*

MAYOR STOCKMANN *(gravely shaking his head)*: Now he's driven her crazy, too.

ACT IV

A large, old-fashioned room in CAPTAIN HORSTER'S *house. Double doors, standing open at the back, lead to an anteroom. Spaced along the wall, left, are three windows. At the middle of the opposite wall a platform has been prepared, with a small table; on it are two candles, a water carafe, a glass, and a bell. The room is mainly illuminated by wall lamps between the windows. In the left foreground stands a table with candles on it, and a chair. Farther forward at the right is a door, with several chairs beside it.*

There is a large assemblage of TOWNSPEOPLE *from all levels of society. Scattered among them are a few* WOMEN *and some* SCHOOL-BOYS. *More and more people gradually crowd in from the rear, until the room is full.*

A CITIZEN *(to another, as he jostles against him)*: Are you here too, Lamstad?

SECOND CITIZEN: I never miss a public meeting.

THIRD CITIZEN: I hope you brought along your whistle?

SECOND CITIZEN: You bet I did. And you?

THIRD CITIZEN: Of course. Skipper Evensen has a whopping big horn he said he'd bring.

SECOND CITIZEN: He's a character, that Evensen.

Laughter among the group.

FOURTH CITIZEN *(joining them)*: Say, tell me, what's going on here tonight?

SECOND CITIZEN: It's Dr. Stockmann; he's giving a speech against the mayor.

FOURTH CITIZEN: But the mayor's his brother.

FIRST CITIZEN: What of it? The doctor isn't afraid.

THIRD CITIZEN: Yes, but he's all wrong. The *Courier* said so.

SECOND CITIZEN: Yes, he really must be this time, because nobody'll rent him a hall—neither the Home Owners Council nor the civic club.

FIRST CITIZEN: Even the hall at the baths wouldn't have him.

SECOND CITIZEN: Well, that you can imagine.

A MAN *(in another group)*: Who are we backing in this?

ANOTHER MAN *(next to him)*: Just watch Aslaksen and do what he does.

BILLING *(with a portfolio under his arm, forcing his way through the crowd)*: Excuse me, gentlemen! If you'll let me by, please? I'm covering this for the *Courier*. Thank you so much! *(He sits at the table on the left.)*

A WORKMAN: Who's he?

ANOTHER WORKMAN: You don't know *him?* That's Billing — writes for Aslaksen's paper.

> CAPTAIN HORSTER *conducts* MRS. STOCKMANN *and* PETRA *in through the door to the right.* EILIF *and* MORTEN *follow.*

HORSTER: I was thinking the family could sit here. If anything should happen, you could slip out quietly.

MRS. STOCKMANN: Do you think there'll be a disturbance?

HORSTER: You never can tell — with so many people. But sit down and rest easy.

MRS. STOCKMANN *(sitting)*: How kind of you to offer Thomas this room.

HORSTER: When nobody else would, then —

PETRA *(who also has seated herself)*: And it was brave of you, too, Captain Horster.

HORSTER: Oh, I don't think it took much courage for that.

> HOVSTAD *and* ASLAKSEN *make their way forward at the same time, but separately, through the crowd.*

ASLAKSEN *(moves across to* HORSTER*)*: Hasn't the doctor come yet?

HORSTER: He's waiting inside.

> *A flurry of activity by the doorway in back.*

HOVSTAD *(to* BILLING*)*: Here's the mayor. Look!

BILLING: Ye gods, he showed up after all!

> The MAYOR *proceeds quietly through the crowd, exchanging polite greetings, and then stations himself by the wall, left. After a moment* DR. STOCKMANN *enters through the door to the right. He is dressed in a black frock coat with a white tie. There is scattered, hesitant applause, which is met by subdued hissing. The room grows silent.*

DR. STOCKMANN *(in an undertone)*: How do you feel, Katherine?

MRS. STOCKMANN: Oh, I'm all right. *(Lowering her voice.)* Now, Thomas, don't fly off the handle.

DR. STOCKMANN: I can manage myself, you know that. *(Looks at his watch, then ascends the platform and bows.)* It's already a quarter past — so I'd like to begin — *(Taking his manuscript out.)*

ASLAKSEN: First, we really ought to elect a chairman.

DR. STOCKMANN: No, that's quite unnecessary.

SEVERAL VOICES (shouting): Yes, yes!

MAYOR STOCKMANN: I also submit that we ought to elect a moderator.

DR. STOCKMANN: But I've called this meeting to present a lecture, Peter!

MAYOR STOCKMANN: The doctor's lecture is likely to arouse some contrary opinions.

MORE VOICES FROM THE CROWD: A chairman! A moderator!

HOVSTAD: The will of the people seems to demand a chairman.

DR. STOCKMANN (restraining himself): All right, then, let the will of the people rule.

ASLAKSEN: Would the mayor agree to accept the chair?

THREE GENTLEMEN (applauding): Bravo! Bravo!

MAYOR STOCKMANN: For certain self-evident reasons, I must decline. But luckily we have in our midst a man whom I think we can all accept. I'm referring to the chairman of the Home Owners Council, Mr. Aslaksen.

MANY VOICES: Yes, yes! Aslaksen! Hurray for Aslaksen!

DR. STOCKMANN puts away his manuscript and leaves the platform.

ASLAKSEN: If my fellow townpeople express their confidence in me, I cannot refuse —

Applause and shouts of approval. ASLAKSEN mounts the platform.

BILLING (writing): So — "Mr. Aslaksen chosen by acclamation — "

ASLAKSEN: And since I'm standing here now in this role, permit me to say a few brief words. I am a man of peace and quiet who's dedicated himself to prudent moderation and to — and to moderate prudence; everyone who knows me can attest to that.

MANY VOICES: Right! You said it, Aslaksen!

ASLAKSEN: I've learned in life's school of experience that moderation is the most rewarding of all virtues for the citizen —

MAYOR STOCKMANN: Hear, hear!

ASLAKSEN: And, moreover, that prudence and temperance are what serve society best. Therefore, I would urge the estimable gentleman who convened this meeting that he make every effort to stay within the bounds of moderation.

A DRUNK (near the door): To the Temperance Union, skoal!

A VOICE: Shut the hell up!

MANY VOICES: Sh, sh!

ASLAKSEN: No interruptions, gentlemen! Does anyone have something to say?

MAYOR STOCKMANN: Mr. Chairman!

ASLAKSEN: The chair recognizes the mayor.

MAYOR STOCKMANN: Considering my close relationship, which you all know, to the present staff physician of the baths, I would very much have wished not to express myself here this evening. But my official connection with the baths, and a due regard for the crucial interests of this town, compel me to present a proposal. I think it safe to assume that not a single citizen here tonight would find it desirable that exaggerated and unreliable charges about the sanitary conditions of the baths should gain currency abroad.

MANY VOICES: No, no, no! Of course not! We protest!

MAYOR STOCKMANN: I therefore move that this gathering refuse to permit the staff physician to read or otherwise report on his version of the matter.

DR. STOCKMANN (*infuriated*): Refuse permission—What's that?

MRS. STOCKMANN (*coughing*): Hm, hm!

DR. STOCKMANN (*controls himself*): Permission refused—all right.

MAYOR STOCKMANN: In my statement to the *People's Courier,* I've acquainted the public with the pertinent facts, so that every right-minded citizen can easily form his own judgment. You'll see there that the doctor's proposal—besides being a vote of no confidence in the leadership of this town—would actually mean afflicting our local taxpayers with a needless expenditure of at least a hundred thousand crowns.

Cries of outrage and the sound of whistles.

ASLAKSEN (*ringing the bell*): Quiet, gentlemen! Allow me to second the mayor's proposal. It's *my* opinion, also, that the doctor's agitation has an ulterior motive. He talks about the baths, but it's a revolution he's after. He wants to put the government into different hands. No one doubts the doctor's honest intentions; Lord knows there's no divided opinion on that. I'm also a friend of self-determination by the people—as long as it doesn't hit the taxpayer too hard. But that exactly would be the case here; and it's why I'll be damned—excuse me—if I can go along with Dr. Stockmann in this. You can pay too much, even for gold; that's *my* opinion.

Lively approval from all sides.

HOVSTAD: Likewise I feel obligated to clarify my own position. Dr. Stockmann's agitation seemed at first to be winning a good deal of acceptance, and I supported it as impartially as I could. But then we began to sense that we'd let ourselves be misled by a false interpretation—

DR. STOCKMANN: False—!

HOVSTAD: A less reliable interpretation, then. The mayor's statement has proved that. I hope no one here tonight would challenge my liberal sentiments; the *Courier*'s policy on our great political issues is well known to all of you. Still, I've learned from men of wisdom and experience that in purely local matters a paper ought to move with a certain caution.

ASLAKSEN: I agree perfectly.

HOVSTAD: And, in the matter in question, it's now indisputable that Dr. Stockmann has the will of the majority against him. But an editor's first and foremost responsibility — what is that, gentlemen? Isn't it to work in collaboration with his readers? Hasn't he received something on the order of an unspoken mandate to strive actively and unceasingly on behalf of those who share his beliefs? Or maybe I'm wrong in this?

MANY VOICES: No, no, no! He's right.

HOVSTAD: It's been a bitter struggle for me to break with a man in whose home I've lately been a frequent guest — a man who, until today, could bask in the undivided esteem of the community — a man whose only fault, or whose greatest fault at least, is that he follows his heart more than his head.

SOME SCATTERED VOICES: That's true! Hurray for Dr. Stockmann.

HOVSTAD: But my duty to society compelled me to break with him. And then there's another consideration that prompts me to oppose him and, if possible, to deter him from the ominous course he's chosen: namely, consideration for his family —

DR. STOCKMANN: Stick to the sewers and water mains!

HOVSTAD: — consideration for his wife and his distressed children.

MORTEN: Is that us, Mother?

MRS. STOCKMANN: Hush!

ASLAKSEN: I hereby put the mayor's proposal to a vote.

DR. STOCKMANN: Never mind that! It's not my intention to speak to-night of all that squalor in the baths. No, you're going to hear something quite different.

MAYOR STOCKMANN *(muttering)*: Now what?

THE DRUNK *(from the main doorway)*: I'm a taxpayer! And, therefore, so I got rights to an opinion! And I have the sotted — solid and incomprehensible opinion that —

SEVERAL VOICES: Quiet over there!

OTHERS: He's drunk! Throw him out!

The DRUNK *is ejected.*

DR. STOCKMANN: Do I have the floor?

ASLAKSEN *(ringing the bell)*: Dr. Stockmann has the floor!

DR. STOCKMANN: If it had been only a few days ago that anyone had tried to gag me like this tonight — I'd have fought for my sacred human rights like a lion! But it doesn't matter to me now. Because now I have greater things to discuss.

The CROWD *presses in closer around him;* MORTEN KIIL *becomes visible among them.*

DR. STOCKMANN *(continuing)*: I've been thinking a lot these past few days—pondering so many things that finally my thoughts began running wild—

MAYOR STOCKMANN *(coughs)*: Hm—!

DR. STOCKMANN: But then I got everything in place again, and I saw the whole structure so distinctly. It's why I'm here this evening. I have great disclosures to make, my friends! I'm going to unveil a discovery to you of vastly different dimension than this trifle that our water system is polluted and that our health spa is built on a muckheap.

MANY VOICES *(shouting)*: Don't talk of the baths! We won't listen! Enough of that!

DR. STOCKMANN: I've said I'd talk about the great discovery I've made these last few days: the discovery that all the sources of our spiritual life are polluted, and that our entire community rests on a muckheap of lies.

STARTLED VOICES *(in undertones)*: What's he saying?

MAYOR STOCKMANN: Of all the insinuations—

ASLAKSEN *(his hand on the bell)*: The speaker is urged to be moderate.

DR. STOCKMANN: I've loved my birthplace as much as any man can. I was barely grown when I left here; and distance and deprivation and memory threw a kind of enchantment over the town, and the people, too.

Scattered applause and cheers.

For many years, then, I practiced in the far north, at the dead end of nowhere. When I came in contact with some of the people who lived scattered in that waste of rocks, I many times thought it would have done those poor starved creatures more good if they'd gotten a veterinary instead of someone like me.

Murmuring among the crowd.

BILLING *(setting down his pen)*: Ye gods, why I never heard such—!

HOVSTAD: That's an insult to the common man!

DR. STOCKMANN: Just a minute—! I don't think anyone could ever say that I'd forgotten my home town up there. I brooded on my egg like an eider duck; and what I hatched—was the plan for the baths.

Applause and objections.

And finally, at long last, when fate relented and allowed me to come back home—my friends, then it seemed as though I had nothing left to wish for in this world. No, I did have one wish: a fierce, insistent, burning desire to contribute to the best of my town and my people.

MAYOR STOCKMANN *(gazing into space)*: It's a funny way to—hm.

DR. STOCKMANN: And so I went around, exulting in my blind happiness. But yesterday morning—no, actually it was the night before last—the eyes of my spirit were opened wide, and the first thing I saw was the consummate stupidity of the authorities—

Confusion, outcries, and laughter. MRS. STOCKMANN *coughs vigorously.*

MAYOR STOCKMANN: Mr. Chairman!

ASLAKSEN *(ringing his bell)*: By the powers vested in me—!

DR. STOCKMANN: It's petty to get hung up on a word, Mr. Aslaksen! I only mean that it came to me then what a consummate mess our local leaders had made out of the baths. Our leaders are one group that, for the life of me, I can't stand. I've had enough of that breed in my days. They're like a pack of goats in a stand of new trees—they strip off everything. They get in a free man's way wherever he turns—and I really don't see why we shouldn't exterminate them like any other predator—

Tumult in the room.

MAYOR STOCKMANN: Mr. Chairman, can you let such a statement pass?

ASLAKSEN *(his hand on the bell)*: Doctor—!

DR. STOCKMANN: I can't imagine why I've only now taken a really sharp look at these gentlemen, because right before my eyes almost daily I've had a superb example—my brother Peter—slow of wit and thick of head—

Laughter, commotion, and whistles. MRS. STOCKMANN *coughs repeatedly.* ASLAKSEN *vehemently rings his bell.*

THE DRUNK *(who has gotten in again)*: Are you referring to me? Yes, my name's Pettersen all right—but I'll fry in hell, before—

ANGRY VOICES: Out with that drunk! Throw him out!

Again the DRUNK *is ejected.*

MAYOR STOCKMANN: Who was that person?

A BYSTANDER: I don't know him, Your Honor.

ANOTHER: He's not from this town.

A THIRD: It must be that lumber dealer from over in— *(The rest is inaudible.)*

ASLAKSEN: The man was obviously muddled on Munich beer. Go on, Dr. Stockmann, but try to be more temperate.

DR. STOCKMANN: So then, my friends and neighbors, I'll say nothing further about our leading citizens. If, from what I've just said, anyone imagines that I'm out to get those gentlemen here this evening, then he's wrong — most emphatically wrong. Because I nourish a benign hope that all those mossbacks, those relics of a dying world of thought, are splendidly engaged in digging their own graves — they don't need a doctor's aid to speed them off the scene. And besides, *They're* not the overwhelming menace to society; *they're* not the ones most active in poisoning our spiritual life and polluting the very ground we stand on; *they're* not the most insidious enemies of truth and freedom in our society.

SHOUTS FROM ALL SIDES: Who, then! Who are they? Name them!

DR. STOCKMANN: Yes, you can bet I'll name them! Because *that's* exactly my great discovery yesterday. *(Raising his voice.)* The most insidious enemy of truth and freedom among us is the solid majority. Yes, the damned, solid, liberal majority — that's it! Now you know.

Wild turmoil in the room. Almost all those present are shouting, stamping, and whistling. Several elderly gentlemen exchange sly glances and appear to be amused. EILIF *and* MORTEN *move threateningly toward the* SCHOOLBOYS, *who are making a disturbance.* ASLAKSEN *rings his bell and calls for order. Both* HOVSTAD *and* BILLING *are talking, without being heard. Finally quiet is restored.*

ASLAKSEN: As chairman, I urge the speaker to withdraw his irresponsible comments.

DR. STOCKMANN: Not a chance, Mr. Aslaksen. It's that same majority in our community that's stripping away my freedom and trying to keep me from speaking the truth.

HOVSTAD: The majority is always right.

BILLING: And it acts for truth. Ye gods!

DR. STOCKMANN: The majority is never right. I say, never! That's one of those social lies that any free man who thinks for himself has to rebel against. Who makes up the majority in any country — the intelligent, or the stupid? I think we've got to agree that, all over this whole wide earth, the stupid are in a fearsomely overpowering majority. But I'll be damned to perdition if it's part of the eternal plan that the stupid are meant to rule the intelligent!

Commotion and outcries.

Oh yes, you can shout me down well enough, but you can't refute me. The majority has the might — unhappily — but it lacks the *right*. The right is with me, and the other few, the solitary individuals. The minority is always right.

Renewed turmoil.

HOVSTAD (*laughs*): So, in a couple of days, the doctor's turned aristocrat.

DR. STOCKMANN: I've told you I'm not going to waste any words on that wheezing, little, narrow-chested pack of reactionaries. The tide of life has already passed them by. But I'm thinking of the few, the individuals among us, who've mastered all the new truths that have been germinating. Those men are out there holding their positions like outposts, so far in the vanguard that the solid majority hasn't even begun to catch up — and *there's* where they're fighting for truths too newly born in the world's consciousness to have won any support from the majority.

HOVSTAD: Well, and now he's a revolutionist!

DR. STOCKMANN: Yes, you're damn right I am, Mr. Hovstad! I'm fomenting a revolution against the lie that only the majority owns the truth. What are these truths the majority flocks around? They're the ones so ripe in age they're nearly senile. But, gentlemen, when a truth's grown that old, it's gone a long way toward becoming a lie.

Laughter and jeers.

Oh yes, you can believe me as you please: but truths aren't at all the stubborn old Methuselahs people imagine. An ordinary, established truth lives, as a rule — let's say — some seventeen, eighteen, at the most twenty years; rarely more. But those venerable truths are always terribly thin. Even so, it's only *then* that the majority takes them up and urges them on society as wholesome spiritual food. But there isn't much nutriment in that kind of diet, I promise you; and as a doctor, I know. All these majority-truths are like last year's salt meat — like rancid, tainted pork. And there's the cause of all the moral scurvy that's raging around us.

ASLAKSEN: It strikes me that the distinguished speaker has strayed rather far from his text.

MAYOR STOCKMANN: I must agree with the chairman's opinion.

DR. STOCKMANN: You're out of your mind, Peter! I'm sticking as close to the text as I can. Because this is exactly what I'm talking about: that the masses, the crowd, this damn solid majority — that *this* is what I say is poisoning our sources of spiritual life and defiling the earth under our feet.

HOVSTAD: And the great liberal-minded majority does this because they're reasonable enough to honor only basic, well-accepted truths?

DR. STOCKMANN: Ah, my dear Mr. Hovstad, don't talk about basic truths! The truths accepted by the masses now are the ones proclaimed basic by the advance guard in our grandfather's time. We fighters on the frontiers today, we no longer recognize them. There's only one truth that's basic in my belief: that no society can live a healthy life on the bleached bones of that kind of truth.

HOVSTAD: Instead of standing there rambling on in the blue, it might be interesting to describe some of those bleached bones we're living on.

Agreement from various quarters.

DR. STOCKMANN: Oh, I could itemize a whole slew of abominations; but to start with, I'll mention just one recognized truth that's actually a vicious lie, though Mr. Hovstad and the *Courier* and all the *Courier's* devotees live on it.

HOVSTAD: That being—?

DR. STOCKMANN: That being the doctrine inherited from your ancestors, which you mindlessly disseminate far and wide—the doctrine that the public, the mob, the masses are the vital core of the people—in fact, that they *are* the people—and that the common man, the inert, unformed component of society, has the same right to admonish and approve, to prescribe and to govern as the few spiritually accomplished personalities.

BILLING: Well, I'll be—

HOVSTAD *(simultaneously, shouting)*: Citizens, did you hear that!

ANGRY VOICES: Oh, we're not the people, uh? So, only the accomplished rule!

A WORKMAN: Out with a man who talks like that!

OTHERS: Out the door! Heave him out!

A MAN *(yells)*: Evensen, blow the horn!

Deep blasts on a horn are heard; whistles and furious commotion in the room.

DR. STOCKMANN *(when the noise has subsided a bit)*: Now just be reasonable! Can't you stand hearing the truth for a change? I never expected you all to agree with me on the spot. But I really did expect that Mr. Hovstad would admit I'm right, after he'd simmered down a little. Mr. Hovstad claims to be a freethinker—

STARTLED VOICES *(in undertones)*: What was that? A freethinker? Hovstad a freethinker?

HOVSTAD *(loudly)*: Prove it, Dr. Stockmann! When have I said that in print?

DR. STOCKMANN *(reflecting)*: No, by God, you're right—you've never had the courage. Well, I don't want to put you in hot water. Let's say I'm the freethinker then. Because I'm going to demonstrate scientifically that the *Courier's* leading you shamelessly by the nose when they say that you—the public, the masses—are the vital core of the people. You see, that's just a journalistic lie! The masses are no more than the raw material out of which a people is shaped.

Mutterings, laughter, and disquiet in the room.

Well, isn't that a fact throughout all the rest of life? What about the difference between a thoroughbred and a hybrid animal? Look at your ordinary barnyard fowl. What meat can you get off such scrawny bones? Not much! And what kind of eggs does it lay? Any competent crow or raven could furnish about the same. But now take a purebred Spanish or Japanese hen, or a fine pheasant or turkey—there's where you'll see the difference! Or again with dogs, a family we humans so closely resemble. First, think of an ordinary stray dog—I mean, one of those nasty, ragged, common mongrels that run around the streets, and spatter the walls of houses. Then set that stray alongside a poodle whose pedigree runs back through a distinguished line to a house where fine food and harmonious voices and music have been the rule. Don't you think the mentality of that poodle will have developed quite differently from the stray's? Of course it will! A young pedigreed poodle can be raised by its trainer to perform the most incredible feats. Your common mongrel couldn't learn such things if you stood him on his head.

Tumult and derision generally.

A CITIZEN (*shouting*): Now you're making us into dogs, uh?

ANOTHER MAN: We're not animals, Doctor!

DR. STOCKMANN: Oh yes, brother, we *are* animals! We're the best animals, all in all, that any man could wish for. But there aren't many animals of quality among us. There's a terrible gap between the thoroughbreds and the mongrels in humanity. And what's amusing is that Mr. Hovstad totally agrees with me as long as we're talking of four-legged beasts—

HOVSTAD: Well, but they're a class by themselves.

DR. STOCKMANN: All right. But as soon as I extend the law to the two-legged animals, Mr. Hovstad stops cold. He doesn't dare think his own thoughts any longer, or follow his ideas to a logical conclusion. So he turns the whole doctrine upside down and declares in the *Courier* that the barnyard fowl and the mongrel dog—that *these* are the real paragons of the menagerie. But that's how it always goes as long as conformity is in your system, and you haven't worked through to a distinction of mind and spirit.

HOVSTAD: I make no claim of any kind of distinction. I was born of simple peasants, and I'm proud that my roots run deep in those masses that he despises.

NUMEROUS WOMEN: Hurray for Hovstad! Hurray, hurray!

DR. STOCKMANN: The kind of commonness I'm talking of isn't only found in the depths: it teems and swarms all around us in society— right up to the top. Just look at your own neat and tidy mayor. My brother Peter's as good a common man as any that walks on two feet—

Laughter and hisses.

MAYOR STOCKMANN: I protest against these personal allusions.

DR. STOCKMANN *(unruffled)*: —and that's not because he's descended, just as I am, from a barbarous old pirate from Pomerania or thereabouts—because so we are—

MAYOR STOCKMANN: A ridiculous fiction. I deny it!

DR. STOCKMANN: —no, he's that because he thinks what the higher-ups think and believes what they believe. The people who do that are the spiritually common men. And that's why my stately brother Peter, you see, is in fact so fearfully lacking in distinction—and consequently so narrowminded.

MAYOR STOCKMANN: Mr. Chairman—!

HOVSTAD: So you have to be distinguished to be liberal-minded in this country. That's a completely new insight.

General laughter.

DR. STOCKMANN: Yes, that's also part of my new discovery. And along with it goes the idea that broadmindedness is almost exactly the same as morality. That's why I say it's simply inexcusable of the *Courier,* day in and day out, to promote the fallacy that it's the masses, the solid majority, who stand as the guardian of tolerance and morality—and that degeneracy and corruption of all kinds are a sort of by-product of culture, filtering down to us like all the pollution filtering down to the baths from the tanneries up at Mølledal.

Turmoil and interruptions.

DR. STOCKMANN *(unfazed, laughing in his enthusiasm)*: And yet this same *Courier* can preach that the deprived masses must be raised to greater cultural opportunities. But, hell's bells—if the *Courier's* assumption holds true, then raising the masses like that would be precisely the same as plunging them smack into depravity! But luckily it's only an old wives' tale—this inherited lie that culture demoralizes. No, it's ignorance and poverty and ugliness in life that do the devil's work! In a house that isn't aired and swept every day—my wife Katherine maintains that the floors ought to be scrubbed as well, but that's debatable—anyway—I say in a house like that, within two or three years, people lose all power for moral thought and action. Lack of oxygen dulls the conscience. And there must be a woeful dearth of oxygen in the houses of this town, it seems, if the entire solid majority can numb their consciences enough to want to build this town's prosperity on a quagmire of duplicity and lies.

ASLAKSEN: It's intolerable—such a gross attack on a whole community.

A GENTLEMAN: I move the chairman rule the speaker out of order.

FURIOUS VOICES: Yes, yes! That's right! Out of order!

DR. STOCKMANN (*vehemently*): Then I'll cry out the truth from every street corner. I'll write to newspapers in other towns! The entire country'll learn what's happened here!

HOVSTAD: It almost looks like the doctor's determined to destroy this town.

DR. STOCKMANN: Yes. I love my home town so much I'd rather destroy it than see it flourishing on a lie.

ASLAKSEN: That's putting it plain.

> *Tumult and whistling.* MRS. STOCKMANN *coughs in vain; the* DOCTOR *no longer hears her.*

HOVSTAD (*shouting above the noise*): Any man who'd destroy a whole community must be a public enemy!

DR. STOCKMANN (*with mounting indignation*): What's the difference if a lying community gets destroyed! It ought to be razed to the ground, I say! Stamp them out like vermin, everyone who lives by lies! You'll contaminate this entire nation in the end, till the land itself deserves to be destroyed. And if it comes to that even, then I say with all my heart: let this whole land be destroyed, let its people all be stamped out!

A MAN: That's talking like a real enemy of the people!

BILLING: Ye gods, but *there's* the people's voice!

THE WHOLE CROWD (*shrieking*): Yes, yes, yes! He's an enemy of the people! He hates his country! He hates all his people!

ASLAKSEN: Both as a citizen and as a human being, I'm profoundly shaken by what I've had to listen to here. Dr. Stockmann has revealed himself in a manner beyond anything I could have dreamed. I'm afraid that I have to endorse the judgment just rendered by my worthy fellow citizens; and I propose that we ought to express this judgment in a resolution, as follows: "This meeting declares that it regards Dr. Thomas Stockmann, staff physician at the baths, to be an enemy of the people."

> *Tumultuous cheers and applause. Many onlookers close in around the* DOCTOR, *whistling at him.* MRS. STOCKMANN *and* PETRA *have risen.* MORTEN *and* EILIF *are fighting with the other* SCHOOLBOYS, *who have also been whistling. Several grown-ups separate them.*

DR. STOCKMANN (*to the hecklers*): Ah, you fools—I'm telling you—

ASLAKSEN (*ringing his bell*): The doctor is out of order! A formal vote is called for; but to spare personal feelings, it ought to be a secret ballot. Do you have any blank paper, Mr. Billing?

BILLING: Here's some blue and white both—

ASLAKSEN (*leaving the platform*): Fine. It'll go faster that way. Cut it in slips—yes, that's it. (*To the gathering.*) Blue means no, white means yes. I'll go around myself and collect the votes.

The MAYOR *leaves the room.* ASLAKSEN *and a couple of other citizens circulate through the crowd with paper slips in their hats.*

A GENTLEMAN *(to* HOVSTAD*)*: What's gotten into the doctor? How should we take this?

HOVSTAD: Well, you know how hot-headed he is.

ANOTHER GENTLEMAN *(to* BILLING*)*: Say, you've visited there off and on. Have you noticed if the man drinks?

BILLING: Ye gods, I don't know what to say. When anybody stops in, there's always toddy on the table.

A THIRD GENTLEMAN: No, I think at times he's just out of his mind.

FIRST GENTLEMAN: I wonder if there isn't a strain of insanity in the family?

BILLING: It's quite possible.

A FOURTH GENTLEMAN: No, it's pure spite, that's all. Revenge for something or other.

BILLING: He was carrying on about a raise at one time — but he never got it.

ALL THE GENTLEMEN *(as one voice)*: Ah, there's the answer!

THE DRUNK *(within the crowd)*: Let's have a blue one! And — let's have a white one, too!

CRIES: There's that drunk again! Throw him out!

MORTEN KIIL *(approaching the* DOCTOR*)*: Well, Stockmann, now you see what your monkeyshines come to?

DR. STOCKMANN: I've done my duty.

MORTEN KIIL: What was that you said about the tanneries at Mølledal?

DR. STOCKMANN: You heard it. I said all the pollution came from them.

MORTEN KIIL: From *my* tannery, too?

DR. STOCKMANN: I'm afraid your tannery's the worst of them.

MORTEN KIIL: You're going to print *that* in the papers?

DR. STOCKMANN: I'm sweeping nothing under the carpet.

MORTEN KIIL: That could cost you plenty, Stockmann. *(He leaves.)*

A FAT GENTLEMAN *(going up to* HORSTER*, without greeting the ladies)*: Well, Captain, so you lend out your house to enemies of the people?

HORSTER: I think I can dispose of my property, sir, as I see fit.

THE MAN: So you'll certainly have no objection if I do the same with mine.

HORSTER: What do you mean?

THE MAN: You'll hear from me in the morning. *(He turns and leaves.)*

PETRA *(to* HORSTER*)*: Doesn't he own your ship?

HORSTER: Yes, that was Mr. Vik.

ASLAKSEN *(ascends the platform with ballots in hand and rings for order)*: Gentlemen, let me make you acquainted with the outcome. All of the votes with one exception —

A YOUNG MAN: That's the drunk!

ASLAKSEN: All of the votes, with the exception of an intoxicated man, are in favor of this assembly of citizens declaring the staff physician of the baths, Dr. Thomas Stockmann, an enemy of the people. *(Shouts and gestures of approval.)* Long live our ancient and glorious community! *(More cheers.)* Long live our capable and effective mayor, who so loyally has suppressed the ties of family! *(Cheers.)* This meeting is adjourned. *(He descends from the platform.)*

BILLING: Long live the chairman!

THE ENTIRE CROWD: Hurray for Aslaksen!

DR. STOCKMANN: My hat and coat, Petra. Captain, have you room for several passengers to the New World?

HORSTER: For you and your family, Doctor, we'll make room.

DR. STOCKMANN *(as* PETRA *helps him on with his coat)*: Good. Come, Katherine! Come on, boys!

He takes his wife by the arm.

MRS. STOCKMANN *(dropping her voice)*: Thomas, dear, let's leave by the back way.

DR. STOCKMANN: No back ways out, Katherine. *(Raising his voice.)* You'll be hearing from the enemy of the people before he shakes this dust off his feet! I'm not as meek as one certain person; I'm not saying, "I forgive them, because they know not what they do."

ASLAKSEN *(in an outcry)*: That's a blasphemous comparison, Dr. Stockmann!

BILLING: That it is, so help me — It's a bit much for a pious man to take.

A COARSE VOICE: And then he threatened us, too!

HEATED VOICES: Let's smash his windows for him! Dunk him in the fjord!

A MAN *(in the crowd)*: Blast your horn, Evensen! Honk, honk!

The sound of the horn; whistles and wild shrieks. The DOCTOR *and his family move toward the exit,* HORSTER *clearing the way for them.*

THE WHOLE CROWD *(howling after them)*: Enemy! Enemy! Enemy of the people!

BILLING *(organizing his notes)*: Ye gods, I wouldn't drink toddy at the Stockmann's tonight!

The crowd surges toward the exit; the noise diffuses outside; from the street the cry continues: "Enemy! Enemy of the people!"

ACT V

DR. STOCKMANN's *study. Bookcases and cabinets filled with various medicines line the walls. In the back wall is a door to the hall; in the foreground,*

left, the door to the living room. At the right, opposite, are two windows, with
all their panes shattered. In the middle of the room is the DOCTOR's *desk,*
covered with books and papers. The room is in disorder. It is morning. DR.
STOCKMANN, *in a dressing gown, slippers, and a smoking cap, is bent down,*
raking under one of the cabinets with an umbrella; after some effort, he sweeps
out a stone.

DR. STOCKMANN *(calling through the open living-room door)*: Katherine, I
found another one.

MRS. STOCKMANN *(from the living room)*: Oh, I'm sure you'll find a lot
more yet.

DR. STOCKMANN *(adding the stone to a pile of others on the table)*: I'm going
to preserve these stones as holy relics. Eilif and Morten have got to see
them every day; and when they're grown, they'll inherit them from
me. *(Raking under a bookcase.)* Hasn't — what the hell's her name — the
maid — hasn't she gone for the glazier yet?

MRS. STOCKMANN *(enters)*: Of course, but he said he didn't know if he
could come today.

DR. STOCKMANN: More likely he doesn't dare.

MRS. STOCKMANN: Yes, Randina thought he was afraid of what the
neighbors might say. *(Speaking into the living room.)* What do you want,
Randina? Oh yes. *(Goes out and comes back immediately.)* Here's a letter
for you, Thomas.

DR. STOCKMANN: Let me see. *(Opens it and reads.)* Of course.

MRS. STOCKMANN: Who's it from?

DR. STOCKMANN: The landlord. He's giving us notice.

MRS. STOCKMANN: Is that true! He's such a decent man —

DR. STOCKMANN *(reading on in the letter)*: He doesn't dare not to, he
says. It pains him to do it, but he doesn't dare not to — in fairness to
his fellow townspeople — a matter of public opinion — not independent — can't affront certain powerful men —

MRS. STOCKMANN: You see, Thomas.

DR. STOCKMANN: Yes, yes, I see very well. They're cowards, all of
them here in town. Nobody dares do anything, in fairness to all the
others. *(Hurls the letter on the table.)* But that's nothing to us, Katherine.
We're off for the New World now —

MRS. STOCKMANN: But, Thomas, is that really the right solution, to
emigrate?

DR. STOCKMANN: Maybe I ought to stay here, where they've pilloried
me as an enemy of the people, branded me, smashed in my windows!
And look at this, Katherine; they even tore my black trousers.

MRS. STOCKMANN: Oh, no — and they're the best you have!

DR. STOCKMANN: One should never wear his best trousers when he
goes out fighting for truth and freedom. It's not that I'm so concerned
about the trousers, you understand; you can always mend them for

me. But what grates is that mob setting on me bodily as if they were my equals — by God, that's the thing I can't bear!

MRS. STOCKMANN: Yes, they've abused you dreadfully in this town, Thomas. But do we have to leave the country entirely because of *that?*

DR. STOCKMANN: Don't you think the common herd is just as arrogant in other towns as well? Why, of course — it's all one and the same. Ahh, shoot! Let the mongrels yap; they're not the worst. The worst of it is that everyone the country over is a slave to party. But *that's* not the reason — it's probably no better in the free United States; I'm sure they have a plague of solid majorities and liberal public opinions and all the other bedevilments. But the scale there is so immense, you see. They might kill you, but they don't go in for slow torture; they don't lock a free soul in the jaws of a vise, the way they do here at home. And, if need be, there's space to get away. *(Pacing the floor.)* If I only knew of some primeval forest, or a little South Sea island at a bargain price —

MRS. STOCKMANN: But, Thomas, think of the boys.

DR. STOCKMANN *(stopping in his tracks)*: You are remarkable, Katherine! Would you rather they grew up in a society like ours? You saw yourself last night that half the population are raging maniacs; and if the other half haven't lost their reason, it's because they're such muttonheads they haven't any reason to lose.

MRS. STOCKMANN: Yes, but dear, you're so intemperate in your speech.

DR. STOCKMANN: Look! Isn't it true, what I'm saying? Don't they turn every idea upside down? Don't they scramble right and wrong completely? Don't they call everything a lie that I know for the truth? But the height of insanity is that here you've got all these full-grown liberals going around in a bloc and deluding themselves and the others that they're independent thinkers! Did you ever hear the like of it, Katherine?

MRS. STOCKMANN: Yes, yes, it's all wrong of course, but —

PETRA *enters from the living room.*

MRS. STOCKMANN: You're back from school already?

PETRA: Yes. I got my notice.

MRS. STOCKMANN: Your notice.

DR. STOCKMANN: You, too!

PETRA: Mrs. Busk gave me my notice, so I thought it better to leave at once.

DR. STOCKMANN: You did the right thing!

MRS. STOCKMANN: Who would have thought Mrs. Busk would prove such a poor human being!

PETRA: Oh, Mother, she really isn't so bad. It was plain to see how miserable she felt, but she said she didn't dare not to. So I got fired.

DR. STOCKMANN *(laughs and rubs his hands)*: She didn't dare not to, either. Oh, that's charming.

MRS. STOCKMANN: Well, after that awful row last night—

PETRA: It was more than just that. Father, listen now!

DR. STOCKMANN: What?

PETRA: Mrs. Busk showed me no less than three letters she'd gotten this morning.

DR. STOCKMANN: Anonymous, of course?

PETRA: Yes.

DR. STOCKMANN: Because they don't *dare* sign their names, Katherine.

PETRA: And two of them stated that a gentleman who's often visited this household had declared in the club last night that I had extremely free ideas on various matters—

DR. STOCKMANN: And that you didn't deny, I hope.

PETRA: No, you know that. Mrs. Busk has some pretty liberal ideas herself, when it's just the two of us talking. But with this all coming out about me, she didn't dare keep me on.

MRS. STOCKMANN: And to think—it was one of our regular visitors! You see, Thomas, there's what you get for your hospitality.

DR. STOCKMANN: We won't go on living in a pigsty like this. Katherine, get packed as soon as you can. Let's get out of here, the quicker the better.

MRS. STOCKMANN: Be quiet—I think there's someone in the hall. Have a look, Petra.

PETRA (*opening the door*): Oh, is it you, Captain Horster? Please, come in.

HORSTER (*from the hall*): Good morning. I thought I ought to stop by and see how things stand.

DR. STOCKMANN (*shaking his hand*): Thanks. That certainly is kind of you.

MRS. STOCKMANN: And thank you, Captain Horster, for helping us through last night.

PETRA: But how did you ever make it home again?

HORSTER: Oh, no problem. I can handle myself pretty well; and they're mostly a lot of hot air, those people.

DR. STOCKMANN: Yes, isn't it astounding, this bestial cowardice? Come here, and I'll show you something. See, here are all the stones they rained in on us. Just look at them! I swear, there aren't more than two respectable paving blocks in the whole pile; the rest are nothing but gravel—only pebbles. And yet they stood out there, bellowing, and swore they'd hammer me to a pulp. But action—action—no, you don't see much of that in this town!

HORSTER: I'd say this time that was lucky for you, Doctor.

DR. STOCKMANN: Definitely. But it's irritating, all the same; because if it ever comes to a serious fight to save this country, you'll see how public opinion is all for ducking the issue, and how the solid majority runs for cover like a flock of sheep. That's what's so pathetic when you think of it; it makes me heartsick—Damn it all, no—this is sheer stupidity; they've labeled me an enemy of the people, so I better act like one.

MRS. STOCKMANN: You never could be that, Thomas.

DR. STOCKMANN: Don't count on it, Katherine. To be called some ugly name hurts like a stabbing pain in the lung. And that damnable label—I can't shake it off; its fixed itself here in the pit of my stomach, where it sits and rankles and corrodes like acid. And there's no magnesia to work against that.

PETRA: Oh, Father, you should just laugh at them.

HORSTER: People will come around in their thinking, Doctor.

MRS. STOCKMANN: As sure as you're standing here, they will.

DR. STOCKMANN: Yes, maybe after it's too late. Well, they've got it coming! Let them stew in their own mess and rue the day they drove a patriot into exile. When are you sailing, Captain Horster?

HORSTER: Hm—as a matter of fact, that's why I stopped by to talk to you—

DR. STOCKMANN: Oh, has something gone wrong with the ship?

HORSTER: No. But it looks like I won't sail with her.

PETRA: You haven't been fired, have you?

HORSTER (smiles): Yes, exactly.

PETRA: You, too.

MRS. STOCKMANN: See there, Thomas.

DR. STOCKMANN: And all this for the truth! Oh, if only I could have foreseen—

HORSTER: Now, don't go worrying about me; I'll find a post with some shipping firm out of town.

DR. STOCKMANN: And there we have Mr. Vik—a merchant, a man of wealth, independent in every way—! What a disgrace!

HORSTER: He's quite fair-minded otherwise. He said himself he'd gladly have retained me if he dared to—

DR. STOCKMANN: But he didn't dare? No, naturally!

HORSTER: It's not so easy, he was telling me, when you belong to a party—

DR. STOCKMANN: There's a true word from the merchant prince. A political party—it's like a sausage grinder; it grinds all the heads up together into one mash, and then it turns them out, link by link, into fatheads and meatheads!

MRS. STOCKMANN: Thomas, really!

PETRA (to HORSTER): If you just hadn't seen us home, things might not have gone like this.

HORSTER: I don't regret it.

PETRA (extending her hand to him): Thank you!

HORSTER (to the DOCTOR): So, what I wanted to say was, if you're still serious about leaving, then I've thought of another plan—

DR. STOCKMANN: Excellent. If we can only clear out of here fast—

MRS. STOCKMANN: Shh! Didn't someone knock?

PETRA: It's Uncle, I'll bet.

DR. STOCKMANN: Aha! *(Calls.)* Come in!

MRS. STOCKMANN: Thomas dear, you must promise me —

The MAYOR *enters from the hall.*

MAYOR STOCKMANN *(in the doorway)*: Oh, you're occupied. Well, then I'd better —

DR. STOCKMANN: No, no, come right in.

MAYOR STOCKMANN: But I wanted to speak to you alone.

MRS. STOCKMANN: We'll go into the living room for a time.

HORSTER: And I'll come by again later.

DR. STOCKMANN: No, you go in with them, Captain Horster. I need to hear something more about —

HORSTER: Oh yes, I'll wait then.

He accompanies MRS. STOCKMANN *and* PETRA *into the living room. The* MAYOR *says nothing, but glances at the windows.*

DR. STOCKMANN: Maybe you find it a bit drafty here today? Put your hat on.

MAYOR STOCKMANN: Thank you, if I may. *(Does so.)* I think I caught cold last night. I was freezing out there —

DR. STOCKMANN: Really? It seemed more on the warm side to me.

MAYOR STOCKMANN: I regret that it wasn't within my power to curb those excesses last evening.

DR. STOCKMANN: Do you have anything else in particular to say to me?

MAYOR STOCKMANN *(taking out a large envelope)*: I have this document for you from the board of directors.

DR. STOCKMANN: It's my notice?

MAYOR STOCKMANN: Yes, effective today. *(Places the envelope on the table.)* This pains us deeply, but — to be quite candid — we didn't dare not to, in view of public opinion.

DR. STOCKMANN *(smiles)*: Didn't dare? Seems as though I've already heard those words today.

MAYOR STOCKMANN: I suggest that you face your position clearly. After this, you mustn't count on any practice whatsoever here in town.

DR. STOCKMANN: To hell with the practice! But how can you be so sure?

MAYOR STOCKMANN: The Home Owners Council is circulating a resolution, soliciting all responsible citizens to dispense with your services. And I venture to say that not one single householder will risk refusing to sign. Quite simply, they wouldn't dare.

DR. STOCKMANN: I don't doubt it. But what of it?

MAYOR STOCKMANN: If I could give you some advice, it would be that you leave this area for a while —

DR. STOCKMANN: Yes, I've been half thinking of just that.

MAYOR STOCKMANN: Good. Then, after you've had some six months, more or less, to reconsider things, if on mature reflection you find yourself capable of a few words of apology, acknowledging your mistakes —

DR. STOCKMANN: Then maybe I could get my job back you mean?

MAYOR STOCKMANN: Perhaps. It's not at all unlikely.

DR. STOCKMANN: Yes, but public opinion? You could hardly dare, in that regard.

MAYOR STOCKMANN: Opinion tends to go from one extreme to another. And to be quite honest, it's especially important to us to get a signed statement to that effect from you.

DR. STOCKMANN: Yes, wouldn't you lick your chinchoppers for that! But, damnation, don't you remember what I already said about that kind of foxy game?

MAYOR STOCKMANN: Your position was much more favorable then. You could imagine then that you had the whole town in back of you —

DR. STOCKMANN: Yes, and I feel now as if the whole town's on my back — (Flaring up.) But even if the devil and his grandmother were riding me — never! Never, you hear me!

MAYOR STOCKMANN: A family provider can't go around risking everything the way you do. You can't risk it, Thomas!

DR. STOCKMANN: Can't risk! There's just one single thing in this world a free man can't risk; and do you know what that is?

MAYOR STOCKMANN: No.

DR. STOCKMANN: Of course not. But I'll tell you. A free man can't risk befouling himself like a savage. He doesn't dare sink to the point that he'd like to spit in his own face.

MAYOR STOCKMANN: This all sounds highly plausible; and if there weren't another prior explanation for your stubborn arrogance — but then of course, there is —

DR. STOCKMANN: What do you mean by that?

MAYOR STOCKMANN: You understand perfectly well. But as your brother and as a man of some discernment, let me advise you not to build too smugly on prospects that might very well never materialize.

DR. STOCKMANN: What in the world are you driving at?

MAYOR STOCKMANN: Are you actually trying to make me believe you're ignorant of the terms of Morten Kiil's will?

DR. STOCKMANN: I know that the little he has is going to a home for destitute craftsmen. But how does that apply to me?

MAYOR STOCKMANN: First of all, the amount under discussion is far from little. Morten Kiil is a rather wealthy man.

DR. STOCKMANN: I hadn't the slightest idea —!

MAYOR STOCKMANN: Hm — really? And you hadn't any idea, either, that a considerable part of his fortune will pass to your children, with you and your wife enjoying the interest for life. He hasn't told you that?

DR. STOCKMANN: Not one blessed word of it! Quite the contrary, he goes on fuming endlessly about the outrageously high taxes he pays. But how do you know this for sure, Peter?

MAYOR STOCKMANN: I have it from a totally reliable source.

DR. STOCKMANN: But, my Lord, then Katherine's provided for — and the children too! I really must tell her — (*Shouts.*) Katherine, Katherine!

MAYOR STOCKMANN (*restraining him*): Shh, don't say anything yet!

MRS. STOCKMANN (*opening the door*): What is it?

DR. STOCKMANN: Nothing, dear. Go back inside.

> MRS. STOCKMANN *shuts the door.*

DR. STOCKMANN (*pacing the floor*): Provided for! Just imagine — every one of them, provided for. And for life! What a blissful feeling, to know you're secure!

MAYOR STOCKMANN: Yes, but that's precisely what you aren't. Morten Kiil can revise his will any time he pleases.

DR. STOCKMANN: But, my dear Peter, he won't do that. The Badger's enraptured by the way I've gone after you and your smart friends.

MAYOR STOCKMANN (*starts and looks penetratingly at him*): Aha, that puts a new light on things.

DR. STOCKMANN: What things?

MAYOR STOCKMANN: So this whole business has been a collusion. These reckless, violent assaults you've aimed, in the name of truth, at our leading citizens were —

DR. STOCKMANN: Yes — were what?

MAYOR STOCKMANN: They were nothing more than a calculated payment for a piece of that vindictive old man's estate.

DR. STOCKMANN (*nearly speechless*): Peter — you're the cheapest trash I've known in all my days.

MAYOR STOCKMANN: Between us, everything is through. Your dismissal is irrevocable — for now we've got a weapon against you. (*He goes.*)

DR. STOCKMANN: Why, that scum — aaah! (*Shouts.*) Katherine! Scour the floors where he's been! Have her come in with a pail — that girl — whozzis, damn it — the one with the smudgy nose —

MRS. STOCKMANN (*in the living-room doorway*): Shh, Thomas. Shh!

PETRA (*also in the doorway*): Father, Grandpa's here and wonders if he can speak to you alone.

DR. STOCKMANN: Yes, of course he can. (*By the door.*) Come in.

> MORTEN KIIL *enters. The* DOCTOR *closes the door after him.*

DR. STOCKMANN: Well, what is it? Have a seat.

MORTEN KIIL: Won't sit. *(Looking about.)* You've made it very attractive here today, Stockmann.

DR. STOCKMANN: Yes, don't you think so?

MORTEN KILL: Really attractive. And fresh air, too. Today you've got enough of that oxygen you talked about yesterday. You must have a marvelous conscience today, I imagine.

DR. STOCKMANN: Yes, I have.

MORTEN KIIL: I can imagine. *(Tapping his chest.)* But do you know what *I* have here?

DR. STOCKMANN: Well, I'm hoping a marvelous conscience, too.

MORTEN KIIL: Pah! No, it's something better than that. *(He takes out a thick wallet, opens it, and displays a sheaf of papers.)*

DR. STOCKMANN *(stares at him, amazed)*: Shares in the baths.

MORTEN KIIL: They weren't hard to get today.

DR. STOCKMANN: And you were out buying —?

MORTEN KIIL: As many as I could afford.

DR. STOCKMANN: But, my dear Father-in-law — with everything at the baths in jeopardy!

MORTEN KIIL: If you go back to acting like a reasonable man, you'll soon get the baths on their feet again.

DR. STOCKMANN: You can see yourself, I'm doing all I can; but the people are crazy in this town.

MORTEN KIIL: You said yesterday that the worst pollution came from my tannery. But now if that *is* true, then my grandfather and my father before me and I myself over numbers of years have been poisoning this town right along, like three angels of death. You think I can rest with that disgrace on my head?

DR. STOCKMANN: I'm afraid you'll have to learn how.

MORTEN KIIL: No thanks. I want my good name and reputation. People call me the Badger, I've heard. A badger's a kind of pig, isn't it? They're not going to be right about that. Never. I want to live and die a clean human being.

DR. STOCKMANN: And how are you going to do that?

MORTEN KIIL: You'll make me clean, Stockmann.

DR. STOCKMANN: I!

MORTEN KIIL: Do you know where I got the money to buy these shares? No, you couldn't know that, but now I'll tell you. It's the money Katherine and Petra and the boys will be inheriting from me someday. Yes, because, despite everything, I've laid a little aside, you see.

DR. STOCKMANN *(flaring up)*: So you went out and spent Katherine's money for *those*!

MORTEN KIIL: Yes, now the money's completely bound up in the baths. And now I'll see if you're really so ranting, raging mad after all, Stockmann. Any more about bugs and such coming down from my tannery, it'll be exactly the same as cutting great strips out of Katherine's skin, and Petra's, and the boys'. But no normal man would do that — he'd *have* to be mad.

DR. STOCKMANN (*pacing back and forth*): Yes, but I *am* a madman; I *am* a madman!

MORTEN KIIL: But you're not so utterly out of your senses as to flay your wife and children.

DR. STOCKMANN (*stopping in front of him*): Why couldn't you talk with me before you went out and bought all that worthless paper?

MORTEN KIIL: When a thing's been done, it's best to hang on.

DR. STOCKMANN (*paces the room restlessly*): If only I weren't so certain in this —! But I'm perfectly sure I'm right.

MORTEN KIIL (*weighing the wallet in his hand*): If you keep on with this foolishness, then these aren't going to be worth much, will they? (*He replaces the wallet in his pocket.*)

DR. STOCKMANN: Damn it, science should be able to provide some counter-agent, some kind of germicide —

MORTEN KIIL: You mean something to kill those little animals?

DR. STOCKMANN: Yes, or else make them harmless.

MORTEN KIIL: Couldn't you try rat poison?

DR. STOCKMANN: Oh, that's nonsense! But — everyone says this is all just imagination. Well, why not? Let them have what they want! Stupid, mean little mongrels — didn't they brand me enemy of the people? And weren't they spoiling to tear the clothes off my back?

MORTEN KIIL: And all the windows they broke for you.

DR. STOCKMANN: And I do have family obligations! I must talk this over with Katherine; she's very shrewd in these things.

MORTEN KIIL: Good. You pay attention to a sensible woman's advice.

DR. STOCKMANN (*turning on him*): And you, too — how could you make such a mess of it! Gambling with Katherine's money; tormenting me with this horrible dilemma! When I look at you, I could be seeing the devil himself —!

MORTEN KIIL: I think I'd better be going. But by two o'clock I want your answer: yes — or no. If it's no, the stock gets willed to charity — and right this very day.

DR. STOCKMANN: And what does Katherine get then?

MORTEN KIIL: Not a crumb.

The hall door is opened. HOVSTAD *and* ASLAKSEN *come into view, standing outside.*

MORTEN KIIL: Well, will you look at *them?*

DR. STOCKMANN (*staring at them*): What —! You still dare to come around here?

HOVSTAD: Of course we do.

ASLAKSEN: You see, we've something to talk with you about.

MORTEN KIIL (*in a whisper*): Yes or no — by two o'clock.

ASLAKSEN *(glancing at* HOVSTAD*)*: Aha!

MORTEN KIIL *leaves.*

DR. STOCKMANN: Well now, what do you want? Cut it short.

HOVSTAD: I can easily realize your bitterness toward us for the posture we took at last night's meeting—

DR. STOCKMANN: You call that a posture! Yes, that was a lovely posture! I call it spinelessness, like a bent old woman—holy God!

HOVSTAD: Call it what you will, we couldn't do otherwise.

DR. STOCKMANN: You didn't *dare,* you mean. Isn't that right?

HOVSTAD: Yes, if you like.

ASLAKSEN: But why didn't you pass us the word beforehand? Just the least little hint to Hovstad or me.

DR. STOCKMANN: A hint? What about?

ASLAKSEN: The reason why.

DR. STOCKMANN: I simply don't understand you.

ASLAKSEN *(nods confidentially)*: Oh, yes, you do, Dr. Stockmann.

HOVSTAD: Let's not make a mystery out of it any longer.

DR. STOCKMANN *(looking from one to the other)*: What in sweet blazes *is* this—!

ASLAKSEN: May I ask—hasn't your father-in-law been combing the town to buy up stock in the baths?

DR. STOCKMANN: Yes, he's bought a few shares today; but—?

ASLAKSEN: It would have been more clever if you'd gotten someone else to do it—someone less closely related.

HOVSTAD: And you shouldn't have moved under your own name. No one had to know the attack on the baths came from you. You should have brought me in on it, Doctor.

DR. STOCKMANN *(stares blankly in front of him; a light seems to dawn on him, and he says as if thunderstruck)*: It's unbelievable! Do these things happen?

ASLAKSEN *(smiles)*: Why, of course they do. But they only happen when you use finesse, if you follow me.

HOVSTAD: And they go better when a few others are involved. The risk is less for the individual when the responsibility is shared.

DR. STOCKMANN *(regaining his composure)*: In short, gentlemen, what is it you want?

ASLAKSEN: Mr. Hovstad can best—

HOVSTAD: No, Aslaksen, you explain.

ASLAKSEN: Well, it's this—that now that we know how it all fits together, we thought we might venture to put the *People's Courier* at your disposal.

DR. STOCKMANN: Ah, so now you'll venture? But public opinion? Aren't you afraid there'll be a storm raised against us?

HOVSTAD: We're prepared to ride out the storm.

ASLAKSEN: And you should be prepared for a quick reversal in position, Doctor. As soon as your attack has served its purpose —

DR. STOCKMANN: You mean as soon as my father-in-law and I have cornered all the stock at a dirt-cheap price —?

HOVSTAD: I suppose it's mostly for scientific purposes that you want control of the baths.

DR. STOCKMANN: Naturally. It was for scientific purposes that I got the old Badger in with me on this. So we'll tinker a bit with the water pipes and dig around a little on the beach, and it won't cost the town half a crown. That ought to do it, don't you think? Hm?

HOVSTAD: I think so — as long as you've got the *Courier* with you.

ASLAKSEN: The press is a power in a free society, Doctor.

DR. STOCKMANN: How true. And so's public opinion. Mr. Aslaksen, I assume you'll take care of the Home Owners Council?

ASLAKSEN: The Home Owners Council and the Temperance Union both. You can count on that.

DR. STOCKMANN: But, gentlemen — it embarrasses me to mention it, but — *your* compensation —?

HOVSTAD: Preferably, of course, we'd like to help you for nothing, as you can imagine. But the *Courier*'s on shaky legs these days; it's not doing too well; and to shut the paper down now when there's so much to work for in the larger political scene strikes me as insupportable.

DR. STOCKMANN: Clearly. That would be a hard blow for a friend of the people like you. *(In an outburst.)* But *I'm* an enemy of the people. *(Lunges about the room.)* Where do I have my stick? Where in hell is that stick?

HOVSTAD: What's this?

ASLAKSEN: You're not going to —?

DR. STOCKMANN *(stops)*: And what if I didn't give you one iota of my shares? We tycoons aren't so free with our money, don't forget.

HOVSTAD: And don't *you* forget that this matter of shares can be posed in two different lights.

DR. STOCKMANN: Yes, you're just the man for that. If I don't bail out the *Courier,* you'll put a vile construction on it all. You'll hound me down — set upon me — try to choke me off like a dog chokes a hare!

HOVSTAD: That's the law of nature. Every animal has to struggle for survival.

ASLAKSEN: We take our food where we can find it, you know.

DR. STOCKMANN: Then see if you can find yours in the gutter! *(Striding about the room.)* Because now we're going to learn, by God, who's the strongest animal among the three of us! *(Finds his umbrella and flourishes it.)* Hi, look out —!

HOVSTAD: Don't hit us!

ASLAKSEN: Watch out with that umbrella!

DR. STOCKMANN: Out of the window with you, Hovstad.

HOVSTAD *(by the hall door)*: Have you lost your mind?

DR. STOCKMANN: Out of the window, Aslaksen! I said, jump! Don't be the last to go.

ASLAKSEN *(running around the desk)*: Moderation, Doctor! I'm out of condition—I'm not up to this— *(Shrieks.)* Help! Help!

MRS. STOCKMANN, PETRA, *and* HORSTER *enter from the living room.*

MRS. STOCKMANN: My heavens, Thomas, what's going on in here?

DR. STOCKMANN *(swinging his umbrella)*: Jump, I'm telling you! Into the gutter!

HOVSTAD: This is unprovoked assault! Captain Horster, I'm calling you for a witness. *(He scurries out down the hall.)*

ASLAKSEN *(confused)*: If I just knew the layout here— *(Sneaks out through the living-room door.)*

MRS. STOCKMANN *(holding onto the* DOCTOR*)*: Now you control yourself, Thomas!

DR. STOCKMANN *(flings the umbrella away)*: Damn, they got out of it after all!

MRS. STOCKMANN: But what did they want you for?

DR. STOCKMANN: You can hear about it later. I have other things to think about now. *(Goes to the desk and writes on a visiting card.)* See, Katherine. What's written here?

MRS. STOCKMANN: *"No,"* repeated three times. Why is that?

DR. STOCKMANN: You can hear about that later, too. *(Holding the card out.)* Here, Petra, tell Smudgy-face to run over to the Badger's with this, quick as she can. Hurry!

PETRA *leaves with the card by the hall door.*

Well, if I haven't had visits today from all the devil's envoys, I don't know what. But now I'll sharpen my pen into a stiletto and skewer them; I'll dip it in venom and gall; I'll sling my inkstand right at their skulls!

MRS. STOCKMANN: Yes, but we're leaving here, Thomas.

PETRA *returns.*

DR. STOCKMANN: Well?

PETRA: It's on its way.

DR. STOCKMANN: Good. Leaving, you say? The hell we are! We're staying here where we are, Katherine!

PETRA: We're staying?

MRS. STOCKMANN: In this town?

DR. STOCKMANN: Exactly. This is the battleground; here's where the fighting will be; and here's where I'm going to win! As soon as I've got my trousers patched, I'm setting out to look for a house. We'll need a roof over our heads by winter.

HORSTER: You can share mine.

DR. STOCKMANN: I can?

HORSTER: Yes, perfectly well. There's room enough, and I'm scarcely ever home.

MRS. STOCKMANN: Oh, how kind of you, Horster.

PETRA: Thank you!

DR. STOCKMANN (*shaking his hand*): Many, many thanks! So that worry is over. Now I can make a serious start right today. Oh, Katherine, it's endless, the number of things that need looking into here! And it's lucky I have so much time now to spend — yes, because, I meant to tell you, I got my notice from the baths —

MRS. STOCKMANN (*sighing*): Ah me, I've been expecting it.

DR. STOCKMANN: And then they want to take my practice away, too. Well, let them! I'll keep the poor people at least — the ones who can't pay at all; and, Lord knows, they're the ones that need me the most. But, by thunder, they'll have to hear me out. I'll preach to them in season and out of season, as someone once said.

MRS. STOCKMANN: But, dear, I think you've seen how much good preaching does.

DR. STOCKMANN: You really are preposterous, Katherine. Should I let myself be whipped from the field by public opinion and the solid majority and other such barbarities? No, thank you! Besides, what I want is so simple and clear and basic. I just want to hammer into the heads of these mongrels that the so-called liberals are the most insidious enemies of free men — that party programs have a way of smothering every new, germinal truth — that acting out of expediency turns morality and justice into a hollow mockery, until it finally becomes monstrous to go on living. Captain Horster, don't you think I could get people to recognize that?

HORSTER: Most likely. I don't understand much about such things.

DR. STOCKMANN: Don't you see — let me explain! The party leaders have to be eradicated — because a party leader's just like a wolf, an insatiable wolf that needs so and so many smaller animals to feed off per annum, if he's going to survive. Look at Hovstad and Aslaksen! How many lesser creatures haven't they swallowed up — or they maul and mutilate them till they can't be more than home owners and subscribers to the *Courier!* (*Sitting on the edge of the desk.*) Ah, come here, Katherine — look at that sunlight, how glorious, the way it streams in today. And how wonderful and fresh the spring air is.

MRS. STOCKMANN: Yes, if we only could live on sunlight and spring air, Thomas.

DR. STOCKMANN: Well, you'll have to skimp and save a bit here and there — it'll turn out. That's my least concern. No, what's worse is that

I don't know any man who's free-spirited enough to carry my work
on after me.

PETRA: Oh, don't think of that, Father; you've lots of time. Why, look—
the boys, already.

EILIF *and* MORTEN *come in from the living room.*

MRS. STOCKMANN: Did you get let out early?

MORTEN: No. We had a fight with some others at recess—

EILIF: That isn't true; it was the others that fought us.

MORTEN: Yes, and so Mr. Rørland said we'd better stay home for a few
days.

DR. STOCKMANN *(snapping his fingers and jumping down off the desk)*: I've
got it! So help me, I've got it! You'll never set foot in school again.

THE BOYS: No more school?

MRS. STOCKMANN: But, Thomas—

DR. STOCKMANN: I said, never! I'll teach you myself—by that, I mean,
you won't learn a blessed fact—

THE BOYS: Hurray!

DR. STOCKMANN: But I'll make you into free-spirited and accomplished
men. Listen, you have to help me, Petra.

PETRA: Yes, of course I will.

DR. STOCKMANN: And the school—that'll be held in the room where
they assailed me as an enemy of the people. But we have to be more. I
need at least twelve boys to begin with.

MRS. STOCKMANN: You'll never get them from this town.

DR. STOCKMANN: Let's see about that. *(To the* BOYS) Don't you know
any boys off the street—regular little punks—

MORTEN: Sure, I know lots of them!

DR. STOCKMANN: So, that's fine. Bring around a few samples. I want
to experiment with mongrels for a change. There might be some
fantastic minds out there.

MORTEN: But what'll we do when we've become free-spirited and accomplished men?

DR. STOCKMANN: You'll drive all the wolves into the Far West, boys!

EILIF *looks somewhat dubious;* MORTEN *jumps about and cheers.*

MRS. STOCKMANN: Ah, just so those wolves aren't hunting you anymore, Thomas.

DR. STOCKMANN: Are you utterly mad, Katherine! Hunt *me* down!
Now, when I'm the strongest man in town!

MRS. STOCKMANN: The strongest—now?

DR. STOCKMANN: Yes, I might go further and say that now I'm one of
the strongest men in the whole world.

MORTEN: You mean it?

DR. STOCKMANN *(lowering his voice)*: Shh, don't talk about it yet — but I've made a great discovery.

MRS. STOCKMANN: What, again?

DR. STOCKMANN: Yes, why not! *(Gathers them around him and speaks confidentially.)* And the essence of it, you see, is that the strongest man in the world is the one who stands most alone.

MRS. STOCKMANN *(smiling and shaking her head)*: Oh, Thomas, Thomas — !

PETRA *(buoyantly, gripping his hands)*: Father!

LORRAINE HANSBERRY (1930–1965)

A Raisin in the Sun

Characters

RUTH YOUNGER
TRAVIS YOUNGER
WALTER LEE YOUNGER *(brother)*
BENEATHA YOUNGER
LENA YOUNGER *(Mama)*
JOSEPH ASAGAI
GEORGE MURCHISON
MRS. JOHNSON
KARL LINDNER
BOBO
MOVING MEN

> *The action of the play is set in Chicago's Southside, sometime between World War II and the present.*

Act I
Scene I: *Friday morning.*
Scene II: *The following morning.*

Act II
Scene I: *Later, the same day.*
Scene II: *Friday night, a few weeks later.*
Scene III: *Moving day, one week later.*

Act III
An hour later.

ACT I

Scene I

(The Younger living room would be a comfortable and well-ordered room if it were not for a number of indestructible contradictions to this state of being. Its furnishings are typical and undistinguished and their primary feature now is that they have clearly had to accommodate the living of too many people for too many years — and they are tired. Still, we can see that at some time, a time probably no longer remembered by the family [except perhaps for MAMA*], the furnishings of this room were actually selected with care and love and even hope — and brought to this apartment and arranged with taste and pride.)*

(That was a long time ago. Now the once loved pattern of the couch upholstery has to fight to show itself from under acres of crocheted doilies and couch covers which have themselves finally come to be more important than the upholstery. And here a table or a chair has been moved to disguise the worn places in the carpet; but the carpet has fought back by showing its weariness, with depressing uniformity, elsewhere on its surface.)

(Weariness has, in fact, won in this room. Everything has been polished, washed, sat on, used, scrubbed too often. All pretenses but living itself have long since vanished from the very atmosphere of this room.)

(Moreover, a section of this room, for it is not really a room unto itself, though the landlord's lease would make it seem so, slopes backward to provide a small kitchen area, where the family prepares the meals that are eaten in the living room proper, which must also serve as dining room. The single window that has been provided for these "two" rooms is located in this kitchen area. The sole natural light the family may enjoy in the course of a day is only that which fights its way through this little window.)

(At left, a door leads to a bedroom which is shared by MAMA *and her daughter,* BENEATHA. *At right, opposite, is a second room [which in the beginning of the life of this apartment was probably a breakfast room] which serves as a bedroom for* WALTER *and his wife,* RUTH.*)*

(Time: Sometime between World War II and the present.)

(Place: Chicago's Southside.)

(At rise: It is morning dark in the living room TRAVIS *is asleep on the make-down bed at center. An alarm clock sounds from within the bedroom at right and presently* RUTH *enters from that room and closes the door behind her. She crosses sleepily toward the window. As she passes her sleeping son she reaches down and shakes him a little. At the window she raises the shade and a dusky Southside morning light comes in feebly. She fills a pot with water and puts it on to boil. She calls to the boy, between yawns, in a slightly muffled voice.)*

*(*RUTH *is about thirty. We can see that she was a pretty girl, even exceptionally so, but now it is apparent that life has been little that she expected, and disappointment has already begun to hang in her face. In a few years, before thirty-five even, she will be known among her people as a "settled woman.")*

(She crosses to her son and gives him a good, final rousing shake.)

RUTH: Come on now, boy, it's seven thirty! *(Her son sits up at last, in a stupor of sleepiness.)* I say hurry up, Travis! You ain't the only person in the world got to use a bathroom! *(The child, a sturdy, handsome little boy of ten or eleven, drags himself out of the bed and almost blindly takes his towels and "today's clothes" from drawers and a closet and goes out to the bathroom, which is in an outside hall and which is shared by another family or families on the same floor.* RUTH *crosses to the bedroom door at right and opens it and calls in to her husband.)* Walter Lee! . . . It's after seven thirty! Lemme see you do some waking up in there now! *(She waits.)* You better get up from there, man! It's after seven thirty I tell you. *(She waits again.)*

All right, you just go ahead and lay there and next thing you know Travis be finished and Mr. Johnson'll be in there and you'll be fussing and cussing round here like a madman! And be late too! *(She waits, at the end of patience.)* Walter Lee—it's time for you to GET UP!

(She waits another second and then starts to go into the bedroom, but is apparently satisfied that her husband has begun to get up. She stops, pulls the door to, and returns to the kitchen area. She wipes her face with a moist cloth and runs her fingers through her sleep-disheveled hair in a vain effort and ties an apron around her housecoat. The bedroom door at right opens and her husband stands in the doorway in his pajamas, which are rumpled and mismated. He is a lean, intense young man in his middle thirties, inclined to quick nervous movements and erratic speech habits—and always in his voice there is a quality of indictment.)

WALTER: Is he out yet?

RUTH: What you mean *out?* He ain't hardly got in there good yet.

WALTER *(wandering in, still more oriented to sleep than to a new day)*: Well, what was you doing all that yelling for if I can't even get in there yet? *(Stopping and thinking.)* Check coming today?

RUTH: They *said* Saturday and this is just Friday and I hopes to God you ain't going to get up here first thing this morning and start talking to me 'bout no money—'cause I 'bout don't want to hear it.

WALTER: Something the matter with you this morning?

RUTH: No—I'm just sleepy as the devil. What kind of eggs you want?

WALTER: Not scrambled. *(RUTH starts to scramble eggs.)* Paper come? *(RUTH points impatiently to the rolled up Tribune on the table, and he gets it and spreads it out and vaguely reads the front page.)* Set off another bomb yesterday.

RUTH *(maximum indifference)*: Did they?

WALTER *(looking up)*: What's the matter with you?

RUTH: Ain't nothing the matter with me. And don't keep asking me that this morning.

WALTER: Ain't nobody bothering you. *(Reading the news of the day absently again.)* Say Colonel McCormick is sick.

RUTH *(affecting tea-party interest)*: Is he now? Poor thing.

WALTER *(sighing and looking at his watch)*: Oh, me. *(He waits.)* Now what is that boy doing in that bathroom all this time? He just going to have to start getting up earlier. I can't be being late to work on account of him fooling around in there.

RUTH *(turning on him)*: Oh, no he ain't going to be getting up no earlier no such thing! It ain't his fault that he can't get to bed no earlier nights 'cause he got a bunch of crazy good-for-nothing clowns sitting up running their mouths in what is supposed to be his bedroom after ten o'clock at night . . .

WALTER: That's what you mad about, ain't it? The things I want to talk about with my friends just couldn't be important in your mind, could they?

(He rises and finds a cigarette in her handbag on the table and crosses to the little window and looks out, smoking and deeply enjoying this first one.)

RUTH *(almost matter of factly, a complaint too automatic to deserve emphasis)*: Why you always got to smoke before you eat in the morning?

WALTER *(at the window)*: Just look at 'em down there . . . Running and racing to work . . . *(He turns and faces his wife and watches her a moment at the stove, and then, suddenly.)* You look young this morning, baby.

RUTH *(indifferently)*: Yeah?

WALTER: Just for a second — stirring them eggs. Just for a second it was — you looked real young again. *(He reaches for her; she crosses away. Then, drily.)* It's gone now — you look like yourself again!

RUTH: Man, if you don't shut up and leave me alone.

WALTER *(looking out to the street again)*: First thing a man ought to learn in life is not to make love to no colored woman first thing in the morning. You all some eeeevil people at eight o'clock in the morning.

(TRAVIS appears in the hall doorway, almost fully dressed and quite wide awake now, his towels and pajamas across his shoulders. He opens the door and signals for his father to make the bathroom in a hurry.)

TRAVIS *(watching the bathroom)*: Daddy, come on!

(WALTER gets his bathroom utensils and flies out to the bathroom.)

RUTH: Sit down and have your breakfast, Travis.

TRAVIS: Mama, this is Friday. *(Gleefully.)* Check coming tomorrow, huh?

RUTH: You get your mind off money and eat your breakfast.

TRAVIS *(eating)*: This is the morning we supposed to bring the fifty cents to school.

RUTH: Well, I ain't got no fifty cents this morning.

TRAVIS: Teacher say we have to.

RUTH: I don't care what teacher say. I ain't got it. Eat your breakfast, Travis.

TRAVIS: I *am* eating.

RUTH: Hush up now and just eat!

(The boy gives her an exasperated look for her lack of understanding and eats grudgingly.)

TRAVIS: You think Grandmama would have it?

RUTH: No! And I want you to stop asking your grandmother for money, you hear me?

TRAVIS *(outraged)*: Gaaaleee! I don't ask her, she just gimme it sometimes!

RUTH: Travis Willard Younger—I got too much on me this morning to
be—

TRAVIS: Maybe Daddy—

RUTH: *Travis!*

(The boy hushes abruptly. They are both quiet and tense for several seconds.)

TRAVIS *(presently):* Could I maybe go carry some groceries in front of the
supermarket for a little while after school then?

RUTH: Just hush, I said. *(TRAVIS jabs his spoon into his cereal bowl viciously
and rests his head in anger upon his fists.)* If you through eating, you can
get over there and make up your bed.

*(The boy obeys stiffly and crosses the room, almost mechanically, to the bed
and more or less folds the bedding into a heap, then angrily gets his books
and cap.)*

TRAVIS *(sulking and standing apart from her unnaturally):* I'm gone.

RUTH *(looking up from the stove to inspect him automatically):* Come here. *(He
crosses to her and she studies his head.)* If you don't take this comb and fix
this here head, you better! *(TRAVIS puts down his books with a great sigh
of oppression and crosses to the mirror. His mother mutters under her breath
about his "slubbornness.")* 'Bout to march out of here with that head
looking just like chickens slept in it! I just don't know where you get
your slubborn ways . . . And get your jacket, too. Looks chilly out
this morning.

TRAVIS *(with conspicuously brushed hair and jacket):* I'm gone.

RUTH: Get carfare and milk money—*(waving one finger)*—and not a single
penny for no caps, you hear me?

TRAVIS *(with sullen politeness):* Yes'm.

*(He turns in outrage to leave. His mother watches after him as in his
frustration he approaches the door almost comically. When she speaks to him,
her voice has become a very gentle tease.)*

RUTH *(mocking; as she thinks he would say it):* Oh, Mama makes me so mad
sometimes, I don't know what to do! *(She waits and continues to his back
as he stands stock-still in front of the door.)* I wouldn't kiss that woman
good-bye for nothing in this world this morning! *(The boy finally turns
around and rolls his eyes at her, knowing the mood has changed and he is
vindicated; he does not however, move toward her yet.)* Not for nothing in
this world! *(She finally laughs aloud at him and holds out her arms to him
and we see that it is a way between them, very old and practiced. He crosses to
her and allows her to embrace him warmly but keeps his face fixed with
masculine rigidity. She holds him back from her presently and looks at him and
runs her fingers over the features of his face. With utter gentleness—)* Now—
whose little old angry man are you?

TRAVIS *(the masculinity and gruffness start to fade at last)*: Aw gaalee— Mama . . .

RUTH *(mimicking)*: Aw—gaaaaalleeeee, Mama! *(She pushes him, with rough playfulness and finality toward the door.)* Get on out of here or you going to be late.

TRAVIS *(in the face of love, new aggressiveness)*: Mama, could I *please* go carry groceries?

RUTH: Honey, it's starting to get so cold evenings.

WALTER *(coming in from the bathroom and drawing a make-believe gun from a make-believe holster and shooting at his son)*: What is it he wants to do?

RUTH: Go carry groceries after school at the supermarket.

WALTER: Well, let him go . . .

TRAVIS *(quickly, to the ally)*: I *have* to—she won't gimme the fifty cents . . .

WALTER *(to his wife only)*: Why not?

RUTH *(simply, and with flavor)*: 'Cause we don't have it.

WALTER *(to RUTH only)*: What you tell the boy things like that for? *(Reaching down into his pants with a rather important gesture.)* Here, son—

(He hands the boy the coin, but his eyes are directed to his wife's. TRAVIS takes the money happily.)

TRAVIS: Thanks, Daddy.

(He starts out. RUTH watches both of them with murder in her eyes. WALTER stands and stares back at her with defiance and suddenly reaches into his pocket again on an afterthought.)

WALTER *(without even looking at his son, still staring hard at his wife)*: In fact, here's another fifty cents . . . Buy yourself some fruit today—or take a taxicab to school or something!

TRAVIS: Whoopee—

(He leaps up and clasps his father around the middle with his legs, and they face each other in mutual appreciation; slowly WALTER LEE peeks around the boy to catch the violent rays from his wife's eyes and draws his head back as if shot.)

WALTER: You better get down now—and get to school, man.

TRAVIS *(at the door)*: O.K. Good-bye.

(He exits.)

WALTER *(after him, pointing with pride)*: That's *my* boy. *(She looks at him in disgust and turns back to her work.)* You know what I was thinking 'bout in the bathroom this morning?

RUTH: No.

WALTER: How come you always try to be so pleasant!

RUTH: What is there to be pleasant 'bout!

WALTER: You want to know what I was thinking 'bout in the bathroom or not!

RUTH: I know what you thinking 'bout.

WALTER *(ignoring her)*: 'Bout what me and Willy Harris was talking about last night.

RUTH *(immediately — a refrain)*: Willy Harris is a good-for-nothing loud-mouth.

WALTER: Anybody who talks to me has got to be a good-for-nothing loudmouth, ain't he? And what you know about who is just a good-for-nothing loudmouth? Charlie Atkins was just a "good-for-nothing loudmouth" too, wasn't he! When he wanted me to go in the dry-cleaning business with him. And now — he's grossing a hundred thousand a year. A hundred thousand dollars a year! You still call *him* a loudmouth!

RUTH *(bitterly)*: Oh, Walter Lee . . .

(She folds her head on her arms over the table.)

WALTER *(rising and coming to her and standing over her)*: You tired, ain't you? Tired of everything. Me, the boy, the way we live — this beat-up hole — everything. Ain't you? *(She doesn't look up, doesn't answer.)* So tired — moaning and groaning all the time, but you wouldn't do nothing to help, would you? You couldn't be on my side that long for nothing, could you?

RUTH: Walter, please leave me alone.

WALTER: A man needs for a woman to back him up . . .

RUTH: Walter —

WALTER: Mama would listen to you. You know she listen to you more than she do me and Bennie. She think more of you. All you have to do is just sit down with her when you drinking your coffee one morning and talking 'bout things like you do and — *(He sits down beside her and demonstrates graphically what he thinks her methods and tone should be.)* — you just sip your coffee, see, and say easy like that you been thinking 'bout that deal Walter Lee is so interested in, 'bout the store and all, and sip some more coffee, like what you saying ain't really that important to you — And the next thing you know, she be listening good and asking you questions and when I come home — I can tell her the details. This ain't no fly-by-night proposition, baby. I mean we figured it out, me and Willy and Bobo.

RUTH *(with a frown)*: Bobo?

WALTER: Yeah. You see, this little liquor store we got in mind cost seventy-five thousand and we figured the initial investment on the place be 'bout thirty thousand, see. That be ten thousand each. Course, there's a couple of hundred you got to pay so's you don't spend your life just waiting for them clowns to let your license get approved —

RUTH: You mean graft?

WALTER *(frowning impatiently)*: Don't call it that. See there, that just goes to show you what women understand about the world. Baby, don't *nothing* happen for you in this world 'less you pay *somebody* off!

RUTH: Walter, leave me alone! *(She raises her head and stares at him vigor-ously — then says, more quietly.)* Eat your eggs, they gonna be cold.

WALTER *(straightening up from her and looking off)*: That's it. There you are. Man say to his woman: I got me a dream. His woman say: Eat your eggs. *(Sadly, but gaining in power.)* Man say: I got to take hold of this here world, baby! And a woman will say: Eat your eggs and go to work. *(Passionately now.)* Man say: I got to change my life, I'm choking to death, baby! And his woman say — *(in utter anguish as he brings his fists down on his thighs)* — Your eggs is getting cold!

RUTH *(softly)*: Walter, that ain't none of our money.

WALTER *(not listening at all or even looking at her)*: This morning, I was lookin' in the mirror and thinking about it . . . I'm thirty-five years old; I been married eleven years and I got a boy who sleeps in the living room — *(very, very quietly)* — and all I got to give him is stories about how rich white people live . . .

RUTH: Eat your eggs, Walter.

WALTER *(slams the table and jumps up)*: —DAMN MY EGGS—DAMN ALL THE EGGS THAT EVER WAS!

RUTH: Then go to work.

WALTER *(looking up at her)*: See—I'm trying to talk to you 'bout myself— *(Shaking his head with the repetition)* — and all you can say is eat them eggs and go to work.

RUTH *(wearily)*: Honey, you never say nothing new. I listen to you every day, every night and every morning, and you never say nothing new. *(Shrugging.)* So you would rather *be* Mr. Arnold than be his chauffeur. So—I would *rather* be living in Buckingham Palace.

WALTER: That is just what is wrong with the colored woman in this world . . . Don't understand about building their men up and making 'em feel like they somebody. Like they can do something.

RUTH *(drily, but to hurt)*: There *are* colored men who do things.

WALTER: No thanks to the colored woman.

RUTH: Well, being a colored woman, I guess I can't help myself none.

(She rises and gets the ironing board and sets it up and attacks a huge pile of rough-dried clothes, sprinkling them in preparation for the ironing and then rolling them into tight fat balls.)

WALTER *(mumbling)*: We one group of men tied to a race of women with small minds!

(His sister BENEATHA enters. She is about twenty, as slim and intense as her brother. She is not as pretty as her sister-in-law, but her lean, almost intellectual face has a handsomeness of its own. She wears a bright red flannel

nightie, and her thick hair stands wildly about her head. Her speech is a mixture of many things; it is different from the rest of the family's insofar as education has permeated her sense of English — and perhaps the Midwest rather than the South has finally — at last — won out in her inflection; but not altogether, because over all of it is a soft slurring and transformed use of vowels which is the decided influence of the Southside. She passes through the room without looking at either RUTH *or* WALTER *and goes to the outside door and looks, a little blindly, out to the bathroom. She sees that it has been lost to the* JOHNSONS. *She closes the door with a sleepy vengeance and crosses to the table and sits down a little defeated.)*

BENEATHA: I am going to start timing those people.

WALTER: You should get up earlier.

BENEATHA *(Her face in her hands. She is still fighting the urge to go back to bed)*: Really — would you suggest dawn? Where's the paper?

WALTER *(pushing the paper across the table to her as he studies her almost clinically, as though he has never seen her before)*: You a horrible-looking chick at this hour.

BENEATHA *(drily)*: Good morning, everybody.

WALTER *(senselessly)*: How is school coming?

BENEATHA *(in the same spirit)*: Lovely. Lovely. And you know, biology is the greatest *(Looking up at him.)* I dissected something that looked just like you yesterday.

WALTER: I just wondered if you've made up your mind and everything.

BENEATHA *(gaining in sharpness and impatience)*: And what did I answer yesterday morning — and the day before that?

RUTH *(from the ironing board, like someone disinterested and old)*: Don't be so nasty, Bennie.

BENEATHA *(still to her brother)*: And the day before that and the day before that!

WALTER *(defensively)*: I'm interested in you. Something wrong with that? Ain't many girls who decide —

WALTER AND BENEATHA *(in unison)*: — "to be a doctor."

(Silence.)

WALTER: Have we figured out yet just exactly how much medical school is going to cost?

RUTH: Walter Lee, why don't you leave that girl alone and get out of here to work?

BENEATHA *(exits to the bathroom and bangs on the door)*: Come on out of there, please!

(She comes back into the room.)

WALTER *(looking at his sister intently)*: You know the check is coming tomorrow.

BENEATHA *(turning on him with a sharpness all her own)*: That money belongs to Mama, Walter, and it's for her to decide how she wants to use it. I don't care if she wants to buy a house or a rocketship or just nail it up somewhere and look at it. It's hers. Not ours — *hers.*

WALTER *(bitterly)*: Now ain't that fine! You just got your mother's interest at heart, ain't you, girl? You such a nice girl — but if Mama got that money she can always take a few thousand and help you through school too — can't she?

BENEATHA: I have never asked anyone around here to do anything for me!

WALTER: No! And the line between asking and just accepting when the time comes is big and wide — ain't it!

BENEATHA *(with fury)*: What do you want from me, Brother — that I quit school or just drop dead, which!

WALTER: I don't want nothing but for you to stop acting holy 'round here. Me and Ruth done made some sacrifices for you — why can't you do something for the family?

RUTH: Walter, don't be dragging me in it.

WALTER: You are in it — Don't you get up and go work in somebody's kitchen for the last three years to help put clothes on her back?

RUTH: Oh, Walter — that's not fair . . .

WALTER: It ain't that nobody expects you to get on your knees and say thank you, Brother; thank you, Ruth; thank you, Mama — and thank you, Travis, for wearing the same pair of shoes for two semesters —

BENEATHA *(dropping to her knees)*: Well — I *do* — all right? — thank everybody! And forgive me for ever wanting to be anything at all! *(Pursuing him on her knees across the floor.)* FORGIVE ME, FORGIVE ME, FORGIVE ME!

RUTH: Please stop it! Your mama'll hear you.

WALTER: Who the hell told you you had to be a doctor? If you so crazy 'bout messing 'round with sick people — then go be a nurse like other women — or just get married and be quiet . . .

BENEATHA: Well — you finally got it said . . . It took you three years but you finally got it said. Walter, give up; leave me alone — it's Mama's money.

WALTER: *He was my father, too!*

BENEATHA: So what? He was mine, too — and Travis' grandfather — but the insurance money belongs to Mama. Picking on me is not going to make her give it to you to invest in any liquor stores — *(underbreath, dropping into a chair)* — and I for one say, God bless Mama for that!

WALTER *(to RUTH)*: See — did you hear? Did you hear!

RUTH: Honey, please go to work.

WALTER: Nobody in this house is ever going to understand me.

BENEATHA: Because you're a nut.

WALTER: Who's a nut?

BENEATHA: You — you are a nut. Thee is mad, boy.

WALTER *(looking at his wife and his sister from the door, very sadly)*: The world's most backward race of people, and that's a fact.

BENEATHA *(turning slowly in her chair)*: And then there are all those prophets who would lead us out of the wilderness — *(WALTER slams out of the house)* — into the swamps!

RUTH: Bennie, why you always gotta be pickin' on your brother? Can't you be a little sweeter sometimes? *(Door opens. WALTER walks in. He fumbles with his cap, starts to speak, clears throat, looks everywhere but at RUTH. Finally.)*

WALTER *(to RUTH)*: I need some money for carfare.

RUTH *(looks at him, then warms; teasing, but tenderly)*: Fifty cents? *(She goes to her bag and gets money.)* Here — take a taxi!

(WALTER exits. MAMA enters. She is a woman in her early sixties, full-bodied and strong. She is one of those women of a certain grace and beauty who wear it so unobtrusively that it takes a while to notice. Her dark brown face is surrounded by the total whiteness of her hair, and, being a woman who has adjusted to many things in life and overcome many more, her face is full of strength. She has, we can see, wit and faith of a kind that keep her eyes lit and full of interest and expectancy. She is, in a word, a beautiful woman. Her bearing is perhaps most like the noble bearing of the women of the Hereros of Southwest Africa — rather as if she imagines that as she walks she still bears a basket or a vessel upon her head. Her speech, on the other hand, is as careless as her carriage is precise — she is inclined to slur everything — but her voice is perhaps not so much quiet as simply soft.)

MAMA: Who that 'round here slamming doors at this hour?

(She crosses through the room, goes to the window, opens it, and brings in a feeble little plant growing doggedly in a small pot on the window sill. She feels the dirt and puts it back out.)

RUTH: That was Walter Lee. He and Bennie was at it again.

MAMA: My children and they tempers. Lord, if this little old plant don't get more sun that it's been getting it ain't never going to see spring again. *(She turns from the window.)* What's the matter with you this morning, Ruth? You looks right peaked. You aiming to iron all them things? Leave some for me. I'll get to 'em this afternoon. Bennie honey, it's too drafty for you to be sitting 'round half dressed. Where's your robe?

BENEATHA: In the cleaners.

MAMA: Well, go get mine and put it on.

BENEATHA: I'm not cold, Mama, honest.

MAMA: I know — but you so thin . . .

BENEATHA *(irritably)*: Mama, I'm not cold.

MAMA *(seeing the make-down bed as* TRAVIS *has left it)*: Lord have mercy, look at that poor bed. Bless his heart — he tries, don't he?

(She moves to the bed TRAVIS *has sloppily made up.)*

RUTH: No — he don't half try at all 'cause he knows you going to come along behind him and fix everything. That's just how come he don't know how to do nothing right now — you done spoiled that boy so.

MAMA *(folding bedding)*: Well — he's a little boy. Ain't supposed to know 'bout housekeeping. My baby, that's what he is. What you fix for his breakfast this morning?

RUTH *(angrily)*: I feed my son, Lena!

MAMA: I ain't meddling — *(Underbreath; busybodyish.)* I just noticed all last week he had cold cereal, and when it starts getting this chilly in the fall a child ought to have some hot grits or something when he goes out in the cold —

RUTH *(furious)*: I gave him hot oats — is that all right!

MAMA: I ain't meddling. *(Pause.)* Put a lot of nice butter on it? *(*RUTH *shoots her an angry look and does not reply.)* He likes lots of butter.

RUTH *(exasperated)*: Lena —

MAMA *(To* BENEATHA. MAMA *is inclined to wander conversationally sometimes.)*: What was you and your brother fussing 'bout this morning?

BENEATHA: It's not important, Mama.

(She gets up and goes to look out at the bathroom, which is apparently free, and she picks up her towels and rushes out.)

MAMA: What was they fighting about?

RUTH: Now you know as well as I do.

MAMA *(shaking her head)*: Brother still worrying hisself sick about that money?

RUTH: You know he is.

MAMA: You had breakfast?

RUTH: Some coffee.

MAMA: Girl, you better start eating and looking after yourself better. You almost thin as Travis.

RUTH: Lena —

MAMA: Un-hunh?

RUTH: What are you going to do with it?

MAMA: Now don't you start, child. It's too early in the morning to be talking about money. It ain't Christian.

RUTH: It's just that he got his heart set on that store —

MAMA: You mean that liquor store that Willy Harris want him to invest in?

RUTH: Yes —

MAMA: We ain't no business people, Ruth. We just plain working folks.

RUTH: Ain't nobody business people till they go into business. Walter Lee say colored people ain't never going to start getting ahead till they start gambling on some different kinds of things in the world—investments and things.

MAMA: What done got into you, girl? Walter Lee done finally sold you on investing.

RUTH: No. Mama, something is happening between Walter and me. I don't know what it is—but he needs something—something I can't give him anymore. He needs this chance, Lena.

MAMA *(frowning deeply)*: But liquor, honey—

RUTH: Well—like Walter say—I spec people going to always be drinking themselves some liquor.

MAMA: Well—whether they drinks it or not ain't none of my business. But whether I go into business selling it to 'em *is,* and I don't want that on my ledger this late in life. *(Stopping suddenly and studying her daughter-in-law.)* Ruth Younger, what's the matter with you today? You look like you could fall over right there.

RUTH: I'm tired.

MAMA: Then you better stay home from work today.

RUTH: I can't stay home. She'd be calling up the agency and screaming at them, "My girl didn't come in today—send me somebody! My girl didn't come in!" Oh, she just have a fit . . .

MAMA: Well, let her have it. I'll just call her up and say you got the flu—

RUTH *(laughing)*: Why the flu?

MAMA: 'Cause it sounds respectable to 'em. Something white people get, too. They know 'bout the flu. Otherwise they think you been cut up or something when you tell 'em you sick.

RUTH: I got to go in. We need the money.

MAMA: Somebody would of thought my children done all but starved to death the way they talk about money here late. Child, we got a great big old check coming tomorrow.

RUTH *(sincerely, but also self-righteously)*: Now that's your money. It ain't got nothing to do with me. We all feel like that—Walter and Bennie and me—even Travis.

MAMA *(thoughtfully, and suddenly very far away)*: Ten thousand dollars—

RUTH: Sure is wonderful.

MAMA: Ten thousand dollars.

RUTH: You know what you should do, Miss Lena? You should take yourself a trip somewhere. To Europe or South America or someplace—

MAMA *(throwing up her hands at the thought)*: Oh, child!

RUTH: I'm serious. Just pack up and leave! Go on away and enjoy yourself some. Forget about the family and have yourself a ball for once in your life—

MAMA *(drily)*: You sound like I'm just about ready to die. Who'd go with me? What I look like wandering 'round Europe by myself?

RUTH: Shoot—these here rich white women do it all the time. They don't think nothing of packing up they suitcases and piling on one of them big steamships and—swoosh!—they gone, child.

MAMA: Something always told me I wasn't no rich white woman.

RUTH: Well—what are you going to do with it then?

MAMA: I ain't rightly decided. *(Thinking. She speaks now with emphasis.)* Some of it got to be put away for Beneatha and her schoolin'—and ain't nothing going to touch that part of it. Nothing. *(She waits several seconds, trying to make up her mind about something, and looks at* RUTH *a little tentatively before going on.)* Been thinking that we maybe could meet the notes on a little old two-story somewhere, with a yard where Travis could play in the summertime, if we use part of the insurance for a down payment and everybody kind of pitch in. I could maybe take on a little day work again, few days a week—

RUTH *(studying her mother-in-law furtively and concentrating on her ironing, anxious to encourage without seeming to)*: Well, Lord knows, we've put enough rent into this here rat trap to pay for four houses by now . . .

MAMA *(looking up at the words "rat trap" and then looking around and leaning back and sighing—in a suddenly reflective mood—)*: "Rat trap"—yes, that's all it is. *(Smiling.)* I remember just as well the day me and Big Walter moved in here. Hadn't been married but two weeks and wasn't planning on living here no more than a year. *(She shakes her head at the dissolved dream.)* We was going to set away, little by little, don't you know, and buy a little place out in Morgan Park. We had even picked out the house. *(Chuckling a little.)* Looks right dumpy today. But Lord, child, you should know all the dreams I had 'bout buying that house and fixing it up and making me a little garden in the back—*(She waits and stops smiling.)* And didn't none of it happen.

(Dropping her hands in a futile gesture.)

RUTH *(keeps her head down, ironing)*: Yes, life can be a barrel of disappointments, sometimes.

MAMA: Honey, Big Walter would come in here some nights back then and slump down on that couch there and just look at the rug, and look at me and look at the rug and then back at me—and I'd know he was down then . . . really down. *(After a second very long and thoughtful pause; she is seeing back to times that only she can see.)* And then, Lord, when I lost that baby—little Claude—I almost thought I was going to lose Big Walter too. Oh, that man grieved hisself! He was one man to love his children.

RUTH: Ain't nothin' can tear at you like losin' your baby.

MAMA: I guess that's how come that man finally worked hisself to death like he done. Like he was fighting his own war with this here world that took his baby from him.

RUTH: He sure was a fine man, all right. I always liked Mr. Younger.

MAMA: Crazy 'bout his children! God knows there was plenty wrong with Walter Younger—hardheaded, mean, kind of wild with women—plenty wrong with him. But he sure loved his children. Always wanted them to have something—be something. That's where Brother gets all these notions, I reckon. Big Walter used to say, he'd get right wet in the eyes sometimes, lean his head back with the water standing in his eyes and say, "Seem like God didn't see fit to give the black man nothing but dreams—but He did give us children to make them dreams seem worthwhile." *(She smiles.)* He could talk like that, don't you know.

RUTH: Yes, he sure could. He was a good man, Mr. Younger.

MAMA: Yes, a fine man—just couldn't never catch up with his dreams, that's all.

(BENEATHA comes in, brushing her hair and looking up to the ceiling, where the sound of a vacuum cleaner has started up.)

BENEATHA: What could be so dirty on that woman's rugs that she has to vacuum them every single day?

RUTH: I wish certain young women 'round here who I could name would take inspiration about certain rugs in a certain apartment I could also mention.

BENEATHA *(shrugging)*: How much cleaning can a house need, for Christ's sakes.

MAMA *(not liking the Lord's name used thus)*: Bennie!

RUTH: Just listen to her—just listen!

BENEATHA: Oh, God!

MAMA: If you use the Lord's name just one more time—

BENEATHA *(a bit of a whine)*: Oh, Mama—

RUTH: Fresh—just fresh as salt, this girl!

BENEATHA *(drily)*: Well—if the salt loses its savor—

MAMA: Now that will do. I just ain't going to have you 'round here reciting the scriptures in vain—you hear me?

BENEATHA: How did I manage to get on everybody's wrong side by just walking into a room?

RUTH: If you weren't so fresh—

BENEATHA: Ruth, I'm twenty years old.

MAMA: What time you be home from school today?

BENEATHA: Kind of late. *(With enthusiasm.)* Madeline is going to start my guitar lessons today.

(MAMA and RUTH look up with the same expression.)

MAMA: Your *what* kind of lessons?

BENEATHA: Guitar.

RUTH: Oh, Father!

MAMA: How come you done taken it in your mind to learn to play the guitar?

BENEATHA: I just want to, that's all.

MAMA (*smiling*): Lord, child, don't you know what to do with yourself? How long it going to be before you get tired of this now—like you got tired of that little play-acting group you joined last year? (*Looking at* RUTH.) And what was it the year before that?

RUTH: The horseback-riding club for which she bought that fifty-five-dollar riding habit that's been hanging in the closet ever since!

MAMA (*to* BENEATHA): Why you got to flit so from one thing to another, baby?

BENEATHA (*sharply*): I just want to learn to play the guitar. Is there anything wrong with that?

MAMA: Ain't nobody trying to stop you. I just wonders sometimes why you has to flit so from one thing to another all the time. You ain't never done nothing with all that camera equipment you brought home—

BENEATHA: I don't flit! I—I experiment with different forms of expression—

RUTH: Like riding a horse?

BENEATHA: —People have to express themselves one way or another.

MAMA: What is it you want to express?

BENEATHA (*angrily*): Me! (MAMA *and* RUTH *look at each other and burst into raucous laughter.*) Don't worry—I don't expect you to understand.

MAMA (*to change the subject*): Who you going out with tomorrow night?

BENEATHA (*with displeasure*): George Murchison again.

MAMA (*pleased*): Oh—you getting a little sweet on him?

RUTH: You ask me, this child ain't sweet on nobody but herself—*Underbreath.*) Express herself!

(*They laugh.*)

BENEATHA: Oh—I like George all right, Mama. I mean I like him enough to go out with him and stuff, but—

RUTH (*for devilment*): What does *and stuff* mean?

BENEATHA: Mind your own business.

MAMA: Stop picking at her now, Ruth. (*She chuckles—then a suspicious sudden look at her daughter as she turns in her chair for emphasis.*) What DOES it mean?

BENEATHA (*wearily*): Oh, I just mean I couldn't ever really be serious about George. He's—he's so shallow.

RUTH: Shallow—what do you mean he's shallow? He's *Rich!*

MAMA: Hush, Ruth.

BENEATHA: I know he's rich. He knows he's rich, too.

RUTH: Well—what other qualities a man got to have to satisfy you, little girl?

BENEATHA: You wouldn't even begin to understand. Anybody who married Walter could not possibly understand.

MAMA *(outraged)*: What kind of way is that to talk about your brother?

BENEATHA: Brother is a flip—let's face it.

MAMA *(To RUTH, helplessly)*: What's a flip?

RUTH *(glad to add kindling)*: She's saying he's crazy.

BENEATHA: Not crazy. Brother isn't really crazy yet—he—he's an elaborate neurotic.

MAMA: Hush your mouth!

BENEATHA: As for George. Well. George looks good—he's got a beautiful car and he takes me to nice places and, as my sister-in-law says, he is probably the richest boy I will ever get to know and I even like him sometimes—but if the Youngers are sitting around waiting to see if their little Bennie is going to tie up the family with the Murchisons, they are wasting their time.

RUTH: You mean you wouldn't marry George Murchison if he asked you someday? That pretty, rich thing? Honey, I knew you was odd—

BENEATHA: No I would not marry him if all I felt for him was what I feel now. Besides, George's family wouldn't really like it.

MAMA: Why not?

BENEATHA: Oh, Mama—The Murchisons are honest-to-God-real-*live*-rich colored people, and the only people in the world who are more snobbish than rich white people are rich colored people. I thought everybody knew that. I've met Mrs. Murchison. She's a scene!

MAMA: You must not dislike people 'cause they well off, honey.

BENEATHA: Why not? It makes just as much sense as disliking people 'cause they are poor, and lots of people do that.

RUTH *(A wisdom-of-the-ages manner. To MAMA.)*: Well, she'll get over some of this—

BENEATHA: Get over it? What are you talking about, Ruth? Listen, I'm going to be a doctor. I'm not worried about who I'm going to marry yet—if I ever get married.

MAMA AND RUTH: *If!*

MAMA: Now, Bennie—

BENEATHA: Oh, I probably will . . . but first I'm going to be a doctor, and George, for one, still thinks that's pretty funny. I couldn't be bothered with that. I am going to be a doctor and everybody around here better understand that!

MAMA *(kindly)*: 'Course you going to be a doctor, honey, God willing.

BENEATHA *(drily)*: God hasn't got a thing to do with it.

MAMA: Beneatha—that just wasn't necessary.

BENEATHA: Well—neither is God. I get sick of hearing about God.

MAMA: Beneatha!

BENEATHA: I mean it! I'm just tired of hearing about God all the time. What has He got to do with anything? Does he pay tuition?

MAMA: You 'bout to get your fresh little jaw slapped!

RUTH: That's just what she needs, all right!

BENEATHA: Why? Why can't I say what I want to around here, like everybody else?

MAMA: It don't sound nice for a young girl to say things like that — you wasn't brought up that way. Me and your father went to trouble to get you and Brother to church every Sunday.

BENEATHA: Mama, you don't understand. It's all a matter of ideas, and God is just one idea I don't accept. It's not important. I am not going out and be immoral or commit crimes because I don't believe in God. I don't even think about it. It's just that I get tired of Him getting credit for all the things the human race achieves through its own stubborn effort. There simply is no blasted God — there is only man and it is *he* who makes miracles!

(MAMA *absorbs this speech, studies her daughter and rises slowly and crosses to* BENEATHA *and slaps her powerfully across the face. After, there is only silence and the daughter drops her eyes from her mother's face, and* MAMA *is very tall before her.*)

MAMA: Now — you say after me, in my mother's house there is still God. (*There is a long pause and* BENEATHA *stares at the floor wordlessly.* MAMA *repeats the phrase with precision and cool emotion.*) In my mother's house there is still God.

BENEATHA: In my mother's house there is still God.

(*A long pause.*)

MAMA (*Walking away from* BENEATHA, *too disturbed for triumphant posture. Stopping and turning back to her daughter.*): There are some ideas we ain't going to have in this house. Not long as I am at the head of this family.

BENEATHA: Yes, ma'am.

(MAMA *walks out of the room.*)

RUTH (*almost gently, with profound understanding*): You think you a woman, Bennie — but you still a little girl. What you did was childish — so you got treated like a child.

BENEATHA: I see. (*Quietly.*) I also see that everybody thinks it's all right for Mama to be a tyrant. But all the tyranny in the world will never put a God in the heavens!

(*She picks up her books and goes out. Pause.*)

RUTH (*goes to* MAMA*'s door*): She said she was sorry.

MAMA (*coming out, going to her plant*): They frightens me, Ruth. My children.

RUTH: You got good children, Lena. They just a little off sometimes — but they're good.

MAMA: No—there's something come down between me and them that don't let us understand each other and I don't know what it is. One done almost lost his mind thinking 'bout money all the time and the other done commence to talk about things I can't seem to understand in no form or fashion. What is it that's changing, Ruth.

RUTH *(soothingly, older than her years)*: Now . . . you taking it all too seriously. You just got strong-willed children and it takes a strong woman like you to keep 'em in hand.

MAMA *(looking at her plant and sprinkling a little water on it)*: They spirited all right, my children. Got to admit they got spirit—Bennie and Walter. Like this little old plant that ain't never had enough sunshine or nothing—and look at it . . .

(She has her back to RUTH, *who has had to stop ironing and lean against something and put the back of her hand to her forehead.)*

RUTH *(trying to keep* MAMA *from noticing)*: You sure . . . sure . . . loves that little old thing, don't you? . . .

MAMA: Well, I always wanted me a garden like I used to see sometimes at the back of the houses down home. This plant is close as I ever got to having one. *(She looks out the window as she replaces the plant.)* Lord, ain't nothing as dreary as the view from this window on a dreary day, is there? Why ain't you singing this morning, Ruth? Sing that "No Ways Tired." That song always lifts me up so—*(She turns at last to see that* RUTH *has slipped quietly to the floor, in a state of semiconsciousness.)* Ruth! Ruth honey—what's the matter with you . . . Ruth!

Scene II *(It is the following morning; a Saturday morning, and house cleaning is in progress at the Youngers'. Furniture has been shoved hither and yon and* MAMA *is giving the kitchen-area walls a washing down.* BENEATHA, *in dungarees, with a handkerchief tied around her face, is spraying insecticide into the cracks in the walls. As they work, the radio is on and a Southside disk jockey program is inappropriately filling the house with a rather exotic saxophone blues.* TRAVIS, *the sole idle one, is leaning on his arms, looking out of the window.)*

TRAVIS: Grandmama, that stuff Bennie is using smells awful. Can I go downstairs, please?

MAMA: Did you get all them chores done already? I ain't seen you doing much.

TRAVIS: Yes'm—finished early. Where did Mama go this morning?

MAMA *(looking at* BENEATHA*)*: She had to go on a little errand.

(The phone rings. BENEATHA *runs to answer it and reaches it before Walter, who has entered from bedroom.)*

TRAVIS: Where?

MAMA: To tend to her business.

BENEATHA: Haylo . . . *(Disappointed.)* Yes, he is. *(She tosses the phone to* WALTER, *who barely catches it.)* It's Willie Harris again.

WALTER *(as privately as possible under* MAMA's *gaze)*: Hello, Willie. Did you get the papers from the lawyer? . . . No, not yet. I told you the mailman doesn't get here till ten-thirty . . . No, I'll come there . . . Yeah! Right away. *(He hangs up and goes for his coat.)*

BENEATHA: Brother, where did Ruth go?

WALTER *(as he exits)*: How should I know!

TRAVIS: Aw come on, Grandma. Can I go outside?

MAMA: Oh, I guess so. You stay right in front of the house, though, and keep a good lookout for the postman.

TRAVIS: Yes'm. *(He darts into bedroom for stickball and bat, reenters, and sees* BENEATHA *on her knees spraying under sofa with behind upraised. He edges closer to the target, takes aim, and lets her have it. She screams.)* Leave them poor little cockroaches alone, they ain't bothering you none! *(He runs as she swings the spraygun at him viciously and playfully.)* Grandma! Grandma!

MAMA: Look out there, girl, before you be spilling some of that stuff on that child!

TRAVIS *(safely behind the bastion of* MAMA*)*: That's right — look out, now! *(He exits.)*

BENEATHA *(drily)*: I can't imagine that it would hurt him — it has never hurt the roaches.

MAMA: Well, little boys' hides ain't as tough as Southside roaches. You better get over there behind the bureau. I seen one marching out of there like Napoleon yesterday.

BENEATHA: There's really only one way to get rid of them, Mama —

MAMA: How?

BENEATHA: Set fire to this building! Mama, where did Ruth go?

MAMA *(looking at her with meaning)*: To the doctor, I think.

BENEATHA: The doctor? What's the matter? *(They exchange glances.)* You don't think —

MAMA *(with her sense of drama)*: Now I ain't saying what I think. But I ain't never been wrong 'bout a woman neither.

(The phone rings.)

BENEATHA *(at the phone)*: Hay-lo . . . *(Pause, and a moment of recognition.)* Well — when did you get back! . . . And how was it? . . . Of course I've missed you — in my way . . . This morning? No . . . house cleaning and all that and Mama hates it if I let people come over when the house is like this . . . You *have?* Well, that's different . . . What is it — Oh, what the hell, come on over . . . Right, see you then. *Arrividerci.*

(She hangs up.)

MAMA *(who has listened vigorously, as is her habit)*: Who is that you inviting over here with this house looking like this? You ain't got the pride you was born with!

BENEATHA: Asagai doesn't care how houses look, Mama—he's an intellectual.

MAMA: *Who?*

BENEATHA: Asagai—Joseph Asagai. He's an African boy I met on campus. He's been studying in Canada all summer.

MAMA: What's his name?

BENEATHA: Asagai, Joseph. Ah-sah-guy . . . He's from Nigeria.

MAMA: Oh, that's the little country that was founded by slaves way back . . .

BENEATHA: No, Mama—that's Liberia.

MAMA: I don't think I never met no African before.

BENEATHA: Well, do me a favor and don't ask him a whole lot of ignorant questions about Africans. I mean, do they wear clothes and all that—

MAMA: Well, now, I guess if you think we so ignorant 'round here maybe you shouldn't bring your friends here—

BENEATHA: It's just that people ask such crazy things. All anyone seems to know about when it comes to Africa is Tarzan—

MAMA *(indignantly)*: Why should I know anything about Africa?

BENEATHA: Why do you give money at church for the missionary work?

MAMA: Well, that's to help save people.

BENEATHA: You mean save them from *heathenism*—

MAMA *(innocently)*: Yes.

BENEATHA: I'm afraid they need more salvation from the British and the French.

(RUTH comes in forlornly and pulls off her coat with dejection. They both turn to look at her.)

RUTH *(dispiritedly)*: Well, I guess from all the happy faces—everybody knows.

BENEATHA: You pregnant?

MAMA: Lord have mercy, I sure hope it's a little old girl. Travis ought to have a sister.

(BENEATHA and RUTH give her a hopeless look for this grandmotherly enthusiasm.)

BENEATHA: How far along are you?

RUTH: Two months.

BENEATHA: Did you mean to? I mean did you plan it or was it an accident?

MAMA: What do you know about planning or not planning?

BENEATHA: Oh, Mama.

RUTH *(wearily)*: She's twenty years old, Lena.

BENEATHA: Did you plan it, Ruth?

RUTH: Mind your own business.

BENEATHA: It is my business—where is he going to live, on the *roof?* *(There is silence following the remark as the three women react to the sense of it.)* Gee—I didn't mean that, Ruth, honest. Gee, I don't feel like that at all. I—I think it is wonderful.

RUTH *(dully)*: Wonderful.

BENEATHA: Yes—really.

MAMA *(looking at* RUTH, *worried)*: Doctor say everything going to be all right?

RUTH *(far away)*: Yes—she says everything is going to be fine . . .

MAMA *(immediately suspicious)*: "She"—What doctor you went to?

*(*RUTH *folds over, near hysteria.)*

MAMA *(worriedly hovering over* RUTH*)*: Ruth honey—what's the matter with you—you sick?

*(*RUTH *has her fists clenched on her thighs and is fighting hard to suppress a scream that seems to be rising in her.)*

BENEATHA: What's the matter with her, Mama?

MAMA *(working her fingers in* RUTH's *shoulders to relax her)*: She be all right. Women gets right depressed sometimes when they get her way. *(Speaking softly, expertly, rapidly.)* Now you just relax. That's right . . . just lean back, don't think 'bout nothing at all . . . nothing at all—

RUTH: I'm all right . . .

(The glassy-eyed look melts and then she collapses into a fit of heavy sobbing. The bell rings.)

BENEATHA: Oh, my God—that must be Asagai.

MAMA *(to* RUTH*)*: Come on now, honey. You need to lie down and rest awhile . . . then have some nice hot food.

(They exit, RUTH's *weight on her mother-in-law.* BENEATHA, *herself profoundly disturbed, opens the door to admit a rather dramatic-looking young man with a large package.)*

ASAGAI: Hello, Alaiyo—

BENEATHA *(holding the door open and regarding him with pleasure)*: Hello . . . *(Long pause.)* Well—come in. And please excuse everything. My mother was very upset about my letting anyone come here with the place like this.

ASAGAI *(coming into the room)*: You look disturbed too . . . Is something wrong?

BENEATHA *(still at the door, absently)*: Yes . . . we've all got acute ghetto-itus. *(She smiles and comes toward him, finding a cigarette and sitting.)* So—sit down! No! Wait! *(She whips the spraygun off sofa where she had left it and puts the cushions back. At last perches on arm of sofa. He sits.)* So, how was Canada?

ASAGAI *(a sophisticate)*: Canadian.

BENEATHA *(looking at him)*: Asagai, I'm very glad you are back.

ASAGAI *(looking back at her in turn)*: Are you really?

BENEATHA: Yes — very.

ASAGAI: Why? — you were quite glad when I went away. What happened?

BENEATHA: You went away.

ASAGAI: Ahhhhhhhh.

BENEATHA: Before — you wanted to be so serious before there was time.

ASAGAI: How much time must there be before one knows what one feels?

BENEATHA *(Stalling this particular conversation. Her hands pressed together, in a deliberately childish gesture)*: What did you bring me?

ASAGAI *(handing her the package)*: Open it and see.

BENEATHA *(eagerly opening the package and drawing out some records and the colorful robes of a Nigerian woman)*: Oh, Asagai! . . . You got them for me! . . . How beautiful . . . and the records too! *(She lifts out the robes and runs to the mirror with them and holds the drapery up in front of herself.)*

ASAGAI *(coming to her at the mirror)*: I shall have to teach you how to drape it properly. *(He flings the material about her for the moment and stands back to look at her.)* Ah — Oh-pay-gay-day, oh-gbah-mu-shay. *(A Yoruba exclamation for admiration.)* You wear it well . . . very well . . . mutilated hair and all.

BENEATHA *(turning suddenly)*: My hair — what's wrong with my hair?

ASAGAI *(shrugging)*: Were you born with it like that?

BENEATHA *(reaching up to touch it)*: No . . . of course not.

(She looks back to the mirror, disturbed.)

ASAGAI *(smiling)*: How then?

BENEATHA: You know perfectly well how . . . as crinkly as yours . . . that's how.

ASAGAI: And it is ugly to you that way?

BENEATHA *(quickly)*: Oh, no — not ugly . . . *(More slowly, apologetically.)* But it's so hard to manage when it's, well — raw.

ASAGAI: And so to accommodate that — you mutilate it every week?

BENEATHA: It's not mutilation!

ASAGAI *(laughing aloud at her seriousness)*: Oh . . . please! I am only teasing you because you are so very serious about these things. *(He stands back from her and folds his arms across his chest as he watches her pulling at her hair and frowning in the mirror.)* Do you remember the first time you met me at school? . . . *(He laughs.)* You came up to me and you said — and I thought you were the most serious little thing I had ever seen — you said: *(He imitates her.)* "Mr. Asagai — I want very much to talk with you. About Africa. You see, Mr. Asagai, I am looking for my *identity!*"

(He laughs.)

BENEATHA *(turning to him, not laughing)*: Yes —

(Her face is quizzical, profoundly disturbed.)

ASAGAI *(still teasing and reaching out and taking her face in his hands and turning her profile to him)*: Well . . . it is true that this is not sc much a profile of a Hollywood queen as perhaps a queen of the Nile — *(A mock dismissal of the importance of the question.)* But what does it matter? Assimilationism is so popular in your country.

BENEATHA *(wheeling, passionately, sharply)*: I am not an assimilationist!

ASAGAI *(the protest hangs in the room for a moment and* ASAGAI *studies her, his laughter fading)*: Such a serious one. *(There is a pause.)* So — you like the robes? You must take excellent care of them — they are from my sister's personal wardrobe.

BENEATHA *(with incredulity)*: You — you sent all the way home — for me?

ASAGAI *(with charm)*: For you — I would do much more . . . Well, that is what I came for. I must go.

BENEATHA: Will you call me Monday?

ASAGAI: Yes . . . We have a great deal to talk about. I mean about identity and time and all that.

BENEATHA: Time?

ASAGAI: Yes. About how much time one needs to know what one feels.

BENEATHA: You see! You never understood that there is more than one kind of feeling which can exist between a man and a woman — or, at least, there should be.

ASAGAI *(shaking his head negatively but gently)*: No. Between a man and a woman there need be only one kind of feeling. I have that for you . . . Now even . . . right this moment . . .

BENEATHA: I know — and by itself — it won't do. I can find that anywhere.

ASAGAI: For a woman it should be enough.

BENEATHA: I know — because that's what it says in all the novels that men write. But it isn't. Go ahead and laugh — but I'm not interested in being someone's little episode in America or — *(with feminine vengeance)* — one of them! *(*ASAGAI *has burst into laughter again.)* That's funny as hell, huh!

ASAGAI: It's just that every American girl I have known has said that to me. White — black — in this you are all the same. And the same speech, too!

BENEATHA *(angrily)*: Yuk, yuk, yuk!

ASAGAI: It's how you can be sure that the world's most liberated women are not liberated at all. You all talk about it too much!

*(*MAMA *enters and is immediately all social charm because of the presence of a guest.)*

BENEATHA: Oh—Mama—this is Mr. Asagai.

MAMA: How do you do?

ASAGAI *(total politeness to an elder)*: How do you do, Mrs. Younger. Please forgive me for coming at such an outrageous hour on a Saturday.

MAMA: Well, you are quite welcome. I just hope you understand that our house don't always look like this. *(Chatterish.)* You must come again. I would love to hear all about—*(not sure of the name)*—your country. I think it's so sad the way our American Negroes don't know nothing about Africa 'cept Tarzan and all that. And all that money they pour into these churches when they ought to be helping you people over there drive out them French and Englishmen done taken away your land.

(The mother flashes a slightly superior look at her daughter upon completion of the recitation.)

ASAGAI *(taken aback by this sudden and acutely unrelated expression of sympathy)*: Yes . . . yes . . .

MAMA *(smiling at him suddenly and relaxing and looking him over)*: How many miles is it from here to where you come from?

ASAGAI: Many thousands.

MAMA *(looking at him as she would WALTER)*: I bet you don't half look after yourself, being away from your mama either. I spec you better come 'round here from time to time to get yourself some decent home-cooked meals . . .

ASAGAI *(moved)*: Thank you. Thank you very much. *(They are all quiet, then—)* Well . . . I must go. I will call you Monday, Alaiyo.

MAMA: What's that he call you?

ASAGAI: Oh—"Alaiyo." I hope you don't mind. It is what you would call a nickname, I think. It is a Yoruba word. I am a Yoruba.

MAMA *(looking at BENEATHA)*: I—I thought he was from—*(Uncertain.)*

ASAGAI *(understanding)*: Nigeria is my country. Yoruba is my tribal origin—

BENEATHA: You didn't tell us what Alaiyo means . . . for all I know, you might be calling me Little Idiot or something . . .

ASAGAI: Well . . . let me see . . . I do not know how just to explain it . . . The sense of a thing can be so different when it changes languages.

BENEATHA: You're evading.

ASAGAI: No—really it is difficult . . . *(Thinking.)* It means . . . it means One for Whom Bread—Food—Is Not Enough. *(He looks at her.)* Is that all right?

BENEATHA *(understanding, softly)*: Thank you.

MAMA *(looking from one to the other and not understanding any of it)*: Well . . . that's nice . . . You must come see us again—Mr.—

ASAGAI: Ah-sah-guy . . .

MAMA: Yes . . . Do come again.

ASAGAI: Good-bye.

(He exits.)

MAMA *(after him)*: Lord, that's a pretty thing just went out here! *(Insinuatingly, to her daughter.)* Yes, I guess I see why we done commence to get so interested in Africa 'round here. Missionaries my aunt Jenny!

(She exits.)

BENEATHA: Oh, Mama! . . .

(She picks up the Nigerian dress and holds it up to her in front of the mirror again. She sets the headdress on haphazardly and then notices her hair again and clutches at it and then replaces the headdress and frowns at herself. Then she starts to wriggle in front of the mirror as she thinks a Nigerian woman might. TRAVIS *enters and stands regarding her.)*

TRAVIS: What's the matter, girl, you cracking up?

BENEATHA: Shut up.

(She pulls the headdress off and looks at herself in the mirror and clutches at her hair again and squinches her eyes as if trying to imagine something. Then, suddenly, she gets her raincoat and kerchief and hurriedly prepares for going out.)

MAMA *(coming back into the room)*: She's resting now. Travis, baby, run next door and ask Miss Johnson to please let me have a little kitchen cleanser. This here can is empty as Jacob's kettle.

TRAVIS: I just came in.

MAMA: Do as you told. *(He exits and she looks at her daughter.)* Where you going?

BENEATHA *(halting at the door)*: To become a queen of the Nile!

(She exits in a breathless blaze of glory. RUTH *appears in the bedroom doorway.)*

MAMA: Who told you to get up?

RUTH: Ain't nothing wrong with me to be lying in no bed for. Where did Bennie go?

MAMA *(drumming her fingers)*: Far as I could make out — to Egypt. *(*RUTH *just looks at her.)* What time is it getting to?

RUTH: Ten twenty. And the mailman going to ring that bell this morning just like he done every morning for the last umpteen years.

*(*TRAVIS *comes in with the cleanser can.)*

TRAVIS: She say to tell you that she don't have much.

MAMA *(angrily)*: Lord, some people I could name sure is tight-fisted! *(Directing her grandson.)* Mark two cans of cleanser down on the list there. If she that hard up for kitchen cleanser, I sure don't want to forget to get her none!

RUTH: Lena — maybe the woman is just short on cleanser —

MAMA *(not listening)*: — Much baking powder as she done borrowed from me all these years, she could of done gone into the baking business!

(The bell sounds suddenly and sharply and all three are stunned — serious and silent — mid-speech. In spite of all the other conversations and distractions of the morning, this is what they have been waiting for, even TRAVIS, who looks helplessly from his mother to his grandmother. RUTH is the first to come to life again.)

RUTH *(to TRAVIS)*: *Get down them steps, boy!*

(TRAVIS snaps to life and flies out to get the mail.)

MAMA *(her eyes wide, her hand to her breast)*: You mean it done really come?

RUTH *(excited)*: Oh, Miss Lena!

MAMA *(collecting herself)*: Well . . . I don't know what we all so excited about 'round here for. We known it was coming for months.

RUTH: That's a whole lot different from having it come and being able to hold it in your hands . . . a piece of paper worth ten thousand dollars . . . *(TRAVIS bursts back into the room. He holds the envelope high above his head, like a little dancer, his face is radiant and he is breathless. He moves to his grandmother with sudden slow ceremony and puts the envelope into her hands. She accepts it, and then merely holds it and looks at it.)* Come on! Open it . . . Lord have mercy, I wish Walter Lee was here!

TRAVIS: Open it, Grandmama!

MAMA *(staring at it)*: Now you all be quiet. It's just a check.

RUTH: Open it . . .

MAMA *(still staring at it)*: Now don't act silly . . . We ain't never been no people to act silly 'bout no money —

RUTH *(swiftly)*: We ain't never had none before — OPEN IT!

(MAMA finally makes a good strong tear and pulls out the thin blue slice of paper and inspects it closely. The boy and his mother study it raptly over MAMA's shoulders.)

MAMA: *Travis!* (She is counting off with doubt.) Is that the right number of zeros.

TRAVIS: Yes'm . . . ten thousand dollars. Gaalee, Grandmama, you rich.

MAMA *(She holds the check away from her, still looking at it. Slowly her face sobers into a mask of unhappiness)*: Ten thousand dollars. *(She hands it to RUTH.)* Put it away somewhere, Ruth. *(She does not look at RUTH; her eyes seem to be seeing something somewhere very far off.)* Ten thousand dollars they give you. Ten thousand dollars.

TRAVIS *(to his mother, sincerely)*: What's the matter with Grandmama — don't she want to be rich?

RUTH *(distractedly)*: You go on out and play now, baby. *(TRAVIS exits. MAMA starts wiping dishes absently, humming intently to herself. RUTH turns to her, with kind exasperation.)* You've gone and got yourself upset.

MAMA *(not looking at her)*: I spec if it wasn't for you all . . . I would just put that money away or give it to the church or something.

RUTH: Now what kind of talk is that. Mr. Younger would just be plain mad if he could hear you talking foolish like that.

MAMA *(stopping and staring off)*: Yes . . . he sure would. *(Sighing.)* We got enough to do with that money, all right. *(She halts then, and turns and looks at her daughter-in-law hard;* RUTH *avoids her eyes and* MAMA *wipes her hands with finality and starts to speak firmly to* RUTH.*)* Where did you go today, girl?

RUTH: To the doctor.

MAMA *(impatiently)*: Now, Ruth . . . you know better than that. Old Doctor Jones is strange enough in his way but there ain't nothing 'bout him make somebody slip and call him "she" — like you done this morning.

RUTH: Well, that's what happened — my tongue slipped.

MAMA: You went to see that woman, didn't you?

RUTH *(defensively, giving herself away)*: What woman you talking about?

MAMA *(angrily)*: That woman who —

*(*WALTER *enters in great excitement.)*

WALTER: Did it come?

MAMA *(quietly)*: Can't you give people a Christian greeting before you start asking about money?

WALTER *(to* RUTH*)*: Did it come? *(*RUTH *unfolds the check and lays it quietly before him, watching him intently with thoughts of her own.* WALTER *sits down and grasps it close and counts off the zeros.)* Ten thousand dollars — *(He turns suddenly, frantically to his mother and draws some papers out of his breast pocket.)* Mama — look. Old Willy Harris put everything on paper —

MAMA: Son — I think you ought to talk to your wife . . . I'll go on out and leave you alone if you want —

WALTER: I can talk to her later — Mama, look —

MAMA: Son —

WALTER: WILL SOMEBODY PLEASE LISTEN TO ME TODAY!

MAMA *(quietly)*: I don't 'low no yellin' in this house, Walter Lee, and you know it — *(*WALTER *stares at them in frustration and starts to speak several times.)* And there ain't going to be no investing in no liquor stores.

WALTER: But, Mama, you ain't even looked at it.

MAMA: I don't aim to have to speak on that again.

(A long pause.)

WALTER: You ain't looked at it and you don't aim to have to speak on that again? You ain't even looked at it and *you* have decided — *(Crumpling his papers.)* Well, *you* tell that to my boy tonight when you put him to sleep on the living room couch . . . *(Turning to* MAMA *and speaking directly to her.)* Yeah — and tell it to my wife, Mama, tomorrow when she has to go out of here to look after somebody else's kids. And tell it to *me,* Mama, every time we need a new pair of curtains and I have to watch *you* go out and work in somebody's kitchen. Yeah, you tell me then!

(WALTER *starts out.*)

RUTH: Where you going?

WALTER: I'm going out!

RUTH: Where?

WALTER: Just out of this house somewhere —

RUTH *(getting her coat)*: I'll come too.

WALTER: I don't want you to come!

RUTH: I got something to talk to you about, Walter.

WALTER: That's too bad.

MAMA *(still quietly)*: Walter Lee — *(She waits and he finally turns and looks at her.)* Sit down.

WALTER: I'm a grown man, Mama.

MAMA: Ain't nobody said you wasn't grown. But you still in my house and my presence. And as long as you are — you'll talk to your wife civil. Now sit down.

RUTH *(suddenly)*: Oh, let him go on out and drink himself to death! He makes me sick to my stomach! *(She flings her coat against him and exits to bedroom.)*

WALTER *(violently flinging the coat after her)*: And you turn mine too, baby! *(The door slams behind her.)* That was my biggest mistake —

MAMA *(still quietly)*: Walter, what is the matter with you?

WALTER: Matter with me? Ain't nothing the matter with *me!*

MAMA: Yes there is. Something eating you up like a crazy man. Something more than me not giving you this money. The past few years I been watching it happen to you. You get all nervous acting and kind of wild in the eyes — (WALTER *jumps up impatiently at her words.*) I said sit there now, I'm talking to you!

WALTER: Mama — I don't need no nagging at me today.

MAMA: Seem like you getting to a place where you always tied up in some kind of knot about something. But if anybody ask you 'bout it you just yell at 'em and bust out the house and go out and drink somewheres. Walter Lee, people can't live with that. Ruth's a good, patient girl in her way — but you getting to be too much. Boy, don't make the mistake of driving that girl away from you.

WALTER: Why — what she do for me?

MAMA: She loves you.

WALTER: Mama — I'm going out. I want to go off somewhere and be by myself for a while.

MAMA: I'm sorry 'bout your liquor store, son. It just wasn't the thing for us to do. That's what I want to tell you about —

WALTER: I got to go out, Mama—

(*He rises.*)

MAMA: It's dangerous, son.

WALTER: What's dangerous?

MAMA: When a man goes outside his home to look for peace.

WALTER (*beseechingly*): Then why can't there never be no peace in this house then?

MAMA: You done found it in some other house?

WALTER: No—there ain't no woman! Why do women always think there's a woman somewhere when a man gets restless. (*Picks up the check.*) Do you know what this money means to me? Do you know what this money can do for us? (*Puts it back.*) Mama—Mama—I want so many things . . .

MAMA: Yes, son—

WALTER: I want so many things that they are driving me kind of crazy . . . Mama—look at me.

MAMA: I'm looking at you. You a good-looking boy. You got a job, a nice wife, a fine boy and—

WALTER: A job. (*Looks at her.*) Mama, a job? I open and close car doors all day long. I drive a man around in his limousine and I say, "Yes, sir; no, sir; very good, sir; shall I take the Drive, sir?" Mama, that ain't no kind of job . . . that ain't nothing at all. (*Very quietly.*) Mama, I don't know if I can make you understand.

MAMA: Understand what, baby?

WALTER (*quietly*): Sometimes it's like I can see the future stretched out in front of me—just plain as day. The future, Mama. Hanging over there at the edge of my days. Just waiting for me—a big, looming blank space—full of *nothing*. Just waiting for *me*. But it don't have to be. (*Pause. Kneeling beside her chair.*) Mama—sometimes when I'm downtown and I pass them cool, quiet-looking restaurants where them white boys are sitting back and talking 'bout things . . . sitting there turning deals worth millions of dollars . . . sometimes I see guys don't look much older than me—

MAMA: Son—how come you talk so much 'bout money?

WALTER (*with immense passion*): Because it is life, Mama!

MAMA (*quietly*): Oh—(*Very quietly.*) So now it's life. Money is life. Once upon a time freedom used to be life—now it's money. I guess the world really do change . . .

WALTER: No—it was always money, Mama. We just didn't know about it.

MAMA: No . . . something has changed. (*She looks at him.*) You something new, boy. In my time we was worried about not being lynched and getting to the North if we could and how to stay alive and still have a pinch of dignity too . . . Now here come you and Beneatha—talking 'bout things we ain't never even thought about hardly, me and your daddy. You ain't satisfied or proud of nothing we done. I mean that you had a home; that we kept you out of trouble till you was grown; that you don't have to ride to work on the back of nobody's streetcar — You my children — but how different we done become.

WALTER *(A long beat. He pats her hand and gets up.)*: You just don't understand, Mama, you just don't understand.

MAMA: Son — do you know your wife is expecting another baby? *(WAL-TER stands, stunned, and absorbs what his mother has said.)* That's what she wanted to talk to you about. *(WALTER sinks down into a chair.)* This ain't for me to be telling — but you ought to know. *(She waits.)* I think Ruth is thinking 'bout getting rid of that child.

WALTER *(slowly understanding)*: — No — no — Ruth wouldn't do that.

MAMA: When the world gets ugly enough — a woman will do anything for her family. *The part that's already living.*

WALTER: You don't know Ruth, Mama, if you think she would do that.

(RUTH opens the bedroom door and stands there a little limp.)

RUTH *(beaten)*: Yes I would too, Walter. *(Pause.)* I gave her a five-dollar down payment.

(There is total silence as the man stares at his wife and the mother stares at her son.)

MAMA *(presently)*: Well — *(Tightly.)* Well — son, I'm waiting to hear you say something . . . *(She waits.)* I'm waiting to hear how you be your father's son. Be the man he was . . . *(Pause. The silence shouts.)* Your wife says she going to destroy your child. And I'm waiting to hear you talk like him and say we a people who give children life, not who destroys them — *(She rises.)* I'm waiting to see you stand up and look like your daddy and say we done give up one baby to poverty and that we ain't going to give nary another one . . . I'm waiting.

WALTER: Ruth — *(He can say nothing.)*

MAMA: If you a son of mine, tell her! *(WALTER picks up his keys and his coat and walks out. She continues, bitterly.)* You . . . you are a disgrace to your father's memory. Somebody get me my hat!

ACT II

Scene I

(Time: Later the same day.)

(At rise: RUTH *is ironing again. She has the radio going. Presently* BE-NEATHA's *bedroom door opens and* RUTH's *mouth falls and she puts down the iron in fascination.)*

RUTH: What have we got on tonight!

BENEATHA *(emerging grandly from the doorway so that we can see her thoroughly robed in the costume* ASAGAI *brought):* You are looking at what a well-dressed Nigerian woman wears — *(She parades for* RUTH, *her hair completely hidden by the headdress; she is coquettishly fanning herself with an ornate oriental fan, mistakenly more like Butterfly than any Nigerian that ever was.)* Isn't it beautiful? *(She promenades to the radio and, with an arrogant flourish, turns off the good loud blues that is playing.)* Enough of this assimilationist junk! *(*RUTH *follows her with her eyes as she goes to the phonograph and puts on a record and turns and waits ceremoniously for the music to come up. Then, with a shout —)* OCOMOGOSIAY!

*(*RUTH *jumps. The music comes up, a lovely Nigerian melody.* BENEATHA *listens, enraptured, her eyes far away — "back to the past." She begins to dance.* RUTH *is dumfounded.)*

RUTH: What kind of dance is that?

BENEATHA: A folk dance.

RUTH *(Pearl Bailey):* What kind of folks do that, honey?

BENEATHA: It's from Nigeria. It's a dance of welcome.

RUTH: Who you welcoming?

BENEATHA: The men back to the village.

RUTH: Where they been?

BENEATHA: How should I know — out hunting or something. Anyway, they are coming back now . . .

RUTH: Well, that's good.

BENEATHA *(with the record):* Alundi, alundi
Alundi alunya
Jop pu a jeepua
Ang gu sooooooooooo

Ai yai yae . . .
Ayehaye — alundi . . .

*(*WALTER *comes in during this performance; he has obviously been drinking. He leans against the door heavily and watches his sister, at first with distaste. Then his eyes look off — "back to the past" — as he lifts both his fists to the roof, screaming.)*

WALTER: YEAH . . . AND ETHIOPIA STRETCH FORTH HER HANDS AGAIN! . . .

RUTH *(drily, looking at him):* Yes — and Africa sure is claiming her own tonight. *(She gives them both up and starts ironing again.)*

WALTER *(all in a drunken, dramatic shout):* Shut up! . . . I'm digging them drums . . . them drums move me! . . . *(He makes his weaving way to his wife's face and leans in close to her.)* In my *heart of hearts* — *(He thumps his chest)* — I am much warrior!

RUTH *(without even looking up):* In your heart of hearts you are much drunkard.

WALTER (*coming away from her and starting to wander around the room, shouting*): Me and Jomo . . . (*Intently, in his sister's face. She has stopped dancing to watch him in this unknown mood.*) That's my man, Kenyatta. (*Shouting and thumping his chest.*) FLAMING SPEAR! HOT DAMN! (*He is suddenly in possession of an imaginary spear and actively spearing enemies all over the room.*) OCOMOGOSIAY . . .

BENEATHA (*to encourage* WALTER, *thoroughly caught up with this side of him*): OCOMOGOSIAY, FLAMING SPEAR!

WALTER: THE LION IS WAKING . . . OWIMOWEH! (*He pulls his shirt open and leaps up on the table and gestures with his spear.*)

BENEATHA: OWIMOWEH!

WALTER (*On the table, very far gone, his eyes pure glass sheets. He sees what we cannot, that he is a leader of his people, a great chief, a descendant of* CHAKA, *and that the hour to march has come.*): Listen, my black brothers —

BENEATHA: OCOMOGOSIAY!

WALTER: —Do you hear the waters rushing against the shores of the coastlands —

BENEATHA: OCOMOGOSIAY!

WALTER: —Do you hear the screeching of the cocks in yonder hills beyond where the chiefs meet in council for the coming of the mighty war —

BENEATHA: OCOMOGOSIAY!

(*And now the lighting shifts subtly to suggest the world of* WALTER's *imagination, and the mood shifts from pure comedy. It is the inner* WALTER *speaking: the Southside chauffeur has assumed an unexpected majesty.*)

WALTER: —Do you hear the beating of the wings of the birds flying low over the mountains and the low places of our land —

BENEATHA: OCOMOGOSIAY!

WALTER: —Do you hear the singing of the women, singing the war songs of our fathers to the babies in the great houses? Singing the sweet war songs! (*The doorbell rings.*) OH, DO YOU HEAR, MY *BLACK* BROTHERS!

BENEATHA (*completely gone*): We hear you, Flaming Spear —

(RUTH *shuts off the phonograph and opens the door.* GEORGE MURCHISON *enters.*)

WALTER: Telling us to prepare for the GREATNESS OF THE TIME! (*Lights back to normal. He turns and sees* GEORGE.) Black Brother!

(*He extends his hand for the fraternal clasp.*)

GEORGE: Black Brother, hell!

RUTH (*having had enough, and embarrassed for the family*): Beneatha, you got company — what's the matter with you? Walter Lee Younger, get down off that table and stop acting like a fool . . .

(WALTER *comes down off the table suddenly and makes a quick exit to the bathroom.*)

RUTH: He's had a little to drink . . . I don't know what her excuse is.

GEORGE *(to* BENEATHA*)*: Look honey, we're going to the theater — we're not going to be *in* it . . . so go change, huh?

(BENEATHA *looks at him and slowly, ceremoniously, lifts her hands and pulls off the headdress. Her hair is close-cropped and unstraightened. George freezes mid-sentence and* RUTH's *eyes all but fall out of her head.)*

GEORGE: What in the name of —

RUTH *(touching* BENEATHA's *hair)*: Girl, you done lost your natural mind? Look at your head!

GEORGE: What have you done to your head — I mean your hair!

BENEATHA: Nothing — except cut it off.

RUTH: Now that's the truth — it's what ain't been done to it! You expect this boy to go out with you with your head all nappy like that?

BENEATHA *(looking at* GEORGE*)*: That's up to George. If he's ashamed of his heritage —

GEORGE: Oh, don't be so proud of yourself, Bennie — just because you look eccentric.

BENEATHA: How can something that's natural be eccentric?

GEORGE: That's what being eccentric means — being natural. Get dressed.

BENEATHA: I don't like that, George.

RUTH: Why must you and your brother make an argument out of everything people say?

BENEATHA: Because I hate assimilationist Negroes!

RUTH: Will somebody please tell me what assimila-whoever means!

GEORGE: Oh, it's just a college girl's way of calling people Uncle Toms — but that isn't what it means at all.

RUTH: Well, what does it mean?

BENEATHA *(cutting* GEORGE *off and staring at him as she replies to* RUTH*)*: It means someone who is willing to give up his own culture and submerge himself completely in the dominant, and in this case *oppressive* culture!

GEORGE: Oh, dear, dear, dear! Here we go! A lecture on the African past! On our Great West African Heritage! In one second we will hear all about the great Ashanti empires; the great Songhay civilizations: and the great sculpture of Bénin — and then some poetry in the Bantu — and the whole monologue will end with the word *heritage! (Nastily.)* Let's face it, baby, your heritage is nothing but a bunch of raggedy-assed spirituals and some grass huts!

BENEATHA: GRASS HUTS! (RUTH *crosses to her and forcibly pushes her toward the bedroom.)* See there . . . you are standing there in your splendid ignorance talking about people who were the first to smelt iron on the face of the earth! (RUTH *is pushing her through the door.)* The Ashanti were performing surgical operations when the English — (RUTH *pulls the door to, with* BENEATHA *on the other side, and smiles graciously at* GEORGE. BENEATHA *opens the door and shouts the end of the sentence*

defiantly at GEORGE) — were still tatooing themselves with blue drag-
ons! *(She goes back inside.)*

RUTH: Have a seat, George. *(They both sit.* RUTH *folds her hands rather
primly on her lap, determined to demonstrate the civilization of the family.)*
Warm, ain't it? I mean for September. *(Pause.)* Just like they always say
about Chicago weather: If it's too hot or cold for you, just wait a
minute and it'll change. *(She smiles happily at this cliché of clichés.)*
Everybody say it's got to do with them bombs and things they keep
setting off. *(Pause.)* Would you like a nice cold beer?

GEORGE: No, thank you. I don't care for beer. *(He looks at his watch.)* I
hope she hurries up.

RUTH: What time is the show?

GEORGE: It's an eight-thirty curtain. That's just Chicago, though. In New
York standard curtain time is eight forty.

(He is rather proud of this knowledge.)

RUTH *(properly appreciating it)*: You get to New York a lot?

GEORGE *(offhand)*: Few times a year.

RUTH: Oh — that's nice. I've never been to New York.

*(*WALTER *enters. We feel he has relieved himself, but the edge of unreality is
still with him.)*

WALTER: New York ain't got nothing Chicago ain't. Just a bunch of
hustling people all squeezed up together — being "Eastern."

(He turns his face into a screw of displeasure.)

GEORGE: Oh — you've been?

WALTER: *Plenty* of times.

RUTH *(shocked at the lie)*: Walter Lee Younger!

WALTER *(staring her down)*: Plenty! *(Pause.)* What we got to drink in this
house? Why don't you offer this man some refreshment. *(To*
GEORGE.*)* They don't know how to entertain people in this house,
man.

GEORGE: Thank you — I don't really care for anything.

WALTER *(feeling his head; sobriety coming)*: Where's Mama?

RUTH: She ain't come back yet.

WALTER *(looking* MURCHISON *over from head to toe, scrutinizing his carefully casual tweed sports jacket over cashmere V-neck sweater over soft eyelet
shirt and tie, and soft slacks, finished off with white buckskin shoes)*: Why all
you college boys wear them faggoty-looking white shoes?

RUTH: Walter Lee!

*(*GEORGE MURCHISON *ignores the remark.)*

WALTER *(to* RUTH*)*: Well, they look crazy as hell — white shoes, cold as
it is.

RUTH *(crushed)*: You have to excuse him—

WALTER: No he don't! Excuse me for what? What you always excusing me for! I'll excuse myself when I needs to be excused! *(A pause.)* They look as funny as them black knee socks Beneatha wears out of here all the time.

RUTH: It's the college *style*, Walter.

WALTER: Style, hell. She looks like she got burnt legs or something!

RUTH: Oh, Walter—

WALTER *(an irritable mimic)*: Oh, Walter! Oh, Walter! *(To* MURCHISON.*)* How's your old man making out? I understand you all going to buy that big hotel on the Drive? *(He finds a beer in the refrigerator, wanders over to* MURCHISON, *sipping and wiping his lips with the back of his hand, and straddling a chair backward to talk to the other man.)* Shrewd move. You old man is all right, man. *(Tapping his head and half winking for emphasis.)* I mean he knows how to operate. I mean he thinks *big,* you know what I mean, I mean for a *home,* you know? But I think he's kind of running out of ideas now. I'd like to talk to him. Listen, man, I got some plans that could turn this city upside down. I mean think like he does. *Big.* Invest big, gamble big, hell, lose *big* if you have to, you know what I mean. It's hard to find a man on this whole Southside who understands my kind of thinking—you dig? *(He scrutinizes* MURCHISON *again, drinks his beer, squints his eyes, and leans in close, confidential, man to man.)* Me and you ought to sit down and talk sometimes, man. Man, I got me some ideas . . .

MURCHISON *(with boredom)*: Yeah—sometimes we'll have to do that, Walter.

WALTER *(understanding the indifference, and offended)*: Yeah—well, when you get the time, man. I know you a busy little boy.

RUTH: Walter, please—

WALTER *(bitterly, hurt)*: I know ain't nothing in this world as busy as you colored college boys with your fraternity pins and white shoes . . .

RUTH *(covering her face with humiliation)*: Oh, Walter Lee—

WALTER: I see you all all the time—with the books tucked under your arms—going to your *(British A—a mimic)* "clahsses." And for what! What the hell you learning over there? Filling up your heads—*(counting off on his fingers)*—with the sociology and the psychology—but they teaching you how to be a man? How to take over and run the world? They teaching you how to run a rubber plantation or a steel mill? Naw—just to talk proper and read books and wear them faggoty-looking white shoes . . .

GEORGE *(looking at him with distaste, a little above it all)*: You're all wacked up with bitterness, man.

WALTER *(intently, almost quietly, between the teeth, glaring at the boy)*: And you—ain't you bitter, man? Ain't you just about had it yet? Don't you see no stars gleaming that you can't reach out and grab? You happy?—

You contented son-of-a-bitch — you happy? You got it made? Bitter? Man, I'm a volcano. Bitter? Here I am a giant — surrounded by ants! Ants who can't even understand what it is the giant is talking about.

RUTH *(passionately and suddenly)*: Oh, Walter — ain't you with nobody!

WALTER *(violently)*: No! 'Cause ain't nobody with me! Not even my own mother!

RUTH: Walter, that's a terrible thing to say!

(BENEATHA enters, dressed for the evening in a cocktail dress and earrings, hair natural.)

GEORGE: Well — hey — *(Crosses to BENEATHA; thoughtful, with emphasis, since this is a reversal.)* You look great!

WALTER *(seeing his sister's hair for the first time)*: What's the matter with your head?

BENEATHA *(tired of the jokes now)*: I cut it off, Brother.

WALTER *(coming close to inspect it and walking around her)*: Well, I'll be damned. So that's what they mean by the African bush . . .

BENEATHA: Ha ha. Let's go, George.

GEORGE *(looking at her)*: You know something? I like it. It's sharp. I mean it really is. *(Helps her into her wrap.)*

RUTH: Yes — I think so, too. *(She goes to the mirror and starts to clutch at her hair.)*

WALTER: Oh no! You leave yours alone, baby. You might turn out to have a pin-shaped head or something!

BENEATHA: See you all later.

RUTH: Have a nice time.

GEORGE: Thanks. Good night. *(Half out the door, he reopens it. To WALTER.)* Good night, Prometheus!

(BENEATHA and GEORGE exit.)

WALTER *(to RUTH)*: Who is Prometheus?

RUTH: I don't know. Don't worry about it.

WALTER *(in fury, pointing after GEORGE)*: See there — they get to a point where they can't insult you man to man — they got to go talk about something ain't nobody never heard of!

RUTH: How do you know it was an insult? *(To humor him.)* Maybe Prometheus is a nice fellow.

WALTER: Prometheus! I bet there ain't even no such thing! I bet that simple-minded clown —

RUTH: Walter —

(She stops what she is doing and looks at him.)

WALTER *(yelling)*: Don't start!

RUTH: Start what?

WALTER: Your nagging! Where was I? Who was I with? How much money did I spend?

RUTH *(plaintively)*: Walter Lee — why don't we just try to talk about it . . .

WALTER *(not listening)*: I been out talking with people who understand me. People who care about the things I got on my mind.

RUTH *(wearily)*: I guess that means people like Willy Harris.

WALTER: Yes, people like Willy Harris.

RUTH *(with a sudden flash of impatience)*: Why don't you all just hurry up and go into the banking business and stop talking about it!

WALTER: Why? You want to know why? 'Cause we all tied up in a race of people that don't know how to do nothing but moan, pray, and have babies!

(The line is too bitter even for him and he looks at her and sits down.)

RUTH: Oh, Walter . . . *(Softly.)* Honey, why can't you stop fighting me?

WALTER *(without thinking)*: Who's fighting you? Who even cares about you?

(This line begins the retardation of his mood.)

RUTH: Well — *(She waits a long time, and then with resignation starts to put away her things.)* I guess I might as well go on to bed . . . *(More or less to herself.)* I don't know where we lost it . . . but we have . . . *(Then, to him.)* I — I'm sorry about this new baby, Walter. I guess maybe I better go on and do what I started . . . I guess I just didn't realize how bad things was with us . . . I guess I just didn't really realize — *(She starts out to the bedroom and stops.)* You want some hot milk?

WALTER: Hot milk?

RUTH: Yes — hot milk.

WALTER: Why hot milk?

RUTH: 'Cause after all that liquor you come home with you ought to have something hot in your stomach.

WALTER: I don't want no milk.

RUTH: You want some coffee then?

WALTER: No, I don't want no coffee. I don't want nothing hot to drink. *(Almost plaintively.)* Why you always trying to give me something to eat?

RUTH *(standing and looking at him helplessly)*: What *else* can I give you, Walter Lee Younger?

(She stands and looks at him and presently turns to go out again. He lifts his head and watches her going away from him in a new mood which began to emerge when he asked her "Who cares about you?")

WALTER: It's been rough, ain't it, baby? *(She hears and stops but does not turn around and he continues to her back.)* I guess between two people there ain't never as much understood as folks generally thinks there is. I mean like between me and you — *(She turns to face him.)* How we gets to the place where we scared to talk softness to each other. *(He waits, thinking hard himself.)* Why you think it got to be like that? *(He is thoughtful, almost as a child would be.)* Ruth, what is it gets into people ought to be close?

RUTH: I don't know, honey. I think about it a lot.

WALTER: On account of you and me, you mean? The way things are with us. The way something done come down between us.

RUTH: There ain't so much between us, Walter . . . Not when you come to me and try to talk to me. Try to be with me . . . a little even.

WALTER *(total honesty)*: Sometimes . . . sometimes . . . I don't even know how to try.

RUTH: Walter —

WALTER: Yes?

RUTH *(coming to him, gently and with misgiving, but coming to him)*: Honey . . . life don't have to be like this. I mean sometimes people can do things so that things are better . . . You remember how we used to talk when Travis was born . . . about the way we were going to live . . . the kind of house . . . *(She is stroking his head.)* Well, it's all starting to slip away from us . . .

(He turns her to him and they look at each other and kiss, tenderly and hungrily. The door opens and MAMA *enters —* WALTER *breaks away and jumps up. A beat.)*

WALTER: Mama, where have you been?

MAMA: My — them steps is longer than they used to be. Whew! *(She sits down and ignores him.)* How you feeling this evening, Ruth?

*(*RUTH *shrugs, disturbed at having been interrupted and watching her husband knowingly.)*

WALTER: Mama, where have you been all day?

MAMA *(still ignoring him and leaning on the table and changing to more comfortable shoes)*: Where's Travis?

RUTH: I let him go out earlier and he ain't come back yet. Boy, is he going to get it!

WALTER: Mama!

MAMA *(as if she has heard him for the first time)*: Yes, son?

WALTER: Where did you go this afternoon?

MAMA: I went downtown to tend to some business that I had to tend to.

WALTER: What kind of business?

MAMA: You know better than to question me like a child, Brother.

WALTER *(rising and bending over the table)*: Where were you, Mama? *(Bringing his fists down and shouting.)* Mama, you didn't go do something with that insurance money, something crazy?

(The front door opens slowly, interrupting him, and TRAVIS *peeks his head in, less than hopefully.)*

TRAVIS *(to his mother)*: Mama, I—

RUTH: "Mama I" nothing! You're going to get it, boy! Get on in that bedroom and get yourself ready!

TRAVIS: But I—

MAMA: Why don't you all never let the child explain hisself.

RUTH: Keep out of it now, Lena.

(MAMA *clamps her lips together, and* RUTH *advances toward her son menacingly.)*

RUTH: A thousand times I have told you not to go off like that—

MAMA *(holding out her arms to her grandson)*: Well—at least let me tell him something. I want him to be the first one to hear . . . Come here, Travis. *(The boy obeys, gladly.)* Travis—*(she takes him by the shoulder and looks into his face)*—you know that money we got in the mail this morning?

TRAVIS: Yes'm—

MAMA: Well—what you think your grandmama gone and done with that money?

TRAVIS: I don't know, Grandmama.

MAMA *(putting her finger on his nose for emphasis)*: She went out and she bought you a house! *(The explosion comes from* WALTER *at the end of the revelation and he jumps up and turns away from all of them in a fury.* MAMA *continues, to* TRAVIS.*)* You glad about the house? It's going to be yours when you get to be a man.

TRAVIS: Yeah—I always wanted to live in a house.

MAMA: All right, gimme some sugar then—*(*TRAVIS *puts his arms around her neck as she watches her son over the boy's shoulder. Then, to* TRAVIS, *after the embrace.)* Now when you say your prayers tonight, you thank God and your grandfather—'cause it was him who give you the house—in his way.

RUTH *(taking the boy from* MAMA *and pushing him toward the bedroom)*: Now you get out of here and get ready for your beating.

TRAVIS: Aw, Mama—

RUTH: Get on in there—*(Closing the door behind him and turning radiantly to her mother-in-law.)* So you went and did it!

MAMA *(quietly, looking at her son with pain)*: Yes, I did.

RUTH *(raising both arms classically)*: PRAISE GOD! *(Looks at* WALTER *a moment, who says nothing. She crosses rapidly to her husband.)* Please, honey— let me be glad . . . you be glad too. *(She has laid her hands on his shoulders, but he shakes himself free of her roughly, without turning to face her.)* Oh, Walter . . . a home . . . a home. *(She comes back to* MAMA.*)* Well—where is it? How big is it? How much it going to cost?

MAMA: Well—

RUTH: When we moving?

MAMA *(smiling at her)*: First of the month.

RUTH *(throwing back her head with jubilance)*: Praise God!

MAMA *(tentatively, still looking at her son's back turned against her and RUTH)*: It's—it's a nice house too . . . *(She cannot help speaking directly to him. An imploring quality in her voice, her manner, makes her almost like a girl now.)* Three bedrooms—nice big one for you and Ruth . . . Me and Beneatha still have to share our room, but Travis have one of his own—and *(with difficulty)* I figure if the—new baby—is a boy, we could get one of them double-decker outfits . . . And there's a yard with a little patch of dirt where I could maybe get to grow me a few flowers . . . And a nice big basement . . .

RUTH: Walter honey, be glad—

MAMA *(still to his back, fingering things on the table)*: 'Course I don't want to make it sound fancier than it is . . . It's just a plain little old house—but it's made good and solid—and it will be *ours*. Walter Lee—it makes a difference in a man when he can walk on floors that belong to *him* . . .

RUTH: Where is it?

MAMA *(frightened at this telling)*: Well—well—it's out there in Clybourne Park—

(RUTH's radiance fades abruptly, and WALTER finally turns slowly to face his mother with incredulity and hostility.)

RUTH: Where?

MAMA *(matter-of-factly)*: Four o six Clybourne Street, Clybourne Park.

RUTH: Clybourne Park? Mama, there ain't no colored people living in Clybourne Park.

MAMA *(almost idiotically)*: Well, I guess there's going to be some now.

WALTER *(bitterly)*: So that's the peace and comfort you went out and bought for us today!

MAMA *(raising her eyes to meet his finally)*: Son—I just tried to find the nicest place for the least amount of money for my family.

RUTH *(trying to recover from the shock)*: Well—well—'course I ain't one never been 'fraid of no crackers mind you—but—well, wasn't there no other houses nowhere?

MAMA: Them houses they put up for colored in them areas way out all seem to cost twice as much as other houses. I did the best I could.

RUTH *(struck senseless with the news, in its various degrees of goodness and trouble, she sits a moment, her fists propping her chin in thought, and then she starts to rise, bringing her fists down with vigor, the radiance spreading from cheek to cheek again)*: Well—well—All I can say is—if this is my time in life—MY TIME—to say good-bye—(and she builds with momentum as she*

starts to circle the room with an exuberant, almost tearfully happy release) —
to these Goddamned cracking walls! — *(she pounds the walls)* — and these
marching roaches! — *(she wipes at an imaginary army of marching
roaches)* — and this cramped little closet which ain't now or never was
no kitchen! . . . then I say it loud and good, HALLELUJAH! AND GOOD-
BYE MISERY . . . I DON'T NEVER WANT TO SEE YOUR UGLY FACE
AGAIN! *(She laughs joyously, having practically destroyed the apartment, and
flings her arms up and lets them come down happily, slowly, reflectively, over
her abdomen, aware for the first time perhaps that the life therein pulses with
happiness and not despair.)* Lena?

MAMA *(moved, watching her happiness)*: Yes, honey?

RUTH *(looking off)*: Is there — is there a whole lot of sunlight?

MAMA *(understanding)*: Yes, child, there's a whole lot of sunlight.

> *(Long pause.)*

RUTH *(collecting herself and going to the door of the room* TRAVIS *is in)*: Well —
I guess I better see 'bout Travis. *(To* MAMA.*)* Lord, I sure don't feel
like whipping nobody today!

> *(She exits.)*

MAMA *(the mother and son are left alone now and the mother waits a long time,
considering deeply, before she speaks)*: Son — you — you understand what I
done, don't you? *(WALTER is silent and sullen.)* I — I just seen my
family falling apart today . . . just falling to pieces in front of my eyes
. . . We couldn't of gone on like we was today. We was going backwards 'stead of forwards — talking 'bout killing babies and wishing
each other was dead . . . When it gets like that in life — you just got to
do something different, push on out and do something bigger . . .
(She waits.) I wish you say something, son . . . I wish you'd say how
deep inside you you think I done the right thing —

WALTER *(crossing slowly to his bedroom door and finally turning there and speaking measuredly)*: What you need me to say you done right for? *You* the
head of this family. You run our lives like you want to. It was your
money and you did what you wanted with it. So what you need for
me to say it was all right for? *(Bitterly, to hurt her as deeply as he knows is
possible.)* So you butchered up a dream of mine — you — who always
talking 'bout your children's dreams . . .

MAMA: Walter Lee —

> *(He just closes the door behind him.* MAMA *sits alone, thinking heavily.)*

Scene II *(Time: Friday night. A few weeks later.)*

(At rise: Packing crates mark the intention of the family to move. BE-
NEATHA *and* GEORGE *come in, presumably from an evening out again.)*

GEORGE: O.K. . . . O.K., whatever you say . . . *(They both sit on the couch. He tries to kiss her. She moves away.)* Look, we've had a nice evening; let's not spoil it, huh? . . .

(He again turns her head and tries to nuzzle in and she turns away from him, not with distaste but with momentary lack of interest; in a mood to pursue what they were talking about.)

BENEATHA: I'm *trying* to talk to you.

GEORGE: We always talk.

BENEATHA: Yes—and I love to talk.

GEORGE *(exasperated; rising)*: I know it and I don't mind it sometimes . . . I want you to cut it out, see—The moody stuff, I mean. I don't like it. You're a nice-looking girl . . . all over. That's all you need, honey, forget the atmosphere. Guys aren't going to go for the atmosphere— they're going to go for what they see. Be glad for that. Drop the Garbo routine. It doesn't go with you. As for myself, I want a nice— *(groping)*—simple *(thoughtfully)*—sophisticated girl . . . not a poet— O.K.?

(He starts to kiss her, she rebuffs him again, and he jumps up.)

BENEATHA: Why are you angry, George?

GEORGE: Because this is stupid! I don't go out with you to discuss the nature of "quiet desperation" or to hear all about your thoughts— because the world will go on thinking what it thinks regardless—

BENEATHA: Then why read books? Why go to school?

GEORGE *(with artificial patience, counting on his fingers)*: (It's simple. You read books—to learn facts—to get grades—to pass the course—to get a degree. That's all—it has nothing to do with thoughts.

(A long pause.)

BENEATHA: I see. *(He starts to sit.)* Good night, George.

(GEORGE looks at her a little oddly and starts to exit. He meets MAMA coming in.)

GEORGE: Oh—hello, Mrs. Younger.

MAMA: Hello, George, how you feeling?

GEORGE: Fine—fine, how are you?

MAMA: Oh, a little tired. You know them steps can get you after a day's work. You all have a nice time tonight?

GEORGE: Yes—a fine time. A fine time.

MAMA: Well, good night.

GEORGE: Good night. *(He exits.* MAMA *closes the door behind her.)*

MAMA: Hello, honey. What you sitting like that for?

BENEATHA: I'm just sitting.

MAMA: Didn't you have a nice time?

BENEATHA: No.

MAMA: No? What's the matter?

BENEATHA: Mama, George is a fool — honest. *(She rises.)*

MAMA *(Hustling around unloading the packages she has entered with. She stops.)*: Is he, baby?

BENEATHA: Yes.

(BENEATHA makes up TRAVIS' bed as she talks.)

MAMA: You sure?

BENEATHA: Yes.

MAMA: Well — I guess you better not waste your time with no fools.

(BENEATHA looks up at her mother, watching her put groceries in the refrigerator. Finally she gathers up her things and starts into the bedroom. At the door she stops and looks back at her mother.)

BENEATHA: Mama —

MAMA: Yes, baby —

BENEATHA: Thank you.

MAMA: For what?

BENEATHA: For understanding me this time.

(She exits quickly and the mother stands, smiling a little, looking at the place where BENEATHA just stood. RUTH enters.)

RUTH: Now don't you fool with any of this stuff, Lena —

MAMA: Oh, I just thought I'd sort a few things out. Is Brother here?

RUTH: Yes.

MAMA *(with concern)*: Is he —

RUTH *(reading her eyes)*: Yes.

(MAMA is silent and someone knocks on the door. MAMA and RUTH exchange weary and knowing glances and RUTH opens it to admit the neighbor, MRS. JOHNSON, who is a rather squeaky wide-eyed lady of no particular age, with a newspaper under her arm.)

MAMA *(changing her expression to acute delight and a ringing cheerful greeting)*: Oh — hello there, Johnson.

JOHNSON *(this is a woman who decided long ago to be enthusiastic about EVERYTHING in life and she is inclined to wave her wrist vigorously at the height of her exclamatory comments)*: Hello there, yourself! H'you this evening, Ruth?

RUTH *(not much of a deceptive type)*: Fine, Mis' Johnson, h'you?

JOHNSON: Fine. *(Reaching out quickly, playfully, and patting RUTH's stomach.)* Ain't you starting to poke out none yet! *(She mugs with delight at the over-familiar remark and her eyes dart around looking at the crates and packing preparation; MAMA's face is a cold sheet of endurance.)* Oh, ain't we getting ready round here, though! Yessir! Lookathere! I'm telling

you the Youngers is really getting ready to "move on up a little
higher!" — Bless God!

MAMA *(a little drily, doubting the total sincerity of the Blesser)*: Bless God.

JOHNSON: He's good, ain't He?

MAMA: Oh yes, He's good.

JOHNSON: I mean sometimes He works in mysterious ways . . . but He
works, don't He!

MAMA *(the same)*: Yes, he does.

JOHNSON: I'm just soooooo happy for y'all. And this here child — *(about
RUTH)* looks like she could just pop open with happiness, don't she.
Where's all the rest of the family?

MAMA: Bennie's gone to bed —

JOHNSON: Ain't no . . . *(the implication is pregnancy)* sickness done hit
you — I hope . . . ?

MAMA: No — she just tired. She was out this evening.

JOHNSON *(all is a coo, an emphatic coo)*: Aw — ain't that lovely. She still
going out with the little Murchison boy?

MAMA *(drily)*: Ummmm huh.

JOHNSON: That's lovely. You sure got lovely children, Younger. Me and
Isaiah talks all the time 'bout what fine children you was blessed with.
We sure do.

MAMA: Ruth, give Mis' Johnson a piece of sweet potato pie and some milk.

JOHNSON: Oh honey, I can't stay hardly a minute — I just dropped in to
see if there was anything I could do. *(Accepting the food easily.)* I guess
y'all seen the news what's all over the colored paper this week . . .

MAMA: No — didn't get mine yet this week.

JOHNSON *(lifting her head and blinking with the spirit of catastrophe)*: You mean
you ain't read 'bout them colored people that was bombed out their
place out there?

(RUTH straightens with concern and takes the paper and reads it.
JOHNSON notices her and feeds commentary.)

JOHNSON: Ain't it something how bad these here white folks is getting
here in Chicago! Lord, getting so you think you right down in Mississippi! *(With a tremendous and rather insincere sense of melodrama.)* 'Course
I thinks it's wonderful how our folks keeps on pushing out. You hear
some of these Negroes round here talking 'bout how they don't go
where they ain't wanted and all that — but not me, honey! *(This is a
lie.)* Wilhemenia Othella Johnson goes anywhere, any time she feels
like it! *(With head movement for emphasis.)* Yes I do! Why if we left it up
to these here crackers, the poor niggers wouldn't have nothing — *(She
clasps her hand over her mouth.)* Oh, I always forgets you don't 'low that
word in your house.

MAMA *(quietly, looking at her)*: No — I don't 'low it.

JOHNSON *(vigorously again)*: Me neither! I was just telling Isaiah yesterday
 when he come using it in front of me—I said, "Isaiah, it's just like Mis'
 Younger says all the time—"
MAMA: Don't you want some more pie?
JOHNSON: No—no thank you; this was lovely. I got to get on over home
 and have my midnight coffee. I hear some people say it don't let them
 sleep but I finds I can't close my eyes right lessen ⎯ done had that
 laaaast cup of coffee . . . *(She waits. A beat. Undaunted.)* My Good-
 night coffee, I calls it!
MAMA *(with much eye-rolling and communication between herself and* RUTH*)*:
 Ruth, why don't you give Mis' Johnson some coffee.

(RUTH *gives* MAMA *an unpleasant look for her kindness.)*

JOHNSON *(accepting the coffee)*: Where's Brother tonight?
MAMA: He's lying down.
JOHNSON: Mmmmmmm, he sure gets his beauty rest, don't he? Good-
 looking man. Sure is a good-looking man! *(Reaching out to pat* RUTH*'s
 stomach again.)* I guess that's how come we keep on having babies
 around here. *(She winks at* MAMA.*)* One thing 'bout Brother, he always know how to have a *good* time. And soooooo ambitious! I bet it
 was his idea y'all moving out to Clybourne Park. Lord—I bet this
 time next month y'all's names will have been in the papers plenty—
 *(Holding up her hands to mark off each word of the headline she can see in front
 of her.)* "NEGROES INVADE CLYBOURNE PARK—BOMBED!"
MAMA *(she and* RUTH *look at the woman in amazement)*: We ain't exactly
 moving out there to get bombed.
JOHNSON: Oh, honey—you know I'm praying to God every day that
 don't nothing like that happen! But you have to think of life like it is—
 and these here Chicago peckerwoods is some baaaad peckerwoods.
MAMA *(wearily)*: We done thought about all that Mis' Johnson.

(BENEATHA *comes out of the bedroom in her robe and passes through to the
 bathroom.* MRS. JOHNSON *turns.)*

JOHNSON: Hello there, Bennie!
BENEATHA *(crisply)*: Hello, Mrs. Johnson.
JOHNSON: How is school?
BENEATHA *(crisply)*: Fine, thank you. *(She goes out.)*
JOHNSON *(insulted)*: Getting so she don't have much to say to nobody.
MAMA: The child was on her way to the bathroom.
JOHNSON: I know—but sometimes she act like ain't got time to pass the
 time of day with nobody ain't been to college. Oh—I ain't criticizing
 her none. It's just—you know how some of our young people gets
 when they get a little education. (MAMA *and* RUTH *say nothing, just
 look at her.)* Yes—well. Well, I guess I better get on home. *(Unmoving.)*

'Course I can understand how she must be proud and everything—being the only one in the family to make something of herself. I know just being a chauffeur ain't never satisfied Brother none. He shouldn't feel like that, though. Ain't nothing wrong with being a chauffeur.

MAMA: There's plenty wrong with it.

JOHNSON: What?

MAMA: Plenty. My husband always said being any kind of a servant wasn't a fit thing for a man to have to be. He always said a man's hands was made to make things, or to turn the earth with—not to drive nobody's car for 'em—or—*(she looks at her own hands)* carry they slop jars. And my boy is just like him—he wasn't meant to wait on nobody.

JOHNSON *(rising, somewhat offended)*: Mmmmmm-mmm. The Youngers is too much for me! *(She looks around.)* You sure one proud-acting bunch of colored folks. Well—I always thinks like Booker T. Washington said that time—"Education has spoiled many a good plow hand"—

MAMA: Is that what old Booker T. said?

JOHNSON: He sure did.

MAMA: Well, it sounds just like him. The fool.

JOHNSON *(indignantly)*: Well—he was one of our great men.

MAMA: Who said so?

JOHNSON *(nonplussed)*: You know, me and you ain't never agreed about some things, Lena Younger. I guess I better be going—

RUTH *(quickly)*: Good night.

JOHNSON: Good night. Oh—*(Thrusting it at her.)* You can keep the paper! *(With a trill.)* 'Night.

MAMA: Good night, Mis' Johnson.

(MRS. JOHNSON exits.)

RUTH: If ignorance was gold . . .

MAMA: Shush. Don't talk about folks behind their backs.

RUTH: You do.

MAMA: I'm old and corrupted. *(BENEATHA enters.)* You was rude to Mis' Johnson, Beneatha, and I don't like it at all.

BENEATHA *(at her door)*: Mama, if there are two things we, as a people, have got to overcome, one is the Klu Klux Klan—and the other is Mrs. Johnson. *(She exits.)*

MAMA: Smart aleck.

(The phone rings.)

RUTH: I'll get it.

MAMA: Lord, ain't this a popular place tonight.

RUTH *(at the phone)*: Hello—Just a minute. *(Goes to door.)* Walter, it's Mrs. Arnold. *(Waits. Goes back to the phone. Tense.)* Hello. Yes, this is his wife speaking . . . He's lying down now. Yes . . . well, he'll be in tomorrow. He's been very sick. Yes—I know we should have called, but we were so sure he'd be able to come in today. Yes—yes, I'm very sorry. Yes . . . Thank you very much. *(She hangs up.* WALTER *is standing in the doorway of the bedroom behind her.)* That was Mrs. Arnold.

WALTER *(indifferently)*: Was it?

RUTH: She said if you don't come in tomorrow that they are getting a new man . . .

WALTER: Ain't that sad—ain't that crying sad.

RUTH: She said Mr. Arnold has had to take a cab for three days . . . Walter, you ain't been to work for three days! *(This is a revelation to her.)* Where you been, Walter Lee Younger? (WALTER *looks at her and starts to laugh.)* You're going to lose your job.

WALTER: That's right . . . *(He turns on the radio.)*

RUTH: Oh, Walter, and with your mother working like a dog every day—

(A steamy, deep blues pours into the room.)

WALTER: That's sad too—Everything is sad.

MAMA: What you been doing for these three days, son?

WALTER: Mama—you don't know all the things a man what got leisure can find to do in this city . . . What's this—Friday night? Well— Wednesday I borrowed Willy Harris' car and I went for a drive . . . just me and myself and I drove and drove . . . Way out . . . way past South Chicago, and I parked the car and I sat and looked at the steel mills all day long. I just sat in the car and looked at them big black chimneys for hours. Then I drove back and I went to the Green Hat. *(Pause.)* And Thursday—Thursday I borrowed the car again and I got in it and I pointed it the other way and I drove the other way—for hours—way, way up to Wisconsin, and I looked at the farms. I just drove and looked at the farms. Then I drove back and I went to the Green Hat. *(Pause.)* And today—today I didn't get the car. Today I just walked. All over the Southside. And I looked at the Negroes and they looked at me and finally I just sat down on the curb at Thirty-ninth and South Parkway and I just sat there and watched the Negroes go by. And then I went to the Green Hat. You all sad? You all depressed? And you know where I am going right now—

(RUTH goes out quietly.)

MAMA: Oh, Big Walter, is this the harvest of our days?

WALTER: You know what I like about the Green Hat? I like this little cat they got there who blows a sax . . . He blows. He talks to me. He ain't but 'bout five feet tall and he's got a conked head and his eyes is always closed and he's all music—

MAMA *(rising and getting some papers out of her handbag)*: Walter—

WALTER: And there's this other guy who plays the piano . . . and they got a sound. I mean they can work on some music . . . They got the best little combo in the world in the Green Hat . . . You can just sit there and drink and listen to them three men play and you realize that don't nothing matter worth a damn, but just being there —

MAMA: I've helped do it to you, haven't I, son? Walter I been wrong.

WALTER: Naw — you ain't never been wrong about nothing, Mama.

MAMA: Listen to me, now. I say I been wrong, son. That I been doing to you what the rest of the world been doing to you. *(She turns off the radio.)* Walter — *(She stops and he looks up slowly at her and she meets his eyes pleadingly.)* What you ain't never understood is that I ain't got nothing, don't own nothing, ain't never really wanted nothing that wasn't for you. There ain't nothing as precious to me . . . There ain't nothing worth holding on to, money, dreams, nothing else — if it means — if it means it's going to destroy my boy. *(She takes an envelope out of her handbag and puts it in front of him and he watches her without speaking or moving.)* I paid the man thirty-five hundred dollars down on the house. That leaves sixty-five hundred dollars. Monday morning I want you to take this money and take three thousand dollars and put it in a savings account for Beneatha's medical schooling. The rest you put in a checking account — with your name on it. And from now on any penny that come out of it or that go in it is for you to look after. For you to decide. *(She drops her hands a little helplessly.)* It ain't much, but it's all I got in the world and I'm putting it in your hands. I'm telling you to be the head of this family from now on like you supposed to be.

WALTER *(stares at the money)*: You trust me like that, Mama?

MAMA: I ain't never stop trusting you. Like I ain't never stop loving you.

(She goes out, and WALTER *sits looking at the money on the table. Finally, in a decisive gesture, he gets up and, in mingled joy and desperation, picks up the money. At the same moment,* TRAVIS *enters for bed.)*

TRAVIS: What's the matter, Daddy? You drunk?

WALTER *(sweetly, more sweetly than we have ever known him)*: No, Daddy ain't drunk. Daddy ain't going to never be drunk again . . .

TRAVIS: Well, good night, Daddy.

(The father has come from behind the couch and leans over, embracing his son.)

WALTER: Son, I feel like talking to you tonight.

TRAVIS: About what?

WALTER: Oh, about a lot of things. About you and what kind of man you going to be when you grow up . . . Son — son, what do you want to be when you grow up?

TRAVIS: A bus driver.

WALTER *(laughing a little)*: A what? Man, that ain't nothing to want to be!

TRAVIS: Why not?

WALTER: 'Cause, man—it ain't big enough—you know what I mean.

TRAVIS: I don't know then. I can't make up my mind. Sometimes Mama asks me that too. And sometimes when I tell her I just want to be like you—she says she don't want me to be like that and sometimes she says she does . . .

WALTER *(gathering him up in his arms)*: You know what, Travis? In seven years you going to be seventeen years old. And things is going to be very different with us in seven years, Travis . . . One day when you are seventeen I'll come home—home from my office downtown somewhere—

TRAVIS: You don't work in no office, Daddy.

WALTER: No—but after tonight. After what your daddy gonna do tonight, there's going to be offices—a whole lot of offices. . . .

TRAVIS: What you gonna do tonight, Daddy?

WALTER: You wouldn't understand yet, son, but your daddy's gonna make a transaction . . . a business transaction that's going to change our lives. . . . That's how come one day when you 'bout seventeen years old I'll come home and I'll be pretty tired, you know what I mean, after a day of conferences and secretaries getting things wrong the way they do . . . 'cause an executive's life is hell, man—*(The more he talks the farther away he gets.)* And I'll pull the car up on the driveway . . . just a plain black Chrysler, I think, with white walls—no—black tires. More elegant. Rich people don't have to be flashy . . . though I'll have to get something a little sportier for Ruth—maybe a Cadillac convertible to do her shopping in. . . . And I'll come up the steps to the house and the gardener will be clipping away at the hedges and he'll say, "Good evening, Mr. Younger." And I'll say "Hello, Jefferson, how are you this evening?" And I'll go inside and Ruth will come downstairs and meet me at the door and we'll kiss each other and she'll take my arm and we'll go up to your room to see you sitting on the floor with the catalogues of all the great schools in America around you. . . . All the great schools in the world! And—and I'll say, all right son—it's your seventeenth birthday, what is it you've decided? . . . Just tell me where you want to go to school and you'll *go*. Just tell me, what it is you want to be—and you'll *be* it. . . . Whatever you want to be—Yessir! *(He holds his arms open for* TRAVIS.*)* You just name it, son . . . *(*TRAVIS *leaps into them)* and I hand you the world!

*(*WALTER's *voice has risen in pitch and hysterical promise and on the last line he lifts* TRAVIS *high.)*

Scene III *(Time: Saturday, moving day, one week later.)*

(Before the curtain rises, RUTH's *voice, a strident, dramatic church alto, cuts through the silence.)*

(It is, in the darkness, a triumphant surge, a penetrating statement of expectation: "Oh, Lord, I don't feel no ways tired! Children, oh, glory hallelujah!")

(As the curtain rises we see that RUTH *is alone in the living room, finishing up the family's packing. It is moving day. She is nailing crates and tying cartons.* BENEATHA *enters, carrying a guitar case, and watches her exuberant sister-in-law.)*

RUTH: Hey!

BENEATHA *(putting away the case)*: Hi.

RUTH *(pointing at a package)*: Honey — look in that package there and see what I found on sale this morning at the South Center. *(RUTH gets up and moves to the package and draws out some curtains.)* Lookahere — hand-turned hems!

BENEATHA: How do you know the window size out there?

RUTH *(who hadn't thought of that)*: Oh — Well, they bound to fit something in the whole house. Anyhow, they was too good a bargain to pass up. *(RUTH slaps her head, suddenly remembering something.)* Oh, Bennie — I meant to put a special note on that carton over there. That's your mama's good china and she wants 'em to be very careful with it.

BENEATHA: I'll do it.

(BENEATHA finds a piece of paper and starts to draw large letters on it.)

RUTH: You know what I'm going to do soon as I get in that new house?

BENEATHA: What?

RUTH: Honey — I'm going to run me a tub of water up to here . . . *(With her fingers practically up to her nostrils.)* And I'm going to get in it — and I am going to sit . . . and sit . . . and sit in that hot water and the first person who knocks to tell *me* to hurry up and come out —

BENEATHA: Gets shot at sunrise.

RUTH *(laughing happily)*: You said it, sister! *(Noticing how large* BENEATHA *is absent-mindedly making the note.)* Honey, they ain't going to read that from no airplane.

BENEATHA *(laughing herself)*: I guess I always think things have more emphasis if they are big, somehow.

RUTH *(looking up at her and smiling)*: You and your brother seem to have that as a philosophy of life. Lord, that man — done changed so 'round here. You know — you know what we did last night? Me and Walter Lee?

BENEATHA: What?

RUTH *(smiling to herself)*: We went to the movies. *(Looking at* BENEATHA *to see if she understands.)* We went to the movies. You know the last time me and Walter went to the movies together?

BENEATHA: No.

RUTH: Me neither. That's how long it been. *(Smiling again.)* But we went last night. The picture wasn't much good, but that didn't seem to matter. We went — and we held hands.

BENEATHA: Oh, Lord!

RUTH: We held hands — and you know what?

BENEATHA: What?

RUTH: When we come out of the show it was late and dark and all the stores and things was closed up . . . and it was kind of chilly and there wasn't many people on the streets . . . and we was still holding hands, me and Walter.

BENEATHA: You're killing me.

(WALTER *enters with a large package. His happiness is deep in him; he cannot keep still with his newfound exuberance. He is singing and wiggling and snapping his fingers. He puts his package in a corner and puts a phonograph record, which he has brought in with him, on the record player. As the music, soulful and sensuous, comes up he dances over to* RUTH *and tries to get her to dance with him. She gives in at last to his raunchiness and in a fit of giggling allows herself to be drawn into his mood. They dip and she melts into his arms in a classic, body-melding "slow drag.")*

BENEATHA (*regarding them a long time as they dance, then drawing in her breath for a deeply exaggerated comment which she does not particularly mean*): Talk about — oldddddddddd-fashioneddddddd — Negroes!

WALTER (*stopping momentarily*): What kind of Negroes?

(*He says this in fun. He is not angry with her today, nor with anyone. He starts to dance with his wife again.*)

BENEATHA: Old-fashioned.

WALTER (*as he dances with* RUTH): You know, when these *New Negroes* have their convention — (*pointing at his sister*) — that is going to be the chairman of the Committee on Unending Agitation. (*He goes on dancing, then stops.*) Race, race, race! . . . Girl, I do believe you are the first person in the history of the entire human race to successfully brainwash yourself. (BENEATHA *breaks up and he goes on dancing. He stops again, enjoying his tease.*) Damn, even the N double A C P takes a holiday sometimes! (BENEATHA *and* RUTH *laugh. He dances with* RUTH *some more and starts to laugh and stops and pantomimes someone over an operating table.*) I can just see that chick someday looking down at some poor cat on an operating table and before she starts to slice him, she says . . . (*pulling his sleeves back maliciously*) "By the way, what are your views on civil rights down there? . . ."

(*He laughs at her again and starts to dance happily. The bell sounds.*)

BENEATHA: Sticks and stones may break my bones but . . . words will never hurt me!

(BENEATHA *goes to the door and opens it as* WALTER *and* RUTH *go on with the clowning.* BENEATHA *is somewhat surprised to see a quiet-looking middle-aged white man in a business suit holding his hat and a briefcase in his hand and consulting a small piece of paper.*)

MAN: Uh—How do you do, miss. I am looking for a Mrs. — *(he looks at the slip of paper)* Mrs. Lena Younger? *(He stops short, struck dumb at the sight of the oblivious* WALTER *and* RUTH.*)*

BENEATHA *(smoothing her hair with slight embarrassment)*: Oh—yes, that's my mother. Excuse me. *(She closes the door and turns to quiet the other two.)* Ruth! Brother! *(Enunciating precisely but soundlessly: "There's a white man at the door!" They stop dancing,* RUTH *cuts off the phonograph,* BENEATHA *opens the door. The man casts a curious quick glance at all of them.)* Uh—come in please.

MAN *(coming in)*: Thank you.

BENEATHA: My mother isn't here just now. Is it business?

MAN: Yes . . . well, of a sort.

WALTER *(freely, the Man of the House)*: Have a seat. I'm Mrs. Younger's son. I look after most of her business matters.

*(*RUTH *and* BENEATHA *exchange amused glances.)*

MAN *(regarding Walter, and sitting)*: Well—My name is Karl Lindner . . .

WALTER *(streching out his hand)*: Walter Younger. This is my wife — *(*RUTH *nods politely)* — and my sister.

LINDNER: How do you do.

WALTER *(amiably, as he sits himself easily on a chair, leaning forward on his knees with interest and looking expectantly into the newcomer's face)*: What can we do for you, Mr. Lindner!

LINDNER *(some minor shuffling of the hat and briefcase on his knees)*: Well—I am a representative of the Clybourne Park Improvement Association—

WALTER *(pointing)*: Why don't you sit your things on the floor?

LINDNER: Oh—yes. Thank you. *(He slides the briefcase and hat under the chair.)* And as I was saying—I am from the Clybourne Park Improvement Association and we have had it brought to our attention at the last meeting that you people—or at least your mother—has bought a piece of residential property at — *(he digs for the slip of paper again)* — four o six Clybourne Street . . .

WALTER: That's right. Care for something to drink? Ruth, get Mr. Lindner a beer.

LINDNER *(upset for some reason)*: Oh—no, really. I mean thank you very much, but no thank you.

RUTH *(innocently)*: Some coffee?

LINDNER: Thank you, nothing at all.

*(*BENEATHA *is watching the man carefully.)*

LINDNER: Well, I don't know how much you folks know about our organization. *(He is a gentle man; thoughtful and somewhat labored in his manner.)* It is one of these community organizations set up to look after—oh, you know, things like block upkeep and special projects and we also have what we call our New Neighbors Orientation Committee . . .

BENEATHA *(drily)*: Yes — and what do they do?

LINDNER *(turning a little to her and then returning the main force to* WALTER*)*: Well — it's what you might call a sort of welcoming committee, I guess. I mean they, we — I'm the chairman of the committee — go around and see the new people who move into the neighborhood and sort of give them the lowdown on the way we do things out in Clybourne Park.

BENEATHA *(with appreciation of the two meanings, which escape* RUTH *and* WALTER*)*: Un-huh.

LINDNER: And we also have the category of what the association calls — *(he looks elsewhere)* — uh — special community problems . . .

BENEATHA: Yes — and what are some of those?

WALTER: Girl, let the man talk.

LINDNER *(with understated relief)*: Thank you. I would sort of like to explain this thing in my own way. I mean I want to explain to you in a certain way.

WALTER: Go ahead.

LINDNER: Yes. Well. I'm going to try to get right to the point. I'm sure we'll all appreciate that in the long run.

BENEATHA: Yes.

WALTER: Be still now!

LINDNER: Well —

RUTH *(still innocently)*: Would you like another chair — you don't look comfortable.

LINDNER *(more frustrated than annoyed)*: No, thank you very much. Please. Well — to get right to the point I — *(a great breath, and he is off at last)* I am sure you people must be aware of some of the incidents which have happened in various parts of the city when colored people have moved into certain areas — *(*BENEATHA *exhales heavily and starts tossing a piece of fruit up and down in the air.)* Well — because we have what I think is going to be a unique type of organization in American community life — not only do we deplore that kind of thing — but we are trying to do something about it. *(*BENEATHA *stops tossing and turns with a new and quizzical interest to the man.)* We feel — *(gaining confidence in his mission because of the interest in the faces of the people he is talking to)* — we feel that most of the trouble in this world, when you come right down to it — *(he hits his knee for emphasis)* — most of the trouble exists because people just don't sit down and talk to each other.

RUTH *(nodding as she might in church, pleased with the remark)*: You can say that again, mister.

LINDNER *(more encouraged by such affirmation)*: That we don't try hard enough in this world to understand the other fellow's problem. The other guy's point of view.

RUTH: Now that's right.

> (BENEATHA *and* WALTER *merely watch and listen with genuine interest.*)

LINDNER: Yes—that's the way we feel out in Clybourne Park. And that's why I was elected to come here this afternoon and talk to you people. Friendly like, you know, the way people should talk to each other and see if we couldn't find some way to work this thing out. As I say, the whole business is a matter of *caring* about the other fellow. Anybody can see that you are a nice family of folks, hard-working and honest I'm sure. (BENEATHA *frowns slightly, quizzically, her head tilted regarding him.*) Today everybody knows what it means to be on the outside of *something.* And of course, there is always somebody who is out to take advantage of people who don't always understand.

WALTER: What do you mean?

LINDNER: Well—you see our community is made up of people who've worked hard as the dickens for years to build up that little community. They're not rich and fancy people; just hard-working, honest people who don't really have much but those little homes and a dream of the kind of community they want to raise their children in. Now, I don't say we are perfect and there is a lot wrong in some of the things they want. But you've got to admit that a man, right or wrong, has the right to want to have the neighborhood he lives in a certain kind of way. And at the moment the overwhelming majority of our people out there feel that people get along better, take more of a common interest in the life of the community, when they share a common background. I want you to believe me when I tell you that race prejudice simply doesn't enter into it. It is a matter of the people of Clybourne Park believing, rightly or wrongly, as I say, that for the happiness of all concerned that our Negro families are happier when they live in their *own* communities.

BENEATHA *(with a grand and bitter gesture):* This, friends, is the Welcoming Committee!

WALTER *(dumfounded, looking at* LINDNER*):* Is this what you came marching all the way over here to tell us?

LINDNER: Well, now we've been having a fine conversation. I hope you'll hear me all the way through.

WALTER *(tightly):* Go ahead, man.

LINDNER: You see—in the face of all the things I have said, we are prepared to make your family a very generous offer . . .

BENEATHA: Thirty pieces and not a coin less!

WALTER: Yeah!

LINDNER *(putting on his glasses and drawing a form out of the briefcase):* Our association is prepared, through the collective effort of our people, to buy the house from you at a financial gain to your family.

RUTH: Lord have mercy, ain't this the living gall!

WALTER: All right, you through?

LINDNER: Well, I want to give you the exact terms of the financial arrangement—

WALTER: We don't want to hear no exact terms of no arrangements. I
want to know if you got any more to tell us 'bout getting together?

LINDNER (*taking off his glasses*): Well—I don't suppose that you feel . . .

WALTER: Never mind how I feel—you got any more to say 'bout how
people ought to sit down and talk to each other? . . . Get out of my
house, man.

(*He turns his back and walks to the door.*)

LINDNER (*looking around at the hostile faces and reaching and assembling his hat
and briefcase*): Well—I don't understand why you people are reacting
this way. What do you think you are going to gain by moving into a
neighborhood where you just aren't wanted and where some elements—well—people can get awful worked up when they feel that
their whole way of life and everything they've ever worked for is
threatened.

WALTER: Get out.

LINDNER (*at the door, holding a small card*): Well—I'm sorry it went like this.

WALTER: Get out.

LINDNER (*almost sadly regarding* WALTER): You just can't force people to
change their hearts, son.

(*He turns and put his card on a table and exits.* WALTER *pushes the door
to with stinging hatred, and stands looking at it.* RUTH *just sits and*
BENEATHA *just stands. They say nothing.* MAMA *and* TRAVIS *enter.*)

MAMA: Well—this is all the packing got done since I left out of here this
morning. I testify before God that my children got all the energy of
the *dead!* What time the moving men due?

BENEATHA: Four o'clock. You had a caller, Mama.

(*She is smiling, teasingly.*)

MAMA: Sure enough—who?

BENEATHA (*her arms folded saucily*): The Welcoming Committee.

(WALTER *and* RUTH *giggle.*)

MAMA (*innocently*): Who?

BENEATHA: The Welcoming Committee. They said they're sure going to
be glad to see you when you get there.

WALTER (*devilishly*): Yeah, they said they can't hardly wait to see your face.

(*Laughter.*)

MAMA (*sensing their facetiousness*): What's the matter with you all?

WALTER: Ain't nothing the matter with us. We just telling you 'bout the gentleman who came to see you this afternoon. From the Clybourne Park Improvement Association.

MAMA: What he want?

RUTH (*in the same mood as* BENEATHA *and* WALTER): To welcome you, honey.

WALTER: He said they can't hardly wait. He said the one thing they don't have, that they just *dying* to have out there is a fine family of fine colored people! (*To* RUTH *and* BENEATHA.) Ain't that right!

RUTH (*mockingly*): Yeah! He left his card—

BENEATHA (*handing card to* MAMA): In case.

(MAMA *reads and throws it on the floor—understanding and looking off as she draws her chair up to the table on which she has put her plant and some sticks and some cord.*)

MAMA: Father, give us strength. (*Knowingly—and without fun.*) Did he threaten us?

BENEATHA: Oh—Mama—they don't do it like that anymore. He talked Brotherhood. He said everybody ought to learn how to sit down and hate each other with good Christian fellowship.

(*She and* WALTER *shake hands to ridicule the remark.*)

MAMA (*sadly*): Lord, protect us . . .

RUTH: You should hear the money those folks raised to buy the house from us. All we paid and then some.

BENEATHA: What they think we going to do—eat 'em?

RUTH: No, honey, marry 'em.

MAMA (*shaking her head*): Lord, Lord, Lord . . .

RUTH: Well—that's the way the crackers crumble. (*A beat.*) Joke.

BENEATHA (*laughingly noticing what her mother is doing*): Mama, what are you doing?

MAMA: Fixing my plant so it won't get hurt none on the way . . .

BENEATHA: Mama, you going to take *that* to the new house?

MAMA: Un-huh—

BENEATHA: That raggedy-looking old thing?

MAMA (*stopping and looking at her*): It expresses ME!

RUTH (*with delight, to* BENEATHA): So there, Miss Thing!

(WALTER *comes to* MAMA *suddenly and bends down behind her and squeezes her in his arms with all his strength. She is overwhelmed by the suddenness of it and, though delighted, her manner is like that of* RUTH *and* TRAVIS.)

MAMA: Look out now, boy! You make me mess up my thing here!

WALTER (*his face lit, he slips down on his knees beside her, his arms still about her*): Mama . . . you know what it means to climb up in the chariot?

MAMA *(gruffly, very happy)*: Get on away from me now . . .

RUTH *(near the gift-wrapped package, trying to catch* WALTER's *eye)*: Psst—

WALTER: What the old song say, Mama . . .

RUTH: Walter—Now?

(She is pointing at the package.)

WALTER *(speaking the lines, sweetly, playfully, in his mother's face)*: I got wings
 . . . you got wings . . .
 All God's Children got wings . . .

MAMA: Boy—get out of my face and do some work . . .

WALTER: When I get to heaven gonna put on my wings,
 Gonna fly all over God's heaven . . .

BENEATHA *(teasingly, from across the room)*: Everybody talking 'bout
 heaven ain't going there!

WALTER *(to* RUTH, *who is carrying the box across to them)*: I don't know,
 you think we ought to give her that . . . Seems to me she ain't been
 very appreciative around here.

MAMA *(eyeing the box, which is obviously a gift)*: What is that?

WALTER *(taking it from* RUTH *and putting it on the table in front of* MAMA*)*:
 Well—what you all think? Should we give it to her?

RUTH: Oh—she was pretty good today.

MAMA: I'll good you—

(She turns her eyes to the box again.)

BENEATHA: Open it, Mama.

*(She stands up, looks at it, turns, and looks at all of them, and then presses
her hands together and does not open the package.)*

WALTER *(sweetly)*: Open it, Mama. It's for you. (MAMA *looks in his eyes. It
 is the first present in her life without its being Christmas. Slowly she opens her
 package and lifts out, one by one, a brand-new sparkling set of gardening tools.*
 WALTER *continues, prodding.)* Ruth made up the note—read it . . .

MAMA *(picking up the card and adjusting her glasses)*: "To our own Mrs.
 Miniver—Love from Brother, Ruth and Beneatha." Ain't that lovely
 . . .

TRAVIS *(tugging at his father's sleeve)*: Daddy, can I give her mine now?

WALTER: All right, son. (TRAVIS *flies to get his gift.)*

MAMA: Now I don't have to use my knives and forks no more . . .

WALTER: Travis didn't want to go in with the rest of us, Mama. He got
 his own. *(Somewhat amused.)* We don't know what it is . . .

TRAVIS *(racing back in the room with a large hatbox and putting it in front of his
 grandmother)*: Here!

MAMA: Lord have mercy, baby. You done gone and bought your grandmother a hat?

TRAVIS *(very proud)*: Open it!

(She does and lifts out an elaborate, but very elaborate, wide gardening hat, and all the adults break up at the sight of it.)

RUTH: Travis, honey, what is that?

TRAVIS *(who thinks it is beautiful and appropriate)*: It's a gardening hat! Like the ladies always have on in the magazines when they work in their gardens.

BENEATHA *(giggling fiercely)*: Travis—we were trying to make Mama Mrs. Miniver—not Scarlett O'Hara!

MAMA *(indignantly)*: What's the matter with you all! This here is a beautiful hat! *(Absurdly.)* I always wanted me one just like it!

(She pops it on her head to prove it to her grandson, and the hat is ludicrous and considerably oversized.)

RUTH: Hot dog! Go, Mama!

WALTER *(doubled over with laughter)*: I'm sorry, Mama—but you look like you ready to go out and chop you some cotton sure enough!

(They all laugh except MAMA, out of deference to TRAVIS' feelings.)

MAMA *(gathering the boy up to her)*: Bless your heart—this is the prettiest hat I ever owned—(WALTER, RUTH, and BENEATHA *chime in—noisily, festively, and insincerely congratulating* TRAVIS *on his gift.)* What are we all standing around here for? We ain't finished packin' yet. Bennie, you ain't packed one book.

(The bell rings.)

BENEATHA: That couldn't be the movers . . . it's not hardly two good yet—

*(BENEATHA *goes into her room.* MAMA *starts for door.)*

WALTER *(turning, stiffening)*: Wait—wait—I'll get it.

(He stands and looks at the door.)

MAMA: You expecting company, son?

WALTER *(just looking at the door)*: Yeah—yeah . . .

*(MAMA *looks at* RUTH, *and they exchange innocent and unfrightened glances.)*

MAMA *(not understanding)*: Well, let them in, son.

BENEATHA *(from her room)*: We need some more string.

MAMA: Travis—you run to the hardware and get me some string cord.

*(MAMA *goes out and* WALTER *turns and looks at* RUTH. TRAVIS *goes to a dish for money.)*

RUTH: Why don't you answer the door, man?

WALTER *(suddenly bounding across the floor to embrace her):* 'Cause sometimes
  it hard to let the future begin! *(Stooping down in her face.)*
  I got wings! You got wings!
  All God's children got wings!
  *(He crosses to the door and throws it open. Standing there is a very slight little
  man in a not too prosperous business suit and with haunted frightened eyes and
  a hat pulled down tightly, brim up, around his forehead.* TRAVIS *passes
  between the men and exits.* WALTER *leans deep in the man's face, still in his
  jubilance.)*
  When I get to heaven gonna put on my wings,
  Gonna fly all over God's heaven . . .
  (The little man just stares at him.)
  Heaven —
  (Suddenly he stops and looks past the little man into the empty hallway.)
  Where's Willy, man?
BOBO: He ain't with me.
WALTER *(not disturbed):* Oh — come on in. You know my wife.
BOBO *(dumbly, taking off his hat):* Yes — h'you, Miss Ruth.
RUTH *(quietly, a mood apart from her husband already, seeing* BOBO*):* Hello,
  Bobo.
WALTER: You right on time today . . . Right on time. That's the way! *(He
  slaps* BOBO *on his back.)* Sit down . . . lemme hear.

  *(*RUTH *stands stiffly and quietly in back of them, as though somehow she
  senses death, her eyes fixed on her husband.)*

BOBO *(his frightened eyes on the floor, his hat in his hands):* Could I please get
  a drink of water, before I tell you about it, Walter Lee?

  *(*WALTER *does not take his eyes off the man.* RUTH *goes blindly to the tap
  and gets a glass of water and brings it to* BOBO*.)*

WALTER: There ain't nothing wrong, is there?
BOBO: Lemme tell you —
WALTER: Man — didn't nothing go wrong?
BOBO: Lemme tell you — Walter Lee. *(Looking at* RUTH *and talking to her
  more than to* WALTER*.)* You know how it was. I got to tell you how it
  was. I mean first I got to tell you how it was all the way . . . I mean
  about the money I put in, Walter Lee . . .
WALTER *(with taut agitation now):* What about the money you put in?
BOBO: Well — it wasn't much as we told you — me and Willy — *(He stops.)*
  I'm sorry, Walter. I got a bad feeling about it. I got a real bad feeling
  about it . . .
WALTER: Man, what you telling me about all this for? . . . Tell me what
  happened in Springfield . . .
BOBO: Springfield.

RUTH *(like a dead woman)*: What was supposed to happen in Springfield?

BOBO *(to her)*: This deal that me and Walter went into with Willy—Me and Willy was going to go down to Springfield and spread some money 'round so's we wouldn't have to wait so long for the liquor license . . . That's what we were going to do. Everybody said that was the way you had to do, you understand, Miss Ruth?

WALTER: Man—what happened down there?

BOBO *(a pitiful man, near tears)*: I'm trying to tell you, Walter.

WALTER *(screaming at him suddenly)*: THEN TELL ME, GODDAMMIT . . . WHAT'S THE MATTER WITH YOU?

BOBO: Man . . . I didn't go to no Springfield, yesterday.

WALTER *(halted, life hanging in the moment)*: Why not?

BOBO *(the long way, the hard way to tell)*: 'Cause I didn't have no reasons to . . .

WALTER: Man, what are you talking about!

BOBO: I'm talking about the fact that when I got to the train station yesterday morning—eight o'clock like we planned . . . Man—*Willy didn't never show up.*

WALTER: Why . . . where was he . . . where is he?

BOBO: That's what I'm trying to tell you . . . I don't know . . . I waited six hours . . . I called his house . . . and I waited . . . six hours . . . I waited in that train station six hours . . . *(Breaking into tears.)* That was all the extra money I had in the world . . . *(Looking up at* WALTER *with the tears running down his face.)* Man, *Willy is gone.*

WALTER: Gone, what you mean Willy is gone? Gone where? You mean he went by himself. You mean he went off to Springfield by himself—to take care of getting the license—*(Turns and looks anxiously at* RUTH.*)* You mean maybe he didn't want too many people in on the business down there? *(Looks to* RUTH *again, as before.)* You know Willy got his own ways. *(Looks back to* BOBO.*)* Maybe you was late yesterday and he just went on down there without you. Maybe—maybe—he's been callin' you at home tryin' to tell you what happened or something. Maybe—maybe—he just got sick. He's somewhere—he's got to be somewhere. We just got to find him—me and you got to find him. *(Grabs* BOBO *senselessly by the collar and starts to shake him.)* We got to!

BOBO *(in sudden angry, frightened agony)*: What's the matter with you, Walter! *When a cat take off with your money he don't leave you no road maps!*

WALTER *(turning madly, as though he is looking for Willy in the very room)*: Willy! . . . Willy . . . don't do it . . . Please don't do it . . . Man, not with that money . . . Man, please, not with that money . . . Oh, God . . . Don't let it be true . . . *(He is wandering around, crying out for Willy and looking for him or perhaps for help from God.)* Man . . . I trusted you . . . Man, I put my life in your hands . . . *(He starts to crumple down on the floor as* RUTH *just covers her face in horror.* MAMA *opens the door and comes into the room, with* BENEATHA *behind her.)* Man . . . *(He starts to*

pound the floor with his fists, sobbing wildly.) THAT MONEY IS MADE OUT
OF MY FATHER'S FLESH——

BOBO *(standing over him helplessly)*: I'm sorry, Walter . . . *(Only* WALTER's
sobs reply. BOBO *puts on his hat.)* I had my life staked on this deal,
too . . .

(He exits.)

MAMA *(to* WALTER*)*: Son— *(She goes to him, bends down to him, talks to his
bent head.)* Son . . . Is it gone? Son, I gave you sixty-five hundred
dollars. Is it gone? All of it? Beneatha's money too?

WALTER *(lifting his head slowly)*: Mama . . . I never . . . went to the bank
at all . . .

MAMA *(not wanting to believe him)*: You mean . . . your sister's school
money . . . you used that too . . . Walter? . . .

WALTER: Yessss! All of it . . . It's all gone . . .

(There is total silence. RUTH *stands with her face covered with her hands;*
BENEATHA *leans forlornly against a wall, fingering a piece of red ribbon
from the mother's gift.* MAMA *stops and looks at her son without recognition
and then, quite without thinking about it, starts to beat him senselessly in the
face.* BENEATHA *goes to them and stops it.)*

BENEATHA: Mama!

*(*MAMA *stops and looks at both of her children and rises slowly and wanders
vaguely, aimlessly away from them.)*

MAMA: I seen . . . him . . . night after night . . . come in . . . and look at
that rug . . . and then look at me . . . the red showing in his eyes . . .
the veins moving in his head . . . I seen him grow thin and old before
he was forty . . . working and working and working like somebody's
old horse . . . killing himself . . . and you—you give it all away in a
day— *(She raises her arms to strike him again.)*

BENEATHA: Mama—

MAMA: Oh God . . . *(She looks up to Him.)* Look down here—and show
me the strength.

BENEATHA: Mama—

MAMA *(folding over)*: Strength . . .

BENEATHA *(plaintively)*: Mama . . .

MAMA: Strength!

ACT III

(An hour later.)

    *At curtain, there is a sullen light of gloom in the living room, gray light not
unlike that which began the first scene of Act I. At left we can see* WALTER *within
his room, alone with himself. He is stretched out on the bed, his shirt out and open,*

his arms under his head. He does not smoke, he does not cry out, he merely lies there,
looking up at the ceiling, much as if he were alone in the world.)

> *(In the living room* BENEATHA *sits at the table, still surrounded by the now*
almost ominous packing crates. She sits looking off. We feel that this is a mood struck
perhaps an hour before, and it lingers now, full of the empty sound of profound
disappointment. We see on a line from her brother's bedroom the sameness of their
attitudes. Presently the bell rings and BENEATHA *rises without ambition or interest*
in answering. It is ASAGAI, *smiling broadly, striding into the room with energy*
and happy expectation and conversation.)

ASAGAI: I came over . . . I had some free time. I thought I might help
with the packing. Ah, I like the look of packing crates! A household
in preparation for a journey! It depresses some people . . . but for me
. . . it is another feeling. Something full of the flow of life, do you
understand? Movement, progress . . . It makes me think of Africa.

BENEATHA: Africa!

ASAGAI: What kind of a mood is this? Have I told you how deeply you
move me?

BENEATHA: He gave away the money, Asagai . . .

ASAGAI: Who gave away what money?

BENEATHA: The insurance money. My brother gave it away.

ASAGAI: Gave it away?

BENEATHA: He made an investment! With a man even Travis wouldn't
have trusted with his most worn-out marbles.

ASAGAI: And it's gone?

BENEATHA: Gone!

ASAGAI: I'm very sorry . . . And you, now?

BENEATHA: Me? . . . Me? . . . Me, I'm nothing . . . Me. When I was
very small . . . we used to take our sleds out in the wintertime and the
only hills we had were the ice-covered stone steps of some houses
down the street. And we used to fill them in with snow and make
them smooth and slide down them all day . . . and it was very dangerous, you know . . . far too steep . . . and sure enough one day a kid
named Rufus came down too fast and hit the sidewalk and we saw his
face just split open right there in front of us . . . And I remember
standing there looking at his bloody open face thinking that was the
end of Rufus. But the ambulance came and they took him to the
hospital and they fixed the broken bones and they sewed it all up . . .
and the next time I saw Rufus he just had a little line down the middle
of his face . . . I never got over that . . .

ASAGAI: What?

BENEATHA: That that was what one person could do for another, fix him
up — sew up the problem, make him all right again. That was the most
marvelous thing in the world . . . I wanted to do that. I always

thought it was the one concrete thing in the world that a human being could do. Fix up the sick, you know—and make them whole again. This was truly being God . . .

ASAGAI: You wanted to be God?

BENEATHA: No—I wanted to cure. It used to be so important to me. I wanted to cure. It used to matter. I used to care. I mean about people and how their bodies hurt . . .

ASAGAI: And you've stopping caring?

BENEATHA: Yes—I think so.

ASAGAI: Why?

BENEATHA *(bitterly)*: Because it doesn't seem deep enough, close enough to what ails mankind! It was a child's way of seeing things—or an idealist's.

ASAGAI: Children see things very well sometimes—and idealists even better.

BENEATHA: I know that's what you think. Because you are still where I left off. You with all your talk and dreams about Africa! You still think you can patch up the world. Cure the Great Sore of Colonialism— *(loftily, mocking it)* with the Penicillin of Independence—

ASAGAI: Yes!

BENEATHA: Independence *and then what?* What about all the crooks and thieves and just plain idiots who will come into power and steal and plunder the same as before—only now they will be black and do it in the name of the new Independence—WHAT ABOUT THEM?!

ASAGAI: That will be the problem for another time. First we must get there.

BENEATHA: And where does it end?

ASAGAI: End? Who even spoke of an end? To life? To living?

BENEATHA: An end to misery! To stupidity! Don't you see there isn't any real progress, Asagai, there is only one large circle that we march in, around and around, each of us with our own little picture in front of us—our own little mirage that we think is the future.

ASAGAI: That is the mistake.

BENEATHA: What?

ASAGAI: What you just said—about the circle. It isn't a circle—it is simply a long line—as in geometry, you know, one that reaches into infinity. And because we cannot see the end—we also cannot see how it changes. And it is very odd but those who see the changes—who dream, who will not give up—are called idealists . . . and those who see only the circle—we call *them* the "realists"!

BENEATHA: Asagai, while I was sleeping in that bed in there, people went out and took the future right out of my hands! And nobody asked me, nobody consulted me—they just went out and changed my life!

ASAGAI: Was it your money?

BENEATHA: What?

ASAGAI: Was it your money he gave away?

BENEATHA: It belonged to all of us.

ASAGAI: But did you earn it? Would you have had it at all if your father had not died?

BENEATHA: No.

ASAGAI: Then isn't there something wrong in a house — in a world — where all dreams, good or bad, must depend on the death of a man? I never thought to see *you* like this, Alaiyo. You! Your brother made a mistake and you are grateful to him so that now you can give up the ailing human race on account of it! You talk about what good is struggle, what good is anything! Where are we all going and why are we bothering!

BENEATHA: AND YOU CANNOT ANSWER IT!

ASAGAI (*shouting over her*): I LIVE THE ANSWER! (*Pause.*) In my village at home it is the exceptional man who can even read a newspaper . . . or who ever sees a book at all. I will go home and much of what I will have to say will seem strange to the people of my village. But I will teach and work and things will happen, slowly and swiftly. At times it will seem that nothing changes at all . . . and then again the sudden dramatic events which make history leap into the future. And then quiet again. Retrogression even. Guns, murder, revolution. And I even will have moments when I wonder if the quiet was not better than all that death and hatred. But I will look about my village at the illiteracy and disease and ignorance and I will not wonder long. And perhaps . . . perhaps I will be a great man . . . I mean perhaps I will hold on to the substance of truth and find my way always with the right course . . . and perhaps for it I will be butchered in my bed some night by the servants of empire . . .

BENEATHA: *The martyr!*

ASAGAI (*he smiles*): . . . or perhaps I shall live to be a very old man, respected and esteemed in my new nation . . . And perhaps I shall hold office and this is what I'm trying to tell you, Alaiyo: Perhaps the things I believe now for my country will be wrong and outmoded, and I will not understand and do terrible things to have things my way or merely to keep my power. Don't you see that there will be young men and women — not British soldiers then, but my own black countrymen — to step out of the shadows some evening and slit my then useless throat? Don't you see they have always been there . . . that they always will be. And that such a thing as my own death will be an advance? They who might kill me even . . . actually replenish all that I was.

BENEATHA: Oh, Asagai, I know all that.

ASAGAI: Good! Then stop moaning and groaning and tell me what you plan to do.

BENEATHA: Do?

ASAGAI: I have a bit of a suggestion.

BENEATHA: What?

ASAGAI *(rather quietly for him)*: That when it is all over — that you come home with me —

BENEATHA *(staring at him and crossing away with exasperation)*: Oh — Asagai — at this moment you decide to be romantic!

ASAGAI *(quickly understanding the misunderstanding)*: My dear, young creature of the New World — I do not mean across the city — I mean across the ocean: home — to Africa.

BENEATHA *(slowly understanding and turning to him with murmured amazement)*: To Africa?

ASAGAI: Yes! . . . *(Smiling and lifting his arms playfully.)* Three hundred years later the African Prince rose up out of the seas and swept the maiden back across the middle passage over which her ancestors had come —

BENEATHA *(unable to play)*: To — to Nigeria?

ASAGAI: Nigeria. Home. *(Coming to her with genuine romantic flippancy.)* I will show you our mountains and our stars; and give you cool drinks from gourds and teach you the old songs and the ways of our people — and in time, we will pretend that — *(very softly)* — you have only been away for a day. Say that you'll come — *(He swings her around and takes her full in his arms in a kiss which proceeds to passion.)*

BENEATHA *(pulling away suddenly)*: You're getting me all mixed up —

ASAGAI: Why?

BENEATHA: Too many things — too many things have happened today. I must sit down and think. I don't know what I feel about anything right this minute. *(She promptly sits down and props her chin on her fist.)*

ASAGAI *(charmed)*: All right, I shall leave you. No — don't get up. *(Touching her, gently, sweetly.)* Just sit awhile and think . . . Never be afraid to sit awhile and think. *(He goes to door and looks at her.)* How often I have looked at you and said, "Ah — so this is what the New World hath finally wrought . . ."

(He exits. BENEATHA sits on alone. Presently WALTER enters from his room and starts to rummage through things, feverishly looking for something. She looks up and turns in her seat.)

BENEATHA *(hissingly)*: Yes — just look at what the New World hath wrought! . . . Just look! *(She gestures with bitter disgust.)* There he is! *Monsieur le petit bourgeois noir°* — himself! There he is — Symbol of a Rising Class! Entrepreneur! Titan of the system! *(WALTER ignores her completely and continues frantically and destructively looking for something and hurling things to floor and tearing things out of their place in his search.*

ACT III. *Monsieur . . . noir:* Mr. Black Middle Class.

BENEATHA *ignores the eccentricity of his actions and goes on with the monologue of insult.)* Did you dream of yachts on Lake Michigan, Brother? Did you see yourself on that Great Day sitting down at the Conference Table, surrounded by all the mighty bald-headed men in America? All halted, waiting, breathless, waiting for your pronouncements on industry? Waiting for you—Chairman of the Board! *(WALTER finds what he is looking for—a small piece of white paper—and pushes it in his pocket and puts on his coat and rushes out without ever having looked at her. She shouts after him.)* I look at you and I see the final triumph of stupidity in the world!

(The door slams and she returns to just sitting again. RUTH comes quickly out of MAMA's room.)

RUTH: Who was that?

BENEATHA: Your husband.

RUTH: Where did he go?

BENEATHA: Who knows—maybe he has an appointment at U.S. Steel.

RUTH *(anxiously, with frightened eyes)*: You didn't say nothing bad to him, did you?

BENEATHA: Bad? Say anything bad to him? No—I told him he was a sweet boy and full of dreams and everything is strictly peachy keen, as the ofay° kids say!

(MAMA enters from her bedroom. She is lost, vague, trying to catch hold, to make some sense of her former command of the world, but it still eludes her. A sense of waste overwhelms her gait; a measure of apology rides on her shoulders. She goes to her plant, which has remained on the table, looks at it, picks it up and takes it to the window sill and sits it outside, and she stands and looks at it a long moment. Then she closes the window, straightens her body with effort, and turns around to her children.)

MAMA: Well—ain't it a mess in here, though? *(A false cheerfulness, a beginning of something.)* I guess we all better stop moping around and get some work done. All this unpacking and everything we got to do. *(RUTH raises her head slowly in response to the sense of the line; and BENEATHA in similar manner turns very slowly to look at her mother.)* One of you all better call the moving people and tell 'em not to come.

RUTH: Tell 'em not to come?

MAMA: Of course, baby. Ain't no need in 'em coming all the way here and having to go back. They charges for that too. *(She sits down, fingers to her brow, thinking.)* Lord, ever since I was a little girl, I always remembers people saying, "Lena—Lena Eggleston, you aims too high all the time. You needs to slow down and see life a little more like it is. Just

---

ofay: White person, usually a derogatory term. "Foe" in pig latin.

slow down some." That's what they always used to say down home —
"Lord, that Lena Eggleston is a high-minded thing. She'll get her due
one day!"

RUTH: No, Lena . . .

MAMA: Me and Big Walter just didn't never learn right.

RUTH: Lena, no! We gotta go. Bennie — tell her . . . *(She rises and crosses to*
BENEATHA *with her arms outstretched.* BENEATHA *doesn't respond.)*
Tell her we can still move . . . the notes ain't but a hundred and
twenty-five a month. We got four grown people in this house — we
can work . . .

MAMA *(to herself)*: Just aimed too high all the time —

RUTH *(turning and going to* MAMA *fast — the words pouring out with urgency
and desperation)*: Lena — I'll work . . . I'll work twenty hours a day in
all the kitchens in Chicago . . . I'll strap my baby on my back if I have
to and scrub all the floors in America and wash all the sheets in America if I have to — but we got to MOVE! We got to get OUT OF HERE!!

(MAMA reaches out absently and pats RUTH's hand.)

MAMA: No — I sees things differently now. Been thinking 'bout some of
the things we could do to fix this place up some. I seen a second-hand
bureau over on Maxwell Street just the other day that could fit right
there. *(She points to where the new furniture might go.* RUTH *wanders away
from her.)* Would need some new handles on it and then a little varnish
and it look like something brand-new. And — we can put up them new
curtains in the kitchen . . . Why this place be looking fine. Cheer us
all up so that we forget trouble ever come . . . *(To* RUTH.*)* And you
could get some nice screens to put up in your room round the baby's
bassinet . . . *(She looks at both of them, pleadingly.)* Sometimes you just
got to know when to give up some things . . . and hold on to what
you got . . .

*(WALTER enters from the outside, looking spent and leaning against the
door, his coat hanging from him.)*

MAMA: Where you been, son?

WALTER *(breathing hard)*: Made a call.

MAMA: To who, son?

WALTER: To The Man. *(He heads for his room.)*

MAMA: What man, baby?

WALTER *(stops in the door)*: The Man, Mama. Don't you know who The
Man is?

RUTH: Walter Lee?

WALTER: *The Man.* Like the guys in the streets say — The Man. Captain
Boss — Mistuh Charley . . . Old Cap'n Please Mr. Bossman . . .

BENEATHA *(suddenly)*: Lindner!

WALTER: That's right! That's good. I told him to come right over.

BENEATHA (*fiercely, understanding*): For what? What do you want to see him for!

WALTER (*looking at his sister*): We going to do business with him.

MAMA: What you talking 'bout, son?

WALTER: Talking 'bout life, Mama. You all always telling me to see life like it is. Well—I laid in there on my back today . . . and I figured it out. Life just like it is. Who gets and who don't get. (*He sits down with his coat on and laughs.*) Mama, you know it's all divided up. Life is. Sure enough. Between the takers and the "tooken." (*He laughs.*) I've figured it out finally. (*He looks around at them.*) Yeah. Some of us always getting "tooken." (*He laughs.*) People like Willy Harris, they don't never get "tooken." And you know why the rest of us do? 'Cause we all mixed up. Mixed up bad. We get to looking 'round for the right and the wrong; and we worry about it and cry about it and stay up nights trying to figure out 'bout the wrong and the right of things all the time . . . And all the time, man, them takers is out there operating, just taking and taking. Willy Harris? Shoot—Willy Harris don't even count. He don't even count in the big scheme of things. But I'll say one thing for old Willy Harris . . . he's taught me something. He's taught me to keep my eye on what counts in this world. Yeah— (*Shouting out a little.*) Thanks, Willy!

RUTH: What did you call that man for, Walter Lee?

WALTER: Called him to tell him to come on over to the show. Gonna put on a show for the man. Just what he wants to see. You see, Mama, the man came here today and he told us that them people out there where you want us to move—well they so upset they willing to pay us *not* to move! (*He laughs again.*) And—and oh, Mama—you would of been proud of the way me and Ruth and Bennie acted. We told him to get out . . . Lord have mercy! We told the man to get out! Oh, we was some proud folks this afternoon, yeah. (*He lights a cigarette.*) We were still full of that old-time stuff . . .

RUTH (*coming toward him slowly*): You talking 'bout taking them people's money to keep us from moving in that house?

WALTER: I ain't just talking 'bout it, baby—I'm telling you that's what's going to happen!

BENEATHA: Oh, God! Where is the bottom! Where is the real honest-to-God bottom so he can't go any farther!

WALTER: See—that's the old stuff. You and that boy that was here today. You all want everybody to carry a flag and a spear and sing some marching songs, huh? You wanna spend your life looking into things and trying to find the right and the wrong part, huh? Yeah. You know what's going to happen to that boy someday—he'll find himself sitting in a dungeon, locked in forever—and the takers will have the key!

Forget it, baby! There ain't no causes—there ain't nothing but taking in this world, and he who takes most is smartest—and it don't make a damn bit of difference *how.*

MAMA: You making something inside me cry, son. Some awful pain inside me.

WALTER: Don't cry, Mama. Understand. That white man is going to walk in that door able to write checks for more money than we ever had. It's important to him and I'm going to help him . . . I'm going to put on the show, Mama.

MAMA: Son—I come from five generations of people who was slaves and sharecroppers—but ain't nobody in my family never let nobody pay 'em no money that was a way of telling us we wasn't fit to walk the earth. We ain't never been that poor. *(Raising her eyes and looking at him.)* We ain't never been that—dead inside.

BENEATHA: Well—we are dead now. All the talk about dreams and sunlight that goes on in this house. It's all dead now.

WALTER: What's the matter with you all! I didn't make this world! It was give to me this way! Hell, yes, I want me some yachts someday! Yes, I want to hang some real pearls 'round my wife's neck. Ain't she supposed to wear no pearls? Somebody tell me—tell me, who decides which women is suppose to wear pearls in this world. I tell you I am a *man*—and I think my wife should wear some pearls in this world!

(This last line hangs a good while and WALTER *begins to move about the room. The word "Man" has penetrated his consciousness; he mumbles it to himself repeatedly between strange agitated pauses as he moves about.)*

MAMA: Baby, how you going to feel on the inside?

WALTER: Fine! . . . Going to feel fine . . . a man . . .

MAMA: You won't have nothing left then, Walter Lee.

WALTER *(coming to her)*: I'm going to feel fine, Mama. I'm going to look that son-of-a-bitch in the eyes and say—*(he falters)*—and say, "All right, Mr. Lindner—*(he falters even more)*—that's *your* neighborhood out there! You got the right to keep it like you want! You got the right to have it like you want! Just write the check and—the house is yours." And—and I am going to say—*(His voice almost breaks.)* "And you—you people just put the money in my hand and you won't have to live next to this bunch of stinking niggers! . . ." *(He straightens up and moves away from his mother, walking around the room.)* And maybe—maybe I'll just get down on my black knees . . . *(He does so;* RUTH *and* BENNIE *and* MAMA *watch him in frozen horror.)* "Captain, Mistuh, Bossman—*(Groveling and grinning and wringing his hands in profoundly anguished imitation of the slow-witted movie stereotype.)* A-hee-hee-hee! Oh, yassuh boss! Yassssssuh! Great white—*(voice breaking, he forces himself to go on)*—Father, just gi' ussen de money, fo' God's sake, and we's—we's

ain't gwine come out deh and dirty up yo' white folks neighborhood
. . ." *(He breaks down completely.)* And I'll feel fine! Fine! FINE! *(He gets
up and goes into the bedroom.)*

BENEATHA: That is not a man. That is nothing but a toothless rat.

MAMA: Yes—death done come in this here house. *(She is nodding, slowly,
reflectively.)* Done come walking in my house on the lips of my children. You what supposed to be my beginning again. You—what supposed to be my harvest. *(To BENEATHA.)* You—you mourning your
brother?

BENEATHA: He's no brother of mine.

MAMA: What you say?

BENEATHA: I said that that individual in that room is no brother of mine.

MAMA: That's what I thought you said. You feeling like you better than
he is today? *(BENEATHA does not answer.)* Yes? What you tell him a
minute ago? That he wasn't a man? Yes? You give him up for me? You
done wrote his epitaph too—like the rest of the world? Well, who give
you the privilege?

BENEATHA: Be on my side for once! You saw what he just did, Mama!
You saw him—down on his knees. Wasn't it you who taught me to
despise any man who would do that? Do what he's going to do?

MAMA: Yes—I taught you that. Me and your daddy. But I thought I taught
you something else too . . . I thought I taught you to love him.

BENEATHA: Love him? There is nothing left to love.

MAMA: There is *always* something left to love. And if you ain't learned
that, you ain't learned nothing. *(Looking at her.)* Have you cried for
that boy today? I don't mean for yourself and for the family 'cause we
lost the money. I mean for him: what he been through and what it
done to him. Child, when do you think is the time to love somebody
the most? When they done good and made things easy for everybody?
Well then, you ain't through learning—because that ain't the time at
all. It's when he's at his lowest and can't believe in hisself 'cause the
world done whipped him so! When you starts measuring somebody,
measure him right, child, measure him right. Make sure you done
taken into account what hills and valleys he come through before he
got to wherever he is.

(TRAVIS bursts into the room at the end of the speech, leaving the door open.)

TRAVIS: Grandmama—the moving men are downstairs! The truck just
pulled up.

MAMA *(turning and looking at him)*: Are they, baby? They downstairs?

*(She sighs and sits. LINDNER appears in the doorway. He peers in and
knocks lightly, to gain attention, and comes in. All turn to look at him.)*

LINDNER *(hat and briefcase in hand)*: Uh—hello . . .

(RUTH *crosses mechanically to the bedroom door and opens it and lets it swing open freely and slowly as the lights come up on* WALTER *within, still in his coat, sitting at the far corner of the room. He looks up and out through the room to* LINDNER.)

RUTH: He's here.

(*A long minute passes and* WALTER *slowly gets up.*)

LINDNER (*coming to the table with efficiency, putting his briefcase on the table and starting to unfold papers and unscrew fountain pens*): Well, I certainly was glad to hear from you people. (WALTER *has begun the trek out of the room, slowly and awkwardly, rather like a small boy, passing the back of his sleeve across his mouth from time to time.*) Life can really be so much simpler than people let it be most of the time. Well—with whom do I negotiate? You, Mrs. Younger, or your son here? (MAMA *sits with her hands folded on her lap and her eyes closed as* WALTER *advances.* TRAVIS *goes closer to* LINDNER *and looks at the papers curiously.*) Just some official papers, sonny.

RUTH: Travis, you go downstairs—

MAMA (*opening her eyes and looking into* WALTER'S): No. Travis, you stay right here. And you make him understand what you doing, Walter Lee. You teach him good. Like Willy Harris taught you. You show where our five generations done come to. (WALTER *looks from her to the boy, who grins at him innocently.*) Go ahead, son—(*She folds her hands and closes her eyes.*) Go ahead.

WALTER (*at last crosses to* LINDNER, *who is reviewing the contract*): Well, Mr. Lindner. (BENEATHA *turns away.*) We called you—(*there is a profound, simple groping quality in his speech*)—because, well, me and my family (*he looks around and shifts from one foot to the other*) Well—we are very plain people . . .

LINDNER: Yes—

WALTER: I mean—I have worked as a chauffeur most of my life—and my wife here, she does domestic work in people's kitchens. So does my mother. I mean—we are plain people . . .

LINDNER: Yes, Mr. Younger—

WALTER (*really like a small boy, looking down at his shoes and then up at the man*): And—uh—well, my father, well, he was a laborer most of his life . . .

LINDNER (*absolutely confused*): Uh, yes—yes, I understand. (*He turns back to the contract.*)

WALTER (*a beat; staring at him*): And my father—(*With sudden intensity.*) My father almost *beat a man to death* once because this man called him a bad name or something, you know what I mean?

LINDNER (*looking up, frozen*): No, no, I'm afraid I don't—

WALTER (*A beat. The tension hangs; then* WALTER *steps back from it.*): Yeah. Well — what I mean is that we come from people who had a lot of *pride.* I mean — we are very proud people. And that's my sister over there and she's going to be a doctor — and we are very proud —

LINDNER: Well — I am sure that is very nice, but —

WALTER: What I am telling you is that we called you over here to tell you that we are very proud and that this — (*Signaling to* TRAVIS.) Travis, come here. (TRAVIS *crosses and* WALTER *draws him before him facing the man.*) This is my son, and he makes the sixth generation our family in this country. And we have all thought about your offer —

LINDNER: Well, good . . . good —

WALTER: And we have decided to move into our house because my father — my father — he earned it for us brick by brick. (MAMA *has her eyes closed and is rocking back and forth as though she were in church, with her head nodding the Amen yes.*) We don't want to make no trouble for nobody or fight no causes, and we will try to be good neighbors. And that's *all* we got to say about that. (*He looks the man absolutely in the eyes.*) We don't want your money. (*He turns and walks away.*)

LINDNER (*looking around at all of then*): I take it then — that you have decided to occupy . . .

BENEATHA: That's what the man said.

LINDNER (*to* MAMA *in her reverie*): Then I would like to appeal to you, Mrs. Younger. You are older and wiser and understand things better I am sure . . .

MAMA: I am afraid you don't understand. My son said we was going to move and there ain't nothing left for me to say. (*Briskly.*) You know how these young folks is nowadays, mister. Can't do a thing with 'em! (*As he opens his mouth, she rises.*) Goodbye.

LINDNER (*folding up his materials*): Well — if you are that final about it . . . there is nothing left for me to say. (*He finishes, almost ignored by the family, who are concentrating on* WALTER LEE. *At the door* LINDNER *halts and looks around.*) I sure hope you people know what you're getting into.

(*He shakes his head and exits.*)

RUTH (*looking around and coming to life*): Well, for God's sake — if the moving men are here — LET'S GET THE HELL OUT OF HERE!

MAMA (*into action*): Ain't it the truth! Look at all this here mess. Ruth, put Travis' good jacket on him . . . Walter Lee, fix your tie and tuck your shirt in, you look like somebody's hoodlum! Lord have mercy, where is my plant? (*She flies to get it amid the general bustling of the family, who are deliberately trying to ignore the nobility of the past moment.*) You all start on down . . . Travis child, don't go empty-handed . . . Ruth, where did I put that box with my skillets in it? I want to be in charge of it myself . . . I'm going to make us the biggest dinner we ever ate tonight . . . Beneatha, what's the matter with them stockings? Pull them things up, girl . . .

(The family starts to file out as two moving men appear and begin to carry out the heavier pieces of furniture, bumping into the family as they move about.)

BENEATHA: Mama, Asagai asked me to marry him today and go to Africa —

MAMA *(in the middle of her getting-ready activity)*: He did? You ain't old enough to marry nobody — *(Seeing the moving men lifting one of her chairs precariously.)* Darling, that ain't no bale of cotton, please handle it so we can sit in it again! I had that chair twenty-five years . . .

(The movers sigh with exasperation and go on with their work.)

BENEATHA *(girlishly and unreasonably trying to pursue the conversation)*: To go to Africa, Mama — be a doctor in Africa . . .

MAMA *(distracted)*: Yes, baby —

WALTER: *Africa!* What he want you to go to Africa for?

BENEATHA: To practice there . . .

WALTER: Girl, if you don't get all them silly ideas out your head! You better marry yourself a man with some loot . . .

BENEATHA *(angrily, precisely as in the first scene of the play)*: What have you got to do with who I marry!

WALTER: Plenty. Now I think George Murchison —

BENEATHA: *George Murchison!* I wouldn't marry him if he was Adam and I was Eve!

(WALTER and BENEATHA go out yelling at each other vigorously and the anger is loud and real till their voices diminish. RUTH stands at the door and turns to MAMA and smiles knowingly.)

MAMA *(fixing her hat at last)*: Yeah — they something all right, my children . . .

RUTH: Yeah — they're something. Let's go, Lena.

MAMA *(stalling, starting to look around at the house)*: Yes — I'm coming. Ruth —

RUTH: Yes?

MAMA *(quietly, woman to woman)*: He finally come into his manhood today, didn't he? Kind of like a rainbow after the rain . . .

RUTH *(biting her lip lest her own pride explode in front of MAMA)*: Yes, Lena.

(WALTER's voice calls for them raucously.)

WALTER *(offstage)*: Y'all come on! These people charges by the hour, you know!

MAMA *(waving* RUTH *out vaguely)*: All right, honey — go on down. I be down directly.

*(*RUTH *hesitates, then exits.* MAMA *stands, at last alone in the living room, her plant on the table before her as the lights start to come down. She looks around at all the walls and ceilings and suddenly, despite herself, while the children call below, a great heaving thing rises in her and she puts her fist to her mouth to stifle it, takes a final desperate look, pulls her coat about her, pats her hat, and goes out. The lights dim down. The door opens and she comes back in, grabs her plant, and goes out for the last time.)*

An Introduction to Nonfiction

Nonfiction is often defined as prose works that are factual. Under this definition, all prose works other than imaginative literature (novels, short stories, poetry, and drama) are considered nonfiction. Essays, transcriptions of speeches, letters, documents, and journals are nonfiction. So are recipes, corporate reports, and grant proposals. But are all of these forms literature?

For centuries, most readers and scholars have agreed that one particular type of essay — the **belle lettre** (French for "beautiful letter") — deserves to be called literature. These essays often pursue philosophical subjects using language with the figures we traditionally think of as literary, such as metaphor, simile, and personification. Loren Eiseley's "The Hidden Teacher" (page 747) exemplifies the *belle lettre* essay.

But what about other forms of nonfiction? Most people would immediately reject recipes, corporate reports, and grant proposals as examples of literature, perhaps because these forms of writing are meant simply to convey information rather than to intrigue both the minds and emotions of readers; perhaps because these forms deal primarily with facts rather than ideas, ideals, and emotions; perhaps because the language of these forms is usually literal rather than figurative; perhaps because these forms tend to avoid ambiguity and complication rather than suggest them; perhaps because these forms generally provide answers and certainties rather than raising questions and possibilities.

This series of "perhaps," then, suggests a possible definition for literary works.

1. They deal with ideas, ideals, and emotions.
2. Their language is often figurative.
3. They suggest ambiguity and complication.
4. They raise questions and possibilities.

It is important to realize that readers and scholars have proposed many different definitions of literature. (During your lifetime of reading, you may develop your own definition of literature, and it may be different both from the one suggested here and from those of other readers.) Many forms that have not traditionally been called literary meet the four criteria in the preceding list. Certain transcriptions of speeches, letters, documents, and journals may be read as literature.

Consider, for example, Lincoln's Gettysburg Address or John F. Kennedy's Inaugural Address. What makes these speeches memorable and important? (Consider not only their original audiences but also those who hear them repeated or who read transcripts.) The answer is complex: Certainly the sensitive and striking choice of language (Lincoln, for example, begins with "Fourscore and seven years ago" rather than with the more common "eighty-seven years ago"); certainly the powerful rhythm (both Lincoln and Kennedy make use of parallel structure: "Government of the people, by the people, for the people shall not perish from the earth" and "Ask not what your country can do for you; ask what you can do for your country"); certainly the thought-provoking themes offered and the complex questions raised. We might say, then, that these speeches can be called literature.

SUGGESTIONS FOR READING SPEECHES

When you read speeches, try to picture the original audience. How has the speech-giver chosen his or her words to reach that audience? Imagine the possible responses of that audience to the speech. Consider, too, that many speakers are aware that their speeches will be reported by the press or — at the very least — repeated by those who have heard them. What elements of the speech might appeal to an even wider audience than those originally addressed? Keep in mind, too, that one of the best ways to appreciate a transcript of a speech is to read it aloud — or to listen to it being read aloud.

SUGGESTIONS FOR READING LETTERS

Like speeches, letters are addressed to an audience. When you read letters, keep in mind the original audience. Some letters were intended to be read by only one other person. Others, like "Letter from Birmingham Jail" (page 1498) by Martin Luther King, Jr., were written for a far larger audience. Consider how the different audiences affect how the writer treats his or her subject. For example, how might King's description have differed if he were explaining the same events in a letter to be read only by his family or close friends?

SUGGESTIONS FOR READING DOCUMENTS

As you read a document, consider its purpose. What, for example, do you think the "Declaration of Sentiments and Resolutions" (page 1511) was intended to accomplish? Consider also how effective you think the document might have been in accomplishing that purpose.

Ask yourself, also, how responses to the document may have changed from the time it was written to the present. Consider why and how readers' responses might have changed (or stayed nearly the same).

SUGGESTIONS FOR READING JOURNALS AND DIARIES

Unlike nearly any other writings, journals and diaries were usually originally composed for an audience of only one: the writer. Journals may jump from subject to subject without any clear connection because the writer is not trying to communicate ideas or emotions to a group of readers but is, instead, exploring those ideas or emotions for personal reasons.

Reading journals and diaries gives us the opportunity to look directly into the hearts and minds of writers; to observe the ideas, images, and emotions they treasure for themselves; and to see the early stages of the creative process. Shonagon's *Pillow Book* (an excerpt is on page 1515) is an example of the personal journal.

SUGGESTIONS FOR READING ESSAYS

As you respond to an essay, consider what its central purpose seems to be. Is it written primarily to describe a person or place? Or does it, perhaps, tell a true story (a **narrative**)? What significance do you see in the description or in the narrative? How does that description or narrative relate to your own observations and experiences?

An essay may make significant comparisons or contrasts; it may explain the reasons something happened or explore the effects of a particular event or action. Some essays contemplate or speculate on an idea, exploring many possibilities without insisting on one final conclusion. Many other essays, in one way or another, argue for or against a point of view, a solution to a problem, or a new way of thinking about the world.

Whatever the essay's purpose, look carefully at the writer's choice of words as well as the way he or she structures both the essay itself and its sentences and paragraphs. Then consider how well you believe the writer has fulfilled his or her purpose. Consider also the details, reasons, and examples the writer supplies to support generalizations. Do you find them convincing? Intriguing? Weak? Insufficient?

Notice the questions and complexities stated or implied by the writer as well as answers or solutions that are offered. Think carefully about your own response to these questions, complexities, answers, and solutions.

Guidelines: Nonfiction

Speeches

1. Imagine that you are a member of the audience first hearing the speech. Describe the setting, the speaker, and your response to the speech.
2. Write a speech in response to the speech you have read. In your speech, pose questions or suggest alternatives to the views you have read.

Letters

1. Assume that you are the person (or one of the persons) to whom the letter was originally addressed. Write a response to the writer. Refer to specific details in the letter as you plan your response.
2. Write a character sketch of the person who wrote the letter. What do the details of the letter (content as well as style) suggest to you about this person? Use specific examples from the letter to support your character analysis.

Documents

1. Imagine that you are one of the drafters of the document. Describe the process of planning and writing the document. Project the arguments and disagreements that might have been part of this process and explain how they were resolved. (You may want to research some of the historical background relating to the document.)
2. Write a document styled on the one you read, but relating to a current political issue.

Journals

1. Write the entry (or series of entries) you imagine might follow the one(s) you have read. Try to capture the writer's style as you build on his or her ideas and emotions.
2. Write a letter to the journal's author explaining your responses to what you have read.

Essays

1. Explain what you see as the author's purpose in writing the essay. How effectively has the author accomplished that purpose? Explain.
2. Find a passage or sentence you find particularly thought-provoking. Copy the passage or sentence and then write your response to it.

3. Identify the point of view taken by the writer. Compose a response written from a different point of view.

4. Describe the values you believe are exemplified by the points raised, the questions asked, or the views asserted in the essay. Write an evaluation of those values, explaining how they compare or contrast to your own.

5. Write a letter to the author of the essay explaining your response to specific parts of the essay (for instance, to specific examples or to a specific argument or proposal). Begin this assignment by making a list of five to ten questions you would like to ask the author if you could speak to him or her privately.

SOJOURNER TRUTH (1797–1883)

Ain't I a Woman?

> *Sojourner Truth was born into slavery in 1797. Originally called Isabella, she took the name by which she is now known to symbolize both her journeys and their purpose. After escaping to freedom in 1827, Sojourner Truth spoke often on spiritual and social issues, including racial equality and women's rights. She is reported to have been an incredibly effective speaker with a wide range of audiences — white and black, liberal and conservative, hostile and friendly.*

Well, children, where there is so much racket there must be something out of kilter. I think that 'twixt the negroes of the South and the women at the North, all talking about rights, the white men will be in a fix pretty soon. But what's all this here talking about?

That man over there says that women need to be helped into carriages, and lifted over ditches, and to have the best place everywhere. Nobody ever helps me into carriages, or over mud-puddles, or gives me any best place! And ain't I a woman? Look at me! Look at my arm! I have ploughed and planted, and gathered into barns, and no man could head me! And ain't I a woman? I could work as much and eat as much as a man — when I could get it — and bear the lash as well! And ain't I a woman? I have borne thirteen children, and seen them most all sold off to slavery, and when I cried out with my mother's grief, none but Jesus heard me! And ain't I a woman?

Then they talk about this thing in the head; what's this they call it? (Intellect, someone whispers.) That's it, honey. What's that got to do with women's rights or negro's rights? If my cup won't hold but a pint, and yours holds a quart, wouldn't you be mean not to let me have my little half-measure full?

Then that little man in black there, he says women can't have as much rights as men, 'cause Christ wasn't a woman! Where did your Christ come from? Where did your Christ come from? From God and a woman! Man had nothing to do with Him.

If the first woman God ever made was strong enough to turn the world upside down all alone, these women together ought to be able to turn it back, and get it right side up again! And now they is asking to do it, the men better let them.

Obliged to you for hearing me, and now old Sojourner ain't got nothing more to say.

CHIEF SEATTLE (1786–1866)

My People

> *Chief of the Suquamish and leader of other tribes in what is now Washington State, Chief Seattle was born around 1786. In 1854, the governor of Washington Territories, Isaac Stevens, proposed to buy two million acres of land from the tribes Seattle led. This speech is Seattle's reply to the offer. His words offer a chilling prediction of the massacres and relocations that decimated native American tribes beginning in the 1860s.*

Yonder sky that has wept tears upon my people for centuries untold, and which to us appears changeless and eternal, may change. Today is fair. Tomorrow may be overcast with clouds. My words are like the stars that never change. Whatever Seattle says the great chief at Washington can rely upon with as much certainty as he can upon the return of the sun or the seasons. The White Chief says that Big Chief at Washington sends us greetings of friendship and goodwill. That is kind of him for we know he has little need of our friendship in return. His people are many. They are like the grass that covers vast prairies. My people are few. They resemble the scattering trees of a storm-swept plain. The great, and — I presume — good, White Chief sends us word that he wishes to buy our lands but is willing to allow us enough to live comfortably. This indeed appears just, even generous, for the Red Man no longer has rights that he need respect, and the offer may be wise also, as we are no longer in need of an extensive country. . . . I will not dwell on, nor mourn over, our untimely decay, nor reproach our paleface brothers with hastening it, as we too may have been somewhat to blame.

Youth is impulsive. When our young men grow angry at some real or imaginary wrong, and disfigure their faces with black paint, it denotes that their hearts are black, and then they are often cruel and relentless, and our old men and old women are unable to restrain them. Thus it has ever been. Thus it was when the white men first began to push our forefathers further westward. But let us hope that the hostilities between us may never return. We would have everything to lose and nothing to gain. Revenge by young men is considered gain, even at the cost of their own lives, but old men who stay at home in times of war, and mothers who have sons to lose, know better.

Our good father at Washington — for I presume he is now our father as well as yours, since King George has moved his boundaries further north — our great good father, I say, sends us word that if we do as he desires he will protect us. His brave warriors will be to us a bristling wall of strength, and his wonderful ships of war will fill our harbors so that our ancient enemies far to the northward — the Hydas and Tsimpsians — will cease to frighten our women, children, and old men. Then in reality will he be our father and we his children. But can that ever be? Your God is not our God! Your God loves your people and hates mine. He folds his strong and protecting arms lovingly about the paleface and leads him by the hand as a father leads his infant son — but He has forsaken His red children — if they really are his. Our God, the Great Spirit, seems also to have forsaken us. Your God makes your people wax strong every day. Soon they will fill the land. Our people are ebbing away like a rapidly receding tide that will never return. The white man's God cannot love our people or He would protect them. They seem to be orphans who can look nowhere for help. How then can we be brothers? How can your God become our God and renew our prosperity and awaken in us dreams of returning greatness? If we have a common heavenly father He must be partial — for He came to his paleface children. We never saw Him. He gave you laws but He had no word for His red children whose teeming multitudes once filled this vast continent as stars fill the firmament. No; we are two distinct races with separate origins and separate destinies. There is little in common between us.

To us the ashes of our ancestors are sacred and their resting place is hallowed ground. You wander far from the graves of your ancestors and seemingly without regret. Your religion was written upon tables of stone by the iron finger of your God so that you could not forget. The Red Man could never comprehend nor remember it. Our religion is the traditions of our ancestors — the dreams of our old men, given them in solemn hours of night by the Great Spirit; and the visions of our sachems°; and it is written in the hearts of our people.

Your dead cease to love you and the land of their nativity as soon as   5
they pass the portals of the tomb and wander way beyond the stars. They are soon forgotten and never return. Our dead never forget the beautiful world that gave them being.

Day and night cannot dwell together. The Red Man has ever fled the approach of the White Man, as the morning mist flees before the morning sun. However, your proposition seems fair and I think that my people will accept it and will retire to the reservation you offer them. Then we will dwell apart in peace, for the words of the Great White Chief seem to be the words of nature speaking to my people out of dense darkness.

It matters little where we pass the remnant of our days. They will not be many. A few more moons; a few more winters — and not one of the descendants of the mighty hosts that once moved over this broad land or lived in happy homes, protected by the Great Spirit, will remain to mourn over the graves of a people once more powerful and hopeful than yours. But why should I mourn at the untimely fate of my people? Tribe follows tribe, and nation follows nation, like the waves of the sea. It is the order of nature, and regret is useless. Your time of decay may be distant, but it will surely come, for even the White Man whose God walked and talked with him as

sachems: Tribal chiefs.

friend with friend, cannot be exempt from the common destiny. We may be brothers after all. We will see.

We will ponder your proposition, and when we decide we will let you know. But should we accept it, I here and now make this condition that we will not be denied the privilege without molestation of visiting at any time the tombs of our ancestors, friends and children. Every part of this soil is sacred in the estimation of my people. Every hillside, every valley, every plain and grove, has been hallowed by some sad or happy event in days long vanished. . . . The very dust upon which you now stand responds more lovingly to their footsteps than to yours, because it is rich with the blood of our ancestors and our bare feet are conscious of the sympathetic touch. . . . Even the little children who lived here and rejoiced here for a brief season will love these somber solitudes and at eventide they greet shadowy returning spirits. And when the last Red Man shall have perished, and the memory of my tribe shall have become a myth among the White Men, these shores will swarm with the invisible dead of my tribe, and when your children's children think themselves alone in the field, the store, the shop, upon the highway, or in the silence of the pathless woods, they will not be alone. . . . At night when the streets of your cities and villages are silent and you think them deserted, they will throng with the returning hosts that once filled and still love this beautiful land. The White Man will never be alone.

Let him be just and deal kindly with my people, for the dead are not powerless. Dead, did I say? There is not death, only a change of worlds.

MARTIN LUTHER KING, JR. (1929–1968)

Letter from Birmingham Jail

> *The son of a Baptist minister, Martin Luther King, Jr., was born in 1929 in Atlanta, Georgia. He first became known as a civil rights activist in 1955 when he led an effective boycott against the segregated bus system in Montgomery, Alabama. Several years later, while in jail in Birmingham, Alabama, for committing civil disobedience, King wrote this reply, on April 16, 1963, to eight clergymen who had published in a local paper a letter disagreeing with King's actions. As King wrote, he had in mind not only the eight clergymen to whom the letter is addressed, but also other people—both sympathetic and unsympathetic—who would read his words when they were published.*

My Dear Fellow Clergymen:

While confined here in the Birmingham city jail, I came across your recent statement calling my present activities "unwise and untimely." Seldom do I pause to answer criticism of my work and ideas. If I sought to answer all the criticisms that cross my desk, my secretaries would have little time for anything other than such correspondence in the course of the day, and I would have no time for constructive work. But since I feel that you are men of genuine good will and that your criticisms are sincerely set forth, I want to try to answer your statement in what I hope will be patient and reasonable terms.

I think I should indicate why I am here in Birmingham, since you have been influenced by the view which argues against "outsiders coming in." I have the honor of serving as president of the Southern Christian Leadership Conference, an organization operating in every southern state, with headquarters in Atlanta, Georgia. We have some eighty-five affiliated organizations across the South, and one of them is the Alabama Christian Movement for Human Rights. Frequently we share staff, educational, and financial resources with our affiliates. Several months ago the affiliate here in Birmingham asked us to be on call to engage in a nonviolent direct-action program if such were deemed necessary. We readily consented, and when the hour came we lived up to our promise. So I, along with several members of my staff, am here because I was invited here. I am here because I have organizational ties here.

But more basically, I am in Birmingham because injustice is here. Just as the prophets of the eighth century B.C. left their villages and carried their "thus saith the Lord" far beyond the boundaries of their home towns, and just as the Apostle Paul left his village of Tarsus and carried the gospel of Jesus Christ to the far corners of the Greco-Roman world, so am I compelled to carry the gospel of freedom beyond my own home town. Like Paul, I must constantly respond to the Macedonian call for aid.

Moreover, I am cognizant of the interrelatedness of all communities and states. I cannot sit idly by in Atlanta and not be concerned about what happens in Birmingham. Injustice anywhere is a threat to justice everywhere. We are caught in an inescapable network of mutuality, tied in a single garment of destiny. Whatever affects one directly, affects all indirectly. Never again can we afford to live with the narrow, provincial, "outside agitator" idea. Anyone who lives inside the United States can never be considered an outsider anywhere within its bounds.

You deplore the demonstrations taking place in Birmingham. But your statement, I am sorry to say, fails to express a similar concern for the conditions that brought about the demonstrations. I am sure that none of you would want to rest content with the superficial kind of social analysis that deals merely with effects and does not grapple with underlying causes. It is unfortunate that demonstrations are taking place in Birmingham, but it is even more unfortunate that the city's white power structure left the Negro community with no alternative.

In any nonviolent campaign there are four basic steps: collection of the facts to determine whether injustices exist; negotiation; self-purification; and direct action. We have gone through all these steps in Birmingham. There can be no gainsaying the fact that racial injustice engulfs this community. Birmingham is probably the most thoroughly segregated city in the United States. Its ugly record of brutality is widely known. Negros have experienced grossly unjust treatment in courts. There have been more unsolved bombings of Negro homes and churches in Birmingham than in any other city in the nation. These are the hard, brutal facts of the case. On the basis of these conditions, Negro leaders sought to negotiate with the city fathers. But the latter consistently refused to engage in good-faith negotiation.

Then, last September, came the opportunity to talk with leaders of Birmingham's economic community. In the course of the negotiations, certain promises were made by the merchants — for example, to remove the stores' humiliating racial signs. On the basis of these promises, the Reverend Fred Shuttlesworth and the leaders of the Alabama Christian Movement for Human Rights agreed to a moratorium on all demonstrations. As the weeks and months went by, we realized that we were the victims of a broken promise. A few signs, briefly removed, returned; the others remained.

As in so many past experiences, our hopes had been blasted, and the shadow of deep disappointment settled upon us. We had no alternative except to prepare for direct action, whereby we would present our very bodies as means of laying our case before the conscience of the local and the national community. Mindful of the difficulties involved, we decided to undertake a process of self-purification. We began a series of workshops on nonviolence, and we repeatedly asked ourselves: "Are you able to accept blows without retaliating?" "Are you able to endure the ordeal of jail?" We decided to schedule our direct-action program for the Easter season, realizing that except for Christmas, this is the main shopping period of the year.

Knowing that a strong economic-withdrawal program would be the by-product of direct action, we felt that this would be the best time to bring pressure to bear on the merchants for the needed change.

Then it occurred to us that Birmingham's mayoral election was coming up in March, and we speedily decided to postpone action until after election day. When we discovered that the Commissioner of Public Safety, Eugene "Bull" Connor, had piled up enough votes to be in the run-off, we decided again to postpone action until the day after the run-off so that the demonstrations could not be used to cloud the issues. Like many others, we waited to see Mr. Connor defeated, and to this end we endured postponement after postponement. Having aided in this community need, we felt that our direct-action program could be delayed no longer.

You may well ask, "Why direct action? Why sit-ins, marches, and so   10
forth? Isn't negotiation a better path?" You are quite right in calling for negotiation. Indeed, this is the very purpose of direct action. Nonviolent direct action seeks to create such a crisis and foster such a tension that a community which has constantly refused to negotiate is forced to confront the issue. It seeks so to dramatize the issue that it can no longer be ignored. My citing the creation of tension as part of the work of the nonviolent-resister may sound rather shocking. But I must confess that I am not afraid of the word "tension." I have earnestly opposed violent tension, but there is a type of constructive, nonviolent tension which is necessary for growth. Just as Socrates felt that it was necessary to create a tension in the mind so that individuals could rise from the bondage of myths and half-truths to the unfettered realm of creative analysis and objective appraisal, so must we see the need for nonviolent gadflies to create the kind of tension in society that will help men rise from the dark depths of prejudice and racism to the majestic heights of understanding and brotherhood.

The purpose of our direct-action program is to create a situation so crisis-packed that it will inevitably open the door to negotiation. I therefore concur with you in your call for negotiation. Too long has our beloved Southland been bogged down in a tragic effort to live in monologue rather than dialogue.

One of the basic points in your statement is that the action that I and my associates have taken in Birmingham is untimely. Some have asked: "Why didn't you give the new city administration time to act?" The only answer that I can give to this query is that the new Birmingham administration must be prodded about as much as the outgoing one, before it will act. We are sadly mistaken if we feel that the election of Albert Boutwell as mayor will bring the millennium to Birmingham. While Mr. Boutwell is a much more gentle person than Mr. Connor, they are both segregationists, dedicated to maintenance of the status quo. I have hoped that Mr. Boutwell will be reasonable enough to see the futility of massive resistance to desegregation. But he will not see this without pressure from devotees of civil rights. My friends, I must say to you that we have not made a single gain in civil rights without determined legal and nonviolent pressure. Lamentably, it is an historical fact that privileged groups seldom give up their privileges voluntarily. Individuals may see the moral light and voluntarily give up their unjust posture; but, as Reinhold Niebuhr° has reminded us, groups tend to be more immoral than individuals.

We know through painful experience that freedom is never voluntarily given by the oppressor; it must be demanded by the oppressed. Frankly, I have yet to engage in a direct-action campaign that was "well timed" in the view of those who have not suffered unduly from the disease of segregation. For years now I have heard the word "Wait!" It rings in the ear of every Negro with piercing familiarity. This "Wait" has almost always meant "Never." We must come to see, with one of our distinguished jurists, that "justice too long delayed is justice denied."

We have waited for more than 340 years for our constitutional and God-given rights. The nations of Asia and Africa are moving with jetlike speed toward gaining political independence, but we still creep at horse-and-buggy pace toward gaining a cup of coffee at a lunch counter. Perhaps it is easy for those who have never felt the stinging darts of segregation to say, "Wait." But when you have seen vicious mobs lynch your mothers and fathers at will and drown your sisters and brothers at whim; when you have seen hate-filled policemen curse, kick, and even kill your black brothers and sisters; when you see the vast majority of your twenty million Negro brothers smothering in an airtight cage of poverty in the midst of an affluent society; when you suddenly find your tongue twisted and your speech stammering as you seek to explain to your six-year-old daughter why she can't go to the public amusement park that has just been advertised on television, and see tears welling up in her eyes when she is told that Funtown is closed to colored children, and see ominous clouds of inferiority beginning to form in her little mental sky, and see her beginning to distort her personality by developing an unconscious bitterness toward white people; when you have to concoct an answer for a five-year-old son who is asking, "Daddy, why do white people treat colored people so mean?"; when you take a cross-country drive and find it necessary to sleep night after night in the uncomfortable corners of your automobile because no motel will accept you; when you are humiliated day in and day out by nagging signs reading "white" and "colored"; when your first name becomes "nigger," your middle name becomes "boy" (however old you are) and your last name becomes "John," and your wife and mother are never given the respected title "Mrs."; when you are harried by day and haunted by night by the fact that you are a Negro, living constantly at tiptoe stance, never quite knowing what to expect next, and are plagued with inner fears and outer resentments; when you are forever fighting a degenerating sense of "nobodiness" — then you will understand why we find it difficult to wait. There comes a time when the cup of endurance runs over, and men are no longer willing to be plunged

---

Reinhold Niebuhr: (1892–1971) An American theologian who believed in the establishment of a code of ethics based on religious convictions.

into the abyss of despair. I hope, sirs, you can understand our legitimate and unavoidable impatience.

You express a great deal of anxiety over our willingness to break laws. 15 This is certainly a legitimate concern. Since we so diligently urge people to obey the Supreme Court's decision of 1954 outlawing segregation in the public schools, at first glance it may seem rather paradoxical for us consciously to break laws. One may well ask: "How can you advocate breaking some laws and obeying others?" The answer lies in the fact that there are two types of laws: just and unjust. I would be the first to advocate obeying just laws. One has not only a legal but a moral responsibility to obey just laws. Conversely, one has a moral responsibility to disobey unjust laws. I would agree with St. Augustine that "an unjust law is no law at all."

Now, what is the difference between the two? How does one determine whether a law is just or unjust? A just law is a manmade code that squares with the moral law or the law of God. An unjust law is a code that is out of harmony with the moral law. To put it in the terms of St. Thomas Aquinas: An unjust law is a human law that is not rooted in eternal law and natural law. Any law that uplifts human personality is just. Any law that degrades human personality is unjust. All segregation statutes are unjust because segregation distorts the soul and damages the personality. It gives the segregator a false sense of superiority and the segregated a false sense of inferiority. Segregation, to use the terminology of the Jewish philosopher Martin Buber, substitutes an "I–it" relationship for an "I–thou" relationship and ends up relegating persons to the status of things. Hence segregation is not only politically, economically, and sociologically unsound, it is morally wrong and sinful. Paul Tillich has said that sin is separation. Is not segregation an existential expression of man's tragic separation, his awful estrangement, his terrible sinfulness? Thus it is that I can urge men to obey the 1954 decision of the Supreme Court, for it is morally right; and I can urge them to disobey segregation ordinances, for they are morally wrong.

Let us consider a more concrete example of just and unjust laws. An unjust law is a code that a numerical or power majority group compels a minority group to obey but does not make binding on itself. This is *difference* made legal. By the same token, a just law is a code that a majority compels a minority to follow and that it is willing to follow itself. This is *sameness* made legal.

Let me give another explanation. A law is unjust if it is inflicted on a minority that, as a result of being denied the right to vote, had no part in enacting or devising the law. Who can say that the legislature of Alabama which set up that state's segregation laws was democratically elected? Throughout Alabama all sorts of devious methods are used to prevent Negroes from becoming registered voters, and there are some counties in which, even though Negroes constitute a majority of the population, not a single Negro is registered. Can any law enacted under such circumstances be considered democratically structured?

Sometimes a law is just on its face and unjust in its application. For instance, I have been arrested on a charge of parading without a permit. Now, there is nothing wrong in having an ordinance which requires a permit for a parade. But such an ordinance becomes unjust when it is used to maintain segregation and to deny citizens the First Amendment privilege of peaceful assembly and protest.

I hope you are able to see the distinction I am trying to point out. In   20 no sense do I advocate evading or defying the law, as would the rabid segregationist. That would lead to anarchy. One who breaks an unjust law must do so openly, lovingly, and with a willingness to accept the penalty. I submit that an individual who breaks a law that conscience tells him is unjust, and who willingly accepts the penalty of imprisonment in order to arouse the conscience of the community over its injustice, is in reality expressing the highest respect for law.

Of course, there is nothing new about this kind of civil disobedience. It was evidenced sublimely in the refusal of Shadrach, Meshach, and Abednego to obey the laws of Nebuchadnezzar, on the ground that a higher moral law was at stake. It was practiced superbly by the early Christians, who were willing to face hungry lions and the excruciating pain of chopping blocks rather than submit to certain unjust laws of the Roman Empire. To a degree, academic freedom is a reality today because Socrates practiced civil disobedience. In our own nation, the Boston Tea Party represented a massive act of civil disobedience.

We should never forget that everything Adolf Hitler did in Germany was "legal" and everything the Hungarian freedom fighters did in Hungary was "illegal." It was "illegal" to aid and comfort a Jew in Hitler's Germany. Even so, I am sure that, had I lived in Germany at the time, I would have aided and comforted my Jewish brothers. If today I lived in a Communist country where certain principles dear to the Christian faith are suppressed, I would openly advocate disobeying that country's antireligious laws.

I must make two honest confessions to you, my Christian and Jewish brothers. First, I must confess that over the past few years I have been gravely disappointed with the white moderate. I have almost reached the regrettable conclusion that the Negro's great stumbling block in his stride toward freedom is not the White Citizen's Counciler or the Ku Klux Klanner, but the white moderate, who is more devoted to "order" than to justice; who prefers a negative peace which is the absence of tension to a positive peace which is the presence of justice; who constantly says, "I agree with you in the goal you seek, but I cannot agree with your methods of direct action"; who paternalistically believes he can set the timetable for another man's freedom; who lives by a mythical concept of time and who constantly advises the Negro to wait for a "more convenient season." Shallow understanding from people of good will is more frustrating than absolute misunderstanding from people of ill will. Lukewarm acceptance is much more bewildering than outright rejection.

I had hoped that the white moderate would understand that law and order exist for the purpose of establishing justice and that when they fail in this purpose they become the dangerously structured dams that block the flow of social progress. I had hoped that the white moderate would understand that the present tension in the South is a necessary phase of the transition from an obnoxious negative peace, in which the Negro passively accepted his unjust plight, to a substantive and positive peace, in which all men will respect the dignity and worth of human personality. Actually, we who engage in nonviolent direct action are not the creators of tension. We merely bring to the surface the hidden tension that is already alive. We bring it out in the open, where it can be seen and dealt with. Like a boil that can never be cured so long as it is covered up but must be opened with all its ugliness to the natural medicines of air and light, injustice must be exposed, with all the tension its exposure creates, to the light of human conscience and the air of national opinion, before it can be cured.

In your statement you assert that our actions, even though peaceful,   25
must be condemned because they precipitate violence. But is this a logical assertion? Isn't this like condemning a robbed man because his possession of money precipitated the evil act of robbery? Isn't this like condemning Socrates because his unswerving commitment to truth and his philosophical inquiries precipitated the act by the misguided populace in which they made him drink hemlock? Isn't this like condemning Jesus because his unique God-consciousness and never-ceasing devotion to God's will precipitated the evil act of crucifixion? We must come to see that, as the federal courts have consistently affirmed, it is wrong to urge an individual to cease his efforts to gain his basic constitutional rights because the quest may precipitate violence. Society must protect the robbed and punish the robber.

I had also hoped that the white moderate would reject the myth concerning time in relation to the struggle for freedom. I have just received a letter from a white brother in Texas. He writes: "All Christians know that the colored people will receive equal rights eventually, but it is possible that you are in too great a religious hurry. It has taken Christianity almost two thousand years to accomplish what it has. The teachings of Christ take time to come to earth." Such an attitude stems from a tragic misconception of time, from the strangely irrational notion that there is something in the very flow of time that will inevitably cure all ills. Actually, time itself is neutral; it can be used either destructively or constructively. More and more I feel that the people of ill will have used time much more effectively than have the people of good will. We will have to repent in this generation not merely for the hateful words and actions of the bad people, but for the appalling silence of the good people. Human progress never rolls in on wheels of inevitability; it comes through the tireless efforts of men willing to be co-workers with God, and without this hard work, time itself becomes an ally of the forces of social stagnation. We must use time creatively, in the knowledge that the time is always ripe to do right. Now is the time to make real the promise of democracy and transform our pending national elegy into a creative psalm of brotherhood. Now is the time to lift our national policy from the quicksand of racial injustice to the solid rock of human dignity.

You speak of our activity in Birmingham as extreme. At first I was rather disappointed that fellow clergymen would see my nonviolent efforts as those of an extremist. I began thinking about the fact that I stand in the middle of two opposing forces in the Negro community. One is a force of complacency, made up in part of Negroes who, as a result of long years of oppression, are so drained of self-respect and a sense of "somebodiness" that they have adjusted to segregation; and in part of a few middle-class Negroes who, because of a degree of academic and economic security and because in some ways they profit by segregation, have become insensitive to the problems of the masses. The other force is one of bitterness and hatred, and it comes perilously close to advocating violence. It is expressed in the various black nationalist groups that are springing up across the nation, the largest and best-known being Elijah Muhammad's Muslim movement. Nourished by the Negro's frustration over the continued existence of racial discrimination, this movement is made up of people who have lost faith in America, who have absolutely repudiated Christianity, and who have concluded that the white man is an incorrigible "devil."

I have tried to stand between these two forces, saying that we need emulate neither the "do-nothingism" of the complacent nor the hatred and despair of the black nationalist. For there is the more excellent way of love and nonviolent protest. I am grateful to God that, through the influence of the Negro church, the way of nonviolence became an integral part of our struggle.

If this philosophy had not emerged, by now many streets of the South would, I am convinced, be flowing with blood. And I am further convinced that if our white brothers dismiss as "rabble-rousers" and "outside agitors" those of us who employ nonviolent direct action, and if they refuse to support our nonviolent efforts, millions of Negroes will, out of frustration and despair, seek solace and security in black-nationalist ideologies — a development that would inevitably lead to a frightening racial nightmare.

Oppressed people cannot remain oppressed forever. The yearning for   30
freedom eventually manifests itself, and that is what has happened to the American Negro. Something within has reminded him of his birthright of freedom, and something without has reminded him that it can be gained. Consciously or unconsciously, he has been caught up by the *Zeitgeist*, and with his black brothers of Africa and his brown and yellow brothers of Asia, South America, and the Caribbean, the United States Negro is moving with a sense of great urgency toward the promised land of racial justice. If one recognizes this vital urge that has engulfed the Negro community, one should readily understand why public demonstrations are taking place. The Negro has many pent-up resentments and latent frustrations, and he must release them. So let him march; let him make prayer pilgrimages to the city

hall; let him go on freedom rides—and try to understand why he must do so. If his repressed emotions are not released in nonviolent ways, they will seek expression through violence; this is not a threat but a fact of history. So I have not said to my people, "Get rid of your discontent." Rather, I have tried to say that this normal and healthy discontent can be channeled into the creative outlet of nonviolent direct action. And now this approach is being termed extremist.

But though I was initially disappointed at being categorized as an extremist, as I continued to think about the matter I gradually gained a measure of satisfaction from the label. Was not Jesus an extremist for love: "Love your enemies, bless them that curse you, do good to them that hate you, and pray for them which despitefully use you, and persecute you." Was not Amos an extremist for justice: "Let justice roll down like waters and righteousness like an ever-flowing stream." Was not Paul an extremist for the Christian gospel: "I bear in my body the marks of the Lord Jesus." Was not Martin Luther an extremist: "Here I stand; I cannot do otherwise, so help me God." And John Bunyan: "I will stay in jail to the end of my days before I make a butchery of my conscience." And Abraham Lincoln: "This nation cannot survive half slave and half free." And Thomas Jefferson: "We hold these truths to be self-evident, that all men are created equal. . . . " So the question is not whether we will be extremists, but what kind of extremists we will be. Will we be extremists for hate or for love? Will we be extremists for the preservation of injustice or for the extension of justice? In that dramatic scene on Calvary's hill three men were crucified. We must never forget that all three were crucified for the same crime—the crime of extremism. Two were extremists for immorality, and thus fell below their environment. The other, Jesus Christ, was an extremist for love, truth, and goodness, and thereby rose above his environment. Perhaps the South, the nation, and the world are in dire need of creative extremists.

I had hoped that the white moderate would see this need. Perhaps I was too optimistic; perhaps I expected too much. I suppose I should have realized that few members of the oppressor race can understand the deep groans and passionate yearnings of the oppressed race, and still fewer have the vision to see that injustice must be rooted out by strong, persistent, and determined action. I am thankful, however, that some of our white brothers in the South have grasped the meaning of this social revolution and committed themselves to it. They are still all too few in quantity, but they are big in quality. Some—such as Ralph McGill, Lillian Smith, Harry Golden, James McBride Dabbs, Ann Braden, and Sarah Patton Boyle—have written about our struggle in eloquent and prophetic terms. Others have marched with us down nameless streets of the South. They have languished in filthy, roach-infested jails, suffering the abuse and brutality of policemen who view them as "dirty nigger-lovers." Unlike so many of their moderate brothers and sisters, they have recognized the urgency of the moment and sensed the need for powerful "action" antidotes to combat the disease of segregation.

Let me take note of my other major disappointment. I have been so greatly disappointed with the white church and its leadership. Of course, there are some notable exceptions. I am not unmindful of the fact that each of you has taken some significant stands on this issue. I commend you, Reverend Stallings, for your Christian stand on this past Sunday, in welcomings Negroes to your worship service on a nonsegregated basis. I commend the Catholic leaders of this state for integrating Spring Hill College several years ago.

But despite these notable exceptions, I must honestly reiterate that I have been disappointed with the church. I do not say this as one of those negative critics who can always find something wrong with the church. I say this as a minister of the gospel, who loves the church; who was nurtured in its bosom; who has been sustained by its spiritual blessings and who will remain true to it as long as the cord of life shall lengthen.

When I was suddenly catapulted into the leadership of the bus protest   35 in Montgomery, Alabama, a few years ago, I felt we would be supported by the white church. I felt that the white ministers, priests, and rabbis of the South would be among our strongest allies. Instead, some have been outright opponents, refusing to understand the freedom movement and misrepresenting its leaders; all too many others have been more cautious than courageous and have remained silent behind the anesthetizing security of stained-glass windows.

In spite of my shattered dreams, I came to Birmingham with the hope that the white religious leadership of this community would see the justice of our cause and, with deep moral concern, would serve as the channel through which our just grievances could reach the power structure. I had hoped that each of you would understand. But again I have been disappointed. . . .

There was a time when the church was very powerful—in the time when the early Christians rejoiced at being deemed worthy to suffer for what they believed. In those days the church was not merely a thermometer that recorded the ideas and principles of popular opinion; it was a thermostat that transformed the mores of society. Whenever the early Christians entered a town, the people in power became disturbed and immediately sought to convict the Christians for being "disturbers of the peace" and "outside agitators." But the Christians pressed on, in the conviction that they were "a colony of heaven," called to obey God rather than man. Small in number, they were big in commitment. They were too God-intoxicated to be "astronomically intimidated." By their effort and example they brought an end to such ancient evils as infanticide and gladitorial contests.

Things are different now. So often the contemporary church is a weak, ineffectual voice with an uncertain sound. So often it is an arch-defender of the status quo. Far from being disturbed by the presence of the church, the power structure of the average community is consoled by the church's silent—and often even vocal—sanction of things as they are.

But the judgment of God is upon the church as never before. If today's church does not recapture the sacrificial spirit of the early church, it will lose its authenticity, forfeit the loyalty of millions, and be dismissed as an irrelevant social club with no meaning for the twentieth century. Every day I meet young people whose disappointment with the church has turned into outright disgust.

Perhaps I have once again been too optimistic. Is organized religion too inextricably bound to the status quo to save our nation and the world? Perhaps I must turn my faith to the inner spiritual church, the church within the church, as the true *ekklesia* and the hope of the world. But again I am thankful to God that some noble souls from the ranks of organized religion have broken loose from the paralyzing chains of conformity and joined us as active partners in the struggle for freedom. They have left their secure congregations and walked the streets of Albany, Georgia, with us. They have gone down the highways of the South on torturous rides for freedom. Yes, they have gone to jail with us. Some have been dismissed from their churches, have lost the support of their bishops and fellow ministers. But they have acted in the faith that right defeated is stronger than evil triumphant. Their witness has been the spiritual salt that has preserved the true meaning of the gospel in these troubled times. They have carved a tunnel of hope through the dark mountain of disappointment.

I hope the church as a whole will meet the challenge of this decisive hour. But even if the church does not come to the aid of justice, I have no despair about the future. I have no fear about the outcome of our struggle in Birmingham, even if our motives are at present misunderstood. We will reach the goal of freedom in Birmingham and all over the nation, because the goal of America is freedom. Abused and scorned though we may be, our destiny is tied up with America's destiny. Before the pilgrims landed at Plymouth, we were here. Before the pen of Jefferson etched the majestic words of the Declaration of Independence across the pages of history, we were here. For more than two centuries our forebears labored in this country without wages; they made cotton king; they built the homes of their masters while suffering gross injustice and shameful humiliation — and yet out of a bottomless vitality they continued to thrive and develop. If the inexpressible cruelties of slavery could not stop us, the opposition we now face will surely fail. We will win our freedom because the sacred heritage of our nation and the eternal will of God are embodied in our echoing demands.

Before closing I feel impelled to mention one other point in your statement that has troubled me profoundly. You warmly commended the Birmingham police force for keeping "order" and "preventing violence." I doubt that you would have so warmly commended the police force if you had seen its dogs sinking their teeth into unarmed, nonviolent Negroes. I doubt that you would so quickly commend the policemen if you were to observe their ugly and inhumane treatment of Negroes here in the city jail; if you were to watch them push and curse old Negro women and young

Negro girls; if you were to see them slap and kick old Negro men and young boys; if you were to observe them, as they did on two occasions, refuse to give us food because we wanted to sing our grace together. I cannot join you in your praise of the Birmingham police department.

It is true that the police have exercised a degree of discipline in handling the demonstrators. In this sense they have conducted themselves rather "nonviolently" in public. But for what purpose? To preserve the evil system of segregation. Over the past few years I have consistently preached that nonviolence demands that the means we use must be as pure as the ends we seek. I have tried to make clear that it is wrong to use immoral means to attain moral ends. But now I must affirm that it is just as wrong, or perhaps even more so, to use moral means to preserve immoral ends. Perhaps Mr. Connor and his policemen have been rather nonviolent in public, as was Chief Pritchett in Albany, Georgia, but they have used the moral means of nonviolence to maintain the immoral end of racial injustice. As T. S. Eliot has said, "The last temptation is the greatest treason: To do the right deed for the wrong reason."

I wish you had commended the Negro sit-inners and demonstrators of Birmingham for their sublime courage, their willingness to suffer, and their amazing discipline in the midst of great provocation. One day the South will recognize its real heroes. They will be the James Merediths,° with the noble sense of purpose that enables them to face jeering and hostile mobs, and with the agonizing loneliness that characterizes the life of the pioneer. They will be old, oppressed, battered Negro women, symbolized in a seventy-two-year-old woman in Montgomery, Alabama, who rose up with a sense of dignity and with her people decided not to ride segregated buses, and who responded with ungrammatical profundity to one who inquired about her weariness: "My feets is tired, but my soul is at rest." They will be the young high school and college students, the young ministers of the gospel and a host of their elders, courageously and nonviolently sitting in at lunch counters and willingly going to jail for conscience' sake. One day the South will know that when these disinherited children of God sat down at lunch counters, they were in reality standing up for what is best in the American dream and for the most sacred values in our Judaeo-Christian heritage, thereby bringing our nation back to those great wells of democracy which were dug deep by the founding fathers in their formulation of the Constitution and the Declaration of Independence.

Never before have I written so long a letter. I'm afraid it is much too 45 long to take your precious time. I can assure you that it would have been much shorter if I had been writing from a comfortable desk, but what else can one do when he is alone in a narrow jail cell, other than write long letters, think long thoughts, and pray long prayers?

James Meredith: The first black student to enroll at the University of Mississippi. His 1961 enrollment led to protests and controversy.

If I have said anything in this letter that overstates the truth and indicates an unreasonable impatience, I beg you to forgive me. If I have said anything that understates the truth and indicates my having a patience that allows me to settle for anything less than brotherhood, I beg God to forgive me.

I hope this letter finds you strong in the faith. I also hope that circumstances will soon make it possible for me to meet each of you, not as an integrationist or a civil-rights leader but as a fellow clergyman and a Christian brother. Let us all hope that the dark clouds of racial prejudice will soon pass away and the deep fog of misunderstanding will be lifted from our fear-drenched communities, and in some not too distant tomorrow the radiant stars of love and brotherhood will shine over our great nation with all their scintillating beauty.

Yours for the cause of Peace and Brotherhood,

MARTIN LUTHER KING, JR.

ELIZABETH CADY STANTON (1815–1902)

Declaration of Sentiments and Resolutions
Adopted by the Seneca Falls Convention,
July 19–20, 1848

> *Born in 1815, Elizabeth Cady Stanton worked tirelessly for social causes such as temperance and the abolition of slavery. Her primary concern, however, was for the rights of women. In July of 1848, Stanton and others organized a convention of men and women sympathetic to these issues, where she read her "Declaration of Sentiments," a document patterned on the Declaration of Independence and intended to rally supporters to adopt a series of resolutions drafted by the rally's organizers.*

When, in the course of human events, it becomes necessary for one portion of the family of man to assume among the people of the earth a position different from that which they have hitherto occupied, but one to which the laws of nature and of nature's God entitle them, a decent respect to the opinions of mankind requires that they should declare the causes that impel them to such a course.

We hold these truths to be self-evident: that all men and women are created equal; that they are endowed by their Creator with certain inalienable rights; that among these are life, liberty, and the pursuit of happiness; that to secure these rights governments are instituted, deriving their just powers from the consent of the governed. Whenever any form of government becomes destructive of these ends, it is the right of those who suffer from it to refuse allegiance to it, and to insist upon the institution of a new government, laying its foundation on such principles, and organizing its powers in such form, as to them shall seem most likely to effect their safety and happiness. Prudence, indeed, will dictate that governments long established should not be changed for light and transient causes; and accordingly all experience hath shown that mankind are more disposed to suffer, while evils are sufferable, than to right themselves by abolishing the forms to which they are accustomed. But when a long train of abuses and usurpations, pursuing invariably the same object, evinces a design to reduce them under absolute despotism, it is their duty to throw off such government, and to provide new guards for their future security. Such has been the patient sufferance of the women under this government, and such is now the necessity which constrains them to demand the equal station to which they are entitled.

The history of mankind is a history of repeated injuries and usurpations on the part of man toward woman, having in direct object the establishment of an absolute tyranny over her. To prove this, let facts be submitted to a candid world.

He has never permitted her to exercise her inalienable right to the elective franchise.

He has compelled her to submit to laws, in the formation of which she   5
had no voice.

He has withheld from her rights which are given to the most ignorant
and degraded men — both natives and foreigners.

Having deprived her of this first right of a citizen, the elective franchise, thereby leaving her without representation in the halls of legislation,
he has oppressed her on all sides.

He has made her, if married, in the eye of the law, civilly dead.

He has taken from her all right in property, even to the wages she
earns.

He has made her, morally, an irresponsible being, as she can commit   10
many crimes with impunity, provided they be done in the presence of her
husband. In the covenant of marriage, she is compelled to promise obedience
to her husband, he becoming to all intents and purposes, her master — the
law giving him the power to deprive her of her liberty, and to administer
chastisement.

He has so framed the laws of divorce, as to what shall be the proper
causes, and in case of separation, to whom the guardianship of the children
shall be given, as to be wholly regardless of the happiness of women — the
law, in all cases, going upon a false supposition of the supremacy of man,
and giving all power into his hands.

After depriving her of all rights as a married woman, if single, and the
owner of property, he has taxed her to support a government which recognizes her only when her property can be made profitable to it.

He has monopolized nearly all the profitable employments, and from
those she is permitted to follow, she receives but a scanty remuneration. He
closes against her all the avenues to wealth and distinction which he considers most honorable to himself. As a teacher of theology, medicine, or law,
she is not known.

He has denied her the facilities for obtaining a thorough education, all
colleges being closed against her.

He allows her in Church, as well as State, but a subordinate position   15
claiming Apostolic authority for her exclusion from the ministry, and, with
some exceptions, from any public participation in the affairs of the Church.

He has created a false public sentiment by giving to the world a different code of morals for men and women, by which moral delinquencies
which exclude women from society, are not only tolerated, but deemed of
little account in man.

He has usurped the prerogative of Jehovah himself, claiming it as his
right to assign for her a sphere of action, when that belongs to her conscience
and to her God.

He has endeavored, in every way that he could, to destroy her confidence in her own powers, to lessen her self-respect, and to make her willing
to lead a dependent and abject life.

Now, in view of this entire disfranchisement of one-half the people of
this country, their social and religious degradation — in view of the unjust

laws above mentioned, and because women do feel themselves aggrieved, oppressed, and fraudulently deprived of their most sacred rights, we insist that they have immediate admission to all the rights and privileges which belong to them as citizens of the United States.

In entering upon the great work before us, we anticipate no small   20
amount of misconception, misrepresentation, and ridicule; but we shall use every instrumentality within our power to effect our object. We shall employ agents, circulate tracts, petition the State and National legislatures, and endeavor to enlist the pulpit and the press in our behalf. We hope this Convention will be followed by a series of Conventions embracing every part of the country.

[The following resolutions were discussed by Lucretia Mott, Thomas and Mary Ann McClintock, Amy Post, Catharine A. F. Stebbins, and others, and were adopted:]

WHEREAS, the great precept of nature is conceded to be, that "man shall pursue his own true and substantial happiness." Blackstone° in his Commentaries remarks, that this law of Nature being coeval° with mankind, and dictated by God himself, is of course superior in obligation to any other. It is binding over all the globe, in all countries and at all times; no human laws are of any validity if contrary to this, and such of them as are valid, derive all their force, and all their validity, and all their authority. mediately and immediately, from this original; therefore,

Resolved, That such laws as conflict, in any way, with the true and substantial happiness of woman, are contrary to the great precept of nature and of no validity, for this is "superior in obligation to any other."

Resolved, That all laws which prevent woman from occupying such a station in society as her conscience shall dictate, or which place her in a position inferior to that of man, are contrary to the great precept of nature, and therefore of no force or authority.

Resolved, That woman is man's equal — was intended to be so by the   25
Creator, and the highest good of the race demands that she should be recognized as such.

Resolved, That the women of this country ought to be enlightened in regard to the laws under which they live, that they may no longer publish their degradation by declaring themselves satisfied with their present position, nor their ignorance, by asserting that they have all the rights they want.

Resolved, That inasmuch as man, while claiming for himself intellectual superiority, does accord to woman moral superiority, it is preeminently his duty to encourage her to speak and teach, as she has an opportunity, in all religious assemblies.

Sir William Blackstone: (1723–1780) British legal scholar whose writings form the foundation for legal studies in England.   *coeval:* Existing at the same time.

Resolved, That the same amount of virtue, delicacy, and refinement of behavior that is required of woman in the social state, should also be required of man, and the same transgressions should be visited with equal severity on both man and woman.

Resolved, That the objection of indelicacy and impropriety, which is so often brought against woman when she addresses a public audience, comes with a very ill-grace from those who encourage, by their attendance, her appearance on the stage, in the concert, or in feats of the circus.

Resolved, That woman has too long rested satisfied in the circum- 30
scribed limits which corrupt customs and a perverted application of the Scriptures have marked out for her, and that it is time she should move in the enlarged sphere which her great Creator has assigned her.

Resolved, That it is the duty of the women of this country to secure to themselves their sacred right to the elective franchise.

Resolved, That the equality of human rights results necessarily from the fact of the identity of the race in capabilities and responsibilities.

Resolved, therefore, That, being invested by the Creator with the same capabilities, and the same consciousness of responsibility for their exercise, it is demonstrably the right and duty of woman, equally with man, to promote every righteous cause by every righteous means; and especially in regard to the great subjects of morals and religion, it is self-evidently her right to participate with her brother in teaching them, both in private and in public, by writing and by speaking, by any instrumentalities proper to be used, and in any assemblies proper to be held; and this being a self-evident truth growing out of the divinely implanted principles of human nature, any custom or authority adverse to it, whether modern or wearing the hoary sanction of antiquity, is to be regarded as a self-evident falsehood, and at war with mankind.

[At the last session Lucretia Mott offered and spoke to the following resolution:]

Resolved, That the speedy success of our cause depends upon the zeal- 35
ous and untiring efforts of both men and women, for the overthrow of the monopoly of the pulpit, and for the securing to woman an equal participation with men in the various trades, professions, and commerce.

SEI SHONAGON (963–?)

From The Pillow Book

> *Sei Shonagon was twenty-seven years old when she came to court to serve as lady-in-waiting to the fifteen-year-old Empress Sadako in tenth-century Japan. Pillow books, represented by the excerpt printed here, were journals commonly kept by ladies of the court. Their writing — prolific, informative, and detailed — has provided historians with most of what is known about the Japanese Heian period.*

For secret meetings summer is best. It is true that the nights are terribly short and it begins to grow light before one has had a wink of sleep. But it is delightful to have all the shutters open, so that the cool air comes in and one can see into the garden. At last comes the time of parting, and just as the lovers are trying to finish off all the small things that remain to be said, they are suddenly startled by a loud noise just outside the window. For a moment they make certain they are betrayed; but it turns out only to be a crow that cried as it flew past.

But it is pleasant, too, on very cold nights to lie with one's lover, buried under a great pile of bed-clothes. Noises such as the tolling of a bell sound so strange. It seems as though they came up from the bottom of a deep pit. Strange, too, is the first cry of the birds, sounding so muffled and distant that one feels sure their beaks are still tucked under their wings. Then each fresh note gets shriller and nearer. . . .

It is very tiresome when a lover who is leaving one at dawn says that he must look for a fan or pocket-book that he left somewhere about the room last night. As it is still too dark to see anything, he goes fumbling about all over the place, knocking into everything and muttering to himself, "How very odd!" When at last he finds the pocket-book he crams it into his dress with a great rustling of the pages; or if it is a fan he has lost, he swishes it open and begins flapping it about, so that when he finally takes his departure, instead of experiencing the feelings of regret proper to such an occasion, one merely feels irritated at his clumsiness. . . .

It is important that a lover should know how to make his departure. To begin with, he ought not to be too ready to get up, but should require a little coaxing: "Come, it is past daybreak. You don't want to be found here . . ." and so on. One likes him, too, to behave in such a way that one is sure he is unhappy at going and would stay longer if he possibly could. He should not pull on his trousers the moment he is up, but should first of all come closer to one's ear and in a whisper finish off whatever was left half-said in the course of the night. But though he may in reality at these moments be doing nothing at all, it will not be amiss that he should appear to be buckling his belt. Then he should raise the shutters, and both lovers should go out together at the double-doors, while he tells her how much he dreads the day that is before him and longs for the approach of night. Then, after he has slipped away, she can stand gazing after him, with charming recollections of those last moments. Indeed, the success of a lover depends greatly on his method of departure. If he springs to his feet with a jerk and at once begins fussing around, tightening in the waist-band of his breeches, or adjusting the sleeves of his Court robe, hunting jacket or what not, collecting a thousand odds and ends, and thrusting them into the folds of his dress, or pulling in his over-belt — one begins to hate him.

I like to think of a bachelor — an adventurous disposition has left him   5
single — returning at dawn from some amorous excursion. He looks a trifle sleepy; but, as soon as he is home, draws his writing-case towards him, carefully grinds himself some ink and begins to write his next-morning letter — not simply dashing off whatever comes into his head, but spreading himself to the task and taking trouble to write the characters beautifully. He should be clad in an azalea-yellow or vermilion cloak worn over a white robe. Glancing from time to time at the dewdrops that still cling to the thin white fabric of his dress, he finishes his letter, but instead of giving it to one of the ladies who are in attendance upon him at the moment, he gets up, and choosing from among his page-boys one who seems to him exactly appropriate to such a mission, calls the lad to him, and whispering something in his ear puts the letter in his hand; then sits gazing after him as he disappears into the distance. While waiting for the answer he will perhaps quietly murmur to himself this or that passage from the *Sutras*. . . .

HENRY DAVID THOREAU (1817–1862)

From Journals

> *Born in 1817, Henry David Thoreau spent much of his life contemplating his natural surroundings — plants, rivers, animals, seasonal changes — and pondering human nature. He was deeply concerned about the political issues of his time and is noted for his essay, "Resistance to Civil Government" (sometimes called "Civil Disobedience"). During his life, Thoreau kept many journals, which suggest the wide range of his thoughts and interests. Often the ideas which were developed in his books and essays began as journal entries. For instance,* Slavery in Massachusetts *draws on the entry of June 16, 1854.*

[Writing "with Gusto"]

[September 2, 1851] We cannot write well or truly but what we write with gusto. The body, the senses, must conspire with the mind. Expression is the act of the whole man, that our speech may be vascular. The intellect is powerless to express thought without the aid of the heart and liver and of every member. Often I feel that my head stands out too dry, when it should be immersed. A writer, a man writing, is the scribe of all nature; he is the corn and the grass and the atmosphere writing. It is always essential that we love to do what we are doing, do it with a heart. The maturity of the mind, however, may perchance consist with a certain dryness.

[The Wisdom of Writing on Many Subjects]

[September 4, 1851] It is wise to write on many subjects, to try many themes, that so you may find the right and inspiring one. Be greedy of occasions to express your thought. Improve the opportunity to draw analogies. There are innumerable avenues to a perception of the truth. Improve the suggestion of each object however humble, however slight and transient the provocation. What else is there to be improved? Who knows what opportunities he may neglect? It is not in vain that the mind turns aside this way or that: follow its leading; apply it whither it inclines to go. Probe the universe in a myriad points. Be avaricious of these impulses. You must try a thousand themes before you find the right one, as nature makes a thousand acorns to get one oak. He is a wise man and experienced who has taken many views; to whom stones and plants and animals and a myriad objects have each suggested something, contributed something.

[Illegally Helping a Fugitive Slave]

[October 1, 1851] 5 P.M. — Just put a fugitive slave, who has taken the name of Henry Williams, into the cars for Canada. He escaped from Stafford County, Virginia, to Boston last October; has been in Shadrach's place at the Cornhill Coffee-House, had been corresponding through an agent with

his master, who is his father, about buying himself, his master asking $600, but he having been able to raise only $500. Heard that there were writs out for two Williamses, fugitives, and was informed by his fellow-servants and employer that Auger-hole Burns and others of the police had called for him when he was out. Accordingly fled to Concord last night on foot, bringing a letter to our family from Mr. Lovejoy of Cambridge and another which Garrison had formerly given him on another occasion. He lodged with us, and waited in the house till funds were collected with which to forward him. Intended to dispatch him at noon through to Burlington, but when I went to buy his ticket, saw one at the depot who looked and behaved so much like a Boston policeman that I did not venture that time. An intelligent and very well-behaved man, a mulatto.

There is art to be used, not only in selecting wood for a withe, but in using it. Birch withes are twisted, I suppose in order that the fibres may be less abruptly bent; or is it only by accident that they are twisted?

The slave said he could guide himself by many other stars than the north star, whose rising and setting he knew. They steered for the north star even when it had got round and appeared to them to be in the south. They frequently followed the telegraph when there was no railroad. The slaves bring many superstitions from Africa. The fugitives sometimes superstitiously carry a turf in their hats, thinking that their success depends on it.

These days when the trees have put on their autumnal tints are the gala days of the year, when the very foliage of trees is colored like a blossom. It is a proper time for a yearly festival, an agricultural show.

[The Purpose of a Journal]

[July 13, 1852] A journal, a book that shall contain a record of all your joy, your ecstasy.

[Writers of Torpid Words]

[July 14, 1852] A writer who does not speak out of a full experience uses torpid words, wooden or lifeless words, such words as "humanitary," which have a paralysis in their tails.

[Living with 706 Copies of A Week]

[October 28, 1853] For a year or two past, my *publisher,* falsely so called, has been writing from time to time to ask what disposition should be made of the copies of "A Week on the Concord and Merrimack Rivers" still on hand, and at last suggesting that they had use for the room they occupied in his cellar. So I had them all sent to me here, and they have arrived to-day by express, filling the man's wagon, — 706 copies out of an edition of 1000 which I bought of Munroe four years ago and have been ever since paying for, and have not quite paid for yet. The wares are sent to me at last, and I

have an opportunity to examine my purchase. They are something more substantial than fame, as my back knows, which has borne them up two flights of stairs to a place similar to that to which they trace their origin. Of the remaining two hundred and ninety and odd, seventy-five were given away, the rest sold. I have now a library of nearly nine hundred volumes, over seven hundred of which I wrote myself. Is it not well that the author should behold the fruits of his labor? My works are piled up on one side of my chamber half as high as my head, my *opera omnia*. This is authorship; these are the work of my brain. There was just one piece of good luck in the venture. The unbound were tied up by the printer four years ago in stout paper wrappers, and inscribed, —

H.D. Thoreau's.

Concord River

50 cops.

So Munroe had only to cross out "River" and write "Mass." and deliver them to the expressman at once. I can see now that I write for, the result of my labors.

Nevertheless, in spite of this result, sitting beside the inert mass of my works, I take up my pen to-night to record what thought or experience I may have had, with as much satisfaction as ever. Indeed, I believe that this result is more inspiring and better for me than if a thousand had bought my wares. It affects my privacy less and leaves me freer.

[Up Railroad — Odors of Nature and Men]

[*June 16, 1854*] 5 A.M. — Up railroad.

As the sun went down last night, round and red in a damp misty atmosphere, so now it rises in the same manner, though there is no dense fog. Poison-dogwood yesterday, or say day before, *i.e.,* 14th. *Rubus hispidus*, perhaps yesterday in the earliest place, over the sand. Mullein, perhaps yesterday.

Observed yesterday the erigeron with a purple tinge. I cannot tell whether this, which seems in other respects the same with the white, is the *strigosus* or *annuus*. The calla which I plucked yesterday sheds pollen to-day; say to-day, then. A *Hypericum perforatum* seen last night will probably open to-day. I see on the *Scirpus lacustris* and pontederia leaves black patches for some days, as if painted, of minute closely placed ova, above water. I suspect that what I took for milfoil is a sium. Is not that new mustard-like plant behind Loring's, and so on down the river, *Nasturtium hispidum;* or hairy cress? Probably the first the 19th. Heart-leaf. *Nymphæa odorata*. Again I scent a white water-lily, and a season I had waited for is arrived. How indispensable all these experiences to make up the summer! It is the emblem of purity, and its scent suggests it. Growing in stagnant and muddy [water], it bursts up so pure and fair to the eye and so sweet to the scent, as if to show us what purity and sweetness reside in, and can be extracted from, the slime and muck of earth. I think I have plucked the first one that has opened for a mile at least. What confirmation of our hopes is in the fragrance of the water-lily! I shall not soon despair of the world for it, notwithstanding slavery, and the cowardice and want of principle of the North. It suggests that the time may come when man's deeds will smell as sweet. Such, then, is the odor our planet emits. Who can doubt, then, that Nature is young and sound? If Nature can compound this fragrance still annually, I shall believe her still full of vigor, and that there is virtue in man, too, who perceives and loves it. It is as if all the pure and sweet and virtuous was extracted from the slime and decay of earth and presented thus in a flower. The resurrection of virtue! It reminds me that Nature has been partner to no Missouri compromise. I scent no compromise in the fragrance of the white water-lily. In it, the sweet, and pure, and innocent are wholly sundered from the obscene and baleful. I do not scent in this the time-serving irresolution of a Massachusetts Governor, nor of a Boston Mayor. All good actions have contributed to this fragrance. So behave that the odor of your actions may enhance the general sweetness of the atmosphere, that, when I behold or scent a flower, I may not be reminded how inconsistent are your actions with it; for all odor is but one form of advertisement of a moral quality. If fair actions had not been performed, the lily would not smell sweet. The foul slime stands for the sloth and vice of man; the fragrant flower that springs from it, for the purity and courage which springs from its midst. It is these sights and sounds and fragrances put together that convince us of our immortality. No man believes against all evidence. Our external senses consent with our internal. This fragrance assures me that, though all other men fall, one shall stand fast; though a pestilence sweep over the earth, it shall at least spare one man. The genius of Nature is unimpaired. Her flowers are as fair and as fragrant as ever.

JONATHAN SWIFT (1667–1745)

A Modest Proposal

> *Jonathan Swift's essay criticizes the suggestions of the "projectors" who, during the eighteenth century, published proposals for alleviating the chronic poverty of the Irish. The projectors, sympathetic with the ruling British government, which imposed stiff taxes on the suffering Irish, suggested solutions that seemed to Swift uncaring and inhumane. His outrageous — and certainly not modest — proposal satirizes both the projectors and their proposals.*

It is a melancholy object to those who walk through this great town or travel in the country, when they see the streets, the roads, and cabin doors, crowded with beggars of the female sex, followed by three, four, or six children, all in rags and importuning every passenger for an alms. These mothers, instead of being able to work for their honest livelihood, are forced to employ all their time in strolling to beg sustenance for their helpless infants, who, as they grow up, either turn thieves for want of work, or leave their dear native country to fight for the Pretender in Spain, or sell themselves to the Barbadoes.

I think it is agreed by all parties that this prodigious number of children in the arms, or on the backs, or at the heels of their mothers, and frequently of their fathers, is in the present deplorable state of the kingdom a very great additional grievance; and therefore whoever could find out a fair, cheap, and easy method of making these children sound, useful members of the commonwealth would deserve so well of the public as to have his statue set up for a preserver of the nation.

But my intention is very far from being confined to provide only for the children of professed beggars; it is of a much greater extent, and shall take in the whole number of infants at a certain age who are born of parents in effect as little able to support them as those who demand our charity in the streets.

As to my own part, having turned my thoughts for many years upon this important subject, and maturely weighed the several schemes of other projectors, I have always found them grossly mistaken in their computation. It is true, a child just dropped from its dam may be supported by her milk for a solar year, with little other nourishment; at most not above the value of two shillings, which the mother may certainly get, or the value in scraps, by her lawful occupation of begging; and it is exactly at one year old that I propose to provide for them in such a manner as instead of being a charge upon their parents or the parish, or wanting food and raiment for the rest of their lives, they shall on the contrary contribute to the feeding, and partly to the clothing, of many thousands.

There is likewise another great advantage in my scheme, that it will   5
prevent those involuntary abortions, and that horrid practice of women

murdering their bastard children, alas, too frequent among us, sacrificing the poor innocent babes, I doubt, more to avoid the expense than the shame, which would move tears and pity in the most savage and inhuman breast.

The number of souls in this kingdom being usually reckoned one million and a half, of these I calculate there may be about two hundred thousand couples whose wives are breeders, from which number I subtract thirty thousand couples who are able to maintain their own children, although I apprehend there cannot be so many under the present distress of the kingdom; but this being granted, there will remain an hundred and seventy thousand breeders. I again subtract fifty thousand for those women who miscarry, or whose children die by accident or disease within the year. There only remain an hundred and twenty thousand children of poor parents annually born. The question therefore is, how this number shall be reared and provided for, which, as I have already said, under the present situation of affairs, is utterly impossible by all the methods hitherto proposed. For we can neither employ them in handicraft nor agriculture; we neither build houses (I mean in the country) nor cultivate land. They can very seldom pick up livelihood by stealing till they arrive at six years old, except where they are of towardly parts, although I confess they learn the rudiments much earlier, during which time they can however be looked upon only as probationers, as I have been informed by a principal gentleman in the county of Cavan, who protested to me that he never knew above one or two instances under the age of six, even in a part of the kingdom so renowned for the quickest proficiency in that art.

I am assured by our merchants that a boy or a girl before twelve years old is no salable commodity; and even when they come to this age, they will not yield above three pounds, or three pounds and half a crown at most on the Exchange; which cannot turn to account either to the parents or the kingdom, the charge of nutriment and rags having been at least four times that value.

I shall now therefore humbly propose my own thoughts, which I hope will not be liable to the least objection.

I have been assured by a very knowing American of my acquaintance in London, that a young healthy child well nursed is at a year old a most delicious, nourishing, and wholesome food, whether stewed, roasted, baked, or boiled; and I make no doubt that it will equally serve in fricassee or a ragout.

I do therefore humbly offer it to public consideration that of the hundred and twenty thousand children, already computed, twenty thousand may be reserved for breed, whereof only one fourth part to be males, which is more than we allow to sheep, black cattle, or swine; and my reason is that these children are seldom the fruits of marriage, a circumstance not much regarded by our savages, therefore one male will be sufficient to serve four females. That the remaining hundred thousand may at a year old be offered

10

in sale to the persons of quality and fortune through the kingdom, always advising the mother to let them suck plentifully in the last month, so as to render them plump and fat for a good table. A child will make two dishes at an entertainment for friends; and when the family dines alone, the fore or hind quarter will make a reasonable dish, and seasoned with a little pepper or salt will be very good boiled on the fourth day, especially in winter.

I have reckoned upon a medium that a child just born will weigh twelve pounds, and in a solar year if tolerably nursed increaseth to twenty-eight pounds.

I grant this food will be somewhat dear, and therefore very proper for landlords, who, as they have already devoured most of the parents, seem to have the best title to the children.

Infant's flesh will be in season throughout the year, but more plentiful in March, and a little before and after. For we are told by a grave author, an eminent French physician, that fish being a prolific diet, there are more children born in Roman Catholic countries about nine months after Lent, than at any other season; therefore, reckoning a year after Lent, the markets will be more glutted than usual, because the number of popish infants is at least three to one in this kingdom; and therefore it will have one other collateral advantage, by lessening the number of Papists among us.

I have already computed the charge of nursing a beggar's child (in which list I reckon all cottagers, laborers, and four fifths of the farmers) to be about two shillings per annum, rags included; and I believe no gentleman would repine to give ten shillings for the carcass of a good fat child, which, as I have said, will make four dishes of excellent nutritive meat, when he hath only some particular friend or his own family to dine with him. Thus the squire will learn to be a good landlord, and grow popular among the tenants; the mother will have eight shillings net profit, and be fit for work till she produces another child.

Those who are more thrifty (as I must confess the times require) may flay the carcass; the skin of which artifically dressed will make admirable gloves for ladies, and summer boots for fine gentlemen. 15

As to our city of Dublin, shambles° may be appointed for this purpose in the most convenient parts of it, and butchers we may be assured will not be wanting; although I rather recommend buying the children alive, and dressing them hot from the knife as we do roasting pigs.

A very worthy person, a true lover of his country, and whose virtues I highly esteem, was lately pleased in discoursing on this matter to offer a refinement upon my scheme. He said that many gentlemen of his kingdom, having of late destroyed their deer, he conceived that the want of venison might be well supplied by the bodies of young lads and maidens, not exceeding fourteen years of age nor under twelve, so great a number of both

shambles: Slaughterhouses.

sexes in every county being now ready to starve for want of work and service; and these to be disposed of by their parents, if alive, or otherwise by their nearest relations. But with due deference to so excellent a friend and so deserving a patriot, I cannot be altogether in his sentiments; for as to the males, my American acquaintance assured me from frequent experience that their flesh was generally tough and lean, like that of our schoolboys, by continual exercise, and their taste disagreeable; and to fatten them would not answer the charge. Then as to the females, it would, I think with humble submission, be a loss to the public, because they soon would become breeders themselves; and besides, it is not improbable that some scrupulous people might be apt to censure such a practice (although indeed very unjustly) as a little bordering upon cruelty; which, I confess, hath always been with me the strongest objection against any project, how well soever intended.

But in order to justify my friend, he confessed that this expedient was put into his head by the famous Psalmanazar, a native of the island Formosa, who came from thence to London above twenty years ago, and in conversation told my friend that in his country when any young person happened to be put to death, the executioner sold the carcass to the persons of quality as a prime dainty; and that in his time the body of a plump girl of fifteen, who was crucified for an attempt to poison the emperor, was sold to his Imperial Majesty's prime minister of state, and other great mandarins of the court, in joints from the gibbet, at four hundred crowns. Neither indeed can I deny that if the same use were made of several plump young girls in this town, who without one single groat to their fortunes cannot stir abroad without a chair, and appear at the playhouse and assemblies in foreign fineries which they never will pay for, the kingdom would not be the worse.

Some persons of a desponding spirit are in great concern about that vast number of poor people who are aged, diseased, or maimed, and I have been desired to employ my thoughts what course may be taken to ease the nation of so grievous an encumbrance. But I am not in the least pain upon that matter, because it is very well known that they are every day dying and rotting by cold and famine, and filth and vermin, as fast as can be reasonably expected. And as to the younger laborers, they are now in almost as hopeful a condition. They cannot get work, and consequently pine away for want of nourishment to a degree that if any time they are accidentally hired to common labor, they have not strength to perform it; and thus the country and themselves are happily delivered from the evils to come.

I have too long digressed, and therefore shall return to my subject. I think the advantages by the proposal which I have made are obvious and many, as well as of the highest importance.

For first, as I have already observed, it would greatly lessen the number of Papists, with whom we are yearly overrun, being the principal breeders of the nation as well as our most dangerous enemies; and who stay at home on purpose to deliver the kingdom to the Pretender, hoping to take

20

their advantage by the absence of so many good Protestants, who have chosen rather to leave their country than to stay at home and pay tithes against their conscience to an Episcopal curate.

Secondly, the poorer tenants will have something valuable of their own, which by law may be made liable to distress, and help to pay their landlord's rent, their corn and cattle being already seized and money a thing unknown.

Thirdly, whereas the maintenance of an hundred thousand children, from two years old and upwards, cannot be computed at less than ten shillings a piece per annum, the nation's stock will be thereby increased fifty thousand pounds per annum, besides the profit of a new dish introduced to the tables of all gentlemen of fortune in the kingdom who have any refinement in taste. And the money will circulate among ourselves, the goods being entirely of our own growth and manufacture.

Fourthly, the constant breeders, besides the gain of eight shillings per annum by the sale of their children, will be rid of the charge for maintaining them after the first year.

Fifthly, this food would likewise bring great custom to taverns, where   25
the vintners will certainly be so prudent as to procure the best receipts for dressing it to perfection, and consequently have their houses frequented by all the fine gentlemen, who justly value themselves upon their knowledge in good eating; and a skillful cook, who understands how to oblige his guests, will contrive to make it as expensive as they please.

Sixthly, this would be a great inducement to marriage, which all wise nations have either encouraged by rewards or enforced by laws and penalties. It would increase the care and tenderness of mothers toward their children, when they were sure of a settlement for life to the poor babes, provided in some sort by the public, to their annual profit instead of expense. We should see an honest emulation among the married women, which of them could bring the fattest child to the market. Men would become as fond of their wives during the time of pregnancy as they are now of their mares in foal, their cows in calf, or sows when they are ready to farrow; nor offer to beat or kick them (as is too frequent a practice) for fear of a miscarriage.

Many other advantages might be enumerated. For instance, the addition of some thousand carcasses in our exportation of barreled beef, the propagation of swine's flesh, and improvements in the art of making good bacon, so much wanted among us by the great destruction of pigs, too frequent at our tables, which are no way comparable in taste or magnificence to a well-grown, fat, yearling child, which roasted whole will make a considerable figure at a lord mayor's feast or any other public entertainment. But this and many others I omit, being studious of brevity.

Supposing that one thousand families in this city would be constant customers for infants' flesh, besides others who might have it at merry meetings, particularly weddings and christenings, I compute that Dublin would take off annually about twenty thousand carcasses, and the rest of the kingdom (where probably they will be sold somewhat cheaper) the remaining eighty thousand.

I can think of no one objection that will possibly be raised against this proposal, unless it should be urged that the number of people will be thereby much lessened in the kingdom. This I freely own, and it was indeed one principal design in offering it to the world. I desire the reader will observe; that I calculate my remedy for this one individual kingdom of Ireland and for no other that ever was, is, or I think ever can be upon earth. Therefore, let no man talk to me of other expedients: of taxing our absentees at five shillings a pound: of using neither clothes nor household furniture except what is of our own growth and manufacture: of utterly rejecting the materials and instruments that promote foreign luxury: of curing the expensiveness of pride, vanity, idleness, and gaming in our women: of introducing a vein of parsimony, prudence, and temperance: of learning to love our country, in the want of which we differ even from Laplanders and the inhabitants of Topinamboo: of quitting our animosities and factions, nor acting any longer like the Jews, who were murdering one another at the very moment their city was taken: of being a little cautious not to sell our country and conscience for nothing: of teaching landlords to have at least one degree of mercy toward their tenants: lastly, of putting a spirit of honesty, industry, and skill into our shopkeepers; who, if a resolution could now be taken to buy only our native goods, would immediately unite to cheat and exact upon us in the price, the measure, and the goodness, nor could ever yet be brought to make one fair proposal of just dealing, though often and earnestly invited to it.

Therefore, I repeat, let no man talk to me of these and the like expedients, till he hath at least some glimpse of hope that there will ever be some hearty and sincere attempt to put them in practice. 30

But as to myself, having been wearied out for many years with offering vain, idle, visionary thoughts, and at length utterly despairing of success, I fortunately fell upon this proposal, which, as it is wholly new, so it hath something solid and real, of no expense and little trouble, full in our own power, and whereby we can incur no danger in disobliging England. For this kind of commodity will not bear exportation, the flesh being of too tender a consistence to admit a long continuance in salt, although perhaps I could name a country which would be glad to eat up our whole nation without it.

After all, I am not so violently bent upon my own opinion as to reject any offer proposed by wise men, which shall be found equally innocent, cheap, easy, and effectual. But before something of that kind shall be advanced in contradiction to my scheme, and offering a better, I desire the author or authors will be pleased maturely to consider two points. First, as things now stand, how they will be able to find food and raiment for an hundred thousand useless mouths and backs. And secondly, there being a round million of creatures in human figure throughout this kingdom, whose sole subsistence put into a common stock would leave them in debt two millions of pounds sterling, adding those who are beggars by profession to the bulk of farmers, cottagers, and laborers, with their wives and children who are beggars in effect; I desire those politicians who dislike my overture, and may perhaps be so bold to attempt an answer, that they will first ask the parents of these mortals whether they would not at this day think it a great happiness to have been sold for food at a year old in this manner I prescribe, and thereby have avoided such a perpetual scene of misfortunes as they have since gone through by the oppression of landlords, the impossibility of paying rent without money or trade, the want of common sustenance, with neither house nor clothes to cover them from the inclemencies of the weather, and the most inevitable prospect of entailing the like or greater miseries upon their breed forever.

I profess, in the sincerity of my heart, that I have not the least personal interest in endeavoring to promote this necessary work, having no other motive than the public good of my country, by advancing our trade, providing for infants, relieving the poor, and giving some pleasure to the rich. I have no children by which I can propose to get a single penny; the youngest being nine years old, and my wife past childbearing.

GEORGE ORWELL (1903–1966)

Shooting an Elephant

> *George Orwell, author of the well-known satirical novel 1984 (1949), also published numerous essays including "Shooting an Elephant" (1950), which reflects his experiences as a member of the Indian imperial police in Burma during the time that this country was a British possession.*

In Moulmein, in Lower Burma, I was hated by large numbers of people — the only time in my life that I have been important enough for this to happen to me. I was sub-divisional police officer of the town, and in an aimless, petty kind of way anti-European feeling was very bitter. No one had the guts to raise a riot, but if a European woman went through the bazaars alone somebody would probably spit betel juice over her dress. As a police officer I was an obvious target and was baited whenever it seemed safe to do so. When a nimble Burman tripped me up on the football field and the referee (another Burman) looked the other way, the crowd yelled with hideous laughter. This happened more than once. In the end the sneering yellow faces of young men that met me everywhere, the insults hooted after me when I was at a safe distance, got badly on my nerves. The young Buddhist priests were the worst of all. There were several thousand of them in the town and none of them seemed to have anything to do except stand on street corners and jeer at Europeans.

All this was perplexing and upsetting. For at that time I had already made up my mind that imperialism was an evil thing and the sooner I chucked up my job and got out of it the better. Theoretically — and secretly, of course — I was all for the Burmese and all against their oppressors, the British. As for the job I was doing, I hated it more bitterly than I can perhaps make clear. In a job like that you see the dirty work of Empire at close quarters. The wretched prisoners huddling in the stinking cages of the lock-ups, the grey, cowed faces of the long-term convicts, the scarred buttocks of the men who had been flogged with bamboos — all these oppressed me with an intolerable sense of guilt. But I could get nothing into perspective. I was young and ill-educated and I had had to think out my problems in the utter silence that is imposed on every Englishman in the East. I did not even know that the British Empire is dying, still less did I know that it is a great deal better than the younger empires that are going to supplant it. All I knew was that I was stuck between my hatred of the empire I served and my rage against the evil-spirited little beasts who tried to make my job impossible. With one part of my mind I thought of the British Raj as an unbreakable tyranny, as something clamped down, in *saecula saeculorum,*° upon the will of prostrate peoples; with another part I thought that the greatest joy in the world would be to drive a bayonet into a Buddhist priest's

---

saecula saeculorum: For generation after generation.   *in terrorem:* As a scare tactic.

guts. Feelings like these are the normal by-products of imperialism; ask any Anglo-Indian official, if you can catch him off duty.

One day something happened which in a roundabout way was enlightening. It was a tiny incident in itself, but it gave me a better glimpse than I had had before of the real nature of imperialism — the real motives for which despotic governments act. Early one morning the sub-inspector at a police station the other end of the town rang me up on the 'phone and said that an elephant was ravaging the bazaar. Would I please come and do something about it? I did not know what I could do, but I wanted to see what was happening and I got on to a pony and started out. I took my rifle, an old .44 Winchester and much too small to kill an elephant, but I thought the noise might be useful *in terrorem.*° Various Burmans stopped me on the way and told me about the elephant's doings. It was not, of course, a wild elephant, but a tame one which had gone "must." It had been chained up, as tame elephants always are when their attack of "must" is due, but on the previous night it had broken its chain and escaped. Its mahout, the only person who could manage it when it was in that state, had set out in pursuit, but had taken the wrong direction and was now twelve hours' journey away, and in the morning the elephant had suddenly reappeared in the town. The Burmese population had no weapons and were quite helpless against it. It had already destroyed somebody's bamboo hut, killed a cow and raided some fruit-stalls and devoured the stock; also it had met the municipal rubbish van and, when the driver jumped out and took to his heels, had turned the van over and inflicted violences upon it.

The Burmese sub-inspector and some Indian constables were waiting for me in the quarter where the elephant had been seen. It was a very poor quarter, a labyrinth of squalid bamboo huts, thatched with palm-leaf, winding all over a steep hillside. I remember that it was a cloudy, stuffy morning at the beginning of the rains. We began questioning the people as to where the elephant had gone and, as usual, failed to get any definite information. That is invariably the case in the East; a story always sounds clear enough at a distance, but the nearer you get to the scene of events the vaguer it becomes. Some of the people said that the elephant had gone in one direction, some said that he had gone in another, some professed not even to have heard of any elephant. I had almost made up my mind that the whole story was a pack of lies, when we heard yells a little distance away. There was a loud, scandalized cry of "Go away, child! Go away this instant!" and an old woman with a switch in her hand came round the corner of a hut, violently shooing away a crowd of naked children. Some more women followed, clicking their tongues and exclaiming; evidently there was something that the children ought not to have seen. I rounded the hut and saw a man's dead body sprawling in the mud. He was an Indian, a black Dravidian coolie, almost naked, and he could not have been dead many minutes. The people said that the elephant had come suddenly upon him round the corner of the hut, caught him with its trunk, put its foot on his back and ground him into the earth. This was the rainy season and the ground was soft, and his face had scored a trench a foot deep and a couple of yards long. He was lying on his belly with arms crucified and head sharply twisted to one side. His face was coated with mud, the eyes wide open, the teeth bared and grinning with an expression of unendurable agony. (Never tell me, by the way, that the dead look peaceful. Most of the corpses I have seen looked devilish.) The friction of the great beast's foot had stripped the skin from his back as neatly as one skins a rabbit. As soon as I saw the dead man I sent an orderly to a friend's house nearby to borrow an elephant rifle. I had already sent back the pony, not wanting it to go mad with fright and throw me if it smelt the elephant.

The orderly came back in a few minutes with a rifle and five cartridges,   5 and meanwhile some Burmans had arrived and told us that the elephant was in the paddy fields below, only a few hundred yards away. As I started forward practically the whole population of the quarter flocked out of the houses and followed me. They had seen the rifle and were all shouting excitedly that I was going to shoot the elephant. They had not shown much interest in the elephant when he was merely ravaging their homes, but it was different now that he was going to be shot. It was a bit of fun to them, as it would be to an English crowd; besides they wanted the meat. It made me vaguely uneasy. I had no intention of shooting the elephant—I had merely sent for the rifle to defend myself if necessary—and it is always unnerving to have a crowd following you. I marched down the hill, looking and feeling a fool, with the rifle over my shoulder and an ever-growing army of people jostling at my heels. At the bottom, when you got away from the huts, there was a metalled road and beyond that a miry waste of paddy fields a thousand yards across, not yet ploughed but soggy from the first rains and dotted with coarse grass. The elephant was standing eight yards from the road, his left side towards us. He took not the slightest notice of the crowd's approach. He was tearing up bunches of grass, beating them against his knees to clean them and stuffing them into his mouth.

I had halted on the road. As soon as I saw the elephant I knew with perfect certainty that I ought not to shoot him. It is a serious matter to shoot a working elephant—it is comparable to destroying a huge and costly piece of machinery—and obviously one ought not to do it if it can possibly be avoided. And at that distance, peacefully eating, the elephant looked no more dangerous than a cow. I thought then and I think now that his attack of "must" was already passing off; in which case he would merely wander harmlessly about until the mahout came back and caught him. Moreover, I did not in the least want to shoot him. I decided that I would watch him for a little while to make sure that he did not turn savage again, and then go home.

But at that moment I glanced round at the crowd that had followed me. It was an immense crowd, two thousand at the least and growing every minute. It blocked the road for a long distance on either side. I looked at the sea of yellow faces above the garish clothes—faces all happy and excited over this bit of fun, all certain that the elephant was going to be shot. They were watching me as they would watch a conjurer about to perform a trick. They did not like me, but with the magical rifle in my hands I was momentarily worth watching. And suddenly I realized that I should have to shoot the elephant after all. The people expected it of me and I had got to do it; I could feel their two thousand wills pressing me forward, irresistibly. And it was at this moment, as I stood there with the rifle in my hands, that I first grasped the hollowness, the futility of the white man's dominion in the East. Here was I, the white man with his gun, standing in front of the unarmed native crowd — seemingly the leading actor of the piece; but in reality I was only an absurd puppet pushed to and fro by the will of those yellow faces behind. I perceived in this moment that when the white man turns tyrant it is his own freedom that he destroys. He becomes a sort of hollow, posing dummy, the conventionalized figure of a sahib. For it is the condition of his rule that he shall spend his life in trying to impress the "natives," and so in every crisis he has got to do what the "natives" expect of him. He wears a mask, and his face grows to fit it. I had got to shoot the elephant. I had committed myself to doing it when I sent for the rifle. A sahib has got to act like a sahib; he has got to appear resolute, to know his own mind and do definite things. To come all that way, rifle in hand, with two thousand people marching at my heels, and then to trail feebly away, having done nothing — no, that was impossible. The crowd would laugh at me. And my whole life, every white man's life in the East, was one long struggle not to be laughed at.

But I did not want to shoot the elephant. I watched him beating his bunch of grass against his knees, with that preoccupied grandmotherly air that elephants have. It seemed to me that it would be murder to shoot him. At that age I was not squeamish about killing animals, but I had never shot an elephant and never wanted to. (Somehow it always seems worse to kill a *large* animal.) Besides, there was the beast's owner to be considered. Alive, the elephant was worth at least a hundred pounds; dead, he would only be worth the value of his tusks, five pounds, possibly. But I had got to act quickly. I turned to some experienced-looking Burmans who had been there when we arrived, and asked them how the elephant had been behaving. They all said the same thing: he took no notice of you if you left him alone, but he might charge if you went too close to him.

It was perfectly clear to me what I ought to do. I ought to walk up to within, say, twenty-five yards of the elephant and test his behavior. If he charged, I could shoot; if he took no notice of me, it would be safe to leave him until the mahout came back. But also I knew that I was going to do no such thing. I was a poor shot with a rifle and the ground was soft mud into which one would sink at every step. If the elephant charged and I missed him, I should have about as much chance as a toad under a steam-roller. But even then I was not thinking particularly of my own skin, only of the watchful yellow faces behind. For at that moment, with the crowd watching me, I was not afraid in the ordinary sense, as I would have been if I had been alone. A white man mustn't be frightened in front of "natives"; and so, in general, he isn't frightened. The sole thought in my mind was that if anything went wrong those two thousand Burmans would see me pursued, caught, trampled on and reduced to a grinning corpse like that Indian up the hill. And if that happened it was quite probable that some of them would laugh. That would never do. There was only one alternative. I shoved the cartridges into the magazine and lay down on the road to get a better aim.

The crowd grew very still, and a deep, low, happy sigh, as of people   10
who see the theatre curtain go up at last, breathed from innumerable throats. They were going to have their bit of fun after all. The rifle was a beautiful German thing with cross-hair sights. I did not then know that in shooting an elephant one would shoot to cut an imaginary bar running from ear-hole to ear-hole. I ought, therefore, as the elephant was sideway on, to have aimed straight at his ear-hole; actually I aimed several inches in front of this, thinking the brain would be further forward.

When I pulled the trigger I did not hear the bang or feel the kick — one never does when a shot goes home — but I heard the devilish roar of glee that went up from the crowd. In that instant, in too short a time, one would have thought, even for the bullet to get there, a mysterious, terrible change had come over the elephant. He neither stirred nor fell, but every line of his body had altered. He looked suddenly stricken, shrunken, immensely old, as though the frightful impact of the bullet had paralyzed him without knocking him down. At last, after what seemed a long time — it might have been five seconds, I dare say — he sagged flabbily to his knees. His mouth slobbered. An enormous senility seemed to have settled upon him. One could have imagined him thousands of years old. I fired again into the same spot. At the second shot he did not collapse but climbed with desperate slowness to his feet and stood weakly upright, with legs sagging and head drooping. I fired a third time. That was the shot that did for him. You could see the agony of it jolt his whole body and knock the last remnant of strength from his legs. But in falling he seemed for a moment to rise, for as his hind legs collapsed beneath him he seemed to tower upward like a huge rock toppling, his trunk reaching skywards like a tree. He trumpeted, for the first and only time. And then down he came, his belly towards me, with a crash that seemed to shake the ground even where I lay.

I got up. The Burmans were already racing past me across the mud. It was obvious that the elephant would never rise again, but he was not dead. He was breathing very rhythmically with long rattling gasps, his great mound of a side painfully rising and falling. His mouth was wide open — I could see far down into caverns of pale pink throat. I waited a long time for him to die, but his breathing did not weaken. Finally I fired my two remaining shots into the spot where I thought his heart must be. The thick blood welled out of him like red velvet, but still he did not die. His body did not even jerk when the shots hit him, the tortured breathing continued without a pause. He was dying, very slowly and in great agony, but in some world remote from me where not even a bullet could damage him further. I felt that I had got to put an end to that dreadful noise. It seemed dreadful to see the great beast lying there, powerless to move and yet powerless to die, and not even to be able to finish him. I sent back for my small rifle and poured shot after shot into his heart and down his throat. They seemed to make no impression. The tortured gasps continued as steadily as the ticking of a clock.

In the end I could not stand it any longer and went away. I heard later that it took him half an hour to die. Burmans were bringing dahs and baskets even before I left, and I was told they had stripped the body almost to the bones by the afternoon.

Afterwards, of course, there were endless discussions about the shooting of the elephant. The owner was furious, but he was only an Indian and could do nothing. Besides, legally I had done the right thing, for a mad elephant has to be killed, like a mad dog, if its owner fails to control it. Among the Europeans opinion was divided. The older men said I was right, the younger men said it was a damn shame to shoot an elephant for killing a coolie, because an elephant was worth more than any damn Coringhee coolie. And afterwards I was very glad that the coolie had been killed; it put me legally in the right and it gave me a sufficient pretext for shooting the elephant. I often wondered whether any of the others grasped that I had done it solely to avoid looking a fool.

JEANNE WAKATSUKI HOUSTON (1935–   )
and JAMES D. HOUSTON (1933–   )

Arrival At Manzanar

> *Born in California in 1935, Jeanne Wakatsuki was among thousands of Americans of Japanese descent who were rounded up and sent to internment camps during World War II (following the Japanese attack on Pearl Harbor in December 1941). She remained at the camp from the age of seven to the age of eleven. Later, while studying journalism at San Jose State University, she met her future husband, novelist James D. Houston. Together, the Houstons wrote* Farewell to Manzanar *to document her life there and to describe the impact of the internment on the Wakatsuki family as well as other families who spent the duration of the war at the camp.*

In December of 1941 Papa's disappearance didn't bother me nearly so much as the world I soon found myself in.

He had been a jack-of-all-trades. When I was born he was farming near Inglewood. Later, when he started fishing, we moved to Ocean Park, near Santa Monica, and until they picked him up, that's where we lived, in a big frame house with a brick fireplace, a block back from the beach. We were the only Japanese family in the neighborhood. Papa liked it that way. He didn't want to be labeled or grouped by anyone. But with him gone and no way of knowing what to expect, my mother moved all of us down to Terminal Island. Woody already lived there, and one of my older sisters had married a Terminal Island boy. Mama's first concern now was to keep the family together; and once the war began, she felt safer there than isolated racially in Ocean Park. But for me, at age seven, the island was a country as foreign as India or Arabia would have been. It was the first time I had lived among other Japanese, or gone to school with them, and I was terrified all the time.

This was partly Papa's fault. One of his threats to keep us younger kids in line was "I'm going to sell you to the Chinaman." When I had entered kindergarten two years earlier, I was the only Oriental in the class. They sat me next to a Caucasian girl who happened to have very slanted eyes. I looked at her and began to scream, certain Papa had sold me out at last. My fear of her ran so deep I could not speak of it, even to Mama, couldn't explain why I was screaming. For two weeks I had nightmares about this girl, until the teachers finally moved me to the other side of the room. And it was still with me, this fear of Oriental faces, when we moved to Terminal Island.

In those days it was a company town, a ghetto owned and controlled by the canneries. The men went after fish, and whenever the boats came back — day or night — the women would be called to process the catch while it was fresh. One in the afternoon or four in the morning, it made no difference. My mother had to go to work right after we moved there. I can still hear the whistle — two toots for French's, three for Van Camp's — and she and Chizu would be out of bed in the middle of the night, heading for the cannery.

The house we lived in was nothing more than a shack, a barracks with single plank walls and rough wooden floors, like the cheapest kind of migrant workers' housing. The people around us were hard-working, boisterous, a little proud of their nickname, *yo-go-re*, which meant literally *uncouth one*, or roughneck, or dead-end kid. They not only spoke Japanese exclusively, they spoke a dialect peculiar to Kyushu, where their families had come from in Japan, a rough, fisherman's language, full of oaths and insults. Instead of saying *ba-ka-ta-re*, a common insult meaning *stupid*, Terminal Islanders would say *ba-ka-ya-ro*, a coarser and exclusively masculine use of the word, which implies gross stupidity. They would swagger and pick on outsiders and persecute anyone who didn't speak as they did. That was what made my own time there so hateful. I had never spoken anything but English, and the other kids in the second grade despised me for it. They were tough and mean, like ghetto kids anywhere. Each day after school I dreaded their ambush. My brother Kiyo, three years older, would wait for me at the door, where we would decide whether to run straight home together, or split up, or try a new and unexpected route.

None of these kids every actually attacked. It was the threat that frightened us, their fearful looks, and the noises they would make, like miniature Samurai, in a language we couldn't understand.

At the time it seemed we had been living under this reign of fear for years. In fact, we lived there about two months. Late in February the navy decided to clear Terminal Island completely. Even though most of us were American-born, it was dangerous having that many Orientals so close to the Long Beach Naval Station, on the opposite end of the island. We had known something like this was coming. But, like Papa's arrest, not much could be done ahead of time. There were four of us kids still young enough to be living with Mama, plus Granny, her mother, sixty-five then, speaking no English, and nearly blind. Mama didn't know where else she could get work, and we had nowhere else to move *to*. On February 25 the choice was made for us. We were given forty-eight hours to clear out.

The secondhand dealers had been prowling around for weeks, like wolves, offering humiliating prices for goods and furniture they knew many of us would have to sell sooner or later. Mama had left all but her most valuable possessions in Ocean Park, simply because she had nowhere to put them. She had brought along her pottery, her silver, heirlooms like the kimonos Granny had brought from Japan, tea sets, lacquered tables, and one fine old set of china, blue and white porcelain, almost translucent. On the day we were leaving, Woody's car was so crammed with boxes and luggage and kids we had just run out of room. Mama had to sell this china.

One of the dealers offered her fifteen dollars for it. She said it was a full setting for twelve and worth at least two hundred. He said fifteen was his top price. Mama started to quiver. Her eyes blazed up at him. She had been packing all night and trying to calm down Granny, who didn't understand why were moving again and what all the rush was about. Mama's nerves were shot, and now navy jeeps were patrolling the streets. She didn't say another word. She just glared at this man, all the rage and frustration channeled at him through her eyes.

He watched her for a moment and said he was sure he couldn't pay   10
more than seventeen fifty for that china. She reached into the red velvet case, took out a dinner plate and hurled it at the floor right in front of his feet.

The man leaped back shouting, "Hey! Hey, don't do that! Those are valuable dishes!"

Mama took out another dinner plate and hurled it at the floor, then another and another, never moving, never opening her mouth, just quivering and glaring at the retreating dealer, with tears streaming down her cheeks. He finally turned and scuttled out the door, heading for the next house. When he was gone she stood there smashing cups and bowls and platters until the whole set lay in scattered blue and white fragments across the wooden floor.

The name Manzanar meant nothing to us when we left Boyle heights. We didn't know where it was or what it was. We went because the government ordered us to. And, in the case of my older brothers and sisters, we went with a certain amount of relief. They had all heard stories of Japanese homes being attacked, of beatings in the streets of California towns. They were as frightened of the Caucasians as Caucasians were of us. Moving, under what appeared to be government protection, to an area less directly threatened by the war seemed not such a bad idea at all. For some it actually sounded like a fine adventure.

Our pickup point was a Buddhist church in Los Angeles. It was very early, and misty, when we got there with our luggage. Mama had bought heavy coats for all of us. She grew up in eastern Washington and knew that anywhere inland in early April would be cold. I was proud of my new coat, and I remember sitting on a duffel bag trying to be friendly with the Greyhound driver. I smiled at him. He didn't smile back. He was befriending no one. Someone tied a numbered tag to my collar and to the duffel bag (each family was given a number, and that became our official designation until the camps were closed), someone else passed out box lunches for the trip, and we climbed aboard.

I had never been outside Los Angeles County, never traveled more   15
than ten miles from the coast, had never even ridden on a bus. I was full of excitement, the way any kid would be, and wanted to look out the window. But for the first few hours the shades were drawn. Around me other people played cards, read magazines, dozed, waiting. I settled back, waiting too, and finally fell asleep. The bus felt very secure to me. Almost half its passengers were immediate relatives. Mama and my older brothers had succeeded

in keeping most of us together, on the same bus, headed for the same camp. I didn't realize until much later what a job that was. The strategy had been, first, to have everyone living in the same district when the evacuation began, and then to get all of us included under the same family number, even though names had been changed by marriage. Many families weren't as lucky as ours and suffered months of anguish while trying to arrange transfers from one camp to another.

We rode all day. By the time we reached our destination, the shades were up. It was late afternoon. The first thing I saw was a yellow swirl across a blurred, reddish setting sun. The bus was being pelted by what sounded like splattering rain. It wasn't rain. This was my first look at something I would soon know very well, a billowing flurry of dust and sand churned up by the wind through Owens Valley.

We drove past a barbed-wire fence, through a gate, and into an open space where trunks and sacks and packages had been dumped from the baggage trucks that drove out ahead of us. I could see a few tents set up, the first rows of black barracks, and beyond them, blurred by sand, rows of barracks that seemed to spread for miles across this plain. People were sitting on cartons or milling around, with their backs to the wind, waiting to see which friends or relatives might be on this bus. As we approached, they turned or stood up, and some moved toward us expectantly. But inside the bus no one stirred. No one waved or spoke. They just stared out the windows, ominously silent. I didn't understand this. Hadn't we finally arrived, our whole family intact? I opened a window, leaned out, and yelled happily. "Hey! This whole bus is full of Wakatsukis!"

Outside, the greeters smiled. Inside there was an explosion of laughter, hysterical, tension-breaking laughter that left my brothers choking and whacking each other across the shoulders.

We had pulled up just in time for dinner. The mess halls weren't completed yet. An outdoor chow line snaked around a half-finished building that broke a good part of the wind. They issued us army mess kits, the round metal kind that fold over, and plopped in scoops of canned Vienna sausage, canned string beans, steamed rice that had been cooked too long, and on top of the rice a serving of canned apricots. The Caucasian servers were thinking the fruit poured over rice would make a good dessert. Among the Japanese, of course, rice is never eaten with sweet foods, only with salty or savory foods. Few of us could eat such a mixture. But at this point no one dared protest. It would have been impolite. I was horrified when I saw the apricot syrup seeping through my little mound of rice. I opened my mouth to complain. My mother jabbed me in the back to keep quiet. We moved on through the line and joined the others squatting in the lee of half-raised walls, dabbing courteously at what was, for almost everyone there, an inedible concoction.

After dinner we were taken to Block 16, a cluster of fifteen barracks that had just been finished a day or so earlier — although finished was hardly the word for it. The shacks were built of one thickness of pine planking   20 covered with tarpaper. They sat on concrete footings, with about two feet of open space between the floorboards and the ground. Gaps showed between the planks, and as the weeks passed and the green wood dried out, the gaps widened. Knotholes gaped in the uncovered floor.

Each barracks was divided into six units, sixteen by twenty feet, about the size of a living room, with one bare bulb hanging from the ceiling and an oil stove for heat. We were assigned two of these for the twelve people in our family group; and our official family "number" was enlarged by three digits — 16 plus the number of this barracks. We were issued steel army cots, two brown army blankets each, and some mattress covers, which my brothers stuffed with straw.

The first task was to divide up what space we had for sleeping. Bill and Woody contributed a blanket each and partitioned off the first room: one side for Bill and Tomi, one side for Woody and Chizu and their baby girl. Woody also got the stove, for heating formulas.

The people who had it hardest during the first few months were young couples like these, many of whom had married just before the evacuation began, in order not to be separated and sent to different camps. Our two rooms were crowded, but at least it was all in the family. My oldest sister and her husband were shoved into one of those sixteen-by-twenty-foot compartments with six people they had never seen before — two other couples, one recently married like themselves, the other with two teenage boys. Partitioning off a room like that wasn't easy. It was bitter cold when we arrived, and the wind did not abate. All they had to use for room dividers were those army blankets, two of which were barely enough to keep one person warm. They argued over whose blanket should be sacrificed and later argued about noise at night — the parents wanted their boys asleep by 9:00 P.M. — and they continued arguing over matters like that for six months, until my sister and her husband left to harvest sugar beets in Idaho. It was grueling work up there, and wages were pitiful, but when the call came through camp for workers to alleviate the wartime labor shortage, it sounded better than their life at Manzanar. They knew they'd have, if nothing else, a room, perhaps a cabin of their own.

That first night in Block 16, the rest of us squeezed into the second room — Granny, Lillian, age fourteen, Ray, thirteen, May, eleven, Kiyo, ten, Mama, and me. I didn't mind this at all at the time. Being youngest meant I got to sleep with Mama. And before we went to bed I had a great time jumping up and down on the mattress. The boys had stuffed so much straw into hers, we had to flatten it some so we wouldn't slide off. I slept with her every night after that until Papa came back.

ANNIE DILLARD (1945–   )

Football and Snowballs

> *Born in 1945, Annie Dillard is a patient, careful observer of events and scenes, both past and present. In "Football and Snowballs" she looks back at a childhood memory and ponders its significance.*

Some boys taught me to play football. This was fine sport. You thought up a new strategy for every play and whispered it to the others. You went out for a pass, fooling everyone. Best, you got to throw yourself mightily at someone's running legs. Either you brought him down or you hit the ground flat out on your chin, with your arms empty before you. It was all or nothing. If you hesitated in fear, you would miss and get hurt: you would take a hard fall while the kid got away, or you would get kicked in the face while the kid got away. But if you flung yourself wholeheartedly at the back of his knees—if you gathered and joined body and soul and pointed them diving fearlessly—then you likely wouldn't get hurt, and you'd stop the ball. Your fate, and your team's score, depended on your concentration and courage. Nothing girls did could compare with it.

Boys welcomed me at baseball, too, for I had, through enthusiastic practice, what was weirdly known as a boy's arm. In winter, in the snow, there was neither baseball nor football, so the boys and I threw snowballs at passing cars. I got in trouble throwing snowballs, and have seldom been happier since.

On one weekday morning after Christmas, six inches of new snow had just fallen. We were standing up to our boot tops in snow on a front yard on trafficked Reynolds Street, waiting for cars. The cars traveled Reynolds Street slowly and evenly; they were targets all but wrapped in red ribbons, cream puffs. We couldn't miss.

I was seven; the boys were eight, nine, and ten. The oldest two Fahey boys were there—Mikey and Peter—polite blond boys who lived near me on Lloyd Street, and who already had four brothers and sisters. My parents approved Mikey and Peter Fahey. Chickie McBride was there, a tough kid, and Billy Paul and Mackie Kean too, from across Reynolds, where the boys grew up dark and furious, grew up skinny, knowing, and skilled. We had all drifted from our houses that morning looking for action, and had found it here on Reynolds Street.

It was cloudy but cold. The cars' tires laid behind them on the snowy 5 street a complex trail of beige chunks like crenellated castle walls. I had stepped on some earlier; they squeaked. We could have wished for more traffic. When a car came, we all popped it one. In the intervals between cars we reverted to the natural solitude of children.

I started making an iceball—a perfect iceball, from perfectly white snow, perfectly spherical, and squeezed perfectly translucent so no snow remained all the way through. (The Fahey boys and I considered it unfair actually to throw an iceball at somebody, but it had been known to happen.)

I had just embarked on the iceball project when we heard tire chains come clanking from afar. A black Buick was moving toward us down the street. We all spread out, banged together some regular snowballs, took aim, and, when the Buick drew nigh, fired.

A soft snowball hit the driver's windshield right before the driver's face. It made a smashed star with a hump in the middle.

Often, of course, we hit our target, but this time, the only time in all of life, the car pulled over and stopped. Its wide black door opened; a man got out of it, running. He didn't even close the car door.

He ran after us, and we ran from him, up the snowy Reynolds side-   10
walk. At the corner, I looked back; incredibly, he was still after us. He was in city clothes: a suit and tie, street shoes. Any normal adult would have quit, having sprung us into flight and made his point. This man was gaining on us. He was a thin man, all action. All of a sudden, we were running for our lives.

Wordless, we split up. We were on our turf; we could lose ourselves in the neighborhood backyards, everyone for himself. I paused and considered. Everyone had vanished except Mikey Fahey, who was just rounding the corner of a yellow brick house. Poor Mikey, I trailed him. The driver of the Buick sensibly picked the two of us to follow. The man apparently had all day.

He chased Mikey and me around the yellow house and up a backyard path we knew by heart: under a low tree, up a bank, through a hedge, down some snowy steps, and across the grocery store's delivery driveway. We smashed through a gap in another hedge, entered a scruffy backyard and ran around its back porch and tight between houses to Edgerton Avenue; we ran across Edgerton to an alley and up our own sliding woodpile to the Halls' front yard; he kept coming. We ran up Lloyd Street and wound through mazy backyards toward the steep hilltop at Willard and Lang.

He chased us silently, block after block. He chased us silently over picket fences, through thorny hedges, between houses, around garbage cans, and across streets. Every time I glanced back, choking for breath, I expected he would have quit. He must have been as breathless as we were. His jacket strained over his body. It was an immense discovery, pounding into my hot head with every sliding, joyous step, that this ordinary adult evidently knew what I thought only children who trained at football knew: that you have to fling yourself at what you're doing, you have to point yourself, forget yourself, aim, dive.

Mikey and I had nowhere to go, in our own neighborhood or out of it, but away from this man who was chasing us. He impelled us forward; we compelled him to follow our route. The air was cold; every breath tore my throat. We kept running, block after block; we kept improvising, back-yard after backyard, running a frantic course and choosing it simultaneously, failing always to find small places or hard places to slow him down, and discovering always, exhilarated, dismayed, that only bare speed could save us—for he would never give up, this man—and we were losing speed.

He chased us through the backyard labyrinths of ten blocks before he   15
caught us by our jackets. He caught us and we all stopped.

We three stood staggering, half blinded, coughing, in an obscure hilltop backyard: a man in his twenties, a boy, a girl. He had released our jackets, our pursuer, our captor, our hero: he knew we weren't going anywhere. We all played by the rules. Mikey and I unzipped our jackets. I pulled off my sopping mittens. Our tracks multiplied in the backyard's new snow. We had been breaking new snow all morning. We didn't look at each other. I was cherishing my excitement. The man's lower pants legs were wet; his cuffs were full of snow, and there was a prow of snow beneath them on his shoes and socks. Some trees bordered the little flat backyard, some messy winter trees. There was no one around: a clearing in a grove, and we the only players.

It was a long time before he could speak. I had some difficulty at first recalling why we were there. My lips felt swollen; I couldn't see out of the sides of my eyes; I kept coughing.

"You stupid kids," he began perfunctorily.

We listened perfunctorily indeed, if we listened at all, for the chewing out was redundant, a mere formality, and beside the point. The point was that he had chased us passionately without giving up, and so he had caught us. Now he came down to earth. I wanted the glory to last forever.

But how could the glory have lasted forever? We could have run   20
through every backyard in North America until we got to Panama. But when he trapped us at the lip of the Panama Canal, what precisely could he have done to prolong the drama of the chase and cap its glory? I brooded about this for the next few years. He could only have fried Mikey Fahey and me in boiling oil, say, or dismembered us piecemeal, or staked us to anthills. None of which I really wanted, and none of which any adult was likely to do, even in the spirit of fun. He could only chew us out there in the Panamanian jungle, after months or years of exalting pursuit. He could only begin, "You stupid kids," and continue in his ordinary Pittsburgh accent with his normal righteous anger and the usual common sense.

If in that snowy backyard the driver of the black Buick had cut off our heads, Mikey's and mine, I would have died happy, for nothing has required so much of me since as being chased all over Pittsburgh in the middle of winter—running terrified, exhausted—by this sainted, skinny, furious redheaded man who wished to have a word with us. I don't know how he found his way back to his car.

ALICE WALKER (1944–   )

In Search of Our Mothers' Gardens

*I described her own nature and temperament. Told how they
needed a larger life for their expression. . . . I pointed out
that in lieu of proper channels, her emotions had overflowed
into paths that dissipated them. I talked, beautifully I
thought, about an art that would be born, an art that would
open the way for women the likes of her. I asked her to hope,
and build up an inner life against the coming of that
day. . . . I sang, with a strange quiver in my voice, a
promise song.*

> "Avey," Jean Toomer, *Cane*
> *The poet speaking to a prostitute who falls
> asleep while he's talking*

When the poet Jean Toomer walked through the South in the early
twenties, he discovered a curious thing: black women whose spirituality
was so intense, so deep, so *unconscious,* they were themselves unaware of the
richness they held. They stumbled blindly through their lives: creatures so
abused and mutilated in body, so dimmed and confused by pain, that they
considered themselves unworthy even of hope. In the selfless abstractions
their bodies became to the men who used them, they became more than
"sexual objects," more even than mere women: they became "Saints." Instead of being perceived as whole persons, their bodies became shrines: what
was thought to be their minds became temples suitable for worship. These
crazy Saints stared out at the world, wildly, like lunatics — or quietly, like
suicides; and the "God" that was in their gaze was as mute as a great stone.

Who were these Saints? These crazy, loony, pitiful women?

Some of them, without a doubt, were our mothers and grandmothers.

In the still heat of the post-Reconstruction South, this is how they
seemed to Jean Toomer: exquisite butterflies trapped in an evil honey, toiling
away their lives in an era, a century, that did not acknowledge them, except
as "the *mule* of the world." They dreamed dreams that no one knew — not
even themselves, in any coherent fashion — and saw visions no one could
understand. They wandered or sat about the countryside crooning lullabies
to ghosts, and drawing the mother of Christ in charcoal on courthouse
walls.

They forced their minds to desert their bodies and their striving spirits   5
sought to rise, like frail whirlwinds from the hard red clay. And when those
frail whirlwinds fell, in scattered particles, upon the ground, no one
mourned. Instead, men lit candles to celebrate the emptiness that remained,
as people do who enter a beautiful but vacant space to resurrect a God.

Our mothers and grandmothers, some of them: moving to music not yet written. And they waited.

They waited for a day when the unknown thing that was in them would be made known; but guessed, somehow in their darkness, that on the day of their revelation they would be long dead. Therefore to Toomer they walked, and even ran, in slow motion. For they were going nowhere immediate, and the future was not yet within their grasp. And men took our mothers and grandmothers, "but got no pleasure from it." So complex was their passion and their calm.

To Toomer, they lay vacant and fallow as autumn fields, with harvest time never in sight: and he saw them enter loveless marriages, without joy; and become prostitutes, without resistance; and become mothers of children, without fulfillment.

For these grandmothers and mothers of ours were not Saints, but Artists; driven to a numb and bleeding madness by the springs of creativity in them for which there was no release. They were Creators, who lived lives of spiritual waste, because they were so rich in spirituality — which is the basis of Art — that the strain of enduring their unused and unwanted talent drove them insane. Throwing away this spirituality was their pathetic attempt to lighten the soul to a weight their work-worn, sexually abused bodies could bear.

What did it mean for a black woman to be an artist in our grandmothers' time? In our great-grandmothers' day? It is a question with an answer cruel enough to stop the blood.

10

Did you have a genius of a great-great-grandmother who died under some ignorant and depraved white overseer's lash? Or was she required to bake biscuits for a lazy backwater tramp, when she cried out in her soul to paint watercolors of sunsets, or the rain falling on the green and peaceful pasturelands? Or was her body broken and forced to bear children (who were more often than not sold away from her) — eight, ten, fifteen, twenty children — when her one joy was the thought of modeling heroic figures of rebellion, in stone or clay?

How was the creativity of the black woman kept alive, year after year and century after century, when for most of the years black people have been in America, it was a punishable crime for a black person to read or write? And the freedom to paint, to sculpt, to expand the mind with action did not exist. Consider, if you can bear to imagine it, what might have been the result if singing, too, had been forbidden by law. Listen to the voices of Bessie Smith, Billie Holiday, Nina Simone, Roberta Flack, and Aretha Franklin, among others, and imagine those voices muzzled for life. Then you may begin to comprehend the lives of our "crazy," "Sainted" mothers and grandmothers. The agony of the lives of women who might have been Poets, Novelists, Essayists, and Short-Story Writers (over a period of centuries), who died with their real gifts stifled within them.

And, if this were the end of the story, we would have cause to cry out in my paraphrase of Okot p'Bitek's great poem:

O, my clanswomen
Let us all cry together!
Come,
Let us mourn the death of our mother,
The death of a Queen
The ash that was produced
By a great fire!
O, this homestead is utterly dead
Close the gates
With *lacari* thorns,
For our mother
The creator of the Stool is lost!
And all the young men
Have perished in the wilderness!

But this is not the end of the story, for all the young women — our mothers and grandmothers, *ourselves* — have not perished in the wilderness. And if we ask ourselves why, and search for and find the answer, we will know beyond all efforts to erase it from our minds, just exactly who, and of what, we black American women are.

One example, perhaps the most pathetic, most misunderstood one, can provide a backdrop for our mothers' work: Phillis Wheatley, a slave in the 1700s.

Virginia Woolf, in her book *A Room of One's Own*, wrote that in order for a woman to write fiction she must have two things, certainly: a room of her own (with key and lock) and enough money to support herself.

What then are we to make of Phillis Wheatley, a slave, who owned not even herself? This sickly, frail black girl who required a servant of her own at times — her health was so precarious — and who, had she been white, would have been easily considered the intellectual superior of all the women and most of the men in the society of her day.

Virginia Woolf wrote further, speaking of course not of our Phillis, that "any woman born with a great gift in the sixteenth century [insert "eighteenth century," insert "black woman," insert "born or made a slave"] would certainly have gone crazed, shot herself, or ended her days in some lonely cottage outside the village, half witch, half wizard [insert "Saint"], feared and mocked at. For it needs little skill and psychology to be sure that a highly gifted girl who had tried to use her gift of poetry would have been so thwarted and hindered by contrary instincts [add "chains, guns, the lash, the ownership of one's body by someone else, submission to an alien religion"], that she must have lost her health and sanity to a certainty."

The key words, as they relate to Phillis, are "contrary instincts." For when we read the poetry of Phillis Wheatley — as when we read the novels of Nella Larsen or the oddly false-sounding autobiography of that freest of all black women writers, Zora Hurston — evidence of "contrary instincts" is everywhere. Her loyalties were completely divided, as was, without question, her mind.

But how could this be otherwise? Captured at seven, a slave of wealthy, doting whites who instilled in her the "savagery" of the Africa they "rescued" her from . . . one wonders if she was even able to remember her homeland as she had known it, or as it really was.

Yet, because she did try to use her gift for poetry in a world that made her a slave, she was "so thwarted and hindered by . . . contrary instincts, that she . . . lost her health. . . ." In the last years of her brief life, burdened not only with the need to express her gift but also with a penniless, friendless "freedom" and several small children for whom she was forced to do strenuous work to feed, she lost her health, certainly. Suffering from malnutrition and neglect and who knows what mental agonies, Phillis Wheatley died.

So torn by "contrary instincts" was black, kidnapped, enslaved Phillis that her description of "the Goddess" — as she poetically called the Liberty she did not have — is ironically, cruelly humorous. And, in fact, has held Phillis up to ridicule for more than a century. It is usually read prior to hanging Phillis's memory as that of a fool. She wrote:

> The Goddess comes, she moves divinely fair,
> Olive and laurel binds her *golden* hair.
> Wherever shines this native of the skies,
> Unnumber'd charms and recent graces rise. [My italics]

It is obvious that Phillis, the slave, combed the "Goddess's" hair every morning; prior, perhaps, to bringing in the milk, or fixing her mistress's lunch. She took her imagery from the one thing she saw elevated above all others.

With the benefit of hindsight we ask, "How could she?"

But at last, Phillis, we understand. No more snickering when your stiff, struggling, ambivalent lines are forced on us. We know now that you were not an idiot or a traitor; only a sickly little black girl, snatched from your home and country and made a slave; a woman who still struggled to sing the song that was your gift, although in a land of barbarians who praised you for your bewildered tongue. It is not so much what you sang, as that you kept alive, in so many of our ancestors, *the notion of song.*

Black women are called, in the folklore that so aptly identifies one's status in society, "the *mule* of the world," because we have been handed the burdens that everyone else — *everyone* else — refused to carry. We have also been called "Matriarchs," "Superwomen," and "Mean and Evil Bitches." Not to mention "Castraters" and "Sapphire's Mama." When we have pleaded for understanding, our character has been distorted; when we have asked for simple caring, we have been handed empty inspirational appellations, then stuck in the farthest corner. When we have asked for love, we have been given children. In short, even our plainer gifts, our labors of fidelity and love, have been knocked down our throats. To be an artist and a black woman, even today, lowers our status in many respects, rather than raises it: and yet, artists we will be.

Therefore we must fearlessly pull out of ourselves and look at and identify with our lives the living creativity some of our great-grandmothers were not allowed to know. I stress *some* of them because it is well known that the majority of our great-grandmothers knew, even without "knowing" it, the reality of their spirituality, even if they didn't recognize it beyond what happened in the singing at church—and they never had any intention of giving it up.

How they did it—those millions of black women who were not Phillis Wheatley, or Lucy Terry or Frances Harper or Zora Hurston or Nella Larsen or Bessie Smith; or Elizabeth Catlett, or Katherine Dunham, either—brings me to the title of this essay, "In Search of Our Mothers' Gardens," which is a personal account that is yet shared, in its theme and its meaning, by all of us. I found, while thinking about the far-reaching world of the creative black woman, that often the truest answer to a question that really matters can be found very close.

In the late 1920s my mother ran away from home to marry my father. Marriage, if not running away, was expected of seventeen-year-old girls. By the time she was twenty, she had two children and was pregnant with a third. Five children later, I was born. And this is how I came to know my mother: she seemed a large, soft, loving-eyed woman who was rarely impatient in our home. Her quick, violent temper was on view only a few times a year, when she battled with the white landlord who had the misfortune to suggest to her that her children did not need to go to school.

She made all the clothes we wore, even my brothers' overalls. She   30
made all the towels and sheets we used. She spent the summers canning vegetables and fruits. She spent the winter evenings making quilts enough to cover all our beds.

During the "working" day, she labored beside—not behind—my father in the fields. Her day began before sunup, and did not end until late at night. There was never a moment for her to sit down, undisturbed, to unravel her own private thoughts; never a time free from interruption—by work or the noisy inquiries of her many children. And yet, it is to my mother—and all our mothers who were not famous—that I went in search of the secret of what has fed that muzzled and often mutilated, but vibrant, creative spirit that the black woman has inherited, and that pops out in wild and unlikely places to this day.

But when, you will ask, did my overworked mother have time to know or care about feeding the creative spirit?

The answer is so simple that many of us have spent years discovering it. We have constantly looked high, when we should have looked high — and low.

For example: in the Smithsonian Institution in Washington, D.C., there hangs a quilt unlike any other in the world. In fanciful, inspired, and yet simple and identifiable figures, it portrays the story of the Crucifixion. It is considered rare, beyond price. Though it follows no known pattern of quiltmaking, and though it is made of bits and pieces of worthless rags, it is obviously the work of a person of powerful imagination and deep spiritual feeling. Below this quilt I saw a note that says it was made by "an anonymous Black woman in Alabama, a hundred years ago."

If we could locate this "anonymous" black woman from Alabama, she   35
would turn out to be one of our grandmothers — an artist who left her mark in the only materials she could afford, and in the only medium her position in society allowed her to use.

As Virginia Woolf wrote further, in *A Room of One's Own:*

> Yet genius of a sort must have existed among women as it must have existed among the working class. [Change this to "slaves" and "the wives and daughters of sharecroppers."] Now and again an Emily Brontë or a Robert Burns [change this to "a Zora Hurston or a Richard Wright"] blazes out and proves its presence. But certainly it never got itself on to paper. When, however, one reads of a witch being ducked, of a woman possessed by devils [or "Sainthood"], of a wise woman selling herbs [our root workers], or even a very remarkable man who had a mother, then I think we are on the track of a lost novelist, a suppressed poet, or some mute and inglorious Jane Austen. . . . Indeed, I would venture to guess that Anon, who wrote so many poems without signing them, was often a woman. . . .

And so our mothers and grandmothers have, more often than not anonymously, handed on the creative spark, the seed of the flower they themselves never hoped to see: or like a sealed letter they could not plainly read.

And so it is, certainly, with my own mother. Unlike "Ma" Rainey's songs, which retained their creator's name even while blasting forth from Bessie Smith's mouth, no song or poem will bear my mother's name. Yet so many of the stories that I write, that we all write, are my mother's stories. Only recently did I fully realize this: that through years of listening to my mother's stories of her life, I have absorbed not only the stories themselves, but something of the manner in which she spoke, something of the urgency that involves the knowledge that her stories — like her life — must be recorded. It is probably for this reason that so much of what I have written is about characters whose counterparts in real life are so much older than I am.

But the telling of these stories, which came from my mother's lips as naturally as breathing, was not the only way my mother showed herself as an artist. For stories, too, were subject to being distracted, to dying without conclusion. Dinners must be started, and cotton must be gathered before the big rains. The artist that was and is my mother showed itself to me only after many years. This is what I finally noticed:

Like Mem, a character in *The Third Life of Grange Copeland,* my mother   40
adorned with flowers whatever shabby house we were forced to live in. And not just your typical straggly country stand of zinnias, either. She planted ambitious gardens — and still does — with over fifty different varieties of plants that bloom profusely from early March until late November. Before she left home for the fields, she watered her flowers, chopped up the grass, and laid out new beds. When she returned from the fields she might divide clumps of bulbs, dig a cold pit, uproot and replant roses, or prune branches from her taller bushes or trees — until night came and it was too dark to see.

Whatever she planted grew as if by magic, and her fame as a grower of flowers spread over three counties. Because of her creativity with her flowers, even my memories of poverty are seen through a screen of blooms — sunflowers, petunias, roses, dahlias, forsythia, spirea, delphiniums, verbena . . . and on and on.

And I remember people coming to my mother's yard to be given cuttings from her flowers; I hear again the praise showered on her because whatever rocky soil she landed on, she turned into a garden. A garden so brilliant with colors, so original in its design, so magnificent with life and creativity, that to this day people drive by our house in Georgia — perfect strangers and imperfect strangers — and ask to stand or walk among my mother's art.

I notice that it is only when my mother is working in her flowers that she is radiant, almost to the point of being invisible — except as Creator: hand and eye. She is involved in work her soul must have. Ordering the universe in the image of her personal conception of Beauty.

Her face, as she prepares the Art that is her gift, is a legacy of respect she leaves to me, for all that illuminates and cherishes life. She has handed down respect for the possibilities — and the will to grasp them.

For her, so hindered and intruded upon in so many ways, being an   45
artist has still been a daily part of her life. This ability to hold on, even in very simple ways, is work black women have done for a very long time.

This poem is not enough, but it is something, for the woman who literally covered the holes in our walls with sunflowers:

They were women then
My mama's generation
Husky of voice — Stout of
Step
With fists as well as
Hands
How they battered down

Doors
And ironed
Starched white
Shirts
How they led
Armies
Headragged Generals
Across mined
Fields
Booby-trapped
Kitchens
To discover books
Desks
A place for us
How they knew what we
Must know
Without knowing a page
Of it
Themselves.

Guided by my heritage of a love of beauty and a respect for strength — in search of my mother's garden, I found my own.

And perhaps in Africa over two hundred years ago, there was just such a mother; perhaps she painted vivid and daring decorations in oranges and yellows and greens on the walls of her hut; perhaps she sang — in a voice like Roberta Flack's — *sweetly* over the compounds of her village; perhaps she wove the most stunning mats or told the most ingenious stories of all the village storytellers. Perhaps she was herself a poet — though only her daughter's name is signed to the poems that we know.

Perhaps Phillis Wheatley's mother was also an artist.

Perhaps in more than Phillis Wheatley's biological life is her mother's   50
signature made clear.

Appendix
MLA Documentation

Whenever you use someone else's words or ideas, either by paraphrasing or quoting directly, you must provide documentation to acknowledge your source. There are many different formats for providing such documentation. When you are writing a paper for a course in one of the humanities (art, literature, music, or history, for example), use the format established by the Modern Languages Association (MLA).

USING AND DOCUMENTING THE SOURCE

The following list suggests some ways of incorporating someone else's words or ideas into the body of your paper. Items 1–4 illustrate these ways by reference to this source material by Nancie Atwell:

Like writing, reading becomes meaningful only when it involves the particular response of an individual — one's own ways of perceiving reality through the prism of written language. And, like writing, reading generates its most significant meanings when the reader engages in a process of discovery, weaving and circling among the complex of behaviors that characterizes genuine participation in written language. (From *In the Middle* by Nancie Atwell, Boynton–Cook Publishers, Portsmouth, N.H., 1987, p. 155.)

Item 5 in the list refers to this original source:

New evidence suggests that at least two theaters used during Shakespeare's time may have been uncovered at a London construction site. One theater, the Swan, is believed to be at least 350 years old. (From: "Shakespearean Theaters Reborn," *New York Times,* August 19, 1987, p. 56.)

1. A brief quotation, including the author's name.

Nancie Atwell believes that meaningful reading and writing both require "the particular response of an individual" (155).

Because the author's name appears in the introduction to the quotation, document it simply by giving the page number where the original quotation appears. Place the page number in parentheses before the ending punctuation.

2. A brief quotation without the author's name.

"The particular response of an individual" gives meaning to both reading and writing (Atwell 155).

Because the author's name does not appear in the text, you must provide it, along with the page number. Give the author's last name only. (However, if in your paper you cite two or more authors with the same last name, use both first and last name.) If you cite more than one source by the same author, use an abbreviated title (one or two significant words) to identify the work, for example, (Atwell, *Middle* 155).

3. A paraphrase or summary.

Nancie Atwell suggests that both reading and writing gain meaning only when they involve the unique reaction of one person — an individual's special way of understanding his or her world through the prism of literature (155).

Even though Atwell's sentences and phrases are not directly cited, the writer uses this author's ideas. (Note particularly the use of the prism image.) Therefore, the source must be documented. Because Atwell's name is mentioned, only the page number (in parentheses, before the final punctuation) is required. When the author's name is not mentioned, his or her last name appears within the parentheses just before the page number, for example, (Atwell 155).

4. A long quotation.

Those interested in the importance of the reader's response to literature should consider Nancie Atwell's thoughts:

> Like writing, reading becomes meaningful only when it involves the particular response of an individual — one's own ways of perceiving reality through the prism of written language. And, like writing, reading generates its most significant meanings when the reader engages in a process of discovery, weaving and circling among the complex of behaviors that characterizes genuine participation in written language. (155)

When you quote four or more typed lines, indent the quotation several spaces from the left margin. Use the normal right margin. *Do not use quotation marks.* Provide documentation within parentheses *after* the final mark of punctuation.

If you do not cite the author's name in the introduction to the quotation, you must include it in the parenthetical documentation. If you do cite the author's name in the introduction to the quotation, provide only the page number.

5. A quotation from an unsigned source (for instance, an unsigned newspaper article).

The *New York Times* noted that a theater uncovered at a construction site in London "is believed to be at least 350 years old" ("Shakespearean" 56).

When the article has no author's byline, use an abbreviated title (often the first word other than "a," "an," or "the") and the page number in parentheses.

6. A source written by two or more people.

If the source is written by two or three people, use all authors' names. For instance, if your source is *No Man's Land* by Sandra Gilbert and Susan Gubar, you could cite it in either of these ways:

The writer's pen may be considered by some to be "a metaphorical pistol" (Gilbert and Gubar 3).

or

Gilbert and Gubar note that some consider the writer's pen to be "a metaphorical pistol" (3).

If the source is written by four or more authors, give only the name of the first author, followed by et al. Note that *et,* the Latin word for "and," is not an abbreviation and therefore requires no period. *Al.* is the abbreviation for the Latin *alia* — others — and does require a period. For instance, if the source is *Women's Ways of Knowing* by Mary Field Belenky, Blythe McVicker Clinchy, Nancy Rule Goldberger, and Jill Mattuck Tarule, you could cite it in either of these ways:

Instructors should consider studies suggesting "that women cultivate their capacities for listening while encouraging men to speak" (Belenky et al. 45).

or

As Belenky et al. remind us, instructors should consider studies suggesting "that women cultivate their capacities for listening while encouraging men to speak" (45).

COMPILING A LIST OF WORKS CITED

Documentation in the text of a paper and in parenthetical citations leads readers to a list of works cited. This list appears at the end of the paper. Arrange entries in the list of works cited alphabetically so that the reader can find the full reference quickly.

Note: You may have previously learned the old MLA format, in which the list of works cited included *all* materials consulted, paraphrased, or quoted. In the new MLA format, the list includes only those works that are actually paraphrased or quoted.

The following list of sample entries illustrates the MLA bibliographic style. If you are using a type of source not included in this list, consult a more complete handbook or style guide.

1. Book by one author.

Atwell, Nancie. *In the Middle*. Portsmouth: Boynton, 1987.

2. Book by two or three authors.

Gilbert, Sandra M. and Susan Gubar. *No Man's Land*. New Haven: Yale UP, 1988.

3. Book by four or more authors.

Belenky, Mary Field et al. *Women's Ways of Knowing*. New York: Basic, 1986.

4. Book with an editor.

Gill, Elaine, ed. *Mountain Moving Day: Poems by Women*. Trumansburg: Crossing, 1973.

5. Two or more books by the same authors (list in alphabetical order by title).

Gilbert, Sandra M. and Susan Gubar. *The Madwoman in the Attic.* New Haven: Yale UP, 1979.

————. *No Man's Land.* New Haven: Yale UP, 1988.

6. Works in an anthology or collection.

Atwood, Margaret. "Fishbowl." *Mountain Moving Day: Poems by Women.* Ed. Elaine Gill. Trumansburg: Crossing, 1973.

7. Multivolume work.

Graves, Robert. *The Greek Myths.* 2 vols. New York: Braziller, 1967. Vol. 2.

8. Article from a professional journal that paginates each issue separately (each new issue begins with page 1).

Johnson, Gale. "Ibsen's Tragic Comedies." *The Center Magazine* 12.2 (1979): 15–21.

9. Article from a professional journal that paginates issues continuously throughout the year. For instance, the first issue of 1991 might begin with page 1 and end with page 330. The second issue, then, would begin with page 331, and so on.

Heilman, Robert B. "Charlotte Brontë, Reason, and the Moon." *Nineteenth-Century Fiction* 14 (1960): 283–302.

10. Article in a newspaper.

Signed

Paulsen, Karen. "Poetry for the '90's." *Boston Globe* 12 Sept. 1990: A55.

Unsigned

"Shakespearean Theaters Reborn." *New York Times* 19 Aug. 1987: 56.

ASSEMBLING THE LIST OF WORKS CITED

Arrange the entries in the list of works cited alphabetically according to the first word of the entry. Here is how the examples listed above would appear in a list of works cited:

Works Cited

Atwell, Nancie. *In the Middle.* Portsmouth: Boynton, 1987.

Atwood, Margaret. "Fishbowl." *Mountain Moving Day: Poems by Women.* Ed. Elaine Gill. Trumansburg: Crossing, 1973.

Belenky, Mary Field et al. *Women's Ways of Knowing.* New York: Basic, 1986.

Gilbert, Sandra M. and Susan Gubar. *The Madwoman in the Attic.* New Haven: Yale UP, 1979.

————. *No Man's Land.* New Haven: Yale UP, 1988.

Gill, Elaine, ed. *Mountain Moving Day: Poems by Women.* Trumansburg: Crossing, 1973.

Graves, Robert. *The Greek Myths.* 2 vols. New York: Braziller, 1967. Vol. 2.

Heilman, Robert B. "Charlotte Brontë, Reason, and the Moon." *Nineteenth-Century Fiction* 14 (1960): 283–302.

Johnson, Gale. "Ibsen's Tragic Comedies." *The Center Magazine* 12.2 (1979): 15–21.

Paulsen, Karen. "Poetry for the '90's." *Boston Globe* 12 Sept. 1990: A55.

"Shakespearean Theaters Reborn." *New York Times* 19 Aug. 1987: 56.

Guidelines for List of Works Cited

- Double space entries.
- Begin the first line of each entry at the left margin.
- Indent the second and subsequent lines five spaces.
- Arrange entries in alphabetical order, according to the first word of the entry (excluding "a" "an" or "the").

INDEX OF FIRST LINES

INDEX OF AUTHORS AND TITLES